WILLIAM BLAKE'S
WRITINGS

❦

VOLUME II

Writings in Conventional Typography
and in Manuscript

WILLIAM BLAKE'S WRITINGS

EDITED BY

G. E. BENTLEY, Jr.

·c⪯⪰⪯⪰·

VOLUME I
Engraved and Etched Writings

VOLUME II
*Writings in Conventional Typography
and in Manuscript*

·c⪯⪰⪯⪰·

VOLUME II

OXFORD
AT THE CLARENDON PRESS
1978

Oxford University Press, Walton Street, Oxford OX2 6DP

OXFORD LONDON GLASGOW
NEW YORK TORONTO MELBOURNE WELLINGTON
KUALA LUMPUR SINGAPORE JAKARTA HONG KONG TOKYO
DELHI BOMBAY CALCUTTA MADRAS KARACHI
IBADAN NAIROBI DAR ES SALAAM CAPE TOWN

ISBN 0 19 811885 6

© Oxford University Press 1978

Printed in Great Britain
at the University Press, Oxford
by Eric Buckley
Printer to the University

CONTENTS

VOLUME II

WRITINGS IN CONVENTIONAL TYPOGRAPHY AND IN MANUSCRIPT

Contents

Contents

Contents

TABLE OF REPRODUCTIONS

(Between pp. 874 and 875)

WRITINGS IN
CONVENTIONAL
TYPOGRAPHY

POETICAL SKETCHES

POETICAL SKETCHES.

By W. B.

LONDON:

Printed in the Year M DCC LXXXIII.

[Page i]

ADVERTISEMENT.[1]

[¶*1*] THE following Sketches were the production of untutored youth, commenced in his twelfth, and occasionally resumed by the author till his twentieth year; since which time, his talents having been wholly directed to the attainment of excellence in his profession, hc has been deprived of the leisure requisite to such a revisal of these sheets, as might have rendered them less unfit to meet the public eye.

[¶*2*] Conscious of the irregularities and defects to be found in almost every page, his friends have still believed that they possessed a poetical originality, which merited some respite from oblivion. These their opinions remain, however, to be now reproved or confirmed by a less partial public.

'Advertisement' [1] According to J. T. Smith (1828), Mrs. Anthony Stephen Mathew persuaded 'her husband, to join Mr. Flaxman in . . . defraying the expense of printing [*the* POETICAL SKETCHES, *and he also*,] . . . with his usual urbanity, wrote the following advertisement' (*Blake Records*, 456).

[*Page 1*]
MISCELLANEOUS POEMS.

TO SPRING.

O THOU, with dewy locks, who lookest down
Thro' the clear windows of the morning; turn
Thine angel eyes upon our western isle,
Which in full choir hails thy approach, O Spring!

The hills tell each other, and the list'ning   [*5*]
Vallies hear; all our longing eyes are turned
Up to thy bright pavillions: issue forth,
And let thy holy feet visit our clime.

Come o'er the eastern hills, and let our winds
Kiss thy perfumed garments; let us taste   [*10*]
Thy morn and evening breath; scatter thy pearls
Upon our love-sick land that mourns for thee.
[*Page*] 2
O deck her forth with thy fair fingers; pour
Thy soft kisses on her bosom; and put
Thy golden crown upon her languish'd head,   [*15*]
Whose modest tresses were bound up for thee!   [*16*]

TO SUMMER.

O THOU, who passest thro' our vallies in
Thy strength, curb thy fierce steeds, allay the heat
That flames from their large nostrils! thou, O Summer,
Oft pitched'st here thy golden tent, and oft
Beneath our oaks hast slept, while we beheld   [*5*]
With joy, thy ruddy limbs and flourishing hair.

Beneath our thickest shades we oft have heard
Thy voice, when noon upon his fervid car

'To Spring'   George Cumberland marked the poem '*fine*' in his copy (D).

'To Summer'   l. 6: 'flourishing' was changed to 'flowing' in copy W in an un-
Blakelike hand.

Rode o'er the deep of heaven; beside our springs
Sit down, and in our mossy vallies, on   [*10*]
Some bank beside a river clear, throw thy
Silk draperies off, and rush into the stream:
Our vallies love the Summer in his pride.

Our bards are fam'd who strike the silver wire:
Our youth are bolder than the southern swains: [*15*]
Our maidens fairer in the sprightly dance:
We lack not songs, nor instruments of joy,
Nor echoes sweet, nor waters clear as heaven,
Nor laurel wreaths against the sultry heat.   [*19*]

[*Page*] [3]
TO AUTUMN.

O autumn, laden with fruit, and stained
With the blood of the grape, pass not, but sit
Beneath my shady roof, there thou may'st rest,
And tune thy jolly voice to my fresh pipe;
And all the daughters of the year shall dance!   [*5*]
Sing now the lusty song of fruits and flowers.

'The narrow bud opens her beauties to
'The sun, and love runs in her thrilling veins;
'Blossoms hang round the brows of morning, and
'Flourish down the bright cheek of modest eve,   [*10*]
'Till clust'ring Summer breaks forth into singing,
'And feather'd clouds strew flowers round her head.

'The spirits of the air live on the smells
'Of fruit; and joy, with pinions light, roves round

'To Autumn' ll. 7–15: *All* the quotation marks here and throughout *Poetical Sketches* are in the 1783 printed text—that is, in 'To Autumn' ll. 7–15, 'Fair Elenor' ll. 21–5,'32, 39–52, 61–8, 'Gwin' ll. 29–32, 34–6, 62, 67–8, 'Blind-Man's Buff' ll. 21, 24–5, 29–*30*, 37–8, *40*–2, 49, 'King Edward the Third' iii, ll. 155, 158–9, 164–6, vi, ll. 15–*18*, 39–60, 'Prologue to King John', 'The Couch of Death', '*Contemplation*', 'Samson' (*italics* identify exceptions)—except for 'Blind-Man's Buff' l. 30 (closing quote), l. 40 (closing quote), 'King Edward the Third' vi, l. 18 (closing quote), 'Contemplation' (in left margin for first speech), where they are added by GEB.

751

'The gardens, or sits singing in the trees.' [*15*]
Thus sang the jolly Autumn as he sat,
Then rose, girded himself, and o'er the bleak
Hills fled from our sight; but left his golden load. [*18*]

[*Page*] [4]
TO WINTER.

O WINTER! bar thine adamantine doors:
The north is thine; there hast thou built thy dark
Deep-founded habitation. Shake not thy roofs,
Nor bend thy pillars with thine iron car.

He hears me not, but o'er the yawning deep [*5*]
Rides heavy; his storms are unchain'd; sheathed
In ribbed steel, I dare not lift mine eyes;
For he hath rear'd his sceptre o'er the world.

Lo! now the direful monster, whose skin clings
To his strong bones, strides o'er the groaning rocks: [*10*]
He withers all in silence, and his hand
Unclothes the earth, and freezes up frail life.

He takes his seat upon the cliffs, the mariner
Cries in vain. Poor little wretch! that deal'st
With storms; till heaven smiles, and the monster [*15*]
Is driv'n yelling to his caves beneath mount Hecla. [*16*]

[*Page*] [5]
TO THE
EVENING STAR.

THOU fair-hair'd angel of the evening,
Now, whilst the sun rests on the mountains, light
Thy bright torch of love; thy radiant crown

'To Winter' ll. 6–8: Perhaps the intention is: 'his storms are unchain'd, sheathed In ribbed steel; I dare not lift mine eyes, For he hath rear'd his sceptre o'er the world.'

l. 11: 1783: 'in his hand'; the 'in' is deleted in copies B, C, E, F, O, Q, S, T, V, W.

'To the Evening Star' l. 2: 'whilst' is altered to 'while' in copy Q.

Put on, and smile upon our evening bed!
Smile on our loves; and, while thou drawest the   [5]
Blue curtains of the sky, scatter thy silver dew
On every flower that shuts its sweet eyes
In timely sleep. Let thy west wind sleep on
The lake; speak silence with thy glimmering eyes,
And wash the dusk with silver. Soon, full soon,   [10]
Dost thou withdraw; then the wolf rages wide,
And the lion glares thro' the dun forest:
The fleeces of our flocks are cover'd with
Thy sacred dew: protect them with thine influence.   [14]

[Page] [6]

TO MORNING.

O HOLY virgin! clad in purest white,
Unlock heav'n's golden gates, and issue forth;
Awake the dawn that sleeps in heaven; let light
Rise from the chambers of the east, and bring
The honied dew that cometh on waking day.   [5]
O radiant morning, salute the sun,
Rouz'd like a huntsman to the chace; and, with
Thy buskin'd feet, appear upon our hills.   [8]

[Page] [7]

FAIR ELENOR.

THE bell struck one, and shook the silent tower;
The graves give up their dead: fair Elenor
Walk'd by the castle gate, and looked in.
A hollow groan ran thro' the dreary vaults.

She shriek'd aloud, and sunk upon the steps   [5]
On the cold stone her pale cheek. Sickly smells
Of death, issue as from a sepulchre,
And all is silent but the sighing vaults.

'Fair Elenor' l. 2: 'give' should be 'gave', as a contemporary hand noted in ink
in the margin of copy F.
    l. 6: 1783: 'cheeks'; the 's' is deleted in copies C, E, Q, S, V.

Chill death withdraws his hand, and she revives;
Amaz'd, she finds herself upon her feet,   [*10*]
And, like a ghost, thro' narrow passages
Walking, feeling the cold walls with her hands.

Fancy returns, and now she thinks of bones,
And grinning skulls, and corruptible death,
Wrap'd in his shroud; and now, fancies she hears   [*15*]
Deep sighs, and sees pale sickly ghosts gliding.

At length, no fancy, but reality
Distracts her. A rushing sound, and the feet
Of one that fled, approaches—Ellen stood,
Like a dumb statue, froze to stone with fear.   [*20*]

[*Page*] 8

The wretch approaches, crying, 'The deed is done;
'Take this, and send it by whom thou wilt send;
'It is my life—send it to Elenor:—
'He's dead, and howling after me for blood!

'Take this,' he cry'd; and thrust into her arms   [*25*]
A wet napkin, wrap'd about; then rush'd
Past, howling: she receiv'd into her arms
Pale death, and follow'd on the wings of fear.

They pass'd swift thro' the outer gate; the wretch,
Howling, leap'd o'er the wall into the moat,   [*30*]
Stifling in mud. Fair Ellen pass'd the bridge,
And heard a gloomy voice cry, 'Is it done?'

As the deer wounded Ellen flew over
The pathless plain; as the arrows that fly
By night; destruction flies, and strikes in darkness,   [*35*]
She fled from fear, till at her house arriv'd.

Her maids await her; on her bed she falls,
That bed of joy, where erst her lord hath press'd:
'Ah, woman's fear!' she cry'd; 'Ah, cursed duke!
'Ah, my dear lord! ah, wretched Elenor!   [*40*]

'My lord was like a flower upon the brows
'Of lusty May! Ah, life as frail as flower!

[*Page*] 9

'O ghastly death! withdraw thy cruel hand,
'Seek'st thou that flow'r to deck thy horrid temples?

'My lord was like a star, in highest heav'n   [*45*]
'Drawn down to earth by spells and wickedness;
'My lord was like the opening eyes of day,
'When western winds creep softly o'er the flowers:

'But he is darken'd; like the summer's noon,
'Clouded; fall'n like the stately tree, cut down;   [*50*]
'The breath of heaven dwelt among his leaves.
'O Elenor, weak woman, fill'd with woe!'

Thus having spoke, she raised up her head,
And saw the bloody napkin by her side,
Which in her arms she brought; and now, tenfold   [*55*]
More terrified, saw it unfold itself.

Her eyes were fix'd; the bloody cloth unfolds,
Disclosing to her sight the murder'd head
Of her dear lord, all ghastly pale, clotted
With gory blood; it groan'd, and thus it spake: [*60*]

'O Elenor, behold thy husband's head,
'Who, sleeping on the stones of yonder tower,
'Was 'reft of life by the accursed duke!
'A hired villain turn'd my sleep to death!

'O Elenor, beware the cursed duke,   [*65*]
'O give not him thy hand, now I am dead;
[*Page*] 10
'He seeks thy love; who, coward, in the night,
'Hired a villain to bereave my life.'

l. 61: 1783: 'I am thy husband's head'; 'I am' was erased and 'behold' neatly
written in its place in copies B, D, E, F, O, Q, S, W.
l. 68: is repeated in 'On H———ys Friendship' l. 6 (*Notebook*, p. 35 (p. 947 below)).

She sat with dead cold limbs, stiffen'd to stone;
She took the gory head up in her arms; [70]
She kiss'd the pale lips; she had no tears to shed;
She hugg'd it to her breast, and groan'd her last. [72]

❖—❖—❖—❖—❖—❖—❖—❖—❖—❖—❖—❖

SONG.

How sweet I roam'd from field to field,
    And tasted all the summer's pride,
'Till I the prince of love beheld,
    Who in the sunny beams did glide!

He shew'd me lilies for my hair, [5]
    And blushing roses for my brow;
He led me through his gardens fair,
    Where all his golden pleasures grow.

With sweet May dews my wings were wet,
    And Phœbus fir'd my vocal rage; [10]
He caught me in his silken net,
    And shut me in his golden cage.

He loves to sit and hear me sing,
    Then, laughing, sports and plays with me;
Then stretches out my golden wing, [15]
    And mocks my loss of liberty. [16]

[*Page*] [11]
SONG.

My silks and fine array,
    My smiles and languish'd air,
By love are driv'n away;
    And mournful lean Despair
Brings me yew to deck my grave: [5]
Such end true lovers have.

'Song [How sweet I roam'd]' l. 1: According to Malkin (1806), this poem 'was written before the age of fourteen', that is, by 1772 (*Blake Records*, 428).

His face is fair as heav'n,
  When springing buds unfold;
O why to him was't giv'n,
  Whose heart is wintry cold?   [*10*]
His breast is love's all worship'd tomb,
Where all love's pilgrims come.

Bring me an axe and spade,
  Bring me a winding sheet;
When I my grave have made,   [*15*]
  Let winds and tempests beat:
Then down I'll lie, as cold as clay.
True love doth pass away!   [*18*]

[*Page*] [12]
SONG.

LOVE and harmony combine,
And around our souls intwine,
While thy branches mix with mine,
And our roots together join.

Joys upon our branches sit,   [*5*]
Chirping loud, and singing sweet;
Like gentle streams beneath our feet
Innocence and virtue meet.

Thou the golden fruit dost bear,
I am clad in flowers fair;   [*10*]
Thy sweet boughs perfume the air,
And the turtle buildeth there.

There she sits and feeds her young,
Sweet I hear her mournful song;
And thy lovely leaves among,   [*15*]
There is love: I hear her tongue.

'Song [Love and harmony combine]' l. 16: 1783: 'her'; altered to 'his' in copies
C, Q, V.

There his charming nest doth lay,
There he sleeps the night away;
There he sports along the day,
And doth among our branches play.   [*20*]

[*Page*] [13]
SONG.

I LOVE the jocund dance,
  The softly-breathing song,
Where innocent eyes do glance,
  And where lisps the maiden's tongue.

I love the laughing vale,   [*5*]
  I love the echoing hill,
Where mirth does never fail,
  And the jolly swain laughs his fill.

I love the pleasant cot,
  I love the innocent bow'r,   [*10*]
Where white and brown is our lot,
  Or fruit in the mid-day hour.

I love the oaken seat,
  Beneath the oaken tree,
Where all the old villagers meet,   [*15*]
  And laugh our sports to see.

I love our neighbours all,
  But, Kitty, I better love thee;
And love them I ever shall;
  But thou art all to me.   [*20*]

[*Page*] [14]
SONG.

MEMORY, hither come,
  And tune your merry notes;
And, while upon the wind,
  Your music floats,

'Song [I love the jocund dance]' l. 8: 'his fill' is altered to 'still' in ink in a con-
temporary hand in the margin of copy F.

758

I'll pore upon the stream, [5]
Where sighing lovers dream,
And fish for fancies as they pass
Within the watery glass.

I'll drink of the clear stream,
    And hear the linnet's song; [10]
And there I'll lie and dream
    The day along:
And, when night comes, I'll go
    To places fit for woe;
Walking along the darken'd valley, [15]
    With silent Melancholy. [16]

[*Page*] (15)
MAD SONG.

THE wild winds weep,
    And the night is a-cold;
Come hither, Sleep,
    And my griefs infold:
But lo! the morning peeps [5]
    Over the eastern steeps,
And the rustling birds of dawn
The earth do scorn.

Lo! to the vault
    Of paved heaven, [10]
With sorrow fraught
    My notes are driven:
They strike the ear of night,
    Make weep the eyes of day;
They make mad the roaring winds, [15]
    And with tempests play.

'Mad Song' l. 4: 1783: 'unfold'; mended to 'infold' in copies B, E, F, O, Q, S, and W.
    l. 7: 1783: 'beds'; deleted and 'birds' inserted in its place in copies B, C, D, E, F, O, Q, S, T, V, W.

Like a fiend in a cloud
  With howling woe,
After night I do croud,
  And with night will go;   [20]
I turn my back to the east,
From whence comforts have increas'd;
For light doth seize my brain
With frantic pain.   [24]

[*Page*] (16)
SONG.

FRESH from the dewy hill, the merry year
Smiles on my head, and mounts his flaming car;
Round my young brows the laurel wreathes a shade,
And rising glories beam around my head.

My feet are wing'd, while o'er the dewy lawn,   [5]
I meet my maiden, risen like the morn:
Oh bless those holy feet, like angels' feet;
Oh bless those limbs, beaming with heav'nly light!

Like as an angel glitt'ring in the sky,
In times of innocence, and holy joy;   [10]
The joyful shepherd stops his grateful song,
To hear the music of an angel's tongue.

So when she speaks, the voice of Heaven I hear:
So when we walk, nothing impure comes near;
Each field seems Eden, and each calm retreat;   [15]
Each village seems the haunt of holy feet.

But that sweet village where my black-ey'd maid,
Closes her eyes in sleep beneath night's shade:
Whene'er I enter, more than mortal fire
Burns in my soul, and does my song inspire.   [20]

[*Page*] [17]

SONG.

WHEN early morn walks forth in sober grey;
Then to my black ey'd maid I haste away,
When evening sits beneath her dusky bow'r,
And gently sighs away the silent hour;
The village bell alarms, away I go;   [5]
And the vale darkens at my pensive woe.

To that sweet village, where my black ey'd maid
Doth drop a tear beneath the silent shade,
I turn my eyes; and, pensive as I go,
Curse my black stars, and bless my pleasing woe.   [10]

Oft when the summer sleeps among the trees,
Whisp'ring faint murmurs to the scanty breeze,
I walk the village round; if at her side
A youth doth walk in stolen joy and pride,
I curse my stars in bitter grief and woe,   [15]
That made my love so high, and me so low.

O should she e'er prove false, his limbs I'd tear,
And throw all pity on the burning air;
I'd curse bright fortune for my mixed lot,
And then I'd die in peace, and be forgot.   [20]

[*Page*] [18]

TO THE MUSES.

WHETHER on Ida's shady brow,
  Or in the chambers of the East,
The chambers of the sun, that now
  From antient melody have ceas'd;

Whether in Heav'n ye wander fair,   [5]
  Or the green corners of the earth,
Or the blue regions of the air,
  Where the melodious winds have birth;

'Song [When early morn walks forth in sober grey]' l. 10: 'black' is altered to
'ill' in ink in a contemporary hand in the margin of copy F.

'To the Muses' l. 6: Blake never corrected the misprinted 'greeen'.

Whether on crystal rocks ye rove,
   Beneath the bosom of the sea   [*10*]
Wand'ring in many a coral grove,
   Fair Nine, forsaking Poetry!

How have you left the antient love
   That bards of old enjoy'd in you!
The languid strings do scarcely move!   [*15*]
   The sound is forc'd, the notes are few! [*16*]

[*Page*] [19]
GWIN, KING OF NORWAY.

COME, Kings, and listen to my song,
   When Gwin, the son of Nore,
Over the nations of the North
   His cruel sceptre bore:

The Nobles of the land did feed   [*5*]
   Upon the hungry Poor;
They tear the poor man's lamb, and drive
   The needy from their door!

The land is desolate; our wives
   And children cry for bread;   [*10*]
Arise, and pull the tyrant down;
   Let Gwin be humbled.

l. 9: Blake never corrected the archaic 'chrystal' printed in the text to the standard 18th-century spelling 'crystal'.

l. 13: Cf. *Notebook* p. 49 (p. 1060), ll. 49–52: 'Come Ye forth Fallen Fiends of Heavnly birth That have forgot your Ancient Love And driven away my trembling Dove'.

'Gwin, King of Norway' l. 8: Cf. Chatterton's 'Bristowe Tragedie', in which Sir Charles Bawdin says that his noble father taught him

     To feede the hungrie poore,
   Ne lett mye servants dryve awaie
     The hungrie fromme my doore

(*Poems*, supposed to have been written . . . by Thomas Rowley, and Others [1778], 52; Blake owned this edition).

Gordred the giant rous'd himself
   From sleeping in his cave;
He shook the hills, and in the clouds   [*15*]
   The troubl'd banners wave.

Beneath them roll'd, like tempests black,
   The num'rous sons of blood;
Like lions' whelps, roaring abroad,
   Seeking their nightly food.   [*20*]

[*Page*] 20
Down Bleron's hills they dreadful rush,
   Their cry ascends the clouds;
The trampling horse, and clanging arms
   Like rushing mighty floods!

Their wives and children, weeping loud,   [*25*]
   Follow in wild array,
Howling like ghosts, furious as wolves
   In the bleak wintry day.

'Pull down the tyrant to the dust,
   'Let Gwin be humbled,'   [*30*]
They cry; 'and let ten thousand lives
   'Pay for the tyrant's head.'

From tow'r to tow'r the watchmen cry,
   'O Gwyn, the son of Nore,
'Arouse thyself! the nations black,   [*35*]
   'Like clouds, come rolling o'er!'

Gwin rear'd his shield, his palace shakes,
   His chiefs come rushing round;
Each, like an awful thunder cloud,
   With voice of solemn sound: [*40*]

   ll. 23–4: 'and clanging arms Like rushing' is deleted in copy W and '[Th]eir hauberks / [*word trimmed off*; ?(flas)h;] the tram / [p]ling horse / Rush on like mighty floods' inserted in an un-Blakelike hand.

Like reared stones around a grave
   They stand around the King;
Then suddenly each seiz'd his spear,
   And clashing steel does ring.

[*Page*] 21

The husbandman does leave his plow,   [*45*]
   To wade thro' fields of gore;
The merchant binds his brows in steel,
   And leaves the trading shore:

The shepherd leaves his mellow pipe,
   And sounds the trumpet shrill;   [*50*]
The workman throws his hammer down
   To heave the bloody bill.

Like the tall ghost of Barraton,
   Who sports in stormy sky,
Gwin leads his host as black as night,   [*55*]
   When pestilence does fly.

With horses and with chariots—
   And all his spearmen bold,
March to the sound of mournful song,
   Like clouds around him roll'd.   [*60*]

Gwin lifts his hand—the nations halt;
   'Prepare for war,' he cries—
Gordred appears!—his frowning brow
   Troubles our northern skies.

The armies stand, like balances   [*65*]
   Held in th' Almighty's hand;—
'Gwin, thou hast filld thy measure up,
   'Thou'rt swept from out the land.'

[*Page*] 22

And now the raging armies rush'd,
   Like warring mighty seas;   [*70*]

l. 56: The full stop may be a typographical error.

The Heav'ns are shook with roaring war,
  The dust ascends the skies!

Earth smokes with blood, and groans, and shakes,
  To drink her children's gore,
A sea of blood; nor can the eye   [75]
  See to the trembling shore!

And on the verge of this wild sea
  Famine and death doth cry;
The cries of women and of babes
  Over the field doth fly.   [80]

The King is seen raging afar,
  With all his men of might;
Like blazing comets, scattering death
  Thro' the red fev'rous night.

Beneath his arm like sheep they die,   [85]
  And groan upon the plain;
The battle faints, and bloody men
  Fight upon hills of slain.

Now death is sick, and riven men
  Labour and toil for life;   [90]
Steed rolls on steed, and shield on shield,
  Sunk in this sea of strife!

                   [*Page*] 23

The god of war is drunk with blood,
  The earth doth faint and fail;
The stench of blood makes sick the heav'ns;   [95]
  Ghosts glut the throat of hell!

O what have Kings to answer for,
  Before that awful throne!
When thousand deaths for vengeance cry,
  And ghosts accusing groan!   [100]

ll. 78, 80: Blake never corrected 'doth' to 'do'.

Like blazing comets in the sky,
  That shake the stars of light,
Which drop like fruit unto the earth,
  Thro' the fierce burning night;

Like these did Gwin and Gordred meet,   [*10*
  And the first blow decides;
Down from the brow unto the breast
  Gordred his head divides!

Gwin fell; the Sons of Norway fled,
  All that remain'd alive;   [*11*
The rest did fill the vale of death,
  For them the eagles strive.

The river Dorman roll'd their blood
  Into the northern sea;
Who mourn'd his sons, and overwhelm'd   [*11*
  The pleasant south country.   [*11*

[*Page*] [24]

AN

IMITATION of SPENCER.

GOLDEN Apollo, that thro' heaven wide
  Scatter'st the rays of light, and truth's beams!
In lucent words my darkling verses dight,
  And wash my earthy mind in thy clear streams,
  That wisdom may descend in fairy dreams: [*5*]
All while the jocund hours in thy train
Scatter their fancies at thy poet's feet;
  And when thou yields to night thy wide domain,

'Imitation of Spencer': Blake never corrected the spelling of his title or running
head to 'Spenser'.
  l. 4: 'And' is deleted and 'thou' inserted in ink in a contemporary hand in copy
F, to make it read 'wash thou my earthy mind . . .'.
  l. 8: 'yields' was correctly emended to 'yield'st' in ink in a contemporary hand
in copy F.

Let rays of truth enlight his sleeping brain.

For brutish Pan in vain might thee assay   [*10*]
  With tinkling sounds to dash thy nervous verse,
Sound without sense; yet in his rude affray,
    (For ignorance is Folly's leesing nurse,
    And love of Folly needs none other curse;)
Midas the praise hath gain'd of lengthen'd ears,   [*15*]
  For which himself might deem him ne'er the worse
  To sit in council with his modern peers,
And judge of tinkling rhimes, and elegances terse.

And thou, Mercurius, that with winged brow
  Dost mount aloft into the yielding sky,   [*20*]
And thro' Heav'n's halls thy airy flight dost throw,

                                        [*Page*] 25

Entering with holy feet to where on high
Jove weighs the counsel of futurity;
  Then, laden with eternal fate, dost go
Down, like a falling star, from autumn sky,   [*25*]
And o'er the surface of the silent deep dost fly.

  If thou arrivest at the sandy shore,
Where nought but envious hissing adders dwell,
  Thy golden rod, thrown on the dusty floor,
Can charm to harmony with potent spell;   [*30*]
Such is sweet Eloquence, that does dispel
  Envy and Hate, that thirst for human gore:
And cause in sweet society to dwell
Vile savage minds that lurk in lonely cell.

  O Mercury, assist my lab'ring sense,   [*35*]
That round the circle of the world wou'd fly!
  As the wing'd eagle scorns the tow'ry fence
Of Alpine hills round his high aery,

l. 14: The printed 's' of 'others' is deleted in copies T and V.
l. 15: The printed 'cares' (for 'ears') is emended in ink to 'Eares' and 'eares' in the text of copies F, Q, and T and to 'eares' in the margin in a contemporary hand in copy F. The change is a great improvement in terms of rhyme and sense.

And searches thro' the corners of the sky,
  Sports in the clouds to hear the thunder's sound,   [*40*]
And see the winged lightnings as they fly,
  Then, bosom'd in an amber cloud, around
Plumes his wide wings, and seeks Sol's palace high.

And thou, O warrior, maid invincible,
Arm'd with the terrors of Almighty Jove!   [*45*]
  Pallas, Minerva, maiden terrible,
Lov'st thou to walk the peaceful solemn grove,
  In solemn gloom of branches interwove?

[*Page*] 26

Or bear'st thy Egis o'er the burning field,
  Where, like the sea, the waves of battle move?   [*50*]
Or have thy soft piteous eyes beheld
  The weary wanderer thro' the desert rove?
Or does th' afflicted man thy heav'nly bosom move?   [*53*]

BLIND-MAN'S BUFF.

WHEN silver snow decks Susan's cloaths,
And jewel hangs at th' shepherd's nose,
The blushing bank is all my care,
With hearth so red, and walls so fair;
'Heap the sea-coal; come, heap it higher,   [*5*]
'The oaken log lay on the fire:'
The well-wash'd stools, a circling row,
With lad and lass, how fair the show!
The merry can of nut-brown ale,
The laughing jest, the love-sick tale,   [*10*]
'Till tir'd of chat, the game begins,
The lasses prick the lads with pins;
Roger from Dolly twitch'd the stool,
She falling, kiss'd the ground, poor fool!

l. 44: 'warrior, maid invincible' was altered to 'warrior maid, invincible' in copy Q.

'Blind-Man's Buff' ll. 1–2 are adapted in 'Song 3ᵈ by an old Shepherd' (1787) ll. 1–2 (p. 901).

l. 1: 1783 capitalizes 'Snow', probably erroneously.

She blush'd so red, with side-long glance   [*15*]
At hob-nail Dick, who griev'd the chance.
But now for Blind-man's Buff they call;
Of each incumbrance clear the hall—
Jenny her silken 'kerchief folds,
And blear-ey'd Will the black lot holds;   [*20*]

[*Page*] 27

Now laughing, stops, with 'Silence! hush!'
And Peggy Pout gives Sam a push.——
The Blind-man's arms, extended wide,
Sam slips between;—'O woe betide
Thee, clumsy Will!'—but titt'ring Kate   [*25*]
Is pen'd up in the corner strait!
And now Will's eyes beheld the play,
He thought his face was t'other way.——
'Now, Kitty, now; what chance hast thou,
'Roger so near thee, Trips; I vow!'   [*30*]
She catches him—then Roger ties
His own head up—but not his eyes;
For thro' the slender cloth he sees,
And runs at Sam, who slips with ease
His clumsy hold; and, dodging round,   [*35*]
Sukey is tumbled on the ground!——
'See what it is to play unfair!
'Where cheating is, there's mischief there.'
But Roger still pursues the chace,—
'He sees! he sees!' cries softly Grace;   [*40*]
'O Roger, thou, unskill'd in art,
'Must, surer bound, go thro' thy part!'
Now Kitty, pert, repeats the rhymes,
And Roger turns him round three times;
Then pauses ere he starts—but Dick   [*45*]
Was mischief bent upon a trick:
Down on his hands and knees he lay,
Directly in the Blind-man's way—
Then cries out, 'Hem!' Hodge heard, and ran
With hood-wink'd chance—sure of his man;   [*50*]

l. 49: 'Hodge' is apparently the same as Roger.

But down he came.—Alas, how frail
Our best of hopes, how soon they fail!
With crimson drops he stains the ground,
Confusion startles all around!
Poor piteous Dick supports his head,
And fain would cure the hurt he made;
But Kitty hasted with a key,
And down his back they strait convey
The cold relief—the blood is stay'd,
And Hodge again holds up his head.
Such are the fortunes of the game,
And those who play should stop the same
By wholesome laws; such as all those
Who on the blinded man impos*e*,
Stand in his stead; as long a-gone
When men were first a nation grown,
Lawless they liv'd—till wantonness
And liberty began t'increase;
And one man lay in another's way,
Then laws were made to keep fair play.

[*55*]

[*60*]

[*65*]

[*70*]

[*Page*] [29]

KING EDWARD THE THIRD.

PERSONS.

King Edward.	*Sir Walter Manny.*
The Black Prince.	*Lord Audley.*
Queen Philippa.	*Lord Percy.*
Duke of Clarence.	*Bishop.*
Sir John Chandos.	*William,* Dagworth's Man.
Sir Thomas Dagworth.	*Peter Blunt,* a common Soldier.[1]

ll. 64–5: The printed text, 'impose. Stand in his stead as' was persuasively altered in copy Q to 'impose, Stand in his stead; as'.

l. 66: In the 1783 text, the line ends, probably erroneously, with a semicolon.

'Edward III' [1] The Minstrel and the Warriors of Scene vi are omitted from the Dramatis Personae.

SCENE [*i*],

The Coast of France, King Edward and Nobles.[2] *The Army.*

King.

O THOU, to whose fury the nations are
But as dust! maintain thy servant's right.
Without thine aid, the twisted mail, and spear,
And forged helm, and shield of seven times beaten brass,
Are idle trophies of the vanquisher.   [*5*]
When confusion rages, when the field is in a flame,
When the cries of blood tear horror from heav'n,
And yelling death runs up and down the ranks,
Let Liberty, the charter'd right of Englishmen,
Won by our fathers in many a glorious field,   [*10*]

[*Page*] 30

Enerve my soldiers; let Liberty
Blaze in each countenance, and fire the battle.
The enemy fight in chains, invisible chains, but heavy;
Their minds are fetter'd; then how can they be free,
While, like the mounting flame,   [*15*]
We spring to battle o'er the floods of death?
And these fair youths, the flow'r of England,
Vent'ring their lives in my most righteous cause,
O sheathe their hearts with triple steel, that they
May emulate their fathers' virtues.   [*20*]
And thou, my son, be strong; thou fightest for a crown
That death can never ravish from thy brow,
A crown of glory: but from thy very dust
Shall beam a radiance, to fire the breasts
Of youth unborn! Our names are written equal   [*25*]
In fame's wide trophied hall; 'tis ours to gild
The letters, and to make them shine with gold
That never tarnishes: whether Third Edward,
Or the Prince of Wales, or Montacute, or Mortimer,
Or ev'n the least by birth, shall gain the brightest fame,   [*30*]
Is in his hand to whom all men are equal.

---

[2] The printed text had, eccentrically, '*Nobles before it*'; '*before it*' is deleted in copy S.

The world of men are like the num'rous stars,
That beam and twinkle in the depth of night,
Each clad in glory according to his sphere;—
But we, that wander from our native seats,   [*35*]
And beam forth lustre on a darkling world,
Grow larger as we advance! and some perhaps
The most obscure at home, that scarce were seen

                                        [*Page*] 31

To twinkle in their sphere, may so advance,
That the astonish'd world, with up-turn'd eyes,   [*40*]
Regardless of the moon, and those that once were bright,
Stand only for to gaze upon their splendor!

[*He here knights the Prince, and other young Nobles.*][3]

Now let us take a just revenge for those
Brave Lords, who fell beneath the bloody axe
At Paris. Thanks, noble Harcourt, for 'twas   [*45*]
By your advice we landed here in Brittany—
A country not yet sown with destruction,
And where the fiery whirlwind of swift war
Has not yet swept its desolating wing.——
Into three parties we divide by day,   [*50*]
And separate march, but join again at night:
Each knows his rank, and Heav'n marshall all.   [*52*]

                                            [*Exeunt.*

SCENE [*ii*], *English Court*; *Lionel, Duke of Clarence*;
Queen Philippa, Lords, Bishop, &c.

Clarence.

MY Lords, I have, by the advice of her
Whom I am doubly bound to obey, my Parent
And my Sovereign, call'd you together.
My task is great, my burden heavier than
My unfledg'd years;   [*5*]
Yet, with your kind assistance, Lords, I hope
England shall dwell in peace; that while my father
Toils in his wars, and turns his eyes on this
His native shore, and sees commerce fly round

---

[3] The stage direction after l. 42 is Blake's.

[*Page*] 32

With his white wings, and sees his golden London,   [*10*]
And her silver Thames, throng'd with shining spires
And corded ships; her merchants buzzing round
Like summer bees, and all the golden cities
In his land, overflowing with honey,
Glory may not be dimm'd with clouds of care.   [*15*]
Say, Lords, should not our thoughts be first to commerce?
My Lord Bishop, you would recommend us agriculture?
  Bishop. Sweet Prince! the arts of peace are great,
And no less glorious than those of war,
Perhaps more glorious in the ph[*i*]losophic mind.   [*20*]
When I sit at my home, a private man,
My thoughts are on my gardens, and my fields,
How to employ the hand that lacketh bread.
If Industry is in my diocese,
Religion will flourish; each man's heart   [*25*]
Is cultivated, and will bring forth fruit:
This is my private duty and my pleasure.
But as I sit in council with my prince,
My thoughts take in the gen'ral good of the whole,
And England is the land favour'd by Commerce;   [*30*]
For Commerce, tho' the child of Agriculture,
Fosters his parent, who else must sweat and toil,
And gain but scanty fare. Then, my dear Lord,
Be England's trade our care; and we, as tradesmen,
Looking to the gain of this our native land.   [*35*]

[*Page*] 33

  Clar. O my good Lord, true wisdom drops like honey
From your tongue, as from a worship'd oak!
Forgive, my Lords, my talkative youth, that speaks
Not merely what my narrow observation has
Pick'd up, but what I have concluded from your lessons: [*40*]
Now, by the Queen's advice, I ask your leave
To dine to-morrow with the Mayor of London:
If I obtain your leave, I have another boon
To ask, which is, the favour of your company;
I fear Lord Percy will not give me leave.   [*45*]
  Percy. Dear Sir, a prince should always keep his state,

773

And grant his favours with a sparing hand,
Or they are never rightly valued.
These are my thoughts, yet it were best to go;
But keep a proper dignity, for now   [*50*]
You represent the sacred person of
Your father; 'tis with princes as 'tis with the sun,
If not sometimes o'er-clouded, we grow weary
Of his officious glory.
   Clar. Then you will give me leave to shine sometimes, [*55*]
My Lord?
   Lord. Thou hast a gallant spirit, which I fear
Will be imposed on by the closer sort!   [*Aside.*
   Clar. Well, I'll endeavour to take
Lord Percy's advice; I have been used so much   [*60*]
To dignity, that I'm sick on't.

[*Page*] 34

   Queen Phil. Fie, Fie, Lord Clarence; you proceed not to
      business,
But speak of your own pleasures.
I hope their Lordships will excuse your giddiness.
   Clar. My Lords, the French have fitted out many   [*65*]
Small ships of war, that, like to ravening wolves,
Infest our English seas, devouring all
Our burden'd vessels, spoiling our naval flocks.
The merchants do complain, and beg our aid.
   Percy. The merchants are rich enough;   [*70*]
Can they not help themselves?
   Bish. They can, and may; but how to gain their will,
Requires our countenance and help.
   Percy. When that they find they must, my Lord, they will:
Let them but suffer awhile, and you shall see   [*75*]
They will bestir themselves.
   Bish. Lord Percy cannot mean that we should suffer
This disgrace; if so, we are not sovereigns
Of the sea; our right, that Heaven gave
To England, when at the birth of nature   [*80*]
She was seated in the deep, the Ocean ceas'd
His mighty roar; and, fawning, play'd around

Her snowy feet, and own'd his awful Queen.
Lord Percy, if the heart is sick, the head
Must be aggriev'd; if but one member suffer,   [*85*]
The heart doth fail. You say, my Lord, the merchants
Can, if they will, defend themselves against

[*Page*] 35

These rovers: this is a noble scheme,
Worthy the brave Lord Percy, and as worthy
His generous aid to put it into practice.   [*90*]
  Percy. Lord Bishop, what was rash in me, is wise
In you; I dare not own the plan. 'Tis not
Mine. Yet will I, if you please,
Quickly to the Lord Mayor, and work him onward
To this most glorious voyage, on which cast   [*95*]
I'll set my whole estate.
But we will bring these Gallic rovers under.
  Queen Phil. Thanks, brave Lord Percy; you have the
    thanks
Of England's Queen, and will, ere long, of England.   [*99*]
                                                    [*Exeunt.*

        S C E N E [*iii*], *At Cressey.*[1] *Sir Thomas Dagworth and*
                    Lord Audley, meeting.

  Aud. Good morrow, brave Sir Thomas; the bright morn
Smiles on our army, and the gallant sun
Springs from the hills like a young hero
Into the battle, shaking his golden locks
Exultingly; this is a promising day.   [*5*]
  Dagw. Why, my Lord Audley, I don't know.
Give me your hand, and now I'll tell you what
I think you do not know—Edward's afraid of Philip.
  Aud. Ha, Ha, Sir Thomas! you but joke;
[*Page*] 36

Did you e'er see him fear? At Blanchetaque,   [*10*]

Scene ii   ll. 96–7: Perhaps the intention was: 'I'll set my whole estate That we
will bring these Gallic rovers under'.
  Scene iii   [1] *'Cressey'* should be *'Cressy'*.
    l. 10: 1783: 'ere'.
    l. 10: Blanchetaque is a ford on the Somme near Abbeville where Edward
forced a triumphant crossing on 24 August 1347, just before the Battle of Crécy.

When almost singly he drove six thousand
French from the ford, did he fear then?
 Dagw. Yes, fear; that made him fight so.
 Aud. By the same reason I might say, 'tis fear
That makes you fight.
 Dagw. Mayhap you may; look upon Edward's face— [*15*]
No one can say he fears. But when he turns
His back, then I will say it to his face,
He is afraid; he makes us all afraid.
I cannot bear the enemy at my back.
Now here we are at Cressy; where, to-morrow, [*20*]
To-morrow we shall know. I say, Lord Audley,
That Edward runs away from Philip.
 Aud. Perhaps you think the Prince too is afraid?
 Dagw. No; God forbid! I'm sure he is not—
He is a young lion. O I have seen him fight, [*25*]
And give command, and lightning has flashed
From his eyes across the field; I have seen him
Shake hands with death, and strike a bargain for
The enemy; he has danc'd in the field
Of battle, like the youth at morrice play. [*30*]
I'm sure he's not afraid, nor Warwick, nor none,
None of us but me; and I am very much afraid.
 Aud. Are you afraid too, Sir Thomas?
I believe that as much as I believe
The King's afraid; but what are you afraid of? [*35*]

               [*Page*] 37

 Dagw. Of having my back laid open; we turn
Our backs to the fire, till we shall burn our skirts.
 Aud. And this, Sir Thomas, you call fear? Your fear
Is of a different kind then from the King's;
He fears to turn his face, and you to turn your back.— [*40*]
I do not think, Sir Thomas, you know what fear is.

    Enter Sir John Chandos.

 Chand. Good morrow, Generals; I give you joy:
Welcome to the fields of Cressy. Here we stop,
And wait for Philip.
 Dagw. I hope so. [*45*]

Aud. There, Sir Thomas; do you call that fear?
Dagw. I don't know; perhaps he takes it by fits.
Why, noble Chandos, look you here—
One rotten sheep spoils the whole flock;
And if the bell-weather is tainted, I wish   [*50*]
The Prince may not catch the distemper too.
Chand. Distemper, Sir Thomas! what distemper?
I have not heard.
Dagw. Why, Chandos, you are a wise man,
I know you understand me; a distemper   [*55*]
The King caught here in France of running away.
Aud. Sir Thomas, you say, you have caught it too.
[*Page*] 38
Dag. And so will the whole army; 'tis very catching,
For when the coward runs, the brave man totters.
Perhaps the air of the country is the cause.—   [*60*]
I feel it coming upon me, so I strive against it;
You yet are whole, but after a few more
Retreats, we all shall know how to retreat
Better than fight.—To be plain, I think retreating
Too often, takes away a soldier's courage.   [*65*]
Chand. Here comes the King himself; tell him your
    thoughts
Plainly, Sir Thomas.
Dagw. I've told him before, but his disorder
Makes him deaf.

      Enter King Edward and Black Prince.

King. Good morrow, Generals; when English courage
    fails,   [*70*]
Down goes our right to France;   `
But we are conquerors every where; nothing
Can stand our soldiers; each man is worthy
Of a triumph. Such an army of heroes
Ne'er shouted to the Heav'ns, nor shook the field.   [*75*]
Edward, my son, thou art
Most happy, having such command; the man
Were base who were not fir'd to deeds
Above heroic, having such examples.

Prince. Sire! with respect and deference I look [*80*]
Upon such noble souls, and wish myself
Worthy the high command that Heaven and you

[*Page*] 39

Have given me. When I have seen the field glow,
And in each countenance the soul of war
Curb'd by the manliest reason, I have been wing'd [*85*]
With certain victory; and 'tis my boast,
And shall be still my glory. I was inspir'd
By these brave troops.
    Dagw. Your Grace had better make
Them all Generals. [*90*]
    King. Sir Thomas Dagworth, you must have your joke,
And shall, while you can fight as you did at
The Ford.
    Dagw. I have a small petition to your Majesty.
    King. What can Sir Thomas Dagworth ask, that Edward [*95*]
Can refuse?
    Dagw. I hope your Majesty cannot refuse so great
A trifle; I've gilt your cause with my best blood,
And would again, were I not forbid
By him whom I am bound to obey: my hands [*100*]
Are tied up, my courage shrunk and wither'd,
My sinews slacken'd, and my voice scarce heard;
Therefore I beg I may return to England.
    King. I know not what you could have ask'd, Sir Thomas,
That I would not have sooner parted with [*105*]
Than such a soldier as you have been, and such a friend;
Nay, I will know the most remote particulars

[*Page*] 40

Of this your strange petition; that, if I can,
I still may keep you here.
    Dagw. Here on the fields of Cressy we are settled, [*110*]
'Till Philip springs the tim'rous covey again.
The Wolf is hunted down by causeless fear;
The Lion flees, and fear usurps his heart;
Startled, astonish'd at the clam'rous Cock;
The Eagle, that doth gaze upon the sun, [*115*]

Fears the small fire that plays about the fen;
If, at this moment of their idle fear,
The Dog doth seize the Wolf, the Forester the Lion,
The Negro in the crevice of the rock,
Doth seize the soaring Eagle; undone by flight,   [*120*]
They tame submit: such the effect flight has
On noble souls. Now hear its opposite:
The tim'rous Stag starts from the thicket wild,
The fearful Crane springs from the splashy fen,
The shining Snake glides o'er the bending grass,   [*125*]
The Stag turns head! and bays the crying Hounds;
The Crane o'ertaken, fighteth with the Hawk;
The Snake doth turn, and bite the padding foot;
And, if your Majesty's afraid of Philip,
You are more like a Lion than a Crane: [*130*]
Therefore I beg I may return to England.
   King. Sir Thomas, now I understand your mirth,
Which often plays with Wisdom for its pastime,
And brings good counsel from the breast of laughter,

                                           [*Page*] 41
I hope you'll stay, and see us fight this battle,   [*135*]
And reap rich harvest in the fields of Cressy;
Then go to England, tell them how we fight,
And set all hearts on fire to be with us.
Philip is plum'd, and thinks we flee from him,
Else he would never dare to attack us. Now,   [*140*]
Now the quarry's set! and Death doth sport
In the bright sunshine of this fatal day.
   Dagw. Now my heart dances, and I am as light
As the young bridegroom going to be married.
Now must I to my soldiers, get them ready,   [*145*]
Furbish our armours bright, new plume our helms,
And we will sing, like the young housewives busied
In the dairy; my feet are wing'd, but not
For flight, an please your grace.
   King. If all my soldiers are as pleas'd as you,   [*150*]
'Twill be a gallant thing to fight or die;
Then I can never be afraid of Philip.
   Dagw. A raw-bon'd fellow t'other day pass'd by me;

I told him to put off his hungry looks—
He answer'd me, 'I hunger for another battle.'   [*155*
I saw a little Welchman with a fiery face;
I told him he look'd like a candle half
Burn'd out; he answer'd, he was 'pig enough
'To light another pattle.' Last night, beneath
The moon I walk'd abroad, when all had pitch'd   [*160*
Their tents, and all were still,
I heard a blooming youth singing a song
He had compos'd, and at each pause he wip'd

[*Page*] 42

His dropping eyes. The ditty was, 'if he
'Return'd victorious, he should wed a maiden   [*165*
'Fairer than snow, and rich as midsummer.'
Another wept, and wish'd health to his father.
I chid them both, but gave them noble hopes.
These are the minds that glory in the battle,
And leap and dance to hear the trumpet sound.   [*170*
　　King. Sir Thomas Dagworth, be thou near our person;
Thy heart is richer than the vales of France:
I will not part with such a man as thee.
If Philip came arm'd in the ribs of death,
And shook his mortal dart against my head,   [*175*
Thoud'st laugh his fury into nerveless shame!
Go now, for thou art suited to the work,
Throughout the camp; enflame the timorous,
Blow up the sluggish into ardour, and
Confirm the strong with strength, the weak inspire,   [*180*
And wing their brows with hope and expectation:
Then to our tent return, and meet to council.
　　　　　　　　　　　　　　　　[*Exit Dagworth.*
　　Chand. That man's a hero in his closet, and more
A hero to the servants of his house
Than to the gaping world; he carries windows   [*185*
In that enlarged breast of his, that all
May see what's done within.
　　Prince. He is a genuine Englishman, my Chandos,
And hath the spirit of Liberty within him.

Forgive my prejudice, Sir John; I think   [*190*]
My Englishmen the bravest people on
The face of the earth.
   Chand. Courage, my Lord, proceeds from self-dependence;
Teach man to think he's a free agent,
Give but a slave his liberty, he'll shake   [*195*]
Off sloth, and build himself a hut, and hedge
A spot of ground; this he'll defend; 'tis his
By right of nature: thus set in action,
He will still move onward to plan conveniences,
'Till glory fires his breast to enlarge his castle,   [*200*]
While the poor slave drudges all day, in hope
To rest at night.
   King. O Liberty, how glorious art thou!
I see thee hov'ring o'er my army, with
Thy wide-stretch'd plumes; I see thee   [*205*]
Lead them on to battle;
I see thee blow thy golden trumpet, while
Thy sons shout the strong shout of victory!
O noble Chandos! think thyself a gardener,
My son a vine, which I commit unto   [*210*]
Thy care; prune all extravagant shoots, and guide
Th' ambitious tendrils in the paths of wisdom;
Water him with thy advice, and Heav'n
Rain fresh'ning dew upon his branches. And,
O Edward, my dear son! learn to think lowly of   [*215*]
Thyself, as we may all each prefer other—
'Tis the best policy, and 'tis our duty.
                     [*Exit*² *King Edward.*

   Prince. And may our duty, Chandos, be our
     pleasure—
Now we are alone, Sir John, I will unburden,
And breathe my hopes into the burning air,   [*220*]
Where thousand deaths are posting up and down,
Commission'd to this fatal field of Cressy;

1783: '*Exeunt*'.

781

Methinks I see them arm my gallant soldiers,
And gird the sword upon each thigh, and fit
Each shining helm, and string each stubborn bow,   [*225*]
And dance to the neighing of our steed;.
Methinks the shout begins, the battle burns;
Methinks I see them perch on English crests,
And roar the wild flame of fierce war, upon
The thronged enemy! In truth, I am too full;   [*230*]
It is my sin to love the noise of war.
Chandos, thou seest my weakness; strong nature
Will bend or break us; my blood, like a spring-tide,
Does rise so high, to overflow all bounds
Of moderation; while Reason, in his   [*235*]
Frail bark, can see no shore or bound for vast
Ambition. Come, take the helm, my Chandos,
That my full-blown sails overset me not
In the wild tempest; condemn my 'ventrous youth,
That plays with danger, as the innocent child,   [*240*]
Unthinking, plays upon the viper's den:
I am a coward, in my reason, Chandos.

[*Page*] 45

   Chand. You are a man, my prince, and a brave man,
If I can judge of actions; but your heat
Is the effect of youth, and want of use;   [*245*]
Use makes the armed field and noisy war
Pass over as a summer cloud, unregarded,
Or but expected as a thing of course.
Age is contemplative; each rolling year
Brings forth fruit to the mind's treasure-house;   [*250*]
While vacant youth doth crave and seek about
Within itself, and findeth discontent:
Then, tir'd of thought, impatient takes the wing,
Seizes the fruits of time, attacks experience,
Roams round vast Nature's forest, where no bounds   [*255*]
Are set, the swiftest may have room, the strongest
Find prey; till tir'd at length, sated and tired
With the changing sameness, old variety,

l. 235: The printed 'her' is changed to 'his' in copies T and V.

We sit us down, and view our former joys
With distaste and dislike. [*260*]
   Prince. Then if we must tug for experience,
Let us not fear to beat round Nature's wilds,
And rouze the strongest prey; then if we fall,
We fall with glory; I know the wolf
Is dangerous to fight, not good for food, [*265*]
Nor is the hide a comely vestment; so
We have our battle for our pains. I know
That youth has need of age to point fit prey,
And oft the stander-by shall steal the fruit
Of th' other's labour. This is philosophy; [*270*]
These are the tricks of the world; but the pure soul

[*Page*] 46

Shall mount on native wings, disdaining
Little sport, and cut a path into the heaven of glory,
Leaving a track of light for men to wonder at.
I'm glad my father does not hear me talk; [*275*]
You can find friendly excuses for me, Chandos;
But do you not think, Sir John, that if it please
Th' Almighty to stretch out my span of life,
I shall with pleasure view a glorious action,
Which my youth master'd. [*280*]
   Chand. Considerate age, my Lord, views motives,
And not acts; when neither warbling voice,
Nor trilling pipe is heard, nor pleasure sits
With trembling age; the voice of Conscience then,
Sweeter than music in a summer's eve, [*285*]
Shall warble round the snowy head, and keep
Sweet symphony to feather'd angels, sitting
As guardians round your chair; then shall the pulse
Beat slow, and taste, and touch, and sight, and sound, and
     smell,
That sing and dance round Reason's fine-wrought throne, [*290*]
Shall flee away, and leave him all forlorn;
Yet not forlorn if Conscience is his friend. [*292*]
                   [*Exeunt.*

l. 291: The printed 'them' is changed to 'him' in copies T and V.

[*Page*] 47

SCENE [*iv*] *in Sir Thomas Dagworth's Tent. Dagworth and*
William his Man.

Dagw. Bring hither my armour, William;
Ambition is the growth of ev'ry clime.
Will. Does it grow in England, Sir?
Dagw. Aye, it grows most in lands most cultivated.
Will. Then it grows most in France; the vines here   [*5*]
Are finer than any we have in England.
Dagw. Aye, but the oaks are not.
Will. What is the tree you mentioned? I don't think
I ever saw it.
Dagw. Ambition.   [*10*]
Will. Is it a little creeping root that grows in ditches?
Dagw. Thou dost not understand me, William.
It is a root that grows in every breast;
Ambition is the desire or passion that one man
Has to get before another, in any pursuit after glory;   [*15*]
But I don't think you have any of it.   [*16*]
Will. Yes, I have; I have a great ambition to know every
thing, Sir.
Dagw. But when our first ideas are wrong, what follows
must all be wrong of course; 'tis best to know a little, and to
know that little aright.
Will. Then, Sir, I should be glad to know if it was not am-
bition that brought over our King to France to fight for his
right?

[*Page*] 48

Dagw. Tho' the knowledge of that will not profit thee much,
yet I will tell you that it was ambition.
Will. Then if ambition is a sin, we are all guilty in coming
with him, and in fighting for him.
Dagw. Now, William, thou dost thrust the question home;
but I must tell you, that guilt being an act of the mind, none
are guilty but those whose minds are prompted by that same
ambition.
Will. Now I always thought, that a man might be guilty of
doing wrong, without knowing it was wrong.

784

Dagw. Thou art a natural philosopher, and knowest truth by instinct; while reason runs aground, as we have run our argument. Only remember, William, all have it in their power to know the motives of their own actions, and 'tis a sin to act without some reason.

Will. And whoever acts without reason, may do a great deal of harm without knowing it.

Dagw. Thou art an endless moralist.

Will. Now there's a story come into my head, that I will tell your honour, if you'll give me leave.

Dagw. No, William, save it till another time; this is no time for story-telling; but here comes one who is as entertaining as a good story.

[*Page*] 49

Enter Peter Blunt.

Peter. Yonder's a musician going to play before the King; it's a new song about the French and English,[1] and the Prince has made the minstrel a 'squire, and given him I don't know what, and I can't tell whether he don't mention us all one by one; and he is to write another about all us that are to die, that we may be remembered in Old England, for all our blood and bones are in France; and a great deal more that we shall all hear by and by; and I came to tell your honour, because you love to hear war-songs.

Dagw. And who is this minstrel, Peter, do'st know?

Peter. O aye, I forgot to tell that; he has got the same name as Sir John Chandos, that the prince is always with—the wise man, that knows us all as well as your honour, only e'nt so good natur'd.

Dagw. I thank you, Peter, for your information, but not for your compliment, which is not true; there's as much difference between him and me, as between glittering sand and fruitful mold; or shining glass and a wrought diamond, set in rich gold, and fitted to the finger of an emperor: such is that worthy Dhandos.

Scene iv [1] Perhaps the 'war-song' referred to is the separately printed 'War Song to Englishmen' (p. 792, below) (as suggested by D. V. Erdman, *Blake: Prophet Against Empire* [1954], 69), though neither this nor the Minstrel's 'Song' in Scene vi is really 'about the French and English'.

Peter. I know your honour does not think any thing of your-
self, but every body else does.

Dagw. Go, Peter, get you gone; flattery is delicious, even
from the lips of a babbler.   [*Exit Peter.*

[*Page*] 50

Will. I never flatter your honour.

Dagw. I don't know that.

Will. Why you know, Sir, when we were in England, at
the tournament at Windsor, and the Earl of Warwick was
tumbled over, you ask'd me if he did not look well when he
fell? and I said, No, he look'd very foolish; and you was very
angry with me for not flattering you.

Dagw. You mean that I was angry with you for not flattering
the Earl of Warwick.

                                            [*Exeunt.*

SCENE [*v*], *Sir Thomas Dagworth's Tent. Sir Thomas Dagworth.*
To him enter Sir Walter Manny.[2]

Sir Walter. Sir Thomas Dagworth, I have been weeping
Over the men that are to die to-day.

Dagw. Why, brave Sir Walter, you or I may fall.

Sir Walter. I know this breathing flesh must lie and rot,
Cover'd with silence and forgetfulness.—   [5]
Death wons in cities' smoke, and in still night,
When men sleep in their beds, walketh about!
How many in walled cities lie and groan,
Turning themselves upon their beds,
Talking with death, answering his hard demands!   [10]
How many walk in darkness, terrors are round

                                            [*Page*] 51

The curtains of their beds, destruction is
Ready at the door! How many sleep
In earth, cover'd with stones and deathy dust,
Resting in quietness, whose spirits walk   [15]
Upon the clouds of heaven, to die no more!
Yet death is terrible, tho' borne on angels' wings!

Scene v   [2] 1783: '. . . *Tent. Sir Tho-* | *mas Dagworth—to him.* | *Enter Sir Walter*
Manny.'

How terrible then is the field of death,
Where he doth rend the vault of heaven,
And shake the gates of hell!   [20]
O Dagworth, France is sick! the very sky,
Tho' sunshine light it, seems to me as pale
As the pale fainting man on his death-bed,
Whose face is shewn by light of sickly taper!
It makes me sad and sick at very heart,   [25]
Thousands must fall to-day!
   Dagw. Thousands of souls must leave this prison-house,
To be exalted to those heavenly fields,
Where songs of triumph, palms of victory,
Where peace, and joy, and love, and calm content,   [30]
Sit singing in the azure clouds, and strew
Flowers of heaven's growth over the banquet-table:
Bind ardent Hope upon your feet like shoes,
Put on the robe of preparation,
The table is prepar'd in shining heaven,   [35]
The flowers of immortality are blown;
Let those that fight, fight in good stedfastness,
And those that fall shall rise in victory.
[*Page*] 52
   Sir Walter. I've often seen the burning field of war,
And often heard the dismal clang of arms;   [40]
But never, till this fatal day of Cressy,
Has my soul fainted with these views of death!
I seem to be in one great charnel-house,
And seem to scent the rotten carcases!
I seem to hear the dismal yells of death,   [45]
While the black gore drops from his horrid jaws:
Yet I not fear the monster in his pride.——
But O the souls that are to die to-day!
   Dagw. Stop, brave Sir Walter; let me drop a tear,
Then let the clarion of war begin;   [50]

l. 22: Cunningham (1830) plausibly emended the punctuation to: 'Though sunshine light, it seems to me . . .' (*Blake Records*, 479).

l. 29: 'psalms of victory' is the attractive reading given by Cunningham (1830) (*Blake Records*, 480).

l. 44: 'seem' is plausibly emended to 'e'[e]n' in pencil in a contemporary hand in copy F.

I'll fight and weep, 'tis in my country's cause;
I'll weep and shout for glorious liberty.
Grim war shall laugh and shout, decked in tears,
And blood shall flow like streams across the meadows,
That murmur down their pebbly channels, and   [55
Spend their sweet lives to do their country service:
Then shall England's verdure shoot, her fields shall smile,
Her ships shall sing across the foaming sea,
Her mariners shall use the flute and viol,
And rattling guns, and black and dreary war,   [60
Shall be no more.
    Sir Walter. Well; let the trumpet sound, and the drum
      beat;
Let war stain the blue heavens with bloody banners,

                                         [*Page*] 53

I'll draw my sword, nor ever sheath it up,
'Till England blow the trump of victory,   [65
Or I lay stretch'd upon the field of death!   [66
                        Exeunt.

SCENE [*vi*], *in the Camp. Several of the Warriors met at the King's Tent with a Minstrel, who sings the following Song*:

O sons of Trojan Brutus, cloath'd in war,
Whose voices are the thunder of the field,
Rolling dark clouds o'er France, muffling the sun
In sickly darkness like a dim eclipse,
Threatening as the red brow of storms, as fire   [5
Burning up nations in your wrath and fury!

Your ancestors came from the fires of Troy,
(Like lions rouz'd by light'ning from their dens,
Whose eyes do glare against the stormy fires)
Heated with war, fill'd with the blood of Greeks,   [10
With helmets hewn, and shields covered with gore,
In navies black, broken with wind and tide!

They landed in firm array upon the rocks
Of Albion; they kiss'd the rocky shore;

'Be thou our mother, and our nurse,' they said;   [*15*]
'Our children's mother, and thou shalt be our grave;
'The sepulchre of ancient Troy, from whence
'Shall rise cities, and thrones, and arms, and awful pow'rs.'

[*Page*] 54

Our fathers swarm from the ships. Giant voices
Are heard from the hills, the enormous sons   [*20*]
Of Ocean run from rocks and caves: wild men,
Naked and roaring like lions, hurling rocks,
And wielding knotty clubs, like oaks entangled
Thick as a forest, ready for the axe.

Our fathers move in firm array to battle,   [*25*]
The savage monsters rush like roaring fire;
Like as a forest roars with crackling flames,
When the red lightning, borne by furious storms,
Lights on some woody shore; the parched heavens
Rain fire into the molten raging sea!   [*30*]

The smoaking trees are strewn upon the shore,
Spoil'd of their verdure! O how oft have they
Defy'd the storm that howled o'er their heads!
Our fathers, sweating, lean on their spears, and view
The mighty dead: giant bodies, streaming blood,   [*35*]
Dread visages, frowning in silent death!

Then Brutus spoke, inspir'd; our fathers sit
Attentive on the melancholy shore:——
Hear ye the voice of Brutus—'The flowing waves
'Of time come rolling o'er my breast,' he said;   [*40*]
'And my heart labours with futurity:
'Our sons shall rule the empire of the sea.

'Their mighty wings shall stretch from east to west,
'Their nest is in the sea; but they shall roam

[*Page*] 55

'Like eagles for the prey; nor shall the young   [*45*]
'Crave or be heard; for plenty shall bring forth,

789

'Cities shall sing, and vales in rich array
'Shall laugh, whose fruitful laps bend down with fulness.

'Our sons shall rise from thrones in joy,
'Each one buckling on his armour; Morning   [50]
'Shall be prevented by their swords gleaming,
'And Evening hear their song of victory!
'Their towers shall be built upon the rocks,
'Their daughters shall sing, surrounded with shining spears!

'Liberty shall stand upon the cliffs of Albion,   [55]
'Casting her blue eyes over the green ocean;
'Or, tow'ring, stand upon the roaring waves,
'Stretching her mighty spear o'er distant lands;
'While, with her eagle wings, she covereth
'Fair Albion's shore, and all her families.'   [60]

[*Page*] [56]

PROLOGUE,

INTENDED FOR A DRAMATIC PIECE OF

KING EDWARD THE FOURTH.

O For a voice like thunder, and a tongue
To drown the throat of war!—When the senses
Are shaken, and the soul is driven to madness,
Who can stand? When the souls of the oppressed
Fight in the troubled air that rages, who can stand?   [5]
When the whirlwind of fury comes from the
Throne of God, when the frowns of his countenance
Drive the nations together, who can stand?
When Sin claps his broad wings over the battle,
And sails rejoicing in the flood of Death;   [10]
When souls are torn to everlasting fire,
And fiends of Hell rejoice upon the slain,
O who can stand? O who hath caused this?
O who can answer at the throne of God?
The Kings and Nobles of the Land have done it!   [15]
Hear it not, Heaven, thy Ministers have done it!   [16]

'Prologue to Edward IV' ll. 2–3: 'When the senses are shaken / And the soul is
driven to madness Page 56' is the first title of 'The Accusers' (p. 162, above).

[*Page*] [57]

PROLOGUE TO KING JOHN.

JUSTICE hath heaved a sword to plunge in Albion's breast; for Albion's sins are crimson dy'd, and the red scourge follows her desolate sons! Then Patriot rose; full oft did Patriot rise, when Tyranny hath stain'd fair Albion's breast with her own children's gore. Round his majestic feet deep thunders roll; each heart does tremble, and each knee grows slack. The stars of heaven tremble: the roaring voice of war, the trumpet, calls to battle! Brother in brother's blood must bathe, rivers of death! O land, most hapless! O beauteous island, how forsaken! Weep from thy silver fountains; weep from thy gentle rivers! The angel of the island weeps! Thy widowed virgins weep beneath thy shades! Thy aged fathers gird themselves for war! The sucking infant lives to die in battle; the weeping mother feeds him for the slaughter![1] The husbandman doth leave his bending harvest! Blood cries afar! The land doth sow itself! The glittering youth of courts must gleam in arms! The aged senators their ancient swords assume! The trembling sinews of old age must work the work of death against their progeny; for Tyranny hath stretch'd his purple arm, and 'blood,' he cries; 'the chariots and the

[*Page*] 58

'horses, the noise of shout, and dreadful thunder of the battle heard afar!'—Beware, O Proud! thou shalt be humbled; thy cruel brow, thine iron heart is smitten, though lingering Fate is slow. O yet may Albion smile again, and stretch her peaceful arms, and raise her golden head, exultingly! Her citizens shall throng about her gates, her mariners shall sing upon the sea, and myriads shall to her temples crowd! Her sons shall joy as in the morning! Her daughters sing as to the rising year!

'Prologue to King John'   [1] Cf. *The French Revolution* (1791), l. 210: 'the pale mother nourishes her child to the deadly slaughter'.

A WAR SONG
TO ENGLISHMEN.

PREPARE, prepare, the iron helm of war,
Bring forth the lots, cast in the spacious orb;
Th' Angel of Fate turns them with mighty hands,
And casts them out upon the darken'd earth!
                              Prepare, prepare. [5]

Prepare your hearts for Death's cold hand! prepare
Your souls for flight, your bodies for the earth!
Prepare your arms for glorious victory!
Prepare your eyes to meet a holy God!
                              Prepare, prepare. [10]
                              [*Page*] 59

Whose fatal scroll is that? Methinks 'tis mine!
Why sinks my heart, why faultereth my tongue?
Had I three lives, I'd die in such a cause,
And rise, with ghosts, over the well-fought field.
                              Prepare, prepare. [15]

The arrows of Almighty God are drawn!
Angels of Death stand in the low'ring heavens!
Thousands of souls must seek the realms of light,
And walk together on the clouds of heaven!
                              Prepare, prepare. [20]

Soldiers, prepare! Our cause is Heaven's cause;
Soldiers, prepare! Be worthy of our cause:
Prepare to meet our fathers in the sky:
Prepare, O troops, that are to fall to-day!
                              Prepare, prepare. [25]

Alfred shall smile, and make his harp rejoice;
The Norman William, and the learned Clerk,
And Lion Heart, and black-brow'd Edward, with
His loyal queen shall rise, and welcome us!
                              Prepare, prepare. [30]

'A War Song to Englishmen' For a possible context see 'Edward III', Scene iv,
and its footnote (p. 785).

THE
COUCH OF DEATH.

THE veiled Evening walked solitary down the western hills, and Silence reposed in the valley; the birds of day were heard in their nests, rustling in brakes and thickets; and the owl and bat flew round the darkening trees: all is silent when Nature takes her repose.—In former times, on such an[1] evening, when the cold clay breathed with life, and our ancestors, who now sleep in their graves, walked on the stedfast globe, the remains of a family of the tribes of Earth, a mother and a sister were gathered to the sick bed of a youth: Sorrow linked them together, leaning on one another's necks alternately—like lilies, dropping tears in each other's bosom, they stood by the bed like reeds bending over a lake, when the evening drops trickle down. His voice was low as the whisperings of the woods when the wind is asleep, and the visions of Heaven unfold their visitation. 'Parting is hard, and death is terrible; I seem to 'walk through a deep valley, far from the light of day, alone 'and comfortless! The damps of death fall thick upon me! 'Horrors stare me in the face! I look behind, there is no

'returning; Death follows after me; I walk in regions of Death, 'where no tree is; without a lantern to direct my steps, without 'a staff to support me.'—Thus he laments through the still evening, till the curtains of darkness were drawn! Like the sound of a broken pipe, the aged woman raised her voice. 'O 'my son, my son, I know but little of the path thou goest! 'But lo, there is a God, who made the world; stretch out thy 'hand to Him.' The youth replied, like a voice heard from a sepulchre, 'My hand is feeble, how should I stretch it out? 'My ways are sinful, how should I raise mine eyes? My voice 'hath used deceit, how should I call on Him who is Truth? 'My breath is loathsome, how should he not be offended? If I 'lay my face in the dust, the grave opens its mouth for me; if I 'lift up my head, sin covers me as a cloak! O my dear friends, 'pray ye for me! Stretch forth your hands, that my helper may

'The Couch of Death' [1] 1783: 'on'.

793

'come! Through the void space I walk between the sinful
'world and eternity! Beneath me burns eternal fire! O for a
'hand to pluck me forth!' As the voice of an omen heard in
the silent valley, when the few inhabitants cling trembling
together; as the voice of the Angel of Death, when the thin
beams of the moon give a faint light, such was this young
man's voice to his friends! Like the bubbling waters of the brook
in the dead of night, the aged woman raised her

[*Page*] 62

cry, and said, 'O Voice, that dwellest in my breast, can I not cry,
'and lift my eyes to Heaven? Thinking of this, my spirit is turned
'within me into confusion! O my child, my child! is thy breath
'infected? So is mine. As the deer, wounded by the brooks of
'water, so the arrows of sin stick in my flesh; the poison hath
'entered into my marrow.'—Like rolling waves, upon a desert
shore, sighs succeeded sighs; they covered their faces, and wept!
The youth lay silent—his mother's arm was under his head;
he was like a cloud tossed by the winds, till the sun shine, and
the drops of rain glisten, the yellow harvest breathes, and the
thankful eyes of the villagers are turned up in smiles. The
traveller that hath taken shelter under an oak, eyes the distant
country with joy! Such smiles were seen upon the face of the
youth! a visionary hand wiped away his tears, and a ray of
light beamed around his head! All was still. The moon hung
not out her lamp, and the stars faintly glimmered in the
summer sky; the breath of night slept among the leaves of the
forest; the bosom of the lofty hill drank in the silent dew, while
on his majestic brow the voice of Angels is heard, and stringed
sounds ride upon the wings of night. The sorrowful pair lift
up their heads, hovering Angels are around them, voices of
comfort are heard over the Couch of Death, and the youth
breathes out his soul with joy into eternity.

[*Page*] [63]

CONTEMPLATION.

WHO is this, that with unerring step dares tempt the wilds,
where only Nature's foot hath trod? 'Tis Contemplation,
daughter of the grey Morning! Majestical she steppeth, and

with her pure quill on every flower writeth Wisdom's name.
Now lowly bending, whispers in mine ear, 'O man, how great,
'how little thou! O man, slave of each moment, lord of eternity!
'seest thou where Mirth sits on the painted cheek? doth it not
'seem ashamed of such a place, and grow immoderate to brave
'it out? O what an humble garb true Joy puts on! Those who
'want Happiness must stoop to find it; it is a flower that grows
'in every vale.[1] Vain foolish man, that roams on lofty rocks!
'where, 'cause his garments are swoln with wind, he fancies he
'is grown into a giant! Lo then, Humility, take it, and wear it
'in thine heart; lord of thyself, thou then art lord of all. Clamour
'brawls along the streets, and destruction hovers in the city's
'smoak; but on these plains, and in these silent woods, true
'joys descend: here build thy nest; here fix thy staff; delights
'blossom around; numberless beauties blow; the green grass
'springs in joy, and the nimble air kisses the leaves; the brook
'stretches its arms along the velvet meadow,

[*Page*] 64

'its silver inhabitants sport and play; the youthful sun joys like
'a hunter rouzed to the chace: he rushes up the sky, and lays
'hold on the immortal coursers of day; the sky glitters with
'the jingling trappings! Like a triumph, season follows season,
'while the airy music fills the world with joyful sounds.' I
answered, 'Heavenly goddess! I am wrapped in mortality, my
'flesh is a prison, my bones the bars of death, Misery builds
'over our cottage roofs, and Discontent runs like a brook. Even
'in childhood, Sorrow slept with me in my cradle; he followed
'me up and down in the house, when I grew up[2] he was my
'school-fellow: thus he was in my steps and in my play, till
'he became to me as my brother. I walked through dreary
'places with him, and in church-yards; and I oft found myself
'sitting by Sorrow on a tomb-stone!'

'Contemplation'   [1] George Cumberland marked 'Contemplation' as 'Beautiful—
G. C.' in his copy (D).
     The printed text of the first speech on pp. 63–4 omits quotation marks in the
left margin, though the second speech, on p. 64, has them.
     [2] The semicolon after 'grew up' is deleted in copies T and V. In copy V a
semicolon is added after 'house'. The punctuation of 'house, when I grew up, he
was' is an editorial emendation.

SAMSON.

SAMSON, the strongest of the children of men, I sing; how he was foiled by woman's arts, by a false wife brought to the gates of death! O Truth, that shinest with propitious beams, turning our earthly night to heavenly day, from presence of the Almighty Father! thou visitest our darkling world with blessed feet, bringing good news of Sin and Death destroyed! O white-robed

[*Page*] 65

Angel, guide my timorous hand to write as on a lofty rock with iron pens the words of truth, that all who pass may read.—Now Night, noon-tide of damned spirits, over the silent earth spreads her pavilion, while in dark council sat Philista's lords; and where strength failed, black thoughts in ambush lay. Their helmed youth and aged warriors in dust together ly, and Desolation spreads his wings over the land of Palestine; from side to side the land groans, her prowess lost, and seeks to hide her bruised head under the mists of night, breeding dark plots. For Dalila's fair arts have long been tried in vain; in vain she wept in many a treacherous tear. 'Go on, fair traitress; 'do thy guileful work; ere once again the changing moon her 'circuit hath performed, thou shalt overcome, and conquer him 'by force unconquerable, and wrest his secret from him. Call 'thine alluring arts and honest-seeming brow, the holy kiss 'of love, and the transparent tear; put on fair linen, that with 'the lily vies, purple and silver; neglect thy hair, to seem more 'lovely in thy loose attire; put on thy country's pride, deceit; 'and eyes of love decked in mild sorrow, and sell thy Lord for 'gold.'—For now, upon her sumptuous couch reclined, in gorgeous pride, she still intreats, and still she grasps his vigorous knees with her fair arms.—'Thou lov'st me not! thou'rt war, 'thou art not love! O foolish Dalila! O weak woman! it is death

[*Page*] 66

'cloathed in flesh thou lovest, and thou hast been incircled in 'his arms!—Alas, my Lord, what am I calling thee? Thou art 'my God! To thee I pour my tears for sacrifice morning and 'evening: My days are covered with sorrow! Shut up; darkened: 'By night I am deceived! Who says that thou wast born of 'mortal kind? Destruction was thy father, a lioness suckled

'thee, thy young hands tore human limbs, and gorged human
'flesh! Come hither, Death; art thou not Samson's servant?
"Tis Dalila that calls; thy master's wife; no, stay, and let thy
'master do the deed: one blow of that strong arm would ease
'my pain; then should I lay at quiet, and have rest. Pity forsook
'thee at thy birth! O Dagon furious, and all ye gods of Palestine,
'withdraw your hand! I am but a weak woman. Alas, I am
'wedded to your enemy! I will go mad, and tear my crisped
'hair; I'll run about, and pierce the ears o'th'gods! O Sam-
'son, hold me not; thou lovest me not! Look not upon me
'with those deathful eyes! Thou wouldst my death, and death
'approaches fast.'—Thus, in false tears, she bath'd his feet,
and thus she day by day oppressed his soul; he seemed a moun-
tain, his brow among the clouds; she seemed a silver stream,
his feet embracing. Dark thoughts rolled to and fro in his mind,
like thunder clouds, troubling the sky; his visage was troubled;
his soul was distressed.—'Though I should tell her all my

[*Page*] 67

'heart, what can I fear? Though I should tell this secret of my
'birth, the utmost may be warded off as well when told as now.'
She saw him moved, and thus resumes her wiles.—'Samson,
'I'm thine; do with me what thou wilt; my friends are enemies;
'my life is death; I am a traitor to my nation, and despised;
'my joy is given into the hands of him who hates me, using
'deceit to the wife of his bosom. Thrice hast thou mocked me,
'and grieved my soul. Didst thou not tell me with green with[*e*]s
'to bind thy nervous arms, and after that, when I had found
'thy fals[*e*]hood, with new ropes to bind thee fast? I knew thou
'didst but mock me. Alas, when in thy sleep I bound thee
'with them to try thy truth, I cried, The Philistines be upon
'thee, Samson! Then did suspicion wake thee; how didst thou
'rend the feeble ties! Thou fearest nought, what shouldst thou
'fear? Thy power is more than mortal, none can hurt thee;
'thy bones are brass, thy sinews are iron! Ten thousand spears
'are like the summer grass; an army of mighty men are as
'flocks in the vallies; what canst thou fear? I drink my tears
'like water; I live upon sorrow! O worse than wolves and tygers,
'what canst thou give when such a trifle is denied me? But O

797

'at last thou mockest me to shame my over-fond inquiry!
'Thou toldest me to weave thee to the beam by thy strong
[*Page*] 68
'hair; I did even that to try thy truth: but when I cried, The
'Philistines be upon thee, then didst thou leave me to bewail
'that Samson loved me not.'—He sat, and inward griev'd,
he saw and lov'd the beauteous suppliant, nor could conceal
aught that might appease her; then, leaning on her bosom,
thus he spoke: 'Hear, O Dalila! doubt no more of Samson's
'love; for that fair breast was made the ivory palace of my
'inmost heart, where it shall lie at rest; for sorrow is the lot of
'all of woman born: for care was I brought forth, and labour
'is my lot: nor matchless might, nor wisdom, nor every gift
'enjoyed, can from the heart of man hide sorrow.—Twice was
'my birth foretold from heaven, and twice a sacred vow en-
'joined me that I should drink no wine, nor eat of any unclean
'thing, for holy unto Israel's God I am, a Nazarite even from
'my mother's womb. Twice was it told, that it might not be
'broken, Grant me a son, kind Heaven, Manoa cried; but
'Heaven refused! Childless he mourned, but thought his God
'knew best. In solitude, though not obscure, in Israel he lived,
'till venerable age came on: his flocks increased, and plenty
'crowned his board: beloved, revered of man! But God hath
'other joys in store. Is burdened Israel his grief? The son of
'his old age shall set it free! The venerable sweetner of his life
'receives the promise first from Heaven. She saw the maidens

[*Page*] 69

'play, and blessed their innocent mirth; she blessed each
'new-joined pair; but from her the long-wished deliverer shall
'spring. Pensive, alone she sat within the house, when busy
'day was fading, and calm evening, time for contemplation,
'rose from the forsaken east, and drew the curtains of heaven;
'pensive she sat, and thought on Israel's grief, and silent prayed
'to Israel's God; when lo, an angel from the fields of light
'entered the house! His form was manhood in the prime, and
'from his spacious brow shot terrors through the evening shade!
'But mild he hailed her——Hail, highly favoured! said he; for
'lo, thou shalt conceive, and bear a son, and Israel's strength

'shall be upon his shoulders, and he shall be called Israel's De-
'liverer! Now therefore drink no wine, and eat not any unclean
'thing, for he shall be a Nazarite to God.—Then, as a neighbour
'when his evening tale is told, departs, his blessing leaving;
'so seemed he to depart: she wondered with exceeding joy,
'nor knew he was an angel. Manoa left his fields to sit in the
'house, and take his evening's rest from labour—the sweetest
'time that God has allotted mortal man. He sat, and heard
'with joy, and praised God who Israel still doth keep. The time
'rolled on, and Israel groaned oppressed. The sword was
'bright, while the plow-share rusted, till hope grew feeble, and
'was ready to give place to doubting: then

[*Page*] 70

'prayed Manoa—O Lord, thy flock is scattered on the hills!
'The wolf teareth them, Oppression stretches his rod over our
'land, our country is plowed with swords, and reaped in blood!
'The echoes of slaughter reach from hill to hill! Instead of peace-
'ful pipe, the shepherd bears a sword; the ox goad is turned into
'a spear! O when shall our Deliverer come? The Philistine riots on
'our flocks, our vintage is gathered by bands of enemies! Stretch
'forth thy hand, and save.— —Thus prayed Manoa. The aged
'woman walked into the field, and lo, again the angel came!
'Clad as a traveller fresh risen on his journey, she ran and called
'her husband, who came and talked with him.——O man of
'God, said he, thou comest from far! Let us detain thee while
'I make ready a kid, that thou mayest sit and eat, and tell us of
'thy name and warfare;[1] that when thy sayings come to pass,
'we may honour thee. The Angel answered, My name is
'wonderful; enquire not after it, seeing it is a secret: but, if
'thou wilt, offer an offering unto the Lord.'

THE END.

'Samson'   [1] 'warfare' may be a misprint for 'wayfare', as Keynes suggests (*The
Complete Writings of William Blake* [1957], 40).

THE FRENCH REVOLUTION

THE

FRENCH REVOLUTION.

A POEM,

IN SEVEN BOOKS.

BOOK THE FIRST.

LONDON:

PRINTED FOR J. JOHNSON, Nº 72, ST PAUL'S CHURCH-YARD.

M DCC XCI.

[PRICE ONE SHILLING.]

[Page i]

ADVERTISEMENT.

The remaining Books of this Poem are finished, and will be
published in their Order.[1]

[Page 1]

THE

FRENCH REVOLUTION.

BOOK THE FIRST.

THE dead brood over Europe, the cloud and vision descends
over chearful France;
O cloud well appointed! Sick, sick: the Prince on his couch,
wreath'd in dim

---

[1] No other contemporary reference to the remaining books of *The French
Revolution* is known.

And appalling mist; his strong hand outstretch'd, from his
    shoulder down the bone
Runs aching cold into the scepter too heavy for mortal grasp.
    No more
To be swayed by visible hand, nor in cruelty bruise the mild
    flourishing mountains. [*5*]

Sick the mountains, and all their vineyards weep, in the eyes of
    the kingly mourner;
Pale is the morning cloud in his visage. Rise, Necker: the
    ancient dawn call us
To awake from slumbers of five thousand years. I awake, but
    my soul is in dreams;
From my window I see the old mountains of France, like aged
    men, fading away.

[Page] [2]

Troubled, leaning on Necker, descends the King, to his cham-
    ber of council; shady mountains [*10*]
In fear, utter voices of thunder; the woods of France embosom
    the sound;
Clouds of wisdom prophetic reply, and roll over the palace
    roof heavy.
Forty men: each conversing with woes in the infinite shadows
    of his soul,
Like our ancient fathers in regions of twilight, walk, gathering
    round the King;
Again the loud voice of France cries to the morning, the morn-
    ing prophecies to its clouds. [*15*]

For the Commons convene in the Hall of the Nation. France
    shakes! And the heavens of France
Perplex'd vibrate round each careful countenance! Darkness of
    old times around them
Utters loud despair, shadowing Paris; her grey towers groan,
    and the Bastile trembles.
In its terrible towers the Governor stood, in dark fogs list'ning
    the horror;
A thousand his soldiers, old veterans of France, breathing red
    clouds of power and dominion, [*20*]

Sudden seiz'd with howlings, despair, and black night, he stalk'd like a lion from tower

To tower, his howlings were heard in the Louvre; from court to court restless he dragg'd

His strong limbs; from court to court curs'd the fierce torment unquell'd,

Howling and giving the dark command; in his soul stood the purple plague,

Tugging his iron manacles, and piercing through the seven towers dark and sickly, [25]

Panting over the prisoners like a wolf gorg'd; and the den nam'd Horror held a man

Chain'd hand and foot, round his neck an iron band, bound to the impregnable wall.

In his soul was the serpent coil'd round in his heart, hid from the light, as in a cleft rock;

And the man was confin'd for a writing prophetic: in the tower nam'd Darkness, was a man

Pinion'd down to the stone floor, his strong bones scarce cover'd with sinews; the iron rings [30]

Were forg'd smaller as the flesh decay'd, a mask of iron on his face hid the lineaments

[Page] [3]

Of ancient Kings, and the frown of the eternal lion was hid from the oppressed earth.

In the tower named Bloody, a skeleton yellow remained in its chains on its couch

Of stone, once a man who refus'd to sign papers of abhorrence; the eternal worm

Crept in the skeleton. In the den nam'd Religion, a loathsome sick woman, bound down [35]

To a bed of straw; the seven diseases of earth, like birds of prey, stood on the couch,

And fed on the body. She refus'd to be whore to the Minister, and with a knife smote him.

In the tower nam'd Order, an old man, whose white beard cover'd the stone floor like weeds

On margin of the sea, shrivel'd up by heat of day and cold of night; his den was short

And narrow as a grave dug for a child, with spiders' webs wove,
   and with slime   [*40*]
Of ancient horrors cover'd, for snakes and scorpions are his
   companions; harmless they breathe
His sorrowful breath: he, by conscience urg'd, in the city of
   Paris rais'd a pulpit,
And taught wonders to darken'd souls. In the den nam'd
   Destiny a strong man sat,
His feet and hands cut off, and his eyes blinded; round his
   middle a chain and a band
Fasten'd into the wall; fancy gave him to see an image of
   despair in his den,   [*45*]
Eternally rushing round, like a man on his hands and knees,
   day and night without rest.
He was friend to the favourite. In the seventh tower, nam'd the
   tower of God, was a man
Mad, with chains loose, which he dragg'd up and down; fed
   with hopes year by year, he pined
For liberty; vain hopes: his reason decay'd, and the world of
   attraction in his bosom
Center'd, and the rushing of chaos overwhelm'd his dark soul.
   He was confin'd   [*50*]
For a letter of advice to a King, and his ravings in winds are
   heard over Versailles.

But the dens shook and trembled, the prisoners look up and
   assay to shout; they listen,
Then laugh in the dismal den, then are silent, and a light walks
   round the dark towers.

[Page] [4]

For the Commons convene in the Hall of the Nations, like
   spirits of fire in the beautiful
Porches of the Sun, to plant beauty in the desart craving
   abyss, they gleam   [*55*]
On the anxious city; all children new-born first behold them;
   tears are fled,

And they nestle in earth-breathing bosoms. So the city of
  Paris, their wives and children,
Look up to the morning Senate, and visions of sorrow leave
  pensive streets.

But heavy brow'd jealousies lower o'er the Louvre, and terrors
  of ancient Kings
Descend from the gloom and wander thro' the palace, and
  weep round the King and his Nobles. [60
While loud thunders roll, troubling the dead, Kings are sick
  throughout all the earth.
The voice ceas'd: the Nation sat: And the triple forg'd fetters of
  times were unloos'd.
The voice ceas'd: the Nation sat: but ancient darkness and
  trembling wander thro' the palace.

As in day of havock and routed battle, among thick shades of
  discontent,
On the soul-skirting mountains of sorrow cold waving: the
  Nobles fold round the King, [65
Each stern visage lock'd up as with strong bands of iron, each
  strong limb bound down as with marble,
In flames of red wrath burning, bound in astonishment a
  quarter of an hour.

Then the King glow'd: his Nobles fold round, like the sun of
  old time quench'd in clouds;
In their darkness the King stood, his heart flam'd, and utter'd
  a with'ring heat, and these words burst forth:

'The nerves of five thousand years ancestry tremble, shaking the
  heavens of France; [70
Throbs of anguish beat on brazen war foreheads, they descend
  and look into their graves.

[*Page*] [5]

'I see thro' the darkness, thro' clouds rolling round me, the
  spirits of ancient Kings

Shivering over the bleached bones; round them their counsel-
lors look up from the dust,
Crying: "Hide from the living! Our bonds and our prisoners
shout in the open field,
Hide in the nether earth! Hide in the bones! Sit obscured in
the hollow scull.   *[75]*
Our flesh is corrupted, and we wear away. We are not num-
bered among the living. Let us hide
In stones, among roots of trees. The prisoners have burst their
dens,
Let us hide; let us hide in the dust, and plague and wrath and
tempest shall cease." '

He ceas'd, silent pond'ring, his brows folded heavy, his forehead
was in affliction,
Like the central fire: from the window he saw his vast armies
spread over the hills,   *[80]*
Breathing red fires from man to man, and from horse to horse;
then his bosom
Expanded like starry heaven, he sat down: his Nobles took
their ancient seats.

Then the ancientest Peer, Duke of Burgundy, rose from the
Monarch's right hand, red as wines
From his mountains, an odor of war, like a ripe vineyard, rose
from his garments,
And the chamber became as a clouded sky; o'er the council he
stretch'd his red limbs,   *[85]*
Cloth'd in flames of crimson, as a ripe vineyard stretches over
sheaves of corn,
The fierce Duke hung over the council; around him croud,
weeping in his burning robe,

l. 74: Perhaps 'bonds' is a misprint for 'bands' (as D. V. Erdman, *Blake: Prophet Against Empire* [1954], 152 n. 41, suggests).

l. 76: The printed 'were away' appears to be a misprint of 'wear away'.

l. 83: The printed 'antientest' is apparently erroneous; cf. 'ancient', ll. 82, 93, 101, 118.

The 'Duke of Burgundy' seems to be distinct from 'the Earl of Borgogne' (l. 169). Many of the noble names and actions of the poem are fictitious. For the historical background, see D. V. Erdman, *Blake: Prophet Against Empire* (1954).

A bright cloud of infant souls; his words fall like purple autumn on the sheaves.

'Shall this marble built heaven become a clay cottage, this earth an oak stool, and these mowers
From the Atlantic mountains, mow down all this great starry harvest of six thousand years? [9c
And shall Necker, the hind of Geneva, stretch out his crook'd sickle o'er fertile France,

[*Page*] [6]

Till our purple and crimson is faded to russet, and the kingdoms of earth bound in sheaves,
And the ancient forests of chivalry hewn, and the joys of the combat burnt for fuel;
Till the power and dominion is rent from the pole, sword and scepter from sun and moon,
The law and gospel from fire and air, and eternal reason and science [9:
From the deep and the solid, and man lay his faded head down on the rock
Of eternity, where the eternal lion and eagle remain to devour?
This to prevent, urg'd by cries in day, and prophetic dreams hovering in night,
To enrich the lean earth that craves, furrow'd with plows; whose seed is departing from her;
Thy Nobles have gather'd thy starry hosts round this rebellious city, [1
To rouze up the ancient forests of Europe, with clarions of cloud breathing war;
To hear the horse neigh to the drum and trumpet, and the trumpet and war shout reply;
Stretch the hand that beckons the eagles of heaven; they cry over Paris, and wait
Till Fayette point his finger to Versailles; the eagles of heaven must have their prey.'

He ceas'd, and burn'd silent, red clouds roll round Necker, a weeping is heard o'er the palace; [1
Like a dark cloud Necker paus'd, and like thunder on the just man's burial day he paus'd;

806

Silent sit the winds, silent the meadows, while the husbandman
    and woman of weakness
And bright children look after him into the grave, and water
    his clay with love,
Then turn towards pensive fields; so Necker paus'd, and his
    visage was cover'd with clouds.

The King lean'd on his mountains, then lifted his head and
    look'd on his armies, that shone   [*110*]
Through heaven, tinging morning with beams of blood, then
    turning to Burgundy troubled:
                [*Page*] [7]
'Burgundy, thou wast born a lion! My soul is o'ergrown with
    distress
For the Nobles of France, and dark mists roll round me and
    blot the writing of God
Written in my bosom. Necker rise, leave the kingdom, thy
    life is surrounded with snares;
We have call'd an Assembly, but not to destroy; we have given
    gifts, not to the weak;   [*115*]
I hear rushing of muskets, and bright'ning of swords, and visages
    redd'ning with war,
Frowning and looking up from brooding villages and every
    dark'ning city;
Ancient wonders frown over the kingdom, and cries of women
    and babes are heard,
And tempests of doubt roll around me, and fierce sorrows,
    because of the Nobles of France;
Depart, answer not, for the tempest must fall, as in years that
    are passed away.'   [*120*]

Dropping a tear the old man his place left, and when he was
    gone out

ll. 110–20: A plausible argument that these lines were intended to follow l. 104, and were accidentally misplaced, is made by W. F. Halloran, 'William Blake's *The French Revolution*: A Note on the Text and a Possible Emendation', *Bulletin of the New York Public Library*, lxxii (1968), 3–18.

ll. 114, 125: The printed 'Neckar' is elsewhere (e.g. ll. 105, 109) correctly spelled 'Necker'.

l. 116: 'rushing of muskets' may be a misprint for 'rattling of muskets'.

He set his face toward Geneva to flee, and the women and children of the city
Kneel'd round him and kissed his garments and wept; he stood a short space in the street,
Then fled; and the whole city knew he was fled to Geneva, and the Senate heard it.

But the Nobles burn'd wrathful at Necker's departure, and wreath'd their clouds and waters   [12]
In dismal volumes; as risen from beneath the Archbishop of Paris arose,
In the rushing of scales and hissing of flames and rolling of sulphurous smoke.

'Hearken, Monarch of France, to the terrors of heaven, and let thy soul drink of my counsel;
Sleeping at midnight in my golden tower, the repose of the labours of men
Wav'd its solemn cloud over my head. I awoke; a cold hand passed over my limbs, and behold   [13]
An aged form, white as snow, hov'ring in mist, weeping in the uncertain light,

[*Page*] [8]

Dim the form almost faded, tears fell down the shady cheeks; at his feet many cloth'd
In white robes, strewn in air censers and harps, silent they lay prostrated;
Beneath, in the awful void, myriads descending and weeping thro' dismal winds,
Endless the shady train shiv'ring descended, from the gloom where the aged form wept.   [13]
At length, trembling, the vision sighing, in a low voice, like the voice of the grasshopper whisper'd:
"My groaning is heard in the abbeys, and God, so long worshipp'd, departs as a lamp
Without oil; for a curse is heard hoarse thro' the land, from a godless race
Descending to beasts; they look downward and labour and forget my holy law;

The sound of prayer fails from lips of flesh, and the holy hymn
    from thicken'd tongues: [*140*]
For the bars of Chaos are burst; her millions prepare their
    fiery way
Thro' the orbed abode of the holy dead, to root up and pull
    down and remove,
And Nobles and Clergy shall fail from before me, and my cloud
    and vision be no more;
The mitre become black, the crown vanish, and the scepter and
    ivory staff
Of the ruler wither among bones of death; they shall consume
    from the thistly field,   [*145*]
And the sound of the bell, and voice of the sabbath, and singing
    of the holy choir,
Is turn'd into songs of the harlot in day, and cries of the virgin
    in night.
They shall drop at the plow and faint at the harrow, un-
    redeem'd, unconfess'd, unpardon'd;
The priest rot in his surplice by the lawless lover, the holy
    beside the accursed,
The King, frowning in purple, beside the grey plowman, and
    their worms embrace together."   [*150*]
The voice ceas'd, a groan shook my chamber; I slept, for the
    cloud of repose returned,
But morning dawn'd heavy upon me. I rose to bring my Prince
    heaven utter'd counsel.
Hear my counsel, O King, and send forth thy Generals, the
    command of heaven is upon thee;
Then do thou command, O King, to shut up this Assembly in
    their final home;
[Page] [9]

Let thy soldiers possess this city of rebels, that threaten to
    bathe their feet   [*155*]
In the blood of Nobility; trampling the heart and the head; let
    the Bastile devour
These rebellious seditious; seal them up, O Anointed, in ever-
    lasting chains.'
He sat down, a damp cold pervaded the Nobles, and monsters
    of worlds unknown

Swam round them, watching to be delivered; when Aumont, whose chaos-born soul

Eternally wand'ring a Comet and swift-falling fire, pale enter'd the chamber;   [1

Before the red Council he stood, like a man that returns from hollow graves.

'Awe surrounded, alone thro' the army a fear and a with'ring blight blown by the north;

The Abbe de Seyes from the Nation's Assembly. O Princes and Generals of France,

Unquestioned, unhindered, awe-struck are the soldiers; a dark shadowy man in the form

Of King Henry the Fourth walks before him in fires, the captains like men bound in chains   [1

Stood still as he pass'd, he is come to the Louvre, O King, with a message to thee;

The strong soldiers tremble, the horses their manes bow, and the guards of thy palace are fled.'

Up rose awful in his majestic beams Bourbon's strong Duke; his proud sword from his thigh

Drawn, he threw on the Earth! the Duke of Bretagne and the Earl of Borgogne

Rose inflam'd, to and fro in the chamber, like thunder-clouds ready to burst.   [1

'What damp all our fires, O spectre of Henry,' said Bourbon; 'and rend the flames

From the head of our King! Rise, Monarch of France; command me, and I will lead

This army of superstition at large, that the ardor of noble souls quenchless,

---

l. 159: 1791 capitalizes 'When', evidently erroneously.
ll. 162–4: Perhaps this should read:

    Awe surrounded, alone thro' the army, a fear and a with'ring blight
      blown by the north,
    The Abbé de Sieyès from the Nation's Assembly, O Princes and Generals
      of France,
    Unquestioned, unhindered; awe-struck are the soldiers . . . .

May yet burn in France, nor our shoulders be plow'd with the
   furrows of poverty.'

[Page] [10]

Then Orleans generous as mountains arose, and unfolded his
   robe, and put forth   [*175*]
His benevolent hand, looking on the Archbishop, who, changed
   as pale as lead,
Would have risen but could not, his voice issued harsh grating;
   instead of words harsh hissings
Shook the chamber; he ceas'd abash'd. Then Orleans spoke,
   all was silent,
He breath'd on them, and said, 'O princes of fire, whose
   flames are for growth not consuming,
Fear not dreams, fear not visions, nor be you dismay'd with
   sorrows which flee at the morning;   [*180*]
Can the fires of Nobility ever be quench'd, or the stars by a
   stormy night?
Is the body diseas'd when the members are healthful? can the
   man be bound in sorrow
Whose ev'ry function is fill'd with its fiery desire? can the
   soul whose brain and heart
Cast their rivers in equal tides thro' the great Paradise, languish
   because the feet
Hands, head, bosom, and parts of love, follow their high breath-
   ing joy?   [*185*]
And can Nobles be bound when the people are free, or God
   weep when his children are happy?
Have you never seen Fayette's forehead, or Mirabeau's eyes,
   or the shoulders of Target,
Or Bailly the strong foot of France, or Clermont the terrible
   voice, and your robes
Still retain their own crimson? mine never yet faded, for fire
   delights in its form.
But go, merciless man! enter into the infinite labyrinth of
   another's brain   [*190*]
Ere thou measure the circle that he shall run. Go, thou cold
   recluse, into the fires

l. 176: The punctuation of 1791 is 'who changed pale as lead;'.

Of another's high flaming rich bosom, and return unconsum'd,
and write laws.
If thou canst not do this, doubt thy theories, learn to consider
all men as thy equals,
Thy brethren, and not as thy foot or thy hand, unless thou
first fearest to hurt them.'

The Monarch stood up, the strong Duke his sword to its
golden scabbard return'd,   [19
The Nobles sat round like clouds on the mountains, when the
storm is passing away.

[Page] [11]

'Let the Nation's Ambassador come among Nobles, like incense
of the valley.'

Aumont went out and stood in the hollow porch, his ivory
wand in his hand;
A cold orb of disdain revolv'd round him, and covered his
soul with snows eternal.
Great Henry's soul shuddered, a whirlwind and fire tore
furious from his angry bosom;   [20
He indignant departed on horses of heav'n. Then the Abbe de
Seyes rais'd his feet
On the steps of the Louvre, like a voice of God following a
storm, the Abbe follow'd
The pale fires of Aumont into the chamber; as a father that
bows to his son,
Whose rich fields inheriting spread their old glory, so the voice
of the people bowed
Before the ancient seat of the kingdom and mountains to be
renewed.   [20

'Hear, O Heavens of France, the voice of the people, arising
from valley and hill,
O'erclouded with power. Hear the voice of valleys, the voice of
meek cities,

l. 203: In 1791, the comma and semicolon are interchanged.
l. 207: In 1791, the Blakean 'vallies' was not corrected to 'valleys', as it was in
ll. 220, 224.

Mourning oppressed on village and field, till the village and
    field is a waste.

For the husbandman weeps at blights of the fife, and blasting of
    trumpets consume

The souls of mild France; the pale mother nourishes her child
    to the deadly slaughter.   [*210*]

When the heavens were seal'd with a stone, and the terrible sun
    clos'd in an orb, and the moon

Rent from the nations, and each star appointed for watchers of
    night,

The millions of spirits immortal were bound in the ruins of
    sulphur heaven

To wander inslav'd; black, deprest in dark ignorance, kept in
    awe with the whip,

To worship terrors, bred from the blood of revenge and breath
    of desire,   [*215*]

In beastial forms; or more terrible men, till the dawn of our
    peaceful morning,

Till dawn, till morning, till the breaking of clouds, and swelling
    of winds, and the universal voice,

[Page] [12]

Till man raise his darken'd limbs out of the caves of night, his
    eyes and his heart

Expand: where is space! where O Sun is thy dwelling! where
    thy tent, O faint slumb'rous Moo*n*!

Then the valleys of France shall cry to the soldier, throw down
    thy sword and musket,   [*220*

And run and embrace the meek peasant. Her nobles shall hear
    and shall weep, and put off

The red robe of terror, the crown of oppression, the shoes of
    contempt, and unbuckle

The girdle of war from the desolate earth; then the Priest in his
    thund'rous cloud

Shall weep, bending to earth embracing the valleys, and putting
    his hand to the plow,

Shall say, "no more I curse thee; but now I will bless thee:
    No more in deadly black   [*225*]

l. 210: Cf. 'Prologue to King John' (*Poetical Sketches* [1783], p. 57): 'the weeping
mother feeds him [The sucking infant] for the slaughter'.

Devour thy labour; nor lift up a cloud in thy heavens, O
  laborious plow,
That the wild raging millions, that wander in forests, and howl
  in law blasted wastes,
Strength madden'd with slavery, honesty, bound in the dens of
  superstition,
May sing in the village, and shout in the harvest, and woo in
  pleasant gardens,
Their once savage loves, now beaming with knowledge, with
  gentle awe adorned;   [23
And the saw, and the hammer, the chisel, the pencil, the pen,
  and the instruments
Of heavenly song sound in the wilds once forbidden, to teach
  the laborious plowman
And shepherd deliver'd from clouds of war, from pestilence,
  from night-fear, from murder,
From falling, from stifling, from hunger, from cold, from
  slander, discontent and sloth;
That walk in beasts and birds of night, driven back by the
  sandy desert   [23
Like pestilent fogs round cities of men: and the happy earth
  sing in its course,
The mild peaceable nations be opened to heav'n, and men
  walk with their fathers in bliss."
Then hear the first voice of the morning: "Depart, O clouds of
  night, and no more
Return; be withdrawn cloudy war, troops of warriors depart,
  nor around our peaceable city
Breathe fires, but ten miles from Paris, let all be peace, nor a
  soldier be seen." '   [24
[*Page*] [13]
He ended; the wind of contention arose and the clouds cast
  their shadows, the Princes
Like the mountains of France, whose aged trees utter an awful
  voice, and their branches
Are shatter'd, till gradual a murmur is heard descending into
  the valley,
Like a voice in the vineyards of Burgundy, when grapes are
  shaken on grass;

Like the low voice of the labouring man, instead of the shout of
   joy; [*245*]
And the palace appear'd like a cloud driven abroad; blood ran
   down the ancient pillars,
Thro' the cloud a deep thunder, the Duke of Burgundy, delivers
   the King's command.

'Seest thou yonder dark castle, that moated around, keeps this
   city of Paris in awe.
Go command yonder tower, saying, "Bastile depart, and take
   thy shadowy course.
Overstep the dark river, thou terrible tower, and get thee up
   into the country ten miles. [*250*]
And thou black southern prison, move along the dusky road to
   Versailles; there
Frown on the gardens," and if it obey and depart, then the
   King will disband
This war-breathing army; but if it refuse, let the Nation's
   Assembly thence learn,
That this army of terrors, that prison of horrors, are the bands
   of the murmuring kingdom.'

Like the morning star arising above the black waves, when a
   shipwreck'd soul sighs for morning, [*255*]
Thro' the ranks, silent, walk'd the Ambassador back to the
   Nation's Assembly, and told
The unwelcome message; silent they heard; then a thunder
   roll'd round loud and louder,
Like pillars of ancient halls, and ruins of times remote they sat.
Like a voice from the dim pillars Mirabeau rose; the thunders
   subsided away;
[*Page*] [14]
A rushing of wings around him was heard as he brighten'd,
   and cried out aloud, [*260*]
'Where is the General of the Nation?' the walls re-echo'd:
   'Where is the General of the Nation?'

Sudden as the bullet wrapp'd in his fire, when brazen cannons
   rage in the field,

Fayette sprung from his seat saying, 'Ready!' then bowing like
  clouds, man toward man, the Assembly
Like a council of ardors seated in clouds, bending over the
  cities of men,
And over the armies of strife, where their children are mar-
  shall'd together to battle;   [26]
They murmuring divide, while the wind sleeps beneath, and
  the numbers are counted in silence,
While they vote the removal of War, and the pestilence
  weighs his red wings in the sky.

So Fayette stood silent among the Assembly, and the votes were
  given and the numbers numb'red;
And the vote was, that Fayette should order the army to
  remove ten miles from Paris.

The aged sun rises appall'd from dark mountains, and gleams
  a dusky beam   [27]
On Fayette, but on the whole army a shadow, for a cloud on the
  eastern hills
Hover'd, and stretch'd across the city and across the army, and
  across the Louvre,
Like a flame of fire he stood before dark ranks, and before
  expecting captains.
On pestilent vapours around him flow frequent spectres of
  religious men weeping;
In winds driven out of the abbeys, their naked souls shiver in
  keen open air,   [275]
Driven out by the fiery cloud of Voltaire, and thund'rous
  rocks of Rousseau,
They dash like foam against the ridges of the army, uttering
  a faint feeble cry.

[Page] [15]

Gleams of fire streak the heavens, and of sulphur the earth, from
  Fayette as he lifted his hand;
But silent he stood, till all the officers rush round him like
  waves

l. 274: In 1791, the line has no terminal punctuation.

Round the shore of France, in day of the British flag, when
heavy cannons   [*280*]
Affright the coasts, and the peasant looks over the sea and wipes
a tear;
Over his head the soul of Voltaire shone fiery, and over the
army Rousseau his white cloud
Unfolded, on souls of war, living terrors silent list'ning toward
Fayette,
His voice loud inspir'd by liberty, and by spirits of the dead,
thus thunder'd.

'The Nation's Assembly command, that the Army remove ten
miles from Paris;   [*285*]
Nor a soldier be seen in road or in field, till the Nation com-
mand return.'

Rushing along iron ranks glittering the officers each to his
station
Depart, and the stern captain strokes his proud steed, and in
front of his solid ranks
Waits the sound of trumpet; captains of foot stand each by his
cloudy drum;
Then the drum beats, and the steely ranks move, and trumpets
rejoice in the sky.   [*290*]
Dark cavalry like clouds fraught with thunder ascend on the
hills, and bright infantry, rank
Behind rank, to the soul shaking drum and shrill fife along the
roads glitter like fire.

The noise of trampling, the wind of trumpets, smote the palace
walls with a blast.
Pale and cold sat the king in midst of his peers, and his noble
heart sunk, and his pulses
Suspended their motion, a darkness crept over his eye-lids,
and chill cold sweat   [*295*]
Sat round his brows faded in faint death, his peers pale like
mountains of the dead,

l. 283: 1791: 'war-living'.

Cover'd with dews of night, groaning, shaking forests and
floods. The cold newt

[*Page*] [16]

And snake, and damp toad, on the kingly foot crawl, or croak
on the awful knee,

Shedding their slime, in folds of the robe the crown'd adder
builds and hisses

From stony brows; shaken the forests of France, sick the kings
of the nations,   [3

And the bottoms of the world were open'd, and the graves of
arch-angels unseal'd;

The enormous dead, lift up their pale fires and look over the
rocky cliffs.

A faint heat from their fires reviv'd the cold Louvre; the frozen
blood reflow'd.

Awful up rose the king, him the peers follow'd, they saw the
courts of the Palace

Forsaken, and Paris without a soldier, silent, for the noise was
gone up   [3

And follow'd the army, and the Senate in peace, sat beneath
morning's beam.   [3

END OF THE FIRST BOOK.

COMMENT ON THE DRAWINGS OF
THOMAS HEATH MALKIN IN
BENJ. HEATH MALKIN,

A FATHER'S MEMOIRS OF HIS CHILD

———

'THEY are all firm, determinate outline, or identical form.
Had the hand which executed these little ideas been that of a
plagiary, who works only from the memory, we should have
seen blots, called masses; blots without form, and therefore
without meaning. These blots of light and dark, as being the

result of labour, are always clumsy and indefinite; the effect of
rubbing out and putting in, like the progress of a blind man,
or of one in the dark, who feels his way, but does not see it.
These are not so. Even the copy from Raphael's Cartoon of
St. Paul preaching, is a firm, determinate outline, struck at
once, as Protogenes struck his line, when he meant to make
himself known to Apelles. The map of Allestone[1] has the same
character of the firm and determinate. All his efforts prove this
little boy to have had that greatest of blessings, a strong imagina-
tion, a clear idea, and a determinate vision of things in his own
mind.'

'TO THE QUEEN' (APRIL 1807) FROM BLAIR'S *GRAVE*

═══════

TO

THE QUEEN.

The Door of Death is made of Gold,
That Mortal Eyes cannot behold;
But, when the Mortal Eyes are clos'd,
And cold and pale the Limbs repos'd,
The Soul awakes; and, wond'ring, sees   [5]
In her mild Hand the golden Keys:
The Grave is Heaven's golden Gate,
And rich and poor around it wait;
O Shepherdess of England's Fold,
Behold this Gate of Pearl and Gold!   [10]

To dedicate to England's Queen
The Visions that my Soul has seen,

Malkin's *Memoirs*
   [1] The map of the imaginary country of Allestone is reproduced with Malkin's
text, but St. Paul Preaching is not.
'To the Queen'
   l. 12: For Blake's poem beginning 'The Visions of the Grave Ive seen', see
Notebook p. 87 (pp. 962–3).

And, by Her kind permission, bring
What I have borne on solemn Wing,
From the vast regions of the Grave,   [*1*
Before Her Throne my Wings I wave;
Bowing before my Sov'reign's Feet,
'The Grave produc'd these Blossoms sweet
'In mild repose from Earthly strife;
'The Blossoms of Eternal Life!'   [*2*

WILLIAM BLAKE.

'EXHIBITION OF PAINTINGS IN FRESCO, POETICAL AND HISTORICAL INVENTIONS'

═══════

EXHIBITION

OF

𝔓aintings in 𝔉resco,

Poetical and Historical Inventions,

By. Wm. BLAKE.

────────

[¶*1*] THE ANCIENT BRITONS—Three Ancient Britons overthrowing the Army of armed Romans; the Figures full as large as Life—From the Welch Triades.[1]

In the last Battle that Arthur fought, the most Beautiful was one
That return'd, and the most Strong another: with them also return'd

'To the Queen'
l. 18: 'sweet;' in the 1813 folio.
ll. 18–20: The quotation marks appear in the 1808 printed text.

'Exhibition of Paintings in Fresco'
    [1] These lines may derive from *The Bardic Museum*, ed. Edward Jones (1802), ii. 25: The 'Three Warriors [*who*] escaped from the battle of *Camlan*, where all their fellow-soldiers were slain' were '*Sanndev*, [*remarkable*] on account of his beauty, *Morvran*, for his ugliness and deformity; and *Glewlwyd*, for his gigantic size, strength, and civility'. A similar Triad (pointed out by S. F. Damon, *A Blake Dictionary* [1965], 443) is given in Welsh only in *The Myvyrian Archaiology of Wales*, Being a Collection of Historical Documents from Ancient Manuscripts [ed. William Owen, Owen Jones, and Edward Williams] (1801), ii. 18. Perhaps, as Crabb Robinson (1810) and Southey (1847) suggest (*Blake Records*, 451; 226, 399), Blake's information came through William Owen.

The most Ugly, and no other beside return'd from the bloody Field.

The most Beautiful, the Roman Warriors trembled before and worshipped: The most Strong, they melted before him and dissolved in his presence: The most Ugly they fled with outcries and contortion of their Limbs.

2] THE CANTERBURY PILGRIMS from *Chaucer*—a cabinet Picture in Fresco—Thirty Figures[2] on Horse-back, in a brilliant Morning Scene.

3] Two Pictures, representing grand Apotheoses of NELSON and PITT, with variety of cabinet Pictures, unchangeable and permanent in Fresco, and Drawings for Public Inspection and for Sale by Private Contract, at

No. 28, Corner of BROAD STREET, Golden-Square.[3]

4] *'Fit Audience find tho' few'* MILTON.[4]

5] Admittance 2s. 6d. each Person, a descriptive Catalogue included.[5]

6] Watts & Co. Printers, Southmolton St.

[*Page 2*]

THE INVENTION OF A PORTABLE FRESCO.

7] A Wall on Canvas or Wood, or any other portable thing, of dimensions ever so large, or ever so small, which may be removed with the same convenience as so many easel Pictures; is worthy the consideration of the Rich and those who have the direction of public Works. If the Frescos of APELLES, of PROTOGENES, of RAPHAEL, or MICHAEL ANGELO could have been removed, we might, perhaps, have them now in England. I

---

[2] In the *Descriptive Catalogue* (1809) itself, the picture is described as having twenty-nine figures (¶13, p. 831).

[3] At this address Blake's brother James had the family hosiery shop.

[4] The quotation marks appear in the 1809 printed text.

[5] In both surviving copies of the flyer, Blake added the words Containing / Ample Illustrations / on Art at the bottom of the page. The printed text just above reads 'discriptive'.

According to the advertisement for 'A Descriptive Catalogue' (p. 825), admission without the catalogue was 1s., '*an Index to the Catalogue gratis*'.

could divide Westminster Hall, or the walls of any other great Building, into compartments and ornament them with Frescos, which would be removable at pleasure.

[¶8] Oil will not drink or absorb Colour enough to stand the test of very little Time and of the Air; it grows yellow, and at length brown. It was never generally used till after VANDYKE's time. All the little old Pictures, called cabinet Pictures, are in Fresco, and not in Oil.

[¶9] Fresco Painting is properly Miniature, or Enamel Painting; every thing in Fresco is as high finished as Miniature or Enamel, although in Works larger than Life. The Art has been lost: I have recovered it. How this was done, will be told, together with the whole Process, in a Work on Art, now in the Press.[6] The ignorant Insults of Individuals will not hinder me from doing my duty to my Art. Fresco Painting, as it is now practised, is like most other things, the contrary of what it pretends to be.

[¶10] The execution of my Designs, being all in Water-colours, (that is in Fresco) are regularly refused to be exhibited by the *Royal Academy*, and the *British Institution* has, this year, followed its example, and has effectually excluded me by this Resolution; I therefore invite those Noblemen and Gentlemen,[7] who are its Subscribers, to inspect what they have excluded: and those who have been told that my Works are but an unscientific and irregular Eccentricity, a Madman's Scrawls, I demand of them to do me the justice to examine before they decide.

[¶11] There cannot be more than two or three great Painters or Poets in any Age or Country; and these, in a corrupt state of Society, are easily excluded, but not so easily obstructed. They have ex[c]luded Water-colours; it is therefore become necessary that I should exhibit to the Public, in an Exhibition of my own, my Designs, Painted in Water-colours. If Italy is enriched and made great by RAPHAEL, if MICHAEL ANGELO is its supreme

---

[6] For this unknown 'Work on Art', see pp. 1680–2.
[7] 1809: 'Gentleman'.

glory, if Art is the glory of a Nation, if Genius and Inspiration are the great Origin and Bond of Society, the distinction my Works have obtained from those who best understand such things, calls for my Exhibition[8] as the greatest of Duties to my Country.[9]

WILLIAM BLAKE.

'BLAKE'S CHAUCER: THE CANTERBURY PILGRIMS'

===

BLAKE's CHAUCER, *THE CANTERBURY PILGRIMS.*

THE FRESCO PICTURE,

Representing CHAUCER's Characters, painted by

WILLIAM BLAKE,

As it is now submitted to the Public,

[1]   THE Designer proposes to Engrave, in a correct and finished Line manner of Engraving, similar to those original Copper Plates of ALBERT DURER, LUCAS, HISBEN, ALDEGRAVE[1] and the old original Engravers, who were great Masters in Painting and Designing, whose method, alone, can delineate Character as it is in this Picture, where all the Lineaments are distinct.

'Exhibition of Paintings in Fresco'
   [8] 1809: 'Exhibition'.
   [9] Under the last line Blake wrote in both surviving copies of the flyer: 'May 15. 1809'.

'Blake's Chaucer: The Canterbury Pilgrims'
   [1] Albrecht Dürer (1471–1528), painter and engraver; Lucas van Leyden (1494–1533), Dutch painter and engraver; Hans Sebald Beham (1500–50) called Hisben, German engraver; Heinrich Aldegrever (1502–62), painter and engraver, pupil of Dürer.

[¶2]   It is hoped that the Painter will be allowed by the Public (notwithstanding artfully disseminated[2] insinuations to the contrary) to be better able than any other to keep his own Characters and Expressions; having had sufficient evidence in the Works of our own HOGARTH, that no other Artist can reach the original Spirit so well as the Painter himself, especially as Mr. B. is an old well-known and acknowledged Engraver.

[¶3]   The size of the Engraving will be 3-feet 1-inch long, by 1-foot high.—The Artist engages to deliver it, finished, in One Year from September next.[3]—No Work of Art, can take longer than a Year: it may be worked backwards and forwards without end, and last a Man's whole Life; but he will, at length, only be forced to bring it back to what it was, and it will be worse than it was at the end of the first Twelve Months. The Value of this Artist's Year is the Criterion of Society: and as it is valued, so does Society flourish or decay.

[¶4]   The Price to Subscribers—FOUR GUINEAS,[4] Two to be paid at the time of Subscribing, the other Two, on delivery of the Print.

[¶5]   Subscriptions received at No. 28, Corner of BROAD-STREET, GOLDEN-SQUARE; where the Picture is now Exhibiting, among other Works, by the same Artist.

[¶6]   The Price will be considerably raised to Non-subscribers.

May 15th. 1809.

Printed by Watts & Bridgewater, Southmolton-Street.

[2] 1809: 'dissemminated'.
[3] It is dated 8 Oct. 1810.
[4] In 1810 the price was lowered to three guineas (see p. 863).

'A DESCRIPTIVE CATALOGUE OF BLAKE'S EXHIBITION'

―――

A DESCRIPTIVE CATALOGUE

OF

BLAKE's EXHIBITION,

At No. 28, Corner of

BROAD-STREET,

GOLDEN-SQUARE.

¶*1*]   THE grand Style of Art restored; in FRESCO, or Water-colour Painting, and England protected from the too just imputation of being the Seat and Protectress of bad (that is blotting and blurring) Art.

¶*2*]   In this Exhibition will be seen real Art, as it was left us by *Raphael* and *Albert Durer, Michael Angelo,* and *Julio Romano*; stripped from the Ignorances of *Rubens* and *Rembrandt, Titian* and *Correggio*;

BY WILLIAM BLAKE.

¶*3*]   The Descriptive Catalogue, Price 2s. 6d. containing Mr. B's Opinions and Determinations on Art, very necessary to be known by Artists and Connoisseurs of all Ranks⌊.⌋ Every Purchaser of a Catalogue will be entitled, at the time of purchase, to view the Exhibition.

¶*4*]   These Original Conceptions on Art, by an Original Artist, are Sold only at the

Corner of BROAD STREET.

Admittance to the Exhibition 1 *Shilling; an Index to the Catalogue gratis.*

―――

Printed by Watts & Bridgewater, Southmolton-Street.

A

DESCRIPTIVE CATALOGUE

OF

PICTURES,

Poetical and Historical Inventions,

PAINTED BY

WILLIAM BLAKE,

IN

WATER COLOURS,

BEING THE ANCIENT METHOD OF

FRESCO PAINTING RESTORED:

AND

DRAWINGS,

FOR PUBLIC INSPECTION,

AND FOR

𝕾𝖆𝖑𝖊 𝖇𝖞 𝕻𝖗𝖎𝖇𝖆𝖙𝖊 𝕮𝖔𝖓𝖙𝖗𝖆𝖈𝖙,[1]

LONDON:

Printed by D. N. SHURY, 7,[2] Berwick-Street, Soho,
for J. BLAKE, 28, Broad-Street, Golden-Square.

1809.

Title-page [1] Under 'Sale by Private Contract,' Blake wrote
  At N 28 Corner of Broad Street Golden Square
on copies C, D, F, G, H, J, K, and O. The J. Blake at this address is the poet's
brother.
  [2] The address of Daniel Nathan Shury from 1801 to 1822 was apparently 17
(not 7) Berwick Street, Soho (according to W. B. Todd, *A Directory of Printers and
Others in Allied Trades* [*in*] *London and Vicinity 1800–1840* [1972], 174).

[*Page ii*]

CONDITIONS OF SALE.

1]   I. *One third of the price to be paid at the time of Purchase, and the remainder on Delivery.*

2]   II. *The Pictures and Drawings to remain in the Exhibition till its close, which will be the* 29th *of September* 1809;[1] *and the Picture of the Canterbury Pilgrims, which is to be engraved, will be Sold only on condition of its remaining in the Artist's hands twelve months, when it will be delivered to the Buyer.*

[*Page iii*]

PREFACE.

3]   THE eye that can prefer the Colouring of Titian and Rubens to that of Michael Angelo and Rafael, ought to be modest and to doubt its own powers. Connoisseurs talk as if Rafael and Michael Angelo had never seen the Colouring of Titian or Correggio: They ought to know that Correggio was born two years before Michael Angelo, and Titian but four years after.[1] Both Rafael and Michael Angelo knew the Venetian, and contemned and rejected all he did with the utmost disdain, as that which is fabricated for the purpose to destroy art.

4]   Mr. B. appeals to the Public, from the judgment of those narrow blinking eyes, that have too long governed art in a dark corner. The eyes of stupid cunning never will be

[*Page*] iv

pleased with the work any more than with the look of self- devoting genius. The quarrel of the Florentine with the Venetian is not because he does not understand Drawing, but because he does not understand Colouring. How should he[1] who does not know how to draw a hand or a foot, know how to colour i*t*?

¶2   [1] The exhibition clearly stayed open after 29 Sept. 1809, for the first independent reference to it is Robert Hunt's review of it in the *Examiner* for 17 Sept. 1809, George Cumberland, Jr. evidently saw it in Oct. 1809, H. C. Robinson went to it on 23 April 1810, and on 11 June 1810 he took Charles and Mary Lamb to see it (*Blake Records*, 215–19, 225, 226).

¶3   [1] Correggio (1494–1534), Michelangelo (1475–1564), Titian (*c.* 1490–1576). The erroneous facts about Michelangelo and Correggio are also given in Blake's notes (?1808) to Reynolds's *Works* (1798) p. 159 (p. 1489).

¶4   [1] 1809: 'How should he? he who . . .'

[¶*5*]   Colouring does not depend on where the Colours are put, but on where the lights and darks are put, and all depends on Form or Outlin*e*, on where that is put;[1] where that is wrong, the Colouring never can be right; and it is always wrong in Titian and Correggio, Rubens and Rembrandt. Till we get rid of Titian and Correggio, Rubens and Rembrandt, *we* never shall equal Rafael and Albert Durer, Michael Angelo, and Julio Romano.

[Page 1]

DESCRIPTIVE CATALOGUE,

&c. &c.

NUMBER I.

[¶*6*] *The spiritual form of Nelson guiding Leviathan, in whose wreathings are infolded the Nations of the Earth.*[1]

[¶*7*] CLEARNESS and precision have been the chief objects in painting these Picture*s*: Clear colours unmudded by oil, and firm and determinate lineaments unbroken by shadows, which ought to display and not to hide form, as is the practice of the latter Schools of Italy and Flanders.

[Page] 2

NUMBER II, ITS COMPANION

[¶*8*] *The spiritual form of Pitt, guiding Behemoth; he is that Angel who, pleased to perform the Almighty's orders, rides on the whirlwind, directing the storms of war: He is ordering the Reaper to reap the*

¶5 [1] 1809: 'Outline. On where that is put;'
¶6 [1] This picture, which is now in the Tate Gallery, was described in the *Catalogue of the Fifth Annual Exhibition of the Associated Painters in Water Colours* At the Society's Rooms, No. 16, Old Bond Street (1812) as 'The *S*piritual *F*orm of Nelson guiding Leviathan, in whose wreathings are *u*nfolded the Nations of the Earth' (differences from the 1809 text are indicated by italics).

On the back of his sketch for this design, Blake wrote: 'The Spirit of Nelson guiding Leviathan, in whose folds are entangled the Nations of the Earth' (according to Francis Harvey, who offered it in a catalogue of about 1864). It is apparently still another sketch (acquired by John Defett Francis in 1834 and given by him to the British Museum Print Room in 1873) which is inscribed: 'The Spirit of Nelson guiding Leviathan / in whose folds are intangled the Nations of the Ear[*th*]'. Cf. *Jerusalem* pl. 91, ll. 38–40, where the Spectre forms 'Leviathan And Behemoth: the War by Sea enormous & the War By Land astounding' (p. 621).

Vine of the Earth, and the Plowman to plow up the Cities and Towers.[1]

>] THIS Picture also is a proof of the power of colours unsullied with oil or with any cloggy vehicle. Oil has falsely been supposed to give strength to colours: but a little consideration must shew the fallacy of this opinion. Oil will not drink or absorb colour enough to stand the test of very little time and of the air. It deadens every colour it is mixed with, at its first mixture, and in a little time becomes a yellow mask over all that it touches. Let the works of modern Artists since Rubens' time

[*Page*] 3

witness the villa[i]ny of some one at that time, who first brought oil Painting into general opinion and practice: since which we have never had a Picture painted, that could shew itself by the side of an earlier production. Whether Rubens or Vandyke, or both, were guilty of this villa[i]ny, is to be enquired in another work on Painting, and who first forged the silly story and known fals[e]hood, about John of Bruges inventing oil colours:[1] in the mean time let it be observed, that before Vandyke's time, and in his time all the genuine Pictures are on Plaster or Whiting grounds and none since.

>] The two Pictures of Nelson and Pitt are compositions of a mythological cast, similar to those Apotheoses of Persian,

¶8 [1] The verso of the painting (now in the Tate Gallery) is inscribed as in the *Descriptive Catalogue*, with the following exceptions: ' "The *Spiritual Form* of Pitt [*no comma*] . . . Behemoth. *He* . . . angel . . . war. *He* is *commanding* the *reaper* . . . plough*man* to plough . . . *c*ities and *t*owers". / William Blake. / 1805'. (*N.B.* Pitt died on 23 Jan. 1806.) The description of the picture when it was exhibited in 1812 at the Water Colour Society was like that in the *Descriptive Catalogue*, except for 'The *Spiritual Form* of Pitt [*no comma*] guiding Behemoth: . . . rides *in* the *W*hirlwind . . . Storms of *W*ar; he . . . Reap . . . Plough*man* to *P*lough' (*Blake Records*, 231).
  Blake is silently quoting Addison's 'The Campaign' (1704), in which the 'godlike' Marlborough when in battle is compared to

> an angel [*who*] by divine command
> With rising tempests shakes a guilty land, . . .
> And, pleas'd th'Almighty's orders to perform,
> Rides in the whirlwind, and directs the storm.
> > (*The Miscellaneous Works* . . . [*of*]
> > *Joseph Addison* [1766], i. 89, 98.)

¶9 [1] For a discussion of this unpublished work see 'A Work on Art' (pp. 1680–2).

Hindoo, and Egyptian Antiquity, which are still preserved on rude monuments, being copies from some stupendous originals now lost or perhaps buried till some happier age. The Artist having been

[*Page*] 4

taken in vision into the ancient republics, monarchies, and patriarchates of Asia, has seen those wonderful originals called in the Sacred Scriptures the Cherubim, which were sculptured and painted on walls of Temples, Towers, Cities, Palaces, and erected in the highly cultivated states of Egypt, Moab, Edom, Aram, among the Rivers of Paradise, being originals from which the Greeks and Hetrurians copied Hercules Farnese,[1] Venus of Medicis, Apollo Belvidere, and all the grand works of ancient art. They were executed in a very superior style to those justly admired copies, being with their accompaniments terrific and grand in the highest degree. The Artist has endeavoured to emulate the grandeur of those seen in his vision, and to apply it to modern Heroes, on a smaller scale.

[¶*11*]　　No man can believe that either Homer's Mythology, or Ovid's, were the production of Greece, or of Latium; neither will any one

[*Page*] 5

believe, that the Greek statues, as they are called, were the invention of Greek Artists; perhaps the Torso is the only original work remaining; all the rest are evidently copies, though fine ones, from greater works of the Asiatic Patriarchs. The Greek Muses are daughters of Mnemosyne, or Memory, and not of Inspiration or Imagination, therefore not authors of such sublime conceptions. Those wonderful originals seen in my visions, were some of them one hundred feet in height; some were painted as pictures, and some carved as basso relievos, and some as groupes of statues, all containing mythological and recondite meaning, where more is meant than meets the eye. The Artist wishes it was now the fashion to make such monuments, and then he should not doubt of having a national commission to execute these two Pictures on a scale that is

¶10　[1] Blake's text was misprinted 'Hercules, Farnese'.

suitable to the grandeur of the nation, who is the parent of his heroes, in high

[*Page*] 6

finished fresco, where the colours would be as pure and as permanent as precious stones though the figures were one hundred feet in height.

2] All Frescos are as high finished as miniatures or enamels, and they are known to be unchangeable; but oil being a body itself, will drink or absorb very little colour, and changing yellow,[1] and at length brown, destroys every colour it is mixed with, especially every delicate colour. It turns every permanent white to a yellow and brown putty, and has compelled the use of that destroyer of colour, white lead; which, when its protecting oil is evaporated, will become lead again. This is an awful thing to say to oil Painters; they may call it madness, but it is true. All the genuine old little Pictures, called Cabinet Pictures, are in fresco and not in oil. Oil was not used except by blundering ignorance, till after Vandyke's time, but the art of fresco painting

[*Page*] 7

being lost, oil became a fetter to genius, and a dungeon to art. But one convincing proof among many others, that these assertions are true is, that real gold and silver cannot be used with oil, as they are in all the old pictures and in Mr. B.'s frescos.

NUMBER III.

3] *Sir Jeffery Chaucer and the nine and twenty Pilgrims on their journey to Canterbury.*[1]

4] THE time chosen is early morning, before sunrise, when the jolly company are just quitting the Tabarde Inn. The Knight and Squire with the Squire's Yeoman lead the Procession,

¶12 [1] Blake's intention may have been to write 'changing to yellow'.
¶13 [1] The number was incorrectly given when the picture (now in Pollok House) was exhibited at the Water Colour Society in 1812 as 'Sir Jeoffrey Chaucer and the Twenty-seven Pilgrims leaving the Tabarde Inn, in the Borough, on their Way to Canterbury, Morning' (*Blake Records*, 230).
Blake's engraving of the scene is inscribed: 'Chaucers Canterbury Pilgrims', 'Painted in Fresco by William Blake & by him Engraved & Published October 8

next follow the youthful Abbess, her nun and three priests; her greyhounds attend her.

> 'Of small hounds had she that she fed
> 'With roast flesh, milk and wastel bread.'[1]

Next follow the Friar and Monk; then the Tapiser, the Pardoner, and the Somner and Manciple. After these 'Our Host,' who oc-

[*Page*] 8

cupies the center of the cavalcade,[2] directs them to the Knight as the person who would be likely to commence their task of each telling a tale in their order. After the Host follow the Shipman, the Haberdasher, the Dyer, the Franklin, the Physician, the Plowman, the Lawyer, the poor Parson, the Merchant, the Wife of Bath, the Miller, the Cook, the Oxford Scholar, Chaucer himself, and the Reeve comes as Chaucer has described:

> 'And ever he rode hinderest of the rout.'[3]

These last are issuing from the gateway of the Inn; the Cook and the Wife of Bath are both taking their morning's draught

---

1810, at N° 28 Corner of Broad Street Golden Square'. To the left of the title in the third state is:

> A Morrow when the day began to spring
> Up rose our host and was our alder cocke
> The use of Money & its Wars.　　　　　　　　　　　　[*3*]

To the right of the title:

> An Allegory of Idolatry or Politics
> And gadrede us together on a flock　　　　　　　　　[*5*]
> Lets see now: who shall tell the first tale ⌊?⌋　　　[*6*]

(ll. 1–2, 5–6 are from the Author's Prologue, ll. 822–4, 831.)

After the date is: 'Ye gon to Canterbury God mote you spede.' (Author's Prologue, l. 769.)

¶14　[1] The old-spelling edition of Chaucer which Blake was using seems to have been that edited by Thomas Speght (1602)—see the note to ¶15 below. The identifications of the quotations below give in italics the differences between Speght's text and Blake's. The passage above is from the Author's Prologue, ll. 146–7 ('ro*st*', 'waste*ll*').

All the quotation marks here and throughout the *Descriptive Catalogue* are in the 1809 printed text—that is, in ¶14–15, 19, 21, 26, 28–9, 34–5, 38–9, 43–5, 51, 53, 54–5, 57–9, 62, 69, 84, 108—except for ¶54 (closing quote), where it is added by GEB.

[2] 1809 has an erroneous semicolon.

[3] Author's Prologue, l. 622 ('ro*ute*').

of comfort. Spectators stand at the gateway of the Inn, and are composed of an old Man, a Woman and Children.[4]

] The Landscape is an eastward view of the country, from the Tabarde Inn, in Southwark, as it may be supposed to have appeared in

[*Page*] 9

Chaucer's time; interspersed with cottages and villages; the first beams of the Sun are seen above the horizon; some buildings and spires indicate the situation of the great City, the Inn is a gothic building, which Thynne in his Glossary says was the lodging of the Abbot of Hyde, by Winchester.[1] On the Inn is inscribed its title, and a proper advantage is taken of this circumstance to describe the subject of the Picture. The words written over the gateway of the Inn, are as follow: 'The Tabarde Inn, by Henry Baillie, the lodgynge-house for Pilgrims, who journey to Saint Thomas's Shrine at Canterbury.'[2]

] The characters of Chaucer's Pilgrims are the characters which compose all ages and nations: as one age falls, another rises, different to mortal sight, but to immortals only the same; for we see the same characters repeated again and again, in animals, vegetables, minerals, and in men; nothing new occurs in iden-

---

[4] The characters are identified in Blake's engraving as

Reeve Chaucer Clerk of Oxenford Cook Miller Wife of Bath Merchant Parson Man of Law Plowman Physician Franklin 2 Citizens Shipman The Host Sompnour Maniciple Pardoner Monk Friar a Citizen Lady Abbess Nun 3 Priests, Squires Yeoman Knight Squire

In his description Blake omits a girl with a bottle, a boy with a jug, and a Black dog.

¶15 [1] The 'Tabard . . . is the signe of an Inne in Southwarke by London, within which was the lodging of the Abbot of Hyde by Winchester'—*The Workes of Our Ancient and Learned English Poet, Geffrey Chaucer* [ed. T. Speght] (1602), a note, perhaps by Francis Thynne [see A. Wood, *Alumni Oxonienses* (1721), i, col. 376], in the list of 'old and obscure words in Chaucer explained'. (For a confused but not implausible 'surmise that Blake used the Tyrwhitt edition' [1532 ff.], see K. Kiralis, 'William Blake as an intellectual and spiritual Guide to Chaucer's *Canterbury Pilgrims*', *Blake Studies*, i [1969], 167–74.)

[2] 'The inscription in the print is the same, except that the owner's name is given as 'Bailly'. In Blake's time the Gateway of the Inn was inscribed: 'THIS IS THE INN WHERE GEOFFREY CHAUCER, KNIGHT, AND NINE AND TWENTY PILGRIMS, LODGED IN THEIR JOURNEY TO CANTERBURY IN 1383' (according to a letter from P. in the *Gentleman's Magazine*, lxxxii [Sept. 1812], 217). The same source said that 'A well-painted Sign [*perhaps a misprint for* design] by Mr. Blake represents Chaucer and his merry Company setting out on their journey.'

[*Page*] 10

tical existence; Accident ever varies, Substance can never suffer change nor decay.[1]

[¶*17*]   Of Chaucer's characters, as described in his Canterbury Tales, some of the names or titles are altered by time, but the characters themselves for ever remain unaltered,[1] and consequently they are the physiognomies or lineaments of universal human life, beyond which Nature never steps. Names alter, things never alter. I have known multitudes of those who would have been monks in the age of monkery, who in this deistical age are deists. As Newton numbered the stars, and as Linneus numbered the plants, so Chaucer numbered the classes of men.[2]

[¶*18*]   The Painter has consequently varied the heads and forms of his personages into all Nature's varieties; the Horses he has also varied to accord to their Riders, the Costume is correct according to authentic monuments.[1]

[¶*19*]   The Knight and Squire with the Squire's

[*Page*] 11

Yeoman lead the procession, as Chaucer has also placed them first in his prologue. The Knight is a true Hero, a good, great, and wise man; his whole length portrait on horseback, as written by Chaucer, cannot be surpassed. He has spent his life in the field; has ever been a conqueror, and is that species of character which in every age stands as the guardian of man against the

¶16 [1] ¶13–16 were adapted in Blake's *Notebook* pp. 117–19 (pp. 1004–6) for a prospectus of the engraving from the painting of the Canterbury Pilgrims; for the printed prospectus see pp. 863–6.

¶17 [1] This sentence is quoted by the anonymous editor of *The Prologue and Characters of Chaucer's Pilgrim* (1812), published apparently to advertise Blake's Chaucer (see *Blake Records*, 230).

[2] Hazlitt echoed this passage in his *Lectures on the English Poets* (1818), 50: 'Chaucer, it has been said, numbered the classes of men, as Linnaeus numbered the plants. Most of them remain to this day: others that are obsolete, and may well be dispensed with, still live in his description of them.'

¶18 [1] At the back of the edition of Blair's *Grave* (1808) with etchings of Blake's designs is a 'PROSPECTUS' for the engraving of Stothard's picture of 'THE PROCESSION OF CHAUCER'S PILGRIMS TO CANTERBURY' (referred to by Blake in ¶52 as 'my rival's prospectus'), which asserts that in Stothard's painting 'The costume of each Person is correct with an antiquarian exactness' (p. 38). Here and elsewhere Blake's description of his 'Canterbury Pilgrims' seems to be aimed at an audience familiar with the claims made for Stothard in this Prospectus.

oppressor. His son is like him with the germ of perhaps greater perfection still, as he blends literature and the arts with his warlike studies. Their dress and their horses are of the first rate, without ostentation, and with all the true grandeur that unaffected simplicity when in high rank always displays. The Squire's Yeoman is also a great character, a man perfectly knowing in his profession:

'And in his hand he bare a mighty bow.'[1]

Chaucer describes here a mighty man; one who in war is the worthy attendant on noble heroes.

[*Page*] 12

The Prioress follows these with her female chaplain.

'Another Nonne also with her had she,
'That was her Chaplaine and Priests three.'[1]

This Lady is described also as of the first rank; rich and honoured. She has certain peculiarities and little delicate affectations, not unbecoming in her, being accompanied with what is truly grand and really polite; her person and face, Chaucer has described with minuteness; it is very elegant, and[1] was the beauty of our ancestors, till after Elizabeth's time, when voluptuousness and folly began to be accounted beautiful.

Her companion and her three priests were no doubt all perfectly delineated in those parts of Chaucer's work which are now lost; we ought to suppose them suitable attendants on rank and fashion.

[*Page*] 13

The Monk follows these with the Friar. The Painter has also grouped with these, the Pardoner and the Sompnour and the Manciple, and has here also introduced one of the rich citizens of London, Characters likely to ride in company, all being above the common rank in life or attendants on those who were so.

For the Monk is described by Chaucer, as a man of the first rank in society, noble, rich, and expensively attended: he is a leader of the age, with certain humourous accompaniments

¶19 [1] Author's Prologue, l. 108 ('might*ie*').
¶21 [1] Author's Prologue, ll. 163–4 ('chapl*ei*ne').
¶22 [1] Perhaps the intention here was: 'they are very elegant, as was the beauty of our ancestors . . .'.

in his character, that do not degrade, but render him an object of dignified mirth, but also with other accompaniments not so respectable.

[¶*26*]   The Friar is a character also of a mixed kind.

'A friar there was, a wanton and a merry.'[1]

[*B*]ut in his office he is said to be a 'full solemn man:'[2] eloquent, amorous, witty, and satyri-

[*Page*] 14

cal; young, handsome, and rich; he is a complete rogue; with constitutional gaiety enough to make him a master of all the pleasures of the world.

'His neck was white as the flour de lis,
Thereto strong he was as a champioun.'[3]

[¶*27*]   It is necessary here to speak of Chaucer's own character, that I may set certain mistaken critics right in their conception of the humour and fun that occurs on the journey. Chaucer is himself the great poetical observer of men, who in every age is born to record and eternize its acts. This he does as a master, as a father, and superior, who looks down on their little follies from the Emperor to the Miller; sometimes with severity, oftener with joke and sport.

[¶*28*]   Accordingly Chaucer has made his Monk a great tragedian, one who studied poetical art.

[*Page*] 15

So much so, that the generous Knight is, in the compassionate dictates of his soul, compelled to cry out

'Ho quoth the Knyght, good Sir, no more of this,
That ye have said, is right ynough I wis;
And mokell more, for little heaviness,
Is right enough for much folk as I guesse.
I say for me, it is a great disease,
Whereas men have been in wealth and ease;
To heare of their sudden fall alas,
And the contrary is joy and solas.'[1]

¶26   [1] Author's Prologue, l. 208 ('Fr*ere*').
      [2] Author's Prologue, l. 209 ('solem*pne*').
      [3] Author's Prologue, ll. 237–8 ('floure de*lice*').
¶28   [1] Nun's Priest's Tale, ll. 3952–9 ('q*d.* the knight', 'iwis', 'mokel', '*i*nough', 'folk*e*', 'gesse', 'be in welth', 'her suddaine').

9]   The Monk's definition of tragedy in the proem to his tale is
worth repeating:

> 'Tragedie is to tell a certain story,
> As old books us maken memory;
> Of hem that stood in great prosperity.
> And be fallen out of high degree,
> Into miserie and ended wretchedly.'¹   [5]

[*Page*] 16

0]   Though a man of luxury, pride and pleasure, he is a master
of art and learning, though affecting to despise it. Those who
can think that the proud Huntsman, and noble Housekeeper,
Chaucer's Monk, is intended for a buffoon or burlesque charac-
ter, know little of Chaucer.

1]   For¹ the Host who follows this group, and holds the center of
the cavalcade, is a first rate character, and his jokes are no
trifles; they are always, though uttered with audacity, and
equally free with the Lord and the Peasant, they are always
substantially and weightily expressive of knowledge and ex-
perience; Henry Baillie, the keeper of the greatest Inn, of the
greatest City; for such was the Tabarde Inn in Southwark, near
London: our Host was also a leader of the age.

2]   By way of illustration, I instance Shakspeare's Witches in
Macbeth. Those who dress

[*Page*] 17

them for the stage, consider them as wretched old women, and
not as Shakspeare intended, the Goddesses of Destiny; this
shews how Chaucer has been misunderstood in his sublime
work. Shakspeare's Fairies also are the rulers of the vegetable
world, and so are Chaucer's; let them be so considered, and
then the poet will be understood, and not else.

3]   But I have omitted to speak of a very prominent character,
the Pardoner, the Age's Knave, who always commands and
domineers over the high and low vulgar. This man is sent in
every age for a rod and scourge, and for a blight, for a trial of
men, to divide the classes of men, he is in the most holy sanc-

¶29   ¹ Monk's Tale, ll. 3132–6 ('certain*e*', 'book*es*', 'memor*ie*', 'prosperit*ie*', 'hie').
¶31   ¹ This 'For' seems to serve no purpose.

tuary, and he is suffered by Providence for wise ends, and has also his great use, and his grand leading destiny.

[¶*34*] His companion the Sompnour, is also a Devil of the first magnitude, grand, terrific, rich and honoured in the rank of which he holds

[*Page*] 18

the destiny. The uses to society are perhaps equal of the Devil and of the Angel, their sublimity who can dispu*te*?

'In daunger had he at his own gise,
The young girls of his diocese,
And he knew well their counsel, &c.'¹   [.

[¶*35*] The principal figure in the next groupe, is the Good Parson; an Apostle, a real Messenger of Heaven, sent in every age for its light and its warmth. This man is beloved and venerated by all, and neglected by all: He serves all, and is served by none; he is, according to Christ's definition, the greatest of his age. Yet he is a Poor Parson of a town. Read Chaucer's description of the Good Parson, and bow the head and the knee to him, who, in every age sends us such a burning and a shining light. Search O ye rich and powerful, for these men and obey their counsel, then

[*Page*] 19

shall the golden age return: But alas! you will not easily distinguish him from the Friar or the Pardoner, they also are 'full solemn men,' and their counsel, you will continue to follow.

[¶*36*] I have placed by his side, the Sergeant at Lawe, who appears delighted to ride in his company, and between him and his brother, the Plowman; as I wish men of Law would always ride with them, and take their counsel, especially in all difficult points. Chaucer's Lawyer is a character of great venerableness, a Judge, and a real master of the jurisprudence of his age.

[¶*37*] The Doctor of Physic is in this groupe, and the Franklin, the voluptuous country gentleman, contrasted with the Physician, and on his other hand, with two Citizens of London. Chaucer's characters live age after age. Every age is a Canterbury Pilgrimage; we all pass on, each sustaining one or other

¶34 ¹ Author's Prologue, ll. 663–5 ('owne', 'yong girl*es*', 'Diocise', 'knew *her* counsaile, and *was of her red*'). The terminal double quotation mark in 1809 is an apostrophe and a single quotation mark.

[*Page*] 20

of these characters; nor can a child be born, who is not one of these characters of Chaucer. The Doctor of Physic is described as the first of his profession; perfect, learned, completely Master and Doctor in his art. Thus the reader will observe, that Chaucer makes every one of his characters perfect in his kind, every one is an Antique Statue; the image of a class, and not of an imperfect individual.

38]   This groupe also would furnish substantial matter, on which volumes might be written. The Franklin is one who keeps open table, who is the genius of eating and drinking, the Bacchus; as the Doctor of Physic is the Esculapius, the Host is the Silenus, the Squire is the Apollo, the Miller is the Hercules, &c. Chaucer's characters are a description of the eternal Principles that exist in all ages. The Franklin is voluptuousness itself most nobly pourtrayed:

[*Page*] 21

'It snewed in his house of meat and drink.'[1]

39]   The Plowman is simplicity itself, with wisdom and strength for its stamina. Chaucer has divided the ancient character of Hercules between his Miller and his Plowman. Benevolence is the plowman's great characteristic, he is thin with excessive labour, and not with old age, as some have supposed.

> 'He would thresh and thereto dike and delve
> For Christe's sake, for every poore wight,
> . Withouten hire, if it lay in his might.'[1]   [*3*]

40]   Visions of these eternal principles or characters of human life appear to poets, in all ages; the Grecian gods were the ancient Cherubim of Phœnicia; but the Greeks, and since them the Moderns, have neglected to subdue the gods of Priam. These Gods are visions of the eternal attributes, or divine names, which, when

[*Page*] 22

erected into gods, become destructive to humanity. They ought to be the servants, and not the masters of man, or of society. They ought to be made to sacrifice to Man, and not man

¶38   1 Author's Prologue, l. 345 ('meat*e* and drink*e*').
¶39   1 Author's Prologue, ll. 536–9 ('di*lf*e').

compelled to sacrifice to them; for when separated from man or humanity, who is Jesus the Saviour, the vine of eternity, they are thieves and rebels, they are destroyers.

[¶*41*]   The Plowman of Chaucer is Hercules in his supreme eternal state, divested of his spectrous shadow; which is the Miller, a terrible fellow, such as exists in all times and places, for the trial of men, to astonish every neighbourhood, with brutal strength and courage, to get rich and powerful to curb the pride of Man.

[¶*42*]   The Reeve and the Manciple are two characters of the most consummate worldly wisdom. The Shipman, or Sailor, is a similar genius of Ulyssean art; but with the highest courage superadded.

[¶*43*]   The Citizens and their Cook are each leaders

[*Page*] 23

of a class. Chaucer has been somehow made to number four citizens,[1] which would make his whole company, himself included, thirty-one. But he says there was but nine and twenty in his company.

'Full nine and twenty in a company.'[2]

[¶*44*]   The Webbe, or Weaver, and the Tapiser, or Tapestry Weaver, appear to me to be the same person; but this is only an opinion, for full nine and twenty may signify one more or less. But I dare say that Chaucer wrote 'A Webbe Dyer,' that is a Cloth Dyer.

'A Webbe Dyer and a Tapiser,'[1]

[¶*45*]   The Merchant cannot be one of the Three Citizens, as his dress is different, and his character is more marked, whereas Chaucer says of his rich citizens:

[*Page*] 24

'All were yclothed in o liverie.'[1]

¶43   [1] The Stothard Prospectus in Blair's *Grave* (1808), p. 39, says: 'The last group of this motley Calvalcade is composed of *the Goldsmith, the Weaver, the Haberdasher, the Dyer*, and *the Tapestry Merchant*, all citizens of London'.
   [2] Author's Prologue, l. 24 ('Well nine and twent*ie*').
¶44   [1] Author's Prologue, l. 362 ('a webbe, *a* d*ie*r').
¶45   [1] Author's Prologue, l. 83 ('l*yu*ere').

6]   The characters of Women Chaucer has divided into two classes, the Lady Prioress and the Wife of Bath. Are not these leaders of the ages of men? The lady prioress, in some ages, predominates; and in some the wife of Bath, in whose character Chaucer has been equally minute and exact; because she is also a scourge and a blight. I shall say no more of her, nor expose what Chaucer has left hidden; let the young reader study what he has said of her: it is useful as a scare-crow. There are of such characters born too many for the peace of the world.

7]   I come at length to the Clerk of Oxenford. This character varies from that of Chaucer, as the contemplative philosopher varies from the poetical genius. There are always these two classes of learned sages, the poetical and the philosophical. The painter has put them side by side, as if the youthful clerk had put him-

[*Page*] 25

self under the tuition of the mature poet. Let the Philosopher always be the servant and scholar of inspiration and all will be happy.

8]   Such are the characters that compose this Picture, which was painted in self-defence against the insolent and envious imputation of unfitness for finished and scientific art; and this imputation, most artfully and industriously endeavoured to be propagated among the public by ignorant hirelings.¹ The painter courts comparison with his competitors, who, having received fourteen hundred guineas and more from the profits of his designs, in that well-known work, Designs for Blair's Grave, have left him to shift for himself, while others, more obedient to an employer's opinions and directions, are employed, at a great expence, to produce works, in succession to his, by which they acquired public patronage.² This has hitherto been his lot—to get patronage for others and then to be left and neglected, and his work, which gained

¶48   ¹ These imputations were made in reviews of his *Grave* designs (1808) in the *Examiner, Antijacobin Review*, and *Monthly Review (Blake Records*, 195–7, 199–210).

    ² The competitors here are Robert Hartley Cromek, who had commissioned Blake's *Grave* designs and Stothard's rival painting of the Canterbury Pilgrims, and Louis Schiavonetti, who engraved the first (1808) and was engaged on the second at his death.

[Page] 26

that patronage, cried down as eccentricity and madness; as unfinished and neglected by the artist's violent temper. He[3] is sure the works now exhibited, will give the lie to such aspersions.

[¶*49*] Those who say that men are led by interest are knaves. A knavish character will often say, of what interest is it to me to do so and so? I answer, of none at all, but the contrary, as you well know. It is of malice and envy that you have done this; hence I am aware of you, because I know that you act not from interest but from malice, even to your own destruction. It is therefore become a duty which Mr. B. owes to the Public, who have always recognized him, and patronized him, however hidden by artifices, that he should not suffer such things to be done or be hindered from the public Exhibition of his finished productions by any calumnies in future.

[¶*50*] The character and expression in this picture could never have been produced with Rubens'[1]

[Page] 27

light and shadow, or with Rembrandt's, or any thing Venetian or Flemish. The Venetian and Flemish practice is broken lines, broken masses, and broken colours. Mr. B.'s practice is unbroken lines, unbroken masses, and unbroken colours. Their art is to lose form, his art is to find form, and to keep it. His arts are opposite to theirs in all things.

[¶*51*] As there is a class of men, whose whole delight is in the destruction of men,[1] so there is a class of artists, whose whole art and science is fabricated for the purpose of destroying art. Who these are is soon known: 'by their works ye shall know them.' All who endeavour to raise up a style against Rafael, Mich. Angelo, and the Antique; those who separate Painting from Drawing; who look if a picture is well Drawn; and, if it is, immediately cry out, that it cannot be well Coloured—those are the men.

[¶*52*] But to shew the stupidity of this class of

¶48   3 1809: 'temper, he'.
¶50   1 1809: 'Ruben's'.
¶51   1 Cf. *Milton* pl. 2, Preface: 'there is a Class of Men whose whole delight is in Destroying'.

[*Page*] 28

men, nothing need be done but to examine my rival's prospectus.[1]

53]   The two first characters in Chaucer, the Knight and the Squire, he has put among his rabble; and indeed his prospectus calls the Squire the fop of Chaucer's age.[1] Now hear Chaucer.

> 'Of his Stature, he was of even length,
> And wonderly deliver, and of great strength;
> And he had be sometime in Chivauchy,
> In Flanders, in Artois, and in Picardy,
> And borne him well as of so litele space.'[2]   [5]

54]   Was this a fop?

> 'Well could he sit a horse, and faire ride,
> He could songs make, and eke well indite
> Just, and eke dance, pourtray, and well write.'[1]

55]   Was this a fop?

[*Page*] 29

> 'Curteis he was, and meek, and serviceable;
> And kerft before his fader at the table.'[1]

56]   Was this a fop?

57]   It is the same with all his characters; he has done all by chance, or perhaps his fortune, money, money. According to his prospectus he has Three Monks;[1] these he cannot find in Chaucer, who has only One Monk, and that no vulgar character, as he has endeavoured to make him. When men cannot read they should not pretend to paint. To be sure Chaucer is a little difficult to him who has only blundered over novels and catchpenny trifles of book-sellers.[2] Yet a little pains ought to be

---

¶52 [1] The Prospectus for Stothard's picture of 'The Procession of Chaucer's Pilgrims to Canterbury' printed at the back of the edition of Blair's *Grave* (1808) with etchings after Blake's designs.

¶53 [1] '*The Fop of Chaucer's Age* [*evidently the knight, who*] is exhibited as making a display of his riding', is with his Squire in the middle of the crowd (Blair's *Grave* [1808], 38).

   [2] Author's Prologue, ll. 83-7 ('*chiuauchie*', 'Flaunders', 'and Picard*ie*').

¶54 [1] Author's Prologue, ll. 94-6 ('si*te on* a', 'coud', '*endite*', 'da*u*nce', 'portray').

¶55 [1] Author's Prologue, ll. 99-100 ('he was, *lowly*, and ser*ui*sable', 'kerf*te*').

¶57 [1] The Prospectus in Blair's *Grave* (1808), 38, numbers three monks.

   [2] Stothard was perhaps the most popular book illustrator of his time and had made hundreds of designs, not only for novels, annuals, and diaries, but for poets

taken even by the ignorant and weak. He has put *the* Reeve, a vulgar fellow, between his Knight and Squire,[3] as if he was resolved to go contrary in every thing to Chaucer, who says of the Reeve:

[*Page*] 30

'And ever he rode hinderest of the rout.'[4]

[¶*58*] In this manner he has jumbled his dumb dollies together, and is praised by his equals for it; for both himself and his friend are equally masters of Chaucer's language. They both think that the Wife of Bath is a young beautiful blooming damsel; and H—— says, that she is the Fair Wife of Bath, and that the Spring appears in her Cheeks.[1] Now hear what Chaucer has made her say of herself, who is no modest one,

'But Lord when it remembereth me
Upon my youth and on my jollity,
It tickleth me about the heart root.
Unto this day it doth my heart boot,
That I have had my world as in my time;
But age, alas, that all will envenime,
Hath me bireft, my beauty and my pith
Let go; farewell: the devil go therewith,

[*Page*] 31

The flower is gone, there is no more to tell.
The bran, as best, I can, I now mote sell;
And yet, to be right merry, will I fond,
Now forth to tell of my fourth husband.'[2]

as well. Blake himself had engraved one of Stothard's designs for an edition of Chaucer of 1783.

[3] '*Betwixt* these two figures [The Young Squire *and* the Knight] is seen *the Reve*' in Stothard's picture (Blair's *Grave*, 39).

[4] Author's Prologue, l. 622 ('rout*e*').

¶58 [1] In a letter reprinted from *The Artist* for 30 May 1807 in Blair's *Grave* (1808), 40, John Hoppner said of Stothard's painting:

He has expressed too, with great vivacity and truth, the freshness of morning, at that season, when Nature herself is most fresh and blooming—the Spring; and it requires no great stretch of fancy to imagine we perceive the influence of it on the cheeks of the Fair Wife of Bath . . . .

[2] Wife of Bath's Tale, ll. 469–80 ('lord *Christ*', 'remembreth', 'and my *iolit*e', 'hart', 'woll', 'Hath *me* bireft', 'Devil*l*', 'gon', 'there *n*is', '[as best I can] now mote *I* sell', '*But* yet', 'mery w*o*ll', 'husb*o*nd').

59] 　　She has had four husbands, a fit subject for this painter; yet the painter ought to be very much offended with his friend H——, who has called his 'a common scene,' 'and very ordinary forms;'¹ which is the truest part of all, for it is so, and very wretchedly so indeed. What merit can there be in a picture of which such words are spoken with tru*th*?

61] 　　But the prospectus says that the Painter has represented Chaucer himself as a knave, who thrusts himself among honest people, to make game of and laugh at them;¹ though I must do justice to the painter, and say that he has made him look more like a fool than a knave. But it appears, in all the writings of Chaucer, and particularly in his Canterbury Tales, that

[*Page*] 32

he was very devout, and paid respect to true enthusiastic superstition. He has laughed at his knaves and fools as I do now. But he has respected his True Pilgrims, who are a majority of his company, and are not thrown together in the random manner that Mr. S—— has done. Chaucer has no where called the Plowman old, worn out with age and labour, as the prospectus has represented him, and says, that the picture has done so too.² He is worn down with labour, but not with age. How spots of brown and yellow, smeared about at random, can be either young or old, I cannot see. It may be an old man, it may be a young one; it may be any thing that a prospectus pleases. But I know that where there are no lineaments there can be no character. And what connoisseurs call touch, I know by experience, must be the destruction of all character and expression, as it is of every lineament.

1] 　　The scene of Mr. S——'s Picture is by

[*Page*] 33

Dulwich Hills,¹ which was not the way to Canterbury; but,

¶59 　¹ In the letter cited above, Hoppner claims that '*the painter has ingeniously contrived to give a value to a common scene and very ordinary forms, that would hardly be found, by unlearned eyes, in the natural objects*' (Blair's *Grave*, 40).

¶60 　¹ The Stothard Prospectus (Blair's *Grave* [1808], 38) says: 'The covert ridicule on these eccentric excursions [*Pilgrimages*], which Chaucer intended, is very happily preserved in his Face'.

　² The Stothard Prospectus (Blair's *Grave*, 38) refers to 'the *old Ploughman*, worn down with age and labour'.

¶61 　¹ According to the Prospectus, 'The Scene of the Picture is laid in that part

perhaps the painter thought he would give them a ride round about, because they were a burlesque set of scare-crows, not worth any man's respect or care.

[¶*62*] But the painter's thoughts being always upon gold, he has introduced a character that Chaucer has not; namely, a Goldsmith; for so the prospectus tells us.[1] Why he has introduced a Goldsmith, and what is the wit of it, the prospectus does not explain. But it takes care to mention the reserve and modesty of the Painter;[2] this makes a good epigram enough.

> 'The fox, the owl, the spider, and the mole,
> By sweet reserve and modesty get fat.'[3]　　　　　　[*2*]

[¶*63*] But the prospectus tells us, that the painter has introduced a Sea Captain;[1] Chaucer has a Ship-man, a Sailor, a Trading Master of a Ves-

[*Page*] 34

sel, called by courtesy Captain, as every master of a boat is; but this does not make him a Sea Captain. Chaucer has purposely omitted such a personage, as it only exists in certain periods: it is the soldier by sea. He who would be a Soldier in inland nations is a sea captain in commercial nations.

[¶*64*] All is misconceived, and its mis-execution is equal to its misconception. I have no objection to Rubens and Rembrandt being employed, or even to their living in a palace; but it shall not be at the expence of Rafael and Michael Angelo living in a cottage, and in contempt and derision. I have been scorned long enough by these fellows, who owe to me all that they have; it shall be so no longer.

> I found them blind, I taught them how to see;
> And, now, they know me not, nor yet themselves.[1]　　　[*2*]

of the road to Canterbury which commands a view of the Dulwich Hills' (Blair's *Grave* [1808], 38).

¶62　[1] Stothard's Prospectus does refer to '*the Goldsmith*' (Blair's *Grave* [1808], 39).

　[2] According to the Prospectus, 'The Proprietor of this undertaking [*Cromek*] finds it difficult to express his own and the general sense of Mr Stothard's qualifications, without violating that admirable Artist's known reserve and modesty of nature' (Blair's *Grave*, 39).

　[3] This couplet is given in a somewhat different form in the *Notebook*, p. 36 (p. 947).

¶63　[1] The Prospectus says that '*the Sea Captain* bestrides his Nag with the usual awkwardness of the Sailor' (Blair's *Grave* [1808], 38).

¶64　[1] This couplet is given in a somewhat different form on *Notebook* p. 34 (p. 945).

[*Page*] 35
NUMBER IV.

The Bard, from Gray.[1]

55]
On a rock, whose haughty brow
Frown'd o'er old Conway's foaming flood,
Robed in the sable garb of woe,
With haggard eyes the Poet stood,
Loose his beard, and hoary hair   [*5*]
Stream'd like a meteor to the troubled air.

Weave the warp, and weave the woof,
The winding sheet of Edward's race.   [*8*]

56] Weaving the winding sheet of Edward's race by means of sounds of spiritual music and its accompanying expressions of articulate speech is a bold, and daring, and most masterly conception, that the public have embraced and approved with avidity. Poetry consists in these conceptions; and shall Painting be confined to the sordid drudgery of fac-simile re-

[*Page*] 36

presentations of merely mortal and perishing substances, and not be as poetry and music are, elevated into its own proper sphere of invention and visionary conception? No, it shall not be so! Painting, as well as poetry and music, exists and exults in immortal thoughts. If Mr. B.'s Canterbury Pilgrims had been done by any other power than that of the poetic visionary, it would have been as dull as his adversary's.

57] The Spirits of the murdered bards assist in weaving the deadly woof.

With me in dreadful harmony they join,
And weave, with bloody hands, the tissue of thy line.

58] The connoisseurs and artists who have made objections to Mr. B.'s mode of representing spirits with real bodies,[1] would

¶65   [1] The tempera of 'The Bard' is now in the Tate Gallery. It must have been a different drawing of 'The Bard, from Gray' that Blake exhibited at the Royal Academy in 1785. His designs for Gray (1797) include fourteen for 'The Bard'.
¶68   [1] Blake was probably thinking of Robert Hunt's review of 'Blake's Edition of Blair's Grave' in the *Examiner* for 7 Aug. 1808, which proclaimed 'The utter impossibility of representing the *Spirit to the eye*' (see *Blake Records*, 195–7).

do well to consider that the Venus, the Minerva, the Jupiter, the Apollo, which they admire in Greek sta-

[*Page*] 37

tues, are all of them representations of spiritual existences of gods[2] immortal, to the mortal perishing organ of sight; and yet they are embodied and organized in solid marble. Mr. B. requires the same latitude and all is well. The Prophets describe what they saw in Vision as real and existing men whom they saw with their imaginative and immortal organs; the Apostles the same; the clearer the organ the more distinct the object. A Spirit and a Vision are not, as the modern philosophy supposes, a cloudy vapour or a nothing: they are organized and minutely articulated beyond all that the mortal and perishing nature can produce. He who does not imagine in stronger and better lineaments, and in stronger and better light than his perishing mortal eye can see does not imagine at all. The painter of this work asserts that all his imaginations appear to him infinitely more perfect and more minutely organized than any thing seen by his mortal eye. Spi-

[*Page*] 38

rits are organized men: Moderns wish to draw figures without lines, and with great and heavy shadows; are not shadows more unmeaning than lines, and more heavy? O who can doubt this?[3]

[¶69] King Edward and his Queen Elenor are prostrated, with their horses, at the foot of a rock on which the Bard stands; prostrated by the terrors of his harp on the margin of the river Conway, whose waves bear up a corse of a slaughtered bard at the foot of the rock. The armies of Edward are seen winding among the mountains.

'He wound with toilsome march his long array.'

[¶70] Mortimer and Gloucester lie spell bound behind their king.
[¶71] The execution of this picture is also in Water Colours, or Fresco.

¶68   [2] 1809: 'God's'.   [3] 1809: 'this!'.

848

[*Page*] 39
NUMBER V.

The Ancient Britons.

In the last Battle of King Arthur only Three Britons escaped, these were the Strongest Man, the Beautifullest Man, and the Ugliest Man; these three marched through the field unsubdued, as Gods, and the Sun of Britain set,[1] but shall arise again with tenfold splendor when Arthur shall awake from sleep, and resume his dominion over earth and ocean.[2]

The three general classes of men who are represented by the most Beautiful, the most Strong, and the most Ugly, could not be represented by any historical facts but those of our own country, the Ancient Britons; without violating costume. The Britons (say historians[1]) were naked civilized men, learned, studious, abstruse in thought and contemplation; naked, simple, plain, in their acts and manners;

[*Page*] 40

wiser than after-ages. They were overwhelmed by brutal arms all but a small remnant; Strength, Beauty, and Ugliness escaped the wreck, and remain for ever unsubdued, age after age.

The British Antiquities are now in the Artist's hands; all his visionary contemplations, relating to his own country and its ancient glory, when it was as it again shall be, the source of learning and inspiration. Arthur was a name for the constellation Arcturus, or Bootes, the Keeper of the North Pole. And all the fables of Arthur and his round table; of the warlike naked Britons; of Merlin; of Arthur's conquest of the whole world; of his death, or sleep, and promise to return again; of the Druid monuments, or temples; of the pavement of Watling-street; of London stone; of the caverns in Cornwall, Wales, Derbyshire, and Scotland; of the Giants of Ireland and Britain; of the elemental beings, called

[*Page*] 41

by us by the general name of Fairies; and of these three who

¶72   [1] 1809: 'sat'.
     [2] For the literary origin of this design see the advertisement for the Exhibition (p. 820). This enormous drawing, with its life-size figures, is now lost.
¶73   [1] 1809: 'histori ans'.

escaped, namely, Beauty, Strength, and Ugliness. Mr. B. has in his hands poems of the highest antiquity. Adam was a Druid, and Noah; also Abraham was called to succeed the Druidical age, which began to turn allegoric and mental signification into corporeal command, whereby human sacrifice would have depopulated the earth. All these things are written in Eden. The artist is an inhabitant of that happy country; and if every thing¹ goes on as it has begun, the world of vegetation and generation may expect to be opened again to Heaven, through Eden, as it was in the beginning.

[¶75]   The Strong man represents the human sublime. The Beautiful man represents the human pathetic, which was in the wars of Eden divided into male and female. The Ugly man represents the human reason. They were originally one man, who was fourfold; he was self-divided, and

[*Page*] 42

his real humanity slain on the stems of generation, and the form of the fourth was like the Son of God. How he became divided is a subject of great sublimity and pathos. The Artist has written it under inspiration, and will, if God please, publish it;¹ it is voluminous, and contains the ancient history of Britain, and the world of Satan and of Adam.

[¶76]   In the mean time he has painted this Picture, which supposes that in the reign of that British Prince, who lived in the fifth century, there were remains of those naked Heroes, in the Welch Mountains; they are there now, Gray saw them in the person of his bard on Snowdon; there they dwell in naked simplicity; happy is he who can see and converse with them above the shadows of generation and death. The giant Albion, was Patriarch of the Atlantic, he is the Atlas of the Greeks, one of those the Greeks called Titans. The stories of Arthur are the acts of Albion, ap-

[*Page*] 43

plied to a Prince of the fifth century, who conquered Europe,

¶74   ¹ 1809: 'thin g'.
¶75   ¹ This seems to refer to *Jerusalem* (1804–?20); 'the form of the fourth is like the Son of God' is from Daniel 3: 25.

and held the Empire of the world in the dark age, which the Romans never again recovered. In this Picture, believing with Milton, the ancient British History, Mr. B. has done, as all the ancients did, and as all the moderns, who are worthy of fame, given the historical fact in its poetical vigour; so as it always happens, and not in that dull way that some Historians pretend, who being weakly organized themselves, cannot see either miracle or prodigy; all is to them a dull round of probabilities and possibilities; but the history of all times and places, is nothing else but improbabilities and impossibilities; what we should say, was impossible if we did not see it always before our eyes.

The antiquities of every Nation under Heaven, is no less sacred than that of the Jews. They are the same thing as Jacob Bryant,[1]

[*Page*] 44

and all antiquaries have proved. How other antiquities came to be neglected and disbelieved, while those of the Jews are collected and arranged, is an enquiry, worthy of both the Antiquarian and the Divine. All had originally one language, and one religion, this was the religion of Jesus, the everlasting Gospel. Antiquity preaches the Gospel of Jesus. The reasoning historian, turner and twister of causes and consequences, such as Hume, Gibbon and Voltaire,[2] cannot with all their artifice, turn or twist one fact or disarrange self evident action and reality. Reasons and opinions concerning acts, are not history. Acts themselves alone are history, and these are neither the exclusive property of Hume, Gibbon nor Voltaire, Echard, Rapin, Plutarch, nor Herodotus. Tell me the Acts, O historian, and leave me to reason upon them as I please; away with your reasoning and your rubbish. All that is not action is not

[*Page*] 45

worth reading. Tell me the What; I do not want you to tell me the Why, and the How; I can find that out myself, as well

---

¶77   [1] Jacob Bryant, *A New System, or, an Analysis of Ancient Mythology*, 3 vols. (1774–6), for which Blake probably designed and engraved some plates signed by his master Basire.
   [2] 1809: 'Voltaire;'.

as you can, and I will not be fooled by you into opinions, that you please to impose, to disbelieve what you think improbable or impossible. His opinion,[3] who does not see spiritual agency, is not worth any man's reading; he who rejects a fact because it is improbable, must reject all History and retain doubts only.

[¶78]   It has been said to the Artist, take the Apollo for the model of your beautiful Man and the Hercules for your strong Man, and the Dancing Fawn for your Ugly Man. Now he comes to his trial. He knows that what he does is not inferior to the grandest Antiques. Superior they cannot be, for human power cannot go beyond either what he does, or what they have done, it is the gift of God, it is inspiration and vision. He had resolved to emulate those

[Page] 46

precious remains of antiquity ⌊;⌋ he has done so and the result you behold; his ideas of strength and beauty have not been greatly different. Poetry as it exists now on earth, in the various remains of ancient authors, Music as it exists in old tunes or melodies, Painting and Sculpture as it exists in the remains of Antiquity and in the works of more modern genius, is Inspiration, and cannot be surpassed; it is perfect and eternal. Milton, Shakspeare, Michael Angelo, Rafael, the finest specimens of Ancient Sculpture and Painting, and Architecture, Gothic, Grecian, Hindoo and Egyptian, are the extent of the human mind. The human mind cannot go beyond the gift of God, the Holy Ghost. To suppose that Art can go beyond the finest specimens of Art that are now in the world, is not knowing what Art is; it is being blind to the gifts of the spirit.

[Page] 47

[¶79]   It will be necessary for the Painter to say something concerning his ideas of Beauty, Strength and Ugliness.

[¶80]   The Beauty that is annexed and appended to folly, is a lamentable accident and error of the mortal and perishing life; it does but seldom happen; but with this unnatural mixture the sublime Artist can have nothing to do; it is fit for the burlesque. The Beauty proper for sublime art, is lineaments, or forms and features that are capable of being the

¶77   [3] The *s* of 'opinions' printed in 1809 is deleted in copy K.

receptacles of intellect; accordingly the Painter has given in his beautiful man, his own idea of intellectual Beauty. The face and limbs that deviates or alters least, from infancy to old age, is the face and limbs of greatest Beauty and perfection.

❧] The Ugly likewise, when accompanied and annexed to imbecility and disease, is a subject for burlesque and not for historical grandeur; the Artist has imagined his Ugly man; one

[*Page*] 48

approaching to the beast in features and form, his forehead small, without frontals; his jaws large; his nose high on the ridge, and narrow; his chest and the stamina of his make, comparatively little, and his joints and his extremities large; his eyes with scarce any whites, narrow and cunning, and every thing tending toward what is truly Ugly; the incapability of intellect.

❧] The Artist has considered his strong Man as a receptacle of Wisdom, a sublime energizer; his features and limbs do not spindle out into length, without strength, nor arc they too large and unwieldy for his brain and bosom. Strength consists in accumulation of power to the principal seat, and from thence a regular gradation and subordination; strength is compactness, not extent nor bulk.

❧] The strong Man acts from conscious superiority, and marches on in fearless dependance on the divine decrees, raging with the inspira-

[*Page*] 49

tions of a prophetic mind. The Beautiful Man acts from duty, and anxious solicitude for the fates of those for whom he combats. The Ugly Man acts from love of carnage, and delight in the savage barbarities of war, rushing with sportive precipitation into the very teeth of the affrighted enemy.

❧] The Roman Soldiers rolled together in a heap before them: 'Like the rolling thing before the whirlwind;'[1] each shew a different character, and a different expression of fear, or revenge, or envy, or blank horror, or amazement, or devout wonder and unresisting awe.

¶84 [1] Isaiah 17: 13: 'The nations . . . shall be chased . . . like a rolling thing before the whirlwind.'

[¶85]   The dead and the dying, Britons naked, mingled with armed Romans, strew the field beneath. Among these, the last of the Bards who were capable of attending warlike deeds, is seen falling, outstretched among the dead and the dying; singing to his harp in the pains of death.

[*Page*] 50

[¶86]   Distant among the mountains, are Druid Temples, similar to Stone Henge. The Sun sets behind the mountains, bloody with the day of battle.

[¶87]   The flush of health in flesh, exposed to the open air, nourished by the spirits of forests and floods, in that ancient happy period, which history has recorded, cannot be like the sickly daubs of Titian or Rubens. Where will the copier of nature, as it now is, find a civilized man, who has been accustomed to go nake*d*? Imagination only, can furnish us with colouring appropriate, such as is found in the Frescos of Rafael and Michael Angelo: the disposition of forms always directs colouring in works of true art. As to a modern Man stripped from his load of cloathing, he is like a dead corpse. Hence Rubens, Titian, Correggio, and all of that class, are like leather and chalk; their men are like leather, and their women like chalk, for the disposition of their

[*Page*] 51

forms will not admit of grand colouring; in Mr. B.'s Britons, the blood is seen to circulate in their limbs; he defies competition in colouring.

NUMBER VI.[1]

[¶88]   *A Spirit vaulting from a cloud to turn and wind a fiery Pegasus—Shakspeare.[2] The Horse of Intellect is leaping from the cliffs of Memory and Reasoning; it is a barren Rock: it is also called the Barren Waste of Locke and Newton.*

[¶89]   THIS Picture was done many years ago, and was one of the

¶88   [1] Drawing VI is now lost.
    [2] See *1 Henry IV*, iv. i. 104–10: Young Harry

> vaulted with such ease into his seat,
> As if an angel dropp'd down from the clouds,
> To turn and wind a fiery Pegasus,
> And witch the world with noble horsemanship.

Blake copied the drawing in the water-colour (inscribed 'W Blake 1809') in the second folio that he helped to illustrate for the Revd. Mr. Joseph Thomas.

first Mr. B. ever did in Fresco; fortunately or rather providentially he left it unblotted and unblurred, although molested continually by blotting and blurring demons; but he was also compelled to leave it unfinished for reasons that will be shewn in the following.[1]

[*Page*] 52

NUMBER VII.[1]

)]

√] *The Goats, an experiment Picture.*

√] T HE subject is taken from the Missionary Voyage and varied from the literal fact, for the sake of picturesque scenery. The savage girls had dressed themselves with vine leaves, and some goats on board the missionary ship stripped them off presently.[1] This Picture was painted at intervals, for experiment, with the colours, and is laboured to a superabundant blackness; it has however that about it, which may be worthy the attention of the Artist and Connoisseur for reasons that follow.[2]

NUMBER VIII.[1]

?]

¡] *The spiritual Preceptor, an experiment Picture.*

¡] T HIS subject is taken from the visions of Emanuel Swedenborg. Universal Theology,

[*Page*] 53

No. 623. The Learned, who strive to ascend into Heaven by means of learning, appear to Children like dead horses, when repelled by the celestial spheres.[1] The works of this

¶89   [1] See ¶95–8.
¶90   [1] This drawing is now lost.
¶91   [1] According to James Wilson, *A Missionary Voyage to the Southern Pacific Ocean* (1799), 129–30, when the ship Duff was in the Marquesas in June 1797, 'Seven beautiful young women, [*came*] swimming [*round the ship*] quite naked, except a few green leaves tied around their middle . . . calling Waheine! ["We are women!"] . . . [*When they came on board*] our mischievous goats [*did not*] even suffer them to keep their green leaves, but as they turned to avoid them they were attacked on each side alternately, and completely stripped naked.'
  [2] The 'reasons that follow' are apparently those in ¶95–9.
¶92   [1] This drawing is now lost.
¶93   [1] Emanuel Swedenborg, *True Christian Religion*; Containing The Universal Theology of the New Church [tr. J. Clowes] (1781), i. 237: 'It was once given to me to see Three Hundred . . . Men of reputed Learning and Erudition . . . ascend into . . . Heaven . . . [*but soon*] they cast themselves down headlong . . . . There were

visionary are well worthy the attention of Painters and Poets; they are foundations for grand things; the reason they have not been more attended to, is, because corporeal demons have gained a predominance; who the leaders of these are, will be shewn below. Unworthy Men who gain fame among Men, continue to govern mankind after death, and in their spiritual bodies, oppose the spirits of those, who worthily are famous; and as Swedenborg observes, by entering into disease and excrement, drunkenness and concupiscence, they possess themselves of the bodies of mortal men, and shut the doors of mind and of thought, by placing Learning above Inspiration. O Artist! you may disbelieve all this, but it shall be at your own peril.

[*Page*] 54

NUMBER IX.

[¶*94*] *Satan calling up his Legions, from Milton's Paradise Lost; a composition for a more perfect Picture, afterward executed for a Lady of high rank.*[1] *An experiment Picture.*

[¶*95*] THIS Picture was likewise painted at intervals, for experiment on colours, without any oily vehicle; it may be worthy of attention, not only on account of its composition, but of the great labour which has been bestowed on it, that is, three or four times as much as would have finished a more perfect Picture; the labour has destroyed the lineaments, it was with difficulty brought back again to a certain effect, which it had at first, when all the lineaments were perfect.

[¶*96*]   These Pictures, among numerous others painted for experiment, were the result of

[*Page*] 55

temptations and perturbations, labouring to destroy Imaginative power, by means of that infernal machine, called Chiaro

some young Children below who saw them descending, and in their Descent supposed them to be dead Horses'. 'The Reason of their appearing like dead Horses in their descent was, because the Understanding of Truth appears by Correspondence like a Horse, and the Understanding of Truth annihilated, like a dead Horse.'

¶94 [1] The 'Picture afterward executed' is now in Petworth House, and was probably commissioned by the wife of the third Earl of Egremont (see Blake's letter of 18 Jan. 1808, pp. 1637–41). The drawing exhibited in 1809 is now in the Victoria and Albert Museum.

Oscuro, in the hands of Venetian and Flemish Demons; whose enmity to the Painter himself, and to all Artists who study in the Florentine and Roman Schools, may be removed by an exhibition and exposure of their vile tricks. They cause that every thing in art shall become a Machine. They cause that the execution shall be all blocked up with brown shadows. They put the original Artist in fear and doubt of his own original conception. The spirit of Titian was particularly active, in raising doubts concerning the possibility of executing without a model, and when once he had raised the doubt, it became easy for him to snatch away the vision time after time, for when the Artist took his pencil, to execute his ideas, his power of imagination weakened so much, and darkened, that memory of nature and of Pictures

[*Page*] 56

of the various Schools possessed his mind, instead of appropriate execution, resulting from the inventions; like walking in another man's style, or speaking or looking in another man's style and manner, unappropriate and repugnant to your own individual character; tormenting the true Artist, till he leaves the Florentine, and adopts the Venetian practice, or does as Mr. B. has done, has the courage to suffer poverty and disgrace, till he ultimately conquers.

7]   Rubens is a most outrageous demon, and by infusing the remembrances of his Pictures, and style of execution, hinders all power of individual thought: so that the man who is possessed by this demon, loses all admiration of any other Artist, but Rubens, and those who were his imitators and journeymen, he causes to the Florentine and Roman Artist fear to execute; and though the original conception was all fire and animation, he loads it with

[*Page*] 57

hellish brownness, and blocks up all its gates of light, except one, and that one he closes with iron bars, till the victim is obliged to give up the Florentine and Roman practice, and adopt the Venetian and Flemish.

8]   Correggio is a soft and effeminate and consequently a most cruel demon, whose whole delight is to cause endless labour to whoever suffers him to enter his mind. The story that is told in all Lives of the Painters about Correggio being poor and but badly paid for his Pictures, is altogether false; he was a petty Prince, in Italy, and employed numerous Journeymen in manufacturing (as Rubens and Titian did) the Pictures that go under his name. The manual labour in these Pictures of Correggio is immense, and was paid for originally at the immense prices that those who keep manufactories of art always charge to their employers, while they themselves pay their journeymen little enough. But though

[*Page*] 58

Correggio was not poor, he will make any true artist so, who permits him to enter his mind, and take possession of his affections; he infuses a love of soft and even tints without boundaries, and of endless reflected lights, that confuse one another, and hinder all correct drawing from appearing to be correct; for if one of Rafael or Michael Angelo's figures was to be traced, and Correggio's reflections and refractions to be added to it, there would soon be an end of proportion and strength, and it would be weak, and pappy, and lumbering, and thick headed, like his own works; but then it would have softness and evenness, by a twelvemonth's labour, where a month would with judgment have finished it better and higher; and the poor wretch who executed it, would be the Correggio that the life writers have written of: a drudge and a miserable man, compelled to softness by poverty. I say again, O Artist, you may disbe-

[*Page*] 59

lieve all this, but it shall be at your own peril.

[¶99]   Note. These experiment Pictures have been bruized and knocked about, without mercy, to try all experiments.

NUMBER X.

[¶*100*]   *The Bramins.—A Drawing.*[1]

[¶*101*] The subject is, Mr. Wilkin, translating the Geeta; an ideal design, suggested by the first publication of that part of the

¶100   [1] This drawing is now lost.

Hindoo Scriptures, translated by Mr. Wilkin.¹ I understand that my Costume is incorrect, but in this I plead the authority of the ancients, who often deviated from the Habits, to preserve the Manners, as in the instance of Laocoon, who, though a priest, is represented naked.

[*Page*] 60

NUMBER XI.

2] *The body of Abel found by Adam and Eve; Cain, who was about to bury it, fleeing from the face of his Parents.—A Drawing.*¹

NUMBER XII.

3] *The Soldiers casting lots for Christ's Garment.—A Drawing.*¹

NUMBER XIII.

4] *Jacob's Ladder.—A Drawing.*¹

NUMBER XIV.

5] *The Angels hovering over the Body of Jesus in the Sepulchre.—A Drawing.*¹

6] The above four drawings the Artist wishes were in Fresco, on an enlarged scale to orna-

[*Page*] 61

ment the altars of churches, and to make England like Italy, respected by respectable men of other countries on account of Art. It is not the want of genius, that can hereafter be laid to our charge, the Artist who has done these Pictures and Drawings

¶101 ¹ *The Bhăgvăt-Gēētā*, or Dialogues of Krĕĕshnă and Ărjŏŏn, tr. Charles Wilkins (1785).

¶102 ¹ The copy of 'The Body of Abel found by Adam and Eve' exhibited in 1809 is in the Fogg Museum, a copy by Blake (*c.* 1826) is in the Tate Gallery (both reproduced in *William Blake's Illustrations to the Bible*, ed. G. Keynes [1957], pl. 15 a–b), and Linnell made a copy *c.* 1821, perhaps that in the Keynes collection. The incident does not appear in the Bible, but the scene is described in Blake's *Ghost of Abel* pl. 1 (p. 670).

¶103 ¹ 'The Soldiers casting lots for Christ's Garment' is now in the Fitzwilliam Museum (reproduced in D. Bindman, *William Blake* [1970], pl. 10).

¶104 ¹ 'Jacob's Ladder' is now in the British Museum Print Room.

¶105 ¹ 'The Angels hovering over the Body of Jesus in the Sepulchre' is now in private hands.

will take care of that; let those who govern the Nation, take care of the other. The times require that every one should speak out boldly; England expects that every man should do his duty,[1] in Arts, as well as in Arms, or in the Senate.

NUMBER XV.

[¶*107*]   *Ruth.—A Drawing.*[1]

[¶*108*] THIS Design is taken from that most pathetic passage in the Book of Ruth, where Naomi having taken leave of her daughters in law, with intent to return to her own country; Ruth cannot leave her, but says, 'Whither

[*Page*] 62

thou goest I will go; and where thou lodgest I will lodge, thy people shall be my people, and thy God my God: where thou diest I will die, and there will I be buried; God do so to me and more also, if ought but death part thee and me.'[1]

[¶*109*]   The distinction that is made in modern times between a Painting and a Drawing proceeds from ignorance of art. The merit of a Picture is the same as the merit of a Drawing. The dawber dawbs his Drawings; he who draws his Drawings draws his Pictures. There is no difference between Rafael's Cartoons and his Frescos, or Pictures, except that the Frescos, or Pictures, are more finished. When Mr. B. formerly painted in oil colours his Pictures were shewn to certain painters and connoisseurs, who said that they were very admirable Drawings on canvass; but not Pictures: but they said the same of Rafael's Pictures.

[*Page*] 63

Mr. B. thought this the greatest of compliments, though it was meant otherwise. If losing and obliterating the outline constitutes a Picture, Mr. B. will never be so foolish as to do one. Such art of losing the outlines is the art of Venice and Flanders; it loses all character, and leaves what some

¶106   [1] This is Nelson's Order of the Day to the fleet before the battle of Trafalgar (1805): 'England expects that every man will do his duty'.
¶107   [1] 'Ruth' (1803) is now in the Southampton Art Gallery.
¶108   [1] Ruth 1: 16–17.

people call, expression: but this is a false notion of expression; expression cannot exist without character as its stamina; and neither character nor expression can exist without firm and determinate outline. Fresco Painting is susceptible of higher finishing than Drawing on Paper, or than any other method of Painting. But he must have a strange organization of sight who does not prefer a Drawing on Paper to a Dawbing in Oil by the same master, supposing both to be done with equal care.

•]   The great and golden rule of art, as well as of life, is this: That the more distinct, sharp,

[*Page*] 64

and wirey the bounding line, the more perfect the work of art; and the less keen and sharp, the greater is the evidence of weak imitation, plagiarism, and bungling. Great inventors, in all ages, knew this: Protogenes and Apelles knew each other by this line. Rafael and Michael Angelo, and Albert Durer, are known by this and this alone. The want of this determinate and bounding form evidences the idea of want[1] in the artist's mind, and the pretence of the plagiary in all its branches. How do we distinguish the oak from the beech, the horse from the ox, but by the bounding outline? How do we distinguish one face or countenance from another, but by the bounding line and its infinite inflexions and movements? What is it that builds a house and plants a garden, but the definite and determinate? What is it that distinguishes honesty from knavery, but the hard and wirey line of rectitude and certainty

[*Page*] 65

in the actions and intention*s*? Leave out this l[*i*]ne and you leave out life itself; all is chaos again, and the line of the almighty must be drawn out upon it before man or beast can exist. Talk no more then of Correggio, or Rembrandt, or any any other of those plagiaries of Venice or Flanders. They were but the lame imitators of lines drawn by their predecessors, and their works prove themselves contemptible dis-arranged imitations and blundering misapplied copies.

¶110   [1] 'of want' is deleted in 1809 and 'want of' inserted over a caret before 'idea' in copies B–D, F–H, J, L, and O.

NUMBER XVI.

[¶*111*] *The Penance of Jane Shore in Saint Paul's Church.—A Drawing.*[1]

[¶*112*] THIS Drawing was done above Thirty Years ago, and proves to the Author, and he thinks will prove to any discerning eye, that the productions of our youth and of our maturer age

[*Page*] 66

are equal in all essential points. If a man is master of his profession, he cannot be ignorant that he is so; and if he is not employed by those who pretend to encourage art, he will employ himself, and laugh in secret at the pretences of the ignorant, while he has every night dropped into his shoe, as soon as he puts it off, and puts out the candle, and gets into bed, a reward for the labours of the day, such as the world cannot give, and patience and time await to give him all that the world can give.

FINIS.

D. N. SHURY, PRINTER, BERWICK-STREET,
SOHO, LONDON.

[*Page 67*]
INDEX
TO THE
CATALOGUE.

[*Page in
present text*]

¶111 [1] 'The Penance of Jane Shore' is now in the Tate Gallery (reproduced in M. Butlin, *William Blake* [1971], 33) and a later version is in the Verney Collection.

'BLAKE'S CHAUCER: AN ORIGINAL ENGRAVING . . .'

———

𝔅𝔩𝔞𝔨𝔢'𝔰 ℭ𝔥𝔞𝔲𝔠𝔢𝔯 :¹

1] An Original Engraving by him from his Fresco Painting of
Sir Jeffery Chaucer and his Nine and Twenty Pilgrims setting
forth from Southwark on their Journey to Canterbury.

2]   Three Feet 1 Inch long, and 1 Foot high:²
                Price Three Guineas.

———

Index ¹ Page '30' should be '39'.

Blake's Chaucer
   ¹ This prospectus combines elements from the draft in the *Notebook*, pp. 117–19
(pp. 1004–6), and from the *Descriptive Catalogue* (1809), ¶14–15, 17, from which
in turn the *Notebook* draft derives. The printed prospectus adds to the *Notebook*

[*See overleaf for note 1 cont. and note 2*]

[¶3] THE time chosen is early morning before sun-rise when the Jolly Company are just quitting the Tabarde Inn. The Knight and Squire with the Squire's Yeoman³ lead the Procession; then the youthful Abbess, her Nun and three Priests: her Grey-hounds attend her

'Of small hounds had she, that she fed
With roast flesh, milk and wastel bread.'

[¶4] Next follow the Friar and Monk, then the Tapster,⁴ the Pardoner, the Sompnour and the Manciple. After these 'Our Host,' who occupies the Center of the Cavalcade, directs them to the Knight as the person who will be likely to commence their Task of each telling a Tale in their order. After the Host follow the Shipman, the Haberdasher, the Dyer, the Franklin, the Physician, the Plowman, the Lawyer, the Parson, the Merchant, the Wife of Bath, the

([*Page*] 2)

Cook, the Oxford Scholar, Chaucer himself, and the Reeve comes as Chaucer has described:

'And ever he rode hinderest of the rout.'

version ¶6-7, 9-10, and the price, and in ¶1 alters 'William Blake' to 'him'. The prospectus follows the *Notebook* rather than the *Descriptive Catalogue* in giving 'in Gothic letters' and 'Bailly' in ¶8 and in erroneously omitting 'the Miller' after 'the Wife of Bath' in ¶4; it follows the *Descriptive Catalogue* rather than the *Notebook* in giving 'first' ('The first beams of the sun') and 'of the Inn' in ¶8, and it takes ¶9 from *Descriptive Catalogue* ¶17-18.

These differences suggest that the manuscript from which the printer worked was a version of the *Notebook* draft expanded by further reference to the *Descriptive Catalogue* account.

The sources of the quotations are given in the annotations to the *Descriptive Catalogue* (pp. 832-3, 844).

² Stothard's picture of 'The Procession of Chaucer's Pilgrims to Canterbury' and the engraving after it were each exactly the same size as Blake's, '3 Feet 1 Inch long, and 1 Foot high', according to the Prospectus in Blair's *Grave* (1808), 40.

³ The erroneous reading in the 1810 text 'Squires and Yeoman' does not appear in the manuscript draft in the *Notebook*, p. 118, or in the similar paragraph in the *Descriptive Catalogue*, ¶14 (pp. 1005, 831).

All the quotation marks—that is, in ¶3-4, 6, 8—appear in the 1810 printed text.

⁴ 'Tapster' (one who draws beer or wine) is a misprint for the correct 'Tapiser' (weaver) in the drafts in the *Notebook*, p. 118, and the *Descriptive Catalogue*, ¶14 (pp. 1005, 832).

5] These last are issuing from the Gateway of the Inn. The Cook and the Wife of Bath are both taking their morning's draught of comfort. Spectators stand at the Gateway of the Inn, and are composed of an Old Man, a Woman and Children.

1] This Inn is yet extant under the name of the Talbot, and the Landlord, Robert Bristow, Esq. of Broxmore near Rumsey, has continued a board over the Gateway, inscribed 'This is the Inn from which Sir Jeffery Chaucer and his Pilgrims set out for Canterbury.'

1] St. Thomas's Hospital which is situated near to it, is one of the most amiable features of the Christian Church, it belonged to the Monastery of[5] St. Mary Overies and was dedicated to Thomas a Becket. The Pilgrims, if sick or lame, on their Journey to and from his Shrine, were received at this House. Even at this day every friendless wretch who wants the succour of it, is considered as a Pilgrim travelling through this Journey of Life.

3] The Landscape is an eastward view of the Country from the Tabarde Inn in Southwark as it may be supposed to have appeared in Chaucer's time; interspersed with Cottages and Villages. The first beams of the sun are seen above the horizon:[6] some Buildings and Spires indicate the situation of the Great City. The Inn is a Gothic Building which Thynne in his Glossary says was the Lodging of the

([Page] 3)

Abbot of Hyde by Winchester. On the Inn is inscribed its Title, and a proper advantage is taken of this circumstance to describe the subject of the Picture. The words written in Gothic Letters over the Gateway of the Inn are as follow: 'The Tabarde Inn by Henry Bailly. The Lodging House for Pilgrims who Journey to St. Thomas's Shrine at Canterbury.'

1] Of Chaucer's Characters as described in his Canterbury Tales, some of the Names are altered by Time, but the Characters themselves for ever remain unaltered and[7] consequently they are the Physiognomies or Lineaments[8] of Universal Human Life beyond which Nature never steps. The Painter has conse-

[5] 1810: 'ef'. [6] 1810: 'horrizon'.
[7] 1810: 'end'. [8] 1810: 'Leneaments'.

quently varied the heads and forms of his Personages into all Nature's varieties. The Horses he has varied to accord to their riders, the Costume is correct according to authentic Monuments.

[¶*10*]   Subscriptions received at No. 28, Corner of Broad Street, Golden Square.

G. Smeeton, Printer, 17, St. Martin's Lane, London

WRITINGS IN
MANUSCRIPT

'THEN SHE BORE PALE DESIRE'

[*Page 1*]

then she bore Pale desire⌐,⌐ father of Curiosity⌐,⌐ a Virgin
ever young. And after, Leaden Sloth from whom came Ig-
norance, who brought forth wonder. These are the Gods which
came from fear, ∧for Gods like these nor male nor female are but
Single Pregnate or if they list together mingling bring forth
mighty powrs⌐.⌐¹ She knew them not yet they all war with
Shame and Strengthen her weak arm. [Now day arose, the
Golden Sun his mighty Race began Refreshing the Cold earth
with beaming Joy. *del*] But Pride awoke nor knew that Joy was
born, and taking Poisnous Seed from her own Bowels in the
Monster Shame infusd. Forth Came Ambition Crawling like a
toad⌐.⌐ Pride Bears it in her Bosom and the Gods all bow to it.
So Great its Power, that Pride inspird by it Prophetic saw the
Kingdoms of the World & all their Glory, Giants of Mighty
arm before the flood, Cains City built with Murder. Then
Babel mighty Reard him to the Skies, Babel with thousand
tongues⌐.⌐ Confusion it was calld and Givn to Shame. This
Pride observ[d and *del*]ing inly Grievd, but knew not that the
rest was Givn to Shame as well as this. [for all the . . . *del*]²
   Then Nineve[h] & Babylon & costly Tyre and evn Jerusalem
was shewn the holy City. Then Athens Learning & the Pride
of Greece and further from

[*Page 2*]

the Rising Sun was Rome Seated on Seven hills⌐,⌐ the mistress of

---

¹ 'for Gods like these . . . bring forth mighty powrs' is written below, between
'Now day' and 'arose'; the passage is separated from the rest of the text by strokes
across the page and headed by an 'X' corresponding to the 'X' at 'She knew them
not'.
² For the deletion I cannot read, Erdman ('A Blake Manuscript in the Berg
Collection: "then She bore Pale desire" and "Woe cried the Muse" ', *Bulletin of
the New York Public Library*, lxii [1958]) makes out 'for all she xxx fear and
adxxx lf x the xxth xxx', though in 1967 (p. 766) he does not guess at what follows
'and'.

the world, Emblem of Pride⌐.⌐ She Saw the Arts their treasures Bring and luxury his bounteous table Spread. But now a Cloud oer casts and back to th'East, to Constantines Great City Empire fled, ⌐Ere long to bleed & die⌐,⌐ A sacrifice done by a Priestly hand⌐.⌐⌐³ So once the Sun his Chariot drew back to prolong a Good kings life⌐.⌐ The Cloud oer past & Rome now shone again⌐,⌐ Miterd & Crown'd with triple crown. Then Pride was better Pleasd⌐.⌐ She Saw the World fall down in Adoration [Nor could Refrain but Cry'd this is the blest time when Pride shall hold the Sway. del] But now full to the Setting Sun a Sun arose out of the Sea⌐;⌐ it rose & shed Sweet Influence oer the Earth⌐.⌐ Pride feared for her City, but not long, for looking Stedfastly She saw that Pride Reignd here⌐.⌐ Now Direful Pains accost her and Still pregnant. So[?] Envy came & Hate, twin progeny⌐.⌐ Envy hath a serpents head of fearful bulk hissing with hundred tongues⌐;⌐ her poisnous breath breeds Satire⌐,⌐ foul Contagion from which none are free. Oer whelmd by ever During Thirst she Swalloweth her own Poison which Consumes her nether Parts, from Whence a River Springs. Most Black & loathsom through the land it Runs Rolling with furious

[Page 3]

Noise, but at the last it Settles in a lake Called Oblivion. Tis at this Rivers fount where evry mortals Cup is Mix't⌐.⌐ My Cup is filld with Envy's Rankest Draught [and Death is in the Pot del]⌐;⌐⁴ a miracle No less can set me Right⌐.⌐ Desire Still pines but for one Cooling Drop and tis Deny'd while others in Contentments downy Nest do sleep. It is the Cursed thorn wounding my breast that makes me sing. However sweet⌐,⌐ tis Envy that Inspires my Song. Prickt by the fame of others how I mourn and my complaints are Sweeter than their Joys but O could I at Envy Shake my hands, my notes Should Rise to meet the New born Day. Hate⌐,⌐ Meager hag⌐,⌐ Sets Envy on unable to Do ought herself, but Worn away⌐,⌐ a Bloodless

---

³ 'Ere long . . . Priestly hand' is added in a paragraph break. It is boxed to separate it from the rest of the text, and an 'X' before 'Ere' and after 'Empire fled' indicates its position.

⁴ 'death was in the Pot' appears again in 'And his legs carried it like a fork' l. 28 on *Notebook* p. 22 (p. 936). Cf. 2 Kings 4: 40: 'there is death in the pot'.

Daemon⌞.⌟ The Gods all Serve her at her will⌞;⌟ so great her
Power is⌞,⌟ like fabled *H*ecate she doth bind them to her law.
Far in a Direful Cave She lives unseen Closd from the Eye of
Day, to the hard Rock transfixt by fate and here She works
her witcheries that when She Groans She shakes the Solid
Ground⌞.⌟ Now Envy She controlls with numming trance &
Melancholy Sprung from her dark womb⌞.⌟ There is a Melan-
choly, O how lovely tis⌞,⌟ whose heaven is in the heavenly
Mind for she from heaven came and where She goes[5] heaven
still doth follow her. She

[*Page 4*]

brings true Joy once fle*d*, & Contemplation is her Daughter.
Sweet Contemplation. [She teacheth knowledge how to know.
del] She brings humility to man [& *del*.] 'Take her' She Says
'& wear her in thine heart⌞,⌟ lord of thy Self⌞,⌟ thou then art
lord of all.' [humilit*y*, her Daughter, *del*] Tis Contemplation
teacheth knowled[ge] truly how to know—&ᶜ &ᶜ[6] and Re-
instates him on his throne⌞,⌟ once lost⌞;⌟ how lost I'll tell. But
Stop the motley Song⌞.⌟ I'll She*w* how Conscience Came from
heaven. But O who listens to his Voice. T'was Conscience who
brought Melancholy down⌞,⌟ Conscience was sent⌞,⌟ a Guard
to Reaso*n*, Reason once fairer than the light till fould in
Knowledges dark Prison house. For knowledge drove sweet
Innocence awa*y*, and Reason would have followd but fate
sufferd not. Then down Came Conscience with his lovely
band⌞.⌟ The Eager Song Goes on telling how Pride against her
father Warrd & Overcame. Down his white Beard the silver
torrents Roll, and Swelling Sighs burst forth⌞,⌟ his Children all
in arms appear to tear him from his throne⌞.⌟ Black was the
dee*d*, most Black. Shame in a Mist Sat Round his troubled
hea*d*, & filld him with Confusion. Fear as a torrent wild
Roard Round his throne⌞;⌟ the mighty pillars shake⌞.⌟ [and
del] Now all the Gods in blackning Ranks appea*r*, like a
tempestuous thunder Cloud⌞.⌟ Pride lead*s* them on. Now they

---

[5] The words 'for she from heaven came and where She goes' are over an erased
passage.

[6] 'She brings humility . . . truly how to know—&ᶜ &ᶜ' is written and bracketed
on p. 7 and is headed with an 'X' corresponding to the 'X' after 'Sweet Contempla-
tion' on p. 4.

Surround the Go*d* and bind him fast. Pride bound him, [and *del*] then usurpd oer all the Gods. She Rode upon the Swelling wind and Scatterd all who durst t'oppos*e*, but Shame opposing fierce and hoverin*g* over her in the darkning Storm_{L,J} She brought forth Rage [then *del*] And Shame bore honour & made league with Pride_{L.J}⁷ Mean while Strife Mighty Prince was born_{L.J} Envy in direful Pains him bore, then Envy brought forth Care. Care Sitteth in the wrinkled brow. Strife Shapeless Sitteth under thrones of kings, like Smouldring fir*e*, or in the Buzz of Cities flies abroad_{L.J} Care brought forth Covet_{L,J} Eyeless & prone to th'

[*Page 5*]

Earth, and Strife brought forth Revenge. Hate brooding in her Dismal den grew Pregnant & [brought forth *del*] bore Scorn & Slander. Scorn waits on Prid*e*, but Slande*r* flies around the World to do the Work of hate her drudge & El*f*, but Policy doth drudge for hate as well as Slande*r*, & oft makes use of he*r*, Policy Soṅ of Shame. Indeed hate Controlls all the God*s* at will. Policy brought forth Guile & fraud. *T*hese Gods last namd live in the Smoke of Cities, on Dusky wing breathing forth Clamour & Destruction, alas in Cities wheres the man whose face is not a mask unto his heart_L?_J Pride made a Goddes*s* fair or Image rather till knowledge animated it, 'twas Calld Self-love. The Gods admiring loaded her with Gifts as once Pandora_{L.J} She 'mongst men was Sen*t*, and worser ills attended her by far. She was a Goddess Powerful & bore Concei*t* ∧& Emulation [& suspition Mixt *del*]∧⁸ & Policy doth dwell with her by Whom She had a Son Called suspition_{L.J} Go See the

⁷ '[then *del*] And Shame bore honour & made league with Pride' is written on p. 7 (below the note for p. 5) and headed with an 'A' corresponding to the 'A' after 'Rage' on p. 4. At some indeterminate stage in the composition, an ambiguous line was drawn from this insertion ('A And Shame . . .') to the insertion intended for p. 5 (see below), so that the reading could have been either 'Conceit And Shame bore honour & made league with Pride & Mistrust & Suspition . . .' or 'Conceit & Mistrust & Suspition And Shame bore honour & made league with Pride_L ;_J by Shame She had a Son . . .'.

⁸ '& Emulation & suspition Mixt' are inserted in pencil over a caret, probably as the first in a series of revisions whose order must now be hypothetical. Perhaps the next stage was the replacement of this addition with a passage in pencil on p. 7 (below that for p. 4) which read

Conceit & Mistrust & Suspition_{L.J}

City₍ₗ,₎ friends Join'd Hand in Hand. Go See the Natural tie of flesh & blood. Go See more strong the ties of marriage love, thou Scarce Shall find but Self love Stands Between₍ₗ.₎

'WOE CRIED THE MUSE'

———

[Page 6]

Woe cried the muse₍ₗ,₎ tears Started at the Sound. Grief perch't upon my brow and thought Embracd Her. 'What does this mean' I cried, 'when all around Summer hath Spre'd her Plumes and tunes her [?Chauntant *del*] Notes, When Buxom Joy doth fan his wings & Golden Pleasures Beam around my head? *Why* Grief dost thou accost m*e*?' The Muse then Struck her Deepest [note *del*] string & Sympathy Came forth. She Spred her [Shadowy *del*] awful Wings & gave me up. *My* Nerves with trembling Curdle all my blood, & ev'ry piece of flesh doth Cry out 'Woe'. [?hark *del*] *H*ow soon the Winds Sing round the Darkning Storm ere while so fair, and now they fall & beg the Skies will weep. *A* Day like this laid Elfrid in the Dus*t*, Sweet Elfrid fairer than the Beaming Sun₍ₗ,₎ O Soon cut off i th morning of her days, twas the Rude thunder Stroke that Closd her Eyes, and laid her lilied Beauties on the Green, The

This may have been continued immediately with the passage just below it:

> by Shame She had a Son calld Honour who bore Revenge. Then Self love bore a Daughter Called Emulatio*n*, wh*o* married honour₍ₗ ;₎ these follow her around the World₍ₗ.₎

The next stage may have been the addition, above 'Conceit & Mistrust & Suspition' but not clearly marked for entry, of

> & Policy doth dwell with her by whom she

apparently to be continued (after the deletion of 'by Shame She had a Son Calld Honour who bore Revenge' and 'Self love') with 'Then bore a Daughter . . . around the world'. (At some stage the addition for p. 4—see above—was inserted in these changes.) Finally this additional matter on p. 7 was abandoned, though not deleted; the 'suspition Mixt' on p. 5 was deleted in pencil and below, after the last line of ink text on p. 5 ('love Stands Between'), was added in pencil '& Policy . . . had a Son Called suspition' with a stroke connecting it to 'Conceit & Emulation'; and in the pencil insertion above '& Emulation &' was confirmed in ink to read '& Emulation'.

dance was broke⌊,⌋ the Circle just Begun⌊;⌋ the flower was Pluckd & yet it was not blown; 'But what art thou!' I could no mor*e*, till mute attention Struck my [trembling *del*] listning Ear. It spoke⌊:⌋ 'I come my friend to take my last farewell, Sunk by the hand of Death in Watry tomb⌊.⌋ Oer yonder [ruffling *del*] lake [while his . . .¹ Clay Cold Corpse Corse *del*] swift as the Nightly Blast that Blights the Infant Bud² the winds their Sad complainings bea*r* fo*r* Conrade lost⌊,⌋ untimely lost⌊,⌋ thy Conrade once. When living thee I lovd ev'n unto Death⌊;⌋ now Dea*d*, I⌈'⌉ll guard thee from approaching ill, farewell my time is gone,⌈'⌉' it Said no mor*e*, but vanishe*d* ever from my Sight⌊.⌋

'Woe cried the muse'   ¹ For 'his . . .' Erdman (p. 766) reads 'living[?]'.

² 'swift as the Nightly Blast that Blights the Infant Bud' is written on p. 7 in a position exactly opposite the deleted phrase on p. 6 ('while his . . . Clay Cold Corpse Corse'), which, as Erdman (loc. cit.) points out, suggests that it was intended to replace the deletion.

POETICAL

SKETCHES.

By W. B.

LONDON:

Printed in the Year M DCC LXXXIII.

Poetical Sketches (1783) copy S, title-page (Huntington Library)

THE

FRENCH REVOLUTION.

A   P   O   E   M,

By Wm BLAKE

IN SEVEN BOOKS.

BOOK THE FIRST.

LONDON:

PRINTED FOR J. JOHNSON, N° 72, ST PAUL'S CHURCH-YARD.

MDCCXCI.

[PRICE ONE SHILLING.]

The French Revolution (1791) copy A, title-page (Huntington Library)

Facing page:
A Descriptive Catalogue (1809) copy H, title-page (Bodleian Library)

A

DESCRIPTIVE CATALOGUE

OF

PICTURES,

Poetical and Historical Inventions,

PAINTED BY

WILLIAM BLAKE,

IN

WATER COLOURS,

BEING THE ANCIENT METHOD OF

FRESCO PAINTING RESTORED:

AND

DRAWINGS,

FOR PUBLIC INSPECTION,

AND FOR

Sale by Private Contract,

At No. 28 Corner of Broad Street Golden Square.

LONDON:

Printed by D. N. SHURY, 7, Berwick-Street, Soho,
for J. BLAKE, 28, Broad-Street, Golden-Square.

1809.

In the Moon, is a certain Island near by a mighty continent, which small island seems to have some affinity to England, & what is more extraordinary the people are so much alike & their language so much the same that you would think you was among your friends. in this Island dwells three Philosophers — Suction the Epicurean, Quid the Cynic, & Sipsop the Pythagorean. I call them by the names of those sects tho the sects are not ever mentiond there as being quite out of date however the things still remain, and the vanities are the same. the three Philosophers sat together thinking of nothing. in comes Etruscan Column the Antiquarian & after an abundance of Enquiries to no purpose sat himself down & described something that nobody listend to so they were employd when Mrs Gimblet came in the corners of her mouth seemd I dont know how but very odd as if she hoped you had not an ill opinion of her. to be sure we are all poor creatures. well she seated & seemd to listen with great attention while the Antiquarian seemd to be talking of virtuous cats but it was not so. she was thinking of the shape of her eyes & mouth & he was thinking of his eternal fame the three Philosophers at this time were each endeavouring to conceal his laughter (not at them but at her own imagination) this was the situation of this improving company. when in a great hurry, Inflammable Gass the Windfinder enterd. they seemd to rise & salute each other Etruscan Column & Inflammable Gass fixd their eyes on each other. their tongues went in question & answer but their thoughts were otherwise employd I dont like his eyes said Etruscan Column. he's a fool said Inflammable Gass. smiling on him. the 3 Philosophers the Cynic smiling the Epicurean seeming studying the flame of the candle & the Pythagorean playing with the cat. listend with open mouths to the edifying discourses.

Sir said the Antiquarian I have seen these works & I do affirm that they are no such thing. they seem to one to be the most wretched paltry flimsy stuff that ever — What dye say What dye say said Inflammable Gass, why why I wish I could see you write so. Sir said the Antiquarian. according to my opinion. the author is an arrant blockhead — Your reason Your reason said Inflammable Gass — why why I think it very abominable to call a man a blockhead that you know nothing of — Reason Sir said the Antiquarian I'll give you an example for your reason As I was walking along the street I saw a vast number of swallows on the rails of an old Gothic square. they seemd to be going on their passage, as Pliny says. as I was looking up. a little outre' fellow pulling me by the sleeve cries pray Sir who do all they belong to. I turnd my self about with great

An Island in the Moon (?1784) p. 1 (Fitzwilliam Museum)

And Aged Tiriel. stood before the Gates of his beautiful palace

With Myratana. once the Queen of all the western plains
But now his eyes were darkned. & his wife fading in death
They stood before their once delightful palace. & thus the Voice
Of aged Tiriel. arose. that his sons might hear in their gates

Accursed race of Tiriel. behold your father
Come forth & look on her that bore you. come you accursed sons.
In my weak arms. I here have borne your dying mother
Come forth sons of the Curse come forth. see the death of Myratana

His sons ran from their gates. & saw their aged parents stand
And thus the eldest son of Tiriel raisd his mighty voice

Old man unworthy to be called. the father of Tiriels race
For every one of those thy wrinkles. each of those grey hairs
Are cruel as death. & as despirate as the devouring pit
Why should thy sons care for thy curses thou accursed man
Were we not slaves till we rebeld. Who cares for Tiriels curse
His blessing was a cruel curse. His curse may be a blessing

He ceast the aged man & raisd up his right hand to the heavens
His left supported Myratana shrinking in pangs of death
The orbs of his large eyes he opend. & thus his voice went forth

Serpents not sons. wreathing around the bones of Tiriel
Ye worms of death feasting upon your aged parents flesh
Listen & hear your mothers groans. No more accursed Sons
She bears. she groans not at the birth of Heuxos or Yuva
These are the groans of death ye serpents These are the groans of death
Nourishd with milk ye serpents. nourishd with mothers tears & cares
Look at my eyes blind as the orbless skull among the stones
Look at my bald head. Hark listen ye serpents listen
What Myratana. What my wife O Soul O Spirit O fire
What Myratana. art thou dead. Look here ye serpents look
The serpents sprung from her own bowels have draind her dry as this

Tiriel (?1789) p. 1 (British Museum MSS Department)

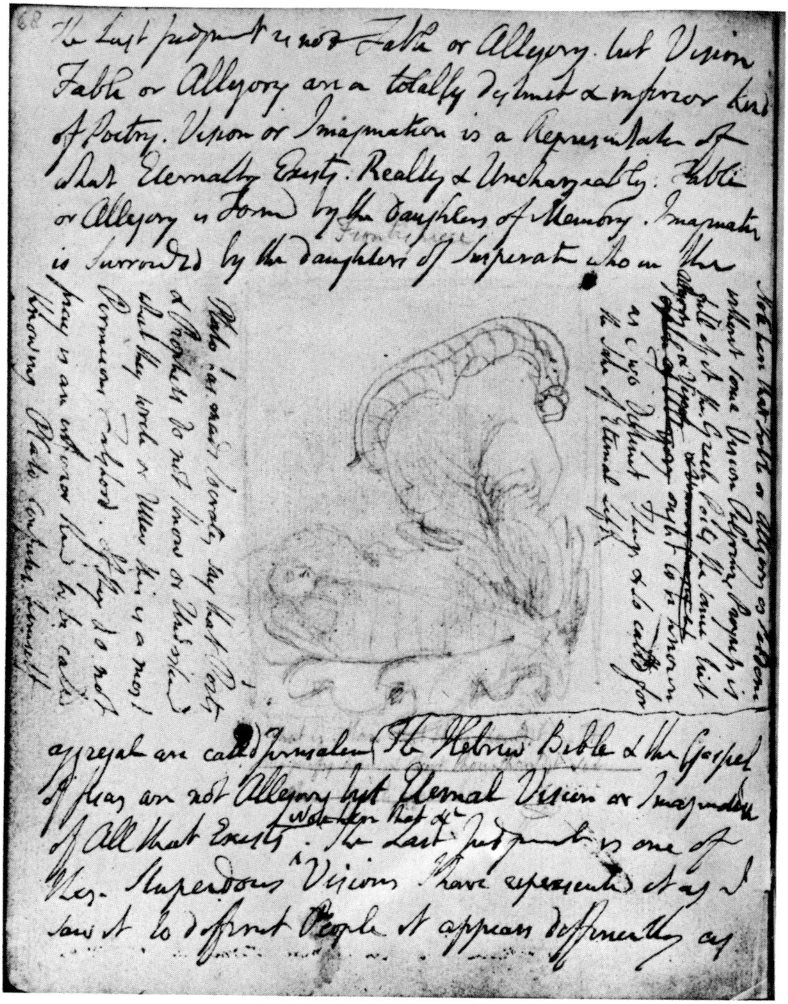

Notebook p. 68, 'Vision of the Last Judgment' (?1810)
(British Museum MSS Department)

Vala or *The Four Zoas* (?1796–?1807) p. 1, title-page
(British Museum MSS Department)

The Smile

There is a Smile of Love
And there is a Smile of Deceit
And there is a Smile of Smiles
In which these two Smiles meet

And there is a Frown of Hate
And there is a Frown of Disdain
And there is a Frown of Frowns
Which you strive to forget in vain

For it sticks in the Hearts deep Core
And it sticks in the deep Back bone
And no Smile that ever was smild
But only one Smile alone

That betwixt the Cradle & Grave
It only once Smild can be
But when it once is Smild
Theres an end to all Misery

The Golden Net

Three Virgins at the break of day
Whither young Man whither away
Alas for woe alas for woe '
They cry & tears for ever flow

AN ISLAND IN THE MOON

1] In the Moon is a certain Island near by a mighty continent, which small island seems to have some affinity to England, & what is more extraordinary the people are so much alike & their language so much the same that you would think you was among your friends. *I*n this Island dwells three Philosophers Suctio*n*, the Epicurean, Quid the Cynic, & Sipsop the Pythagorean. I call them by the names of those sects tho the sects are not ever mentiond there as being quite out of date⌊;⌋ however the things still remain, and the vanities are the same. *T*he three Philosophers sat together thinking of nothing. *I*n come*s* Etruscan Column the Antiquarian & after an abundance of Enquiries to no purpose sat himself down & described something that nobody listend to⌊;⌋ so they were employd when Mrs Gimblet came in [*illeg word*[1] *del*]⌊;⌋ the corners of her mouth seemd I dont know ho*w*, but very odd as if she hoped you had not an ill opinion of her. *T*o be sure we are all poor creatures. *W*ell she seated & [listend *del*] seemd to listen with great attention while the Antiquarian seemd to be talking of virtuous cat*s*, but it was not so. *S*he was thinking of the shape of her eyes & mouth & he was thinking of his eternal fame⌊.⌋ *T*he three Philosophers at this time were each endeavouring[2] to conceal [the *blotted*] his laughte*r* (not at them but) at his own imagination, this was the situation of this improving compan*y*, when in a great hurr*y* Inflammable Gass the Wind finder enterd. *T*hey seemd to rise & salute each other⌊.⌋

2] Etruscan Column & Inflammable Gass fixd their eyes on each other. *T*heir tongues went in question & answe*r*, but their

---

Chap. 1   [1] The deleted word Erdman (p. 440) reads as 'tipsy[?]'.
   [2] Under 'endeavouring' Erdman (p. 767) makes out 'endeavoured'.

thoughts were otherwise employd$_{\llcorner\lrcorner}$ 'I dont like his eyes' said Etruscan Column. '*He*s a foolish puppy' said Inflammable Gas*s*, smiling on him. *T*he 3 Philosophers [Quid *del*]³ the Cynic smiling$_{\llcorner,\lrcorner}$ the Epicurean seeming [not *del*] studying the flame of the candle & the Pythagorean playing with the ca*t*, listend with open mouths to the edifying discourses.

[¶*3*] 'Sir' said the Antiquarian 'I have seen these works & I do affirm that they are no such thing. *T*hey seem to me to be the most wretched paltry flimsy stuff that ever——$_{\llcorner.\lrcorner}$' 'What d'ye say What dye say$_{\llcorner}$?$_{\lrcorner}$' said Inff[*l*]ammable Gass, 'why why I wish I could see you write so.' 'Sir' said the Antiquaria*n*, 'according to my opinio*n*, the author is an errant blockhead.—' 'Your reason Your reason' said Inflammable Gass— 'why why I think it very abominable to call a man a blockhead that you know nothing of.—' 'Reason Sir$_{\llcorner}$?$_{\lrcorner}$' said the Antiquarian$_{\llcorner};\lrcorner}$ 'I'll give you an example for your reason$_{\llcorner.\lrcorner}$ As I was walking along⁴ the street I saw a ʌvastʌ number of swallows on the [top of an house *del*] rails of an old Gothic square$_{\llcorner};\lrcorner}$ they seemd to be going on their passage as Pliny says$_{\llcorner};\lrcorner}$ as I was looking u*p*, a little outrè fellow pulling me by the sleeve cries "pray Sir who do all they belong *t*o?" I turnd my self about with great

[*Page 2*]

contempt. Said *I*, "Go along you fool—$_{\llcorner.\lrcorner}$" "Fool$_{\llcorner}!\lrcorner$" said he$_{\llcorner};\lrcorner}$ "who do you call fool$_{\llcorner}$?$_{\lrcorner}$ I only asked you a civil question$_{\llcorner.\lrcorner}$" [—— had(?)⁵ the *del*] I had a great mind to have thrashd the fellow only he was bigger than I—$_{\llcorner.\lrcorner}$' *H*ere Etruscan *C*olumn left off— Inflammable Gas*s* recollecting himself 'Indeed I do not think the man was a fool for he seems to me to have been desirous of enquiring into the works of nature—$_{\llcorner.\lrcorner}$' 'Ha Ha Ha' said the Pythagorean. It was reechod by [the *del*] Inflammable Gass to overthrow the argument— Etruscan Column then staring up & clenching both his fists was prepared to give a formal answer to the company But Ob[*t*]use Angl*e* entering the room having made a gentle bow,

---

³ The deleted word Erdman (p. 440) deciphers as '[ʌtheʌ old(?) *del*]'.
⁴ 'along' is accidentally deleted with a blob of ink.
⁵ For 'had' Erdman (p. 441) reads 'here'.

proceeded to empty his pockets of a vast number of paper*s*, turned about & sat down₍ₗ,₎ wiped his [head *del*] ˄face˄ with his pocket handkercheif & shutting his eyes began to scratch his head— '*W*ell gentlemen' said he 'what is the cause of strife₍ₗ?₎' *T*he *C*ynic answer*d*, 'they are only quarreling about Voltaire—₍ₗ.₎' 'Yes' said the Epicurean '& having a bit of fun with him,' 'And' said the Pythagorean 'endeavoring to incorporate their souls with their bodies₍ₗ.₎' Obtuse Angle giving a grin said 'Voltaire understood nothing of the Mathematics and a man must be a fool ifaith not to understand the Mathematics₍ₗ.₎' Inflammable *G*ass turning round hastily in his chair said 'Mathematics₍ₗ!₎ *H*e found out a number of Queries in Philosophy,' Obtuse Angle shutting his eyes & saying that he always understood better when he shut his eyes '[It is not of use to make *del*][6] In the first place it is of no use for a man to make Queries but to solve them, for a man may be a fool & make Queries but a man must have good sound sense to solve them. *A* query & an answer are as different as a strait line & a crooked one, secondly I, I, I.' '*A*ye Secondl*y*, Voltaire's a foo*l*,' says the Epicurean—. 'Pooh' says the Mathematician scratching his head with double violence, 'it is not worth Quarrelling about,—' The Antiquarian here got up—& hemming twice to shew the strength of his Lungs said 'but my Good Sir, Voltaire was immersed in matte*r* & seems to have understood very little but what he saw before his eyes like the Animal upon the Pythagoreans lap always playing with its own tail.' 'Ha Ha Ha' said Inflammable Gass₍ₗ,₎ 'he was the Glory of France— I have got a bottle of air that would spread a Plague.' *H*ere the Antiquarian shrugged up his shoulders & was silent [talkd for half an hour *del*] while Inflammable Gass talkd for half an hour₍ₗ.₎

¶] When Steelyard ˄the *L*awgiver˄ coming in stalking—with an act of parliament in his hand said that it was a shameful thing that acts of parliament should be in a free stat*e*, it had so engrossed his mind that he did not salute the company₍ₗ.₎ M**rs** *G*imblet drew her mouth downwards₍ₗ.₎

[6] For this long deletion Erdman (p. 441) reads merely '˄said˄'.

877

[*Page 3*]
Chap 2^d

[¶5] Tilly Lally the Siptippidist⌞,⌟ Aradobo, the dean of Morocco, [and(?) *del*] Miss Gittipin [& *del*] Mrs Nannicantipot⌞,⌟ [& the three Philosophers *word illeg*¹ Quid the Cynic, Sipsop the Pythagorean Suction² the Epicurean enterd(?) the room *del*] Mrs Sistagatist³ Gibble Gabble the wife of Inflammable Gass— [enterd(?) the room *del*] & Little Scopprell enterd the room⌞·⌟

[¶6] (If I have not presented you with every character in the piece call me [Ass *del*] [Arse *del*] Ass—[)]

Chap 3^d

[¶7] In the Moon as Phebus stood over his oriental Gardening 'O ay come Ill sing you a song' said the Cynic, 'the trumpeter shit in his hat' said the Epicurean '& clapt it on his head' said the Pythagorean⌞·⌟

[¶8] 'Ill begin again' said the Cynic⌞:⌟

> Little Phebus came strutting in
> With his fat belly & his round chin
> What is it you wants¹ please to have
> Ho ho
> I wont let it go at only so & so

[¶9] Mrs Gimblet lookd as if they meant her. Tilly Lally laughd² like a cherry·clapper. Aradobo áskd who was Phebus⌞·⌟ 'Sir,' Obtuse Angle answer*d* quickl*y*, 'He was the God of Physi*c*, Painting Perspective geometry Geography Astronom*y*, Cookery Chymistry [Comparative(?) *del*]³ Mechanic*s*, Tactics Pathology

---

Chap. 2 ¹ For the illegible word Erdman (p. 767) reads 'com[*in*]g'.
  ² Erdman (p. 767) reads '& Suction'.
  ³ Erdman (p. 442) gives 'Sigtagatist' throughout.

Chap. 3 ¹ For 'wants' Erdman (p. 442) reads 'would'.
  ² For 'laughd' Erdman (p. 442) gives 'laught'.
  ³ The deleted word Erdman (p. 442) reads as 'Conjunctives'.

Phraseology Theology Mythology Astrology Osteolog*y*, Soma-
tology⌐‚⌐ in short every art & science adornd him as beads
around his neck.' *H*ere Aradobo lookd Astonishd & askd if he
understood Engraving— Obtuse Angle Answerd 'indeed he
did.—' 'Well' said the other 'he was as great as Chatterton.'
Tilly Lally turnd round to Obtuse Angle & askd who it was
that was as great as Chatterton. [Obtuse Angle answerd *del*]
'Ha*y*, how should I know⌐?‚⌐' Answerd Obtuse Angle⌐;⌐ 'who
was It Aradob*o*?' '*W*hy sir' said he 'the Gentleman that the
song was about.' 'Ah' said Tilly Lally 'I did not hear it. *W*hat
was it Obtuse Angl*e*?' 'Pooh' said he 'Nonsense.' 'Mhm' said
Tilly Lally— '*I*t was Phebus' said the Epicurean⌐‚⌐ [*word del*]
'Ah that was the Gentleman' said Aradobo. 'Pray Sir' said
Tilly Lally 'who was Phebu*s*?' Obtuse Angle answerd 'the
heathens in the old ages usd to have Gods that they worshipd &
they usd to sacrifice to them⌐;⌐ you have read about that in the
bible.' 'Ah' said Aradobo 'I thought I had read of Phebus in the
Bible.'— 'Aradobo you should always think [of what you *del*]
before you speak' said Obtuse Angle— ‸'Ha Ha Ha he means
Pharoah' said Tilly Lally— 'I am ashamd of you making
                            [*Page 4*]
use of the name [of *del*] in the Bible' said Mrs Sistagatist. 'Ill
tell you what Mrs Sinagain⌐.‚⌐ I dont think theres any harm in
i*t*,' said Tilly Lally—— 'No' said Inflammable Gass. 'I have
got a camera obscura at home⌐;⌐ what was it you was talking
about,' 'Law' said Tilly Lally⌐;⌐ 'what has that to do with
Pharoah—⌐?‚⌐' 'Pho nonsense hang Pharo[*a*]h & all his host'
said the Pythagorean⌐;⌐ 'sing away Quid—⌐.‚⌐'

⌐] Then the Cynic sung
        Honour & Genius is all I ask
        And I ask the Gods no more[4]

[4] Perhaps this is an echo of the Song in [James Harris], *Daphnis and Amaryllis,*
The Music by Mr. Handel, And other Eminent Masters (1766), 5:
            A bleating flock, an humble Cot,
              Of simple food a Store,
            These are a blest unenvy'd Lot.—
              We ask the Gods no more.

(See M. W. England, 'The Satiric Blake: Apprenticeship at the Haymarket?
Part II', *Bulletin of the New York Public Library*, lxxiii [1969], 537.)

No more No more⎱   the three Philosophers
No more No more⎰   bear Chorus

[¶*11*] Here Aradobo suckd his under lip⌊.⌋

Chap 4

[¶*12*] 'Hang names' said the Pythagorean⌊;⌋' whats Pharo[a]h better than Phebus or Phebus than Pharo[a]h?' '*H*ang them both' Said the Cynic⌊.⌋ 'Dont be prophane' said Mrs Sistagatist, 'Why' said Mrs Nannicantipot 'I dont think its prophane to say hang Pharo[a]h.' '*A*h' said Mrs Sinagain, 'Im sure you ought to hold your tongu*e*, for you never say any thing about the scriptures & you hinder your husband from going to church.—' 'Ha Ha' said Inflammable Gass 'what dont you like to go to chur*ch*?' '*N*o' said Mrs Nannicantipot⌊,⌋ 'I think a person may be as good at home.' 'If I had not a place of profit that forces me to go to church' said Inflammable Gas*s*, 'Id see the parsons all hangd⌊;⌋ a parcel of lying——⌊.⌋' 'O' said Mrs Sistagatist 'if it was not for church & chapels I should not have livd so long— there was I up in a Morning at four o clock when I was a Girl. I would run like the dickins till I was all in a heat. I would stand till I was ready to sink into the earth, ah Mr Huffcap would kick the bottom of the Pulpit ou*t* with Passio*n*, would tear off the sleave of his Gown, & set his wig on fire & throw it at the people⌊;⌋ hed cry & stamp & kick & sweat and all for the good of their souls.—' 'I'm sure he must be a wicked villain' said Mrs Nannicantipot⌊,⌋ 'a passionate wretch. If I was a man Id wait at the bottom of the pulpit stairs & knock him down & run away.—' 'You would⌊,⌋ You Ignorant jade⌊?⌋ I wish I could see you hit any of the ministers. *Y*ou deserve to have your ears boxed you do.—' 'Im sure this is not religion' answers the

[*Page 5*]

other— Then Mr Inflammable Gass ran & shovd his head into the fire & set his [head *del*] hair all in a flame & ran about the room— No No he did not⌊,⌋ I was only making a fool of you.

Chap 5

3] Obtuse Angle Scopprell Aradobo & Tilly Lally are all met in

4] Obtuse Angles study—
'Pray' said Aradobo 'is Chatterton a Mathematician?' 'No'
said Obtuse Angle 'how ⌃can you⌃ be so foolish as to think he
was?' 'Oh I did not think he was⌞;⌟ I only askd' said Aradobo,
'How could you think he was not, & ask if he was⌞?⌟' said
Obtuse Angle.— ⌃'Oh no Sir⌃ I did think he was before you
told me but afterwards I thought he was not⌞.⌟' Obtuse Angle
said 'in the first place you thought he was [not *del*] & then
afterwards when I said he was not you thought he was not⌞!⌟
[*word del* I know that *del*] ⌃Why I know that⌃——⌞.⌟' 'Oh no
sir I thought that he was not but I askd to know whether he
was.—' 'How can that be⌞?⌟' said Obtuse Angle⌞;⌟ 'how could
you ask & think that he was not⌞?⌟'— '*Why*' said h*e*, 'It came
into my head that he was not⌞.⌟'—'Why then' said Obtuse
Angle 'you said that he was.' 'Did I say so⌞?⌟ Law I did not
think I said that⌞.⌟'— 'Did not he⌞?⌟' said Obtuse Angle⌞.⌟
'Yes' said Scopprell. 'But I meant' said Aradobo 'I I I cant
think⌞.⌟ Law Sir I wish youd tell m*e* how it is⌞!⌟' Then Obtuse
Angle put his chin in his hand & said 'whenever you think you
must always think for yourself⌞.⌟'— 'How Sir⌞?⌟' said Aradob*o*;
'whenever I think I must think myself— I think I do— In the
first place' said he with a grin— 'Poo Poo⌞!⌟' said Obtuse
Angle⌞,⌟ 'dont be a fool⌞!⌟'—

5] Then Tilly Lally took up a Quadrant & ask*d*, '[what is this
gim(?) used[1] for *del*] Is not this a sun dia*l*?' 'Yes' said Scopprel*l*,
'but its broke⌞.⌟'— *A*t this moment the three Philosophers
enterd and lowring darkness hoverd oer the assembly,

5] 'Come' said the Epicurean 'lets have some rum & water &
hang the mathematics⌞;⌟ come Aradobo say some thing⌞!⌟'
*T*hen Aradobo began 'In the first place I think I think in the
first place that Chatterton was clever at Fissic Follogy, Pistino-
log*y*, Aridology, Arograph*y*, Transmography Phizograph*y*,
Hagamy Hatom*y*, & hall that but ⌃in the first place⌃ he eat

Chap. 5   [1] For 'used' Erdman (p. 444) makes out 'crank'.

wery little wickly that is he slept very little which he brought
into a consumsio*n*, & what was that that he took [*word del*]
Fissic or somethink & so died⌊.⌋’

[¶*17*]
So all the people in the book enterd into the room & they
could not talk any more to the present purpose⌊.⌋

[*Page 6*]

Chap 6

[¶*18*] They all went home & left the Philosophers. *T*hen Suction
Askd if Pindar was not a better Poet than Ghiotto was a
Painter⌊.⌋ ‘Plutarch has not the life of Ghiotto’ said Sipsop⌊.⌋
‘*N*o’ said Quid ‘to be sure he was an Italian.’ ‘*W*ell’ said
Suction⌊,⌋ ‘that is not any proof,’ ‘Plutarch was a nasty ignorant
puppy’ said Quid⌊.⌋ ‘I hate your sneaking rascals, theres
Aradobo in [*word del*]¹ ten or twelve years will be a far superior
genius.’ ‘Ah’ said the Pythagorean ‘Aradobo will make a very
clever fellow.’ ‘*W*hy’ said Quid ‘I think that [a *del*] ∧any∧
natural fool would make a clever fellow if he was properly
brought up⌊.⌋’— ‘Ah hang your reasoning’ said the Epicurean⌊;⌋
‘I hate reasoning⌊.⌋ I do every thing by my feelings⌊.⌋’—

[¶*19*] ‘Ah’ said Sipsop. ‘I only wish Jack [Hunter(?) *del*]² Tearguts had
had the cutting of Plutarch⌊;⌋ he understands anatomy better
than any of the Ancients⌊;⌋ he⌈’⌉ll plunge his knife up to the
hilt in a single drive and thrust his fist in, and all in the space
of a Quarter of an hour. *H*e does not mind their crying——
*T*ho they cry ever so he⌈’⌉ll Swear at them & keep them down.
with his fist & tell them that he⌈’⌉ll scrape their bones if they
dont lay still & be quiet— Wha*t* the devil should the people in
the hospital that have it done for nothing, make such a piece
of work for⌊?⌋’

[¶*20*] ‘Hang them’ said Suction ‘let us have a song⌊!⌋’

Chap 6.   ¹ For the deleted word Erdman (p. 444) reads ‘twen[*ty*]’.
² John Hunter (1728–93), the great anatomist and surgeon, familiarly known
as ‘Jack Hunter’, took as his ‘favourite pupil’ William Henry Mathew, the son of
Blake’s patron A. S. Mathew (see ‘A. S. Mathew, Patron of Blake and Flaxman’,
Notes and Queries, cciii [1958], 169, 176–7).

Then [Sipsop sang *del*] the Cynic sung

[*1*]

When old corruption first begun
Adornd in yellow vest
He committed on flesh a whoredom╷;╵
O what a wicked beast╷!╵

2

From them a callow babe did spring   [*5*]
And old corruption smild
To think his race should never end
For now he had a child╷.╵

3

He calld him Surgery & fed
The babe with his own milk   [*10*]
For flesh & he could neer agree╷;╵
She would not let him suck

[*Page 7*]

4

And this he always kept in mind
And formd a crooked knife
And ran about with bloody hands   [*15*]
To seek his mothers life

5

And as he ran to seek his mother
He met with a dead woman╷.╵
He fell in love & married her╷,╵
A deed which is not common╷.╵   [*20*]

6

She soon grew pregnant & brought forth
Scurvy & spotted fever╷.╵
The father grind & skipt about
And said 'I'm made for ever

883

7

'For now I have procured these imps
Ill try experiments∟·⌋'
With that he tied poor scurvy down
& stopt up all its vents

8

And when the child began to swell
He shouted out aloud
'Ive found the dropsy out & soon
Shall do the world more good∟·⌋'

9

He took up fever by the neck
And cut out all its spots
And thro the holes which he had made
He first discoverd guts∟·⌋

[¶22] 'Ah' said Sipsop 'you think we are rascals & we think you are rascals. I do as I chuse∟;⌋ what is it to any body what I do∟?⌋ I am always unhappy too. When I think of Surgery—I dont know∟,⌋ I do it because I like it∟·⌋ My father does what he likes & so do I. I think some how Ill leave it off∟;⌋ there was a woman having her cancer cut & she shriekd *so*, that I was quite sick∟·⌋'

Chap 7

[¶23] 'Good night' said Sipsop, 'Good night' said the other two∟;⌋ then [they *del*] Quid & Suction were left alone. *T*hen said Quid 'I think that Homer is bombast & Shakespeare is too wild & Milton has no feelings∟;⌋ they might be easily outdone∟·⌋ Chatterton never writ those poems. *A* parcel of fools going to Bristol∟·⌋[1] *If* I was to go Id find it out in a minut*e*, but Ive found it out already∟·⌋'— 'If I dont knock them all up next year in the Exhibition[2] Ill be hangd' said Suction.

Chap. 7   [1] Blake owned a copy of Thomas Chatterton's *Poems*, Supposed to have been written at Bristol, by Thomas Rowley, and Others, in the Fifteenth Century, The Third Edition (1778).
   [2] Probably the spring exhibition of the Royal Academy.

'*H*ang Philosophy_L;_J I would not give a farthing for it_L;_J do all by your feelings and never think at all about it. Im hangd if I dont get up tomorrow morning by four o clock & work Sir Joshua_L._J'— 'Before ten years are at an end' Said Quid_L,_J 'how I will work those poor milk

[*Page 8*]

sop devil*s*, an ignorant pack of wretches_L._J'

So they went to bed_L._J

Chap 8

Steelyard the Lawgive*r* sitting at his table taking extracts from Herveys Meditations among the tombs[1] & Youngs Night thoughts.[2] [This is *words illeg*[3] *del*] 'He is not able to hurt me' (said he) 'more than making me Constable or taking away the parish business. Hah!

[O what a scene is here What a disguise *del*]
My crop of corn is but a field of tares[4]

'Says Jerome happiness is not for us poor crawling reptiles of the earth_L._J[5] [*word del*] Talk of happiness & happiness its no such thing—every person has a something_L._J

 Hear then the pride & knowledge of a Sailor_L,_J
 His sprit sail fore sail main sail & his mizin_L;_J
 A poor frail man god wot I know none frailer_L;_J
 I know no greater sinner than John Taylor_L._J[6]   [4]

Chap. 8   [1] James Hervey's *Meditations and Contemplations* (1746–7) were the subject of Blake's 'Epitome of Hervey's *Meditations among the Tombs*' (1807–10)—see p. 1332.
  [2] Edward Young's *The Complaint: or, Night Thoughts on Life, Death, and Immortality* (1742–7) was lavishly illustrated by Blake in an edition published in 1797.
  [3] The first word, illegible to me, Erdman (p. 446) reads as 'unfair'.
  [4] In Henry Wotton's *Reliquiae Wottonianae*, The Fourth Edition (1685), 395–[6], are given three untitled stanzas by 'Chidick Tychborn [*Chidiock Tichborne*] (*being young and then in the Tower*) *the Night before his Execution*[*for treason*]', the first of which is:

  My prime of Youth, is but a Frost of Cares,
  My Feast of joy, is but a Dish of pain,
  My Crop of Corn is but a Field of Tares,
  And all my good is but vain hope of gain:
  The day is past, and yet I saw no Sun,
  And now I live, and now my life is done.

  [5] The sentiment is similar to those in Ecclesiastes.
  [6] 'John Taylor' is apparently a fictitious name.

'If I had only myself to care for I'd soon make Double Elephant look foolis*h*, & Filligree work I hope shall live to see—

The wreck of matter & the crush of worlds
as Younge says[.]'[7]

[¶26] Obtuse Angle enterd the Room. 'What news M*r* Steelyard∟?⌐' — 'I am Reading Theron & Aspasio,'[8] said he. Obtuse Angle took up the books one by one∟·⌐ 'I dont find it here' said he. 'Oh no' said the other∟,⌐ 'it was the meditations,' Obtuse Angle took up the book & read till the other was quite tird out∟·⌐

[¶27] Then Scopprell & Miss Gittipin coming in Scopprell took up a book & read the following passage∟:⌐

An Easy of [Human *altered to*:] Huming Understanding by John Lookye [*word illeg* man[9] *del*] Gent

'John Locke' said Obtuse Angle. 'O ay Lock' said Scopprell. [*three words del*] 'Now here' said Miss Gittipin 'I never saw such company in my life. *Y*ou are always talking of your books∟·⌐ I like to be where we talk— *Y*ou had better take a wal*k* that we may have some pleasure∟·⌐ I am sure I never see any pleasure. *T*heres Double Elephants Girls∟,⌐ they have their own wa*y*, & theres Miss Filligreework∟,⌐ she goes out in her coach & her footman & her maids & Stormonts & Balloon hats & a pair of Gloves every day & the sorrows of Werter & Robinsons & the Queen of Frances Puss colour[10] & my Cousin Gibble Gabble says that I am like nobody else∟·⌐ I might as well be in a nunnery∟·⌐ There they go in Post chaises & Stages to Vauxhall & Ranelagh.[11] And I hardly know what a coach i*s*, except when I go to

[7] This quotation is not from Young but from Joseph Addison, *Cato*, A Tragedy (1713), Act V, Scene i, Cato solus: 'And I shall never die. The soul . . . [*shall*] flourish in immortal youth, Unhurt amidst the war of elements, The wrecks of matter, and the crush of worlds.'

[8] James Hervey's *Theron and Aspasio*, or a Series of Dialogues and Letters upon the Most Important and Interesting Subjects (3 vols.) was first published in 1755.

[9] Keynes (1957, p. 52) reads the deletion as 'pantryman'.

[10] For the fashions in this sentence, see pp. 1698–9.

[11] The public pleasure-gardens.

[*Page 9*]

Mr Jacko's_L,_J ¹² he knows what riding is & [he does not *del*] & his wife is the most agreeable woman_L,_J you hardly know she has a tongue in her head and he is the funniest fello*w*, & I do believe he⌐˥ll go in partnership with his maste*r*, & they have black servants lodge at their house_L,_J I never saw such a place in my life_L;_J he says he has Six & twenty rooms in his house and I believe it & he is not such a liar as Quid thinks he is.' [but he is always Envying *del*] 'Poo Poo hold your tongue hold your tongue' said the Lawgiver. *T*his quite provokd Miss Gittipin_L,_J to interrupt her in her favourite topic & she proceded to use every Provoking speech that ever she coul*d*, & he bore it ˄more˄ like a Saint than a Lawgiver and with great Solemnity he addressd the company in these words_L:_J 'They call women the weakest vessel but I think they are the strongest_L._J A girl has always more tongue than a boy_L._J I have seen a little brat no higher than a nettle & she had as much tongu*e* as a city clark but a boy would be such a fool_L,_J not have any thing to say and if any body askd him a question he would put his head into a hole & hide it, I am sure I take but little pleasure_L;_J you have as much pleasure as I have. *T*here I stand & bear every fools insult. *I*f I had only myself to care for I'd ring off their noses_L._J'

To this Scopprell answer*d*, 'I think the Ladies discourses Mr Steelyard are some of them more improving than any book, that is the way I have got some of my knowledge_L._J'

Then said Miss Gittipin . 'Mr Scopprell do you know the song of Phebe and Jellic*o*?' '*N*o Miss' said *S*copprell— *T*hen she repeated these verses while *S*teelyard walkd about the room_L:_J

> Phebe drest like beauties Queen_L,_J
> Jellicoe in faint pea green

---

[12] Mr. Jacko is apparently related both to Jacko, the famous monkey brought to Astley's Circus in 1784 (M. D. George, *Catalogue of Political and Personal Satires Preserved in the Department of Prints and Drawings in the British Museum* [1938], vi, no. 6715) and to Richard Cosway the fashionable miniaturist (D. V. Erdman, *Blake: Prophet Against Empire* [1954], 88).

Sitting all beneath a grot
Where the little lambkins[13] trot_{L,⌋}

Maidens dancing_{L,⌋} loves a sporting_{L,⌋}   ⌊
All the country folks a courting_{L,⌋}
Susan Johnny Bob & Joe
Lightly tripping on a row_{L.⌋}

Happy people who can be
In happiness compard with ye_L?_⌋   ⌊
The Pilgrim with his crook & hat
Sees your happiness compleat_{L.⌋}   ⌊

[¶*30*] 'A charming Song indeed miss_{L,⌋}' said Scopprell_{L.⌋} [that was all for *del*] *H*ere they receivd a Summons for a merry making at the Philosophers house_{L.⌋}

[*Page 10*]
Chap 9

[¶*31*] 'I say_{L,⌋} this evening we'll all get drunk, I say dash. *A*n Anthem an Anthem,' said Suction_{L.⌋}

Lo the Bat with Leathern wing
Winking & blinking
Winking & blinking
Winking & blinking
Like Doctor Johnson_{L.⌋}[1]   ⌊

Quid——'Oho' said Doctor Johnson
To Scipio Africanus
'If you dont own me a Philosopher
Ill kick your Roman Anus_{L.⌋}'

Suction–'A ha' To Doctor Johnson
Said Scipio Africanus_{L,⌋}

[13] Under 'lambkins' Erdman (p. 767) reads 'lambs do'.

Chap. 9 [1] Cf. 'the weak-eyed bat . . . on leathern wing' in William Collins, 'Ode to Evening', ll. 9–10. Dr. Johnson died on 13 Dec. 1784.

'Lift up my Roman Petticoat
And kiss my Roman Anus_L._J'
And the Cellar goes down with a Step (Grand Chorus_L)_J   [*14*]

?] 'Ho Ho Ho Ho Ho Ho Ho Hooooo my poooooor siiides_L,_J I I
should die if I was to live here_L,_J' said Scopprell_L,_J 'Ho Ho Ho
Ho Ho_L!_J'

1st Vo[*ice*]	Want Matches
2d Vo	Yes Yes Yes
1 V°	Want Matches
2d V°	No ———————

1st Vo	Want Matches	[*5*]
2d V°	Yes Yes Yes	
1st Vo	Want Matches	
2d V°	N° —————	[*8*]

] Here was great confusion & disorder_L._J Aradobo said that the
boys in the street sing something very pretty & funny [about
London *del*] [O no *del*] about Matches_L._J Then Mrs Nanni-
cantipot sung

I cry my matches as far as Guild hall_L._J
God bless the duke & his alderman all_L._J   [*2*]

] Then sung Scopprell

I ask the Gods no more
no more no more_L._J   [*2*]

] Then Said *S*uction 'come Mr Lawgiver your song' and the
Lawgiver

sung As I walkd forth one *M*ay morning
To see the fields so pleasant & so gay_L,_J
O there did I spy a young maiden sweet
[*Page 11*]
Among the Violets that smell so sweet
Smell so sweet   [*5*]
Smell so sweet
Among the Violets that smell so sweet_L._J   [*7*]

[¶*36*] 'Hang your Violets∟;⌐ heres your Rum & water∟·⌐' [*word del*][2]
'O ay' said Tilly Lally. 'Joe Bradley & I was going along one
day in the Sugar house∟,⌐ Joe Bradley saw∟,⌐ for he had but one
eye [*word del*,] saw a treacle Jar So he goes of his blind side &
dips his hand up to the shoulder in treacle. "*H*ere lick lick lick"
said he∟·⌐ Ha Ha Ha Ha Ha For he had but one eye∟·⌐ Ha Ha
Ha Ho∟!⌐' *T*hen sung Scopprell

> And I ask the Gods no more
> no more no more
> no more no more∟·⌐   [

[¶*37*] 'Miss Gittipin' said he 'you sing like a harpsichord, let your
bounty descend to our fair ears and favour us with a fine
song∟·⌐'

> *T*hen she sung   This frog he would a wooing ride
> Kitty alone Kitty alone
> This frog he would a wooing ride
> Kitty alone & I
> Sing cock[3] I cary Kitty alone   [
> Kitty Alone Kitty alone
> Cock I cary Kitty alone
> Kitty alone & I∟·⌐[4]   [

[¶*38*] 'Charming∟,⌐ truly elegant∟,⌐' said Scopprell∟,⌐

> And I ask the gods no more∟·⌐   •

---

[2] The deleted word Erdman (p. 449) makes out as 'sweeter'. 'As I walked out
one May morning' is a traditional ballad; only ll. 5–7 of the version above may
be Blake's—see J. Adlard, *The Sports of Cruelty* (1972), 22.

[3] Under 'Sing cock' Erdman (p. 767) reads 'This frog'.

[4] The second stanza of 'The Frog and Mouse' is given thus in *Gammer Gurton's
Garland*: or the Nursery Parnassu*s*, A choice Collection of pretty Songs and Verse*s*,
For the Amusement of all little good Children, Who can neither read nor run [ed.
Joseph Ritson, 1783]:

> This frog he would a wooing ride,
> Kitty alone, Kitty alone,
> This frog he would a wooing ride,
> And on a snail he got astride,
> Cock me cary, Kitty alone,
> Kitty alone and I.

(The refrains, represented in this second stanza by '&c.', I have repeated from the
first stanza.)

'Hang your Serious Song*s*,' said Sipsop & he sung as follows₎:₎

Fa ra so bo ro
Fa ra bo ra
Sa ba ra ra ba rare roro
Sa ra ra ra bo ro ro ro
Radara
Sarapodo no flo ro

                      [*5*]
                      [*6*]

'Hang Italian songs₎,₎ lets having English₎,₎' said Quid₎;₎
[sing a Mathematical Song Obtuse Angle then he Sung *del*]
'English Genius forever₎;₎ here I go₎:₎

Hail Matrimony made of Love₎!₎
To thy wide gates how great a drove
On purpose to be yok'd do come₎,₎
Widows & maids & Youths also
That lightly trip on beauty's toe   [*5*]
Or sit on beauty's bum₎.₎

———

Hail fingerfooted lovely Creatures₎,₎
The females of our human Natures
Formed to suckle all Mankind₎;₎
Tis you that come in time of need₎;₎   [*10*]
Without you we should never Breed
Or any Comfort find—

———

For if a Damsel's blind or lame
Or Nature's hand has crooked her frame

[Page 12]

Or if she's deaf or is wall eyed   [*15*]
Yet if her heart is well inclined
Some tender lover she shall find
That panteth⁵ for a Bride₎.₎

———

The universal Poultice this
To ease whatever is amiss   [*20*]

⁵ Under 'panteth' Erdman (p. 767) discerns 'panted'.

In damsel or in widow gay_L;_J
It makes them smile_L,_J it makes them skip_L;_J
Like Birds just cured of the pip
They chirp & hop away_L._J

_____

Then come ye maidens_L,_J come ye Swains_L,_J   [
Come & be eased of all your pains
In Matrimony's Golden cage_L._J'   [

[¶*41*] 'I [None of *del*] Go & be hanged' said Scopprell_L,_J 'how can you have the face to make game of matrimony_L?_J'— [What you skipping flea How dare ye? Ill dash you through your chair says the cynic This Quid (cries out Miss Gittipin) allways spoils good Company in this manner & its a shame *del*]

[¶*42*] Then Quid calld upon Obtuse Angle for a Song & he wiping his face & looking on the corner of the cieling sang

To be or not to be
Of great capacity
Like Sir Isaac Newton
Or Locke or Doctor South
Or Sherlock upon death[6]
Id rather be Sutton[7]

For he did build a house
For aged man & youth
With walls of brick & stone_L;_J
He furnishd it within
With whatever he could win
And all his own_L._J

---

[6] Robert South, D.D. (1634–1716) was a controversial Anglican divine and pamphleteering enemy of William Sherlock, D.D. (?1641–1707), Dean of St. Paul's, author of *A Practical Discourse Concerning Death*, which was repeatedly reprinted from 1689 on.

[7] This is probably Thomas Sutton (1532–1611), founder of Charterhouse, rather than Sir Richard Sutton (d. 1524), co-founder of Brasenose College, Oxford. The earliest accounts of Charterhouse (e.g. Samuel Herne, *Domus Carthusiana* [1677], or Philip Bearcroft, *An Historical Account of Thomas Sutton Esq; And of His Foundation in Charter-House* [1737]) give none of the precise details in the poem such as the name of the bricklayer or the number of chimneys.

He drew out of the Stocks
His money in a box
And sent his servant   [*15*]
To Green the Bricklayer
And to the Carpenter
He was so fervent∟·⌋

The [windows *del*] chimneys were three score∟,⌋
The [chi *del*] windows many more   [*20*]
And for convenience
He sinks & gutters made
And all the way he pavd
To hinder pestilence∟·⌋

Was not this a good man   [*25*]
Whose life was but a span
Whose name was Sutton

                    [*Page 13*]
As Locke or Doctor South
Or Sherlock upon Death
Or Sir Isaac Newton∟?⌋   [*30*]

The Lawgiver was very attentive & begd to have it sung over
again & again till the company were tired & insisted on the
Lawgiver singing a song himself which he readily complied
with∟:⌋

This city & this country has brought forth many mayors
To sit in state & give forth laws out of their old oak chairs
With face as brown as any nut with drinking strong ale∟;⌋
Good English hospitality∟,⌋ O then it did not fail,

With Scarlet gowns & broad gold lace would make a yeoman
     sweat∟,⌋   [*5*]
With stockings rolld above their knees & shoes as black as jet∟,⌋
With eating beef & drinking beer O they were stout & hale∟;⌋
Good English hospitality O then it did not fail∟!⌋

Thus sitting at the table wide the Mayor & Aldermen
Were fit to give law to the city∟;⌋ each eat as much as ten∟;⌋ [*10*]

The hungry poor enterd the hall to eat good beef & ale∟;⌐
Good English hospitality O then it did not fail∟!⌐

[¶44] Here they give a shout & the company broke up∟.⌐

Chap 10

[¶45] Thus these happy Islanders spent their time but felicity does not last long, for being met at the house of Inflammable Gass the windfinder, the following affairs happend.

[¶46] 'Come Flammable∟,⌐' said Gibble Gabble∟,⌐ '& lets enjoy ourselves∟;⌐ bring the Puppets.' 'Hay Hay!' said he, 'you sho. why ya ya. How can you be so foolish— Ha Ha Ha she calls the experiments puppets∟!⌐' Then he went up stairs & loaded the maid with glasses, & brass tubes, & magic pictures∟.⌐

[¶47] 'Here ladies & gentlemen∟,⌐' said he∟,⌐ 'Ill shew you a louse [*word del*][1] or a flea or a butterfly or a cockchafer∟,⌐ the blade bone of a tittle back,[2] no no heres a bottle of wind that I took up in the bog house.[3] O dear o dear the waters got into the sliders. Look here Gibble Gabble— Lend me your handkerchief, Tilly Lally∟.⌐' Tilly Lally took out his handkerchief which smeard the glass worse than ever. Then he screwd it on∟,⌐ then he took the slides & then he set up the glasses for the Ladies to view the pictures∟;⌐ thus he was employd & quite out of breath∟.⌐

[¶48] While Tilly Lally & Scopprell were pumping at the air pump Smack went the glass— 'Hang∟!⌐' said Tilly Lally∟.⌐ Inflammable Gass turnd short round & threw down the table & Glasses & Pictures & broke the bottles of wind & let out the Pestilence∟.⌐ He saw the Pestilence fly out of the bottle & cried out

Chap. 10 [1] The deleted word Erdman (p. 452) reads as 'climing'.
  [2] Tittleback is a childish form of 'stickleback', a small fish with spiny fins; the first reference to 'tittleback' in the *Oxford English Dictionary* is from 1820.
  [3] A bog house is a privy, or, as Dr. Johnson says primly in his *Dictionary*, 'a house of office'.

[Page 14]

while he ran out of the roo*m*, [he *del*] 'come out come out [you are *del*] we are putrified‸,‿ we are corrupte*d*, our lungs are destroyd with the Flogiston‸,‿⁴ this will spread a plague all thro the Island‸.‿' *He* was down the stairs the very first‸;‿ on the back of him came all the others in a heap‸.‿

So they need not bidding go‸.‿

Chap 11

Another merry meeting at the house of Steelyard the Lawgiver‸.‿ After Supper Steelyard & Obtuse Angl*e* had pumped In-flammable Gass quite dry. *T*hey playd at forfeits & tryd every method to get good humour. *S*aid Miss Gittipin‸,‿ 'pray Mʳ Obtuse Angle sing us a song‸.‿' *T*hen he sung

Upon a holy *T*hursday their innocent faces clean
The children walking two & two in grey & blue & green‸,‿
Grey headed beadles walkd before with wands as white as snow
Till into the high dome of Pauls they like *T*hames waters
    flow‸.‿

O what a multitude they seemd, these flowers of London
    town‸!‿   [*5*]
Seated in companies they sit with radiance all their own‸.‿
The hum of multitudes were there but multitudes of lambs‸,‿
[And all in order sit waiting the chief chanters commands *del*]
Thousands of little girls & boys raising their innocent hands‸.‿¹
[Then like a mighty wind they raise to heavn the voice of song [*10*]
[Or like harmonious thunderings the seats of heavn among
[When the whole multitude of innocents their voices raise
[Like angels on the throne of heavn raising the voice of praise
    del]

[Let cherubim & seraphim now raise their voices high *del*]

⁴ Phlogiston is a hypothetical substance containing the principle of inflam-mability.

Chap. 11   ¹ l. 9 is written in the stanza-break left between ll. 8 and 10. This is the earliest-known draft of 'Holy Thursday', later etched in *Innocence* (1789) pl. 19 (see p. 41).

Then like a mighty wind their raise to heavn the voice of song [
Or like harmonious thunderings the seats of heavn among_L;_J
Beneath them sit the revrend men_L,_J the guardians of the
poor_L;_J
Then cherish pity lest you drive an angel from your door_L._J [

[¶*51*] After this they all sat silent for a quarter of an hour [& M^{rs}
Sistagatist *del*] ˄& Mrs Nannicantipot˄ said 'it puts me in Mind
of my [Grand *del*] mothers song[:]'

[The voice *del*]
When the tongues of children are heard on the green
And laughing ˄is heard˄ [up *del*] on the hill
My heart is at rest within my breast
And every thing else is still_L._J   [

'Then come home ˄my˄ children_L,_J the sun is ˄gone˄ down
And the dews of night arise_L;_J
Come Come leave off play & let us away
Till the morning appears in the skies_L._J'

[*Page 15*]
'No No let us play for it is yet day
And we cannot [go to *del*] ˄go to˄ sleep [till its dark *del*.]
[The flocks are at play & we cant go away *del*]
Besides ˄in˄ the Sky the little birds fly
And the meadows are coverd with Sheep_L._J'

'Well Well go & play till the light fades away
And then go home to bed_L._J'
The little ones leaped & shouted & laughd
And all the hills ecchoed_L._J[2]

[¶*52*] Then [Miss Gittipin Tilly Lally sung Quid *del*] Sung Quid_L:_J

'O father father where are you going_L?_J
O do not walk so fast_L!_J
O speak father speak to your little boy
Or else I shall be lost_L!_J'

[2] This is the earliest-known draft of 'Nurse's Song' etched later for *Innocence*
pl. 24 (p. 47).

The night it was dark & no father was there   [*5*]
And the child was wet with dew_{ʟ·」}
The mire was deep & the child did weep
And away the vapour flew_{ʟ·」}³   [*8*]

3] Here nobody could sing any longe*r*, till Tilly Lally pluckd up
a spirit & he sun*g*:

O I say you Joe_{ʟ,」}
Throw us the ball_{ʟ·」}
Ive a good mind to go
And leave you all_{ʟ·」}
I never saw saw such a bowler   [*5*]
To bowl the ball on a [turd *del*] tansy
And to clean it with my handkercher
Without saying a word_{ʟ·」}

That Bills a foolish fellow_{ʟ;」}
[He hit me with the bat *del*]   [*10*]
He has given me a black eye_{ʟ,」}
He does not know how to handle a bat
Any more than a [d he *del*]⁴ ˄dog or a˄ cat_{ʟ·」}
He has knockd down the wicket
And broke the stumps   [*15*]
And runs without shoes to save his pumps_{ʟ·」}   [*16*]

] Here a laugh began and Miss Gittipin sung_{ʟ:」}

Leave O leave [me *omitted*] to my sorrows_{ʟ;」}
Here Ill sit & fade away
Till Im nothing but a spirit
And I lose this form of clay_{ʟ·」}

[*Page 16*]

Then if chance along this forest   [*5*]
Any walk in pathless ways_{ʟ,」}
Thro the gloom he⌐¬ll see my shadow_{ʟ,」}
Hear my voice upon the Breeze_{ʟ·」}   [*8*]

³ This first draft known of 'The Little Boy Lost' was etched by Blake for *In-
nocence* pl. 13 (see p. 34). There is a stanza-break between l. 4 and l. 5.
⁴ Erdman (p. 767) reads the deletion as 'a[ny bird the *del*]'.

[¶55] The Lawgiver all the while sat delighted to see them in such a serious humour⌊.⌋ 'Mr Scopprell' said he⌊,⌋ 'you must be acquainted with a good many songs.' 'O dear sir Ho Ho Ho I am no singer⌊!⌋ I must beg one of these tender hearted ladies to sing for me⌊.⌋'— *T*hey all declined & he was forced to sing himself[:]

> Theres Doctor Clash
> And Signior Falalasole⌊;⌋
> O they sweep in the cash
> Into their purse hole⌊.⌋
> Fa me la sol La me fa Sol

> [If(?) we(?) manage(?) Blackamoors
> [Will sing with their thick lips *del*]⁵

> Great A little A
> Bouncing B
> Play away Play away
> Your out of the key⌊.⌋⁶
> Fa me la sol La me fa sol

> Musicians should have
> A pair of very good ears
> And Long fingers & thumbs
> And not like clumsy bears⌊.⌋
> Fa me la sol La me fa sol

> Gentlemen Gentlemen
> Rap Rap Rap
> Fiddle Fiddle Fiddle
> Clap Clap Clap⁷
> Fa me la sol La me fa sol

⁵ For this couplet Erdman (p. 768) reads rather more plausibly:
> [(If *del*) How many Blackamoors
> Could sing with their thick lips *del*]

⁶ In *Gammer Gurton's Garland* [ed. J. Ritson, 1783], the nursery song is given as:
> Great A, little a,
> Bouncing B;
> The cat's in the cupboard,
> And she can't see.

⁷ It has been suggested that this odd stanza represents the conductor addressing his orchestra, rapping for attention with his baton, and then the performance followed by applause.

5] 'Hm' said the Lawgiver, 'funny enough; lets have *H*andels waterpiece_L!』'⁸ *T*hen Sipsop sung_L:」

  A crowned king
  On a white horse sitting
  With his trumpets sounding
  And Banners flying
  Thro the clouds of smoke he makes his way   [5]
  And the shout of his thousands fills his heart with rejoicing
   & victory_L,」
  And the shout of his thousands fills his heart with rejoicing
   & victory_L.」
  Victory Victory_L!」 twas William the prince of Orange_L!」 [8]
[. . . .]⁹

      [*Page A*]

] thus Illuminating the Manuscript_L.」'—'Ay_L,」' said she 'that would be excellent.' '*T*hen' said he 'I would have all the writing Engraved instead of Printed & at every other [*word del*] leaf a high finishd print_L,」 all in three Volumes folio, & sell them a hundred pounds a piece. *T*hey would Print off two thousand_L.」'¹ '*T*hen' said she 'whoever will not have them will be ignorant fools & will not deserve to live_L.」' '*D*ont you think I have something of the Goa*t*s face_L?」' says he. 'Very like a Goats face' she answerd— 'I think your face' said he 'is like that noble beast the Tyger— Oh I was at Mʳˢ Sicknackers & I was speaking of my abilities but their nasty hearts poor devils are eat up with envy— they envy me my abilities & all the Women envy your abilities_L,」 my dear they hate people who are of higher abi[*li*]ties than their nasty filthy [Souls *del*] Selves but do you outface them & then Strangers will see you have an opinion— *N*ow I think we should do as much good

⁸ Handel's non-vocal *Water Music* was written for a party on the Thames for George I in 1715.
⁹ Four or more pages seem to be missing from the manuscript at this point—see the Note, pp. 1699–1700.

Page A ¹ Blake's friend George Cumberland had been experimenting with a similar method, and in January 1784 he sent his brother 'a specimen of my new mode of Printing [*from etched copper*]—it is the amusement of an evening and is capable of Printing 2000' (BM Add. MSS 36494, ff. 231–2). In October 1784 he printed a description of his 'New Mode of Printing' in *A New Review* (iv, 318–19), though without specifying how many copies could be printed.

as we can when we are at Mr Femality's$_{\llcorner}$;$_{\lrcorner}$ do you snap & take
me up— and I will fall into such a passion$_{\llcorner}$!$_{\lrcorner}$ Ill hollow and
stamp & frighten all the People there & show them what
truth is$_{\llcorner}$.$_{\lrcorner}$'— At this Instant Obtuse Angle came in$_{\llcorner}$.$_{\lrcorner}$ 'Oh I am
glad you are come' said Quid$_{\llcorner}$.$_{\lrcorner}$

'SONGS BY SHEPHERDS', MS POEMS IN
POETICAL SKETCHES

[*f. 1^v*]
Songs by Mr Blake
Song 1st by a Shepherd

1st

Welcome stranger to this place,
Where joy doth sit on Every bough,
Paleness flies from every face,
We reap not, what we do not sow.

2^d

Innocence doth like a Rose,
Bloom on every Maidens cheek;
Honor twines around her brows,
The jewel Health adorns her neck.

[*f. 2^r*]
Song 2^d by a Young Shepherd[1]

1st

'When the trees do laugh with our merry Wit,
And the green hill laughs with the noise of it,
When the meadows laugh with lively green
And the grasshopper laughs in the merry sçene,

'Songs by Shepherds'
[1] 'Song 2^d by a Young Shepherd': 'Young' is actually spelled 'Yound'. The
poem is an early version of the 'Laughing Song' in *Innocence* (1789) pl. 15 (p. 36).

2^d

'When the greenwood laughs with the voice of joy, [5]
And the dimpling stream runs laughing by,
When Edessa, & Lyca, & Emilie,
With their sweet round mouths sing ha, ha, he,

3^d

'[Where *corrected to*] When the painted Birds laugh in the
  shade,
Where our table with cherries & nuts is spread; [10]
Come live & be merry & join with me
To sing the sweet chorus of ha, ha, he.'² [12]

[*f. 2ᵛ*]

Song 3^d by an old Shepherd

1st

When silver snow decks Sylvio's cloaths
And jewel hangs at shepherds nose,³
We can abide life's pelting storm
That makes our limbs quake, if our hearts be warm.

2^d

Whilst Virtue is our walking staff, [5]
And truth a lantern to our path;
We can abide life's pelting storm
That makes our limbs quake, if our hearts be warm.

3^d

Blow boisterous Wind, stern Winter frown,
Innocence is a winter's gown; [10]
So clad, we'll abide life's pelting storm
That makes our limbs quake, if our hearts be warm. [12]

² The closing quotation mark is Blake's.
³ ll. 1–2 are a variant of ll. 1–2 of 'Blind-Man's Buff' from *Poetical Sketches* (1783)
(p. 768).

TIRIEL

[*Page 1*]

I

And Aged Tirie*l* stood before the Gates of his beautiful palace
[But dark were his once piercing eyes *del*]
With Myratan*a*, once the Queen of all the western plains⌐,˩
But now his eyes were darkne*d*, & his wife fading in death⌐.˩
They stood before their once delightful palac*e*, & thus the
    Voice   [
Of aged Tirie*l* aros*e*, that his sons might hear in their gates⌐:˩

'Accursed race of Tirie*l*, behold your [aged *del*] father⌐.˩
Come forth & look on her that bore you. *C*ome you accursed
    sons.
In my weak [aged *del*] arm*s* I here have borne your dying
    mother⌐.˩
Come forth sons of the Curse come fort*h*, see the death of
    Myratana⌐.˩'   [

His sons ran from their gate*s* & saw their aged parents stand
And thus the eldest son of Tiriel raisd his might*y* voice⌐:˩

'Old man unworthy to be call*d* the father of Tiriels race⌐,˩
For every one of those thy wrinkle*s*, each of those grey hairs .
Are cruel as deat*h* & as obdurate as the devouring pit⌐.˩   [
Why should thy sons care for thy curses thou accursed man⌐?˩
Were we not slaves till we rebel*d*? Who cares for Tiriels curse⌐?˩
His blessing was a cruel curse. His curse may be a blessing⌐.˩'

He ceast⌐;˩ the aged man raisd up his right hand to the
    heavens⌐;˩

l. 1: 'Tiriel [*is*] The Intelligence of *Mercury*' in Cornelius Agrippa, *Three Books of Occult Philosophy*, tr. J. F. (1651), 243.
ll. 19–20 are illustrated by *Drawing 1*, which shows Tiriel supporting the dying

His left supported Myratana [Living(?) *del*] ⁀shrinking⁀ in
   pangs of death_{⌐⌐} [*20*]
The orbs of his large eyes he open*d*, & thus his voice went forth_⌐:_⌐

'Serpents not son*s*, wreathing around the bones of Tiriel_{⌐,⌐}
Ye worms of death feasting upon your aged parents flesh_{⌐,⌐}
Listen & hear your mothers groans. No more accursed Sons
She bears. *S*he groans not at the birth of Heuxos or Yuva_⌐._⌐ [*25*]
These are the groans of death_{⌐,⌐} ye serpents_{⌐,⌐} These are the
   groans of death_⌐._⌐
Nourishd with milk ye serpent*s*, nourishd with mothers tears
   & cares_⌐._⌐
Look at my eyes blind as the orbless scull among the stones_{⌐,⌐}
Look at my bald head. Hark listen ye serpents [all(?) *del*]
   listen_⌐!_⌐
What Myratana. What my wife O Soul O Spirit O fire_⌐!_⌐ [*30*]
What Myratana. *A*rt thou dea*d*? Look here ye serpents look_⌐!_⌐
The serpents sprung from her own bowels have draind her dry
   as this_⌐._⌐

            [*Page 2*]
Curse on your ruthless head*s*, for I will bury her even here_⌐._⌐'

So saying he began to dig a grave with his aged hands
But Heuxos call*d* a son of Zaze*l* to dig their mother a grave_⌐._⌐ [*35*]

'Old cruelty_{⌐,⌐} desist & let us dig a grave for thee_⌐._⌐
Thou hast refus*d* our charity_{⌐,⌐} thou hast refus*d* our food_{⌐,⌐}
Thou hast refus*d* our clothes our beds our houses for thy dwell-
   ing
Chusing to wander like a Son of Zazel in the rocks_⌐._⌐
Why dost thou curs*e*; is not the cur*s*e now come upon your
   head_⌐?_⌐ [*40*]
Was it not you enslav*d* the sons of Zaze*l*, & they have curs*d*

Myratana with his left hand, while with his right hand he gestures at three men,
one clad in a mantle and vine leaves, one in a skirt and bay leaves, and one (Heuxos)
in a robe, mantle, and crown. In the background are four smooth round columns,
a river, and, beyond it, a pyramid.

  l. 20: For the added word, Erdman (p. 735) reads '?shriecking'.
  l. 35: 'Zazel [*is*] The spirit of *Saturn*' in Agrippa, above.

And now you feel it. Dig a grave & let us bury our mother∟·⌋'

'There take the bod*y*, cursed son*s*, & may the heavens rain
    wrath
As thick as northern fog*s* around your gate*s* to choke you up
That you may lie as now your mother lie*s*, like dog*s* cast out∟,⌋ [4
The stin*k* of your dead carcase*s* annoying man & beast
Till your white bones are bleachd with age for a memorial∟·⌋
No your remembrance shall peris*h*, for when your carcases
Lie stinking on the eart*h*, the buriers shall arise from the east
An*d* not a bone of all the sons of Tiriel remain∟·⌋   [5
Bury your mother but you cannot bury the curse of Tiriel∟·⌋'

He ceast & darkling oer the mountains sought his pathless
    way∟·⌋

[*Page 3*]

2

He wanderd day & night∟;⌋ to him both day & night were
    dark∟·⌋
The sun he felt but the bright moon was now a useless globe∟·⌋
Oer mountains & thro vales of wo*e*, the blind & aged man   [5
Wanderd till he that leadeth al*l* led him to the vales of Har

And Har & Heva like two children sat beneath the Oak∟·⌋
Mnetha now aged waited on the*m*, & brought them food &
    clothing
But they were as the shadow of Ha*r*, & as the years forgotten∟,⌋
Playing with flower*s* & running after birds they spent the day [6
And in the night like infants slept delighted with infant dreams∟·⌋

Soon as the blind wanderer enterd the pleasant gardens of Har
[The aged father & mother saw him as they sat at play *del*]

  l. 56: 'Har' means 'mountain' in Hebrew (see J. Bryant, *A New System, or, an
Analysis of Ancient Mythology* [1774], i. 94).
  ll. 59–60 may be illustrated in *Drawing 2*, which shows Har and Heva apparently
sitting naked in a shallow stream with their foreheads pressed together. On the
bank behind them lies Mnetha in a belted, ankle-length gown which leaves
her right breast free. In the background are vertical shapes which may represent
a forest.

They ran weeping like frighted infants for refuge in Mnethas
    arms₎.₎
The blind man felt his way & cried 'Peace to these open doors₎.₎ [65]
Let no one fear₎,₎ for poor blind Tiriel hurts none but himself₎.₎
Tell me O friends where I am no*w*, & in what pleasant place₎.₎'

'This is the valley of Har₎,₎' said Mnetha '& this the tent of
    Har₎.₎
Who art thou poor blind ma*n*, that takest the name of Tiriel on
    thee₎?₎
Tiriel is king of all the west. *W*ho art thou₎?₎ I am Mnetha [70]
And this is Har & Hev*a*, trembling like infants by my side₎.₎'

'I know Tiriel is king of the west & there he lives in joy₎.₎
No matter who I am O Mnetha. *I*f thou hast any food
Give it m*e*, for I cannot stay₎;₎ my journey is far from hence₎.₎'

Then Har said 'O my mother Mnetha venture not so near him [75]
For he is the king of rotten wood & of the bones of death₎.₎
He wander*s* without eye*s* & passes thro thick walls & doors₎.₎
Thou shalt not smite my mother Mnetha O thou eyeless man₎.₎'

[O venerable O most piteous O most woeful day *del*]
'A wander*er*, I beg for food. *Y*ou see I cannot weep₎.₎ [80]
[But I can kneel down at your door. I am a harmless man *del*]
I cast away my staff the kind companion of my travel
And I kneel down that you may see I am a harmless man₎.₎'

                [*Page 4*]
He kneeled down & Mnetha said 'Come Har & Heva rise₎.₎

---

ll. 75–85 are probably alluded to in *Drawing 3* which, according to Rossetti,
represents Har 'blessing or advising a Damsel' (?Mnetha, 'whose back is turned'
and who 'is robed in a richly-patterned dress'), with Heva by his side, 'all three
kneeling on a bed'.

ll. 84–6 are depicted in *Drawing 4*, in which Tiriel kneels at the left in front of
Har, who bends slightly forward with both hands on Tiriel's bald head, while to
the right Heva grasps Mnetha fearfully around the waist and rests her head on
Mnetha's breasts. To the right of Mnetha (who is in shiny slippers, a dress with a
foliage pattern, and a mob-cap), is a wicker chair and table, and to the left of
Har are thin trees and distant mountains.

He is an innocent old man & hungry with his travel⌊.⌋'   [

Then Har arose & laid his hand upon old Tiriels head⌊.⌋

'God bless thy poor bald pate. God bless thy hollow winking
    eyes⌊.⌋
God bless thy shriveld beard. God bless thy many [wrik(?) *del*]
    wrinkled forehead⌊.⌋
Thou hast no teeth old man & thus I kiss thy sleek bald head⌊.⌋
Heva come kiss his bald head for he will not hurt us Heva⌊.⌋' [

Then Heva came & took old Tiriel in her mothers arms⌊.⌋

'Bless thy poor eyes old man, & bless the old father of Tiriel⌊.⌋
Thou art my Tiriels old father. I know thee thro thy wrinkles
Because thou smellest like the figtree, thou smellest like ripe
    figs⌊.⌋
How didst thou lose thy eyes old Tiriel? Bless thy wrinkled
    face⌊.⌋'   ⌊

[The aged Tiriel could not speak his heart was full of grief
He strove against his rising passions. but still he could not speak
    del]

Mnetha said 'come in aged wanderer⌊,⌋ tell us of thy name⌊.⌋
Why shouldest thou conceal thyself from those of thine own
    flesh⌊?⌋'

'I am not of this region' said Tiriel dissemblingly⌊.⌋
[Fearing to tell them who he was. because of the weakness of
    Har *del*]
'I am an aged wanderer once father of a race
Far in the north, but they were wicked & were all destroyd
And I their father sent an outcast. I have told you all⌊.⌋
Ask me no more I pray for grief hath seald my precious sight⌊.⌋'

'O Lord⌊,⌋' said Mnetha 'how I tremble⌊;⌋ are there then more
    people

More human creatures on this earth beside the sons of Har_L?_J'

'No more_L,_J' said Tiriel 'but I remain on all this globe
And I remain an outcast. *H*ast thou any thing to drink_L?_J'

Then Mnetha gave him milk & fruits, & they sat down together_{L·J} [*110*]

[*Page 5*]

3

They sat & eat & Har & Heva smild on Tiriel_{L·J}

'Thou art a very old old man but I am older than thou_{L·J}
How came thine hair to leave thy forehead_L?_J *H*ow came thy
   face so brown_L?_J
My hair is very long_L,_J my bear*d* doth cover all my breast_{L·J}
God bless thy piteous face. *T*o count the wrinkles in thy face [*115*]
Would puzzle [Har(?) *del*] Mnetha. *B*less thy face for thou art
   Tiriel_{L·J}'

[Tiriel could scarce dissemble more & his tongue could scarce
   refrain
But still he feard that Har & Heva would die of joy & grief *del*]

'Tiriel I never saw but once_{L·J} I sat with him & eat_{L·J}
He was as chearful as a prince & gave me entertainment [*120*]
But long I staid not at his palace for I am forcd to wander_{L·J}'

'What wilt thou leave us too_L?_J' said Heva 'thou shalt not leave
   us too
For we have many sports to shew thee & many songs to sing
And after dinner we will walk into the cage of Har
And thou shalt help us to catch bird*s* & gather them ripe
   cherries_{L·J} [*125*]
Then let thy name be Tiriel & never leave us more_{L·J}'

'If thou dost go_L,_J' said Har 'I wish thine eyes may see thy
   folly_{L·J}

l. 123 may be illustrated in *Drawing 5*, which, according to Rossetti, shows Har
and Heva 'playing Harps'.

My sons have left me_L;_⌐ did thine leave thee_L?_⌐ O twas very cruel_L!_⌐'

'No venerable man_L,_⌐' said Tiriel 'ask me not such things
For thou dost make my heart to bleed_L;_⌐ my sons were not like thine   [*ı*
But worse_L._⌐ O never ask me more or I must flee away_L._⌐'

'Thou shalt not go_L,_⌐' said Heva 'till thou hast seen our singing birds
And [H *del*] heard Har sing in the great cage & slept upon our fleeces_L._⌐
Go not for thou art so like Tirie*l*, that I love thine head
Tho it is wrinkled like the earth parchd with the summer heat_L._⌐'   [*ı*

Then Tiriel rose up from the seat & said 'god bless these tents_L._⌐
[God bless my benefactors for I cannot tarry longer *del*]
My Journey is oer rocks & mountain*s*, not in pleasant vales_L._⌐
I must not sleep nor rest because of madness & dismay_L._⌐'

[Then Mnetha led him to the door & gave to him his staff *del*] [*ı*
[Page 6]
[And Har & Heva stood & watchd him till he enterd the wood
[And then they went & wept to Mnetha but they soon forgot their tears *del*]
[But *del*] ⌃And⌃ Mnetha said 'Thou must not go to wander dar*k* alone
But dwell with us & let us be to thee instead of eyes
And I will bring thee food old ma*n*, till death shall call thee hence_L._⌐'   [*ı*

Then Tiriel frownd & answer*d*: 'Did I not command you saying
Madness & deep dismay possess the heart of the blind man
The wanderer who [runs *del*] seeks the woods leaning upon his staff_L?_⌐'

Then Mnetha trembling at his frowns led him to the tent door

And gave to him his staff & blest him. *H*e went on his way_{L·」} [*150*]

But Har & Heva stood & watchd him till he enterd the wood
And then they went & wept to Mnetha, but they soon forgot
   their tears_{L·」}

[*Page 7*]

4

Over the weary hills the blind man took his lonely way_{L·」}
To him the day & night alike was dark & desolate
But far he had not gone when Ijim from his woods come down [*155*]
Met him at entrance of the forest in a dark & lonely way_{L·」}

'Who art thou Eyeless wretch that thus obstructst the lions
   path_L?_」
Ijim shall rend thy feeble joints thou tempter of dark Ijim_{L·」}
Thou hast the form of Tiriel but I know thee well enough_{L·」}
Stand from my path foul fiend_L;_」 is this the last of thy deceits [*160*]
To be a hypocrite & stand in shape of a blind beggar_L?_」'

The blind man heard his brothers voice & kneeld down on his
   knee_{L·」}

'O brother Ijim if it is thy voice that speaks to me
Smite not thy brother Tiriel tho weary of his life_{L·」}
My sons have smitten me already, and if thou smitest me [*165*]
The curse that rolls over their heads will rest itself on thine_{L·」}
˄Tis now seven years since in my palace I beheld thy face_{L·」}'
[Seven years of sorrow then the curse of Zazel *del*]˄

'Come thou dark fiend I dare thy cunning_L;_」 know that Ijim
   scorns
To smite the[*e*] in the form of helpless age & eyeless policy_{L·」} [*170*]
Rise up for I discern thee & I dare thy eloquent tongue_{L·」}

l. 151 is illustrated in *Drawing 6*, which shows Har and Heva standing in a
doorway as they watch blind Tiriel grope his way toward a young forest with the
aid of a long, straight staff. In the distance are what appear to be mountains.
   l. 155: 'Ijim' is translated in the King James Bible (Isaiah 13: 21) as 'satyrs'
(N. Frye, *Fearful Symmetry* [1947], 242–3) and is used by Swedenborg (*True Christian
Religion*, tr. J. Clowes [1781], 65–6) to represent 'diabolical Love' or 'Love of Self'.
   ll. 167–8 are written in the right margin after l. 166.

Come I will lead thee on thy way & use thee as a scoff_L._」'

'O Brother Ijim thou beholdest wretched Tiriel_L._」
Kiss me my brother & then leave me to wander desolate_L._」'

'No artful fien*d*, but I will lead thee_L ;_」 dost thou want to go_L ?_」 [*I*
Reply not lest I bind thee with the green flags of the brook_L._」
Ay now thou art discoverd I will use thee like a slave_L._」'

When Tiriel heard the words of Ijim he sought not to reply_L._」
He knew twas vain for Ijims words were as the voice of Fate_L._」

And they went on together over hills thro woody dales   [*I*
Blind to the pleasures of the sight & deaf to warbling birds_L._」
All day they walkd & all the night beneath the pleasant Moon
Westwardly journeying till Tiriel grew weary with his travel_L._」

'O Ijim I am faint & weary for my knees forbid
To bear me further. *U*rge me not lest I should die with travel_L._」 [*I*

[*Page 8*]

A little rest I crave a little water from a brook
Or I shall soon discover that I am a mortal man
And you will lose your once lovd Tiriel_L ;_」 alas how faint I am_L !_」'

'Impudent fiend_L,_」' said Ijim 'hold thy glib & eloquent
   tongue_L._」
Tiriel is a king & thou the tempter of dark Ijim_L._」   [*I*
Drink of this ⌃running⌃ broo*k*, & I will bear thee on my
   shoulders_L._」'

He drank & Ijim raisd him up & bore him on his shoulders_L._」
All day he bore him & when evening drew her solemn curtain

ll. 192–233 are illustrated in *Drawing 7*, which shows Ijim, naked and Black-
bearded, seated on a step, holding on his shoulders Tiriel, who raises his left
hand to curse his three daughters clinging to one another, and his three kneeling sons,
one of them (Heuxos) virtually prostrate in a mantle and crown. On the ground is
Tiriel's curved staff.

Enterd the gates of Tiriels palac*e*, & stood & calld aloud˻:˼

'Heuxos come forth I here have brought the fiend that troubles
    Ijim˻!˼   [*195*]
Look knowst thou ought of this grey bear*d*, or of these blinded
    eyes˻?˼'

Heuxos & Lotho ran forth at the sound of Ijims voice
And saw their aged father borne upon his mighty shoulders˻.˼
Their eloquent tongues were dumb & sweat stood on their
    trembling limbs˻.˼
They knew twas vain to strive with Ijim˻;˼ they bowd & silent
    stood˻.˼   [*200*]

'What Heuxos call thy father for I [must *del*] mean to sport to
    night˻.˼
This is the hypocrite that sometimes roars a dreadful lion˻.˼
Then I have rent his limbs & left him rotting in the forest
For birds to eat but I have scarce departed from the place
But like a tyger he would come & so I rent him too˻.˼   [*205*]
Then like a river he would seek to drown me in his waves
But soon I buffetted the torrent˻;˼ anon like to a cloud
Fraught with the swords of lightnin*g*, but I bravd the vengeance
    too˻.˼
Then he would creep like a bright serpent till around my neck
While I was Sleeping he would twine˻;˼ I squeezd his poisnous
    soul˻.˼   [*210*]
Then like a toad or like a new*t* would whisper in my ears
Or like a rock stood in my wa*y*, or like a poisnous shrub˻.˼
At last I caught him in the form of Tiriel blind & old
And so Ill keep him˻;˼ fetch your father fetch forth Myratana˻.˼'

They stood confounde*d*, and Thus Tiriel raisd his silver
    voice˻:˼   [*215*]

'Serpents not sons [you see *word illeg* your father *del*]
                  ˻why do you stand˻?˼ fetch hither Tiriel˻!˼˼

1. 203: 'rent' is mended from 'rend'.
1. 216: Erdman (p. 736) reads the illegible part of the deletion as 'and know'.

[*Page 9*]

Fetch hither Myratana & delight yourselves with scoffs
For poor blind Tiriel is returnd & this much[?] injurd head
Is ready for your bitter taunts. Come forth sons of the curse⌞!⌟'

Mean time the other sons of Tiriel ran around their father⌞·⌟   [≛
Confounded at the terrible strength of Ijim they knew twas
    vain⌞;⌟
Both spear & shield were useless & the coat of iron mail
When Ijim stretchd his mighty arm. The arrow from his limbs
Rebounded & the piercing sword broke on his naked [limbs
    del] ∧flesh⌞·⌟∧

[Then Ijim said Lotho Clithyma(?). Makuth fetch your father [≛
[Why do you stand confounded thus. Heuxos why art thou
    Silent

[O noble Ijim thou hast brought our father to (the gates *del*)
    our eyes
[That we may tremble & repent before thy mighty knees
[O we are but the slaves of Fortune. & that most cruel man
[Desires our deaths. O Ijim (tis one whose aged tongue   [≛
[(Decieve the noble & *word illeg; del*) if the eloquent voice of
    Tiriel
[Hath workd our ruin we submit nor strive against stern fate

[He spoke & kneeld upon his knee. Then Ijim on the pavement
[Set aged Tiriel. in deep thought whether these things were so
    del]

'Then is it true Heuxos that thou hast turnd thy aged parent   [≛
To be the sport of wintry wind*s*?' (said Ijim) 'is this tru*e*?
It is a lie & I am [torn like *del*] ∧like∧ the tree torn by the wind⌞·⌟
Thou eyeless fien*d* & you dissemblers. Is this Tiriels house⌞?⌟
It is as false & [*for* as] Math*a* & as dark as vacant[?] Orcus⌞·⌟
Escape ye fiends for Ijim will not lift his hand against ye⌞·⌟'   [≛

So sayin*g*, Ijim gloomy turnd his back & silent sought

ll. 225–34 are deleted with five vertical strokes.

The [gloom *del*] secret forests & all night wanderd in desolate
　ways

[*Page 10*]

5

And aged Tiriel stood & said 'where does the thunder sleep∟?」
Where doth he hide his terrible head & his swift & fiery
　daughters∟?」
Where do they shroud their fiery wings & the terrors of their
　hair∟?」　　　　　　　　　　　　　　　　　　　　　　　　　　　[245]
Earth thus I stamp thy bosom∟;」 rouse the earthquake from his
　den
[Display thy *del*] To raise his dark & burning visage thro the
　cleaving [world *del*] ⌃ground⌃
To thrust these towers with his shoulders. Let his fiery dogs
Rise from the center belching flames & roarings, dark smoke∟·」
Where art thou Pestilence that bathest in fogs & standing
　lakes∟?」　　　　　　　　　　　　　　　　　　　　　　　　　　　[250]
Rise up thy sluggish limbs, & let the loathsomest of poisons
Drop from thy garments as thou walkest wrapt in yellow
　clouds∟·」
Here take thy seat in this wide court. Let it be strown with dead
And sit & smile upon these cursed sons of Tiriel∟·」
Thunder & fire & pestilence, here [*for* hear] you not Tiriels
　curse∟?」'　　　　　　　　　　　　　　　　　　　　　　　　　　[255]

He ceast∟;」 the heaving clouds confusd rolld round the lofty
　towers
Discharging their enormous voices. At the fathers curse

l. 244: The 's' of 'daughters' is mended from an accidental 'd'.
ll. 246-9: Elements of this metaphor appear in *Vala* p. 91, ll. 6-9 (p. 1212).
ll. 257-61 are illustrated in *Drawing 8*, which shows a garland of five weeping
and gesticulating daughters kneeling round Tiriel, who stands with both arms out-
stretched towards four men at the right, including Heuxos.
　A related drawing in the Whitworth Institute (reproduced in *Pencil Drawings*,
ed. G. Keynes [1927], pl. 10) represents (1) an old man, with two women bowed
at his feet, gesturing towards (2) three unarmed men in long robes, the one at the
right crowned, while behind him is (3) a woman crouched as if in despair. No. 1
here is adapted in *Europe* pl. 11; no. 2 is copied in 'The Accusers'; and no. 3 is used
in *Europe* pl. 9. Another related drawing of 'Joseph making himself known to his
brethren' (1785) (reproduced in *William Blake*: Catalogue of the Collection in the

913

The earth trembled_{L,⌋} fires belched from the yawning clefts
And when the shaking ceast a fog possesst the accursed clime_{L·⌋}

The cry was great in Tiriels palace_{L;⌋} his five daughters ran   [
And caught him by the garments weeping with cries of bitter
    woe_{L·⌋}

'Aye now you feel the curse_{L,⌋} you cr*y*, but may all ears be deaf
As Tiriels & all eyes as blind as Tiriels to your woes_{L·⌋}
May never stars shine on your roofs_{L;⌋} may never [plea(*?*) *del*]
    sun nor moon
Visit you but eternal fogs hover around your walls_{L·⌋}   [
Hela my youngest daughter you shall lead me from this place
And let the curse fall on the rest & wrap them up together_{L·⌋}'

He ceast & Hela led her father from the noisom place_{L·⌋}
In haste they fled while all the sons & daughters of Tiriel
Chaind in thick darkness utterd cries of mourning all the night [
And in the morning Lo an hundred men in ghastly death_{L·⌋}
The four daughters [& all the children in their silent beds
[*words illeg; all del*] stretchd on the marble pavement silent all
[And *del*] falln by the pestilence_{L,⌋} the rest moped round in
    [ghastly fe *del*] ⌄guilty fears⌄

And all the children in their beds were cut off in one night_{L·⌋}   ▸
Thirty of Tiriels sons remain*d*, to wither in the palace
Desolat*e*, Loathe*d*, Dumb [Con *del*] Astonishd waiting for black
    death_{L·⌋}

Fitzwilliam Museum, ed. D. Bindman [1970], pl. 3) shows Joseph with open arms
before his eleven kneeling brothers, one of them in virtually the position of the
left daughter in the *Tiriel* drawing.

    l. 264: For 'plea' Erdman (p. 736) reads 'slee[p]'.
    l. 266: Here and in ll. 268, 278, 280, 283, the 'e' of 'Hela' is faulty, as if it were
an 'a' which has been written over. Thereafter, in ll. 293, 306, 317, 323, 346, the
'Hela' is quite plain. Hela is 'the Goddess of Death' in Scandinavian mythology
(*Poems by Mr Gray* [1776], 105).
    ll. 271-7 are apparently represented in *Drawing 9*, which, according to Rossetti,
represents 'Figures kneeling near some richly-sculptured columns, seemingly in
awe at some impending catastrophe' (1863) or 'The Death of Tiriel's Sons' (1880).

[*Page 11*]

6

And Hela led her father thro the silent of the night
Astonishd silen*t*, till the morning beams began to spring⌊·⌋

'Now Hela I can go with pleasure & dwell with Har & Heva⌊,⌋ [*280*]
Now that the curse shall clean devour all those guilty sons⌊·⌋
This is the right & ready way⌊,⌋ I know it by the sound
That our feet make. Remember Hela I have savd thee from
    death⌊·⌋
Then be obedient to thy father for the curse is taken off thee⌊·⌋
I dwelt with Myratana five years in the desolate rock [*285*]
And all that time we waited for the fire to fall from heaven
Or for the torrents of the sea to overwhelm you all
But now my wife is dead & all the time of grace is past
You see the parents curse. Now lead me where I have com-
    manded⌊·⌋'

'O Leagued with evil spirits thou accursed man of sin⌊!⌋ [*290*]
True I was born thy [child *del*] slave⌊;⌋ who askd thee to save
    me from death⌊?⌋
Twas for thy self thou cruel man because thou wantest eyes⌊·⌋'

'True Hela this is the desert of all those cruel ones⌊·⌋
Is Tiriel cruel⌊?⌋ Look. *H*is daughter & his youngest daughter
Laughs at affection⌊,⌋ glories in rebellio*n*, scoffs at Love! [*295*]
I have not eat these two days⌊;⌋ lead me to Har & Hevas tent
Or I will wrap the[*e*] up in such a terrible fathers curse
That thou shalt feel worms in thy marrow creeping thro thy
    bones
Yet thou shalt lead me. Lead me I command to Har & Heva⌊·⌋'

'O cruel O destroyer O consumer O avenger⌊!⌋ [*300*]
To Har & Heva I will lead thee⌊;⌋ then would that they would
    curse⌊·⌋
Then would they curse as thou hast cursed but they are not
    like thee⌊·⌋
O they are hol*y* & forgiving⌊,⌋ filld with loving mercy
Forgetting the offences of their most rebellious children

915

Or else thou wouldest not have livd to curse thy helpless
children∟•⌟’   [

'Look on my eyes Hela & see for thou hast eyes to see
The tears swell from my stony fountains. *W*herefore do I weep∟?⌟
Wherefore from my blind orbs art thou not siezd with poisnous
    stings∟?⌟
Laugh serpent youngest venomous reptile of the flesh of Tiriel∟•⌟

[*Page 12*]

Laug*h*, for thy father Tiriel shall give the[*e*] cause to laugh
Unless thou lead me to the tent of Har child of the curse∟•⌟’

'Silence thy evil tongue thou murderer of thy helpless children∟•⌟
I lead thee to the tent of Har∟,⌟ not that I mind thy curse
But that I feel they will curse thee & hang upon thy bones
Fell shaking agonie*s* & in each wrinkle of that face
Plant worms of death to feast upon the tongue of terrible
    curses∟•⌟’

'Hela my daughter listen. *T*hou [child(?) *del*] art the daughter
    of Tiriel∟•⌟
Thy father calls. Thy father lifts his hand into the [air *del*]
    ∧heavens∧
For thou hast laughed at my tear*s* & curst thy aged father∟•⌟
Let snakes rise from thy bedded locks & laugh among thy
    curls∟•⌟’

He ceast∟;⌟ her dark hair upright stood while snakes infolded
    round
Her madding brows. *H*er shrieks appalld the soul of Tiriel∟•⌟

'What have I done Hela my daughter∟?⌟ *F*earst thou now the
    curse
Or wherefore dost thou cry∟?⌟ Ah wretch to curse thy aged
    father∟!⌟

ll. 321–7 are illustrated in *Drawing 10*, in which Hela, with four snakes rising
from her dark hair, walks into a forest with blind Tiriel, who grasps her firmly by
the right arm. In the background are a plain and mountains.

Lead me to Har & Heva & the curse of Tiriel [325]
Shall fail. If thou refuse howl in the desolate mountains∟˩’

[*Page 13*]

7

She howling led him over mountains & thro frighted vales
Till to the caves of Zazel they approachd at even tide∟˩

Forth from their caves [the sons of Zazel *del*] ˄old Zazel & his
sons˄ ra*n* [& *del*] when they saw
Their tyrant prince blind & his daughter howling & leading
him∟˩ [330]

They laughd & mocked∟;˩ some threw dirt & stones as they
passd by
But when Tiriel turnd around & raisd his awful voice
[They *del*] ˄Some˄ fled away [& hid themselves *del*] but [some
del] ˄Zazel˄ stood still & thus [scoffing *del*] ˄begun∟:˩˄
'Bald tyrant. Wrinkled cunning [wretch *del*] listen to Zazels
chains∟˩
Twas thou that chaind thy brother Zazel∟˩ *W*here are now
thine eyes∟?˩ [335]
Shout beautiful daughter of Tiriel. *T*hou singest a sweet
song∟!˩
Where are you goin*g*? *C*ome & eat some roots & drink some
water∟˩
Thy crown is bald old man∟;˩ the sun will dry thy brains away
And thou wilt be as foolish as thy foolish brother Zazel∟˩’

The blind man hear*d* & smote his breast & trembling passed
on∟˩ [340]
They threw dirt after the*m*, till to the covert of a wood
[They *del*] The howling maiden led her father where wild
beasts resort
Hoping to end her [life *del*] woe*s*, but from her cries the tygers
fled∟˩
All night they wanderd thro the wood & when the sun arose

---

1. 326: The original word 'fall' has been converted to 'fail' by erasing the top of
the first 'l'.

They enterd on the mountains of Har₍ₗ₎;₍ₗ₎ at Noon the happy
    tents   [
Were frighted by the dismal cries of Hela on the mountains

But Har & Heva slept fearless as babe*s* on loving breasts₍ₗ₎·₍ₗ₎
Mnetha awoke₍ₗ₎;₍ₗ₎ she ran & stood at the tent door [in *del*] &
    saw
The aged wanderer led towards the tents₍ₗ₎;₍ₗ₎ she took her bow
And chose her arrows₍ₗ₎,₍ₗ₎ then advancd to meet the terrible
    pair₍ₗ₎·₍ₗ₎   ⌐

[*Page 14*]

8

And Mnetha hasted & met them at the gate of the lower
    garden₍ₗ₎·₍ₗ₎

'Stand still or from my bow recieve a sharp & winged death₍ₗ₎·₍ₗ₎'

. Then Tiriel stoo*d*, saying 'what soft voice threatens such bitter
    things₍ₗ₎?₍ₗ₎
Lead me to Har & Heva₍ₗ₎·₍ₗ₎ I am Tiriel King of the west₍ₗ₎!₍ₗ₎'

And Mnetha led them to the tent of Ha*r*, and Har & Heva
Ran to the door. *W*hen Tiriel felt the ankles of aged Har
He sai*d*, 'O weak mistaken father of a lawless race₍ₗ₎,₍ₗ₎
Thy laws O Har & Tiriels wisdom end together in a curse₍ₗ₎·₍ₗ₎
[Thy God of Love thy heaven of joy *del*]
Why is one law given to the lion & the [Ox *del*] patient Ox₍ₗ₎?₍ₗ₎
[Dost thou not see that men cannot be formed all alike *del*]
ᴧAnd why men bound beneath the heavens in a reptile form₍ₗ₎,₍ₗ₎
A worm of sixty winters creeping on the dusky ground₍ₗ₎?₍ₗ₎ᴧ

ll. 347–8 may be represented in *Drawing 11*, which shows Har sleeping on an
enormous bolster with his arm round Heva. Over them is a flowered bedspread,
and behind them Mnetha watches protectively. At the head of the bed is what
appears to be an unfigured bed-curtain, and at the left is a rather vaguely ex-
pressed tapestry, with foliage, and, in the centre, a flying child.
    ll. 355–93 are written with a sharper pen. It has been suggested, with little
evidence, that they were written at a later date.
    l. 360 appears in a slightly different form in *The Marriage* pl. 24, ¶90 and in
Visions pl. 7, l. 108 (pp. 97, 110).
    ll. 362–3 are written in the margin as a continuation of l. 361.

[Some nostrild wide breathing out blood. Some close shut up
[In silent deceit. poisons inhaling from the morning rose   [*365*]
[With daggers hid beneath their lips & poison in their tongue
[Or eyed with little sparks of Hell or with infernal brands
[Flinging flames of discontent & plagues of dark despair
[Or those whose mouths are graves whose teeth the gates of
   eternal death
[Can wisdom be put in a silver rod or love in a golden bowl   [*370*]
[Is the son of a king warmed without wool or does he cry with a
   voice
[Of thunder does he look upon the sun & laugh or stretch
[His little hands into the depths of the sea to bring forth
[The deadly cunning of the scaly tribe ⌃(flatterer[?] *del*)⌃ &
   spread it to the morning *del*]
The child springs from the womb. *T*he father ready stands to
   form   [*375*]
The infant head while the mother idle plays with her dog on her
   couch⌊·⌋
The young bosom is cold for lack of mothers nourishment & milk
Is cut off from the weeping mouth with difficulty & pain⌊·⌋
The little lids are lifted & the little nostrils opend⌊·⌋
The father forms a whip to rouze the sluggish senses to act   [*380*]
And scourges off all youthful fancies from the newborn man⌊·⌋
⌃Then walks the weak infant in sorrow compelld to number
   footsteps
Upon the sand, &ᶜ⌃
And when the [foolish crawling *del*]drone has reachd his
   crawling length
Black berries appear that poison all around him. Such [is *del*]
   was Tiriel⌊,⌋   [*385*]
[Hypocrisy the idiots wisdom & the wise mans folly *del*]

[*Page 15*]

Compelld to pray repugnant & to humble the immortal spirit
Till I am subtil as a serpent in a paradise
Consuming all both flowers & fruits insects & warbling birds

ll. 364–74 were each deleted individually.
l. 370 appears in *Thel* pl. 1, ll. 3–4 (p. 62).
ll. 382–3 are written in the right margin at the end of l. 381, with an angle
bracket to show where they should come in.

And now my paradise is falln & a drear sandy plain   [3
Returns my thirsty hissings in a curse on thee O Har
Mistaken father of a lawless race my voice is past⌊.⌋'

He ceast outstretchd at Har & Hevas feet in awful death⌊.⌋   [3

l. 393 is illustrated in *Drawing 12*, which shows Tiriel rigidly outstretched at the
edge of a clump of young trees and Hela standing at his head with her hands in
her hair as if in horror. Just beyond Tiriel's body are rows of thickly set young
trees, with grapes in heavy fruit twining round them.

NOTEBOOK

[*Page 3*]

1

My Spectre around me night & day
Like a Wild beast guards my way⌊·⌋
[E *del*] My Emanation far within
Weeps incessantly for my Sin⌊·⌋

[(Her *del*) ⌃Thy⌃ weeping (she *del*) ⌃thou⌃ shall neer give oer   [*5*]
I Sin against (her *del*) ⌃thee⌃ more & more
And never will from sin be free
Till she forgives & comes to me *del*]

2

[⌃A deep winter (night *del*) dark ⌃⌃&⌃⌃ cold⌃
(In *del*) a (dark cold winter night *del*)   [*10*]
(Within my [loves *del*] Heart *del*)
Within my heart thou didst unfold

Pages 3–2: Order of Composition: Page 3: (**1**) ll. 1–8, 19–22, 27–30, 35–42, 47–50
were written first in a column of seven stanzas at the left; (**2**) The second stanza
(ll. 5–8) was deleted, and two more stanzas (ll. 9–18) were drafted in the top right
corner to replace it, a stanza was added in the middle of the right margin of the
page (ll. 31–4) marked to come between ll. 30 and 35, and another was added at
the bottom right corner (ll. 43–6) marked to come between ll. 42 and 47; the
stanzas were numbered 1–10 in the new order (ll. 1–4, 9–22, 27–50); (**3**) A stanza
(ll. 23–6) was drafted, using ll. 13–14, to replace ll. 9–14 which were deleted with
a stroke, and ll. 23–6, 31–4, 15–22, 27–30 were renumbered as stanzas 2–6; (**4**)
Three stanzas (ll. 15–22, 31–4) were deleted, and ll. 27–30, 35–50 were numbered
as stanzas 3–7; (**5**) Blake marked ll. 31–4 'To come in' again, and renumbered
ll. 31–50 as stanzas 4–8; (**6**) The direction 'To come in' was deleted, thus removing
the last numbered '4' in the stanza-numbering system;

Page 2: (**7**) Evidently at this point Blake began on p. 2, adding ll. 51–66 at the
corners of the page and numbering them as stanzas 9–12; (**8**) ll. 67–70 appear to be
in a later, browner ink, at the foot of the page, and the number '13' is in pencil, as
is the rest of the writing on the page; (**9**) Stanza 14 (ll. 71–4) is written in the last
available blank space at the bottom right of the design; (**10**) ll. 75–90 are written
above stanza 14 and then in the left margin, and ll. 79–82 seem to be squeezed in,
above l. 83; ll. 75–90 may be a new, prematurely abandoned redraft of the poem.

Page 3 ll. 5–6 and the first word of l. 7 are written over an illegible erasure.

ᴧAᴧ Fathomless & boundless deep
There we wander there we weep *del*]

[3 *del*] 4
[1 When my Love did first begin   [ᴧ
2 Thou didst call that Love a Sin
3 (Secret trembling night & day *del*)
4 (Driving all my Loves away *del*) *del*]

[4 *del*] [5 *del*]
[Thou hast parted from my side
Once thou wast a virgin bride   [ᴧ
Never shalt thou a (lover *del*) ᴧtrue loveᴧ find
My Spectre follows thee Behind *del*]

2
A Fathomless & boundless deepᴸ,ᴶ
There we wanderᴸ,ᴶ there we weep
On the hungry craving wind   [
My Spectre follows thee behindᴸ·ᴶ

[5 *del*] [6 *del*] 3
He scents thy footsteps in the snow
Wheresoever thou dost go
Thro the wintry hail & rainᴸ;ᴶ
When wilt thou return againᴸ?ᴶ   [

[6 *del*] [3 *del*] 4
[(Didst *del*) ᴧDostᴧ thou not in Pride & scorn
Fill with tempests all my morn
And with jealousies & fears
Fill my pleasant nights with tears *del*]

[7 *del*] [4 *del*] 5
Seven of my sweet loves thy knife
Has bereaved of their lifeᴸ·ᴶ
Their marble tombs I built with tears
And with cold & shuddering fearsᴸ·ᴶ

922

[8 *del*] [5 *del*] 6

Seven more loves weep night & day
Round the tombs where my loves lay   [*40*]
And seven more loves attend each night
Around my couch with torches bright_L·_J

[9(?)*del*] [6 *del*] 7

And Seven more Loves in my bed
Crown with wine my mournful head_{L,J}
Pitying & forgiving all   [*45*]
Thy transgressions great & small_L·_J

[10 *del*] [7 *del*] 8

When wilt thou return & view
My loves & them to life renew_L?_J
When wilt thou return & live_L?_J
When wilt thou pity [& *del*] ∧as I∧ forgive[?]   [*50*]

[*Page 2*]

9

Never Never I return_L·_J
Still for Victory I burn_{L,J}
Living thee alone Ill have
And when dead Ill be thy Grave_L·_J

10

Thro the Heavn & Earth & Hell   [*55*]
Thou shalt never never quell_L·_J
I will fly & thou pursue_{L,J}
Night & Morn the flight renew_L·_J

11

Till [thou *del*] ∧I∧ turn from Female Love
And [dig *del*] root up the Infernal Grove   [*60*]
[Thou *del*] ∧I∧ [shalt *altered to*] shall never worthy be
To Step into Eternity

l. 44 is written over an erased line, the first word of which Erdman (p. 774) reads
as 'Pity' or 'Pitying'.

12

[& *del*] ∧And∧ to end thy cruel mocks
Annihilate thee on the rocks
And another form create   [
To be subservient to my Fate⌊.⌋

13

Let us agree to give up Love
And root up the infernal grove⌊.⌋
Then shall we return & see
The worlds of happy Eternity   [

14

∧&∧ Throughout all Eternity
I forgive you⌊,⌋ you forgive me⌊,⌋
As our dear Redeemer said
This the Wine & this the Bread⌊.⌋

[1]Oer [thy *del*] ∧my∧ Sins ∧Thou∧ Sit & moan⌊.⌋   [
[Have *altered to*] Hast [I *del*] ∧thou∧ no Sins of [my *altered to*]
   thy own⌊?⌋
Oer [thy *del*] ∧my∧ Sins [I *del*] ∧thou∧ sit & weep
And lull [my *del*] ∧thy∧ own Sins fast asl[eep.]

[2]What Transgressions I commit
Are for thy Transgressions fit⌊,⌋
They thy Harlots⌊,⌋ thou their Slave   ▮
And my Bed becomes their Grave⌊.⌋
Poor pale pitiable form
That I follow in a Storm⌊,⌋
Iron tears & groans of lead   ▮
Bind around my aking head

And let us go to the high[?] downs
With many pleasing wiles⌊.⌋
The Woman that does not love your Frowns
Will never embrace your smiles⌊.⌋

Page 2 l. 68: 'grove' was first miswritten 'grave'.
   l. 87: For 'high' Erdman (p. 468) reads 'highest'.
   ll. 89–90: Cf. *Jerusalem* pl. 95, l. 24: 'She who adores not your frowns will only
loathe your smiles' (p. 630).

[*Page 4*]

When a Man has Married a Wife he finds out whether
Her knees & elbows are only glued together⌊·⌋   [*2*]

[*Page 5*]

When Klopstock England defied
Uprose William Blake in his pride
For old Nobodaddy aloft
Farted & Belchd & coughd⌊,⌋
Then swore a great oath that made heaven quake   [*5*]
And calld aloud to English Blake⌊·⌋
Blake was giving his body ease
At Lambeth beneath the poplar trees⌊·⌋
From his seat then started he
And turned him⌃self⌃ round three times three⌊·⌋   [*10*]
The Moon at that sight blushd scarlet red⌊,⌋
The stars threw down their cups & fled
⌃And all the devils that were in hell
Answered with a ninefold yell⌊·⌋⌃
Klopstock felt the [ninefold *del*] ⌃intripled⌃ turn   [*15*]
And all his bowels began to [burn *del*] churn
[⌃And⌃ They *del*] ⌃And his bowels⌃ turned round three times
    three
And Lockd in his soul with a ninefold key
That from his body it neer could be parted
Till to the last trumpet it was farted⌊·⌋   [*20*]

Then again old Nobodaddy swore
He neer had seen such a thing before

Page 4 l. 2: The poem may be connected with the pencil sketch on the same page
of a woman lying in bed and a man sitting on the edge of the bed apparently
taking off long stockings. Neither poem nor drawing seems very closely connected
with the words 'Ideas / of / Good & Evil' which are partly obliterated by the
sketch.

Page 5 The whole page is written in very faint pencil.
ll. 3–5: Compare 'Let the Brothels of Paris be opend' ll. 9–10, 16 (*Notebook* p. 99
[p. 971]), where virtually the same words appear.
l. 8: Blake lived in Lambeth from September 1790 to September 1800.
ll. 13–14 are written in the right margin and are scarcely legible now.
l. 17: 'round' was first written 'around' and then the initial letter was deleted.

Since Noah was shut in the ark⌊,⌋
Since Eve first chose her hell fire Spark⌊,⌋
Since twas the fashion to go naked⌊,⌋
Since the old anything was created
And so feeling he begd him to turn again
And ease poor Klopstock's ninefold pain⌊.⌋
From [anger(?) *del*] ∧pity then∧ he returnd round
And the ∧ninefold[?]∧ spell unwound⌊.⌋
[If thus Blake could Shite
What Klopstock did write *del*]
∧If Blake could do this when he [sat down to *del*] rose up from
  shite
What might he not do if he sat down to write⌊?⌋∧

[*Page 6*]

On the Virginity of the Virgin Mary & Johanna Southcott

Whateer is done to her she cannot know
And if youll ask her she will [tell you *del*] ∧swear it∧ so⌊;⌋
Whether tis good or evil none's to blame⌊,⌋
No one can take the pride⌊,⌋ no one the shame⌊.⌋

[*Page 7*]

Mock on Mock on Voltaire Rousseau⌊,⌋
Mock on Mock on: tis all in vain!
You throw the sand against the wind
[The *del*] And the wind blows it back again

And every sand becomes a Gem

ll. 29–30: '[Then *del*] From [after *del*] ∧pity then∧ he redend round
              And the Spell ∧removed∧ unwound'
is the tempting reading of D. V. Erdman (*Blake Newsletter*, No. 4 [1968], 8).
      ll. 31–2 are almost illegible, and only 'If' and 'What Klopstock' can I read with
anything approaching confidence. For ll. 31–2 Erdman somewhat awkwardly
gives:
              'It spun Back on the Stile
              [What did *del*] Whereat Klopstock did smile'.
      ll. 33–4 are written sideways in the left margin and are not marked for entry.
Page 6 The title seems to be squeezed in as an afterthought.
      Joanna Southcott (1750–1814) announced in October 1802 that she would
bring forth Shiloh, and in 1813 she said she was actually pregnant by the Holy
Ghost.
      l. 2: Blake added an extra 'so' (when he emended the line) which I have omitted.

Reflected in the beams divine∟;⌐
Blown back they [mo *del*] blind the [mockers *mended to*] mocking
  Eye
But still in Israels paths they shine∟·⌐

The Atoms of Democritus
And Newtons Particles of light   [*10*]
Are sands upon the Red sea shore
Where Israels tents do shine so bright∟·⌐   [*12*]

[*Page 10*]
Tuesday Jan^ry· 20, 1807 between Two & Seven in the Evening—
  Despair∟·⌐

I say I shant live five years
And if I live one it will be a Wonder∟·⌐ June 1793[1]

Memorandum[2]

To Engrave on Pewter: Let there be first a drawing made
correctly with black lead penci*l*, let nothing be to see*k*, then
rub it off on the plate coverd with white wax, or perhaps pass
it thro press. *T*his will produce certain & determind forms on
the plate & time will not be wasted in seeking them afterwards∟·⌐

Memorandum

To Wood cut on Pewter: lay a ground on the Plate & smoke it
as for Etching. *T*hen trace your outlines [& draw them in with
a needle. *del*] and beginning with the spots of light on each
object with an oval pointed needle scrape off the groun*d*
[& instead of etching the shadowy strokes *del*] as a direction
for your graver∟,⌐ then proceed to graving with the ground
on the plate being as careful as possible not to hurt the ground

---

Page 10 ¹ 'I say . . . 1793' is in pencil. The ink of the note at the top is Black, that
of the bottom is Brown.
  ² Perhaps the Memoranda were written for Robert Blake when he was using
the *Notebook* and the poet was instructing him about engraving *c.* 1787, though they
appear to be written later than the 1793 Memorandum. The directions 'To Wood
cut on Copper' are apparently those followed by Blake in his own works in Illu-
minated Printing.

because it being black will shew perfectly what is wanted [to read(*?*) *del*]ʟ·ʌ³

Memorandum

To Wood cut on Copper Lay a ground as for Etchi*n*g, trace &ᶜ & instead of Etching the blacks Etch the whites & bite it inʟ·ʌ

[*Page 12*]

1 I saw a Monk of [Constantine *del*] ˄Charlemaine˄
Arise before my sightʟ·ʌ
I talkd to the Grey Monk where he stood
In beams of infernal lightʟ·ʌ

2 Gibbon arose with a lash of steel
And Voltaire with a wracking wheelʟ·ʌ
[Charlemaine & his barons bold *del*]
˄The Schools in clouds of Learning rolld˄
Arose with War in iron & goldʟ·ʌ

Gibbon plied his lash of Steelʟ,ʌ

³ For 'to read' Erdman (p. 673) reads 'towards[?]'.

Page 12: Order of Composition: (1) 'I saw a Monk . . .' ll. 1–9, 22–9, 'I die I die . . .', 'I saw a Monk . . .' ll. 30–7, 48–51, 'Morning', 'Terror in the house . . .', 'I saw a Monk . . .' ll. 38–41, 'This world . . .' ll. 1–4 were written in that order in two columns (dividing after 'I die I die . . .' l. 22), with strokes drawn after 'I saw a Monk . . .' ll. 29, 37, 41, 51, 'I die I die . . .' ll. 25, 30, 'Morning', 'Terror in the house . . .', suggesting that 'I die I die . . .' ll. 26–9; 'I saw a Monk . . .' ll. 1–9, 22–9; 30–7; 38–41; 48–51, were each separate poems like 'Morning' and 'Terror in the house . . .'; (2) A stroke was drawn indicating that l. 30 of 'I saw a Monk . . .' should follow l. 29; (3) 'I saw a Monk . . .' ll. 42–7 were written sideways in the right margin beside 'Morning' and not yet marked for entry, and 'This world . . .' ll. 5–7 were written below 'I saw a Monk . . .' ll. 42–7 and also not marked for entry—they may belong to another poem; (4) 'I saw a Monk . . .' was amplified by the addition sideways of ll. 10–13 (between columns, beside ll. 1–9, 21), 14–17 (to the right margin beside ll. 30–7, 48–51), 18–20 (between columns, beside 'I die I die . . .' ll. 1–11), none of these passages being marked for entry, and each of them evidently being redrafts of ll. 5–9; (5) 'This world . . .' and 'I saw a Monk . . .' were revised, 'I saw a Monk . . .' ll. 1–9, 21–9, 38–46, 48–51 were numbered as stanzas 1–7 (the corner of the page, where the '1' should be, is torn off now, but the number '1' seems to be visible in the 1935 facsimile, where the corner is present, and is so given in the 1935 Keynes transcript), and in this revised form the two poems were etched in *Jerusalem* (1804–?20) pl. 41, 52 (pp. 502, 529).

'I saw a Monk . . .' ll. 6, 11, 31 are substituted for illegible erased lines.

l. 7: Every word in this deleted line is read doubtfully.

Voltaire turnd his wracking wheel_L,_J
Charlemaine & his barons bold
Stood by & mockd in iron & gold_L._J

The Wheel of Voltaire whirld on high_L,_J
Gibbon aloud his lash does ply_L,_J   [*15*]
Charlemaine & his clouds of War
Muster around the Polar Star_L._J

A Grecian Scoff is a wracking wheel_L,_J
[A *del*] The Roman pride is a sword of steel_L,_J
[Vic *del*] Glory & Victory a [*illeg* ing *del*] [plaited(?) *del*] plaited
    Whip   [*20*]
[Seditious *del*] ∧'Thou Lazy∧ Monk'[said Charlemaine *del*] ∧they
    sound afar∧
[The Glory of War thou condemnst in vain *del*]
∧'In vain condemning Glorious War∧
And in thy Cell thou shalt ever dwell_L._J
Rise War & bind him in his Cell_L!_J'   [*25*]

The blood red ran from the Grey monks side_L,_J
His hands & feet were wounded wide_L._J
His body bent_L,_J his arms & knees
Like to the roots of ancient trees_L,_J

Untill the Tyrant himself relent_L,_J   [*30*]
The Tyrant who first the black bow bent_L,_J
Slaughter shall heap the bloody plain_L,_J
Resistance & war is the Tyrants gain

But The Tear of Love & forgiveness sweet
And submission to death beneath his feet_L,_J   [*35*]
The Tear shall melt the sword of steel
And every wound it has made shall heal_L._J

When Satan first the black bow bent
And the Moral Law from the Gospel rent

l. 20: '[Ron(?)*del*] [Trojan(?)*del*] [plaited *del*] phallic' is the reading of Erdman
(p. 733).

He forg'd the Law into a Sword
And [spilt *altered to*] spilld the blood of Mercys Lord⌊.⌋   [

---

6 [O Charlemaine O Charlemaine *del*]
∧Titu*s*, Constantine Charlemaine∧
O Voltaire Rousseau Gibbon vain
Your [mocks & scorn *del*] ∧Grecian mocks∧ & Roman Sword   [
Against this image of his Lord⌊.⌋

A tear is an &ᶜ

7 For the tear is an intellectual thing
And a Sigh is the Sword of an Angel King
And the bitter groan [for another's *del*] ∧of the Martyrs∧ woe   [
Is an arrow from the Almighties bow.   [

'I die I die' the Mother said⌊,⌋
'My Children will die for lack of bread⌊!⌋
What more has the merciless tyrant said⌊?⌋'
The Monk sat down on her stony bed⌊.⌋

His Eye was dry⌊,⌋ no tear could flow⌊.⌋   [
A hollow groan first spoke his woe⌊.⌋
[From his aking tongue these accents flow *del*]
He trembled & shudderd upon the bed⌊.⌋
At length with a feeble cry he said

'When God commanded this hand to write
In the studious hours of deep midnight
He told me that All I wrote should prove
The bane of all that on Earth I love⌊.⌋

'My brother starvd between two walls⌊,⌋
His childrens cry my soul appalls⌊.⌋

l. 41: 'Mercys' is written over an illegible erasure.
'I die I die . . .' ll. 1–4, 'I saw a Monk . . .' ll. 26–9, 'I die I die . . .' ll. 5–6, 8–25,
'I saw a Monk . . .' ll. 48–51, 'I die I die . . .' ll. 26–8, 30 were fairly copied in
the 'Ballads MS' (pp. 1310–11) as 'The Grey Monk'.
'I die I die . . .' l. 7: For 'aking' Erdman (p. 778) reads 'dry'.

[But(?) *del*] I mockd at the wrack & griding chain₎,₎
My bent body mocks at their torturing pain₎.₎

'Thy father drew his sword in the north₎,₎
With his thousands strong he is marched forth₎.₎
Thy brother has armed himself in steel   [*20*]
To revenge the wrongs thy Children feel₎.₎

'But vain the sword & vain the bow₎,₎
They never can work wars overthrow₎!₎
The Hermits prayer & the widows tear
Alone can free the world from fear₎.₎'   [*25*]

The hand of vengeance sought the bed
To which the purple tyrant fled₎.₎
The iron hand crushd the tyrants head
[And usurpd the tyrants throne & bed *del*]
And became a tyrant in his stead₎.₎   [*30*]

      Morning
To find the western path
Right thro the Gates of Wrath
I urge my way₎.₎
Sweet Mercy leads me on
With soft repentant moan   [*5*]
I see the break of day₎.₎

The war of swords & spears
Melted by dewy tears
Exhales on high₎.₎
The sun is freed from fears   [*10*]
And with soft grateful tears
Ascends the Sky₎.₎   [*12*]

Terror in the house does roar
But Pity stands before the door₎.₎   [*2*]

'Morning' title is squeezed in as if it were an afterthought.

931

[4 *del*] [This world *del*] ⌃Each Man⌃ is in [the *del*] ⌃his⌃ Spectres
power
[3 *del*] Untill the arrival of that hour
[1 *del*] [Untill *del*] ⌃When⌃ [the *del*] ⌃his⌃ Humanity awake
[2 *del*] And cast [the *del*] ⌃his own⌃ Spectre into the Lake

And there to Eternity aspire   [.
The Selfhood in a flame of fire
Till then the Lamb of God   [.

[*Page 14*]   W Bl

⌃Beneath the white thorn lovely May⌊,⌋⌃
[Three Virgins at the Break of day *del*]
[Whither Young Man whither away *del*]
⌃'Alas for wo alas for wo alas for wo'
They cry & tears for ever flow⌊·⌋⌃   [
3 The one was clothd in flames of fire⌊,⌋
4 The other [in d(?) *del*] clothd in [sweet desire *del*] ⌃Iron wire⌃
5 The other clothd in [sighs *del*] & tears & sighs
6 Dazzling bright before my Eyes
1 They bore a Net of Golden twine   [
2 To hang upon the branches fine
7 [Pitying I wept to see the woe
8 That Love & Beauty undergo
9 To be consumd in burning fires
And in Ungratified desires *del*]   [
[Wings they had (& when they chose *del*) ⌃that soft inclose⌃

'This world . . .' ll. 1–4 were engraved for *Jerusalem* (1804–?20) pl. 41 (p. 502).

Page 14 'W Blake' is written in the top right corner in pencil.

  Order of Composition: (1) 'Three Virgins . . .' ll. 2–3, 6–15, 20–31 were written in
Black ink in the left margin; (2) ll. 4–5 were written beside ll. 3, 6, and the poem
in this form (ll. 2–15, 20–31) was fairly copied as 'The Golden Net' in the 'Ballads
MS' (pp. 1302–3); (3) Perhaps at this point l. 2 was deleted and ll. 10–11, 6–9, 12–14
were numbered as ll. 1–9 in Black ink; (4) ll. 12–15 were deleted and ll. 16–19 were
written, evidently as substitutes, beside them, and then ll. 16–19 were also deleted
—all in Black ink; (5) l. 3 was deleted, l. 1 was written beside l. 2 and evidently
intended to precede it, ll. 1–2, 6–9 were copied as ll. 32–7 and deleted, and 'The
Birds' was written below l. 19—all in Grey ink; (6) ll. 7, 35 were similarly altered
in Black ink.
  'Three Virgins' ll. 2–3 were deleted separately; the redraft of the lines below
indicates that l. 2 was deleted first.

932

Round their body when they chose
They would let them down at will
Or make translucent *del*]
And in tears clothd night & day   [*20*]
Melted all my soul away⌊·⌋
When they saw my tears a smile
That did heaven itself beguile
Bore the Golden net aloft
As by downy pinions soft   [*25*]
Oer the morning of my day⌊·⌋
Underneath the net I stray
Now intreating flaming fire⌊,⌋
Now intreating [sweet desire *del*] iron wire⌊,⌋
Now intreating tears & sighs⌊·⌋   [*30*]
[When *del*] O when will ⌃the⌃ Morning rise⌊?⌋

[Beneath the white thorn lovely may
Three Virgins at the break of day
The one was clothd in flames of fire
The other clothd in (sweet desire *del*) ⌃iron wire⌃   [*35*]
The other clothd in tears & sighs
Dazzling bright before my eyes *del*]   [*37*]

The Birds

He.　Where thou dwellest⌊,⌋ in what grove⌊,⌋
　　　Tell me Fair one⌊,⌋ tell me love
　　　Where thou thy charming Nest does build⌊,⌋
　　　O thou pride of every field⌊·⌋

She.　Yonder stands a lonely tree⌊,⌋   [*5*]
　　　There I live & mourn for thee⌊·⌋
　　　Morning drinks my Silent tear
　　　And Evning winds my sorrows bear⌊·⌋

He.　O thou Summers harmony⌊,⌋
　　　I have livd & mournd for thee⌊·⌋   [*10*]

ll. 28–30: 'intreating' in each of these lines may be written over an illegible erasure.

Each day I mourn along the wood
And night hath heard my sorrows loud⌊.⌋

She   Dost thou truly long for me
And am I thus sweet to thee⌊?⌋
Sorrow now is at an End   [
O my Lover & my Friend⌊.⌋

He   Come⌊,⌋ on wings of joy we⌈'⌉ll fly
To where my Bower hangs on high⌊.⌋
Come & make thy calm retreat
Among green leaves & blossoms sweet⌊.⌋   [

[*Page 21*]

No real Style of Colouring ever appears
But advertising in the News Papers⌊.⌋
Look there youll see Sʳ Joshuas Colouring⌊.⌋
Look at his Pictures⌊,⌋ [tis quite another Thing *del*]
    All has taken Wing⌊.⌋   [

You dont believe⌊,⌋ I [would *mended to*] wont attempt to make
   ye⌊.⌋
You are asleep⌊,⌋ I wont attempt to wake ye⌊.⌋
Sleep on Sleep on while in your pleasant dreams
Of Reason you may drink of Lifes clear streams⌊.⌋
Reason and Newton they are quite two things   ▮
For so the Swallow & the Sparrow sings⌊.⌋
Reason Says Miracle⌊,⌋ Newton Says Doubt⌊.⌋
Aye thats the way to make all Nature out⌊.⌋
Doubt Doubt & dont believe without experiment⌊,⌋
That is the very thing that Jesus meant   ▮
When he said [Beli *del*] Only Believe Believe & try
Try Try & never mind the Reason why⌊.⌋

Page 21: Order of Composition: (**1**) 'Public Address' part uu, below the sketch, continued from p. 20, was probably the first writing on the page; (**2**) 'No real Style . . .' is written to the right of the sketch of a bearded profile; (**3**) 'You dont believe . . .' is written sideways to the right and (after l. 6) left of the central sketch.

'You dont believe . . .' l. 11 For 'Beli[*eve*]' Erdman (p. 781) reads 'Rich'.

Notebook p. 22

[*Page 22*]
And his legs carried it like a long fork
Reachd all the way from Chichester to York∟,⌟
From York all across Scotland to the Sea∟;⌟
This was a Man of Men as seems to me∟.⌟
Not only in his Mouth his own Soul lay   [*5*]
But my Soul also would he bear away∟.⌟
Like as a Pedlar bears his weary Pack
[He would bear my soul *del*] ˄So Stewhards Soul he˄ buckled to
    his Back
But once alas committing a Mistake
He bore the wicked Soul of *William* Blake   [*10*]
That he might turn it into Eggs of Gold
But neither Back nor mouth those Eggs could hold∟.⌟
His under jaw dropd as those Eggs he laid
And [all my *del*] ˄Stewhards˄ Eggs are addled & decayd∟.⌟
The Examiner whose very name is Hunt   [*15*]
Calld Death a Madman [Deadly the affront *del*] ˄trembling for
    the affront˄
Like trembling Hare sits on his weakly paper
On which he usd to dance & sport & caper∟.⌟
[And *del*] Yorkshire Jack Hemp & gentle blushing Daw

Page 22 l. 1 'He' is Bob Screwmuch, that is, Robert Cromek (1770–1812), who
journeyed from Chichester to York and Scotland soliciting subscriptions to Blair's
Grave (1808) with Blake's designs etched by Louis Schiavonetti. The reference to
Cromek's death (l. 46) suggests that the poem was written in or after 1812.
 l. 4: ll. 8, 14, 51 show that the speaker is Stewhard, i.e. Thomas Stothard. Blake
claimed that Cromek stole Blake's idea of illustrating Chaucer's *Canterbury Tales*
and commissioned Stothard to paint a similar picture, which proved very popular.
 l. 15: The *Examiner* was edited by Leigh Hunt, his brother Robert contributed
articles on art, and his brother John helped with the editing and printed the work.
ll. 15–16 are written sideways from the bottom left margin, with a stroke in-
dicating that they are to follow l. 14 (another stroke to l. 35 is deleted). ll. 17–19
are written to their right, and ll. 20–30 continue down the top margin over the
large smudge (which was perhaps made by rubbing a pencil to sharpen it).
 l. 16: 'R[obert] H[unt]' called Blake 'an unfortunate lunatic' in the *Examiner*
on 17 Sept. 1809 (*Blake Records*, 216).
 l. 17: 'trembling Hare' is Prince Hoare (1755–1834), painter, popular dramatist,
Honorary Secretary of the Royal Academy, author of *Academic Correspondence*
(1804) and *An Inquiry into . . . the Arts of Design in England* (1806) with plates by
Blake; he edited the weekly journal called the *Artist* from its inception on 14 March
1807 until its demise in mid 1809.
 l. 19: 'Yorkshire Jack Hemp' is John Flaxman, who was born in York. 'Daw'
has not been identified.

935

Clapd Death into the corner of their jaw   [⸱
And Felpham Billy rode out every morn
Horseback with Death over the fields of corn
[And *del*] ⌃Who⌃ with iron hand cuffd in the afternoon
The Ears of Billys Lawyer & Dragoon
And Cur my Lawyer & Dadymus[?] Jack Hemps Parson   [⸱
Both went to Law with Death to keep our Ears on
For how to Starve Death we had laid a plot
Against his Price but death was in the Pot⌞·⌟
He made them pay his Price⌞,⌟ alack a day⌞,⌟
He knew both Law & Gospel better than they⌞·⌟   [⸱
O that I neer has [*for* had] seen that William Blake
Or could from death Assassinetti wake:
We thought⌞,⌟ Alas that such a thought should be⌞,⌟
That Blake would etch for him & draw for me
For twas a kind of Bargain Screwmuch made   [⸱
That Blakes designs should be by us displayd

l. 21 'Felpham Billy' is William Hayley of Felpham riding regularly across the fields with Blake to collect the mail in Lavant.

l. 24 'Billys Lawyer' is presumably Samuel Rose, whom Hayley hired to defend Blake at Blake's treason trial in January 1804. 'Billys . . . dragoon' must be either John Scolfield, the private who accused Blake of treason, or 'George Hulton a Lieutenant in the First Regiment of Dragoons', his commanding officer, who actually preferred the charge. In his deposition, Private Scolfield said that he 'was sent by his Captain on Esquire Hayley to hear what he had to say' about the charges (*Blake Records*, 124–30).

l. 25: Stothard (Stewhard) is not known to have had a legal encounter with Blake, and consequently 'Cur my Lawyer' cannot be identified. 'Dadymus Jack Hemps Parson' (Erdman [p. 782] reads 'Dady my Parson' as an undeleted first draft) may perhaps be the Revd. Joseph Thomas, Rector of Epsom, whom Blake identified in his letter to Flaxman of 19 Oct. 1801 as 'your friend to whom you was so kind as to make honourable mention of me', and for whom Blake executed several commissions, including his *Comus* designs and others of about 1805–9 (see *Blake Records*, 164).

l. 28: 'Death is in the Pot' appeared in 'then she bore Pale desire' (p. 870); cf. 2 Kings 4: 40.

l. 29: This enigmatic line might refer to the facts that: (1) Hayley apparently paid Blake's lawyer (see Blake's letter of 27 Jan. 1804); (2) Blake replied to public criticism of himself in his published *Descriptive Catalogue* (1809) and his unpublished 'Public Address'; or (3) after legal action Blake 'made me [*Charles Henry Bellenden Ker*] pay 30 Guineas for 2 Drawings' (*Blake Records*, 228). Ker's lawyer was named Davis.

l. 32: 'Assassinetti' is Louis Schiavonetti, who died on 10 June 1810. Blake claimed that Cromek gave to Schiavonetti the commission to engrave Blake's designs (1805) for Blair's *Grave* (1808) which Cromek had promised to Blake.

Because he makes designs so very cheap∟⌋
Then Screwmuch at Blakes Soul took a long leap∟⌋
Twas not a Mouse∟,⌋ twas Death in a disguise
And I alas live to weep out mine Eyes   ⌊*40*⌋
And death Sits [mocking *del*] ∧Laughing∧ on their Monuments
On which he s written 'Recievd the Contents∟.⌋'
¹But I have writ/ ⁴[with *del*] ∧for my∧ tears [of *del*] ∧are∧ aqua
     fortis
³His Epitaph/ ²so sorrowful my thought is∟:⌋
'[Ye *del*] ∧Come∧ Artists knock your heads against this stone   ⌊*45*⌋
For Sorrow that [your *del*] ∧our∧ friend Bob Screwmuchs gone'
And now the Men upon me smile & Laugh
Ill also write my own dear Epitaph
And Ill be buried near a Dike
That my friends may weep as much as they like∟:⌋   ⌊*50*⌋
'Here lies Stewhard [Lord(?) of *del*] the Friend of All' &ᶜ∟.⌋   ⌊*51*⌋

[*Page 23*]

Was I angry with Hayley who usd me so ill
Or can I be angry with Felphams old Mill
[Or angry with Boydell or Bowyer or Ba *del*]
Or angry with Flaxman or Cromek or Stothard
Or poor Schiavonetti whom they to death botherd   ⌊*5*⌋
Or angry with [Boydell or Bowyer(?) or Basire(?) *del*] Macklin or
     Boydel or Bowyer
[Mirth all your sufferings convey sir *del*]
∧Because they did not say 'O what a Beau ye are'∟?⌋∧

ll. 38–42 are written sideways in the right margin, apparently as a continuation
of l. 37.

ll. 43–8 are written parallel to ll. 38–42. The intention in ll. 43–4 is apparently
> But I have writ, so sorrowful my thought is,
> His Epitaph with tears of aqua fortis.

ll. 49–51 are written between ll. 1–11 on the left and ll. 38–48 on the right.

l. 50: See *Notebook* p. 37 (p. 948), where a variant appears.

l. 51: See *Notebook* p. 37 (p. 948), where a variant appears.

Page 23 'Was I angry . . .' ll. 3, 6: Thomas Macklin (d. 1800), John Boydell
(1719–1804), and Robert Bowyer (1758–1834), the most ambitious print-sellers
of their day, published respectively the Bible (completed 1800), *The Dramatic
Works of Shakspeare* (completed 1803), and Hume's *History of England* (completed
1806), each with scores of folio engravings.

l. 7: I can only make out with confidence the first two words of this reading by
Erdman (p. 783).

At a Friends Errors Anger Shew_{L,⌋}
Mirth at the Errors of a Foe_{L.⌋}   [

Anger & wrath my bosom rends_{L;⌋}
I thought them the Errors of friends
But all my limbs with warmth glow_{L;⌋}
I find them the Errors of the foe_{L.⌋}

[*Page 24*]

The Sussex Men are Noted Fools
And weak is their brain pan_{L.⌋}
I wonder if H—— the painter
Is not a Sussex Man_{L.⌋}

[*Line erased*]
                ^old acquaintance well renew_{L.⌋}^
Prospero had One Caliban & I have Two_{L.⌋}

[*Page 25*]

Madman I have been calld[,] Fool they Call thee_{L.⌋}
I wonder which they Envy Thee or Me_{L.⌋}

To H

You think Fuseli is not a Great Painter_{L.⌋} Im Glad_{L!⌋}
This is one of the best compliments he ever had_{L.⌋}

'Anger & wrath . . .' These four lines are written sideways to the left of the poem above.

Page 24 'The Sussex Men . . .' l. 3: 'H——' may be William Haines (1778–1848), engraver and painter, who was brought up in Chichester, Sussex. He was in Cape Town 1800–5 and engraved a plate for Hayley's *Romney* (1809) which Blake may well have expected to be given.

'old acquaintance . . .' l. 1 For the erased line Erdman (p. 786) reads 'Look[?] xxx xxxxx Flaxman & Stothard do'; of this I can read only 'Stothard' with confidence.

Page 25 'Madman I have been calld . . .': The similarity of this poem to the ones 'To F——' on pp. 26 and 35 (pp. 939, 946) suggests that it may be addressed to Flaxman.

'To H' should be 'To Robert Hunt', who said that Fuseli's 'Muse has been on the verge of insanity' ('Mr. Blake's Exhibition', *Examiner*, 17 Sept. 1809, p. 605; see *Blake Records*, 215).

[*Page 26*]

To F—

I mock thee not tho I by thee am Mocked⌊.⌋
Thou callst me Madman but I call thee Blockhead⌊.⌋   [2]

Can there be any thing more mean⌊,⌋
More Malice in disguise⌊,⌋
Than Praise a Man for doing [that *del*] what
[Which he *del*] ⌃That Man⌃ does most despise⌊?⌋
[This *del*] Reynolds Lectures [plainly shew *del*] Exactly So   [5]
When he praises Michael Angelo⌊.⌋   [6]

[*Page 27*]

S—— in Childhood on the Nursery floor
Was extreme old & most extremely poor⌊.⌋
He is grown old & rich & what he will⌊,⌋
He is extreme old & extreme poor still⌊.⌋   [4]

To Nancy F——

How can I help thy Husbands copying Me⌊?⌋
Should that make difference twixt me & Thee⌊?⌋   [2]

Of H s birth this was the happy lot⌊:⌋
His Mother on his Father him begot⌊.⌋   [2]

[*Page 28*]

Sir Joshua praises Michael Angelo⌊.⌋
[And counts it courage *del*] ⌃[Is it Politeness *del*]⌃ [thus to praise his foe *del*]

Page 26 'To F——' is probably 'To Flaxman'. Though Flaxman is not known to have called Blake a 'Madman', he certainly warned Hayley in 1805 of Blake's eccentricity and unworldliness (see *Blake Records*, 167, 172).

Page 27 'S—— in Childhood . . .' l. 1: 'S——' is probably 'Stothard'.

'To Nancy F——': 'Nancy F——' is Nancy Flaxman, the sculptor's wife.

'Of H s birth . . .': 'H' may be Hayley.

ˍTis Christian Mildness when [fools *del*] ˄˄Knaves˄˄ Praise a
Foeˍ
ˍButˍ Twould be Madness [that we all must *del*] all the World
would say
[All *del*] ˍ[If *del*]ˍ ˄˄Should˄˄ Michael Angelo [praising *del*]
ˍpraiseˍ Sir Joshuaₗ•ₗ   [
Christ usd the Pharisees in a rougher wayₗ•ₗ   [

Hes a Blockhead who wants a proof of what he Can't Percieve
And he's a Fool who [seeks *del*] ˍtriesˍ to make such a Blockhead
believeₗ•ₗ   [

[*Page 29*]

Cr—— loves artists as he loves his Meatₗ;ₗ
[Cr—— *del*] ˍHeˍ loves ˍtheˍ Art but [it is(?) *del*] ˍtisˍ the
Art to Cheatₗ•ₗ   [

A Petty sneaking Knave I knewₗ•ₗ
'O Mʳ Cr—— how do ye doₗ?ₗ'   [

Sir Jo[*s*]hua praised Rubens with a Smile
By Calling his the ornamental Style
[But in *del*] ˍAnd yetˍ his praise of Flaxman was the smartest
When he calld him the Ornamental Artist
But sure such ornaments we well may spare   [
[Like a filthy infectious head of hair *del*]
[A Crooked Stick & Louzy head of hair *del*]
As Crooked limbs & louzy heads of hairₗ•ₗ   [

He is a Cock [won't *altered to*] would
And would be a [Crow *altered to*] Cock if he couldₗ•ₗ   ▌

Page 28 'Sir Joshua praises . . .' l. 4 is written over an erased line, which may
begin (as Erdman [p. 788] says) 'Printing his praises . . .'.

Page 29 'Cr—— loves artists . . .' l. 1: 'Cr——' here and in the poem below is
Cromek.

'He is a Cock . . .' l. 1: Perhaps the reference is to Private Cock, who joined
Private Scolfield in accusing Blake of sedition in 1803. The couplet is written
sideways in the right margin.

[*Page 30*]

He has observd the Golden Rule
Till hes become the Golden Fool⌊.⌋   [2]

To S——d

[He *del*] ∧You∧ All [his *del*] ∧Your∧ Youth observed the Golden
  Rule
Till [hes *del*] ∧youre∧ at last become the [old(?) *del*] golden
  Fool⌊.⌋
I sport with Fortune Merry Blithe & Gay
Like to the Lion Sporting with his Prey⌊.⌋
[He has *del*] ∧[Make(?) thou *del*]∧ ∧∧Take you∧∧ the hide &
  horns which [he may wear *del*] ∧[thou maist *del*]∧ you may
  wear⌊,⌋   [5]
Mine is the flesh⌊,⌋ the bones may be [his *del*] ∧[thy *del*]∧ ∧∧your∧∧
  Share⌊.⌋   [6]

[*Page 31*]

[Mr Cromek to *del*] Mr Stothard to Mr Cromek

For Fortunes favours you your riches bring
But Fortune says she gave you no such thing⌊.⌋
Why should you be ungrateful to your friends
Sneaking & [Calumny *del*] Back biting & Odds & Ends⌊?⌋   [4]

Page 30 'He has observd . . .': This couplet is written over drafts of two couplets
which were deleted before they were erased; they may have read

                    The Golden Fool[?]
          Sporting[?] with[?] fortune [*words illeg*] gay
          Like to the Lion[?] sporting with[?] his[?] prey
          With air[?] I sport merry[?] blithe & gay
          Like to the Lion Sporting with[?] his prey
                    Sparrow
(ll. 1, 3 of this erasure are read hesitantly by Erdman [p. 785] as
          I sport [*or* He sports] with Fortune merry Blithe & gay
          . . . .
          With Fortune sporting Merry Blithe & gay)
The couplet was used as ll. 3–4 of 'To S—d' below.
'To S——d' 'S——d' must be Stothard.
  ll. 3–4 may have been written before ll. 1–2, 5–6, for they carefully avoid the
pencil inscription for the picture over which ll. 1–2 are written, and they were first
drafted above the design (see the note above).
  ll. 5–6 are written with a sharper pen than the other lines.

Mr Cromek to Mr Stothard

Fortune favours the Brave old Proverbs say
But not with Money. *T*hat is not the way⌊·⌋
Turn back turn back⌊,⌋ you travel all in vain⌊;⌋
Turn thro the Iron gate down Sneaking lane⌊·⌋   [

I am no Homers Hero you all know⌊·⌋
I profess not Generosity to a Foe⌊·⌋
My Generosity is to my Friends
That for their Friendship I may make amends⌊·⌋
The Genrous to Enemies promotes their Ends   [.
And becomes the Enemy & Betrayer of his Friends⌊·⌋   [

[*Page 32*]

The Angel that presided oer my birth
Said 'Little creature [thou art *del*] formd [for *del*] of ⌃Joy &
[of *del*]⌃ Mirth

Page 31 'Fortune favours the Brave . . .' l. 3: 'travel' might equally well be read
as 'travil', i.e. 'travail'.

l. 4: Sneaking Alley was in the Tower of London (see J. Adlard, *The Sports
of Cruelty* [1972], 110, 145–6), where the Mint was, the south-eastern entrance
of which was called The Iron Gate.

'I am no Homers Hero . . .' ll. 5–6 appear to be an addition in a browner ink.
The whole poem is written sideways to the left of the sketch.

Page 32: Order of Composition: (**1**) 'The Angel . . .' and 'Sir Joshua . . .' (before its
Black ink title of 'Florentine Ingratitude' was written over the design) ll. 1–6 (plus
four lines later erased and now illegible) were written in the same large hand and
brownish ink respectively above and below the central pencil sketch; (**2**) They
may have been followed immediately by ll. 19–20, 27–30 (ll. 27–30 written as two
lines) in the same ink sideways in the right margin; (**3**) ll. 12–13 were perhaps
written next in Black ink (like the rest of the lines) sideways in the left margin in a
large hand; (**4**) 'These Verses . . .' (which may be either a separate poem or the
conclusion of 'Florentine Ingratitude') were probably written next in a large
hand in the last clearly free space above the design and below 'The Angel . . .';
(**5**) 'Florentine Ingratitude' ll. 7–11 (written over the previous illegible erasure),
21–4 (written below l. 11 and squeezed in as two lines at the bottom of the page over
an illegible erasure in Brown ink), 18–20 (written sideways in the right margin),
14–15 (written small and sideways in the right margin above ll. 18–20), 16–17
(written to the right of l. 15, l. 16 as a continuation of l. 15), l. 19 (substituted
for l. 18), ll. 25–6 (squeezed in as one line in the right margin above ll. 27–8) can
only quite tentatively be said to have been written in this order.

The smudge over ll. 23–5 may not be connected with the text at all.

'The Angel . . .' l. 1: Compare 'So spoke an Angel at my birth . . .', *Notebook*
p. 79 (p. 962).

Go live without the help of any [Thing [*altered to*] King[*?*] on
Earth⌊·⌋   [*3*]

These Verses were written by a very Envious Man
Who whatever likeness he may have to Michael Angelo
Never can have any to Sir Jehoshuan⌊·⌋   [*3*]

Florentine Ingratitude

Sir Joshua Sent his own Portrait to
The birth Place of Michael Angelo
And in the hand of the Simpering fool
He put a dirty paper scroll
And on the paper to be polite   [*5*]
Did 'Sketches by Michael Angelo' write⌊,⌋
[They said Thus Learning ∧& Politeness∧ from England ∧(&
    Politeness *del*)∧ we fetch
([I *del*] ∧We∧ thought Michael Angelo did never *del*) ∧For No
    good artist will or Can∧ Sketch
And tis English Politeness as fair as [my *del*] ∧your∧ Aunt   [*10*]
(To [say *del*] ∧speak∧ Michael Angelo & [mean *del*] ∧act∧
    Rembrandt *del*)
To speak Michael Angelo & mean Rembrandt *del*]
The Florentines said 'Tis a Dutch English bore⌊,⌋
Michael Angelos Name writ on Rembrandts door'⌊·⌋
The Florentines call it an English Fetch
For Michael Angelo did never Sketch⌊·⌋   [*15*]
Every line of his has Meaning
And needs neither Suckling nor Weaning⌊·⌋
[Is(?) This (?) Politeness or is it Cant *del*]
∧Tis the trading English Venetian Cant∧
To Speak Michael Angelo & Act Rembrandt⌊·⌋   [*20*]

'These Verses . . .' l. 1: 'These Verses' are probably 'Florentine Ingratitude'
below.

'Florentine Ingratitude' l. 1: Sir Joshua Reynolds (1723–92) sent his portrait to
the Uffizi Gallery in Florence in 1776, with a long letter.
    l. 7: Under 'we fetch' Erdman (p. 788) reads 'was sent'.
    l. 8: Under 'Sketch' Erdman (p. 788) reads 'Paint'.
    ll. 9–10: Beside ll. 9–10 in the left margin is '[Angelo *del*]', but its significance is
not clear.

Ghiottos Circle or Apelles Line
Were not the Work of Sketchers drunk with Wine
Nor of the City Clarks warm[?] Hearted Fashion
Nor of Sir Isaac Newtons Calculation
Nor of the City Clarks Idle Facilities   [⸱
Which sprang from Sir Isaac Newtons great Abilities
2 But You must not bring in your hand a Lie
  If you mean ˄that˄ the Florentines [to *del*] ˄should˄ buy⌊·⌋
1 It will set his Dutch friends all in a roar
  To write Mch Ang on Rembrandts door⌊·⌋   [

[*Page 33*]
A[Pitiable *altered to*] Pitiful Case

The Villa[i]n at the Gallows tree
When he is doomd to die
To assuage his misery
In Virtues praise does cry⌊·⌋

So Reynolds when he came to die   [
To assuage his bitter woe:
Thus aloud [was heard to *del*] ˄did howl &˄ cry
'Michael Angelo Michael Angelo⌊!⌋'   [

To the Royal Academy
A Strange Erratum in all the Editions
Of Sir Joshua Reynolds⌈'⌉s Lectures
Should be corrected by the Young Gentlemen

ll. 21–30: Erdman (p. 504) gives the order as ll. 29–30, 27–8, 21–6, and 'These Verses . . .' as ll. 31–3.

l. 23: For 'warm' Erdman (p. 504) reads confidently 'merry'.

Page 33: Order of Composition: (**1**) First 'The Villa[i]n . . .' and 'A Strange Erratum . . .' were written respectively above and below the pencil sketch, ll. 9–10 of 'A Strange Erratum . . .' to the right of ll. 7–8, and the titles in a slightly different ink; (**2**) Then probably 'The Everlasting Gospel' part e was written sideways from the right margin to the sketch, (**3**) Followed by 'If it is True . . .' written sideways from the left margin to and over (ll. 11–14) the sketch, ll. 1–8 as four lines, ll. 11–12 run on.

'A Pitiful Case' l. 8: An allusion to the conclusion of Reynolds's last Discourse to the Royal Academy (Dec. 1790): 'I should desire that the last words which I should pronounce in this Academy, and from this place, might be the name of—MICHAEL ANGELO' (*The Works of Sir Joshua Reynolds, Knight*, ed. E. Malone [1798], ii. 217–18).

Notebook p. 34

And the Royal Academys directors⌊·⌋

Instead of Michael Angelo   [5]
Read Rembrandt [& you will know *del*] ˄for it is fit˄
[That Sir Joshua never wishd to Speak
Of Michael Angelo *del*]
To make [either sense or *del*] ˄meer common˄ honesty
In all that he has writ⌊·⌋   [*10*]

If it is True What the Prophets write
That the heathen Gods are all stocks & stones
Shall we for the sake of being Polite
Feed them with the juice of our marrow bones
And if Bezaliel & Aholiab drew   [5]
What the Finger of God pointed to their View
Shall we Suffer the Roman & Grecian Rods
To compell us to worship them as Gods⌊?⌋
They Stole them from the Temple of the Lord
And Worshippd them [to *del*] ˄that they might˄ make Inspired
  Art Abhorrd⌊·⌋   [*10*]
The Wood & Stone were calld The Holy Things—
And their Sublime Intent given to their Kings⌊,⌋
All the Atonements of Jehovah spurnd
And Criminals to Sacrifices Turnd⌊·⌋   [*14*]

[*Page 34*]
[To *del*] ˄On˄ F—— & S——

I found [thee *altered to*] them blind⌊,⌋ I taught [thee *altered to*]
  them how to see
And now [thou *del*] ˄they˄ know[st *del*] neither [thyself *del*]
  ˄themselves˄ nor me⌊·⌋

'If it is True . . .' l. 5: Exodus 36: 1: 'Then wrought Bezaleel and Aholiab, and
every wise hearted man, in whom the Lord put wisdom and understanding to
know how to work all manner of work for the service of the sanctuary . . .'; for
Bezaleel see also Exodus 31–8.

Page 34 'On F—— & S——'; The title may have been written as two stages of
afterthoughts, first 'To F——' and then 'On F—— and S——'. 'F—— & S——'
are probably Flaxman & Stothard.

ll. 1–2 These two lines are found in a slightly different form in the *Descriptive
Catalogue* ¶64 (p. 846).

945

Tis excellent to turn a thorn to a pin⌊,⌋
A [knave *del*] ∧Fool∧ to a bolt⌊,⌋ a [fool *del*] ∧Knave∧ to a glass
of gin⌊.⌋   [

P—— loved me not as he lovd his Friends
For he lovd them for gain to serve his Ends⌊.⌋
[But *del*] He loved me [but *del*] ∧and∧ for no Gain at all
But to rejoice & triumph in my fall⌊.⌋   [

To forgive Enemies H. does pretend
Who never in his Life forgave a friend⌊.⌋   [

[*Page 35*]

To F——

You call me Mad⌊,⌋ tis Folly to do so
To seek to turn a Madman to a Foe⌊.⌋
If you think as you speak you are an Ass⌊;⌋
If you do not you are [just *del*] ∧but∧ what you was⌊.⌋   [

On H——ys Friendship

When H——y finds out what you cannot do
That is the very thing he⌈'⌉ll set you to⌊.⌋
If you break not your Neck tis not his fault
[A *del*] ∧But∧ pecks of poison ∧are∧ not [a *del*] pecks of salt

'P—— loved me not . . .' l. 1: 'P——' is probably Richard Phillips, Blake's
employer in his engravings for Hayley's *Ballads* (1805) and Prince Hoare's *Inquiry
into the . . . Arts of Design in England* (1806).

'To forgive Enemies . . .' This poem is written in a blacker ink than the poems
above it. In other respects it appears to be a continuation of 'P—— loved me . . .'.
'H.' is probably Hayley.

Page 35 'To F——' and 'On H——ys Friendship' The titles appear to be in a
later, darker ink. 'F——' is probably Flaxman and 'H——y' Hayley.

'On H——ys Friendship' ll. 3–4 are written over two illegible erased lines which
may end in 'fire'. The 's' in both 'pecks' in l. 4 appears to have been added later,
and 'poison' was originally 'poisons'.

And when he could not act upon my wife   [5]
Hired a Villain to bereave my Life⌞.⌟   [6]

[*Page 36*]
Some Men created for destruction come
Into the World & make the World their home⌞.⌟
[Friend Caiaphas is one do what he can *del*]
ⱯBe they as Vile & Base as Eer they can⌞,⌟Ɐ
[He(')ll *del*] ⱯTheyllⱯ still be called The Worlds' honest man⌞.⌟ [5]

On S

You say reserve & modesty he has
[His *del*] ⱯWhoseⱯ heart is iron⌞,⌟ his head wood & his face brass⌞.⌟
The Fox the Owl the Beetle & the Bat
[Say *del*] ⱯByⱯ sweet reserve & modesty [feed Fat *del*] get Fat⌞.⌟ [4]

[*Page 37*]
Imitation of Pope⌞:⌟ A Compliment to the Ladies

Wondrous the Gods⌞,⌟ more wondrous are the Men⌞,⌟
More Wondrous Wondrous Still the Cock & Hen⌞,⌟
More wondrous Still the Table Stool & Chair
But Ah More wondrous still the Charming Fair⌞.⌟ [4]

To H——

Thy Friendship oft has made my heart to ake⌞;⌟
Do be my Enemy for Friendships sake⌞.⌟   [2]

---

ll. 5–6 are written in a later, blacker ink. The Hired Villain is presumably John Scolfield, who accused Blake of sedition in 1803. l. 6 is repeated from 'Fair Elenor' l. 68 (p. 755).

Page 36 'Some Men . . .' ll. 3–4: The additions are made with a distinctly blacker ink in a smaller hand.

'On S' 'S' is probably Stothard.

ll. 3–4 are given in a slightly different form in *Descriptive Catalogue* ¶62 (p. xxx).

Page 37: Order of Composition: (1) 'Imitation of Pope' and 'To H——' are written in a brownish ink in a large hand above and below the pencil sketch ('A Compliment to the Ladies' rather browner than the others); (2) Below 'To H——' is 'Cosway Frazer . . .' in Black ink (like the rest of the page) ll. 1–6, apparently completed by ll. 7–8 written sideways in the right margin; (3) The epitaphs are written sideways from the left margin over part of the design.

'To H——' 'H——' is probably Hayley.

Cosway Frazer & Baldwin of Egypts Lake
Fear to Associate with Blake⌊·⌋
This Life is a Warfare against Evils⌊;⌋
They heal the sick⌊,⌋ he casts out devils⌊·⌋
Hayley Flaxman & Stothard are also in doubt   [⸱
Lest their Virtue should be put to the rout⌊·⌋
One grins⌊,⌋ [one *del*] ∧tother∧ Spits & in corners hides
And all the [Righteous *del*] ∧Virtuous∧ have shewn their back- [⸱
sides⌊·⌋

An Epitaph

Come knock your heads against this Stone
For Sorrow that poor John Thompsons gone⌊·⌋   [

another

I was buried near this Dike
That my Friends may weep as much as they like⌊·⌋   [

another

Here lies John Trot the Friend of all mankind⌊·⌋
He has not left one Enemy behind⌊·⌋
Friends were quite hard to find old authors say
But now they stand in every bodies way⌊·⌋   [

[*Page 38*]

My title as an [Artist *del*] ∧Genius∧ thus is provd⌊,⌋
Not Praisd by Hayley nor by Flaxman lovd⌊·⌋   ▮

'Cosway Frazer . . .' l. 1: Richard Cosway (1740–1821), fashionable miniaturist and occultist, was a friend of Blake; George Baldwin (d. 1818), mystical writer, explorer of the Red Sea, consul-general in Egypt, became interested there in magnetic influences, and evidently returned to England after 1801. The *Notebook* reference to Baldwin is his only known association with Blake. Frazer has not been identified.

'I was buried . . .' See *Notebook* p. 22, ll. 49–50 (p. 937), where a variant appears.

'Here lies John Trot . . .' l. 1: See *Notebook* p. 22, l. 51 (p. 937), where a variant appears.

Page 38: Order of Composition: (1) First, written in the largest hand, were probably 'My title . . .' and 'Rubens had been . . .' above the sketch and 'Nature & Art . . .' (before the titles) below it; (2) Perhaps they were followed in the last obviously clear space by 'To English Connoisseurs' ll. 1–4 below 'Rubens had been . . .',

ʌIʌ Rubens [had been *del*] ʌamʌ a Statesman [or *del*] & a
   Saintʟ·˩
[He mixd them both & so he learnd to Paint *del*]
ʌDeceptions? O no & So I'll learn to Paintʟ·˩ʌ   [*3*]

To English Connoisseurs

You must agree that Rubens was a Fool
And yet you make him master of Your School
And give more money for his Slobberings
Than you will give for Rafaels finest Thingsʟ·˩
I understood Christ was a Carpenter   [*5*]
And not a Brewers Servant my good Sirʟ·˩
Swelld limbs with no outline that you can descry
That Stink in the Nose of a Stander by
But all the Pulp washd painted finishd with labour
Of an hundred Journeymens how dye Do Neighbourʟ·˩   [*10*]

[A Pretty Epigram for ʌthe Entertainment ofʌ those who
have given high Prices for Bad Pictures *del*]
[And(?) have(?) *del*] Pretty Epigram for [those *del*] the
            Entertainment of those
Who [pay *del*] ʌhave Paidʌ Great Sums in the Venetian &
   Flemish Ooze

Nature & Art in this together Suitʟ,˩
What is Most Grand is always most Minuteʟ·˩
Rubens thinks Table Chairs & Stools are Grand
But Rafael thinks A Head a foot a handʟ·˩   [*4*]

l. 4 impinging on the sketch; (**3**) 'Public Address' part ccc is written boldly across
the sketch; (**4**) 'To English Connoisseurs' ll. 5–6 are written as one line squeezed
between l. 4 and the 'Public Address'; (**5**) Perhaps they were continued directly
with ll. 7–10 (which may alternatively be a separate poem) written between the
prose and the title of 'A Pretty Epigram . . .' (ll. 9–10 written as one line); (**6**) 'Let
it be told . . .' was perhaps next written at the bottom of the page, ll. 1–4 written
in two columns terminated by a stroke across the page, supplemented by ll. 5–6
written as one line below the stroke, ll. 7–8 written sideways to the bottom left
margin, the first words of l. 1 altered, and the lines renumbered.

'Pretty Epigram' Erdman (p. 789) reads a first title of 'To——' (which I cannot
find), and a second of 'Major testament of ——', misreading (I believe) 'the Enter-
tainment of' over the caret (which he seems to ignore).

3[Let it be told *del*] ⌃The Swallow sings⌃ in Courts of Kings
That Fools have their high finishings
And this the Princes golden rule
The Laborious stumble of a Fool⌞·⌟
1 These are the Idiots chiefest Arts
2 To blend & not define the Parts⌞·⌟
To make out the parts is the wise mans aim
But to lose them the Fool makes his foolish Game⌞·⌟

[

[

[*Page 39*]
The Hebrew Nation did not write it⌞,⌟
Avarice & Chastity did Shite it⌞·⌟

[

If I eer Grow to Mans Estate
O Give to me a Womans fate⌞,⌟
May I govern all both great & small⌞,⌟
Have the last word & take the wall⌞·⌟

[

The Cripple every Step drudges & labours
And says 'come learn to walk of me Good Neighbours'⌞·⌟
Sir Joshua in astonishment cries out⌞,⌟
[His pains are more than others theres no doubt *del*]
⌃'See what Great Labour Pain[?] him & Modest doubt⌞·⌟'⌃
Newton & Bacon cry being badly Nurs*t*,
'He is all Experiments from last to first⌞·⌟

'Let it be told . . .' l. 8: 'them' is clearly written as 'then'.

Page 39: Order of Composition: (1) First came the pencil lines 'The Hebrew Nation . . .'
at the top of the page, (2) Probably followed by 'If I eer . . .' in the large vacant
space below the sketch; (3) 'Rafael Sublime . . .' ll. 1–4 ('Public Address' part ddd)
between the pencil lines at the top and the sketch, and 'The Cripple . . .' ll. 1–3, 5
at the bottom were probably next; (4) 'Public Address' part eee is written side-
ways from the left margin to the right, avoiding (after 'understand Graving')
the pencil sketch and the top poetry ('The Hebrew Nation . . .' and 'Rafael
Sublime . . .'), and continued (after 'to the Subject') *upside-down* in the top margin
on top of the pencil lines; (5) 'Rafael Sublime . . .' and 'The Cripple . . .' were
probably then amplified with the alteration of l. 4 of 'The Cripple . . .', ll. 6–7
squeezed in as one line at the foot of the page, ll. 8–9 written sideways in the bottom
right margin and carefully avoiding the prose, 'Rafael Sublime . . .' continued with
a passage to its right partially erased, emended to include ll. 5 and 7, and l. 6
written under 'I must grant / Learn the Laborious' *upside-down* (its place in the
poem is therefore somewhat conjectural).

'The Cripple . . .' l. 4: 'pains are more than others' is written over an illegible
erasure.

He walks & stumbles as if he Crep
And how high labourd is every step∟⌐⌐'   [9]

[*Page 40*]
On the Great Encouragement [giving(?)
mended to]
Given by English Nobility & Gentry to Correggio
Rubens Rembrand[*t*] Reynolds Gainsborough Catalani
DuCrowe & Dilbury Doodle
As the Ignorant Savage will sell his own Wife
For a [Button *del*] ∧Sword or∧ a [Bauble a Bead or *del*] ∧[Buckle
del] cutlass a dagger∧ [a *mended to*] or Knife∟⌐⌐
So the [wise *del*] ∧[Learned *del*] Taught∧ Savage Englishman
[gives *del*] ∧spends∧ his whole Fortune
[For *del*] ∧On∧ a smear [& *del*] ∧or∧ a squall [that is not *del*] ∧to
destroy∧ Picture [Nor *del*] ∧or∧ Tune
And I call upon Colonel Wardle   [5]
To give these Rascals a dose of Cawdle∟⌐⌐   [6]

Give pensions to the Learned Pig
Or the Hare playing [a *del*] on a Tabor∟⌐⌐
Anglus can never see Perfection
But in the Journeymans Labour∟⌐⌐   [4]

The Cunning sures & the aim at yours

All Pictures thats Pa[*i*]nted with Sense & with Thought
Are Painted by Madmen as sure as a Groat
For the Greater the Fool in the Pencil more blest
And when they are drunk they always pa[*i*]nt best∟⌐⌐

Page 40: Order of Composition: (1) 'As the Ignorant Savage . . .' (before its title)
was written above the sketch; (2) 'Give pensions . . .', 'The Cunning sures . . .'
(both written over the central sketch), and 'All Pictures . . .' written over the
scratched-out portrait at the bottom were perhaps next.

'On the Great Encouragement . . .' Angélique Catalani (1782–1849) was an
Italian singer immensely successful in Paris, London (about 1807–15), and else-
where. Pierre Ducros (1745–1810) was a Swiss painter and engraver of popular
landscapes whose example George Cumberland urged Blake to follow in Dec. 1808
(*Blake Records*, 211). 'Dilbury' might also be 'Dilberry'; he has not been identified.
  l. 5: Lt.-Col. Gwyllym Lloyd Wardle (1762?–1833) brought forward a motion in
the House of Commons on 27 Jan. 1809 concerning the official corruption of the
Duke of York, which necessitated the Duke's retirement. Wardle's great but brief
popularity was in the spring of 1809.

They never Can Rafael it Fuseli *it*, nor Blake it⌐;⌐   ⌐
If they cant see an outline pray how can they make it⌐?⌐
When Men will draw outlines begin you to Jaw them⌐;⌐
Madmen see outlines & therefore they draw them⌐.⌐   [

[*Page 41*]

On H——— the Pick thank
I write the Rascal Thanks till he & I
With Thanks & Compliments are quite drawn dry⌐.⌐   [

Cromek Speaks

I always take my judgment from a Fool
Because [I know he always judges *del*] ˄his Judgment is so
very˄ Cool⌐,⌐
Not prejudicd by feelings great or Small⌐.⌐
[Because we know *del*] ˄Amiable state⌐,⌐˄ he cannot feel at all⌐.⌐ |

English Encouragement of Art
Cromeks opinions put into Rhyme

If you mean to Please Every body you will
[Set to work *del*] ˄Mennywouver˄ both [Ignorance *del*]
˄Bunglishness˄ & skill
For a great [multitud(*e*) *del*] ˄[Madjority *del*] Conquest˄ are
[Ignorant *del*] Bunglery
And [skill *del*] [to them *del*] [seems *del*] [raving & rant *del*]
˄Jenous looks to him [looks *del*] like mad Rantery⌐,⌐˄
Like [*putting *del*] ˄displaying˄ oil & water into a lamp⌐,⌐
Twill [make a great *del*] ˄hold forth a huge˄ splutter with smoke
& damp

Page 41: Order of Composition: (**1**) The two couplets at the top of the page ('I write the Rascal Thanks . . .' and 'I always take . . .' ll. 1–2) were probably,written first, above the sketch; (**2**) 'If you mean to Please . . .' ll. 1–8 were written below the sketch, followed by 'When you look at a picture . . .' ll. 1–4 written sideways from the left margin and ll. 5–8 written sideways to the right margin; each of the titles may be an afterthought.

'On H—— the Pick thank' 'H——' is probably Hayley.

'Cromek Speaks' ll. 1–2 are essentially repeated on *Notebook* p. 70 (p. 960).

'English Encouragement of Art . . .' l. 4: For 'him' Erdman (p. 501) reads 'ham'.

    l. 6: Under 'damp' is an undeleted and illegible scribbled word apparently unrelated to any other writing on this page.

For [there is no use *del*] ˄its all sheer loss˄ as it seems to me
Of [Lighting a Lamp *del*] ˄displaying[*?*] up a light˄ when [you
   dont wish *del*] ˄we want not˄ to see⌊.⌋   [*8*]

When you look at a picture you always can see
If a Man of Sense has Painted he⌊.⌋
Then never flinch but keep up a Jaw
About freedom & Jenny Suck awa'

And when it smells of the Lamp we [all *del*] can   [*5*]
Say all was owing to the Skilful Man
For the smell of water is but small⌊;⌋
So een let Ignorance do it all⌊.⌋   [*8*]

[*Page 42*]
You say their Pictures well Painted be
And yet they are Blockheads you all agree⌊.⌋
Thank God I never was sent to school
[To learn to admire the works of a Fool *del*]
To be Flogd into following the Style of a Fool⌊.⌋   [*5*]

The Errors of a Wise Man make your Rule
Rather than the Perfections of a Fool⌊.⌋   [*2*]

The Washer Womans Song
I washd them out & washd them in
And they told me it was a great Sin⌊.⌋   [*2*]

[*Page 43*]
When I see a ˄Rubens˄ Rembran[*d*]t [or *del*] Correggio
I think of the Crippled Harry & Slobbering Joe
And then I [say to myself *del*] ˄question thus⌊:⌋˄ are artists rules
To be drawn from the works of two manifest fools⌊?⌋

'When you look at a picture . . .' is written in Cromek's Yorkshire dialect and may
have been intended as part of 'English Encouragement of Art . . .'.

Page 42: Order of Composition: (1) 'You say . . .' is written boldly above the sketch,
and below it 'The Washer Womans Song' is written the same size; (2) 'The Errors
of a Wise Man . . .' seems somewhat smaller and just fills the space between the
sketch and 'The Washer Womans Song'.

Then God defend us from the Arts I say⌊·⌋   [⸀
Send Battle Murder Sudden death [we *del*] ∧O∧ pray⌊·⌋
Rather than [let *del*] be such a ∧blind∧ Human Fool
Id be an Ass a Hog a worm a Chair a Stool⌊·⌋   [⸀

    Great things are done when Men & Mountains meet⌊·⌋
    This is not done by Jostling in the Street⌊·⌋   L⸀

[*Page 46*]

I [have givn *del*] ∧give∧ you the end of a golden string⌊,⌋
Only wind it into a ball⌊:⌋
It will lead you in at Heavns Gate
Built in Jerusalems wall⌊·⌋   [

[*Page 47*]

If you play a Game of Chance⌊,⌋ know before you begin
If you are benevolent you will never win⌊·⌋   [

[*Page 50*]

The only Man that eer I knew
Who did not make me almost spew
Was Fuseli⌊,⌋ he was both Turk & Jew
And so [Sweet *del*] ∧dear∧ Christian[s *del*] ∧Friends∧ how do you
do⌊?⌋   [

Page 43 'Great things are done . . .' may be either a separate poem or the conclusion of 'When I see . . .'.

Page 46 The poem as revised was etched in *Jerusalem* pl. 77 (p. 587).

Page 50: Order of Composition: (1) The lines about Cowper below the sketch were probably written first; (2) They were evidently continued by 'For this is being a Friend . . .' (ll. 5–8) at the bottom of the page and ll. 9–16 sideways from the left margin to the sketch; (3) Before the 'Cowper' passage was erased, a stroke was drawn from the end of that passage to l. 13 (indicating that it should precede ll. 5–8 above), and later the stroke seems to have been negated in Grey wash; (4) The 'Cowper' passage was erased and 'The only Man . . .' was written in its place (between the title 'William Cowper Esqre' and ll. 5–8 below it) but apparently unrelated in subject to the 'Cowper' poem; (5) 'The Everlasting Gospel' part f, ll. 53–64, 69–71 are written across the top of the page and descending down the right margin (ll. 57–8 and 59–60 as single lines) carefully avoiding the sketch and all the 'Cowper' lines; (6) ll. 65–8 were written in the only significant blank remaining, at the top right corner, and a stroke brings them in after l. 64.

William Cowper Esqre

[Stanza erased.]

For this is being a Friend just in the nick   ⌊*5*⌋
Not when hes well but waiting till hes Sick⌊.⌋
He calls you to his help⌊,⌋ be you not movd
Untill by being Sick his wants are provd⌊.⌋

You see him spend his Soul in Prophecy⌊,⌋
Do you believe it a Confounded lie   [*10*]
Till some Bookseller & the Public Fame
Proves there is truth in his extravagant claim

For tis [most wicked *del*] ⌃atrocious⌃ in a Friend[*?*] you love
To tell you any thing that he cant prove
And tis most wicked in a Christian Nation   [*15*]
For any Man to pretend to Inspiration⌊.⌋   [*16*]

[*Page 52*]
I will tell you what Joseph of Arimathea
Said to my Fairy⌊,⌋ was not it ⌃very⌊?⌋⌃ queer⌊?⌋

'William Cowper Esqre' Erdman (p. 784) reads an erasure to the left of the title as 'Epitaph for'.

ll. 1–4: The 4 erased lines may have read in part:

	E	ternal
	&	story
[. . . .]		
It		ment

Erdman (p. 784) makes out the first two lines in part as:
Here lies the Man
Hayley & History [*or* Victory]
ll. 7–8: 'movd' and 'provd' were crudely mended from 'moved' and 'proved'.

Page 52: Order of Composition: (1) 'Public Address' part b, 'of my work . . . as a draughtsman' was written above the sketch, followed by 'The manner . . . your Friend' below it; (2) 'Public Address' part b was supplemented with the parenthetical passage 'We all know . . . Subjects' written at the bottom of the page (after 'your Friend') and ending below the bottom prose on p. 53 ('upon these ungracious Subjects') with a + after 'Beaufort Buildings' and another before 'We all know' to show its place—this passage was probably continued directly on p. 53 ('Flaxman cannot . . .'); (3) Next 'The Everlasting Gospel' part f, ll. 93–4 were added and numbered ('94 lines'); (4) Next probably 'The Everlasting Gospel' part g was written below ll. 93–4 above; (5) 'The Everlasting Gospel' part k, ll. 1–2, 5–21, 25

Pliny & Trajan₍ₗ₎ what₍ₗ₎ are You here₍ₗ₎?₍₎
Come listen to Joseph of Arimathea₍ₗ₎·₍₎
Listen patient & when Joseph has done   [
Twill make a Fool laugh & a Fairy Fun₍ₗ₎·₍₎   [

[*Page 54*]
Grown old in Love from Seven till Seven times seven
I oft have wishd for Hell for Ease from Heaven₍ₗ₎·₍₎

[*Page 56*]
Why was Cupid a Boy
And why a boy was he₍ₗ₎?₍₎
He should have been a Girl
For ought that I can see

For he shoots with his bow
And the Girl shoots with her Eye
And they both are merry & glad
And laugh when we do cry

[Then *del*] ˄And˄ to make Cupid a Boy
Was [surely a Womans *del*] ˄the Cupid Girls mocking˄ plan

were written in the last clear space to the right of the sketch avoiding the top and
bottom prose, and supplemented with ll. 3–4 written to the left and marked with
two strokes for insertion here; (**6**) 'The Everlasting Gospel' part f, ll. 95–6 were
added *on top of the sketch* and clearly marked by two strokes for insertion after l. 94;
(**7**) 'I will tell you . . .' is written sideways to the left margin, ll. 2–4 as one line,
ll. 5–6 continuing round the bottom of the page also as one line; (**8**) 'The Ever-
lasting Gospel' part k, ll. 21–4 are written just below part g in a much darker ink
and smaller hand, ll. 23–4 as one line avoiding the bottom prose—they are not
marked for entry.

Page 54: Order of Composition: (**1**) 'Grown old in Love . . .' is written in pencil above
the three sketches; (**2**) 'The Everlasting Gospel' part k, ll. 84–6, 91–108 were
written in the left margin carefully avoiding all the sketches; (**3**) 'The Everlasting
Gospel' part k, ll. 87–90, part 1 and 'Was Jesus Chaste or did he &ᶜ' were written
at indeterminate times to the right (ll. 87–90 over the sketched woman's head)
and a stroke joins 'Was Jesus Chaste or did he &ᶜ' to l. 108.

'Grown old in Love . . .' l. 1: If literally true, this passage must have been written
in 1806–7.

Page 56: Order of Composition: (**1**) 'Why was Cupid a Boy . . .' was written first in
the right margin; (**2**) 'Public Address' part a was written next in the top left
corner, (**3**) Followed by part b below the sketch continuing from p. 55; (**4**) Part d
was next written sideways from the left margin between the top and bottom
prose—its relation to the other prose is uncertain.

For a boy [never learns so much *del*] ‸cant interpret the thing‸
Till he is become a man

And then hes so piercd with care
And wounded with arrowy smarts
That the whole business of his life   [*15*]
Is to pick out the heads of the darts⌊·⌋

Twas the Greeks love of war
Turnd Love into a Boy
And Woman into a Statue of Stone
And away fled every Joy⌊·⌋   [*20*]

[*Page 59*]
From Bells Weekly Messenger Aug^st 4, 1811.[1]

'Salisbury July 29
A Bill of Indictment was preferred against Peter Le Cave for
Felony but returnd Ignoramus by the Grand Jury. It appeard
that he was in extreme indigence but was an Artist of very
superior Merit⌊;⌋ while he was in Wilton [Jail *del*] Goal he
painted many Pieces in the Style of Morland⌊,⌋ some of which
are stated to be even Superior to the performances of that
Artist, with whom Le Cave lived many years as a Professional
Assistant & he states that many Paintings of his were only
Varnished over by Morland & sold by that Artist as his own.
Many of the Principal Gentlemen of the County have visited
Le Cave in the Goal & declared his drawings & Paintings in
many instances to excel Morlands. The Writer of this Article
has seen many of Le Caves Works & tho he does not pretend
to the Knowledge of an artist yet he considers them as Chaste
delineations of Rural Objects.'
     Such is the Paragraph⌊·⌋ It confirms the Suspition I enter-
taind concerning those two [Prints *del*] I Engraved From for

Page 59: Order of Composition: (1) Probably 'Public Address' part g was written
first above the main sketch of Ugolino in prison, for *For Children* pl. 14, (2) Followed
by the passage 'From Bells Weekly Messenger' to the left and below the main
sketch, and over that at the bottom.
     1 Except for minor particulars of capitalization, and spelling (e.g. 'gaol' for
Blake's 'Goal'), the account in *Bell's Weekly Messenger* for 4 Aug. 1811 is just as
Blake gives it.

J. R. Smit*h*,[2] That Morland could not have Painted them as
they were the works of a Correct Mind & no Blurrer∟•⌟

[*Page 60*]

I askd my dear Friend Orator Prigg
'Whats the first part of Oratory∟?⌟' he said 'a great wig'∟•⌟
'And what is the second∟?⌟' then dancing a jig
And bowing profoundly he said 'a great wig'∟•⌟
'And what is the third∟?⌟' then he snord like a pig
And [smild like a Cherub & said *del*] ⁁puffing his cheeks he
    replied⁁ 'a Great wig'∟•⌟
So if a Great Painter with Questions you push
'Whats the first Part of Painting∟?⌟' he⌐¬ll say 'a Paint brush'∟•⌟
'And what is the Second∟?⌟' with most modest blush
He ll [nod wink & *del*] smile [& reply *del*] ⁁like a cherub & say⁁
    'a paint Brush'∟•⌟
'And what is the third∟?⌟' he ll bow like a rush∟,⌟
With a lear in his Eye he⌐¬ll reply 'a Paint brush'∟•⌟
Perhaps this is all a Painter can want
But look yonder that house is the house of Rembran[*d*]t &ᶜ
        to come in Barry a Poem

That God is Colouring Newton does shew
And the devil is a Black outline all of us know∟•⌟
Perhaps this little Fable &ᶜ

[*Page 61*]

To Venetian Artists

Perhaps this little Fable may make us merry∟•⌟
A dog went over the water without a wherry∟•⌟

---

² Blake's engravings of the 'Industrious Cottager' and 'The Idle Laundress'
are both inscribed 'Painted by G. Morland' and 'Publish'd May 12ᵗʰ 1788, by
J. R. Smith'.

Page 60: Order of Composition: (**1**) First came 'Public Address' part h in a large hand
above the sketch, (**2**) Probably followed by part i just below the sketch; (**3**) 'I
askd my dear Friend . . .' ll. 1–12 were next written in blacker ink with a sharper
pen to the left of the sketch; (**4**) The rest of the writing comes to the right; 'I
askd my dear Friend . . .' is evidently the work 'to come in Barry a Poem' (other-
wise unknown), for 'That God . . . Fable &ᶜ' is written in a smaller hand than the
direction.

Page 61: Order of Composition: (**1**) First came 'Public Address' part i below the sketch;
(**2**) Followed by 'Perhaps this little Fable . . .' ll. 4–15 (later entitled 'To Venetian

A bone which he had stoln he had in his mouth
He cared not whether the wind was north or south‚ₗ.ⱼ
As he swam he saw the reflection of the bone‚ₗ.ⱼ
'This is quite Perfection [heres two for *del*] one [what a brilliant
   tone *del*] ‸Generalizing Tone‚ₗ.ⱼ‸
Outline‚ₗ!ⱼ theres no outline‚ₗ,ⱼ theres no such thing‚ₗ;ⱼ   [*10*]
All is Chiaro Scuro Poco Pen‚ₗ;ⱼ [& *del*] ‸its all‸ Colouring‚ₗ.ⱼ'
[‸Then‸ He snapd & *del*] ‸Sna*p*! Snap! he has‸ lost shadow &
   substance too‚ₗ.ⱼ
He had them both before‚ₗ,ⱼ now how do ye do‚ₗ?ⱼ
'A great deal better than I was before‚ₗ.ⱼ
[Ive tasted shadow & *del*] ‸Those who taste‸ ‸ Colouring‸ love
   it more & more‚ₗ.ⱼ'   [*15*]

[Then Reynolds said O Woman most Sage *del*]
'O dear Mother outline [be not in a Rage *del*] ‸of Knowledge
   most Sage‸
Whats the First Part of Painting‚ₗ?ⱼ' she said 'Patronage‚ₗ!ⱼ'
'And what is the Second‚ₗ?ⱼ to Please & Engage‚ₗ?ⱼ'
She frownd like a Fury & Said 'Patronage‚ₗ!ⱼ'   [*5*]
'And what is the Third‚ₗ?ⱼ' She put off Old Age
And smild like a Syren & said 'Patronage‚ₗ!ⱼ'   [*7*]

[*Page 63*]

Great Men & Fools [of *del*] do often me Inspire
But the Greater Fool the Greater Liar‚ₗ.ⱼ   [*2*]

Artists') at the top and partly over the sketch, with ll. 10–11 written sideways from
the right margin and clearly marked for entry with a stroke; (3) Last came 'Then
Reynolds said . . .' to the left of the sketch; this last poem might alternatively
belong with 'I askd my dear Friend Orator Prigg' on the facing p. 60.

Page 63: Order of Composition: Each passage is written with so much room to spare
that it is difficult to be confident of the order. (**1**) 'Public Address' part l is written
in a large hand at the top of the page, and part m is below the sketch; (**2**) Part j,
ll. 15–16 are written below the prose and evidently intended for the poem on
p. 62; (**3**) Parts t and u are written at the left and right of the sketch; (**4**) 'Great
Men & Fools . . .' is written *upside-down* in the broad space at the bottom of the
page.

[*Page 64*]

From Cratelos

Me Time has Crook'd. *No* good workman
Is he. Infirm is all that he does⌞.⌟   [

I always thought that Jesus Christ was a Snubby or I should not
have worshipd him if I had thought he had been one of those
long spindle nosed rascals⌞.⌟

[*Page 65*]

If Men will act like a maid smiling over a Churn
They ought not when it comes to anothers turn
To grow sower at what a friend may utter
Knowing & feeling that we all have need of Butter⌞.⌟

False Friends [O no *del*] ⌃fie fie⌃ our Friendship [neer shall
del] ⌃you shant⌃ sever⌞,⌟   [
[For now *del*] ⌃In spite⌃ we will be greater friends than ever⌞.⌟ [

[*Page 67*]

23 May 1810 found the Word Golden⌞.⌟

[*Page 70*]

Some people admire the work of a Fool
For its sure to keep your Judgment cool⌞.⌟

Page 64: Order of Composition: The three passages (including 'Public Address'
part n) are written with much room to spare in an indeterminate order.

'From Cratelos' l. 2: This couplet is evidently a translation from the Greek or
Latin ('Me tempus incurvavit, egregius faber, / Sed qui imbecilliora reddit omnia')
of Crates, probably as printed in the anthology of John Stobaeus (e.g. *Dicta
Poetarvm qvæ apvd Stobævm exstant*, ed. H. Grotio [Paris, 1623], Title 116 [here
misprinted cxviii], p. 482). The identification was made by W. H. Stevenson,
'Blake's "From Cratetos": A Source and a Correction', *Notes & Queries*, ccxiii
(1968), 21.

Page 65: Order of Composition: (1) First came 'Public Address' part p at the top,
leaving much free space, (2) Followed by part q, ll. 1–15 below the sketch, con-
tinued by ll. 16–22 written sideways to the right margin; (3) 'If Men will act . . .'
is written sideways from the left margin to the sketch.

Page 67 '23 May 1810 . . .' is written sideways from the left margin just below
the stroke connecting 'Public Address' part z on p. 67 with part v on p. 66, and
may be associated with it.

Page 70: Order of Composition: (1) 'Vision of the Last Judgment' part d continuing
from p. 69 was written first at the bottom of the page; (2) This was perhaps followed

It does not reproach you with want of wit⌞,⌟
It is not like a lawyer serving a writ⌞.⌟ [*4*]

[*Page 72*]

Jesus does not trea[*t*] [?]   he makes a Wide distinction
between the Sheep & the Goats⌞,⌟ consequently he is Not
Charitable⌞.⌟

[*Page 73*]

To God

If you have formd a Circle to go into
Go into it yourself & see how you would do⌞.⌟ [*2*]

Since all the Riches of this [Earth *del*] World
May be gifts from the Devil & Earthly Kings
I should suspect that I worshipd the Devil
If I thankd my God for [Worldly *del*] [Earthly *del*] ⌃Wordly⌃
things⌞.⌟ [*4*]

[*Page 78*]

To Chloes breast young Cupid slily Stole
But he crept in at Myras pocket hole⌞.⌟ [*2*]

[*Page 79*]

[When(?) *del*] 'Now Art has lost its mental Charms
France shall subdue the World in arms⌞.⌟'

by the title of part f in a bold hand between the sketches at the top of the page;
(3) The rest of part f was written sideways from the sketch to the right margin,
evidently intended to follow the title; (4) 'Some people admire . . .' is written
sideways from the left margin.

'Some people admire . . .' ll. 1–2 are essentially repeated on *Notebook* p. 41 (p. 952),
'I always take . . .' ll. 1–2.

Page 72   'Jesus does not trea[*t*] . . . Charitable': This passage may be connected
with 'The Everlasting Gospel' (see part k, l. 4, p. 1065). The gap was caused when
the corner of the leaf was cut off. The missing letters might be 'all alike'.

Page 73   'Since all the Riches . . .' is written *upside-down* at the bottom of the page
in pencil.

Page 79: Order of Composition: (1) Probably 'Now Art has lost . . .' was written first,
and perhaps ll. 13–14 were written immediately thereafter, though they may
alternatively be part of a separate poem; (2) 'Vision of the Last Judgment' part r
was written at the bottom in the same Black ink, sharp pen, and small hand, and
probably at the same time, as part s at the bottom of p. 78; (3) 'Nail his neck to the
Cross . . .' was probably written after all the other space was filled.

So spoke an Angel at my birth⌞,⌟
Then Said 'Descend thou upon Earth⌞,⌟
Renew the Arts on Britains Shore   [⸢
And France shall fall down & adore⌞.⌟
With works of Art their Armies meet
And [Armies *del*] ⌃War⌃ shall sink beneath thy feet
But if thy Nation Arts refuse
And if they Scorn the immortal Muse   [
France shall the arts of Peace restore
And save [thy works *del*] ⌃thee⌃ from [Britains *del*] ⌃the Un-
  grateful⌃ Shore⌞.⌟'

Spirit who lovst Brittannias [Shore *del*] Isle
Round which the Fiends of Commerce [roar *del*] smile [. . . .] [

Nail his neck to the Cross⌞,⌟ nail it with a nail⌞;⌟
Nail his neck to the Cross⌞,⌟ ye all have power over his tail⌞.⌟ [

[*Page 87*]

The [Visions *del*] ⌃Caverns⌃ of the Grave Ive seen
And these I shewd to Englands Queen
[Shed(?) *del*] ⌃But⌃ now the Caves of Hell I view⌞:⌟
Who shall I dare to shew them to⌞?⌟
[Egr(?) *del*] What mighty Soul in Beautys form   [
Shall [dare to *del*] ⌃dauntless⌃ View the Infernal Storm⌞?⌟
Egremonts Countess [dares *del*] can Controll
The [waves *del*] ⌃flames⌃ of Hell that round me roll⌞.⌟
If she refuse I still go on
Till the Heavens & Earth are gone   ▶

'Now Art has lost . . .' l. 3: Cf. 'The Angel that presided oer my birth' on *Note-book* p. 32 (p. 942).
  l. 14 The rest of this sentence is not known.

Page 87, Order of Composition: (1) 'The Visions of the Grave . . .' was written first, going straight over the very faint sketch; (2) 'Vision of the Last Judgment' part z was written sideways in a large hand from the right margin and presumably con-tinued by (3) 'Those who . . . Intention' sideways to the left margin; (4) 'The Modern . . . Downwards' is written sideways in the last available space in the top left margin.
  l. 2: See 'To the Queen' (pp. 819–20), Blake's dedication to his *Grave* designs (1808).
  ll. 5, 7: Lord Egremont did not marry the mother of his children for many years, and he separated from her not long after they were married. His wife does not seem to have been generally known as the 'Countess'.

Still admird by [worthy *del*] ⌄Noble⌄ minds└,┘
Followd by Envy on the winds└.┘
Reengravd Time after Time└,┘
Ever in their Youthful prime
My Designs [shall still *del*] ⌄unchangd⌄ remain└.┘   [*15*]
Time may rage but rage in vain
For above Times troubled Fountains
On the Great Atlantic Mountains
In my Golden House on high
There they Shine Eternally└.┘   [*20*]

[*Page 88*]
South Molton Street

Sunda*y* Augus*t* 1807   My Wife was told by a Spirit to look for her fortune by opening by chance a book which She had in her hand└;┘ it was Bysshes art of Poetry. She opend the following└:┘

    I saw 'em kindle with desire
    While with soft sighs they blew the fire└,┘
    Saw the approaches of their joy└,┘
    He growing more fierce & she less coy└,┘
    Saw how they mingled melting rays   [*5*]
    Exchanging Love a thousand ways└.┘
    Kind was the force on every side└;┘ ⎫
    Her new desire she could not hide ⎬
    Nor would the Shepherd be denied└.┘ ⎭
    The blessed minute he pursud   [*10*]
    Till She transported in his arms
    Yields to the Conqueror all her charms└.┘
    His panting breast to hers now joind
    They feast on raptures unconfind

Page 88   The quotations from Edward Bysshe's *Art of English Poetry* come from sections entitled 'Enjoyment' (or, as a passage from Dryden there quoted specifies, 'The secret Joys of sweet Coition') and 'Oak', which are in separate volumes in the two-volume editions of 1714, 1718, 1739, 1762. Since the Blakes were using 'a book', they probably had one of the one-volume editions (1702, 1705, 1708, 1710, 1724, 1725, 1737). Three of Blake's verbal changes ('every' for 'either' in l. 7 of the first passage, 'bear' and 'tear' for 'bend' and 'rend' in ll. 3–4 of the second) do not seem to be justified by any edition of the book, but his alteration of 'Far' to 'For' in the penultimate line seems to point to the third edition of 1708, which is evidently the only edition in which this variant is found.

Vast & luxuriant such as prove   [1

The immortality of Love

For who but a Divinity ⎫

Could mingle souls to that degree ⎬

And melt them into Extasy⌊?⌋ ⎭

Now like the Phoenix both expire ⎫   [2

While from the ashes of their fire ⎬

Spring up a new & soft desire⌊.⌋ ⎭

Like charmers thrice they did invoke

The God & thrice new Vigor took⌊.⌋   [3

Behn

I was so well pleased with her Luck that I thought I would try
my own & opend the following⌊:⌋

As when the winds their airy quarrel try⌊,⌋

Justling from every quarter of the Sky⌊,⌋

This way & that the Mountain oak they bear⌊,⌋

His boughs they shatter & his branches tear⌊.⌋

[Page 89]

With leaves & falling mast they spread the Ground⌊;⌋   [

The hollow Valleys Eccho [the(?) *del*] to the Sound⌊.⌋

Unmovd the royal plant their fury mocks

Or shaken clings more closely to the rocks

For as he shoots his lowring head on high

So deep in earth his fixd foundations lie⌊.⌋   [

Drydens Virgil

I rose up at the dawn of day⌊:⌋

'Get thee away get thee away⌊!⌋

Prayst thou for Riches⌊?⌋ away away⌊!⌋

This is the Throne of Mammon grey⌊.⌋'

Page 89: Order of Composition: (1) The end of the poem beginning on p. 88 was almost
certainly copied first at the top of the page above the sketch; (2) Next came 'I rose
up . . .' ll. 1–12, 21–4 written over the sketch; (3) ll. 13–16 were written sideways
to the right margin and a stroke embracing them indicates that they should come
after l. 12; (4) ll. 17–20 were almost certainly written later, ll. 17–18 as one line
below l. 16, ll. 19–20 angling across the top right corner; (5) ll. 25–8 were written
at the bottom of the page in a smaller hand than ll. 1–12, 21–4, and are probably
a later addition.

Said I 'this sure is very odd_{L·J}   [5]
I took it to be the throne of God_{L·J}
For every Thing besides I have_{L,J}
It is only for Riches that I can crave_{L·J}

'I have Mental Joy & Mental Health
And Mental [Friendshi(?) *del*] Friends & Mental wealth_{L,J}   [*10*]
Ive a Wife I love & that loves me_{L,J}
Ive all But Riches Bodily_{L·J}

'I am in Gods presence night & day
And he never turns his face away_{L·J}
The accuser of sins by my side does Stand   [*15*]
And he holds my money bag in his hand_{L·J}

'For [all that *del*] my worldly things God makes him pay
And hed pay for more if to him I would pray
And so you may do the worst you can do
Be assurd Mr Devil I wont pray to you_{L·J}   [*20*]

'Then If for Riches I must not Pray
God knows I little of Prayers need say
So [as sure(?) *del*] as a Church is known by its Steeple
If I pray it must be [of *del*] for other People_{L·J}

'He says if I do not worship him for a God   [*25*]
I shall eat coarser food & go worse shod
So as I dont value such things as these
You must do Mr Devil just as God please_{L·J}'   [*28*]

[*Page 92*]

Every thing that is in harmony with me[?] I call In Harmony—
But there may be things which are Not in harmony with Me &
yet are in a More perfect Harmony_{L·J}[1]

Page 92   [1] This passage is written in pencil *upside-down* under 'Vision of the Last Judgment' part x and below the sketch.

[*Page 93*]
A Woman Scaly & a Man all Hairy
Is such a Match as he who dares
Will find the Womans Scales Scrape off the Mans Hairs⌊·⌋   ⌊

[*Page 96*]
Lines
Written on hearing the Surrender of Copenhagen
The Glory of Albion is tarnishd with Shame
And the field of her might is the bourn of her fame⌊·⌋
Her giant strength blesses the Nations no more
And the race of the Sun of her honour is oer⌊·⌋

Like an Eagle she soard in the youth of her pride
And her joy was the Battle of Freedom to guide⌊·⌋
As the fate bearing lightning she sped on the wind
And her young in the shade of her pinions reclind⌊·⌋

Her haunt was the rocks & she chased in dismay
The vulture & Wolf from her Eyrie away
And when the wild tempest howld over the wave
Her delight was the weak from its fury to save

But her giant strength blesses the nations no more
And the race of the Sun of her honour is oer⌊·⌋
She hath tasted of blood & her anger hath hurld
The flame shaft of war oer a desolate world⌊·⌋

O England, when mercy soft murmurd her prayer
And bade the blood of the nations to spare
Thy soul was for War & thy haughty behest
Chast the Seraph of Peace from thy merciless breast⌊·⌋

[*Page 97*]
The seraph of Peace from thy fury had fled⌊;⌋
In the gloom of the North she had pillowd her head

Page 93   The poem is written in pencil underneath 'Vision of the Last Judgment' part x.

Page 96,   title: The occasion was probably the British bombardment, brief invasion, and pillaging of neutral Copenhagen on 2–4 Sept. 1807. (Another such attack had taken place in April 1801.)

Notebook p. 99

But thy vengeance pursud her bewilderd with care⌐;⌐
She awoke to fierce havoc⌐,⌐ to groans & despair⌐.⌐

O bring not the laurel wreath constant to fame   [*25*]
And rend not heavens concave with shouts of acclaim
When the spoil & the plunder shall rise on the wave⌐,⌐
The plunder of friends & the spoil of the brave⌐,⌐

For the triumph which Liberty hallowd is fled
And the night of the Tyrant has raged in its stead   [*30*]
And changd is the radiance that streamd oer the heath
To the warning of Nation*s*, the meteor of death⌐.⌐   [*32*]
Birmingham   I.

[*Page 99*]
Several Questions Answerd
[4 *del*] What is it men in women do require⌐?⌐
The Lineaments of Gratifid Desire⌐.⌐

Page 97 l. 32: The identity of the author ('I' or 'J' of Birmingham) is not known.
D. V. Erdman ('Blake's Transcript of Bisset's "Lines written on hearing the sur-
render of Copenhagen" ', *Bulletin of the New York Public Library*, lxxii [1968],
518–21) suggests plausibly but with precious little evidence that the author was
James Bisset (?1762–1832), radical, painter, and bookseller. Another possibility
is James Freeth (1730–1808), the 'poetical landlord' of a coffee-house in Birming-
ham, author of *The Political Songster* (1790) (see [Watkins & Shoberl] *Biographical
Dictionary* [1816], 431, 123).

Pages 99–98: Order of Composition: (1) The five 'Questions Answerd' poems were
probably written first on p. 99 in pencil *upside-down* (like the rest of the page)
in the right margin (left when reversed) partly over the erased sketch; (2) 'Let the
Brothels . . .' was written in ink (like the rest of pp. 99–98) in a column beside the
'Questions Answerd', and ll. 13–15, 22–3, 25 were probably individually deleted
almost immediately; (3) ll. 1–4, 9–12, 16–19, 5–8 were numbered as stanzas 1–4,
and probably later ll. 1–4, 16–17, 11–12, 5–8 were renumbered as ll. 1–12;
(4) ll. 9–19 were deleted together with three strokes (perhaps when ll. 9–10, 16
were re-used on p. 5, ll. 3–5 [p. 925,]); (5) 'Fayette . . .' ll. 1–12 were written
below the 'Questions Answerd' on p. 99, followed by ll. 13–16 below the stroke
terminating 'Let the Brothels . . .'; (6) ll. 1–8 were deleted with five strokes, and
Blake unsuccessfully tried to redraft them with ll. 17–19 written *upside-down* (like
the rest of the poem) in the bottom right corner (top left when reversed) of p. 98,
                                                    [*Note continued overleaf*]

Page 99 'Several Questions Answerd': These five poems may be gathered for
etching on one plate; see p. 101 (p. 973).
    'What is it men . . .' The draft of this poem is on p. 103 (p. 974).
    ll. 2, 4 'The Lineaments of Gratifid Desire' also appear in 'The sword sung . . .'
l. 8 on p. 105 and *Europe* pl. 17, l. 236 (pp. 978, 220, 235).

What is it women do in men require⌐?⌐
The lineaments of Gratifid desire⌐·⌐   [4

---

2   The look of love alarms
     Because tis filld with fire
     But the look of soft deceit
     Shall Win the lovers hire⌐·⌐   [4

---

3   Soft deceit & Idleness⌐,⌐
     These are Beautys sweetest dress⌐·⌐   [4

---

1   He who bends to himself a joy
     Does the winged life destroy
     But he who kisses the joy as it flies
     Lives in Eternitys sun rise⌐·⌐   [

---

and then he deleted ll. 17–19; (**7**) ll. 20–3 were drafted below l. 19, redrafted as
ll. 24–5 (probably deleted immediately), drafted again in ll. 26–9; (**8**) ll. 13–16
on p. 99 were deleted and redrafted as ll. 30–3 below l. 29 on p. 98, ll. 9–12, 26–9,
30–3 were numbered as stanzas 1–3 and a box was drawn round ll. 26–33 to show
that they were the lines to stand at this point; (**9**) Perhaps at this stage Blake
deleted ll. 26–9 (with two strokes) and the stanza number '3' by ll. 30–3, replaced
the number with a '1' at the head of the stanza, copied out ll. 9–12 as ll. 34–7
below l. 33, numbered ll. 34–7, 20–3 as stanzas '2' and '3' (making the order 30–3,
26–9, 20–3), then deleted the '3' and copied ll. 20–3 as ll. 38–41 below l. 37 and
numbered them as stanza '3'; (**10**) Finally he deleted ll. 30–3 (number '1') with a
stroke, changed the '3' by ll. 38–41 to '1', and added ll. 42–5 in the bottom left
corner (top right when reversed) and numbered it stanza '3'—the poem as it last
stood consisted of ll. 38–41, 34–7, 42–5, and is quite separate from 'Let the
Brothels . . .'—the order of construction of 'Fayette' is rather conjectural; (**11**)
'The Everlasting Gospel' part j, ll. 1–18, 23–8, 33–44 were written right way up in
a column on the left of p. 98, ll. 29–32 and 45–9 were written with the same pen
sideways in the middle of the page (the former beside l. 28) and in the top right
corner of the page; (**12**) ll. 19–22, 50–1 were written with a sharper pen, ll. 19–22
clearly marked with two strokes to follow l. 18, ll. 50–1 well below l. 49 in the
last blank space—ll. 50–1 might be taken as a detached fragment of a poem were
they not so clearly integrated with this poem when it was copied on pp. 52–4
(ll. 81–2) (p. 1068).

'The look of love . . .' is also transcribed on p. 103.

'Soft deceit . . .' is copied from p. 103.

'He who bends . . .' l. 4: 'sunrise', which is now so faint as to be illegible, I have
taken from the transcript by Keynes in his 1935 facsimile; see the draft on p. 105
(p. 979).

5   An ancient Proverb

Remove away that blackning church⌞,⌟
Remove away that marriage hearse⌞,⌟
Remove away that — of blood⌞,⌟
Youll quite remove the ancient curse⌞.⌟   [*4*]

[Fayette beside King Lewis stood⌞,⌟
He saw him sign his hand
And soon he saw the famine rage
About the fruitful land⌞.⌟ *del*

[Fayette beheld the Queen to smile   [*5*]
And wink her lovely eye
And soon he saw the pestilence
From street to street to fly⌞.⌟ *del*]

[1 *del*] Fayette beheld the King & Queen
In tears & iron bound   [*10*]
But meek Fayette wept tear for tear
And guarded them around⌞.⌟

[Fayette Fayette thourt bought & sold
For well I see thy tears
Of Pity are exchangd for those   [*15*]
Of selfish slavish fears *del*]

[*Page 98*]

[Fayette beside his banner stood
His captains false around
Thourt bought & sold *del*]

[3 *del*] Who will exchange his own fire side   [*20*]
For the steps of anothers door⌞?⌟
Who will exchange his wheaten loaf
For the links of a dungeon floor⌞?⌟

'An ancient Proverb' For an earlier draft, see p. 107 (p. 985).
'Fayette . . .' l. 1: In revolutionary etiquette, honorific titles, such as the 'La' in 'Lafayette', were omitted.

[Who will exchange his own hearts blood
For the drops of a harlots eye *del*]   [

[2   Will the mother exchange her new born babe
For the dog at the wintry door⌐?⌐
Yet thou dost exchange thy pitying tears
For the links of a dungeon floor *del*

I

[(3 *del*)   Fayette Fayette thourt bought & sold   [
And sold is thy happy morrow⌐.⌐
Thou givest the tears of Pity away
In exchange for the tears of sorrow *del*]

2   Fayette beheld the King & Queen
In [tears *del*] ∧curses∧ & iron bound
But mute Fayette wept tear for tear
And guarded them around⌐.⌐

[3 *del*] 1 Who will exchange his own fire side
For the [steps *del*] ∧stone∧ of anothers door⌐?⌐
Who will exchange his wheaten loaf
For the links of a dungeon floor⌐?⌐

[3 *del*] O who would smile on the wintry seas
[Or *del*] ∧&∧ Pity the stormy roar
Or who will exchange his newborn child
For the dog at the wintry door⌐?⌐

[*Page 99*]

1 1 'Let the Brothels of Paris be opend
   2 With many an alluring dance
   3 To awake the [Pestilence *del*] ∧Physicians∧ thro the city⌐,⌐'
   4 Said the beautiful Queen of France⌐.⌐

4 9 The King awoke on his couch of gold
  10 As soon as he heard these tidings told⌐.⌐

Page 98: 'Fayette . . .' l. 45: See 'The Dog at the wintry door' on *Urizen* pl. 25,
26 (pp. 277, 280).

11 'Arise & come⌊,⌋ both fife & drum⌊,⌋
12 And the [Famine *del*] shall eat both crust & crumb⌊.⌋'

[2   Then old Nobodaddy aloft
     Farted & belchd & coughd   [*10*]
7 And Said 'I love hanging & drawing & quartering
8 (To[?] *del*) Every bit as well as war & slaughtering⌊.⌋' *del*]

[(Damn praying & singing
Unless they will bring in
The blood of ten thousand by fighting or swinging *del*)   [*15*]

[3 5 Then he swore a great ∧& solemn∧ Oath⌊:⌋
   6 'To kill the people I am loth
     But If they rebel they must go to hell⌊;⌋
     They shall have a Priest & a passing bell⌊.⌋' *del*]

The Queen of France just touchd this Globe   [*20*]
And the Pestilence darted from her robe
[But the bloodthirsty people across the water
Will not submit to the gibbet & halter *del*]
But our good Queen quite grows to the ground
[There is just such a tree at Java found *del*]   [*25*]
And a great many suckers grow all around⌊.⌋   [*26*]

[*Page 100*]

Her whole Life is an Epigram smart[?] smooth & neatly[?]
pen'd⌊,⌋
Platted quite neat to catch applause with a sliding noose at the
end⌊.⌋   [*2*]

Page 99 'Let the Brothels . . .' ll. 9-10, 16: Cf. 'When Klopstock England defied
. . .' ll. 3–5 (*Notebook* p. 5—p. 925), where virtually the same words appear.

l. 20 seems to allude to a passage in Edmund Burke's *Reflections on the Revolution
in France* (London, 1791 [Second Edition, first impression], 112)—'surely never
lighted on this orb, which she hardly seemed to touch, a more delightful vision'
than 'the queen of France' (as D. V. Erdman, *Blake: Prophet Against Empire* [1954],
169, points out).

Page 100: Order of Composition: (**1**) 'Her whole Life . . .' is written *upside-down* in the
bottom margin, avoiding the full-page sketch; (**2**) 'O I cannot . . .' was written
in a large hand, also *upside-down*, below 'Her whole Life . . .'; (**3**) 'The Everlasting
Gospel' part i was written right way up in two columns at the top of the page
(ll. 1–18 in a column to the left of ll. 19–37).

'Her whole Life . . .' l. 1: Erdman (p. 508) reads 'smart' as 'smack'.

2 O I cannot cannot find
  The undaunted courage of a Virgin Mind
  For [I in *del*] ˏEarlyˏ I in Love was crost
  Before my flower of love was lost⌊·⌋

1 An Old maid early eer I knew   [ᴬ
  Ought but the love that on me grew
  And now Im coverd oer & oer
  And wish that I had been a Whore⌊·⌋   [⸰

[*Page 101*]

[Woe alas my guilty hand
 Brushd across thy summer joy
 All thy gilded painted pride
 Shatterd fled *del*]
1 Little fly   ⌊ˏ
  Thy summer play
  My [guilty hand *del*] thoughtless hand
  Hath brushd away⌊·⌋

[The cut worm
 Forgives the plow
 And dies in peace   [
 And so do thou *del*]

2 Am not I
  A fly like thee

'O I cannot . . .' The numbers by the stanzas are in pencil.

Page 101: Order of Composition: (1) Probably 'Woe alas . . .' was drafted first *upside-down* in a very small hand in the right margin (left when reversed); (2) Next may have been the pencil directions for what to put 'on 1 Plate' *upside-down* in the bottom left corner (top right when reversed); (3) The 'Motto to the Songs of Innocence & of Experience' is written *upside-down* at the top of the page (bottom when reversed) below a stroke separating it from the sketch; (4) 'Who shall chain the' (unfinished and unattached) is *upside-down* at the top of the page (bottom when reversed); (5) 'The Everlasting Gospel' part i, ll. 38–59, continued from p. 100, are written right way up below the dividing stroke at the top of the page and going partly over both the sketch and the directions in 2 above.

'Woe alas . . .' For the final version of 'The Fly', see *Songs* pl. 40 (p. 182).
    ll. 9–10 This is the fifth Proverb in the *Marriage* pl. 7: 'The cut worm forgives the plow' (p. 81).

Or art not thou   [*15*]
A man like me

3 For I dance
  And drink & sing
  Till some blind hand
  Shall brush my wing⌊.⌋   [*20*]

5 Then am I
  A happy fly
  If I live
  Or if I die⌊.⌋

[4 Thought is life   [*25*]
  And strength & breath
  But the want (of *del*)
  Of Thought is death *del*]

4 If thought is life
  And strength & breath   [*30*]
  And the want [of *del*]
  Of Thought is death⌊.⌋   [*32*]

Who shall chain[?] the

              ⌜O Lapwing &ᶜ
              | An answer to the Parson
              | ——————————
              | Experiment
on 1 Plate⟨ ——————————
              | Riches[?]
              | ——————————
              ⌞If you trap &
              ——————————

'Who shall chain the' is perhaps a draft of *Europe* pl. 5: 'And who shall bind the infinite with an eternal band' (p. 225).

'O Lapwing &ᶜ' For 'O Lapwing' (four lines) see p. 113 (p. 995); for 'An answer to the Parson' (two lines) and 'Riches' (four lines) see p. 103 (p. 975); for 'If you trap (four lines) see p. 105 (pp. 978–9); for 'Experiment' Erdman (p. 770) suggests 'Thou hast a lap full . . .' on p. 111 (pp. 990–1), though at ten lines it seems rather long. Only pl. 43 of the *Songs* carries more than one poem, with 'My pretty Rose Tree' (eight lines), 'Ah! Sun-Flower' (eight lines), and 'The Lilly' (four lines).

Motto to the Songs of Innocence & of Experience

The Good are attracted by Mens perceptions
And Think not for themselves
Till Experience teaches them to catch
And to Cage the Fairies & Elves

And then the Knave begins to snarl   [5
And the Hypocrite to howl
And all his good Friends shew their private ends
And the Eagle is known from the Owl∟⌐⌐   [8

[*Page 103*]
The Question Answerd

What is it men [of *del*] ⌃in⌃ women do require∟?⌐
The lineaments of Gratified Desire∟⌐⌐
What is it women [of *del*] ⌃in⌃ men require∟?⌐
The lineaments of Gratified Desire∟⌐⌐   [4

[Because I was happy upon the heath
And Smild among the winters (wind *del*) snow
They clothed me in the clothes of death
And taught me to sing the notes of woe *del*

[And because I am happy & dance & sing   [
They think they have done me no injury
And are gone to praise God & his Priest & King
(Who wrap themselves up in our misery *del*)
Who make up a heaven of our misery∟⌐⌐ *del*]   [

Page 103: *Order of Composition*: (1) 'The Angel', 'The look of love . . .', and 'Which
are beauties . . .' are written in pencil *upside-down* (like the rest of the page) on the
left side (right reversed); (2) 'The Question Answerd', 'Because I was happy . . .',
'Lacedemonian Instruction', 'Riches', 'An answer to the parson', and 'Holy
Thursday' are written in a column down the right side of the page (left reversed),
'Holy Thursday' making two columns at the bottom of the column.

'The Question Answerd' The poem as corrected was copied on p. 99 (pp. 967–8).
    ll. 1, 3 The corrections are in pencil.

'Because I was happy . . .' For the first stanza of 'The Chimney Sweeper' see p. 106
(p. 982); for the etched version, see *Songs* pl. 37 (p. 179). The two stanzas were
deleted with a single stroke.

Lacedemonian Instruction

'Come hither my boy⌊,⌋ tell me what thou seest there⌊.⌋'
'A fool tangled in a religious snare⌊.⌋' [2]

Riches

The [*word illeg del*] [count(?) *del*] Countless gold of a merry
heart⌊,⌋
The rubies & pearls of a loving eye⌊,⌋
The [idle man *del*] ⌃indolent⌃ never can bring to the mart
Nor the [cunning *del*] ⌃secret⌃ hoard up in his treasury⌊.⌋ [4]

An answer to the parson

'Why of the sheep do you not learn peace⌊?⌋'
'Because I dont want you to shear my fleece⌊!⌋' [2]

Holy Thursday

Is this a holy thing to see
In a rich & fruitful land⌊,⌋
Babes reducd to misery⌊,⌋
Fed with cold & usurous hand⌊?⌋

Is that trembling cry a song⌊?⌋ [5]
Can it be a song of joy⌊?⌋
And so great a number poor⌊?⌋
Tis a land of poverty

And their sun does never shine
And their fields are bleak & bare [10]

'Lacedemonian Instruction' The title is written in blacker ink (all the rest of the page save the title to 'Riches' is in Brown) squeezed in as an afterthought. Lacedaemon is the area of which Sparta was the capital.

'Riches' The title is squeezed in as an afterthought in Black ink. Directions for etching 'Riches' are on p. 101 (p. 973).

l. 1: For the deletions Erdman (p. 770) reads '[we *del*] [count *del*] [weal *del*]'.

'An answer to the parson' Directions for etching 'An answer to the parson' are on p. 101 (p. 973).

'Holy Thursday' was scarcely changed when etched for *Songs* pl. 33 (p. 178).

And their ways are filld with thorns⌊.⌋
Tis Eternal winter there

But wherever the sun does Shine
And wherever the rain does fall
Babe can never hunger there   [1
Nor poverty the mind appall⌊.⌋   [1

The Angel

[I dreamt a dream⌊,⌋ what can it mean⌊?⌋
And that I was a maiden queen
Guarded by an angel mild⌊.⌋
Witless woe was neer beguild⌊!⌋ *del*

[And I wept both night & day   [5
And he wiped my tears away
And I wept both day & night
And hid from him my hearts delight *del*

[So he took his wings & fled⌊;⌋
Then the morn blushd rosy red⌊.⌋   [1
I dried my tears & armd my fears
With ten thousand shields & spears⌊.⌋ *del*

[Soon my angel came again
I was armed⌊,⌋ he came in vain
(But *del*) ⌃For⌃ the time of youth was fled   [1
And grey hairs were on my head *del*]   [1

The look of love alarms
Because tis filld with fire
But the look of soft deceit
Shall win the lovers hire⌊.⌋   [

ll. 13–14: For 'wherever' Erdman (p. 716) reads 'whereeer'.

'The Angel' The title is written with a much blunter pencil than that for the text which follows it and appears to be squeezed in as an afterthought. The poem was deleted with a single stroke, probably when it was etched for *Songs* pl. 41 (p. 184).

'The look of love . . .' is written among 'Several Questions Answerd' on p. 99 (p. 968).

[Which are beauties sweetest dress *del*]
Soft deceit & idleness
[These are beauties sweetest dress *del*]   [3]

[*Page 105*]
Day

[The (day *del*) ∧Sun∧ arises in the East
Clothd in robes of blood & gold⌊·⌋
Swords & spears & wrath increast
All around his (ancles *del*) ∧bosom∧ rolld
Crownd with warlike fires & raging desires⌊·⌋ *del*]   [5]

[The Marriage Ring *del*] The Fairy
'Come hither my sparrows⌊,⌋
My little arrows⌊!⌋
If a tear or a smile
Will a man beguile ⌊,⌋
If an amorous delay   [5]
Clouds a sunshiny day⌊,⌋
If the [tread *del*] ∧step∧ of a foot
Smites the heart to its root⌊,⌋
Tis the marriage ring

'Which are beauties . . .' ll. 2–3 are copied on p. 99 (p. 968).

Page 105: Order of Composition: The page is written *upside-down* in two columns, the one to the right (left reversed) in Brown ink and the one to the left in pencil. Since the pencil poems are corrected in Brown ink and the Brown ink poems are corrected in pencil, it is very difficult to establish precedence, but perhaps the ink passages came first.

(1) 'Day', 'The Marriage Ring', 'The sword sung . . .', 'Abstinence . . .', and 'In a wife . . .' are written in a column to the right of the page (left reversed) in Brown ink; (2) 'If you trap . . .', 'He who bends . . .', 'The Kid', and 'The Little Vagabond' were drafted in pencil in a column at the left of the page (right reversed); (3) Changes in 'The little Vagabond' ll. 4, 14, 'The Marriage Ring' ll. 21–2 (l. 22 written as a continuation of the deleted l. 20), and the deletion of 'Day' were made in Brown ink; (4) The title of 'The little Vagabond' was squeezed in, l. 18 was written to the left of l. 17 to replace it, the title of 'The Marriage Ring' was altered to 'The Fairy', 'The 'Fairy' l. 21 was deleted, all in pencil, and l. 19 was written as a continuation of l. 18; (5) 'The Fairy' ll. 21–2 were deleted, l. 19 was altered and confirmed, and the title 'Eternity' was added, all in Black ink.

'Day' was not etched, as were many of the other poems deleted (like it) with a single pencil stroke.

Makes each fairy a King⌞.⌟'   [⸢

So a fairy sung⌞.⌟
From the leaves I sprung⌞.⌟
He leapd from the spray
To flee away
[And *del*] But in my hat caught   [⸢
He soon shall be taught⌞.⌟
Let him laugh⌞,⌟ let him cry
Hes my butterfly
[& *del*] For I've pulld out the Sting
[And a *del*] ^Of^ the marriage ring⌞.⌟   [
[Is a foolish thing *del*]
[Is a childs plaything *del*]   [

The sword sung on the barren heath⌞,⌟
The sickle [on *del*] in the fruitful field⌞.⌟
The sword he sung a song of death
But could not make the sickle yield⌞.⌟   [

Abstinence sows sand all over
The ruddy limbs & flourishing hair
But desire Gratified
Plants fruits of life & beauty there⌞.⌟   ▪

In a wife I would desire
What in whores is always found⌞,⌟
The lineaments of Gratified desire⌞.⌟

If you [catch *del*] ^[trap(?) *del*] ^trap^ the moment before its
rip⌞e⌟
The tears of repentance youll certainly wip⌞e⌟

'Abstinence . . .' l. 2: 'flourishing hair' seems to be written over something else.
Erdman (p. 465) reads 'flourishing' as 'flaming'.

'In a wife . . .' l. 3: 'The lineaments of Gratified desire' also appear in the first
'Question Answerd' on p. 99 (p. 967). 'The' in this line may have been deleted.

'If you trap . . .' l. 1: 'trap' is written below the line because the ill-written and
deleted 'trap[?]' filled the space above the line.

ll. 1–2: The last part of the last words in ll. 1 and 2 are torn off at the margin.

But if once you let the ripe moment go
You[ll *del*] ˄can˄ never wipe off the tears of woe└·┘ [*4*]

Eternity
He who bends ˄to˄ himself [to *del*] a joy
Does the winged life destroy
But he who [just *del*] kisses the joy as it fl[ies]
Lives in [an eternal *del*] ˄eternity's˄ sun rise└·┘ [*4*]

The Kid
Thou little kid didst play
&ᶜ

˄The little˄ [A pretty *del*] Vagabond
Dear Mother Dear Mother the Church is cold
But the alehouse is healthy & pleasant & warm└·┘
Besides I can tell [where *mended to*] when I am usd well└·┘
[Such usage in heaven makes all go to hell *del*]
˄The poor parsons with wind like a blown bladder swell└·┘˄ [*5*]

But if at the Church they would give us some Ale
And a pleasant fire our souls to regail
We'd sing and we'd pray all the live long day
Nor ever once wish from the Church to stray└·┘

Then the parson might preach & drink & sing [*10*]
And we⌐¬d be as happy as birds in the spring
And Modest dame Lurch who is always at Church
Would not have bandy children nor fasting nor birch└·┘

Then God like a father [that joys for *del*] ˄rejoicing˄ to see
His children as pleasant & happy as he [*15*]

l. 4: Directions for etching this poem are on p. 101 (p. 973).
'Eternity' was copied on p. 99 (p. 968).
l. 1: The 'dot on the *i*' of 'binds', which 'is visible in strong light' to Erdman (p. 770), is invisible to me in a strong light and through a magnifying glass.
'The Kid' No more of 'The Kid' is known, but it may be related to 'The Fly' ll. 5–6 on p. 101 (p. 972): 'Little fly Thy summer play . . .'
'The little Vagabond' was etched as *Songs* pl. 45 (p. 189).

Would have no more quarrel with the Devil or the Barrel
[But shake hands & kiss him & thered be no more hell *del*]
ʌBut kiss him & give him both [food *del*] ʌʌdrinkʌʌ & apparelʟˌʟ ʌ [ʌ

[*Page 106*]
[O how sick & weary I
Underneath my Mirtle lie *del*]

To my Mirtle
5 Why should I be bound to thee
6 O my lovely mirtle treeʟ?ˌ
   [Love free love cannot be bound   [
   [To any tree that grows on ground *del*]

1 To a lovely mirtle boundʟˌˌ
2 Blossoms showring all aroundʟˌˌ
   [Like to dung upon the ground
   Underneath my mirtle bound *del*]   [
3 O how sick & weary I
4 Underneath my mirtle lieʟˌˌ   [

'Nought loves another as itself
Nor venerates another soʟˌˌ
Nor is it possible to Thought
A greater than itself to know

'[Then *del*] ʌAndʌ father [I cannot *del*] ʌhow can Iʌ love you
[Nor *del*] ʌOrʌ any of my brothers moreʟ?ˌ

Page 106: Order of Composition: The text is all written *upside-down* over the sketch, and it is very difficult to be confident of the order in which the passages were written. (1) 'O how sick . . .' ll. 1–12, 'Nought loves another . . .' ll. 1–15, 20–5 were drafted on the right side of the page (left reversed), ll. 16–19, 26–9 were written to their right, and 'Merlins prophecy' was written beside ll. 1–4, all in Brown ink; (2) 'Deceit to secresy . . .' and the first stanza of the 'Chimney Sweeper' were written in the bottom left corner (top right when reversed).

'O how sick . . .' ll. 1–2 were evidently deleted when the ink was still wet, creating a smudge.

'To my Mirtle' is copied from 'in a mirtle shade' ll. 7–8, 1–6, 9–10, 7–8 on p. 111 (p. 980).

I love [myself so does the bird *del*] you like the little bird
That picks up crumbs around the door_{L.⌋}'

The Priest sat by and heard the child_{L;⌋}
In trembling zeal he siezd his hair_{L.⌋}   [*10*]
[The mother followd weeping loud
O that I such a fiend should bear *del*]
[Then *del*] ⌃He⌃ led him by his little coat
[To show his zealous priestly care *del*]
And all admird his priestly care   [*15*]

And standing on the altar high
'Lo what a fiend is here_L!⌋' said he_{L,⌋}
'One who sets reason up for judge
Of our most holy mystery_L!⌋'

The weeping child could not be heard_{L,⌋}   [*20*]
The weeping parents wept in vain_{L.⌋}
[They bound his little ivory limbs *del*]
[In a cruel Iron chain *del*]
[And *del*] ⌃They⌃ strip'd him to his little shirt
& bound him in an iron chain   [*25*]

[They *del*] ⌃And⌃ burnd him in a holy [fire *del*] place
Where many had been burnd before_{L.⌋}
The weeping parents wept in vain_{L.⌋}
⌃Are⌃ Such things [are *del*] done on Albions shore_L?⌋   [*29*]

Deceit to secresy [inclind *del*] confind_{L,⌋}
[Modest prudish & confind *del*]
⌃Lawful cautious [& confind *del*] & refind_{L,⌋⌃}
[Never is to *del*] ⌃To every thing but⌃ interest blind
[And chains in fetters every mind *del*]   [*5*]
And forges fetters for the mind_{L.⌋}   [*6*]

'Nought loves another . . .' ll. 16–19, 26–9 are written to the right of ll. 14–15, 20–5
and are not marked for entry, but their position as above may be inferred from
their position and from the etched version of the poem as 'A Little Boy Lost'
in *Songs* pl. 50 (pp. 195–6).
    ll. 24–5 are hand-printed, not in cursive writing like all the rest of the *Notebook*.
'Deceit to secresy . . .' may have been considered as a continuation or a redraft of
'Love to faults . . .' on p. 107 (p. 984).
    l. 5: For 'in' Erdman (p. 772) reads '&'.

Chimney Sweeper

[A little black thing among the snow
Crying 'weep weep' in notes of woe
'Where are thy father & mother say⌊?⌋'
'They are both gone up to Church to pray⌊·⌋' *del*]   [

Merlins prophecy

The harvest shall flourish in wintry weather
When two virginities meet together⌊·⌋

The King & the Priest must be tied in a tether
Before two virgins can meet together⌊·⌋   [

[*Page 107*]

[How came pride in Man
From Mary it began
How Contempt & scorn *del*]

[What a world is Man
His Earth *del*]

The human Image

[(Mercy *del*) ⌃Pity⌃ could be no more
(If there was nobody poor *del*)

'Chimney Sweeper' For the draft of the next two stanzas of 'The Chimney Sweeper', see p. 103 (p. 974); for the etched version, see *Songs* pl. 37 (pp. 178–9).

'Merlins prophecy' Merlin's gnomic prophecy to Vortigern is given at length in Geoffrey of Monmouth's *Historie of the Kings of Britain*, Book VII, chap. 3–4, Book VIII, chap. 1.

Page 107: Order of Composition: (1) 'How came pride . . .' and 'The human Image' ll. 1–25, 27–8 (the title almost as a continuation of the last line of 'How came pride . . .') were written *upside-down* (like the rest of the page) in a column to the right (left reversed) of the page, and were probably followed by a parallel column of 'There souls of men . . .', 'The wild flowers Song', 'The sick rose', 'Soft Snow', and 'An ancient Proverb', all in Brown ink; (2) 'How to know Love from Deceit' was written in the bottom left corner (top right reversed, just above 'There souls of men . . .'), and 'The human Image' l. 26. 'The sick rose' ll. 9–10, 'Soft Snow' l. 5 were written, and the corresponding lines deleted, in pencil.

'The human Image' was deleted with a pencil stroke, probably because it was etched for *Songs* pl. 47 (p. 192).

ll. 1–4 were adapted from 'I heard an Angel singing . . .' ll. 11–14 on p. 114 (p. 997).

ˏIf we did not make somebody poorˏ
And Mercy no more could be
If all were as happy as we *del*   [*5*]

[And mutual fear brings Peace
Till the selfish Loves increase˪;˩
Then Cruelty knits a snare
And spreads his (seeds[?] *del*) baits with care˪.˩ *del*

[He sits down with holy fears   [*10*]
And waters the ground with tears˪.˩
Then humility takes its root
Underneath his foot˪.˩ *del*

[Soon spreads the dismal shade
Of Mystery over his head   [*15*]
And the catterpiller & fly
Feed on the Mystery *del*

[And it bears the fruit of deceit
Ruddy & sweet to eat
And the raven his nest has made   [*20*]
In its thickest shade˪.˩ *del*

[The Gods of the Earth & Sea
Sought thro nature to find this tree
But their search was all in vain˪,˩
(Till they sought in the human brain *del*)   [*25*]
There grows one in the human brain˪.˩ *del*

[They said this mystery never shall cease
The priest (loves *del*) ˏ(promotes(?) *heavily smudged*)ˏ ˏpromotesˏ
    war & the soldier peace *del*]   [*28*]

l. 9: For 'seeds' Erdman (p. 719) reads 'nets'.
l. 28 seems to come from 'The modest rose . . .' l. 5 on p. 109 (p. 988). When
'loves' was deleted and 'promotes[?]' written above it, the latter was badly smudged,
so 'promotes' was written clearly below the deletion.

[How to know Love from Deceit *del*]
Love to faults is always blind﹐﹐
Always is to joy inclind﹐﹐
ᴧLawlessᴧ *Always* wingd & unconfind
And breaks all chains from every mind﹐.﹐   [

There souls of men are bought & sold
And [cradled *del*] ᴧmilkfedᴧ infancy [is sold *del*] for gold
And youth to slaughter houses led
And [maidens *del*] ᴧbeautyᴧ for a bit of bread﹐.﹐   [

The wild flowers Song
As I wanderd the forest
The green leaves among
I heard a wild [thistle *del*] flower
Singing a song﹐.﹐

I slept in the [dark *del*] ᴧEarthᴧ &ᶜ   [

The sick rose
[O rose thou art sick﹐﹐
The invisible worm
That flies in the night
In the howling storm *del*

[Hath found out thy bed   ▮
Of crimson joy

'How to know Love from Deceit' may be continued by 'Deceit to secresy . . .' on
p. 106 (p. 981).
    l. 3: Blake has accidentally underlined 'Always' instead of deleting it.
'There souls of men . . .' l. 2: Under 'And' Erdman (p. 719) reads '[There *del*]'.
    l. 3: 'youth' was mended from 'youths'. The poem may be a part of 'The human
Image'.
'The wild flowers Song' The title is squeezed in as an afterthought. The poem
is continued on p. 109 (p. 987).
'The sick rose' The title seems to be added in a rather paler ink than that of the
text. The poem was deleted with a single stroke in pencil, presumably when it was
etched for *Songs* pl. 39 (pp. 181–2).

(O dark secret love *del*)
ᴧAnd (his *del*) ᴧᴧherᴧᴧ dark secret loveᴧ
(Doth life destroy *del*)
ᴧDoes thy life destroyʟ·ᴌᴧ *del*]   [*10*]

Soft Snow

[I walked abroad in a snowy dayʟ·ᴌ
I askd the soft snow with me to playʟ·ᴌ
She playd & she melted in all her prime
(Ah that sweet love should be thought a crime *del*)
And the winter calld it a dreadful crimeʟ·ᴌ *del*]   [*5*]

An ancient Proverb

Remove away that blackning churchʟ,ᴌ
Remove away that marriage hearseʟ,ᴌ
Remove away that [place *del*] ᴧmanᴧ of bloodʟ,ᴌ
[Twill *del*] ᴧYou'llᴧ quite remove the ancient curseʟ·ᴌ   [*4*]

[*Page 109*]
London
[I wander thro each dirty street
Near where the dirty Thames does flow

ll. 7–8 were deleted and their substitutes (ll. 9–10) written to their right in pencil, and then 'his' was altered to 'her' in the Brown ink of the main text.

'Soft Snow' The title seems to be added in a rather paler ink than that of the text, written through the stroke separating it from 'The sick rose'. 'Soft Snow' was not, like other poems similarly deleted with a single pencil stroke, etched for *Songs*.

l. 4: This line was repeated in 'A Little Girl Lost' (*Songs* pl. 51 [p. 196]), l. 4: 'Know that in a former time / Love! sweet Love! was thought a crime.'

'An ancient Proverb' The title seems to be an afterthought written partly through the stroke dividing it from 'Soft Snow'. For a fairer copy, see p. 99 (p. 969).

Pages 109–108: Order of Composition: (1) 'London' ll. 1–12, 'I slept . . .', 'To Nobodaddy', 'The modest rose . . .' were written *upside-down* (like the rest of the page) in the right margin (left when reversed) in a column on page 109, each poem in
[*Note continued overleaf*]

'London' The titles 'London', 'To Nobodaddy', and 'The Tyger' seem to be squeezed in as afterthoughts.

ll. 1–13 are deleted with a single pencil stroke, presumably because they were etched for *Songs* pl. 46 (p. 191).

And (see *del*) ˄mark˄ in every face I meet
Marks of weakness marks of woe⌊·⌋ *del*

[In every cry of every man⌊,⌋   [
In (every voice of every child *del*) ˄every infants cry of fear⌊,⌋˄
In every voice⌊,⌋ in every ban
The (german *del*) ˄mind˄ forgd (links I hear *del*) ˄manacles I
  hear⌊,⌋˄ *del*

[(But most *del*) ˄How˄ the chimney sweepers cry
(Blackens oer the churches walls *del*)   [
˄Every blackning church appals˄
And the hapless soldiers sigh
Runs in blood down palace walls⌊·⌋ *del*

[But most the midnight harlots curse
From every dismal street I hear   [
Weaves around the marriage hearse
And blasts the new born infants tear⌊·⌋ *del*]

But most [from every *del*] ˄thro wintry˄ streets I hear
How the midnight harlots curse
Blasts the new born infants tear   ▮
And [hangs *del*] ˄smites˄ with plagues the marriage hearse

this and the next column in a slightly different shade of ink, (2) Followed by
'When the voices of children . . .', 'Are not the joys . . .', 'The Tyger' ll. 1–21,
27–30 in a column on p. 109 beside 1 above; (3) ll. 22–6 of 'The Tyger' were drafted
upside-down (like the rest of the page) on the right side of p. 108 (left reversed), the
lines were renumbered, and then ll. 1–12, 18–30 were numbered as stanzas 1–6
(during the course of which the possibly ambiguous line number '3' of l. 22 was
deleted); (4) The confusing draft of 'The Tyger' was straightened out by copying
ll. 1–4, 9–12, 25–6, 22, 24, 27–30 out as ll. 31–4, 39–50 in the left margin (right
reversed) of p. 108; (5) ll. 5–8, omitted in the copy above, were written out as
ll. 35–8 above l. 22; (6) A last stanza for 'London' was drafted and redrafted as
ll. 14–23, squeezed in the middle of p. 109 carefully avoiding 'I slept . . .' on their
left and 'Are not the joys . . .' and 'The Tyger' ll. 1–4 on their right. *N.B.* Nos.
4, 5, and 6 above could well have been composed in a different order.

  l. 8: 'forgd' was corrected from 'forged'.
  l. 11 is written to the right of the line it displaces.
  l. 18: 'streets' was mended from 'street'.

But most the shrieks of youth I hear
But most thro midnight &
   How the youthful   [*24*]

   I [was fond *del*] ⌄slept⌄ in the dark
   In the silent night⌞‚⌟
   I murmurd my fears
   And I felt delight⌞.⌟

   In the morning I went   [*5*]
   As rosy as morn
   To seek for new joy
   But I met with scorn⌞.⌟   [*8*]

            To Nobodaddy
  [Why art thou silent & invisible
  (Man *del*) ⌄Father⌄ of Jealousy⌞?⌟
  Why dost thou hide thyself in clouds
  From every searching Eye⌞?⌟ *del*

  [Why darkness & obscurity   [*5*]
  In all thy words & laws
  That none dare eat the fruit but from
  The ̣wily serpents jaws
  Or is it because Secrecy
  gains (feminine *del*) ⌄females loud⌄ ̣applause⌞?⌟ *del*] [*10*]

[The (rose *del*) ⌄modest (lustful *del*) rose⌄ (puts *del*) (envious
   del) puts forth a thorn⌞‚⌟
The (coward *del*) ⌄humble⌄ sheep a threatning horn

'I slept . . .' The first stanza is given in 'The wild flowers song' on p. 107 (p. 984).
  l. 1: 'fond' may have been intended for 'found'.

'To Nobodaddy' was not, like other poems deleted as it is with a pencil slash, etched
for the *Songs*.
  ll. 9–10 are written in pencil as a single line.

'The modest rose . . .' was deleted with a single stroke, presumably because it was
etched as 'The Lilly' for *Songs* pl. 43 (p. 187).

While the lilly white shall in love delight
(And the lion increase freedom & peace *del*)
(The pri[e]st loves war & the soldier peace *del*)   [
Nor a thorn nor (t *del*) a threat stain her beauty bright⌊.⌋   [

When the voices of children are heard on the green
And whisprings are in the dale
The [desires *del*] ∧days∧ of youth rise fresh in my mind⌊,⌋
My face turns green & pale⌊.⌋

Then come home my children⌊,⌋ the sun is gone down
And the dews of night arise⌊.⌋
Your spring & your day are wasted in play
And your winter & night in disguise⌊.⌋

[Are not the joys of morning sweeter
Than the joys of night
And are the vigrous joys of youth
Ashamed of the light⌊?⌋ *del*

[Let age & sickness silent rob
The vineyards in the night
But those who burn with vigrous youth
Pluck fruits before the light⌊.⌋ *del*]

The Tyger
1 [Tyger Tyger burning bright
In the forests of the night⌊,⌋
What immortal hand (& *del*) or eye
(Could *del*) ∧(Dare *del*)∧ frame thy fearful symmetry⌊?⌋ *del*

l. 5 is also in 'The human Image' l. 28 on p. 107 (p. 983).

'When the voices . . .' was etched as 'Nurses Song' for *Songs* pl. 38 (p. 180).

l. 3: 'days' was written twice in pencil, once above the word deleted in pencil, and once to the left of the line.

'Are not the joys . . .' was deleted with a single pencil stroke, but it was not etched for *Songs*.

'The Tyger' was etched for *Songs* pl. 42 (pp. 185–6).

2 [(In what *del*) ⌃(Burnt in *del*)⌃ distant deeps or Skies   [5]
(Burnt the *del*) ⌃(The cruel *del*)⌃ fire of thine eyes∟?⌋
On what wings dare he aspire∟?⌋
What the hand dare seize the fire∟?⌋ *del*

3 [And what shoulder & what art
Could twist the sinews of thy heart   [*10*]
And when thy heart began to beat
What dread hand & what dread feet *del*

[(Could fetch it from the furnace deep *del*)
(And in [the *altered to*] thy horrid ribs dare steep *del*)
(In the well of sanguine woe *del*)   [*15*]
(In what clay & in what mould *del*)
(Were thy eyes of fury rolld *del*) *del*

4 [(What *del*) ⌃Where⌃ the hammer∟,⌋ (what *del*) ⌃where⌃ the
    chain∟,⌋
In what furnace was thy brain∟?⌋
What the anvil∟?⌋ what (the arm *del*) (arm *del*) (grasp *del*)
    (clasp *del*) ⌃dread grasp⌃   [*20*]
(Could *del*) ⌃Dare⌃ its deadly terrors (clasp *del*) (grasp *del*)
    clasp∟?⌋ *del*]

[*Page 108*]

] And [(is *altered to*) did he laugh *del*] ⌃dare he [smile *del*]
    [laugh *del*]⌃ his work to see
[What the (Shoulder *del*) ⌃ankle∟,⌋⌃ what the knee *del*]
4 [Did *del*] ⌃Dare⌃ he who made the lamb make thee∟?⌋
1 When the stars threw down their spears   [*25*]
2 And waterd heaven with their tears

[*Page 109*]

6 [Tyger Tyger burning bright
In the forests of the night∟,⌋
What immortal hand & eye
Dare (form *del*) ⌃frame⌃ thy fearful symmetry∟?⌋ *del*]   [*30*]

[*Page 108*]
[Tyger Tyger burning bright
In the forests of the night₍ₗ,₎
What immortal hand & eye
Dare frame thy fearful symmetry₍ₗ?₎ *del*

[Burnt in distant deeps or skies
The cruel fire of thine eyes₍ₗ?₎
Could heart descend or wings aspire₍ₗ?₎
What the hand dare sieze the fire *del*

[And what shoulder & what art
Could twist the sinews of thy heart
And when thy heart began to beat
What dread hand & what dread feet₍ₗ?₎ *del*

[When the stars threw down their spears
And waterd heaven with their tears₍ₗ,₎
Did he smile his work to see₍ₗ?₎
Did he who made the Lamb make thee₍ₗ?₎ *del*

[Tyger Tyger burning bright
In the forests of the night₍ₗ,₎
What immortal hand & eye
Dare frame thy fearful symmetry₍ₗ?₎ *del*]

[*Page 111*]
['Thou hast a lap full of seed
And this is a fine country₍ₗ.₎

Page 111: *Order of Composition*: (**1**) 'Thou hast a lap . . .', 'Earths Answer' ll. 1–15,
21–5, and 'in a mirtle shade' ll. 5–10 were written *upside-down* (like the rest of the
page) in a column on the right of p. 111 (left reversed); (**2**) 'in a mirtle shade'
ll. 1–4, 11–19 were written in a column to the left of the first (right reversed), and
ll. 1–4, 7–14 were numbered as stanzas 1–3; (**3**) 'Earths Answer' ll. 11–15 were
deleted with five slanting strokes, ll. 16–20 were drafted over the sketch as if to
replace them, and two strokes indicate that they are to follow l. 15—all these
changes being made with a pen with a broader point than that used elsewhere on
the page. Each poem (except 'Earths Answer' ll. 16–20) was deleted with a single
pencil stroke (of course 'in a mirtle shade' required two strokes since it was in two
columns).

'Thou hast a lap . . .' Directions for etching 'Experiment' on p. 101 (p. 973) may
refer to 'Thou hast a lap . . .'.

Why dost thou not cast thy seed
And live in it merrily⌊?⌋' *del*

['(Oft Ive *del*) ∧Shall I∧ cast it on the sand   [*5*]
And (turnd *del*) ∧turn∧ it into fruitful land
(But *del*) ∧For∧ on no other ground (can *del*)
Can I sow my seed
Without (pulling *del*) ∧tèaring∧ up
Some stinking weed⌊.⌋' *del*]   [*10*]

[the *del*] Earths Answer
[Earth raisd up her head
From the darkness dread & drear⌊;⌋
Her (eyes *del*) ∧(orbs *del*)∧ (fled *del*) (dead *del*) light fled
Stony dread;
And her locks coverd with gray despair: *del*   [*5*]

['Prisond on watry shore
(Starry *del*) ∧Starry∧ jealousy does keep my den⌊,⌋
Cold & hoar
Weeping oer
I hear the (father of the *del*) ancient ∧(father of *del*)∧ men⌊.⌋ *del* [*10*]

['(Cruel *del*) ∧Selfish∧ father of men⌊,⌋
Cruel jealous (wintry *del*) ∧selfish∧ fear⌊,⌋
Can delight
(Closd *del*) ∧Chaind∧ in night
The virgins of youth & morning bear⌊?⌋ *del*   [*15*]

'Does spring hide its [delight *del*] joy
When buds & blossoms grow⌊?⌋
Does the sower [sow *del*]
[His seed *del*] ∧Sow∧ by night
Or the plowman in darkness plow⌊?⌋   [*20*]

'Earths Answer' was etched as *Songs* pl. 31 (pp. 175–6).
l. 3: The alterations are in pencil.

['Break this heavy chain
That does (close *del*) ⌃freeze⌃ my bones around⌊!⌋ *del*
Selfish vain
(Thou my *del*) ⌃Eternal⌃ bane
(Hast *del*) ⌃That⌃ (my *del*) ⌃free⌃ love with bondage bound⌊.⌋' *del*] [.

---

in a mirtle shade
[1 Why should I be bound to thee
O my lovely mirtle tree⌊?⌋
Love free love cannot be bound
To any tree that grows on ground⌊.⌋ *del*

[(To a lovely mirtle bound *del*)
(Blossoms showring all around *del*)
2 O how sick & weary I
Underneath my mirtle lie
Like to dung upon the ground
Underneath my mirtle bound⌊.⌋ *del*

[3 Oft my mirtle sighd in vain
To behold my heavy chain⌊.⌋
Oft (the priest beheld *del*) ⌃my father saw⌃ us sigh
And laughd at our simplicity *del*

[So I smote him & his gore
Staind the roots my mirtle bore
But the time of youth is fled
And grey hairs are on my head⌊.⌋ *del*]

[*Page 113*]
I feard the [roughness *del*] ⌃fury⌃ of my wind
Would blight all blossoms fair & true

'in a mirtle shade' ll. 7–8 (immediately deleted), 1–6, 9–10, 7–8 were copied as 'To my Mirtle' on p. 106 (p. 980).

ll. 15–19 were used in 'Infant Sorrow' ll. 37–40 on p. 113 (p. 995), and ll. 17–18 were used in 'The Angel' in *Songs* pl. 41, ll. 15–16 (p. 184).

Page 113: Order of Composition: (1) 'I feard . . .' and 'Silent Silent Night . . .' were written *upside-down* (like the rest of the page) in orangish-Brown ink like that of pp. 114–15 in parallel columns at the bottom (top reversed) of the page, with

And my sun it shind & shind
[But *del*] ⌃And⌃ my wind it never blew

But a blossom fair or true   [*5*]
Was not found on any tree
For all blossoms grew & grew
Fruitless false tho˙fair to see⌞.⌟   [*8*]

[Why should I care for the men of *T*hames
Or the cheating waves of charterd streams
Or shrink at the little blasts of fear
That the hireling blows into my ear⌞?⌟ *del*

[Tho born on the cheating banks of Thames⌞,⌟   [*5*]
Tho his waters bathed my infant limbs
(I spurnd his waters away from me *del*)
⌃The Ohio shall wash his stains from me⌞,⌟⌃
I was born a slave but I (long *del*) ⌃go⌃ to be free⌞.⌟ *del*] [*9*]

Infant Sorrow

[My mother groand⌞,⌟ my father wept⌞,⌟
Into the dangerous world I leapt

orangish-Brown strokes terminating them; (2) 'Why should I care . . .' and 'O
lapwing . . .' ll. 1–2 were written as a continuation of these columns, 'I feared . . .'
l. 1 was corrected, and a stroke terminating 'Why should I care . . .' was made,
all in a very Black ink; (3) 'O lapwing . . .' ll. 3–4 and 'Infant Sorrow' ll. 1–8,
13–40 were written (a second column of the latter beginning after l. 23), with
terminating strokes after the respective last lines, all in a distinct Grey ink; (4)
'Infant Sorrow' ll. 13, 15, 21, 23–4, 26, 28, 30, 32–6 were altered and added, ll. 33–6
were renumbered and then the numbers were smudged while still wet, ll. 9–12, were
written below l. 36, and two strokes, apparently embracing ll. 29–40, 9–12 were
drawn evidently to indicate that ll. 9–12 should succeed l. 8, all in a slightly
darker ink and with a rather sharper pen than the preceding lines; (5) 'Why
should I care . . .' and 'Infant Sorrow' ll. 1–8 were deleted with a single pencil
stroke each, ll. 13–23 were deleted with an ink cross, and, in the next column,
ll. 24–40, 9–12 were deleted with four vertical ink strokes.

'Infant Sorrow' The title is squeezed in as an afterthought in a browner ink than
that of the poem.

ll. 1–8 were deleted with a pencil stroke probably when they were etched for
Songs pl. 48 (p. 193).

Helpless naked piping loud
Like a fiend hid in a cloud⌊·⌋ *del*

[Struggling in my fathers hands   [
Striving against my swaddling bands
Bound & weary I thought best
To sulk upon my mothers breast⌊·⌋ *del*

[When I saw that rage was vain
And to sulk would nothing gain   [
(I began to so *del*) (seeking many an artful wile *del*) ∧Turning
    many a∧ trick & wile
I began to soothe & smile⌊·⌋ *del*

[And I (grew *del*) ∧(smild *del*) Soothd∧ day after day
Till upon the ground I stray
And I (grew *del*) ∧smild∧ night after night   [
Seeking only for delight *del*

[(But upon the nettly[?] ground *del*)
(No delight was to be found *del*)
And I saw before me shine
Clusters of the wandring vine   [
(And beyond a mirtle tree *del*]
And many a lovely flower & tree
Stretchd (its *del*) ∧their∧ blossoms out to me⌊·⌋ *del*

[(But a *del*) ∧(But many a *del*)∧ (Priest *del*) ∧My father then∧
    with holy look
In his ∧(their *del*)∧ hands a holy book
Pronouncd curses on (his *del*) ∧my∧ head
(Who the fruit or blossoms shed *del*)
And bound me in a mirtle shade⌊·⌋ *del*

[(I beheld the Priests by night *del*)
(They embracd my mirtle *del*) ∧the blossoms∧ (bright *del*)

l. 25: The 's' of 'hands' is an addition.
ll. 37–40 were used in 'in a mirtle shade' ll. 15–19 on p. 111 (p. 992). ll. 39–40
were etched in 'The Angel', *Songs* pl. 41, ll. 15–16 (p. 184).

(I beheld the Priests by day *del*)
(Where [beneath my *del*] ˄underneath the˄ vines [he *del*] ˄they˄
   lay *del*) *del*

Like ˄to˄ a serpents in the night *del*)
[They *del*] He embracd my [mirtle *del*] ˄blossoms˄ bright *del*)
Like ˄to˄ (a *del*) (serpent in the *del*) ˄holy men by˄ day   [*35*]
Underneath (my *del*) ˄the˄ vines he ˄they˄ lay *del*

[So I smote them & (his *del*) ˄their˄ gore
Staind the roots my mirtle bore
But the time of youth is fled
And grey hairs are on my head˪.˩ *del*]   [*40*]

Silent Silent Night
Quench the holy light
Of thy torches bright

For possessd of Day
Thousand spirits stray   [*5*]
That sweet joys betray˪.˩

Why should joys be sweet
Used with deceit
Nor with sorrows meet˪?˩

But an honest joy   [*10*]
Does itself destroy
For a harlot coy˪.˩   [*12*]

O lapwing thou fliest around the heath
Nor seest the net that is spread beneath˪.˩
Why dost thou not fly among the corn fields˪?˩
They cannot spread nets where a harvest yields˪.˩   [*4*]

'O lapwing . . .' Directions for etching 'O lapwing . . .' are on p. 101 (p. 973).

[*Page 114*]

[I asked a thief (if he'd *del*) ‸to‸ steal me a peach⌞;⌟
(And h *del*) He turned up his eyes⌞.⌟
I askd a lithe lady to lie her down⌞;⌟
(And h *del*) Holy & meek she cries⌞.⌟ *del*

[As soon as I went an angel came⌞.⌟   [
(And h *del*) He winkd at the thief
And (he *del*) smild at the dame
And without one word (spoke *del*) said
Had a peach from the tree
(And twixt earnest & joke *del*)
‸And still as a maid‸
(He e *del*) Enjoyd the Lady⌞.⌟ *del*]

[I heard an Angel singing
When the day was springing
'Mercy Pity (& *del*) Peace
Is the worlds release⌞.⌟' *del*

[Thus he sung all day
Over the new mown hay

Page 114: *Order of Composition*: (1) 'I asked a thief . . .' and 'I heard an Angel singing . . .' ll. 1–24 were written *upside-down* (like the rest of the page) on the right side (left reversed), ll. 25–8 were written in the middle of the page beside ll. 21–4, 'A cradle song' and 'I was angry . . .' were written in a parallel column, 'A cradle song' ll. 1–2, 5, 7 were renumbered, and ll. 1–2, 5, 7, 18–21, 10–17, 24–7 were numbered as stanzas 1–5—all in the same orangish-Brown ink used on pp. 113, 115; (2) 'I heard an Angel singing . . .' ll. 15, 17 were corrected, 'A cradle song' ll. 3, 21, 'I heard an Angel singing . . .' ll. 27–8 were deleted, ll. 29–30 and 'A cradle song' ll. 4, 22 were added (l. 22 as a continuation of l. 21), and the title 'Christian forbearance' was added—all in Grey ink; (3) 'I asked a thief . . .' and 'I heard an Angel singing . . .' were deleted with a single pencil stroke and 'Christian forbearance' with another.

'I asked a thief . . .' was fairly copied on a separate sheet of paper—see p. 1071.
    ll. 10, 12: Erdman (p. 769) reads 'game' and 'dame' under 'joke' and 'Lady'.
    l. 11 is written as a continuation of l. 10.

'I heard an Angel singing . . .' ll. 11–14 were adapted as ll. 1–4 of 'The human Image' on p. 107 and 'The Human Abstract' in *Songs* pl. 47; cf. 'A Divine Image' in *Songs* pl. b (see pp. 192, 200).
    l. 3: For a song 'To Mercy Pity Peace', see 'The Divine Image' in *Songs* pl. 18 (p. 40).

Till the sun went down
And haycocks looked brown⌊·⌋ *del*

[I heard a Devil curse
Over the heath & the furze   [*10*]
'Mercy could be no more
If there was nobody poor *del*

['And pity no more could be
If all were as happy as we⌊·⌋'
(Thus he sang & *del*) ⌄At his curse⌄ the sun went down   [*15*]
And the heavens gave a frown⌊·⌋ *del*

[([And d *del*] Down pourd the heavy rain *del*)
(Over the new reapd grain *del*
([And *del*] Mercy & Pity & Peace descended *del*)
(The Farmers were ruind & harvest was ended *del*) *del*   [*20*]

[(And Mercy Pity [& *del*] Peace *del*)
(Joyd at their increase *del*)
(With Povertys Increase *del*)
(Are *del*) *del*

[(And ⌄by⌄ distress increase *del*)   [*25*]
(Mercy Pity Peace *del*)
(By Misery to increase *del*)
(Mercy Pity Peace *del*) *del*

[And Miseries increase
Is Mercy Pity Peace *del*]   [*30*]

1 A cradle song

3 Sleep sleep; in thy sleep
4 [Thou wilt every secret keep *del*]

'A cradle song' The title is written, presumably as an afterthought, well to the right of the number '1' heading stanza 1. Cf. 'A Cradle Song' in *Songs* pl. 16–17 (pp. 37, 38).
   l. 2 is deleted in orangish-Brown ink and l. 3 is written as a continuation in the same ink; l. 3 is corrected from 'Canst thou' to 'Thou canst' in pencil and then deleted in the same dark Grey ink in which l. 4 is written above it.

ʌ[(Canst *del*) Thou ʌcanstʌ any secret keep *del*]ʌ
Little sorrows sit & weep_L.」

1 Sleep Sleep beauty bright
[Thou shalt taste the joys of night *del*]
2 Dreaming of the joys of night_L.」

[Yet a little while the moon
Silent *del*]
3 As thy softest limbs I [touch *del*] [stroke *del*] feel
Smiles as of the morning [broke *del*] steal
Oer thy cheek & oer thy breast
When thy little heart does rest_L.」

4 O the cunning wiles that creep
On thy little heart asleep_L.」
When thy little heart does wake
Then the dreadful lightnings break_L.」

---

2 Sweet Babe in thy face
Soft desires I can trace_L.」
Secret joys & secret smiles
[Such as burning youth beguiles *del*]
ʌlittle pretty infant wiles_L.」ʌ

[O the cunning wiles that creep *del*]
5 From thy cheek & from thy eye
Oer the youthful harvests nigh
[Female *del*] ʌInfantʌ wiles & [female *del*] ʌinfantʌ smiles
Heaven & Earth of peace beguiles_L.」

Christian forbearance
[I was angry with my friend_L,」
I told my wrath_L,」 my wrath did end_L.」
I was angry with my foe_L,」
I told it not_L,」 my wrath did grow *del*

'Christian forbearance' was deleted presumably when it was etched as 'A Poison
Tree' for *Songs* pl. 49 (pp. 194–5).

[And I waterd it in fears   [5]
Night & morning with my tears
And I sunned it with smiles
And with soft deceitful wiles *del*

[And it grew by day & night
Till it bore an apple bright   [10]
(And I gave it to my foe *del*)
And my foe beheld it shine
And he knew that it was mine *del*

[And into my garden stole
When the night had veild the pole⌊·⌋   [15]
In the morning Glad I see
My foe outstretchd beneath the tree⌊·⌋ *del*]   [17]

[Page 115]

[A flower was offerd to me⌊,⌋
Such a flower as *M*ay never bore
But I said 'Ive a pretty rose tree'
And I passed the sweet flower oer⌊·⌋ *del*

[Then I went to my pretty rose tree   [5]
(In the silent of the night *del*)
ᴧTo tend it by day & by nightᴧ
But my rose (was turned from me *del*) ᴧ(was filld *del*) turnd
    away with Jealousyᴧ
And her thorns were my only delight⌊·⌋ *del*]   [9]

Page 115: *Order of Composition*: (1) 'A flower . . .', 'Never seek . . .', 'Love seeketh . . .'
were written *upside-down* (like the rest of the page) in a column on the right side
(left reversed), and 'I laid me down . . .', 'I went to the garden of love . . .', 'I
saw a chapel . . .' ll. 1–8, 10–17 were written in a parallel column in the orangish-
Brown ink used also on pp. 113–14: (2) 'A flower . . .' l. 8 was corrected and 'I saw
a chapel . . .' l. 8 was deleted and l. 9 inserted to replace it, all in Grey ink; (3) 'A
flower . . .', 'Love seeketh . . .', and 'I saw a chapel . . .' were individually deleted
with single pencil strokes.

'A flower . . .' was deleted presumably when it was etched as 'My Pretty Rose
Tree' for *Songs* pl. 43 (p. 186).

[Never (seek *del*) ^pain^ to tell thy love *del*]
[Love that never told can be *del*]
[For the gentle wind does move *del*]
[Silently invisibly *del*]

I told my love_{L,J} I told my love_{L,J}   [5
I told her all my heart_{L.J}
Trembling cold in ghastly fears
Ah she doth depart_{L.J}

Soon as she was gone from me
A traveller came by_{L.J}   [1
Silently invisibly
[He took her with a sigh *del*]
^O was no deny_{L.J}^   [

['Love seeketh not itself to please
Nor for itself hath any care
But for another gives its ease
And builds a heaven in hells despair_{L.J}' *dei*

[So sung a little clod of clay   [
Trodden with the cattles feet
But a pebble of the brook
Warbled out these metres meet_{L:J} *del*

['Love seeketh only self to please_{L,J}
To bind anothers to its delight_{L,J}   [
Joys in anothers loss of ease
And builds a hell in heavens despite_{L.J}' *del*]   [

I laid me down upon a bank
Where love lay sleeping_{L.J}
I heard among the rushes dank
Weeping Weeping_{L.J}

'Love seeketh not . . .' was deleted presumably when it was etched as 'The Clod
& the Pebble' for *Songs* pl. 32 (pp. 176–7).

Then I went to the heath & the wild⌊,⌋   [5]
To the thistles & thorns of the waste
And they told me how they were beguild
Driven out & compeld to be chaste⌊.⌋   [8]

I went to the garden of love
And [I *del*] saw what I never had seen⌊:⌋
A chapel was built in the midst
Where I used to play on the green

And the gates of the chapel were shut   [5]
And 'thou shalt not' writ over the door
[And *del*] ⌃So⌃ I turnd to the garden of love
That so many sweet flowers bore

And I saw it was filled with graves
And tomb-stones where flowers should be   [10]
And priests in black gounds were walking their rounds
And binding with briars my joys & desires⌊.⌋   [12]

[I saw a chapel all of gold
That none(?) did dare to enter in
And many weeping stood without
Weeping mourning worshipping⌊.⌋ *del*

[I saw a serpent rise between   [5]
The white pillars of the door
And he forcd & forcd & forcd⌊,⌋
(Till he broke the pearly door *del*)
⌃Down the golden hinges tore *del*⌃

'I went to the garden of love . . .' was etched as 'The Garden of Love' for *Songs* pl. 44 (p. 188).
  l. 2: The letter I read as '[I *del*]' (as in the etched version) Erdman (p. 718) reads as '[a *del*] I'.
  l. 3: 'built' was first spelt 'build'.
  l. 5: Erdman (p. 718) believes 'gates . . . were' originally read 'gates . . . was'.
  l. 7: The correction is in pencil.
  l. 11 'gounds' was correctly etched as 'gowns'.

[And along the pavement sweet
Set with pearls & rubies bright
All his slimy length he drew
Till upon the altar white *del*

[Vomiting his poison out
On the bread & on the wine⌊.⌋
So I turnd into a sty
And laid me down among the swine⌊.⌋ *del*]

[*Page 116*]

1 Giants ancient inhabitants of England[1]
2 The Landing of Brutus[2]
3 Corinius Throws Gogmagog the Giant into the sea[3]
4 King Lear[4]

Page 116: Order of Composition: (1) Nos. 1–20 were written first before deletions or additions; (2) Nos. 16–18 were renumbered 17–18, 16; (3) New nos. 17–18 were added to the left and the old nos. 19–20 were numbered 21–22; (4) No. 5 and new nos. 17–18 were deleted, no. 5 was called 'The Frontispiece', these two words were deleted, 'The Britons distress and depopulation' and 'Women fleeing from War' were added to the right of no. 8, and two strokes were drawn to indicate that they were to follow no. 8, then 'Women in a Siege' was added below them; (5) The pencil subjects were added at the bottom of the page; (6) In the bottom right corner (top left reversed) was written *upside-down* the puzzling word 'Franks[?]'

[1] This list of subjects is probably for 'The History of England, a small book of Engravings. Price 3*s*.' which Blake advertised in his Prospectus of 10 October 1793 (p. 203) but which he never completed.

[2] According to Geoffrey of Monmouth, Brutus, the grandson of Aeneas, led the Trojans to England, where they rid the land of giants, settled the country, and named it after their leader, Britain. Small drawings ($5\frac{1}{4} \times 7\frac{1}{4}''$) known as 'The Landing of Brutus' and the 'Landing of Julius Caesar' belong to Mr. Robert Taylor of Princeton, and the second is reproduced in C. Ryskamp, *William Blake Engraver* (1969), pl. 1. No drawings have been traced for most of the subjects, but other drawings similar in historical subject and in date (*c.* 1779) are 'St. Augustine Converting Ethelbert of Kent' (Collection of Gwen Lady Melchett), 'The Death of Earl Goodwin' (BMPR, exhibited at the Royal Academy in 1780), and 'The Finding of the Body of Harold' (untraced)—see Butlin below.

[3] Gogmagog was one of the giants of Britain defeated in combat by Brutus' follower Corineus and thrown from a high rock into the sea, according to Milton, *History of Britain* (1670), 20.

[4] 'Lear and Cordelia in Prison' (?1779) probably derives from Milton's *History of Britain* rather than from Shakespeare's *King Lear*, where the scene depicted does not appear, or from Nahum Tate's adaptation (1681) of Shakespeare's play. Blake's drawing is reproduced in M. Butlin, *William Blake: a complete catalogue of the works in the Tate Gallery* (1971), 25.

[5 *del*] The Ancient Britons according to Caesar [The Frontis-
piece *del*]
6 The Druids
7 [C *del*] The Landing of Julius Caesar[1]
8 Boadicea inspiring the Britons against the Romans
The Britons distress & depopulation
Women fleeing from War
Women in a Siege
9 Alfred in the countrymans house
10 Edwin & Morcar stirring up the Londoners to resist W the
Conq[r2]
11 W the Conq Crownd
12 King John & Mag Charta[3]
A Famine occasiond by the Popish interdict[4]
13 Edward at Calais[5]
14 Edward the Black Prince brings his Captives to his father
15 The Penance of Jane Shore[6]
17 [The Reformation of H VIII. *del*]
18 [Ch I beheaded *del*]
[16 *del*] [17 *del*] 19 The Plague[7]
[17 *del*] [18 *del*] 20 The fire of London
[18 *del*] 16 The Cruelties used by Kings & Priests [whose
rule(?)[8] *del*]

[1] See note 2 opposite.
[2] In 1068 Edwin and Morcar, sons of the Earl of Mercia, raised a rebellion
against William the Conqueror.
[3] Blake's water-colour of 'The Making of Magna Charta' is in the Collection of
Mr. Robert N. Essick.
[4] The Interdict was probably that of 1209 by which Innocent III forced King
John to acknowledge that he held England and Ireland as fiefs from the Holy See.
[5] Edward III besieged Calais in 1346 and took it in 1347. Blake's water-colour
of 'The Keys of Calais' is described in *The Blake Collection of W. Graham Robertson*,
ed. K. Preston (1952), 174, and is now in Yale.
[6] 'The Penance of Jane Shore in St. Paul's' (*c*. 1779, Sir Edmund Verney
Collection) derives from the account (probably by Rapin) of the punishment of
Jane Shore by Richard III for having been the mistress of Edward IV and of the
public favour she won by her modesty and beauty. The drawing was later repeated
in the design (now in the Tate) described in Blake's *Descriptive Catalogue* (1809),
¶112 (p. 862).
[7] There are five versions of 'Plague', the earliest of *c*. 1779, in the Collection of
Mr. Donald Davidson reproduced in *Blake Newsletter*, VII (1973), 4 and cover;
four later ones of 1780–4, 1790–5, 1795–1800, 1805 are reproduced in G. Keynes,
William Blake's Illustrations to the Bible (1957), no. 38 a, b, d, c.
[8] For 'rule' Erdman (p. 616) reads 'arts'.

[19 *del*] 21 A prospect of Liberty
[20 *del*] 22 A Cloud

[Exodus VII]

1 Aaron[?] [*word illeg*]
2   [*word illeg*]
3 [River] [*word illeg*]
  [blood(?)]
4 Frogs
5 Lice
6 [Flies *del*] Swarms [of
  flies]
7 Murrain of [Beasts]

8 Boils & B[lains]
9 Hail
10 Locusts

11 [Darkness]
12 [First] born
13 Red Sea [Egyptians
  Drownd]¹

[*Page 117*]

Blakes Chaucer²

[¶*1*]   An Original Engraving by William Blake, ∧from
his Fresco Painting of Chaucers Canterbury Pilgrims∧

[¶*2*]   Mʳ B having from early Youth cultivated the two Arts
Painting & Engraving & during a Period of forty Years never
suspended his Labours on Copper for a single day³ Submits

¹ This list, written in extremely faded pencil, is apparently taken from Exodus 7: 17–21 (the river of blood), 8: 2–14 (the plague of frogs), 16–18 (the plague of lice), 21–4, 29–31 (the plague of flies), 9: 3–7 (the murrain of beasts), 9–11 (the plague of boils and blains), 18–34 (the plague of hail), 10: 4–6, 12–19 (the plague of locusts), 21–3 (the plague of darkness), 11: 5–7, 12: 12–13, 29–30 (the death of the first-born), 14: 16, 21–9 (the Egyptians drowned in the Red Sea).

The words printed within square brackets, which are quite illegible to me, are transcribed from Erdman, p. 661.

Page 117 ² This advertisement for Blake's engraving of Chaucer is adapted almost word for word from the description of the painting of the same subject in the *Descriptive Catalogue* (1809) ¶13–18 (pp. 831–4), except that the MS *adds* two parenthetical phrases in ¶5, 'in Gothic Letters' in ¶7, and all of ¶1–2; the MS *omits* 'the Miller' (after 'the Wife of Bath', presumably by accident) in ¶5, and 'of the Inn' after 'Gateway' in ¶7. The *Notebook* draft was itself adapted in the printed prospectus (pp. 863–6).

For notes on some of the factual matter in this *Notebook* draft, see *Descriptive Catalogue* pp. 831–4.

³ The 'forty Years' is evidently from 1772 (4 Aug.), when Blake was apprenticed as an engraver, until about 1812, though the 'Canterbury Pilgrims' plate was published in 1810.

with Confidence to Public Patronage & requests the attention of the Amateur in a Large [Work *del*] ∧Stroke Engraving∧ 3 feet 1 inch long by one foot high[1] Containing Thirty original high finishd whole Length Portraits on Horseback Of Chaucers Characters, Where every Character & every Expressio*n*, every Lineament of Head Hand & Foo*t*, every particular of dress or Costum*e*, where every Horse is appropriate to his Rider & the Scene or Landscape with its Villages Cottages Churches & the Inn in Southwark is minutely labour*d* not by the hands of Journeymen but by the Original Artist himself even to the Stuff*s* & Embroidery of the Garment*s*, the hair upon the Horses⌊,⌋ the Leaves upon the Tree*s*, & the Stones & Gravel upon the road: the Great Strength of Colouring & depth of work peculiar to M[r] B's Prints will be here found accompanied by a Precision not to be seen but in the work of an Original Artist⌊.⌋

]   Sir Jeffery Chaucer & the nine & twenty Pilgrims on their Journey to Canterbury⌊.⌋

]   The time chosen is early morning before Sun ris*e*, when

[*Page 118*]

the jolly Company are just quitting the Tabarde Inn. The Knight & Squire with the Squires Yeoman lead the Procession: then the Youthful Abess⌊,⌋ her Nun & three Priest*s*, her Grey-hounds attend her.

'Of small Hounds had she that she fed .
With roast flesh milk & wastel bread'[2]

]   Next follow the Friar & Mon*k*, then the Tapiser the Pardoner, the Sompnour & the Manciple. After these 'Our Host' who occupies the Center of the cavalcade (the Fun afterwards exhibited on the road may be seen depicted in his jolly face) directs them to the Knight (whose solemn gallantry no less fixes attention) as the person who will be likely to commense their Task of each telling a Tale in their order. After the Host, follow, the Shipman, the Haberdasher, the Dyer, the

---

[1] The engraved surface is 3 feet 1⅜ inches wide by 1 foot 1½ inches high (31 × 95·5 cm, according to G. Keynes, *Engravings by William Blake: The Separate Plates* [1956], 47), though the platemark is somewhat larger (35·5 × 97·5 cm).

Page 118   [2] *All* the quotation marks in ¶4 and 5 are Blake's.

Franklin, the Physician the Plowman, the Lawyer, the Poor Parson, the Merchant, the Wife of Bath the Coo*k*, the Oxford Schola*r*, Chaucer himself⌊,⌋ & the Reeve comes as Chaucer has described

'and ever he rode hinderest of the rout⌊.⌋'

[¶6]   These last are issuing from the Gateway of the Inn⌊;⌋ the Cook & Wife of Bath are both taking their mornings draught of comfort. Spectators stand at the Gateway of the Inn & are composed of an old man⌊,⌋ a woman & children⌊.⌋

[¶7]   The Landscape is an Eastward view of the Country from the Tabarde Inn in Southwark as it may be supposed to have appeard in Chaucers

[*Page 119*]

tim*e*, interspersed with Cottages & Villages, the beams of the Sun, are seen above the Horizon. *S*ome buildings & spires indicate the Situation of the Great City. The Inn is a Gothic Building which Thynne in his Glossary says was the Lodging of the Abbot of Hyde by Winchester.[1] On the Inn is inscribed its title & a proper advantage is taken of this circumstance to describe the Subject of the Picture. *T*he Words written in Gothic Letters over the Gateway are as follows⌊:⌋ 'The Tabardé Inne by Henry Bailly the Lodgynge House for Pilgrims who Journey to Saint Thomas s Shrine at Canterbury⌊.⌋'[2]

[¶8]   The Characters of Chaucers Pilgrims are the Characters that compose all ages & Nations; as one Age falls another rises, different to Mortal Sight but to Immortals only the same, for we see the same Characters repeated again & again in Animals in Vegetables in Minerals & in Men. Nothing new occurs in Identical Existence ∴ Accident ever Varies⌊.⌋ Substance can never suffer change nor decay⌊.⌋

Page 119 [1] Blake is probably quoting Chaucer's *Works* [ed. T. Speght] (1602)— see *Descriptive Catalogue* ¶15, n. 1.

[2] The opening quotation mark is Blake's, but he forgot the closing one.

('VISION OF THE LAST JUDGMENT')

[*Page 70, part f*]

For the Year 1810
Additions
to Blakes Catalogue
of Pictures &ᶜ

The Last Judgment [*will be*] when all those are Cast away who trouble Religion with Questions concerning Good & Evil or Eating of the Tree of those Knowledges or Reasonings which hinder the Vision of God turning all into a Consuming fire⌊.⌋ ⌃When⌃ Imaginative Art & Science & all Intellectual Gifts⌊,⌋ all the Gifts of the Holy Ghost are [despisd *del*] lookd upon as of no use & only Contention remains to Man then the Last Judgment begins & its Vision is seen by the [Imaginative Eye *del*] of Every one according to the Situation he holds⌊.⌋

[*Page 68, part a*]

The Last Judgment is not Fable or Allegory, but Vision⌊.⌋ Fable or Allegory are a totally distinct & inferior kind of Poetry. Vision or Imagination is a Representation of what Eternally Exists, Really & Unchangeably. Fable or Allegory is Formd by the Daughters of Memory. Imagination is Surrounded

---

'Vision of the Last Judgment', part f, p. 70 'For the Year . . . Pictures &ᶜ' is written at the top of the page, and the rest of part f is written sideways to the right margin, with no indication of its position. For the Order of Composition, see p. 960.

Pages 68–69: Order of Composition: (1) Parts a–b–c are written above and below the sketch on p. 68 (divided after 'who in the'); (2) The passage was continued by the rest of this paragraph and the whole of the next (part c) on p. 69 and by part d, each with a slightly different ink and pen, the second paragraph of part c ending to the left of the sketch and with considerable space left below it; (3) Part h is written sideways from the right margin of p. 68 to the sketch and keyed to its proper position in the paragraph with the words 'Note here that &ᶜ'; (4) This was probably followed immediately by part i written sideways from the sketch on p. 68 to the left margin; (5) Part g is written sideways beside the sketch on p. 69 towards the right margin, and a stroke clearly indicates its intended position on p. 68; (6) Part j begins ('the Writings of the Prophets') perhaps as an addition, and continues to the left of the sketch, stopping well above part d.

by the daughters of Inspiration who in the aggregate are calld Jerusalem⌊.⌋

[*Page 69, part g*]

Fable is Allegory but what Critics call The Fable is Vision itself⌊.⌋

[*Page 68, part b*]

The Hebrew Bible & the Gospel of Jesus are not Allegory but Eternal Vision or Imagination of All that Exists. ∧Note here that &ᶜ∧

[*Part h*]

Note here that Fable or All[*e*]gory is Seldom without some Vision⌊.⌋ Pilgrims Progress is full of it⌊,⌋ the Greek Poets the same but [Fable & Allegory *del*] ∧Allegory & Vision∧ ∧[& Visions of Imagination]∧ ought to be known as Two Distinct Things & so calld for the Sake of Eternal Life⌊.⌋

[*Part i*]

Plato has made Socrates say that Poets & Prophets do not Know or Understand what they write or Utter⌊;⌋[1] this is a most Pernicious Fals[*e*]hood. If they do not pray is an inferior Kind to be calld Knowing⌊?⌋ Plato Confutes himself⌊.⌋

[*Part c*]

The Last Judgment is one of these Stupendous Visions⌊.⌋ I have represented it as I Saw it⌊;⌋ to different People it appears differently as

[*Page 69*]

every thing else does for tho on Earth things seem Permanent they are less permanent than a Shadow as we all know too well⌊.⌋

The Nature of Visionary Fancy or Imagination is very little known & the Eternal nature & permanence of its ever [*illeg word del*] Existent Images is considerd as less permanent than the things of Vegetable & Generative Nature⌊,⌋ yet the Oak dies as well as the Lettuce but Its Eternal Image & Individuality never die*s*, but renews by its See*d*, just [as *del*] ∧So∧ the

Part i   [1] Blake was evidently thinking of 'The Apology of Socrates': 'I discovered ... [*that*] the poets ... like prophets ... say many and beautiful things, but they understand nothing of what they say' (*The Works of Plato*, tr. Thomas Taylor & F. Sydenham [1804], iv. 205; the passage is pointed out by K. Raine, *Blake and Tradition* [1968], i. 411).

Imaginative Image returns [according to *del*] by the Seed of Contemplative Thought$_L$;$_J$

[*Part j*]

the Writings of the Prophets illustrate these conceptions of the Visionary Fancy by their various sublime & divine Images as seen in the Worlds of Vision$_L$.$_J$

[*Page 71, part e*]

The Learned m[1]
[of *del*] or Heroes [it *del*] ∧this is n[?]∧ an
& not Spiritu
while the Bibl
of Virtue & Vic
as they are Ex
is the Real Di
Things The
when they Assert that Jupiter usurped the Throne of his Father Saturn & brought on an Iron Age & Begat on Mnemosyne or Memory The Greek Muses which are not Inspiration as the Bible is. Reality was Forgot & the Vanities of Time & Space only Rememberd & calld Reality$_L$.$_J$ Such is the Mighty difference between Allegoric Fable & Spiritual Mystery$_L$.$_J$ Let *it* here be Noted that the Greek Fables originated in Spiritual Mystery ∧& Real Vision∧

[*Page 72*]

∧and Real Vision∧ Which are lost & clouded in Fable & Allegory [which *del*] ∧while∧ the Hebrew Bible & the Greek Gospel are Genuine Preservd by the Saviours Mercy$_L$.$_J$ The Nature of my Work is Visionary or Imaginative$_L$;$_J$ it is an Endeavour to Restore ∧what the Ancients calld∧ the Golden Age$_L$.$_J$ [the Females behind them represent the Females belonging to Such States Who are under perpetual terrors vain dreams plots

Page 71: Order of Composition: (1) Part e is written above and below the sketch (divided after 'Father'); (2) 'Public Address' part bb is written sideways from the left margin, and part cc is written sideways from the sketch to the right margin, perhaps as a continuation. (2) is written in a different ink and pen from (1).
[1] The top right corner of the page was cut out, leaving a column of unfinished lines at the left.

Page 72, part e The deleted passage does not seem to be connected with any other passage on this page. It was later added to p. 78 (part s) (p. 1014).

& secret deceit those who descend into the flames before Cai[*a*]phas & Pi *del*]

[*Page 69, part d*]

This world of Imagination is the World of Eternity$_{L}$;$_{\rfloor}$ it is the divine bosom into which we shall all go after the death of the Vegetated body$_{L}$.$_{\rfloor}$ This World ∧of Imagination∧ is Infinite & Eternal whereas the world of Generation or Vegetation is Finite & [for a small moment *del*] Temporal$_{L}$.$_{\rfloor}$ There Exist in that Eternal World the Permanent Realities of Every Thing which we see reflected in this Vegetable Glass of Nature$_{L}$.$_{\rfloor}$ All Things are comprehended in their Eternal Forms in the divine

[*Page 70*]

body of the Saviour$_{L}$,$_{\rfloor}$ the True Vine of Eternity$_{L}$,$_{\rfloor}$ The Human Imagination who appeard to Me as Coming to Judgmen*t* among his Saints & throwing off the Temporal that the Eternal might be Establishd. *A*round him were seen the Images of Existences according to [their Aggregate Signification(*?*) *del*] a certain order Suited to my Imaginative Eye [In the following order *del*] ∧as follows$_{L}$.$_{\rfloor}$∧

Query$_{L}$:$_{\rfloor}$ the Above ought to follow the description$_{L}$.$_{\rfloor}$

Here follows the description of the Picture$_{L}$:$_{\rfloor}$[1]

[*Page 76, part k*]

Jesus seated between the Two Pillars Jachin & Boaz[2] with the Word of ∧divine∧ Revelation on his Knee ∧& on each side the four & twenty Elders sitting in Judgment$_{L}$.$_{\rfloor}$∧ *T*he Heavens opening around him by unfolding the clouds around his throne$_{L}$,$_{\rfloor}$ ∧the Old H & old Earth are passing away & the N H & N Earth descending$_{L}$.$_{\rfloor}$∧ [as on a Scroll *del*] The Just arise on his right & the wicked on his Left hand$_{L}$.$_{\rfloor}$ ∧A Sea of fire Issues from before the throne$_{L}$.$_{\rfloor}$∧ Adam & Eve appear first before the [throne *del*] ∧Judgment Seat∧ in humilation. Abel surrounded by Innocents & Cain ∧with the flint in his hand

Page 70, part d [1] 'Query . . . the description' and 'Here follows . . . the Picture' are squeezed in at the bottom of the page as afterthoughts, the first probably after the second. For the Order of Composition, see p. 960.

Page 76, part k [2] 1 Kings 7: 21: Solomon 'set up the pillars in the porch of the temple: and he set up the right pillar and called the name thereof Jachin: and he set up the left pillar, and called the name thereof Boaz.' See also 2 Chronicles 53: 17.

with which he slew his brother⌃ falling with the head down-
ward⌊.⌋ From the Cloud on which Eve stands Satan is seen
falling headlong wound round by the tail of the serpent whose
bulk naild to the Cross round which he wreathes is falling into
the Abyss⌊.⌋ Sin is also represented as a female bound in one
of the Serpents folds surrounded by her fiends⌊.⌋ Death is
Chaind to the Cross & Time falls together with death dragged
down by [an Angel *del*] a demon crownd with Laurel⌊;⌋ another
demon with a Key has the charge of Sin & is dragging her
down by the hair⌊;⌋ beside them a [Scaled *del*] figure is Seen
scaled with iron scales from head to feet [with *del*] precipitating
himself into the Abyss with the Sword & Balances⌊;⌋ he is
Og King of Bashan⌊.⌋

⌃On the Right⌃[1] Beneath the Cloud on which Abel Kneels
is Abraham with Sarah & Isaac⌊,⌋ also Hagar & Ishmael⌊.⌋
⌃Abel kneels on a bloody Cloud &ᶜ to come in here ⌃⌃as⌃⌃
two leaves forward⌊.⌋[2]

[Page 80, part q]

Abel kneels on a bloody cloud descriptive of those Churches
before the flood that they were filld with blood & fire &
vapour of Smoke⌊,⌋ even till Abrahams time the vapor & heat
was not extinguishd⌊;⌋ these States Exist now⌊.⌋ Man Passes
on but States remain for Ever⌊;⌋ he passes thro them like a
traveller who may as well suppose that the places he has passd
thro exist no more as a Man may suppose that the States he
has passd thro Exist no more⌊.⌋ Every thing is Eternal⌊.⌋

[Page 79, part r]

In Eternity one Thing never Changes into another Thing⌊.⌋
Each Identity is Eternal⌊;⌋ consequently Apuleius's Golden
Ass & Ovids Metamorphosis & others of the like kind are
Fable⌊,⌋ yet they contain Vision in a Sublime degree being
derived from real Vision in More Ancient Writings⌊∴⌋ Lots

---

[1] The directions 'On the Right' in part k and 'on the left' in part l were probably
made at the same time, before the other changes on this page.

[2] 'Abel kneels . . . leaves forward' is written sideways from the left margin and is
inserted by a stroke.

Page 80, part q is written sideways from the left margin carefully avoiding part p.

Page 79, part r is written in the small hand, Black ink, sharp pen, and probably at
the same time as part s on p. 78. For the Order of Composition, see p. 961.

Wife being Changed into [*a*] Pillar of Salt[1] alludes to the Mortal Body being renderd a Permanent Statue but not Changed or Transformd into Another Identity while it retains its own Individuality. A Man can never become Ass nor Horse∟;⌐ some are born with shapes of Men who may be both but Eternal Identity is one thing & Corporeal Vegetation is another thing∟.⌐ Changing Water into Wine by Jesus & into Blood by Moses relates to Vegetable Nature also∟.⌐

[Page 76, part l]

[*Beneath*] ∧Ishmael is Mahomet∧ ∧on the left∧[2] & beneath the falling figure of Cain is Moses casting his tables of Stone into the deeps. *I*t ought to be understood that the Persons Moses & Abraham are not here meant but the States Signified by those Names∟,⌐ the Individuals being representatives or Visions of those States as they were reveald to Mortal Man in the Series of Divine Revelation*s*, as they are written in the Bible∟;⌐ these various States I have seen in my Imagination∟;⌐ when distant they appear as One Man but as you approach they appear Multitudes of Nations. Abraham hovers above his posterity which appear as Multitudes of Children ascending from the Earth surrounded by Stars as it was said 'As the stars of Heaven for Multitude∟.⌐'[3] Jacob & [their *del*] his Twelve Sons hover beneath the feet of Abraham & recieve their children from the Earth∟.⌐ ∧I have Seen when at a distance Multitudes of Men in Harmony appear like a Single Infant Sometimes in the Arms of a Female∟;⌐ this represented the Church∟.⌐∧

But to proceed With the Description of those on the Left Han*d*: beneath the Cloud on which Moses Kneels is two figures∟,⌐ a Male & Female chaind [to *del*]

[Page 77]

together by the feet∟,⌐ they represent those who perishd by the flood∟;⌐ beneath them a multitude of their associates are seen falling headlong∟;⌐ by the Side of them is a Mighty fiend with

---

[1] Genesis 19: 26: 'his [*Lot's*] wife looked back from behind him, and she became a pillar of salt.'

Page 76, part l [2] 'on the left' was probably written at the same time as 'On the Right' in part k, and before the other changes on the page were made.

[3] Deuteronomy 1: 10; 10: 22; 28: 62: 'as the stars of heaven for multitude'; see also Hebrews 11: 12.

a Book in his hand which is Shut⌊;⌋ he represents the person namd in Isaiah XXII. c & 20 *v*,[1] Eliakim the Son of Hilkiah⌊;⌋ he drags Satan down headlong⌊;⌋ he is crownd with oak [& has *del*]⌊;⌋ by the side of the Scaled figure representing Og King of Bashan[2] is a Figure with a Basket emptiing out the vanities of Riches & Worldly Honours⌊;⌋ ∧he is Araunah the Jebusite master of the threshing floor⌊;⌋∧[3] above him are two figures ∧elevated on a Cloud∧ representing the Pharisees who plead their own Righteousness before the throne. *T*hey are weighed down by two fiends⌊.⌋ Beneath the Man with the Basket are three fiery fiends with grey beards & scourges of fire⌊;⌋ they represent Cruel Laws⌊;⌋ they scourge a groupe of figures down into the deeps⌊;⌋ beneath them are various figures in attitudes of contention representing various States of Misery which alas every one on Earth is liable to enter into & against which we should all watch⌊.⌋

The Ladies will be pleasd to see that I have represented the Furies by Three Men & not by three Women⌊.⌋ It is not because I think the Ancients wrong but they will be pleasd to remember that mine is Vision & not Fable⌊.⌋ The Spectator may suppose them Clergymen in the Pulpit Scourging Sin instead of forgiving it⌊.⌋[4]

The Earth beneath these falling Groupes of figures is rocky & burning and seems as if convulsd by Earthquakes⌊;⌋ a Great City ∧on fire∧ is seen in the distance⌊;⌋ ∧the armies are fleeing upon the Mountains⌊.⌋∧ On the foreground Hell is opened & many figures are descending into it down stone steps & beside a Gate beneath a rock ∧where Sin & Death are to be closed Eternally by that Fiend who carries the Key [& drags *del*] in one hand & drags them down with the other∧ [howling & lamenting *del*]⌊.⌋ On the rock & above the Gate a fiend with wings [de *del*] urges [them *del*] ∧the wicked∧ onwards with

Page 77 [1] Isaiah 22: 20: 'And it shall come to pass that day, that I will call my servant Eliakim the son of Hilkiah'.

[2] Og King of Bashan was a giant enemy of Israel; see Deuteronomy 3.

[3] In 2 Samuel 16–24 the plague stops at 'the threshing-place of Araunah the Jebusite', which is therefore bought for an altar.

[4] 'Laws they scourge . . . should all watch' and 'The Earth beneath these falling' are written to the left of the sketch; 'The Ladies . . . forgiving it' to the right has no indication of its position except the sense. It was probably written after 'all watch'.

fiery darts⌐;⌐ he [represents the Assyrian *del*] ^is Hazael the Syrian^[1] who drives abroad all those who rebell against their Saviour⌐;⌐ beneath the Steps [*is*] Babylon represented by a King crownd Grasping his Sword & his Sceptre⌐;⌐ he is just awakend out of his Grave⌐;⌐ around him are other Kingdoms arising to Judgmen*t*, represented in this Picture [as in the Prophets *del*] as Single Personages according to the descriptions in the Prophets⌐.⌐ The Figure dragging up a Woman by her hair represents the Inquisition as do those contending on the Sides of the Pit & in Particular the Man Strangling two Women represents a Cruel Church⌐.⌐[2]

[Page 78, part s]

Two persons one in Purple the other in Scarlet are descending [into Hell *del*] ^down the Steps into the Pit⌐.⌐^ These are Cai[*a*]phas & Pilate⌐,⌐ Two States where all those reside who Calumniate & Murder ^under Pretence of Holiness & Justice^. Cai[*a*]phas has a Blue Flame like a Miter on his head⌐.⌐ Pilate has bloody hands that never can be cleansed⌐;⌐ the Females behind them represent the Females belonging to such States who are under perpetual terrors & vain dreams plots & secret deceit. Those figures that descend into the Flames before Cai[*a*]phas & Pilate[3] are Judas & those of his Class⌐.⌐ Achitophel is also here with the cord in his hand⌐.⌐

[Page 80, part m]

Between the Figures of Adam & Eve appears a fiery Gulph descending from the Sea of fire Before the throne⌐;⌐ in this

---

[1] 'Hazael king of Syria' appears especially in 2 Kings 8–13.

[2] 'on the Sides . . . Cruel Church' trail sideways up the right margin.

Page 78, part s [3] 'the Females behind them . . . Cai[*a*]phas & Pilate' was first inexplicably drafted on p. 72.

Page 80: Order of Composition: (1) Parts m and n were written straight through before any additions were made, carefully avoiding the sketch; (2) Part t was added first between lines and then (after 'The wreathed') bending sideways in a column from the right margin to the sketch; (3) This was perhaps continued with part p (not marked for entry) written to the left of the sketch and below the prose; (4) The addition to part n 'he has . . . before him' begins above the line and continues sideways to the right margin carefully avoiding addition 2; (5) The addition to part n 'who have . . . Seven Headed Kingdoms' begins above the line, continues (after 'Ezekiel') sideways from the right margin and then (after 'with') bends *upside-down* into the right margin; (6) Part q is written sideways from the left margin carefully avoiding both the sketch and addition 3 above.

'Last Judgment' (*Notebook* p. 80)

Cataract Four Angels descend headlong with four trumpets to awake the dead. *B*eneath these is the Seat of the Harlot ˄namd˄ Mystery¹ in the Revelations.² She is [bound *del*] siezed by Two Beings each with three heads⌞;⌟ [representing *del*] ˄they Represent˄ Vegetative Existence; ˄as˄ it is written in Revelations they strip her naked & burn her with fire.

[*Part t*]

*I*t represents the Eternal Consummation of Vegetable Life & Death with its Lusts⌞.⌟ The wreathed Torches in their hands represents Eternal Fire which is the fire of Generation or Vegetation⌞;⌟ it is an Eternal Consummation⌞.⌟ Those who are blessed with Imaginative Vision See This Eternal Female & tremble at what others fear not while they ˄despise &˄ laugh at what others fear⌞.⌟

[*Part p*]

Her Kings & Councellors & Warriors³ descend in Flames Lamenting & looking upon her in astonishment & Terro*r*, & Hell is opend beneath her Seat on the Left hand⌞.⌟

[*Part n*]

*B*eneath her feet is a flaming Cavern in which is Seen the Great Red Dragon with Seven heads & ten horns⌞;⌟ [who *del*] ˄he has Satans book of Accusations lying on the Rock open before him⌞;⌟˄⁴ ˄he˄ is bound in chains by Two Strong demons⌞;⌟ they are Gog & Magog⁵ ˄who have been compelld

---

Part m ¹ Revelation 17:5: 'upon her forehead was a name written, MYSTERY, BABYLON THE GREAT, THE MOTHER OF HARLOTS AND ABOMINA-TIONS OF THE EARTH.'

² Revelation 17: 16: 'the ten horns which thou sawest upon the beast, these shall hate the whore, and shall make her desolate and naked, and shall eat her flesh, and burn her with fire.'

Part t begins ('*I*t represents . . . The wreathed') as an addition to part m and clearly continues sideways from the right margin, avoiding the addition to part n.

Part p is to the left of the sketch and is not marked for entry.

³ One of Blake's designs (1805) for Blair's *Grave* (1808) was entitled 'The King, Counsellor, Warrior, Mother & Child in the Tomb.'

Part n ⁴ 'he has Satans . . . before him' begins above the line and continues up the margin.

⁵ Revelation 20: 8: Satan 'shall go out to deceive the nations which are in the four quarters of the earth, Gog and Magog, to gather them together to battle . . .'.

to subdue their Master [(]Ezekiel xxxviii c. 8 v¹[)] with their Hammers & Tongs about to new Create the Seven Headed Kingdoms∧.² The Graves beneath are opend & the dead awake & obey the call of the Trumpet⌐;⌐ those on the Right hand awaken in joy⌐,⌐ those on the Left in Horror. *B*eneath the dragons Cavern a Skeleton begins to Animate Starting into life at the trumpets Sound while the Wicked contend with each other on the brink of

[*Page 81*]

perdition. ∧On the Right∧ a Youthful couple are awaked by their Children⌐;⌐ an Aged patriarch is awaked by his aged wife⌐.⌐ ∧[They *del*] He is Albion our Ancester⌐,⌐ ∧∧Patriarch of the Atlantic Continent∧∧ whose History Preceded that of the Hebrews & in whose Sleep ∧∧or chaos∧∧ Creation began, [his Emanation or Wife is Jerusalem *del*] ∧∧[who is about to be recievd into the Bride of the *del*]∧∧ at their head the Aged Woman is Britannica the Wife of Albion⌐;⌐ Jerusalem is their daughter⌐.⌐∧ *L*ittle Infants creep out of the [ground³ *del*] flowery mould into the Green fields of the blessed who in various Joyful companies embrace & ascend to meet Eternity⌐.⌐

The Persons who ascend to Meet the Lord coming in the Clouds with power & great Glory are representations of those States described in the Bible under the Names of the Fathers before & after the Flood⌐.⌐ Noah is seen in the Midst of these Canopied by a Rainbow, on his right hand Shem & on his

---

¹ Ezekiel 38: 8: 'After many days thou shalt be visited: in the latter years thou shalt come into the land that is brought back from the sword, and is gathered out of many people, against the mountains of Israel, which have been always waste; but it is brought forth out of the nations, and they shall dwell safely all of them.'

² 'who have been . . . Headed Kingdoms' begins above the line, continues (at 'xxxviii') sideways in the right margin, and concludes ('with their Hammers') *upside-down* at the bottom of the page.

Page 81: Order of Composition: (1) First came part n before additions, 'perdition . . . Sweep away' above the sketch, 'Above Noah . . . under her feet' to the left of it, 'The Aged . . . Oaks of Albion' to its right, and 'Around Noah . . . the Hebrew' below it—the self-contained passages on either side could have been later additions; (2) The addition 'He is Albion . . . at their head' begins between the lines and bends (after 'Hebrews') sideways from the right margin; (3) It appears to be continued with the sentence 'the Aged Woman . . . daughter' written *upside-down* at the top of the page and not marked for entry.

³ Under 'ground' Erdman (p. 548) reads '[mould *del*]'.

Left Japhet_L;_J[1] these three Persons represent Poetry Painting & Music_{L,J} the three Powers ˄in Man˄ of conversing with Paradise which the flood did not Sweep away_L._J Above Noah is the Church Universal represented by a Woman Surrounded by Infants_L._J There is Such a State in Eternity_L;_J it is composed of the Innocent ˄civilized[?]˄ Heathen & the Uncivilized Savages who having not the Law do by Nature the things contain in the Law. This State appears like a Female crownd with Stars driven into the Wilderness_L._J She has the Moon under her feet_L._J The Aged Figure with Wings having a writing tablet & taking account of the numbers who arise is That Angel of the Divine Presence mentiond in Exodus XIVc 19v[2] & in other Places_L;_J this Angel is frequently calld by the Name of Jehovah Elohim_{L,J} The 'I am' of the Oaks of Albion_L._J Around Noah & beneath him are various figures Risen into the Air_L;_J ˄among˄ these are Three Females representing those who are not of the dead but of those found alive at the Last Judgment_L;_J they appear to be innocently gay & thoughtless_{L,J} not ˄being˄ among the Condemnd because ignorant of crime in the midst of a corrupted Age_L;_J ˄the Virgin Mary was of this Class˄. A Mother Meets her ˄numerous˄ Family in the Arms of their Father_L;_J these are representations of the Greek Learned & Wise as also of those of other Nations such as Egypt & Babylon in which were multitudes who shall meet the Lord coming in the Clouds_L._J

The Children of Abraham or Hebrew Church are represented as a Stream of [Light *del*] ˄Figures˄ in which are seen Stars somewhat like the Milky way_L;_J they ascend from the Earth where Figures kneel Embracing above the Graves & Represent Religion or Civilized Life such as it is in the Christian Church who are the Offspring of the Hebrew_L._J

[*Page 82*]

Just above the graves & above the spot where the Infants creep

[1] Genesis 9: 18: 'the sons of Noah, that went forth of the ark, were Shem, and Ham, and Japheth . . . .'

[2] Exodus 14: 19: 'And the angel of God, which went before the camp of Israel, removed and went behind them, and the pillar of the cloud went from before their face, and stood behind them . . . .'

Page 82: Order of Composition: (1) Part n before additions carefully skirts the sketch; (2) The addition, which may begin at 'Calld Gothic', continues and turns sideways out of the Ground Stand two_{L,J} a Man & Woman_{L;J} these are the Primitive Christians_{L.J} The two Figures in ⌃purifying⌃ flames by the Side of the Dragons cavern represents the Latter State of the Church when on the verge of Perdition yet protected by a Flaming Sword. Multitudes are seen ascending from the Green fields of the blessed in which a Gothic Church is representative of true Art ⌃Calld Gothic in All Ages by those who follow ⌃⌃the⌃⌃ Fashion as that is calld which is without Shape or Fashion_{L.J} [By *del*] On the right hand of Noah a Woman with Children represents the State Calld Laban the Syrian_{L;J}¹ it is the Remains of Civilization in the State from whence Abraham was taken_{L.J}⌃

Also On the right hand of Noah A Female descends to meet her Lover or Husband representative of that Love calld Friendship which Looks for no other heaven than their Beloved & in him Sees all reflected as in a Glass of Eternal Diamond_{L.J}

On the right hand of these rise the diffident & Humble & on their left a ⌃Solitary⌃ Woman with her infant_{L;J} these are caught up by three aged Men who appear as suddenly emerging from the blue sky for their help. These three Aged Men represent Divine Providence as oppos'd to & distinct from divine vengeance represented by three Aged men on the Side of the Picture among the Wicked with Scourges of fire_{L.J}

If the Spectator could Enter into these Images in his Imagination approaching them on the Fiery Chariot of his Contemplative Thought_{L,J} if he could Enter into Noahs Rainbow or into his bosom or could make a Friend & Companion of one of these Images of wonder which always intreats him to leave mortal things_{L,J} as he must know_{L,J} then would he arise from his Grave_{L,J} then would he meet the Lord in the Air & then he would be happy_{L.J} General Knowledge is Remote Knowledge_{L;J} it is in Particulars that Wisdom consists & Happiness too, Both in Art & in Life_{L.J} General Masses are as Much Art as a Pasteboard Man is Human_{L.J} Every Man has Eyes Nose

---

(after 'Fashion') from the right margin, goes on (with a stroke clearly indicating the sequence after 'Shape or Fashion') to the right of the sketch; (3) After the addition of 'By the right hand of Noah . . .' an 'Also' had to be added to the paragraph already beginning 'On the right hand of Noah'.

¹ Laban the Syrian is the father of Leah and Rachel and the uncle of Jacob (Genesis 29–31).

& Mouth﹍, this Every Idiot knows but he who enters into & discriminates most minutely the Manners & Intentions﹍,

[*Page 83*]

the [Expression *del*] Characters in all their branches﹍, is the alone Wise or Sensible Man & on this discrimination All Art is founded. I intreat then that the Spectator will attend to. the Hands & Feet﹍, to the Lineaments of the Countenances﹍; they are all descriptive of Character & not a line is drawn without intention & that most discriminate & particular﹍. ⌃As Poetry admits not a Letter that is Insignificant So Painting admits not a Grain of Sand or a Blade of Grass ⌃⌃Insignificant﹍,⌃⌃ much less an Insignificant Blur or Mark﹍.⌃[1]

Above the Head of Noah is Seth﹍; this State calld Seth is Male & Female in a higher State of Happiness & wisdom than Noah being nearer the State of Innocence﹍; beneath the feet of Seth two figures represent the two Seasons of Spring & Autum*n*, while beneath the feet of Noah Four Seasons represent [our present changes of Extremes *del*] the Changed State made by the flood.

By the side of Seth is Elijah﹍; he comprehends all the Prophetic Characters﹍; he is seen on his fiery Chariot bowing before the throne of the Saviour. *I*n like manner The figures of Seth & his wife Comprehends the Fathers before the flood & their Generations﹍; when Seen remote they appear as One Man. *A* little below Seth on his right are Two Figures﹍, a Male & Female with numerous Children﹍; these represent those who were not in the Line of the Church & yet were Saved from among the Antediluvians who Perished. *B*etween Seth & these a female figure [with the back turnd *del*] represents the Solitary State of those who previous to the Flood walked with God﹍.

All these arise toward the opening Cloud before the Throne led onward by triumphant Groupes of Infants ⌃& the Morning Stars sang together⌃. Between Seth & Elijah three Female Figures crownd with Garlands Represent Learning & Science which accompanied Adam out of Eden﹍.

The Cloud that opens rolling apart before the throne &

Page 83, part n 	[1] 'As Poetry . . . or Mark' is written in a break between paragraphs and continues (after 'Blade') sideways from the right margin.

before the New Heaven & the New Earth is Composed of Various Groupes of Figures particularly the Four Living Creatures mentiond in Revelations as Surrounding the Throne_L;_J¹ these I suppose to have the chief agency in removing the [former *del*]

[*Page 84*]

old heavens & the old Earth to make way for the New Heaven & the New Earth to descend from the throne of God & of the Lamb. *T*hat Living Creature on the Left of the Throne Gives to the Seven Angels the Seven Vials of the wrath of God ˄with˄ which they hovering over the deeps beneath pour out upon the wicked their Plagues_L;_J the Other Living Creatures are descending with a Shout & with the Sound of the Trumpet directing² the Combats in the upper Elements [where Appolyon *del*] ˄in the two Corners of the Picture_L;_J˄ on the Left hand ˄Apollyon˄ is foiled before the Sword of Michael & on the Right the Two Witnesses ˄are˄ subduing their Enemies_L._J

[Around the Throne Heaven is opened *del*] On the Cloud are opend the Books of Remembrance of Life & of Death_L;_J before that of Life ˄on the Right˄ some figures [for(?) *del*] bow in humiliation_L;_J before that of death ˄on the Left˄ the Pharisees are pleading their own Righteousness_L;_J the one Shines with beams of Light_L,_J the other utters Lightnings & tempests_L._J

A Last Judgment is Necessary because Fools flourish_L._J˄ Nations Flourish under Wise Rulers & are depressd under foolish Rulers_L;_J it is the same with Individuals as Nations_L;_J works of Art can only be producd in Perfection where the Man is either in Affluence or is Above the Care of it_L._J Poverty is the Fools Rod which at last is turned upon his own back_L;_J this is A Last Judgment when Men of Real Art Govern & Pretenders Fall_L._J Some People & not a few Artists have asserted that the Painter of this Picture would not have done so well if he had been properly [patr *del*] Encouragd_L;_J Let those who

¹ Revelation 4: 6–8: 'round about the throne were four beasts full of eyes before and behind. And the first beast was like a lion, and the second beast was like a calf, and the third beast had a face as a man, and the fourth beast was like a flying eagle. And the four beasts had each of them six wings about him; and they were full of eyes within . . . .'

Page 84 ² Blake actually wrote here, apparently meaninglessly, 'Trumpet & with directing'; perhaps he accidentally omitted a word after 'with'.

think So reflect on the State of Nations under Poverty & their
incapability of Art∟;⌐ tho art is Above Either the Argument is
better for Affluence than Poverty & tho he would not have been
a greater Artist yet he would have producd Greater works of
art in proportion to

[*Page 85*]

his means∟.⌐ A Last Judgment is not for the purpose of making
Bad Men better but for the Purpose of hindering them from
op[*p*]ressing the Good with Poverty & Pain by means of such
Vile Arguments & Insinuations∟.⌐¹

[*Page 84*]

Around the Throne Heaven is opend & the Nature of
Eternal Things Displayd∟,⌐ All Springing from the Divine
Humanity∟.⌐ All beams from him∟,⌐ ∧Because *del*]∧ [& as he
himself has Said All dwells in him *del*] He is the Bread & the
Wine∟,⌐² he is the Water of Life∟;⌐ accordingly on Each Side of
the opening Heaven appears an Apostle∟,⌐ [one *del*] ∧that on
the Right∧ Represents Baptism∟,⌐ [& the other *del*] ∧that on the
Left Represents∧ the Lords Supper∟.⌐ All Life consists of these
Two Throwing off Error ∧& Knaves from our company∧ con-
tinually & Recieving Truth ∧or Wise Men into our Company∧
Continually∟;⌐ he who is out of the Church & opposes it is no
less an agent of Religion than he who is in it. To be an Error
& to be Cast out is a part of Gods design∟.⌐ No man can Em-
brace True Art till he has explord & Cast out False Art∟,⌐
∧such is the Nature of Mortal Things∟,⌐∧ or he will be himself
Cast out by those who have Already Embraced True Art∟.⌐
Thus My Picture is a History of Art & Science∟,⌐ [& its *del*]
∧the Foundation of Society∧ Which is Humanity itself. What
are all the Gifts of the Spirit but Mental Gifts∟?⌐ Whenever

¹ 'this is A Last Judgment . . . Insinuations' is apparently a single addition, be-
ginning at the end of a paragraph, continuing (**a**) after 'when', sideways along the
right margin to the bottom right corner, (**b**) after 'Fall', sideways in the opposite
direction to the top right corner and not marked for entry; (**c**) after 'Picture',
upside-down at the top of the page, (**d**) after 'reflect', sideways to the left margin,
(**e**) after 'Affluence than Poverty', right way up in the bottom margin, (**f**) after
'proportion to', right way up below the text on p. 85, (**g**) after 'hindering them',
upside-down between the last two lines of prose on p. 85.

² John 7: 56: 'He that eateth of my flesh, and drinketh of my blood, dwelleth
in me, and I in him.'

any Individual Rejects Error & Embraces Truth a Last Judgment passes upon that Individual_L._

[Page 85]

Over the Head of the Saviour & Redeemer The Holy Spirit like a Dove is Surrounded by a blue Heaven in which are the two Cherubim that bowd over the Ark for here the temple is opend in Heaven & the Ark of the Covenant is as a Dove of Peace_L._ The Curtains are drawn apart_L,_ Christ having rent the Veil_L,_ The Candlestick & the Table of Shew bread appear_L,_ on Each side a Glorification of Angels with Harps surround the dove_L._

The Temple Stands on the Mount of God_L;_ from it flows on each Side the River of Life on whose banks Grows the tree of Life among whose branches temples & Pinnacles tents & pavilions Gardens & Groves display Paradise with its Inhabitants walking up & down in Conversations concerning Mental Delights_L._ Here they are &c as three leaves on_L:_

[Page 90, part v]

Here they are no longer talking of what is Good & Evil or of what is Right or Wrong & puzzling themselves in Satans [Maze *del*] Labyrinth But are Conversing with Eternal Realities as they Exist in the Human Imagination_L._ We are in a World of Generation & death & this world we must cast off if we would be Painters

[Page 91]

Such as Rafa[*e*]l Mich Angelo & the Ancient Sculptors. *If* we do not cast off this world we Shall be only Venetian Painters Who will be cast off & Lost from Art_L._

[Page 85, part o]

Jesus is surrounded by Beams of Glory in which are seen all around him Infants emanating from him_L;_ these represent the Eternal Births of Intellect from the divine Humanity_L._ A Rainbow surrounds the throne & the Glory in which youthful Nuptials recieve the infants in their hands_L._ In Eternity Woman is the Emanation of Man_L,_ she has No Will of her own_L._ There is no such thing in Eternity as a Female Will_L._[1]

Page 85, part o   [1] 'In Eternity . . . Female Will' begins in a paragraph break and continues (after 'In Eternity') sideways down the right margin.

'Last Judgment' (*Notebook* p. 86)

On the Side next Baptism are Seen those calld in the Bible Nursing Fathers & Nursing Mothers⌐;⌐[1] ∧[they have Crowns the Spectator may suppose them to be (the *del*) good *Kings del*]∧ ∧& Queens [of England *del*]∧[2] ∧they represent Education⌐.⌐ On the Side next the Lords Supper [*is*] The Holy Family consisting of Mary Joseph John the Baptist Zacharias & Elizabeth recieving the Bread & Wine among other Spirits of ∧the∧ Just made perfect. [Just *del*] Beneath these a Cloud of Women & Children are taken up fleeing from the rolling Cloud which separates the Wicked from the Seats of Bliss. These represent those who tho willing were too weak to Reject Error without the Assistance & Countenance of those Already in the Truth for a Man Can only Reject Error by the Advice of a Friend or by the Immediate Inspiration of God⌐;⌐ it is for this Reason among many others that I have put the Lords Supper on the Left Hand of the [Picture *del*] Throne for it appears so at the Last Judgment for a Protection.

[Page 86, part u]

The Combats of Good & Evil [& of Truth & Error which are the Same thing *del*] ∧is Eating of the Tree of Knowledge. The Combats of Truth & Error is Eating of the tree of Life;[3] ∧these∧ are not only Universal but Particular. Each are Personified⌐.⌐ There is not an Error but it has a Man for its [Actor *del*] Agent⌐,⌐ that is it is a Man. There is not a truth but it has also a Man⌐;⌐ ∧Good & Evil are Qualities in Every Man whether ∧∧a∧∧ Good or Evil Man⌐.⌐∧ These are Enemies & destroy one another by every Means in their power both of deceit & of open Violence⌐.⌐ The Deist & the Christian are but the Results of these Opposing Natures⌐.⌐ Many are Deists who would in certain Circumstances have been Christians in

---

[1] Isaiah 49: 23: 'kings shall be thy nursing fathers, and their queens thy nursing mothers . . .'

[2] '& Queens [of England *del*]' is written sideways in the right margin as a continuation of the sentence but after 'Female Will' above, after which Keynes prints it.

Page 86, part u at the bottom of the page is separated from 'Public Address' part ee by a stroke and in turn is deleted by two strokes.

[3] 'is Eating . . . of Life' begins above the line and continues (after 'Error is') sideways in the right margin.

outward appearance∟.⌐ Voltaire was one of this number∟;⌐ he was as intolerant as an Inquisitor∟.⌐ Manners make the Man not Habits. It is the Same in Art∟,⌐ by their Works ye

[*Page 90*]

Shall know them∟;⌐ the Knave who is Converted to [Christianity *del*] ∧Dcism∧ & the Knave who is Converted to Christianity is still a Knave but he himself will not know it tho Every body else does∟.⌐ Christ comes as he came at first to deliver those who were bound under the Knave∟,⌐ not to deliver the Knave∟;⌐ he Comes to Deliver Man the [*illeg word*[1] *del*] Accused & not Satan the Accuser∟;⌐ we do not find any where that Satan is Accused of Sin∟;⌐ he is only accused of Unbelief & thereby drawing Man into Sin that he may accuse him. Such is the Last Judgment∟,⌐ a Deliverance from Satans Accusation∟.⌐ Satan thinks that Sin is displeasing to God∟;⌐ he ought to know that Nothing is displeasing to God but Unbelief & Eating of the Tree of Knowledge of Good & Evil∟.⌐

[*Page 87, part z*]

Men are admitted into Heaven not because they have ∧Curbed &∧ governd their Passions or have No Passions but because they have Cultivated Their Understandings. The Treasures of Heaven are not Negations of Passion but Realities of Intellect from which All the Passions Emanate ∧Uncurbed∧ in their Eternal Glory∟.⌐ The Fool shall not enter into Heaven let him be ever so Holy. Holiness is not The Price of Enterance into Heaven∟.⌐ ∧Those who are cast out Are All Those who having no Passions of their own because No Intellec*t*, Have spent their lives in Curbing & Governing other Peoples by the various arts of Poverty & Cruelty of all Kinds∟.⌐ Wo Wo Wo to You Hypocrites∟.⌐ Even Murder the Courts of Justice∟,⌐ ∧∧more merciful than the Church∟,⌐∧∧ are compelld to allow is not done in Passion but in Cool Blooded design & Intention∟.⌐ ∧[2]

Page 90, part u   is deleted by a single stroke.
   [1] The deleted word Erdman (p. 553) reads as 'Forgiven'.

Page 87, part z   [2] 'Men are admitted . . . Enterance into Heaven' is written sideways to the right margin, and (on the other side of 'The Caverns of the Grave . . .')
'Those who are . . . Intention' appears sideways to the left margin. For the Order of Compositions, see p. 962.

ˏThe Modern Church Crucifies Christ with the Head Down-
wardsʟ·ˌˏ¹

[*Page 92, part x*]

Many Persons such as Paine & Voltaire ˏwith ˏˏsome ofˏˏ
the Ancient Greeksˏ say 'we will not Converse concerning
Good & Evilʟ,ˌ we will live in Paradise & Libertyʟ·ˌ' You may
do So in Spirit but not in the ˏMortalˏ Body as you [pre *del*]
pretend till after the Last Judgment for in Paradise they have no
Corporeal ˏ& Mortalˏ Bodyʟ;ˌ that originated with the Fall
& was calld Death & cannot be removed but by a Last Judg-
mentʟ;ˌ while we are in the world of Mortality we Must
Sufferʟ·ˌ The Whole Creation Groans to be deliverdʟ;ˌ there
will always be as many Hypocrites born as Honest Men &
they will always have superior Power in Mortal Thingsʟ·ˌ
You cannot have Liberty in this World without ˏwhat you
callˏ Moral Virtue & you cannot have Moral Virtue without
the Slavery of [half *del*] that half of the Human Race who
hate ˏwhat you Callˏ Moral Virtueʟ·ˌ

The Nature of Hatred & Envy & of All the Mischiefs in the
World are here depictedʟ·ˌ No one Envies or Hates one of his
Own Partyʟ;ˌ even the devils love one another in their wayʟ;ˌ
they torment one another for other reasons than Hate or
Envyʟ;ˌ these are only employd against the Just. Neither can
Seth Envy Noah or Elijah Envy Abraham but they may both
of them Envy The Success

[*Page 93*]

of Satan or of Og or Molechʟ·ˌ The Horse never Envies the
Peacock nor the Sheep the Goat but they Envy a Rival in Life
& Existence whose ways & means exceed their ownʟ,ˌ let him
be of what Class of Animals he willʟ;ˌ a dog will envy a Cat
who is pamperd at [his *del*] ˏtheˏ expense of his comfort as I

---

¹ 'The Modern . . . Downwards' is written sideways in the last available space
in the top left corner and is not marked for entry.

Pages 92–93 For the Orders of Composition, see pp. 965–6.

Page 91, Order of Composition: (1) Part v at the top of the page above the sketch was
probably written first, (2) Followed by part w in a smaller hand below the sketch;
(3) Part y ¶1 is written sideways from the left margin to the sketch, (4) Followed
by ¶2 written sideways to the right margin, neither passage being clearly con-
nected with any other.

have often seen₎.₎ The Bible never tells us that Devils torment
one another thro Envy₎;₎ it is ∧thro∧ this that [makes *del*] they
torment the Just but for what do they torment one another₎?₎
I answer For the Coercive Laws of Hell₎,₎ Moral Hypocrisy.
They torment a Hypocrite when he is discoverd₎,₎ they Punish
a Failure in the tormentor who has sufferd the Subject of his
torture to Escape₎.₎ In Hell all is Self Righteousness₎;₎ there is
no such thing there as Forgiveness of Sin₎;₎ he who does For-
give Sin is Crucified as an Abettor of Criminals & he who
performs Works of Mercy in Any shape whatever is punishd &
if possible destroyd not thro envy or Hatred or Malice but
thro Self Righteousness that thinks it does God Service₎,₎ which
God is Satan₎.₎ ∧They do not Envy one another₎.₎ They con-
temn ∧∧& despise∧∧ one another₎.₎∧ Forgiveness of Sin is only
at the Judgment Seat of Jesus the Saviour where the Accuser
is cast out not because he Sins but because he torments the
Just & makes them do what he condemns as Sin & what he
knows is opposite to their own Identity₎.₎

It is not because Angels are Holier than Men or Devils that
makes them Angels but because they do not Expect Holiness
from one another but from God only₎.₎

The Player is a liar when he Says 'Angels are happier than

[*Page 94*]

Men because they are better'₎.₎ Angels are happier than Men
∧& Devils∧ because they are not always Prying after Good &
Evil in one another & eating the Tree of Knowledge for Satans
Gratification₎.₎

Thinking as I do that the Creator of this World is a very
Cruel Being & being a Worshipper of Christ I cannot help
saying 'the Son O how unlike the Father₎!₎ First God Almighty
comes with a Thump on the Head₎,₎ Then Jesus Christ comes
with a balm to heal it₎.₎'

Page 94, Order of Composition: (1) The top paragraph continuing from p. 93 was
written first with space to spare above the sketches; (2) The prose at the bottom
('The Last Judgment . . . Last Judgment &') is in the same hand and ink as 1
above and may have been written at the same time; (3) 'Thinking as I do . . .
heal it' is written in a larger, freer hand with a browner ink than 1 and 2 above,
goes across the top and to the left of the sketch, and was probably written rather
later.

The Last Judgment is an Overwhelming of Bad Art & Science. Mental Things are alone Real_L;⌋ what is Calld Corporeal Nobody Knows of its Dwelling Place_L;⌋ ᴧit᷃ is in Fallacy & its Existence an Imposture_L.⌋ Where is the Existence Out of Mind or Thought_L?⌋ Where is it but in the Mind of a Fool_L?⌋ Some People flatter themselves that there will be No Last Judgment &

[*Page 95*]

that Bad Art will be adopted & mixed with Good Art_L,⌋ That Error or Experiment will make a Part of Truth & they Boast that it is its Foundation_L;⌋ these People flatter themselves_L.⌋ I will not flatter them_L.⌋ Error is Created_L,⌋ Truth is Eternal_L.⌋ Error or Creation will be Burned up & then & not till Then Truth or Eternity will appear_L.⌋ It is Burnt up the Moment Men cease to behold it_L.⌋ I assert for My Self that I do not behold the outward Creation & that to me it is hindrance & not Action_L;⌋ it is as the Dirt upon my feet_L,⌋ No part of Me. 'What' it will be Questiond 'When the Sun rises do you not See a round Disk of fire somewhat like a Guinea_L?⌋' O no no I see an Innumerable company of the Heavenly host crying 'Holy Holy Holy is the [G *del*] Lord God Almighty_L!⌋' I question not my Corporeal or Vegetative Eye any more than I would Question a Window concerning a Sight_L.⌋ I look thro it & not with it_L.⌋

[*Page 91, part w*]

Many Suppose that before [Adam *del*] [Th *del*] ᴧthe Creationᴧ All was Solitude & Chaos_L.⌋ This is the most pernicious Idea that can enter the Mind as it takes away all Sublimity from the Bible & Limits All Existence to Creation & to Chaos_L,⌋ To the Time & Space fixed by the Corporeal Vegetative Eye & leaves the Man who entertains such an Idea the habitation of Unbelieving Demons_L.⌋ Eternity Exists and All things in Eternity Independent of Creation which was an act of Mercy_L.⌋ I have

[*Page 92*]

represented those who are in Eternity by some in a Cloud within the Rainbow that Surrounds the Throne_L;⌋ [they *del*] they merely appear as in a Cloud when any thing of Creation

1027

Redemption or Judgment are the Subjects of Contemplation
tho their Whole Contemplation is Concerning these thingsₗ;⅃
the Reason they so appear is The Humiliation of ∧the Reason
& doubting∧ Selfhood & the Giving all up to Inspirationₗ.⅃
By this it will be seen that I do not consider either the Just or
the Wicked to be in a Supreme State but to be every one of
them States of the Sleep [of *del*] which the Soul may fall into
in its deadly dreams of Good & Evil when it leaves Paradise
[with *del*] ∧following∧ the Serpentₗ.⅃

[Page 91, part y]

The Greeks represent Chronos or Time as a very aged Manₗ;⅃
this is Fable but the Real Vision of Time is in Eternal Youthₗ.⅃
I have ∧however∧ Somewhat accomodated my Figure of Time
to ∧the∧ Common opinion as I myself am also infected with
it & my Visions also infected & I see Time Agedₗ,⅃ alas too
much soₗ.⅃

Allegories are things that Relate to Moral Virtuesₗ.⅃ Moral
Virtues do not Existₗ;⅃ they are Allegories & dissimulations
But Time & Space are Real Beings ₗ,⅃ a Male & a Femaleₗ.⅃
Time is a Manₗ,⅃ Space is a Woman & her Masculine Portion
is Deathₗ.⅃

[End of the VISION OF THE LAST JUDGMENT.]

('PUBLIC ADDRESS')

[*Page 65, part p*]

Chaucers Canterbury Pilgrims
Being a Complete Index of Human Characters as
they appear Age after Age

[*Page 56, part a*]

This Day is Publishd Advertizements to Blakes Canterbury
Pilgrims from Chaucer, Containing Anecdotes of Artists. Price
6ᵈ

[*Page 1, part ff*]

If Men of weak Capacities [in Art *del*] have alone the Power
of Execution in Art Mʳ B has now put to the test. If to Invent
& to draw well hinders the Executive Power in Art & his
Strokes are still to be Condemnd because they are unlike those
of Artists who are Unacquainted with drawing [& the ac-
companying *del*] is now to be decided by The Public⌊.⌋ Mʳ B s
Inventive Powers & his Scientific knowledge of drawing is on
all hands acknowledgd⌊;⌋ it only remains to be Certified whether
[The Fools hand or the *del*] Physiognomic Strength & Power is
to give Place to Imbecility⌊.⌋ ∧In a Work of Art it is not fine
tints that are required but Fine Forms⌊.⌋ Fine Tints without
Fine Forms are always the Subterfuge of the Blockhead⌊.⌋∧¹
Raphael Sublime &ᶜ

[*Page 39, part ddd*]

Raphael Sublime Majestic Graceful Wise
His [Execution *altered to*] Executive Power must I despise⌊?⌋
Rubens Loud Vulgar Stupid Ignorant
His power of Execution I must grant⌊?⌋

'Public Address' *Pages 65, 56* For the Orders of Composition, see pp. 960, 956.

Page 1, parts ff, gg ¹ 'In a Work of Art . . . Subterfuge of the Blockhead' and 'In
a Work of Art . . . are loathsom' are additions in Brown ink; the rest of the page is
in Black ink.

Learn the [*illeg words del*] Laborious stumble of a Fool
And from an Idiots Actions form my rule∟?⌐
Go Send your Children to the Slobbering School∟!⌐

[*Page 1, part gg*]

[and whether (an unending[?] and an¹ *del*) an unabated Study
& practise of forty Years for I devoted myself to Engraving
in my Earliest Youth are sufficient to elevate me above the
Mediocrity to which I have hitherto been the victim *del*] ∧In
a Work of Art it is not Fine Tints that are required but Fine
Form, fine Tints without, are loathsom∟.⌐∧

I account it a Public Duty respectfully to address myself to
The chalcographic Society² & to Express to them my opinion
the result of the incessant Practise & Experience of Many
Years that Engraving [is *altered to*] as [in a most wretched
state *del*] [of *del*] [arising from an *del*] an ∧Art is Lost in England∧
∧owing to an artfully propagated∧ opinion that drawing spoils
an Engraver∟.⌐ [which opinion has been held out to (my *del*)
me by such men as Flaxman Romney Stothard &ᶜ *del*] I
request the society to inspect my Print of which drawing is the
Foundation & indeed the Superstructure∟;⌐ it is drawing on
Copper as Painting ought to be drawing on Canvas or any
other [table *del*] ∧Surface∧ & nothing Else∟.⌐+³ I request
likewise that the Society will compare the Prints of Bartol-
louzzi Woolett Strange &c with the Old English Portraits∟,⌐
that is ∧compare the Modern Art∧ with the Art as it Existed
Previous to the Enterance of Vandyke & Rubens into this

Page 39, part ddd l. 5 is written as an extension of l. 4; l. 7 is written below it
(avoiding part eee, 'I do not condemn Pope . . .'), and l. 6 appears *upside-down*
between them. For the Order of Composition, see p. 950.

'Laborious stumble' is written over an illegible erasure which in turn is over part
of perhaps three illegible erased lines, beside which are a series of about 31 tiny
blind strokes in two columns made as if with a knife blade (perhaps a metal pro-
jection of an erasing instrument). Parts of the lines may be very tentatively read
as

Learn[?]	led
Stumble[?]	

Page 1, part gg   ¹ For the deletion Erdman (p. 560) reads 'an artist who has carried
on'.

² Presumably this is the Society of Engravers, whose President was at one time
Blake's former fellow-apprentice and partner James Parker. Blake does not appear
in the membership list printed in their *Rules, Orders, and Regulations* (1804).

³ The '+' suggests that an unidentified passage should be entered here.

Country ˄since which English Engraving is Lost˄ & I am sure [of the *del*] [*the*] Result ˄of this Comparison˄ will be that the Society must be of my Opinion that Engraving by Losing drawing has Lost all character & all Expression without which ˄The˄ Art is Lost⌊.⌋

[*Page 51, part b*]

In this Plate Mʳ B has resumed the Style with which he set out in life [& *del*] of which Heath & Stothard were the awkward imitators at that time, it is the Style of Alb Durers Hist[o]ries[?] & the old Engravers which cannot be imitated by any one who does not understand drawing & which according to *H*eath & Stothard Flaxman & even Romney Spoils an Engraver for Each of these Men have repeatedly asserted this Absurdity to me in Condemnation

[*Page 52*]

of my Work & approbation of He˄a˄ths lame imitation⌊,⌋ Stothard being such a fool as to suppose that his blundering blurs can be made out & delineated by any Engraver who knows how to cut dots & lozenges equally well with those little prints which I engraved after him five & twenty years ago & by which he got his reputation as a draughtsman⌊.⌋[1]

The manner in which my Character both as an artist & a Man ˄has been blasted these thirty years˄ may be seen particu-

---

Page 51: Order of Composition: (1) Illegible pencil lines at the top of the page were probably the first words on it; (2) Part b was written at the bottom carefully avoiding both sketches; (3) 'The Everlasting Gospel' part f, ll. 72–9 were written below the pencil passage down the left margin, and ll. 80–4, 91–3 down the right margin, both carefully skirting the sketches and stopping above the bottom prose; (4) ll. 85–6 were added at the top of the right column (above l. 80) with a stroke to show they should come in after l. 84; (5) ll. 87–90 were written on top of the top pencil lines, and a stroke clearly indicates that they are to follow l. 86.

Page 52, part b For the Order of Composition, see p. 955.

[1] Blake engraved small plates after Stothard in 1780 (for W. Enfield, *The Speaker*), 13 in 1782 (for *Poetical Works of John Scott, Esq.*, J. Bonnycastle's *Introduction to Mensuration, Poetical Works of Geoff. Chaucer*, the *Lady's Pocket Book*, the *Novelist's Magazine* vols. viii–ix), and 13 in 1783 (for the *Novelist's Magazine* vol. x, *A Select Collection of English Songs* [ed. J. Ritson], Ariosto's *Orlando Furioso*, tr. J. Hoole), as well as 3 large plates for D. Fenning and J. Collyer, *A New System of Geography* (1785), E. Kimpton, *A New and Complete History of the Holy Bible* (?1781), and *The Genuine and Complete Works of Flavius Josephus* (?1786). Blake's reference to 'those little prints which I engraved after him five & twenty years ago' suggests that the time of writing is about 1808.

'Heath' is the engraver James Heath (1757–1834).

larly in a Sunday Paper cal[*l*]d the Examiner[1] Publishd in
Beaufort Building*s*[2] ˄(We all know that Editors of Newspapers
trouble their heads very little about art & science & that they
are always paid for wh[at] they put [in] [up]on these ungracious
Subjects˪)˩,˄ & the manner in which I have routed out the
nest of villains will be seen in a Poem concerning my Three
years ˄Herculean˄ Labours at Felpham[3] which I will soon
publish.[4] Secret Calumny & open Professions of Friendship are
common enough all the world over but have never been so good
an occasion of Poetic Imagery˪.˩ When a Base Man means to
be your Enemy he always begins with being your Friend˪.˩

[*Page 53*]

Flaxman cannot deny that one of the very first Monuments he
did I gratuitously designd for him[5] ˄at the same time he was
blasting my character as an Artist to Macklin my Employer[6]
as Macklin told me at the time˪;˩˄[7] how much of his Homer

[1] Blake is described as an 'absurd' artist, a 'Quack', and 'an unfortunate
lunatic' in articles by Leigh and Robert Hunt dealing with his *Grave* designs and
his exhibition in the *Examiner* for 7 and 28 Aug. 1808 and 17 Sept. 1809 (*Blake
Records*, 195–8, 215–18).

[2] A cross after 'Beaufort Buildings' is repeated before 'We all know . . . upon
these ungracious Subjects', which is written at the bottom of the page, the last
four words continued on p. 53.

[3] Blake lived under the patronage of William Hayley at Felpham in Sussex
from Sept. 1800 to Sept. 1803.

[4] *Jerusalem* (1804–?20), the work apparently intended here, begins: 'After my
three years slumber on the banks of the Ocean, I again display my Giant forms to
the Public' (pl. 3). In it appears 'Hand', evidently so named from the pointing hand
used in the *Examiner* to identify the editor's pieces by Leigh Hunt, who, with his
brothers Robert and John, is probably intended by Blake's 'nest of villains'. No
surviving copy of *Jerusalem* can be dated earlier than 1818, but Blake seems to have
thought of the work as finished about 1810.

Page 53: Order of Composition: (1) Part b at the top ('Flaxman cannot . . . will know',
the insertion made before the last four words were written) and bottom ('Many
People . . . that Wooletts') were written after the sketch; (2) 'The Everlasting
Gospel' part k, ll. 26–83 (see pp. 1066–8) were written next.

[5] After he had been in Rome five years, 'J. Flaxman [*made sketches*] from memory
of three drawings of Blake June 1792', according to the note he made on the page
(reproduced in *Blake Records*, pl. vi). No other evidence concerning this allegation
is known.

[6] Blake engraved 'Morning [*and*] Evening Amusement', 'Robin Hood and
Clorinda', and 'The Fall of Rosamond' for Thomas Macklin on 10, 21 Aug. 1782,
30 March, and 1 Oct. 1783.

[7] A '+' after 'designd for him' links it with another before 'at the same time . . .
at the time' written between two dividing strokes two lines below.

& Dante he will allow to be mine I do not know as he went far enough off to Publish them ʟ,ʟ even to Italy,[1] but the Public will know & Posterity will know ʟ.ʟ

Many People are So foolish [*as*] to think that they can wound Mʳ Fuseli over my Shoulder ʟ;ʟ[2] they will find themselves mistaken ʟ;ʟ they could not wound even Mʳ Barry So ʟ.ʟ[3]

A Certain Portrait Painter said To me in a boasting way 'Since I have Practisd Painting I have lost all idea of Drawing.' Such a Man must know that I lookd upon him with contempt ʟ;ʟ he did not care for this any more than West did who hesitated & equivocated with me upon the same Subject at which time he asserted that Wooletts

[*Page 55*]

Prints were superior to Basires[4] because they had more Labour & Care ʟ;ʟ now this is contrary to the truth ʟ.ʟ Woolett did not know how to put so much labour into a head or a foot as Basire did ʟ;ʟ he did not know how to draw the Leaf of a tree ʟ;ʟ all his Study was clean strokes & mossy tints ʟ;ʟ how then shall he be able to make use of either Labour or Care unless the Labour & Care of Imbecillity ʟ?ʟ The Lifes Labour of Mental Weakness scarcely Equals one Hour of the Labour of Ordinary Capacity like the full Gallop of the Gouty Man to the ordinary walk of youth & health ʟ.ʟ I allow that there is such a thing as high finishd Ignorance as there may be a fool or a Knave in an Embroiderd Coat but I say that the Embroidery of the Ignorant finisher is not like a Coat made by another but is an Emanation from Ignorance itself & its finishing is like its

[1] Flaxman's *Iliad*, *Odyssey*, and Dante designs were made in Rome in 1793, plates were engraved after all three sets at the same time, but though the first two sets were published in Rome in 1793, the Dante plates were not published until they appeared in Paris in 1802 and London in 1807 (see G. E. Bentley, Jr., *The Early Engravings of Flaxman's Classical Designs* [1964]).

[2] Blake may have been thinking of Robert Hunt's reviews of his *Grave* designs (1808) and his exhibition (1809) in the *Examiner* for 7 Aug. 1808 and 17 Sept. 1809, in which Fuseli is described as 'a frantic' 'on the verge of insanity', partly because of his printed recommendation of Blake's *Grave* designs (*Blake Records*, 195, 215).

[3] I do not know the significance of this comment. No known published or manuscript contemporary reference to Blake links Blake with Barry.

Page 55 [4] William Woollett engraved 'The Death of General Wolf' (1776) and 'The Battle of La Hogue' (1781) after Benjamin West (1738–1820).

master⌊,⌋ The Lifs Labour of Five Hundred Idiots⌊,⌋ for he never does the Work Himself⌊.⌋¹

What is Calld the English Style of Engraving such as proceeded from the Toilettes of Woolett & Strange (for theirs were ⌃Fribbles⌃ Toilettes) can never produce Character & Expression. I knew the Men intimately from their Intimacy with Basire my Master & knew them both to be heavy lumps of Cunning & Ignorance as their works Shew to all the Continent who Laugh at the Contemptible Pretences of Englishmen to Improve Art before they even know the first [lines *del*] ⌃Beginnings⌃ of Art⌊.⌋ I hope this Print will redeem my Country from this Coxcomb Situation & shew that it is only some Englishmen

[*Page 56*]

and not All who are thus ridiculous in their Pretences⌊.⌋ Advertizements in Newspapers are no proofs of Popular approbation but often the Contrary⌊.⌋ A Man who Pretends to Improve Fine Art does not know what Fine Art is⌊.⌋ Ye English Engravers must come down from your high flights⌊,⌋ ye must condescend to study Marc Antonio & Albert Durer⌊.⌋ Ye must begin before you attempt to finish or improve & when you have begun you will know better than to think of improving what cannot be improvd⌊.⌋ It is very true what you have said

[*Page 57*]

for these thirty two Years⌊.⌋ I am Mad or Else you are So⌊;⌋ both of us cannot be in our right Senses⌊.⌋ Posterity will judge by our Works⌊.⌋ Wooletts & Stranges works are like those of Titian & Correggio⌊,⌋ the Lifs Labour of Ignorant journeymen⌊,⌋ Suited to the Purposes of Commerce no doubt⌊,⌋ for Commerce Cannot endure Individual Merit⌊;⌋ its insatiable Maw must be fed by What All Can do Equally well⌊;⌋ at least

¹ 'I allow . . . Work Himself' seems to be written smaller than the preceding and succeeding passages and may be an addition squeezed in at a later date.

Page 56 For the Order of Composition, see p. 956.

Page 57: Order of Composition: (1) Parts b and c were written first, above and below the pencil sketch (divided after 'as I have'); (2) They were continued probably with part e written sideways from the sketch to the right margin, and (3) Completed by part f written in a paler ink to the left of the sketch and not clearly placed in the text.

'Public Address' (*Notebook* p. 60)

it is so in England as I have found to my Cost these Forty Years⌊·⌋

Wooletts best works were Etchd by Jack Brown⌊·⌋[1] Woolett Etchd very bad himself. Stranges Prints were when I knew him all done by Aliamet[2] & his french journeyman whose name I forget.

[*Part e*]

'The Cottagers' & 'Jocund Peasants'⌊,⌋ the 'Views in Kew Gardens'⌊,⌋ 'Foots Cray'⌊,⌋ & 'Diana & Acteon'⌊,⌋[3] & in short all that are Calld Wooletts were Etchd by Jack Browne & in Wooletts works the Etching is All tho even in these a single leaf of a tree is never correct⌊·⌋

[*Page 56, part d*]

Such Prints as Woolett & Strange producd will do for those who choose to purchase the lifes labour of Ignorance & Imbecillity in Preference to the Inspired Moments of Genius & Animation⌊·⌋

[*Page 60, part h*]

I also knew something of Tom Cooke who engraved after Hogarth⌊·⌋[4] Cooke wished to give to Hogarth what he could take from Rafael⌊,⌋ that is Outline & Mass & Colour but he could not⌊·⌋ [& Hogarth with all his Merit *word illeg*[5] *del*]

---

[1] John Browne (1741–1801) was apprenticed as an engraver to Woollett, and some of the landscapes on which the two men collaborated acknowledge that the preliminary etching work was Browne's.

[2] François Germain Aliamet (1734–90), French engraver.

[3] 'The Cottagers' (1765) and 'The Jocund Peasants' (1767), both etched by Browne and engraved by Woollett after Cornelius Du Sart, 'A View of Foots-Craye Place in Kent, the Seat of Bourchier Cleeve Esqʳ' (1760), 'Diana and Acteon' (1764) after Filippo Lauri are all separate plates; 'A View of the Palace at Kew, from the Lawn', 'North Prospect of the Ruin in the Gardens of Kew', and 'A View of the South Side of the Ruins at Kew' after Jos: Kirby appeared in William Chambers, *Plans, Elevations, Sections, and Perspective Views of the Gardens ana Buildings At Kew in Surry*, The Seat of Her Royal Highness The Princess Dowager of Wales (1763), nos. 36, 41, 42, all engraved by Woollett.

Page 56 Part d is written sideways in the right margin and is not marked for entry.

Page 60 Part h is written in a large hand at the top of the page and is not marked for entry. For the Order of Composition, see p. 958.

[4] Thomas Cook (1744?–1818) engraved 160 plates for *The Genuine Works of William Hogarth*, ed. J. Nichols & G. Steevens, 2 vols. (1808–10).

[5] For the illegible word Erdman (p. 563) reads 'never g'.

[*Part 57, part f*]

I do not pretend to Paint better than Rafael or Mch Angelo ⌃or Julio Romano or Alb Durer⌃ but I do Pretend to Paint finer than Rubens or Remb^t or Correggio or Titian. I do not Pretend to Engrave finer than Alb *D*urer Goltzius Sadeler or Edelinck but I do pretend to Engrave finer than Strange Woolett Hall¹ or Bartolozzi, ⌃& All⌃ because I understand drawing which they understood not⌐.⌐

[*Page 39, part eee*]

I do not condemn Rubens Rembran[*d*]t or Titian because they did not understand Drawing but because they did not Understand Coloring⌐;⌐ how long shall I be forced to beat this into Mens Ears⌐?⌐ I do not condemn [Bartolozzi *del*] ⌃Strange⌃ or Woolett because they did not understand Drawing but because they did not understand [col *del*] Graving⌐.⌐ I do not condemn Pope or Dryden because they did not Understand Imagination but because they did not understand Verse⌐.⌐ Their Colouring Graving & Verse can never be applied to Art⌐.⌐ That is not either colouring Graving or Verse which is Unappropriate to the Subject⌐.⌐ He who makes a design must know the Effect & Colouring Proper to be put to that design & will never take that of Rubens Rembrandt or Titian to [put *del*] ⌃turn⌃ that which [a *del*] is Soul & Life into a Mill or Machine⌐.⌐

[*Page 46, part ggg*]

They say there is no Strait Line in Nature⌐;⌐ this Is a Lie like all that they say. For there is Every Line in Nature But I will tell them what is Not in Nature. An Even Tint is not in Nature⌐;⌐ it produces Heaviness. Natures Shadows ⌃are⌃ Ever

Page 57 Part f is written, in a paler ink than the rest of the page, to the left of the sketch, and is not marked for entry.

¹ Henri Goltzius (1558–1617), or perhaps Hubert Goltzius (1526–83), both Dutch painters and engravers; Jean Sadeler (d. 1600), or conceivably his brothers Raphael (b. 1555) or Gilles (1570–1629), all Flemish engravers; Gerard Edelinck (1640–1707), celebrated Belgian engraver, inventor of the lozenge-dotted style; John Hall (1739–97), English engraver.

Page 39 'I do not . . . to the Subject' is written sideways from the left margin to the right, skirting part ddd above, and 'If I eer grow . . . .'. 'He who makes . . . Machine' continues the part *upside-down* at the top above the page above part ddd. For the Order of Composition, see p. 950.

'Public Address' (*Notebook* p. 57)

varying, & a Ruled Sky that is quite Even never can Produce a Natural Sky⌊,⌋ the same with every Object in a Picture⌊;⌋ its Spots are its beauties⌊.⌋ Now Gentlemen Critics how do you like this⌊?⌋ You may rage but what I say I will prove by Such Practise & have already done so that you will rage to your own destruction⌊.⌋ Woolett I knew very intimately by his intimacy with Basire & I knew him to be one of the most ignorant fellows that I ever knew. A Machine is not a Man nor a Work of Art⌊,⌋ it is destructive of Humanity & of Art⌊.⌋ the word Machination [*illeg word*[1] *del*]

> Delicate Hands & Heads will never appear
> While Titians &ᶜ as in the Book of Moonlight p 5⌊.⌋[2]

Woolett I know did not know how to Grind his Graver⌊.⌋ I know this⌊;⌋ he has often proved his Ignorance before me at Basires by laughing at Basires Knife tools &[3]

[*Page 47*]

ridiculing the Forms of Basires other Gravers till Basire was quite dashd & out of Conceit with what he himself knew but his Impudence had a Contrary Effect on me⌊.⌋ Englishmen have been so used to Journeymens undecided bungling that they cannot bear the firmness of a Masters Touch⌊.⌋ Every Line is the Line of Beauty⌊;⌋ it is only fumble & Bungle which cannot draw a Line⌊,⌋ this only is Ugliness⌊.⌋ That is not a Line which Doubts & Hesitates in the Midst of its Course⌊.⌋

[*Page 57, part c*]

Commerce is so far from being beneficial to Arts or to Empire that it is destructive of both ʌas all their History Shewsʌ for the above Reason of Individual Merit being its Great

---

Page 46 [1] The illegible deletion, which appears at the end of the line, is read as 'seems' by Erdman (p. 564).

[2] In the space between the end of one line ('Machination') and the beginning of the next ('Woolett I know') is 'Delicate Hands . . . Book of Moonlight p 5'. Its appearance on the page does not distinguish it from the preceding and succeeding passages. It may have preceded the surrounding prose and have no connection with it.

No other reference to the 'Book of Moonlight' is known.

[3] 'Woolett I know . . . tools &' is in a browner ink than the words above.

Page 47 'ridiculing the Forms . . . Masters Touch' is written below 'If you play a Game' (from which it is separated by a stroke across the page—see p. 954) and is continued sideways from the right margin with 'Every Line . . . of its Course'.

hatred. Empires flourish till they become Commercial & then they are scatterd abroad to the four winds⌊.⌋

[*Page 58*]

In this manner the English Public have been imposed upon for many Years under the impression that Engraving & Painting are somewhat Else besides drawing⌊.⌋ Painting is Drawing on Canvas & Engraving is drawing on Copper & Nothing Else & he who pretends to be either Painter or Engraver without being a Master of Drawing is an Impostor. We may be Clever as Pugilists but as Artists we are & have long been the Contempt of the Continent⌊.⌋ [*Illeg word*[1] *del*.] Gravelot once Said to My Master Basire [you *del*] '∧de∧ English may be very clever in [your *del*] ∧deir∧ own opinions but [you *del*] ∧dey∧ do not draw [th *del*] de draw⌊.⌋'[2]

Resentment for Personal Injuries has had some share in this Public address But Love to My Art & Zeal for my Country a much Greater.

[*Page 59, part g*]

Men think they can Copy Nature as Correctly as I copy Imagination⌊;⌋[3] this they will find Impossib*le*, & all the Copies or Pretended Copiers of Nature from Rembra[*nd*]t to Reynolds Prove that Nature becomes [tame(?) *del*] to its Victim nothing but Blots & Blurs. Why are Copiers of Nature Incorrect while Copiers of Imagination are Correct⌊?⌋ *T*his is manifest to all⌊.⌋

[*Page 60, part i*]

The Originality of this Production makes it necessary to say a few words⌊.⌋ While the Works [of Translators *del*] of Pope & Dryden are lookd upon as [in the Same class of *del*] the Same Art with those of Milton & Shakespeare⌊,⌋ while the works of Strange & Woollett are lookd upon as the Same Art with those

---

Page 58 [1] For the illegible word Erdman (p. 563) reads 'Aliamet'.

[2] Blake cannot have been a witness to this encounter, for Hubert François Gravelot (1699–1773), draughtsman and book illustrator, was apparently not in England after 1754, nor was Blake ever in France.

Page 59 For the Order of Composition, see p. 957.

[3] ' "To learn the language of art, copy for ever, is my rule," said he. But he never painted his pictures from models. "Models are difficult—enslave one—efface from one's mind a conception or reminiscence which was better" ' (Gilchrist [1863], i. 370).

of Rafael & Albert Durer there can be no Art in a Nation but such as is Subservient to the interest of the Monopolizing Trader⌐.⌐[whose *illeg word del*] ∧[*illeg word del*]∧ ([who Manufactures Art by the Hands of Ignorant Journeymen till at length Christian Charity is held out as a Motive to encourage a Blockhead & he is Counted the Greatest Genius who can sell a Good for Nothing Commodity for a Great Price⌐.⌐ Obedience to the Will of the Monopolist is calld Virtue *del*]

[*Page 61*]

[And the really ∧Industrious∧ Virtuous & Independent Barry is driven out to make room for a pack of Idle Sycophants with whitlors on their fingers *del*]) Englishmen rouze yourselve*s* from the fatal Slumber into which Booksellers & Trading Dealers have thrown you Under the artfully propagated pretense that a Translation or a Copy of any kind can be as honourable to a Nation as An Original⌐,⌐ [Belying *del*] Be-lying the English Character in that well known Saying 'Englishmen Improve what others Invent⌐.⌐' This Even Hogarths Works Prove

[*Page 62*]

a detestable Fals[*e*]hood⌐.⌐ No Man Can Improve An Original Invention. [Since Hogarths time we have had very few Efforts of Originality *del*] ∧Nor can an Original Invention Exist without Execution Organized & minutely delineated & Articulated Either by God or Man⌐.⌐∧

Page 61 For the Order of Composition, see p. 958.

Page 62: Order of Composition: (**1**) The blank page was first filled straight through with part i, ll. 1–4, 7–8, 19–22 and part k; (**2**) These were probably followed by the substitution of 'Nor can an Original Invention . . . God or Man' inserted above the poem and bending round (after 'Organized') sideways from the right margin; (**3**) Part o, *upside-down* at the bottom of the page, the last two words bending into the left margin, is not marked for entry; (**4**) Part r was written sideways from the left margin beside the poem and not marked for entry; (**5**) Part f, written sideways from the poem to the right margin, is not marked for entry; (**6**) The poem in part j was renumbered before the first additions were made to it; (**7**) ll. 5–6, 9–10, 17–18 (each couplet written as one line) were added, carefully avoiding the marginal prose passages; (**8**) ll. 11–12 were written as one line below l. 20 and were deleted without being marked for entry (their position here is therefore conjectural); (**9**) 'Blakes apology for his Catalogue' is squeezed between ll. 20 and 11–12 and may be intended to head the poem (where the prose additions left no room for a title)—see p. 65 (p. 1041) where two new lines (ll. 21–2) added to this poem contain Blake's 'sweet apology'; (**10**) ll. 15–16, written on p. 63, were entered after l. 14 in the copy made on p. 65.

[*Part r*]

I do not mean Smoothd up & Niggled & Poco Pend [but *del*]
ˏand all the beauties pickd out [*illeg word del*] & blurrd &
blotted butˏ Drawn with a firm hand ˏ& decidedˏ¹ at once
[with all its Spots & Blemishes which are beauties & not faults
del] like Fuseli & Michael Angeloʟˏ، Shakespeare & Miltonʟˏ،

[*Part j*]

Blakes apology for his Catalogue

3 Dryden in Rhyme cries 'Milton only Plannd'ʟ;،
4 Every Fool shook his bells throughout the Landʟ;،
5 Tom Cooke cut Hogarth down with his clean gravingʟ;،
6 [How many *del*] Thousands ˏofˏ Connoisseurs ˏwith joyˏ
  ran ravingʟ!،

Having Given great offence by writing in Prose
Ill write in Rhymes as Soft as [feather Bows(?) *del*] ˏBar-
tollozeˏʟˏ،

1 Some blush at what others can see no crime in
2 But Nobody [at all *del*] sees ˏanyˏ harm in Rhymingʟˏ،
13 Poor Schiavonetti died of the Cromekʟˏ،
14 A thing thats tied about the Examiners neckʟˏ،
[*W*ho cries all art is fraud(?) & Genius a trick
And Blake is an unfortunate Lunatic *del*]
7 Thus Hayley on his toilette seeing the Sope
8 Says 'Homer is very much improved by Pope[.]'

[*Page 63*]

Ive given great provision to my Foes
And now Ill lead my false friends by the Noseʟˏ،

---

¹ '& decided' is written below the line because the previous addition took up the space above the line.

l. 1: 'Milton only Plannd'; cf. part q, l. 5 (p. 1041), where this mistake is repeated, and part vv (p. 1049) where the idea is correctly attributed to Nat Lee.

l. 6: 'Bartolloze' means in the style of the engraver Francesco Bartollozzi (1727–1815).

l. 9: Schiavonetti died 10 June 1810.

l. 10: Blake may have been thinking of R. H. Cromek's obituary 'Account of Mr. Schiavonetti' in the *Examiner* (1 July 1810), 412–14, in which the works by Schiavonetti which Cromek owned were especially praised.

l. 12: In an unsigned review of 'Mr. Blake's Exhibition' in the *Examiner* (17 Sept. 1809, pp. 605–6: see *Blake Records*, 216), Robert Hunt described Blake as 'an unfortunate lunatic, whose personal inoffensiveness secures him from confinement'.

ll. 13–14, 19–22: Numbers 7–12 may all have been different originally.

[*Page 62*]

Flaxman & Stothard smelling a sweet savour
Cry 'Blakified drawing spoils painter & Engraver'⌊,⌋
9 While I looking up to my Umbrella⌊,⌋
10 Resolvd to be a very Contrary Fellow⌊,⌋   [*20*]
11 Cry [Tom Cooke proves *del*] ˄Looking up˄ from [Circum-
    ference *del*] ˄Skumference˄ to Center
12 'No one can finish so high as the original Inventor⌊.⌋'   [*22*]

[*Page 65, part q*]

Having given great offence by writing in Prose
Ill write in Verse as soft as Bartelloze⌊.⌋
Some blush at what others can see no harm in
But nobody sees any harm in Rhyming⌊.⌋
Dryden in Rhyme cries 'Milton only plannd⌊;⌋'   [*5*]
Every Fool shook his bells throughout the land⌊;⌋
Tom Cooke cut Hogarth down with his clean graving⌊;⌋
Thousands of Connoisseurs with joy ran raving⌊.⌋
˄Thus˄ Hayley on his Toillette seeing his Sope
Cries 'Homer is very much improvd by Pope⌊.⌋'   [*10*]
˄Some say˄ Ive given great Provision to my foes
And ˄that˄ now I lead my false friends by the nose⌊.⌋
Flaxman & Stothard Smelling a sweet savour
Cry 'Blakified drawing spoils painter & Engraver⌊,⌋'
While I looking up to my Umbrella⌊,⌋   [*15*]
Resolved to be a very contrary fellow⌊,⌋
Cry looking quite from Skumference to Center
'No one can finish so high as the original Inventor⌊!⌋'
Thus Poor Schiavonetti died of the Cromek⌊,⌋
A thing that is tied around the Examiners neck⌊.⌋   [*20*]
This is my sweet apology to my friends
That I may put them in mind of their latter ends⌊.⌋   [*22*]

[*Page 62, part k*]

I have heard many People say 'Give me the Ideas. It is no
matter what words you put them into' & others say 'Give me
the Design⌊,⌋ it is no matter for the Execution.' These People
Know ˄Enough of Artifice but˄ Nothing Of Art. Ideas cannot

Page 65 ll. 1–15 are at the bottom of the page, and ll. 16–22 are written sideways
to the right margin. All are in a smaller hand than the rest of the page.

be Given but in their minutely Appropriate Words nor Can a
Design be made without its minutely Appropriate Execution∟˩
The unorganized Blots & Blurs of Rubens & Titian are not Art
nor can their Method ever express Ideas or Imaginations any
more than Popes Metaphysical Jargo[n] of Rhyming∟˩

[*Part o*]

Unappropriate Execution is the Most nauseous ∧of all∧ affecta-
tion & foppery∟˩

[*Part f*]

He who copies does not Execute∟;˩ he only Imitates what is
already Executed∟˩ Execution is only the result of Invention∟˩

[*Page 63, part 1*]

Whoever looks at any of the Great & Expressive Works ∧of
engraving∧ that have been Publishd by English Traders must
feel a Loathing & disgust & accordingly most Englishmen have
a Contempt for Art [which is the *del*] which is the Greatest
Curse that can fall upon a Nation∟˩

[*Part m*]

He who could represent Christ uniformly like a Drayman must
have Queer Conceptions∟,˩ consequently his Executi[o]n must
have been as Queer & those must be Queer fellows who give
great Sums for such nonsense & think it fine Art∟˩

[*Part u*]

The ∧Modern Chalcographic∧ Connoisseurs & Amateurs ad-
mire only the work of the journeyman Picking out of whites &
blacks in what is calld Tints∟;˩ they despise drawing which
despises them in retur*n*; they see only whether every thing is
coverd down but one spot of light∟˩

[*Part t*]

M^r B submits to a more severe tribunal∟;˩ he invites the ad-
mirers of old English Portraits to look at his Print∟˩

[*Page 64, part m*]

I do not know whether Homer is a Liar & that there is no
Such thing as Generous Contention∟˩ I know that all those

Page 63 Parts t and u are written to the left and right of the sketch, between parts
l and m, and are not marked for entry.

Pages 63–65 For the Orders of Composition, see pp. 959–60.

with whom I have Contended in Art have strove not to Excell but to Starve me out by Calumny & the Arts of Trading Combination⌊.⌋

[Page 66, part x]

It is Nonsense for Noblemen & Gentlemen to offer Premiums for the Encouragement of Art when such Pictures as these can be done without Premiums⌊;⌋ let them Encourage what Exists Already & not endeavour to counteract by tricks⌊;⌋ let it no more be said that Empires Encourage Arts for it is Arts that Encourage Empires⌊.⌋ Arts & Artists are Spiritual & laugh at Mortal Contingencies⌊.⌋ It is in their Power to hinder Instruction but not to Instruct just as it is in their Power to Murder a Man but not to make a Ma⌊n.⌋

[Part w]

Let us teach Buonaparte & whomsoever else it may concern That it is not Arts that follow & attend upon Empire[s *del*] but Empire[s *del*] that attends upon & follows [wherever(?) Art leads *del*] The Arts⌊.⌋

[Page 67, part z]

No Man of Sense[1] can think that an Imitation of the Objects of Nature is The Art of Painting or that such Imitation which any one may easily perform is worthy of Notice much less that such an Art should be the Glory [of *del*] & Pride of a Nation⌊.⌋ [& that the man who does this is *del*] The Italians laugh at English Connoisseurs who are [All *del*] ∧most of them∧ such silly Fellows as to believe this⌊.⌋

[Part aa]

A Man Sets himself down with Colours & with all the Articles of Painting⌊,⌋ he puts a Model before him & he Copies that so neat as to make it a Deception⌊;⌋ now let any Man of Sense ask himself one Question⌊:⌋ Is this Ar*t*? *C*an it be worthy of admiration to any body of Understandin*g*? Who could not

---

Page 66 Parts v, w, x are written over the sketch, and each is in a slightly different ink and pen.

Page 67 A stroke from 'No Man . . .' to the end of the first line of part v on p. 66 seems to indicate that part z should precede part v. Part aa is written sideways from the sketch to the right margin and was probably intended to follow part z.

[1] Cf. part y (p. 1044).

do this_L?_⌋ *W*hat man who has eyes and an ordinary share of patience cannot do this neatl*y*? Is this Art_L?_⌋ Or is it glorious to a Nation to produce such contemptible Copies_L?_⌋ Countrymen Countrymen do not suffer yourselves to be disgracd_L·_⌋

[*Page 66, part v*]

The English Artist may be assured that he is doing an injury & injustice to his Country while he studies & imitates the Effects of Nature. England will never rival Italy while we servilely cop*y* what the Wise Italians Rafael & Michael Angelo scorned_L,_⌋ nay abhorred as Vasari tells us_L·_⌋

> Call that the Public Voice which is their Error
> Like [to *del*] ˄as˄ a Monkey peeping in a Mirror
> Admires all his colours brown & warm
> And never once percieves his ugly form_L·_⌋   [*4*]

What kind of Intellects must he have who sees only the Colours of things & not the forms of Things_L?_⌋

[*Page 71, part bb*]

A Jockey that is any thing of a Jockey will never buy a Horse by the Colour & a Man who has got any brains will never buy a Picture by the Colour_L·_⌋

[*Part cc*]

When I tell any Truth it is not for the Sake of Convincing those who do not know it but for the Sake of defending those who Do_L·_⌋

[*Page 76, part y*]

No Man of Sense ever Supposes that Copying from Nature is the Art of Painting_L;_⌋ if the Art is no more than this it is no better than any other⌐˥s Manual Labour_L,_⌋ any body may do it & the fool often will do it best as it is a work of no Mind_L·_⌋

[*Page 78, part dd*]

The Greatest part of what are calld in England Old Pictures are Oil Colour Copies from Fresco originals_L;_⌋ the Comparison

Page 71 Parts bb and cc are written sideways to the left and right of the sketch. For the Order of Composition, see p. 1009.

Page 76 Part y is squeezed in above 'Vision of the Last Judgment' part k as two lines, the second curving round at the margin and returning *upside-down*. It has no clear connection with anything else on the page, but seems to be a draft of part z above (p. 1043).

'Public Address' (*Notebook* p. 18)

is Easily made & the Copy Detected⌐.⌐ Note I mean Fresco
Easel or Cabinet Pictures on Canvas & wood & Copper &ᶜ⌐.⌐

[*Page 86, part ee*]

The Painter hopes that his Friends Anytus [& *del*] Melitus ⌃&
Lycon⌃¹ will percieve that they are not now in Ancient Greece
& tho they can use the Poison of Calumny the English Public
will be convincd that such a Picture as this Could never be
Painted by a Madman or by one in a State of Outrageous
manners as these [Villains *del*] ⌃Bad Men⌃ both Print &
Publish by all the means in their Power. *T*he Painter begs
Public Protection & all will be well⌐.⌐

[*Page 17, part hh*]

I wonder who can say 'Speak no Ill of the dead' when it is
asserted in the Bible that the name of the Wicked shall Rot⌐.⌐²
It is Deistical Virtue I suppose but as I have none of this I
will pour Aqua fortis on the Name of the Wicked & turn it
into an Ornament & an Example to be Avoided by Some &
Imitated by Others if they Please⌐.⌐

Columbus discoverd America but Americus Vesputius finishd
& smoothd it over like an English Engraver or Corregio &
Titian⌐.⌐³

[*Page 18, part ii*]

What Man of Sense will lay out his Money upon the Lifes
Labours of Imbecillity & Imbecillitys Journeymen or think to
Educate a[n Idiot *del*] Fool how to build a Universe with
Farthing Balls⌐?⌐ The Contemptible Idiots who have been

Page 86 ¹ Anytus the tanner, Meletus the poet, and Lycon the orator, the accusers
of Socrates, apparently here represent John, Leigh, and Robert Hunt, in whose
Examiner Blake was attacked on 7 and 28 Aug. 1808 and 17 Sept. 1809 (*Blake
Records*, 195–8, 215–18). Cf. the design on *Jerusalem* pl. 93 (p. 624).

Page 17 ² Proverbs 10: 7: 'The memory of the just is blessed: but the name of the
wicked shall rot.'

³ 'Columbus discoverd . . . Corregio & Titian' are squeezed in, 'it over . . .
Titian' continuing up the side of the page.

Pages 18–19 Parts ii–kk are written in a large hand above and below the designs
on pp. 18–19 and to the left of that on p. 19; part ll is to the right of the sketch on
p. 19; parts mm and nn fill part of the space to the left and right of the sketch
on p. 18; part oo is squeezed in at the top of p. 18, and part pp goes over the central
design; parts qq and rr are written below parts mm and nn and are separated from
them by strokes; part ss is written sideways from the top left corner on p. 19 in the
last remaining space. None is clearly marked for entry.

calld Great Men of late Years ought to rouze the Public In-
dignation of Men of Sense in all Professions┗.┛

[*Part oo*]

There is not because there cannot be any difference of Effect
in the Pictures of Rubens & Rembrandt┗;┛ when you have seen
one of their Pictures you have seen all┗.┛ It is not so with Rafael
Julio Romano Alb d Mich Ang┗.┛ Every Picture of theirs has
a different & appropriate effect┗.┛

[*Part pp*]

Yet I do not shrink from the Comparison in Either Relief or
Strength of Colour with either Rembrand[*t*] or Rubens┗,┛ on
the Contrary I court the Comparison & fear not the Result but
not in a dark Corner┗;┛ their Effects are in Every Picture the
Same┗.┛ Mine are in every Picture different┗.┛

[*Part jj*]

I hope my Countrymen will excuse me if I tell them a
Wholesom truth┗.┛ Most Englishmen when they look at a
Picture immediately set about searching for Points of Light
[this in *del*] ∧& clap the Picture into a Dark Corner┗;┛ this
when done by∧ Grand Works is like looking for Epigrams in
Homer┗.┛ A point of light is a Witticism┗;┛ many are destruc-
tive of all Art┗,┛ ∧one is an Epigram only∧ & no Grand work
can have them┗;┛ ∧they Produce System & Monotony┗.┛∧[1]

[*Part qq*]

Rafael Mich Ang Alb. d Jul Rom are accounted[?] ignorant of
that Epigrammatic Wit in Art because they avoid it as a de-
structive Machine as it is┗.┛

[*Part rr*]

That Vulgar Epigram in Art Rembrandts Hundred Guilders
has intirely put an End to all Genuine & appropriate Effect┗;┛
all both Morning & Night is now a dark cavern┗;┛ it is the
Fashion┗.┛[2]

Page 18 [1] 'they Produce System & Monotony' trails sideways down the right
margin, and ends ('& Monotony') *upside-down* at the bottom.
 [2] 'all both Morning . . . is now' is squeezed in, perhaps as an addition, and the
rest of the sentence continues sideways down the right margin.
 'it is the Fashion' is covered by the stub of the page, and I have therefore read it
from the 1935 facsimile, where it is clear.

[*Page 19, part ss*]

When you view a Collection of Pictures painted since Venetian Art was the Fashion or Go into a Modern Exhibition with a Very few Exceptions Every Picture has the Same Effect, a Piece of Machinery of Points of Light to be put into a dark hole∟⌐

[*Part ll*]

Who that has Eyes cannot see that Rubens & Correggio must have been very weak & Vulgar fellows & ∧we∧ are [we *del*] to imitate their Execution. *T*his is [as if *del*] ∧like what∧ Sʳ Francis Bacon [should downright assert *del*] ∧says∧ that a healthy Child should be taught & compelld to walk like a Cripple while the Cripple must be taught to walk like healthy people∟⌐ O rare wisdom∟!⌐

[*Page 38, part ccc*]

There is just the same Science in Lebrun or Rubens or even Vanloo that there is in Rafael or Mich Angelo but not the same Genius∟⌐ Science is soon got∟,⌐ the other never can be acquired but must be Born∟⌐

[*Page 44, part fff*]

Let a Man who has made a drawing go on & on & he will produce a Picture or Painting but if he chooses to leave off[1] before he has spoild it he will [a *del*] do a Better Thing∟⌐[2]

[*Page 18, part kk*]

Mʳ B repeats that there is not one Character or Expression in this Print which could be Produced with the Execution of Titian Rubens Cor[r]eggio Rembrandt or any of that Class∟⌐ Character & Expression can only be Expressed by those who Feel Them∟⌐ Even Hogarths Execution cannot be Copied or Improved. Gentlemen of Fortune who give great Prices for Pictures should consider the following∟:⌐

[*Page 19*]

Rubens s Luxembourg Gallery[3] is Confessd on all hands [be-

Page 38   For the Order of Composition, see p. 948.

Page 44   [1] 'off' is read by Erdman (p. 565) as 'it'.

    [2] He 'was wont to affirm: "First thoughts are best in art, second thoughts in other matters" ' (A. Gilchrist [1863], i. 370).

Page 19   [3] *La Gallerie du Palais du Luxembourg* peinte par Rubens, Dessinée par Les. S. Nattier, et gravée Par Les plus Illustres Graveurs du Temps (Paris, 1710), an enormous folio which Blake probably saw at the Royal Academy (see p. 1456).

cause it bears the evidence at first view *del*] to be the work of
a Blockhead∟;⌐ ⌐it bears this Evidence in its face∟;⌐⌐ how can its
Execution be any other than the Work of a Blockhea*d*? ⌐Bloated
[awkward *del*] Gods⌐ Mercury Juno Venus & the rattle traps
of Mythology & the lumber of an [old *del*] awkward French
Palace are [de(*?*) *del*] thrown together around ⌐Clumsy &
Ricketty⌐ Princes & Princesses higgledy piggledy∟·⌐ On the
Contrary Julio Rom ⌐Palace of T at Mantua⌐[1] is allowd on all
hands to be ⌐the Production of⌐ a Man of the Most Profound
sense & Genius & Yet his Execution is pronouncd by English
Connoisseurs & Reynolds their doll to be unfit for the Study
of the Painter. Can I speak with too great Contempt of such
Contemptible fellow*s*? If all the Princes in Europe ⌐like Louis
XIV & Charles the first⌐ were to Patronize such Blockheads I
William Blake a Mental Prince should decollate & Hang their
Souls as Guilty of Mental High Treason∟·⌐

[*Page 18, part mm*]

Princes appear to me to be Fools∟,⌐ Houses of Commons &
Houses of Lords appear to me to be fools∟;⌐ they seem to me to
be something Else besides Human Life∟·⌐

[*Part nn*]

I am really sorry to see my Countrymen trouble themselves
about Politics. If men were wise ⌐the Most arbitrary⌐ Princes
Could not hurt them∟·⌐ If they are not Wise the Freest Govern-
ment is compelld to be a Tyranny∟·⌐

[*Page 20, Part tt*]

The wretched state of the Arts in this Country & in Europe
originating in the Wretched State of Political Science which is
the Science of Sciences Demands a firm & determinate conduct
on the part of Artists to Resist the Contemptible Counter
Arts [set on foot *del*] ⌐Established⌐ by Such contemptible
Politicians as Lewis XIV & [but *del*] originally set on foot by
Venetian Picture traders Music traders & Rhime traders to
the destruction of all true art as it is this day.

---

[1] *Sigismundi Augusti Mantuam Adventis Profectio ac Triumphus* . . . Opus ex Arche-
type Iulii Romani a Francisco Primaticio Mantuae in Ducali Palatio quod del T.
nuncupatur (Roma [1680]), a folio which Blake probably saw at the Royal
Academy. The plates are engraved by P. S. Bartolus.

[*Part vv*]

An example of these Contrary Arts is given us in the Characters
of Milton & Dryden as they are written in a Poem Signed with
the name of Nat Lee which perhaps he never wrote & perhaps
he wrote in a paroxysm of insanity In which it is said that
Miltons Poem is a rough Unfinishd Piece & Dryden has
finishd it∟˩¹ Now let Drydens Fall & Miltons Paradise be
read & I will assert that every Body of Understanding [can(?)
del] [will *del*] ˄must˄ cry out Shame on such Niggling & Poco
Pen as dryden has degraded Milton with But at the same time
I will allow that Stupidity will Prefer Dryden because it is in
Rhyme [but for no other cause *del*] ˄& Monotonous Sing Song
Sing Song˄ from beginning to end∟˩ Such are Bartollozzi
Woolett & Strange∟˩

[*Part uu*]

To recover Art has been the business of my life to the Florentine
Original & if possible to go beyond that Original∟;˩ ˄this˄ I
thought the only pursuit worthy of [an Englishman *del*] ˄a
Man˄. To Imitate I abhorr∟˩ I obstinately adhere to the true
Style of Art such as Michael Angelo Rafael Jul Rom Alb
Durer left it∟˩ [the Art of Invention not of Imitation. *del*]
[Imagination is My World this world of Dross is beneath my
Notice & beneath the Notice of the Public *del*] I demand
therefore of the Amateurs of

[*Page 21*]

art the Encouragement which is my due∟;˩ if they ˄continue to˄
refuse theirs is the loss∟,˩ not mine ˄—& theirs is the Contempt
of Posterity∟˩˄ I have enough in the˄Approbation of fellow

Page 20   Part vv is written sideways on both sides of the central sketch and is not
marked for entry.

¹ In the prefatory poem to Dryden's *The State of Innocence, and Fall of Man*: An
Opera (1677), Nat Lee wrote:

> To the dead Bard, your fame a little owes,   ⎫
> For *Milton* did the Wealthy Mine disclose,   ⎬
> And rudely cast what you cou'd well dispose: ⎭
> He roughly drew, on an old fashion'd ground,
> A Chaos, for no perfect World was found,
> Till through the heap, your mighty Genius shin'd;
> His was the Golden Orĕ which you refin'd.

In parts j and q (pp. 1040, 1041), Blake carelessly attributed these ideas to Dryden.

Page 21   For the Order of Composition, see p. 934.

labourers_L;_J this is my glory & exceeding great reward. I go on & nothing can hinder my course

and in Melodious accents I
Will sit me down & Cry *I*, I.

[Page 23, part ww]

[That Painted as well as Sculptured Monuments were common among the Ancients is evident from the words of our Savants who compared Those Sepulchers Painted on the outside with others only of stone   Their Beauty is confessd even by the Lips of Pasch(*?*)[1] himself *del*][2] The Painters of England are unemployd in Public work*s*, while the Sculptors have continual & Superabundant employment_L._J Our Churches & Abbeys are treasures of [Spiritual riches(*?*) *del*] their producing for ages back While Painting is excluded_L._J Painting the Principal Art has no place [in our *del*] ∧among our almost∧ only public works. [while *del*] ∧Yet∧ it is more adapted to solemn ornament than [dull(*?*)[3] *del*] Marble can be as it is capable of being Placd on any heighth & indeed would make a Noble finish ∧Placed∧ above the Great Public Monuments in Westminster St Pauls & other Cathedrals. To the Society for Encouragement of Arts[4] I address myself with [duty & *del*] Respectful duty [& *del*] requesting their Consideration of my Plan[5] as a Great

part ww [1] If the very difficult proper name has been correctly deciphered, it seems likely that Blake's information came from C. G. Heyne's *The Pretended Tomb of Homer* [discovered by Pasch] (1795), which discusses, not very respectfully, Pasch's discoveries and opinions, rather than Conte [Enrico Leonardo] Pasch di Krienen, *Breve Descrizione dell'Arcipelago* . . . Con un ragguaglio . . . specialmente del sepolcro d'Omero (Livorno, 1773), since Blake probably could not read Italian when he wrote the deleted passage above. In all accounts, Pasch is enthusiastic about the beauty and authenticity of the works he discovered.

Page 23 [2] For 'our Savants . . . Sepulchers' Erdman (p. 570) reads 'the Savants . . . Sepolchures'. The words 'our Savants . . . compared Those Sepulchers Painted on the outside with others only of stone' all seem exceedingly doubtful (though possible) to me. The deletion of these lines turns curiously from loops into words:

Thomas James Robert

Hands

Horses

Blake John Thomas

[3] For 'dull' Erdman (p. 570) reads 'dead'.

[4] The Society for the Encouragement of Arts, Manufactures, and Commerce, founded in 1754.

[5] In his letter to Cumberland of 19 Dec. 1808 (p. 1645), Blake refers to his 'plan of publishing'.

Public [deed(?) *del*] means of advancing Fine Art in Protestant Communities ⌊.⌋ Monuments to the dead Painted by Historical & Poetical Artists like Barry & Mortimer[1]—I forbear to name [a li *del*] living Artists tho equally worthy[—] I say Monuments So Painted must make England What Italy is ⌊,⌋ an Envied Storehouse of Intellectual Riches ⌊.⌋

[Page 24, part xx]

It has been said of late years The English Public have no Taste for Painting ⌊.⌋ This is a Fals[*e*]hood ⌊.⌋ The English are as Good Judges of Painting as of Poetry & they prove it in their Contempt for Great Collections of all the Rubbish of the Continent brought here by Ignorant Picture dealers ⌊;⌋ an Englishman may well say 'I am no Judge of Painting' when he is shewn these Smears & Dawbs at an immense price & told that such is the Art of Painting ⌊.⌋ I say the English Public are true Encouragers of Great[2] Art while they discourage & look with contempt on False Art ⌊.⌋[3]

[Page 25, part yy]

In a Commercial Nation Impostors are abroad in all Professions ⌊,⌋ these are the greatest Enemies of Genius ⌊.⌋ [Mʳ B thinks it his duty to Caution the Public against a Certain Impostor who *del*] In [our Art *del*] the Art of Painting these Impostors Sedulously propagate an Opinion that Great Inventors Cannot Execute ⌊;⌋ this Opinion is as destructive of the true Artists as it is false by all experience ⌊.⌋ Even Hogarth cannot be either Copied or Improved ⌊.⌋ Can Anglus[4] never Discern Perfection but in the Journeymans Labour ⌊?⌋[5]

---

[1] James Barry (1741–22 Feb. 1806) and John Hamilton Mortimer (1741–79) were both historical painters.

part xx [2] 'Great' has been written over, perhaps (as Erdman [p. 570] suggests) to make it read 'real'.

[3] 'I say . . . on False Art' is written sideways up the right margin, and only the ascenders of the last three words are visible, for the paper has broken off.

[4] 'Anglus' may be Robert Hunt, who wrote anonymously in the *Examiner* (7 Aug. 1808, 17 Sept. 1809): 'Mr Schiavonetti has done more than justice to Mr. Blake's [*GRAVE*] designs', which owe 'their best popularity to . . . the unrivalled graver of L. Schiavonetti', who bestowed 'an exterior charm on deformity and nonsense' (*Blake Records*, 195, 197, 216).

Page 25 [5] This sentence is written very small, perhaps as an addition.

[*Page 24, part aaa*]

I know my Execution is not like Any Body Else∟⌐ I do not intend it should be so∟⌐ ∧None but Blockheads Copy one another∟⌐∧ My Conception & Invention are on All hands Allowd to be Superior∟⌐ My Execution will be found so too∟⌐ To what is it that Gentlemen of the first Rank both in Genius & Fortune have subscribed their Names∟?⌐ To My Inventions∟!⌐ The Executive part they never Disputed∟;⌐

[*Page 25, part bbb*]

the Lavish praise I have recievd from all Quarters for Invention & Drawing has generally been accompanied by this∟:⌐ 'he can concieve but he cannot Execute∟⌐' This Absurd assertion has done me & may still do me the greatest mischief∟⌐ I call for Public protection against these Villains∟⌐ I am like others∟,⌐ Just Equal in Invention & in Execution as my works Shew∟⌐ I in my own defence Challenge a Competition with the finest Engravings & defy the most critical judge to ∧make∧ the Comparison Honestly∟,⌐

[*Page 24*]

asserting in my own Defence that This Print is the Finest that has been done or is likely to be done in England where drawing∟,⌐ ∧its foundation∟,⌐∧ is Contemnd and absurd Nonsense about Dots & Lozenges & Clean Strokes made to occupy the attention to the Neglect of all real Art∟⌐ I defy any Man to Cut Cleaner Strokes than I do or rougher where I please & assert that he who thinks he can Engrave or Paint either without being a Master of Drawing is a Fool. [who(?) *del*] Painting is Drawing on Canvas & Engraving is Drawing on Copper & nothing Else∟⌐ ∧Drawing is Execution & nothing Else∧ & he who draws best must be the best Artist∟;⌐ [& *del*] to this I subscribe my name as a Public Duty

William Blake

Pages 24–25 Parts aaa and bbb are written sideways to the right of the sketches on pp. 24 and 25. At the end of part bbb, 'Shew . . . Honestly' is written *upside-down* at the top of p. 25, continues to the left margin of p. 24 ('Nonsense . . . Neglect of all'), and then sideways from the right margin of p. 24 the other way up ('real Art . . . William Blake'). 'as a Public Duty' is squeezed over the signature as if an afterthought.

'Public Address' (*Notebook* p. 25)

[*Page 25, part zz*]

P.S I do not believe that this Absurd opinion ever was set on foot till in my Outset into life it was artfully publishd both in whispers & in print by Certain persons whose robberies from me made it necessary to them that I should be [left *del*] hid in a corner ; ¦[1] it never was supposed that a Copy Could be better than an original or near so Good till a few Years ago it became the interest of certain envious Knaves .

[*End of THE PUBLIC ADDRESS*]

Page 25   Part zz is written sideways from the left margin beside the sketch and is not marked for entry.

[1] Cf. 'I am hid' on the title-page of Blake's Reynolds marginalia (p. 1450).

('THE EVERLASTING GOSPEL')

[Page 1, part a]

There is not one Moral Virtue that Jesus Inculcated but Plato
& Cicero did Inculcate before him⌞;⌟ what then did Christ
Inculcate⌞?⌟ Forgiveness of Sins⌞!⌟ This alone is the Gospel &
this is the Life & Immortality brought to light by Jesus, Even
the Covenant of Jehovah which is This⌞:⌟ If you forgive one
another your Trespasses so shall Jehovah forgive you That he
himself may dwell among you but if you Avenge you Murder
the Divine Image & he cannot dwell among you⌞:⌟ [together(?)[1]
del] because you Murder him he arises Again & you deny that
he is Arisen & are blind to Spirit⌞.⌟

[Page 2, part b]

2[2]

What can this Gospel of Jesus be⌞,⌟
What Life & Immortality⌞?⌟
What was it that he brought to Light
That Plato & Cicero did not write⌞?⌟
The Heathen Deities wrote them all⌞,⌟
These Moral Virtues great & small⌞.⌟
What is the Accusation of Sin
But Moral Virtues deadly Gin⌞?⌟
The Moral Virtues in their Pride
Did oer the World triumphant ride
In Wars & Sacrifice for Sin
And Souls to Hell ran trooping in⌞.⌟
The Accuser Holy God of All
This Pharisaic Worldly Ball

'The Everlasting Gospel' *page 1 part a* [1] The deleted word might be 'by his', as
Erdman (p. 792) suggests.

Page 2 part b [2] The '2' was added when part c was moved before part b.

Page 2 ll. 9–10 are written at the bottom of the page; their position between
ll. 8 and 11 is indicated by a bracket.

Amidst them in his Glory Beams   [*15*]
Upon the Rivers & the Streams⌊.⌋
Then Jesus rose & said to [men *altered to*] Me
'Thy Sins are all forgiven thee⌊.⌋'
Loud Pilate Howld⌊,⌋ loud Cai[*a*]phas yelld
When they the Gospel Light beheld⌊.⌋   [*20*]
[Jerusalem he said to me *del*]

[*Page 3*]

It was when Jesus said to Me
'Thy Sins are all forgiven thee⌊.⌋'
The Christian trumpets loud proclaim
Thro all the World in Jesus name   [*25*]
Mutual forgiveness of each Vice
And oped the Gates of Paradise⌊.⌋
The Moral Virtues in great fear
Formed the Cross & Nails & Spear
And the Accuser standing by   [*30*]
Cried out 'Crucify Crucify⌊!⌋
Our Moral Virtues neer can be
Nor Warlike pomp & Majesty
For Moral Virtues all begin
In the Accusations of Sin   [*35*]
And [Moral *del*] ⌃all the⌃ Heroic Virtues [all *del*] End
In destroying the Sinners Friend⌊.⌋
Am I not Lucifer the Great
And you my daughters in Great State
The fruit of my Mysterious Tree   [*40*]
Of Good & Evil & Misery

[*Page 4*]

And death & Hell which now begin
On every one who Forgives Sin⌊?⌋'   [*43*]

ll. 19–22 are written sideways in the right margin as two lines; their position
between ll. 18 and 23 is indicated by a bracket.

Page 3 ll. 26–7: Cf. 'Mutual Forgiveness of each Vice⌊;⌋ Such are the Gates of
Paradise' (*For the Sexes*, pl. 2 [p. 645]).

ll. 36–7 are written in the right margin; their position between ll. 35 and 38
is shown by a stroke.

[*Part c*]

1　This to come first⌊:⌋

If Moral Virtue was Christianity
Christs Pretensions were all Vanity
And Cai[*a*]phas & Pilate Men
[Of God (*?*) *del*] Praise Worthy & the Lions Den
And not the Sheepfold Allegories
Of God & Heaven & their Glories⌊.⌋
The Moral Christian is the Cause
Of the Unbeliever & his Laws⌊.⌋
The Roman Virtues⌊,⌋ Warlike Fame⌊,⌋
Take Jesus & Jehovahs Name
For what is Antichrist but those
Who against Sinners Heaven close
With Iron bars in Virtuous State
And Rhadamanthus at the Gate⌊?⌋

[*Page 120, part d*]

Was Jesus Born of a Virgin Pure
With narrow Soul & looks demure⌊?⌋
If he intended to take on Sin
The Mother Should an Harlot been⌊,⌋
Just such a one as Magdalen
With Seven devils in her Pen
Or were Jew Virgins still more Curst
And more sucking devils nurst
Or what was it which he took on
That he might bring Salvation⌊?⌋

Page 4 l. 2: Cf. 'Laocoon': 'If Morality was Christianity Socrates was the Saviour' (p. 664).
　　l. 4: The deletion may be 'Of Moral', as Erdman (p. 793) reads it.

Page 120: *Order of Composition*: (1) ll. 1–6, 9–20, 27–49 were written in two columns (divided after l. 27) in Black ink, with a stroke dividing the columns; (2) Then Blake added ll. 7–8 (as one line inserted above l. 9, the last two words bent sideways when they came to the inter-columnar strokes), ll. 21–4 (at the bottom right corner below l. 49, ll. 21–3 as two lines, a bracket embracing these lines headed by an asterisk leads by a stroke—later deleted—to an asterisk after l. 16, but apparently. they were intended to go with the other asterisk following l. 20 just facing it), ll. 25–6 (written sideways to the right margin, not marked for entry, perhaps intended to follow l. 24), altered the first 'his' to 'Earths' in l. 35, all in the same greyish-Brown ink; (3) Finally he altered the second 'his' to 'Earths' in l. 35 in pencil.

A Body subject to be Tempted⌊,⌋
From neither pain nor grief Exempted
Or such a body as must not feel
The passions that with Sinners deal⌊?⌋
Yes but they say he never fell⌊.⌋ [*15*]
Ask Caiaphas for he can tell⌊.⌋
He mockd the Sabbath & he mockd
The Sabbaths God & he unlockd
The Evil spirits from their Shrines
And turnd Fishermen to Divines⌊,⌋ [*20*]
[End(?) *del*] ⌃Oerturnd⌃ the Tent of Secret Sins
& its golden cords & Pins⌊.⌋
Tis the Bloody Shrine of War
Pinnd around from Star to Star⌊,⌋
Halls of Justice hating Vice [*25*]
Where the devil Combs his Lice⌊.⌋
He turnd the Devils into Swine
That he might tempt thc Jews to Dine
Since which a Pig has got a look
That for a Jew may be mistook⌊.⌋ [*30*]
'Obey your Parents⌊!⌋' *W*hat says he⌊?⌋
'Woman what have I to do with thee⌊?⌋
No Earthly Parents I confess⌊;⌋
I am doing my Fathers Business⌊.⌋'
He scornd [his *del*] ⌃Earths⌃ Parents⌊,⌋ Scornd [his *del*] ⌃Earths⌃
   God [*35*]
And mockd the one & the others Rod⌊,⌋
His Seventy Disciples sent
Against Religion & Government⌊.⌋
They by the Sword of Justice fell
And him their Cruel Murderer tell⌊.⌋ [*40*]
He left his Fathers trade to roam
A wandring Vagrant without Home
And thus he others labour stole
That he might live above controll⌊.⌋

ll. 17–18, 43–4, 47–8: Cf. *Marriage* pl. 23, ¶86: 'did he not mock at the sabbath, and so mock the sabbaths God? . . . turn away the law from the woman taken in adultery? steal the labor of others to support him?' (p. 96).
l. 32: 'What have I to do with thee' is repeated in 'To Tirzah' (*Songs* pl. 52) ll. 4, 16 and in 'William Bond' ('Ballads [Pickering] MS') (pp. 198, 1317).

The Publicans & Harlots he   [
Selected for his Company
And from the Adulteress turnd away
Gods righteous Law that lost its Prey⌊·⌋   [

[Page 33, part e]

The Vision of Christ that thou dost See
Is my Visions greatest Enemy⌊·⌋
Thine has a great hook nose like thine⌊,⌋
Mine has a snub nose like to mine⌊·⌋
Thine is the friend of All Mankind⌊,⌋
Mine speaks in Parables to the Blind⌊·⌋
Thine loves the same world that mine hates⌊,⌋
[It(?) *del*] Thy Heaven doors are my Hell Gates⌊·⌋
Socrates taught what Meletus
Loathd as a Nations bitterest Curse
And Cai[*a*]phas was in his own Mind
A benefactor to Mankind⌊·⌋
Both read the Bible day & night
But thou readst black where I read White⌊·⌋

[Page 48, part f]

Was Jesus Chaste or did he
Give any Lessons of Chastity⌊?⌋
The morning blushd fiery red⌊,⌋
Mary was found in Adulterous bed⌊·⌋
Earth groand beneath & Heavn above
Trembled at discovery of Love⌊·⌋
Jesus was sitting in Moses Chair⌊;⌋
They brought the trembling Woman There⌊·⌋
Moses commands she be stoned to death⌊;⌋
What was the [words *del*] ⌃Sound⌃ of Jesus breath⌊?⌋
He laid his hand on Moses Law⌊,⌋
The ancient Heavens in Silent awe
Writ with Curses from Pole to Pole
All away began to roll⌊;⌋

Page 33 Part e is written in two columns (1–6, 7–14) sideways from the right margin to the central sketch, following 'The Villa[*i*]n at the Gallows tree' and 'To the Royal Academy' and probably preceding 'If it is True What the Prophets write' (pp. 944, 945).
    l. 9: Meletus the poet was one of the three accusers of Socrates.

The Earth trembling & Naked lay   [*15*]
In secret bed of Mortal Clay
On Sinai felt the hand divine
Putting back the bloody shrine
And She heard the breath of God
As she heard by Edens flood⌊:⌋   [*20*]
'[God *altered to*] Good & Evil are no more⌊!⌋
Sinais trumpets cease to roar⌊!⌋
Cease finger of God to Write⌊!⌋
The Heavens are not clean in thy Sight⌊.⌋
Thou art Good & thou Alone   [*25*]
Nor may the sinner cast one Stone⌊.⌋

[*Page 49*]

To be Good only is to be
A God ⌃Devil⌃ or else a Pharisee⌊.⌋
Thou Angel of the Presence divine
That didst create this Body of Mine⌊,⌋   [*30*]
Wherefore has[*t*] thou writ these Laws
And Created Hells dark Jaws⌊?⌋
My Presence I will take from thee⌊,⌋
A Cold Leper thou shalt be
Tho thou wast so pure & bright   [*35*]
[The *mended to*] That Heaven was Impure in thy Sight⌊,⌋
Tho thy Oath turnd Heaven Pale⌊,⌋
Tho thy Covenant built Hells Jail⌊,⌋
Tho [G(?) *del*] thou didst all to Chaos roll
With the Serpent for its soul⌊,⌋   [*40*]
Still the breath divine does move
And the breath divine is Love⌊.⌋
Mary Fear Not⌊!⌋ Let me See
The Seven Devils that torment thee⌊!⌋
Hide not from my Sight thy Sin   [*45*]
That forgiveness thou maist win⌊.⌋
Has no Man Condemned thee⌊?⌋'
'No Man Lord!' '*T*hen what is he

l. 24: 'the heavens are not clean in his sight' is from Job 15: 15; cf. 25: 5.

Page 49 ll. 27–8 are written sideways from the right margin, and two strokes clearly indicate that they are to go at the top of the page.

l. 28: 'Devil' is inserted in pencil, but 'God' was not deleted.

Who shall Accuse the*e*? Come Ye forth
Fallen Fiends of Heavnly birth
That have forgot our Ancient Love
And driven away my trembling Dove∟·⌟

[*Page 50*]

You Shall bow before her feet∟,⌟
You shall lick the dust for Meat
And tho you cannot Love but Hate
Shall be beggars at Loves Gate∟!⌟
What was thy love∟?⌟ Let me See it∟!⌟
Was it Love or dark Deceit∟?⌟'
'Love too long from Me has fled.
Twas dark deceit to Earn my bread∟·⌟
Twas Covet or Twas Custom or
[Twas *del*] Some trifle not worth caring for
That they may call a [crime *del*] ∧shame∧ & Sin
[The *del*] ∧Loves∧ Temple [where *del*] ∧that∧ God dwelleth in
And hide in Secret hidden Shrine
   The Naked Human form divine
And render that a Lawless thing
   On which the Soul Expands its wing
But this O Lord this was my Sin
When first I let these Devils in
In dark pretence to Chastity

[*Page 51*]

Blaspheming Love∟,⌟ blaspheming thee∟·⌟
Thence Rose Secret Adulteries

l. 51: Compare 'To the Muses' (p. 762): 'How have you left the antient love
That bards of old enjoy'd in you'.

Page 50   ll. 53–64, 69–71 are written across the top of the page and descending
down the right margin (ll. 57–8, 59–60 as single lines), carefully avoiding the
'Cowper' lines and the sketch; ll. 65–8 are written in the only significant remaining
blank at the top right corner, and a stroke brings them in after l. 64. For the
Order of Composition, see p. 954.

Page 51   The 'Everlasting Gospel' lines follow the illegible pencil lines at the top
of the page, and the 'Public Address' prose at the bottom. ll. 72–9 were written
below the pencil passage down the left margin, and ll. 80–4, 91–3 go down the
right margin, both carefully skirting the sketches and stopping above the bottom
prose. ll. 85–6 were added at the top of the right column (above l. 80), with a
stroke to show they should come after l. 84. ll. 87–90 were written on top of the
top pencil lines, and a stroke clearly indicates they are to follow l. 86.

And thence did Covet also rise∟·⌐

My Sin thou hast forgiven me∟·⌐ [*75*]

Canst thou forgive my Blasphemy∟?⌐

Canst thou return to this dark Hell

And in my burning bosom dwell

And canst thou die that I may live

And canst thou Pity & forgive∟?⌐' [*80*]

Then Rolld the Shadowy Man away

From the Limbs of Jesus to make them his prey∟,⌐

An Ever devo[*u*]ring appetite

Glittering with festering Venoms bright

Crying [Ive found *del*] '∧Crucify∧ [the *altered to*] this cause of
distress [*85*]

[You *del*] ∧Who∧ dont keep the secrets of Holiness∟!⌐

All Mental Powers by Diseases we bind

But he heals the Deaf & the Dumb & the Blind∟·⌐

Whom God has afflicted for Secret Ends

He Comforts & Heals & calls them Friends∟·⌐' [*90*]

But when Jesus was Crucified

Then was perfected his glittring pride

In three Nights

[*Page 52*]

In three Nights he devourd his prey

And still he devours the Body of Clay

94 lines

For dust & Clay is the Serpents meat [*95*]

Which never was made for Man to Eat∟·⌐ [*96*]

[*Part g*]

Seeing this False Christ In fury & Passion

I made my Voice heard all over the Nation∟:⌐

'What are those' &ᶜ [*3*]

l. 85: For 'the' Erdman (p. 796) reads 'hi[*m*]'.

Page 52 ll. 93–4 were written to the left of the sketch, followed by part g; then ll. 95–6 were written on top of the sketch and clearly marked for insertion after l. 94. For the Order of Composition of p. 52, see p. 955.

 ll. 93–4: Cf. *Jerusalem* pl. 89, l. 13 (p. 615): 'In three nights he devourd the rejected corse of death'.

 l. 3: The continuation implied by the '&ᶜ' has not survived.

[*Page 48, part h*]

This was Spoke by My Spectre to Voltaire Bacon &ᶜ

Did Jesus teach doubt or did he
Give any lessons of Philosophy ͺ,͵
Charge Visionaries with decieving
Or call Men wise for not Believing ͺ? ͵   [

[*Page 100, part i*]

Was Jesus gentle or did he
Give any marks of Gentility ͺ? ͵
When twelve years old he ran away
And left his Parents in dismay ͺ. ͵
When after three days sorrow found ͺ,͵   [
Loud as Sinai's trumpet sound ͺ: ͵
'No Earthly Parents I confess[—]
My Heavenly Fathers business ͺ. ͵
Ye understand not what I say
And angry force me to obey ͺ. ͵'   [
Obedience is a duty then
And favour gains with God & Men ͺ. ͵
John from the Wilderness loud cried ͺ; ͵
Satan gloried in his Pride ͺ. ͵
'Come' Said Satan 'come away ͺ. ͵
Ill soon see if youll obey ͺ. ͵
John for disobedience bled
But you can turn the stones to bread ͺ. ͵
Gods high King & Gods high Priest
Shall Plant their Glories in your breast ͺ. ͵
If Caiaphas you will obey ͺ,͵
If Herod you with bloody Prey
Feed with the Sacrifice & be
Obedient ͺ,͵ fall down ͺ,͵ worship me ͺ! ͵'

Page 48   This line was written at the top of the page above part f (which is in ink), but it is in pencil like part h, which is written sideways from the right margin to the sketch. Blake's intention for the position of the passage is therefore obscure. The '&ᶜ' suggests it was to be continued by a passage now lost.

Pages 100–101   Two columns (ll. 1–18, 19–37) were written on p. 100 below the much earlier drafts of 'Her whole Life . . .' and 'An old maid . . .' (see p. 972), and these were continued with ll. 38–59 on p. 101 below a stroke dividing them from the 'Motto to the Songs of Innocence & of Experience' and to the left of the draft of 'The Fly'. For the Order of Composition, see pp. 971, 972.

Thunders & lightnings broke around   [*25*]
And Jesus voice in thunders sound_L:_J
'Thus I sieze the Spiritual Prey_L!_J
Ye Smiters with disease_L,_J make way_L!_J
I come Your King & God to sieze_L·_J
Is God a Smiter with disease_L?_J'   [*30*]
The God of this World raged in vain_L·_J
He bound Old Satan in his Chain
And bursting forth [with *del*] ˄his˄ furious ire
Became a Chariot of fire_L·_J
Throughout the land he took his course   [*35*]
And traced diseases to their Source_L·_J
He cursd the Scribe & Pharisee

[*Page 101*]

Trampling down Hipocrisy_L·_J
Where eer his Chariot took its way_L,_J
There Gates of death let in the day_L,_J   [*40*]
Broke down from every Chain & Bar
And Satan in his Spiritual War
Dragd at his Chariot wheels_L;_J loud howld
The God of this World_L;_J louder rolld
The Chariot Wheels & louder Still   [*45*]
His voice was heard from Zions hill
And in his hand the Scourge shone bright_L·_J
He Scourgd the Merchant Canaanite
From out the Temple of his Mind
And in his Body tight does bind   [*50*]
Satan & all his Hellish Crew
And thus with wrath he did subdue
The Serpent Bulk of Natures dross
Till he had naild it to the Cross_L·_J
[He took on Sin in the Virgins Womb   [*55*]
And on the Cross he Seald its doom *del*]
He took on Sin in the Virgins Womb
And put it off on the Cross & Tomb
To be Worshipd by the Church of Rome_L·_J   [*59*]

Page 101 l. 38: Oddly enough, Blake had spelled 'Hypocrite' correctly on this page many years previously (see the 'Motto to the Songs of Innocence & of Experience', p. 974).

[Page 98, part j]

Was Jesus Humble or did he
Give any proofs of Humility∟?˩
When but a Child he ran away
And left his Parents in dismay∟.˩
When they had wanderd three days long
These were the words upon his Tongue∟:˩
'No Earthly Parents I confess∟.˩
I am doing my Fathers business∟.˩'
When the rich learned Pharisee
1 Came to consult him secretly
4 He was too Proud to take a bribe∟.˩
5 He spoke with authority∟,˩ not like a Scribe∟.˩
2 [And(?) on *del*] Upon his heart with Iron pen
3 He wrote 'Ye must be born again∟!˩'
6 He says with most consummate Art
'Follow me∟,˩ I am meek & lowly of heart'
As that is the only way to Escape
The Misers net & the Gluttons trap∟.˩
He who loves his Enemies hates his Friends∟.˩
This is surely not what Jesus intends∟.˩
He must mean the meer love of Civility
And so he must mean concerning Humility
But he acts with triumphant honest pride
And this is the Reason Jesus died∟.˩
If he had been [the *del*] ⌃Antichrist⌃ Creeping Jesus
Hed have done any thing to please us∟,˩
Gone sneaking into the Synagogues
And not used the Elders & Priests like dogs

Page 98 ll. 1–18, 23–8, 33–44 were written in a column on the left of p. 98 in the space left from 'Let the Brothels . . .'; ll. 29–32 and 45–9 were written with the same pen sideways in the middle of the page (the former beside l. 28) and in the top right corner of the page. ll. 19–22, 50–1 were written with a sharper pen; ll. 19–22, sideways at the top of the space left between the two columns, are clearly marked to follow l. 18; ll. 50–1 are written in the stanza-break between ll. 33 and 34 of 'Let the Brothels . . .' (p. 970) and might be taken as a detached fragment were they not clearly integrated in the poem when it was copied on pp. 52–4 (part k, ll. 85–6, p. 1068). For the Order of Composition, see p. 967.

ll. 1–20, 23–36, 39–47 were transcribed, after ll. 11–16 were rearranged, on pp. 52–4 (part k, ll. 1–2, 5–20, 25–6, 29–30, 59–68, 71–6, 79–86, pp. 1065–8).

l. 5: 'wanderd' looks rather like 'wonderd', but when it was transcribed on p. 52 (part k, l. 7, p. 1066) it was written clearly as 'wanderd'.

But humble as a Lamb or an Ass
Obey himself to Caiaphas⌊.⌋   [*30*]
God wants not Man to humble himself⌊.⌋
This is the Trick of the Ancient Elf⌊.⌋
Humble toward God⌊,⌋ Haughty toward Man⌊,⌋
This is the Race [wh(?) *del*] ⌃that⌃ Jesus ran
And when he humbled himself to God   [*35*]
Then descended the Cruel Rod⌊.⌋
[Why dost thou humble thyself to me
Thou Also dwelst in Eternity *del*]
'If thou humblest thyself thou humblest me⌊.⌋
Thou also dwelst in Eternity⌊.⌋   [*40*]
Thou art a Man⌊,⌋ God is no more⌊!⌋
Thine own Humanity learn to Adore
And thy Revenge Abroad display
In terrors at the Last Judgment day⌊!⌋
Gods Mercy & Long Suffering   [*45*]
Are but the Sinner to Judgment to bring⌊.⌋
Thou on the Cross for them shalt pray
[Whom thou shalt Torment at the Last Day *del*]
And take Revenge at the last Day⌊.⌋'

Do what you will⌊,⌋ this Lifes a Fiction   [*50*]
And is made up of Contradiction⌊.⌋   [*51*]

[*Page 52, part k*]
The Everlasting Gospel

Was Jesus Humble or did he
Give any Proofs of Humility⌊,⌋
Boast of high Things with Humble tone
And give with Charity a Stone⌊?⌋
When but a Child he ran away   [*5*]
And left his Parents in dismay⌊.⌋

l. 30: When Blake copied out this line on p. 53 (part k, l. 64, p. 1067), he corrected the grammar by writing 'Obeyd'.

Page 52 ll. 1–2, 5–20, 25–6, 29–30, 59–68, 71–6, 79–86 were copied from p. 98 (part j, ll. 1–20, 23–36, 39–47, 49–51, pp. 1064–5). Part k was written on p. 52 after 'Public Address' part b and 'The Everlasting Gospel' parts f and g had filled all the page except to the right of the sketch, ll. 3–4 being written later to the left and marked for entry with two strokes; ll. 21–4 (ll. 23–4 as one line) were squeezed between part g, l. 3, and the 'Public Address' and not marked for entry. See p. 955.

When they had wanderd three days long
These were the words upon his tongue⌊:⌋
'No Earthly Parents I confess⌊!⌋
I am doing my Fathers business⌊!⌋'   [
When the rich learned Pharisee
Came to consult him secretly
Upon his heart with Iron pen
He wrote 'Ye must be born again⌊.⌋'
He was too proud to take a bribe⌊.⌋   [
He spoke with authority⌊,⌋ not like a Scribe⌊.⌋
He says with most consummate Art
'Follow me⌊,⌋ I am meek & lowly of heart'
As that is the only way to escape
The Misers net & the Gluttons trap⌊.⌋   [
What can be done with such desperate Fools
Who follow after the Heathen Schools⌊?⌋
I was standing by when Jesus died⌊.⌋
What I calld Humility they calld Pride⌊.⌋
He who loves his Enemies [hates *del*] ⌃betrays⌃ his Friends⌊;⌋   [

[*Page 53*]

This Surely is not what Jesus intends
But the Sneaking Pride of Heroic Schools
And the Scribes & Pharisees Virtuous Rules
For he acts with honest triumphant Pride
And this is the cause that Jesus died⌊.⌋   ▮
He did not die with Christian Ease
Asking Pardon of his Enemies⌊.⌋
If he had Cai[*a*]phas would forgive⌊;⌋
Sneaking submission can always live⌊.⌋
He had only to say that God was the devil

Page 53 ll. 26–30, 51–63 were written in the space left from 'Public Address' part b
(pp. 1032–3), to the left of the sketch; ll. 64–83 are to its right, and ll. 31–48 (ll. 39–48
with a blunter pen) were written straight over the sketch and marked for insertion
by two strokes; ll. 49–50 were added above the line sideways in the right margin
and clearly joined to l. 48 by a stroke.

ll. 27–8 are written over an erasure of which only enough can now be made out
to allow one to say that they may be the same as those drafted in this place in the
poem on p. 98 (p. 1064):

He [must mean the meer love of Civility]
And [so he must mean concernin]g [Humilit]y

And the devil was God like a Christian Civil_{L,⌋}
Mild Christian regrets to the devil Confess
For affronting him ⌃thrice[?]⌃ in the Wilderness
Like d^r Priestly & ⌃Bacon &⌃ [Sir Isaac *del*] Newton
Poor[?] Spiritual Knowledge is not worth a button   [*40*]
He had soon been bloody Caesars Elf
And at last he would have been Caesar himself
[As *del*] ⌃For⌃ thus the Gospel Sr Isaac confutes_{L:⌋}
'God can only be known by his Attributes
And as for[?] the indwelling of the Holy Ghost   [*45*]
Or of Christ & his Father its all a boast
And Pride & Vanity of ⌃the⌃ imagination[?]
That disdains to follow this Worlds Fashion_{L.⌋}'
To teach doubt & Experiment
Certainly was not what Christ meant_{L.⌋}   [*50*]
What was he doing all that time
From twelve years old to manly prime_{L?⌋}
Was he then Idle or the Less
About his Fathers business
Or was his wisdom held in Scorn   [*55*]
Before his wrath began to burn
In Miracles throughout the Land
That quite unnervd the Caiaphas[?] hand_{L?⌋}
If he had been [the *del*] ⌃Antichrist⌃ Creeping Jesus
Hed have done any thing to please us_{L,⌋}   [*60*]
Gone Sneaking into Synagogues
And not usd the Elders & Priests like dogs
But Humble as a Lamb or Ass
Obeyd himself to Caiaphas_{L.⌋}
God wants not Man to Humble himself_{L;⌋}   [*65*]
This is the trick of the ancient Elf_{L.⌋}
This is the Race that Jesus ran_{L:⌋}
Humble to God_{L,⌋} Haughty to Man_{L,⌋}

ll. 45–7 are written over an illegible erasure.
  l. 58: 'the Caiaphas' is written over an erasure which may (as Erdman, p. 796, suggests) be 'the guilty'. It is difficult to say whether 'the' was intended to stand or not.
  l. 59: 'Creeping Jesus' was evidently a proverbial Sussex expression meaning a favour-seeking hypocrite (see J. J. Robinson, 'A Creeping Jesus', *Times Literary Supplement*, 27 Aug. 1925, p. 557).

Cursing the Rulers before the People
Even to the temples highest Steeple
And when he Humbled himself to God
Then descended the Cruel Rod⌞.⌟
'If thou humblest thyself thou humblest me⌞!⌟
Thou also dwellst in Eternity⌞!⌟
Thou art a Man⌞,⌟ God is no more⌞!⌟
Thy own humanity learn to adore
For that is my Spirit of Life⌞.⌟
Awake⌞,⌟ arise to Spiritual Strife
And thy Revenge abroad display
In terrors at the Last Judgment day⌞!⌟
Gods Mercy & Long Suffering
Is but the Sinner to Judgment to bring⌞.⌟
Thou on the Cross for them shalt pray

[*Page 54*]

And take Revenge at the last day⌞.⌟'
[This Corporeal All lifes a fiction
And is made up of Contradiction *del*]
Jesus replied & thunders hurld⌞:⌟
'I never will Pray for the World⌞!⌟
Once a [*for* I?] did so when I prayd in the Garden⌞;⌟
I wishd to take with me a Bodily Pardon⌞.⌟'
Can that which was of woman born
In the absence of the Morn
When the Soul fell into Sleep
And Archangels round it weep
Shooting out against the Light
Fibres of a deadly night
Reasoning upon its own dark Fiction

l. 82: The verb was 'Are' in the original of this passage on p. 98 (part j, l. 46—
p. 1065).

Page 54 ll. 84–6, 91–108 were written to the left of the central sketch; ll. 87–90
were written beside ll. 84–6, 91 over a sketch (l. 87 as a continuation of l. 84),
perhaps as a substitute for ll. 85–6 which were deleted. For the Order of Com-
position see above.

l. 85: The descenders and ascenders still visible in the illegible words erased
under 'This Corporeal All' are consistent with 'Do what you will' in the passage
from which this line was copied on p. 98 (p. 1065); Erdman (p. 596) reads them as
'All Corporeal lifes a'.

In doubt which is Self Contradiction⌊?⌋
Humility is only doubt
And does the Sun & Moon blot out   [*100*]
Rooting over with thorns & stems
The buried Soul & all its Gems⌊·⌋
This Lifes dim Windows of the Soul
Distorts the Heavns from Pole to Pole
And leads you to Believe a Lie   [*105*]
When you see wit*h*, not thro the Eye
That was born in a night to perish in a night
When the Soul Slept in the beams of light⌊·⌋
                              78 lines
Was Jesus Chaste or did he &ᶜ   [*109*]
                    [*Part l*]
Im Sure This Jesus will not do
Either for Englishman or Jew⌊·⌋   [*2*]

[*End of THE EVERLASTING GOSPEL*]

ll. 97–8: Cf. *For the Sexes* pl. 19, ll. 13–14 (p. 659), which repeats l. 98.
ll. 105–8 are a variant of ll. 125–8 of 'Auguries of Innocence' from the 'Ballads MS' (p. 1315).
l. 108: '78 lines' counts the first four columns written on pp. 52–54 before any of the additions (i.e. before ll. 3–4, 21–4, 31–50, 87–90).
l. 109: 'Was Jesus Chaste . . .', written to the right and joined to l. 108 by a stroke, refers to part f (p. 1058), written before part k was begun.
'Im Sure . . .' evidently refers to part k, by the last line of which it is written.

'A FAIRY LEAPT'

A Fairy leapt ^Stept^ upon my knee
Singing & dancing merrily⌊.⌋
I said 'Thou thing of patches rings
Pins Necklaces & Such like things
Disgu[i]ser of the Female Form⌊,⌋
Thou paltry gilded poisnous[?] worm⌊!⌋'
Weeping he fell upon my thigh
And thus in tears did soft reply⌊:⌋
'Knowest thou not O Fairies Lord
How much by us Contemnd Abhorrd
Whatever hides the Female form
That cannot bear the Mental Storm⌊?⌋
Therefore in Pity still we give
Our lives to make the Female live
And what would turn into disease
We turn to what will joy & please⌊.⌋'

l. 1: 'Stept' is written above 'leapt', which has not been deleted.

'I ASKED A THIEF'

———

I askéd a thief to steal me a peach ;
He turned up his eyes .
I asked a lithe lady to lie her down ;
Holy & meek she cries—

As soon as I went   [5]
An angel came .
He wink'd at the thief
And smil'd at the dame—

And without one word said
Had a peach from the tree   [10]
And still as a maid
Enjoy'd the lady.   [12]
       W Blake
       Lambeth
       1796

VALA OR THE FOUR ZOAS

———

[Page 1]

^^*The Four Zoas^^

[VALA del]

[or del]

^^*The torments of Love & Jealousy in^^

The Death and

Judgement

of ^^*Albion^^ the

[Eternal del] ^Ancient^ Man

[A DREAM

of Nine Nights del]

by William Blake 1797

[Page 2]

*Rest before Labour

Page 1   DESIGN: A rough sketch represents a naked figure plunging down the right margin with his back to us, a trumpet to his lips, and his right leg curved over the writing at the top of the page. (The trumpeter is just like the figure illustrating *Night Thoughts* p. 19, except that the *Vala* figure has his back to us, while the *Night Thoughts* figure has his front to us.) He seems to be trumpeting to about ten figures whose heads may be seen at the bottom of the page looking up; a horse, a bird, and perhaps a Wizard-of-Oz lion are among these figures. Some figures at the bottom look demonic, and some fingers and hooves appear above the ground. A serpent seems to rise in the left margin. (The design may illustrate a passage such as p. 122, ll. 34–5: 'Numerous as the leaves of autumn every species Flock to the trumpet muttring over the sides of the grave'.)

The 'torments of love and jealousy' are in *Jerusalem* pl. 69, l. 7 (p. 569).

Page 2   DESIGN: The page is almost entirely occupied by a naked man lying on his back with his body curved to the left, both knees bent, and his left arm behind his head as if in sleep. He might alternatively be soaring upward. (An analogous figure is on p. 139 and a soaring man with a broken chain on *America* pl. 5 is similar

1072

Οτι ουκ εστιν ημιν η παλη προς αιμα και ϛαρκα. αλλα προς τας αρχας, προς τας εξθξιας, προς τθς κοϛμοκρατορας τθ ϛκοτθς τθ αιωνος τθτθ, προς τα πνευματικα της πονηριας εν τοις επουρανιοις.

Εφες: 5 ˏviˏ κεφ 12 ver

VALA

Night the First

ˏThe Song of the Aged Motherˏ which shook the heavens
with wrath   [1 *del*] ˏˏ*1ˏˏ
ˏ[Hearing the march of long resounding strong heroic Verse   [2 *del*]

from the waist up.) A chain or rope seems to descend from his right arm, and his right foot may be a cloven hoof. Both legs were roughly sketched outstretched (?standing). Many other vague strokes, particularly above his head, are indecipherable.

Page 3 DESIGN: At the foot of the·page is a nude reclining woman (perhaps Vala) with her right knee bent sharply, her right arm behind her head, looking up. An erased ink stroke put her right arm farther back, and another made her rest on this arm. Pencil strokes show a raised left(?) leg, and blurred and obscured ink and water-colour strokes show this leg semi-extended with the heel on the ground.

By 'VALA' at the top of the page is a figure in ink with its back to us which seems to be soaring away with its arms outspread; this drawing is very firm and sure. The background has been indicated in wash which surrounds and partly covers the text, both erased and present. There are numerous other vague strokes.

Above the title: The Greek is for:
For we wrestle not against flesh and blood, but against principalities, against powers, against the rulers of the darkness of this world, against spiritual wickedness in high places.

Ephes vi chap. 12 ver

The whole text is written over about twelve erased Copperplates lines, the third of which may end 'Round' and the sixth 'Dream'. These were replaced by lines in the Copperplate Hand, now erased, the first five of which may read:
This is the [Dirge of Eno *del*] ˏSong[?] of Enitharmonˏ which shook the heavens
   with wrath
And thus beginneth the Book of Vala which Whosoever reads
If with his Intellect he comprehend the terrible Sentence
The heavens shall quak*e*, the earth shall move & shudder & the mountains
With all their woods, the streams & valleys: wail in dismal fear
ll. 2–3 are deleted with a pencil scrawl, as are the ink numbers which were written in the left margin.
ll. 2, 6: Cf. Pope's 'Epistle to Augustus' ll. 267–9 (*The Works of Alexander Pope* [1787], ii. 276):
<blockquote>
Dryden taught to join
The varying verse, the full resounding line,
The long majestic March, and Energy divine.
</blockquote>

ʌMarshalld in order for the day of Intellectual Battle *del*]ʌ

The heavens [shall *del*] quak*e*, the earth [shall *del*] ʌwasʌ

moveʌdʌ & shudderʌdʌ & the mountains

With all their woods, the streams & valleys: wailʌdʌ in dismal fearₗ·₊

ʌʌ[(To hear *del*) ʌʌʌHearingʌʌʌ the (Sound *del*) ʌʌʌmarchʌʌʌ of Long resounding strong heroic verse

ʌʌ[Marshalld in order for the day of intellectual battle *del*]ʌʌ

Four Mighty Ones are in every Man: a Perfect Unity John XVII
                                                    22 &23

Cannot Exis*t*, but from the Universal Brotherhood of John 1 c.

Eden   εσκηνωσεν

The Universal Ma*n*, To Whom be Glory Evermore Amenₗ·₊

ʌʌ*What are the Natures of those Living Creatures the Heavenly Father only

ʌʌ*Knowethₗ,₊ ʌʌʌ*noʌʌʌ *del*] [Man *del*] Knoweth [not *del*] nor Can know in all Eternityₗ·₊ʌʌ

Los was the fourth immortal starry one, & in the Earth

Of a bright Univers*e* Empery attended day & nightₗ,₊

Days & nights of revolving joy, Urthona was his name

[*Page 4*]

In Eden; in the Auricular Nerves of Human Life

Which is the Earth of Eden, he his Emanations propagatedₗ,₊

l. 4: The verb tense was altered from future ('shall quake . . . shall move & shudder') to present ('quake . . . moves & shudders') to past ('quake . . . moved & shudderd').

ll. 6–7 are connected by two strokes with the space after l. 3.

l. 8: John 17: 21–3: '[*Jesus said, I pray*] that they all may be one; as thou, Father, art in me, and I in thee, that they also may be as one in us: that the world may believe that thou hast sent me. And the glory which thou gavest me I have given them; that they may be one, even as we are one: I in them, and thou in me, that they may be made perfect in one; and that the world may know that thou hast sent me, and hast loved them, as thou hast loved me.'

ll. 10–11: John 1: 14: 'And the Word was made flesh, and dwelt among us'; the last phrase Blake gives in Greek.

ll. 11–12 are written in a stanza-break.

Page 4 DESIGN: At the foot of the page, a winged(?) man (?Tharmas) kneeling on the coils of a sea serpent draws a bow to his ear and aims at the lower right corner. (Cf. the archers on pp. 19, 40, 108.) The bowman's elbow was erased with the last line of the erased text, and the serpent has alternate heads at the top of the page and in the left margin. Perhaps an erased coil of the serpent covered several textual lines. The bow covers the catchwords, both erased and current. There are pencil swirls over the serpent. (The serpent is much like all Blake's serpents—cf. *Marriage* pl. 20, p. 93—but in particular its head resembles that of

Vala p. 4

[Like Sons & Daughters, *del*] ∧∧*Fairies of Albion_L,」 after-
wards Gods of the Heathen_L.」∧∧ Daughter of Beulah Sing
His fall into Division & his Resurrection to Unity_L.」
∧[His fall into the Generation of Decay & Death & his   [5]
  ∧[Regeneration by the Resurrection from the dead *del*]∧
Begin with Tharmas Parent power darkning in the West_L.」

'Lost! Lost! Lost! are my Emanations_L.」 Enion [come forth
  del] ∧O Enion_L.」∧

[I am *del*] ∧We are∧ become a Victim to the Living_L.」 [I *del*]
  ∧We∧ hide in secret_L.」
I have hidden [thee Enion in Jealous Despair *del*] ∧Jerusalem
  in Silent Contrition_L.」∧∧ O Pity Me_L.」∧   [10]
I will build thee a Labyrinth [where we may remain for ever
  alone *del*] ∧also_L.」 O pity me O Enion_L.」∧
∧Why has[t] thou taken sweet Jerusalem from my inmost
  Soul_L?」

the monster in Blake's *Night Thoughts* drawing [?1796] No. 349, which is identified
in Young's text as Leviathan; it is ridden by a scaled man with a pope's hat and
pastoral crook.)
ll. 1–15, 18–26 (a single block) cover about nineteen erased Copperplate lines.
Some may be very tentatively read: l. 2 'Saying . . . of . . . for . . . of Eternal
Life'; l. 3 'Song of . . .'; l. 6 'Rejoicing so amongst . . .'; l. 7 'The . . . faded . . .
slept . . .'; l. 8 'Till far dismal . . . four . . . all . . .'; l. 9 '. . . a pleasing'; l. 10
'Enion . . . of slavery . . .'; l. 12 '. . . cloud'; l. 18 '. . . Enion'; l. 19 '. . . the light
of day'. Because of the multiple erasures which (under ll. 12–15) have almost
worn through the paper, the counting of the lines erased and the interpretation of
the whole page are exceptionally difficult.
ll. 5–6 are inserted in a stanza-break.
l. 10: The alteration first read in pencil 'Enitharmon in Silent[?] Contrition';
then 'Enitharmon' was changed in pencil to 'Jerusalem'; and then the whole was
darkened in ink. The deleted words are crossed out in pencil.
l. 11: The words deleted were crossed out in pencil and 'also pity me O Enion'
written above them; the addition was then confirmed in ink, with the added
addition of 'O'.
ll. 12–15, 18–26 (a single block) seem to be written over about eleven erased
Modified Copperplate lines which had been written over the erased Copperplate
lines. The Modified Copperplate lines begin farther to the left than those in
the Copperplate Hand. The tenth begins 'Arise O[?] Enion' and the thirteenth
may conclude: 'for Lo! I have calmd my seas', as on p. 129, ll. 24–7 and p. 6,
under ll. 10–38.
ll. 12–15 seem to be written over the same thing in pencil (with the exception
of l. 12), which were written over erased Modified Copperplate lines, which in
turn were written over erased Copperplate writing. l. 12 read in pencil:
  Why hast thou taken [Enitharmon *del*] ∧Jerusalem∧ from my inmost soul

ʌLet her Lay secret in the Soft recess of darkness & silenceʟ·」
ʌIt is not Love I bear to Enitharmonʟ·」 It is Pityʟ·」
ʌShe hath taken refuge in my bosom & I cannot cast her out.ʌ   [ˌ

ʌʌʌ'The Men have recieved their death wounds & their Emanations are fled
ʌʌʌTo me for refuge & I cannot turn them out for Pitys Sakeʟ·」'ʌʌʌ
ʌEnion said—'[His *del*] ʌʌThyʌʌ fear has made me trembleʟ;」 thy terrors have surrounded meʟ·」
ʌAll Love is lostʟ!」 Terror succeeds & Hatred instead of Love
ʌAnd stern demands of Right & Duty instead of Libertyʟ·」   [
ʌOnce thou wast to Me the loveliest son of heaven—But now
ʌWhy art thou Terrible and yet I love thee in thy terror till
ʌI am almost Extinct & soon shall be a Shadow in Oblivion
ʌUnless some way can be found that I may look upon thee & liveʟ·」
ʌHide me some Shadowy semblanc*e*, secret whispring in my Ear   [
ʌIn secret of soft Wing*s*, in mazes of delusive beautyʟ·」ʌ
ʌʌI have lookd into the secret soul of him I lovd
ʌʌAnd in the Dark recesses found Sin & cannot returnʟ·」'ʌʌ

ʌʌTrembling & pale sat Tharmas weeping in his cloudsʟ·」ʌʌ   ▮

ʌʌ'Why wilt thou Examine every little fibre of my soulʟ,」
ʌʌSpreading them out before the Sun like Stalks of flax to dryʟ?」
ʌʌThe infant joy is beautiful but its anatomy
ʌʌHorrible Ghast & Deadlyʟ!」 nought shalt thou find in it
ʌʌBut Death Despair & Everlasting brooding Melan- cholyʟ!」ʌʌ

ll. 16–17 are written sideways in the left margin over the same thing in pencil (except that 'Men' had a lower-case 'm'). They are in no way marked for entry, and their present position in this stanza break is therefore conjectural. Both the pencil and the ink lines seem to be written over part of the drawing.

ll. 18–21, 27–8, 30–4 are in *Jerusalem* pl. 22, ll. 1, 10–12, 14–15, 20–4 (pp. 460–1).

ll. 30–4 are written sideways at the top of the right margin beside ll. 42–6 and are in no way marked for entry. After l. 34 is a stanza-break.

ᐱᐱThou wilt go mad with horror if thou Dost Examine thus   [*35*]
ᐱᐱEvery moment of my secret hours⌞.⌟ Yea I know
ᐱᐱThat I have sinnd & that my Emanations are become
   harlots⌞.⌟
ᐱᐱI am already distracted at their deeds & if I look
ᐱᐱUpon them more Despair will bring self murder on my
   soul⌞.⌟
ᐱᐱO Enion thou art thyself a root growing in hell   [*40*]
ᐱᐱTho thus heavenly beautiful to draw me to destruction⌞.⌟ᐱᐱ

ᐱᐱ*Sometimes I think thou art a flower expanding⌞;⌟
ᐱᐱ*Sometimes I think thou art fruit breaking from its bud
ᐱᐱ*In dreadful dolor & pain & I am like an atom⌞,⌟
ᐱᐱ*A Nothing left in darkness yet I am an identity⌞.⌟   [*45*]
ᐱᐱ*I wish & feel & weep & groan⌞.⌟ Ah terrible terrible⌞!⌟'ᐱᐱ   [*46*]

[*Page 5*]

ᐱIn [Beulah *del*] ᐱᐱEdenᐱᐱ Females sleep the winter in soft
   silken veils
ᐱWoven by their own hands to hide them in the darksome
   grave
ᐱBut Males immortal live renewd by female death*s*; in soft
ᐱDelight they die & they revive in spring with music &
   songs⌞.⌟
ᐱEnion said 'Farewell I die⌞.⌟ I hide from thy searching
   eyes⌞.⌟'ᐱ
      [*5*]

So saying—From her bosom weaving soft in Sinewy threads
A tabernacle [of delight *del*] ᐱᐱ*for [Enitharmon *del*]ᐱᐱ
   ᐱᐱᐱJerusalemᐱᐱᐱ She sat among the Rocks

ll. 35–41 are written sideways in the right margin beside ll. 30–4 over the ends
of several erased Copperplate lines and are in no way marked for entry.
   ll. 42–6 are written at the top of the page above the main text and are in no
way marked for entry.

Page 5 DESIGN: At the foot of the page is a winged figure, up to its chest in a
Grey sea or cloud, with its face bowed in its hands. (Probably he is 'Tharmas . . .
among his Clouds Weeping', ll. 8–9.) Blue sky around the text and over the present
ll. 1–9 seems to surround just the original text, particularly in the right margin
where the border is irregular.

Singing her Lamentation. Tharmas groand among his
  Clouds
Weeping, [and *del*] ˄then˄ bending from his Clouds he
  stoopd his [holy *del*] ˄innocent˄ head   [˙
And stretching out his holy hand in the vast deep sublime   [˙
Turnd round the circle of Destiny with tears & bitter sighs
And sai*d*: 'Return O Wanderer when the day of Clouds is
  oer∟˙」'
  ˄So saying he sunk down into the sea a pale white
  corse∟˙」˄
[So saying *del*] ˄In torment˄ he sunk down & flowd among
  her filmy Woof∟ˬ」
  ˄His Spectre issuing from his feet in flames of fire˄   [
In [dismal *del*] ˄gnawing˄ pain drawn out by her lovd
  fingers∟ˬ」 every nerve
She counte*d*, every vein & lacteal threading them among
Her woof of terror. Terrified & drinking tears of woe
Shuddring she wove nine days & nights Sleepless∟;」 her food
  was tears∟˙」
  ˄Wondring she saw her woof begin to animate & not   [
  ˄As garments woven subservient to her hands but having
  a will
  ˄Of its own perverse & wayward∟˙」 Enion lovd & wept∟˙」˄
Nine days she labourd at her work & nine dark sleepless
  nights
But on the tenth [bright(?) *del*] ˄trembling˄ morn∟ˬ」 the
  Circle of Destiny Complete∟ˬ」
Round rolld the Sea Englobing in a watry Globe self
  balancd∟˙」
A Frowning Continent appeard Where Enion in the desart
Terrified in her own Creation viewing her woven shadow

ll. 9–20, 23–8, 46–57 (a single block to the bottom of the page) are written over
about eighteen erased Copperplate lines, divided into stanzas of five, three, four,
one, two, and three lines.
  ll. 9–13, 25 may have been written under p. 7, ll. 1–18.
  l. 13 is inserted in a stanza-break.
  l. 16: 'gnawing' is written below the line, presumably because the insertion of
l. 15 left no room above the line.
  ll. 20–2: l. 20 is inserted in a stanza-break; l. 21 continues after it up the right
margin and is separated from l. 20 by a stroke; and l. 22 is written below l. 21
in the right margin.

Sat in a [sweet *del*] ˄dread˄ intoxication of [false *del*] ˄Self˄
[woven *del*] [bliss *del*] ˄[sorrow *del*] Repentance & Con-
trition˪.˩˄

˄[He spurnd Enion with his foot˪,˩ he sprang aloft in Clouds
˄[(Alighting down from *del*) Alighting in his drunken joy in
a far distant Grove *del*]   [*30*]

˄˄There is from Great Eternity a mild & pleasant rest
˄˄Namd Beulah˪,˩ a Soft Moony Universe feminine lovely
˄˄Pure mild & Gentle given in Mercy to those who sleep
˄˄Eternall*y*, Created by the Lamb of God around
˄˄On all sides within & without the Universal Man˪.˩   [*35*]
˄˄The daughters of Beulah follow sleepers in all their Dreams
˄˄Creating Spaces lest they fall into Eternal Death˪.˩
˄˄The Circle of Destiny complete they gave it to a Space
˄˄And namd the Space Ulro & brooded over it in care &
love˪.˩˄˄

˄˄˄They said 'The Spectre is in every man insane & most   [*40*]
˄˄˄Deformd˪.˩ Thro the three heavens des[*c*]ending in fury
& fire
˄˄˄We meet it with our Songs & loving blandishments & give
˄˄˄To it a form of vegetation But this spectre of Tharmas
˄˄˄Is Eternal Death˪.˩ What shall We do˪?˩ O God [help
del] pity & help˪.˩'
˄˄˄So spoke they & closd the Gate of [Auricular *del*] [power
del] ˄˄˄˄nerves˄˄˄˄ ˄˄˄˄the Tongue˄˄˄˄ in trembling
fear˪.˩˄˄˄   [*45*]

ll. 29–30 are inserted in a stanza-break and are deleted by separate strokes and
by a smudge.
l. 31 is in *Milton* pl. 30, l. 14 (p. 385).
ll. 31–9 are written sideways in the right corner in the Modified Copperplate
Hand over the same thing in pencil, except that the last word of l. 36, now
'Dreams', was 'wanderings'. All the other additions to this page are in the Usual
Hand. Pencil strokes (which go under ll. 40–5) seem to indicate that ll. 31–9 should
follow l. 30, but it is quite possible that these directional strokes were inserted
before ll. 29–30 were written.
ll. 40–1 are on p. 84, ll. 38–9 and *Jerusalem* pl. 37, l. 4 (pp. 1196, 495).
ll. 40–5 are written sideways beside ll. 31–9, but no position is indicated for
them.

['What have I done_L?_J' said Enion_L,_J 'accursed wretch! What
deed?

[Is this a deed of Love_L?_J I know what I have done. I know

[Too late now to repent. Love is changd to deadly Hate_L,_J

[A life is blotted out & I alone remain possessd with Fears_L._J

[I see the (remembrance *del*) ^Shadow^ of the dead within my
(eyes *del*) ^Soul^ wandering

[In darkness & solitude forming Seas of (Trouble *del*)
^Doubt^ & rocks of (sorrow *del*) ^Repentance_L._J^

[Already are my Eyes reverted; all that I behold

[Within my Soul has lost its splendor & a brooding Fear

[Shadows me oer & drives me outward to a world of woe_L._J'

[So waild she trembling before her own Created Phantasm
^^[*Who animating times on times by the Force of her sweet
song^^

[But standing on the Rocks her woven shadow glowing
bright *all del*]

[*Page 6*]

^She drew the spectre forth from Tharmas in [her silken
del] her shining[?] loom

^Of Vegetation weeping in wayward infancy & sullen
youth_L;_J^

^^*Listning to her soft lamentations soon his tongue began

^^*To Lisp out words & soon in masculine strength aug-
menting he^^

Reard up a form of gold & stood upon the glittering rock

A shadowy human form winged & in his depths

The dazzlings as of gems shone clear, rapturous in [joy
del] fury_L,_J

ll. 46–55 are circled and deleted with three slanting strokes. The erased Copper-
plate lines beneath them lap outside this circle. The circle seems to have been
erased when ll. 29–30 were written.

l. 56 is inserted in a stanza-break.

Page 6 DESIGN: At the foot of the page is a large, firm sketch of a winged man
sleeping with his legs curled under him. Five of the present and erased lines go
over a wing, which was erased. Very vague pencil strokes seem to surround the
rest of the text in the left margin, somewhat like an arching tree; they are apparently
under the added lines at the top of the page.

l. 1 is so close to the top of the page that several letters disappear off the
paper.

Vala p. 6

Glorying in his own eyes⌐,⌐ Exalted in terrific Pride⌐,⌐

⁴[Searching for glory⌐,⌐ wishing that the heavens had eyes to
See
[And courting that the Earth would ope her Eyelids & be-
hold   [*10*]
[Such wondrous beauty repining in the midst of all his glory
[That nought but Enion could be found to praise adore &
love⌐.⌐
[Three days in self admiring raptures on the rocks he flamd
[And three dark nights repind the solitude, but the third
morn
[Astonishd he found Enion hidden in the darksom Cave⌐.⌐
all del]   [*15*]

[She spoke⌐:⌐ 'What am I⌐?⌐ wherefore was I put forth on
these rocks
[Among the Clouds to tremble in the wind in solitude⌐?⌐
[Where is the voice that lately woke the desart⌐?⌐ Where the
Face
[That wept among the clouds & where the voice that shall
reply⌐?⌐
[No other living thing is here. The Sea the Earth, the
Heaven   [*20*]
[And Enion desolate⌐;⌐ where art thou Tharmas⌐?⌐ O
return⌐!⌐' *all del*]

[Three days she waild & three dark nights sitting among the
Rocks
[While the bright spectre hid himself among the backing(?)
clouds⌐.⌐

ll. 9–25 are deleted in Grey wash. ll. 9–12, 15, 22–5 were also deleted with
individual strokes; ll. 16–21 are deleted by six slanting strokes.
    ll. 10–38 cover about seventeen erased Copperplate lines which were in stanzas
of two, nine, two, and four lines; l. 1 reads: 'When[?] . . . golden day'; l. 2 '. . .
seas', and l. 3 '. . . crystal sky', suggesting that the first two may be the same as
p. 129, ll. 26–7 and p. 4, under ll. 1–15, 18–26; cf. also p. 130, l. 14. The Copper-
plate lines had been added to and altered before they were erased.
    Beside l. 22, in the left margin, '*the Jealous' is legible though erased and may
have been part of the original additions to the Copperplate text. It may have con-
tinued as a whole line.

[Then sleep fell on her eyelids in a Chasm of the Valley⌐·⌐

[The sixteenth morn the spectre stood before her manifest⌐·⌐ *all*

[The Spectre thus spok*e*: (Art thou not my slave & shalt thou
   dare

[(To smite me with thy tongue⌐?⌐ beware lest I sting also
   thee, *del*)
      ∧'Who art thou Diminutive husk & shell⌐?⌐∧

   ∧[(Broke from my bonds I scorn my prison⌐·⌐ I scorn &
   yet I love *del*)∧

   ∧[If thou hast sinnd & art polluted know that I am pure

   ∧[And unpolluted & will bring to rigid strict account

   ∧[All thy past deeds⌐;⌐∧ hear what I tell thee∧!∧ mark it
   well! remember!

[This world is (Mine *del*) ∧Thine∧ in which thou dwellest⌐;⌐
   that within thy soul

[That dark & dismal infinite where Thought roams up &
   down

[Is (thine *del*) Mine & there thou goest when with one
   Sting of my tongue

[Envenomd thou rollst inwards to the place (of death & hell
   del) ∧∧*whence I emergd⌐·⌐'∧∧

[She trembling answerd⌐:⌐ 'Wherefore was I born & what
   am I⌐?⌐

[A sorrow & a fear⌐,⌐ a living torment & naked Victim⌐·⌐

   ∧[I thought to weave a Covering (from *del*) ∧∧for∧∧ my
   Sins from wrath of Tharmas' *all del*]∧

---

ll. 26, 28–38 (a single block) have a rectangle drawn round them and are deleted
by two vertical strokes. l. 37 is separately deleted as well. The rectangle surrounds
the added lines, but some erased Copperplate words were outside it, as were the
pencil 'I emergd' (l. 35) and part of l. 38. The deleting strokes were partly erased
when the lines under ll. 29–30, 38 were erased.

ll. 26–8: 'Art thou . . . sting also' (ll. 26–7) were deleted in pencil; 'Who art . . .
shell' was inserted over a caret above 'Art thou not my slave &' (l. 26) and con-
tinued up the right margin with l. 28, which was later deleted in pencil. Over l. 28
is an erased pencil line which may begin 'Behold I'.

ll. 29–30 seem to be written over two erased lines of the first series of additions.

[*Page 7*]

∧∧['Examining the sins of Tharmas I (have *del*) ∧∧∧soon∧∧∧
found my own∟·⌐

∧∧[O Slay me not∟!⌐ thou art his Wrath embodied in
Deceit∟·⌐

∧∧[I thought Tharmas a Sinner & I murderd his Emana-
tions∟,⌐∧∧

   ∧∧∧[His secret loves & Graces∟·⌐ Ah me wretched∟!⌐
What have I done∟?⌐∧∧∧

∧[(But *del*) ∧∧∧For∧∧∧ now I find that all those Emanations   5
were my Childrens Souls∧∧   [*5*]

   ∧∧∧[And I have murderd them with Cruelty above
atonement∟·⌐∧∧∧

∧∧[Those that remain have fled from my cruelty into the
desarts

∧∧[(Among wild beasts to roam *del*) And thou the delusive
tempter ∧∧∧to these deeds∧∧∧ sittest before me∟·⌐∧∧   ∧∧100∧∧

∧[(But where is *del*) ∧∧(Thou art not *del*) ∧∧ ∧∧∧And art thou∧∧∧
Tharmas∟?⌐ all thy soft delusive beauty cannot

∧[Tempt me to *del*] ∧∧murder∧∧ (honest love *del*) ∧∧my own
soul∧∧ & wipe my tears & smile   [*10*]

∧∧*This line to come in∧∧

∧[In this thy world (for ah! how *del*) ∧∧not mine tho∧∧ dark
I feel my world within∟·⌐' *all del*]∧

∧[The Spectre said∟:⌐ 'Thou sinful Woma*n*, was it thy desire

Page 7 DESIGN: At the foot of the page is a naked male(?) figure on his left side
in the sea holding his head in his hands and looking up the right margin. His
legs were later turned into a coiling serpent. (He may be related to the serpent-
man on p. 144, and both probably represent the 'monster' 'Twisting in fearful
forms & howling', ll. 26, 19.) The sea swirls around him, and his head may be in
flames. A Grey wash covers all the drawing but avoids all but the last four words of
the text.

l. 1: The quotation mark is Blake's.

ll. 1–18 cover two stanzas (about seven lines) of Copperplate writing; they may
read: l. 1 '. . . head [?]'; l. 3 'T . . . Destiny[?]'; l. 4 'And said Return . . . of
clouds is o'er'; l. 5 'So . . .'; l. 6 '. . . balanc'd', as in p. 5, ll. 9–13, 25.

ll. 1–18 also cover six or more erased pencil lines which went above them to
the top of the page. ll. 1–16 were deleted with two strokes; ll. 1–2, 16–18 were
deleted individually with a single stroke apiece; ll. 9–11 were deleted in pencil; and
ll. 1–2 were deleted in Grey wash.

ll. 1–11 cover about five erased added lines. This group of lines (1–11) is circled
in ink. Under l. 1 the last erased word is legible: 'threatening'.

ʌ[That I should hide thee with my power & delight thee
with my beauty
ʌ[And now thou darknest in my presenc*e*, never from my
sight
ʌ[Shalt thou depart to weep in secret. In my jealous wings
ʌ[I evermore will hold thee when thou goest out or comest
inₗ·ⱼ
ʌ[Tis thou hast darkend all My World O Woman lovely
baneₗ·ⱼ' *all del*]

ʌ[Thus they contended all the day among the Caves of
Tharmasʌ
[Twisting in fearful forms & howling ʌhowling harsh shriek-
ingʌ
ʌ[Howlingʌ harsh shrieking, mingling their bodies join in
burning anguish *all del*]
Mingling his [horrible *del*] ʌterrible *del*]ʌ brightness with her
tender limbs; then high she soar'd
ʌ[Shrieking *del*]ʌ Above the ocean; a bright wonder [that
(Beulah *del*) ʌʌNatureʌʌ shudderd at *del*]
Half Woman & half [Spirit(?) *del*] ʌSpectreʌ, all his lovely
changing colours mix
With her fair crystal clearness; in her lips & cheeks his
poisons rose
In blushes like the morning, and his scaly armour softening
A monster lovely in the heavens or wandering on the
earth,
[With (Spirit[?] *del*) ʌSpectreʌ voice incessant wailing, in
incessant thirstₗ,ⱼ

l. 13: sideways, ending in the right margin by l. 13, are several rubbed but not
erased lines which may read:

			veiny pipes[?]
Enion	d	torrent floods melting [away *del*]	
		white rocks	
		from heaven to heaven	
		fills *A*lbion[?]	

ll. 13–14, 20–8, p. 8, ll. 12, 20 are copied on p. 144, ll. 1–2, p. 143, ll. 1–10,
14–15.
ll. 19–28 are apparently represented in the design.
l. 23: Cf. the design on p. 26.

[Beauty all blushing with desire mocking her fell despair∟.」

[Wandering desolate, a wonder abhorr'd by Gods & Men
  all del]   [*29*]

[Page 8]

6
Till with fierce pain she brought forth on the rocks her
  sorrow & woe∟;」
Behold two [little Infants wept *del*] ᐱᐱ[*figures(?) of(?) howld
  del]ᐱᐱ upon the desolate wind.

ᐱThe first state weeping they began & helpless as a wave
ᐱBeaten along its sightless way growing enormous in / its
  motion to
ᐱIts utmost goal, till strength from Enion / like ᐱᐱrichestᐱᐱ
  summer shining   [*5*]
ᐱRaised the [bright *del*] ᐱᐱ*fierceᐱᐱ boy & girl with glories
  from their heads out beaming∟,」
ᐱDrawing forth drooping mothers pity∟,」 drooping mothers
  sorrow ᐱ
ᐱᐱ[But those in Great Eternity Met in the Council of God
ᐱᐱ[As One Man hovering over Gilead & Hermon∟.」
    ᐱᐱ[He is the Good Shepherd∟,」 He is the Lord &
      Master   [*10*]
    ᐱᐱ[To Create Man Morning by Morning∟,」 to Give
      gifts at Noon day∟.」ᐱᐱ

Page 8   DESIGN: At the foot of the page, a woman in a loose garment leans against
the left margin; she is holding two naked nursing babies who are facing each other
and at whom she is looking. One baby appears to be a boy. (They seem to represent
Enion with the 'two little Infants' Los and Enitharmon as 'They sulk upon her
breast', ll. 2, 21.) Vague strokes behind the woman up the margin and above
the text may be meant to represent a tree. Similarly, there may be insects hovering
over her head and grass by her legs.
  ll. 3–7 are written in the Modified Copperplate Hand over five erased Copper-
plate lines.
  l. 5: Originally 'shining' was 'shines'.
  ll. 8–20 were deleted with Grey wash; ll. 8–12, 20 were deleted individually
with a stroke apiece; and ll. 12–20 were deleted with a single stroke.
  ll. 8–9 are repeated on p. 21, ll. 1–2, 7 and on p. 99, ll. 1–2.
  ll. 8–11 are in a stanza break. ll. 10–11 are written progressively smaller, prob-
ably because of the shrinking space.
  l. 10 is in *Jerusalem* pl. 38, l. 23 (p. 496), q.v.
  ll. 10–11 may be under p. 99, ll. 4–9.

[Enion brooded, oer the rocks, the rough rocks (*word del*)
ˆgroaning vegetate⌊·⌋ˆ
 ˆ[Such power was given to the Solitary wanderer.ˆ
[The barked Oak, the long limbd Beach; the Ches'nut
 tree; the Pin*e*,
[The Pear tree mild, the frowning Walnut, the sharp Crab,
 & Apple sweet,
[The rough bark opens; twittering peep forth little beaks &
 wings⌊,⌋
[The Nightingale, the Goldfinch, Robin, Lark, Linnet &
 Thrush⌊·⌋
[The Goat leap'd from the craggy (*word del*) ˆcliff,ˆ the
 Sheep awoke from the mould⌊,⌋
[Upon its green stalk rose the Corn, waving innumerable⌊,⌋
[Infolding the bright Infants from the desolating winds⌊·⌋
 all del]

 ˆThey sulk upon her breast⌊,⌋ her hair became like snow
 on mountains⌊,⌋
ˆWeaker & weaker, weeping woful, wearier and wearier⌊,⌋ˆ
ˆˆFaded & her bright Eyes decayd melted with pity & loveˆˆ

[Page 9]

ˆAnd then they wanderd far away⌊;⌋ she sought for them in
 vain⌊;⌋

l. 20 is largely repeated on p. 143, l. 15.
ll. 21–2 are written over an erased Copperplate line.

Page 9   DESIGN: At the foot of the page, a woman with closed eyes stumbles and almost falls as she follows a boy and a girl who are about ten years old. All are loosely clothed, and both children are in the left corner looking back, the boy skipping from the woman's reach and the girl reaching up the margin. The boy's head is under the last line of the text, but no other part of the drawing impinges on the writing. (The design clearly represents Enion as 'In weeping blindness stumbling she followd' Los and Enitharmon, l. 2; it was etched, reversed, with 'the children somewhat altered, in *Jerusalem* pl. 87—p. 611.)
 In the centre of the top margin, over the erased pencil text (I think), is a vague pencil sketch of a circle with a Christ-like figure in it looking pathetic, with his arms down, his hands out to the sides, standing on a semi-circle which may be the world. This sketch goes over the first erased ink line.
 ll. 1–3 partly cover three erased Copperplate lines and perhaps three erased pencil lines. Above these lines, at the top of the page, are several (perhaps four) erased pencil lines, *under* ll. 12–13 and the sketch. The second was the same as l. 2, but nothing else is legible.

7

˄In weeping blindness stumbling she followd them oer rocks
& mountains˄
˄˄*Rehumanizing from the Spectre in pangs of maternal
love˪·˩˄˄
Ingrate they wanderd scorning her [*word del*] ˄drawing˄ her
[life; ingrate *del*] ˄˄[*Spectrous Life *del*]˄˄
Repelling her away [from them (?) *del*] ˄& away˄ by a dread   ˄˄*100˄˄
repulsive power   [5]
Into Non Entity revolving round in dark despai*r*,
˄˄*And drawing in the Spectrous life in pride & haughty
joy˪·˩˄˄
˄˄*Thus Enion gave them all her Spe[*c*]terous life [in Deep
Despair *del*]
˄˄*Then [Ona (?) *del*] ˄˄˄*Eno˄˄˄ a daughter of Beulah took
a Moment of Tim*e*,
˄˄*And drew it out to [twenty years *del*] ˄˄˄*Seven thousand
years˄˄˄ with much care & affliction   [*10*]
˄˄*And many tears & in the [twenty *del*] ˄˄˄*Every˄˄˄ years
[gave visions toward(?) heaven *del*] ˄˄˄*made windows
into Eden˪·˩˄˄˄
˄˄˄*She also took an atom of space & opend its centre
˄˄˄*Into Infinitude & ornamented it with wondrous
art˪·˩˄˄˄
˄˄*Astonishd sat her Sisters of Beulah to see her soft affec-
tions
˄˄*To Enion & her children & they ponderd these things
wondring   [*15*]
˄˄*And they Alternate kept watch over the Youthful
terrors˪·˩
˄˄*They saw not yet the Hand Divine for it was not yet
reveald
˄˄*But they went on in Silent Hope & Feminine repose˄˄

l. 7 is written over an erased Copperplate line: 'Till they . . . quite away from
Enion'.
ll. 8–11, 14–18 are written sideways in a block in the left margin, and a bracket
going round all but l. 8 points to the space after l. 7.
ll. 9–11: The idea is used in *Jerusalem* pl. 48, ll. 30–1 (p. 519).
ll. 12–13 are written slanting in the top left corner of the page, near l. 9, and
are in no way marked for entry.

^^But Los & Enitharmon delighted in the Moony
spaces of [Ona del]^^ ^^^*Eno_L.J^^^

Nine Times they livd among the forests, feeding on sweet
fruits
And nine bright Spaces wandered [*words del*] ^weaving
mazes of delight_L.J^
Snaring the wild Goats for their milk_L,J they eat the flesh of
Lambs_L,J
A male & female naked & ruddy as the pride of summer_L.J

Alternate Love & Hate his breast; hers Scorn & Jealousy
In embryon passion*s*; they kiss'd not nor embrac'd for shame
& fear_L.J
His head beamd light & in his vigorous voice was prophecy_L.J
He could controll the times & seasons, & the days & years_L;J
She could controll the spaces, regions, desart, flood & forest
    ^But had no power to weave a Veil of covering for her
    Sins_L.J
    ^She drave the Females all away from Los
    ^[& *del*] ^^And^^ Los drave all the Males from her
    away_L.J^
They wanderd long, till they sat down upon the margind
se*a*,
    ^Conversing with the visions of Beulah in dark slumber-
    ous bliss_L.J
    ^[Nine years they view the gleaming(?) spheres (of
    Beulah[?] *del*) ^^leading^^ the Visions of Beulah *del*]

l. 19 is inserted in a stanza break.
l. 25: There are perhaps one-and-a-half lines of erased pencil words above
and below this line.
ll. 30–1 are written as a continuation of l. 29 up the right margin, with only the
unnecessary capitals to separate them. They are adapted on p. 10, ll. 22, 25–6, and
p. 30, ll. 51–2.
l. 33 is written in a stanza-break over several erased pencil words.
l. 34 is written in a stanza-break, and the words 'of Beulah' were separately
deleted when they were replaced by 'leading'. Below l. 34 is l. 35, which seems
to be a continuation of l. 34 but is not crossed out.
l. 34 is deleted by a pencil stroke and an ink stroke which continue into the
right margin, and above this dividing line in the right margin is written 'Night
the Second'. Blake evidently intended to begin Night II here, but he never con-
firmed the intention by deleting 'End of The First Night' on p. 18 and p. 19 or the
whole Second Night heading on p. 23, or by renumbering the Night.

ʌBut the two Youthful wonders wanderd in the world of
    Tharmas⌞.⌟ʌ   [*35*]
'Thy name is Enitharmon;' said the [bright *del*] ʌʌ*fierceʌʌ
    prophetic boy⌞.⌟
ʌʌ'While thy mild voice fills all these Caverns with sweet
    harmony
ʌO how [thy *del*] ʌʌourʌʌ Parents sit & [weep *del*] ʌʌmournʌʌ
    in their silent secret bowers⌞.⌟'   [*38*]

[*Page 10*]

8

But Enitharmon answerd with a dropping tear & [smiling
    del] ʌfrowningʌ
[Bright *del*] ʌDarkʌ as a dewy morning when the crimson
    light appears⌞:⌟

'To make us happy [how they *del*] ʌʌ*let themʌʌ weary their
    immortal powers
While we draw in their sweet delights ʌwhile we return them
    scorn
ʌOn scorn to feed our discontentʌ for if we grateful prove   [*5*]
They will withhold sweet love, whose food is thorns & bitter
    roots.
ʌWe hear the warlike clarions⌞,⌟ we view the turning spheres
ʌYet Thou in indolence reposest holding me in bonds⌞.⌟ʌ
Hear! [*words del*] ʌI will sing a Song ofʌ Death! it is a [*word
del*] ʌSongʌ of Vala!

ll. 37–8 cover an erased Copperplate line and a catchword. Above l. 37 is an
erased pencil line in which 'While they' and 't Harmony' may be deciphered.

Page 10 DESIGN: In each bottom corner is a rough pencil sketch of an angelic
figure. There are many other vague strokes below the text and surrounding it.

l. 1: 'smiling' was deleted and '*frowning' written above it; then both words
were erased and 'frowning' was written in ink where 'smiling' had been.

l. 3: 'let them' is written below the line, presumably because ll. 7–8 left no room
for it above the line.

ll. 4–5: The additions to these lines seem to be written over the same thing in
pencil, which is written over the erasure.

ll. 7–8 were written in a stanza-break between l. 2 and l. 3 over the same thing
in pencil (except that 'Thou' was 'thou'); later a bracket was put beside them
pointing to an 'X', referring to another 'X' in the mouth of a sideways 'V' pointing
between l. 6 and l. 9, indicating where ll. 7–8 should be moved.

ll. 9–24 have an erased circle around them.

l. 9: Above the line are some erased pencil words which could be 'Hear I will
sing a Song of'. The word under the second added 'Song' could be 'Dirge'.

The [Eternal(?) *del*] ∧Fallen∧ Man takes his repose: Urizen
sleeps in the porch∟·₁   [
Luvah and Vala [wake *del*] ∧∧*woke∧∧ & [fly *del*] ∧∧*flew∧∧
up from the Human Heart
Into the Brain; from thence upon the Pillow Vala slumber'd.
And Luvah siez'd the Horses of Light, & rose into the Chariot
of Day∟·₁
∧Sweet laughter siezd me in my sleep! silent & close I laughd∧
[*word del*] ∧For∧ in the visions of Vala [*words del*] ∧I walkd
with the mighty Fallen One∟·₁
[*words del*] ∧I heard his voice∧ among the branches, &
among sweet flowers.
Why is the light of [*word del*] ∧Enith armon∧ darken'd in
[her *del*] dewy morn∟?₁
Why is the silence of [*words del*] ∧Enitharmon a [Cloud *del*]∧
∧∧terror∧∧ & her smile a whirlwind
Uttering this darkness in my halls? in the pillars of my
Holy-ones∟?₁
Why dost thou weep [*word del*] ∧as∧ Vala? & wet thy veil
with dewy tear*s*,
In slumbers of my night-repose, infusing a false morning∧?∧
    ∧∧Driving the Female Emanations all away from Los∧∧
∧I have refusd to look upon the Universal Vision
∧And wilt thou slay with death him who devotes himself to
thee∟?₁∧

∧∧[If thou drivst all the (Males *del*) ∧∧∧Females∧∧∧ away from
(Vala *del*) ∧∧Luvah∧∧ I will drive all

ll. 10–11: '*woke' was written above 'wake'; then the pencil '*woke' was erased
and the ink 'wake' altered to 'woke'. '*flew' was written above 'fly' and later
erased, presumably when 'fly' was altered in ink to 'flew', but later the ink 'ew'
was altered to 'y' in pencil again.
    l. 17: The original name was deleted and '*Enitharmon' was written above it;
then both words were erased and 'Enith' and 'armon' written over them.
    l. 18: 'Cloud' is deleted in pencil, and 'terror' is written over the same thing in
pencil.
    ll. 22, 25–6: cf. p. 9, ll. 30–1; p. 30, ll. 51–2, where they are adapted.
    ll. 23–6 are written over two erased Copperplate lines.
    l. 25: 'Males' and 'Vala' were separately deleted and replaced above by
'Females' and 'Luvah', but when the line as a whole was deleted the last two
words were left standing.

⌃⌃[The Males away from thee *all del.*]

+ ⌃⌃Once born for the sport & amusement of Man⌞,⌟ now
born to drink up ⌃⌃⌃all⌃⌃⌃ his Powers⌞!⌟⌃⌃   [27]

[*Page 11*]   9

I heard the sounding sea: I heard the voice weaker and
weaker:

The voice came & went like a dream, I awoke in my sweet
bliss.'

⌃⌃*Then Los smote her upon the Earth⌞;⌟ twas long eer
she revivd⌞.⌟⌃⌃

[Los *del*] ⌃⌃*He⌃⌃ answer'd, darkning ⌃⌃*more⌃⌃ with [foul
del] indignation hid in smiles⌞:⌟

⌃'I die not Enitharmon [thou *del*] ⌃⌃tho⌃⌃ thou singst thy
Song of death   [5]

⌃Nor shalt thou me torment For I behold the [Eternal *del*]
⌃⌃Fallen⌃⌃ Man⌞.⌟⌃

Seeking to comfort Vala, [*word del*] she will not be com-
forted⌞.⌟

She rises from his throne and seeks the shadows of her
garden

Weeping for Luvah [*words del*] ⌃lost in the bloody beams of
your false morning⌞.⌟⌃

Sickning lies the [Eternal *del*] ⌃Fallen⌃ Man⌞,⌟ his head
sick⌞,⌟ his heart faint⌞;⌟   [10]

⌃Mighty atchievement of your power! Beware the
punishment⌞!⌟⌃

l. 27 is adapted on p. 133, l. 7.

Page 11 D E S I G N: At the bottom corners of the page, very rough pencil sketches
of angelic figures seem almost to mirror those on p. 10, which they face. There is
no other hint of a sketch.

ll. 1–2 have an erased pencil circle around them.

l. 3 is added in a stanza-break; it is apparently illustrated on p. 12.

ll. 5–11, 21–2 (a single block) have an erased pencil circle around them.

ll. 5–6 are written over two erased Copperplate lines. Above l. 5 is an erased
pencil line in which the words 'I', 'singst thy', and 'of death' are legible. In the
margin to the right of l. 6 'Man' was written in pencil and erased; perhaps all l. 6
was written under it in pencil.

l. 9: Above 'your' is '⌃⌃[*your del*]⌃⌃'.

l. 11 seems to be written over the same thing in pencil. There is a stanza-break
between l. 11 and l. 12.

ᴧ['Refusing to behold the Divine image which all behold
ᴧ[And live thereby, he is sunk down into a deadly sleep
ᴧ[But we immortal in our own strength survive by stern debate
ᴧ[Till we have drawn the Lamb of God into a mortal form   [ɪ
ᴧ[And that he must be born is certain for One must be All
ᴧ[And comprehend within himself all things both small & great∟·⌐
ᴧ[We therefore for whose sake all things aspire to be & live
ᴧ[Will so recieve the Divine Image that amongst the Reprobate
ᴧ[He may be devoted to Destruction from his mothers womb *all del.*]ᴧ   [ₐ

'I see, invisible descend into the Gardens of Vala
Luvah walking on the winds, ᴧI see the invisible knife∟,⌐
ᴧI see the shower of blood: I see the swords & spears of futurity∟·⌐ᴧ
[*word del*] ᴧThoᴧ in the Brain of Man we live, & in his circling Nerves,
[*word del*] ᴧTho'ᴧ this bright world of all our joy is in the Human Brain,   [ₐ
[*word del*] ᴧWhereᴧ Urizen & all his Hosts hang their immortal lamps∟,⌐
[*words del*] ᴧThou neer shalt leave thisᴧ cold expanse where watry Tharmas mourns∟·⌐'
ᴧᴧSo spoke Los. Scorn & Indignation rose upon Enitharmon∟·⌐ᴧᴧ
ᴧThen Enitharmon reddning fierce stretchd her immortal hands∟:⌐ᴧ
ᴧᴧ[Threaten not me O visionary thine the punishment *del*]ᴧᴧ   [

ll. 12–20 are written sideways in the top right margin and are deleted with a single stroke. There are large Xs after l. 11 and before l. 12, evidently indicating the position of this section.
ll. 22–3 are written over one-and-a-half erased Copperplate lines.
l. 28 is added in a stanza-break.
ll. 28–32 are written over two erased Copperplate lines and two or perhaps more erased pencil lines. All this erasure has almost worn through the page. In the first pencil line 'Then Enitharmon reddning' and 'hands' are legible; and the second ends with 'ots'.

⌐'Descend O Urizen descend with horse & chariots⌐!⌐⌐

⌐⌐Threaten not me O visionary⌐;⌐ thine the punishment⌐.⌐⌐⌐

⌐The Human Nature shall no more remain nor Human acts

⌐Form the [free *del*] ⌐⌐rebellious⌐⌐ Spirits of Heave*n*, but War & Princedom & Victory & Blood⌐.⌐'⌐   [*34*]

[*Page 12*]

⌐Night darkend as she spoke; a shuddring ran from East to West⌐;⌐

⌐A Groan was heard on high. The warlike clarions ceas*t*, the Spirits   ⌐200⌐

⌐Of Luvah & Vala shudderd in their Orb: an orb of blood:⌐

⌐Eternity groand & was troubled at the Image of Eternal Death⌐.⌐⌐

The [*word del*] ⌐Wandering⌐ Man bow'd his [*word del*] ⌐faint⌐ head and Urizen descended   [*5*]

⌐⌐⌐And⌐⌐⌐ ⌐⌐*the one must have murderd the Man if he had not descended⌐;⌐⌐⌐

Indignant muttering low thunders; [*words del*] ⌐Urizen descende*d*,

⌐Gloomy sounding, 'Now I am God from Eternity to Eternity⌐.⌐'

⌐Sullen sat Los plotting Revenge. Silent he [Urizen *del*] eye'd⌐ ⌐⌐the Prince

l. 34: 'War & Princedom & Victory' is repeated in *Jerusalem* pl. 4, l. 31 (p. 422).

Page 12   DESIGN: At the foot of the page is a very rough pencil sketch of a man and a woman. The woman, with her hands lifted as in horror or pain toward the man, has half fallen. The man is in a duelling stance, but has no sword. Between them is a circle, perhaps for a head, and some strokes go up the right margin below the marginal addition. (The design probably represents p. 11, l. 3: 'Los smote her [*Enitharmon*] upon the Earth'; cf. p. 12, l. 40.)

ll. 1–3 are written over an erasure of two lines in the Copperplate Hand.

l. 4, which is written over the same thing in pencil, is repeated on p. 18, l. 9, and in *Jerusalem* pl. 48, l. 12 (p. 518).

l. 5: 'Wandering' is written over the same thing in pencil, which is written over an erasure.

l. 6 is written with a thick pencil or crayon, and the first word was darkened in ink.

ll. 8–9 are written over two erased Copperplate lines. There is a atanza-break between l. 9 and l. 10.

ᴧᴧOf Light. Silent the prince of Light viewd Lo*s*; at length
a brooded   [
ᴧᴧSmile broke from Urizen for Enitharmon brightend
more & more﹂.﹂
ᴧᴧSullen he lowerd on Enitharmon but he smild on Losᴧᴧ

ᴧᴧSaying 'Thou art the Lord of Luvah﹂;﹂ into thine hands I
give
ᴧᴧThe prince of love﹂,﹂ the murderer﹂;﹂ his soul is in thine
hands﹂.﹂
ᴧᴧPity not Vala for she pitied not the Eternal Man   [
ᴧᴧNor pity thou the cries of Luvah. Lo these starry hosts﹂,﹂
ᴧᴧThey are thy servants if thou wilt obey my awful Law﹂.﹂'ᴧᴧ

ᴧᴧSo spoke the Prince of Light & sat beside the Seat of Los﹂.﹂
ᴧᴧUpon the sandy shore rested his chariot of fire﹂.﹂
ᴧᴧLos answerd furious﹂:﹂ 'art thou one of those who when
most complacent ·   [
ᴧᴧMean mischief mos*t*? If you are such Lo! I am also such﹂.﹂
ᴧᴧOne must be master; [the(*?*) *del*] try thy Arts﹂.﹂ I also will
try mineᴧᴧ
        ᴧᴧᴧFor I percieve Thou hast Abundance which I claim
        as mine﹂.﹂'ᴧᴧᴧ
ᴧᴧUrizen startled stood but not Long﹂;﹂ soon he cried
ᴧᴧ'Obey my voice young Demon﹂;﹂ I am God from Eternity
to Eternity﹂.﹂ᴧᴧ   [
ᴧᴧ*Art thou a visionary of Jesus the soft delusion of Eter-
nity﹂?﹂
ᴧᴧ*Lo I am God the terrible destroyer & not the Saviour﹂.﹂
ᴧᴧ*Why should the Divine Vision compell the sons of Eden to
forego[*?*] each his own delight to warr against his spectre﹂?﹂

ll. 10–19 are written sideways in the left margin, and a stroke goes from the
beginning of l. 10 to the stanza-break after l. 9.
ll. 20–9 are written at the top of the page above l. 1. All the writing in these
lines is approximately the same size. A connecting stroke goes from l. 17 to l. 21,
but the sense indicates the order as printed here.
l. 23 is written in a stanza-break.
ll. 25–8, 30 are written over several, perhaps five, erased pencil lines.
ll. 26–9 are written after l. 30, but the sense indicates that they should precede
l. 30.
l. 28 begins three words out in the left margin and continues into the right margin.

ᵔᵔ*The Spectre is the Man the rest is only delusion &
  fancy⌞.⌟' ᵔᵔ
ᵔᵔᵔᵔThus Urizen spoke collected in himself in awful
  pride⌞.⌟ᵔᵔᵔᵔ   [30]
Ten thousand thousand were his hosts of spirits on the wind:

Ten thousand thousand glittering Chariots shining in the sky:
They pour upon the golden shore beside the silent ocea*n*,
ᴧRejoicing in the Victory & the heavens were filld with
  blood⌞.⌟ᴧ

The Earth spread forth her table wide; the Night a silver cup   [35]
Fill'd with the wine of [*word del*] ᴧanguishᴧ waited at the
  golden feast
But the bright Sun was not as yet; he filling all the expanse
Slept as a bird in the blue shell that soon shall burst away⌞.⌟
    ᵔᵔ*Los saw the wound of his blow⌞;⌟ he saw⌞,⌟ he
      pitid⌞,⌟ he wept⌞.⌟ᵔᵔ
ᴧLos now repented that he had smitten Enitharmon⌞;⌟ he
  felt love   [40]
ᴧArise in all his Veins⌞;⌟ he threw his arms around her
  loinsᴧ
ᵔᵔ*To heal the wound of his smiting⌞.⌟ᵔᵔ
They eat the [*word del*] ᵔᵔ[*fleshly(?) del*]ᵔᵔ ᴧfleshlyᴧ bread,
  they drank the [*word del*] ᴧ[*bloody del*]ᴧ ᵔᵔnervousᵔᵔ wine⌞;⌟ [43]

[*Page 13*]
                                                                 11
They listend to the Elemental Harps & Sphery Song⌞;⌟
They view'd the dancing Hours, quick sporting thro' the sky

l. 29 meets the end of l. 28 and is written down the right margin.
Above l. 31 are two erased pencil lines.
l. 34 is written over an erased Copperplate line.
Below l. 34 is an erased pencil line which begins with 'A' and may end with 'of
Enitharmon'.
l. 39 is written with an orangish-Brown crayon and fills a stanza-break.
ll. 40–1 fill a stanza break between Copperplate lines.
l. 42 is written (with the same crayon as l. 39) in the right margin after l. 41.
Beside the main text in the right margin are six or more erased pencil lines.
Page 13 DESIGN: At the foot of the page is a head with closed eyes which is resting
on its right ear. Its extended left hand apparently holds a triple-looped horn.
(Perhaps he is one of the 'Elemental Gods [*who*] their thunderous Organs blew',

With winged radiance scattering joys thro the [*word del*]
   ^ever^ changing light

^[The shades(*?*) of(*?*) *del*] ^^But^^ Luvah & Vala standing in
   the bloody sky
^On high remaind alone forsaken in fierce jealousy⌞·⌟   [5
^They stood above the heavens forsaken desolate suspended
   in blood⌞·⌟
^Descend they could no*t*, nor from Each other avert their
   eyes⌞·⌟^
^^Eternity appeard above them as One Man infolded
^^In Luvah['*s*] robes of blood & bearing all his afflictions⌞;⌟
^^As the sun shines down on the misty earth such was the
   Vision^^   [1
[The *del*] ^But^ purple night [the *del*] ^and^ crimson morning
   & [the *del*] golden day [*word del*] ^descending^
[*word del*] ^Thro'^ the clear changing atmosphere display'd
   green fields among
The varying clouds, like paradises stretch'd in the expanse
With towns & villages and temples, tents sheep-folds and
   pastures
Where dwell the children of the elemental worlds in harmony.   [1
Not long in harmony they dwell, their life is drawn away
And wintry woes succeed: successive driven into the Void
Where Enion craves: successive drawn into the golden feast

And Los & Enitharmon sat in discontent & scorn⌞·⌟

l. 22.) There are vague strokes in the left margin as if for a tree or crescent moon,
but they could conceivably refer to the text. All the drawing is quite clear of the
text.

ll. 4–5 are inserted in a stanza-break over several, perhaps four, erased pencil
lines extending into the right margin, which could, from the few letters decipherable,
read as ll. 4–7 do now.

ll. 6–10 are written sideways in the right margin, and l. 6 is clearly joined to the
end of l. 5.

ll. 11–21 seem to have been circled and deleted individually with single strokes,
all in pencil, and then these changes were erased.

Above l. 16 is an erased pencil line which may begin: 'But now strong Urizen'.

Above l. 19 and extending into the right margin (under ll. 6–10) are several,
perhaps three, erased pencil lines which may begin with 'In beauty love[*?*]
&[*?*] scorn'.

ll. 19–21 were once deleted, and the deletion was erased.

l. 19 is repeated on p. 16, l. 18.

The Nuptial Song arose from all the thousand thousand spirits   [20]
Over the joyful Earth & Sea, and ascended into the Heavens
For Elemental Gods their thunderous Organs blew; creating
Delicious Viands. Demons of Waves their watry Eccho's woke!
Bright Souls ᴧᴧ[*Elements(?) *del*]ᴧᴧ of vegetative life, budding
  and blossoming   [24]

[*Page 14*]

Stretch their immortal hands to smite the gold & silver
  Wires
And with immortal Voice soft warbling fill all Earth &
  Heaven.
With doubling Voices and [*word del*] ᴧloudᴧ Horns wound
  round sounding⌐,⌐
Cavernous dwellers fill'd the enormous Revelry, Responsing!
And Spirits of Flaming fire on high, govern'd the mighty   250
  Song.   [5]

ᴧᴧAnd This the Song! sung at The Feast of Los & Enithar-
  mon⌐:⌐ᴧᴧ

ᴧ'[The Mountain *del*] ᴧᴧᴧ*Ephraimᴧᴧᴧ calld out [to the
  Mountain: *del*] ᴧᴧᴧ*to Zionᴧᴧᴧ "Awake O Brother Moun-
  tain⌐!⌐
ᴧLet us refuse the Plow & Spade, the heavy Roller & spiked
ᴧHarrow; burn all these Corn field*s*; throw down all these
  fences⌐!⌐
ᴧFattend on Human blood & drunk with wine of life is better
  farᴧ   [10]

'"ᴧThan all these labours of the harvest & the vintage. See
  the river

Page 14   DESIGN: At the foot of the page are three female heads growing out of
one torso. All the heads are looking up, and a left arm is extended backward with
the palm of the hand open. Vague strokes behind the heads may represent a
serpentine coil. In the left margin by the text, a figure seems to run left with out-
stretched arms; above it another figure flies in the same position. Both these mar-
ginal figures are very rough.
  l. 6 (in the Copperplate Hand) was inserted in an original stanza-break, prob-
ably as the first addition to the page.
  ll. 7–18 are written over an erasure of two stanzas of about nine lines.

˄Red with the blood of Me*n*, swells lustful round my rocky
knees˻·˼
˄My clouds are not the clouds of verdant fields & groves of
fruit
˄But Clouds of Human Soul*s*; my nostrils drink the lives of
Men˻·˼ '''˄

˄'The Villages Lamen*t*; they faint outstretchd upon the
plain˻·˼   [
˄Wailing runs round the Valleys from the Mill & from the
Barn
˄But most the polishd Palaces [weak(*?*) *del*] ˄˄dark˄˄ silent
bow with dread
˄Hiding their books & picture*s* underneath the dens of
Earth˻·˼˄

'˄The Cities send to one another saying "My Sons are Mad
˄With wine of cruelty. [Let(*?*) us(*?*) light(*?*) *del*] ˄˄Let us
plat a˄˄ Scourge O Sister City˻·˼"
˄Children are nourishd for the Slaughter; oñce the Child was
fed
˄With Milk; but wherefore now are Children fed with
blood˻?˼˄

[*Page 15*]

'The Horse is of more value than the Man. The Tyger
fierce
Laughs at the Human for*m*; the Lion mocks & thirsts for
blood˻·˼
They cry "O Spider spread thy web! Enlarge thy bones &
fill'd
With marrow sinews & flesh Exalt thyself˻,˼ attain a voice˻·˼

' "Call to thy dark armd host*s*, for all the Sons of Men
muster together

Page 15   DESIGN: At the foot of the page is the profile of a bearded man with his
right arm extended to the lower left corner and his left arm reaching up the right
margin. In both hands he holds a rope (which continues up the right margin) at
which he is looking. Several other vague strokes do not reveal the position of the
rest of his body. The drawing carefully avoids all but the last words of ll. 18 and
20 and the catchword. The contours of his head and arm are emphasized in Brown
wash.

To desolate their cities! Man shall be no more! Awake O
Hosts₋!₋"
The bow string sang upon the hills! Luvah & Vala ride
Triumphant in the bloody sk*y*, & the Human form is no
more₋·₋

'The listning Stars heard, & the first beam of the morning
started back₋·₋
He cried out to his Father, "depart! depart!" but sudden
[he(?) was(?) siezd(?) *del*] ∧Siez'd∧   [*10*]
And clad in stee*l*, & his Horse proudly neighd; he smelt the
battle
Afar off, Rushing back, reddning with rage the [Eternal
del] ∧Mighty∧ Father

'Siezd his bright Sheephook studded with gems & gold, he
Swung it round
His head shrill sounding in the sky, down rushd the Sun with
noise
Of war, The Mountains fled away₋;₋ they sought a place
beneath₋·₋   [*15*]
Vala remaind in desarts of dark solitud*e*, nor Sun nor Moon

'[To light the(?) *del*] ∧By night nor∧ day to comfort her, she
labourd in thick smoke₋·₋
Tharmas endurd not, he fled howlin*g*; then a barren waste
sunk down
Conglobing in the dark confusion, Mean time Los was born
And [*word del*] ∧Thou∧ O Enitharmon! Hark I hear the
hammers of Los₋·₋   [*20*]
[*Page 16*]
'They melt the bones of Vala, & the bones of Luvah into
wedges₋;₋

Page 16 DESIGN: A pencil sketch which took up the whole page has been erased.
It seems to have represented Christ; his arms are extended, the palms of his hands
face the upper corners of the page, his head is tilted down to his right, and around
him is a ring of clouds which he is pushing back. The outline of his torso is dis-
cernible, and in the lower corners are two kneeling angelic figures. The whole
drawing is very roughly sketched in outline only, but the two angelic figures, parti-
cularly the one on the right, are the clearest parts of the drawing. (The design,

The innumerable sons & daughters of Luvah closd in fur-
naces
Melt into furrow*s*; winter blows his bellows: Ice & Snow
Tend the dire anvils. Mountains mourn & Rivers faint &
fail⌞.⌟

'There is no City nor Corn field nor Orchard! all is Rock &
Sand⌞.⌟   [
There is no Sun nor Moon nor Sta*r*, but rugged wintry rocks
Justling together in the void suspended by inward fires⌞.⌟
Impatience now no longer can endur*e*; distracted Luvah

'Bursting forth from the Loins of Enitharmon, Thou fierce
Terror
Go howl in vain, Smite Smite his fetters⌞!⌟ Smite O wintry
hammers⌞!⌟   [
Smite Spectre of Urthona, mock the fiend who drew us down
From heavens of joy into this deep. Now rage but rage in
vain⌞!⌟'

Thus Sang the demons of the dee*p*; the Clarions of War
blew loud⌞.⌟   ^
The Feast redounds & Crownd with roses & the circling vine
The Enormous Bride & Bridegroom sat, beside them Urizen   [
With faded radiance sighd, forgetful of the flowing wine
And of Ahania his pure Bride but She was distant far

But Los & Enitharmon sat in discontent & scorn
Craving the more the more enjoying, drawing out sweet
bliss

like those on pp. 58, 116, is evidently for Young's *Night Thoughts* [1797] p. 65 and
not for *Vala*.)
  At the foot of the page, not related to the large sketch, is a rough pencil sketch
of two feet walking toward the right. (Cf. p. 31, ll. 9–10: 'I see not Luvah as of old;
I only see his feet Like pillars of fire travelling thro darkness & non entity'; cf.
also *Jerusalem* pl. 62 design—p. 551.) In the bottom left corner, over(?) the Christ,
is an even rougher sketch of a figure facing the feet with hands raised as in horror.
Other vague strokes may have been connected with either the early drawing or the
late one.
  l. 14 may be represented in the design on p. 17.
  l. 18 is repeated on p. 13, l. 19.

From all the turning wheels of heaven & the chariots of the
  Slain⌊.⌋   [20]

At distance Far in Night repell*d*, in direful hunger craving
Summers & Winters round revolving in the frightful dee*p*,   [22]

                [*Page 17*]

                                    13

[And *del*] Enion blind & age-bent wept upon the desolate
  wind⌊:⌋

'Why does the Raven cry aloud and no eye pities her?
Why fall the Sparrow & the Robin in the foodless winter?
ˆFaint! shivering they sit on leafless bush, or frozen stoneˆ
Wearied with seeking food across the snowy waste; the little   [5]
Heart, cold; and the little tongue consum'd, that once in
  thoughtless joy
Gave songs of gratitude to [the *del*] waving corn fields round
  their nest.   ˆˆ*200ˆˆ

'Why howl the Lion & the Wolf? why do they roam abroad?
Deluded by [the *del*] summers heat they sport in enormous
  love
And cast their young out to the [*words del*] ˆhungry wilds &ˆ
  sandy desarts⌊.⌋   [10]

                [*Page 18*]

'Why is the Sheep given to the knife? the Lamb plays in the
  Sun

Page 17 DESIGN: At the foot of the page is a figure with its back to the viewer, its legs trailing off to the right in a skirt(?), facing left with its arms above its head. She seems to have flowers in her flying hair. (Perhaps she is Enitharmon 'Crownd with roses', p. 16, l. 14.) A spiral, perhaps for clouds, covers the first word on the page. Two strokes going from the figure's shoulders to the margins may have stood for outstretched arms, as in the drawing on p. 58.

    l. 4 (in the Copperplate Hand) is written over an erased line which probably began with 'Why'.

    l. 8: 'howl' was at first 'howls'.

    l. 9: 'the' is deleted in pencil.

Page 18 DESIGN: In the left margin is a very rough sketch of a figure plunging down with its arms extended and its hand in the bottom right corner. Its feet are by the first words of the text, and it had to be partly erased to fit in each of the added lines, though it carefully avoids the earliest text. Many vague strokes below the figure and by its hands may represent the same figure kneeling to avoid the additions.

He starts! he hears the foot of Man! he says, "take thou my
  wool
But spare my life," ⌄⌄*but⌄⌄ he knows not that [the *del*]
  winter cometh fast.

'The Spider sits in his labourd Web, eager watching for the
  Fly⌊;⌋
Presently comes a famishd Bird & takes away the Spider⌊;⌋
His Web is left all desolate, that his little anxious heart
So careful wove: & spread it out with sighs and weariness.'

This was the Lamentation of Enion round the golden
  Feast⌊.⌋
⌃Eternity groand & was troubled at the image of Eternal
  Death⌃
    ⌄⌄*Without the body of Man⌊,⌋ an Exudation from his
      sickning limbs⌊.⌋⌄⌄
⌃Now Man was come to the Palm tree & to the Oak of
  Weeping
⌃Which stand upon the Edge of Beulah & he sunk down
⌃From the Supporting arms of the Eternal Saviour; who
  disposd
⌃The pale limbs of his Eternal Individuality
⌃Upon The Rock of Ages, Watching over him with Love &
  Care⌊.⌋⌃

  ⌃End of The First Night⌃

[*Page 21*]

Then those in Great Eternity met in the Council of God
As one Man for Contracting their Exalted Senses

  l. 3: 'the' is deleted in pencil.
  l. 9 is repeated in p. 12, l. 4 (see p. 1093 and note).
  l. 10 is written in a stanza-break.
  ll. 11–12 are written over '[End of the[?] First[?] Night *del*]'. ll. 11–12 are in
a slightly different form in *Jerusalem* pl. 23, ll. 24–5 (p. 463).
  ll. 14–15 are found in part in *Jerusalem* pl. 48, ll. 3–4 (p. 518).

Page 21 DESIGN: A very few pencil strokes in the right margin and at the foot of
the page do not seem to represent anything.
  Pages 21–2, 19 seem to fit better after p. 18 than anywhere else, though their
position even here is awkward.
  ll. 1–2, 7 are repeated on p. 8, ll. 8–9, and on p. 99, ll. 1–2.
  ll. 2–6 are in *Jerusalem* pl. 38, ll. 17–21 (p. 496).

They behold Multitude or Expanding they behold as one∟,⌐
As One Man all the Universal family & that One Man
They Call Jesus the Christ & they in him & he in them   [5]
Live in Perfect harmony in Eden the land of life
Consulting as One Man above [Mount Gilead *del*] ⌐the
    Mountain of Snowdon⌐ Sublime

For messengers from Beulah come in tears & darkning clouds
Saying 'Shiloh is in ruins∟,⌐ our brother is sick∟,⌐ [Shiloh *del*]
    ⌐Albion⌐ He
Whom thou lovest is sick∟,⌐ he wanders from his house of
    Eternity∟.⌐   [10]
The daughters of Beulah terrified have closd the Gate of the
    Tongue∟.⌐
Luvah & Urizen contend in war around the holy tent∟.⌐'

So spoke the Ambassadors from Beulah & with solemn mourn-
    ing
They were introducd to the divine presence & they kneeled
    down
In [Beth Peor *del*] ⌐Conways Vale⌐ thus recounting the
    Wars of Death Eternal∟:⌐   [15]

'The Eternal Man wept in the holy tent∟,⌐ Our Brother in
    Eternity∟,⌐
Even [Shiloh *del*] ⌐Albion⌐ whom thou lovest wept in pain∟;⌐
    his family
Slept round on hills & valleys in the regions of his love
But Urizen awoke & Luvah woke & thus conferrd∟:⌐

' "Thou Luvah" said the Prince of Light "behold our sons &
    daughters   [20]
Reposd on beds; let them sleep on; do thou alone depart
Into thy wished Kingdom where in Majesty & Power
We may erect a throne; deep in the North I place my lot∟.⌐
Thou in the South listen attentive. In silent of this night
I will infold the Eternal tent in clouds opake while thou   [25]
Siezing the chariots of the morning, Go outfleeting ride
Afar into the Zenith high bending thy furious course

1103

Southward with half the tents of men inclosd in clouds
Of Tharmas & Urthona. I remaining in porches of the brain
Will lay my scepter on Jerusalem the Emanation⌐,⌐   [⌐
On all her sons & on thy sons O Luvah & on mine
Till dawn was wont to wake them⌐ ;⌐ then my trumpet sound-
     ing loud
Ravishd away in night⌐ ;⌐ my strong command shall be obeyd
For I have placd my centinels in stations⌐ ;⌐ each tenth man
Is bought & sold & in dim night my Word shall be their
     law⌐.⌐"   [⌐

[*Page 22*]

'Luvah replied "Dictate to thy Equal*s*; am not I
The Prince of all the hosts of Men nor Equal know in
     Heaven⌐?⌐
If I arise into the Zenith leaving thee to watch
The Emanation & her Sons the Satan & the Anak⌐,⌐
Sihon & O*g*, wilt thou not rebel to my laws remain   [⌐
In darkness building thy strong throne & in my ancient night
Daring my power wilt arm my sons against me in the [deep
     del] Atlantic⌐,⌐
My deep⌐,⌐ My night which thou assuming hast assumd my
     Crown⌐?⌐
I will remain as well as thou & here with hands of blood
Smite this dark sleeper in his tent⌐,⌐ then try my strength
     with thee⌐.⌐"   [⌐

'While thus he spoke his fires reddend [round *del*] ⌃oer⌃ the
     holy tent⌐.⌐
Urizen cast deep darkness round him⌐,⌐ silent brooding
     death⌐,⌐

Page 22 DESIGN: *Under* the writing (apparently) and covering the whole page
is a large, clear, pencil sketch evidently made when pp. 19[–20] was the top half of
a sheet of which the bottom was pp. [21–]22; it represents the full face of a bearded
man, his lips at the left edge of p. 22, his wavy beard falling through the text of
p. 22, his nostrils and moustache below the elbow of the woman on p. 19, lines for
his nose rising through the woman, his erased left eye just to her left, his right eye
by p. 19, ll. 8–14, his hair elaborately waving beside a centre part through 'End of
The First Night' on p. 19—strikingly similar (except for age) to the sketch said to
be for Job reproduced in G. Keynes, *Drawings* (1970), pl. 74, as J. E. Grant points
out in 'Visions in *Vala*', *Blake's Sublime Allegory*, ed. S. Curran & J. Wittreich, Jr.
(1973), 149–50.
    ll. 12–15 are adapted from p. 58, ll. 23–5.

Eternal death to Luva*h*; raging Luvah pourd
The Lances of Urizen from chariot*s* round the holy tent⌐.⌐
Discord began & yells & cries shook the wide firmament⌐.⌐   [*15*]

'Beside his anvil stood Urthona dar*k*, a mass of iron
Glowd furious on the anvil prepard for spades & coulters⌐.⌐
   All
His sons fled from his side to join the conflict⌐;⌐ pale he heard
The Eternal voice⌐;⌐ he stood⌐,⌐ the sweat chilld on his
   mighty limbs⌐.⌐
He dropd his hamme*r*; dividing from his aking bosom fled   [*20*]
A portion of his life⌐,⌐ shrieking upon the wind she fled
And Tharmas took her in pitying⌐.⌐ Then Enion in jealous
   fear
Murderd her & hid her in her bosom embalming her for
   fear
She should arise again to life⌐.⌐ Embalmd in Enions bosom
Enitharmon remains a corse⌐;⌐ such thing was never known   [*25*]
   ᴧᴧ*In Eden that one died a death never to be revivd⌐.⌐ᴧᴧ

'Urthona stood in terror but not long⌐;⌐ his Spectre fled
To Enion & his body fell. Tharmas beheld him fall
Endlong a raging Serpent rolling round the holy tent⌐.⌐
The sons of war astonishd at th*c* Glittring mon*s*ter drove   ⌊*30*⌋
Him far into the world of Tharmas into a cavernd rock

'But Urizen with darkness overspreading all the armies
Sent round his heralds secretly commanding to depart
Into the north⌐.⌐ Sudden with thunders sound his multitudes
Retreat from the fierce conflict all the sons of Urizen at once   [*35*]
Mustring together in thick clouds leaving the rage of Luvah
To pour its fury on himself & on the Eternal Man⌐.⌐

'Sudden down fell they all together into an unknown
   Space
Deep horrible without End Separated from Beulah far be-
   neath⌐.⌐

   ll. 16–17: The phrase is repeated on p. 50, l. 8, and p. 84, ll. 16–17.
   ll. 25–6 are in *Jerusalem* pl. 80, ll. 23–4 (p. 596).

The Mans exteriors are become indefinite opend to pain
In a fierce hungring void & none can visit his regions⌊·⌋

[*Page 19*]

'Jerusalem his Emanation [will soon .*del*] ^^*is^^ become a
    ruin⌊,⌋
Her little ones [will be *del*] ^^*are^^ slain on the top of every
    street
And she herself let captive & scatterd into [all nations *del*]
    ^the indefinite⌊·⌋^
Gird on thy sword O thou most mighty in glory & majesty⌊!⌋
Destroy these op[*p*]ressors of Jerusalem & those who ruin
    Shiloh⌊·⌋'

So spoke the Messengers of Beulah. Silently removing
The Family divine drew up the Universal tent
Above [Mount Gilead *del*] ^High Snowdon^ & closd the
    Messengers in clouds around
Till the time of the End. Then they Elected Seve*n*, called the
    Seven
Eyes of God & the Seven lamps of the Almighty⌊·⌋
The Seven are one within the other⌊;⌋ the Seventh is named
    Jesus
The Lamb of God blessed for ever & he followd the Man
Who wanderd in mount Ephraim seeking a Sepulcher⌊,⌋
His inward eyes closing from the Divine vision & all
His children wandering outside from his bosom fleeing
    away⌊·⌋

End of The First Night

Page 19 - DESIGN: For the design apparently *under* the writing, see Page 22 above.
At the foot of the present page, just below the writing, is sketched a winged child
(like those on pp. 4, 40, 108) who has just shot an arrow into the vagina of a naked
woman at the right who reaches for the arrow. A similar winged Cupid at left
shooting at [a butterfly on] the crotch of a nude woman at right appears in Blake's
engraving for Fuseli's 'Falsa ad Coelum' [?1790] reproduced in *Blake Newsletter*
(1972), 238.
    l. 3: Perhaps 'let' was intended for 'led'.
    ll. 9–10 are repeated in *Jerusalem* pl. 55, l. 31 (p. 535). For the 'seven . . . eyes of
the Lord' and 'the seven lamps', see Zechariah 4: 10, 2.

[AN ADDITIONAL FRAGMENT]

[*Page 20*]

*The Daughters of Beulah beheld the Emanation⌐;⌐ they pitied⌐,⌐

*They wept before the Inner gates of Enitharmons bosom

*And of her fine wrought brain & of her bowels within her loins⌐.⌐

*Three gates within Glorious & bright open into [Eternity *del*] Beulah

*From Enitharmons inward parts but the bright female terror [5]

*Refusd to open the bright gates⌐;⌐ she closd & barrd them fast

*Lest Los should enter into Beulah thro her beautiful gates⌐.⌐

*The Emanation stood before the Gates of Enitharmon

*Weepin*g*; the Daughters of Beulah silent in the Porches

*Spread her a Couch unknown to Enitharmon⌐;⌐ here reposd [10]

*Jerusalem in slumbers soft lulld into silent rest⌐.⌐

*Terrific ragd the Eternal Wheels of intellect⌐,⌐ terrific ragd

*The living creatures of the wheels in the Wars of Eternal life

*But perverse rolld the wheels of Urizen & Luvah back reversd

*Downwards & outwards [tending *del*] ^consuming^ in the wars of Eternal Death⌐.⌐ [15]

Page 20 DESIGN: Very vague crayon curves and spirals seem to go *over* the writing. In the bottom right corner is a pencil sketch of an outstretched nude figure, its thighs horizontal, right knee slightly bent, left at a right angle, lying at ease. The figure has clear breasts, a slit for the vulva, and a clear erect penis which is coloured Pink. The figure *could* represent a woman in labour, with the infant's arm protruding as in *Marriage* pl. 3 (p. 77), but this is unlikely.

No satisfactory position has been devised for the text of p. 20; its position on the verso of p. 19 may be coincidental.

VALA

Night the [First *del*] ˄˄*First˄˄

˄˄*Rising upon his Couch of death Albion beheld
his Sons⌊.⌋˄˄
˄Turning his Eyes outward to Self, losing the Divine
Vision˄
[The Man *del*] ˄Albion˄ calld Urizen & sai*d*: 'Behold
these sickning Spheres⌊.⌋
˄Whence is this Voice of Enion that soundeth in my [Ears
del] ˄˄*Porches⌊?⌋˄˄
Take thou possession! take this Scepter! go forth in my
might
For I am wear*y*, & must sleep in the dark sleep of Death⌊.⌋
˄Thy brother Luvah hath smitten me but pity thou his
youth˄
˄˄Tho thou hast not pitid my Age O Urizen Prince of
Light⌊.⌋'˄˄
Urizen rose from the bright Feast like a star thro' the evening
sky
[Exulting *del*] ˄Indignant˄ at the voice that calld him from
the Feast of [envy *del*] ˄love⌊.⌋˄
First he beheld the body of Man pale, cold, ˄the horrors of
death˄
˄Beneath his feet˄ shot thro' him as he stood in the Human
Brain

Page 23   DESIGN: At the foot of the page is a naked bearded man who is leaning
on his right elbow and looking up the margin. Many very vague strokes do not
reveal the position of the rest of his body, except that it was more or less ex-
tended.

ll. 7–8 fill a stanza break. They cover two erased pencil lines, the first of which
was the same as l. 7, and the second of which ended 'fallen man'.

l. 10: 'Exulting' and 'envy' were deleted and 'Indignant' and 'love' written in
the left and right margins with a very sharp instrument (erased pencil). Perhaps
by erasure Blake tried to restore the original readings.

ll. 11–12: The adjoining sections of these lines were first erased and the present
changes made in pencil; later they were confirmed in ink.

And all its golden porches grew pale with his sickening
 light
  ˏNo more Exulting for he saw Eternal Death beneathʟ·ɟˏ [*14*]
Pale he beheld futurity; pale he beheld the Abyss ˏˏ*15ˏˏ
Where Enion blind & age bent wept in direful hunger
 craving
All rav'ning like the hungry worm, & like the silent graveʟ·ɟ [*17*]

    [*Page 24*]

Mighty was the draught of Voidness to draw Existence inʟ·ɟ

Terrific Urizen strode above, in fear & pale dismay
He saw the indefinite space beneath & his soul shrunk with
 horrorʟ,ɟ ˏˏ*20ˏˏ
His feet upon the verge of Non Existence; his voice went
 forthʟ·ɟ

Luvah & Vala trembling & shrinking, beheld the [*words del*]
 ˏgreat Work masterˏ [*5*]
And heard his word! 'Divide ye bands influence by in-
 fluenceʟ·ɟ
Build we a Bower for heavens darling in the grizly deepʟ;ɟ
ˏˏ*Build we the Mundane Shell around the Rock of
 Albionʟ·ɟ'ˏˏ ˏˏ*25ˏˏ
The Bands of Heaven flew thro the air singing & shouting to
 ˏUrizenʟ·ɟˏ
Some fix'd the anvil, some the loom erected, some the plow [*10*]
And harrow formd & framd the harness of silver & ivoryʟ,ɟ
The golden compasses, the quadrant & the rule & balanceʟ·ɟ
They erected the furnaces, they formd the anvils of gold
 beaten in mills ˏˏ*30ˏˏ
Where winter beats incessant, fixing them firm on their
 baseʟ·ɟ

l. 17 is adapted on p. 136, l. 8.

Page 24 DESIGN: At the foot is a figure falling off the page, with its elbows before
its face, its left side to the viewer, its legs horizontal, its skirt flowing, and its left
hand grasping a rope(?) which trails above the figure. In the left margin, an un-
related drawing consists of a dozen strokes outlining the torso and legs of a nude
female standing or leaning with her legs apart.
 After l. 4, in the stanza break, is a *very* long erased pencil line, of which the only
legible word is 'bloody'.

The bellows began to blow & the Lions of Urizen stood
round the anvil   [

[*Page 25*]

And the leopards coverd with skins of beasts tended the
roaring fires∟,⌋
    ∧∧*Sublime distinct their lineaments divine of human
    beauty∟·⌋∧∧
The tygers of wrath called the horses of instruction from
their mangers∟·⌋
They unloos'd them & put on the harness of gold & silver &
ivory∟·⌋
In human forms distinct they stood round Urizen prince of
Light   [
∧Petrifying all the Human Imagination into rock & sand∟·⌋
∧Groans ran along Tyburns brook and along the River of
Oxford∟·⌋
∧Among the druid Temples Albion groand on Tyburns
brook∟·⌋
∧Albion gave his loud death groan∟,⌋ the Atlantic Mountains
trembled∟·⌋
∧Aloft the Moon fled with a Cry∟;⌋ the Sun with streams of
blood
∧From Albions loins fled∟;⌋ all Peoples and Nations of the
Earth [Fled *del*]
∧Fled with the noise of Slaughter & the Stars of heaven
Fled∟·⌋

Page 25 DESIGN: At the foot of the page is a kneeling figure with his back to the
viewer, his right calf beneath his buttock, his left leg extended back, holding three
alternate sets of poles (?huge compasses) which meet in three round objects before
him. All the poles cover the writing.

l. 2 originally seems to have been continued with several, perhaps five, pencil
lines in the right margin. Later the marginal lines were erased and ll. 11–33
written at right angles over them; and l. 2 was darkened in pencil.

l. 3: Cf. *Marriage* pl. 9, proverb 44: 'The tygers of wrath are wiser than the horses
of instruction' (p. 83).

ll. 6–11 are squeezed into a stanza-break as one continuous line, with strokes
after ll. 7, 8, 9, and 10. The division of ll. 6 and 7 is therefore conjectural.

l. 8 is written in a stanza-break.

ll. 9–10: Cf. Jeremiah 4:24–5: 'the mountains . . . trembled . . . and all the birds
of heaven were fled'.

ll. 11–20, 'and Nations of the Earth . . . over the mountains', are written side-
ways in the top right margin and are clearly joined to the previous addition by
a stroke.

ᐱJerusalem came down in a dire ruin over all this Earth[?]ʟ.ᒆ
ᐱShe fell cold from Lambeths Vales in groans & Dewy
death ʟ,ᒆ
ᐱThe dew of anxious Souls ʟ,ᒆ the death-sweat of the dying ʟ,ᒆ   [*15*]
ᐱIn every pillard hall & arched roof of Albions Skies ʟ.ᒆ
ᐱThe brother & the brother bathe in blood upon the
Severn ʟ,ᒆ
ᐱThe Maiden weeping by. The father & the mother with
ᐱThe Maidens father & her mother fainting over the body
ᐱAnd the Young Man the Murderer fleeing over the moun-
tains ʟ.ᒆ ᐱ   [*20*]

ᐱReuben slept on Penmaenmawr & Levi slept on Snowdon ʟ.ᒆ
ᐱTheir eyes their ears nostrils & tongues roll outward ʟ,ᒆ
they behold
ᐱWhat is within now seen without ʟ;ᒆ they are raw to the
hungry wind ʟ.ᒆ
ᐱThey become Nations far remote in a little & dark Land ʟ.ᒆ
ᐱThe daughters of Albion girded around their garments of
Needlework   [*25*]
ᐱStripping Jerusalems curtains from mild demons of the
hills ʟ;ᒆ
ᐱAcross Europe & Asia to China & Japan like lightenings
ᐱThey go forth & return to Albion on his rocky couch ʟ,ᒆ
ᐱGwendolen Ragan Sabrina Gonorill Mehetabel Cordella
ᐱBoadicea Conwenna Estrild Gwinefrid Ignoge Cambel   [*30*]
ᐱBinding Jerusalems children in the dungeons of Babylon ʟ;ᒆ
ᐱThey play before the Armies before the hounds of Nimrod
ᐱWhile the Prince of Light on Salisbury plain among the
druid stones ʟ.ᒆ ᐱ
Rattling the adamantine chains & hooks heave up the ore
In mountainous masses, plung'd in furnaces, & they shut &
seald   [*35*]
The furnaces a time & times; all the while blew the North
His cloudy bellows & the South & East & dismal West

ll. 21–33 are written sideways in the right margin beside ll. 15–20.
ll. 29–30: These Daughters of Albion reappear in *Jerusalem* pl. 5, ll. 41–4
(p. 425), except that Gwineverra is substituted for Boadicea.
l. 33: 'the druid stones' 'on Salisbury plain' are Stonehenge.

And all the while the plow of iron cut the dreadful furrows
ᴧᴧ*In Ulro beneath Beulah where the Dead wail Night &
Day⌞·⌟ᴧᴧ

Luvah was cast into the Furnaces of affliction & sealed   ⌊
And Vala fed in cruel delight, the furnaces with fire⌞·⌟
Stern Urizen beheld urg'd by necessity to keep
The evil day afar, & if perchance with iron power
He might avert his own despair; in woe & fear he saw   [

[*Page 26*]

Vala incircle round the furnaces where Luvah was clos'd⌞·⌟
In joy she heard his howlings, & forgot he was her Luvah
With whom she walk'd in bliss, in times of innocence &
youth⌞!⌟

Hear ye the voice of Luvah from the furnaces of Urizen⌞:⌟

'If I indeed am [Luvahs(?) Lord(?) *del*] ᴧValas Kingᴧ & ye O
sons of Men   ⌊
The workmanship of Luvahs hands; in times of Everlasting
When I calld forth the Earth-worm from the cold & dark
obscure
I nurturd her⌞,⌟ I fed her with my rains & dews, she grew
A scaled Serpent, yet I fed her tho' she hated me⌞;⌟   [
Day after day she fed upon the mountains in Luvahs sight⌞·⌟   ᴧ

l. 39: The phrase is in *Jerusalem* pl. 40, l. 57, and pl. 48, l. 52 (pp. 502, 520).
ll. 40–4 and p. 26, ll. 1–3 are in *Jerusalem* pl. 7, ll. 30–7 (p. 428).

Page 26   DESIGN: There are four apparently unrelated pencil and crayon sketches
in the left margin and at the foot of the page. By the first words in the left margin is
a figure with butterfly wings, a plump human face, hair done in a frizzy eighteenth-
century style, pendulous breasts, an enormous erased vulva extending the length
of her stomach, dangling legs, and hands apparently in her hair. Below this
sketch, still in the margin, is a bat-winged figure with a human head cocked to the
side, arms clasped around something which has been erased, legs dangling, and no
indication of its sex. Just below the writing is a creature with long narrow bat
wings, a bird's head and shoulders, scaled legs joining in a tail, and a clearly em-
phasized vulva. All these are front view. Below them, much larger than the others,
is a side view of a creature with wide powerful bat wings, a swan's neck, a woman's
head and hair, scaled narrow arms extended forward and ending in breasts, three
breasts extending from chest to belly, ineffectual sea-creature legs, and an enormous
heavy serpentine tail that begins to curl up the right margin—all quite clear.
(Perhaps she is the 'Half Woman & half Spectre' of p. 7, l. 23; cf. p. 26, ll. 8–9.)
All these sketches carefully avoid the text, and there are very few waste strokes.

I brought her thro' the Wilderness, a dry & thirsty land
And I commanded springs to rise for her in the black desart
[Till *del*] ∧[But *del*]∧ she became a [de *del*] ∧Dragon∧ winged
   bright & poisonous⌐·⌐
I opend all the floodgates of the heavens to quench her thirst   [*14*]

[*Page 27*]

'And I commanded the Great deep to hide her in his hand
Till she became a little weeping Infant a span long⌐·⌐
I carried her in my bosom as a man carries a lamb⌐;⌐
I loved her⌐,⌐ I gave her all my soul & my delight⌐;⌐
I hid her in soft gardens & in secret bowers of Summer   [*5*]
Weaving mazes of delight along the sunny Paradise⌐,⌐
Inextricable labyrinths, She bore me sons & daughters
And they have taken her away & hid her from my sight⌐·⌐
They have surrounded me with walls of iron & brass,
   [*word del*] ∧O Lamb
∧Of God clothed in Luvahs garments⌐,⌐ little knowest thou   [*10*]
∧Of death Eternal⌐,⌐ that we all go to Eternal Death
∧To our Primeval Chaos in fortuitous concourse of in-
   coherent
∧Discordant principles of Love & Hate⌐·⌐ I suffer affliction∧

'Because I love for I [am *del*] ∧was∧ love [& *del*] ∧but∧ hatred
   [*word del*] ∧awakes∧ in me
     ∧And Urizen∧ ∧∧who was Faith & Certainty is changd to
   Doubt⌐·⌐∧∧   [*15*]
The hand of Urizen is upon me because I blotted out
That Human [terror *del*] ∧delusion∧ to deliver all the sons of
   God

l. 13: 'But' was added and 'Till' deleted in Brown ink. Then both changes were
deleted, leaving a smudge.

Page 27 DESIGN: The sketch at the foot of the page is chiefly in crayon, though
there may be some pencil. At the bottom right is a clear drawing of a nude woman
half reclining on her left elbow, her head on her left shoulder, half smiling. Just be-
low her belly is sketched the upper half of a skeleton with a fleshed and bearded
face, leaning on his right elbow; his right hand seems to be a cloven hoof. (Perhaps
it represents Luvah 'Reasoning from the loins', p. 28, l. 2.)

ll. 9–13: The additions, 'O Lamb . . . suffer affliction', are written over an erasure
of three lines.

Above l. 14 a squeezed-in line was erased; it began 'And Urizen who i'.

l. 17 was first altered in pencil, and the changes were later confirmed in ink.

From bondage of the Human form, O first born Son of
    Light⌊,⌋
O Urizen my enemy I weep for thy stern ambition
But weep in vain⌊.⌋ O when will you return Vala the
    wanderer⌊?⌋'

                [*Page 28*]

These were the words of Luvah patient in afflictions
^Reasoning from the loins in the unreal forms of Ulros night^

And when Luvah age after age was quite melted with woe
The fires of Vala faded like a shadow cold & pale⌊,⌋
An evanescent shado*w*; last she fell a heap of Ashes
Beneath the furnaces⌊,⌋ a woful heap in living death⌊.⌋

Then were the furnaces unseald with spades & pickaxes
Roaring let out the fluid, the molten metal ran in channels
Cut by the plow of ages held in Urizens strong hand
In many a valley, for the Bulls of Luvah dragd the Plow⌊.⌋
^With trembling horror pale aghast the Children of Man
^Stood on the infinite Earth & saw these visions in the air⌊,⌋
^In waters & in Earth beneath⌊;⌋ they cried to one another
^'What are we terrors to one anothe*r*? Come O brethren⌊,⌋
    wherefore
^Was this wide Earth spread all abroa*d*? not for wild beasts
    to roam⌊.⌋'
^But many stood silent & busied in their families
^And many said 'We see no Visions in the darksom air⌊.⌋
^Measure the course of that sulphur orb that lights the
    [dismal *del*] ^^darksom^^ day⌊;⌋
^Set stations on this breeding Earth & let us buy & sell⌊.⌋'

Page 28   DESIGN: In the left margin very vague strokes may represent a woman
cradling a child in her arms. At the bottom, carefully to the right of the added
words, is sketched a nude woman kneeling with her right arm resting in her lap,
her head on her left shoulder, and her left arm over her head; she is looking toward
a naked man whose head is pillowed on the object she is leaning on. He is evidently
asleep with his left arm at his side and his legs slightly apart. Between the two
figures something has been erased.

    l. 2 (which is perhaps represented on p. 27) is written over an erased pencil
line which may begin with 'Los'.

    ll. 11–24 are written in the bottom left corner, and two strokes connect them
with the stanza-break after l. 10.

ʌOthers arose & schools Erected forming Instruments   [20]
ʌTo measure out the course of heaven. Stern Urizen beheld
ʌIn woe his brethren & his Sons in darkning woe lamenting
ʌUpon the winds in clouds involvd⌞,⌟ Uttering his voice in
   thunders⌞,⌟
ʌCommanding all the work with care & power & severity⌞·⌟ʌ

Then siezd the Lions of Urizen their work, & heated in the
   forge
Roar the bright masses, thund'ring beat the hammers, many   [25]
   a [Globe *del*] ʌpyramidʌ
Is form'd & thrown down thund'ring into the deeps of Non
   Entity⌞·⌟
Heated red hot they hizzing rend their way down many a
   league
Till resting, each his [center *del*] ʌ[basement *del*]ʌ finds; sus-
   pended there they stand
Casting their sparkles dire abroad into the dismal deep   [30]
For measurd out in orderd spaces the Sons of Urizen
With compasses divide the deep; they the strong scales erect   [32]

[*Page 29*]

That Luvah rent from the faint Heart of the [Eternal *del*]
   ʌFallenʌ ʌʌ[*Ancient *del*]ʌʌ Man
And weigh the massy [Globes *del*] ʌCubesʌ, then fix them in
   their awful stations

And all the time in Caverns shut, the golden Looms erected
First spun, then wove the Atmospheres, there the Spider &
   Worm
Plied the wingd shuttle piping shrill thro' all the list'ning
   threads⌞;⌟
Beneath the Caverns roll the weights of lead & spindles of   [5]
   iron⌞;⌟

Page 29   DESIGN: At the foot of the page, a naked man(?) squats with his right
leg extended, his left heel under his buttock, his right elbow on his right knee,
and his left arm extended up the right margin, holding in his right hand a net(?)
which is hooked on the toes of his right foot. Lines drop from his left hand to his
right hand. (Perhaps the design illustrates ll. 15–16: 'The threads are spun & the
cords twisted & drawn out . . .'.) If his head had been completed, it would have
impinged on the writing. Curious scrawly hair covers one letter. There are some
undecipherable scrawls in the left margin.

The enormous warp & woof rage direful in the affrighted
    deep

While far into the vast unknown, the strong wing'd Eagles
    bend
Their venturous flight, in Human forms distinct; thro dark-
    ness deep
They bear the woven draperies; on golden hooks they hang
    abroad
The universal curtains & spread out from Sun to Sun
The vehicles of light, they separate the furious particles
Into mild currents as the water mingles with the wine.

While thus the Spirits of strongest wing enlighten the dark
    deep
The threads are spun & the cords twisted & drawn out; then
    the weak
Begin their work; & many a net is netted; many a net

[*Page 30*]

Spread & many a Spirit caught, innumerable the nets⌊ˌ⌋
Innumerable the gins & traps; & many a soothing flute
Is form'd & many a corded lyre, outspread over the im-
    mense⌊·⌋
In cruel delight they trap the listeners, & in cruel delight
Bind them, [together *del*] ⌃condensing⌃ the strong energies
    into little compass⌊·⌋
Some became seed of every plant that shall be planted; some
The bulbous roots, thrown up together into barns & garners⌊·⌋

Then rose the Builders; First the Architect divine his plan
Unfolds, The wondrous scaffold reard all round the in-
    finite⌊·⌋
⌃Quadrangular the building rose⌊ˌ⌋ the heavens squared by
    a line.

l. 11: Cf. Isaiah 40: 22: God 'stretcheth out the heavens as a curtain, and spreadeth them out as a tent to dwell in'.

Page 30 DESIGN: Half a dozen strokes outline a female torso and legs in the left margin.

ll. 10–11 are written as one continuous line into the right margin, with nothing to divide them.

ʌTrigons & cubes divide the elements in finite bonds⌞.⌟ʌ
Multitudes without number work incessant: the hewn stone
Is placd in beds of mortar mingled with the ashes of
   Vala⌞.⌟
Severe the labour, female slaves the mortar trod oppressed⌞.⌟

ʌTwelve halls after the names of his twelve sons composd   [*15*]
ʌThe [golden *del*] ʌʌwondrousʌʌ building & three [halls(*?*)
   of(*?*) *del*] ʌCentral Domesʌ after the Names
ʌOf his three daughters were encompassd by the twelve
   bright halls⌞,⌟
ʌEvery hall surrounded by bright Paradises of Delight
ʌIn which [were *del*] ʌʌareʌʌ towns & Cities Nations Seas
   Mountains & Rivers⌞.⌟
ʌEach Dome opend toward four halls & the Three Domes
   Encompassd   [*20*]
ʌThe Golden Hall of Urizen whose western side glowd
   bright
ʌWith ever streaming fires beaming from his awful limbs⌞.⌟
ʌHis Shadowy Feminine Semblance here reposd in a [bright
   del] ʌʌWhiteʌʌ Couch
ʌOr hoverd oer his Starry head & when he smild she
   brightend
ʌLike a bright Cloud in harves*t*, but when Urizen frownd
   She wept   [*25*]
ʌIn mists over his carved throne & when he turnd his back
ʌUpon his Golden hall & sought the Labyrinthine porches
ʌOf his wide heaven Trembling, cold in paling fears she sat
ʌA Shadow of Despair⌞;⌟ therefore toward the West Urizen
   formd
ʌA recess in the wall for fires to glow upon the pale   [*30*]
ʌFemales limbs in his absence & her Daughters oft upon
ʌA Golden Altar burnt perfumes with Art Celestial formdʌ

ʌFoursquare sculpturd & sweetly Engravd to please their
   shadowy mother⌞.⌟

ll. 15–32 are written in the bottom left corner, and two strokes connect them
with the stanza-break after l. 14.
ll. 33–52 are written in the lower right corner beside ll. 15–32.

ʌAs[c]ending into her [cloudy *del*] ʌʌmistyʌʌ garments the
blue smoke rolld to revive
ʌHer cold limbs in the absence of her Lord. Also her sons
ʌWith lives of Victims sacrificed upon an altar of brass
ʌOn the East sid*e*, Revivd her Soul with lives of beasts &
  birds
ʌSlain on the Altar up ascending into her cloudy bosomʟ·ɹ
ʌOf terrible workmanship the Altar labour of ten thousand
  Slavesʟ;ɹ
ʌOne thousand Men of wondrous power spent their lives in
  its formationʟ·ɹ
ʌIt stood on twelve steps namd after the names of her twelve
  sons
ʌAnd was Erected at the chief entrance of Urizens hallʟ·ɹʌ

ʌWhen Urizen [descended *del*] ʌʌreturndʌʌ from his immense
  labours & travelsʟ,ɹ
ʌDescending She reposd beside him folding him around
ʌIn her bright skirts. Astonishd & Confounded he beheld
ʌHer shadowy form now Separateʟ;ɹ he shudderd & was
  silent
ʌTill her caresses & her tears revivd him to life & joyʟ·ɹ
ʌTwo wills they hadʟ,ɹ two intellects & not as in times of
  oldʟ·ɹ
ʌThis Urizen percievd & silent brooded in darkning Cloudsʟ·ɹ
ʌTo him his Labour was but Sorrow & his Kingdom was
  Repentanceʟ·ɹʌ
ʌʌHe drave the Male Spirits all away from Ahania
ʌʌAnd she drave all the Females from him awayʟ·ɹʌʌ

Los joyd & Enitharmon laughd, saying 'Let us go down
And see this labour & sorrow;' They went down to see the
  woes
Of Vala &ₗthe woes of Luvah, to draw in their delights

And Vala like a shadow oft appeard to Urizenʟ·ɹ

l. 48 is repeated in *Jerusalem* pl. 86, l. 61 (p. 611).
ll. 51–2 are written in different ink. Cf. p. 9, ll. 30–1 and p. 10, ll. 22, 25–6.

[*Page 31*]

The King of Light beheld her mourning among the Brick
kilns compelld
To labour night & day among the fires, her lamenting voice
Is heard when silent night returns & the labourers take their
rest∟:⌋

'O Lord wilt thou not look upon our sore afflictions
Among these flames incessant labouring, our hard masters
laugh   [5]
At all our sorrow. We are made to turn the wheel for water∟,⌋
To carry the heavy basket on our scorched shoulders, to sift
The sand & ashes, & to mix the clay with tears & repen-
tance∟·⌋
  ∧∧*I see not Luvah as of old∟;⌋ I only see his feet
  ∧∧*Like pillars of fire travelling thro darkness & non
  entity∟·⌋∧∧   [10]
The times are now returnd upon us, we have given ourselves
To scorn and now are scorned by the slaves of our enemies∟·⌋
Our beauty is coverd over with clay & ashes, & our backs
Furrowd with whips, & our flesh bruised with the heavy
basket∟·⌋
Forgive us O thou piteous one whom we have offended,
forgive   [15]
The weak remaining shadow of Vala that returns in sorrow
to thee.'

Thus she lamented day & night, compelld to labour &
sorrow∟·⌋

Page 31 DESIGN: At the foot of the page, an egg-shaped figure bows toward a
naked boy in the right corner, who is looking down to the left with his arm behind
him. His torso has been erased, and some vague Grey and brownish water-colour
lines may be meant to re-outline this figure. There is some shading behind the
bowing figure. (A similar kneeling figure is in *Night Thoughts* drawing no. 163
[BMPR].)
  ll. 9–10 are written beside ll. 7–8, 11–12 in the right margin as follows:
        I see not Luvah as of old
        I only see his feet / Like pillars
        of fire travelling thro darkness & non entity
No position is indicated for them. (Cf. the designs on p. 16 and *Jerusalem* pl. 62
[p. 551] and Revelation 10: 1: 'I saw . . . [a] mighty angel['s] . . . feet as pillars of
fire'.)

Luvah in vain her lamentations heard; in vain his love
Brought him in various forms before her still she knew him
   not⌐,⌐   [
                     [*Page 32*]
Still she despisd him, calling on his name & knowing him
   not⌐,⌐
Still hating⌐,⌐ still professing love, still labouring in the smoke

[And Los & Enitharmon joyd, they drank in tenfold joy   ⌐To cc
[From all the sorrow of Luvah & the labour of Urizen *del*]
   ⌐And Enitharmon joyd Plotting to rend the secret
      cloud⌐,⌐   [
   ⌐To plant divisions in the Soul of Urizen & Ahania⌐
[For *del*] ⌐But⌐ infinitely beautiful the wondrous work arose
In [songs & joy *del*] ⌐sorrow & care⌐,⌐⌐ a Golden World
   whose porches round the heavens
And pillard halls & rooms recievd the eternal wandering
   stars⌐,⌐
A wondrous golden Building; many a window many a door   [
And many a division let in & out into the vast unknown
[Circled *del*] ⌐[Cubed(?) *del*]⌐ in [infinite orb *del*] ⌐[window(?)
   square *del*]⌐ immoveable, within its [arches all *del*] ⌐walls
   & cielings⌐
The heavens were closd [*word del*] ⌐and⌐ ⌐⌐[& *del*] spirits
   mournd their bondage night & day⌐⌐
⌐And the Divine Vision appeard in Luvahs robes of blood⌐.⌐⌐
   ⌐⌐*Thus was the Mundane Shell builded by Urizens
   strong power⌐.⌐⌐⌐   [

Page 32 DESIGN: At the foot of the page, a nude woman is outstretched on her
belly (?asleep) in tall grass. Stretched out in the opposite direction is another nude
female (?asleep) on her back who seems to be leaning on another figure lying
face down. By her head is a nude woman walking toward the viewer with her
left hand by her side and her right hand over her vulva. Facing her, but with her
back to us, is another nude (?female) figure with her arms crossed behind her back,
evidently talking. (Two very similar figures are etched, reversed and slightly
altered, in *Jerusalem* pl. 81 [p. 599], where they represent Gwendolen and Cambel.)
Beside this last woman some vague erased perpendicular lines are not decipherable.
Above the head of the first sleeping woman may be a seated nude woman, and
another standing before her; these figures are sketched more lightly than the others
and are partly erased.
    l. 14 is written over an erased line which may end with 'within'.
    l. 15 is written in a stanza-break.

[Then *del*] ∧Sorrowing∧ went the Planters forth to plant, the
   Sowers [forth *del*] to sow∟·⌋   150
They dug the channels for the rivers & they pourd abroad   [*17*]

                     [*Page 33*]

The seas & lakes, they reard the mountains & the rocks &
   hills
On broad pavilions, on pillard roofs & porches & high
   towers
In beauteous order, thence arose soft clouds & exhalations
Wandering even to the sunny [orbs *del*] ∧Cubes∧ of light &
   heat
For many a window ornamented with sweet ornaments   [*5*]
Lookd out into the World of Tharmas, where in ceaseless
   torrents
His billows roll∟,⌋ where monsters wander in the foamy
   paths∟·⌋
On clouds the Sons of Urizen beheld [*words del*] ∧[the heavens
   ∧∧were∧∧ walld *del*]∧ ∧∧∧Heaven walled round∟·⌋∧∧∧
They weighd & orderd all & Urizen ∧∧∧comforted saw∧∧∧
The wondrous work flow forth like visible out of the in-
   visible   [*10*]
∧For the Divine Lamb Even Jesus who is the Divine Vision
∧Permitted all lest Man should fall into Eternal Death
∧For when Luvah sunk down himself put on the robes of
   blood
∧Lest the state calld Luvah should cease & the Divine Vision
∧Walked in robes of blood till he who slept should awake∟·⌋∧   [*15*]

Thus were the stars of heaven created like a golden chain

l. 16: 'Sorrowing' was first written in pencil (in the margin), and then inked
over, but 'Then' and 'forth' are deleted in ink only.

Page 33 DESIGN: In the bottom right corner, carefully avoiding the additions,
are a number of vague undecipherable pencil and crayon strokes which may
delete a sketch.

ll. 8–9: All the erased words in these lines are read with some hesitation. The
words at the end of l. 9 were deleted and 'comforted saw' was written above them;
then both original and added words were erased and 'comforted saw' written in the
place of the original words.

ll. 11–15 are written over an erasure of five lines, the third of which ends 'ing
in triumph' and the last 'Mundane Egg'.

To bind the Body of Man to heaven from falling into the
  Abyss⌞.⌟
Each took his station, & his course began with [songs & joy
  del] ⌃[eternal(?) fear + 1 *del*]⌃ ⌃sorrow & care⌞.⌟⌃

⌃[2 X In sevens & tens & fifties, hundreds, thousands,
  numbered all
⌃According to their various power*s*, Subordinate to Urizen   [
⌃And to his sons in their degrees & to his beauteous daughters⌃
⌃3 Travelling in silent majesty along their orderd ways
⌃In right lined paths outmeasurd by proportions of [weight
  & measure *del*] ⌃⌃number⌃⌃ ⌃⌃weight⌃⌃
⌃And measur*e*, mathematic motion wondrou*s*, along the deep
⌃In fiery pyramid or Cub*e*, or ⌃⌃un⌃⌃ornamented pillar
  [square *del*]   [
⌃Of fire far shinin*g*, travelling along even to its destind
  end⌞,⌟
⌃Then falling dow*n* a terrible space⌞,⌟ recovring in winter
  dire
⌃Its wasted [pow *del*] strengt*h*, it back returns upon a nether
  course
⌃Till fired with ardour fresh recruited in its humble [spring
  del] ⌃⌃season⌃⌃
⌃It rises up on high all summer till its wearied course
⌃Turns into autum*n*; such the periods of many worlds⌞.⌟   [
⌃Others triangular [their *del*] ⌃⌃right angled⌃⌃ course main-
  tai*n*; others obtuse
⌃Acute [& oblong; *del*] ⌃⌃Scalene⌃⌃ in simple path*s*; but
  others move
⌃In intricate ways biquadrat*e*, Trapeziums Rhombs Rhom-
  boids
⌃Paralellogram*s*, triple & quadrupl*e*, polygonic   ▪
⌃In their amazing [fructifying *del*] ⌃⌃hard subdued⌃⌃ course
  in the vast deep⌞.⌟⌃   ▪

l. 17: The initial letter of 'Body' was originally 'f'.
l. 18: The erased words below this line ('eternal fear +1') were underlined.
Presumably a missing section should be inserted at '+1'.
ll. 19–21, 22–36 are put in this order on the basis of the numbers ('2 X' and '3')
which precede them.

[*Page 34*]

And Los & Enitharmon were drawn down by their
desires
Descending sweet upon the wind among soft harps & voices
‸‸‸To plant divisions in the Soul of Urizen & Ahania⌐,⌐
‸‸‸To conduct the Voice of Enion to Ahanias midnight
pillow⌐.⌐‸‸‸

Urizen saw & envied & his imagination was filled⌐.⌐   [*5*]
[Then *del*] ‸Repining‸ he contemplated the past in his bright
sphere   200
Terrified with his heart & spirit at the visions of futurity
That his dread fancy formd before him in the unformd void

[Now *del*] ‸For‸ Los & Enitharmon walkd forth on the dewy
Earth
Contracting or expanding their all flexible senses   [*10*]
At will to murmur in the flowers small as the honey bee⌐,⌐
At will to stretch across the heavens & step from star to star
Or standing on the Earth erect, or on the stormy waves
Driving the storms before them or delighting in sunny
beams
While round their heads the Elemental Gods kept harmony   [*15*]

‸And Los said: 'Lo the Lilly pale & the rose reddning fierce
‸Reproach thee & the beamy gardens sicken at thy beauty⌐.⌐
‸I grasp thy vest in my strong hand in vai*n*, like water springs
‸In the bright sands of Lo*s*, evading my embrac*e*; then I
alone
‸Wander among the virgins of the summer⌐.⌐ Look⌐,⌐ they
cry⌐,⌐   [*20*]

Page 34   ll. 3–4 are written over two erased pencil lines. Two erased pencil words,
the first of which may be 'But', were written in the left margin by the first line.
Under l. 3 the words 'the limbs of Enitharmon' may be conjecturally deciphered.
Crowded in the right margin beside ll. 2–4 is more erased pencil writing, which
may read 'Laughing & mocking Luvah bursting[?] in the womb [*or* woes] of
Vala . . .'.
    ll. 4–8 once had a bracket beside them in the left margin, which was later erased.
    ll. 16–61 are written over seven or more erased pencil lines which were written
directly below the original text.
    ll. 16–36 are written in the bottom left corner, and two strokes clearly indicate
that they should be inserted after l. 15.

ʌThe poor forsaken Los mockd by the worm∟,⌐ the shelly snail∟,⌐

ʌThe Emmet & the beetle∟,⌐ hark∟!⌐ they laugh & mock at Los∟.⌐'ʌ

ʌEnitharmon answerd ʌʌ∟:⌐' Secure now from the smitings of thy Power demon of furyʌʌ If the God Enrapturd me infolds

ʌIn clouds of sweet obscurity my beauteous form dissolving∟,⌐ʌ

[*words del*] ʌʌHowl thou over the body of death∟;⌐ tis thineʌʌ

ʌBut if among the virgins   [

ʌOf summer I have seen thee sleep & turn thy cheek de-lighted

ʌUpon the rose or lilly pal*e*, or on a bank where sleep

ʌThe beamy daughters of the light∟,⌐ starting they rise∟,⌐ they flee

ʌFrom thy fierce love for tho I am dissolvd in the bright God

ʌMy spirit still pursues thy false love over rocks & valleys∟.⌐'ʌ   [

ʌLos answerd∟:⌐ 'therefore fade I thus dissolvd in raptur trance∟.⌐

ʌThou canst repose on clouds of secrecy while oer my limbs

ʌCold dews & hoary frost creeps tho I lie on banks of summer

ʌAmong the beauties of the World∟.⌐ Cold & repining Losʌ

ʌʌStill dies for Enitharmon nor a spirit springs from my dead corse∟.⌐ʌʌ   [

ʌThen I am dead till thou revivest me with thy sweet song∟.⌐ʌ

ʌ'Now taking on Ahanias form & now the form of Enion∟,⌐

ʌI know thee not as once I knew thee in those blessed fields

ʌWhere memory wishes to repose among the flocks of Thar-mas∟.⌐'ʌ

ʌEnitharmon answerd∟:⌐ 'Wherefore didst thou throw thine arms around

ʌAhanias Image∟?⌐ I decievd thee & will still decieve∟.⌐

ʌUrizen saw thy sin & hid his beams in darkning Clouds∟.⌐

l. 27: 'sleep' at first was 'sleeps'.
l. 28: 'flee' looks like 'flie'.
l. 35 is written over an erasure, of which only 'Enitharmon' is legible.
ll. 37–61 are written in the lower right corner beside ll. 16–36.

ᴧI still keep watch altho I tremble & wither across the
  heavens
ᴧIn strong vibrations of fierce jealousy for thou art mineᴧ

   ᴧᴧCreated for my will⌞;⌟ my slave⌞,⌟ tho strong⌞,⌟ tho I
     am weak⌞·⌟ᴧᴧ   [45]
ᴧFarewell the God calls me away⌞·⌟ I depart in my sweet
  bliss⌞·⌟'ᴧ

ᴧShe fled vanishing on the windᴧ ᴧᴧAnd left a dead cold
  corse
ᴧᴧIn Los's arms⌞;⌟ howlings began over the body of death⌞·⌟ᴧᴧ
ᴧLos spok*e*: 'Thy God in vain shall call thee if by my strong
  power
ᴧI can infuse my dear revenge into his glowing breast⌞·⌟   [50]
ᴧThen jealousy shall shadow all his mountains & Ahania
ᴧCurse thee thou plague of woful Los & seek revenge on
  thee⌞·⌟'ᴧ
     ᴧᴧSo saying in deep sobs he languishd till dead he also
       fell⌞·⌟ᴧᴧ
ᴧNight passd & Enitharmon eer the dawn returnd in bliss⌞·⌟
ᴧShe sang Oer Lo*s*, ᴧᴧreviving him to Life⌞;⌟ his groans were
  terribleᴧᴧ   [55]
ᴧᴧBut thus she sang⌞:⌟ᴧᴧ ᴧ'I seize the sphery harp⌞,⌟ I strike
  the strings⌞·⌟ᴧ

ᴧAt the first Sound the Golden sun arises from the deep
ᴧAnd shakes his awful hair⌞;⌟
ᴧThe Eccho wakes the moon to unbind her silver locks⌞;⌟
ᴧThe golden sun bears on my song   [60]
ᴧAnd nine bright spheres of harmony rise round the fiery
  King⌞·⌟ᴧ

ᴧ'The joy of woman is the Death of her most best beloved
ᴧWho dies for Love of her

ll. 47–8: The additions are written over an illegible erasure.
ll. 55–6: The additions to these lines are written over illegible erasures which
were themselves added to l. 55. 'She sang . . . the strings' was originally one line.
ll. 62–6 are written sideways in the bottom right corner, in a larger hand and with
a sharper pen than the rest of the page, and they are not marked in any way for
entry. Their present position is therefore conjectural.

ʌIn torments of fierce jealousy & pangs of adoration∟⌐

ʌThe Lovers night bears on my song   [

ʌAnd the nine Spheres rejoice beneath my powerful con-
   troll∟⌐ʌ

ʌ'They sing unceasing to the notes of my immortal hand∟⌐

ʌThe solemn silent moon

ʌReverberates the living harmony upon my limbs∟;⌐

ʌThe birds & beasts rejoice & play   [

ʌAnd every one seeks for his mate to prove[?] his inmost
   joy∟⌐ʌ

ʌ'Furious & terrible they sport & rend the nether deep∟;⌐

ʌThe deep lifts up his rugged head

ʌAnd lost in infinite hum[m]ing wings vanishes with a cry∟⌐

ʌThe fading cry is ever dying∟,⌐   [

ʌThe living voice is ever living in its inmost joy∟⌐ʌ

ʌ'Arise you little glancing wings & sing your infant joy∟!⌐

ʌArise & drink your bliss

ʌFor every thing that lives is holy∟;⌐ for the source of life

ʌDescends to be a weeping babe∟;⌐   [

ʌFor the Earthworm renews the moisture of the sandy
   plain∟⌐ʌ

ʌ'Now my left hand I stretch to earth beneath

ʌAnd strike the terrible string∟⌐

ʌI wake sweet joy in dens of sorrow & I plant a smile

ʌIn forests of affliction   ▮

ʌAnd wake the bubbling springs of life in regions of dark
   death∟⌐ʌ

ʌ'O I am weary∟!⌐ lay thine hand upon me or I faint∟,⌐

ʌI faint beneath these beams of thine

ll. 67–81 are written sideways in the left margin, and a stroke is drawn from
the end of l. 61 to l. 68.

l. 72: 'deep' may be 'deeps'.

ll. 77–9 are from *Visions* pl. 11, ll. 214–15 (p. 116).

l. 79 is adapted from Lavater's *Aphorisms* (1788) ¶309 ('*all life is holy*'); see
Marriage pl. 27, ¶92 (p. 99), where it also occurs.

ll. 82–95 are written sideways in the left margin beside ll. 67–81.

Vala p. 35

∧For thou hast touchd my five senses & they answerd thee⌞.⌟
∧Now I am nothing & I sink   [90]
∧And on the bed of silence sleep till thou awakest me⌞.⌟'∧

∧Thus sang the Lovely one in Rapturous delusive trance⌞.⌟
∧Los heard [word del] ∧∧[delighted del]∧∧ ∧∧reviving∧∧ he
siezd her in his arms⌞;⌟ delusive hopes
∧Kindling She led him into Shadows & thence fled
outstretchd
∧Upon the immense like a bright rainbow weeping & smiling   ∧71∧
& fading⌞.⌟∧   [95]

Thus [word del] ∧livd∧ Los driving Enion far into the [word
del] ∧∧*deathful∧∧ infinite
∧That he may also draw Ahania's spirit into her Vor-
tex⌞.⌟∧
Ah happy blindness [she del] ∧Enion∧ sees not the terrors of
the uncertain⌞.⌟
[And oft del] ∧[thus del]∧ [she del] ∧∧*Thus Enion∧∧ wails from
the dark deep, the golden heavens tremble⌞:⌟   [99]

[Page 35]

'I am made to sow the thistle for wheat; the nettle for a
nourishing dainty⌞.⌟
I have planted a false oath in the earth, it has brought forth
a poison tree⌞.⌟
I have chosen the serpent for a councellor & the dog
For a schoolmaster to my children⌞.⌟

Above l. 96, in the stanza break and continuing into the left margin, are perhaps
two erased pencil lines, of which the only legible word is 'Urizen'.

Page 35 DESIGN: In the bottom left margin a woman with bare breasts wearing
pyjamas(?) with buttons down the front stands holding a flat-bottomed basket
full of fruit(?) on her head. Below the writing, a nude kneeling woman with her
knees apart seems to pull up plants. Beside her another nude kneeling woman
appears to be watching her. Another nude woman kneeling with her legs apart
and her left arm behind her back also watches; there is an erasure between the
legs of this figure. Behind her is some foliage in which another figure looks over its
shoulder at the group; the lower part of the body is erased. Beside this figure, a
nude girl of about six years old, her vulva carefully emphasized, stands with her
hands up looking on.
l. 1: Cf. Job 31: 40: 'Let thistles grow instead of wheat, and cockle instead of
barley.'
ll. 3–4 are adapted from Visions pl. 8, ll. 119–20 (p. 110).

I have blotted out from light & living the dove & nightingale   [5

And I have caused the earth worm to beg from door to door⌊·⌋

I have taught the thief a secret path into the house of the just⌊·⌋

I have taught pale artifice to spread his nets upon the morning⌊·⌋

My heavens are brass⌊,⌋ my earth is iron⌊,⌋ my moon a clod of clay⌊,⌋

My sun a pestilence burning at noon & a vapour of death in night⌊·⌋   [

'What is the price of Experience⌊?⌋ do men buy it for a song

Or wisdom for a dance in the street? No it is bought with the price

Of all that a man hath⌊,⌋ his house his wife his children⌊·⌋

Wisdom is sold in the desolate market where none come to buy

And in the witherd field where the farmer plows for bread in vain⌊·⌋   [

'It is an easy thing to triumph in the summers sun

And in the vintage & to sing on the waggon loaded with corn⌊·⌋

It is an easy thing to talk of patience to the afflicted⌊,⌋

To speak the laws of prudence to the houseless wanderer⌊,⌋   [

[Page 36]

'To listen to the hungry ravens cry in wintry season

When the red blood is filld with wine & with the marrow of lambs⌊·⌋

'It is an easy thing to laugh at wrathful elements⌊,⌋

To hear the dog howl at the wintry door, the ox in the slaughter house moan⌊,⌋

l. 11: For the 'price' of 'wisdom', see Job 27: 12–28.

Page 36 DESIGN: In the left margin, a figure plunges down with its elbows before its face, its heel by the second stanza, and a long loose dress swirling up.

   The additions to this page are in Brown ink in the Usual Hand.

ll. 3–4 are adapted from *Urizen* pl. 25, ll. 448–9 (p. 277).

To see a god on every wind & a blessing on every blast⌞,⌟ [5]
To hear sounds of love in the thunder storm that destroys our
    enemies house⌞,⌟
To rejoice in the blight that covers his field, & the sickness
    that cuts off his children
While our olive & vine sing & laugh round our door &
    our children bring fruits & flowers⌞.⌟

'Then the groan & the dolor are quite forgotten & the slave
    grinding at the mill
And the captive in chains & the poor in the prison, & the
    soldier in the field [10]
When the shatterd bone hath laid him groaning among the
    happier dead⌞.⌟

'It is an easy thing to rejoice in the tents of prosperity⌞.⌟
Thus could I sing & thus rejoice, but it is not so with me,'

∧Ahania heard the Lamentation & a swift Vibration
∧Spread thro her Golden frame. She rose up eer the dawn of
    day [15]
∧When Urizen slept on his couch; drawn thro unbounded
    space
∧Onto the margin of Non Entity the bright Female came⌞.⌟
∧There she beheld the [terrible *del*] ∧∧*Spectrous∧∧ form of
    Enion in the Void
∧And never from that moment could she rest upon her ∧250∧
    pillow⌞.⌟ [19]
        ∧End of the Second Night∧

l. 13: Cf. Job 9: 34–5: 'Let him [*God*] take his rod away from me, and let not
his fear terrify me. Then would I speak, and not fear him: but it is not so with me.'
    The quotation mark is Blake's.
ll. 14–15 are written over '[End of the Second(?) Night *del*]'.

VALA

Night the [Fourth(?) del] ˄Third˄

Now sat the King of Light on high upon his starry throne
And bright Ahania bow'd herself before his splendid feet∟˩

'O Urizen look on [thy Wife, that *del*] ˄˄*Me∟;˩˄˄ like a
mournful stream
˄˄*I˄˄ Embrace round thy knees & wet [her *del*] ˄˄*My˄˄
bright hair with [her *del*] ˄˄*my˄˄ tears:
Why sighs my Lord! are not the morning stars thy obedient
Sons∟?˩
Do they not bow their bright heads at thy voice? at thy
command
Do they not fly into their stations & return their light to
thee∟?˩
The immortal Atmospheres are thine, there thou art seen in
glory
Surrounded by the ever changing Daughters of the Light∟˩
[Thou sitst in harmony for God hath set thee over all *del*]
˄Why wilt thou look upon futurity darkning present joy∟?˩'˄

She ceas'd∟;˩ the Prince his light obscurd & the splendors of
his crown

Page 37 DESIGN: In the right margin is a vague crayon sketch of a man who is
looking, pop-eyed, across the page. His right knee is lifted, his right foot (a bird-
like claw) is on the head of a female(?) figure who crouches below the writing and
holds his left foot as if to kiss or wash it. The lines of the marginal figure cover(?)
the last words of the text. (They clearly represent Urizen 'upon his starry throne'
and 'Ahania bow'd . . . before his splendid feet', ll. 1–2. An analogous design is
on p. 132.)
    All the deletions on the page are in pencil.
    Above l. 1: Sloss & Wallis (ed., *The Prophetic Writings* [1926]) and Margoliouth
(ed., *Vala* [1956]) report a '*Second' by the heading, but neither I nor half a
dozen others who have examined the manuscript at my request can see any sign
of this whatever.
    l. 4: At first 'Embrace' and 'wet' were 'Embraces' and 'wets'.

[*Page 38*]
Infolded in thick clouds, from whence his mighty voice
  burst forth_L:_J

'O bright [Ahania: *del*] ∧[shadow *del*]∧ a Boy is born of the
  dark Ocean
Whom Urizen doth serve, with Light replenishing his dark-
  ness_L·_J
I am set here a King of trouble commanded here to serve
And do my ministry to those who eat of my wide table_L·_J   [*5*]
All this is mine yet I must serve & that Prophetic boy
Must grow up to command his Prince [& all my Kingly
  power *del*] ∧∧*but hear my determind Decree_L:_J∧∧
[That(?) *del*] ∧But∧ Vala [may(?) *del*] ∧shall∧ become a
  Worm in Enitharmons Womb
Laying her seed upon the fibres soon to issue forth
And Luvah in the loins of Los a dark & furious death_L·_J   [*10*]
Alas for me! what will become of me at that dread time?'

Ahania bow'd her head & wept seven days before the King
And on the eighth day when his clouds unfolded from his
  throne
She rais'd her bright head sweet perfumd & thus with
  heavenly voice_L:_J

'O Prince_L,_J the Eternal One hath set thee leader of his
  hosts_L·_J   [*15*]
[*Page 39*]
'[Raise then thy radiant eyes to him_L,_J raise thy obedient
  hands

Page 38 DESIGN: There is a large erasure in the bottom left corner of the page.
Beside it is a partly erased small figure which hugs another small female figure
from the back. The second figure (which covers the catchword) kneels with her
right knee on the ground and her left knee up, and looks back over her shoulder
as if in horror at the erasure.
    All the textual deletions but the first are in pencil.
    l. 8: Probably 'But' should have been deleted.
Page 39 DESIGN: Vague pencil strokes going up the left margin end in an erasure.
In the bottom left part of the page is a naked boy (whose genitals have been erased),
his head cocked to the left, who is pointing forward. Beside him, a smaller nude
girl (whose genitals have also been erased) raises her arms as if in shock and looks

Vala p. 39

[And comforts shall descend from heaven into thy darkning
clouds *del*]
ʌLeave all futurity to him˪‚˩ resume thy fields of Light˪·˩ʌ
Why didst thou listen to the voice of Luvah that dread
morn
To give the immortal steeds of light to his deceitful hands˪?˩
No longer now obedient to thy will [*words del*] ʌthou art
compell'dʌ
To [*word del*] ʌforgeʌ the curbs of iron & brass˪‚˩ to build the
iron mangers˪‚˩
To feed them with intoxication from the wine presses of
Luvah
ʌTill the Divine Vision & Fruition is quite obliterated˪·˩ʌ
They call thy lions to the fields of blood, they rouze thy
tygers
Out of the halls of justice, till these dens thy wisdom
framd
Golden & beautiful but O how unlike those sweet fields of
bliss
Where liberty was justice & eternal science was mercy˪·˩
Then O my dear lord listen to Ahania, listen to the vision˪‚˩
The vision of Ahania in the slumbers of Urizen
When Urizen slept in the porch & the [Eternal *del*] ʌAncientʌ
Man was smitten˪·˩

'The [Eternal *del*] ʌ[Fallen *del*]ʌ ʌʌDarkningʌʌ Man walkd
on the steps of fire before his halls
And Vala walkd with him in dreams of soft deluding slum-
ber˪·˩
He looked up & saw theʌeʌ Prince of Light [with *del*] ʌthyʌ
splendor faded˪·˩
[But saw not Los nor Enitharmon for Luvah hid them in
shadow

the same way at a large erasure. A nude leg and bent knee extend from the erasure
toward them. The erasure partly covers the last two words of the text.
ll. 1, 2, 10 are deleted in pencil.
l. 9 is written over an erasure.
ll. 17–19, p. 40, ll. 2–11, 13–20, p. 41, ll. 1–4, 10–17, p. 42, ll. 1–6, 9–19 are
repeated, mostly as corrected here in pencil, in *Jerusalem* pl. 29, ll. 33–82 (p. 477).

[*Page 40*]

'[(Of *del*) ∧∧*In∧∧ a soft cloud outstretch'd across, & Luvah
dwelt in the cloud *del*]

'Then Man ascended mourning into the splendors of his
palace_L·」
Above him rose a Shadow from his wearied intellect
Of living gold, pure, perfect, holy; in white linen pure he
hover'd_L,」
A sweet entrancing self delusion, a watry vision of Man   50
Soft exulting in existence_L,」 all the Man absorbing_L!」   [6]

'Man fell upon his face prostrate before the watry shadow
Saying "O Lord whence is this change_L?」 thou knowest I
am nothing_L·」"
And Vala trembled & coverd her face, & her lock*s* were
spread on the pavement_L·」
[I *del*] ∧∧*We∧∧ heard astonishd at the Vision & [my *del*]
∧∧*our∧∧ heart∧∧*s∧∧ trembled within [me *del*] ∧∧*us_L·」∧∧   [10]
[I *del*] ∧∧*We∧∧ heard the voice of the [Eternal· *del*] ∧Slum-
berous∧ Man & thus he spoke
∧Idolatrous to his own Shadow words of Eternity uttering_L:」∧
∧∧[*I heard astonishd at the vision(?) & my(?) heart(?)
trembled(?) within me *del*]∧∧
"O I am nothing when I enter into judgment with thee_L!」
If thou withdraw thy breath I die & vanish into Hades_L;」   [15]
If thou dost lay thine hand upon me behold I am silent_L;」
If thou withhold thine hand I perish like a fallen leaf_L;」

Page 40   DESIGN: At the foot of the page is a vague pencil sketch, largely erased,
of a nude woman lying on her belly, with her arms above her head holding the
hands of a man(?) who is kneeling over her, as in coitus. Riding on the man's hip,
unerased, is a tiny winged figure with spurs; this figure is similar to ones on pp. 4,
19, 108, and *Jerusalem* pl. 46 (p. 516).
   All the deletions on the page are in pencil.
   There are Xs in the left margin above l. 1, above and below l. 6, beside a line
bracketing ll. 10–12, and above l. 20, but no purpose is made clear.
   l. 10 is in Brown ink.
   ll. 12–13: l. 13 was written in a stanza break·and erased so that l. 12 could be
written in the same ·place.
   l. 14: Cf. Job 14:3 ('dost thou . . . [*bring*] me into judgment with thee?) and
Psalm 143: 1–2, 7.

O I am nothing & to nothing must return again⌞;⌟
If thou withdraw thy breath, behold I am oblivion⌞.⌟"

'He ceasd: the shadowy voice was silent; but the cloud
hoverd over their heads ˙   [⁴

[*Page 41*]
'In golden wreathes, the sorrow of Man & the balmy drops
fell down
And Lo that Son of Man, that shadowy Spirit of the [Eternal
del] ˄Fallen˄ One ˄˄*Albion˄˄
Luvah, descended from the cloud; [the Eternal *del*] ˄In
terror˄ [Man *del*] arose ˄˄*Albion rose⌞.⌟˄˄

Indignant rose the [Eternal *del*] ˄[Fallen *del*]˄ ˄˄Awful˄˄
Man & turnd his back on Vala⌞.⌟
I ˄˄*We˄˄ heard the Voice of the [Eternal *del*] ˄[Falln One
del]˄ ˄˄*Albion˄˄ starting from his sleep⌞:⌟   [.

' "Why roll thy clouds in sickning mist*s*? I can no longer hide
The dismal vision of mine Eyes, O love & life & light!
Prophetic dreads urge me to spea*k*: futurity is before me
Like a dark lamp. Eternal death haunts all my expectation⌞.⌟
˄Rent from Eternal Brotherhood we die & are no more.˄   [.

' "Whence is this voice crying Enion that soundeth in my
ears⌞?⌟
O cruel pity! O dark deceit! can Love seek for dominion⌞?⌟"

'And Luvah strove to gain dominion over the [Eternal *del*]
˄Ancient˄ ˄˄*mighty Albion˄˄ Man⌞.⌟

Page 41 DESIGN: At the foot of the page is a voluptuous nude woman lying on her back, her right leg extended, her left leg bent to the side, her back arched, breasts thrust forward, mouth open, who stretches her arms far back to vague (?erased) lines which seem to represent the enormous penis and scrotum of a naked man kneeling behind her. There are a few other vague undecipherable strokes.

l. 3: Clearly 'arose' should also be deleted.

l. 5 was written after l. 10, but a partially erased stroke seems to indicate that it should be entered after l. 4.

ll. 6–10 are bracketed in the left margin, evidently indicating that they should be omitted when the passage on p. 41 was copied on *Jerusalem* pl. 29.

l. 11: The opening outer quotation mark is Blake's.

Vala p. 42

They strove together above the Body where Vala was inclos'd
And the dark Body of [Man *del*] ʌʌ*Albionʌʌ left prostrate
    upon the crystal pavement   [*15*]
Coverd with boils from head to foo*t*: the terrible smitings of
    Luvah∟·⌡

'Then frownd the [Eternal *del*] ʌFallenʌ Man ʌʌ*Albionʌʌ
    & put forth Luvah from his presence
ʌ(I heard him: frown not Urizen: but listen to my Vision)ʌ   [*18*]
                  [*Page 42*]
'Saying, "Go & die the Death of Man for Vala the sweet
    wanderer∟·⌡
I will turn the volutions of your Ears outward; & bend your
    Nostrils
Downward; & your fluxile Eyes englob'd, roll round in
    fear∟;⌡
Your withring Lips & Tongue shrink up into a narrow circle
Till into narrow forms you creep. Go take your fiery way   [*5*]
And learn what 'tis to absorb the Man∟,⌡ you Spirits of
    Pity & Love∟·⌡"
    ʌO Urizen why art thou pale at the visions of Ahania∟?⌡
    ʌListen to her who loves thee lest we also are driven
    away.ʌ
They heard the Voice & ʌʌ[*they del*]ʌʌ fled swift as the
    winters setting sun
And now the Human Blood foamd high, [*words del*] ʌI saw
    thatʌ Luvah & Vala   [*10*]

l. 16: Cf. Job 2:7: Satan 'smote Job with sore boils from the sole of his foot unto
his crown'.
    l. 18, the only writing in Brown ink on the page, is written over the same thing
in pencil.
    Page 42 DESIGN: To the left at the foot of the page, a running nude woman, with
her arms up, chases a bat-winged phallus-like creature off the page. Behind her,
much revised, erased, and blurred, seems to be a kneeling nude woman bending
toward a kneeling nude girl. There is much erasure between them of a drawing
which may have represented another nude child looking at the woman; the
woman's hand is near the child's genitals.
    ll. 7–8 are squeezed into a stanza-break. Under them and in the margin are two
erased pencil lines which may be identical. The marginal line was erased before
the pencil line below it was written over it.
    l. 10: The surviving fragments of the erased words would fit 'the Spirits' which

Went down the Human Heart where Paradise & its joys
abounded
In jealous fears⌊,⌋ in fury & rage, & flames roll'd round their
fervid feet
And the vast form of Nature like a Serpent play'd before
them
And as they went in folding fires & thunders of the deep
Vala shrunk in like the dark sea that leaves its slimy banks   [
And from her bosom Luvah fell far as the east & west
And the vast form of Nature like a Serpent roll'd between.
  ^^*Whether this is Jerusalem or Babylon we know
  not⌊:⌋
  ^^*All is Confusion⌊:⌋ All is tumult & we alone are
  escaped⌊.⌋'^^
She ende*d*, for his wrathful throne burst forth the black hail
storm⌊.⌋

^'Am I not God⌊?⌋' said Urizen. 'Who is Equal to me⌊?⌋
^Do I not stretch the heavens abroad or fold them up like
  a garment⌊?⌋'^
^^He spoke mustering his heavy clouds around him black
  opake⌊.⌋^^

appear in the version of the line Blake etched in *Jerusalem* pl. 29, l. 73. Apparently
'the Spirits' was deleted and '*I saw[?] that' written above it; then both were
erased and 'I saw that' was written in ink where 'the Spirits' had been.
  Beside ll. 11–12 in the left margin is written:

> Albion closd the Western Gate &
> shut America out by the Atlantic
> for a Curse and hidden horror
> and an altar of victims to Sin
> & Repentance

They are not marked for entry; Keynes prints them after l. 20.
  ll. 18–19 are squeezed into a stanza break. They are written over two or more
erased pencil lines, the second of which may have read 'Our[?] hearts[?] sick
      on his Rock'. A third erased line up the right margin may have read
'We fled from Jerusalem[?] . . . Lord & Saviour'.
  l. 19 is repeated in *Jerusalem* pl. 29, ll. 29, 82 (pp. 477, 479); cf. Job: 1 15–17,
19: 'I only am escaped alone'.
  l. 20: 'for' seems to be a mistake for 'from'.
  ll. 21–3 are written over an erasure of the first two lines.
  l. 22: Cf. p. 95, ll. 19–20, *Jerusalem* pl. 91, ll. 33–4 (pp. 1206, 620), and Psalm
104: 2 (My God, thou 'coverest thyself with light as with a garment . . . [*and*]
stretchest out the heavens like a curtain').

Vala p. 43

[*Page 43*]

Then thunders rolld around & lightnings darted to & fro˻.˼
His visage changd to darkness & his strong right hand came
    forth
To cast Ahania to the Earth˻;˼ he siezd her by the hair
And threw her from the steps of ice that froze around his
    throne

Saying 'Art thou also become like Val*a*? thus I cast thee
    out˻!˼   [*5*]
Shall the feminine indolent bli*ss*, the indulgent self of
    weariness˻,˼
The passive idle sleep˻,˼ the enormous night & darkness of
    Death
Set herself up to give her laws to the active masculine
    virtue˻?˼
Thou little diminutive portion that darst be a counterpart˻,˼
Thy passivity˻,˼ thy laws of obedience & insincerity   [*10*]
Are my abhorrence. Wherefore hast thou taken that fair
    form˻?˼
Whence is this power given to thee! once thou wast in my
    breast
A sluggish current of dim water*s*, on whose verdant margin
A cavern shaggd with horrid shade*s*, dark cool & deadl*y*,
    where
I laid my head in the hot noon after the broken clods   [*15*]
Had wearied m*e*; there I laid my plow & there my horses fed
And thou hast risen with thy moist locks into a watry image
Reflecting all my indolence˻,˼ my weakness & my death
To weigh me down beneath the grave into non Entity
Where Luvah strives scorned by Vala age after age wander-
    ing˻,˼   [*20*]
Shrinking & shrinking from her Lord & calling him the
    Tempter
And art thou also become like Vala˻?˼ thus I cast thee out˻!˼'
    ˄So loud in thunders spoke the King folded in dark
        despair˄

Page 43 l. 2: 'hand' was originally 'had'.
ll. 23–4 are squeezed into a stanza-break.

1137

^^And threw Ahania from his bosom obdurate_L·_ She
  fell like lightning_L·_^^
Then fled the Sons of Urizen from his thunderous throne
  petrific_L·_
They fled to East & West & left the North & South of
  Heaven_L·_
A crash ran thro the immense_L·_ The bounds of Destiny were
  broken_L·_
The bounds of Destiny Crashd direful & the swelling Sea
Burst from its bonds in whirlpools fierce roaring with Human
  voice
Triumphing even to the Stars at bright Ahanias fall_L·_

Down from the dismal North the Prince in thunders & thick
  clouds

[*Page 44*]

As when the thunder bolt down falleth on the appointed
  place
Fell down down rushing ruining thundering [darkning *del*]
  shuddering
Into the Caverns of the Grave & places of Human Seed
Where the impressions of Despair ^& Hope^ enroot forever_L,_
A world of Darkness. Ahania fell far into Non Entity_L·_

She Continued falling. Loud the Crash continud loud &
  Hoarse_L·_
From the Crash roared a flame of blue su[l]phuireous fire_L,_
  from the flame

Page 44 DESIGN: In the lower left margin is a very roughly drawn nude armless
woman whose head ends in jagged points which may be a crown. On her belly are
vague lines like a tripartite Gothic shrine. (Cf. *Jerusalem* pl. 88, ll. 17, 19, 39
[pp. 613–14], where Enitharmon says: 'I will Create secret places . . . A triple Female
Tabernacle for Moral Law . . . I will make their places of joy & love excre-
mentitious'. Blake's Design 8 [1797] for Gray's 'Descent of Odin' [reproduced in
I. Tayler, *Blake's Illustrations to the Poems of Gray* (1971)] shows an analogous
woman, clothed and with hands but with similar spiky hair.) At the foot to the right
lies a naked bearded man with a look of pain on his face who is leaning on his left
elbow and reaching up the right margin with his right hand. (He is almost a mirror
image of the *Night Thoughts* engraving opposite him on *Vala* p. 45. Perhaps they
are Ahania and Urizen.)
  l. 3 is repeated on p. 91, l. 1.
  l. 7: At first 'roared' was 'reared'.

A dolorous groan that struck with dumbness all confusion
Swallowing up the horrible din in agony on agony
Thro the Confusion like a crack across from immense to
   immense `⁻10]`
Loud strong a universal groan of death louder
Than all the wracking elements deafend & rended worse
Than Urizen & all his hosts in curst despair down rushing
But from the Dolorous Groan one like a shadow of smoke
   appeard
And human bones rattling together in the smoke & stamping `[15]`
The nether Abyss & gnasshing in fierce despai*r*, panting in
   sobs
Thick short incessant bursting sobbin*g*, deep despairing
   stamping struggling⌊,⌋
[To take the limbs(?) of Man *del*] ∧Struggling to utter the
   voice∧ of Man⌊,⌋ struggling to take the features of Ma*n*,
   Struggling
To take the limbs of Man⌊,⌋ at length emerging from the
   smoke `150`
Of Urizen dashed in pieces from his precipitant fall `[20]`
Tharmas reard up his hands & stood on the affrighted
   Ocean⌊.⌋
The dead reard up his Voice & stood on the resounding
   shore

Crying: 'fury in my limb*s*! destruction in my bones & mar-
   row⌊!⌋
My skull riven into filament*s*, my eyes into sea jellies
Floating upon the tide wander bubbling & bubbling `[25]`
Uttering my lamentations & begetting little monsters
Who sit mocking upon the little pebbles of the tide
In all my rivers & on dried shells that the fish `[28]`

[Page 45]

'Have quite forsaken. O fool⌊!⌋ fool⌊!⌋ to lose my sweetest
   bliss⌊.⌋
Where art thou Enion⌊?⌋ ah too near to cunning⌊,⌋ too far
   off
And yet too near. Dashd down I send thee into distant
   darkness

Far as my strength can hurl thee ͇;͒ wander there & laugh
   & play
Among the frozen arrows ͇;͒ they will tear thy tender flesh ͇·͒
Fall off afar from Tharmas ͇,͒ come not too near my strong
   fury ͇·͒
Scream & fall off & laugh at Tharmas ͇,͒ lovely summer
   beauty ͇,͒
Till winter rends thee into Shivers as thou hast rended me ͇·͒'

So Tharmas bellowd oer the ocean thundring sobbing
   bursting ͇·͒
The bounds of Destiny were broken & hatred now began
Instead of love to Enion. Enion blind & age bent
Plungd into the cold billows living [& *del*] ˄a˄ life in midst of
   waters ͇·͒
In terrors she witherd away to Entuthon Benithon ͇,͒
A world of deep darkness where all things in horrors are
   rooted ͇·͒

These are the words of Enion heard from the cold waves of
   despair ͇:͒
˄'O Tharmas I had lost the*e*, & when I hoped I had found
   thee˄
O Tharmas do not thou destroy me quite but let
A little shado*w*, but a little showery form of Enion
Be near thee ͇,͒ loved Terror; let me still remain & then do
   thou
Thy righteous doom upon m*e*, only let me hear thy voice ͇·͒
Driven by thy rage I wander like a cloud into the deep
Where never yet Existence came, there losing all my life
I back return weaker & weaker, consume me not away
In thy great wra*th*; tho I have sinne*d*, Tho I have rebelld
Make me not like the things forgotten as they had not been ͇·͒
Make not the thing that loveth the*e*, a tear wiped away ͇·͒'

Tharmas replied riding on storms ͇,͒ [the *del*] ˄his˄ voice of
[Tharmas *del*] ˄Thunder˄ rolld ͇:͒

Page 45 l. 16 is inserted in a stanza-break.
l. 27. A stanza-break follows l. 27.

'Image of grief_L,_J thy fading lineaments make my eyelids
  fail_L·_J
What have I done! both rage & mercy are alike to me_L·_J
Looking upon thee_L,_J Image of faint water*s*, I recoil   [*30*]
From my fierce rage into thy semblance. Enion return_L·_J
Why does thy piteous face Evanish like a rainy cloud   [*32*]
                            [*Page 46*]
'Melting, a shower of falling tear*s*, nothing but tears! Enion:
Substanceles*s*, voiceless, weeping, vanish*d*, nothing but tears!
  Enion:
Art thou for ever vanishd from the watry eyes of Tharmas_L?_J
Rage Rage shall never from my boso*m*; winds & waters of
  wo*e*
Consuming all_L,_J to the end consuming_L·_J Love & [Joy *del*]
  ˄Hope˄ are ended_L·_J'   [*5*]

For now no more remaind of Enion in the dismal air_L,_J
Only a voice eternal wailing in the Elements_L·_J

Where Enion blind & age bent wanderd Ahania wanders
  now_L·_J
She wanders in Eternal fear of falling into the indefinite
For her bright eyes behold the Abys*s*; sometimes a little   200
  sleep   [*10*]
Weighs down her eyelids_L;_J then she falls_L,_J then starting
  wakes in fears
Sleepless to wander round repelld on the margin of Non
  Entity_L·_J   [*12*]
            The End of the Third Night

Page 46   DESIGN: At the foot of the page, a nude woman stands with her hands
to her cheeks as if in fear, looking right towards a naked man who seems to have
pushed through six-foot waves (?or grass) to find her. His left hand is above his
head and his right hand is parting the water. His head was erased and redrawn.
(Perhaps thɛy represent Enion 'in midst of waters' as she 'witherd away' from
Tharmas, p. 45, ll. 12–13, or Tharmas as 'in a Wave he rap'd bright Enitharmon
far Apart', p. 49, ll. 4–5.)

VALA

Night The Fourth

But Tharmas rode on the dark Abys*s*; the voice of
    Tharmas rolld
Over the heaving delug*e*; he saw Los & Enitharmon Emerge
In strength & brightness from the Abyss∟;⌐ his bowels yearnd
    over them∟·⌐
They rose in strength above the heaving delug*e*, in mighty
    scorn
Red as the Sun in the hot morning of the bloody day   [
Tharmas beheld them∟,⌐ his bowels yearnd over them

∧And he said∟,⌐ 'Wherefore do I feel such love & pity∟?⌐∧
∧∧Ah Enion∟!⌐ Ah Enion∟!⌐ Ah lovely lovely Enion∟!⌐∧∧
[*words del*] ∧How is this∧ All my hope [*word del*] ∧is gone∟!⌐∧
  ∧∧[Enion *del*]∧∧ for ever [*word del*] ∧fled∟!⌐∧
Like a famishd Eagle Eyeless raging in the vast expanse∟,⌐   [
Incessant tears are now my foo*d*, incessant rage & tears∟·⌐
Deathless for ever now I wander seeking oblivion
In torrents of despair in vai*n*, for if I plunge beneath
Stifling I live. If dashd in pieces from a rocky height
I reunite in endless tormen*t*; would I had never risen
From deaths cold sleep [upon *del*] beneath the bottom of the
    raging Ocean
And cannot those who once have lov*d* ever forget their Love?
Are love & rage the same passion? they are the same in me∟·⌐
Are those who lov*e*, like those who die*d*, risen again from
    death
Immorta*l*, in immortal tormen*t*, never to be deliverd∟?⌐
Is it not possible that one risen again from Death
Can die! When dark despair comes over can I not
Flow down into the sea & slumber in oblivio*n*? Ah Enion∟,⌐

Page 47   ll. 7, 9 are written over two erased lines, which may have read
   He Tharmas thought[?]   thundring[?]   Enveloped[?] thee
   And Tharmas said All my hope I thought for ever gone

[*Page 48*]

'Deformd I see these lineaments of ungratified Desire⌊·⌋
The all powerful curse of an honest man be upon Urizen &
　Luvah
But thou My Son Glorious in brightness⌊,⌋ comforter of
　Tharmas⌊,⌋
Go forth⌊,⌋ Rebuild this Universe beneath my indignant
　power⌊,⌋
A Universe of Death & Decay. Let Enitharmons hands　　　[5]
Weave soft delusive forms of Man above my watry world⌊·⌋
Renew these ruind souls of Men thro Earth Sea Air & Fire
To waste in endless corruptio*n*, renew thou⌊,⌋ I will destroy⌊·⌋
Perhaps Enion may resume some little semblance
To ease my pangs of heart & to restore some peace to
　Tharmas⌊·⌋'　　　　　　　　　　　　　　　　　　　[10]

Los answerd in his furious pride sparks issuing from his
　hair⌊:⌋
'Hitherto shalt thou com*e*, no furthe*r*; here thy proud waves
　cease⌊·⌋
We have drunk up the [Anci *del*] ⌃Eternal⌃ Man by our un-
　bounded power⌊·⌋
Beware lest we also drink up thee⌊;⌋ rough demon of the
　waters⌊·⌋
Our God is Urizen the King, King of the Heavenly hosts⌊·⌋　[15]
We have no other God but he⌊,⌋ thou father of worms &
　clay⌊,⌋
And he is fallen into the Deep⌊,⌋ rough Demon of the
　waters⌊,⌋
And Los remains God over al*l*, weak father of worms &
　clay⌊·⌋
I know I was Urthona⌊,⌋ keeper of the gates of heaven⌊,⌋

Page 48　DESIGN: In the bottom right corner a naked man sits with his legs ex-
tended across the page, leaning on his left hand, with his right hand on his left
breast. Drops fall from beneath his hand, and he is looking up the right margin as
if in agony. (The design, reversed, may be sketched on *Notebook* p. 90.)

l. 12: Cf. Job 38:11: God said to the sea, 'Hitherto shalt thou come, but no
further: and here shall thy proud waves be stayed.'

l. 19 is in *Jerusalem* pl. 82, l. 81 (p. 602).

But now I am all powerful Los & Urthona is but my
shadow⌊·⌋’   [

Doubting stood Tharmas in the [dismal *del*] ∧solemn∧ dark-
ness; his dim Eyes
Swam in red tears; he reard his waves above the head of Los
In wrath, but pitying back withdrew with many a sigh⌊·⌋
Now he resolvd to destroy Los & now his tears flowd down⌊·⌋

In scorn stood Los⌊,⌋ red sparks of blighting from his furious   [
head
Flew over the waves of Tharmas; pitying Tharmas stayd his
Waves

For Enitharmon shriekd amain crying 'O my sweet world
Built by the Architect divine whose love to Los & Enitharmon   ⁵
Thou rash abhorred Demon in thy fury hast oerthrown⌊!⌋’   [

[Page 49]

'What Sovereign Architect' said Tharmas 'dare my will con-
troll
For if I will I urge these waters. If I will they sleep
In peace beneath my awful frown⌊;⌋ my will shall be my
Law⌊·⌋’

So Saying in a Wave he rap'd bright Enitharmon far
Apart from Los, but coverd her with softest brooding care   [
On a broad wave in the warm west, balming her bleeding
wound⌊·⌋

O how Los howld at the rending asunder⌊,⌋ all the fibres
rent
Where Enitharmon joind to his left side in [dismal *del*]
∧griding∧ pain⌊·⌋
He falling on the rocks bellowd his Dolor, till the blood
Stanchd, then in ululation waild his woes upon the wind   ∎

And Tharmas calld to the Dark Spectre who upon the
Shores

Page 49 ll. 7–8 may be represented on p. 52.

With dislocated Limbs had falln. The Spectre rose in pain⌐,⌐
A Shadow blue obscure & disma*l*, like a statue of lead
Bent by its fall from a high tower the dolorous shadow rose⌐·⌐

'Go forth' said Tharmas⌐,⌐ 'works of joy are thine⌐;⌐ obey &
    live⌐,⌐   [*15*]
So shall the spungy marrow issuing from thy splinterd bones
Boni*fy*, & thou shalt have rest when this thy labour is done⌐·⌐
Go forth⌐,⌐ bear Enitharmon back to the Eternal Prophet⌐·⌐
Build her a bower in the midst of all my dashing waves⌐·⌐
Make first a resting place for Los & Enitharmo*n*, then   [*20*]
Thou shalt have rest. If thou refusest dashd abroad on all
My wave*s*, thy limbs shall separate in stench & rotting &
    thou
Become a prey to all my Demons of despair & hope⌐·⌐'

The Spectre of Urthona [answers *del*] ︿seeing︿ Enitharmon
    writhd
His cloudy form in jealous fear & muttering thunders hoarse   [*25*]
And casting round thick glooms, thus utterd his fierce pangs
    of heart⌐:⌐

'Tharmas I know the*e*, how are we alterd⌐,⌐ our beauty
    decayd
But still I know thee tho in this horrible ruin whelmd⌐·⌐
Thou once the mildest son of heaven art now become a
    Rage⌐,⌐
A terror to all living thing*s*; think not that I am ignorant   [*30*]
That thou art risen from the dead or that my power forgot   [*31*]
                [*Page 50*]
'I slumber here in weak repose. I well remember the Day⌐,⌐
The day of terror & abhorrence [eternal *del*]
When fleeing from the battle thou fleeting like the raven
Of dawn outstretching an expanse where neer expanse had
    been

Page 50 DESIGN: At the foot of the page, a voluptuous nude woman lies on her
left side (?in the sea) with her left arm extended, her right arm by her side, and
an unhappy look on her face. Vague lines by her head and feet may be billows.
(Perhaps she is Enitharmon 'issuing down the tide', l. 19.)

Drewst all the Sons of Beulah into thy [great *del*] dread
vortex following
Thy Eddying spirit down the hills of Beulah. All my sons
Stood round me at the anvil where new heated the wedge
Of iron glowd furious prepard for spades & mattocks⌊.⌋
Hearing the symphonies of war loud sounding All my sons
Fled from my side⌊,⌋ then pangs smote me unknown before.
    I saw
ʌMy loins begin to break forth into Veiny pipes & writheʌ
[Before me in the wind englobing trembling with strong
    vibrations(?) *del*]
Before me in the wind englobing⌊,⌋ trembling with strong
    vibrations
The bloody mass began to animate. I bending over
Wept bitter tears incessant. Still beholding how the piteous
    form
Dividing & dividing from my loins⌊,⌋ a weak & piteous
Soft cloud of snow⌊,⌋ a female pale & weak⌊,⌋ I soft embracd
My counter part & calld it Love⌊.⌋ I namd her Enitharmon
But found myself & her together issuing down the tide
Which now our rivers were become delving thro caverns
    huge
Of goary blood strugg[*l*]ing to be deliverd from our bonds⌊.⌋
She strove in vain⌊;⌋ not so Urthona strove for breaking forth
A shadow blue obscure & dismal from the breathing Nostrils
Of Enion I issued into the air divided from Enitharmon⌊.⌋
I howld in sorrow⌊.⌋ I beheld thee rotting upon the Rocks⌊.⌋
I pitying hoverd over thee⌊;⌋ I protected thy ghastly corse
From Vultures of the deep⌊;⌋ then wherefore shouldst thou
    rage
Against me who thee guarded in the night of death from
    harm⌊?⌋'

Tharmas replie*d*: 'Art thou Urthona⌊,⌋ My friend⌊,⌋ my
    old companion,
With whom I livd in happiness before that deadly night
When Urizen gave the horses of Light into the hands of
    Luvah⌊?⌋

l. 8: The phrase is repeated on p. 22, ll. 16–17 and on p. 84, ll. 16–17.

1146

Thou knowest not what Tharmas knows. O I could tell thee
  tales
That would enrage thee as it has Enraged me even
From Death in wrath & fury. But now come bear back
Thy loved Enitharmon. For thou hast her here before thine
  Eyes   [*35*]

[Page 51]

'But my Sweet Enion is Vanishd & I never more
Shall see her unless thou O Shadow, wilt protect this Son
Of Enion & him assist to bind the fallen King
Lest he should rise again from death in all his [dismal *del*]
  ∧dreary∧ power⌞.⌟
Bind him, take Enitharmon for thy sweet reward While I   [*5*]
In vain am driven on false hope, hope sister of despair⌞.⌟'

Groaning the terror rose & drave his solid rocks before
Upon the tide till underneath the feet of Los a World
Dark dreadful rose & Enitharmon lay at Los's feet⌞.⌟
The Dolorous shadow joyd; weak hope appeard around his
  head⌞.⌟   [*10*]

Tharmas before Los stood & thus the Voice of Tharmas
  rolld⌞:⌟

'Now all comes into the power of Tharmas. Urizen is falln
And Luvah hidden in the Elemental forms of Life & Death⌞.⌟
Urthona is My Son⌞.⌟ O Los thou art Urthona & Tharmas
Is God. The Eternal Man is sealed⌞,⌟ never to be deliverd⌞.⌟   [*15*]
I roll my floods over his body⌞,⌟ my billows & waves pass
  over him⌞.⌟
The Sea encompasses him & monsters of the deep are his
  companions⌞.⌟
Dreamer of furious oceans⌞,⌟ cold sleeper of weeds & shells⌞,⌟
Thy Eternal form shall never renew⌞,⌟ my uncertain prevails
  against thee
Yet tho I rage God over al*l*, A portion of my Life   [*20*]
That in Eternal fields in comfort wanderd with my flocks

    Page 51 l. 7: 'solid' was at first 'sold'.
      l. 15 is repeated on p. 103, l. 11.
      l. 16: Cf. Jonah 2:3: 'thy billows and thy waves pass over me'.

At noon & laid her head upon my wearied bosom at night⌞,⌟
She is divided⌞.⌟ She is vanishd even like Luvah & Vala⌞.⌟
O why did foul ambition sieze thee Urizen Prince of Light⌞?⌟
And thee O Luvah prince of Love till Tharmas was divided⌞?⌟
And I⌞,⌟ what can I now behold but an Eternal Death
Before my Eyes & an Eternal weary work to strive
Against the monstrous forms that breed among my silent
waves⌞?⌟
Is this to be A God⌞?⌟ far rather would I be a Man
To know sweet Science & to do with simple companions
Sitting beneath a tent & viewing sheepfolds & soft pastures⌞.⌟
Take thou the hammer of Urthona⌞,⌟ rebuild these furnaces⌞.⌟
Dost thou refuse⌞?⌟ mind I the sparks that issue from thy
hair⌞?⌟

[*Page 52*]

'I will compell thee to rebuild by these my furious waves⌞.⌟
Death choose or life⌞;⌟ thou strugglest in my waters, now
choose life
And all the Elements shall serve thee to their soothing flutes⌞.⌟
Their sweet inspiriting lyres thy labours shall administer
And they to thee⌞;⌟ only remit not⌞,⌟ faint not thou my
Son⌞.⌟
Now thou dost know what tis to strive against the God of
waters⌞.⌟'

So saying Tharmas on his furious chariots of the Deep
Departed far into the Unknown & left a wondrous void
Round Lo*s*; afar his waters bore on all sides round with noise
Of wheels & horses hoofs & Trumpets Horns & Clarions⌞.⌟

Terrified Los beheld the ruins of Urizen beneath⌞,⌟
A horrible Chaos to his eye*s*, a formless unmeasurable Death

l. 23: 'Vala' was 'Valan' at first.
l. 24: Under 'Urizen' Blake originally began a word with 'L'.

Page 52 DESIGN: In the bottom left corner is a kneeling naked man, with his left
arm behind a kneeling nude woman at whom he is looking. She has her right hand
under his left armpit, her left hand on her breast, as if pushing herself away
from him, and she is looking at him (?in terror). There are some undecipherable
strokes behind the man. (Perhaps they represent Los, with Enitharmon 'rent . . .
[*from*] his left side', p. 49, ll. 7–8.)

Whirling up broken rocks on high into the dismal air
And fluctuating all beneath in Eddies of molton fluid_L.

Then Los with terrible hands siezd on the Ruind Furnaces   [*15*]
Of Urizen. Enormous work: he builded them anew_L,
Labour of Ages in the Darkness & the war of Tharmas
And Los formd Anvils of Iron petrific, for his blows
Petrify with incessant beating many a rock, many a planet

But Urizen slept in a stoned stupor in the nether Abyss_L,   [*20*]
A dreamful horrible State in tossings on his icy bed
Freezing to Solid all beneath, his grey oblivious form
Stretchd over the immense heaves in strong shudders, silent
    his voice
In brooding contemplation stretching out from North to
    South
In mighty power. Round him Los rolld furious   [*25*]
His thunderous wheels from furnace to furnace, tending
    diligent
The contemplative terror, frightend in his scornful sphere_L,
Frightend with cold infectious madness; in his hand the
    thundering
Hammer of Urthona, forming under his heavy hand the
    hours   [*29*]

[*Page 53*]

The days & years, in chains of iron round the limbs of
    Urizen
Linkd hour to hour & day to night & night to day & year to
    year
In periods of pulsative furor; mills he formd & works
Of many wheels resistless in the power of dark Urthona

But Enitharmon wrapd in clouds waild loud, for as Los beat   [*5*]
The anvils of Urthona link by link the chains of sorrow
Warping upon the winds & whirling round in the dark deep
Lashd on the limbs of Enitharmon & the sulphur fires
Belchd from the furnaces wreathd round her, chaind in
    ceaseless fire_L.
The lovely female howld & Urizen beneath deep groand   [*10*]

Deadly between the hammers beating grateful to the Ears
Of Lo*s*, absorbd in dire revenge he drank with joy the cries
Of Enitharmon & the groans of Urizen fuel for his wrath
And for his pity secret feeding on thoughts of cruelty⌞·⌟

The Spectre wept at his dire labours when from [ladles(*?*)
  del] Ladles huge
He pourd the molten iron round the limbs of Enitharmon
But when he pourd it round the bones of Urizen he laughd
Hollow upon the hollow win*d*, his shadowy form obeying
The voice of Los⌞,⌟ compelld he labourd round the Furnaces

And thus began the binding Of Urizen day & night in fear⌞·⌟
Circling round the dark Demon with howlings dismay &
  sharp blightings
The Prophet of Eternity beat on his iron links & links of
  brass
And as he beat round the hurtling Demo*n*, terrified at the
  Shapes
Enslavd humanity put on⌞,⌟ he became what he beheld⌞·⌟
Raging against Tharmas his God & uttering
Ambiguous words blasphemous filld with envy⌞,⌟ firm re-
  solvd
On hate Eternal⌞,⌟ in his vast disdain he labourd beating
The Links of fate⌞,⌟ link after link⌞,⌟ an endless chain of
  sorrows⌞·⌟

[*Page 54*]

The Eternal Mind bounded began to roll eddies of wrath
  ceaseless
Round & round & the sulphureous f⌐am surging thick

Page 53   ll. 20-2 are repeated in *The Book of Los* pl. 5, ll. 141-5 (p. 313).
  ll. 23-4 are on p. 55, ll. 47-9.
  l. 24: Variants of 'they became what they behe*l*d' are on p. 55, l. 49; see
Jerusalem pl. 34, ll. 50, 54 (pp. 489, 490).

Page 54   DESIGN: There is a largely undecipherable sketch *under* the text. Two
poles(?) cross at mid-page, and a ball at the foot with vague strokes on it (?a
globe) rests between two mountains. There are many other vague strokes.
  ll. 1-30, p. 55, ll. 1-9, 43-6 are repeated from *Urizen* pl. 10-11, 13 (pp. 253-7);
see *Milton* pl. b, ll. 6, 10-14, 16-27 (pp. 320-1), where the same passage from
Urizen was adapted.

Settled a Lake bright & shining clea*r*: White as the snow[.]

Forgetfulness dumbness necessity in chains of the mind lockd
  up
In fetters of ice shrinkin*g*, disorganizd rent from Eternity[.]   [5]
Los beat on his fetters & [pourd *del*] heated his furnaces
And pourd iron sodor & sodor of brass[.]

Restless the immortal inchaind heaving dolorous
Anguishd unbearable till a roof shaggy wild inclosd
In an orb his fountain of thought[.]   [10]

In a horrible dreamful slumber like the linked chain
A vast spine writhd in torment upon the wind
Shooting pain*d* ribbs like a bending Cavern
And bones of solidness froze over all his nerves of joy[.]
A first age passe*d*, a state of dismal woe[.]   [15]

From the Caverns of his jointed spine down sunk with fright
A red round glob*e*, hot burnin*g*, deep deep down into the
  Abyss[,]
Panting Conglobing trembling Shooting out ten thousand
  branches
Around his solid bones & a Second Age passed over[.]

In harrowing fear rolling his nervous brain shot branches   [20]
[Round the branches of his heart *del*]
On high into two little orbs hiding in two little caves[,]
Hiding carefully from the wind his eyes beheld the deep
And a third age passed[,] a State of dismal woe[.]

The pangs of hope began in heavy pain striving struggling[;]   [25]
Two Ears in close volutions from beneath his orbs of vision
Shot spiring out & petrified [in *del*] ^as^ they grew. And a
  Fourth
Age passed over & a State of dismal woe[.]

In ghastly torment sick hanging upon the wind
Two nostrils bent down to the deeps—   [30]

l. 20: 'brain' was originally 'brains'.

[*Page 55*]
And a fifth age passed & a state of dismal woe⌞·⌟

In ghastly torment sic*k*, within his ribs bloated round
A craving hungry cavern. Thence arose his channeld
Throa*t*; then like a red flame a tongue of hunger
And thirst appeard and a sixth age passed of dismal woe⌞·⌟

Enraged & stifled with torment he threw his right arm to the
 north⌞,⌟
His left arm to the south shooting out in anguish deep
And his feet stampd the nether abyss in trembling howling &
 dismay
And a seventh age passed over & a state of dismal woe⌞·⌟
 ⌃The Council of God &ᶜ as belo*w*, to immensity 31
 lines⌃
⌃The Council of God on high watching over the Body
⌃Of Man clothd in Luvahs robes of blood saw & wept⌞·⌟
⌃Descending over Beulahs mild moon coverd regions
⌃The daughters of Beulah saw the Divine Vision⌞;⌟ they were
 comforted
⌃And as a Double female form⌞,⌟ Loveliness & perfection of
 beauty⌞,⌟
⌃They bowd the head & worshippd & with mild voice spoke
 these words⌞:⌟⌃

[*Page 56*]
'Lor*d*, Saviour if thou hadst been here our brother had not
 died
And now we know that whatsoever thou wilt ask of God
He will give it thee for we are weak women & dare not lift

Page 55 l. 8: For a variant of this line see *Urizen* pl. 13, ll. 251–2 (p. 257).
 After l. 9, the direction, in a stanza-break, refers to ll. 10–42 on pp. 55–6.
 ll. 10–12 are written over '[End of the Fourth Night *del*]'.

Page 56: l. 16 is in *Jerusalem* pl. 50, ll. 10–11 (pp. 523–4).
 ll. 16, 32–3: Cf. John: 10 21–3: 'Then Martha said unto Jesus, Lord, if thou
 hadst been here, my brother had not died. But I know, that even now, whatsoever
 thou wilt ask of God, God will give it thee. Jesus saith unto her, Thy brother shall
 rise again.'

Our eyes to the Divine pavilion*s*; therefore in mercy thou
Appearest clothd in Luvahs garments that we may behold
    thee   [20]
And live. Behold Eternal Death is in Beulah⌊·⌋ Behold
We perish & shall not be found unless thou grant a place
In which we may be hidden under the Shadow of wings
For if we who are but for a time & who pass away in winter
Behold these wonders of Eternity we shall consume⌊·⌋'   [25]

∧Such were the words of Beulah of the Feminine Emana-
    tion⌊·⌋
∧The Empyrean groand throughout⌊·⌋ All Eden was dar-
    kend⌊·⌋
∧The Corse of [Man *del*] ∧∧*Albion∧∧ lay on the Rock⌊;⌋ the
    Sea of Time & Space
∧Beat round the Rock in mighty waves & as a Polypus
∧That vegetates beneath the Sea the limbs of Man vegetated   [30]
∧In monstrous forms of Death⌊,⌋ a Human polypus of
    Death⌊·⌋∧

The Saviour mild & gentle bent over the corse of Death
    ∧Saying 'If Ye will Believe Your brother Shall rise
    again⌊·⌋'∧
And first he found the Limit of Opacity & namd it Satan
    ∧∧*In Albions bosom for in every human[?] bosom these
    limits stand∧∧   [35]
And next he found the Limit of Contraction & namd it
    Adam

ll. 22–5 are in *Milton* pl. 30, ll. 24–7 (p. 385).
ll. 26–31 are written over an erased passage of six lines which may have read in
part:

    A   five days of Great Eternity
    The   Eternal Death

    Then J
    The   tions
    Then all the Space of E
    Witherd beneath the gentle

The first of these was in what is now a stanza-break.
l. 33 is written over an erased added line.
l. 35 is written in the right margin after l. 34.

While yet those beings were not born nor knew of good
or Evil_{L·⌋}

Then wondrously the [Deep beneath *del*] ⌃⌃*Starry Wheels⌃⌃
felt the divine hand. Limit
Was put to Eternal Death_{L·⌋} Los felt the Limit & saw
The Finger of God touch the Seventh furnace in terror
And Los beheld the hand of God over his furnaces
⌃Beneath the Deeps in dismal Darkness beneath immen-
sity_{L·⌋⌃}
  In terrors &c ⌃to Abyss⌃ as 31 lines above

[*Page 55*]

In terrors Los shrunk from his tas*k*; his great hammer
Fell from his hand_{L;⌋} his fires hid their strong limbs in
smoke
For [in *del*] ⌃with⌃ noises ruinous hurtlings & clashings &
groans
The immortal endur*d*, tho bound in a deadly sleep_{L·⌋}
Pale terror siezd the Eyes of Los as he beat round
The hurtling Demo*n*; terrifid at the shapes
Enslavd humanity put on he became what he beheld_{L;⌋}
He became what he was doing_{L;⌋} he was himself transformd_{L·⌋}
  ⌃⌃*Bring in here the Globe of Blood as in the B of
  Urizen⌃⌃

ll. 39–40 are in *Jerusalem* pl. 48, ll. 44–5 (pp. 519–20).
l. 42 is written over '[The End of the Fourth Book(?) *del*]'.

Page 55 ll. 43–58 are bracketed on both sides; Blake clearly meant to transpose
them after p. 56, l. 42.
ll. 46–8 are on p. 53, ll. 23–4, q.v.
l. 49: Variants of 'they became what they beheld' are on p. 53, l. 24, q.v. and
note (p. 1150).
After l. 50, the pencil direction is in a stanza-break; see *Urizen* pl. 18 (p. 265),
which describes the creation of Urizen, first as a 'round globe of blood' and then
as 'the first female now separate';

   Los saw the Female & pitied_{L·⌋}
   He embrac'd her, she wept, she refus'd
   In perverse and cruel delight_{L:⌋}
   She fled from his arms, yet he followd_{L·⌋}

This scene seems to be represented in the full-page sketch on p. 112 (see p. 1728
below).

Spasms siezd his muscular fibres writhing to & fro∟;⌟ his
   pallid lips
Unwilling movd as Urizen howld∟;⌟ his loins wavd like the
   sea
At Enitharmons shriek∟;⌟ his knees each other smote & then
   he lookd
[On *del*] ⌃With⌃ stony Eyes on Urizen & then swift writhd
   his neck
Involuntary to the Couch where Enitharmon lay∟·⌟   [55]
The bones of Urizen hurtle on the wind∟;⌟ the bones of Los
Twinge & his iron sinews bend like lead & fold
Into unusual forms dancing & howling∟,⌟ stamping the   292[290 *del*]
   Abyss∟·⌟   [58]

[Page 56]
End of the Fourth [Book *del*] ⌃Night⌃

l. 51: 'fro' was originally 'from'.
l. 53: 'shriek' at first was 'shrieks'.

Page 56 DESIGN: Below all the writing is a figure with its legs enormously extended across the page. It is leaning forward, its left arm bent, its right arm extended, holding the wrists of a smaller figure in a crawling position who looks half-smiling at the first. Behind this second figure are the very faint head and shoulder of a child facing them.

   Below all the writing at the foot of the page the following line was written very faintly (and erased?):

   Christs Crucifix shall be made an excuse for Executing Criminals

VALA

[Book *del*] ⌃Night⌃ The Fifth

Infected Mad he dancd on his mountains high & dark as
heaven⌞·⌟
Now fixd into one stedfast bulk his features stonify⌞·⌟
From his mouth curses & from his eyes sparks of blighting⌞,⌟
Beside the anvil cold he dancd with the hammer of Urthona
Terrific pale. Enitharmon stretchd on the [dismal *del*]
⌃⌃*Dreary⌃⌃ Earth   [L
Felt her immortal limbs freeze stiffning pale inflexible⌞·⌟
His feet shrink withring from the deep⌞,⌟ shrinking & wither-
ing
And Enitharmon shrunk up all their fibres withring beneath
As plants witherd by winter leaves & stems & roots decaying
Melt into thin air while the seed driven by the furious wind   [*
Rests on the distant Mountains top. So Los & Enitharmon
Shrunk into fixed space stood trembling on a Rocky cliff
Yet mighty bulk & majesty & beauty remaind but un-
expansive⌞·⌟
As far as highest Zenith from the lowest Nader, so far
shrunk
Los from the furnaces⌞,⌟ a Space immense⌞,⌟ & left the cold   [*
Prince of Light bound in chains of intellect among the
furnaces
But all the furnaces were out & the bellows had ceast to
blow⌞·⌟

He stood trembling & Enitharmon clung around his knees⌞·⌟
Their senses unexpansive in one stedfast bulk remain⌞·⌟
The night blew cold & Enitharmon shriekd on the dismal
wind⌞·⌟   [*

[*Page 58*]
Her pale hands cling around her husband & over her weak
head

Page 58 DESIGN: *Underneath* the text is a full-page sketch of Christ, with his hands
at the corners of the page, his body angled, his head looking slightly toward his

Shadows of Eternal Death sit in the leaden air

But the soft pipe the flute the viol organ harp & cymbal
And the sweet sound of silver voices calm the weary couch
Of Enitharmon but her groans drown the immortal harps⌊·⌋   [*5*]
Loud & more loud the living music floats upon the air⌊,⌋
Faint & more faint the daylight wanes. The wheels of turn-
ing darkness
Began in solemn revolutions. Earth convulsd with rending
pangs
Rockd to & fro & cried sore at the groans of Enitharmon⌊·⌋
Still the faint harps & silver voices calm the weary couch   [*10*]
But from the caves of deepest night ascending in clouds of
mist
The winter spread his wide black wings across from pole to
pole⌊·⌋
Grim frost beneath & terrible snow linkd in a marriage chain
Began a dismal dance. The winds around on pointed rocks
Settled like bats innumerable ready to fly abroad⌊·⌋   [*15*]
The groans of Enitharmon shake the skies⌊,⌋ the labring
Earth⌊,⌋
Till from her heart rending his way a terrible Child sprang
forth
In thunder smoke & sullen flames & howlings & fury &
blood⌊·⌋

Soon as his burning Eyes were opend on the Abyss
The horrid trumpets of the deep bellowd with bitter blasts⌊·⌋   [*20*]

right breast, and clouds surging around him. This sketch was not erased. (The
design echoes one by Richard Westall for *The Poetical Works of John Milton*, ed. W.
Hayley [1795], i. 85, and is elaborated in *Vala* p. 116 and in *Night Thoughts* water-
colour f. 108 [BMPR]; angels were added on *Vala* p. 16; and Christ and the angels
were incorporated in *Night Thoughts* water-colour f. 108 verso [BMPR] and copied
in the engraving for *Night Thoughts* [1797] p. 65. The designs on *Vala* pp. 16, 58,
116 seem therefore to have been made for Young's *Night Thoughts* and not for
Vala.)
    At the foot of the page a nude woman (?Enitharmon) lies with her head on her
crossed arms but twists at the hip so that she is on her left side. A fainter sketch
represented her as crouching. At her head stands a naked boy (?Orc) with
his left hand behind her, his right hand on his hip, looking down at her pen-
sively. These figures avoid the text.
    l. 9: The MS has 'fro & & cried'.

The Enormous Demons woke & howld around the [youthful
del] new born king
Crying 'Luvah King of Love thou art the King of rage &
death ∟·⌋'
∧∧[When *del*]∧∧ ∧Urizen cast deep darkness round him ∟;⌋
raging Luvah pourd
∧The spears of Urizen from Chariots round the Eternal
tent ∟·⌋
∧∧[Then *del*]∧∧ Discord began [& *del*] ∧∧then∧∧ yells &
cries shook the wide firma[*m*]ent ∟·⌋∧   [∧

[*Page 59*]

'Where is Sweet Vala ∟,⌋ gloomy prophet ∟?⌋ where the lovely
form
That drew the body of Man from heaven into this dark
Abyss ∟?⌋
Soft tears & sighs where are you ∟?⌋ come forth ∟,⌋ shout on
bloody fields ∟·⌋
Shew thy soul ∟,⌋ Vala ∟!⌋ shew thy bow & quiver of secret
fires ∟·⌋

'Draw thy bow Vala ∟,⌋ from the depths of hell thy black bow   5
draw   [.
And twang the bow string to our howlings ∟,⌋ let thine arrows
black
Sing in the Sky as once they sang upon the hills of Light
When dark Urthona wept in torment of the secret pain ∟·⌋

'He wept & he divided & he laid his gloomy head
Down on the Rock of Eternity on darkness of the deep ∟,⌋   [
Torn by black storms & ceaseless torrents of consuming fire ∟:⌋

ll. 23–5 (which were adapted on p. 22, ll. 12–15) partly cover an erasure of
five lines which were circled in ink and which may read in part:

Then		round his Chariot
In		
This to be? Was Luvah	he stood glowing in the dark flame	
before Around		All his Demons
Of hope & fear	ing th	song around the glowing bed

There was a stanza-break before these lines.
A pencil stroke goes from the '*45' to the third of the erased lines.

Page 59 ll. 5, 19: 'Vala' was originally 'Valan'.
  ll. 11–16 are rearranged in *Jerusalem* pl. 40, ll. 32, 38–42 (p. 501).

Within his breast his fiery sons chaind down & filld with
  cursings

'And breathing terrible blood & vengeance⌞,⌟ gnashing his
  teeth with pain⌞,⌟
Let loose the Enormous spirit in the darkness of the deep
And his dark wife that once fair crystal form divinely clear   [*15*]
Within his ribs producing serpents whose souls are flames of
  fire

'But now the times return upon thee⌞.⌟ Enitharmons womb
Now holds thee soon to issue forth. Sound Clarions of war⌞!⌟
Call Vala from her close recess in all her dark deceit⌞.⌟
Then rage on rage shall fierce redound out of her crystal
  quiver⌞.⌟'   [*20*]

So Sung the Demons [of the deep *del*] ⌃round red Orc⌃ &
  round faint Enitharmon⌞.⌟
Sweat & blood stood on the limbs of Los in globe*s*; his fiery
  Eyelids
Fade*d*; he rouzd⌞,⌟ he siezd the wonder in his hands &
  went
Shuddring & weeping thro the Gloom & down into the
  deeps⌞.⌟

Enitharmon nursd her fiery child in the dark deeps   [*25*]
Sitting in darknes*s*, over her Los mournd in anguish fierce
Coverd with gloo*m*; the fiery boy grew fed by the milk
Of Enitharmon. Los around her builded pillars of iron   [*28*]

[*Page 60*]

And brass & silver & gold fourfold in dark prophetic fear
For now he feard Eternal Death & uttermost Extinction⌞.⌟

l. 21: The erased words are all doubtful readings.

Page 60 DESIGN: At the bottom left a naked man sits on his heels, his arms by his
sides, his hands on the ground, and a band round his chest; he is looking back over
his left shoulder toward a nude woman, half reclining, who seems to be talking to a
naked boy whose legs are intertwined with hers. (The scene clearly represents Los
as he beheld Orc embracing Enitharmon, and 'a tightning girdle grew Around his
bosom like a bloody cord', ll. 7–11.) These figures carefully avoid the text; if the
man's head had been completed, it would have covered part of the last line.

He builded Golgonooza on the Lake of Udan Adan⌊;⌋
Upon the Limit of Translucence then he builded Luban⌊·⌋
Tharmas laid the Foundations & Los finishd it in howling
    woe   [5

But when fourteen summers & winters had revolved over
Their solemn habitation Los beheld the ruddy boy
Embracing his bright mother & beheld malignant fires
In his young eyes discerning plain that Orc plotted his
    death⌊·⌋
Grief rose upon his ruddy brow*s*; a tightning girdle grew   [*
Around his bosom like a bloody cor*d*; in secret sobs
He burst it, but next morn another girdle succeeds
Around his bosom. Every day he viewd the fiery youth
With silent fear & his immortal cheeks grew deadly pale
Till many a morn & many a night passd over in dire woe   [*
Forming a girdle in the day & bursting it at night⌊·⌋
The girdle was formd by day⌊:⌋ by night was burst in twain
Falling down on the rock an iron chain link by link lockd⌊·⌋

Enitharmon beheld the bloody chain of nights & days
Depending from the bosom of Los & how with [dismal
    del] ∧∧*griding∧∧ pain   [*
He went each morning to his labours with the spectre dark⌊,⌋
Calld it the chain of Jealousy. Now Los began to speak
His woes aloud to Enitharmo*n*, since he could not hide
His uncouth plague. He siezd the boy in his immortal hands
While Enitharmon followd him weeping in dismal woe   [*
Up to the iron mountains top & there the Jealous chain
Fell from his bosom on the mountain. The Spectre dark   i*
Held the fierce boy⌊,⌋ Los naild him down binding around his
    limbs
The [dismal *del*] ∧∧*accursed∧∧ chain⌊·⌋ O how bright Eni-
    tharmon howld & cried
Over her Son. Obdurate Los bound down her loved Joy⌊·⌋   [*
[Page 61]
The hammer of Urthona smote the rivets in terro*r*, of brass
Tenfol*d*; the Demons rage flamd tenfold forth rending

ll. 10–13, 16–18 are adapted from *Urizen* pl. 20, ll. 379–90 (pp. 269–70).

Roaring redounding, Loud Loud Louder & Louder & fird
The darkness warring with the waves of Tharmas & Snows
    of Urizen⌞·⌟
Crackling the flames went up with fury from the immortal
    Demon⌞·⌟   [5]
Surrounded with flames the Demon grew loud howling in
    his fires⌞·⌟
Los folded Enitharmon in a cold white cloud in fear⌞,⌟   ∧∧*110∧∧
Then led her down into the deeps & into his labyrinth
Giving the Spectre sternest charge over the howling fiend
    ∧Concenterd into Love of Parent Storgous Appetite
      Craving⌞·⌟∧   [10]
His limbs bound down mock at his chains for over them a
    flame
Of circling fire unceasing plays⌞;⌟ to feed them with life &
    bring
The virtues of the Eternal worlds⌞,⌟ ten thousand thousand
    spirits
Of life [rejoice *del*] ∧lament∧ around the Demon going forth
    & returning⌞·⌟
At his enormous call they flee into the heavens of heavens   [15]
And back return with wine & food. Or dive into the
    deeps
To bring the thrilling joys of sense to quell his ceaseless
    rage⌞·⌟   ∧∧*120∧∧
His eyes the lights of his large soul contract or else expand⌞:⌟
Contracted they behold the secrets of the infinite mountains⌞,⌟
The veins of gold & silver & the hidden things of Vala⌞,⌟   [20]
Whatever grows from its pure bud or breathes a fragrant
    soul⌞;⌟
Expanded they behold the terrors of the Sun & Moon⌞,⌟
The Elemental Planets & the orbs of eccentric fire⌞·⌟
His nostrils breathe [with *del*] ∧a∧ fiery flam*e*; his locks are
    like the forests
Of wild beasts⌞;⌟ there the lion glares⌞,⌟ the tyger & wolf
    howl there   [25]
And there the Eagle hides her young in cliffs & precipices⌞·⌟
His bosom is like starry heaven expanded⌞;⌟ all the stars   ∧∧*130∧∧

Page 61 l. 10 is added in a stanza-break.

Sing roun*d*; there waves the harvest & the vintage rejoice*s*;
the Springs
Flow into rivers of deligh*t*; there the spontaneous flowers
Drink laugh & sin*g*, the grasshopper the Emmet & the Fly∟;⌐
The golden Moth builds there a house & spreads her silken
bed∟·⌐

[*Page 62*]

His loins inwove with silken fires are like a furnace fierce∟,⌐
As the strong Bull in summer time when bees sing round the
heath
Where the herds low after the shadow & after the water
spring∟·⌐
The numrous flocks cover the mountain & shine along the
valley∟·⌐
His knees are rocks of adamant & rubie & emerald∟·⌐
Spirits of strength [rejoice *del*] ∧in∧ Palaces rejoice in golden
armour∟,⌐
Armed with spear & shield they drink & rejoice over the
slain∟·⌐
Such is the Demon∟,⌐ such his terror on the nether deep

But when returnd to Golgonooza Los & Enitharmon
Felt all the sorrow Parents fee*l*, they wept toward one another
And Los repented that he had chaind Orc upon the moun-
tain
And Enitharmons tears prevaild∟;⌐ parental love returnd
Tho terrible his dread of that infernal chain∟·⌐ They rose
At midnight hasting to their much beloved care∟·⌐
Nine days they traveld thro the Gloom of Entuthon Beni-
thon∟·⌐
Los taking Enitharmon by the hand led her along
The dismal vales & up to the iron mountains top where Orc
Howld in the furious wind∟;⌐ he thought to give to Enithar-
mon

Page 62 DESIGN: At the foot of the page a naked man, Los (his head flaming?),
raises his arms above his head as if lamenting. Near him a nude woman, Enithar-
mon, with her hands by her ears, bends as if in agony toward a naked man, Orc,
outstretched before them with his legs apart and his arms outspread. There is
heavy crayon shading above him. (Similar figures are in *America* pl. 3, q.v., p. 120.)

Her son in tenfold joy & to compensate for her tears
Even if his own death resulted⌐,⌐ so much pity him paind   [20]

But when they came to the dark rock & to the spectrous
    cave⌐,⌐
Lo the young limbs had strucken root into the rock & strong
Fibres had from the Chain of Jealousy inwove themselves
In a swift vegetation round the rock & round the Cave
And over the immortal limbs of the terrible fiery boy⌐.⌐   [25]
In vain they strove now to unchain. In vain with bitter tears
To melt the chain of Jealousy; not Enitharmons death   ∧∧*160∧∧
Nor the Consummation of Los could ever melt the chain
Nor unroot the infernal fibres from their rocky bed
Nor all Urthonas strength nor all the power of Luvahs Bulls   [30]
Tho they each morning drag the unwilling Sun out of the
    deep   ∧∧*165∧∧
Could uproot the infernal chain, for it had taken root   [32]

       · [*Page 63*]

Into the iron rock & grew a chain beneath the Earth
Even to the Center wrapping round the Center & the limbs
Of Orc entering with fibres became one with him a living
    Chain
Sustained by the Demons life. Despair & Terror & Woe &
    Rage
Inwrap the Parents in cold clouds as they bend howling   ∧∧*170∧∧
    over   [5]
The terrible boy till fainting by his side the Parents fell⌐.⌐

Not long they lay⌐;⌐ Urthonas spectre found herbs of the
    pit⌐.⌐
Rubbing their temples he revivd them; all their lamentations
I write not here but all their after life was lamentation⌐.⌐

When satiated with grief they returnd back to Golgonooza⌐,⌐   [10]
Enitharmon on the road of Dranthon felt the inmost gate

l. 32: 'it' was originally 'its'.
Page 63   DESIGN: The hair of the woman in the engraving has been touched up
with a pencil.
    l. 3: The 'a' of 'became' is clear, but perhaps the word should be present tense.

Of her bright heart burst open & again close with a [dismal(?) *del*] ˄deadly˄ pain_L·˩
Within her heart Vala began to reanimate in bursting sobs
And when the Gate was open she beheld that [dismal *del*]
˄dreary˄ Deep
Where bright Ahania wept. She also saw the infernal roots   ˄˄
Of the chain of Jealousy & felt the rendings of fierce howling
Orc_L·˩   [

Rending the Caverns like a mighty wind pent in the Earth
[Uri *del*] ˄Tho˄ wide apart as furthest north is from the
furthest south
Urizen trembled where he lay to hear the howling terror_L·˩
The rocks shook_L,˩ the Eternals bars tuggd to & fro were
rifted_L·˩
Outstretchd upon the stones of ice_L,˩ the ruins of his throne_L,˩
Urizen shuddring heard_L,˩ his trembling limbs shook the
strong caves_L·˩

The woes of Urizen shut up in the deep dens of Urthona_L:˩

'Ah how shall Urizen the King submit to this dark mansion_L?˩
Ah how is this! Once on the heights I stretchd my throne   ˄
sublime_L;˩
The mountains of Urizen once of silver where the sons of
wisdom dwelt
And on whose tops the Virgins sang are rocks of Desolation_L·˩

'My fountains once the haunt of Swans now breed the scaly
tortoise_L;˩
The houses of my harpers are become a haunt of crows_L;˩
The gardens of wisdom are become a field of horrid graves
And on the bones I drop my tears & water them in vain_L·˩

[*Page 64*]

'Once how I walked from my palace in gardens of delight_L;˩
The sons of wisdom stood around_L;˩ the harpers followd with
harps_L;˩

l. 13: 'Vala' was originally 'Valan'.

Page 64 DESIGN: At the foot of the page is a pencil and crayon sketch which has
been much modified and erased. A man squats on his heels with his shoulders

Nine virgins clothd in light composd the song to their
   immortal voices
And at my banquets of new wine my head was crownd with
   joy⌞·⌟   200

'Then in my ivory pavilions I slumberd [with *del*] ˄in˄ the
   noon   [5]
And walked in the silent night among sweet smelling flowers
Till on my silver bed I slept & sweet dreams round me hoverd
But now my land is darkend & my wise men are departed⌞·⌟

'My songs are turned to cries of Lamentation
Heard on my Mountains & deep sighs under my palace
   roofs   [10]
Because the Steeds of Urizen once swifter than the light
Were kept back from my Lord & from his chariot of mercies⌞·⌟

'O did I keep the horses of the day in silver pastures⌞?⌟
O I refusd the Lord of day the horses of his prince⌞!⌟   ˄˄*210˄˄
O did I close my treasuries with roofs of solid stone   [15]
And darken all my Palace walls with envyings & hate⌞?⌟

'O Fool to think that I could hide from his all piercing eyes
The gold & silver & costly stones⌞,⌟ his holy workmanship⌞!⌟
O Fool⌞!⌟ could I forget the light that filled my bright
   spheres
Was a reflection of his face who calld me from the deep⌞?⌟   [20]

'I well remember for I heard the mild & holy voice
Saying ˄"O˄ light spring up & shine" & I sprang up from
   the deep⌞·⌟
He gave to me a silver scepter & crownd me with a golden
   crown

bowed and his forearms on his knees. His hips and legs once belonged to a woman(?)
who leaned far back behind him. Now the woman (whose breasts are quite clear in
the additions) leans back to kiss a man holding her from behind; erasures obscure
the rest of her body. The drawing goes *over* the last five lines of text.
   l. 9: 'to' was originally 'into'.
   l. 22: 'O' was originally 'S'.

[Saying *del*] ∧∧*& Said∧∧ "Go forth & guide my Son who ∧∧
wanders on the ocean∟·⌋"

'I went not forth∟·⌋ I hid myself in black clouds of my
wrath∟·⌋   [
I calld the stars around my feet in the night of councils
dark∟·⌋
The stars threw down their spears & fled naked away∟·⌋
We fell. I siezed thee dark Urthona∟·⌋ In my left hand falling

'I siezd thee beauteous Luvah∟;⌋ thou art faded like a flower
And like a lilly is thy wife Vala witherd by winds∟·⌋   [
When thou didst bear the golden cup at the immortal
tables
Thy children smote their fiery wings crownd with the gold ∧∧
of heaven∟·⌋   [

[Page 65]

'Thy pure feet stepd on the steps divin*e*, too pure for other
feet
And thy fair locks shadowd thine eyes from the divine efful- ∧∧
gence∟·⌋
Then thou didst keep with Strong Urthona the living gates
of heaven
But now thou art bound down with him even to the gates of
hell∟·⌋

'Because thou gavest Urizen the wine of the Almighty   [
For steeds of Light that they might run in thy golden chariot
of pride
I gave to thee the Steeds∟,⌋ I pourd the stolen wine
And drunken with the immortal draught fell from my
throne sublime∟·⌋

'I will arise∟,⌋ Explore these dens & find that deep pulsation
That shakes my caverns with strong shudder*s*; perhaps this
is the night

l. 27: Cf. 'The Tyger' (*Songs* pl. 42, p. 186) l. 17: 'the stars threw down their
spears'.

Of Prophecy & Luvah hath burst his way from Enitharmon∟˩
When Thought is closd in Cave*s*, Then love shall shew its ᴧ240ᴧ
    root in deepest Hell∟˩' [*12*]

End of the Fifth [Book *del*] ᴧNightᴧ

Page 66 DESIGN: The page is entirely filled with sketches: (1) In the centre, a trim, naked man standing erect with his back to us holds a large ball on top of his head. Larger balls are also sketched, but there are no arms to hold them. (2) By his waist in the left margin is a naked man with his back to us, his knees flexed, and his arms raised, as if he were swimming to the surface. (3) Below him, by the central man's feet, a nude woman sits sideways, with her hands on the ground behind her supporting her, and her knees close to her breasts. (4) Opposite her, on the other side of the large man, is another sitting (?female) figure with her back to us, her left knee raised, her left hand by her left foot, and her head on her knee. (5) Above her is a figure like the swimmer opposite, but drawn front view and much larger. (A similar figure is in *Urizen* pl. 12—p. 245.)

VALA

Night the Sixth

So Urizen arose & leaning on his Spear explord his dens_L·⌋
He threw his flight thro the dark air to where a river flowd
And taking off his silver helmet filled it & drank
But when unsatiated his thirst he assayd to gather more
Lo three terrific women at the verge of the bright flood
Who would not suffer him to approac*h*, but drove him back
    with storms_L·⌋

Urizen knew them not & thus addressd the spirits of dark-
    ness_L:⌋

'Who art thou Eldest Woman sitting in thy clouds_L?⌋
What is that name written on thy forehead: what art thou?
And wherefore dost thou pour this water forth in sighs &
    care_L?⌋'

She answerd not but filld her urn & pourd it forth abroad_L·⌋

'Answerest thou not_L?⌋' said Urize*n*; 'then thou maist answer
    me
Thou terrible woman clad in blue whose strong attractive
    power
Draws all into a fountain at the rock of thy attraction_L·⌋
With frowning brow thou sittest mistress of these mighty
    waters_L·⌋'

She answerd not but stretchd her arms & threw her limbs.
    abroad_L·⌋

'Or wilt thou answer youngest Woman clad in shining
    green_L?⌋

With labour & care thou dost divide the [river *del*] ^^*cur-
rent^^ into four_L·_
Queen of these dreadful rivers_L,_ speak & let me hear thy
voice_L!_’   [*19*]

[*Page 68*]

^^*1^^   ^^*2^^
[but *del*] They reard up a wall of rocks [Then *del*] ^^*And^^   ^^*20^^
Urizen raisd his spear.
They gave a scream, they knew their father_L,_ Urizen knew
his daughters_L·_
They shrunk into their channel*s*, dry the rocky strand be-
neath his feet_L,_
Hiding themselves in rocky forms from the Eyes of Urizen_L·_

Then Urizen wept & thus his lamentation poured forth_L:_   [*5*]

‘O horrible_L,_ O dreadful state! those whom I loved best_L,_
On whom I pourd the beauties of my light adorning them
With jewels & precious ornament labourd with art divine_L,_
Vests of the radiant colours of heaven & crowns of golden
fire_L;_
I gave sweet lillies to their breasts & roses to their hair_L,_   [*10*]
I taught them songs of sweet delight. I gave their tender   ^^*30^^
voices
Into the blue expanse & I invented with laborious art
Sweet instruments of soun*d*; in pride encompassing my
Knees
They pourd their radiance above al*l*; the daughters of
Luvah Envied
At their exceeding brightness & the sons of eternity sent
them gifts_L·_   [*15*]
Now will I pour my fury on them & I will reverse

Page 68   DESIGN: At the foot of the page is a lovely nude woman with her head
hanging down, her hair falling on the ground, and her arms extended before her
to support her; only the back of her neck, her hair, shoulders, and arms are shown.
(Perhaps she is a daughter of Urizen. She is similar to Eve in the tempera of
‘The Body of Abel Found by Adam and Eve’ [1799].)
   l. 1: The line, originally written ‘Then Urizen . . . wall of rocks’, was later
revised with the numbers as above.
   l. 12: The first letter of ‘expanse’ was originally ‘x’.

The previous benediction; for their colours of loveliness
I will give blackness⌊,⌋ for jewels hoary frost⌊,⌋ for ornament
  deformity⌊,⌋
For crowns wreathd Serpents⌊,⌋ for sweet odors stinking
  corruptibility⌊,⌋
For voices of delight hoarse croakings inarticulate thro
  frost⌊,⌋   [
For labourd fatherly care & sweet instruction, I will give
Chains of dark ignorance & cords of twisted self conceit
And whips of stern repentance & food of stubborn obstinacy
That they may curse Tharmas their God & Los his adopted
  son⌊,⌋
That they may curse & worship the obscure Demon of
  destruction⌊,⌋   [
That they may worship terrors & obey the violent⌊.⌋
Go forth sons of my curse⌊!⌋ Go forth daughters of my
  abhorrence⌊!⌋'

Tharmas heard the deadly scream across his watry world
And Urizens loud sounding voice lamenting on the wind
And he came riding in his fury; froze to solid were his waves⌊;⌋   [
[Page 69]
Silent in ridges he beheld them stand round Urizen⌊,⌋
A dreary waste of Solid waters for the King of Light
Darkend his brows with his cold helmet & his gloomy spear
Darkend before him; silent on the ridgy waves he took
His gloomy way⌊;⌋ before him Tharmas fled & flying fought

Crying: 'What & who art thou Cold Demon? art thou
  Urizen⌊?⌋
Art thou like me risen again from death or art thou death-
  less⌊?⌋
If thou art he my desperate purpose hear & give me death
For death to me is better far than life, death my desire
That I in vain in various paths have sought but still I live⌊.⌋
The Body of Man is given to me⌊.⌋ I seek in vain to destroy
For still it surges forth in fish & monsters of the deeps

l. 26 is adapted from *Visions* pl. 4, l. 23 (p. 104).

And in these monstrous forms I [Lie(?) *del*] Live in an
    Eternal woe
And thou O Urizen art falln never to be deliverd⌐•⌐
Withhold thy light from me for ever & I will withhold   [*15*]
From thee thy food⌐;⌐ so shall we cease to be & all our
    sorrows
[Cease *del*] End & the Eternal Man no more renew beneath
    our power⌐•⌐
If thou refusest in eternal flight thy beams in vain
Shall pursue Tharmas & in vain shalt crave for food⌐•⌐ I will
Pour down my flight thro dark immensity Eternal falling⌐•⌐   [*20*]
Thou shalt pursue me but in vain till starvd upon the void
Thou hangst a dried skin shrunk up weak wailing in the
    wind⌐•⌐'

So Tharmas spoke but Urizen replied not. On his Way
He too*k*, high bounding over hills & desarts floods &
    horrible chasms⌐•⌐
Infinite was his labour⌐,⌐ without end his travel⌐;⌐ he strove   ⌐*25*⌐
In vain for hideous monsters of the deeps annoyd him sore⌐;⌐
Scaled & finn'd with iron & brass they devourd the path
    before him⌐•⌐
Incessant was the conflict. On he bent his weary steps
Making a path toward the dark world of Urthon*a*; he rose
With pain upon the [dismal *del*] ⌃dreary⌃ mountains & with
    pain descended   [*30*]
And saw their grizly fears & his eyes sickend at the Sight⌐:⌐
The howlings gnashings groanings shriekings shudderings
    sobbings burstings
Mingle together to create a world for Los. In cruel delight   [*33*]
[*Page 70*]
Los brooded on the darknes*s*, nor saw Urizen with a Globe of
    fire
Lighting his dismal journey thro the pathless world of death

Page 70 DESIGN: At the foot of the page is a fearsome alligator-dragon with its
jaws open in the right margin at an angle of about 150 degrees, its stubby tail
rising up the left margin, human feet and hands on stubby limbs, short wings, and
a navel, and strokes as of fire from its snout and tail. (He is evidently one of the
'ribbd And scaled monsters', ll. 37–8.)

Writing in bitter tears & groans in books of iron & brass
The enormous wonders of the Abysses⌞,⌟ once his brightest joy
⌃⌃For Urizen beheld the terrors of the Abyss wandring among
⌃⌃The ruind spirits once his children & the children of Luvah⌞.⌟⌃⌃
⌃Scard at the sound of their own sigh that seems to shake the immense
⌃They wander Moping⌞,⌟ in their heart a Sun⌞,⌟ a Dreary moon⌞,⌟
⌃A Universe of fiery constellations in their brain⌞,⌟
⌃An Earth of wintry woe beneath their feet & round their loins
⌃Waters or winds or clouds or brooding lightnings & pestilential plagues⌞.⌟
⌃Beyond the bounds of their own self their senses cannot penetrate
⌃As the tree knows not what is outside of its leaves & bark
⌃And yet it drinks the summer joy & fears the winter sorrow
⌃So in the regions of the grave none knows his dark compeer
⌃Tho he partakes of his dire woes & mutual returns the pang⌞,⌟
⌃The throb⌞,⌟ the dolor⌞,⌟ the convulsion in soul sickening woes⌞.⌟⌃

⌃[Not so closd up the Prince of Light now darkend wandring among *del*]

ll. 5–6 are written in the left margin starting just below l. 4.
ll. 7–18 are written over an erasure of ten lines; l. 18 was probably added at a different time.
In the right margin, beside ll. 10–17, the following couplet is written in crayon and is not marked for entry:

> Till thou dost injure[?]
> the distrest
> Thou shalt never have peace
> within thy breast

Sloss & Wallis (ed., *The Prophetic Writings* [1926], i. 229) comment: 'For the fourth word of the first line, Dr. Sampson reads "conquer". Messrs. Ellis and Yeats print "injure", adding the note: "After fruitless efforts, we reluctantly leave the deciphering of the word that cannot be *injure* to future editors." The present editors can only follow the example of Messrs. Ellis and Yeats.'

Max Plowman (*Bridge into the Future*, ed. D. L. P. [1944], 195) wrote to Geoffrey Keynes: 'I am absolutely satisfied with "*injure* the distrest".'

ʌ[The Ruind Spirits once his Children & the Children of
  Luvah *del*]ʌ
ʌForʌ Urizen beheld the terrors of the Abyss wandring among   [*20*]
The horrid shapes & sights of torment in burning dungeons
  & in
Fetters of red hot iron⌐;⌐ some with crowns of serpents &
  some
With monsters girding round their bosom*s*; Some lying on
  beds of sulphur
On racks & wheels⌐;⌐ he beheld women marching oer burn-
  ing wastes   100
Of Sand in bands of hundreds & of fifties & of thousands
  strucken with   [*25*]
Lightnings which blazed after them upon their shoulders in
  their march
In successive vollies with loud thunders⌐;⌐ swift flew the
  King of Light
Over the burning desarts⌐;⌐ Then the desarts pass*d*, in-
  volvd in clouds
Of smoke with myriads moping in the stifling vapour*s*, Swift
Flew the King tho flagd his powers labrin*g*, till over rocks   [*30*]
And Mountains faint weary he wander*d*, where multitudes
  were shut
Up in the solid mountains & in rocks which heavd with their
  torments⌐.⌐
Then came he among fiery cities & castles built of burning
  steel⌐.⌐
Then he beheld the forms of tygers & of Lions⌐,⌐ dishumanizd
  men⌐.⌐   ʌʌ*110ʌʌ
Many in serpents & in worms stretchd out enormous length   [*35*]
Over the sullen mould & slimy tracks obstruct his way
Drawn out from deep to deep woven by ribbd
And scaled monsters or armd in iron shell or shell of brass
Or gold a glittering torment shining & hissing in eternal
  pain⌐.⌐

ll. 18–48 are bracketed in the left margin, but no purpose is made clear.
l. 20 was deleted, ll. 18–19 were written above and below it and then deleted.
l. 31: The first 'e' of 'were' has a dot perhaps accidentally over it, making it
read 'wire'.

Some [as(?) *del*] columns of fire [& *del*] ˄or˄ of water﹍,﹍ some-
times stretchd out in [length *del*] heighth﹍,﹍   [
Sometimes in [breadth *del*] length﹍,﹍ sometimes englobing﹍,﹍
wandering in vain seeking for ease﹍.﹍
His voice to them was but an inarticulate thunder for their
Ears
Were heavy & dull & their eyes & nostrils closed up﹍.﹍
Oft he stood by a howling victim Questioning in words   ˄˄*12
Soothing or Furious﹍;﹍ no one answerd﹍;﹍ every one wrapd
up
                                                              [
In his own sorrow howld regardless of his words, nor voice
Of sweet response could he obtain tho oft assayd with tears﹍.﹍
˄He knew they were his Children ruind in his ruind world﹍.﹍   [

[*Page 71*]

Oft would he stand & question a fierce scorpion glowing   ˄˄
with gold﹍:﹍
                                                              [
In vain﹍,﹍ the terror heard no*t*; then a lion he would Sieze
By the fierce mane staying [their *del*] ˄his˄ howling course﹍;﹍
in vain the voice   ˄˄
Of Urizen﹍;﹍ in vain the Eloquent tongue. A Rock a Cloud
a Mountain
Were now not Vocal as in Climes of happy Eternity
Where the lamb replies to the infant voice & the lion to the
man of years
Giving them sweet instructions﹍;﹍ Where the Cloud the
River & the Field
Talk with the husbandman & shepherd. But these attackd
him sore
Siezing upon his feet & rending the Sinews that in Caves
He hid to recure his obstructed powers with rest & oblivion﹍.﹍

[*Page 70*]

˄Here he had time enough to repent of his rashly threatend
curse﹍.﹍˄
˄˄*He saw them cursd beyond his Curse﹍;﹍ his soul melted
with fear﹍.﹍˄˄

Page 71 ll. 5–14 have a box drawn round them, apparently to indicate that they
should precede p. 70, l. 49.

[*Page 71*]

He could not take their fetters off for they grew from the
  soul
Nor could he quench the fires for they flamd out from the
  heart
Nor could he calm the Elements because himself was Subject
So he threw his flight in terror & pain & in repentant tears_L·_J   [*4*]

When he had passd these southern terrors he approachd the
  East_L,_J   [*15*]
Void_L,_J pathless_L,_J beaten with [eternal *del*] ⌄iron⌃ sleet &
  eternal hail & [snow *del*] ⌄rain_L·_J⌃
No form was there_L,_J no living thing_L,_J & yet his way lay
  thro
This dismal worl*d*; he stood a while & lookd back oer his
  former   ⌃⌃*140⌃⌃
Terrific voyag*e*, Hills & Vales of torment & despair_L!_J
Sighing & wiping a fresh tea*r*, then turning round he threw   [*20*]
Himself into the dismal voi*d*; falling he fell & fell
Whirling in unresistible revolutions down & down
In the horrid bottomless vacuity falling falling falling
  ⌄Into the Eastern vacuity_L,_J the empty world of Lu-
vah_L·_J⌃
The ever pitying one who seeth all things saw his fall   [*25*]
And in the dark vacuity created a bosom of [slime *del*]
  ⌄clay_L·_J⌃
When wearied dead he fell his limbs reposd in the bosom of
  slime_L;_J
As the seed falls from the sowers hand so Urizen fell & death   150
Shut up his powers in oblivio*n*; then as the seed shoots forth
In pain & sorro*w*, So the slimy bed his limbs renewd_L·_J   [*30*]
At first an infant weakne*ss*; periods passd_L;_J he gatherd
  strength
But still in solitude he sat_L;_J then rising threw his flight
Onward tho falling thro the waste of night & ending in death
And in another resurrection to sorrow & weary travel
But still his books he bore in his strong hands & his iron pen   [*35*]

l. 21 is adapted from *The Book of Los* pl. 4, l. 76 (p. 311).

For when he died they lay beside his grave & when he rose
He siezd them with a [dismal *del*] ˄*gloomy˄ smile for wrapd
   in his death clothes
He hid them when he slept in death∟,⌋ when he revivd the
   clothes   ˄˄
Were rotted by the winds∟,⌋ the books remaind still uncon-
   sumd∟,⌋
Still to be written & interleavd with brass & iron & gold   [₄
Time after time for such a journey none but iron pens
Can write And adamantine leaves recieve nor can the man
   who goes   [₅
                [*Page 72*]
The journey obstinate refuse to write time after time∟.⌋

˄Endless had been his travel but the Divine hand him led
˄For infinite the distance & obscurd by Combustions dire∟,⌋
˄By rocky masses frowning in the abysses revolving erratic
˄Round Lakes of fire in the dark deep∟,⌋ the ruins of Urizens
   world∟.⌋   [∟
˄Oft would he sit in a dark rift & regulate his books   ˄
˄Or sleep such sleep as spirits eternal wearied in his dark
˄Tearful & sorrowful stat*e*; then rise∟,⌋ look out & ponder
˄His dismal voyage eyeing˄ the next sphere tho far remote∟,⌋
Then darting into the Abyss of night his venturous limbs   [₄
Thro lightnings thunders earthquakes & concussions fires &
   floods
Stemming his downward fall∟,⌋ labouring up against futur-
   ity∟,⌋
Creating many a Vortex∟,⌋ fixing many a Science in the deep
And thence throwing his venturous limbs into the Vast
   unknown∟,⌋

l. 36: 'his' was originally 'him'.

Page 72 DESIGN: In the bottom left corner is a nude woman sleeping on her left
side, her right arm extended, facing us. Above and behind her another nude woman
with her back to us leans forward as if in sleep. To the right another nude sleeping
woman facing us is sitting with her knees raised and her head on one side. A tree
to the right bends over them and up the right margin, and shading behind them
may indicate grass.

ll. 2–9 are written over an erasure of seven and a half lines, the sixth of which
may end 'the rivers', and the seventh 'shouted round', perhaps as in p. 70, ll. 34–9,
p. 73, ll. 1–2.

Swift Swift from Chaos to chaos_L,_J from void to void_L,_J
   a road immense   [*15*]

For when he came to where a Vortex ceasd to operate   ^*180^
Nor down nor up remaind_L,_J then if he turnd & lookd back
From whence he came twas upward al*l*, & if he turnd &
   viewd
The unpassd void upward was still his mighty wandring_L,_J
The midst between an Equilibrium grey of air serene   [*20*]
Where he might live in peace & where his life might meet
   repose

But Urizen said 'Can I not leave this world of Cumbrous
   wheels_L,_J
Circle oer Circle_L,_J nor on high attain a void
Where self sustaining I may view all things beneath my
   feet_L?_J
Or sinking thro these Elemental wonders swift to fall   [*25*]
I thought perhaps to find an End_L,_J a world beneath of void-
   ness   ^*190^
Whence I might travel round the outside of this Dark con-
   fusion_L._J
When I bend downward_L,_J bending my head downward into
   the deep_L,_J
Tis upward all which way soever I my course begin
But when A Vortex formd on high by labour & sorrow & care   [*30*]
And weariness begins on all my limbs then sleep revives
My wearied spirits_L;_J waking then tis downward all which
   way
So ever I my spirits turn_L;_J no end I find of all_L._J
O what a world is here_L,_J unlike those climes of bliss
Where my sons gatherd round my knees_L!_J O thou poor
   ruined world_L!_J   [*35*]
Thou horrible ruin_L!_J once like me thou wast all glorious   200
And now like me partaking desolate thy masters lot_L._J
Art thou O ruin[?] the once glorious heaven_L?_J are these thy
   rocks
Where joy sang in the trees & pleasure sported on the rivers   [*39*]

ll. 34–9, p. 73, ll. 1–2 may have been written under p. 72, ll. 2–9.

[*Page 73*]

'And laughter sat beneath the Oaks & innocence sported
    round
Upon the green plains & sweet friendship met in palaces
And books & instruments of song & pictures of delight∟?˩
Where are they∟,˩ whelmd beneath these ruins in horrible
    [confusion *del*] ˄destruction∟?˩˄
And if Eternal falling I repose on the dark bosom
Of winds & waters or thence fall into a Void where air
Is not∟,˩ down falling thro immensity ever & ever
I lose my powers weakend every revolution till a death
Shuts up my powers∟;˩ then a seed in the vast womb of
    darkness
I dwell in dim oblivio*n*; brooding over me the Enormous
    worlds
Reorganize me∟,˩ shooting forth in bones & flesh &
    blood
I am regenerated to fall or rise at will or to remain
A labourer of ages∟,˩ a dire discontent∟,˩ a living woe
Wandring in vain. Here will I fix my foot & here rebuild∟.˩
        ˄Here Mountains of Brass promise much riches in their
            dreadful [bowels *del*] ˄˄bosoms∟.˩'˄˄
So [Saying *del*] he began to [form *del*] ˄dig˄ of gold silver &
    [brass *del*] iron
[*Words del*] ˄And brass vast˄ instruments to measure out the
    immense & fix
The whole into another world better suited to obey
His will where none should dare oppose his will∟,˩ himself
    being King
Of All & all futurity he bound in his vast chain

And all the Sciences were fixd & the Vortexes began to
    operate
On all the sons of men & every human soul terrified
At the turning wheels of heaven Shrunk away inward with-
    ring away

Page 73 l. 15 is squeezed into a stanza-break. ll. 15, 17 are written in the same
ink, which is different from that on the rest of the page.

ᴧGaining a New Dominion over all his sons & Daughters
   & over the Sons & daughters of Luvah in the horrible
   Abyssᴧ

For Urizen lamented over them in a selfish lamentation   [*25*]
Till a white woof coverd his cold limbs from head to feetʟ,ʟ
Hair white as snow coverd him in flaky locks terrific
Overspreading his limbs; in pride he wanderd weeping   ᴧᴧ*230ᴧᴧ
Clothed in aged venerablenessʟ,ʟ obstinately resolvdʟ,ʟ
Travelling thro darkness & whereever he traveld a dire Web   [*30*]
Followd behind him as the Web of a Spider dusky & cold
Shivering across from Vortex to Vortex drawn out from his
   mantle of yearsʟ,ʟ
         ᴧᴧ*A living Mantle adjoind to his life & growing from
         his Soulᴧᴧ
And the Web of Urizen stre[*t*]chd direful shivring in clouds
And uttering such woesʟ,ʟ such bursts[?] such thunderingsʟ·ʟ   [*35*]
The eyelids expansive as morning & the Ears
As a golden ascent winding round to the heavens of heavens   ᴧᴧ*240ᴧᴧ
Within the dark horrors of the Abyssesʟ,ʟ lion or tyger or
   scorpion
                                                                [*38*]
                        [*Page 74*]
For every one opend within into Eternity at will
But they refusd because their outward forms were in the
   Abyss
And the wing like tent of the Universeʟ,ʟ beautiful surround-
   ing all
Or drawn up or let down at the will of the immortal manʟ,ʟ
Vibrated in such anguish the eyelids quiverdʟ,ʟ   [*5*]
Weak & Weaker their expansive orbs began shrinkingʟ;ʟ

l. 24 is squeezed between lines with no indication of where it should be broken.
At 'over the Sons &' it is broken by the side of the page; 'daughters of Luvah'
is written just below this; and the rest is written sideways down the'edge of the
page.
   l. 26: 'feet' was originally 'foot'.
   l. 33 is squeezed into a stanza-break.
   l. 35: 'bursts' seems to have been 'burstings' at first.

Page 74 DESIGN: In the bottom right corner is a bearded man in a long gown,
with his left arm raised up the right margin, carrying a huge ball with his right
hand, and taking an enormous stride off the page. (He is copied from *Urizen*
pl. 23 [p. 275] and evidently represents Urizen 'with his globe of fire immense in
his venturous hand', l. 35.)

Pangs smote thro the brain & a universal shriek
Ran thro the Abysses rending the web torment on torment⌊.⌋

Thus Urizen in sorrows wanderd many a dreary way
Warring with monsters of the Deeps in his most hideous
  pilgrimage
Till his bright hair scatterd in snows⌊,⌋ his skin barkd oer
  with wrinkles⌊,⌋
Four Caverns rooting downwards their foundations⌊,⌋ thrust-
  ing forth
The metal rock & stone in ever painful throes of vegetation⌊.⌋
The Cave of Orc stood to the South⌊,⌋ a furnace of dire
  flames
Quenchless unceasing. In the west the Cave of Urizen
For Urizen fell as the Midday sun falls down into the West⌊.⌋
North stood Urthonas stedfast throne⌊,⌋ a World of Solid
  darkness
Shut up in stifling obstruction rooted in dumb despair⌊.⌋
The East was Void. But Tharmas rolld his billows in cease-
  less eddies⌊,⌋
Void⌊,⌋ pathless⌊,⌋ beat with [Enion(?) *del*] Snows eternal &
  iron hail & rain
All thro the caverns of fire & air & Eart*h*, Seeking
For Enions limbs⌊,⌋ nought finding but ˄the˄ black sea weed
  & sickning slime⌊,⌋
Flying away from Urizen that he might not give him food⌊,⌋
Above⌊,⌋ beneath⌊,⌋ on all sides round in the vast deep of
  immensity⌊,⌋
That he might starve the sons & daughters of Urizen on the
  winds
Making between horrible chasms into the vast unknown⌊.⌋
All these around the world of Los cast forth their monstrous
  births
But in Eternal times the Seat of [*word del*] ˄Urizen˄ is in the
  South⌊,⌋
Urthona in the North⌊,⌋ Luvah in East⌊,⌋ Tharmas in West

And now he came into the Abhorred world of Dark Urthona

At l. 9 the writing seems to change to a smaller hand in Black ink.

By Providence divine conducted not bent from his own will ^^*270^^
Lest death Eternal should be the result for the Will cannot be
    violated⌊·⌋
Into the doleful vales where no tree grew nor river flowd
Nor man nor beast nor creeping thing nor sun nor cloud nor
    star
Still he with his globe of fire immense in his venturous hand [35]

Bore on thro the Affrighted vales ascending & descending⌊,⌋
Oerwearied or in cumbrous flight he venturd oer dark rifts
Or down dark precipices or climbd with pain & labour huge
Till he beheld the world of Los from the Peaked rock of
    Urthona
And heard the howlings of red Orc distincter & distincter⌊·⌋ [40]

[*Page 75*] ^^*279^^

Redoubling his immortal efforts thro the narrow vales ^^*280^^
With difficulty down descending guided by his Ear
And [with *del*] ⌃by⌃ his globe of fire he went down the Vale
    of Urthona
Between the enormous iron walls built by the Spectre dark⌊·⌋
Dark grew his globe reddning with mists & full before his
    path [5]
Striding across the narrow vale the Shadow of Urthona
A Spectre Vast appeard whose feet & legs with iron scaled
Stampd the hard rocks expectant of the unknown wanderer
Whom he had seen wandring his nether world when distant
    far
And watchd his swift approach⌊;⌋ collected⌊,⌋ dark the
    Spectre stood⌊·⌋ [10]
⌃Beside his Tharmas stayd his flight & stood in stern de-
fiance ^^*290^^
⌃Communing with the Spectre who rejoicd along the Vale⌊·⌋⌃
Round his loins a girdle glowd with many colourd fires⌊,⌋
In his hand a knotted Club whose knots like mountains
    frownd

Page 75 l. 6: 'Shadow' at first was 'Shade'.
    ll. 11–12 are written over an erasure of two lines which may have been the same
as ll. 13–14. The first 'his' evidently should be 'him'.

Desart among the Stars them withering with its ridges cold_{ʟ·」}
Black scales of iron arm the dread visage_ʟ;」 iron spikes instead
Of hair shoot from his orbed scul*l*, his glowing eyes
Burn like two fŭrnace*s*; he calld with Voice of Thunder_{ʟ·」}

Four winged heralds mount the furious blasts & blow their
　　trumps_ʟ;」
Gold Silver Brass & iron clangors clamoring rend the [deeps
　　del] ᴧᴧ*shores_{ʟ·」}ᴧᴧ
Like white clouds rising from the Vales his fifty two armies
From the four Cliffs of Urthona rise glowing around the
　　Spectre_{ʟ·」}
Four sons of Urizen the Squadrons of Urthona led in arms
Of gold & silver brass & iron_ʟ;」 he knew his mighty sons_{ʟ·」}

Then Urizen arose upon the wind back many a mile
Retiring into his dire Web scattering fleecy snows_{ʟ,」}
As he ascended howling loud the Web vibrated strong
From heaven to heaven_{ʟ,」} from globe to globe. In vast
　　excentric paths
Compulsive rolld the Comets at his dread command_{ʟ,」} the
　　dreary way
Falling with wheel impetuous down among Urthonas vales
And round red Orc_{ʟ,」} returning back to Urizen gorgd with
　　blood_{ʟ·」}
Slow roll the massy Globes at his command & slow oerwheel
The dismal squadrons of Urthon*a*, weaving the dire Web
In their progressions & preparing Urizens path before him_{ʟ·」}

End of The Sixth Night

ll. 19–22 are adapted from *America* pl. c, ll. 14–17 (p. 159).
l. 31: 'gorgd' was first 'gord'.

Page 76 is entirely filled with a pencil and crayon sketch of a figure in the attitude
of Albion in 'Albion Rose', his arms outstretched, dancing toward us. The arms and
head are *very* rough, and the genitals have been erased and rudimentary breasts
added.

VALA

Night the Seventh [*a*]

Then Urizen arose⌞·⌟ The Spectre fled & Tharmas fled⌞·⌟
The darkning Spectre of Urthona hid beneath a rock⌞·⌟
Tharmas threw his impetuous flight thro the deeps of im-
mensity
Revolving round in whirlpools fierce all round the cavernd
worlds

But Urizen silent descended to the Caves of Orc & saw   [5]
A Cavernd Universe of flaming fire⌞;⌟ the horses of Urizen
Here bound to fiery mangers furious dash their golden hoofs
Striking fierce sparkles from their brazen fetter*s*; fierce his
lions
Howl in the burning dens⌞;⌟ his tygers roam in the redound-
ing smoke
In forests of afflictio*n*; the adamantine scales of justice   [*10*]
Consuming in the raging lamps of mercy pourd in rivers⌞·⌟
The holy oil rages thro all the cavernd rocks⌞;⌟ fierce
flames
Dance on the rivers & the rocks howling & drunk with
fury⌞;⌟
The plow of ages & the golden harrow wade thro fields
Of goary blood⌞;⌟ the immortal seed is nourishd for the
slaughter⌞·⌟   [*15*]
The bulls of Luvah breathing fire bellow on burning pas-
tures
Round howling Orc whose awful limbs cast forth red smoke
& fire
That Urizen approachd not near but took his seat on a rock
ᴧAnd rangd his books around him brooding Envious over
Orc⌞·⌟ᴧ
Howling & rending his dark caves the awful Demon lay⌞·⌟   [*20*]

Page 77 l. 19 is added in a stanza-break.

Pulse after pulse beat on his fetters∟‚⌋ pulse after pulse his
  spirit
Darted & darted higher & higher to the shrine of Enithar-
  mon∟;⌋
As when the thunder folds himself in thickest clouds
The watry nations couch & hide in the profoundest deeps∟‚⌋
Then bursting from his troubled head with terrible Visages
  & flaming hair
His swift wingd daughters sweep across the vast black
  ocean∟.⌋
Los felt the Envy in his limbs like to a blighted tree

[*Page 78*]

For Urizen fixd in Envy sat brooding & coverd with snow∟.⌋
His book of iron on his knees he tracd the dreadful letters
While his snows fell & his storms beat to cool the flames of
  Orc
Age after Age till underneath his heel a deadly root
Struck thro the rock∟‚⌋ the root of Mystery accursed shooting
  up
Branches into the heaven of Los∟‚⌋ they pipe formd bending
  down
Take root again whereever they touch again branching
  forth
In intricate labyrinths oerspreading many a grizly deep∟.⌋

Amazd started Urizen when he found himself compassd
  round
And high roofed over with trees, he arose but the stems
Stood so thick he with difficulty & great pain brought
His books out of the dismal shade, all but the book of iron∟.⌋

Page 78 DESIGN: At the foot of the page is a naked man (?Orc), his left side to
us, outstretched rigidly across the page, his back arched slightly, his head back.
There is much shading above him, and this shading and some erasure obscured
part of the man, particularly above his genitals. An alternative idea put his left
foot beneath his buttock. There are a few other undecipherable vague strokes.
  In the top left margin, *upside-down*, are some vague strokes which seem to
outline a foot. Above them (nearer the top) was
            [*B Blake
                *Catherine Blake *del*]
  ll. 9-12 are repeated from *Ahania* pl. 4-5, ll. 116-22 (p. 301).

Again he took his seat & rangd his ^[Books *del*]^ Books
   around
On a rock of iron frowning over the foaming fires of Orc

And Urizen hung over Orc & viewd his terrible wrath_L;_J   [*15*]
Sitting upon [his *del*] ^an^ iron Crag at length his words
   broke forth_L:_J

'Image of dread_{L,J} whence art thou_L?_J whence is this most
   woful place_L?_J
Whence these fierce fires but from thyself_L?_J No other living
   thing
In all this Chasm I behold. No other living thing
Dare thy most terrible wrath abide_L._J Bound here to waste in
   pain   [*20*]
Thy vital substance in these fires that issue new & new
Around thee_{L,J} sometimes like a flood & sometimes like a
   rock
Of living pangs_{L,J} thy horrible bed glowing with ceaseless
   fires   50
Beneath thee & around_L._J Above a Shower of fire now beats
Moulded to globes & arrowy wedges rending thy bleeding
   limbs   [*25*]
And now a whirling pillar of burning sands to overwhelm
   thee
Steeping thy wounds in salts infernal & in bitter anguish
And now a rock moves on the surface of this[?] lake of fire
To bear thee down beneath the waves in stifling despair_L._J
Pity for thee movd me to break my dark & long repose   [*30*]
And to reveal myself before thee in a form of wisdom
Yet thou dost laugh at all these tortures & this horrible
   place_{L,J}
Yet throw thy limbs these fires abroad that back return upon
   thee
While thou reposest throwing rage on rage_{L,J} feeding thyself
With visions of sweet bliss far other than this burning clime_L._J   [*35*]
Sure thou art bathd in rivers of delight_{L,J} on verdant fields
Walking in joy_{L,J} in bright Expanses sleeping on bright
   clouds

With visions of delight so lovely that they urge thy rage
Tenfold with fierce desire to rend thy chain & howl in fury
And dim oblivion of all woe & desperate repose   [
Or is thy joy founded on torment which others bear for
    thee∟?⌐'

Orc answerd 'curse thy hoary brows. What dost thou in this
    deep∟?⌐
Thy Pity I contemn∟!⌐ scatter thy snows elsewhere∟·⌐   [

[*Page 79*]

'I rage in the deep for Lo my feet & hands are naild to the
    burning rock
Yet my fierce fires are better than thy snows∟·⌐ Shuddring
    thou sittest∟·⌐
Thou art not chaind∟·⌐ Why shouldst thou sit∟,⌐ cold
    grovelling demon of woe∟,⌐
In tortures of dire coldness∟?⌐ now a Lake of waters deep
Sweeps over thee freezing to solid∟;⌐ still thou sitst closd up   [
In that transparent rock as if in joy of thy bright prison
Till overburdend with its own weight drawn out thro im-
    mensity
With a crash breaking across the horrible mass comes down
Thundring∟,⌐ & hail & frozen iron haild from the Element
Rends thy white hair∟,⌐ yet thou dost fixd obdurate brooding
    sit   [
Writing thy books. Anon a cloud filld with a waste of snows
Covers thee still obdurate∟,⌐ still resolvd & writing still
Tho rocks roll oer thee∟,⌐ tho floods pour∟,⌐ tho winds black
    as the Sea
Cut thee in gashes∟,⌐ tho the blood pours down around thy
    ankles
Freezing thy feet to the hard rock∟,⌐ still thy pen obdurate
Traces the wonders of Futurity in horrible fear of the   ▮
    future∟·⌐
I rage furious in the deep for lo my feet & hands are naild
To the hard rock or thou shouldst feel my enmity & hate

Page 79 l. 13: 'roll' at first was 'rolls'.

In all the diseases of man falling upon thy grey accursed
front⌊.⌋'

Urizen answered 'Read my books⌊,⌋ explore my Constella-
tions⌊,⌋   [*20*]
Enquire of my Sons & they shall teach thee how to War⌊.⌋
Enquire of my Daughters who accursd in the dark depths
Kneed bread of Sorrow by my stern command for I am God
Of all this dreadful ruin⌊.⌋ Rise O daughters at my Stern
command⌊!⌋'

Rending the Rocks Eleth & Uveth rose & Ona rose   [*25*]
Terrific with their iron vessels driving them across
In the dim air⌊;⌋ they took the book of iron & placd above
On clouds of death & sang their songs Kneading the bread
of Orc⌊.⌋
Orc listend to the song compelld hungring on the cold wind
That swaggd heavy with the accursed dou*gh*; the hoar frost   100
ragd   [*30*]
Thro Ona's sieve⌊;⌋ the torrent rain pourd from the iron pail
Of Eleth & the icy hands of Uveth kneaded the bread⌊.⌋
The heavens bow with terror underneath their iron hands
Singing at their dire work the words of Urizens book of iron
While the enormous scrolls rolld dreadful in the heavens
above   [*35*]
And still the burden of their song in tears was poured forth⌊:⌋
'The bread is Kneaded⌊,⌋ let us rest O cruel father of Chil-
dren⌊.⌋'

But Urizen remitted not their labours upon his rock   [*38*]
                        [*Page 80*]
And Urizen [*words del*] ⌃Read in his book of brass in sounding
tones⌊:⌋

After l. 19 the writing seems to become more compact and cramped.
  l. 23: Cf. Psalm 127: 2: Without God, 'It is vain for you . . . to eat the bread of
sorrows'.
  ll. 29–30: Cf. *Marriage* pl. 2, ll. 1–2: 'Rintrah roars . . . Hungry clouds swag on
the deep' (p. 75).
  l. 35: Cf. Isaiah 34: 4: 'the heavens shall be rolled together as a scroll'.
Page 80 DESIGN: There are five vague pencil and crayon strokes in the margin.
An erased drawing at the foot of the page was cut off.

ᴧ'Listen O Daughters to my voice_ᴌ!ᴊ Listen to the
  Words of wisdom_ᴌ,ᴊ
ᴧSo Shall be govern over all_ᴌ;ᴊ let Moral Duty tune
  your tongue
ᴧBut be your hearts harder than the nether millstone_ᴌ.ᴊ
ᴧᴧTo bring the shadow of Enitharmon beneath our wondrous
  tree   [
ᴧᴧThat Los may Evaporate like smoke & be no more
ᴧᴧDraw down Enitharmon to the Spectre of Urthona
ᴧᴧAnd let him have dominion over Los the terrible shade_ᴌ.ᴊᴧᴧ
Compell the poor to live upon a Crust of bread by soft mild
  arts_ᴌ:ᴊ
Smile when they frown_ᴌ,ᴊ frown when they smile & when a
  man looks pale   [
With labour & abstinence say he looks healthy & happy
And when his children sicken let them die_ᴌ;ᴊ there are
  enough
Born_ᴌ,ᴊ even too many & our Earth will be overrun
Without these arts_ᴌ.ᴊ If you would make the poor live with
  temper_ᴌ,ᴊ
With pomp give every crust of bread you give_ᴌ;ᴊ with gracious
  cunning   [
Magnify small gifts_ᴌ;ᴊ reduce the man to want a gift & then
  give with pomp_ᴌ.ᴊ
Say he smiles if you hear him sigh_ᴌ;ᴊ If pale say he is ruddy_ᴌ.ᴊ
Preach temperance_ᴌ:ᴊ say he is overgorgd & drowns his wit
In strong drink tho you know that bread & water are all
He can afford_ᴌ.ᴊ Flatter his wife_ᴌ,ᴊ pity his children till we
  can   [
Reduce all to our will as spaniels are taught with art_ᴌ.ᴊ
Lo how the heart & brain are formed in the breeding womb
Of Enitharmon_ᴌ,ᴊ how it buds with life & forms the bones_ᴌ,ᴊ
The little heart_ᴌ,ᴊ the liver & the red blood in its labyrinths_ᴌ;ᴊ

ll. 2–9: l. 2 'is squeezed in above l. 9, l. 3 is squeezed between l. 9 and l. 10; l. 4
is a continuation of l. 3 at the side of the page; and ll. 5–8, which seem to be written
in a different shade of ink, are in verse form below the second line. The sense seems
to dictate the transfer of l. 9 after ll. 3–8.

ll. 3, 16 are in *Jerusalem* pl. 30, ll. 30–1 (p. 481).

l. 3: 'be' must be a mistake for 'you' or 'ye'.

l. 16: 'the' was originally 'them'.

By gratified desire_{L,⌋} by strong devouring appetite she fills   [*25*]
Los with ambitious fury that his race shall all devour_{L.⌋}'

ˆThenˆ Orc [answerd *del*] ˆcriedˆ 'Curse thy Cold hypocrisɣ!
   already round thy Tree
In scales that shine with gold & rubies thou beginnest to
   weaken
My divided Spirit_{L.⌋} Like a worm I rise in peace unbound
From wrath_{L.⌋} Now When I rage my fetters bind me more_{L.⌋}   [*30*]
O torment_L!_⌋ O torment_L!_⌋ A Worm compelld. Am I
   a worm_L?_⌋
Is it in strong deceit that man is bor*n*? In strong deceit
Thou dost restrain my fury that the worm may fold the
   tree_{L.⌋}
Avaunt Cold hypocrite_L!_⌋ I am chaind or thou couldst not
   use me thus_{L.⌋}
The Man shall rage bound with this Chain_{L,⌋} the worm in
   silence creep_{L.⌋}   [*35*]
Thou wilt not cease from rage_{L.⌋} Grey Demon silence all thy
   storms_{L.⌋}
Give me example of thy mildness_{L.⌋} King of furious hail
   storms_{L,⌋}
Art thou the cold attractive power that holds me in this
   chain_L?_⌋
I well remember how I stole thy light & it became fire
Consuming. Thou Knowst me now_{L,⌋} O Urizen Prince of
   Light_{L,⌋}   [*40*]
And I know thee_L!_⌋ is this the triumph_{L,⌋} this the Godlike
   State
That lies beyond the bounds of Science in the Grey ob-
   scure_L?_⌋'
ˆTerrified Urizen heard Orc_{L,⌋} now certain that he was
   Luvahˆ
[So saying *del*] ˆAnd Orcˆ he began to Organize a Serpent
   body_{L,⌋}
Despising Urizens light & turning it into flaming fire_{L,⌋}   [*45*]
Recieving as a poisond Cup Recieves the heavenly wine

      l. 43 was added in a stanza-break.
      l. 44: Blake forgot to delete 'he'.

And turning [wisdom *del*] ∧affection∧ into fury & thought
  into abstraction_L,⌋
A Self consuming dark devourer rising into the heavens_L.⌋

Urizen envious brooding sat & saw the secret terror
Flame high in pride & laugh to scorn the source of his
  deceit
Nor knew the source of his own but thought himself the
  Sole author

[*Page 81*]

Of all his wandering Experiments in the horrible Abyss_L.⌋
He knew that weakness stretches out in breadth & length_L,⌋
  he knew
That wisdom reaches high & deep & therefore he made Orc_L,⌋
In Serpent form compelld_L,⌋ stretch out & up the mysterious
  tree_L.⌋
He sufferd him to Climb that he might draw all human forms
Into submission to his will nor knew the dread result_L.⌋

Los sat in showers of Urizen [cold *del*] watching ∧cold∧
  Enitharmon_L.⌋
His broodings rush down to his feet producing Eggs that
  hatching
Burst forth upon the winds above the tree of Mystery_L.⌋
Enitharmon lay on his knees. Urizen tracd his Verses_L.⌋
In the dark deep the dark tree grew; her shadow was drawn
  down_L,⌋
Down to the roots_L;⌋ it wept over Orc, the Shadow of
  Enitharmon_L.⌋

Los saw her stretchd the image of death upon his witherd
  valleys_L.⌋
Her Shadow went forth & returnd_L.⌋ Now she was pale as
  Snow
When the mountains & hills are coverd over & the paths of
  Men shut up

l. 47: 'wisdom' was first crossed out in pencil and 'affection' written in pencil
above it; later both these changes were inked over.
Page 81 l. 7: 'Urizen' may be 'Urizens'.

But when her spirit returnd as ruddy as a morning when
The ripe fruit blushes into joy in heavens eternal halls
[She Secret joyd to see∟;⌐ She fed herself on his Despair∟.⌐
[She said 'I am avengd for all my sufferings of old∟.⌐' *del*]

Sorrow shot thro him from his feet∟,⌐ it shot up to his head   [*20*]
Like a cold night that nips the root & shatters off the leaves∟.⌐
Silent he stood oer Enitharmon watching her pale face∟.⌐
He spoke not∟,⌐ he was Silent till he felt the cold disease∟.⌐
Then Los mournd on the dismal wind in his jealous lamen-
tation∟:⌐

'Why can I not Enjoy thy beauty Lovely Enitharmon∟?⌐   [*25*]
When I return from clouds of Grief in the wandring Elements
Where thou in thrilling joy∟,⌐ in beaming summer loveliness
Delectable reposest ruddy in my absence flaming with
beauty∟,⌐
Cold pale in sorrow at my approach trembling at my
terrific
Forehead & eyes thy lips decay like roses in [early *del*] ⌃the⌃
spring∟.⌐   [*30*]
How art thou Shrunk∟!⌐ thy grapes that burst in summers
vast Excess
Shut up in little purple covering faintly bud & die∟.⌐
Thy olive trees that pourd down oil upon a thousand hills
Sickly look forth & scarcely stretch their branches to the
plain∟.⌐
Thy roses that expanded in the face of glowing morn   [*35*]
[*Page 82*]
'Hid in a little silken veil scarce breathe & faintly shine∟.⌐
The lillies that gave light what time the morning looked forth
Hid in the Vales faintly lament & no one hears their voice∟.⌐
All things beside the woful Los enjoy the delights of beauty∟!⌐

l. 21: 'root' was 'roots' originally.

Page 82 DESIGN: Below the text is a nude woman taking an enormous step (her
legs make an angle of about 160 degrees, though an alternative right leg shortened
her stride), her body bent horizontal; her arms above and below her head hold
a large circle of stars which disappears off the right margin. There are also several
other vague strokes and heavy shading behind her. (A small related design, re-
versed, is on *Jerusalem* pl. 20.)

Once how I sang & calld the beasts & birds to their delights   [.

Nor knew that I alone exempted from the joys of love

Must war with secret monsters of the animating worlds⌞·⌟

O that I had not seen the day⌞!⌟ then should I be at rest

Nor felt the stingings of desire nor longings after life

For life is Sweet to Los the wretched⌞;⌟ to his winged woes   [

Is given a craving cry that they may sit at night on barren
    rocks

And whet their beaks & snuff the air & watch the opening
    dawn

And Shriek till at the smells of blood they stretch their boney
    wings

And cut the winds like arrows shot by troops of Destiny⌞·⌟'

Thus Los lamented in the night unheard by Enitharmon   [

For the Shadow of Enitharmon descended down the tree of
    Mystery⌞·⌟

The Spectre saw the Shade Shivring over his gloomy rocks   2

Beneath the tree of Mystery which in the dismal Abyss

Began to blossom in fierce pain shooting its writhing buds

In throes of birth & now⌞,⌟ the blossoms falling⌞,⌟ shining
    fruit   [

Appeard of many colours & of various poisonous qualities

Of Plagues hidden in shining globes that grew on the living
    tree⌞·⌟

The Spectre of Urthona saw the Shadow of Enitharmon

Beneath the Tree of Mystery among the leaves & fruit⌞·⌟

Reddning the Demon strong prepard the poison of sweet
    Love⌞·⌟   [

He turnd from side to side in [vain *del*] ^tears⌞;⌟^ he wept &
    he embracd

The fleeting image & in whispers mild wood the faint shade⌞:⌟

'Loveliest delight of M*e*n! Enitharmon shady hiding

In secret places where no eye can trace thy watry way⌞,⌟

Have I found thee⌞?⌟ have I found thee⌞?⌟ tremblest thou in
    fear   [

Because of Orc⌞,⌟ because he rent his discordant way

From thy sweet loins of bli*ss*? red flowd thy blood_L,_⌐
Pale grew thy face_L;_⌐ [thy Smiles(?) *del*] lightnings playd
  around thee_L,_⌐ thunders hoverd
Over thee, & the terrible Orc rent his discordant way
But the next joy of thine shall be in sweet delusion   [35]
And its birth in fainting & sleep & [woe *del*] ⌃Sweet⌃
  delusions of Vala_L._⌐'

The Shadow of Enitharmon answerd 'Art thou terrible
  Shade
Set over this sweet boy of mine to guard him lest he rend   [38]
             [*Page 83*]
'His mother to the winds of heaven_L?_⌐ Intoxicated with
The fruit of this delightful tre*e*, I cannot flee away
From thy embrace_L,_⌐ else be assurd so horrible a form
Should never in my arms repos*e*; now listen_L,_⌐ I will tell
Thee secrets of Eternity which neer before unlockd   [5]
My golden lips nor took the bar from Enitharmons breast_L._⌐
Among the Flowers of Beulah walkd the Eternal Man & Saw
Vala the lilly of the desar*t*, melting in high noon_L._⌐
Upon her bosom in sweet bliss he fainted_L._⌐ Wonder siezd
All heaven_L;_⌐ they saw him dar*k*; they built a golden wall   [10]
Round Beulah_L._⌐ There he reveld in delight among the
  Flowers_L._⌐
Vala was pregnant & brought forth Urizen Prince of Light_L,_⌐
First born of Generation. Then behold a wonder to the Eyes
Of the now fallen Man_L,_⌐ a double form Vala appear*d*, A
  Male
And female_L;_⌐ shuddring pale the Fallen Man recoild   [15]
From the Enormity & calld them Luvah & Val*a*, turning
  down
The vales to find his way back into Heaven but found none
For his frail eyes were faded & his ears heavy & dull_L._⌐

'Urizen grew up in the plains of Beulah_L._⌐ Many Sons
And many daughters flourishd round the holy Tent of Man   [20]
Till he forgot Eternity_L,_⌐ delighted in his sweet joy

     Page 83 l. 12: 'Vala' was at first 'Valan'.

Among his family_L,_J his flocks & herds & tents & pastures

But Luvah close conferrd with Urizen in darksom night
To bind the father & enslave the brethren_L._J Nought he knew
Of sweet Eternity_L ;_J the blood flowd round the holy tent &
    rivn
From its hinges_L,_J uttering its final groan_L,_J all Beulah fell
In dark confusion_L ;_J mean time Los was born & Enitharmon
But how I know not_L ;_J then forgetfulness quite wrapd me up
A period nor do I more remember till I stood
Beside Los in the Cavern dark enslavd to vegetative forms
According to the Will of Luvah who assumd the Place
Of the Eternal Man & smote him. But thou Spectre dark
Maist find a Way to punish Vala in thy fiery South_L,_J
To bring her down subjected to the rage of my fierce boy_L._J'

[*Page 84*]

The Spectre sai*d*: 'Thou lovely ˄Vision_L,_J this˄ delightful
    Tree
Is given us for a Shelter from the tempests of Void & Solid
Till once again the morn of ages shall renew upon us
To reunite in those mild fields of happy Eternity
Where thou & I in undivided Essence[?] walkd about   ˄˄
Imbodie*d*, thou my garden of delight & I the spirit in the
    garden_L._J
Mutual there we dwelt in one anothers joy revolving
Days of Eternity with Tharmas mild & Luvah sweet melo-
    dious
Upon our waters. This thou well rememberest_L ;_J listen_L,_J
    I will tell
What thou forgettest. They in us & we in them alternate
    Livd_L,_J
Drinking the joys of Universal Manhood. One dread morn_L,_J
Listen_L,_J O vision of delight_L,_J One dread morn of goary
    blood

Page 84 DESIGN: Below and around the text is a very roughly drawn naked (?male)
figure, his knees bent double, his thighs horizontal, supporting himself on his
toes and extended right arm, who lifts his left arm well up the margin. An alternative
left arm seems to have supported him also.
l. 10: Under 'Livd' Blake originally began a word with 'f'.

The [*words del*] ^manhood was divided for the^ gentle pas-
sions making way
Thro the infinite labyrinths of the heart & thro the nostrils
issuing   [*14*]
In odorous stupefaction stood before the Eyes of Man   ^^*270^^
A female bright. I stood beside my anvil dark⌊,⌋ a mass
Of iron glowd bright prepard for spades & plowsha*r*es;
sudden down
I sunk with cries of blood issuing downward in the veins
Which now my rivers were become⌊,⌋ rolling in tubelike
forms
Shut up within themselves descending down⌊.⌋ I sunk along   [*20*]
The goary tide even to the place of seed & there dividing
I was divided in darkness & oblivion⌊;⌋ thou an infant woe
And I an infant terror in the womb of Enion⌊.⌋
My masculine spirit scorning the frail body issud forth

^From Enions brain^ In this deformed form leaving thee   ^^*280^^
there   [*25*]
Till times passd over thee but still my spirit returning
hoverd
And formd a Male to be a counterpart to thee⌊,⌋ O Love
Darkend & Lost⌊!⌋ In due time issuing forth from Enions
womb
Thou & that demon Los wert born⌊.⌋ Ah Jealousy &
woe⌊!⌋
Ah poor divided dark Urthona⌊!⌋ now a Spectre wandring   [*30*]
The deeps of Los⌊,⌋ the Slave of that Creation I created⌊.⌋
I labour night & day for Los but listen thou my vision⌊.⌋
I view futurity in thee⌊.⌋ I will bring down soft Vala
To the embraces of this terror & I will destroy
That body I created⌊;⌋ then shall we unite again in bliss   ^^*290^^
For till these terrors planted round the Gates of Eternal life   [*36*]
Are driven away & annihilated we never can repass the   ^^*292^^
Gates⌊.⌋

ll. 16–17: The phrase is repeated on p. 22, ll. 16–17 and p. 50, l. 8.
l. 19: 'tubelike' was originally 'tublike'.
l. 26: 'returning' was first written 'returnd'.
l. 29: 'wert' was originally 'were'.

ˏThou knowest that the Spectre is in Every Man insane ˄˄*o
  brutish
ˏDeformd⌊,⌋ ˄˄[Brutis *del*]˄˄ that I am thus a ravening
  devouring lust continually
ˏCraving & devouring but my Eyes are always upon
  thee O lovely   [
ˏDelusion & I cannot crave for any thing but thee⌊;⌋
  ˏ[& till *del*]˄ ˄˄not so˄˄
ˏ[I have thee in my arms & am again united to Los
ˏ[To be one body & One spirit with him *del*]˄
  ˄˄The spectres of the Dead for I am as the Spectre of
  the Living⌊.⌋'˄˄   [

[*Page 85*]

ˏAstonishd⌊,⌋ filld with tears⌊,⌋ the spirit of Enitharmon
  beheld
ˏAnd heard the Spectre⌊;⌋ bitterly she wept Embracing
  fervent
ˏHer once lovd Lord⌊,⌋ now but a Shade⌊,⌋ herself also
  a shade⌊,⌋
ˏConferring times on times among the branches of that
  Tree⌊.⌋˄
Thus they conferrd among the intoxicating fumes of Mystery   [
Till Enitharmons shadow pregnant in the deeps beneath
Brought forth a wonder horrible. While Enitharmon shriekd
And trembled thro the Worlds above Los wept⌊,⌋ his fierce
  soul was terrifid
At the shrieks of Enitharmon⌊,⌋ at her tossings⌊,⌋ nor could
  his eyes percieve
The cause of her dire anguish for she lay the image of Death   [
Movd by strong shudders till her shadow was deliverd⌊,⌋
  then she ran
Raving about the upper Elements in maddning fury⌊:⌋   :

She burst the Gates of Enitharmons heart with direful Crash

  ll. 38–44 are written sideways in the right margin and are marked for insertion
apparently after l. 35, but the sense seems to fit them best after l. 37.
  ll. 38–9 are in p. 5, ll. 40–1 (see p. 1079 and note).

Page 85: The original text is in the Usual Hand; ll. 1–4, 23–31 are in a slightly
smaller hand; and ll. 32–47 are written smallest of all with a sharper pen. The
writing on pp. 87, 90 is in this smallest hand.

Nor could they ever be Closd again⌐,⌐ the golden hinges were
 broken
And the gates [burst *del*] ˄broke˄ in sunder & their ornaments
 defacd   [*15*]
Beneath the tree of Mystery for the immortal shadow shud-
 dering
Brought forth this wonder horrible⌐,⌐ a Cloud⌐,⌐ she grew &
 grew
Till many of the dead burst forth from the bottoms of their
 tombs
˄In male forms without female counterparts or Emana-
 tions⌐,⌐
˄Cruel & ravening with Enmity & Hatred[?] & War   [*20*]
˄In dreams of Ulro [sweet *del*] ˄˄dark˄˄ delusive drawn by
 the lovely shadow⌐.⌐˄

The Spectre [smild *del*] ˄terrified˄ & gave her Charge over
 the howling Orc⌐.⌐
˄Then took the tree of Mystery root[?] in the World of Los⌐,⌐
˄Its topmost [branches *del*] ˄˄boughs˄˄ shooting a [stem *del*]
 ˄˄fibre˄˄ beneath Enitharmons couch⌐,⌐
˄The double rooted Labyrinth soon wavd around their
 heads˄   [*25*]

˄But then the Spectre enterd Los's bosom⌐.⌐ Every sigh &
 groan
˄Of Enitharmon bore Urthonas Spectre on its wings⌐.⌐
˄Obdurate Los felt Pity⌐,⌐ Enitharmon told the tale
˄Of Urthona. Los Embracd the Spectre first as a brother⌐,⌐
˄Then as another Self; astonishd humanizing & in tears⌐,⌐   [*30*]
˄In Self abasement Giving up his Domineering lust⌐.⌐˄

˄˄'Thou never canst embrace sweet Enitharmon⌐,⌐ terrible
 Demo*n*, Till

l. 18 is adapted on p. 95, l. 11.
ll. 19–20 are written sideways in the margin and are marked for entry in this
position.
l. 21 is written over an erasure.
l. 22: Evidently '&' should also have been deleted.
ll. 26–7 are written over '[End of the Seventh(?) Night *del*]'.

^^Thou art united with thy Spectre [*word del*] ^^^Consummating^^^ by pains & labours

^^[Thy *del*] ^^^That^^^ mortal body & by Self annihilation back returning

^^To Life Eternal﹂;﹂ be assurd I am thy real Self [

^^Tho thus divided from thee & the Slave of Every passion

^^Of thy fierce Soul﹂.﹂ Unbar the Gates of Memory﹂,﹂ look upon me

^^Not as another but as thy real Self﹂.﹂ I am thy Spectre﹂.﹂

^^Thou didst subdue me in old times by thy Immortal Strength

^^When I was a ravening hungering & thirsting cruel lust & murder﹂.﹂ [

^^Tho horrible & Ghastly to thine Eyes﹂,﹂ tho buried beneath

^^The ruins of the Universe, hear what inspird I speak & be silent﹂.﹂

^^If [once *del*] we unite in one another better world will be

^^Opend within your heart & loins & wondrous brain

^^Threefold as it was in Eternity & this the fourth Universe [

^^Will be Renewd by the three & consummated in Mental fires

^^But if thou dost refuse Another body will be prepared^^ [

[*Page 86*]

'For me & thou annihilate evaporate & be no more

For thou art but a form & organ of life & of thyself

Art nothing being Created Continually by Mercy & Love divine﹂.﹂'

Los furious answerd: 'Spectre horrible﹂,﹂ thy words astound my Ear

ll. 37–8, 41 are written over '[The End of the Seventh Night *del*]'; only the last word is clearly legible.

ll. 39–40 are written sideways in the bottom right margin, and no position is indicated for them. The sense seems to sanction their insertion here.

Page 86 DESIGN: Between ll. 1–8 (squeezed at the top of the page) and ll. 9–14 (squeezed at the bottom) is a nude woman on her knees but otherwise erect, looking down to her left, with a hand on each breast outlining the nipple with her fingers as if she were squirting milk. There are swirls around her. She is appropriate to Ahania's words on p. 108, ll. 16–17: ' "I am the nourisher . . . in my bosom is milk & wine And a fountain from my breasts" '.

With irresistible conviction⌊.⌋ I feel I am not one of those   [5]
Who when convincd can still persist tho furious⌊,⌋ controll-
able
By Reasons power. Even I already feel a World within
Opening its gates & in it all the real substances

'Of which these in the outward World are shadows which
  pass away⌊.⌋
Come then into my Bosom & in thy [*word del*] ∧shadowy∧
  arms bring with thee   [*10*]
My lovely Enitharmon. I will quell my fury & teach
Peace to the Soul of dark revenge & repentance to Cruelty⌊.⌋'

So spoke Los & Embracing Enitharmon & the Spectre⌊,⌋
[*words del*] ∧Clouds would have folded round in∧ Extacy &
  Love uniting   [*14*]

                 [*Page 87*]
But Enitharmon trembling fled & hid beneath Urizens
  tree
[Then *del*] ∧But∧ mingling together with his Spectre the
  Spectre of Urthona
[*words del*] ∧Wondering beheld the Center opend⌊;⌋∧ by
  Divine Mercy inspird
∧⌊(⌋He in his turn Gave Tasks to Los Enormous to destroy
∧That body he created but in vain for Los performd   [5]
∧Wonders of labour⌊)⌋∧
∧They∧ Builded Golgonooza⌊,⌋ Los labouring [inspird *del*]
  builded pillars high
And Domes terrific in the nether heavens for beneath
Was opend new heavens & a new Earth beneath & within⌊,⌋
Threefold within the brain⌊,⌋ within the heart⌊,⌋ within the
  loins⌊,⌋   [*10*]
A Threefold Atmosphere Sublime continuous from [Uri-
  zens(?) *del*] ∧Urthonas∧ world

Page 87 l. 3: The words erased under this addition extended to the left margin
and may have begun: 'With love'.

   ll. 4–6 are written as one line squeezed in between l. 3 and l. 7, with a stroke
between the words 'to destroy' and 'That body' and between 'Los performd' and
'Wonders of labour'.

But yet having a Limit Twofold named Satan & Adam

But Los stood on the Limit of Translucence_L,_⌋ weeping &
trembling_L,_⌋
Filled with doubts in self accusation_L,_⌋ [gatherd *del*] ˄beheld˄
the fruit
Of Urizens Mysterious tree For Enitharmon thus spake_L:_⌋

'When In the Deeps beneath I gatherd of this ruddy fruit
It was by that I knew that I had Sinnd & then I knew
That without a ransom I could not be savd from Eternal
death_L,_⌋
That Life lives upon Death & by devouring appetite
All things subsist on one another_L;_⌋ thenceforth in Despair
I spend my glowing time but thou art strong & mighty
To bear this Self conviction_L;_⌋ take then_L,_⌋ Eat thou also of
The fruit & give me proof of life Eternal or I die_L._⌋'

Then Los plucked the fruit & Eat & sat down in Despair
And must have given himself to death Eternal But
Urthonas Spectre in part mingling with him comforted him_L,_⌋
Being a medium between him & Enitharmon But This
Union
Was not to be Effected without Cares & Sorrows & Troubles
Of Six thousand Years of self denial & [many Tears *del*] of
bitter Contrition_L._⌋

Urthonas Spectre terrified beheld the Spectres of the Dead
Each Male ˄formd˄ without a counterpart_L,_⌋ without a con-
centering vision_L._⌋
The Spectre of Urthona wept before Los Saying 'I am the
cause
That this dire state commences_L._⌋ I began the dreadful state
Of Separation & on my dark head the curse & punishment
Must fall unless a way be found [the *del*] to Ransom &
Redeem
˄But I have thee my [Counterpart *del*] ˄˄[Vegetation(*?*)
del]˄˄ miraculous_L._⌋

l. 19: Urizen 'saw that life liv'd upon death' in *Urizen* pl. 23, l. 447 (p. 274).
ll. 36–9 are written in the right margin and are clearly marked for insertion here.

Vala p. 87

ᴧThese Spectres have no [Counter *del*]ₗ,Ↄ therefore they
  ravin
ᴧWithout the food of lifeₗ.Ↄ Let us Create them Coun
ᴧFor without a Created body the Spectre is Eternal Deathₗ.Ↄ'ᴧ

Los trembling answerd 'Now I feel the weight of stern re-
  pentanceₗ.Ↄ   [*40*]
Tremble not so my Enitharmon at the awful gates
Of thy poor broken Heartₗ.Ↄ I see thee like a shadow wither-
  ing
As on the outside of Existence but look! behold! take com-
  fort!
Turn inwardly thine Eyes & there behold the Lamb of God
Clothed in Luvahs robes of blood descending to redeemₗ.Ↄ   [*45*]
O Spectre of Urthonaₗ,Ↄ take comfortₗ!Ↄ O Enitharmonₗ!Ↄ
Couldst thou but cease from terror & trembling & affrightₗ,Ↄ
When I appear before thee.in forgiveness of [former injuries
  del] ᴧancient injuriesₗ,Ↄᴧ
Why shouldst thou remember & be afrai*d*? I surely have died
  in pain
Often enough to convince thy jealousy & fear & terrorₗ.Ↄ   [*50*]
Come hitherₗ;Ↄ be patientₗ;Ↄ let us converse together because
I also tremble at myself & at all my former lifeₗ.Ↄ'

Enitharmon answerd 'I behold the Lamb of God descending
To Meet these Spectres of the Deadₗ.Ↄ I therefore fear that
  he
Will give us to Eternal Deathₗ,Ↄ fit punishment for such   [*55*]
Hideous offendersₗ,Ↄ Uttermost extinction in eternal painₗ,Ↄ
An ever dying life of stifling & obstruction shut out
Of existence to be a sign & terror to all who behold
Lest any should in futurity do as we have done in heavenₗ.Ↄ
ᴧᴧ*Such is our state nor will the Son of God redeem us but
  destroyₗ.Ↄ'ᴧᴧ   [*60*]

ll. 42–5, except for the first five words, are written in Brown ink, while the
rest of the page is in Black ink.
l. 46: The first six words of this line trace in ink the same words written in
pencil.
l. 50: 'enough' was originally 'enought'.

Vala p. 88

[Page 88 has no VALA text]

[Page 89 has no text]

[Page 90]

So Enitharmon spoke trembling & in torrents of tears⌊·⌋

Los [stood(?) *del*] ˄sat˄ in Golgonooza in the Gate of Luban where

He had erected many porches [which . . . *del*] ˄where branchd the Mysterious Tree˄

Where the Spectrous dead wail & sighing thus he spoke to Enitharmon⌊:⌋

'Lovely delight of Men⌊,⌋ Enitharmon⌊,⌋ shady [sweet *del*] refuge from furious war⌊,⌋

Thy bosom translucent is a soft repose for the weeping souls   ⌊

Of those piteous victims of battle⌊;⌋ there they sleep in happy obscurity⌊;⌋

˄They feed upon our life⌊;⌋ we are their victims. Stern desire˄

I feel to fabricate embodied semblances in which the dead

May live before us in our palaces & in our gardens of [pleasure *del*] labour

   ˄Which now opend within the Center we behold spread   ⌊
   abroad˄

To form a world of [life & love *del*] ˄Sacrifice˄ of brothers & sons & daughters

Page 88 is inscribed with words evidently not integral to *Vala*:

> The Christian Religion teaches that No Man is Indifferent to you but that every one is / Either Your friend or your enemy; he must necessarily be either the one [of *del*] or the other / And that he will be equally profitable both ways if you treat him as he deserves⌊·⌋

The third line ('And that . . . deserves') is written with a sharper pen.

Page 89 DESIGN: In the bottom left margin beside the engraving of 'Edward & Elinor' is a very vaguely sketched person kneeling before a standing figure who points with his left hand at the kneeler and with his right hand in the air.

Page 90 is written in a hand somewhat smaller than the Usual Hand. All the additions over erasures are in the Usual Hand with a blunter pen and look as if they were made at the same time. The last stanza (not that in the margin) may be written with a sharper pen in a hand between the small hand above it and the Usual Hand in the margin.

l. 8 is written over an erased line.

l. 12: 'Sacrifice' is written below the line because the added line above left no room above l. 12.

To comfort Orc in his dire sufferings∟;⌐ look∟,⌐ my fires en-
  lume afresh
Before my face ascending with delight as in ancient
  times∟!⌐'

Enitharmon spread her beaming locks upon the wind &
  said∟:⌐   [*15*]
'O [Lovely *del*] ∧Lovely terrible∧ Los∟,⌐ wonder of Eternity∟,⌐
  O Los∟,⌐ my defence & guide∟,⌐
Thy works are all my jo*y*, & in thy fires my soul delights∟.⌐
If mild they burn in just proportion & in secret night
And silence build their day in shadow of soft clouds &
  dews
Then I can sigh forth on the winds of Golgonooza piteous
  forms   [*20*]
That vanish again into my bosom but if thou my Los
Wilt in sweet moderated fur*y* fabricate [sweet *del*] forms
    ∧∧*sublime∧∧
Such as the piteous spectres may assimilate themselves into
∧They shall be ransoms for our Souls that we may live∟.⌐'

So Enitharmon spoke & Los his hands divine inspird began   [*25*]
[To hew the cavernd rocks of Dranthon into forms of beauty
  del]
To modulate his fires∟;⌐ studious the loud roaring flames
He vanquishd with the strength of Art bending their iron
  points
And drawing them forth ∧delighted∧ upon the winds of
  Golgonooza
From out the ranks of Urizens war & from the fiery lake   [*30*]
Of Orc bending down as the binder of the Sheaves follows
The reaper in both arms embracing the furious raging
  flames∟.⌐
Los drew them forth out of the deeps planting his right foot
  firm
Upon the Iron crag of Urizen∟,⌐ thence springing up aloft

        l. 24 is written over an erased line.
        l. 31: 'bending' could be 'binding'.

Into the heavens of Enitharmon in a mighty circle   [

And first he drew a line upon the walls of shining heaven
And Enitharmon tincturd it with beams of blushing love ⌊.⌋
It remaind permanent ⌊,⌋ a lovely form inspird ⌊,⌋ divinely
 human ⌊.⌋
Dividing into just proportions Los unwearied labourd
The immortal lines upon the heavens till with sighs of love   [
Sweet Enitharmon mild Entrancd breathd forth upon the
 wind
The Spectrous dead ⌊.⌋ Weeping the Spectres viewd the im-
 mortal works
Of Los Assimilating to those forms Embodied & Lovely
In youth & beauty in the arms of Enitharmon mild reposing ⌊.⌋

First Rintrah & then Palamabron drawn from out the ranks
 of war
In infant innocence repos'd on Enitharmons bosom ⌊.⌋   [
Orc was comforted in the deeps ⌊;⌋ his soul revivd in them
As the Eldest brother is the [second *del*] fathers image So
 Orc became
As Los a father to his brethren & he joyd in the dark lake
Tho bound with chains of Jealousy & in scales of iron & brass   ▮

But Los loved them & refusd to Sacrifice their infant limbs
And Enitharmons smiles & tears prevaild over self pro-
 tection ⌊.⌋
They rather chose to meet Eternal death than to destroy
The offspring of their Care & Pity ⌊.⌋ Urthonas Spectre was
 comforted
But Tharmas most rejoicd in hope of Enions return   ▮
For he beheld new Female forms born forth upon the air
Who wove soft silken veils of covering in sweet rapturd trance
Mortal & not as Enitharmon without a covering veil ⌊.⌋

ˬFirst his immortal spirit drew Urizen['s] [Spectre *del*]
 ˄˄Shadow˄˄ away

ll. 59–68 are written sideways in the bottom right margin, though there was
room for them to be written in a column parallel to the main text. They are written
with a blunter pen than the rest of the page.

ˆFrom out the ranks of war separating him in sunderʟˏ⌟   [*60*]
ˆLeaving his Spectrous form which could not be drawn
  awayʟ·⌟
ˆThen he divided Thirielʟˏ⌟ the Eldest of Urizens sonsʟ;⌟
ˆUrizen became Rintrahʟˏ⌟ Thiriel became Palamabronʟ·⌟
ˆThus dividing the powers of Every Warrior
ˆStartled was Losʟ;⌟ he found his Enemy Urizen now   [*65*]
ˆIn his hands; he wonderd that he felt love & not hateʟ·⌟
ˆHis whole soul loved himʟ;⌟ he beheld him an infant
ˆLovely breathd from Enitharmonʟ;⌟ he trembled within
  himselfʟ·⌟ˆ   [*68*]

VALA

Night the Seventh[*b*]

∧This Night begins at line 153∟;⌐ the following comes in at
the End∟·⌐∧

∧Beginning of the [Book *del*] Seventh Night∧
But in the Deeps beneath the [tree *del*] ∧Roots∧ of Mystery in
darkest night
When Urizen sat on his rock the Shadow brooded [dismal
del]
Urizen saw & triumphd & he cried to [the Shadowy female
del] ∧his warriors∟:⌐∧
T
'The time of Prophecy is now revolvd & all
This Universal Ornament[?] is mine & in my hands
The ends of heaven like a Garment will I fold them round
me
Consuming what must be consumd∟;⌐ then in power &
majesty
I will walk forth thro those wide fields of endless Eternity∟,⌐
A God & not a Man∟,⌐ a Conqueror in triumphant glory
And all the Sons of Everlasting[?] shall bow down at my
feet∟·⌐'

[The shadowy voice answerd 'O urizen Prince of Light'
del]

Page 95: Blake first wrote Night VIIb on pp. 91–8, numbered the lines in this
order, and wrote 'End of The Seventh Night' on p. 98; then he inserted directions
at the top of p. 91, after p. 95, l. 14, and at the end of p. 98, indicating that the
order should be 95–8, 91–5. Night VIIb is printed here as Blake reorganized it,
but his line-numbers indicate its earlier form.

Page 95 is written with a slightly blunter pen than p. 94.

Above l. 1, the insertion ('This Night . . . at the End') is in a stanza break. In the
left margin, in a hand rather unlike Blake's, is '*Beginning of Night VII', with
strokes pointing to this stanza-break.

After l. 17: The 'T' is evidently an accident.

ll. 19–20: Cf. p. 42, l. 22, *Jerusalem* pl. 91, ll. 33–4, and Psalm 104: 2.

First Trades & Commerce Ships & armed vessels he builded
   laborious
To swim the deep & on the Land children are sold to trades
Of dire necessity⌊,⌋ still laboring day & night till all
Their life extinct they took the spectre form in dark despair
And slaves in myriads in ship loads burden the hoarse
   sounding deep   [*30*]
Rattling with clanking chains⌊,⌋ the Universal Empire
   groans

And he commanded his Sons [*to*] found[*?*] a Center in the   ^^*170^^
   Deep
And Urizen laid the first Stone & all his myriads
Builded a temple in the image of the human heart   [*34*]

[*Page 96*]

And in the inner part of the Temple⌊,⌋ wondrous workman-
   ship⌊,⌋
They formd the Secret place reversing all the order of delight
That whosoever enterd into the Temple might not behold
The hidden wonders allegoric of the Generations
Of secret lust when hid in chambers dark the nightly harlot   [*5*]
Plays in Disguise in whisperd hymn & mumbling prayer⌊·⌋
   The priests
He ordaind & Priestesses clothd in disguises beastial
Inspiring secrecy & lamps they bore⌊,⌋ intoxicating fumes   ^^*180^^
Roll round the Temple & they took the Sun that glowd oer
   Los
And with immense machines down rolli*n*g, the terrific orb   [*10*]
Compelld. The Sun reddning like a fierce lion in his chains
Descended to the sound of instruments that drownd the
   noise
Of the hoarse wheels & the terrific howlings of wild beasts
That dragd the wheels of the Suns chariot & they put the
   Sun
Into the temple of Urizen to give light to the Abyss⌊,⌋   [*15*]
To light the War by day⌊,⌋ to hide his secret beams by night

Page 96 DESIGN: In the bottom left corner is a large pillar-like object, before
which three clothed figures bow abjectly. (Perhaps the scene is part of the rites 'Of
secret lust' of the 'secret religion in his temple', ll. 5, 18.)

For he divided day & night in different orderd portions⌐,⌐
The day for war⌐,⌐ the night for secret religion in his temple⌐.⌐ ‸‸
[Urizen namd it Pande *del*]

Los reard his mighty [forehead *del*] ‸stature⌐;⌐‸ on Earth
  stood his feet. Above   [
The moon his furious forehead circled with black bursting
  thunders⌐,⌐
His naked limbs glittring upon the dark blue sky⌐,⌐ his
  knees
Bathed in bloody clouds, his loins in fires of war where spears
And swords rage⌐,⌐ where the Eagles cry & Vultures laugh
  saying
'Now comes the night of Carnage⌐,⌐ now the flesh of Kings
  & Princes   [
Pamperd in palaces [of *del*] ‸for‸ our food⌐,⌐ the blood of
  Captains nurturd
With lust & murder for our drink⌐;⌐ the drunken Raven
  Shall wander
All night among the slain & mock the wounded that groan
  in the field⌐.⌐'

Tharmas laughd furious among the Banners clothd in blood ‸‸

Crying 'As I will I rend the Nations all asunder⌐,⌐ rending ‸
The People, vain their combinations⌐,⌐ I will scatter them [
But thou⌐,⌐ O Son whom I have crowned & inthrond⌐,⌐ thee
  Strong
I will preserve tho Enemies arise around thee numberless⌐.⌐
I will command my winds & they shall scatter them or call [
[*Page 97*]
'My Waters like a flood around thee⌐;⌐ fear not⌐,⌐ trust in me ‸‸
And I will give thee all the ends of heaven for thy possession⌐.⌐
In war shalt thou bear rule⌐,⌐ in blood shalt thou triumph for
  me
Because in times of Everlasting I was rent in sunder   [
And what I loved best was divided among my Enemies⌐.⌐ ‸‸*

ll. 29–34 are in a much clearer and more upright hand. The rest of the page is
written with a blunter pen.

My little daughters were made captives & I saw them
beaten
With whips along the sultry [roads *del*] sands. I heard those
whom I lovd ∧∧*210∧∧
Crying in secret tents at night & in the morn compelld
To labour & behold my heart sunk down beneath
In sighs & sobbings [till *del*]⌐,⌐ all dividing till I was divided [*10*]
In twain & lo my Crystal form that lived in my bosom
Followd her daughters to the fields of blood⌐;⌐ they left me
naked
Alone & they refusd to return from the fields of the mighty⌐.⌐
Therefore I will reward them as they have rewarded me⌐.⌐
I will divide them in my anger & thou O my King [*15*]
Shalt gather them from out their graves & put thy fetter on
them
And bind them to thee that my crystal form may come to
me⌐.⌐' ∧∧*220∧∧

So cried the Demon of the Waters in the Clouds of Los⌐.⌐
Outstretchd upon the hills lay Enitharmon⌐;⌐ clouds &
tempests
Beat round her head all night⌐;⌐ all day she riots in Excess [*20*]
But [day by *del*] ∧night or∧ day Los follows War & the dismal
moon rolls over her
That when Los warrd upon the South reflected the fierce
fires ∧∧*25∧∧
Of his immortal head into the North upon faint Enithar-
mon⌐.⌐
Red rage the furies of fierce Orc⌐;⌐ black thunders roll round
Los⌐,⌐
Flaming his head like the bright sun seen thro a mist that
magnifies [*25*]
His disk into a terrible vision to the Eyes of trembling mortals

And Enitharmon trembling & in fear utterd these words⌐:⌐ ∧∧*230∧∧

'I put not any trust in thee nor in thy glittring scales⌐.⌐
Thy eyelids are a terror to me & the flaming of thy crest⌐,⌐

Page 97: ll. 19–37 are written in a smaller, more regular hand.

The rushing of thy Scales confound me∟,⌐ thy hoarse rushing
　　scales　　　　　　　　　　　　　　　　　　　　　　[
And if that Los had not built me a tower upon a rock
I must have died in the dark desart among noxious worms∟.⌐
How shall I flee∟?⌐ how shall I flee into the tower of Los∟?⌐
My feet are turned backward & my footsteps slide in clay
And clouds are closd around my tower∟;⌐ my arms labour in
　　vain∟.⌐　　　　　　　　　　　　　　　　　　　　[
Does not the God of waters in the wracking Elements[?]
Love those who hate∟,⌐ rewarding with hate the Loving
　　Soul∟?⌐

　　　　　　　　　[*Page 98*]
'And must not I obey the God∟,⌐ thou Shadow of Jealousy∟?⌐
I cry∟;⌐ the watchman heareth not∟.⌐ I pour my voice in
　　roarings∟.⌐
Watchman∟!⌐ the night is thick & darkness cheats my rayie
　　sight∟.⌐
Lift up∟!⌐ Lift up∟!⌐ O Los∟!⌐ awake my watchman for he
　　sleepeth∟.⌐
Lift up∟!⌐ Lift up∟!⌐ Shine forth, O Light∟!⌐ watchman∟,⌐
　　thy light is out∟!⌐
O Los∟,⌐ unless thou keep my tower the Watchman will be
　　slain∟!⌐'

So Enitharmon cried upon her terrible Earthy bed
While the broad Oak wreathd his roots round her∟,⌐ forcing
　　his dark way
Thro caves of death into Existence∟.⌐ The Beech long limbd
　　advancd
Terrific into the paind heavens∟.⌐ The fruit trees humanizing
Shewd their immortal energies in warlike desperation
Rending the heavens & earths & drinking blood in the hot
　　battle
To feed their fruit∟,⌐ to gratify their hidden Sons & daughters
That far within the close recesses of their secret palaces
Viewd the vast war & joyd∟,⌐ wishing to vegetate

Page 98　DESIGN: At the bottom of the page is a coiled and coiling serpent which
culminates in a man's face in a cobra hood in the right margin. (He must be 'The
Prester Serpent' with a 'Cowl upon my head' of ll. 22–4.)

Into the Worlds of Enitharmon_L·_J Loud the roaring winds
Burdend with clouds howl round the Couch_L;_J sullen the
   wooly sheep
Walks thro the battle_L·_J Dark & fierce the Bull his rage
Propagates thro the warring Earth_L,_J The Lion raging in
   flames_L,_J
The Tyger in redounding smoke_L;_J The Serpent of the woods   ∧∧*260∧∧
And of the waters & the scorpion of the desart irritate   [21]
With harsh songs every living soul. The Prester Serpent runs
Along the ranks crying 'Listen to the Priest of God_L,_J ye
   warriors_L!_J
This Cowl upon my head he placd in times of Everlasting
And said "Go forth & guide my battle*s*; like the jointed
   spine   [25]
Of Man I made thee when I blotted Man from life & light_L·_J
Take thou the seven Diseases of Man_L;_J store them for times
   to come
In store houses in secret places that I will tell the[e] of
To be my great & awful curses at the time appointed_L·_J" '

                                               ∧∧*270∧∧

The Prester serpent ceasd_L;_J the War song sounded loud &
   strong   [30]
Thro all the heavens_L,_J Urizens Web vibrated torment on   272
   torment_L·_J   ∧∧*271∧∧
    ∧∧*Then I heard the Earthquake &^c∧∧
Then follows 'Thus in the Caverns of the Grave' &^c as it
   stands now in the beginning of Night the Seventh

                   [*Page 91*]
Now in the Caverns of the Grave & Places of human seed
The nameless shadowy Vortex stood before the face of Orc_L·_J
The Shadow reard her dismal head over the flaming youth
With sighs & howling & deep sobs_L;_J that he might lose his
   rage
And with, it lose himself in meekness she embracd his fire_L;_J   [5]

ll. 19–20: 'Lion' and 'Tyger' were originally plural.
   After l. 31: 'Then I heard the Earthquake &^c' apparently refers to a lost passage.
'Then follows . . . the beginning of Night the Seventh' refers to p. 91.
   Page 91: l. 1 is repeated on p. 44, l. 3.

As when the Earthquake rouzes from his den⌐,⌐ his shoulders huge
Appear above the crumb[*l*]ing Mountai*n*, Silence waits around him
A moment⌐,⌐ then astounding horror belches from the Center⌐,⌐
The fiery dogs arise⌐,⌐ the shoulders huge appear⌐;⌐
So Orc rolld round his clouds upon the deeps of dark Urthona
  ⌃Knowing the arts of Urizen were Pity & Meek [love *del*] affection
  ⌃And that by these arts the Serpent form exuded from his limbs⌃
Silent as despairing love & strong as Jealousy[—]
⌃Jealous that she was Vala now become Urizens harlot
⌃And the Harlot of Los & the deluded harlot of the Kings of Earth
⌃His soul was gnawn in sunder[—]
The hairy shoulders rend the links⌐,⌐ free are the wrists of fire⌐.⌐
Red rage redounds⌐;⌐ he rouzd his lions from his forests black⌐;⌐
They howl around the flaming youth rending the nameless shadow
And running their immortal course thro solid darkness borne⌐.⌐

Loud Sounds the war song round red Orc in his [blind(?) f th(?) *del*] fury
And round the nameless shadowy Female in her howling terror

ll. 6–9: The metaphor appears in *Tiriel* ll. 246–9 (p. 913).
  ll. 11–12 are written as a continuation of l. 10, up the right margin, and are not clearly marked as separate lines. l. 12 looks as if it were added later than l. 11.
  ll. 13–14 are repeated from *America* pl. 4, ll. 21–2 (p. 138).
  ll. 14–16 are inserted in a stanza-break after l. 20. After 'Urizens harlot' the lines bend up the page. Two Xs connected by a stroke clearly indicate that l. 14 should precede l. 17, and presumably ll. 15–16 should follow l. 14. ll. 15–16, which are very like the addition above, look as if they were added later than l. 14.

Vala p. 92

When all the Elemental Gods joind in the wondrous Song_L:_J

'Sound the War trumpet terrific_L,_J Souls clad in attractive
    steel_L!_J
Sound the shrill fife_L,_J serpents of war! I hear the northern
    drum_L._J   [25]
Awake, I hear the flappings of the folding banners_L._J
The dragons of the North put on their armour_L;_J
Upon the Eastern sea direct they take their course_L._J
The glittring of their horses trappings stains the vault of
    night_L._J

'Stop we the rising of the glorious King; spur spur your
    [steeds *del*] ⁀clouds⁀   [30]

[Page 92]

'Of death_L!_J O northern drum_L,_J awake_L!_J O hand of iron_L,_J
    sound
The northern drum! Now give the charge! bravely obscurd!
With darts of wintry hail. Again the black bow draw_L,_J
Again the Elemental Strings to your right breasts draw
And let the thundring drum speed on the arrows black_L._J'   [5]

The arrows flew from cloudy bow all day, till blood
From east to west flowd like the human veins in rivers
Of life upon the plains of death & valleys of despair_L._J

'Now sound the Clarions of Victory_L,_J now strip the slain_L;_J
[Now *del*] clothe yourselves in golden arms_L,_J brothers of
    war_L._J'   [10]
They sound the clarions strong_L!_J they chain the howling
    captives_L;_J

Page 92 DESIGN: In the bottom right margin is a clothed male(?) figure with
his back to us, half lying down, leaning on his left elbow, his legs extended to the
right, looking toward a nude woman who is kneeling on her heels, her head bowed
in her arms. Above the man's head is a very vague drawing of a tiny floating figure.
Indefinite strokes may represent a large open book between the man and the
woman. Behind the woman a drawing of the back of a nude torso has been crossed
out. Above this is an indecipherable scribble.
    l. 10: 'Now' is deleted in pencil.
    ll. 11–13, 15 to p. 93, l. 19 are in a slightly different form in *Jerusalem* pl. 65,
ll. 6–8, 10–32, 37–55 (pp. 557–9).

[1]They give the Oath of blood[L,], [2]They cast the lots into the
   helmet,
They vote the Death of Luvah & they naild him to the
   tree[L];]
They piercd him with a spear & laid him in a sepulcher
To die a death of Six thousand years bound round with
   desolation[L.]
The sun was black & the moon rolld a useless globe thro
   heaven[L.]

Then left the Sons of Urizen the plow & harrow[L,] the
   loom[L,]
The hammer & the Chisel & the rule & compasses[L;]
They forgd the sword[L,] the chariot of war[L,] the battle ax[L,]
The trumpet fitted to the battle & the flute of summer
And all the arts of life they changd into the arts of death[L.]
The hour glass contemnd because its simple workmanship
Was as the workmanship of the plowman & the water wheel
That raises water into Cisterns broken & burnd in fire
Because its workmanship was like the workmanship of the
   Shepherd
And in their stead intricate wheels invented[L,] Wheel without
   wheel
To perplex youth in their outgoings & to bind to labours
Of day & night the myriads of Eternity, that they might file
And polish brass & iron hour after hour[L;] laborious work-
   manship[L,]
Kept ignorant of the use that they might spend the days of
   wisdom
In sorrowful drudgery to obtain a scanty pittance of bread[L,]
In ignorance to view a small portion & think that All
And call it Demonstration[L,] blind to all the simple rules of
   life[L.]

'Now[L,] now the Battle rages round thy tender limbs O
   Vala[L!]

l. 12 was originally written 'They cast . . . Oath of blood' and then rearranged
as above. The line is not inverted in *Jerusalem* pl. 65 where it also appears.

Now smile among thy bitter tears⌊,⌋ now put on all thy
    beauty⌊·⌋   [*35*]
Is not the wound of the sword Sweet & the broken bone
    delightful⌊?⌋
Wilt thou now smile among the slain when the wounded   ^^*63^^
    groan in the field⌊?⌋   [*37*]

              [*Page 93*]

'Lift up thy blue eyes Vala & put on thy sapphire shoes⌊;⌋ ^^*69^^
    ^O Melancholy Magdalen behold the morning breaks⌊;⌋
Gird on thy flaming Zon*e*, descend into the Sepulcher⌊·⌋
Scatter the blood from thy golden brow⌊,⌋ the tears from thy
    silver locks⌊;⌋
Shake off the waters from thy wings & the dust from thy
    white garments⌊·⌋   [*5*]

'Remember all thy feigned terrors on the secret Couch
When the sun rose in glowing morn with arms of mighty
    hosts
Marching to battle who was wont to rise with Urizens harps
Girt as a Sower with his seed to scatter life abroad⌊·⌋

'Arise O Vala⌊!⌋ bring the bow of Urizen⌊,⌋ bring the swift
    arrows of light⌊·⌋   [*10*]
How ragd the golden horses of Urizen bound to the chariot
    of Love⌊,⌋   ^^*70^^
Compelld to leave the plow to the Ox⌊,⌋ to snuff up the winds
    of desolation⌊,⌋
To trample the corn fields in boastful neighing*s*; this is no
    gentle harp⌊,⌋
This is no warbling brook nor Shadow of a Myrtle tree

'But blood & wounds & dismal cries & clarions of war
And hearts laid open to the light by the broad grizly sword   [*15*]
    ^And bowels hidden [in darkness are *del*] ^^in hammerd
      Steel^^ rippd forth upon the Ground⌊·⌋^
Call forth thy Smiles of soft deceit⌊;⌋ call forth thy cloudy
    tears⌊;⌋

        Page 93   l. 8: 'Marching' at first lacked its 'h'.

We hear thy sighs in trumpets shrill when [*word del*] ∧Morn∧
shall blood renew∟·」'

So sung the demons of the deep∟;」 the Clarions of war blew
loud∟·」   [

Orc rent her & his human form consumd in his own fires
Mingled with her dolorous members strewn thro the abyss∟·」
 ∧She joyd in all the Conflict Gratified & drinking[?]
  tears of woe∟·」∧
No more remaind of Orc but the Serpent round the tree of
Mystery∟·」
The form of Orc was gone∟;」 he reard his serpent bulk among
The stars of Urizen in [fire(?) *del*] ∧Power∟,」∧ rending the
form of life
Into a formless indefinite & strewing her on the Abyss
Like clouds upon the winter sky broken with winds &
thunders∟·」
 ∧This was to her Supreme delight∟;」 the Warriors
  mournd disappointed∟·」∧
 ∧∧They go out to war with Strong Shouts & loud
  Clarions∟·」 O Pity∟!」
 ∧∧They return with lamentations mourning & weep-
  ing∟·」∧∧
Invisible or visible∟,」 drawn out in length or stretchd in
breadth
 ∧The Shadowy Female varied in the War in her de-
 light∟,」∧
Howling in discontent black & heavy∟,」 uttering brute
sounds∟,」
Wading thro fens among the slimy weeds∟,」 making Lamen-
tations

ll. 29–31 are written in the break between stanzas, l. 31 as a continuation of
l. 30, with a stroke to indicate that it is a separate line. ll. 30–1 are written much
smaller than l. 29.
l. 32: 'In visible' is written as two words.
In the left margin is written:
 ∧∧Unorganizd Innocence, an Impossibility∧∧
 Innocence dwells with Wisdom but never with Ignorance

They are not marked for entry and may not be intended as part of *Vala*. A pencil
stroke is drawn from the fourth stanza break *through the middle* of these two lines.

To deceive Tharmas in his rage∟,⌐ to soothe his furious soul∟,⌐
To stay him in his flight that Urizen might live tho in pain∟.⌐
He said 'Art thou bright Enion∟?⌐ is the Shadow of hope
    returnd∟?⌐'

And She said 'Tharmas∟,⌐ I am Vala∟,⌐ bless thy innocent
    face∟!⌐
Doth Enion avoid the sight of thy blue watry eyes∟?⌐   [*40*]
Be not perswaded that the air knows this or the falling
    dew∟.⌐'

Tharmas replid 'O Vala once I livd in a garden of
    delight∟;⌐   [*42*]

           [*Page 94*]

'I wakend Enion in the morning & she turnd away
Among the apple trees & all the gardens of delight   100
Swam like a Dream before my eyes∟.⌐ I went to seek the
    steps
Of Enion in the gardens & the shadows compassd me
And closd me in a watry world of woe where Enion stood   [*5*]
Trembling before me like a shadow∟,⌐ like a mist∟,⌐ like air
And she is gone & here alone I war with darkness & death∟.⌐
I hear thy voice but not thy form se*e*; thou & all delight
And life appear & vanish mocking me with shadows of
    false hope∟.⌐
Hast thou forgot that the air listens thro all its districts telling   [*10*]
The subtlest thoughts shut up from light in chambers of the   ∧∧*110∧∧
    Moon∟?⌐'

   ∧'Tharma*s*, The Moon has Chambers where the babes
      of love lie hid
∧And whence they never can be brought in all Eternity
∧Unless exposd by their vain parents. Lo∟,⌐ him whom I love
∧Is hidden from me & I never in all Eternity   [*15*]

Page 94   DESIGN: Below the text is a nude woman, lying on her right side facing
us, with her right hand to her forehead; she may be falling. (Perhaps she is Vala
'flying furious or falling', l. 31.)
    ll. 12–23 are written sideways in the right margin and are clearly marked for
entry here.

ₐShall see himₗ.ₗ Enitharmon & Ahania combind with
   Enion
ₐHid him in that Outrageous form ₐₐof Orcₐₐ which tor-
   ments me for Sinₗ,ₗ
ₐFor all my Secret faults which he brings forth upon the
   light
ₐOf dayₗ,ₗ in jealousy & blood my Children are led to
   Urizens war
ₐBefore my eyes & for every one of these I am condemnd   [
ₐTo Eternal torment in these flames for tho I have the power
ₐTo rise on high Yet love here binds me down & never never
ₐWill I arise till him I love is loosd from this dark chainₗ.ₗ'ₐ

ₐTharmas replied 'Vala thy Sins have lost us heaven &
   blissₗ.ₗ
ₐThou art our Curse [in *del*] and till I can bring love into the
   light
ₐI never will depart from my great wrathₗ.ₗ'

So Tharmas waild [then furious(?) *del*] ₐwrathfulₗ,ₗₐ ₐthenₐ
   rode upon the Stormy Deep
Cursing the Voice that mockd him with false hopeₗ,ₗ in
   furious moodₗ.ₗ
Then She returns swift as a blight upon the infant bud
Howling in all the notes of woe to stay his furious rageₗ,ₗ
Stamping the hillsₗ,ₗ wading or swimmingₗ,ₗ flying furious
   or falling
Or like an Earthquake rumbling in the bowels of the earth
Or like a cloud beneath & like a fire flaming on highₗ,ₗ
Walking in pleasure of the hills or murmuring in the dales
Like to a rushing torrent beneath & a falling rock aboveₗ,ₗ
A thunder cloud in the south & a lulling voice heard in the
   north

And she went forth & saw the forms of Life & of delight

ll. 24–6 are written in the right margin beside ll. 12–23 but are not marked
for entry. Probably they are the tail of ll. 12–23. ll. 12–26 are written with a
sharper pen and in a clearer hand than the rest of the page.
l. 33: 'in' should be 'on'.

Walking on Mountains or flying in the open expanse ˄of˄
  heaven˻·˼
She heard sweet voices in the winds & in the voices of birds
That rose from waters for the waters were as the voice of
  Luvah˻,˼   [*40*]
Not seen to her like waters or like this dark world of death
Tho all those fair perfections which men know only by name
In beautiful substantial forms appeard & served her
As food or drink or ornament or in delightful works
To build her bowers for the Elements brought forth abun-
  dantly   [*45*]
The living soul in glorious forms & every one came forth   ˄˄*130˄˄
Walking before her Shadowy face & bowing at her feet
But in vain delights were poured forth on the howling melan-
  choly˻·˼
For her delight the horse his proud neck bowd & his white
  mane
And the Strong Lion deignd in his mouth to wear the golden
  bit   [*50*]
While the far beaming Peacock waited on the fragrant wind
To bring her fruits of sweet delight from trees of richest
  wonders
And the strong piniond Eagle bore the fire of heaven in the
  night season˻·˼
Wood & subdud into Eternal[?] death the Demon Lay[?]   [*54*]
In [anguish for *del*] ˄rage against˄ the dark despai*r*, the   ˄˄*140˄˄
  howling Melancholy   ˄˄*with insertion 155˄˄

[*Page 95*]

For far & wide she stretchd thro all the worlds of Urizens
  journey
And was Adjoind to Beulah as the Polypus to the Rock˻·˼   ˄˄*140˄˄
Mo[*u*]rning the daughters of Beulah saw nor could they have
  sustaind
The horrid sight of death & torment But the Eternal Promise
They wrote on all their tombs & pillars & on every Urn   [*5*]
These words 'If ye will believe˻,˼ your B[*r*]other shall rise
  again'
In golden letters ornamented with sweet labours of Love˻,˼

Vala p. 95

Waiting with Patience [of *del*] ˄for˄ the fulfilment of the
　Promise Divine

And all the Songs of Beulah sounded comfortable notes⌞,⌟
Not suffring doubt to rise up from the Clouds of the Shadowy
　Female⌞.⌟　　　　　　　　　　　　　　　　　　　　　　[
Then myriads of the Dead burst thro the bottoms of their
　tombs⌞,⌟
Descending on the shadowy females clouds in Spectrous
　terror　　　　　　　　　　　　　　　　　　　　　　　　　1
Beyond the Limit of Translucence on the Lake of Udan
　Adan⌞.⌟
These they namd Satans & in the Aggregate they namd
　Them Satan⌞.⌟　　　　　　　　　　　　　　　　　　　　[
　　　　　　　　　　　[*Page 98*]

End of The Seventh Night

Page 95　l. 9 is in *Milton* pl. 34, l. 1 (p. 393).
　l. 11 is adapted from p. 85, l. 18.

1220

VALA

Night the Eighth

Then All in Great Eternity [which is called *del*] ∧Met in∧
the Council of God
[Met *del*] as One Man⌐,⌐ Even Jesus⌐,⌐ upon Gilead & Her-
mon⌐,⌐
Upon the Limit of Contraction to create the fallen Man⌐.⌐

∧The [Eternal *del*] ∧∧Fallen∧∧ Man stretchd like a Corse upon
the oozy Rock
∧Washd with the tides⌐,⌐ Pale overgrown with weeds   [5]
∧That movd with horrible dreams & hovring high over his
head
∧Two winged immortal shapes⌐,⌐ one standing at his feet
∧Toward the East⌐,⌐ one standing at his head toward the
west⌐,⌐
∧Their wings joind in the Zenith over head⌐.⌐ [but other
wings *del*]∧

∧[They had which clothd their bodies like a garment of soft
down⌐,⌐   [*10*]

Page 99 DESIGN: A great toe is sketched near that of the engraved figure, and
the engraved toe is circled. Pencil strokes appear to have been added to the legs,
feet, and beard of the engraved figure.
  ll. 1–2 are repeated on p. 8, ll. 8–9 and on p. 21, ll. 1–2, 7.
  l. 2: 'Met' is deleted in pencil.
  ll. 4–9 seem to cover five erased lines, the last four of which may read in part:

> He is the   [*2*]
> He is the Shepherd[?] of Albion he is all in all [*3*]
> In Eden in the Garden   Jerusalem [*4*]
> To create   Day [*5*]

The second and fifth are perhaps as in p. 8, ll. 10–11, and the third, fourth, and
fifth as in *Jerusalem* pl. 38, ll. 23–5, q.v. (p. 496).
  ll. 7–9 describe Blake's drawing of 'The Angels hovering over the Body of
Jesus in the Sepulchre' (listed in his *Descriptive Catalogue* [1809], ¶105–6 and re-
produced in A. Blunt, *The Art of William Blake* [1959], pl. 37b).
  ll. 10–15 are written sideways in the right margin and are clearly marked for
entry here.

ʌ[Silvery white∟,⌐ shining upon the dark blue sky in silence∟.⌐
ʌ[Their wings touchd the heavens∟;⌐ their fair feet hoverd
above
ʌ[The swelling tides∟;⌐ they bent over the dead corse like an
arch
ʌ[Pointed at top in highest heavens of precious stones &
pearl *all del*]
ʌSuch is a Vision of all Beulah hovring over the sleeper∟.⌐ʌ   [

The limit of Contraction now was fixd & Man began
To wake upon the Couch of Death∟;⌐ he sneezed Seven
times∟;⌐
A tear of blood dropped from either eye∟;⌐ again he reposd
In the saviours arm*s*, in the arms of tender mercy & loving
kindness∟.⌐

Then ʌ[first *del*]ʌ Los ʌsaid 'Iʌ behold the Divine vision thro
the broken Gates
Of [Enitharmons *del*] ʌthy poor brokenʌ heart∟,⌐ astonishd∟,⌐
melted into Compassion & Love'

And Enitharmon said ʌ'I seeʌ the Lamb of God upon Mount
Zion∟.⌐'
Wondring with love & [*word del*] ʌAweʌ they felt the divine
hand upon them

For nothing could restrain the dead in Beulah from descend-
ing
Into Ulros night∟;⌐ tempted by the Shadowy females sweet
Delusive cruelty they descend away from the Daughters of
Beulah
And Enter Urizens temple∟,⌐ Enitharmon pitying & her
heart
Gates broken dow*n*; they descend thro the Gate of Pity∟,⌐
The broken heart Gate of Enitharmon∟.⌐ [which joins to
Urizens temple

l. 17: Cf. 2 Kings 4:35: When Elisha restored a dead child to life, 'the child
sneezed seven times, and . . . opened his eyes'.
l. 20: At first 'behold' was 'beheld'.

Vala p. 100

[Which is the Synagogue of Satan *del*] She sighs them forth
   upon the wind   [*30*]
Of Golgonooza_L.₎ Los stood [at the Gate *del*] recieving them
ᴧ_L(₎For Los could enter into Enitharmons bosom & explore
ᴧIts intricate Labyrinths now the Obdurate heart was   ᴧ*26ᴧ
   broken_L)₎ᴧ   [*33*]

[*Page 100*]

From out the War of Urizen & Tharmas_L,₎ recieving them
ᴧLos stood &cᴧ
Into his hands. Then Enitharmon erected Looms in Lubans
   Gate
And calld the Looms Cathedron_L;₎ in these Looms She wove
   the Spectres
Bodies of Vegetation Singing lulling Cadences to drive away
Despair from the poor wondering spectres and Los loved
   them   [*5*]
With a parental love for the Divine hand was upon him
And upon Enitharmon & the Divine Countenance shone
In Golgonooza_L.₎ Looking down the Daughters of Beulah saw
With joy the bright Light & in it a Human form
And knew he was the Saviour_L,₎ Even Jesus_L,₎ & they wor-
   shipped_L.₎   [*10*]

[Astonishd Comforted Delighted the daughters of Beulah
   saw *del*]
Astonishd Comforted Delighted in notes of Rapturous Ex-
   tacy

ll. 32–3 are written over the engraving at the bottom and may be an addition.

Page 100 DESIGN: At the foot of the page a creature with a goat's hind quarters
and legs, stubby wings at the shoulders, and a bearded man's head walks stolidly
toward the left margin. Long vertical strokes in the margin may indicate flames.
Page 100 is very dirty, though the recto (p. 99) is not.
   After l. 1: The added words are written at the side of the page, with strokes
leading between the first two lines of poetry and may refer to p. 99, l. 31 or to
a lost passage.
   l. 4: This or a similar passage may be alluded to in the design which Blake
entitled 'Theotormon Woven' (V & A; *c.* 11·3 × 19·5 cm; reproduced in *Pencil
Drawings*, ed. G. Keynes [1927], pl. 23). It represents a man kneeling towards
the viewer with his head in his hands; on each side of him are four or more stand-
ing and floating figures, and behind him is a large domed building like St. Paul's.
The central kneeling figure appears in a drawing in the collection of Mr. David
J. Black.

All Beulah stood astonishd Looking down to Eternal Death⌊·⌋
They saw the Saviour beyond the Pit of death & destruction
For whether they lookd upward they saw the Divine Vision   [⸀
Or whether they lookd downward still they saw the Divine
    Vision
Surrounding them on all sides beyond sin & death & hell⌊·⌋

Enitharmon wove in tears singing Songs of Lamentation
And pitying comfort as she sighd forth on the wind the
    Spectres⌊,⌋
Also the Vegetated bodies which Enitharmon wove   [⸀
Opend within their hearts & in their loins & in their brain
To Beulah & the Dead in Ulro descended from the War
Or Urizen & Tharmas & from the Shadowy females clouds
And some were woven [One fold *del*] ⌃single⌃ & some two
    fold & some three fold
In Head or Heart or Reins according to the fittest order   ⌃
Of most merciful pity & compassion to the Spectrous dead⌊·⌋   [⸀

[*Page 101*]

When Urizen Saw the Lamb of God clothed in Luvahs
    robes⌊,⌋
Perplexd & terrifid he Stood tho well he knew that Orc
Was Luvah But he now beheld a new Luva*h*, Or one
Who assumd Luvahs form & stood before him opposite
But he saw Orc a Serpent form augmenting times on times   [⸀
In the fierce battle & he saw the Lamb of God & the World
    of Los
Surrounded by his dark machines for Orc augmented swift
In fury⌊,⌋ a Serpent wondrous among the Constellations of
    Urizen⌊·⌋
A crest of fire rose on his forehead red as the carbuncle⌊,⌋   ⌃
Beneath down to his eyelids scales of pearl⌊,⌋ then gold &
    silver   [
Immingled with the ruby overspread his Visage down

ll. 18–19 are on p. 103, ll. 32–3.
ll. 20–2, 24–6 are copied from p. 145, ll. 24–9.
After l. 26 are nine lines with a box drawn round them, indicating that they,
with the first three lines on p. 101 similarly boxed, are to be transferred to p. 101,
l. 29.

His furious neck_L;_J writ[*h*]ing contortive in dire budding
  pains
The scaly armour shot out. Stubborn down his back &
  bosom
The Emerald Onyx Sapphire jasper beryl amethyst
Strove in terrific emulation which should gain a place   [*15*]
[On the immortal fiend *del*] ∧Upon the mighty∧ Fiend_L,_J the
  fruit of the mysterious tree
Kneaded in Uveths kneading trough. Still Orc devourd the
  food
In raging hunger_L._J Still the pestilential food in gems & gold
Exuded round his awful limbs Stretching to serpent length   ∧∧*80∧∧
His human bulk While the dark shadowy female brooding
  over   [*20*]
Measurd his food morning & evening in cups & baskets
  of iron_L._J

With tears of sorrow incessant she labourd the food of Orc
  ∧Compelld by the iron hearted sisters_L,_J Daughters of
    Urizen_L,_J∧
Gathring the fruit of that mysterious tree_L,_J circling its root
She spread herself thro all the branches in the power of Orc_L._J   [*25*]
Thus Urizen in self deci[*e*]t his warlike preparations fabri-
  cated
And when all things were finished sudden wavd [his hurtling
  hand *del*] ∧among the Stars∧
[Among the Stars *del*] ∧His hurtling∧ hand gave the dire
  signal_L;_J thunderous Clarions blow
And all the hollow deep rebellowd with the wonderous   ∧∧*90∧∧
  war
  ∧'But Urizen his mighty rage' comes in here: to 'quench-
    less rage'_L._J∧

Page 101 l. 14: These are half the stones of the breastplate of Aaron (Exodus
28: 18-20, 39: 11-13), repeated as the 'covering' of the King of Tyre (Ezekiel
28: 13, lacking amethyst) and as the foundations of Jerusalem (Revelation 21: 19-20,
with sardonyx substituted for onyx).
  l. 20: 'brooding' was originally 'broods'.
  ll. 20-1 are adapted from *America* pl. 3, ll. 1, 3 (p. 137).
  ll. 24-5 are also on p. 103, ll. 24-5.
  After l. 29: The direction, inserted in a stanza-break, refers to ll. 30-41 trans-
ferred from pp. 100-1 above.

[*Page 100*]

[But in(*?*) *del*] But Urizen his mighty rage let loose in the mid
  deep∟·⌋
Sparkles of Dire affliction issud [from *del*] round his frozen
  limbs∟·⌋
Horrible hooks & nets he formd twisting the cords of iron
And brass & molten metals cast in hollow globes & bor'd
Tubes in petrific steel & rammd combustibles & wheels
And chains & pullies fabricated all round the heavens of
  Los∟,⌋
Communing with the Serpent of Orc in dark dissimulation
And with the Synagogue of Satan in dark Sanhedrem
To undermine the World of Los & tear bright Enitharmon

[*Page 101*]

To the four winds∟,⌋ hopeless of future. All futurity
Seems teeming with Endless destruction never to be ex-
  pelld[*?*]∟;⌋
Desperate remorse swallows the present in a quenchless
  rage∟·⌋
∧Terrified & astonishd Urizen beheld the battle take a form
∧Which he intended not∟,⌋ a Shadowy [male *del*] ∧∧her-
  maphrodite∧∧ black & opake∟;⌋
∧The Soldiers namd it Satan but he was yet unformd &
  vast∟·⌋
∧Hermaphroditic it at length became∟,⌋ hiding the Male
∧Within as in a Tabernacle Abominable Deadly∟·⌋
The battle howls∟,⌋ the terrors fird rage in the work of
  death∟;⌋
∧Enormous Works Los Contemplated inspird by the holy
  Spirit∟·⌋∧
Los builds the walls of Golgonooza against the stirring
  battle
That only thro the Gates of Death they can enter to Enithar-
  mon∟·⌋

Page 100 l. 37: For 'the synagogue of Satan (which say they are Jews, and are
not, but do lie)', see Revelation 3:9, 2:9.

Page 101 ll. 42–6 are written sideways in the left margin and are not marked for
insertion. The sense suggests that they should follow l. 41.

Raging they take the human visage & the human form⌞,⌟

∧Feeling[?] the hand of Los in Golgonooza & the force

∧Attractive of his hammers beating & the Silver looms

∧Of Enitharmon singing lulling cadences on the wind⌞;⌟

∧They humanize in the fierce battle where in direful pain∧   [55]

Troop by troop the beastial droves rend one another sound-
   ing loud

The instruments of sound & troop by troop in human forms
   they urge   [57]

[Page 102]

The dire confusion till the battle faints⌞;⌟ those that remain

Return in pangs & horrible convulsions to their beastial state

For the monsters of the Elements⌞,⌟ lions or Tygers or
   Wolves⌞,⌟

Sound loud the howling music⌞,⌟ ∧Inspird by Los & Enithar-
   mon∧ Sounding loud⌞;⌟ terrific men

They seem to one another laughing terrible among the   ∧∧*old∧∧

   banners   [6]100

And when the revolution of their day of battles over

Relapsing in dire torment[?] they return to forms of woe⌞,⌟

To moping visages returning inanimate tho furious⌞,⌟

No more erect tho strong drawn out in length they ravin

For senseless gratification & their visages thrust forth   [10]

Flatten above & beneath & stretch out into beastial length⌞.⌟

Weakend they stretch beyond their power in dire droves till
   war begins

Or Secret religion in their temples before secret shrines

And Urizen gave life & sense by his immortal power

ll. 52-5 are written sideways in the right margin and are clearly marked for
insertion here; l. 55 is written as a continuation of l. 54 and is separated from it by
a stroke.

   l. 54 is in a slightly different form in *Milton* pl. 4, l. 6 (p. 326).

Page 102 DESIGN: At the foot of the page is a lovely naked figure lying on his(?)
side, back to us, with his left knee bent down and his head on his arms as if in
exhaustion. (A similar design is on p. 120.)

   In the right margin is a faint offset of the cherub in the engraving for *Night
Thoughts* (1797) p. 23. No other portion of this engraving is visible. The impression
is at right angles to the page and the writing.

   l. 7: The ill-written 'torment' may be 'torments'.

To all his Engines of deceit that linked chains might run   [
Thro ranks of war spontaneous & that hooks & boring
  screws
Might act according to their forms by innate cruelty_L·_⌋
He formed also harsh instruments of sound
To grate the soul into destruction or to inflame with fury
The spirits of life_L,_⌋ to pervert all the faculties of sense   [
Into their own destruction if perhaps he might avert
His own despair even at the cost of every thing that
  breathes_L·_⌋

Thus in the temple of the Sun his books of iron & brass
And silver & gold he consecrated reading incessantly
To myriads of perturbed spirits_L;_⌋ thro the universe   [
They propagated the deadly words_L,_⌋ the shadowy Female
  absorbing
The enormous Sciences of Urizen_L,_⌋ ages after ages exploring
The fell destruction. And she said 'O Urizen Prince of Light_L,_⌋
What words of Dread pierce my faint Ear_L!_⌋ what fal[*l*]ing
  snows around
My feeble limbs infold my destind misery_L!_⌋   [
I alone dare the lash abide to sit beneath the blast
Unhurt & dare the inclement forehead of the King of Light_L,_⌋   [
From dark abysses of the times remote fated to be

[Page 103]

'The sorrower of Eternity in love with tears_L;_⌋ Submiss I rear
My Eyes to thy Pavilions_L;_⌋ hear my prayer for Luvahs
  Sake_L·_⌋
I see the murderer of my Luvah clothd in robes of blood_L,_⌋
He who assumd my Luvahs throne in times of Everlasting_L·_⌋
Where hast thou hid him whom I love_L?_⌋ in what remote
  Abyss
Resides that God of my delight_L?_⌋ O might my eyes behold
My Luvah_L,_⌋ then could I deliver all the sons of God
From Bondage of [the human form *del*] ⌃these terrors⌃ &
  with influences sweet_L,_⌋

l. 21: 'avert' was originally 'invert'.
l. 26: 'words' was originally 'world'.

As once in those eternal fields in brotherhood & Love
United⌐,⌐ we should live in bliss as those who sinned not⌐.⌐   [*10*]
The Eternal Man is seald by thee⌐,⌐ never to be deliverd⌐.⌐
We are all servants to thy will⌐.⌐ O King of Light⌐,⌐ relent
Thy furious power⌐;⌐ be our father & our loved King
But if my Luvah is no more⌐,⌐ If [that *word del*] thou hast   ^^*140^^
   smitten him

And laid him in the Sepulcher Or if [that *del*] thou wilt
   revenge   [*15*]
His murder on another⌐,⌐ Silent I bow with dread
But happiness can never to thee⌐,⌐ O King⌐,⌐ nor me
For he was source of every joy that this mysterious tree
Unfolds in Allegoric fruit. When shall the dead revive⌐?⌐
Can that which has existed cease or can love & life Expire⌐?⌐'   [*20*]

Urizen heard the Voice and saw the Shadow underneath
His woven darkness & in laws & deceitful religions
Beginning at the tree of Mystery circling its root   150
She spread herself thro all the branches in the power of
   Orc⌐,⌐
A shapeless & indefinite cloud in tears of sorrow incessant   [*25*]
Steeping the Direful Web of Religion⌐;⌐ swagging heavy it
   fell
From heaven to heaven thro all its meshes altering[?] the
   Vortexes⌐,⌐
Misplacing every Center⌐;⌐ hungry desire & lust began
Gathering the fruit of that Mysterious tree till Urizen
Sitting within his temple furious felt the num[*m*]ing Stupor⌐,⌐   [*30*]
Himself tangled in his own net in sorrow lust repentance⌐.⌐

Enitharmon wove in tears Singing Songs of Lamentations
And pitying comfort as she sighd forth on the wind the
   spectres
And wove them bodies calling them her belovd sons &
   daughters⌐,⌐

Page 103 l. 11 is on p. 51, l. 15.
   l. 17: Presumably the intention is: 'happiness can never [*come*] to thee'.
   ll. 24–5 are on p. 101, ll. 24–5.
   ll. 32–3 are on p. 100, ll. 18–19.

Vala p. 103

Employing the daughters in her looms & Los employd the
 Sons   [35]
In Golgonoozas Furnaces among the Anvils of time &
 space⌊,⌋
Thus forming a Vast family wondrous in beauty & love
And they appeard a Universal female form created
From those who were dead in Ulro from the Spectres of the
 dead   [39]

[*Page 104*]

And Enitharmon namd the Female Jerusa[*le*]m the holy⌊·⌋
Wondring she saw the Lamb of God within Jerusalems
 Veil⌊,⌋
The divine Vision seen within the inmost deep recess
Of fair Jerusalems bosom in a gently beaming fire[?]⌊·⌋

Then sang the Sons of Eden round the Lamb of God &
 said⌊:⌋   [5]
'Glory⌊!⌋ Glory⌊!⌋ Glory⌊!⌋ to the holy Lamb of God
Who now beginneth to put off the dark Satanic body⌊·⌋
Now we behold redemption⌊·⌋ Now we know that life Eternal
Depends alone upon the Universal hand & not in us
Is aught but death In Individual weakness sorrow & pain⌊·⌋   [10]
 ˄We behold with wonder

[*Page 113*]

[Daughter of Beulah describe *del*] ˄'We behold with wonder˄   [11]
Enitharmons Looms & Los's Forges

And the Spindles of Tirzah & Rahab and the Mills of Satan
 & Beelzeboul⌊·⌋
In Golgonooza Los's anvils stand & his Furnaces rage⌊;⌋
[The hard dentant hammers are lulld by the flute lula lula⌊,⌋

Page 104 DESIGN: At the foot of the page a nude woman on her knees seems to
be pushing an enormous wheel of eyes off the right margin. There are other vague
strokes by her.
 l. 6 is in *Milton* pl. 11, l. 28 (p. 342).
 After l. 10: The direction written in the margin refers to the top of p. 113, which
is inserted here.
Page 113 l. 12: 'Beelzeboul' is corrected from 'Baalzebole'.
 ll. 13–15 are in *Milton* pl. 23, ll. 51, 63–4 (pp. 368, 369).

[The bellowing furnaces blare by the long sounding Clarion *del*]   [*15*/

Ten thousand demons labour at the forges Creating Continually

The times & Spaces of Mortal Life⌊,⌋ the Sun⌊,⌋ the Moon⌊,⌋ the Stars⌊,⌋

In periods of Pulsative furor beating into [bars *del*] wedges & bars⌊,⌋

Then drawing into wires the terrific Passions & Affections

Of Spectrous dead. Thence to the Looms of Cathedron conveyd   [*20*]

The Daughters of Enitharmon weave the ovarium & the integument

In soft silk drawn from their own bowels in lascivious delight

With songs of sweetest cadence to the turning spindle & reel⌊,⌋

Lulling the weeping spectres of the dea*d*, Clothing their limbs

With gifts & gold of Eden. Astonishd⌊,⌋ stupified with delight⌊,⌋   [*25*]

The terrors put on their sweet clothing on the banks of ˙[the Moon *del*] Arnon⌊,⌋

Whence they plunge into the river of space for a period till

The dread Sleep of Ulro is past. But Satan [recieves(?) *del*]⌊,⌋ Og & Sihon

Build Mills of resistless wheels to unwind the soft threads & reveal

Naked of their clothing the poor spectres before the accusing heavens   [*30*]

While Rahab & Tirzah far different mantles prepare⌊,⌋ webs of torture⌊,⌋

Mantles of despair⌊,⌋ girdles of bitter compunction⌊,⌋ shoes of indolence⌊,⌋

Veils of ignorance covering from head to feet with a cold web⌊·⌋

ˏWe look down into Ulro⌊;⌋ we behold the Wonders of the Grave⌊·⌋ˏ

---

l. 15: 'blare' looks like 'blone', but the doubtless correct 'blare' is given in *Milton* pl. 23, l. 64.

l. 34 is inserted in a stanza-break.

Eastward of Golgonooza stands the Lake of Udan[?] Adam In

Entuthon Benithon╚,╝ [it is *del*] a Lake not of Waters but of Spaces

Perturbd black & deadly╚;╝ on [the *del*] ˄its˄ Islands & [the *del*] ˄its˄ Margins [of this Lake *del*]

The Mills of Satan & Beelzeboul stand round the roots of Urizens tree

For this Lake is formd from the tears & sighs & death sweat of the Victims

Of Urizens laws to irrigate the roots of the tree of Mystery╚·╝

They unweave the soft threads╚,╝ then they weave them anew in the forms

Of dark death & despair & none [is(?) *del*] ˄from˄ Eternity to Eternity could Escape

But [All *del*] ˄thou O˄ Universal Humanity╚,╝ who is One Man blessed for Ever╚,╝

Recievest the Integuments woven╚·╝ Rahab beholds the Lamb of God╚·╝

She smites with her knife of flint╚,╝ she destroys her own work

Times upon times thinking to destroy the Lamb blessed for Ever╚·╝

He puts off the clothing of blood╚,╝ he redeems the spectres from their bonds╚·╝

He awakes the sleepers in Ulro╚;╝ the daughters of Beulah praise him╚;╝

They anoint his feet with ointment╚,╝ they wipe them with the hair of their head╚·╝

[*Page 104*]

'We now behold the Ends of Beulah & we now behold Where Death Eternal is put off Eternally╚·╝

Assume the dark Satanic body in the Virgins womb╚,╝

O Lamb divin[*e*]╚!╝ it cannot thee annoy╚·╝ O pitying one╚,╝

Thy pity is from the foundation of the World & thy Redemption

l. 35: The 'd' of 'Udan' was originally an 'a'. 'Adam' is hastily written, and Blake may have intended what he usually wrote: 'Udan Adan'.

l. 49: Cf. Luke 7: 38 (and John 12: 3): Mary 'did wipe them [*Jesus' feet*] with the hairs of her head, and kissed his feet, and anointed them with the ointment'.

ˏBegunˏ Already in Eternity[.] Come then[,] O Lamb of
God[,]   [55]
Come Lord Jesus[,] come quickly[.]'

So sang they in Eternity looking down into Beulah[.]

The war roard round Jerusalems Gates[;] it took a hideous
    form
Seen in the aggregate[,] a Vast Hermaphroditic form
[Heaving Tw(?) *del*] Heavd like an Earthquake labring with
    convulsive groans   [60]
Intolerable[;] at length an awful wonder burst
From the Hermaphroditic bosom[.] Satan he was namd[,]
Son of Perdition[;] terrible his form[,] dishumanizd[,]
    monstrous[,]
A male without a female counterpart[,] a howling fiend
Fo[r]lorn of Eden & repugnant to the forms of Life   [65]
    ˏYet hiding the shadowy female Vala as in an ark &
    Curtains[,]ˏ
Abhorrd[,] accursed[,] ever dying an Eternal death[,]

Being multitudes of tyrant Men in union blasphemous
Against the divine imag*e*, Congregated Assemblies of wicked   195
    men[.]
    ˏˏ*Los said to Enitharmon 'Pitying I saw[.]'ˏˏ   [70]
Pitying the Lamb of God Descended thro Jerusalems gates
To put off Mystery time after time & as a Man
Is born on Earth so was he born of Fair Jerusalem
In mysterys woven mantle & in the Robes of Luvah[.]   [200 *del*]

He stood in fair Jerusalem to awake up into Eden   200
The fallen Man but first to [rend(?) *del*] [the Veil of Mystery
    del] ˏGiveˏ ˏhis vegetated bodyˏ   [76]
[And then Call Urizen & Luvah & Tharmas & Urthona
    del]
ˏTo be cut off & separated that the Spiritual body may be
    Reveald[.]ˏ   [78]

Page 104 l. 56: Cf. Revelation 22: 20: 'come Lord Jesus'.
    l. 63: For the 'man of sin . . . the son of perdition', see 2 Thessalonians 2: 3, and
John 17: 12. 'Son' at first was 'Sons' in Blake's text.

[*Page 105*]

The Lamb of God stood before Satan opposite ˄˄*201˄˄ ˄
In Entuthon Benithon in the shadows of torments & woe
Upon the heights of Amalek⌐;⌐ taking refuge in his arms
The Victims fled from punishment for all his words were
    peace⌐·⌐

Urizen calld together the Synagogue of Satan in dire
    Sanhedrim
To Judge the Lamb of God to Death as a murderer &
    robber⌐;⌐
As it is written⌐,⌐ he was numberd among the transgressors⌐·⌐

Cold⌐,⌐ dark⌐,⌐ opake⌐,⌐ the Assembly met twelvefold in
    Amalek⌐,⌐
Twelve rocky unshapd forms terrific⌐,⌐ forms of torture &   ˄
    woe⌐,⌐
Such seemd the Synagogue to distant view⌐;⌐ [around *del*]
    ˄amidst˄ them [stood *del*] ˄beamd˄
˄A False Feminine Counterpart ˄˄of˄˄ Lovely Delusive
    Beauty
˄Dividing & Uniting at will in the Cruelties of Holiness⌐,⌐
    ˄˄Vala drawn down into a Vegetated body now trium-
    phant⌐·⌐˄˄
˄The Synagogue of Satan Clothed her with Scarlet robes &
    Gems
˄And on her forehead was her name written in blood 'Mys-
    tery'⌐·⌐
˄When viewd remote She is One⌐,⌐ when viewd near she
    divides

Page 105   ll. 1–4 are written on the engraving space at the top of the page.
    ll. 1–10, 28–30 are copied from p. 145, ll. 1–13.
    l. 7: Cf. Isaiah 53: 12; Mark 15: 28; Luke 22: 37.
    ll. 11–19 are written sideways in the left margin and are clearly marked for
insertion after l. 10.
    ll. 14–15: Cf. Revelation 17: 4–5: 'the woman was arrayed in purple, and scarlet
colour, and decked with gold and precious stone, and pearls . . . And upon her
forehead was written, MYSTERY, BABYLON THE GREAT, THE MOTHER
OF HARLOTS, AND ABOMINATIONS OF THE EARTH'. In Night VIII
of *Night Thoughts*, design no. 345 (BMPR) represents a woman with 'MYSTERY'
on her forehead.

ˆTo multitude⌊,⌋ as it is in Eden⌊,⌋ so permitted because
ˆIt was the best possible in the State calld Satan to Save
ˆFrom Death Eternal & to put off Satan Eternally⌊.⌋ˆ

ˆThe Synagogue Created her from Fruit of Urizens tree [20]
ˆBy devilish arts abominable unlawful unutterable⌊,⌋
ˆPerpetually vegetating in detestable births
ˆOf Female forms⌊,⌋ beautiful thro poisons hidden in secret
ˆWhich give a tincture to false beauty [therefore they were
    calld *del*]⌊;⌋ ˆˆthen was hidden withinˆˆ
ˆ[The daughters & *del*]ˆ ˆˆThe bosom of Satan The false
    Female as in an ark & veil [25]
ˆˆWhich Christ must rend & her reveal⌊.⌋ Her Daughters are
    Calld
ˆˆTirzah⌊;⌋ She is [calld *del*] namd Rahab⌊;⌋ their various
    divisions are calld
ˆˆThe daughters &cˆˆ
The Daughters of ˆAmalek⌊,⌋ˆ Canaan & Moab⌊,⌋ binding
    on the [Stems *del*] Stones
Their victims & with knives tormenting them⌊,⌋ singing with
    tears
Over their victims⌊.⌋ Hear ye the song of the Females of
    Amalek⌊:⌋ [30]

'O thou poor human form⌊!⌋ O thou poor child of woe⌊!⌋
Why dost thou wander away from Tirzah⌊?⌋ why me com-
    pell to bind thee⌊?⌋
If thou dost go away from me I shall consume upon the
    rocks⌊.⌋
These fibres of thine eyes that used to wander in distant
    heavens
[I have *del*] ˆAwayˆ from me I have bound down with a hot
    iron⌊.⌋ [35]

ll. 20–7 are written sideways in the left margin beside ll. 11–19 and were evi-
dently meant to follow them, though they are not marked for entry.
    ll. 31–54 are adapted from *Jerusalem* pl. 67, ll. 44–50, 52–61, pl. 68, ll. 3–9
(pp. 565–6).
    ll. 32, 45, 49, 51: Mahlah, Noah, Milcah, Hoglah, and Tirzah, the daughters of
Zelophehad (Numbers 26: 33), reappear in *Milton* pl. 16, l. 11 (see p. 350 and
note).

These nostrils that Expanded with delight in morning skies ∧∧
I have bent downward with lead molten in my roaring
furnaces∟˩
My soul is seven furnaces∟,˩ incessant roars the bellows
Upon my terribly flaming heart∟,˩ the molten metal runs
In channels thro my fiery limbs∟˩ O love∟!˩ o pity∟!˩ O
pain∟!˩   [
O the pangs∟,˩ the bitter pangs of love forsaken∟!˩
Ephraim was a wilderness of joy where all my wild beasts
ran∟˩
The river Kanah wanderd by my sweet Manassehs side∟˩
[To see the boy spring into heaven sounding from my sight
del]
Go Noah fetch the girdle of strong brass∟;˩ [pre *del*] heat it
red hot∟;˩   [
Press it around the loins of this expanding cruelty∟˩
Shriek not so my only love∟˩   ∧′
Bind him down Sisters bind him down on Ebal∟,˩ mount of
Cursing∟˩
Malah come forth from Lebanon & Hoglah from Mount
Sinai∟˩
Come circumscribe this tongue of sweets & with a Screw of
iron   [
Fasten this Ear into the Rock∟˩ Milcah the task is thine∟˩
Weep not so sisters∟,˩ weep not so∟;˩ our life depends on
this
Or mercy & truth are fled away from Shechem & Mount
Gilead
Unless my beloved is bound upon the Stems of Vegetation∟˩'

Such are the songs of Tirzah∟,˩ such the loves of Amalek∟˩   ▮
The Lamb of God descended thro the twelve portions of
Luvah
Bearing his sorrows & rec[*iev*]ing all his cruel wounds∟˩   ▮

l. 48: Moses directed Reuben, Gad, Asher, Zebulon, Dan, and Naphtali to
'stand upon Mount Ebal to curse' the people (Deuteronomy 27:13). Ebal is
Hebrew for cursing.

l. 51 'task' looks like 'lash', but the doubtless correct reading of 'task' is given on
Jerusalem pl. 68, l. 6.

[*Page 106*]

Thus was the Lamb of God condemnd to Death_ʟ·ﾞ   ^^*241^^
They naild him upon the tree of Mystery weeping over him
And then mocking & then worshipping_ʟ,ﾞ calling him Lord
& King_ʟ·ﾞ
Sometimes as twelve daughters lovely & sometimes as five
They stood in beaming beauty & sometimes as one_ʟ,ﾞ even
Rahab   [5]
Who is Mystery_ʟ,ﾞ Babylon the Great_ʟ,ﾞ the Mother of
Harlots_ʟ·ﾞ
^[She *del*] ^^Jerusalem^^ Saw the Body dead upon the Cross_ʟ·ﾞ
She fled away
^Saying 'Is this Eternal Death_ʟ?ﾞ Where shall I hide from
Death_ʟ?ﾞ
^Pity me Los_ʟ!ﾞ pity me Urizen & [build *del*] let us build
^A Sepulcher & worship Death in fear while yet we live_ʟ,ﾞ   [10]
^Death! God of All_ʟ!ﾞ from whom we rise_ʟ,ﾞ to whom we all
return
^And Let all Nations [in *del*] ^^of^^ the Earth worship at the
Sepulcher
^With Gifts & Spices_ʟ,ﾞ with lamps rich embossd_ʟ,ﾞ jewels
& gold_ʟ·ﾞ'^

^Los took the Body from the Cross_ʟ,ﾞ Jerusalem weeping
over_ʟ·ﾞ
^They bore it to the Sepulcher which Los had hewn in the
rock   [15]
^Of Eternity for himself_ʟ;ﾞ he hewd it despairing of Life
Eternal^
      ^^'But when Rahab' &c turn back 3 leaves^^

Page 106   DESIGN: At the foot of the page a naked man reclines with his left hand
in the middle of his back. Behind his head a nude woman walks toward him with
her belly thrust forward. Her left hand is between her buttocks, and a *very* vague
figure standing behind her seems to have his hand between her thighs also.
      ll. 1–6, 17–19 are from p. 145, ll. 13–17, 19, 30–2.
      l. 6: The phrase is repeated in *Jerusalem* pl. 75, l. 19 and adapted in pl. 93, l. 25;
see *Vala* p. 105, ll. 14–15 note.
      ll. 7–16: The first line of this addition is inserted in a stanza break, and the
next ten lines, written sideways in the right margin, are clearly marked for
insertion here. The direction refers to the bottom half of p. 113, which is inserted
here.
      ll. 14–16 are adapted from p. 110, ll. 38–40.

[*Page 113*]

ᴧ[And *del*] ᴧᴧBut ᴧᴧ when Rahab had cut off the Mantle of
Luvah from
ᴧThe Lamb of God it rolld apart revealing to all in heaven
ᴧAnd all on Earth the Temple & the Synagogue of Satan &
Mystery∟‚⌋
ᴧEven Rahab in all her turpitude∟·⌋ Rahab divided herself∟;⌋   [·
ᴧShe stood before Los in her Pride [above *del*] among the
Furnaces
ᴧDividing & uniting in Delusive feminine pomp∟‚⌋ question-
ing him∟·⌋ᴧ
ᴧᴧHe answerd her with tenderness & love not un-
inspird∟·⌋ᴧᴧ
Los sat upon his anvil stock∟;⌋ they sat beside the forge∟·⌋

Los wipd the sweat from his red brow & thus began   [
ᴧTo the delusive female forms shining among his
furnaces∟:⌋ᴧ
'I am that shadowy Prophet who six thou[*sa*]nd years ago
Fell from my station in the Eternal bosom∟·⌋ I divided
To multitude & my multitudes are children of Care &
Labour∟·⌋
O Rahab I behold thee∟·⌋ I was once like thee∟‚⌋ a Son   [
Of Pride and I also have piercd the Lamb of God in pride &
wrath∟·⌋
Hear me repeat my Generations that thou mayst also
repent∟·⌋
[*Page 115*]
'And these [were *del*] ᴧareᴧ the Sons of Los & Enitharmon∟:⌋   [
Rintrah Palamabron
Theotormon Bromion Antamon Ananton Ozoth Ohana
Sotha Mydon Ellayol Natho Gon Harhath Satan
Har ᴧOchim Ijimᴧ Adam Reuben Simeon Levi Judah Dan
Naphtali
Gad Asher Issachar Zebulun Joseph Benjamin David
Solomon

Page 113 ll. 17–23 are written over an erasure of six lines.
   ll. 27–8 are in *Milton* pl. 20, ll. 15–16 (p. 361).
Page 115 ll. 5–6 were apparently intended as two lines. The metre would suggest

ˏPaul Constantine Charlemaine Luther Milton∟·⌐ˏ
These [were their *del*] ˏareˏ ˏourˏ daughters∟:⌐ Ocalythron
Elynittria Oothoon Leutha
Elythiria Enanto Manathu Vorcyon Ethinthus Moab Midian
Adah Zillah Caina Naamah Tamar Rahab Tirzah Mary
And myriads more of Sons & daughters to whom [their *del*]
ˏourˏ love increasd   [*10*]
To each according [to *del*] to the multiplication of their
multitudes
But Satan accusd Palamabron before [Los *del*] ˏhis breth-
ren∟,⌐ˏ also he maddend
The horses of *P*alamabrons harrow∟,⌐ wherefor[*e*] Rintrah &
Palamabron
Cut him off from Golgonooza. But Enitharmon in tears
Wept over him∟,⌐ Created him a Space closd with a tender
moon   [*15*]
And he rolld down beneath the fires of Orc∟,⌐ a Globe im-
mense
Crusted with snow in a dim voi*d*; here by the Arts of Urizen
He tempted many of the Sons & Daughters of Los to flee
Away from [Los *del*] ˏMe∟;⌐ˏ first Reuben fled∟,⌐ then Simeon
then Levi then Judah
Then Dan then Naphtali then Gad then Asher then Issachar   [*20*]
Then Zebulun then Joseph then Benjamin∟,⌐ twelve sons of
Los
And this is the manner in which Satan became the Temp-
ter∟·⌐

'There is a State namd Satan∟;⌐ learn distinct to know O
[Mortals *del*] ˏRahabˏ
The Difference between States & Individuals of those States∟·⌐
The State namd Satan never can be redeemd in all Eternity   [*25*]
But when Luvah in Orc became a Serpent he des[*c*]ended
into

that the second should begin with 'David Solomon'. The catalogue of names from
Dan to Zebulun appears in *Jerusalem* pl. 74, l. 50, and 'Paul Constantine Charle-
maine Luther' recur in *Milton* pl. 23, l. 32, pl. 37, ll. 41-2, and *Jerusalem* pl. 75,
ll. 15-16 (pp. 583, 368, 400, 584).
   l. 8: 'Elythiria' was originally 'Elythyria'.
   l. 24 is in *Milton* pl. e, l. 22 (p. 389).

That State calld Satan. Enitharmon breathd forth on the
  Winds
Of Golgonooza her well beloved knowing he was Orc's
  human remains.
She tenderly lovd him above all his brethren; he grew up
In mothers tenderness. The Enormous worlds rolling in
  Urizens power   [
Must have given Satan by these mild arts Dominion over all,
Wherefore [Rintrah & *del*] Palamabron being accusd by
  Satan to Los
Calld down a Great Solemn assembly. Rintrah in fury &
  fire
Defended Palamabron & rage filld the Universal Tent.
      ^Because Palamabron was good naturd Satan supposd
  he feard him^   [
And Satan not having the Science of Wrath but only of Pity
Was soon condemnd & wrath was left to wrath & Pity to
  Pity,
Rintrah & Palamabron Cut sheer off from Golgonooza,
Enitharmons Moony space & in it Satan & his companions.
They rolld down a dim world Crusted with Snow deadly &
  dark.   [
Jerusalem pitying them wove them mantles of life & death
Times after times And those in Eden sent Lucifer for their
  Guard.
Lucifer refusd to die for Satan & in pride he forsook his
  charge.
Then they Sent Molech. Molech was impatient. They
  Sent
Molech impatient. They Sent Elohim who created Adam   [
To die for Satan. Adam refusd but was compelld to die
By Satans arts. Then the Eternals Sent Shaddai.

ll. 33–4 are in *Milton* pl. 6, l. 46 (p. 331).
ll. 36–7 are in a slightly different form in *Milton* pl. 7, ll. 46–7 (p. 334).
ll. 42–4, 47–9 are in a somewhat different form in *Milton* pl. 11, ll. 17–19,
22–4 (pp. 341–2).
ll. 41–51 overlap the engraving at the bottom and may be an addition.
ll. 44–5: 'They Sent Molech impatient' appears to be a redundancy of tran-
scription.
ll. 45–6: The design which Blake called 'Elohim creating Adam' (1795) is
reproduced in M. Butlin's Tate catalogue (*William Blake* [1971], 35).

Vala p. 106

Shaddai was angry$_{L \cdot J}$ Pachad descended$_{L,J}$ Pachad was
terrified
And then they Sent Jehovah who leprous stretchd his hand
to Eternity$_{L \cdot J}$
Then Jesus Came & Died willing beneath Tirzah & Rahab$_{L \cdot J}$ [50]
$_{\wedge}$Thou art that Rahab$_{L \cdot J}$ Lo the Tomb$_{L}!_{J}$ what can we pur-
pose more$_{L}?_{J \wedge}$ [51]

[Page 116]

'Lo Enitharmon$_{L,J}$ terrible & beautiful in Eternal youth$_{L}!_{J}$
Bow down before her$_{L,J}$ you her children & set Jerusalem
free$_{L \cdot J}$'

Rahab burning with pride & revenge departed from Los$_{L \cdot J}$
$_{\wedge}$Los dropd a tear at her departure but he wipd it away
in hope$_{L \cdot J \wedge}$
She went to Urizen in pride$_{L};_{J}$ the Prince of Light beheld   [5]
Reveald before the face of heaven his secret holiness   [6]
    'Darkness & sorrow' &^{c} turn over leaf

[Page 106]

Darkness & sorrow coverd all flesh$_{L \cdot J}$ Eternity was darkend$_{L \cdot J}$
Urizen sitting in his web of dec[i]etful Religion [was dar-
kend(?) del]
[He del] felt the female death$_{L,J}$ a dull & numming stupor   250
such as neer   [35]
Before assaulted the bright human form$_{L};_{J}$ he felt his pores
Drink in the deadly dull delusion$_{L};_{J}$ horrors of Eternal death
Shot thro him$_{L \cdot J}$ Urizen sat Stonied upon his rock$_{L \cdot J}$
Forgetful of his own Laws$_{L,J}$ pitying he began to Embrace
The Shadowy Female$_{L};_{J}$ since life cannot be quenchd Life
exuded$_{L};_{J}$ [40]

Page 116   DESIGN: The page is almost entirely taken up by a naked Christ-like
man whose eyes, nose, and mouth have been emphasized in ink. He is walking to
the right with his arms outstretched, his palms facing out in a traffic-stopping
gesture in the upper corners of the page, pushing back clouds which are roughly
sketched in surrounding him. He is looking slightly down to the left, and erased
strokes represented his left leg farther back and his right arm somewhat lower.
(The design, like that on p. 58, q.v., is evidently for Young's *Night Thoughts* and
not for *Vala*.)
After l. 6: The direction refers to p. 106, l. 33.

His eyes [his *del*] ∧[then *del*]∧ shot outwards⌊,⌋ then his
  breathing nostrils drawn forth⌊,⌋
Scales coverd over a cold forehead & a neck outstretchd
Into the deep to seize the shadow⌊;⌋ scales his neck & bosom
Coverd & scales his hands & feet⌊;⌋ upon his belly falling

Outstretchd [over *del*] ∧thro∧ the immense⌊,⌋ his mouth wide
  opening⌊,⌋ tongueless⌊,⌋
His teeth a triple row⌊,⌋ he strove to sieze the shadow in vain
And his immense tail lashd the Abyss⌊;⌋ his human form a
  Stone⌊,⌋
A form of Senseless Stone remain in terrors on the rock
Abominable to the eyes of mortals who explore his books⌊.⌋
His wisdom still remaind & all his memory stord with woe

And still his stony form remaind in the Abyss immense
∧Like the pale visage in its sheet of lead that cannot follow⌊.⌋∧
Incessant stern disdain his scaly form gnaws inwardly
With deep repentance for the loss of that fair form of Man⌊.⌋
With Envy he saw Los⌊,⌋ with Envy Tharmas & [Urthona
  del] ∧the Spectre⌊,⌋∧
With Envy & in vain he swam around his stony form⌊.⌋

No longer now Erect the King of Light outstretchd in fury
Lashes his tail in the wild deep⌊;⌋ his Eyelids like the Sun
Arising in his pride enlighten all the Grizly deeps⌊,⌋
His scales transparent give forth light like windows of the
  morning⌊,⌋
His neck flames with wrath & majesty⌊,⌋ he lashes the Abyss⌊,⌋
Beating the Desarts & the rocks⌊;⌋ the desarts feel his power⌊;⌋
They shake their slumbers off. They wave in awful fear
Calling the Lion & the Tyger the horse & the wild Stag

[*Page 107*]

The Elephant the wolf the Bear the Lamia the Satyr⌊.⌋
His Eyelids give their light around⌊;⌋ his folding tail aspires

Page 106 l. 47: 'form' is written 'forn'.
l. 52 may be an addition.
l. 58 'wild' was originally 'wide'.

Page 107: l. 1: 'Satyr' was originally 'Satur'.

Among the stars⌞;⌟ the Earth & all the Abysses feel his
    fury
When as the snow covers the mountain⌞,⌟ oft petrific hard-
    ness [covers *del*]
Covers the deeps⌞,⌟ at his vast fury moving in his rock   [5]
Hardens the Lion & the Bear⌞;⌟ trembling in the Solid
    mountain
They view the light & wonder⌞;⌟ crying out in terrible exis-
    tence
Up bound the wild stag & the horse⌞;⌟ behold the King of
    Pride⌞!⌟

Oft doth his Eyes emerge from the Abyss into the realms
Of his Eternal day & memory strives to augment his ruthful-   ᴧᴧ*10ᴧᴧ
    ness⌞.⌟   [*10*]
Then weeping he descends in wrath⌞,⌟ drawing all things in
    his fury
Into obedience to his will & now he finds in vain
That not of his own power he bore the human form erect
Nor of his own will gave his Laws in times of Everlasting
For now fierce Orc in wrath & fury rises into the heavens[?]⌞,⌟   [*15*]
[In forms of priesthood in the dark delusions of repentance(?)
    del]
A King of wrath & fury⌞,⌟ a dark enraged horror
And Urizen ¹repentant ²forgets his wisdom in the abyss
In forms of priesthood⌞,⌟ in the dark delusions of repentance
Repining in his heart & spirit that Orc reignd over all
And that his wisdom servd but to augment the indefinite   ᴧᴧ*20ᴧᴧ
    lust⌞.⌟   [*20*]

Then Tharmas & Urthona felt the stony stupor rise
Into their limbs⌞.⌟ Urthona shot forth a Vast Fibrous form⌞,⌟   300
Tharmas like a pillar of sand rolld round by the whirl-
    wind⌞,⌟

l. 3: 'his' is malformed and could be 'hot'.
l. 5: 'moving' looks rather more like 'moning'.
l. 8: At first 'behold' was 'beholds'.
l. 9: 'Eyes' presumably should be 'Eye'.
l. 18: The order of 'forgets repentant' was reversed with the numbers.

An animated Pillar rolling round & round in incessant rage⌊·⌋   [

Los felt the stony stupor & his head rolld down beneath
Into the Abysses of his bosom⌊;⌋ the vessels of his blood
Dart forth upon the wind in pipes writhing about in the
    Abyss
And Enitharmon pale & cold in milky juices flowd
Into a form of Vegetation⌊,⌋ living⌊,⌋ having a voice⌊,⌋   [
Moving on rootlike fibres⌊,⌋ trembling in fear upon the
    Earth

And Tharmas gave his Power to Los⌊,⌋ Urthona gave his
    strength
Into the youthful prophet for the Love of Enitharmon   ∧
And of the nameless Shadowy female in the nether deep
And for the dread of the dark terrors of Orc & Urizen⌊·⌋   ▌

Thus in a living Death the nameless shadow all things
    bound⌊,⌋
∧All mortal things made permanent that they may be put off
∧Time after time by the Divine Lamb who died for all
∧And all in him die*d*, & he put off all mortality⌊·⌋∧   [

[Page 108]

Tharmas [above *del*] ∧on∧ high rode furious thro the afflicted
    worlds
Pursuing the Vain Shadow of Hope⌊,⌋ fleeing from identity
In abstract false Expanses that he may not hear the Voice
Of Ahania wailing on the winds⌊;⌋ in vain he flies for still   ∧
The voice incessant calls on all the children of Men   ▌
    ∧For she spoke of all in heaven & all upon the Earth
    ∧Saw not as yet the Divine vision⌊;⌋ her Eyes are
        Toward Urizen∧

ll. 37–9: l. 37 is written at the bottom of the page; l. 38 is a continuation of l. 37,
written up the side of the page with nothing to indicate where it begins except the
unnecessary capital; and l. 39 is written below l. 38.

Page 108   DESIGN: At the foot of the page is a nude woman lying on her belly
with her right shoulder raised, her right hand behind her head, her mouth open
as if in agony, resting on her left elbow near what looks like a bolster. Behind her
buttock a child seems to be stringing a bow (cf. the figures on pp. 4, 19, 40).
    l. 5: 'on' looks rather more like 'in'.
    ll. 6–7 are written as one long line, with a stroke to divide them.

And thus Ahania cries aloud to the Caverns of the Grave⌐:⌐

'Will you keep a flock of wolves & lead them⌐?⌐ will you
    take the wintry blast
For a covering to your limbs or the summer pestilence for
    a tent To abide in⌐?⌐   [*10*]
Will you erect a lasting habitation in the mouldering Church
    yard
Or a pillar & palace of Eternity in the jaws of the hungry
    grave⌐?⌐
Will you seek pleasure from the festering wound or marry for
    a Wife
The ancient Leprosy⌐?⌐ that the King & Priest may still
    feast on your decay
And the grave mock & laugh at the plowd field saying   [*15*]
"I am the nourisher⌐,⌐ thou the destroyer⌐;⌐ in my bosom is
    milk & wine   ^^*330^^
And a fountain from my breasts⌐;⌐ to me come all multi-
    tudes⌐;⌐
To my breath they obey⌐;⌐ they worship me⌐.⌐ I am a god-
    dess & queen⌐.⌐"
But listen to Ahania⌐,⌐ O ye sons of the Murderd one⌐;⌐
Listen to her whose memory beholds your ancient days⌐;⌐   [*20*]
Listen to her whose eyes behold the dark body of corruptible
    death
Looking for Urizen in vai*n*; in vain I seek for morning⌐.⌐
The Eternal Man sleeps in the Earth nor feels the vigrous sun
Nor silent moon nor all the hosts of heaven move in his
    body⌐.⌐
His fiery halls are dark & round his limbs the Serpent Orc   [*25*]
Fold without fold encompasses him And his corrupting
    members
Vomit out the Scaly monsters of the restless deep⌐.⌐   ^^*340^^
They come up in the rivers & annoy the nether parts
Of Man who lays upon the Shores leaning[?] his faded head
Upon the Oozy rock inwrapped with the weeds of death⌐.⌐   [*30*]
His eyes sink hollow in his head⌐,⌐ his flesh coverd with slime

ll. 11–12 are adapted from *Visions* pl. 8–9, ll. 152–3 (p. 112).
ll. 16–17: A design appropriate to these lines is on p. 86.

And shrunk up to the bones_L ;_J alas that Man should come to
    this_L!_J
His strong bones beat with snows & hid within the caves of
    night_{L,J}
Marrowless_{L,J} bloodless_{L,J} falling into dust_{L,J} driven by the
    winds_{L.J}
O how the horrors of Eternal Death take hold on Man_L!_J
His faint groans shake the caves & issue thro the desolate
    rocks

[*Page 109*]

'And the Strong Eagle_{L,J} now with numming cold blighted of
    feathers_{L,J}
Once like the pride of the sun_{L,J} now flagging in cold night_{L,J}
Hovers with blasted wings aloft watching with Eager Eye
Till Man shall leave a corruptible body_L ;_J he famishd hears
    him groan
And now he fixes his strong talons in the pointed rock
And now he beats the heavy air with his enormous wings_{L.J}
Beside him lies the Lion dead & in his belly worms
Feast on his death till universal death devours all
And the pale horse seeks for the pool to lie him down & die
But finds the pools filled with serpents devouring one
    another_{L.J}
He droops his head & trembling stands & his bright eyes
    decay_{L.J}
These are the Visions of My Eyes_{L,J} the Visions of Ahania_{L.J}'

Thus cries Ahania_{L.J} Enion replies from the Caverns of the
    Grave_{L:J}

'Fear not_{L,J} O poor forsaken one_L!_J O land of briars &
    thorns
Where once the Olive flourishd & the Cedar spread his
    wings_L!_J
Once I waild desolate like thee_L ;_J my fallow fields in fear
Cried to the Churchyards & the Earthworm came in dismal
    state_{L.J}
I found him in my bosom & I said "the time of Love
Appears upon the rocks & hills in silent shades" but soon

A voice came in the night⌊,⌋ a midnight cry upon the moun-
    tains⌊:⌋
"Awake⌊!⌋ the bridegroom cometh⌊!⌋" I awoke to sleep no
    more   [*20*]
But an Eternal Consummation is dark Enion⌊,⌋
The watry Grave. O thou Corn field⌊!⌋ O thou Vegetater
    happy⌊!⌋
More happy is the dark consumer⌊;⌋ hope drowns all my
    torment
For I am now surrounded by a shadowy vortex drawing
The Spectre quite away from Enion that I die a death
Of bitter hope altho I consume in these raging waters⌊.⌋   [*25*]
The furrowd field replies to the grave⌊.⌋ I hear her reply to
    me⌊:⌋
"Behold the time approaches fast that thou shalt be as
    a thing
Forgotten⌊;⌋ when one speaks of thee he will not be believd⌊.⌋
When the man gently fades away in his immortality⌊,⌋
When the mortal disappears in improved knowledge⌊,⌋ cast   [*30*]
    away
The former things⌊,⌋ so shall the Mortal gently fade away
And so become invisible to those who still remain⌊.⌋
Listen⌊!⌋ I will tell thee what is done in the caverns of the
    grave⌊:⌋
                    [*Page 110*]   382
ᴧ' "The Lamb of God has rent the Veil of Mystery⌊,⌋ soon to   [*35*]
    return
ᴧIn Clouds & Fires around the rock & the Mysterious tree⌊.⌋ᴧ
As the Seed waits Eagerly watching for its flower & fruit⌊,⌋
Anxious its little soul looks out into the clear expanse
To see if hungry winds are abroad with their invisible army⌊,⌋
So Man looks out in tree & herb & fish & bird & beast
Collecting up the scatterd portions of his immortal body   [*5*]

Page 109: l. 21: Cf. the parable of the wise and foolish virgins: 'Behold, the bride-
groom cometh' (Matthew 25 : 6).
Page 110 DESIGN: At the foot of the page an almost prostrate nude woman seems
to be diving toward the bottom right corner, with her legs apart as if she were
kicking. There are a few other vague strokes. The sketch covers the erased 'End of
the Eighth Night'.

Into the Elemental forms of every thing that grows⌞·⌟
He tries the sullen north wind riding on its angry furrows⌞,⌟
The sultry South when the sun rises & the angry east   [
When the sun sets⌞;⌟ when the clods harden & the cattle
   stand
Drooping & the birds hide in their silent nest*s*, he stores his
   thoughts
As in a store house in his memory⌞;⌟ he regulates the forms
Of all beneath & all above & in the gentle West
Reposes where the Suns heat dwells⌞;⌟ he rises to the Sun   [
And to the Planets of the Night & to the stars that gild
The Zodiac & the stars that sullen stand to north & south⌞·⌟
He touches the remotest pole & in the Center weeps
That Man should labour & sorrow & learn & forget &
   return
To the dark valley whence he came to begin his labours
   anew⌞·⌟   [
In pain he sighs⌞,⌟ in pain he labours in his universe⌞,⌟
Screaming in birds over the deep & howling in the Wolf
Over the slain & moaning in the cattle & in the winds
And weeping over Orc & Urizen in clouds & [dismal *del*]
   ʌʌ*flamingʌʌ fires
And in the cries of birth & in the groans of death his voice   [
Is heard throghuout the Universe⌞;⌟ whereever a grass
   grows
Or a leaf buds The Eternal Man is seen⌞,⌟ is heard⌞,⌟ is felt
And all his Sorrows till he reassumes his ancient bliss⌞·⌟ " '
   ʌʌSuch are the words of Ahania & Enion. Los hears &
   weepsʌʌ
ʌ[But Rahab (built *del*) ʌʌhewdʌʌ a Sepulcher in the Rock of
   Eternity   [
ʌ[And⌞,⌟ placing in the Sepulcher the body which she had
   taken
ʌ[From the divine Lamb⌞,⌟ wept over the Sepulcher weaving
ʌ[Her web of Religion around the Sepulcher times after
   times beside Jerusalems Gate
ʌ[But as she wove behold the bottom of the Sepulcher
ʌ[Rent & a door was opend thro the bottom of the Sepulcher   [

ll. 29–31 are written over '[The End of the Eighth Night *del*]'.

ʌ[Into Eternity And as she wove she heard a Voice behind
  her calling herʟ·ᒲ
ʌ[She turnd & saw the Divine Vision & her *all del*]

ʌAnd Los & Enitharmon took the Body of the Lamb
ʌDown from the Cross & placd it in a Sepulcher which Los
  had hewn
ʌFor himself in the Rock of Eternity trembling & in [fear
  del] despairʟ·ᒲ   [*40*]
ʌJerusalem wept over the Sepulcher two thousand   ʌ412ʌ
  Yearsʟ·ᒲʌ   [*41*]

            ʌ[End of the Eighth Night *del*]ʌ

                    [*Page 111*]
Rahab triumphs over allʟ;ᒲ she took Jerusalem
Captiveʟ,ᒲ A Willing Captiveʟ,ᒲ by delusive arts impelld
To worship Urizens Dragon formʟ,ᒲ to offer her own Children
Upon the bloody Altarʟ·ᒲ John Saw these things Reveald in
  Heaven
On Patmos Isle & heard the Souls cry out to be deliverdʟ·ᒲ   [*5*]
He saw the Harlot of the Kings of Earth & saw her Cup
Of fornicationʟ,ᒲ food of Orc & Satan pressd from the fruit of
  Mystery
But when she saw the form of Ahania weeping on the Void
And heard Enions voice sound from the caverns of the Grave
No more spirit remain in herʟ·ᒲ She secretly left the Syna-
  gogue of Satanʟ,ᒲ   [*10*]
She commund with Orc in secretʟ·ᒲ She hid him with the flax
That Enitharmon had numberd away from the Heavensʟ,ᒲ
She gatherd it together to consume her Harlot Robes

ll. 38–40 are adapted on p. 106, ll. 14–16.

Page 111: All but ll. 22–4 are written over the same thing in pencil, with the
following exceptions: l. 12 reads: 'That Enion had numberd away from Heaven';
in l. 13, after 'consume' the two words were deleted and 'her harlot robes' written
after them. Since ll. 22–4 do not ink over pencil lines, they are in effect an addition.

Page 111 does not fit very well after p. 110—or anywhere else.
  ll. 4–7: For John's vision of Babylon and her 'cup . . . full of . . . fornication',
see Revelation 17:4–5.
  l. 5: The allusion seems to be to Revelation 6:9–10.
  l. 11: Rahab 'hid them [*the two Jewish spies*] with the stalks of flax' (Joshua 2:6).

In bitterest Contrition_L,_⌐ sometimes Self condemning re-
  pentant
And Sometimes kissing her Robes & Jewels & weeping
  over them_L,_⌐   [*1*
Sometimes returning to the Synagogue of Satan in Pride
And Sometimes weeping before Orc in humility & trem-
  bling_L._⌐
The Synagogue of Satan therefore uniting against Mystery_L,_⌐
Satan divided against Satan_L,_⌐ resolvd in open Sanhedrim
To burn Mystery with fire & form another from her ashes   [*2*
For God put it into their heart to fulfill all his will_L._⌐

˄The Ashes of Mystery began to animate_L;_⌐ they calld it
  Deism
˄And Natural Religion_L;_⌐ as of old_L,_⌐ so now anew began
˄Babylon again in Infancy Calld Natural Religion_L._⌐˄   [*2*

Page 112 DESIGN: See the note to the direction after p. 55, l. 50, which the design
on p. 112 apparently illustrates.

Page 113 is written in a cramped hand in two sections divided by a stroke across
the page, the top thirty-nine lines transferred to p. 104 and the bottom sixteen
lines transferred to pl. 106.

Page 114 has only the *Night Thoughts* engraving.

Page 115: The text was transferred to p. 106.

Page 116: The text was transferred to p. 106.

VALA

Night the Ninth
Being
The Last Judgment

ᴧAnd Los & Enitharmon builded Jerusalem weeping
ᴧOver the Sepulcher & over the Crucified body
ᴧWhich to their Phantom Eyes appeard still in the Sepulcher
ᴧBut Jesus stood beside them in the Spirit Separating
ᴧTheir Spirit from their body. Terrified at Non Existence⌐,⌐   [*5*]
ᴧFor such they deemd the death of the body⌐,⌐ Los his
   vegetable hands
ᴧOutstretchd⌐;⌐ his right hand branching out in fibrous
   Strength
ᴧSiezd the Su*n*; His left hand like dark roots coverd the
   Moon
ᴧAnd tore them down cracking the heavens across from im-
   mense to immense⌐.⌐
ᴧThen fell the fires of Eternity with loud & shrill   [*10*]
ᴧSound of Loud Trumpet thundering along from heaven to
   heaven
ᴧA mighty sound articulate 'Awake ye dead & come
ᴧTo Judgment from the four winds⌐!⌐ Awake & come
   away⌐!⌐'ᴧ
Folding like scrolls of the Enormous volume of Heaven &
   Earth
With thunderous noise & dreadful shakings racking to &
   fro⌐,⌐   [*15*]
The heavens are shaken & the Earth removed from its
   place⌐,⌐

Page 117: ll. 1–13 are written over about eleven lines of erasure which formed
two separate stanzas; they probably followed from p. 110, l. 28. The present lines
in ink are over the same thing in pencil.

    ll. 12–13 are repeated on p. 118, ll. 17–18. In *Pilgrim's Progress* (ed. Thomas Scott
[1801], 60), the Dreamer in The House of the Interpreter heard 'a voice saying,
"Arise, ye dead, and come to judgment;" and with that the rocks rent, the graves
opened, and the dead that were therein came forth . . .'.

The foundations of the Eternal hills discoverd_L·_
The thrones of Kings are shaken_L_;_ they have lost their
   robes & crowns_L·_
ᴧThe poor Smite their op[p]ressors_L_,_ they awake up to the
   harvest_L_;_ᴧ
The naked warriors rush together down to the sea shore   [
ᴧTrembling before the multitudes of slaves now set at
   liberty_L_;_ᴧ
They are become like wintry flocks_L_,_ like forests stripd of
   leaves_L_;_
ᴧThe op[p]ressed pursue like the wind_L_;_ there is no room for
   escapeᴧ
The Spectre of Enitharmon let loose in the troubled deep
Waild Shrill in the confusion & the Spectre of Urthona   [

[*Page 118*]

Recievd her in the darkning South_L_;_ their bodies lost_L_,_
   they stood
Trembling & weak_L_,_ a faint embrace_L_,_ a fierce desire_L_,_ as
   when
Two shadows mingle on a wall_L_;_ they wail & shadowy tears
Fell down & shadowy forms of joy mixd with despair &
   grief_L_,_
Their bodies buried in the ruins of the Universe_L_,_   [
Mingled with the confusion. Who shall call them from the
   Grave_L_?_
ᴧRahab & Tirzah wail aloud in the wild flames_L_;_ they give
   up themselves to Consummation_L·_ᴧ
The books of Urizen unroll with dreadful noise_L_;_ the folding
   Serpent
Of Orc began to Consume in fierce raving fire_L_;_ his fierce
   flames
Issud on all sides gathring strength in animating volumes_L_,_   [

Page 118 ᴅᴇsɪɢɴ: At the foot of the page is a complex pencil and crayon sketch
of three nude women. One seems to be unhappy because her arms are held behind
her; the woman holding her arms is sitting with one knee and one foot on the
ground (one leg is lightly sketched also raised in the air); and the third woman
is hugging the second woman from behind. There are other vague strokes, and
heavy crayon background shading has partly covered the third woman's raised
knee.
   ᴧ. 7 is inserted in a stanza-break.

Roaming abroad on all the winds⌊,⌋ raging intense⌊,⌋ red-
dening
Into resistless pillars of fire rolling round & round⌊,⌋ gathering
Strength from the Earths consumd & heavens & all hidden
abysses⌊,⌋
Wherever the Eagle has Explord or Lion or Tyger trod
Or where the Comets of the night or stars of [eternal *del*]
^asterial^ day   [*15*]
Have shot their arrows or long beamed spears in wrath &
fury

And all the while the trumpet sounds⌊,⌋ [Awake ye dead &
come
[To Judgment. *del*] from the clotted gore & from the hollow
den
Start forth the trembling millions into flames of mental fire
Bathing their limbs in the bright visions of Eternity⌊.⌋   [*20*]
Then like the doves from pillars of Smoke the trembling
families
Of women & children throughout every nation under heaven
Cling round the men in bands of twenties & of fifties⌊,⌋ pale
As snow that falls around a leafless tree upon the green⌊.⌋
^Their op[*p*]ressors are falln⌊,⌋ they have Stricken them⌊,⌋
they awake to life⌊.⌋^   [*25*]
Yet pale the just man stands erect & looking up to heaven⌊.⌋
Trembling & strucken by the Universal stroke the trees
unroot⌊;⌋
The rocks groan horrible & run about⌊;⌋ the mountains &
Their rivers cry with a dismal cry⌊;⌋ the cattle gather to-
gether⌊;⌋
Lowing they kneel before the heaven*s*; the wild beasts of the   50
forests   [*30*]
Tremble⌊;⌋ the Lion shuddring asks the Leopar*d*: 'Feelest
thou
The dread I feel⌊,⌋ unknown before⌊?⌋ My voice refuses to
roar

ll. 17–18: 'Awake ye dead & come To Judgment' is also on p. 117, ll. 12–13.
ll. 18–20 are repeated on p. 119, ll. 21–3.
l. 26: 'Yet' is written over 'Th'.

And in weak moans I speak to thee_L.⌋ This night
Before the mornings dawn the Eagle called the Vulture_L,⌋
The Raven calld the hawk_L,⌋ I heard them from my forests
black_L,⌋
Saying "Let us go up far for soon I smell upon the wind
A terror coming from the South." The Eagle & Hawk fled
away
At dawn & Eer the sun arose the raven & Vulture followd_L.⌋
Let us flee also to the north.' They fled. The Sons of Men
Saw them depart in dismal droves. ⌃The trumpet sounded
loud
⌃And all the Sons of Eternity Descended into Beulah_L.⌋⌃

[*Page 119*]

⌃In the fierce flames the limbs of Mystery lay consuming with
howling
⌃And deep despair. Rattling go up the flames around the
Synagogue
⌃Of Satan_L.⌋ Loud the Serpent Orc ragd thro his twenty
Seven
⌃Folds. The tree of Mystery went up in folding flames_L.⌋
⌃Blood issud out in mighty volumes pouring in whirlpools
fierce
⌃From out the flood gates of the Sky_L ;⌋ the Gates are burst_L ;⌋
down pours
⌃The torrents black upon the Earth_L ;⌋ the blood pours down
incessant_L.⌋
⌃Kings in their palaces lie drownd_L ;⌋ shepherds_L,⌋ their
flocks_L,⌋ their tents
⌃Roll down the mountains in black torrents_L.⌋ Cities Villages
⌃High spires & Castles drownd in the black deluge_L ;⌋ Shoal
on Shoal

ll. 40–1: These added words are written over an erasure of three-and-a-half lines
—the sketch is over part of the erasure. l. 41 is inked over the same thing in pencil.
Page 119 DESIGN: The leg of the engraved figure has been lightly sketched under
the writing and its foot redrawn.
ll. 1–14 are written over

[Vala
[Night the Ninth
[Being
[The Last Judgment *del*]

ˆFloat the dead carcases of Men & Beasts driven to & fro on
  waves
ˆOf foaming blood beneath the black incessant Sky till all
ˆMysterys tyrants are cut off & not one left on Earth
ˆAnd when all Tyranny was cut off from the face of Earthˆ

ˆAround the Dragon form of Urizen & round his stony form   [*15*]
ˆThe flames rolling intense thro the wide Universe
ˆ[Began to draw near to the Earth *del*] ˆˆBegan to Enter the
  Holy CityᴸˎᴶˆˆEntring the dismal clouds
ˆIn furrowd lightnings break their wayᴸˏᴶ the wild flames
  li[*c*]king[?] up
ˆThe Bloody Delugeᴸˏᴶ living flames winged with intellect
ˆAnd Reasonᴸˏᴶ round the Earth they march in order flame
  by flameᴸˎᴶ   [*20*]
ˆFrom the clotted gore & from the hollow den
ˆStart forth the trembling millions into flames of mental fire
ˆBathing their Limbs in the bright visions of Eternityᴸˎᴶ ˆ
[Without *del*] ˆBeyondˆ this Universal Confusionᴸˏᴶ beyond
  the remotest[?] Polc
Where their vortexes begin to operate there stands   [*25*]
A Horrible rock far in the Southᴸˎᴶ it was forsaken when
Urizen gave the horses of Light into the hands of Luvahᴸˎᴶ

On this rock lay the faded head of the Eternal Man
Enwrapped round with weeds of deathᴸˏᴶ pale cold in sorrow
  & woeᴸˎᴶ
He lifts the blue lamps of his Eyes & cries with heavenly
  voiceᴸˏᴶ   [*30*]
ˆBowing his head over the consuming Universe he criedᴸːᴶˆ
'O weakness & O wearinessᴸˎᴶ O war within my membersᴸˎᴶ
My Sons exiled from my breast pass to & fro before meᴸˏᴶ
My birds are silent on my hillsᴸˏᴶ flocks die beneath my
  branchesᴸˏᴶ

ll. 15–23 are written in the margin and are clearly marked for insertion in the
stanza-break in this position.
  ll. 21–3 are repeated from p. 118, ll. 18–20.
  l. 31 is added in a stanza-break.
  ll. 32–8, 40–3, p. 120, ll. 1–3 are in a slightly different form in *Jerusalem* pl. 19,
ll. 1–7, 9–14 (p. 454).

My tents are fallen_L;_J my trumpets & the sweet sounds of my
    harp
Is silent on my clouded hills that belch forth storms & fire_{L·J}
My milk of cows & honey of bees & fruit of golden harvest
Are gatherd in the scorching heat & in the driving rain_{L·J}
My robe is turned to confusion & my bright gold to stone_{L·J}
Where once I sat I weary walk in misery & pain
For from within my [narrow *del*] ⌃witherd⌃ breast grown
    narrow with my woes
The Corn is turnd to thistles & the apples into poison_{L,J}
The birds of song to murderous crows_{L,J} My joys to bitter
    groans_{L,J}

[*Page 120*]

'The voices of children in my tents to cries of helpless infants
And all exiled from the face of light & shine of morning
In this dark world_{L,J} a narrow House_{L,J} I wander up &
    down_{L·J}
⌃I hear Mystery howling in these flames of Consummation_{L·J}
When shall the Man of future times become as in days of
    old_L?_J
O weary life_L!_J why sit I here & give up all my powers
To indolence_{L,J} to the night of death when indolence &
    mourning
Sit hovring over my dark threshol*d*? tho I arise_{L,J} look out
And scorn the war within my members yet my heart is weak
And my head faint_{L·J} Yet will I look again into the morning_{L·J}
Whence is this sound of rage of Men drinking each others
    blood_{L,J}
Drunk with the smoking gore & red but not with nourishing-
    wine_L?_J'

The Eternal Man sat on the Rocks & cried with awful voice_L:_J

l. 36: 'Is' was correctly given as 'Are' in the corresponding *Jerusalem* passage.

Page 120 DESIGN: At the foot of the page, a lovely reclining nude woman (like
the one on p. 102) leans her head on her arms as if in sorrow. (A similar figure,
reversed, is in 'Satan Calling Up his Legions' [1808] for *Paradise Lost*.) Something
like a drawing-compass is repeated several times above her. A very light small
sketch, which partly overlaps her buttock, seems to represent the torso and legs of
a nude woman.

l. 13 is followed by a stanza-break.

'O Prince of Light∟,⌐ where art thou∟?⌐ I behold thee not as
  once
In those Eternal fields in clouds of morning stepping forth   [*15*]
With harps & songs where bright Ahania sang before thy
  face
And all thy sons & daughters gatherd round my ample
  table∟·⌐
˄See you not all this wracking furious confusion∟?⌐˄
Come forth from slumbers of thy cold abstraction∟,⌐ come
  forth∟!⌐
Arise to Eternal births∟!⌐ shake off thy cold repose∟!⌐   [*20*]
Schoolmaster of souls∟,⌐ great opposer of change∟,⌐ arise
That the Eternal worlds may see thy face in peace & joy∟,⌐
That thou∟,⌐ dread form of Certainty∟,⌐ maist sit in town &
  village
While little children play around thy feet in gentle awe
Fearing thy frown∟,⌐ loving thy smile∟,⌐ O Urizen prince of
  light∟·⌐'   [*25*]

He calld∟;⌐ the deep buried his voice & answer none re-
  turnd∟·⌐

Then wrath burst round∟;⌐ the Eternal Man was wrath∟;⌐
  again he cried∟:⌐

'Arise O stony form of death∟!⌐ O dragon of the Deeps∟!⌐
Lie down before my feet O Dragon∟!⌐ let Urizen arise∟!⌐
˄˄*O how couldst thou deform those beautiful proportions   [*30*]
˄˄*Of life & person for as the Person [is *del*] so is his life
  proportiond∟·⌐˄˄
Let Luvah rage in the dark deep even to Consummation
For if thou feedest not his rage it will subside in peace
But if thou darest obstinate refuse my stern behest
Thy crown & scepter I will sieze & regulate all my members   [*35*]
In stern severity & cast thee out into the indefinite

l. 19: Cf. John 11:43: When Jesus came to the grave-cave of Lazarus, 'he cried
with a loud voice, Lazarus come forth'.
    ll. 30–1 are written as one continuous line, the second up the side of the page,
with only the unnecessary capital to indicate where they separate.

Where nothing lives, there to wande*r*, & if thou returnst
　weary
Weeping at the threshold of Existence I will steel my heart
Against thee to Eternity & never recieve thee more﹂‧﹂
Thy self destroying beast formd Science shall be thy eternal
　lot﹍‧﹂
My anger against thee is greater than against this Luvah
For war is [honest *del*] ∧[an *del*]∧ energy ∧Enslavd∧ but thy
　religion﹍‚﹂
The first author of this war & the distracting of honest minds
Into confused perturbation & strife & honour & pride﹍‚﹂
Is a deciet so detestable that I will cast thee out
If thou repentest not & leave thee as a rotten branch to be
　burned
∧With Mystery the Harlot & with Satan for Ever & Ever﹍‧﹂
∧Error can never be redeemd in all Eternity
∧But Sin﹍‚﹂ Even Rahab﹍‚﹂ is redeemd in blood & fury &
　jealousy﹍‚﹂
∧∧∧That line of blood that stretchd across the windows of the
　morning﹍‚﹂∧∧∧
∧Redeemd from Errors power. Wake﹍‚﹂ thou dragon of the
　deeps﹍!﹂'∧

[*Page 121*]

Urizen wept in the dark deep﹍‚﹂ anxious his Scaly form
To reassume the human & he wept in the dark deep
Saying 'O that I had never drank the wine nor eat the
　bread
Of dark mortality nor cast my view into the [past *del*]
　∧futurity∧ nor turnd
My back﹍‚﹂ darkning the present﹍‚﹂ clouding with a cloud
And building arches high & cities turrets & [high *del*] towers
　& domes

ll. 48–9, 51 are probably but not certainly later additions.
l. 50: The Jewish spies whom the harlot Rahab hid in Jericho directed her to
'bind this line of scarlet thread in the window', that she and her family might be
saved when the city was destroyed 'about the dawning of the day' (Joshua 2: 18,
6: 15).

Page 121 l. 3: The '130' by this line was written by l. 4 but is connected by
a stroke with l. 3.

Whose smoke destroyd the pleasant garden & whose run-
  ning Kennels
Chokd the bright rivers∟,⌐ burdning with my Ships the angry
  deep∟,⌐
Thro Chaos seeking for delight & in spaces remote
Seeking the Eternal which is always present to the wise∟,⌐   [*10*]
Seeking for pleasure which unsought falls round the infants
  path
And on the fleeces of mild flocks who neither care nor labour
But I the labourer of ages whose unwearied hands   ʌʌ[*140(?) *del*]ʌʌ
Are thus deformd with hardness with the [plow(?) *del*]
  sword & with the spear
And with the Chisel & the mallet∟,⌐ I whose labours vast   [*15*]
Order the nations separating family by family
Alone enjoy not∟.⌐ I alone in misery supreme
Ungratifid give all my joy into this Luvah & Vala∟.⌐
Then Go O dark [remembrance *del*] ˄futurity∟!⌐˄ I will cast
  thee forth from these
Heavens of my brain nor will I look upon [Remembrance
  del] ˄futurity˄ more∟.⌐   [*20*]
I cast [remembrance *del*] ˄futurity˄ away & turn my back
  upon that void
Which I have made for lo [Remembrance *del*] ˄futurity˄ is
  in this moment∟.⌐
Let Orc consume∟!⌐ let Tharmas rage∟!⌐ let dark   ʌʌ[*150(?) *del*]ʌʌ
  Urthona give
All strength to Los & Enitharmon & let Los self cursd
Rend down this fabric as a wall ruind & family extinct∟.⌐   [*25*]
Rage Orc∟!⌐ Rage Tharmas∟!⌐ Urizen no longer curbs your
  rage∟.⌐'

So Urizen spoke∟;⌐ he shook his snows from off his Shoulders
  & arose
As on a Pyramid of mist∟,⌐ his white robes scattering   ʌʌ*116ʌʌ
The fleecy white∟;⌐ renewd he shook his aged mantles off
Into the fires∟.⌐ Then glorious bright∟,⌐ Exulting in his joy   [*30*]
He sounding rose into the heavens in naked majesty∟,⌐

    l. 7: 'garden' was originally plural.
    l. 18: 'into' perhaps was meant for 'unto'.

In radiant Yout*h*, when Lo like garlands in the Eastern sky
When vocal *M*ay comes dancing from the East_L,_J   ∧∧[*160(?)
  Ahania came
Exulting in her flight_L,_J as when a bubble rises up
On to the surface of a lak*e*, Ahania rose in joy_L._J   [
Excess of joy is worse than grief—her heart beat high_L,_J her
  blood
Burst its bright Vessels_L;_J She fell down dead at the feet of
  Urizen
Outstretchd_L,_J a Smiling corse_L;_J they buried her in a silent
  cave_L._J
Urizen dropt a tear_L;_J the Eternal Man Darkend with
  sorrow_L._J

  ∧The three daughters of Urizen Guard Ahanias Death
  couch_L,_J   [
  ∧Rising from the confusion in tears & howlings & despair_L,_J
  ∧Calling upon their fathers Name upon their Rivers dark_L._J∧

And the Eternal Man Said 'Hear my [voice *del*] words   ∧∧[*17
  O Prince of Light_L._J   [

[*Page 122*]

'Behold Jerusalem in whose bosom the Lamb of God [is seen
  del]
Is seen_L;_J tho slain before her Gates he self renewd remains
Eternal & I thro him awake to life from deaths dark vale_L._J
The times revolve_L;_J the time is coming when all these
  delights
Shall be renewd & all these Elements that now consume   [
Shall reflourish. Then bright Ahania shall awake from
  death_L,_J

l. 36: Cf. 'excess of joy is like Excess of grief', p. 136, l. 3.
ll. 40–2 are written sideways at the bottom of the page; a pencil stroke seems to indicate that they should follow l. 43, but the sense indicates a place between ll. 39 and 43.
Beside ll. 13, 23, 33 in the left margin are underlined erasures, perhaps of numbers.

Page 122 DESIGN: At the foot of the page is a lovely nude woman sitting on the ground with her left leg outstretched, her right knee drawn up, her head and left arm thrown well back in a reclining position.

A glorious Vision [of *del*] to thine Eyes_L,_J a Self renewing
Vision_L:_J
The spring_L,_J the summer to be thine_L;_J then sleep the wintry
days
In silken garments spun by her own hands against her   ʌʌ[*180(?) *del*]ʌʌ
funeral_L._J
The winter thou shalt plow & lay thy stores into thy barns   [*10*]
Expecting to recieve Ahania in the spring with joy_L._J
Immortal tho*u*, Regenerate She & all the lovely Sex
From her shall learn obedience & prepare for a wintry grave
That spring may see them rise in tenfold joy & sweet de-
light_L._J
Thus shall the male & female live the life of Eternity   [*15*] 200
Because the Lamb of God Creates himself a bride & wife
That we his Children evermore may live in Jerusalem
Which now descendeth out of heaven_L,_J a City yet
a Woman_L,_J
Mother of myriads redeemd & born in her spiritual   ʌʌ[*190(?) *del*]ʌʌ
palaces_L,_J
By a New Spiritual birth Regenerated from Death_L._J'   [*20*]

Urizen Sai*d*: 'I have Erred & my Error remains with me_L._J
What Chain encompasses_L?_J in what Lock is the river of
light confind
That issues forth in the morning by measure & the evening
by carefulness_L?_J
Where shall we take our stand to view the infinite & un-
bounded
Or where are human feet_L?_J for Lo our eyes are in the
heavens_L._J'   [*25*]

He ceasd for rivn link from link the bursting Universe ex-
plodes_L._J
All things reversd flew from their centers_L;_J rattling bones
[to bones *del*]
ʌTo bonesʌ Join, shaking convulsd the shivering clay   ʌʌ[*200(?) *del*]ʌʌ
breathes_L;_J

Beside ll. 9, 14, 19, 38 in the left margin are underlined erasures, as if for numbers.

Each speck of dust to the Earths center nestles round &
   round
In pangs of an Eternal Birth⌊;⌋ in torment & awe & fear   [ɜ
All spirits deceasd let loose from reptile prisons come in
   shoals⌊;⌋
Wild furies from the tygers brain & from the lions Eyes
And from the ox & ass come moping terror*s*, from the Eagle
And raven⌊;⌋ numerous as the leaves of autumn every
   species
Flock to the trumpet muttring over the sides of the grave &
   crying   [ɜ
In the fierce wind round heaving rocks & mountains filld
   with groans⌊.⌋
On rifted rocks suspended in the air by inward fires
Many a woful company & many on clouds & waters⌊,⌋ ⌃⌃[*210(?
Fathers & friends⌊,⌋ Mothers & Infants⌊,⌋ Kings & War-
   riors⌊,⌋
Priests & chaind Captives met together in a horrible fear   [ɜ
And every one of the dead appears as he had livd before   [ɜ

[*Page 123*]

And all the marks remain of the slaves scourge & tyrants
   Crown
And of the Priests oergorged Abdomen & of the merchants thin
Sinewy deception & of the warriors ou[*t*]braving & thought-
   lessness
In lineaments too extended & in bones too strait & long⌊.⌋
They shew their wounds⌊;⌋ they accuse⌊;⌋ they sieze the
   op[*p*]ressor⌊;⌋ howlings began   [
On the golden palace⌊,⌋ Songs & joy on the desart⌊;⌋ the
   Cold babe
Stands in the furious air⌊;⌋ he cries 'the children of six thou-
   sand years
Who died in infancy rage furious⌊;⌋ a mighty multitude   ⌃⌃
   rage furious⌊,⌋
Naked & pale standing in the expecting air to be deliverd⌊,⌋

ll. 34–5 may be illustrated on p. 1.

Page 123 l. 5: Above 'howlings began' the same thing is written somewhat more
clearly in pencil.

Rend limb from limb the Warrior & the tyrant_ʟ,_」 reuniting
   in pain_ʟ._」   [*10*]
The furious wind still rends around_ʟ;_」 they flee in sluggish
   effort_ʟ;_」
ᐱThey beg_ʟ;_」 they intreat in vain now_ʟ;_」 they Listend not to
   intreaty_ʟ;_」ᐱ
They view the flames red rolling on thro the wide universe
From the [black *del*] ᐱdarkᐱ jaws of death beneath & desolate
   shores remote_ʟ,_」
These covering Vaults of heaven & these trembling globes of
   earth_ʟ._」   [*15*]
One Planet [cries *del*] ᐱcallsᐱ to another & one star enquires
   of another_ʟ:_」
'What flames are these coming from the South_ʟ?_」 what
   noise_ʟ,_」 what dreadful rout
As of a battle in the heavens_ʟ?_」 hark_ʟ!_」 heard you not the
   trumpet
As of fierce battle_ʟ?_」' while they spoke the flames come ᐱᐱ[*230(?) del*]ᐱᐱ
   on intense roaring_ʟ._」

They see him whom they have piercd_ʟ,_」 they wail because of
   him_ʟ,_」   [*20*]
They magnify themselves no more against Jerusalem Nor
Against her little ones_ʟ;_」 the innocent_ʟ,_」 accused before the
   Judges_ʟ,_」
Shines with immortal Glory_ʟ;_」 trembling the Judge springs
   from his throne
Hiding his face in the dust beneath [a *del*] ᐱtheᐱ prisoners
   feet & saying
'Brother of Jesus_ʟ,_」 what have I done_ʟ?_」 intreat thy lord for   250
   me_ʟ!_」   [*25*]
Perhaps I may be forgiven_ʟ,_」' while he speaks the flames
   roll on
And after the flames appears the Cloud of the Son of Man

   l. 12 is inserted in a stanza-break.
   l. 20: 'they shall look upon me whom they have pierced' in Zechariah 12:10
(repeated in John 19:37) is paraphrased in Revelation 1:7: '. . . the earth shall
wail because of him'.
   ll. 27–8: Man shall 'see the Son of man coming in a cloud with power and great
glory' (Luke 21:27).

Descending from Jerusalem with power & great Glory⌊·⌋
All nations look up to the Cloud & behold him who was
  Crucified⌊·⌋

˄The Prisoner answers 'you scourgd my father to death
  before my face
˄While I stood bound with cords & heavy chains. Your
  hipocrisy
˄Shall now avail you nought.' So speaking he dashd him
  with his foot⌊·⌋˄

The Cloud is Blood dazling upon the heavens & in the cloud
Above upon its volumes is beheld [as *del*] a throne & [as
  del] a pavement
Of precious stone*s*, surrounded by [twenty four(?) *del*]
  ˄twenty four˄ venerable patriarchs
And these again surrounded [of *del*] by four Wonders of the
  Almighty
Incomprehensibl*e*, pervading all amidst & round about⌊,⌋
Fourfold⌊,⌋ each in the other reflected⌊;⌋ they are named
  Life's in Eternity⌊,⌋
Four Starry Universes going forward from Eternity to
  Eternity
And the Falln Man who was arisen upon the Rock of Ages
[*Page 124*]
Beheld the Vision of God & he arose up from the Rock
And Urizen arose up with him walking thro the flames

ll. 30–2 are written sideways in the right margin and are marked for entry in this
stanza break, though once they seem to have preceded l. 29.
  ll. 34–9: Blake's water-colour of 'The Four and Twenty Elders Casting their
Crowns before the Divine Throne' shows the 'throne . . . surrounded by twenty
four venerable patriarchs And these again surrounded by four Wonders of the
Almighty'. The picture is based on Revelation 4: 6–10, was delivered to Butts on
12 May 1805, and is reproduced in M. Butlin's Tate catalogue (*William Blake*
[1971], 51). The Greek word 'Zoa', meaning 'living creatures' (Ezekiel 1: 5) or
'Lives', is translated as 'beasts' in Revelation 4: 6.

Page 124 DESIGN: At the foot of the page a clothed man leans his forearms on his
stick and looks right towards a lovely nude woman who is sitting in a huge plant
like a lotus with her heels under her, her right arm raised, her left hand on her
breasts, looking toward him. The outlines of these figures are firmly darkened in
crayon. To the right, evidently connected with them, is a tall vague pencil figure

To meet the Lord coming to Judgment but the flames re-
pelld them
Still to the Rock∟;⌐ in vain they strove to Enter the Consum-
mation
Together for the [Fallen *del*] ⌐Redeemd⌐ Man could not
enter the Consummation∟.⌐   [*5*]

Then siezd the Sons of Urizen the Plow∟;⌐ they polishd it
From rust of ages∟;⌐ all its ornaments of Gold & silver &
ivory
Reshone across the field immense where all the nations
Darkend like Mould in the divided fallows where the weed
Triumphs in its own destruction∟;⌐ they took down the
harness   [*10*]
From the blue walls of heaven∟,⌐ starry jingling∟,⌐ orna-
minted
With beautiful art∟,⌐ the study of angels∟,⌐ the workmanship
of Demons
When Heaven & Hell in Emulation strove in sports of Glory∟.⌐

The noise of rural work resounded thro the heavens of
heavens∟;⌐
The horse[*s*] neigh from the battle∟,⌐ the wild bulls from the
sultry waste∟,⌐   [*15*]
The tygers from the forests & the lions [of *del*] from the sandy
desarts∟.⌐
They Sing∟;⌐ they sieze the instruments of harmony∟;⌐ they
throw away
The spear∟,⌐ the bow∟,⌐ the gun∟,⌐ the mortar∟;⌐ they level
the fortifications∟.⌐
They beat the iron engines of destruction into wedges∟;⌐
They give them to Urthonas Sons∟;⌐ ringing the hammers
sound   [*20*]
In dens of death to forge the spade∟,⌐ the mattock & the
ax∟,⌐

in a shroud-like garment, with crayon strokes as of flames going round it and up
the right margin. In the left margin, unconnected with the main sketch, is out-
lined the left leg and torso of a kneeling nude figure. (A similar lotus is in *Jerusalem*
pl. 28, p. 474.)
  l. 18: 'mortar' was originally 'mortal'.

The heavy roller to break the clods₍ᴸ,₎ to pass over the
nations₍ᴸ.₎

The Sons of Urizen Shout₍ᴸ.₎ Their father rose₍ᴸ.₎ The Eternal
horses
Harnessd₍ᴸ,₎ They calld to Urizen₍ᴸ;₎ the heavens moved at
their call₍ᴸ.₎
The limbs of Urizen shone with ardor. [he rose up from the
Rock
[The Fallen Man wondring beheld. *del*] He laid his ha[*n*]d on
the Plow₍ᴸ,₎
Thro dismal darkness drave the Plow of ages over Cities
And all their villages₍ᴸ,₎ over Mountains & all their Vallies₍ᴸ,₎
Over the graves & caverns of the dead₍ᴸ,₎ Over the Planets
And over the void Spaces₍ᴸ;₎ over Sun & moon & star &
constellation₍ᴸ.₎

Then Urizen commanded & they brought the Seed of Men₍ᴸ.₎
The trembling souls of All the Dead stood before Urizen
Weak wailing in the [*word del*] ∧troubled∧ air₍ᴸ.₎ East₍ᴸ,₎ west
& north & south

[*Page 125*]

He turnd the horses loose & laid his Plow in the northern
corner
Of the wide Universal fiel*d*, then Stepd [out *del*] ∧forth∧
into the immense₍ᴸ.₎

Then he began to sow the seed₍ᴸ;₎ he girded round his loins
With a bright girdle & his skirt filld with immortal souls₍ᴸ.₎
Howling & Wailing fly the souls from Urizens strong hand

For from the hand of Urizen the myriads fall like stars
Into their own appointed places₍ᴸ,₎ driven back by the
winds₍ᴸ,₎
The naked warriors rush together down to the sea shores₍ᴸ;₎
They are become like wintry flocks₍ᴸ,₎ like forests stripd of
leaves₍ᴸ.₎

Page 125 l. 16 is written in the right margin as a continuation of l. 15 and is
not distinguished from it except by the unnecessary capital.

The Kings & Princes of the Earth cry with a feeble cry⌞,⌟   [*10*]
Driven on the unproducing sands & on the hardend rocks
And all the while the flames of Orc follow the ventrous feet
Of Urizen & all the while the Trump of Tharmas sounds⌞.⌟
Weeping & wailing fly the souls from Urizens strong hand⌞.⌟
⌃The Daughters of Urizen stand with Cups & measures of
    foaming wine   [*15*]
⌃Immense upon the heavens⌞,⌟ with bread & delicate
    repasts⌞.⌟⌃
Then follows the golden harrow in the midst of Mental
    fires⌞.⌟
To ravishing melody of flutes & harps & softest voice
The seed is harrowd in while flames heat the black mould &
    cause
The human harvest to begin⌞.⌟ Towards the south first
    sprang   [*20*]
The myriads & in silent fear they [f *del*] look out from their
    graves⌞.⌟

Then Urizen sits down to rest & all his wearied Sons
Take their repose on beds⌞;⌟ they drink⌞,⌟ they sing⌞,⌟ they
    view the flames
Of Orc⌞;⌟ in joy they view the human harvest springing up⌞.⌟
A time they give to sweet repose till all the harvest is ripe   [*25*]

And Lo like the harvest Moon Ahania cast off her death
    clothes⌞.⌟
She folded them up in care⌞,⌟ in silence & her brightning
    limbs
Bathd in the clear spring of the rock⌞;⌟ then from her dark-
    some cave
Issud in majesty divine⌞.⌟ Urizen rose up from his couch
On wings of tenfold joy clapping his hands⌞,⌟ his feet⌞,⌟
    his radiant wings   [*30*]
In the immense⌞,⌟ as when the Sun dances upon the moun-
    tains

l. 31: 'Albion rose . . .' illustrates a scene like 'when the Sun dances upon the
mountains'.

A shout of jubilee in lovely notes responding from daughter
  to daughter⌊,⌋
From son to Son as if the Stars beaming innumerable
Thro night should sing soft warbling filling Earth & heaven
And bright Ahania took her seat by Urizen in songs &
  joy⌊·⌋   [

The Eternal Man also sat down upon the Couches of
  Beulah⌊,⌋
Sorrowful that he could not put off his new risen body
In mental flames⌊;⌋ the flames refusd⌊,⌋ they drove him
  back to Beulah⌊·⌋
His body was redeemd to be permanent thro the Mercy
  Divine
                    [*Page 126*]
And now fierce Orc had quite consumd himself in Mental
  flames⌊,⌋
Expending all his energy against the fuel of fire⌊·⌋
The [Ancient Man *del*] ⌃Regenerate Man⌄ stoopd his head
  over the Universe & in
His holy hands recievd the flaming Demon & Demoness of
  Smoke
And gave them to Urizens hands⌊;⌋ the Immortal frownd
  Saying⌊:⌋

'Luvah & Vala⌊,⌋ henceforth you are Servants⌊;⌋ obey &
  live⌊·⌋
You shall forget your former state⌊;⌋ return & Love in peace

Page 126 DESIGN: The drawing on this page seems to consist of four separate
sketches. (1) In the lower left margin is the right side of a standing naked man
with his arms raised, as in a crucifixion. The sketch is largely in crayon, and the
man is incomplete above the neck and elbows and below the knees. (2) Below him
a small figure, holding a pole as a pole-vaulter now does, runs to the right. Behind
him a swirl may represent distant bushes, trees, or hills. (3) In front of him in the
right corner is sketched the naked back and head of a huge man perhaps rising
from within the earth who just avoids the last line of the text. (4) *Over* all the text
and parts of the drawings are a great many uncertain amateurish strokes which
seem to outline a large figure running with immense strides and waving his arms
in the air as if to stop a train. The eyes have been particularly darkened so that
they look like demonic goggles. (This figure might well be a copy of the engraved
figure on p. 109.)
  l. 6: '& live' could be 'O live'.

Into your Place⌊,⌋ the place of seed⌊,⌋ not in the brain or
 heart⌊·⌋
If Gods combine against Man⌊,⌋ Setting their Dominion
 above
The Human form Divin*e*, Thrown down from their high
 Station   [*10*]
In the Eternal heavens of Human [Thought *del*] Imagina-
 tion: buried beneath
In dark oblivion⌊,⌋ with incessant pangs ages on ages⌊,⌋
In Enmity & war first weakend⌊,⌋ then in stern repentance
They must renew their brightness & their disorganizd
 functions
Again reorganize till they resume the image of the human⌊,⌋   [*15*]
Cooperating in the bliss of Man⌊,⌋ obeying his Will⌊,⌋
Servants to the infinite & Eternal of the Human form⌊·⌋'

Luvah & Vala descended & enterd the Gates of Dark
 Urthona
And walkd from the hands of Urizen in the shadows of
 Valas Garden
Where the impressions of Despair & Hope for ever vegetate   [*20*]
In flowers⌊,⌋ in fruits⌊,⌋ in fishes⌊,⌋ birds & beasts & clouds &
 waters⌊,⌋
The land of doubts & shadows⌊,⌋ sweet delusions⌊,⌋ un-
 formd hopes⌊·⌋
They saw no more the terrible confusion of the wracking
 universe⌊·⌋
They heard not⌊,⌋ saw not⌊,⌋ felt not all the terrible con-
 fusion
For in their orbed senses⌊,⌋ within closd up⌊,⌋ they wanderd
 at will   [*25*]
ᴧAnd those upon the Couches viewd them in the dreams of
 Beulah
ᴧAs they reposd from the terrible wide universal harvest⌊·⌋ᴧ
Invisible Luvah in bright clouds hoverd over Valas head
And thus their ancient golden age renewd⌊,⌋ for Luvah
 spoke

ll. 26–7 are written slanting in the margin and are clearly marked for insertion
here.

ˆWith voice mild from his golden Cloud upon the
 breath of morning⌞·⌟ˆ
'Come forth O Vala from the grass & from the silent Dew⌞,⌟
Rise from the dews of death for the Eternal Man is Risen⌞·⌟'

She rises among flowers & looks toward the Eastern clear-
 ness⌞·⌟
She walks⌞,⌟ yea runs⌞,⌟ her feet are wingd on the tops of the
 bending grass⌞,⌟
Her garments rejoice in the vocal wind & her hair glistens
 with dew⌞·⌟

She answerd thus 'Whose voice is this in the voice of the
 nourishing air⌞,⌟
In the spirit of the morning awaking the Soul from its
 grassy bed⌞?⌟

[*Page 127*]

'Where dost thou dwell for it is thee I seek & but for thee
I must have slept Eternally nor have felt the dew of thy
 morning⌞·⌟
Look how the opening dawn advances with vocal harmony⌞!⌟

l. 30 is inserted in a stanza-break.
l. 35: 'vocal' was originally 'vocle'.

Page 128 DESIGN: At the foot of the page, to the left, a nude(?) female, her right
knee bent at a right angle, bends forward to the right, with her right arm stretched
forward and bent up at the elbow. Her right hand meets the hand of a man in a
similar position opposite her except that his left foot and right knee are on the
ground. Behind and beneath them are golfball-like objects, on a firmly drawn flat
surface. At the back of the man, partly obscuring his leg, is a prostrate sleeping
nude woman (?Vala), with her right ankle crossed over her left, her right arm
above her head, her left by her side. She has been quite carefully drawn; both
wrists have pearl-like bracelets, and the left arm may have slave-bands; she has
a curious hat or halo, elegant embroidered shoes, a large pillow, a pearl choker,
and a kind of feathery girdle which does not go as low as her vulva, which has
been carefully outlined in crayon. The background above her was indicated in
Blue wash, and her skin was shaded here and there with Brown, purplish-Pink, and
Blue water-colour. Above her, evidently unconnected with the other drawings, is
a nude woman sitting with her left side to us, her left leg extended, facing us over
her left shoulder, and holding something like a lute with her fingers in position as
if to play. She has a pearl slave-band on her left biceps, a fashionable hair-do,
and a smile. Vague strokes seem to have been first thoughts for another flute
before her, another leg, and another back and head behind her. Vague circles
above her seem to represent a crowd of faces.

Look how the beams foreshew the rising of some glorious
    power⌐!⌐
The sun is thine⌐,⌐ [when *del*] he goeth forth in his majestic
    brightness⌐,⌐   [5]
O thou creating voice that callest & who shall answer thee⌐?⌐'

'Where dost thou flee O fair one⌐?⌐ where dost thou seek thy
    happy place⌐?⌐'

'To yonder brightness⌐,⌐ there I haste for sure I came from
    thence
Or I must have slept eternally nor have felt the dew of
    morning⌐.⌐'

'Eternally thou must have slept nor have felt the morning
    dew   [10]
But for yon nourishing sun⌐;⌐ tis that by which thou art
    arisen⌐.⌐
The birds adore the sun⌐,⌐ the beasts rise up & play in his
    beams
And every flower & every leaf rejoices in his light⌐.⌐
Then O thou fair one⌐,⌐ sit thee down for thou art as the
    grass⌐,⌐
Thou risest in the dew of morning & at night are folded
    up⌐.⌐'   [15]

'Alas am I but as a flower⌐?⌐ then will I sit me down⌐,⌐
Then will I weep⌐,⌐ then Ill complain & sigh for immortality
And chide my maker⌐,⌐ thee O Sun⌐,⌐ that raisedst me to
    fall⌐.⌐'

So saying she sat down & wept beneath the apple trees⌐.⌐

'O be thou blotted out⌐,⌐ thou Sun⌐,⌐ that raisedst me to
    trouble⌐,⌐   [20]
That gavest me a heart to crave & raisedst me thy phantom
To feel thy heat & see thy light & wander here alone⌐,⌐
Hopeless if I am like the grass & so shall pass away⌐.⌐'
'Rise sluggish Soul⌐!⌐ why sitst thou here⌐?⌐ why dost thou
    sit & weep⌐?⌐

Yon Sun shall wax old & decay but thou shalt ever flourish⌞·⌟   [
The fruit shall ripen & fall down & the flowers consume
   away
But thou shalt still survive⌞;⌟ arise⌞,⌟ O dry thy dewy
   tears⌞·⌟'

'Hah! Shall I still survive⌞?⌟ whence came that sweet & com-
   forting voice
And whence that voice of sorrow⌞?⌟ O sun⌞,⌟ thou art
   nothing now to me⌞·⌟
Go on thy course rejoicing & let us both rejoice together⌞·⌟   [
I walk among his flocks & hear the bleating of his lambs⌞·⌟
O that I could behold his face & follow his pure feet⌞!⌟
I walk by the footsteps of his flocks⌞;⌟ come hither tender
   flocks⌞!⌟
Can you converse with a pure Soul that seeketh for her
   maker⌞?⌟   4
You answer not⌞;⌟ then am I set your mistress in this garden⌞·⌟   [
Ill watch you & attend your footsteps⌞;⌟ you are not like the
   birds   [
                        [*Page 128*]
'That sing & fly in the bright air but you do lick my feet
And let me touch your wooly backs⌞;⌟ follow me as I sing
For in my bosom a new song arises to my Lord⌞·⌟

'Rise up O Sun⌞,⌟ most glorious minister & light of day⌞·⌟
Flow on⌞,⌟ ye gentle airs⌞,⌟ & bear the voice of my rejoicing⌞·⌟   [
Wave freshly clear waters flowing around the tender grass
And thou sweet smelling ground⌞,⌟ put forth thy life in
   fruits & flowers⌞·⌟
Follow me⌞,⌟ O my flocks & hear me sing my rapturous
   Song⌞·⌟
I will cause my voice to be heard on the clouds that glitter in
   the sun⌞·⌟
I will call & who shall answer me⌞?⌟ I will sing⌞,⌟ who shall
   reply⌞?⌟   [
For from my pleasant hills behold the living living springs
Running among my green pastures⌞,⌟ delighting among my
   trees⌞·⌟

I am not here alone⌞,⌟ my flocks⌞,⌟ you are my brethren
And you birds that sing & adorn the sky⌞,⌟ you are my
  sisters⌞.⌟
I sing & you reply to my song⌞.⌟ I rejoice & you are glad⌞.⌟   [*15*]
Follow me⌞,⌟ o my flocks⌞;⌟ we will now descend into the
  valley⌞.⌟
O how delicious are the grapes flourishing in the Sun⌞!⌟
How clear the spring of the rock running among the golden
  sand⌞!⌟
How cool the breezes of the vall[*e*]y & the arms of the branch-
  ing trees⌞!⌟
Cover us from the Sun⌞;⌟ come & let us sit in the Shade⌞.⌟   [*20*]
My Luvah here hath placd me in a Sweet & pleasant Land
And given me fruits & pleasant waters & warm hills & cool
  valleys⌞.⌟
Here will I build myself a house & here Ill call on his name⌞.⌟
Here Ill return when I am weary & take my pleasant rest⌞.⌟'

So spoke the Sinless Soul & laid her head on the downy
  fleece   [*25*]
Of a curld Ram who stretchd himself in sleep beside his mis-
  tress
And soft sleep fell upon her eyelids in the silent noon of day⌞.⌟

Then Luvah passed by & saw the sinless Soul
And said 'Let a pleasant house arise to be the dwelling place
Of this immortal Spirit growing in lower Paradise⌞.⌟'   [*30*]

He spoke & pillars were builded & walls as white as ivory⌞.⌟
The grass she slept upon was pavd with pavement as of
  pearl⌞.⌟
Beneath her rose a downy bed & a cieling coverd all⌞.⌟

Vala awoke. 'When in the pleasant gates of sleep I enterd
I saw my Luvah like a spirit stand in the bright air⌞.⌟   [*35*]
Round him stood spirits like me who reard me a bright
  house
And here I see thee⌞,⌟ house⌞,⌟ remain in my most pleasant
  world⌞.⌟   [*37*]

l. 37: 'thee' was originally 'the'.

[*Page 129*]

'My Luvah smild_L,_J I kneeled down_L;_J he laid his hand on
   my head
And when he laid his hand upon me from the gates of sleep I
   came
Into this bodily house to tend my flocks in my pleasant
   garden_L._J'

So saying she arose & walked round her beautiful house
And then from her white door she lookd to see her bleating
   lambs
But her flocks were gone up from beneath the trees into the
   hills_L._J

'I see the hand that leadeth me doth also lead my flocks_L._J'
She went up to her flocks & turned oft to see her shining
   house_L._J
She [d *del*] ⌃stopd⌃ to drink of the clear spring & eat the
   grapes & apples_L._J
She bore the fruits in her lap_L;_J she gatherd flowers for her
   bosom_L._J
She called to her flocks saying 'follow me o my flocks_L!_J'

They followd her to the silent vall[*e*]y beneath the spreading
   trees
And on the rivers margin she ungirded her golden girdle_L._J
She stood in the river & viewd herself within the watry
   glass
And her bright hair was wet with the waters_L;_J she rose up
   from the river
And as she rose her Eyes were opend to the world of waters_L._J
She saw Tharmas sitting upon the rocks beside the wavy
   sea_L._J
He strokd the water from his beard & mour[*n*]d faint·thro
   ⌃the⌃ summer vales
And Vala stood on the rocks of Tharmas & heard his mourn-
   ful voice_L:_J
'O Enion my weary head is in the bed of death
For weeds of death have wrapd around my limbs in the
   hoary deeps_L._J

I sit in the place of shells & mourn & thou art closd in
    clouds$_L._J$
When will the time of Clouds be past & the dismal night of
    Tharmas$_L$?$_J$
⌃Arise O Enion$_L$!$_J$ Arise & Smile upon my head
⌃As thou dost smile upon the barren mountains & they
    rejoice$_L._J$ [25]
⌃When wilt thou smile on Tharmas O thou bringer of
    golden day$_L$?$_J$
⌃Arise O Enion$_{L,J}$ arise$_{L,J}$ for Lo I have calmd my seas$_L._J$'⌃
So saying his faint head he laid upon the Oozy rock
And darkness coverd all the deep$_L$;$_J$ the light of Enion faded
Like a fa[i]nt flame quivering upon the surface of the dark-
    ness$_L._J$ [30]

Then Vala lifted up her hands to heaven to call on Enion$_L._J$
She calld but none could answer her & the Eccho of her
    voice returnd$_L$:$_J$

'Where is the voice of God that calld me from the silent
    dew$_L$?$_J$
Where is the Lord of Vala$_L$?$_J$ dost thou hide in clefts of the
    rock$_L$?$_J$
Why shouldst thou hide thyself from Vala$_{L,J}$ from the soul
    that wanders desolate$_L$?$_J$'   [35]

She ceasd & l[i]ght beamd round her like the glory of the
    morning   [36]
                        [*Page 130*]
And She arose out of the river & girded on her golden girdle

And now her feet step on the grassy bosom of the ground

Page 129 ll. 24–7 are written in a stanza break. ll. 24–6 are written as one con-
tinuous line, with strokes to separate them; and l. 27 is written below l. 26 in the
margin. They may have been written once on p. 4, under ll. 12–15, 18–26 and
again on p. 6, under ll. 10–38.

Page 130 DESIGN: At the foot of the page, a prostrate skeleton-like man raises
his head and shoulders from within the ground and looks up the right margin.
Heavy crayon darkening of the background above his legs may have obscured
a partly raised right leg.

Among her flocks & she turnd her eyes toward her pleasant
house
And saw in the door way beneath the trees two little children
playing⌊·⌋
She drew near to her house & her flocks followd her foot-
steps⌊·⌋
The Children clung around her knees⌊,⌋ she embracd them
& wept over them⌊·⌋

'Thou little Boy art Tharmas & thou bright Girl Enion⌊·⌋
How are ye thus renewd & brought into the Gardens of
Vala⌊?⌋'

She embracd them in tear*s*, till the sun descended the
western hills
And then she enterd her bright house leading her mighty
children
And when night came the flocks laid round the house
beneath the trees⌊·⌋
She laid the Children on the beds which she saw prepard in
the house⌊,⌋
Then last herself laid down & closd her Eyelids in soft
slumbers

And in the morning when the Sun arose in the crystal sky
Vala awoke & calld the children from their gentle slumbers⌊:⌋

'Awake O Enion⌊!⌋ awake & let thine innocent Eyes
Enlighten all the Crystal house of Vala⌊!⌋ awake⌊!⌋ awake⌊!⌋
Awake Tharmas⌊!⌋ awake awake thou child of dewy tears⌊·⌋
Open the orbs of thy blue eyes & smile upon my gardens⌊·⌋'

The Children woke & smild on Vala⌊;⌋ she kneeld by the
golden couch⌊·⌋
She presd them to her bosom & her pearly tears dropd
down⌊·⌋
'O my sweet Children⌊!⌋ Enion⌊,⌋ let Tharmas kiss thy
Cheek⌊·⌋
Why dost thou turn thyself away from his sweet watry
eyes⌊?⌋

Tharmas_{L,J} henceforth in Valas bosom thou shalt find sweet
  peace_{L·J}
O bless the lovely eyes of Tharmas & the Eyes of Enion_L!_J'   [*25*]

They rose_{L,J} they went out wandring_{L,J} sometimes together_{L,J}
  sometimes alone_{L·J}
'Why weepest thou_{L,J} Tharmas_{L,J} Child of tears_{L,J} in the
  bright house of joy_L?_J
Doth Enion avoid the sight of thy blue heavenly Eyes
And dost thou wander with my lambs & [with *del*] ˄wet˄
  their innocent faces   500
With thy bright tears because the steps of Enion are in the
  gardens_L?_J   [*30*]
Arise sweet boy & let us follow the path of Enion_{L·J}'

So saying they went down into the garden among the fruits
And Enion sang among the flowers that grew among the trees
And Vala said 'Go_{L,J} Tharmas_L!_J weep not_L!_J Go to
  Enion_L!_J'   [*34*]
                            [*Page 131*]
He said 'O Vala I am sick & all this garden of Pleasure
Swims like a dream before my eyes but the sweet smelling
  fruit
Revives me to new deaths_{L·J} I fade even like a water lilly
In the suns heat till in the night on the couch of Enion
I drink new life & feel the breath of sleeping Enion   [*5*]
But in the morning she arises to avoid my Eyes_{L;J}
Then my loins fade & in the house I sit me down & weep_{L·J}'

'Chear up thy Countenance bright boy & go to Enion_{L·J}
Tell her that Vala waits her in the shadows of her garden_{L·J}'

He went with timid steps & Enion like the ruddy morn   [*10*]
When infant spring appears in swelling buds & opening
  flowers
Behind her Veil withdraws_{L,J} so Enion turnd her modest
  head

But Tharmas spoke 'Vala seeks thee sweet Enion in the
  shades_{L·J}

Follow the steps of Tharmas∟,⌟ O thou brightness of the
  gardens∟.⌟’
He took her hand∟;⌟ reluctant she followd in infant doubts∟.⌟ [

Thus in Eternal Childhood straying among Valas flocks
In infant sorrow & joy alternate Enion & Tharmas playd
Round Vala in the Gardens of Vala & by her rivers margin∟.⌟
They are the shadows of Tharmas & of Enion in Valas
  world

And the sleepers who rested from their harvest work beheld
  these visions∟.⌟
Thus were the sleepers entertaind upon the Couches of
  Beulah∟.⌟

When Luvah & Vala were closd up in their world of shadowy
  forms
Darkness was all beneath the heavens∟;⌟ only a little light
Such as glows out from sleeping spirits appeard in the deeps
  beneath∟.⌟
As when the wind sweeps over a Corn field∟,⌟ the noise of
  souls
Thro all the immense∟,⌟ borne down by Clouds swagging in
  autumnal heat∟,⌟
Muttering along from heaven to heaven∟,⌟ hoarse roll the
  human forms
Beneath thick clouds∟,⌟ dreadful lightnings burst & thunders
  roll∟,⌟
Down pour the torrent Floods of heaven on all the human
  harvest∟.⌟
Then Urizen sitting at his repose on beds in the bright South
Cried ‘Times are Ended∟!⌟’ he Exulted∟;⌟ he arose in joy∟;⌟
  he exulted∟;⌟
He pourd his light & all his Sons & daughters pourd their
  light
To exhale the spirits of Luvah & Vala thro the atmosphere
And Luvah & Vala saw the Light∟;⌟ their spirits were Exhald
In all their ancient innocence∟;⌟ the floods depart∟;⌟ the
  clouds

Dissipate or sink into the Seas of Tharmas⌊.⌋ Luvah sat
Above on the bright heavens in peac*e*; the Spirits of Men
  beneath
Cried out to be deliverd & the Spirit of Luvah wept
Over the human harvest & over Vala the sweet wanderer⌊.⌋
In pain the human harvest wavd in horrible groans of woe⌊.⌋   [*40*]

[*Page 132*]

The Universal Groan went up⌊;⌋ the Eternal Man was
  Darkend⌊.⌋

Then Urizen arose & took his Sickle in his hand⌊.⌋
There is A brazen sickle & a scythe of iron hid
Deep in the South guarded by a few solitary stars⌊.⌋
This sickle Urizen took⌊;⌋ the scythe his sons embracd   550
And went forth & began to reap & all his joyful sons   [*6*]
Reapd the wide Universe & bound in Sheaves a wondrous
  harvest⌊.⌋
They took them into the wide barns with loud rejoicings &
  triumph
Of flute & harp & drum & trumpet⌊,⌋ horn & clarion⌊.⌋

The feast was spread in the bright South & the Regenerate
  Man   [*10*]
Sat at the feast rejoicing & the wine of Eternity
Was servd round by the flames of Luvah all Day & all the
  Night
    ⌃And when Morning began to dawn upon the distant
      hills⌃
[Then *del*] a whirlwind rose up in the Center & in the
  Whirlwind a shriek
And in the Shriek a rattling of bones & in the rattling of
  bones   [*15*]

Page 132 DESIGN: At the foot of the page a naked(?) man (?Tharmas), half
sitting down, bends as low as possible before a nude woman (?Enion) standing
with her hands at her sides looking down at him. The woman is in pencil, the
man in crayon. (An analogous design is on p. 37.)
  Over the head and *over* all the text is a large ineptly drawn man swinging a
sword over his head at a much larger woman who gestures at him and looks down
the right margin. These two figures are very rough.
  ll. 10–12 are on p. 133, ll. 2–4.

A dolorous groan & from the dolorous groan in tears
Rose Enion like a gentle light & Enion spoke saying_L:_J

'O Dreams of Death_L!_J the human form dissolving com-
panied
[With *del*] By beasts & worms & creeping things & darkness
& despair_L._J
The clouds fall off from my wet brow_L,_J the dust from my
cold limbs
Into the Sea of Tharmas_L._J Soon renewd_L,_J a Golden Moth_L,_J
I shall cast off my death clothes & Embrace Tharmas again
For Lo the winter melted away upon the distant hills
And all the black mould sings.' She speaks to her infant
race_L;_J her milk
Descends [of *del*] down on the san*d*; the thirsty sand drinks &
rejoices
Wondering to behold the Emmet_L,_J the Grasshopper_L,_J the
jointed worm_L._J
The roots shoot thick thro the solid rocks bursting their way_L._J
They cry out in joys of existenc*e*; the broad stems
Rear on the mountains stem after stem_L;_J the scaly newt
creeps
From the stone & the armed fly springs from the rocky
crevice_L;_J
The spide*r*, The bat burst from the hardend slime crying
To one another 'what are we & whence is our joy &
delight_L?_J
Lo the little moss begins to spring & the tender weed
Creeps round our secret nest.' Flocks brighten the Moun-
tains_L,_J
Herds throng up the Valley_L,_J wild beasts fill the forests_L._J

Joy thrilld thro all the Furious form of Tharmas humaniz-
ing_L._J
Mild he Embracd her whom he sought_L;_J he raisd her thro
the heavens_L,_J
Sounding his trumpet to awake the dead_L,_J on high he soard
Over the ruind worlds_L,_J the smoking tomb of the Eternal
Prophet_L._J

[*Page 133*]

The Eternal Man arose_ʟ;_ᴊ he welcomd them to the Feast_{ʟ•ᴊ}
The feast was spread in the bright South & the Eternal‑Man
Sat at the feast rejoicing & the wine of Eternity
Was servd round by the flames of Luvah all day & all the
  night

And Many Eternal Men sat at the golden feast to see   [5]
The female form now separate_{ʟ,ᴊ} They shudderd at the
  horrible thing
    ⌃Not born for the sport & amusement of Man but born
      to drink up all his powers_{ʟ•ᴊ}⌃
[And *del*] ⌃They⌃ wept to see their shadows_ʟ;_ᴊ they said to
  one another 'this is Sin_ʟ;_ᴊ
This is the [Vegetative *del*] ⌃Generative⌃ world_ʟ;_ᴊ' they
  rememberd the Days of old

And One of the Eternals spoke_{ʟ•ᴊ} All was silent at the feast_{ʟ•ᴊ}   [10]

'Man is a Worm_ʟ;_ᴊ wearied with joy he sccks the caves of
  sleep
Among the Flowers of Beulah_{ʟ,ᴊ} in his Selfish cold repose
Forsaking Brotherhood & Universal love_{ʟ,ᴊ} in selfish clay
Folding the pure wings of his mind_{ʟ,ᴊ} seeking the places dark
Abstracted from the roots of [Nature *del*] ⌃Science_ʟ;_ᴊ⌃ then
  inclosd around   [15]
In walls of Gold we cast him like a Seed into the Earth
Till times & spaces have passd over him_ʟ;_ᴊ duly every morn
We visit him covering with a Veil the immortal seed_{ʟ,ᴊ}   600
With windows from the inclement sky we cover him & with
  walls
And hearths protect the Selfish terror till divided all   [20]
In families we see our shadows bor*n*, & thence we know
That Man subsists by Brotherhood & Universal Love_{ʟ•ᴊ}
We fall on one anothers necks_{ʟ,ᴊ} more closely we embrace_{ʟ•ᴊ}

Ephesians
iii c. 10 v

Page 133 ll. 2–4 are on p. 132, ll. 10–12.
  l. 7 is adapted on p. 10, l. 27.
  ll. 21–3: Ephesians 3: 10: Paul preached to the Gentiles, 'that now unto the
principalities and powers in heavenly places might be known by the church the
manifold wisdom of God'.

Not for ourselves but for the Eternal family we live⌊.⌋
Man liveth not by Self alone but in his brothers face   [
Each shall behold the Eternal Father & love & joy abound⌊.⌋'

So spoke the Eternal at the Feast⌊;⌋ they embracd the New
   born Man
Calling him Brother⌊,⌋ image of the Eternal Father; they sat
   down
At the immortal tables sounding loud their instruments of
   joy⌊,⌋
Calling the Morning into Beulah⌊;⌋ the Eternal Man re-
   joicd⌊.⌋   [

When Morning dawnd The Eternals rose to labour at the
   Vintage⌊.⌋
Beneath they saw their sons & daughters wondering in-
   conceivable
At the dark myriads in Shadows in the worlds beneath⌊.⌋

The morning dawnd⌊.⌋ Urizen rose & in his hand the Flail
Sounds on the Floor⌊,⌋ heard terrible by all beneath the
   heavens⌊.⌋   [
Dismal loud redounding the nether floor shakes with the
   sound
            [*Page 134*]
And all Nations were threshed out & the stars threshd from
   their husks⌊.⌋

Then Tharmas took the Winnowing fan⌊;⌋ the winnowing
   wind furious
Above veerd round by the violent whirlwind driven west &
   south
Tossed the Nations like Chaff into the seas of Tharmas⌊.⌋

'O Mystery⌊,⌋' Fierce Tharmas cries 'Behold thy end is
   come⌊!⌋

Page 134 DESIGN: At the foot of the page is a bird with a long body, a dragon
tail, and a woman's head (the hair fashionably done), which is ridden by a tiny
naked boy whose right hand extends forward with a long stick, his left stretched
behind him holding a cup(?).

Art thou she that made the nations drunk with the cup of
Religion␣?␣
Go down ye Kings & Councellors & Giant Warriors␣,␣
Go down into the depths␣,␣ go down & hide yourselves
beneath␣,␣
Go down with horse & Chariots & Trumpets of hoarse war␣.␣

'Lo how the Pomp of Mystery goes down into the Caves␣!␣   [*10*]
Her great men howl & throw the dust & rend their hoary
hair␣.␣
Her delicate women & children shriek upon the bitter wind␣,␣
Spoild of their beauty␣,␣ their hair rent & their skin shrivild
up␣.␣
Lo darkness covers the long pomp of banners on the wind
And black horses & armed men & miserable bound captives␣.␣   [*15*]
Where shall the graves recieve them all & where shall be
their place
And who shall mourn for Mystery who never loosd her
Captives␣?␣
Let the slave grinding at the mill run out into the field␣;␣
Let him look up into the heavens & laugh in the bright air␣;␣
Let the inchaind soul shut up in darkness & in sighing   [*20*]
Whose face has never seen a smile in thirty weary years
Rise & look out␣,␣ his chains are loose␣,␣ his dungeon doors
are open
And let his wife & children return from the op[*p*]ressors
seourge␣;␣
They look behind at every step & believe it is a dream␣.␣
Are these the Slaves that groand along the streets of
Mystery␣?␣   [*25*]
Where are your bonds & task masters␣?␣ are these the
prisoners␣?␣
Where are your chains␣?␣ where are your tears␣?␣ why do
you look around␣?␣
If you are thirsty there is the river␣;␣ go bathe your parched
limbs␣,␣

ll. 18–24 are repeated from *America* pl. 8, ll. 42–8 (pp. 141–2).

l. 20: The *America* passage has 'inchained', which seems to be called for by the
metre.

The good of all the Land is before you for Mystery is no
more∟.⌐'

Then All the Slaves from every Earth in the wide Universe ⌐.
Sing a New song drowning confusion in its happy notes
While the flail of Urizen sounded loud & the winnowing 6
wind of Tharmas
So loud∟,⌐ so clear in the wide heavens & the song that they
sung was this
Composed by an African Black from the little Earth of
Sotha∟:⌐

'Aha∟!⌐ Aha∟!⌐ how came I here so soon in my sweet native
land∟?⌐ ⌐.
How came I here∟?⌐ Methinks I am as I was in my youth ⌐.

[*Page 135*]

'When in my fathers house I sat & heard his chearing voice∟.⌐
Methinks I see his flocks & herds & feel my limbs renewd
And Lo my Brethren in their tents & their little ones around
them∟.⌐'

The song arose to the Golden feast∟;⌐ the Eternal Man
rejoicd∟.⌐
Then the Eternal Man said 'Luvah the Vintage is ripe∟;⌐
arise∟!⌐ ⌐.
The sons of Urizen shall gather the vintage with sharp hooks
And all thy Sons∟,⌐ O Luvah∟,⌐ bear away the families of
Earth∟.⌐
I hear the flail of Urizen∟;⌐ his barns are full∟;⌐ no room
Remains & in the Vineyards stand the abounding sheaves
beneath
The falling Grapes that odorous burst upon the winds.
Arise∟,⌐ [
My flocks & herds trample the Corn∟,⌐ my cattle browze upon
The ripe Clusters∟.⌐ The shepherds shout for Luvah prince
of Love∟.⌐

Page 135 l. 1 is written above the engraved box left for the text and may be
an addition.
l. 8: 'room' is written 'roon'.

Let the Bulls of Luvah tread the Corn & draw the loaded
   waggon
Into the Barn while children glean the Ears around the
   door_{L·⌋}
Then shall they lift their innocent hands & stroke his furious
   nose   [*15*]
And he shall lick the little girls white neck & on her head
Scatter the perfume of his breath while from his mountains
   high
The lion of terror shall come down & bending his bright
   mane
And couching at their side shall eat from the curld boys white
   lap
His golden food and in the evening sleep before the Door_{L·⌋}'   [*20*]

'Attempting to be more than Man We become less' said
   Luvah
As he arose from the bright feast drunk with the wine of
   ages_{L·⌋}
His crown of thorns fell from his head_{L,⌋} he hung his living
   Lyre
Behind the seat of the Eternal Man & took his way
Sounding the Song of Los_{L,⌋} descending to the Vineyards
   bright_{L·⌋}   [*25*]
His sons arising from the feast with golden baskets follow_{L,⌋}
A fiery train as when the Sun sings in the ripe vineyards_{L,⌋}
Then Luvah stood before the wine press_{L;⌋} all his fiery sons
Brought up the loaded Waggons with shoutings_{L;⌋} ramping
   tygers play
In the jingling traces_{L;⌋} furious lions sound the song of joy   [*30*]
To the golden wheels circling upon the pavement of heaven
   & all
The Villages of Luvah ring_{L;⌋} the golden tiles of the villages
Reply to violins & tabors_{L,⌋} to the pipe flute lyre & cymbal_{L·⌋}
Then fell the Legions of Mystery in maddning Confusion
Down_{L,⌋} Down thro the immense with outcry fury & despair   [*35*]
Into the wine presses of Luvah_{L;⌋} howling fell the Clusters
Of human families thro the dee*p*; the wine presses were
   filld_{L;⌋}

The blood of life flowd plentiful∟·₁ Odors of life arose
All round the heavenly arches & the Odors rose singing this
   song∟:₁

[*Page 136*]

'O terrible wine presses of Luvah∟!₁ O caverns of the Grave∟!₁
How lovely the delights of those risen again from death∟!₁
O trembling joy∟!₁ excess of joy is like Excess of grief∟·₁'

So Sung the Human Odors round the wine presses of Luvah

But in the Wine presses is wailing terror & despair∟·₁
Forsaken of their Elements they vanish & are no more∟,₁
No more but a desire of Being∟,₁ a distracted ravening
   desire∟,₁
Desiring like the hungry worm & like the [silent *del*] ˄gaping˄
   grave∟·₁
They plunge into the Elements∟;₁ the Elements cast them
   forth
Or else consume their shadowy semblance∟·₁ Yet they
   obstinate
Tho pained to distraction Cry 'O let us Exist for
This dreadful Non Existence is worse than pains of Eternal
   [death *del*] ˄Birth∟·₁˄
Eternal Death who can Endur*e*? let us consume in fires∟,₁
In waters stifling or in air corroding or in earth shut up∟·₁
The Pangs of Eternal birth are better than the Pangs of
   Eternal Death∟·₁'

How red the Sons & daughters of Luvah∟!₁ how they tread
   the Grapes∟!₁
Laughing & shouting drunk with odors many fall oer-
   wearied∟·₁
Drownd in the wine is many a youth & maiden∟;₁ those
   aroun*d*

Page 136 DESIGN: At the foot of the page is a man's face with flowing moustaches,
small wings meeting on his chest, and large wings growing from his shoulders.
   l. 3: Cf. 'Excess of joy is worse than grief', p. 121, l. 36.
   l. 8 is adapted from p. 23, l. 17.
   ll. 16–40, p. 137, ll. 1–4 are rearranged in *Milton* pl. 24, ll. 2–7, 11–14, 16, 19–20,
25–41 (pp. 369–71).

Lay them on skins of tygers or the spotted Leopard or wild
    Ass
Till they revive or bury them in cool Grots making lamenta-
    tion   [20]

But in the Wine Presses the Human Grapes Sing not nor
    dance⌊·⌋
They howl & writhe in shoals of torment⌊,⌋ in fierce flames
    consuming⌊,⌋
In chains of iron & in dungeons circled with ceaseless fires⌊,⌋
In pits & dens & shades of death⌊,⌋ in shapes of torment &
    woe⌊;⌋
The Plates⌊,⌋ the Screws [the nets *del*] and Racks & [*word*
    del] Saws & cords & fires & floods⌊,⌋   [25]
The cruel joy of Luvahs daughters lacerating with knives
And whips their Victims & the deadly sports of Luvahs
    Sons⌊·⌋

Timbrels & Violins sport round the Wine Presses⌊;⌋ The
    little Seed⌊,⌋
The Sportive root⌊,⌋ the Earthworm⌊,⌋ the small beetle⌊,⌋
    the wise Emmet
Dance round the Wine Presses of Luva*h*; the Centipede is
    there⌊,⌋   [30]
The ground Spider with many Eyes⌊,⌋ the Mole clothed in
    Velvet⌊,⌋
The Earwig armd⌊,⌋ the tender maggot emblem of Im-
    mortality⌊,⌋
The Slow Slug⌊,⌋ the grasshopper that sings & laughs &
    drinks⌊:⌋
The winter comes⌊,⌋ he folds his slender bones without
    a murmur⌊·⌋
There is the Nettle that stings with soft down & there   [35]
The indignant Thistle whose bitterness is bred in his milk
And Who lives in the contempt of his neighbour⌊;⌋ there all
    the idle weeds

        l. 22: 'shoals' could be 'shouts'.
        l. 27: 'whips' (as in *Milton* pl. 24, l. 36) is written 'whipt'.

That creep about the obscure places shew their various
limbs_L,_J
Naked in all their beauty dancing round the Wine Presses_L·_J

They Dance around the Dying & they Drink the howl &
groan_L·_J

[*Page 137*]

They catch the Shrieks in cups of gold_L,_J they hand them to
one another_L·_J
These are the sports of love & these the sweet delights of
amorous play_L,_J
Tears of the grape_L,_J the death sweat of the Cluster_L,_J the
last sigh
Of the mild youth who listens to the luring songs of
Luvah_L·_J
The Eternal Man darkend with Sorrow & a wintry mantle
Coverd the Hills_L·_J He said 'O Tharmas rise & O Urthona_L!_J'

Then Tharmas and Urthona rose from the Golden feast
satiated
With Mirth & Joy_L·_J Urthona limping from his fall on
Tharmas leand_L,_J
In his right hand his hammer_L·_J Tharmas held his Shepherds
crook
Beset with gold_L,_J gold were the ornaments formd by the sons
of Urizen_L·_J

Then Enion & Ahania & Vala & the wife of Dark Urthona
Rose from the feast in joy ascending to their Golden Looms_L·_J
There the wingd shuttle Sang_L,_J the spindle & the distaff &
the Reel
Rang sweet the praise of industry. Thro all the golden rooms
Heaven rang with winged Exultation_L·_J All beneath howld
loud_L;_J

Page 137 DESIGN: In the engraving the box left for the text impinges upon the
picture of two wrestlers. Pencil strokes have been drawn in, perfectly completing
these figures.

ll. 1–4 are written above the engraved box left for the text and may be later
additions.

With tenfold rout & desolation roard the Chasms beneath
Where the wide woof flowd down & where the Nations are   750
  gatherd together_L._J

Tharmas went down to the Wine presses & beheld the sons
  & daughters
Of Luvah quite exhausted with the Labour & quite filld
With new wine, that they began to torment one another & to
  tread [the weak *del*]   [*20*]
The weak. Luvah & Vala slept on the floor oerwearied_L._J

Urthona calld his Sons around him_L;_J Tharmas calld his sons
Numrou*s*; they took the wine_L,_J they separated the Lees
And Luvah was put for dung on the ground by the Sons of
  Tharmas & Urthona_L._J
They formed heavens of sweetest wood_L,_J of gold & silver
  & ivory_L,_J   [*25*]
Of glass & precious stones_L._J They loaded all the waggons of
  heaven
And took away the wine of ages with solemn songs & joy_L._J

Luvah & Vala woke & all the sons & daughters of Luvah
Awoke_L;_J they wept to one another & they reascended
To the Eternal Man in woe_L;_J he cast them wailing into   [*30*]
The world of shadows thro the air till winter is over & gone

But the Human Wine stood wondering_L;_J in all their de-
  lightful Expanses
The Elements subside_L;_J the heavens rolld on with vocal
  harmony_L._J

Then Los who is Urthona rose in all his regenerate power_L._J
The Sea that rolld & foamd with darkness & the shadows of
  death   [*35*]
Vomited out & gave up all_L;_J the floods lift up their hands
Singing & shouting to the Man_L;_J they bow their hoary
  heads
And murmring in their channels flow & circle round his
  feet_L._J   [*38*]

l. 25: 'wood' is spelt 'wodd'.

[*Page 138*]

Then Dark Urthona took the Corn out of the Stores of
Urizen_L;_J
He ground it in his rumbling Mills_L,_J Terrible the distress
Of all the Nations of Earth ground in the Mills of Urthona_L._J
In his hand Tharmas takes the Storm*s*; he turns the whirl-
wind Loose
Upon the wheels_L;_J the stormy seas howl at his dread
command
And Eddying fierce rejoice in the fierce agitation of the
wheels
Of Dark Urthona_L._J Thunders Earthquakes Fires Water
floods
Rejoice to one another_L;_J loud their voices shake the Abyss_L,_J
Their dread forms tending the dire mills_L._J The grey hoar
frost was there
And his pale wife the aged Snow_L;_J they watch over the
fires_L;_J
They build the Ovens of Urthona_L._J Nature in darkness
groans
And Men are bound to sullen contemplations in the night_L._J
Restless they turn on beds of sorro*w*; in their inmost brain
Feeling the crushing Wheels they rise_L,_J they write the bitter
words
Of Stern Philosophy & knead the bread of knowledge with
tears & groans_L._J

Such are the works of Dark Urthona_L._J Tharmas sifted the
corn_L._J
Urthona made the Bread of Ages & he placed it
In golden & in silver baskets in heavens of precious stone
And then took his repose in Winter in the night of Time_L._J

The Sun has left his blackness & has found a fresher morning
[Then *del*] ⌃And⌃ the mild moon rejoices in the clear &
cloudless night

Page 138 DESIGN: At the foot of the page is a lovely nude woman stretched across
the page, leaning on her right side and looking up the left margin.
  ll. 20–1 are from *America* pl. 8, ll. 49–50 (p. 142).

And Man walks forth from midst of the fires﹐;﹐ the evil is all
    coṇsumd﹐.﹐
His eyes behold the Angelic spheres arising night & day﹐,﹐
The stars consumd like a lamp blown out & in their stead
    behold
The Expanding Eyes of Man beholds the depths of wondrous
    worlds﹐,﹐   [25]
⌃One Earth﹐,﹐ one sea beneath nor Erring Globes wander
    but Stars
⌃Of fire rise up nightly from the Ocean & one Sun
⌃Each morning like a New born Man issues with songs &
    Joy
⌃Calling the Plowman to his Labour & the Shepherd to his   800
    rest﹐.﹐
⌃He walks upon the Eternal Mountains raising his heavenly
    voice﹐,﹐   [30]
⌃Conversing with the Animal forms of wisdom night & day
⌃That risen from the Sea of fire renewd walk oer the Earth⌃

⌃For Tharmas brought his flocks upon the hills & in the Vales
⌃Around the Eternal Mans bright tent the little Children
    play
⌃Among the wooly flocks﹐.﹐ The hammer of Urthona Sounds⌃   [35]
In the deep caves beneath﹐;﹐ his limbs renewd﹐,﹐ his Lions
    roar
Around the Furnaces & in Evening sport upon the plains﹐.﹐
They raise their faces from the Earth conversing with the
    Man﹐:﹐

'How is it we have walkd thro fires & yet are not consumd﹐?﹐
How is it that all things are changd even as in ancient
    times﹐?﹐'   [40]
                          [*Page 139*]
The Sun arises from his dewy bed & the fresh airs
Play in his smiling beams giving the seeds of life to grow

l. 25: 'beholds' should be 'behold'.
ll. 26–35 are written over an erasure of nine lines. l. 26 is in a stanza break.

Page 139 DESIGN: At the foot of the page is the back of a naked figure whose
left toe just touches a circle that disappears off the bottom margin. He seems to be

And the fresh Earth beams forth ten thousand thousand
 springs of life∟·⌟
Urthona is arisen in his strength∟,⌟ no longer now
Divided from Enitharmon∟,⌟ no longer the Spectre Los∟·⌝   [∟
Where is the Spectre of Prophecy∟?⌟ where the delusive
 phantom∟?⌟
Departed & Urthona rises from the ruinous walls
In all his ancient strength to form the golden armour of
 science
For intellectual War∟·⌟ The war of swords departed now∟,⌟
The dark Religions are departed & sweet Science reigns∟·⌟   [

End of The Dream

springing upward, bending sinuously and beautifully to the right, and reaching
toward the right margin with his right hand, which may be a cloven hoof. His
wrist goes over the last word, 'Dream'. (He is analogous to the figure on p. 2;
a similar design is on *Night Thoughts* drawing no. 139 [BMPR].)

Page 140 has only the *Night Thoughts* engraving.

[*Page 141*]

Beneath the veil of [*word del*] ⌄Vala⌄ rose Tharmas from
    dewy tears⌊·⌋
The [ancient *del*] ⌄⌄*eternal⌄⌄ man bowd his bright head &
    Urizen prince of light
[Astonishd lookd from his bright Portals calling thus to
    Luvah
[O Luvah in the *del*] ————————————————
Astonishd lookd from his bright portals. Luvah king of Love   [*5*]
Awakend Vala. Ariston ran forth with bright Anana[*?*]
And dark Urthona rouzd his shady bride from her deep
    den⌊·⌋
Pitying they viewd the new born demo*n*, ⌄[Awaking from his
    stony slumber *del*]⌄ for they could not love⌊·⌋
[After(*?*) their(*?*) sin(*?*) *del*] ——————————————
Male formd the demon mild⌊,⌋ athletic force his shoulders
    spread   [*10*]
And his bright feet firm as a brazen alta*r*, bu*t* the parts
To love devote*d*, female, all astonishd stood the hosts
Of heaven, while Tharmas with wingd speed flew to the
    sandy shore ⌄[ocean *del*]⌊·⌋⌄
He rested on the desart wild & on the raging sea
He stood & stretchd his wings &ᶜ———   [*15*]

With printless feet scorning the concave of the joyful sky⌊,⌋
Female her form bright as the summer but the parts of love
Male & her brow radiant as da*y* darted a lovely scorn⌊·⌋
Tharmas beheld from his high rocks &———   [*19*]

Other ADDITIONAL FRAGMENTS not integrated with *Vala* are on pp. 56,
88, and perhaps p. 42.

Page 141 seems to consist of scraps of a previous draft of the poem, as does p. 142.
    l. 8: The words above l. 8 were deleted in pencil.
    l. 9: Only two to four words were written in this line before it was deleted.
They could be: 'After their sin'.
    ll. 15, 19: The '&ᶜ' and '&' presumably refer to passages written elsewhere and
now lost.

[*Page 142*]

*The ocean calm₎,₎ the clouds fold round & fiery flames of love
*Inwrap the immortal limbs struggling in terrific joy₎;₎
*Not long₎;₎ thunders lightnings swift rendings & blasting winds
*Sweep oer the struggling copulatio*n*, in fell writhing pangs
*They lie in twisting agonies beneath the covring heavens₎·₎ [⸏

---

*The womb impressd₎,₎ Enion fled & hid in verdant mountains
*Yet here his heavenly orbs &ᶜ

---

*From Enion pours the seed of life & death in all her limbs
*Frozen₎;₎ in the womb of Tharmas rush the rivers of Enions pain₎·₎
*Trembling he lay swelld with the deluge₎,₎ stifling in the anguish₎·₎ [⸏

[*Page 144*]
That I should hide thee with my power &
And now thou darknest in my presence, never from my sight

[*Page 143*]
[*words del*] ⌃⌃*Opening his rifted rocks₎,₎⌃⌃ mingling [their bodies *del*] ⌃⌃*together they⌃⌃ join in burning anguish₎,₎

Page 144 DESIGN: Below the text, which takes up only the top fraction of the torn page, is a male(?) figure sitting on his heels with his back to us, in the middle of the coils of a snake which is wrapped around his torso. There is a vague, undecipherable sketch crossed out to the right. (He may be related to the serpent-man on p. 7.)

Pages 144, 143 are evidently bound backward, for p. 144, ll. 1–2, p. 143, ll. 1–10, 14–15 are copied from p. 7, ll. 13–14, 20–8, p. 8, ll. 12, 20.

l. 1 was partly torn off, but the loops that come on to the page would fit 'delight thee with my beauty', as on p. 7, l. 13. Similarly, a loop coming down above 'That' would fit 'Spectre' as on p. 7, l. 12.

Page 143 is a small torn scrap of paper, and in the left margin someone has written '(for 1st night varied)'. The ends of ll. 10, 14–15, and perhaps l. 12 were torn off.

l. 1: The first (erased) words of this line could not have been 'Howling harsh shrieking' (as on p. 7, where the line is copied), because of the loops below the line. Similarly, the line above it which was torn off cannot have ended with 'howling harsh shrieking' as on p. 7.

Mingling his horrible [brightness *del*] ∧∧*darkness∧∧ with her
   tender limbs∟;⌄ then high she soard   ∧∧*72∧∧
Shrieking above the ocean: a bright wonder that nature
   shudderd at∟,⌄
Half Woman & half [Serpen*t*, *del*] ∧∧*desart∧∧ all his [lovely
   changing *del*] ∧∧*darkly waving∧∧ colours mix
With her fair crystal clearness∟;⌄ in her lips & cheeks his
   [poisons *del*] ∧metals∧ rose   [*5*]
In blushes like the morning & his [scaly armour *del*] ∧∧*rocky
   features∧∧ softning
A [monster *del*] ∧∧*wonder∧∧ lovely in the heavens or   140
   wandring on the earth
With [*words del*] ∧female∧ voice [*words del*] ∧warbling upon
   the [hills & *del*] hollow vales∟,⌄∧
Beauty all blushing with desire∟,⌄ [*words del*] ∧a Self enjoying
   wonder∧
∧For Enion brooded groaning loud∟,⌄ the rough seas vege-
   tate. Golden rocks rise from the [vorte *del*]∧ ∧∧vast∧∧   [*10*]
And thus her voice; 'Glory, delight & sweet enjoyment born
∧To mild Eternity shut in a threefold shape delightful∧
To wander in [word *del*] ∧sweet∧ solitude [*word del*] ∧en-
   rapturd∧ at every wind
∧[Shining across the ocean / Enion brooded groaning the
   golden rocks vegetate The V
∧to *del*] Infolding the bright woman [from the desolving(?)
   winds / & thus   [*15*]
∧her voice & *del*]∧

[*Page 145*]
   ∧The Lamb of God stood before Urizen opposite∧
In Entuthon Benithon in the Shadows of torment & woe
Upon the heights of [Entuthon that *del*] ∧Amalek∟;⌄∧ taking
   refuge in his arms

    l. 4: 'desart' could be 'beast'.
    l. 8: The loops and bumps of the erased words under this line would fit 'With
Spirit voice incessant wailing in incessant thirst' as on p. 7, l. 27.
    l. 10 is inserted in a stanza-break.
    l. 12 is written over an erasure.
    l. 15: 'desolving' could be 'desolating' (as in p. 8, l. 20, where the line is largely
repeated).

The victims fled from punishmen*t*, [that *del*] ˄for˄ all his words were peace⌞.⌟

[He *del*] ˄Urizen˄ calld together all the synagogue of Satan in dark Sanhedrim   [

To judge the lamb of God to death as a murderer & robber⌞;⌟

As it [*word del*] ˄is˄ written⌞,⌟ He was numberd among the transgressors⌞.⌟

Cold⌞,⌟ dark⌞,⌟ opake the Assembly met twelve fold in Amalek⌞,⌟

Twelve rocky unshapd forms terrific⌞,⌟ forms of torture & woe⌞,⌟

Such seemd the Synagogue to distant view⌞;⌟ around them stood   [

The daughters of Canaan & Moab binding on the Stones

Their victims & with [Songs *del*] ˄Knives˄ tormenting them⌞,⌟ singing with tears

Over their victims. Thus was the Lamb of God condemnd to death⌞.⌟

They naild him upon the tree of Mystery & weeping over him

And mocking & then worshipping⌞,⌟ calling him Lord & King⌞.⌟   [

Sometimes as twelve daughters lovely & sometimes as five

They stood in beaming beauty & sometimes as One⌞,⌟ even Rahab⌞,⌟

[In which is Tirzah untranslucent(?) an opake covering *del*]

Who is Mystery⌞,⌟ Babylon the Great⌞,⌟ Mother of harlots

[And Rahab stripd off Luvahs robes from off the lamb of God⌞.⌟   [

[Then first she saw his glory & her harlot form appeard

[In all its turpitude beneath the divine light & of Luvahs robes

Page 145 ll. 1–17, 19, 30–2: The undeleted lines are on p. 105, ll. 1–10, 28–30 and p. 106, ll. 1–6, 17–19.

l. 18: The first five words were deleted with a scrawl and the last three by several distinctly different straight strokes.

l. 19: In the last word, Blake crossed the wrong ascender, so that it reads 'hartols'.

ll. 20–3 are deleted by three vertical strokes.

[She made herself a Mantle˻.˼

[Also the Vegetated bodies which Enitharmon wove in her
　looms

[Opend within the heart & in the loins & in the brain　　　　[*25*]

[To Beulah & the dead in Beulah descended thro their gates

[And some were woven one fold some two fold & some
　threefold

[In head or heart or reins according to the fittest order

[Of most merciful(?) pity & compassion to the spectrous
　dead *all del*]　　　　　　　　　　　　　　　　　　　 .

Darkness & sorrow coverd all flesh˻ ;˼ eternity was darkend˻.˼　[*30*]

Urizen sitting in his web of deceitful religion was tor-
　mented[?]˻.˼

He felt the female &ᶜ　　　　　　　　　　　　　　　　　　[*32*]

ll. 24–9 are deleted by two vertical strokes and copied on p. 100, ll. 20–2, 24–6.
Page 146 is blank.

———

his wit has not
[*be*]cause he is always thinking of his End
which has brimstone at both Ends
Pair of Spectacles
Ring her hands   [5
the Garden of Eden
Duck
[*wh*]en he calls her A Love lie Girl
t Love Errs
forwards   [*
an Ell taken from London is Undone
because they are [Isinglass *del*] Eyes in Glass   [*

'BLAKE'S MEMORANDUM'

—Blake's Memorandum in Refutation of the Information and Complaint of John Scholfield,[1] a private Soldier, &c

The Soldier has been heard to Say repeatedly, that he did not know how the Quarrel began, which he would not Say if Such seditious words were Spoken.—

Mrs. Haynes Evidences, that she saw me turn him down the Road, & all the while we were at the Stable Door, and that not one word of charge against me was uttered, either relating to Sedition or any thing else; all he did was Swearing and threatening.—

Mr. Hosier heard him Say that he would be revenged, and would have me hanged if he could. He spoke this the Day after my turning him out of the Garden. Hosier says he is ready to give Evidence of this if necessary.—

The Soldier's Comrade Swore before the Magistrates,[2] while I was present, that he heard me utter Seditious words, at the Stable Door, and in particular Said, that he heard me D—n the K—g. Now I have all the Persons who were present at the Stable Door to witness that no Word relating to Seditious Subjects was uttered, either by one Party or the other, and they are ready, on their Oaths, to Say that I did not utter Such Words.—

Mrs. Haynes says very sensibly, that she never heard People quarrel, but they always charged each other with the Offence, and repeated it to those around, therefore as the Soldier charged not me with Seditious Words at that Time, neither did his Comrade, the whole Charge must have been fabricated in the Stable afterwards.—

[1] John Scolfield's 'Information and Complaint' of 15 Aug. 1803 is printed in *Blake Records*, 123–5. For evidence supplementing this 'Refutation' see Blake's letter of 16 Aug. 1803.
[2] No deposition by Private Cock, Scolfield's comrade, is known.

[¶6]   If we prove the Comrade perjured who swore that he heard me D—n the K—g, I believe the whole Charge falls to the Ground.

[¶7]   Mr. Cosens, owner of the Mill at Felpham, was passing by in the Road, and Saw me and the Soldier and William standing near each other; he heard nothing, but Says we certainly were not quarrelling.—

[¶8]   The whole Distance that William could be at any Time of the Conversation between me and the Soldier (Supposing Such Conversation to have existed) is only 12 Yards, & W—— Says that he was backwards and forwards in the Garden. It was a still Day, there was no Wind stirring.

[¶9]   William says on his Oath, that the first Words that he heard me Speak to the Soldier were ordering him out of the Garden; the truth is, I did not Speak to the Soldier till then, & my ordering him out of the Garden was occasioned by his Saying something that I thought insulting.

[¶10]   The Time that I & the Soldier were together in the Garden, was not Sufficient for me to have uttered the Things that he alledged.

[¶11]   The Soldier Said to Mrs. Grinder, that it would be right to have my House Searched, as I might have plans of the Country which I intended to Send to the Enemy; he called me a Military Painter; I suppose mistaking the Words Miniature Painter, which he might have heard me called. I think that this proves, his having come into the Garden, with Some bad Intention, or at least with a prejudiced Mind.[3]

[¶12]   It is necessary to learn the Names of all that were present at the Stable Door, that we may not have any Witnesses brought against us, that were not there.

[¶13]   All the Persons present at the Stable Door were, Mrs. Grinder and her Daughter, all the Time; Mrs. Haynes & her Daughter all the Time; Mr Grinder, part of the Time; Mr Hayley's Gardener part of the Time.— Mrs. Haynes was present from my turning him out at my Gate, all the rest of the time— What passed in the Garden, there is no person but William & the soldier, & myself can know.—

---

[3] At the trial, Blake's lawyer Samuel Rose prudently ignored Blake's allegation of predisposed malignity in Scolfield.

] There was not any body in Grinder's Tap-room, but an Old Man, named Jones, who (Mrs. Grinder Says) did not come out— He is the Same Man who lately hurt his Hand, & wears it in a sling—

] The Soldier after he and his Comrade came together into the Tap-room, threatened to knock William's Eyes out (this was his often repeated Threat to me and to my Wife) because W—— refused to go with him to Chichester, and Swear against me. William Said that he would not take a false Oath, for that he heard me Say nothing of the Kind (i.e. Sedition)⌊·⌋ Mrs. Grinder then reproved the Soldier for threatening William, and Mr. Grinder Said, that W—— should not go, because of those Threats, especially as he was Sure that no Seditious Words were Spoken.—

] William's timidity in giving his Evidence before the Magistrates, and his fear of uttering a Falsehood upon Oath, proves him to be an honest Man, & is to me an host of Strength. I am certain that if I had not turned the Soldier out of my Garden I never should have been free from his Impertinence & Intrusion.

] Mr. Hayley's Gardener came past at the time of the Contention at the Stable Door, & going to the Comrade Said to him, Is your Comrade drunk?—a Proof that he thought the Soldier abusive, & in an Intoxication of Mind.

] If Such a Perjury as this can take effect, any Villain in future may come & drag me and my Wife out of our Home, & beat us in the Garden, or use us as he pleases, or is able, & afterwards go and Swear our Lives away.

] Is it not in the Power of any Thief who enters a Man's Dwelling, & robs him, or misuses his Wife or Children, to go & Swear as this Man has Sworn?—

———

[*Page 1*]

The Smile

There is a Smile of Love
And there is a Smile of Deceit
And there is a Smile of Smiles
In which these two Smiles meet

And there is a Frown of Hate
And there is a Frown of Disdain
And there is a Frown of Frowns
Which you strive to forget in vain

For it sticks in the Hearts deep Core
And it sticks in the deep Back bone
And no Smile that ever was smild
But only one Smile alone

That betwixt the Cradle & Grave
It only once Smild can be
But when it once is Smild
Theres an end to all Misery⌊.⌋

The Golden Net

Three Virgins at the break of day⌊:⌋
'Whither young Man whither away⌊?⌋
Alas for woe! alas for woe!'
They cry & tears for ever flow⌊.⌋

[*Page 2*]

The one was Clothd in flames of fire⌊,⌋
The other Clothd in iron wire⌊,⌋

'The Golden Net' is an improvement of the draft on *Notebook* p. 14 (pp. 932-3).

The other Clothd in tears & sighs
Dazling bright before my Eyes⌞·⌟
They bore a Net of Golden twine
To hang upon the Branches fine⌞·⌟ [*10*]
Pitying I wept to see the woe
That Love & Beauty undergo
To be consumd in burning Fires
And in ungratified Desires
And in tears clothd Night & day [*15*]
Melted all my Soul away⌞·⌟
When they saw my Tears a Smile
That did Heaven itself beguile
Bore the Golden Net aloft
As on downy Pinions soft [*20*]
Over the Morning of my day⌞·⌟
Underneath the Net I stray
Now intreating Burning Fire⌞,⌟
Now intreating Iron Wire⌞,⌟
Now intreating Tears & Sighs⌞·⌟ [*25*]
O when will the morning rise⌞?⌟ [*26*]

[*Page 3*]
The Mental Traveller

I traveld thro' a Land of Men⌞,⌟
A Land of Men & Women too
And heard & saw such dreadful things
As cold Earth wanderers never knew

For there the Babe is born in joy [*5*]
That was begotten in dire woe
Just as we Reap in joy the fruit
Which we in bitter tears did Sow

And if the Babe is born a Boy
He's given to a Woman Old [*10*]

'The Mental Traveller' 1. 8: Cf. Psalm 126: 5: 'They that sow in tears shall reap in joy'.

Who nails him down upon a rock⌊,⌋
Catches his Shrieks in Cups of gold⌊.⌋

She binds iron thorns around his head⌊,⌋
She pierces both his hands & feet⌊,⌋
She cuts his heart out at his side   [
To make it feel both cold & heat⌊.⌋

Her fingers number every Nerve
Just as a Miser counts his gold⌊;⌋
She lives upon his shrieks & cries
And She grows young as he grows old   [

[*Page 4*]

Till he becomes a bleeding youth
And she becomes a Virgin bright⌊;⌋
Then he rends up his Manacles
And binds her down for his delight⌊.⌋

He plants himself in all her Nerves   [
Just as a Husbandman his mould
And She becomes his dwelling place
And Garden fruitful Seventy fold⌊.⌋

An aged Shadow soon he fades
Wandring round an Earthly Cot
Full filled all with gems & gold   [
Which he by industry had got

And these are the gems of the Human Soul⌊,⌋
The rubies & pearls of a lovesick eye⌊,⌋
The countless gold of the akeing heart⌊,⌋   [
The martyrs groan & the lovers sigh⌊.⌋

They are his meat⌊,⌋ they are his drink⌊;⌋
He feeds the Beggar & the Poor
And the way faring Traveller⌊;⌋
For ever open is his door⌊.⌋   [

His grief is their eternal joy⌊;⌋
They make the roofs & walls to ring
Till from the fire on the hearth
A little Female Babe does spring

[*Page 5*]
And she is all of solid fire   [*45*]
And gems & gold that none his hand
Dares stretch to touch her Baby form
Or wrap her in his swaddling-band

But She comes to the Man she loves
If young or old or rich or poor⌊;⌋   [*50*]
They soon drive out the aged Host
A Beggar at anothers door⌊.⌋

He wanders weeping far away
Untill some other take him in
Oft blind & age-bent sore distrest   [*55*]
Untill he can a Maiden win

And to allay his freezing Age
The Poor Man takes her in his arms⌊;⌋
The Cottage fades before his Sight⌊,⌋
The Garden & its lovely Charms⌊.⌋   [*60*]

The Guests are scatterd thro' the land
For the Eye altering alters all⌊;⌋
The Senses roll themselves in fear
And the flat Earth becomes a Ball⌊;⌋

The Stars Sun Moon all shrink away   [*65*]
A desart vast without a bound
And nothing left to eat or drink
And a dark desart all around⌊.⌋

l. 57: 'his freezing Age' is written over an illegible erasure.

[*Page 6*]

The honey of her Infant lips␣,␣
The bread & wine of her sweet smile␣,␣
The wild game of her roving Eye
Does him to Infancy beguile

For as he eats & drinks he grows
Younger & younger every day
And on the desart wild they both
Wander in terror & dismay␣.␣

Like the wild Stag she flees away␣,␣
Her fear plants many a thicket wild
While he pursues her night & day
By various arts of Love beguild␣,␣

By various arts of Love & Hate
Till the wide desart planted oer
With Labyrinths of wayward Love
Where roams the Lion Wolf & Boar

Till he becomes a [weeping(?) *del*] wayward Babe
And she [becomes(?) a(?) *del*] a weeping Woman Old␣.␣
Then many a Lover wanders here␣;␣
The Sun & Stars are nearer rolld␣.␣

The trees bring forth sweet Extacy
To all who in the desart roam
Till many a City there is Built
And many a pleasant Shepherds home

[*Page 7*]

But when they find the frowning Babe
Terror strikes thro the region wide␣;␣
They cry 'the Babe the Babe is Born'
And flee away on Every side

l. 84 is written over an erasure which may begin with 'They'.
l. 87: 'Then' is written over an illegible erasure.
ll. 89–91 are written over three erased lines, the last of which may begin with 'Built'.

For who dare touch the frowning form
His arm is witherd to its root⌊;⌋
Lions Boars Wolves all howling flee
And every Tree does shed its fruit   [*100*]

And none can touch that frowning form
Except it be a Woman Old⌊;⌋
She nails him down upon the Rock
And all is done as I have told⌊.⌋   [*104*]

The Land of Dreams

Awake awake my little Boy⌊!⌋
Thou wast thy Mothers only joy⌊;⌋
Why dost thou weep in thy gentle Sleep⌊?⌋
Awake⌊!⌋ thy Father does thee keep⌊.⌋

'O what Land is the Land of Dreams⌊?⌋   [*5*]
What are its Mountains & what are its Streams⌊?⌋
O Father I saw my Mother there
Among the Lillies by waters fair⌊.⌋

'Among the Lambs clothed in white
She walkd with her Thomas in sweet delight⌊.⌋   [*10*]
                    [*Page 8*]
I wept for joy⌊,⌋ like a dove I mourn⌊;⌋
O when Shall I again return⌊?⌋'

Dear Child I also by pleasant Streams
Have wanderd all Night in the Land of Dreams
But tho calm & warm the waters wide   [*15*]
I could not get to the other side⌊.⌋

'Father O Father what do we here
In this Land of unbelief & fear⌊?⌋
The Land of Dreams is better far
Above the light of the Morning Star⌊.⌋'   [*20*]

Mary

Sweet Mary the first time she ever was there
Came into the Ball room among the Fair⌞;⌟
The young Men & Maidens around her throng
And these are the words upon every tongue⌞:⌟

'An Angel is here from the heavenly Climes
Or again does return the Golden times⌞;⌟
Her eyes outshine every brilliant ray⌞,⌟
She opens her lips tis the Month of May⌞.⌟'

Mary moves in soft beauty & conscious delight
To augment with sweet smiles all the joys of the Night
Nor once blushes to own to the rest of the Fair
That sweet Love & Beauty are worthy our care⌞.⌟

[Page 9]

In the Morning the Villagers rose with delight
And repeated with pleasure the joys of the night
And Mary arose among Friends to be free
But no Friend from henceforward thou Mary shalt see⌞.⌟

Some said She was proud⌞,⌟ some calld her a whore
And some when she passed by shut to the door⌞;⌟
A damp cold came oer her⌞,⌟ her blushes all fled⌞;⌟
Her lillies & roses are blighted & shed⌞.⌟

'O why was I born with a different Face⌞?⌟
Why was I not born like this Envious Race⌞?⌟
Why did Heaven adorn me with bountiful hand
And then set me down in an envious Land⌞?⌟

'To be weak as a Lamb & smooth as a dove
And not to raise Envy is calld Christian Love
But if you raise Envy your Merit⌜'⌝s to blame
For planting such spite in the weak & the tame⌞.⌟

'Mary' ll. 21–2 appear in a slightly different form in Blake's autobiographical
poem in his letter of 16 Aug. 1803 (p. 1580).

'I will humble my Beauty⌊,⌋ I will not dress fine⌊,⌋
I will keep from the Ball & my Eyes shall not shine   [*30*]
And if any Girls Lover forsakes her for me
I'll refuse him my hand & from Envy be free⌊.⌋'

She went out in Morning attird plain & neat⌊;⌋
'Proud Marys gone Mad' said the Child in the Street⌊;⌋
She went out in Morning in plain neat attire   [*35*]
And came home in Evening bespatterd with mire⌊.⌋

[*Page 10*]

She trembled & wept sitting on the Bed side⌊;⌋
She forgot it was Night & she trembled & cried⌊;⌋
She forgot it was Night⌊,⌋ she forgot it was Morn⌊,⌋
Her soft Memory imprinted with Faces of Scorn⌊,⌋   [*40*]

With Faces of Scorn & with Eyes of disdain
Like foul Fiends inhabiting Marys mild Brain⌊;⌋
She remembers no Face like the Human Divine⌊.⌋
All Faces have Envy sweet Mary but thine

And thine is a Face of sweet Love in despair   [*45*]
And thine is a Face of mild sorrow & care
And thine is a Face of wild terror & fear
That shall never be quiet till laid on its bier⌊.⌋   [*48*]

The Crystal Cabinet

The Maiden caught me in the Wild
Where I was dancing merrily⌊;⌋
She put me into her Cabinet
And Lockd me up with a golden Key⌊.⌋

This Cabinet is formd of Gold   [*5*]
And Pearl & Crystal Shining bright
And within it opens into a World
And a little lovely Moony Night⌊.⌋

'The Crystal Cabinet' l. 8: 'lovely' is written over an erased word which may begin with 'fl'.

[*Page 11*]
Another England there I saw⌐,⌐
Another London with its Tower⌐,⌐   [
Another Thames & other Hills
And another pleasant Surrey Bower⌐,⌐

Another Maiden like herself
Translucent lovely shining clear
Threefold each in the other closd⌐;⌐   [
O what a pleasant trembling fear⌐!⌐

O what a smile a threefold Smile
Filld me that like a flame I burnd⌐;⌐
I bent to Kiss the lovely Maid
And found a Threefold Kiss returnd⌐.⌐   [

I strove to sieze the inmost Form
With ardor fierce & hands of flame
But burst the Crystal Cabinet
And like a Weeping Babe became⌐;⌐

A weeping Babe upon the wild   [
And Weeping Woman pale reclind
And in the outward air again
I filld with woes the passing Wind⌐.⌐

[*Page 12*]
The Grey Monk
'I die I die⌐!⌐' the Mother said⌐,⌐
'My Children die for lack of Bread⌐.⌐
What more has the merciless Tyrant said⌐?⌐'
The Monk sat down on the Stony Bed⌐.⌐

The blood red ran from the Grey Monks side⌐,⌐
His hands & feet were wounded wide⌐,⌐
His Body bent⌐,⌐ his arms & knees
Like to the roots of ancient trees⌐.⌐

'The Grey Monk' was drafted on *Notebook* p. 12 and copied on *Jerusalem* pl. 52
(pp. 929-30, 529).

1310

His eye was dry⌐;⌐ no tear could flow⌐;⌐
A hollow groan first spoke his woe⌐.⌐   [*10*]
He trembled & shudderd upon the Bed⌐;⌐
At length with a feeble cry he said

'When God commanded this hand to write
In the Studious hours of deep midnight
He told me the writing I wrote should prove   [*15*]
The Bane of all that on Earth I lovd⌐.⌐

'My Brother starvd between two Walls⌐,⌐
His Childrens Cry my Soul appalls⌐;⌐
I mockd at the wrack & griding chain⌐,⌐
My bent body mocks their torturing pain⌐.⌐   [*20*]

'Thy Father drew his Sword in the North⌐,⌐
With his thousands strong he marched forth⌐;⌐

[*Page 13*]

Thy Brother has armd himself in Steel
To avenge the wrongs thy Children feel

'But vain the Sword & vain the Bow⌐,⌐   [*25*]
They never can work Wars overthrow⌐.⌐
The Hermits Prayer & the Widows tear
Alone can free the World from fear

'For a Tear is an Intellectual Thing
And a Sigh is the Sword of an Angel King   [*30*]
And the bitter groan of the Martyrs woe
Is an Arrow from the Almighties Bow⌐.⌐

'The hand of Vengeance found the Bed
To which the Purple Tyrant fled⌐;⌐
The iron hand crushd the Tyrants Head   [*35*]
And became a Tyrant in his stead⌐.⌐'   [*36*]

Auguries of Innocence

To see a World in a Grain of Sand
And a Heaven in a Wild Flower⌞,⌟
Hold Infinity in the palm of your hand
And Eternity in an hour⌞.⌟
A Robin Red breast in a Cage
Puts all Heaven in a Rage⌞.⌟
A dove house filld with doves & Pigeons

[*Page 14*]

Shudders Hell thro all its regions⌞.⌟
A dog starvd at his Masters gate
Predicts the ruin of the State⌞.⌟
A Horse misusd upon the Road
Calls to Heaven for Human blood⌞.⌟
Each outcry of the hunted Hare
A fibre from the Brain does tear⌞.⌟
A sky lark wounded in the wing⌞,⌟
A Cherubim does cease to sing⌞.⌟
The Game Cock clipd & armd for fight
Does the Rising Sun affright⌞.⌟
Every Wolfs & Lions howl
Raises from Hell a Human Soul⌞.⌟
The wild deer wandring here & there
Keeps the Human Soul from Care⌞.⌟
The Lamb misusd breeds Public strife
And yet forgives the Butchers Knife⌞.⌟
The Bat that flits at close of Eve
Has left the Brain that wont Believe⌞.⌟
The Owl that calls upon the Night
Speaks the Unbelievers fright⌞.⌟
He who shall hurt the little Wren
Shall never be belovd by Men⌞.⌟

[*Page 15*]

He who the Ox to wrath has movd
Shall never be by Woman lovd⌞.⌟
The wanton Boy that kills the Fly
Shall feel the Spiders enmity⌞.⌟

He who torments the Chafers sprite   [35]
Weaves a Bower in endless Night⌊·⌋
The Caterpiller on the Leaf
Repeats to thee thy Mothers grief⌊·⌋
Kill not the Moth nor Butterfly
For the Last Judgment draweth nigh⌊·⌋   [40]
He who shall train the Horse to War
Shall never pass the Polar Bar⌊·⌋
The Beggers Dog & Widows Cat⌊,⌋
Feed them & thou wilt grow fat⌊·⌋
The Gnat that sings his Summers song   [45]
Poison gets from Slanders tongue⌊·⌋
The poison of the Snake & Newt
Is the sweat of Envys Foot⌊·⌋
The Poison of the Honey Bee
Is the Artists Jealousy⌊·⌋   [50]
The Princes Robes & Beggars Rags
Are Toadstools on the Misers Bags⌊·⌋
A truth thats told with bad intent
Beats all the Lies you can invent⌊·⌋

[Page 16]

It is right it should be so⌊;⌋   [55]
Man was made for Joy & Woe
And when this we rightly Know
Thro the World we safely go⌊·⌋
Joy & Woe are woven fine
A Clothing for the soul divine⌊;⌋   [60]
Under every grief & pine
Runs a joy with silken twine⌊·⌋
The Babe is more than Swadling Bands⌊;⌋
Throughout all these Human Lands
Tools were made & Born were hands⌊,⌋   [65]
Every Farmer Understands⌊·⌋
Every Tear from Every Eye
Becomes a Babe in Eternity⌊;⌋
This is caught by Females bright

'Auguries of Innocence' ll. 37–8 are echoed in 'The Keys' to *For the Sexes*, pl. 19,
ll. 1–2 (p. 659), with the alteration of 'Repeats to thee' to 'Reminds thee of'.
    l. 69: 'This is' is written over an illegible erasure.

And returnd to its own delight⌐·⌐   [⸴
The Bleat the Bark Bellow & Roar
Are Waves that Beat on Heavens Shore⌐·⌐
The Babe that weeps the Rod beneath
Writes Revenge in realms of death⌐·⌐
The Beggars Rags fluttering in Air   [⸴
Does to Rags the Heavens tear⌐·⌐
The Soldier armd with Sword & Gun
Palsied strikes the Summers Sun⌐·⌐
The poor Mans Farthing is worth more
Than all the Gold on Africs Shore⌐·⌐   [⸴

[*Page 17*]

One Mite wrung from the Labrers hands
Shall buy & sell the Misers Lands
Or if protected from on high
Does that whole Nation sell & buy⌐·⌐
He who mocks the Infants Faith   [⸴
Shall be mock'd in Age & Death⌐·⌐
He who shall teach the Child to Doubt
The rotting Grave shall neer get out⌐·⌐
He who respects the Infants faith
Triumphs over Hell & Death⌐·⌐   [⸴
The Childs Toys & the Old Mans Reasons
Are the Fruits of the Two seasons⌐·⌐
The Questioner who sits so sly
Shall never Know how to Reply⌐·⌐
He who replies to words of Doubt   [⸴
Doth put the Light of Knowledge out⌐·⌐
The Strongest Poison ever known
Came from Caesars Laurel Crown⌐·⌐
Nought can deform the Human Race
Like to the Armours iron brace⌐·⌐   [⸴
When Gold & Gems adorn the Plow
To peaceful Arts shall Envy Bow⌐·⌐
A Riddle or the Crickets Cry
Is to Doubt a fit Reply⌐·⌐
The Emmets Inch & Eagles Mile   [⸴
Make Lame Philosophy to smile⌐·⌐

[*Page 18*]

He who Doubts from what he sees
Will neer Believe do what you Please⌐·⌐
If the Sun & Moon should doubt
Theyd immediately Go out⌐·⌐   [*110*]
To be in a Passion you Good may do
· But no Good if a Passion is in you⌐·⌐
The Whore & Gambler by the State
Licencd build that Nations Fate⌐·⌐
The Harlots cry from Street to Street   [*115*]
Shall weave Old Englands winding Sheet⌐·⌐
The Winners Shout⌐,⌐ the Losers Curse
Dance before dead Englands Hearse⌐·⌐
Every Night & every Morn
Some to Misery are Born⌐·⌐   [*120*]
Every Morn & every Night
Some are Born to sweet delight⌐,⌐
Some are Born to sweet delight⌐,⌐
Some are Born to Endless Night⌐·⌐
We are led to Believe a Lie   [*125*]
When we see [With *del*] not Thro the Eye
Which was Born in a Night to perish in a Night
When the Soul Slept in Beams of Light⌐·⌐
God Appears & God is Light
To those poor Souls who dwell in Night   [*130*]
But does a Human Form Display
To those who Dwell in Realms of day⌐·⌐   [*132*]

[*Page 19*]

Long John Brown & ⌃Little⌃ Mary Bell

[Pretty *del*] Little Mary Bell had a Fairy in a Nut⌐,⌐
[Young *del*] Long John Brown had the Devil in his Gut⌐;⌐

ll. 125–6 appear in a slightly altered form in 'The Everlasting Gospel', part k (*Notebook* p. 54), ll. 105–8 (p. 1069).

l. 126: The deletion is in Brown ink, though the rest of the line is in Black ink.

l. 127: The gourd which God made to shade Jonah 'came up in a night, and perished in a night' (Jonah 4: 10).

'Long John Brown & Little Mary Bell' title   'Little' is inserted over a caret in Grey ink, as are all the changes in the first stanza of the poem, though the original transcript is in Black ink.

[Young *del*] Long John Brown lovd [Pretty *del*] Little Mary Bell
And the Fairy drew the Devil into the Nut-shell_{L.J}

Her Fairy Skipd out & her Fairy Skipd in_{L;J}   [
He laughd at the Devil Saying 'Love is a Sin_{L.J}'
The Devil he raged & the Devil he was wroth
And the Devil enterd into the Young Mans broth_{L.J}

He was soon in the Gut of the loving Young Swain
For John eat & drank to drive away Loves pain   [
But all he could do he grew thinner & thinner
Tho he eat & drank as much as ten Men for his dinner_{L.J}

Some said he had a Wolf in his stomach day & night_{L,J}
Some said he had the Devil & they guessd right_{L;J}
The fairy skipd about in his Glory Joy & Pride   [
And he laughd at the Devil till poor John Brown died_{L.J}

Then the Fairy skipd out of the old Nut shell
And woe & alack for Pretty Mary Bell
For the Devil crept in when the Fairy skipd out
And there goes Miss Bell with her fusty old Nut_{L.J}   [

[*Page 20*]

William Bond

I wonder whether the Girls are Mad
And I wonder whether they mean to Kill
And I wonder if William Bond will die
For assuredly he is very ill_{L.J}

He went to Church in a May morning   [
Attended by Fairies one two & three
But the Angels of Providence drove them away
And he returnd home in Misery_{L.J}

He went not out to the Field nor Fold_{L,J}
He went not out to the Village nor Town   [
But he came home in a black black cloud
And took to his Bed & there lay down

And an Angel of Providence at his Feet
And an Angel of Providence at his Head
And in the midst a Black Black Cloud [15]
And in the midst the Sick Man on his Bed

And on his Right hand was Mary Green
And on his Left hand was his Sister Jane
And their tears fell thro the black black Cloud
To drive away the sick mans pain⌊·⌋ [20]

[Page 21]
'O William if thou dost another Love⌊,⌋
Dost another Love better than poor Mary⌊,⌋
Go & take that other to be thy Wife
And Mary Green shall her Servant be⌊·⌋'

'Yes Mary I do another Love⌊,⌋ [25]
Another I Love far better than thee
And Another I will have for my Wife⌊;⌋
Then what have I to do with thee⌊?⌋

'For thou art Melancholy Pale
And on thy Head is the cold Moons shine [30]
But she is ruddy & bright as day
And the Sun beams dazzle from her eyne⌊·⌋'

Mary trembled & Mary chilld
And Mary fell down on the right hand floor
That William Bond & his Sister Jane [35]
Scarce could recover Mary more⌊·⌋

When Mary woke & found her Laid
On the Right hand of her William dear⌊,⌋
On the Right hand of his loved Bed⌊,⌋
And saw her William Bond so near [40]

'William Bond' l. 28: 'what have I to do with thee' is repeated in 'To Tirzah'
(*Songs* pl. 52) ll. 4, 16 and in 'The Everlasting Gospel', part d (*Notebook* p. 120),
l. 32 (pp. 1057, 198).

The Fairies that fled from William Bond
Danced around her Shining Head_L;_J
[*Page 22*]
They danced over the Pillow white
And the Angels of Providence left the Bed_L._J

I thought Love livd in the hot sun Shine   ·   [
But O he lives in the Moony light_L!_J
I thought to find Love in the heat of day
But sweet Love is the Comforter of Night_L._J

Seek Love in the Pity of others Woe_L,_J
In the gentle relief of anothers care_L,_J   [
In the darkness of night & the winters snow_L,_J
In the naked & outcast Seek Love there_L!_J   [

'THE ORDER' OF THE SONGS

'Order' of the *Songs*

William Blake₍ₗ,₎ one who is very much delighted with being
in good Company₍ₗ·₎

[*Sketch of a naked floating man.*]

Born 28 Novʳ 1757 in London & has died Several times
Since₍ₗ·₎
January 16
1826

The above was written & the drawing annexed by the desire
of Mʳ Leigh₍ₗ;₎[1] how far it is an Autograph is a Question₍ₗ·₎ I
do not think an Artist can write an Autograph₍ₗ,₎ especially
one who has Studied in the Florentine & Roman Schools₍ₗ,₎ as
such an one will Consider what he is doing but an Autograph
as I understand it, is writ helter skelter like a hog upon a rope or
a Man who walks without Considering whether he shall run
against a Post or a House or a Horse or a Man & I am apt to
believe that what is done without meaning is very different
from that which a Man does with his Thought & Mind &
ought not to be Calld by the Same Name.

I consider the Autograph of Mʳ Cruikshank which very
justly stands first in the Book[2] & that Beautiful Specimen of
Writing by Mʳ Comfield & my own; as standing [*in*] the same
Predicament₍ₗ;₎ they are in some measure Works of Art & not
of Nature or Chance₍ₗ·₎

[1] This is evidently the 'Mʳ [*Samuel*] Leigh Bookseller, [(Strand) *who paid for a*]
Sub[*scription*] for Job' on 10 Jan. 1824 and 29 April 1826 (*Blake Records*, 587, 591).
Leigh was a publisher who specialized in Bibles and Prayer Books (according to
a prospectus of forty-three of his publications [BM 11902 bbb 23]). At his shop at
18 Strand Blake was apparently 'a frequent visitor . . . it was there he drew his
"Demon Flea" [*in Oct. 1819*]' (W. Thornbury, *British Artists from Hogarth to Turner*
[1861], ii. 28).
[2] The autograph of George Cruikshank (1792–1878) is now the frontispiece to
Volume I, whereas Blake's is in the second volume.

Heaven born the Soul a Heavenward Course must hold
For what delights the Sense if False & Weak⌊·⌋
Beyond the Visible World she soars to Seek
Ideal Form, The Universal Mold⌊·⌋
Michael Angelo. Sonnet as Translated by Mr Wordsworth⌊·⌋[3]

[3] Blake copied these lines accurately from Wordsworth's *Poems* (1815), lent to
him by Crabb Robinson in Dec. 1825, except for punctuation, spelling ('Mould'),
and the transposition of the second and third lines. In his annotations to the volume
(p. 1512) he again referred to this sonnet.

MS INSCRIPTIONS ON DESIGNS

The inscriptions printed here are written on the designs themselves.

———

'Father & mother . . .' (?1793)

Father & Mother I return From flames of fire
tried[?] & pure & white⌞.⌟

'The Bible of Hell' (?1793)

The Bible of Hell, in Nocturnal Visions collected.
Vol. I. Lambeth.

'Is all joy forbidden' (?1793)

Is all joy forbidden⌞?⌟

'How I pity' (?1793)

How I pity⌞!⌟

'Visions of Eternity' (?1793)

VISIONS / OF / ETERNITY⌞.⌟

'For Children The Gates of Hell' (?1793)

For Children / The / Gates / of / HELL

'Behold your King' (?1795)

Behold your King⌞.⌟

Descriptions (1797) of Blake's designs for *Poems by Mr. Gray* (1790)

[*Title-page verso:*]

Ode on the Spring

Design[1]

[¶*1*]	1	The Pindaric Genius recieving his Lyre
[¶*2*]	2	Gray writing his Poems
[¶*3*]	3	The Purple Year awaking from the Roots of Nature & The Hours suckling their Flowery Infants
[¶*4*]	4	'With me the Muse shall sit & think At ease reclind in rustic state'
[¶*5*]	5	'Brush'd by the hand of rough Mischance Or childd by Age'
[¶*6*]	6	Summer Flies reproaching the Poet

Around the Springs of Grey my wild root weaves⌞;⌟
Traveller repose & Dream among my leaves.
                              —Will. Blake

[*Page 48*]

Ode on the Death of a Favourite Cat

Design.

[¶*7*]	1.	'Midst the tide Two Angel forms were seen to glide'
[¶*8*]	2.	'Demurest of the Tabby Kind'
[¶*9*]	3	'The pensive Selima⌞. . .⌟ Her Ears of Jet & Emrald Eyes She saw & purr'd applause'

[1] The word 'Design' and the entries for Nos. 3–6 are written in ink over the same thing in pencil.

No. 3: The line with an X is 'And wake the purple year!'

No. 4: *All* the quotation marks are Blake's—viz., on title-page verso and pp. 48, 54, 62, 76, 82, 94, 106, 118, 126, 134, 148—except for the inscriptions on designs 17 (opening quotation marks in second and third lines), 18–21, 25 (quotation marks before and after 'which'; Blake opens with a double quotation mark and closes with a single one), 43 (second line), 45 (Blake opens with a double quotation mark and closes with a single one), 48 (closing quotation mark), 51, 58 (quotation mark after 'Cliffs.'), 69, 96, 97 (closing quotation mark in first line and opening one in second), which are the editor's.

No. 6: The line with an X is 'Thy joys no glitt'ring female meets'.

_0]_   4.   'Still had she gazd but midst the tide
              Two Angel forms were seen to glide. ⌊. . .⌋
              The hapless nymph with wonder saw
              A Whisker first & then a Claw &ᶜ'

_1]_   5.   'Malignant Fate sat by & smild
              The slippery verge her feet beguild
              She tumbled headlong in'

_2]_   6.   'Nine times emerging from the flood
              'She mew'd to every watry God'

[*Page 54*]

Ode on a distant prospect of Eton College

Design

_3]_   1   Windsor terrace, a Boy contemplating a distant view
              of Eton College.

_4]_   2.   A Boy flying a Kite

_5]_   3   Two Boys wandering in the woods by Eton College.
              The Shade of Henry the Sixth is seen among the
              trees.

_6]_   4.   'Say Father Thames for thou hast seen
              Full many a sprightly race ⌊. . .⌋
              Who foremost &ᶜ'

_7]_   5.   'The captive linnet'
              'The rolling circle'
                'murmuring labours' &ᶜ

_8]_   6.   'Yet see how all around them wait ⌊. . .⌋
              The vultures of the Mind'

_9]_   7.   'Ambition this shall tempt to rise
              Then whirl the wretch from high' &ᶜ

[*A new column to the right:*]

Design

_9]_   8.   'Lo in the Vale of Years beneath ⌊. . .⌋
              The painful family of Death'

No. 12: Gray's line reads 'Eight times'. (Only substantial variants are noted here.)
The line illustrated is on the page before the design.

No. 18: The line with an X is: 'These shall the fury passions tear, The vultures of
the mind'.

[¶*21*]   9.   'Where Ignorance is bliss
               Tis folly to be wise'
[¶*22*]   10   Boys playing at Top.

[*Page 62*]

A Long Story

Design

[¶*23*]   1.   A circular Dance
[¶*24*]   2.   Fairies riding on Flies
[¶*25*]   3.   'An ancient Pile of Bui[*l*]ding' which
               'Employd the power of Fairy hands'
[¶*26*]   4.   'The Seals & Maces dancd before him'
[¶*27*]   5.   'A brace of warriors'
[¶*28*]   6   'Bewitchd the children of the Peasants'
[¶*29*]   7.   'Upstairs in a whirlwind rattle'
[¶*30*]   8.   'Out of the window whisk they flew'
[¶*31*]   9.   'At the Chapel door stand centry'
[¶*32*]   10.   'A sudden fit of ague shook him'
[¶*33*]   11.   'My Lady rose & with a grace
               She smild & bid him come to dinner'
[¶*34*]   12.   'Guard us from long winded lubbers
               That to Eternity would sing
               And keep my Lady from her rubbers'

[*Page 76*]

Ode to Adversity

Design

[¶*35*]   1.   A Widower & children
[¶*36*]   2.   Grief among the roots of trees
[¶*37*]   3.   'Purple tyrant vainly groans'
[¶*38*]   4.   'Stern rugged Nurse'
               Virtue Nursd in the Lap of Adversity

No. 22: The design surrounds the contents for 'A Long Story'.

No. 27: The line illustrated is on the previous text page.

No. 32: The line with an X is 'In peaked hoods and mantles tarnish'd'.

No. 38: 'Virtue . . . Adversity' is an afterthought squeezed in following the line above. The line with an X is: 'To thee he gave the heavenly birth'.

5. 'In thy Gorgon terrors clad ⌊. . .⌋
Screaming horrors funeral cry
Despair & Fell Disease & ghastly Poverty'

6. 'Oh gently on thy suppliants head
Dread Goddess lay thy chastening hand'

[*Page 82*]

The Progress of Poesy

1. The Beginning of Poesy. The blind begging Bard
2. Study
3. 'The Laughing flowers that round them blow'
'Drink life & fragrance as they flow'
4. 'Perching on the Scepterd hand
Of Jove, thy magic lulls the featherd King'
5. 'Cythereas Day.'
6. 'Hyperions march they spy & glittering Shafts of war'
7. 'Shaggy forms oer Ice built mountains roam'
8 'Alike they scorn the pomp of Tyrant power
And coward Vice that revels in her chains'
9. 'To him the mighty Mother did unveil
Her awful Face'
10. 'Dryden. ⌊. . .⌋
'Bright Eyd Fancy hovering o'er'
11. 'Oft before his Infant eyes would run
Such forms as glitter in the Muses ray'
12. A Muse.

[*Page 94*]

The Bard.

1. A Welch Bard.
2. The Slaughterd Bards, taken from the line
'The famishd Eagle screams & passes by' Page 98.
3. The Bard weaving Edwards fate

No. 40: The lines illustrated come from the previous text page. The line with an X is 'Thy form benign, oh Goddess, wear'.

No. 41: Since p. 82 has printed lines on it, Blake had to write his descriptions on a separate leaf, which is pasted over the printed p. 82.

No. 52: The design surrounds the contents for 'The Bard'.

No. 55: No line has an X, but there are two Xs above the title at the top of the page.

[¶56]	4.	Edward & his Queen & Nobles astonishd at the Bards Song
[¶57]	5.	'Hark how each Giant Oak & Desart Cave Sigh[s] to the Torrents awful voice beneath'
[¶58]	6.	'On yonder cliffs.' 'I see them Sit'
[¶59]	7.	'Oer thy country hangs The scourge of heaven'
[¶60]	· 8.	The Whirlwind. 'Hushd in grim repose'
[¶61]	9.	'Fell thirst & Famine Scowl A baleful smile upon their baffled guest'
[¶62]	10.	The death of Edwards Queen Eleanor from this line 'Half of thy heart we consecrate'
[¶63]	11.	Elizabeth. 'Girt with many a Baron bold'
[¶64]	12.	Spenser Creating his Fairies.
[¶65]	13.	'Headlong from the Mountains height Deep in the roaring tide he plungd to endless night'
[¶66]	14.	A poor Goatherd in Wales.—

[*Page 106*]

The Fatal Sisters

[¶67]	1.	The Three Fatal Sisters
[¶68]	2.	A Muse
[¶69]	3.	'Sigtryg with the Silken beard'
[¶70]	4.	'Persons of Horseback riding full speed toward a hill & seeming to Enter into it'
[¶71]	5.	'Iron sleet of arrowy shower Hurtles in the darkend air'
[¶72]	6.	'Shafts for shuttle dyed in gore Shoot the trembling cords along'
[¶73]	7.	'We the reins to Slaughter give'
[¶74]	8.	The Fatal Sisters riding thro the Battle. They are calld in Some Northern poems 'Choosers of the Slain'

No. 56: The line with an X is: '[Such were the sounds that o'er the crested pride] Of the first Edward scatter'd wild dismay'.

No. 59: I have omitted Blake's accidental quotation mark after 'hangs'.

No. 64: The line with an X is 'Truth severe, by fairy Fiction drest'.

No. 66: The design surrounds the contents for 'The Fatal Sisters'.

No. 70: The title to No. 70 is on a slip of paper pasted apparently over the passage these words replace. The printed text reads 'on horseback'.

No. 72: The line with an X is 'See the grisly texture grow!'

No. 74: The line with an X is 'Soon a King shall bite the ground.'

[Page 118]

The Descent of Odin

[Page 126]

The Triumphs of Owen

No. 75: No line has an X in the text.
No. 76: The inset page is blank.
Nos. 79, 84: No line has an X.
No. 86: The drawing surrounds the contents of 'The Triumphs of Owen'.
No. 89: The line with an X is 'Owen's praise demands my song'.
Nos. 90–1: No line has an X.
No. 92: The inset page is blank.

[*Page 134*]

Ode for Music.

[¶93]	1.	Fame.
[¶94]	2.	A bird singing
[¶95]	3.	A Genius driving away 'Comus & his midnight crew'
[¶96]	4.	'Milton struck the corded Shell ⌊. . .⌋
		Newtons self bends from his state sublime'
[¶97]	5.	'I ⌊. . .⌋ wood the gleam of Cynthia silver bright'
		'Where willowy Comus lingers with delight'
[¶98]	6.	'Great Edward with the lillies on his brow ⌊. . .⌋
		To hail the festal morning come'
[¶99]	7.	'Leaning from her golden cloud
		The venerable Margaret'
[¶100]	8.	'The Laureate wreathe'
[¶101]	9.	'Nor fear the rocks nor seek the Shore'
[¶102]	10.	Fame.

[*Page 142*]

Epitaph

[¶103]	1.	The mourner at the tomb
[¶104]	2.	Her infant image here below
		Sits smiling on a Fathers woe

[*Page 148*]

Elegy

[¶105]	1.	The author writing
[¶106]	2.	Contemplation among Tombs
[¶107]	3.	'The Plowman homeward plods his weary way
		And leaves the world to darkness & to me'
[¶108]	4.	'For him no more the blazing hearth shall burn ⌊. . .⌋
		Nor children run to lisp their sires return'
[¶109]	5.	'Oft did the Harvest to their sickle yield'
[¶110]	6.	'Chill penury repressd their noble rage'

Nos. 97, 99: No line has an X.
No. 98: Gray's line reads: 'To hail their Fitzroy's festal morning come'.
No. 102: The drawing surrounds the contents for the 'Epitaph'.
No. 108: No line has an X. Gray's line reads 'For them . . . No Children . . .'.

7. 'Some Village Hampden that with dauntless breast
   The little Tyrant of his Fields withstood'
8. 'Many a holy text around she strews'
9. 'Some kindred spirit shall enquire thy fate
   Haply some hoary headed swain may say
   Oft &c'
10. 'Slow thro the Churchway path we saw him borne'
11. A Shepherd reading the Epitaph
12 A Spirit conducted to Paradise

[*Page 158*]

To M⁚ˢ [N(?) *del*] Ann Flaxman

A little Flower grew in a lonely Vale∟;˩
Its form was lively but its colours pale∟·˩
One standing in the Porches of the Sun
When his Meridian Glories were begun
Leapd from the Steps of fire & on the grass   [*5*]
Alighted where this little flower was∟·˩
With hands divine he movd the gentle Sod
And took the Flower up in its native Clod∟·˩
Then planting it upon a Mountains brow∟:˩
'Tis your own fault if you dont flourish now∟·˩   [*10*]

William Blake

Title-page for Blair's *Grave* (1806)

A Series of Designs / Illustrative of / The Grave, / a Poem / by
Robert Blair. / Invented & Drawn by William Blake / 1806∟·˩¹

No. 112: No line has an X. On the drawing illustrating these words is a tomb inscribed

DUST THOU ART / HERE LIETH / WM BLAKE[?] / Aug
[*or* Age] 10

Blake died on 12 August 1827.

Page 158: 'To M⁚ˢ Ann Flaxman': Mrs. Flaxman was ordinarily called Nancy.
   l. 1: Blake described her as 'the flower of Flaxmans joy' in the poem with his
letter of 14 Sept. 1800.

¹ The design is reproduced in C. H. Collins Baker, *Catalogue of William Blake's
Drawings and Paintings in the Huntington Library*, rev. R. R. Wark (1957), pl. xxx.
A different title-page design was published, with the etched title: *THE* / GRAVE, /
A POEM. / *Illustrated by twelve Etchings* / Executed / *by* / LOUIS SCHIAVONETTI, / *From
the Original* / Inventions / *of* / WILLIAM BLAKE. / 1808.

'The Fall of Man' (1807)

The‚ Father indignant at the Fall—the Saviour, while the Evil Angels are driven, gently conducts our first parents out of Eden through a Guard of weeping Angels—Satan now awakes Sin, Death, & Hell, to celebrate with him the birth of war & Misery, while the Lion siezes the Bull, the Tyger the Horse, the Vulture and the Eagle contend for the Lamb⌊.⌋

'Epitome of Hervey's *Meditations among the Tombs*' (after 1808)

[*The words identify characters in the picture, reading from left to right and from bottom (least important) to top.*]

Widow Father Babe Baptism Hervey Angel of Death Virgin Wife Infancy Old Age Husband Angel of Providence Guardian Angel Child Angel of Death Mother Where is your Father The Lost Child Orphans Sophronia died in Childbed¹ She died on the Wedding Day² Orphan Moses Elias JESUS David Solomon Protecting Angel Aaron Abraham believed God These died for Love Ministering Angels Mother of Leah & Rachel Mother of Rebecca Recording Angels Protecting Angel NOAH Enoch Cain Serpent Abel Eve Adam God out of Christ is a Consuming Fire³ MERCY WRATH

Descriptions of *L'Allegro* and *Il Penseroso* Designs (?1816)

[*Leaf 1*]

[Mirth]

Mirth. Allegro

1 Heart easing Mirth.
Haste thee Nymph & bring with thee

¹ The picture is only somewhat distantly related to Hervey's *Meditations*, except for the reference to Sophronia, which comes literally from Hervey (*The Works of . . . James Hervey* [1769], i. 69): '*Sophronia, who died in child-bed*'.

² In Hervey (ibid. 64), it is the bridegroom who is imagined to have died on his wedding day.

³ The words 'God out of Christ is a Consuming Fire' (cf. 'God is a consuming fire', Deuteronomy 4:24; Hebrews 12:29) refer to the godly figure at the top who seems to be the source of the flames which fill the picture.

Jest & Youthful Jollity⌊,⌋
Quips & Cranks & Wanton Wiles⌊,⌋
Nods & Becks & wreathed Smiles⌊,⌋   [5]
Sport that wrinkled Care derides
And Laughter holding both his Sides⌊.⌋
Come & trip it as you go
On the light phantastic toe
And in thy right hand lead with thee   [10]
The Mountain Nymph Sweet Liberty.   [11]

These Personifications are all brought together in the First Design, Surrounding the Principal Figure which is Mirth herself⌊.⌋

[*Leaf 2*]

[The Lark]

2 To hear the Lark begin his flight
And Singing startle the dull Night
From his Watch Tower in the Skies
Till the dappled dawn does rise⌊.⌋   [4]

The Lark is an Angel on the Wing⌊.⌋ Dull Night starts from his Watch Tower on a Cloud. The Dawn with her dappled Horses arises above the Earth⌊.⌋ The Earth beneath awakes at the Larks Voice⌊.⌋

[*Leaf 3*]

[The Sun at his Eastern Gate]

3 Sometime walking not unseen
By hedge row Elms on Hillocks green
Right against the Eastern Gate
Where the Great Sun begins his state
Robed in Flames & amber Light   [5]
The Clouds in thousand Liveries dight
While the Plowman near at hand
Whistles o'er the Furrowd Land
And the Milkmaid Singeth blithe
And the Mower whets his Scythe   [10]
And every Shepherd tells his Tale
Under the Hawthorne in the Dale⌊.⌋   [12]

The Great Sun is represented clothed in Flames Surrounded
by the Clouds in their Liveries, in their various Offices at the
Eastern Gate; beneath in Small Figures Milton walking by
Elms on Hillocks green⌐;⌐ The Plowma*n*, The Milkmaid The
Mower whetting his Scyth*e*, & the Shepherd & his Lass under
a Hawthorne in the dale⌐·⌐

[*Leaf 4*]
[Sunshine Holiday]

4 Sometimes with secure delight
   The upland Hamlets will invite
   When the merry Bells ring round
   And the jocund Rebecks Sound
   To many a youth & many a Maid
   Dancing in the chequerd Shade
   And Young & Old come forth to play
   On a Sunshine Holiday⌐·⌐
In this design is Introduced
   Mountains on whose barren breast
   The Labring Clouds do often rest⌐·⌐
Mountains Clouds Rivers Trees appear Humanized on the
Sunshine Holiday. The Church Steeple with its merry bells⌐·⌐
The Clouds arise from the bosoms of Mountains While Two
Angels Sound their Trumpets in the Heavens to announce the
Sunshine Holiday⌐·⌐

[*Leaf 5*]
[The Goblin]

5 Then to the Spicy Nut brown Ale
   With Stories told of many a Treat
   How Fairy Mab the junkets eat⌐·⌐
   She was pinchd & pulld she said
   And he by Friars Lantern led
   Tells how the drudging Goblin sweat
   To earn his Cream Bowl duly Set
   When in one Night e'er glimpse of Morn
   His shadowy Flail had threshd the Corn
   That ten day labourers could not end⌐;⌐

Then crop-full out of door he flings
E'er the first Cock his Matin rings⌞.⌟   [*12*]

The Goblin crop full flings out of doors from his Laborious
task dropping his Flail & Cream bowl⌞,⌟ yawning & stretching
vanishes into the Sk*y*, in which is Seen Queen Mab Eating the
Junkets. The Sports of the Fairies are seen thro the Cottage
where 'She' lays in Bed 'pinchd & pulld' by Fairies as they
dance on the Bed the Cieling & the Floor & a Ghost pulls the
Bed Clothes at her Feet. 'He' is seen following the Friars
Lantern towards the Convent⌞.⌟[1]

[*Leaf 6*]

[The youthful Poets Dream]

6 There let Hymen oft appear
  In Saffron Robe with Taper clear
  With Mask & antique Pageantry⌞,⌟
  Such Sights as youthful Poets dream
  On Summers Eve by haunted Stream⌞;⌟   [*5*]
  Then to the well trod Stage anon
  If Johnsons learned Sock be on
  Or Sweetest Shakespeare Fancies Child
  Warble his native wood notes wild⌞.⌟   [*9*]

The youthful Poet sleeping on a bank by the Haunted Stream
by Sun Set sees in his dream the more bright Sun of Imagi-
natio*n*, under the auspices of Shakespeare & Johnso*n*,[2] in
which is Hymen at a Marriage & the Antique Pageantry
attending it⌞.⌟

[*Leaf 7*]

[Melancholy]

Melancholy. Pensieroso

7 Come pensive Nun devout & pure
  Sober stedfast & demure
  Still in Robe of darkest grain
  Flowing with magestic train⌞,⌟

---

[1] The quotation marks are Blake's.   [2] That is, Ben Jonson.

Come but keep thy wonted state
With even step & musing gait
   And looks commencing with the Skies
   ———

   And join with thee calm Peace & Quiet
Spare Fast who oft with Gods doth diet
And hears the Muses in a ring
A*y* round about Joves altar Sing
And add to these retired Leisure
Who in trim Gardens takes his pleasure
But first & chiefest with thee bring
Him who yon Soars on golden Wing
Guiding the Fiery wheeled Throne
The Cherub Contemplation⌊·⌋
———

Less Philomel will deign a song
In her sweetest saddest plight
Smoothing the rugged Brow of Night
While Cynthia Checks her dragon yoke
Gently o'er the accustomed[1] Oak⌊·⌋

These Personifications are all brought together in this design surrounding the Principal Figure [of *del*] Who is Melancholy herself⌊·⌋

[*Leaf 8*]
[The Wandring Moon]

8 To behold the wandring Moon
  Riding near her highest Noon
  Like one that has been led astray
  Thro the heaving wide pathless way
  And oft as if her head she bowd
  Stooping thro' a fleecy Cloud⌊·⌋
  Oft on a plat of rising ground
  I hear the far off Curfew sound
  Over Some wide waterd Shore
  Swinging slow with Sullen roar⌊·⌋

Milton in his Character of a Student at Cambridg*e* Sees the Moon terrified as one led astray in the midst of her path thro

---

[1] Blake wrote 'accustoned'.

heaven. The distant Steeple Seen across a wide water indicates
the Sound of the Curfew Bell⌊·⌋

[*Leaf 9*]
[The Spirit of Plato]

9 Where I may oft outwatch the Bear
With thrice great Hermes or unsphear
The Spirit of Plato to unfold
What Worlds or what vast regions hold
The Immortal Mind that has forsook   [*5*]
Its Mansion in this Fleshly nook
And of those Spirits that are found
In Fire, Air, Floo*d* & Underground⌊·⌋   [*8*]

The Spirit of Plato unfolds his Worlds to Milton in Con-
templation. The Three destinies sit on the Circles of Platos
Heavens weaving the Thread of Mortal Life⌊;⌋ these Heavens
are Venus Jupiter & Mars⌊·⌋ Hermes flies before as attending
on the Heaven of Jupiter⌊;⌋ the Great Bear is seen in the Sky
beneath Hermes & The Spirits of Fir*e*, Ai*r*, Water & Earth
Surround Miltons Chair⌊·⌋

[*Leaf 10*]
[The Sun in his Wrath]

10   And when the Sun begins to fling
His flaring Beams me Goddess bring
To arched walks of twilight Groves
And Shadows brown that Sylvan loves⌊·⌋   [*4*]

Milton led by Melancholy into the Groves away from the
Suns flaring Beams who is seen in the Heavens throwing his
darts & flames of fire⌊·⌋ The Spirits of the Trees on each side
are Seen under the domination of Insects raised by the Suns
heat⌊·⌋

[*Leaf 11*]
[Mysterious Dream]

11   There in close Covert by lorne Brook
Where no profaner Eye may look

With such concert as they keep
Entice the dewy featherd Sleep
 And let some strange mysterious dream   [
 Wave on his Wings in airy stream
Of liveliest Portraiture display*d*
On my Sleeping eyelids laid
And as I wake sweet Music breathe
Above; about: or underneath   [
Sent by some Spirit to Mortals good
Or the unseen Genius of the Wood⌊·⌋   [

Milton Sleeping on a Bank. Sleep descending with a Strange Mysterious dream upon his Wings of Scrolls & Nets & Webs unfolded by Spirits in the Air & in the Brook⌊;⌋ around Milton are Six Spirits or Fairies hovering on the air with Instruments of Music⌊·⌋

[*Leaf 12*]

[Milton. Old age]

12 .And may at last my weary Age
 Find out the peaceful Hermitage⌊,⌋
 The hairy Gown⌊,⌋ the mossy Cell
 Where I may sit & rightly spell
 Of every Star that heaven doth shew
 And every Herb that Sips the dew
 Till old Experience do attain
 To somewhat like Prophetic Strain⌊·⌋

Milton in his Old Age sitting in his Mossy Cell Contemplating the Constellation*s*, Surrounded by the Spirits of the Herbs & Flower*s*, bursts forth into a rapturous Prophetic Strain⌊·⌋

'Return Alpheus' (?1816)

Return Alpheus⌊·⌋[1]

---

[1] *Lycidas* ll. 132–5:

> Return *Alpheus*, the dread voice is past,
> That shrunk thy streams; Return *Sicilian Muse*,
> And call the Vales, and bid them hither cast
> Their Bels, and Flourets of a thousand hues.

'All Genius varies . . .' (?1819)

All Genius varies Thus_L;_⌋ Devils are various_L,_⌋
Angels are all alike_L._⌋

List of Apostles (?1823)

1 Peter P
2 Andrew a
3 James J
4 John J
5 Philip P
6 Bartholomew B
7 Thomas M
8 Matthew T[?]
9 James J[?]
10 Taddeus S[?]
11 Judas
12 Simon[1]

Dante Designs (1824–7)

Dante No. 3

At the top of the design is a figure labelled

The Angry God of this World and his throne[?] in Purgatory

and by his outstretched hands is

The THUNDER of[?] Egypt_L._⌋

He is being worshipped by a figure swinging a censer who is labelled

Caesar_L._⌋

Dante No. 4

Above the gate through which Virgil and Dante are passing is an inscription from the *Inferno* and a translation by Blake:

Lasciate ogni Speranza voi che entrate[?]
Leave every Hope you who in Enter_L._⌋

[1] For nos. 1–10, Blake's names correspond to those in Matthew 10: 2–4 and his initials to those in Luke 6: 14–16; nos. 11–12 do not correspond to the order in Matthew, in Luke, or in Mark 3: 16–18. The inscription seems to be written partly over a sketch (?1823) for *Job* pl. 18; B. Lindberg, *William Blake's Illustrations to the Book of Job* (1973), 330–1, suggests that Blake was contemplating identifying the twelve altar-stones of pl. 18 with the initials of the disciples. For no. 10 he reads 'Ze[lotes] Z[?]' and for no. 12 'I[s]c[ariot?]'.

Dante No. 7

The design is a kind of chart of the universe, showing

Homer [*who seems to be identified also as*] Satan[?]

at the centre of seven semicircles numbered:

1st circle / 2nd Circle / 3d Circle / 4th Circle / 5 / 6 / 7

Within them is written:

2nd Circle Every thing in Dantes Comedia shows That for Tyrannical Purposes he has made This World the Foundation of All⌊;⌋ the Goddess Nature Mystery is his Inspirer & not Imagination the Holy Ghost⌊;⌋[1] as Poor Churchill said 'Nature thou art my Goddess⌊.⌋'[2]

Round Purgatory is Paradise & round Paradise is Vacuum or Limbo so that Homer is the Center of All[3]⌊—⌋ I mean the Poetry of the Heathen Stolen & Perverted from the Bible not by Chance but by design by the Kings of Persia & their Generals⌊,⌋ The Greek Heroes & lastly by The Romans⌊.⌋

[1] This line is written:
1 Mystery[?]

Imagination[?]

of All   the Goddess Nature 3 [is(?)*del*] & not the Holy Ghost
[Nature(?) *del*]   2 is his Inspirer

For 'Mystery' Keynes (1957) and Roe read (not unreasonably) 'Mistress'. Keynes gives an ellipsis for 'Imagination' and Roe ignores it. The line may first have read: 'the Goddess Nature is not the Holy Ghost'. Then, with the aid of the numbers, it seems to have been emended to: 'the Goddess Nature [(]¹Mystery[)] ²is his Inspirer ³& not Imagination the Holy Ghost'. Keynes and Roe read: 'he has made This World the Foundation of All & the Goddess Nature Mistress; Nature [*not deleted by Roe*] is his Inspirer & not [*ellipsis in Keynes*] the Holy Ghost.'

[2] Charles Churchill, *The Prophecy of Famine*, A Scots Pastoral (1763), 5–6:

Thou NATURE, art *my* goddess—to thy law
Myself I dedicate—*hence* slavish awe
Which bends to fashion, and obeys the rules
Impos'd at first, and since observ'd by fools.

Keynes (1957) pointed out that Churchill was the intermediary between Blake and *King Lear*, I. ii. 1: 'Thou, Nature, art my Goddess'.

[3] The outermost semicircle is entitled 'Limbo of Weak Shadows', and at the top and right sides, in the '1st circle', is another diagram of creation. In the top right corner is a circle marked 'Purgatory', described below: 'it is an Island in Limbo'. Above 'Purgatory' is 'Terrestrial Paradise', and in the top and right margins are nine concentric arcs (which would, if continued, have overlapped with those in the main design) round 'Purgatory', each series identically marked from 'Purgatory' out: 'Moon / Mercury / Venus / Sun / Mars / Jupi[*te*]r / Saturn / Starry heaven / Vacuum'. The sixth word looks like 'Japan', but Jupiter belongs in this circle, and this reading (which Roe and Keynes do not question) is probable.

3ᵈ Circle   Swedenborg   does   the   same   in   saying   that   in   this World is the Ultimate of Heaven⌊.⌋ This is the most damnable Fals[e]hood of Satan & his Antichrist⌊.⌋

Dante No. *14*

A money-bag is labelled

Money⌊.⌋

Dante No. *15*

The design is entitled

The Stygian Lake⌊.⌋

Dante No. *16*

The design represents the Goddess Fortune in a hole, with the explanation:

The hole of a Shit house⌊:⌋ The Goddess Fortune is the devils Servant ready to Kiss any ones Arse⌊.⌋

Above her are two circles labelled

Celestial Globe / Terrestrial Globe⌊.⌋

Dante No. *17*

The design is entitled

Stygian Lake⌊.⌋

Dante No. *36*

On the verso of No. 36 is an erased pencil passage which may read:

N 61[?] last in the Inferno / unless[?] in[*cluding?*] Dante lifted / by Virgil f[*rom? the? wi*]ndow[?]¹

At the bottom right is 'Hell canto 34', which is in fact the last in the *Inferno*.

Dante No. *51*

A faint sketch on the verso of No. 51 is labelled in pencil

Vanni Fucci² / Hell Canto 24⌊.⌋

---

¹ Design 69, the last in the *Inferno*, represents Lucia carrying Dante in his sleep.
² Vanni Fucci is represented in designs 48 and 49.

Dante No. 56

On the verso of No. 56 is a very faint sketch of No. 10 labelled at the bottom:

One of the Whirlwinds of Love

and in the bottom right corner:

Hell Canto 5 / Paulo & Francesca⌊·⌋[1]

Dante No. 86

The design represents Dante, Statius, and Virgil on the stairs of Purgatory. Above to the right is the moon, within which one woman is looking in a mirror and another woman is standing beneath a tree. There are two exceedingly faint inscriptions, one of which to the right of the mirror may say

Leah and Rachel

and the other, close to the left figure, may be

Dantes Dream⌊·⌋

Dante No. 90

On the verso of No. 90 is written in pencil '24', '96', 'N 43 next at p. 33', and

Vanni Fucci⌊·⌋

Dante No. 99

The design represents the Queen of Heaven in Glory seated on a huge sunflower (like that in *Jerusalem* [1804–?20] pl. 53—p. 530) surrounded by figures. Above her head is

Mary

the fleur-de-lis in her right hand is labelled

Sceptre

and the mirror in her left hand is called

Looking Glass[?]

A circle at the top right seems to be called

Sun [?or Saturn.]

On either side of her are large figures, each with one open book and one closed one. The figure to the left seems to be labelled

Thrones[?]

---

[1] The engraving after this design is labelled in the bottom right:
The Whirlwind of Lovers from Dantes Inferno Canto V⌊·⌋

and his open and closed books are called

Homer [and] corded-round_{⌊·⌋}

The corresponding identifications to the right are:

Dominion / Aristotle / Bible / chaind round_{⌊·⌋}

Dante No. 101

The design is a diagram of the circles of hell, with the circles described in numerical order from the bottom up:

1 Limbo Charon[1]
2 Minos
3 Cerberus
4 Plutus & Phlegyas
5 / City of Dis / furies &   / Queen of Endless Woe[2] / Lesser Circle[3] / Point of the Universe / Canto Eleventh line 68
6 Minotaur⌊·⌋ The City of Dis seems to occupy the Space between the Fifth & Sixth Circles or perhaps it occupies both Circles with its Environs⌊·⌋
7 Centaurs. Most Likely Dante describes the 7 8 & 9 Circles in Canto XI v 18⌊·⌋ 3 Compartments⌊;⌋ Dante calls them Cerchietti⌊·⌋[4]
8 Malebolge Geryon. Containing 10 Gulfs[?]
[9] Containing 9 round[5]

In the left margin is:

It seems as if Dantes Supreme Good was something Superior to the Father or Jesus For if he gives his rain to the Evil & the Good & his Sun to the Just & the Unjust He could never have

---

[1] The order Blake apparently intended for these very rough jottings did not always correspond with the space left for the words. Consequently the order of some of the phrases is somewhat conjectural. In this first line, for instance, the words are actually written 'Limbo 1 Charon'.

[2] The 'queen of endless woe' comes from Hell, Canto IX, l. 45 in H. F. Cary's translation (The Vision; or Hell, Purgatory, and Paradise [1819], i. 74).

[3] The 'lesser circle, Point of the universe, dread seat of Dis' appears in Hell, Canto XI, ll. 68–9 (tr. Cary, i. 94).

[4] Cary (i. 92) translates them as 'close circles' in Hell, Canto XI, l. 19.

[5] Keynes (1957, p. 785) reads 'Lucifer' here, and Roe (p. 199) specifies that the name appears on the left wing of the angel in the ninth circle. I have searched in vain with a magnifying glass for any word in the ninth circle beyond 'Containing 9 round'.

Built Dantes Hell nor the Hell of the Bible neither in the way our Parsons explain it⌞·⌟ It must have been originally Formed by the devil Himself & So I understand it to have been⌞·⌟

In the right margin is:

Whatever Book is for Vengeance for Sin & Whatever Book is Against the Forgiveness of Sins is not of the Father but of Satan the Accuser & Father of Hell⌞·⌟

Sideways in the right margin is:

This is Upside Down when viewed from Hells Gate which ought to be at top [*and upside-down below it*] But right when Viewed from Purgatory after they have passed the Center⌞·⌟ In Equivocal Worlds Up & Down are Equivocal⌞·⌟

Blake's Chapter Titles to his Illuminated Transcription of Genesis (1827)

[*Leaf 3*]
Chap: I   The Creation of the Natural Man.

[*Leaf 6*]
Ch. 2   The Natural Man divided into Male & Female & of the Tree of Life & of the Tree of Good & Evil

[*Leaf 8*]
Ch 3   Of the Sexual Nature & its Fall into Generation & Death

Chap I   The substantive variants from the unrevised King James Version of the Bible are: 1 'heavens'; 11 'grass & the herb . . . after its [his] kind'; 12 'is [was] in itself after its [his] kind'; 14 'firmament of [the] heaven . . . and *for* years'; 17 'firmament of [the] heaven'; 18 '[and God saw that it was good *omitted*]'; 20 'in the [open] firmament'; 25 '[after his kind: and God saw that it was good]' is not inked in; 26 'every [creeping] thing'; 29 'of [all] the earth'.

Chap 2   3 'because [that] in it . . . works'; 4 '*And* these are . . . the day when [the day that]'; 7, 15 over 'man' is written 'Adam'; 13 '*en*compasseth'; 14 'and the name of the P [And the fourth river is Euphrates]'; 15 'into the garden [of Eden] to dress [it] and'; 17 'thou shalt surely *surely* die'; 22 'And *of* the rib'; 24 'leave [his] Father & [his] mother . . . they *twain* shall'.

Chap 3   1 'that [which]'; 5 'thereof [then] your eyes . . . Gods (*Elohim*) knowing'; 12 'gavest *me* to be'; 14 '*ac*cursed'; 15 'he shall bruize . . . bruize [it shall bruize . . . bruize]'; 18 '*unto*'; 19 'the [thy] face'; 22 'Behold Adam [Behold the man]'; 23 'forth at [from] the garden'.

[*Leaf 10*]

Chap IV   How Generation & Death took possession of the Natural Man & of the Forgiveness of Sins written upon the Murderers Forehead

Chap IV   1 'a man from Jehovah [from the Lord]'; 2 'of *the* sheep'; 3 '*for* an[?] offering'; 4 'and [to] his offering'; 8 'with [Abel] his brother'; 15 'unto Cain [unto him] . . . of him [on him] . . . a mark upon Cains forehead [a mark upon Cain, lest any finding him should kill him]'.

MARGINALIA

Words in the printed text which Blake under-
lined are given in *SMALL ITALIC CAPITALS*.

The passage to which Blake's indented mar-
ginal note applies is printed before it in smaller
type. When a printed sentence, or part of it, is
on one printed page, and Blake's note is on the
next, the page given is the one on which Blake's
comment appears.

MARGINALIA

===

MARGINALIA (?1788): Swedenborg, *Heaven and Hell* (1784)

[Half-title]

[In MS.:] 'And as Imagination bodies forth in forms of things unseen—turns them to shape & gives to airy nothing a local habitation & a name.'

Sh. [*A MIDSUMMER NIGHT'S DREAM*, v. i.]
    Thus Fools quote Shakespeare⌊!⌋ The Above Theseus's opinion not Shakespeares⌊.⌋ You might as well quote Satans blasphemies from Milton & give them as Miltons Opinions⌊.⌋

[Page 339]

513. *The angels appointed for instructors are from several societies . . . .

    *See N 73 Worlds in Universe for account of Instructing Spirits⌊.⌋

[Page 389]

There are also Hells under Hells . . . under every mountain, hill, rock, plain, and valley, there were particular Hells of different extent in length, breadth, and depth.

    *U*nder every <u>Good</u> is a hel*l*; i.e. hell is the outward or external of heave*n* & is of the body of the lor*d*, for nothing is destroyd⌊.⌋

Page 339. Swedenborg, *Of the Earths in the Universe and of their Inhabitants*, tr. J. Clowes (1787).

Marginalia: Lavater, *Aphorisms* p. 1

[*Page 1*]

*F*or the reason of these remarks see the last aphorism⌊.⌋ [1]

1.

Know, in the first place, that mankind agree in essence, as they do in their limbs and senses.

2.

Mankind differ as much in essence as they do in form, limbs, and senses— and only so, and not more.

This is true Christian philosophy far above all abstraction⌊.⌋

[*Page 2*]

3.

As in looking upward each beholder thinks himself the centre of the sky; so Nature formed her individuals, that each must see himself the centre of being.

Let me refer here, to a remark on aphorism 533 & another on 630 [*pp.* 1377, 1385 *below*]⌊.⌋

[*Page 4*]

8.

Who pursues means of enjoyment contradictory, irreconcilable, and self-destructive, is a fool, or what is called a sinner—*Sin and destruction of order are the same.*

A golden sentence⌊.⌋

11

The less you *can enjoy, the poorer, the scantier* yourself—the more you *can enjoy,* the richer, the more *vigorous.*

---

[1] The last aphorism (¶643) reads: 'If you mean to know yourself, interline such of these aphorisms as affected you agreeably in reading and set a mark to such as left a sense of uneasiness with you; and then shew your copy to whom you please.' Blake showed his notes 'to Fuseli; who said one could assuredly read their writer's character in *them*' (Gilchrist [1863], i. 62).

[*Page 5*]

You enjoy with wisdom or with folly, as the gratification of your appetites capacitates or unnerves your powers.

[Doubtful(*?*) *del*] *F*alse for weak is the joy that is never wearied⌊·⌋

13.

Joy and grief decide character. What exalts prosperity? what imbitters grief? what leaves us indifferent? what interests us? As the interests of MAN, SO HIS GOD—AS HIS GOD, SO HE.

All Gold⌊!⌋

[*Page 6*]

14.

WHAT IS A MAN'S INTEREST? WHAT CONSTITUTES HIS GOD, THE ULTIMATE of his wishes, his end of existence? Either that which on every occasion he communicates with the most unrestrained cordiality, or hides from every profane eye and ear with mysterious awe; to which he makes every other thing a mere appendix;—the vortex, the centre, the comparative point from which he sets out, on which he fixes, to which he irresistibly returns;—that, at the loss of which you may safely think him inconsolable;—that which he rescues from the gripe of danger with equal anxiety and boldness.

Pure gold⌊!⌋

[*Page 7*]

The story of the painter and the prince is well known: to get at the best piece in the artist's collection, the prince ordered fire to be cried in the neighbourhood—at the first noise the artist abruptly left the prince, and seized his darling—his Titian. The alarm proved a false one, but the object of purchase was fixed. The application is easy: of thousands it may be decided what loss, what gain, would affect them most. And suppose we cannot pronounce on others, cannot we determine on ourselves? This the sage o Nazareth meant when he said, *Where thy treasure is, there will thy heart be also—THE OBJECT OF YOUR LOVE IS YOUR GOD.*

This should be written in gold letters on our temples⌊·⌋

[*Page 8*]

16.

The greatest of characters, no doubt, was he, who, free of all trifling accidental helps, could see objects through one grand immutable medium, always at hand, and proof against illusion and time, reflected by every object, and invariably traced through all the fluctuation of things.

*T*his was Christ⌊·⌋

[Page 10]

20.

Distinguish with exactness, in thyself and others, between *wishes* and *will*, in the strictest sense.

Who has many wishes has generally but little will. Who has energy of will has few diverging wishes. Whose will is bent with energy on *one, must* renounce the wishes for *many* things. Who cannot do this is not stamped with the majesty of human nature.

Admirable!

THE ENERGY OF CHOICE, THE UNISON OF VARIOUS POWERS FOR ONE IS ONLY WILL, BORN UNDER THE AGONIES OF SELF-DENIAL AND RENOUNCED DESIRES.

Regeneration⌊.⌋

[Page 11]

21.

× ˎ Calmness of will is a sign of grandeur. The vulgar, far from hiding their *will*, blab their wishes—a single spark of occasion discharges the child of passions into a thousand crackers of desire.

Uneasy⌊.⌋

[Page 12]

23.

Who in the same given time can produce more than many others, has *vigour*; who can produce more and better, has *talents*; who *CAN PRODUCE WHAT NONE ELSE CAN, HAS GENIUS.*

[Pages 13–14]

28.

THE GLAD GLADDENS—WHO GLADDENS NOT IS NOT GLAD. WHO IS FATAL TO OTHERS IS SO TO HIMSELF—TO HIM, heaven, earth, wisdom, folly, virtue, *VICE, ARE EQUALLY* so—to such an one tell neither good nor bad of yourself.

[Page 15]

32.

× Let the degree of egotism be the measure of confidence.

Uneasy⌊.⌋

[Page 16]

36.

× Who begins with severity, in judging of another, ends commonly with falsehood.

False⌊!⌋ Severity of judgment is a great virtue⌊.⌋

37.

The smiles that encourage severity of judgment, hide malice and in-sincerity.

<u>False</u>⌊!⌋ Aphorisms should be universally true⌊.⌋

[*Page 17*]

39.

Who, without pressing temptation, tells a lie, will, without pressing temptation, act ignobly and meanly.

*U*neasy⌊.⌋
False⌊!⌋ *A* man may lie for his own pleasur*e*, but if any one is hurt by his lying will confess his lie⌊;⌋ see N 124 [*p.* 1358 *below*]⌊.⌋

40.

*W*HO, *UNDER PRESSING TEMPTATIONS TO LIE, ADHERES TO TRUTH, NOR TO THE PROFANE BETRAYS AUGHT OF A SACRED TRUST, IS NEAR THE SUMMIT OF WISDOM AND VIRTUE.*

Excellent⌊.⌋

[*Page 18*]

43.

*A*S *THE PRESENT CHARACTER OF A MAN, SO HIS PAST, SO HIS FUTURE. W*HO *KNOWS INTUITIVELY THE HISTORY OF THE PAST, KNOWS HIS DESTINY TO COME.*

44.

You can depend on no man, on no friend, but him who can depend on himself. *H*E *ONLY* who acts consequentially *TOWARD HIMSELF* will act so toward others, and *vice versa.*

[*Page 19*]

Man is for ever the same; the same under every form, in all situations and relations that admit of free and unrestrained exertion. The same regard which you have for *YOURSELF, YOU HAVE FOR OTHERS, FOR NATURE, FOR THE INVISIBLE NUMEN, WHICH YOU CALL GOD—W*HO *HAS WITNESSED ONE FREE* and unconstrained act of yours, has witnessed all.

¶*40* The spacing indicates that the comment on ¶40 was written after that on ¶39.

[*Page 23*]

54·

×   Frequent laughing has been long called a sign of a little mind—whilst the scarcer smile of harmless quiet has been complimented as the mark of a noble heart—But to abstain from laughing, and exciting laughter, merely not to offend, or to risk giving offence, or not to debase the inward dignity of character—is a power unknown to many a vigorous mind.

I hate scarce smiles ; I love laughing.

[*Page 24*]

59·

A SNEER IS OFTEN THE SIGN OF HEARTLESS MALIGNITY.

Damn Sneerers!

60.

WHO COURTS THE INTIMACY OF A PROFESSED SNEERER, IS A PROFESSED KNAVE.

[*Page 25*]

61.

I know not which of these two I should wish to avoid most; the scoffer at virtue and religion, who, with heartless villany, butchers innocence and truth; *OR THE PIETIST, WHO CRAWLS, GROANS, BLUBBERS, AND SECRETLY SAYS TO GOLD, THOU ART* my hope! and to his belly, thou art my god!

I hate crawlers.

62.

ALL MORAL DEPENDENCE ON HIM, WHO HAS BEEN GUILTY OF ONE ACT OF POSITIVE COOL VILLANY, against an acknowledged, virtuous and noble character, is credulity, imbecility, or insanity.

Is being like him rather.

[*Page 26*]

63.

The most stormy ebullitions of passion, *FROM BLASPHEMY TO MURDER, ARE LESS TERRIFIC THAN ONE SINGLE ACT OF COOL VILLANY: A STILL RABIES IS MORE DANGEROUS THAN THE PAROXISMS OF A FEVER—FEAR THE BOISTEROUS SAVAGE OF PASSION LESS THAN THE SEDATE GRIN OF VILLANY.*

Bravo!

[*Page 27*]

66.

CAN HE LOVE TRUTH WHO CAN TAKE A KNAVE TO HIS BOSOM?

No⌐!⌐

67.

THERE ARE OFFENCES AGAINST INDIVIDUALS, TO ALL APPEARANCE TRIFLING, WHICH ARE CAPITAL OFFENCES AGAINST THE HUMAN RACE—FLY HIM WHO CAN COMMIT THEM.

[*Page 28*]

68.

There ought to be a perpetual whisper in the ear of plain honesty—take heed not even to pronounce the name of a knave—he will make the very sound of his name a handle of mischief. And do you think a knave begins mischief to leave off? Know this—whether he overcomes or be foiled, he will wrangle on.

*T*herefor pronounce him a knave, why should honesty fear a knave⌐?⌐

69.

Humility and love, whatever obscurities may involve religious tenets, constitute the essense of true religion. *THE HUMBLE IS FORMED TO ADORE; THE LOVING TO ASSOCIATE WITH ETERNAL LOVE.*

Sweet.

[*Page 29*]

70.

Have you ever seen a vulgar mind warm or humble? or a proud one that could love?—where pride begins, love ceases—as love, so humility—as both, so the still real power of man.

*P*ride may love⌐.⌐

71.

Every thing may be mimicked by hypocrisy, but humility and love united. The humblest star twinkles most in the darkest night—the more rare humility and love united, the more radiant where they meet.

*A*ll this may be mimicked very well. *T*his Aphorism

¶*69* Catherine Blake transcribed this aphorism on the back of Blake's engraving of Robert Hawker when she sent it as a gift to C. H. Tatham about Aug. 1824 (see p. 165).

¶*70* Under Blake's comment is a three-line erasure which may begin with the word 'Therefor'.

certainly was an oversight for what are all crawlers but mimickers of humility & love⌊?⌋

[*Page 30*]

73·

× Modesty is silent when it would not be improper to speak: the humble, without being called upon, never recollects to say any thing of himself.

Uneasy⌊·⌋

[*Page 32*]

78.

THE WRATH THAT ON CONVICTION SUBSIDES INTO MILDNESS, IS THE WRATH OF A GENEROUS MIND.

[*Page 33*]

80.

Thousands are hated, *WHILST NONE ARE EVER LOVED, WITHOUT A REAL CAUSE. THE AMIABLE ALONE CAN BE LOVED.*

81.

HE WHO IS LOVED AND COMMANDS LOVE, WHEN HE CORRECTS OR IS THE CAUSE OF UNEASINESS, MUST BE LOVELINESS ITSELF; AND

82.

HE WHO CAN LOVE HIM, IN THE MOMENT OF CORRECTION, IS THE MOST AMIABLE OF MORTALS.

83.

HE, TO WHOM YOU MAY TELL ANY THING, MAY SEE EVERY THING, AND WILL BETRAY NOTHING.

[*Page 35*]

86.

× *THE FREER YOU FEEL YOURSELF IN THE PRESENCE OF ANOTHER, THE MORE FREE IS HE: WHO IS FREE MAKES FREE.*

Rather uneasy⌊·⌋

[*Page 36*]

92.

× Who instantly does the best that can be done, what no other could have done, and what all must acknowledge to be the best, is a genius and a hero at once.

Uneasy⌊·⌋

1356

[*Page 37*]

93.

The discovery of truth, by slow progressive meditation, is wisdom—
INTUITION OF TRUTH, NOT PRECEDED BY PERCEPTIBLE MEDITATION, IS GENIUS.

94.

The degree of genius is determined by its velocity, clearness, depth,
simplicity, copiousness, extent of glance (*coup d'oeil*), and instantaneous
intuition of the whole at once.

Copiousness of glance⌞.⌟

[*Page 38*]

96.

Dread more the blunderer's friendship than the calumniator's enmity.

I doubt this⌞.⌟

97.

He only, who can give durability to his exertions, has genuine power and
energy of mind.

Uneasy⌞.⌟ Sterling⌞!⌟

98.

Before thou callest a man hero or genius, investigate whether his exertion
has features of indelibility; for all that is celestial, all genius, IS THE OFFSPRING
OF IMMORTALITY.

Uneasy⌞.⌟ Sterling⌞!⌟

[*Page 39*]

99.

WHO DESPISES ALL THAT IS DESPICABLE, IS MADE TO BE IMPRESSED WITH ALL
THAT IS GRAND.

[*Page 42*]

107.

Who takes from you, ought to give in his turn, or he is a thief; I dis-
tinguish taking and accepting, robbing and receiving: many give already
by the mere wish to give; their still unequivocal wish of improvement and
gratitude, whilst IT DRAWS FROM US, OPENS TREASURES WITHIN US, THAT MIGHT
HAVE REMAINED LOCKED UP, EVEN TO OURSELVES.

Noble & Generous⌞.⌟

[*Page 45*]

114.

WHO WRITES AS HE SPEAKS, SPEAKS AS HE WRITES, LOOKS AS HE SPEAKS AND WRITES—IS HONEST.

115.

A habit of sneering marks the egotist, or the fool, or the knave—or all three.

 —all three⌊!⌋

[*Page 46*]

121.

× Who knows not how to wait with *yes*, will often be with shame reduced to say *no*—Letting '*I dare not* wait upon *I would.*'

 *U*neasy⌊·⌋

124.

WHO HAS A DARING EYE, TELLS DOWNRIGHT TRUTHS AND DOWNRIGHT LIES.

 *C*ontrary to N 39 but <u>most True</u>⌊·⌋

[*Page 53*]

141.

× Many trifling inattentions, neglects, indiscretions—are so many unequivocal proofs of dull frigidity, hardness, or extreme egotism.

 *R*ather uneasy⌊·⌋

[*Page 57*]

150.

× As your enemies and your friends, so are you.

 *V*ery uneasy⌊·⌋

151.

× You may depend upon it that he is a good man whose intimate friends are all good, and whose enemies are characters decidedly bad.

 *U*neasy⌊;⌋ I fear I have not many enemies⌊·⌋

[*Page 59*]

157.

SAY NOT YOU KNOW ANOTHER ENTIRELY, TILL YOU HAVE DIVIDED AN INHERI-
TANCE WITH HIM.

! !

[*Page 61*]

163.

Who, at the pressing solicitation of bold and noble confidence, hesitates
one moment before he consents, proves himself at once inexorable.

*U*neasy⌞;⌟ I do not believe it⌞.⌟

164.

Who, at the solicitations of cunning, self-interest, silliness, or impudence,
hesitates one moment before he refuses, proves himself at once a silly giver.

*U*neasy⌞.⌟

[*Page 64*]

168.

Whenever a man undergoes a considerable change, in consequence of
being observed by others, whenever he assumes another gait, another
language, than what he had before he thought himself observed, be advised
to guard yourself against him.

*R*ather uneasy⌞.⌟

[*Page 65*]

170.

I AM PREJUDICED IN FAVOUR OF HIM WHO CAN SOLICIT BOLDLY, WITHOUT
IMPUDENCE—HE HAS FAITH IN HUMANITY—he has faith in himself. No one,
who is not accustomed to give grandly, can ask nobly and with boldness.

[*Page 67*]

176.

AS A MAN'S SALUTATION, SO THE TOTAL OF HIS CHARACTER: IN NOTHING DO
WE LAY OURSELVES SO OPEN AS IN OUR MANNER OF MEETING AND SALUTATION.

177.

BE AFRAID OF HIM WHO MEETS YOU WITH FRIENDLY ASPECT, AND, IN THE
MIDST OF A FLATTERING SALUTATION, AVOIDS YOUR DIRECT OPEN LOOK.

¶*157* Blake probably divided an inheritance with his three brothers, his sister,
and his mother after his father died in July 1784.

[*Page 70*]

185.

All finery is a sign of littleness.

*N*ot always⌊.⌋

[*Page 71*]

200.

*THE MORE HONESTY A MAN HAS, THE LESS HE AFFECTS THE AIR OF A SAINT—
THE AFFECTATION OF SANCTITY IS A BLOTCH ON THE FACE OF PIETY.*

Bravo⌊!⌋

201.

There are more heroes than saints; (heroes I call rulers over the minds
and destinies of men); more saints than humane characters. Him, who
humanises all that is within and around himself, adore: I know but of one
such by tradition.

Sweet⌊!⌋

[*Page 72*]

203.

*WHO SEEKS THOSE THAT ARE GREATER THAN HIMSELF, THEIR GREATNESS EN-
JOYS, AND FORGETS HIS GREATEST QUALITIES IN THEIR GREATER ONES, IS ALREADY
TRULY GREAT.*

I hope I do not flatter my self that this is pleasant to me⌊.⌋

[*Page 76*]

219.

× None love without being loved; *AND NONE BELOVED IS WITHOUT LOVELINESS.*

[*Page 78*]

225.

The friend of *ORDER HAS MADE HALF HIS WAY TO VIRTUE.*

226.

× There is no mortal truly wise and restless at once—wisdom is the repose
of minds.

*R*ather uneasy⌊.⌋

[*Pages 84–5*]

242.

The connoisseur in painting discovers an original by some great line, though covered with dust, and disguised by daubing; so he who studies man discovers a valuable character by some original trait, though unnoticed, disguised, or debased—ravished at the discovery, he feels it his duty to restore it to its own genuine splendour. *HIM WHO, IN SPITE OF CONTEMPTUOUS PRETENDERS, HAS THE BOLDNESS TO DO THIS, CHOOSE FOR YOUR FRIEND.*

[*Page 85*]

244.

Who writes what he should tell, and dares not tell what he writes, is either like a wolf in sheep's clothing, or like a sheep in a wolf's skin.

Some cannot tell what they can write tho they dare⌞.⌟

[*Page 87*]

248.

Know that the great art to love your enemy consists in never losing sight of *man* in him: humanity has power over all that is human; the most inhuman man still remains man, and never *can* throw off all taste for what becomes a man—but you must learn to wait.

*N*one can see the man in the enemy⌞;⌟ if he is ignorantly so, he is not truly an enemy⌞;⌟ if maliciously not a man⌞.⌟ I cannot love my enemy for my enemy is not man but beast or devil⌞,⌟ if I have any. I can love him as a beast & wish to beat him⌞.⌟

[*Page 89*]

253.

WHO WELCOMES THE LOOK OF THE GOOD IS GOOD HIMSELF.

254.

I know deists, whose religiousness I venerate, and atheists, whose honesty and nobleness of mind I wish for; but I have not yet seen the man who could have tempted *ME TO THINK HIM HONEST WHOM*[1] *I KNEW PUBLICLY ACTED THE CHRISTIAN WHILST PRIVATELY HE WAS A POSITIVE DEIST.*

*B*ravo⌞!⌟

¶*248* The first sentence is written to the left of the printed text, the rest ('I cannot love . . . .') to the right.

¶*254* [1]Blake deleted the '*M*' of '*WHOM*'.

[*Page 90*]

256.

HE WHO LAUGHED AT YOU TILL HE GOT TO YOUR DOOR, FLATTERED YOU AS
YOU OPENED IT—FELT THE FORCE OF YOUR ARGUMENT WHILST HE WAS WITH
YOU—APPLAUDED WHEN HE ROSE, AND, AFTER HE WENT AWAY, BLASTS YOU—
HAS THE MOST INDISPUTABLE TITLE TO AN ARCHDUKEDOM IN HELL.

Such a one I can never forgive while he continues such a
one⌊·⌋

[*Page 92*]

261.

×   Ask not only, am I hated? but, by whom?—*AM I LOVED?* but why?—
AS THE *GOOD* LOVE THEE, THE *BAD* WILL HATE THEE.

Uneasy⌊·⌋

[*Page 95*]

272.

WHO CAN ACT OR PERFORM AS IF EACH WORK OR ACTION WERE THE FIRST, THE
LAST, AND ONLY ONE IN HIS LIFE, IS GREAT [in his sphere *del*].

[*Page 97*]

276.

×   We can do all by speech and silence. He, who understands the double
art of speaking opportunely to the moment, and of saying not a syllable
more or less than it demanded—and he who can wrap himself up in silence
when every word would be in vain—will understand to connect energy
with patience.

Uneasy⌊·⌋

[*Page 98*]

278.

Let the unhappiness you feel at *ANOTHER'S ERRORS, AND THE HAPPINESS YOU
ENJOY IN THEIR PERFECTIONS, BE THE MEASURE OF YOUR PROGRESS IN WISDOM
AND VIRTUE.*

Excellent⌊!⌋

279.

Who becomes every day more sagacious, in observing his own faults,
and the perfections of another, without either envying him or despairing of
himself, is ready to mount the ladder on which angels ascend and descend.

Noble⌊!⌋

[*Page 99*]

282.

THE MORE THERE IS OF MIND IN YOUR SOLITARY EMPLOYMENTS, THE MORE
DIGNITY THERE IS IN YOUR CHARACTER.

[*Page 100*]

285.

HE, WHO CAN AT ALL TIMES SACRIFICE PLEASURE TO DUTY, APPROACHES
SUBLIMITY.

[*Page 101*]

287.

The most eloquent speaker, the most ingenious writer, and the most
accomplished statesman, cannot effect so much as the mere presence of the
man [who tempers his wisdom and his vigour with humanity *del in pencil*].

*U*nsophisticated ⌐!⌐

[*Page 102*]

289.

Between the best and the worst, there are, you say, innumerable degrees—
and you are right; but admit that I am right too, in saying that the best
and the worst differ only in one thing—*IN THE OBJECT OF THEIR LOVE.*

*W*ould to God that every one would consider this ⌐·⌐

290.

What is it you love in him you love? what is it you hate in him you hate?
Answer this closely to yourself, pronounce it loudly, and you will know
yourself and him.

All Gold ⌐·⌐

[*Page 103*]

292.

If you see one cold and vehement at the same time, set him down for a
fanatic.

i.e hypocrite ⌐·⌐

[*Page 104*]

295.

WHO CAN HIDE MAGNANIMITY, STANDS ON THE SUPREME DEGREE OF HUMAN
NATURE, AND IS ADMIRED BY THE WORLD OF SPIRITS.

1363

[*Page 106*]

301.

He has not a little of the devil in him who prays and bites.

There is no other devil, he who bites without praying is only a beast⌊.⌋

302.

He who, when called upon to speak a DISAGREEABLE TRUTH, TELLS IT BOLDLY AND HAS DONE, IS BOTH BOLDER AND MILDER THAN HE WHO NIBBLES IN A LOW VOICE, AND NEVER CEASES NIBBLING.

Damn such⌊!⌋

303.

As the shadow follows the body, so restless [subtleness *del*] ⌃sullenness⌃ the female knave.

[*Page 107*]

305.

BE NOT THE FOURTH FRIEND OF HIM WHO HAD THREE BEFORE AND LOST THEM.

An excellent rule⌊.⌋

[*Page 108*]

308.

×   Want of friends argues either want of humility or courage, or both.

Uneasy⌊.⌋

[*Page 109*]

309.

He who, at a table of forty covers, thirty-nine of which are exquisite, and one indifferent, lays hold of that, and with a 'damn your dinner' dashes it in the landlord's face, should be sent to Bethlem or to Bridewell— and whither he, who blasphemes a book, a work of art, or perhaps a man of nine-and-thirty good and but one bad quality, and calls those fools or flatterers who, engrossed by the superior number of good qualities, would fain forget the bad one ⌃?⌃.

To hell till he behaves better; mark that I do not believe there is such a thing litterally, but hell is the being shut up in the possession of corporeal desires which shortly weary the man for all life is holy⌊.⌋

¶*309* Cf. *Marriage* pl. 27, ¶92, *Visions* pl. 11, l. 215, *America* pl. 10, l. 71, *Vala* p. 34, l. 79 ('every thing that lives is holy', pp. 99, 116, 143, 1126).

[Page 114]

328.

KEEP HIM AT LEAST THREE PACES DISTANT WHO HATES BREAD, MUSIC, AND THE LAUGH OF A CHILD.

The best in the book⌊!⌋

[Page 115]

333.

Between passion and lie there is not a finger's breadth.

Li*e* is the contrary to Passion⌊.⌋

334.

AVOID, LIKE A SERPENT, HIM WHO WRITES IMPERTINENTLY, YET SPEAKS POLITELY.

A dog⌊!⌋ get a stick to him⌊!⌋

[Page 116]

338.

Search carefully if one patiently finishes what he boldly began.

*U*neasy⌊.⌋

[Page 117]

339.

Who comes from the kitchen smells of its smoke; *WHO ADHERES TO A SECT HAS SOMETHING OF ITS CANT*: the college-air pursues the student, and dry inhumanity him who herds with literary pedants.

341.

CALL HIM TRULY RELIGIOUS WHO BELIEVES IN SOMETHING HIGHER, MORE POWERFUL, MORE LIVING, THAN VISIBLE NATURE; AND WHO, CLEAR AS HIS OWN EXISTENCE, FEELS HIS CONFORMITY TO THAT SUPERIOR BEING.

[Page 118]

342.

[Superstition *del*] ∧Hypocrisy∧ always inspires littleness, religion grandeur of mind: the [superstitious *del*] ∧hypocrite∧ raises beings inferiour to himself to deities.

I do not allow that there is such a thing as Superstition taken in the strict sense of the word⌊.⌋

A man must first decieve himself before he is ∧thus∧ Superstitious & so he is a hypocrite⌊·⌋
True superstition is ignorant honesty & this is beloved of god & man⌊·⌋
Hipocris*y* is as distant from superstition, as the wolf from the lamb⌊·⌋
*N*o man was ever truly superstitiou*s* who was not truly religious as far as he knew⌊·⌋

343.

Who are the saints of humanity? those whom perpetual habits of goodness and of grandeur have made nearly unconscious that what they do is good or grand—*HEROES WITH INFANTINE SIMPLICITY.*

*T*his is heavenly⌊·⌋

[*Page 119*]

345.

The jealous is possessed by a 'fine mad devil*' and a dull spirit at once.

*P*ity the jealous⌊!⌋

[*Page 121*]

352.

He alone has *ENERGY THAT CANNOT BE DEPRIVED OF IT*

353.

Sneers are the blasts that precede quarrels.

*H*ate the sneerer⌊!⌋

354.

Who loves will not be adored.

*F*alse⌊!⌋

[*Page 122*]

359.

NO GREAT CHARACTER CAVILS.

[*Page 124*]

365.

HE CAN LOVE WHO CAN FORGET ALL AND NOTHING.

* Shakspeare [*printed footnote to Lavater's text*].

1366

366.

THE PUREST RELIGION IS THE MOST REFINED EPICURISM. HE, WHO IN THE SMALLEST GIVEN TIME CAN ENJOY MOST OF WHAT HE NEVER SHALL REPENT, AND WHAT FURNISHES ENJOYMENTS, still more unexhausted, still less changeable—is the most religious and the most voluptuous of men.

True Christian philosophy⌊·⌋

[*Page 125*]

370.

The generous, who is always just—and the just, who is always generous— *MAY, UNANNOUNCED, APPROACH THE THRONE OF GOD.*

[*Page 127*]

375.

Let me once more, in other words, repeat it—he is the king of kings who longs for nothing, *AND WILLS BUT ONE AT ONCE.*

376.

Spare the lover without flattering his passion; to make the pangs of love the butt of ridicule, is unwise and harsh—soothing meekness and wisdom subdue in else unconquerable things.

*A*nd consider that <u>love is life</u>⌊·⌋

[*Page 128*]

377.

There is none so bad to do the twentieth part of the evil he might, nor any so good as to do the tenth part of the good it is in his power to do. Judge of yourself by the good you might do and neglect—and of others by the evil they might do and omit—and your judgment will be poised between too much indulgence for yourself and too much severity on others.

Most Excellent⌊!⌋

[*Page 129*]

380.

To him who is simple, and inexhaustible, *LIKE NATURE, SIMPLE AND INEX-HAUSTED NATURE RESIGNS HER SWAY.*

[*Page 130*]

383.

How can he be pious who loves not the beautiful, whilst piety is nothing but the love of beauty? Beauty we call the *most varied one* the *most united variety*. Could there be a man who should harmoniously unite each variety of knowledge and of powers—were he not the most beautiful? were he not your *GOD*?

> *T*his is our Lord⌊.⌋

384.

Incredible are his powers who *DESIRES* nothing that he *CANNOT WILL*.

385.

×   The unloved cannot love.

> *D*oubtful⌊.⌋

[*Page 131*]

386.

×   Let the object of love be careful to lose none of its loveliness.

389.

×   We cannot be great, if we calculate how great we and how little others are, and calculate not how great others, how minute, how impotent ourselves.

> *U*neasy⌊.⌋

[*Page 132*]

391.

He loves unalterably who keeps within the bounds of love; who always shews somewhat less than what he *IS POSSESSED OF*—nor ever utters a *SYLLABLE*, or gives a hint, of *MORE THAN* what in fact remains *BEHIND*—is just and friendly in the same degree.

[*Page 134*]

396.

WHO KINDLES LOVE LOVES WARMLY.

[*Page 135*]

400.

There is a manner of forgiving so divine, that you are ready to embrace the offender for having called it forth.

> *T*his I cannot concieve⌊.⌋

401.

Expect the secret resentment of him whom your forgiveness has impressed with a sense of his inferiority; expect the resentment of the woman whose proffered love you have repulsed; yet surer still expect the unceasing rancour of envy against the progress of genius and merit—renounce the hopes of reconciling him: but know, that whilst you steer on, mindless of his grin, allruling destiny will either change his rage to awe, or blast his powers to their deepest root.

If you expect his resentment you do not forgive him now, tho you did once⌊;⌋ forgiveness of enemies can only come upon their repentance⌊.⌋

[*Page 137*]

407.

Whatever is visible is the vessel or veil of the invisible past, present, future—as man penetrates to this more, or perceives it less, he raises or depresses his dignity of being.

A vision of the Eternal Now—

[*Page 138*]

408.

Let none turn over books, or roam the stars IN QUEST OF GOD, WHO SEES HIM NOT IN MAN.

409.

He alone is good, who, though possessed of energy, prefers virtue, WITH THE APPEARANCE OF WEAKNESS, TO THE INVITATION OF ACTING BRILLIANTLY ILL.

Noble⌊!⌋ But Mark⌊!⌋ Active Evil is better than Passive Good.

[*Page 139*]

410.

Clearness, rapidity, comprehension of look, glance (what the French call '*coup d'oeil*'), is the greatest, simplest, most inexhausted gift a mortal can receive from heaven: who has that has all; and who has it not has little of what constitutes the good and great.

*U*neasy⌊;⌋ doubtful⌊.⌋

[*Page 140*]

413.

As the presentiment of the possible, deemed impossible, so genius, so heroism—EVERY GENIUS, EVERY HERO, IS A PROPHET.

414.

× He who goes one step beyond his real faith, or presentiment, is in danger of deceiving himself and others.

Uneasy⌞·⌟

[*Page 141*]

416.

He, who to obtain much will suffer little or nothing, can never be called great; and none ever little, who, to obtain one great object, will suffer much.

The man who does this is a Sectary⌞,⌟ therefore not great⌞·⌟

[*Page 142*]

419.

YOU BEG AS YOU QUESTION; YOU GIVE AS YOU ANSWER.

Excellent⌞!⌟

[*Page 143*]

424.

Love sees what no eye sees; *LOVE HEARS WHAT NO EAR HEARS; AND WHAT NEVER ROSE IN THE HEART OF MAN LOVE PREPARES FOR ITS OBJECT.*

Most Excellent⌞!⌟

426.

Him, who arrays malignity in good nature and treachery in familiarity, a miracle of Omnipotence alone can make an honest man.

No Omnipotence can act against order⌞·⌟

[*Page 144*]

427.

He, who sets fire to one part of a town to rob more safely in another, is, no doubt, a villain: what will you call him, who, to avert suspicion from himself, accuses the innocent of a crime he knows himself guilty of, and means to commit again?

Damn him⌞!⌟

[*Page 146*]

432.

The richer you are, the more calmly you bear the reproach of poverty: *THE MORE GENIUS YOU HAVE, THE MORE EASILY YOU BEAR THE IMPUTATION OF MEDIOCRITY.*

[Page 147]

435.

There is no instance of a miser becoming a prodigal without losing his intellect; but there are thousands of prodigals becoming misers; if, therefore, *YOUR TURN BE PROFUSE, NOTHING IS SO MUCH TO BE AVOIDED AS AVARICE*: and, if you be a miser, procure a physician who can cure an irremediable disorder.

Excellent⌐!⌐

[Page 148]

437.

Avarice has sometimes been the flaw of great men, but never of great minds; great men produce effects that cannot be produced by a thousand of the vulgar; but great minds are stamped *WITH EXPANDED BENEVOLENCE*, unattainable by most.

[Page 149]

440.

He is much greater and more authentic, who produces one thing entire and perfect, than he who does many by halves.

Uneasy⌐·⌐

[Page 150]

444.

Say what you please of your humanity, no wise man will ever believe a syllable while *I* and *mine* are the two only gates at which you sally forth and enter, and through which alone all must pass who seek admittance.

Uneasy⌐·⌐

[Page 151]

447.

Who hides love, to bless with unmixed happiness, is great, like the king of heaven.

I do not understand this or else I do not agree to it⌐·⌐
I know not what hiding love means⌐·⌐

[Page 152]

449.

Trust not him with your secrets, who, when left alone in your room, turns over your papers.

*U*neasy yet I hope I should not do it⌐·⌐

450.

A woman whose ruling passion IS NOT VANITY, IS SUPERIOR TO ANY MAN OF EQUAL FACULTIES.

Such a woman I adore⌊·⌋

451.

He who has but one way of seeing every thing, is as important for him who studies man as fatal to friendship.

*T*his I do not understand⌊·⌋

[*Pages 152–3*]
452.

Who has written will write again, says the Frenchman; [he who has written against you will write against you again; *del*] he who has begun certain things is under the [curse *del*] ∧blessing∧ of leaving off no more.

[*Page 155*]
460.

×   Nothing is more impartial than the stream-like public; always the same and never the same; of whom, sooner or later, each misrepresented character obtains justice, and each calumniated, honour: he who cannot wait for that, is either ignorant of human nature, or feels that he was not made for honour.

*U*neasy⌊·⌋

[*Page 156*]
462.

*T*HE OBSTINACY OF THE INDOLENT AND WEAK IS LESS CONQUERABLE THAN THAT OF THE FIERY AND BOLD.

463.

Who, with calm wisdom alone, imperceptibly directs the obstinacy of others, will be the most eligible friend or the most dreadful enemy.

*T*his must be a grand fellow⌊·⌋

[*Page 157*]
465.

×   He is condemned to depend on no man's modesty and honour who dares not depend on his own.

*U*neasy⌊·⌋

[Page 161]

477.

The frigid smiler, crawling, indiscreet, obtrusive, brazen-faced, is a scorpion-whip of destiny—avoid him!

& never forgive him till he mends⌊·⌋

[Page 163]

486.

Distrust your heart and the durability of your fame, if from the stream of occasion you snatch a handful of foam; deny the stream, and give its name to the frothy bursting bubble.

*U*neasy⌊;⌋ this I lament that I have done⌊·⌋

487.

If you ask me which is the real hereditary sin of human nature, do you imagine I shall answer pride? or luxury? or ambition? or egotism? no; I shall say indolence—who·conquers indolence will conquer all the rest.

Pride⌊,⌋ fullness of bread & <u>abundance of Idleness</u> was the sin of Sodom. See Ezekiel, Ch xvi, 49 ver⌊·⌋

[Page 164]

489.

An entirely honest man, in the severe sense of the word, exists no more than an entirely dishonest knave: the best and the worst are only approximations of those qualities. Who are those that never contradict themselves? yet honesty never contradicts itself: who are those that always contradict themselves? yet knavery is mere self-contradiction. Thus the knowledge of man determines not the things themselves, but their proportions, the quantum of congruities and incongruities.

Man is a twofold bein*g*, one part capable of evil & the other capable of good⌊;⌋ that which is capable of good is not also capable of evi*l*, but that which is capable of evil is also capable of good. *T*his aphorism seems to consider man as simple & yet capable of evil. *N*ow both evil & good cannot exist in a simple bĕing, for thus 2 contraries

¶*487* Ezekieł 16:49: 'Behold, this was the iniquity of thy sister Sodom, pride, fulness of bread, and abundance of idleness was in her and in her daughters, neither did she strengthen the hand of the poor and needy.'

¶*487* has offset to p. 162, but ¶486 has not, suggesting that they were written at distinctly different times.

would spring from one essence which is impossibl*e*; but if man is considered as only evi*l* & god only good, how then is regeneration effected which turns the evil to goo*d*? by casting out the evil, by the goo*d*? See Matthew XII, Ch 26, 27, 28, 29 v⌊·⌋

[*Page 167*]

496.

Sense seeks and finds the thought; the thought seeks and finds genius.

& vic*e* versa. Genius finds thought without seek^g & thought thus producd finds sense⌊·⌋

[*Page 169*]

503.

No wheedler loves.

*N*o fumbler kisses⌊·⌋

[*Page 170*]

506.

The poet, who composes not before THE MOMENT OF INSPIRATION, AND AS THAT LEAVES HIM CEASES—COMPOSES, AND HE ALONE, FOR ALL MEN, ALL CLASSES, ALL AGES.

Most Excellent⌊!⌋

507.

HE, WHO HAS FREQUENT MOMENTS OF COMPLETE EXISTENCE, IS A HERO, THOUGH NOT LAURELLED, IS CROWNED, AND WITHOUT CROWNS, A KING: HE ONLY WHO HAS ENJOYED IMMORTAL MOMENTS CAN REPRODUCE THEM.

O that men would seek immortal moments⌊!⌋ O that men would converse with God⌊!⌋

¶*489* For 'v' Erdman (p. 583) reads '&^c'.
Matthew 12: 26–9:
    And if Satan cast out Satan, he is divided against himself; how shall then his kingdom stand?
    And if I by Beelzebub cast out devils, by whom do your children cast them out? therefore they shall be your judges.
    But if I cast out devils by the Spirit of God, then the kingdom of God is come unto you.
    Or else how can one enter into a strong man's house, and spoil his goods, except he first bind the strong man? and then he will spoil his house.

508.

THE GREATER THAT WHICH YOU CAN HIDE, THE GREATER YOURSELF.

Pleasant∟!⌐

[*Page 172*]

514.

He, who cannot forgive ∧a∧ trespass of malice to his enemy, has never yet tasted the most sublime enjoyment of love.

*U*neasy∟;⌐ this I know not∟.⌐

[*Page 174*]

518.

You may have hot enemies without having a warm friend; but not a fervid friend without a bitter enemy. The qualities of your friends will be those of your enemies: cold friends, cold enemies—half friends, half enemies —fervid enemies, warm friends.

*V*ery Uneasy indeed but truth∟.⌐

[*Page 176*]

521.

HE, WHO REFORMS HIMSELF, HAS DONE MORE TOWARD REFORMING THE PUBLIC THAN A CROWD OF NOISY, IMPOTENT PATRIOTS.

Excellent∟!⌐

[*Page 177*]

523.

He will do great things who can avert his words and thoughts from past irremediable evils.

*N*ot if evils are past sin*s*, for these a man should never avert his thoughts from∟.⌐

[*Page 178*]

526.

He, who is ever intent on great ends, has an eagle-eye for great means, and scorns not the smallest.

Great ends never look at means but produce them spontaneously∟.⌐

[*Page 179*]

532.

Take from *Luther* his roughness and fiery courage; from *Calvin* his hectic obstinacy; from *Erasmus* his timid prudence; hypocrisy and fanaticism from *Cromwell*; from *Henry* IV. his sanguine character; mysticism from *Fenelon*; from *Hume* his all-unhinging wit; love of paradox and brooding suspicion from *Rousseau*; naivetè and elegance of knavery from *Voltaire*; from *Milton* the extravagance of his all-personifying fancy; from *Rafaelle* his dryness and nearly hard precision; and from *Rubens* his supernatural luxury of colours: —deduct this oppressive *exuberance* from each; rectify them according to your own taste—what will be the result? your own correct, pretty, flat, useful—for me, to be sure, quite convenient vulgarity. And why this amongst maxims of humanity? that you may learn to know this *exuberance*, this *leven*, of each great character, and its effects on contemporaries and posterity—that you may know where d, e, f, is, there must be a, b, c: he alone has knowledge of man, who knows the ferment that raises each character, and makes it that which it shall be, and something more or less than it shall be.

Deduct from a rose its redne*ss*, from a lilly its whiteness⌊,⌋ from a diamond its hardness⌊,⌋ from [*a*] spunge its softness⌊,⌋ from an oak its heighth⌊,⌋ from a daisy its lowness & [Chaos *del*] rectify every thing in Nature as the Philosophers d*o*, & then we shall ret*u*rn to Chaos & God will be compelld to be Eccentric if he Creates⌊,⌋ O happy Philosopher⌊.⌋

[*Page 180*]

Variety does not necessarily suppose deformity, for a rose & a lilly are various & both beautiful⌊.⌋

Beauty is exuberant but not of ugliness but of beauty & if ugliness is adjoind to beauty it is not the exuberance of beauty; so if Rafael is hard & dry it is not his genius but an accident acquired for how can Substance & Accident be predicated of the same Essence! I cannot concieve⌊.⌋

But the substance gives tincture to the accident & makes it physiognomic⌊.⌋

Aphorism 47 speaks of the heterogeneous, which all extravagance i*s*, but exuberance not.

¶*532* Aphorism 47 reads:

Man has an inward sense of consequence—of all that is pertinent. This sense is the essence of humanity: this, developed and determined, characterises

[*Page 181*]

533.

I have often, too often, been tempted, at the daily relation of new knaveries, to despise human nature in every individual, till, on minute anatomy of each trick, I found that the knave was only an *enthusiast* or *momentary fool*. This discovery of momentary folly, symptoms of which assail the wisest and the best, has thrown a great consolatory light on my inquiries into man's moral nature: by this the theorist is enabled to assign to each class and each individual its own peculiar fit of vice or folly; and, by the same, he has it in his power to contrast the ludicrous or dismal catalogue with the more pleasing one of sentiment and virtue, more properly their own.

*M*an is the ark of God‸;‿ the mercy seat is above upon the ark‸;‿ cherubims guard it on either side & in the midst is the holy law. *M*an is either the ark of God or a phantom of the earth & of the water‸;‿ if thou seekest by human policy to guide this ark, remember Uzzah‸,‿ II Sam! [*erasure*] vi Ch: Knaveries are not human nature‸;‿ knaveries are knaveries‸.‿ See N 554‸;‿ this aphorism seems to me to want discrimination‸.‿

[*Page 182*]

534.

He, who is master of the fittest moment to crush his enemy, and magnanimously neglects it, is born to be a conqueror.

*T*his was old George the second‸.‿

[*Page 184*]

539.

A great woman not imperious, a fair woman not vain, a woman of common talents not jealous, an accomplished woman, who scorns to

him—this, displayed, is his education. The more strict you are in observing what is pertinent and impertinent, (or heterogeneous) in character, actions, works of art and literature—the wiser, nobler, greater, the more humane yourself.

Blake's comment is written so far into the inner margin that it must have been put on the page before the sheets were bound.

¶*533* 2 Samuel 6:6–7: 'Uzzah put forth his hand to the ark of God, and took hold of it; for the oxen shook it . . . and God smote him for his error; and there he died by the ark of God.'

The first part of the comment is to the left of the printed text, the rest ('Knaveries are not . . .') to the right.

shine—are four wonders, just great enough to be divided among the four quarters of the globe.

Let the men do their duty & the women will be such wonders, the female life lives from the light of the male$_{\llcorner \cdot \lrcorner}$ see a mans female dependants you know the man$_{\llcorner \cdot \lrcorner}$

[*Pages 185–6*]

543.

DEPEND NOT MUCH UPON YOUR RECTITUDE, IF YOU ARE UNEASY IN THE PRESENCE OF THE GOOD;

Easy$_{\llcorner \cdot \lrcorner}$

× nor trust to your humility if you are mortified when you are not noticed.

Uneasy$_{\llcorner \cdot \lrcorner}$

[*Pages 187–8*]

549.

He, who [hates *del*] ∧loves∧ the wisest and best of men, [hates *del*] ∧loves∧ the Father of men; for, where is THE FATHER OF MEN TO BE SEEN BUT IN THE MOST PERFECT OF HIS CHILDREN?

This is true worship$_{\llcorner \cdot \lrcorner}$

[*Page 189*]

552.

HE, WHO ADORES AN IMPERSONAL GOD, HAS NONE; AND, WITHOUT GUIDE OR RUDDER, LAUNCHES ON AN IMMENSE ABYSS THAT FIRST ABSORBS HIS POWERS AND NEXT HIMSELF.

Most superlatively beautiful & Most affectionat[*e*]ly Holy & pure$_{\llcorner ; \lrcorner}$ would to God that all men would consider it$_{\llcorner \cdot \lrcorner}$

[*Page 190*]

554.

The enemy of art is the enemy of nature; art is nothing but the highest sagacity and exertion of human nature; AND WHAT NATURE WILL HE HONOUR WHO HONOURS NOT THE HUMAN?

Human nature is the image of God$_{\llcorner \cdot \lrcorner}$

556.

Where there is much pretension, much has been borrowed—NATURE NEVER PRETENDS.

557.

Do you think *HIM A COMMON MAN WHO CAN MAKE WHAT IS COMMON EXQUISITE?*

[*Page 191*]

559.

WHOSE PROMISE MAY YOU DEPEND ON? HIS WHO DARES REFUSE WHAT HE KNOWS HE CANNOT PERFORM; WHO PROMISES CALMLY, STRICTLY, CONDITIONALLY, AND NEVER EXCITES A HOPE WHICH HE MAY DISAPPOINT.

560.

YOU PROMISE AS YOU SPEAK.

[*Page 192*]

562.

Avoid him *WHO SPEAKS SOFTLY, AND WRITES SHARPLY.*

Ah rogue⌞!⌟ I could be thy hangman⌞!⌟

[*Page 193*]

566.

NEITHER PATIENCE NOR INSPIRATION CAN GIVE WINGS TO A SNAIL—you waste your own force, you destroy what remained of energy in the indolent, by urging him to move beyond his own rate of power.

[*Page 195*]

573.

YOUR HUMILITY IS EQUAL TO YOUR DESIRE OF BEING UNNOTICED, UNOBSERVED IN YOUR ACTS OF VIRTUE.

*T*rue humility⌞.⌟

[*Page 196*]

574.

There are certain light characteristic momentary features of man, which, in spite of masks and all exterior mummery, represent him as he is and shall be. If once in an individual you have discovered one ennobling feature, let him debase it, *LET IT AT TIMES SHRINK FROM HIM, NO MATTER; HE WILL, IN THE END, PROVE SUPERIOR TO THOUSANDS OF HIS CRITICS.*

*T*he wise man falleth 7 times in a day & riseth again &ᶜ⌞.⌟

576.

The man who has and uses but one scale for every thing, for himself and his enemy, the past and the future, the grand and the trifle, for truth and error, virtue and vice, religion, superstition, infidelity; for nature, art, works of genius and art—is truly wise, just, great.

*T*his is most true but how does this agree with 451 [*p. 1372 above*]ᴸ?ᴶ

[*Page 197*]

577.

× The infinitely little constitutes the infinite difference in works of art, and in the degrees of morals and religion; the greater the rapidity, precision, acuteness, with which this is observed and determined, the more authentic, the greater the observer.

*U*neasyᴸ·ᴶ

[*Page 198*]

580.

Range him high amongst your saints, who, with all-acknowledged powers, and his own stedfast scale for every thing, can, on the call of judgment or advice, submit to *TRANSPOSE HIMSELF INTO ANOTHER'S SITUATION, AND TO ADOPT HIS POINT OF SIGHT.*

[*Page 199*]

582.

*N*o *COMMUNICATIONS AND NO GIFTS CAN EXHAUST GENIUS, OR IMPOVERISH CHARITY.*

*M*ost Excellentᴸ!ᴶ

[*Page 200*]

585.

Distrust yourself if you fear the eye of the sincere; *BUT BE AFRAID OF NEITHER GOD OR MAN, IF YOU HAVE NO REASON TO DISTRUST YOURSELF.*

586.

*W*HO COMES AS HE GOES, AND IS PRESENT AS HE CAME AND WENT, IS SINCERE.*

[*Page 201*]

588.

× He loves grandly (I speak of friendship) who is not jealous when he has partners of love.

*U*neasy but I hope to mendᴸ·ᴶ

590.

HE KNOWS HIMSELF GREATLY WHO NEVER OPPOSES HIS GENIUS.

Most Excellent⌊!⌋

[Page 204]

596.

'Love as if you could hate and might be hated;'—a maxim of detested prudence in real friendship, the bane of all tenderness, the death of all familiarity. Consider the *FOOL WHO FOLLOWS IT AS NOTHING INFERIOR TO HIM WHO AT EVERY BIT OF BREAD TREMBLES AT THE THOUGHT OF ITS BEING POISONED.*

Excellent⌊!⌋

597.

'Hate as if you could love or should be loved;'—him who follows this maxim, if all the world were to declare an idiot and enthusiast, I shall esteem, of all men, the most eminently formed for friendship.

Better than Excellent⌊!⌋

[Pages 205–6]

600.

Distinguish with exactness, if you mean to know yourself and others, what is so often mistaken—the *singular*, the *original*, the *EXTRAORDINARY*, THE *GREAT*, AND THE *SUBLIME MAN*: THE *SUBLIME ALONE UNITES THE SINGULAR, ORIGINAL, EXTRAORDINARY, AND GREAT, WITH HIS OWN UNIFORMITY AND SIMPLICITY: THE *GREAT*, WITH MANY POWERS, AND UNIFORMITY OF ENDS, IS DESTITUTE OF THAT SUPERIOR CALMNESS* and inward harmony which soars above the atmosphere of praise: the *extraordinary* is distinguished by copiousness, and a wide range of energy: THE *ORIGINAL NEED NOT BE VERY RICH, ONLY* that which he produces is unique, and has the exclusive stamp of individuality: the *singular*, as such, is placed between originality and whim, and often makes a trifle the medium of fame.

[Page 206]

601.

Forwardness nips affection in the bud.

The more is the pity⌊.⌋

602.

If you mean to be loved, give more than what is asked, but not more than what is wanted [; and ask less than what is expected *del*].

This whole aphorism is an oversight⌊.⌋
This is human policy as it is calld—

¶602 The first sentence is written to the left of the printed text, the rest to the right.

[*Page 207*]

603.

Whom smiles and [tears *altered to* frowns] make equally lovely, [all *altered to* only good] hearts [may *altered to* can or dare] court.

604.

Take here the grand secret—if not of pleasing all, yet of displeasing none—court mediocrity, avoid originality, and sacrifice to fashion.

> & go to hell∟·⌋

605.

He who pursues the glimmering steps of hope, with stedfast, not presumptuous, eye, may pass the gloomy rock, on either side of which [superstition *altered to* hypocrisy] and incredulity their dark abysses spread.

> Superstition has been long a bugbear by reason of its being united with hypocrisy, but let them be fairly seperated & then superstition will be honest feeling, & God who loves all honest me*n*, will lead [them(*?*) *del*] the poor enthusiast in the paths of holiness∟·⌋

[*Page 208*]

606.

The public seldom forgive twice.

> *L*et us take their example∟·⌋

607.

× Him who is hurried on by the furies of immature, impetuous wishes, stern repentance shall drag, bound and reluctant, back to the place from which he sallied: where you hear the crackling of wishes expect intolerable vapours or repining grief.

> *U*neasy∟·⌋

608.

He submits to be seen through a microscope, who suffers himself to be caught in a fit of passion.

> & such a one I dare love∟·⌋

[*Page 209*]

609.

Venerate four characters; the sanguine, who has checked volatility
AND THE RAGE FOR PLEASURE; THE CHOLERIC, WHO HAS SUBDUED PASSION AND

PRIDE; THE PHLEGMATIC, EMERGED FROM INDOLENCE; AND THE MELANCHOLY, WHO HAS DISMISSED AVARICE, SUSPICION, AND ASPERITY.

4 most holy men⌞.⌟

610.

ALL GREAT MINDS SYMPATHIZE.

[*Page 210*]

612.

Men carry their character not seldom in their pockets: you might decide on more than half of your acquaintance, had you will or right to turn their pockets inside out.

I seldom carry money in my pockets⌞;⌟ they are generally full of paper [for *about five words erased.*]

[*Page 211*]

615.

NOT HE WHO FORCES HIMSELF ON OPPORTUNITY, BUT HE WHO WATCHES ITS APPROACH, AND WELCOMES ITS ARRIVAL BY IMMEDIATE USE, IS WISE.

616.

Love and hate are the genius of invention, the parents of virtue and of vice—*FORBEAR TO DECIDE ON YOURSELF TILL YOU HAVE HAD OPPORTUNITIES OF WARM ATTACHMENT OR DEEP DISLIKE.*

True Experience⌞.⌟

[*Page 214*]

619.

Each heart is a world of nations, classes, and individuals; full of friend-ships, enmities, indifferences; . . . the world that surrounds you is the magic glass of the world, and of its forms within you; the brighter you are your-self, so much brighter are your friends—so much more polluted your enemies. Be assured then, that to know yourself perfectly you have only to set down a true statement of those that ever loved or hated you.

*U*neasy because I cannot do this⌞.⌟

[*Page 215*]

623.

Avoid connecting yourself with characters whose good and bad sides are unmixed, and have not fermented together; they resemble phials of vinegar and oil, or pallets set with colours: they are either excellent at

home and intolerable abroad, or insufferable within doors and excellent
in public: they are unfit for friendship, merely because their stamina, their
ingredients of character, are too single, too much apart; let them be finely
ground up with each other, and they will be incomparable.

Most Excellent⌊!⌋

[*Page 216*]
624.

× The fool separates his object from all surrounding ones; all abstraction
is temporary folly.

*U*neasy because I once thought otherwise but now know
it is Truth⌊.⌋

626.

Let me repeat it—He only is great who has the habits of greatness; who,
after performing what none in ten thousand could accomplish, *PASSES ON,
LIKE SAMSON, AND 'TELLS NEITHER FATHER NOR MOTHER OF IT.'*

This is excellent⌊.⌋

[*Page 218*]
630.

A *god*, an *animal*, a *plant*, are not companions of man; nor is the *faultless*—
then judge with lenity of all; the coolest, wisest, best, all without exception,
have their points, their moments of enthusiasm, fanaticism, absence of
mind, faint-heartedness, stupidity—if you allow not for these, your criti-
cisms on man will be a mass of accusations or caricatures.

It is the God in *all* that is our companion & friend, for
our God himself says, 'you are my brother⌊,⌋ my sister
& my mother,' & St John: 'Whoso dwelleth in love dwell-
eth in God & God in him,' & such an one cannot judge
of any but in lov*e*, & his feelings will be attractions or
repulses⌊.⌋ See Aphorisms 549 & 554 [*p. 1378 above*]⌊.⌋

[*Page 219*]
God is in the lowest effects as well as in the highest causes
for he is become a worm that he may nourish the weak⌊.⌋

¶*630* Mark 3:35: 'whosoever shall do the will of God, the same is my brother,
and my sister, and mother' (Matthew 12:50 is almost identical).

1 John 4:16: 'God is love; and he that dwelleth in love dwelleth in God, and
God in him.'

The first part of the paragraph on p. 219 is in one column, the rest ('For let
it . . .') in a second column.

For let it be rememberd that creation *is* God descending according to the weakness of man for our Lord is the word of God & every thing on earth is the word of God & in its essence is God⌐.⌐

631.

GENIUS ALWAYS GIVES ITS BEST AT FIRST, PRUDENCE AT LAST.

[*Pages 220, 221*]
633.

You think to meet with some additions here to your stock of moral knowledge—and not in vain, I hope: but know, a great many rules cannot be given by him who means not to offend, and many of mine have perhaps offended already; believe me, for him who has an open ear and eye, every minute teems with observations of precious import, yet scarcely communicable to the most faithful friend; so incredibly weak, so vulnerable in certain points, is man; forbear to meddle with these at your first setting out, and make amusement the minister of reflection: sacrifice all egotism—sacrifice ten points to one, if that one have the value of twenty; and if you are happy enough to impress your disciple with respect for himself, with probability of success in his exertions of growing better; and, above all, with the idea of your disinterestedness—you may perhaps succeed in making one proselyte to virtue.

[*Page 221*]
—lovely.

[*Page 220*]

Those who are offended [*word del*] with any thing in this book would be offended with the innocence of a child & for the same reason, because it reproaches him with the errors of acquired folly.

[*Page 221*]
635.

Keep your heart from him who begins his acquaintance with you by indirect flattery of your favourite paradox or foible.

*U*nless you find it to be his also, previous to your acquaintance⌐.⌐

636.

Receive no satisfaction for premeditated impertinence—forget it, forgive it—but keep him inexorably at a distance who offered it.

This is a paradox⌐.⌐

[Page 223]

638.

×   Let the cold, who offers the nauseous mimickry of warm affection, meet with what he deserves—a repulse; but from that moment depend on his irreconcilable enmity.

*U*neasy because I do not know how to do this but I will try to [*word del*] do it the first opportunity⌐·⌐

640.

The moral enthusiast, who in the maze of his refinements loses or despises the plain paths of honesty and duty, is on the brink of crimes.

Most True⌐!⌐

[Page 224, the last page]

I hope no one will call what I have written cavilling because he may think my remarks of small consequence For I write from the warmth of my heart, & cannot resist the impulse I feel to rectify what I think false in a book I love so much, & approve so generally⌐·⌐

[First fly-leaf after text, recto]

Man is bad or goo*d* as he unites himself with bad or good spirits. *T*ell me with whom you go & Ill tell you what you do⌐·⌐

As we cannot experience pleasure but by means of others [As(?) we(?) are(?) *del*] who experience either pleasure or pain thro u*s*, And as all of us on earth are united in thought, for it is impossible to think without images of somewhat on earth—So it is impossible to know God or heavenly things without conjunction with those who know God & heavenly thing*s*; therefore all who converse in the spirit, converse with spirits. [& thus are either good or Evil *del*][1] For these reasons I say that this Book is written by consultation with Good Spirits because it is Goo*d* & that the name Lavate*r* is the amulet of those who purify the heart of man.

[1] For this deletion, every word of which I read hesitantly, Erdman (p. 590) reads confidently: '& they converse with the spirit of God'.

[First fly-leaf after text, verso]

There is a strong objection to Lavaters principles (as I understand them) & that is He makes every thing originate in its accident⌊;⌋ he makes the vicious propensity ⌃not only⌃ a leading feature of the man but the stamina on which all his virtues grow. But as I understand Vice it is a Negative—It does not Signify what the laws of Kings & Priests have calld Vice⌊;⌋ we who are philosophers ought not to call the Staminal Virtues of Humanity by the same name that we call the omissions of intellect springing from poverty⌊.⌋

Every mans ⌃leading⌃ propensity ought to be calld his leading Virtue & his good Angel But the Philosophy of Causes & Consequences misled Lavater as it has all his Cotemporaries. Each thing is its own cause & its own effect⌊.⌋ Accident is the omission of act in self & the hindering of act in another, This is Vice but all Act [⌃from Individual propensity⌃ *del*] is Virtue. To hinder another

[Second fly-leaf after text, recto]

is not an act⌊;⌋ it is the contrary⌊;⌋ it is a restraint on action both in ourselves & in the person hinder*d*, for he who hinders another omits his own dut*y* at the time⌊.⌋

Murder is Hindering Another⌊.⌋

Theft is Hindering Another⌊.⌋

Backbitin*g*, Undermining Circumventing & whatever is Negative is Vice⌊.⌋

But the origin of this mistake in Lavater & his cotemporaries, is, They suppose that Womans Love is Sin. *I*n consequence all the Loves & Graces with them are Sin⌊.⌋

Second fly-leaf after text: In *Europe* pl. 8, l. 94 (p. 228), Enitharmon sends Rintrah and Palamabron to 'tell the human race that Womans love is Sin'.

MARGINALIA (?1789): Swedenborg, *Divine Love and Divine Wisdom* (1788)

[*On the fly-leaf:*]

There can be no Good Will⌐.⌐ Will is always Evil⌐;⌐ it is pernicious to others or selfish⌐.⌐ If God is any thing he is Understanding⌐.⌐ He is the Influx from that into the Will⌐;⌐ This Good to others or benevolent Understanding can Work ignorantly but never can the Truth because Man is only Evil [*five words illeg.*]

H & Hell Chapter 425

Understanding or Thought is not natural to Man⌐;⌐ it is acquired by means of Suffering & Distress i e. Experience⌐.⌐ Will Desire Love, Rage, Envy, & all other Affections are Natural but Understanding is Acquired But Observe without these is to be less than Man. Man could never light from heaven without affections⌐;⌐ one would be limited to the five hells in different periods of time⌐.⌐

Wisdom of Angels 10

[*Page 2*]

Doth it not happen that in Proportion as the Affection which is of Love groweth cold, the Thought, Speech and Action grow cold also? And that in Proportion as it is heated, they also are heated? But this a wise Man perceiveth, not from a Knowledge that Love is the Life of Man, but from Experience of this Fact.

They also percieve this from knowledge but not with the natural part⌐.⌐

Fly-leaf: The italicized words below are read by Erdman (p. 591) with much greater confidence than I can muster:

pernicious . . . selfish . . . God . . . he is the . . . the Truth *because Man . . . is not natural . . . Desire . . . Rage . . . all other Affections . . . Understanding is . . . without these is to be less than . . . Man could never light . . . without affections one would be limited to the five hells . . . periods of time Wisdom of Angels . . . .*

Heaven and Hell ¶425 (pp. 272–3 of the 1784 edition) is about 'the conjunction of good [in the will] and truth [in the understanding, *which*] is heaven in the soul'; it says that good-truth and evil-falsehood are united in men on earth.

[*Page 3*]

No one knoweth what is the Life of Man, unless he knoweth that it is Love . . . .

This was known to me & thousands⌞.⌟

[*Page 7*]

That the Divine or God is not in Space . . . cannot be comprehended by any merely natural Idea, but it may by a spiritual Idea: The Reason why it cannot be comprehended by a natural Idea, is, because in that Idea there is Space . . . .

What a natural Idea is—⌞.⌟

Nevertheless, Man may comprehend this by natural Thought, if he will only admit into such Thought somewhat of spiritual Light . . . .

Mark this⌞.⌟

A spiritual Idea doth not derive any Thing from Space, but it derives every Thing appertaining to it from State . . . .

Poetic idea⌞.⌟

[*Pages 8–9*]

Hence it may appear, that Man from a MERELY NATURAL Idea cannot comprehend that the Divine is every where, and yet not in Space; and yet that Angels and Spirits clearly comprehend this; consequently THAT MAN ALSO MAY, if so be he will admit something of spiritual Light into his Thought; the Reason why Man may comprehend it is because his Body doth not think, but his Spirit, therefore not his natural but his spiritual [Part].

Observe the distinction here between Natural & Spiritual as seen by Man⌞.⌟ Man may comprehen*d*, but not the natural or external man⌞.⌟

[*Page 10*]

It hath been said, that in the spiritual World Spaces appear equally as in the natural World . . . . Hence it is that the Lord, although he is in the Heavens with the Angels every where, nevertheless appears high above them as a Sun: And whereas the Reception of Love and Wisdom constitutes Affinity with him, therefore those Heavens appear nearer to him where the Angels are in a nearer Affinity from Reception, than where they are in a more remote Affinity . . . .

He who Loves feels love descend into him & if he has wisdom may percieve it is from the Poetic Genius which is the Lord⌞.⌟

[*Page 11*]

In all the Heavens there is no other Idea of God than that of a Man . . . .

Man can have no idea of any thing greater than Man as a cup cannot contain more than its capaciousness⌊·⌋
But God is a man not because he is so percievd by man but because he is the creator of man⌊·⌋

[*Page 12*]

The Gentiles, particularly the Africans . . . entertain an Idea of God as of a Man, and say that no one can have any other Idea of God: When they hear that many form an Idea of God as existing in the Midst of a Cloud, they ask where such are . . . .

Think of a white clou*d* as being holy⌊,⌋ you cannot love it but think of a holy man within the cloud⌊,⌋ love springs up in your thought*s*, for to think of holiness distinct from man is impossible to the affections. *T*hought alone can make monster*s*, but the affections cannot⌊·⌋

[*Page 13*]

. . . they who are wiser than the common People pronounce God to be invisible . . . .

Worldly wisdom or demonstration by the senses is the cause of this⌊·⌋

[*Page 14*]

. . . the Negation of God constitutes Hell, and in the Christian World the Negation of the Lord's Divinity.

*T*he Negation of the Poetic Genius⌊·⌋

[*Page 15*]

. . . when Love is in Wisdom, then it existeth. These two are such a ONE, that they may be distinguished indeed in Thought, but not in Act.

Thought without affection makes a distinction between Love & Wisdom as it does between body & Spirit⌊·⌋

[*Page 24*]

What Person of Sound Reason doth not perceive, that the Divine is not divisible . . . ? If another, who hath no Reason, should say that it is possible there may be several Infinites, Uncreates, Omnipotents and Gods, provided they have the same Essence, and that thereby there is one Infinite,

Uncreate, Omnipotent and God—is not one and the same Essence one and the same Identity?

> Answer⌞:⌟ Essence is not Identity but from Essence proceeds Identity & from one Essence may proceed many Identities as from one Affection may proceed many thoughts⌞.⌟ Surely this is an oversight⌞.⌟ That there is but one Omnipotent Uncreate & God I agree but that there is but one Infinite I do not, for if all but God is not Infinite they shall come to an End which God forbid⌞.⌟ If the Essence was the same as the Identity there could be but one Identity, which is false— Heaven would upon this plan be but a Clock⌞;⌟ but one & the same Essence is therefore Essence & not Identity⌞.⌟

[*Page 33*]

Appearances are the first Things from which the human Mind forms it's Understanding, and . . . it cannot shake them off but by an Investigation of the Cause, and if the Cause lies very deep, it cannot investigate it, *WITHOUT KEEPING THE UNDERSTANDING SOME TIME IN SPIRITUAL LIGHT* . . . .

> This Man can do while in the body.

. . . it cannot be demonstrated except by such Things as a Man can perceive by his bodily Senses . . . .

> Demonstration is only by bodily Senses.

[*Page 40*]

With respect to God, it is not possible that he can love and be reciprocally beloved by others, in whom there is . . . any Thing Divine; for if there was any Thing . . . Divine in them, then it would not be beloved by others, but it would love itself . . . .

> False⌞.⌟ Take it so or the contrary it comes to the same for if a thing loves it is infinite⌞;⌟ perhaps we only differ in the meaning of the words Infinite & Eternal⌞.⌟

[*Page 56*]

Man is only a Recipient of Life. From this Cause it is, that Man, from his own hereditary Evil, reacts against God; but so far as he believes that all his Life is from God, and every Good of Life from the Action of God, and every Evil of Life from the Reaction of Man, Reaction thus becomes correspondent with Action, and Man acts with God as from himself.

Good & Evil are here both Good & the two contraries Married⌐·⌐

[*Page 57*]

But he who knows how to elevate his Mind above the Ideas of Thought which are derived from Space and Time, such a Man passes from Darkness to Light, and becomes wise in Things spiritual and Divine . . . and then by Virtue of that Light he shakes off the Darkness of natural Light, and removes *IT'S FALLACIES* from the Center to the Circumference.

When the fallacies of darkness are in the circumference they cast a bound about the infinite⌐·⌐

[*Page 58*]

Now inasmuch as the Thoughts of the Angels derive nothing from Space and Time, but from States of Life, it is evident that they do not comprehend what is meant when it is said, that the Divine fills Space, for they do not know what Space is, but that they comprehend clearly, when it is said, without any Idea of Space, that the Divine fills all Things.

Excellent⌐!⌐

[*Page 131*]

That without two Suns, the one living and the other dead, there can be no Creation.

False philosophy according to the letter but true according to the spirit⌐·⌐

[*Page 133*]

. . . it follows that the one Sun is living and that the other Sun is dead, also that the dead Sun itself was created by the living Sun from the Lord.

How could Life create death⌐?⌐

The reason why a dead Sun was created is to the End that in the Ultimates all Things may be fixed . . . . On this and no other Ground Creation is Founded: The terraqueous Globe . . . is as it were the Basis and Firmament . . . .

*T*hey exist literally about the sun & not about the earth⌐·⌐

Page 56: It has been suggested that this sentence and the one on p. 458 were the genesis of *The Marriage of Heaven and Hell* (?1790–3).

That all Things were created from the Lord by the living Sun, AND NOTHING BY THE DEAD SUN, may appear from this Consideration . . . .

⌐The dead Sun is only a phantasy of evil Man⌐.⌐

[*Page 146*]

It is the same upon Earth with Men, but with this Difference, that the Angels feel that Heat, and see that Light, whereas Men do not . . . .

He speaks of Men as meer earthly Men not as receptacles of spirit, or else he contradicts N 257 [*p. 220—p. 1395 below.*]

Man, whilst he is in natural Heat and Light, knoweth nothing of spiritual Heat and Light in himself, and this cannot be known but by Experience from the spiritual World . . . .

This is certainly not to be understood according to the letter for it is false by all experience⌐;⌐ who does not or may not Know of love & wisdom in himself⌐?⌐

[*Page 181*]

From these Considerations a Conclusion was drawn, that the Whole of Charity and Faith is in Works, and that Charity and Faith without Works are like Rainbows about the Sun, which vanish and are dissipated by a Cloud; wherefore Works are so often mentioned in the Word, and it is said we are to do them, and that the Salvation of Man depends upon them; moreover he who doeth them is called a wise Man, and he who doeth them not is called a foolish Man. But it is to be observed, that by Works here are meant Uses, which are actually performed; for in them and according to them is the Whole of Charity and Faith; there is this Correspondence with Uses, because this Correspondence is spiritual, but it is effected by Substances and Matters, which are it's subjects.

The Whole of the New Church is in the Active Life & not in Ceremonies at all⌐.⌐

[*Pages 195–6*]

These three Degrees of Altitude are named Natural, Spiritual and Celestial . . . . Man, at his Birth, first comes into the natural Degree, and this increases in him by Continuity according to the Sciences, and according to the Understanding acquired by them, to the Summit of Understanding which is called Rational . . . .

Study Sciences till you are blind⌐,⌐ Study intellectuals till

Page *181*: Blake and his wife supported the resolution adopted unanimously at the first session of the New Church on 13 April 1789 affirming that God's Kingdom is one of uses (*Blake Records*, 37).

you are cold Yet science cannot teach intellect⌐,⌐ Much less can intellect teach Affection⌐.⌐

How foolish then is it to assert that Man is born in only one degree when that one degree is reception of the 3 degree*s*, two of which he must destroy or close up or they will descend, if he closes up the two superior then he is not truly in the 3ᵈ but descends out of it into meer Nature or Hell⌐.⌐

See N 239 [*p. 198.*]

Is it not also evident that one degree will not open the other & that science will not open intellect but that they are discrete & not continuous so as to explain each other except by correspondence which has nothing to do with demonstration for you cannot demonstrate one degree by the other for how can science be brought to demonstrate intellect, without making them continuous & not discrete⌐?⌐

[*Page 196*]

Man, so long as he lives in the World, does not know any Thing of the opening of these Degrees in himself . . . .

See N 239 [*p. 198.*]

[*Page 198*]

. . . in every Man there is a natural, spiritual and celestial Will and Understanding, in Power from his Birth, and in Act whilst they are opening.

Mark this⌐;⌐ it explains N 238 [*p. 196.*]

In a Word the Mind of Man . . . is of three Degrees, so that . . . a Man thereby may be elevated to Angelic Wisdom, and possess it, while he lives in the World, but nevertheless he does not come into it till after Death, if he becomes an Angel, AND THEN HE SPEAKS *THINGS INEFFABLE AND IN-COMPREHENSIBLE TO THE NATURAL MAN*.

Not to a Man but to the natural Man⌐.⌐

[*Page 200*]

Every one who consults his Reason, *WHILST IT IS IN THE LIGHT*, may see, that Man's Love is the End of all Things appertaining to him . . . .

[*Page 204*]

And hence it also follows, that the Understanding does not lead the Will, or that Wisdom does not produce Love, but that it only teaches and shows the Way, it teaches how a Man ought to live, and shows the Way in which he ought to walk.

Mark this⌊.⌋

[*Page 219*]

From this it is evident, that Man, SO LONG AS HE LIVES IN THE WORLD, AND IS THEREBY IN THE NATURAL DEGREE, cannot be elevated into Wisdom itself . . . .

See Sect. 4 of the next Number [*below.*]

[*Page 220*]

4. That human Wisdom, which is natural so long as a Man lives in the World, can by no means be exalted into Angelic Wisdom, but only into a certain Image thereof; the Reason is, because the Elevation of the human Mind is affected by Continuity, as from Shade to Light, or from dense to more pure. But still Man, in whom the spiritual Degree is open, comes into that Wisdom when he dies, and may also come into it by laying asleep the Sensations of the Body, and by Influx from above at the same Time into the Spirituals of his Mind.

[*Note to 'when he dies':*] This is while in the Body⌊.⌋ This is to be understood as unusual in our time but common in ancient⌊.⌋

5. The natural Mind of Man consists of spiritual Substances, and at the same Time of natural Substances; from its SPIRITUAL SUBSTANCES Thought is produced, but not from its NATURAL SUBSTANCES . . . .

Many perversely understand him, as if man while in the body was only conversant with natural Substance*s*, because themselves are mercenary & worldly & have no idea of any but worldly gain⌊.⌋

[*Page 233*]

. . . for the natural Man can elevate his Understanding to superior Light as far as he desires it, but he who is principled in Evils and thence in Things false, does not elevate it higher than to the superior Region of his natural Mind . . . .

Who shall dare to say after this that all elevation is of self & is Enthusiasm & Madness & is it not plain that self derived intelligence is worldly demonstration⌊?⌋

[Page 268]

Things, which constitute the Sun of the spiritual World, are from the
Lord, and not the Lord, therefore they are not Life in itself . . . .

This assertion that the spiritual Sun is not Life explains
how the natural Sun is dead⌊.⌋

This is an Arcanum, which the Angels by their spiritual Ideas can see in
Thought, and also express in Speech, but not Men by their *NATURAL IDEAS* . . . .

How absurd then would it be to say that no man on
earth has a spiritual idea after reading N 257 [*p. 220.*]

[Page 269]

That there is such a Difference between the Thoughts of Angels and Men,
was made known to me by this Experience: They were told to think of
something spiritually, and afterwards to tell me what they thought of;
when this was done and they would have told me, they could not . . . .

*T*hey could not tell him in natural ideas⌊;⌋ how absurd
must men be to understand him as if he said the angels
could not express themselves at all to him⌊.⌋

[Page 276]

Forasmuch as there is such a Progression of the Fibres and Vessels in a
Man from first Principles to Ultimates, therefore there is a similar Pro-
gression of their States; their States are the Sensations, Thoughts and
Affections; these also from their first Principles *WHERE THEY ARE IN THE LIGHT*,
pervade to their Ultimates, where they are in Obscurity; or from their first
Principles, where they are in Heat, to their Ultimates where they are not
in heat.

We see here that the cause of an ultimate is the absence
from heat & light⌊.⌋

[Page 285]

It is to be observed, that the Heat, Light and Atmospheres of the natural
World conduce nothing to this Image of Creation . . . .

Therefore the Natural Earth & Atmosphere is a Phantasy⌊.⌋

The Heat, Light and Atmospheres of the natural World only open Seeds . . .
but this not by Powers derived from their own Sun . . . .

Mark this⌊.⌋

[*Page 286*]

. . . but by Powers from the spiritual Sun, . . . FOR THE IMAGE OF CREATION IS SPIRITUAL, nevertheless that it may appear, and furnish Use IN THE NATURAL WORLD . . . it must be clothed in Matter . . . as there is a Resemblance of Creation in the Forms of Vegetables, so there is also in the Forms of Animals, viz. that there is a Progression from first Principles to Ultimates, and from Ultimates to first Principles.

A Going forth & returning⌊.⌋

[*Page 295*]

. . . there doth not exist any Thing in the created Universe, which hath not Correspondence with something of Man, not only with his Affections and his Thoughts thence derived, but also with the Organs and Viscera of his Body, not with them as Substances, but with them as Uses.

Uses & substances are so different as not to correspond⌊.⌋

[*Pages 410–11*]

THOUGHT INDEED EXISTS FIRST, BECAUSE IT IS OF THE NATURAL MIND, BUT THOUGHT FROM THE Perception of Truth, which is from the Affection OF TRUTH, EXISTS LAST; THIS THOUGHT is the THOUGHT OF WISDOM, BUT THE OTHER is THOUGHT FROM THE MEMORY BY THE SIGHT OF THE NATURAL MIND.

Note this⌊.⌋

[*Page 421*]

FROM THESE THINGS IT MAY BE seen, THAT LOVE OR THE WILL JOINS itself to WISDOM OR THE UNDERSTANDING, and not that WISDOM OR THE UNDER-STANDING joins itself to LOVE OR THE WILL . . . .

Mark this⌊.⌋

[*Page 422*]

. . . the Perception of Truth which it acquires from the Affection of under-standing, and Thought which it acquires from the Affection of seeing that which it knows and understands, are not of the Understanding, but are of Love. Thoughts, Perceptions, and Knowledge thence derived, flow in indeed from the spiritual World, BUT STILL THEY ARE NOT RECEIVED BY THE UNDERSTANDING, BUT BY THE LOVE ACCORDING TO ITS AFFECTIONS IN THE UNDERSTANDING.

Mark this⌊.⌋

It appears as if the Understanding received them, and not Love or the Will, but it is a Fallacy: It appears also as if the Understanding joined itself to Love or the Will, BUT THIS ALSO IS A FALLACY; Love or the Will joins itself to the Understanding, and causeth the Understanding to be reciprocally joined to it . . . .

Mark this⌊.⌋

[*Page 423*]

For the Life of Man is his Love, as was shewn above, and his Life is according as he has exalted his Affections by Truths, that is according as he has perfected his Affections from Wisdom; for the Affections of Love are exalted and perfected by Truths, thus by Wisdom; and in such Case Love acts in Conjunction with Wisdom, as it were from Wisdom, but it acts from itself by Wisdom, as by it's Form, which derives nothing at all from the Understanding, but every Thing from some Determination of the Love, which is called Affection.

Mark this⌊.⌋

[*Page 424*]

From these Considerations it is also evident, THAT LOVE JOINS ITSELF TO THE UNDERSTANDING, AND NOT VICE VERSA . . . .

Mark this⌊.⌋

[*Page 425*]

He who knows all the Fabric of the Lungs from Anatomy, if he compares them with the Understanding, may clearly see that the UNDERSTANDING DOES NOTHING FROM ITSELF, that it does not PERCEIVE NOR THINK FROM ITSELF, BUT ALL FROM AFFECTIONS WHICH ARE OF THE LOVE, which in the Understanding are called the Affection of knowing, of understanding, and of seeing it . . . .

Mark⌊.⌋

[*Page 426*]

From the Structure of the Lungs, which was known to me, I WAS FULLY CONVINCED THAT THE LOVE BY IT'S AFFECTIONS JOINS ITSELF TO THE UNDERSTANDING, AND THAT THE UNDERSTANDING DOES NOT JOIN ITSELF TO ANY AFFECTION OF THE LOVE . . . .

Mark this⌊.⌋

[*Pages 426–7*]

THAT WISDOM OR THE UNDERSTANDING BY MEANS OF THE POWER GIVEN IT BY LOVE, CAN BE ELEVATED, AND RECEIVE THE THINGS WHICH ARE OF THE LIGHT FROM HEAVEN, AND PERCEIVE THEM.

Mark this⌊.⌋

[Page 429]

... when Man shuns Evils as Sins, therefore by these Means Love or the Will also can be elevated, and without these Means it cannot ....

Is it not false then, that love recieves influx thro the understandᵍ as was asserted in the society⌊?⌋

[Page 435]

... this Love became impure by Reason of the Separation of celestial Love from it in the Parents.

Therefore it was not created impure & is not naturally so.

[Page 436]

... so far the Love is purged of its Uncleannesses, and purified, that is, so far it is elevated into the Heat of Heaven, and joined to the Light of Heaven, in which the Understanding is ....

Therefore it does not recieve influx thro the understanding⌊.⌋

[Page 440]

THAT LOVE OR THE WILL IS DEFILED IN THE UNDERSTANDING, AND BY IT, IF THEY ARE NOT ELEVATED TOGETHER ....

Mark this⌊;⌋ they are elevated together⌊.⌋

[Page 441]

THE UNDERSTANDING IS NOT MADE SPIRITUAL AND CELESTIAL, BUT THE LOVE IS ....

[Page 458]

Moreover it was shown in the Light of Heaven ... that the interior Compages of this little Brain was ... in the Order and Form of Heaven; and that it's exterior Compages was in Opposition to that Order and Form.

Heaven & Hell are born together⌊.⌋

Page 429: Probably this is the first session of the general conference of the New Church which Blake and his wife attended on 13 April 1789 (*Blake Records*, 35, 37).

[Page v of (Translator's) PREFACE]

For if we allow a *general* Providence, and yet deny a *particular* one, or if we allow a *particular* one, and yet deny a *singular* one, that is, one extending to Things and Circumstances most *singular* and minute, what is this but denying a *general* Providence?

Is not this Predestination˻?˼

[Page xix]

. . . if he [*the reader*] be one of a sincere and humble Mind . . . his Humility and Sincerity will teach him, that Nothing doth *in general* so contradict Man's natural and favourite Opinions as *Truth*, and that all the grandest and purest Truths of Heaven must needs seem obscure and perplexing to the natural Man at first View,

Lies & Priestcraft˻.˼ Truth is Nature˻.˼

UNTIL HIS INTELLECTUAL EYE BECOMES ACCUSTOMED TO THE LIGHT, AND CAN THEREBY BEHOLD IT WITH SATISFACTION.

That is: till he agrees to the Priests interest˻.˼

[Page 82 of text]

69. But the Man who doth not suffer himself to be led to, and enrolled in Heaven, is prepared for his Place in Hell;

What is Enrolling but Predestination˻?˼

for Man from himself continually tends to the lowest Hell, but is continually with-held by the Lord; and he, who cannot be with-held, is prepared for a certain Place there, in which he is also enrolled immediately after his Departure out of the World; and this Place there is opposite to a certain Place in Heaven, for Hell is in Opposition to Heaven; wherefore as a Man Angel, according to the Affection of Good and Truth, hath his Place assigned him in Heaven, so a Man Devil, according to the Affection of Evil and the False, hath his Place assigned him in Hell; for two Opposites, disposed in a similar Situation against each other, are contained in Connection. This is the *intimum* of the Divine Providence concerning Hell.

Query does he also occupy that place in Heaven— See N 185 & 329 at the End˻.˼ See 277, & 307, & 203 where he says that a Place for Every Man is Foreseen and at the same time provided⌊.⌋

[*Page 254*]

185. That this is the Case, cannot better be known than from the Case of Men after Death in the spiritual World, where the greatest Part of those, who in the natural World became great and rich, and in Honours respected themselves alone, and also in Riches, at first speak of God, and of the Divine Providence, as if they acknowledged them in their Hearts; But whereas they then manifestly see the Divine Providence, and from it their final Portion, which is that they are to be in Hell, they connect themselves with Devils there, and then not only deny God, but also blaspheme . . . .

What could Calvin Say more than is Said in this Number⌊?⌋ Final Portion is Predestination⌊.⌋ See N 69 & 329 at the End & 277 & 203 Where he says A Place for Each Man is Foreseen & at the same time Provided⌊.⌋

[*Page 281*]

203. Since every Man therefore lives after Death to Eternity, and according to his Life here hath his Place assigned to him either in Heaven or in Hell, and both these, as well Heaven as Hell, must be in such a Form as to act as one, as was said before; and no one can occupy any other Place in that Form, but his own, it follows, that the human Race throughout the whole World is under the Auspices of the Lord, and that every one, from his Infancy even to the End of his Life, is led of Him in the most minute Particulars, and his *PLACE FORESEEN*, and at the same *TIME PROVIDED*.

Devils & Angels are Predestinated⌊.⌋

[*Page 317*]

220. . . . Dignities with their Honours are natural and temporary, when a Man personally respects himself in them, and not the State and Uses, for then a Man cannot but think interiorly with himself, that the State was made for him, and not he for the State; he is like a King who thinks his Kingdom and all the Men in it are for him, *AND NOT HE FOR THE* Kingdom and all the Men of which it consists.

He says at N 201 No King hath such a Government as this for all Kings are Universal in their Government⌊,⌋ otherwise they are No Kings⌊.⌋

¶220 ¶201 is:

. . . . If it should be alledged, that the Divine Providence is an universal Government, and that not any Thing is governed, but only kept in it's Connection,

[Page 426]

224. . . . *it was not known heretofore, that Man liveth after Death; and this was not discovered till now.* The Reason why this was not known, is, because in those who do not shun Evils as Sins, there lieth inwardly concealed a Belief, that Man doth not live after Death, and therefore they think it of no Importance, whether it be said that Man liveth after Death, or that he will rise again at the Day of Judgment; and if he happens to have any belief in a Resurrection, he saith to himself, I shall not fare worse than others, for if I go to Hell, I shall have many to accompany me, and if to Heaven, it will be the same. But yet all who have any Religion, *HAVE IN THEM* an inherent Knowledge, that Men live after Death; the Idea that they live as Souls, and not as Men, takes Place only with those who are infatuated by their own Self-derived Intelligence, and with no others.

It was not Known & yet All Know⌊.⌋

[Page 434]

277. That Man is to be withdrawn from Evil, in Order that he may be reformed, is evident without Explanation; for he who is in Evil in the World, the same is in Evil after he goes out of *THE WORLD; WHEREFORE IF EVIL BE NOT REMOVED* in the *WORLD, IT CANNOT BE REMOVED AFTERWARDS;*

Cursed Folly⌊!⌋

where the Tree falls, there it lieth; so also it is with the Life of Man; as it was at his Death, such it remaineth; every one also is judged according to his Actions, not that they are enumerated, but because he returns to them, and does the like again; for Death is a Continuation of Life, with this Difference, that then Man cannot be reformed.

Predestination after this Life is more Abominable than Calvins & Swedenborg is Such a Spiritual Predestinarian⌊,⌋ witness this Number & many others⌊;⌋ See 69 & 185 & 329 & 307⌊.⌋

[Page 497]

307. . . . in the World . . . Man is continually in a State of Reformation, wherefore according to his Life and the Changes thereof, he is translated by the Lord from one Society of Hell to another, if he is wicked; but if he

and the Things which relate to Government . . . are disposed by others, can this be called an universal Government? No King hath such a Government as this; for if a King were to allow his Subjects to govern every Thing in his Kingdom, he would no longer be a King, but would only be called a King, therefore would have only a nominal Dignity and no real Dignity: Such a King cannot be said to hold the Government, much less universal Government.

suffers himself to be reformed, he is led out of Hell and introduced into Heaven, and there also he is translated from one Society to another, and this until the Time of his Death, after which he is no longer carried from one Society to another, because he is then no longer in any State of Reformation, but remains in that in which he is according to his Life; wherefore when a Man dies, he is inscribed in his own Place.

Predestination⌊!⌋

[Page 566]

329. . . . there is not wanting to any Man a Knowledge of the Means whereby he may be saved, nor the Power of being saved if he will; from which it follows, that all are predestined or intended for Heaven, and none for Hell. But forasmuch as there prevails among some a Belief in Predestination to no Salvation, which is Predestination to Damnation, and such a Belief is hurtful, and cannot be dispelled, unless Reason also sees the Madness and Cruelty of it, therefore it shall be treated of in the following Series. 1. That any other Predestination, than Predestination to Heaven, is contrary to the Divine Love and it's Infinity. 2. That any other Predestination, than Predestination to Heaven, is contrary to the Divine Wisdom and it's Infinity. 3. That it is an insane Heresy, to suppose that they only are saved who are born within the Church. 4. That it is a cruel Heresy, to suppose that any of the human Race are predestined to be damned.

Read N 185 & There See how Swedenborg contradicts himself & N 69⌊.⌋ See also 277 & 203 where he Says that a Place for Each Man is foreseen & at the same time provided⌊.⌋

[*Title-page verso*]
Notes on the B of L's Apology for the Bible
by William Blake₍.₎

To defend the Bible in this year 1798 would cost a man his life₍.₎
[The Beast & the Whore rule without control *del*]
It is an easy matter for a Bishop to triumph over Paines attack but it is not so easy for one who loves the Bible₍.₎
The Perversions of Christs words & acts are attacked by Paine & also the perversions of the Bible; Who Dare defend [them *del*] either the Acts of Christ or the Bible Unperverted? But to him who sees this mortal pilgrimage in the light that I see i*t*, Duty to [my *del*] his country is the first consideration & safety the last₍.₎

Read patiently₍;₎ take not up this Book in an idle hour₍;₎ the consideration of these things is the [most(?) *del*] whole duty of man & the affairs of life & death trifles₍,₎ sports of time₍.₎ ∧But∧ these considerations [are the *omitted*] business of Eternity₍.₎

I have been commanded from Hell not to print this as it is what our Enemies wish₍.₎

[*Page i, Preface*]
THIS edition of the Apology for the Bible is published, in compliance with the earnest solicitations of many serious persons of all ranks. They have remarked to me, that the deistical writings of Mr. Paine are circulated, with great and pernicious industry, amongst the unlearned part of the community, especially in large manufacturing towns; and they have been pleased to think, that this Defence of Revealed Religion might, if generally distributed, be efficacious in stopping the torrent of infidelity which endangers alike the future happiness of individuals, and the present safety of all *CHRISTIAN STATES*.

Paine has not Attacked Christianity₍.₎ Watson has Defended Antichrist₍.₎

Title-page verso. The sentence beginning 'The Beast' is deleted in pencil.

[*Page ii*]

[*A list of books by Bishop Watson*]

Read the XXIII Chap of Matthew & then condemn
Paines hatred of Priests if you dare⌊.⌋

7. The WISDOM and GOODNESS of GOD, in having made both RICH
and POOR: a SERMON, preached before the Stewards of WEST-
MINSTER DISPENSARY, at the Anniversary Meeting in Charlotte-
street Chapel . . . .

God made Man happy & Rich but the Subtil made the
innocent Poor⌊.⌋ This must be a most wicked & blas-
phemous book⌊.⌋

[*Page 1*]

LETTER I.

If this first Letter is written without Railing & Illiberality
I have never read one that is. To me it is all Daggers &
Poison. The sting of the serpent is in every Sentence as
well as the glittering Dissimulation⌊.⌋ Achilles' wrath is
blunt abuse⌊,⌋ Thersites' Sly insinuation⌊;⌋ Such is the
Bishops⌊.⌋ If such is the characteristic of a modern polite
gentleman we may hope to see Christs discourses Ex-
pung'd⌊.⌋ I have not the Charity for the Bishop that he
pretends to have for Paine. I believe him to be a State
trickster⌊.⌋

SIR,

I HAVE lately met with a book of your's, entitled—THE AGE OF REASON,
part the second, being an investigation of true and of fabulous theology;—
and I think it not inconsistent with my station, and the duty I owe to society,
to trouble you and the world with some observations on so extraordinary
a performance. Extraordinary I esteem it; not from any novelty in the
objections which *YOU HAVE PRODUCED AGAINST REVEALED RELIGION, (FOR
I FIND LITTLE OR NO NOVELTY IN THEM,)*

Dishonest Misrepresentation⌊.⌋

Page ii 'Charlotte-street Chapel' was the chapel of Blake's early patron A. S.
Mathew.

Page 1 In his notes to Lavater's *Aphorisms* (1788), ¶342 (p. 1365), Blake carefully
substitutes the word 'Hipocrisy' for 'Superstition'.

but from the zeal with which you labour to disseminate your opinions, and from the confidence with which you esteem them true. You perceive, by this, that I give you credit for your sincerity, HOW MUCH SOEVER I MAY QUESTION YOUR WISDOM,

Priestly Impudence⌊.⌋

in writing in such a manner on such a subject: and I have no reluctance in acknowledging, that you possess a considerable share of energy of language, and acuteness of investigation; though I must be allowed to lament, that these TALENTS HAVE NOT BEEN APPLIED IN A MANNER MORE USEFUL TO HUMAN KIND, AND MORE CREDITABLE TO YOURSELF.

Contemptible Fals[e]hood & Detraction⌊.⌋

I begin with your preface. You therein state—that you had long had an intention of publishing your thoughts upon religion, but that you had originally reserved it to a later period in life.—I hope there is no want of charity in saying, that it would have been fortunate for the christian world, HAD YOUR LIFE BEEN TERMINATED BEFORE YOU HAD FULFILLED YOUR INTENTION.

Presumptuous Murder⌊;⌋ dost thou O Priest wish thy brothers death when God has preserved him⌊?⌋

In accomplishing your purpose you will have unsettled the faith of thousands; rooted from the minds of the unhappy virtuous all their comfortable assurance of a future recompence; have annihilated in the minds of the flagitious all their fears of future punishment; you will have given the reins to the domination of every passion, and have thereby contributed to the introduction of the public insecurity, and of the private unhappiness usually and almost necessarily accompanying a state of corrupted morals.

Mr Paine has not extinguishd & cannot Extinguish Moral rectitude. He has Extinguishd Superstition which took the Place of Moral Rectitude⌊;⌋ what has Moral Rectitude to do with Opinions concerning historical fact⌊?⌋

[*Page 2*]

No one can think worse of confession to a priest and subsequent absolution, as practised in the church of Rome, than I do: but I cannot, with you, attribute the guillotine-massacres to that cause.

To what does the Bishop attribute the English Crusade against Franc*e*? *Is* it not to State Religio*n*? blush for shame⌊!⌋

Men's minds were not prepared, as you suppose, for the commission of all manner of crimes, by any doctrines of the church of Rome, corrupted as I esteem it, *BUT BY THEIR NOT THOROUGHLY BELIEVING EVEN THAT RELIGION. WHAT MAY NOT SOCIETY EXPECT FROM THOSE, WHO SHALL IMBIBE THE PRIN-CIPLES OF YOUR BOOK?*

> Folly & Impudence! Does the thorough belief of Popery hinder crimes or can the man who writes the latter sentiment be in the good humour the bishop Pretends to be? If we are to expect crimes from Paine & his followers, are we to believe that Bishops do not Rail⌊?⌋ I should Expect that the man who wrote this sneaking sentence would be as good an inquisitor as any other Priest⌊.⌋

A fever, which you and those about you expected would prove mortal, made you remember, with renewed satisfaction, that you had written the former part of your Age of Reason—and you know therefore, you say, by experience, the conscientious trial of your own principles. I admit this declaration to be a proof of the sincerity of your persuasion, but I cannot admit it to be any proof of the truth of your principles. What is conscience? Is it, as has been thought, an internal monitor implanted in us by the *SUPREME BEING*, and dictating to us, on all occasions, what is *RIGHT OR WRONG? OR IS IT MERELY* our own judgment of the moral rectitude or turpi-tude of our own actions? I *TAKE THE WORD* (with Mr. Locke) in the latter, *AS IN THE ONLY INTELLIGIBLE* sense.

> Conscience in those that have it is unequivocal, it is the voice of God⌊.⌋ Our judgment of right & wrong is Reason⌊.⌋ I believe that the Bishop laught at the Bible in his slieve & so did Locke⌊.⌋

Now who sees not that our judgments of virtue and vice, right and wrong, are not always formed from an enlightened and dispassionate use of our reason, in the investigation of truth? They are more generally formed from the nature of the religion we profess; from the quality of the civil govern-ment under which we live; from the general manners of the age, or the particular manners of the persons with whom we associate; from the educa-tion we have had in our youth; from the books we have read at a more advanced period; and from other accidental causes. Who sees not that, on this account, conscience may be conformable or repugnant to the law of nature?—may be certain, or doubtful?—and that it can be no criterion of moral rectitude, even when it is certain, because the certainty of an opinion is no proof of it's being a right opinion?

> Virtue is not Opinion⌊.⌋

[*Page 3*]

If Conscience is not a Criterion of Moral Rectitude
What is it? He who thinks that Honesty is changeable
knows nothing about it⌞.⌟

A man may be certainly persuaded of an error in reasoning, or of an
untruth in matters of fact. It is a maxim of every law, human and divine,
that a man ought never to act in opposition to his conscience: but it will
not from thence follow, that he will, in obeying the dictates of his conscience,
ON ALL OCCASIONS ACT RIGHT.

*Always, or the Bible is false⌞.⌟

An inquisitor, who burns jews and heretics; a Robespierre, who massacres
innocent and harmless women; a robber, who thinks that all things ought
to be in common, and that a state of property is an unjust infringement of
natural liberty:—these, and a thousand perpetrators of different crimes,
may all follow *THE DICTATES OF CONSCIENCE;*

ᴧContemptibleᴧ Fals[e]hood & Wickedness⌞.⌟
Virtue & honesty or the dictates of Conscience are of no
doubtful Signification to any one⌞.⌟
Opinion is one thing, Principle another. No Man can
change his Principles⌞.⌟ Every Man changes his opinions.
He who supposes that his Principles are to be changed is
a Dissembler who Disguises his Principles & calls that
change⌞.⌟

and may, at the real or supposed approach of death, remember 'with re-
newed satisfaction' the worst of their transactions, and experience, without
dismay, 'a conscientious trial of their principles.' But this their conscientious
composure can be no proof to others of the rectitude of their principles,
and ought to be no pledge to themselves of their innocence, in adhering to
them.

I have thought fit to make this remark, with a view of suggesting to you
a consideration of great importance—whether you have examined calmly,
and according to the best of your ability, the arguments by which the truth .
of revealed religion may, in the judgment of learned and impartial men,
be established?

Paine is either a Devil or an Inspired man. Men who
give themselves tò their Energetic Genius in the manner
that Paine does [is *del*] are no [modest(?) Enquirers *del*]

Page 3 'Contemptible' is written later with a blacker ink.

ˏExaminersˏ. If they are not determinately wrong they must be Right or the Bible

[*Page 4*]

is false. *As* to [modest Enquirers *del*] ˏExaminersˏ in these points they will [always be found to be neither cold nor hot & will *del*] be spewed out. *The* Man who pretends to be a modest enquirer into the truth of a self evident thing is a Knaveʟˌ The truth & certainty of Virtue & Honesty i.e. Inspiration needs no one to prove itʟ;ˌ it is Evident as the Sun & Moonʟˌ [*Six words del*] He who stands doubting of what he intends whether it is Virtuous or Vicious knows not what Virtue means *N*o man can do a Vicious action & think it to be Virtuous. *N*o man can take darkness for light. *H*e may pretend to do so & may pretend to be a modest Enquirer, but he is a Knaveʟˌ

[*Page 3*]

. . . If you have made the best examination you can, and yet reject revealed religion as an imposture, I pray that God may pardon what I esteem your error. And whether you have made this examination or not, does not become me or any man to determine. That gospel, which you despise, has taught me this moderation; it has said to me—'Who art thou that judgest another man's servant? To his own master he standeth or falleth.'—I think that you are in an error; but whether that error be to you a vincible or an invincible error, I presume not to determine.

Serpentine Dissimulationʟˌ

[*Page 5*]

. . . You hold it impossible that the Bible can be the Word of God, because it is therein said, that the Israelites destroyed the Canaanites by the express command of God: and to believe the Bible to be true, we must, you affirm, unbelieve all our belief of the moral justice of God; for wherein, you ask, could crying or smiling infants offend?

To me who believe the Bible & profess myself a Christian a defence of the Wickedness of the Israelites in murdering so many thousands under pretence of a command from

Page 4 The erased passage looks rather as follows, with the most doubtful letters *in italics*: '   self / to *where* / men *blest* / it   / *Em*   *Tension*'. Erdman (p. 603) reads without hesitation: 'What doubt is virtuous even Honest that depends upon Examination.'

God is altogether Abominable & Blasphemous╷.╵ Where-
fore did Christ come╷?╵ was it not to abolish the Jewish
Imposture╷?╵ Was not Christ marterd because he taught
that God loved all Men & was their father & forbad all
contention for Wordly prosperity in opposition to the
Jewish Scriptures which are only an Example of the
wickedness & deceit of the Jews & were written as an
Example of the possibility of Human Beastliness in all
its branches? Christ died as an Unbeliever & if the
Bishops had their will so would Pain*e*; ˄see page 1╷;╵˄
but he who speaks a word against the Son of man shall
be forgiven╷;╵ let the Bishop prove that he has not spoken
against

[*Page 6*]

the Holy Ghost who in Paine strives with Christendom as
in Christ he strove with the Jews╷.╵

I am astonished that so acute a reasoner should attempt to disparage
the Bible, by bringing forward this exploded and frequently refuted objec-
tion of Morgan, Tindal, and Bolingbroke. You profess yourself to be a deist,
and to believe that there is a God, who created the universe, and established
the laws of nature, by which it is sustained in existence. You profess that
from the contemplation of the works of God, you derive a knowledge of his
attributes; and you reject the Bible, because it ascribes to God things in-
consistent (as you suppose) with the attributes which you have discovered
to belong to him; in particular, you think it repugnant to his moral justice,
that he should doom to destruction the crying or smiling infants of the
Canaanites.—Why do you not maintain it to be repugnant to his moral
justice, that he should suffer crying or smiling infants to be swallowed up
by an earthquake, drowned by an inundation, consumed by a fire, starved
by famine, or destroyed by a pestilence? The Word of God is in perfect
harmony with his work; crying or smiling infants are subjected to death in
both. We believe that the earth, at the express command of God, opened her
mouth, and swallowed up Korah, Dathan, and Abiram, with their wives,
their sons, and their little ones. This you esteem so repugnant to God's
moral justice, that you spurn, as spurious, the book in which the circum-
stance is related. When Catania, Lima, and Lisbon, were severally destroyed
by earthquakes, men with their wives, their sons, and their little ones, were
swallowed up alive:—why do you not spurn, as spurious, the book of nature,
in which this fact is certainly written, and from the perusal of which you
infer the moral justice of God? You will, probably, reply, that the evils

Page 5 For 'marterd' Erdman (p. 604) reads 'murderd'.

which the Canaanites suffered from the express command of God, were different from those which are brought on mankind by the operation of the laws of nature.—Different! in what?—Not in the magnitude of the evil—not in the subjects of sufferance—not in the author of it—for my philosophy, at least, instructs me to believe, that God not only primarily formed, but that he hath through all ages executed, the laws of nature; and that he will through all eternity administer them, for the general happiness of his creatures, whether we can, on every occasion, discern that end or not.

The Bible says that God formed Nature perfect but that Man perverted the order of Nature since which time the Elements are filld with the Prince of Evil who has the power of the air⌊.⌋

I am far from being guilty of the impiety of questioning the existence of the moral justice of God, as proved either by natural or revealed religion; what I contend for is shortly this—that you have no right, in fairness of reasoning, to urge any apparent deviation from moral justice, as an argument against revealed religion, because you do not urge an equally apparent deviation from it, as an argument against natural religion: you reject the former, and admit the latter, without considering that, as to your objection, they must stand or fall together.

Natural Religion is the voice of God & not the result of reasoning on the Powers of Satan⌊.⌋

As to the Canaanites, it is needless to enter into any proof of the depraved state of their morals; they were a wicked people in the time of Abraham, and they, even then, were devoted to destruction by God; but their iniquity was not then full. In the time of Moses, they were idolaters; sacrificers of their own crying or smiling infants; devourers of human flesh; addicted to unnatural lust; immersed in the filthiness of all manner of vice. Now, I think, it will be impossible to prove, that it was a *PROCEEDING CONTRARY TO GOD'S MORAL JUSTICE, TO EXTERMINATE SO WICKED A PEOPLE.*

Horrible⌊!⌋ the Bishop is an Inquisitor⌊.⌋ God never makes one man murder another nor one nation⌊.⌋

He made the Israelites the executors of his vengeance; and, in doing this, he gave such an evident and terrible proof of his abomination of vice, as could not fail to strike the surrounding nations with astonishment and terror, and to impress on the minds of the Israelites what they were to expect, if they followed the example of the nations whom he commanded them to cut off. 'Ye shall not commit any of these abominations—that the land spue not you out also, as it spued out the nations that were before

Page 6 For 'the prince of the power of the air', see Ephesians 2: 2. Cf. *There is No Natural Religion* (pp. 3–14).

you.' How strong and descriptive this language! the vices of the inhabitants were so abominable, that the very land was sick of them, and forced to vomit them forth, as the stomach disgorges a deadly poison.

[*Page 7*]

There is a vast difference between an accident brought on by a mans own carelessness & a destruction from the designs of another. The Earthquakes at Lisbon &ᶜ were the Natural result of Si*n*, but the distruction of the Canaanites by Joshua was the Unnatural design of wicked men⌊.⌋ / To Extirpate a nation by means of another is as wicked as to destroy an individual by means of another individual which God considers (in the Bible) as Murder & commands that it shall not be done⌊.⌋ Therefore the Bishop has not answerd Paine⌊.⌋

I have often wondered what could be the reason that men, not destitute of talents, should be desirous of undermining the authority of revealed religion, and studious in exposing, with a malignant and illiberal exultation, every little difficulty attending the scriptures, to popular animadversion and contempt. I am not willing to attribute this strange propensity to what Plato attributed the atheism of his time—to profligacy of manners—to affectation of singularity—to gross ignorance, assuming the semblance of deep research and superior sagacity;—I had rather refer it to an impropriety of judgment, respecting the manners, and mental acquirements, of human kind in the first ages of the world. Most unbelievers argue as if they thought that man, in remote and rude antiquity, in the very birth and infancy of our species, had the same distinct conceptions of one, eternal, invisible, incorporeal, infinitely wise, powerful, and good God, which they themselves have now. This I look upon as a great mistake, and a pregnant source of infidelity. Human kind, by long experience; by the institutions of civil society; by the cultivation of arts and sciences; by, as I believe, divine instruction actually given to some, and traditionally communicated to all; *IS IN A FAR MORE DISTINGUISHED SITUATION, AS TO THE POWERS* of the mind, than it was in the childhood of the world.

That mankind are in a less distinguished Situation with regard to mind than they were in the time of Homer Socrates Phidias, Glyco*n*, Aristotle &ᶜ let all their works witness⌊.⌋ [the Deists *del*] ∧Paine∧ say∧s∧ that Christianity put a stop to improvement & the Bishop has not shewn the contrary⌊.⌋

Page 7 English preachers frequently used the Lisbon earthquake of 1755 as an example of divine punishment for Popish sin.

[*Page* 8]

. . . It appears incredible to many, that God Almighty should have had colloquial intercourse with our first parents; that he should have contracted a kind of friendship for the patriarchs, and entered into covenants with them;

> That God does & always did converse with honest Men Paine never denies. *H*e only denies that God conversed with Murderers & Revengers such as the Jews wer*e*, & of course he holds that the Jews conversed with their own [self will *del*] State Religion which they calld God & so were liars as Christ says⌊.⌋

that he should have suspended the laws of nature in Egypt; should have been so apparently partial, as to become the God and governor of one particular nation;

> That the Jews assumed a right ⌃Exclusively⌃ to the benefits of Go*d* will be a lasting witness against them, & the same will it be [of *del*] against Christians⌊.⌋

and should have so far demeaned himself, as to give to that people a burdensome ritual of worship, statutes and ordinances, many of which seem to be beneath the dignity of his attention, unimportant and impolitic. . . . I own to you, that when I consider how nearly man, *IN A SAVAGE STATE, APPROACHES TO THE BRUTE CREATION*, as to intellectual excellence;

> Read the Edda of Iceland⌊,⌋ the Songs of Fingal⌊,⌋ the accounts of North American Savages (as they are calld)⌊.⌋ Likewise read Homers Ilia*d*; he was certainly a Savag*e*, in the Bishops sense. He knew nothing of Go*d*, in the Bishops sense of the word & yet he was no fool⌊.⌋

[*Page 9*]

and when I contemplate his miserable attainments, as to the knowledge of God, in a civilized state, when he has had no divine instruction on the subject, or when that instruction has been forgotten, (for all men have known something of God from tradition,) I cannot but admire the wisdom and goodness of the Supreme Being, in having let himself down to our apprehensions; in having given to mankind, in the earliest ages, sensible and extraordinary proofs of his existence and attributes; in having made the jewish and christian dispensations mediums to convey to all men, through

Page 8 The 'Songs of Fingal' are MacPherson's Ossianic forgeries.

all ages, that knowledge concerning himself, which he had vouchsafed to give immediately to the first.

The Bible or ⌃Peculiar⌃ Word of God, Exclusive of Conscience or the Word of God Universal, is that Abomination which like the Jewish ceremonies is for ever removed & henceforth every man may converse with God & be a King & Priest in his own house⌞.⌟

I own it is strange, very strange, that he should have made an immediate manifestation of himself in the first ages of the world; but what is there that is not strange? It is strange that you and I are here—that there is water, and earth, and air, and fire—that there is a sun, and moon, and stars—that there is generation, corruption, reproduction.

It is strange that God should speak to man formerly & not now, because it is not true but the Strangeness of Sun Moon or Stars is Strange on a contrary account⌞.⌟

I can account ultimately for none of these things, without recurring to him who made every thing. I also am his workmanship, and look up to him with hope of preservation through all eternity; I adore him for his word as well as for his work; his work I cannot comprehend, but his word hath assured me of all that I am concerned to know—that he hath prepared everlasting happiness for those who love and obey him. This you will call preachment:—I will have done with it; but the subject is so vast, and the PLAN OF PROVIDENCE, in my opinion, so obviously WISE AND GOOD, that I can never think of it without having my mind filled with piety, admiration, and gratitude.

The Bible tells me that the plan of Providence was Subverted at the Fall of Adam & that it was not restored till [we in *del*] Christ [were(?) restored(?) *del.*]

In addition to the moral evidence (as you are pleased to think it) against the Bible, you threaten, in the progress of your work, to produce such other evidence as even a priest cannot deny. A philosopher in search of truth forfeits with me all claim to candour and impartiality, when he introduces railing for reasoning, vulgar and illiberal sarcasm in the room of argument. I will not imitate the example you set me; but examine what you shall produce, with as much coolness and respect, as if you had given the priests no provocation; AS IF YOU WERE A MAN OF THE MOST UNBLEMISHED CHARACTER, subject to no prejudices, actuated by no bad designs, not liable to have abuse retorted upon you with success.

Is not this Illiberal⌞?⌟ has not the Bishop given himself the lie in the moment the first words were out of his mouth⌞?⌟

Can any man who writes so pretend that he is in a good humour? Is not this the Bishops cloven foo*t*? has he not spoild the hasty pudding⌐?⌐

[*Page 10*]

LETTER II. ...

The trifles which the Bishop has combated in the following Letters are such as do nothing against Paines Arguments none of which the Bishop has dared to Consider⌐.⌐ One for instance which is That the books of the Bible were never believd willingly by any nation & that none but designing Villains ever pretended to believe⌐;⌐ That the Bible is all a State Trick thro which tho' the People at all times could see they never ha*d* the power to throw off⌐.⌐ Another Argument is that all the Commentators on the Bible are Dishonest Designing Knaves who in hopes of a good living adopt the State religion⌐;⌐ this he has shewn with great force which calls upon His Opponent loudly for an answer. I could name an hundred such⌐.⌐

[*Page 11*]

This distinction between the genuineness and authenticity of a book, will assist us in detecting the fallacy of an argument, which you state with great confidence in the part of your work now under consideration, and which you frequently allude to, in other parts, as conclusive evidence against the truth of the Bible. Your argument stands thus—If it be found that the books ascribed to Moses, Joshua, and Samuel, were not written by Moses, Joshua, and Samuel, every part of the authority and authenticity of these books is gone at once.—I presume to think otherwise. The genuineness of these books (in the judgment of those who say that they were written by these authors) will certainly be gone; but their authenticity may remain; they may still contain a true account of real transactions, though the names of the writers of them should be found to be different from what they are generally esteemed to be.

He who writes things for true which none could writ*e* but the acto*r*—such are most of the acts of Mose*s*—must either be the actor or a fable writer or a liar. If Moses did not write the history of his act*s*, it takes away the authority altogether⌐;⌐ it ceases to be history & becomes a Poem of probable impossibilities fabricated for pleasure as moderns say but I say by Inspiration⌐.⌐

1415

[*Page 12*]

Had, indeed, Moses said that he wrote the five first books of the Bible; and had Joshua and Samuel said that they wrote the books which are respectively attributed to them; and had it been found, that Moses, Joshua, and Samuel, did not write these books; then, I grant, the authority of the whole would have been gone at once; these men would have been found liars, as to the genuineness of the books; and this proof of their want of veracity, in one point, would have invalidated their testimony in every other; these books would have been justly stigmatized, as neither genuine nor authentic. . . .

If Paine means that a history tho true in itself is false When it is attributed to a wrong author, he's a fool. But he says that Moses being proved not the author of that history which is written in his name & in which he says I did so & so Undermines the veracity intirely⌞;⌟ the writer says he is Moses⌞;⌟ if this is proved false the history is false[—] Deut XXXI v 24⌞.⌟ But perhaps Moses is not the author & then the Bishop loses his Author⌞.⌟

As to your assertion, that the miracles recorded in Tacitus, and in other profane historians, are quite as well authenticated as those of the Bible—it, being a mere assertion destitute of proof, may be properly answered by a contrary assertion. I take the liberty then to say, that the evidence for the miracles recorded in the Bible is, both in kind and degree, so greatly superior to that for the prodigies mentioned by Livy, or the miracles related by Tacitus, as to justify us in giving credit to the one as the work of God, and in with-holding it from the other as the effect of superstition and imposture. This method of derogating from the credibility of christianity, by opposing to the miracles of our Saviour, the tricks of ancient impostors, seems to have originated with Hierocles in the fourth century; and it has been adopted by unbelievers from that time to this; with this difference, indeed, that the heathens of the third and fourth century admitted that Jesus wrought miracles; but lest that admission should have compelled them to abandon their gods and become christians, they said, that their *Apollonius*, their *Apuleius*, their *Aristeas*, did as great: whilst modern deists deny the fact of Jesus having ever wrought a miracle.

Jesus could not do miracles where unbelief hinderd⌞;⌟ hence we must conclude that the man who holds miracles to be ceased puts it out of his own power to ever witness one⌞.⌟ The manner of a miracle being performd is in modern times considerd as an arbitrary command of the agent upon the patient but this is an impossibility not a miracle⌞,⌟ neither did Jesus ever do such a miracle. Is it

a greater miracle to feed five thousand men with five
loaves than to overthrow all

[*Page 13*]

the armies of Europe with a small pamphle*t*? *L*ook over the
events of your own life & if you do not find that you have
both done such miracles & lived by such you do not see
as I do ⌞.⌟ True I cannot do a miracle thro experiment &
to domineer over & prove to others my superior power
as neither could Christ But I can & do work such as both
astonish & comfort me & mine⌞.⌟ How can Paine the
worker of miracles ever doubt Christs in the above sense
of the word miracle⌞?⌟ But how can Watson ever believe
the above sense of a miracle who considers it as an arbi-
trary act of the agent upon an unbelieving patient whereas
the Gospel says that Christ could not do a miracle because
of Unbelief⌞?⌟

[*Page 14*]

If Christ could not do miracles because of Unbelief the
reason alledged by Priests for miracles is false for those who
believe want not to be confounded by miracles. Christ
& his Prophets & Apostles were not Ambitious miracle
mongers⌞.⌟

. . . The Bible is not the only book which has undergone the fate of being
reprobated as spurious, after it had been received as genuine and authen-
tic for many ages. It has been maintained that the history of *Herodotus* was
written in the time of *Constantine*; and that the Classics are forgeries of the
thirteenth or fourteenth century. These extravagant reveries amused the
world at the time of their publication, and have long since sunk into
oblivion. You esteem all prophets to be such lying rascals, that I dare not
venture to predict the fate of your book.

Prophets in the modern sense of the word have never
existed⌞.⌟ Jonah was no prophet in the modern Sense for
his prophecy of Nineveh failed⌞.⌟ Every honest man is a
Prophet⌞;⌟ he utters his opinion both of private & public
matters / Thus / If you go on So / the result is So⌞.⌟ / He

Page 13 Jesus 'did not many mighty works there because of their unbelief'
(Matthew 13: 58).

never says Such a thing shall happen let you do what you will. *A Prophet is a Seer not an Arbitrary Dictator.* It is mans fault if God is not able to do him goo*d*, for he gives to the just & to the unjust but the unjust reject his gift⌞.⌟

[*Page 15*]

. . . What if I should grant all you undertake to prove (the stupidity and ignorance of the writer excepted)?—What if I should admit, that *Samuel*, or *Ezra*, or some other learned jew, composed these books, from public records, many years after the death of Moses? Will it follow, that there was no truth in them? According to my logic, it will only follow, that they are not genuine books; every fact recorded *IN THEM MAY BE TRUE*, whenever, or by whomsoever they were written.

Nothing can be more contemptible than to suppose Public RECORDS to be True⌞.⌟ Read them & Judge if you are not a Fool⌞.⌟
Of what consequence is it whether Moses wrote the Pentateuch or n*o*? If Paine trifles in some of his objections it is folly to confute him so seriously in them & leave his more material ones unanswered⌞.⌟ Public Records⌞!⌟ As If Public Records were True⌞!⌟ Impossible⌞;⌟ for the facts are such as none but the actor could tell, if it is True Moses & none but he could write it unless we allow it to be Poetry & that poetry inspired⌞.⌟

[*Page 16*]

It cannot be said that the jews had no public records; the Bible furnishes abundance of proof to the contrary. I by no means admit, that these books, as to the main part of them, were not written by Moses; but I do contend, that a book may contain a true history, though we know not the author of it, or though we may be mistaken in ascribing it to a wrong author.

If historical facts can be written by inspiration Miltons Paradise Lost is as true as Genesi*s* or Exodu*s*; but the Evidence is nothing for how can he who writes what he has neither seen nor heard o*f* be an Evidence of The Truth of his history⌞?⌟

Page 15 A stroke leads from the printed text which Blake marked to the MS addition at the top of the page. The order in which Blake's notes were written on this page is quite uncertain.

[*Page 17*]

. . . I do not call you a vain and arrogant coxcomb for vindicating your
character, when in the latter part of this very work you boast, and I hope
truly, 'that the man does not exist that can say I have persecuted him, or
any man, or any set of men, in the American revolution, or in the French
revolution; or that I have in any case returned evil for evil.' I know not
what kings and priests may say to this; you may not have returned to them
evil for evil, because they never, I believe, did you any harm; but you
have done them all the harm you could, and that without provocation.

Paine says that Kings & Priests have done him harm from
his birth⌊.⌋

[*Page 22*]
LETTER III.

HAVING done with what you call the grammatical evidence that Moses
was not the author of the books attributed to him, you come to your his-
torical and chronological evidence; and you begin with Genesis.

I cannot concieve the Divinity of the ⌃books in the⌃ Bible
to consist either in who they were written by or at what
time or in the historical evidence which may be all false
in the eyes of one man & true in the eyes of another but in
the Sentiments & Examples which whether true or Para-
bolic are Equally useful as Examples given to us of the
perverseness of some & its consequent evil & the honesty
of others & its consequent good⌊.⌋ This sense of the Bible is
equally true to all & equally plain to all. None can doubt
the impression which he recieves from a book of Examples.
If he is good he will abhor wickedness in David or Abra-
ham⌊;⌋ if he is wicked he will make their wickedness an
excuse for his & so he would do by any other book⌊.⌋

[*Page 25*]

The destruction of the Canaanites exhibits to all nations, in all ages, a sig-
nal proof of God's displeasure against sin; it has been to others, and it is
to ourselves, a benevolent warning. Moses would have been the wretch
you represent him, had he acted by his own authority alone; but you may
as reasonably attribute cruelty and murder to the judge of the land in
condemning criminals to death, as butchery and massacre to Moses in
executing the command of God.

All Penal Laws court Transgression & therefore are
cruelty & Murder⌊.⌋

The laws of the Jews were (both ceremonial & real) the basest & most oppressive of human code*s* & being like all other codes given under pretence of divine command were what Christ pronounced them⌊,⌋ The Abomination that maketh desolat*e*, i.e State Religion, which is the Source of all Cruelty⌊.⌋[1]

[*Page 29*]

LETTER IV.

And who told you that the jews had no records, or that they did not preserve them with singular care? . . . If any one, having access to the journals of the lords and commons, to the books of the treasury, war-office, privy council, and other public documents, should at this day write an history of the reigns of George the first and second, and should publish it without his name, would any man, three or four hundreds or thousands of years hence, question the authority of that book, when he knew that the whole British nation had received it as an authentic book, from the time of it's first publication to the age in which he lived? . . .

Hundreds or Thousands of Years⌊!⌋ O very fine Records⌊!⌋ as if he Knew that there were Records⌊!⌋ *T*he Ancients Knew Better⌊.⌋

If I am right in this reasoning, (and I protest to you that I do not see any error in it,) all the arguments you adduce in proof that the book of Joshua was not written by Joshua, nor that of Samuel by Samuel, are nothing to the purpose for which you have brought them forward: these books may be books of authority, though all you advance against the genuineness of them should be granted.

*A*s if Reasoning was of any Consequence to a Question⌊!⌋ Downright Plain Truth is Something but Reasoning is Nothing⌊.⌋

[*Page 31*]

Whoever wrote the gospel of St. Matthew, it was written not many centuries, probably (I had almost said certainly) not a quarter of one century after the death of Jesus . . . .

There are no Proofs that Mathew⌊,⌋ the Earliest of all the Writings of the New Testament⌊,⌋ was written within the First Century⌊.⌋ See p 94 & 95⌊.⌋

[*Page 25*] [1] 'is the Source of all Cruelty' is on p. 26.

[*Page 34*]

It seems to me that you do not perfectly comprehend what is meant by the expression—the Word of God—or the divine authority of the scriptures:—I will explain it to you in the words of Dr. Law, late bishop of Carlisle, and in those of St. Austin. . . . 'God . . . interfered upon particular occasions, by giving express commissions to some persons . . . .'

They seem to Forget that there is a God of This World, A God Worshipd in this World as God & Set above all that is calld God⌞.⌟

[*Page 35*]

The two books of Samuel come next under your review. You proceed to shew that these books were not written by Samuel, that they are anonymous, and thence you conclude without authority.

Who gave them the Name of Books of Samuel⌞?⌟ *It* is not of Consequence⌞.⌟

[*Page 36*]

Very little certainty, I think, can at this time be obtained on this subject: but that you may have some knowledge of what has been conjectured by men of judgment, I will quote to you a passage from Dr. Hartley's Observations on Man. . . .

Hartley a Man of Judgment⌞!⌟ Then Judgment was a Fool⌞.⌟ What Nonsense⌞!⌟

[*Page 48*]

As to the sins and debaucheries of Solomon, we have nothing to do with them but to avoid them; and to give full credit to his experience, when he preaches to us his admirable sermon on the vanity of every thing but piety and virtue.

Piety & Virtue⌞!⌟ *Is* Seneca Classical O Fine Bishop⌞?⌟

[*Page 49*]

I shall never cease to believe that the Eternal alone, by whom things future are more distinctly known than past or present things are by man, that the eternal God alone could have dictated to the prophet Isaiah the subject of the burden of Babylon.

The Bishop never saw the Everlasting Gospel any more than Tom Paine⌞.⌟

Page 36   Blake engraved the frontispiece to David Hartley, *Observations on Man* (1791).

[*Page 95*]

LETTER IX. . . .

Did you ever read the apology for the christians, which Justin Martyr presented to the emperor Antoninus Pius, to the senate, and people of Rome? I should sooner expect a falsity in a petition, which any body of persecuted men, imploring justice, should present to the king and parliament of Great Britain, than in this apology.—Yet in this apology, which was presented not fifty years after the death of St. John, not only parts of *all the four gospels are quoted,*

A: D: 150.

but it is expressly said, that on the day called Sunday, a portion of them was read in the public assemblies of the christians. I forbear pursuing this matter farther; else it might easily be shewn, that PROBABLY the GOSPELS, and certainly some of St. Paul's epistles, were known to *Clement, Ignatius,* and *Polycarp,* contemporaries with the apostles. These men could not quote or refer to books which did not exist: and therefore, though you could make it out that the book called the New Testament did not formally exist under that title, till 350 years after Christ; YET I HOLD IT TO BE A CERTAIN FACT, THAT ALL THE BOOKS, of which it is composed, were written, and most of them received by all christians, within a few years after his death.

This is No Certain Fact⌊.⌋ Presumption is no Proof⌊.⌋

[*Page 108*]

LETTER X. . . .

The moral precepts of the gospel are so well fitted to promote the happiness of mankind in this world, and to prepare human nature for the future enjoyment of that blessedness, of which, in our present state, we can form no conception, that I had no expectation they would have met with your disapprobation.

The Gospel is Forgiveness of Sins & has No Moral Precepts⌊;⌋ these belong to Plato & Seneca & Nero⌊.⌋

[*Page 109*]

Two precepts you particularize as inconsistent with the dignity and the nature of man—that of not resenting injuries, and that of loving enemies.

Well done Paine⌊!⌋

—Who but yourself ever interpreted literally the proverbial phrase—'If a man smite thee on thy right cheek, turn to him the other also?'—Did

Page 108 This sentiment is one which Blake expressed frequently about 1818 in *For the Sexes*, 'The Everlasting Gospel', and 'Laocoon' (pp. 645, 1054–69, 664).

Jesus himself turn the other CHEEK WHEN THE OFFICER OF THE HIGH PRIEST
SMOTE him?

Yes I have no doubt he Did⌞.⌟

It is evident, that a patient acquiescence under SLIGHT personal injuries
is here enjoined; and that a proneness to revenge, which instigates men
to savage acts of brutality, for every trifling offence, is forbidden.

O Fool⌞!⌟ Slight Hypocrite & Villain⌞!⌟

[*Page 117*]

The importance of revelation is by nothing rendered more apparent, than
by the discordant sentiments of learned and good men (for I speak not of the
IGNORANT AND IMMORAL) on this point.

O how Virtuous⌞!⌟ Christ came not to call the Virtuous⌞.⌟

[*Page 118*]

We are all, of every rank and condition, equally concerned in knowing—
what will become of us after death;—and, if we are to live again, we are
interested in knowing—whether it be possible for us to do any thing whilst
we live here, which may render that future life an happy one.—

Do or Act to Do Good or to do Evil⌞.⌟ Who Dare to
Judge but God alone⌞?⌟

Now, 'that thing called christianity,' as you scoffingly speak—that last
best gift of Almighty God, as I esteem it, the gospel of Jesus Christ, has
given us the most clear and satisfactory information on both these points.
It tells us, what deism never could have told us, that we shall certainly be
raised from the dead—that, whatever be the nature of the soul, we shall
certainly live for ever—and that, whilst we live here, it is possible for us to
do much towards the rendering that everlasting life an happy one.—These
are tremendous truths to bad men; they cannot be received and reflected
on with indifference by the best; and they suggest to all such a cogent motive
to virtuous action, as deism could not furnish even to *Brutus* himself.

Who does the Bishop call Bad Men⌞?⌟ Are they the Pub-
licans & Sinners that Christ loved to associate with⌞?⌟
Does God Love the Righteous according to the Gospel or
does he cast them off⌞?⌟

[*Page 119*]

Some men have been warped to infidelity by viciousness of life; and
some may have hypocritically professed Christianity from prospects of

temporal advantage: but, being a stranger to your character, I neither impute the former to you, nor can admit the latter as operating on myself. The generality of unbelievers are such, from want of information on the subject of religion; having been engaged from their youth in struggling for worldly distinction, or perplexed with the incessant intricacies of business, or bewildered in the pursuits of pleasure, they have neither ability, inclination, nor leisure, to enter into critical disquisitions concerning the truth of christianity.

For who is really Righteous⌊?⌋ It is all Pretension⌊.⌋

[*Page 120, the last page*]

It appears to me Now that Tom Paine is a better Christian than the Bishop⌊.⌋

I have read this Book with attention & find that the Bishop has only hurt Paines heel while Paine has broken his head⌊;⌋ the Bishop has not answerd one of Paines grand objections⌊.⌋

MARGINALIA (?1798): Bacon, *Essays* (1798)

[Half-title top]

Is it True or is it False that the Wisdom of this World is Foolishness with God ?

[Half-title bottom]

This is Certain : If what Bacon says Is True what Christ says Is False If Caesar is Right Christ is Wrong both in Politics & Religion since they will divide them in Two .

[Title-page]

Good Advice for Satans Kingdom .

[Page i, Editor's Preface]

I am astonishd how such Contemptible Knavery & Folly as this Book contains can ever have been calld Wisdom by Men of Sense but perhaps this never was the Case & all Men of Sense have dispised the Book as Much as I do .
Per[?] William Blake

[Page iv]

But these Essays, written at a period of better taste, and on subjects of immediate importance to the conduct of common life, 'such as come home to men's BUSINESS AND BOSOMS,' are still read with pleasure . . . .

Erratum : to Mens Pockets .

[Page xii]

Every Body Knows that this is Epicurus and Lucretius & Yet Every Body Says that it is Christian Philosophy ; how is this Possible ? Every Body must be a Liar & deciever, but Every Body does not do this But The Hirelings of Kings & Courts who make themselves Every Body & Knowingly propagate Fals[e]hood .

It was a Common opinion in the Court of Queen Elizabeth that Knavery Is Wisdom. Cunning Plotters were considerd as wise Machiavels .

[*Page 1, OF TRUTH*]

Self Evident Truth is one Thing and Truth the result
of Reasoning is another Thing⌊.⌋ Rational Truth is not
the Truth of Christ but of Pilate⌊.⌋ It is the Tree of the
Knowledge of Good & Evil⌊.⌋

What is truth? said jesting Pilate, and would not stay for an answer.
Certainly there be that delight in giddiness, and count it a bondage to fix
a belief; affecting free-will in thinking, as well as in acting: and, though
the sects of philosophers of that kind be gone, yet there remain certain
discoursing wits which are of the same veins, though there be not so much
blood in them as was in those of the ancients.

But more Nerve if by Ancients he means Heathen
Authors⌊.⌋

[*Page 2*]

But it is not only the difficulty and labour which men take in finding out of
truth; nor again, that, when it is found, it imposeth upon men's thoughts,
that doth bring lies in favour; but a natural, though corrupt love of the lie
itself. One of the later school of the Grecians examineth the matter, and is
at a stand to think what should be in it, that men should love lies, where
neither they make for pleasure, as with poets; nor for advantage, as with
the merchant; but for the lie's sake. But I cannot tell: this same truth is a
naked and open daylight, that doth not shew the masques, and mummeries,
and triumphs of the world half so stately and daintily as candlelights.

What Bacon calls Lies is Truth itself⌊.⌋

[*Page 3*]

But howsoever these things are thus in men's depraved judgments and
affections, yet truth, which only doth judge itself, teacheth that the inquiry
of truth, which is the love-making, or wooing of it; the knowledge of truth,
which is the presence of it; and the belief of truth, which is the enjoying of
it, is the sovereign good of human nature. The first creature of God, in the
works of the days, was the light of the sense; the last was the light of reason;
and his sabbath work, ever since, is the illumination of his Spirit.

Pretence to Religion to destroy Religion⌊.⌋

[*Page 4*]

To pass from theological and philosophical truth to the truth of civil
business, it will be acknowledged, even by those that practise it not, that

Page 3: Cf. *Jerusalem* pl. 43, l. 36 (p. 509): 'a pretence of Religion to destroy Re-
ligion'.

clear and round dealing is the honour of man's nature, and that mixture of falsehood is like allay in coin of gold and silver . . . .

> Christianity is Civil Business Only∟.⌋ There is & can Be No Other to Man∟.⌋ What Else Can Be∟?⌋ Civil is Christianity or Religion or whatever is Humane∟.⌋

[*Page 5*]

Surely the wickedness of falsehood and breach of faith cannot possibly be so highly expressed as in that it shall be the last peal to call the judgments of God upon the generations of men: it being foretold, that when 'Christ cometh,' he shall not 'find faith upon earth.'

> Bacon put an End to Faith∟.⌋

[*Page 6, OF DEATH*]

You shall read in some of the friars books of mortification, that a man should think with himself what the pain is, if he have but his finger's end pressed, or tortured, and thereby imagine what the pains of death are when the whole body is corrupted and dissolved; when many times death passeth with less pain than the torture of a limb; for the most vital parts are not the quickest of sense: and by him that spake only as a philosopher and natural man, it was well said, 'Pompa mortis magis terret, quam mors ipsa.'

> Bacon Supposes all Men alike∟.⌋

Revenge triumphs over death; love flights it; honour aspireth to it; grief flieth to it; fear pre-occupieth it; nay, we read, after Otho the emperor had slain himself, pity (which is the tenderest of affections) provoked many to die out of mere compassion to their sovereign, and as the truest sort of followers.

> One Mans Revenge or Love is not the Same as Anothers∟.⌋
> The tender Mercies of some Men are Cruel∟.⌋

[*Page 8, OF UNITY IN RELIGION*]

Religion being the chief band of human society, it is a happy thing when itself is well contained within the true band of unity. The quarrels and divisions about religion were evils UNKNOWN TO THE HEATHEN.

> False O Satan∟.⌋

The reason was, because the religion of the heathen consisted rather in rites and ceremonies, than in any constant belief: for you may imagine what kind of faith theirs was, when the chief doctors and fathers of their church were the POETS.

> Prophets∟.⌋

[Page 9]

The fruits of unity (next unto the well-pleasing of God, which is all in all) are two; the one towards those that are without the church; the other towards those that are within. For the former, it is certain, that heresies and schisms are of all others the greatest scandals; yea more than corruption of manners: for as in the natural body a wound or solution of continuity is worse than a corrupt humour, so in the spiritual . . . .

False⌐!⌐

[Page 10]

The doctor of the Gentiles (the propriety of whose vocation drew him to have a special care of those without) saith, 'If an heathen come in, and hear 'you speak with several tongues, will he not say that you are mad?' and, certainly, it is little better: when atheists and profane persons do hear of so many discordant and contrary opinions in religion, it doth avert them from the church, and maketh them 'to sit down in the chair of the scorners.' It is but a light thing to be vouched in so serious a matter, but yet it expresseth well the deformity.

Trifling Nonsense⌐!⌐

[Page 12]

Men ought to take heed of rending God's church by two kinds of controversies; the one is, when the matter of the point controverted is too small and light, not worth the heat and strife about it, kindled only by contradiction; for, as it is noted by one of the fathers, Christ's coat indeed had no seam, but the church's vesture was of divers colours; whereupon he saith, 'in 'veste varietas sit, scissura non sit,' they be two things, unity and uniformity: the other is when the matter of the point controverted is great, but it is driven to an over-great subtility and obscurity, so that it becometh a thing rather ingenious than substantial.

Lame Reasoning upon Premises⌐.⌐ This Never can Happen⌐.⌐

[Page 14]

It was great blasphemy when the devil said, 'I will ascend and be like the 'Highest;' but it is greater blasphemy to personate God, and bring him in saying, 'I will descend, and be like the prince of darkness' . . . .

Did not Jesus descend & become a Servant⌐?⌐ The Prince of darkness is a Gentleman & not a Man⌐;⌐ he is a Lord Chancellor⌐.⌐

[*Page 17, OF REVENGE*]

This is certain, that a man that studieth revenge keeps his own wounds green, which otherwise would heal and do well. Public revenges are for the most part fortunate . . . .

A Lie⌞!⌟

[*Page 22, OF SIMULATION AND DISSIMULATION*]

In a few words, mysteries are due to secrecy. Besides (to say truth) NAKEDNESS IS UNCOMELY, as well in mind as in body . . . .

This is Folly Itself⌞.⌟

[*Page 32, OF ENVY*]

A man that hath no virtue in himself ever envieth virtue in others: for men's minds will either feed upon their own good, or upon others evil; and who wanteth the one will prey upon the other; and whoso is out of hope to attain to another's virtue, will seek to come at even hand by depressing another's fortune.

What do these Knaves mean by Virtue⌞?⌟ Do they mean War & its horrors & its Heroic Villains⌞?⌟

[*Page 37*]

Lastly, to conclude this part, as we said in the beginning that the act of envy had somewhat in it of witchcraft, so there is no other cure of envy but the cure of witchcraft; and that is, to remove the lot, (as they call it), and to lay it upon another; for which purpose, the wiser sort of great persons bring in ever upon the stage somebody upon whom to derive the envy that would come upon themselves . . . .

Politic Foolery & most contemptible Villainy & Murder⌞!⌟

Now to speak of public envy: there is yet some good in public envy, whereas in private there is none; for public envy is as an ostracism, that eclipseth men when they grow too great . . . .

Foolish & tells into the hands of a Tyrant⌞.⌟

[*Page 38*]

This public envy seemeth to beat chiefly upon principal officers or ministers, rather than upon kings and estates themselves.

A Lie⌞!⌟ Every Body hates a King⌞.⌟ Bacon was afraid to say that the Envy was upon a King but is This Envy or Indignation⌞?⌟

[*Page 44, OF GREAT PLACE*]

But power to do good is the true and lawful end of aspiring; for good thoughts, (though God accept them), yet towards men are little better than good dreams, except they be put in act . . . .

Thought Is Act. Christs Acts were Nothing to Caesars if this is not so∟.⌋

[*Page 45*]

In the discharge of thy place set before thee the best examples; for imitation is a globe of precepts; and after a time set before thee thine own example; and examine thyself strictly whether thou didst not best at first.

Here is nothing of Thy own Original Genius but only Imitation∟;⌋ what Folly∟!⌋

[*Page 48*]

Be not too sensible or too remembering of thy place in conversation and private answers to suitors; but let it rather be said, 'When he sits in place 'he is another man.'

A Flogging Magistrate∟!⌋ I have seen many such fly blows of Bacon∟.⌋

[*Page 54, OF GOODNESS AND GOODNESS OF NATURE*]

And beware how in making the portrait thou breakest the pattern: for divinity maketh the love of ourselves the pattern; the love of our neighbours but the portraiture: 'Sell all thou hast, and give it to the poor, and follow 'me:' but sell not all thou hast, except thou come and follow me; that is, except thou have a vocation wherein thou mayest do as much good with little means as with great . . . .

Except is Christ∟.⌋ You Lie Except did any one ⌃Ever⌃ do this & not follow Christ Who Does by Nature∟.⌋

[*Page 55, OF A KING*]

[*An erased sketch of buttocks(?), with an erased identification:*] The Devils arse[(?). *From these depend a chain, at the bottom of which is:*] A King∟.⌋

[*Page 56*]

A KING is a mortal god on earth, unto whom the living God hath lent his own name as a great honour. . . .

O Contemptible & Abject Slave∟!⌋

[*Page 58*]

That king which is not feared is not loved; and he that is well seen in his craft must as well study to be feared as loved; yet not loved for fear, but feared for love.

Fear Cannot Love⌞.⌟

[*Page 60*]

He then that honoureth him [*the King*] not is next an atheist, wanting the fear of God in his heart.

Blasphemy⌞!⌟

[*OF NOBILITY*]

We will speak of nobility first as a portion of an estate, then as a condition of particular persons.

Is Nobility a portion of a State i.e Republic⌞?⌟

A monarchy, where there is no nobility at all, is ever a pure and absolute tyranny, as that of the Turks; for nobility attempers sovereignty, and draws the eyes of the people somewhat aside from the line royal: but for DEMO-CRACIES THEY NEED it not; and they are COMMONLY MORE QUIET, AND LESS subject to sedition, than where there are stirps of nobles . . . .

Self Contradiction⌞!⌟ Knave & Fool⌞!⌟

[*Page 62*]

Those that are first raised to nobility, are commonly more virtuous, but less innocent, than their descendants; for there is rarely any rising but by acommixture of good and evil arts . . . .

Virtuous I Supposed to be Innocent⌞:⌟ was I Mistaken or is Bacon a Liar⌞?⌟

On the other side, nobility extinguisheth the passive envy from others to-wards them, because they are in possession of honour. Certainly, kings that have able men of their nobility shall find ease in employing them, and a better slide into their business; for people naturally bend to them as born in some sort to command.

Nonsense⌞!⌟

[*Page 63, OF SEDITIONS AND TROUBLES*]

This Section contradicts the Preceding⌞.⌟

1431

SHEPHERDS of all people had need know the calendars of tempests in state, which are commonly greatest when things grow to EQUALITY. . . .

What Shepherds does he mean∟?⌐ Such as Christ describes by Ravening Wolves∟?⌐

[*Page 65*]

Also, when discords, and quarrels, and factions are carried openly and audaciously, it is a sign the reverence of government is lost . . . .

When the Reverence of Government is Lost it is better than when it is found∟.⌐ Reverence is all For Reverence∟.⌐

[*Page 66*]

So when any of the four pillars of government are mainly shaken, or weakened, (which are religion, justice, counsel, and treasure,) men had need to pray for fair weather.

Four Pillars of different heights & Sizes∟.⌐

The matter of seditions is of two kinds, much poverty and much discontentment.

These are one Kind Only∟.⌐

[*Page 67*]

As for discontentments, they are in the politic body like to humours in the natural, which are apt to gather a preternatural heat and to enflame; and let no prince measure the danger of them by this, whether they be just or unjust . . . .

A Tyrant is the Worst disease & the Cause of all others∟.⌐

. . . in great oppressions, the same things that provoke the patience, do withal mate the courage . . . .

A lie∟!⌐

[*Page 69*]

The first remedy or prevention is to remove by all means possible that material cause of sedition whereof we speak, which is want and poverty in the estate; to which purpose serveth the opening and well balancing of trade; the cherishing of manufactures; the banishing of idleness; the repressing of waste and excess by sumptuary laws; the improvement and husbanding of the soil; the regulating of prices of things vendible; the moderating of taxes and tributes, and the like.

You cannot regulate the price of Necessaries without destruction∟.⌐ All False∟!⌐

It is likewise to be remembered, that, forasmuch as the increase of any estate must be upon the foreigner, (for whatsoever is somewhere gotten is somewhere lost,) there be but three things which one nation selleth unto another; the commodity as nature yieldeth it; the manufacture; and the vecture or carriage: so that if these two wheels go, wealth will flow as in a spring tide . . . .

The Increase of a State as of a Man is from Internal Improvement or Intellectual Acquirement. Man is not Improved by the hurt of another⌊.⌋ States are not Improved at the Expense of Foreigners⌊.⌋

[*Page 70*]

Bacon has no notion of any thing but Mammon⌊.⌋

[*Page 71*]

The poets feign that the rest of the Gods would have bound Jupiter, which he hearing of by the counsel of Pallas, sent for Briareus with his hundred hands to come in to his aid: an emblem, no doubt, to shew how safe it is for monarchs to make sure of the good will of common people.

Good Advice for the Devil⌊.⌋

[*Page 72*]

Certainly, the politic and artificial nourishing and entertaining of hopes, and carrying men from hopes to hopes is one of the best antidotes against the poison of discontentments . . . .

Subterfuges⌊!⌋

[*Page 74*]

Lastly, let princes against all events, not be without some great person, one or rather more, of military valour, near unto them, for the repression of seditions in their beginnings . . . .

Contemptible Knave⌊!⌋ Let the People look to this⌊!⌋

. . . but let such military persons be assured and well reputed of, rather than factious and popular . . . .

Factious is Not Popular & never can be except Factious is Christianity⌊.⌋

[*Page 75, OF ATHEISM*]

I HAD rather believe all the fables in the legend, and the Talmud, and the Alcoran than that this universal frame is without a MIND: and, therefore,

God never wrought miracle to convince atheism, because his ordinary works convince it.

The devil is the Mind of the Natural Frame∟·」

It is true that a little philosophy inclineth man's mind to atheism; but depth in philosophy bringeth men's minds about to religion; for while the mind of man looketh upon second causes scattered, it may sometimes rest in them and go no farther . . . .

There is no Such Thing as a Second Cause nor as a Natural Cause for any Thing in any Way∟·」

[*Page 76*]

He who says there are Second Causes has already denied a First∟·」 The Word Cause is a foolish Word∟·」

[*Page 77*]

The contemplative atheist is rare, a Diagoras, a Bion, a Lucian perhaps, and some others . . . .

A Lie! Few believe it is a New Birth∟·」 Bacon was a Contemplative Atheist∟,」 Evidently an Epicurean∟·」 Lucian disbelievd Heathen Gods∟;」 he did not perhaps disbelieve for all that∟·」 Bacon did∟·」

[*Page 79*]

The causes of atheism are, divisions in religion, if they be many . . . another is, scandal of priests . . . a third is, a custom of profane scoffing in holy matters . . . and, lastly, learned times, especially with peace and prosperity; for troubles and *ADVERSITIES* do more bow men's minds to religion.

A Lie∟!」

They that deny a God destroy man's nobility; for certainly man is of kin to the beasts by his body; and, if he be not of kin to God by his spirit, he is a base and ignoble creature.

An artifice∟!」

It destroys likewise magnanimity, and the raising of human nature; for take an example of a dog, and mark what a generosity and courage he will put on when he finds himself maintained by a man, who to him is instead of a god, or 'melior natura;' which courage is manifestly such as that creature, without that confidence of a better nature than his own, could never attain.

Self Contradiction∟!」

. . . therefore, as atheism is in all respects hateful, so in this, that it depriveth human nature of the means to exalt itself above human frailty.

An Atheist pretending to talk against Atheism∟!」

[*Page 79, OF SUPERSTITION*]

It were better to have no opinion of God at all, than such an opinion as is unworthy of him . . . .

Is this true∟?」 is it better∟?」

[*Page 80*]

. . . as the contumely is greater TOWARDS GOD, SO THE DANGER is greater towards men. Atheism LEAVES a man to sense, to philosophy, to natural PIETY, to laws, to reputation; all which may BE GUIDES to an outward moral virtue, though religion were not;

Praise of Atheism∟!」

but superstition dismounts all these, and erecteth an absolute monarchy in the minds of men: THEREFORE ATHEISM did NEVER PERTURB states; for it makes men wary of themselves, as looking no farther, and we see the times inclined to atheism, (as the time of Augustus Caesar,) were civil times . . . .

Atheism is thus the best of all∟.」 Bacon fools us∟.」

The master of superstition is the people, and in all superstition wise men follow fools; and arguments are fitted to practise in a reversed order.

What must our Clergy be who Allow Bacon to be Either Wise or even of Common Capacity∟?」 I cannot∟.」

[*Page 82*]

There is a superstition in avoiding superstition, when men think to do best if they go farthest from the superstition formerly received; therefore care should be had that, (as it fareth in ill purgings,) the good be not taken away with the bad, which commonly is done when the PEOPLE is the reformer.

Who is to be the Reformer∟?」 Bacons Villain[1] is a King or Who∟?」

[1] Erdman suggests that a caret between 'Bacons' and 'Villain' pointing to 'Reformer' just above indicates that the phrase should read 'Bacons Reformer Villain' (Erdman, p. 801).

[*Page 83, OF TRAVEL*]

The things to be seen and observed are the courts of princes, especially when they give audience to ambassadors; the courts of justice . . . the churches and monasteries . . . the walls and fortifications . . . the havens and harbours, antiquities and ruins, libraries, colleges, disputations, and lectures where any are; shipping and navies; houses and gardens of state and pleasure near great cities; armories, arsenals, magazines, exchanges, burses, warehouses, exercises of horsemanship, fencing, training of soldiers, and the like; comedies . . . treasuries of jewels and robes; cabinets and rarieties . . . .

The Things worthy to be seen are all the Trumpery he could rake together⌊.⌋
Nothing of Arts or Artists or Learned Men or of Agriculture or any Useful Thing⌊.⌋ His Business & Bosom was to be Lord Chancellor⌊.⌋

[*Page 84*]

As for triumphs, masks, feasts, weddings, funerals, capital executions, and such shews, men need not to be put in mind of them; yet are they not to be neglected.

Bacon supposes that the dragon Beast & Harlot are worthy of a Place in the New Jerusalem⌊.⌋ Excellent Traveller Go on & be damnd⌊!⌋

If you will have a young man to put his travel into a little room, and in short time to gather much, this you must do . . . let him not stay long in one city or town, more or less as the place deserveth, but not long; nay, when he stayeth in one city or town, let him change his lodging from one end and part of the town to another, which is a great adamant of acquaintance;

Harum Scarum⌊;⌋ who Can do this⌊?⌋

let him sequester himself from the company of his countrymen, and diet in such places where there is good company of the nation where he travelleth; let him upon his removes from one place to another procure recommendation to some person of QUALITY residing in the place whither he removeth . . . .

The Contrary is the best Advice⌊.⌋

[*Page 85*]

As for the acquaintance which is to be sought in travel, that which is most of all profitable is acquaintance with the secretaries and employed men of ambassadors . . . .

Acqua[i]ntance with Knaves⌊.⌋

[*Page 86, OF EMPIRE*]

It is a miserable state of mind to have few things to desire, and many things to fear . . . .

He who has few Things to desire cannot have many to fear⌊.⌋

[*Page 87*]

. . . the mind of man is more cheered and refreshed by profiting in small things, than by standing at a stay in great.

A Lie⌊!⌋

[*Page 98, OF COUNSEL*]

For weakening of authority the fable sheweth the remedy: nay, the majesty of kings is rather exalted than diminished when they are in the chair of council; neither was there ever prince bereaved of his dependances by his council, except where there hath been either an over-greatness in one counsellor, or an over-strict combination in divers, which are things soon found and holpen.

Did he mean to Ridicule a King & his Council⌊?⌋

[*Page 101*]

In choice of committees for ripening business for the council, it is better to choose indifferent persons, than to make an indifferency by putting in those that are strong on both sides.

better choose Fools at once⌊!⌋

[*Page 104, OF CUNNING*]

There be that can pack the cards, and yet cannot play well; so there are some that are good in canvasses and factions, that are otherwise weak men.

Nonsense⌊!⌋

Again, it is one thing to understand persons, and another thing to understand matters . . . .

Nonsense⌊!⌋

Such men are fitter for practice than for counsel, and they are good but in their own ally . . . .

How Absurd⌊!⌋

[*Page 105*]

If a man would cross a business that he doubts some other would hand-somely and effectually move, let him pretend to wish it well, and move it himself in such sort as may foil it.

None but a Fool can act so⌐·⌐

[*Page 107*]

I knew one that, when he wrote a letter, he would put that which was most material in the post-script, as if it had been a bye matter.

I knew another that, when he came to have speech, he would pass over that that he intended most; and go forth, and come back again, and speak of it as of a thing that he had almost forgot.

What Fools⌐!⌐

[*Page 108*]

It is a point of cunning to let fall those words in a man's own name which he would have another man learn and use, and thereupon take advantage. I knew two that were competitors for the secretary's place in queen Eliza-beth's time . . . one of them said, that to be a secretary in the declination of a monarchy was a ticklish thing, and that he did not affect it: the other straight way caught up those words, and discoursed with divers of his friends, that he had no reason to desire to be secretary in the declination of a monarchy. The first man took hold of it, and found means it was told the queen; who, hearing of a declination of a monarchy, took it so ill, as she would never after hear of the other's suit.

This is too Stupid to have been True⌐·⌐

[*Page 113, OF INNOVATIONS*]

As the births of living creatures at first are ill shapen, so are all innova-tions, which are the births of time . . . .

What a Cursed Fool is this⌐?⌐ Ill Shapen⌐!⌐ are Infants or Small Plants ill shapen because they are not yet come to their maturity⌐?⌐ What a Contemptible Fool is This Bacon⌐!⌐

[*Page 124, OF FRIENDSHIP*]

L. Sylla, when he commanded Rome, raised Pompey . . . to that height, that Pompey vaunted himself for Sylla's over-match . . . . With Julius Caesar Decimus Brutus had obtained that interest as he set him down in his testament for heir in remainder after his nephew . . . . Augustus raised Agrippa, (though of mean birth,) to that height, as, when he consulted

Mecænas about the marriage of his daughter Julia, Mecænas took the liberty to tell him, that he must either marry his daughter to Agrippa, or take away his life . . . .

The Friendship of these Roman Villains is a strange Example to alledge for our imitation & approval∟!⌐

[*Page 133, OF EXPENSE*]

Certainly, if a man will keep but of even hand, his ordinary expenses ought to be but to the half of his receipts; and if he think to wax rich, but to the third part.

If this is advice to the Poor it is mocking them∟;⌐
If to the Rich it is worse still∟;⌐ it is The Miser∟;⌐
If to the Middle Class it is the direct Contrary to Christs advice∟.⌐

[*Page 134*]

He that can look into his estate but seldom, it behoveth him to turn all to *CERTAINTIES*.

Nonsense∟!⌐

[*Page 135, OF THE TRUE GREATNESS OF KINGDOMS AND ESTATES*]

The speech of Themistocles the Athenian, which was haughty and arrogant in taking so much to himself, had been a grave and wise observation and censure, applied at large to others. Desired at a feast to touch a lute, he said, 'he could not fiddle, but yet he could make a small town a great city.' These words, (holpen a little with a metaphor,) may express two differing abilities in those that deal in business of estate . . . .

A Lord Chancellors opinions as different from Christ as those of Cai[*a*]phas or Pilate or Herod∟;⌐ what such Men call Great is indeed detestable∟.⌐

[*Page 136*]

. . . let us speak of the work; that is, the true greatness of kingdoms and estates; and the means thereof. An argument fit for great and mighty *PRINCES* to have in their hand; and to the end, that neither by over-measuring their forces they lose themselves in vain enterprises . . . .

Princes Powers∟!⌐ Powers of darkness∟!⌐

[*Page 137*]

The kingdom of heaven is compared, not to any great kernal or nut but, to a grain of mustard seed; which is one of the least grains, but hath in it a property and spirit hastily to get up and spread.

The Kingdom of Heaven is the direct Negation of Earthly domination⌞.⌟

[*Page 138*]

Walled towns, stored arsenals and armories, goodly races of horse, chariots of war, elephants, ordnance, artillery, and the like; all this is but a sheep in lion's skin, except the breed and disposition of the people be stout and warlike. Nay, number (itself) in armies importeth not much, where the people is of weak courage . . . . The army of the Persians, in the plains of Arbela was such a vast sea of people as it did somewhat astonish the commanders in Alexander's army, who came to him therefore, and wished him to set upon them by night; but he answered, he would not pilfer the victory; and the defeat was easy.

Bacon knows the Wisdom of War if it is Wisdom⌞.⌟

[*Page 142*]

Never any state was, in this point, so open to receive strangers into their body as were the Romans; therefore it sorted with them accordingly, for they grew to the GREATEST MONARCHY.

Is this Great⌞?⌟ Is this Christian⌞?⌟ No⌞!⌟

[*Page 144*]

It is certain, that sedentary and within-door arts, and delicate manufactures, (that require rather the finger than the arm,) have in their nature a contrariety to a military disposition .·. . therefore it was great advantage in the ancient states of Sparta, Athens, Rome, and others, that they had the use of slaves, which commonly did rid those manufactures; but that is abolished, in greatest part, by the christian law. That which cometh nearest to it is, to leave those arts chiefly to strangers . . . and to contain the principal bulk of the vulgar natives within those three kinds, tillers of the ground, free servants, and handicraftsmen of strong and manly arts; as smiths, masons, carpenters, &c. not reckoning professed soldiers.

Bacon calls Intellectual Arts Unmanly⌞.⌟ Poetry Painting Music are in his opinion Useless & so they are for Kings & Wars & shall in the End Annihilate them⌞.⌟

[*Page 147*]

No body can be healthful without exercise, neither natural body nor politic: and, certainly, to a kingdom or estate a just and honourable war is the true exercise.

Is not this the Greatest Folly_L?_J

[*Page 149*]

There be now, for martial encouragement, some degrees and orders of chivalry, which, nevertheless, are conferred promiscuously upon soldiers and no soldiers, and some remembrance perhaps upon the escutcheon . . . .

What can be worse than this or more foolish_L?_J

[*Page 151, OF REGIMEN OF HEALTH*]

. . . strength of nature in youth passeth over many excesses which are owing a man till his age.

Excess in Youth is Necessary to Life_L._J

Beware of sudden change in any great point of diet, and if necessity enforce it, fit the rest to it;

Nonsense_L!_J

for it is a secret both in nature and state, that it is safer to change many things than one.

False_L!_J

[*Page 152*]

If you fly physic in health altogether, it will be too strange for your body when you shall need it . . . .

Very Pernicious Advice_L._J The work of a Fool to use Physic but for necessity_L._J

[*Page 153*]

In sickness, respect health principally; and in health, action: for those that put their bodies to endure in health, may in most sicknesses which are not very sharp, be cured only with diet and tendering.

Those that put their Bodies to Endure are Fools_L._J

Celsus could never have spoken it as a physician, had he not been a wise man withal, when he giveth it for one of the great precepts of health and lasting, that a man do vary and interchange contraries; but with an inclination to the more benign extreme: use fasting and full eating, but rather full eating; watching and sleep, but rather sleep; sitting and exercise, but rather exercise, and the like: so shall nature be cherished, and yet taught masteries.

Celsus was a bad adviser⌞.⌟
Nature taught to Ostentation⌞.⌟

[*Page 154, OF SUSPICION*]

SUSPICIONS amongst thoughts are like bats amongst birds, they ever fly by twilight: certainly they are to be repressed, or, at the least, well guarded . . . .

What is Suspition in one Man is Caution in Another & Truth or Discernment in Another & in Some it is Folly⌞.⌟

[*Page 156, OF DISCOURSE*]

SOME in their discourse desire rather commendation of wit, in being able to hold all arguments, than of judgment, in discerning what is true; as if it were a praise to know what might be said, and not what should be thought.

Surely the Man who wrote this never talked to any but Coxcombs⌞.⌟

[*Page 158*]

Discretion of speech is more than eloquence; and to speak agreeably to him with whom we deal, is more than to speak in good words, or in good order.

Bacon hated Talents of all Kinds⌞.⌟ Eloquence is discretion of Speech⌞.⌟

[*Page 169, OF RICHES*]

Be not penny-wise; riches have wings, and sometimes they fly away of themselves, sometimes they must be set flying to bring in more.

Bacon was always a poor devil if History says true⌞;⌟ how should one So foolish know about Riches Except Pretence to be Rich if that is it⌞?⌟

[*Page 182, OF NATURE IN MEN*]

Neither is the ancient rule amiss, to bend nature as a wand to a contrary extreme, whereby to set it right; understanding it where the contrary extreme is no vice.

Very Foolish⌞.⌟

[*Page 187, OF FORTUNE*]
It cannot be denied but outward accidents conduce much to fortune; favour, opportunity, death of others, occasion fitting virtue: but chiefly, the mould of a man's fortune is in his own hands . . . .

What is Fortune but an outward Accident for a few years⌊,⌋ Sixty at most⌊,⌋ & then gone⌊?⌋

[*Page 190, OF USURY*]
Bacon was a Usurer⌊.⌋

[*Page 191*]
The discommodities of usury are, first, that it makes fewer merchants; for were it not for this lazy trade of usury, money would not lie still, but would in great part be employed upon merchandizing . . . .

A Lie⌊;⌋ it makes Merchants & nothing Else⌊.⌋

[*Page 192*]
On the other side, the commodities of usury are first, that howsoever usury in some respect hindereth merchandizing, yet in some other it advanceth it . . . .

Commodities of Usury⌊?⌋ can it Be⌊?⌋

[*Page 193*]
I remember a cruel monied man in the country, that would say, 'The devil 'take this usury, it keeps us from forfeitures of mortgages and bonds.'

It is not True what a Cruel Man says⌊.⌋

To speak now of the reformation and reglement of usury; how the discommodities of it may be best avoided, and the commodities retained.

Bacon is in his Element on Usury⌊;⌋ it is himself & his Philosophy⌊.⌋

[*Page 197, OF YOUTH AND AGE*]
The errors of young men are the ruin of business; but the errors of aged men amount but to this, that more might have been done, or sooner.

Bacons Business is not Intellect or Art⌊.⌋

[*Page 198*]
. . . age doth profit rather in the powers of understanding, than in the virtues of the will and affections.

A Lie⌊!⌋

[Page 199]

There be some have an over-early ripeness in their years, which fadeth betimes: these are, first, such as have brittle wits, the edge whereof is soon turned; such as was Hermogenes the rhetorician, whose books are exceeding subtile, who afterwards waxed stupid . . . .

Such was Bacon ; Stupid Indeed !

[Page 202, OF DEFORMITY]

Certainly there is a consent between the body and the mind, and where nature erreth in the one, she ventureth in the other . . . .

False ! Contemptible !

Whosoever hath any thing fixed in his person that doth induce contempt, hath also a perpetual spur in himself to rescue and deliver himself from scorn; therefore all deformed persons are extreme bold . . . .

Is not this Very Very Contemptible ? Contempt is the Element of the Contemptible.

[Page 203]

Kings in ancient times, (and at this present in some countries,) were wont to put great trust in eunuchs, because they that are envious towards all are more obnoxious and officious towards one . . . .

*B*ecause Kings do it is it Wisdom ?

[Page 206, OF BUILDING]

First, therefore, I say you cannot have a perfect PALACE, except you have two several sides; a side for the banquet, as is spoken of in the book of Esther, and a side for the household . . . .

What Trifling Nonsense & Self Conceit !

[Page 235, OF FACTION]

The even carriage between two factions proceedeth not always of moderation, but of a trueness to a man's self, with end to make use of both. Certainly, in Italy they hold it a little suspect in popes, when they have often in their mouth 'PADRE COMMUNE;' and take it to be a sign of one that meaneth to refer all to the greatness of his own house.

None but God is This.

Page 202: Cf. *Marriage* pl. 10 (p. 83): 'As the air to a bird or the sea to a fish, so is contempt to the contemptible.'

Kings had need beware how they side themselves . . . . The motions of factions under Kings, ought to be like the motions, (as the astronomers speak,) of the inferior orbs; which may have their proper motions, but yet still are quietly carried by the higher motion of 'primum mobile.'

King James was Bacons Primum Mobile⌊.⌋

[*Page 236, OF CEREMONIES AND RESPECTS*]

. . . the proverb is true, 'That light gains make heavy purses;' for light gains come thick, whereas great come but now and then: so it is true, that SMALL MATTERS win great commendation, because they are continually in use and in note . . . .

Small Matters⌊!⌋ What are They⌊?⌋ Caesar seems to me a Very Small Matter & so he seemd to Jesus⌊;⌋ is the devil Great⌊?⌋ Consider⌊.⌋

[*Page 239, OF PRAISE*]

PRAISE is the reflection of virtue; but it is as the glass or body which giveth the reflection: if it be from the COMMON PEOPLE, it is commonly false and nought, and rather followeth vain persons, than virtuous . . . .

Villain⌊!⌋ did Christ Seek the Praise of the Rulers⌊?⌋

MARGINALIA (?1800): Dante, *Inferno*, tr. Boyd (1785)

[*Page 35, A COMPARATIVE VIEW OF THE INFERNO*, With some other *POEMS* relative to the *ORIGINAL PRINCIPLES* of *HUMAN NATURE*, on which they are founded, or to which they appeal:]

[But *del*] the most daring flights of fancy, the most accurate delineations of character, and the most artful conduct of fable, are [not, even *del*] when combined together, sufficient of themselves to make a poem interesting.

[*Page 36*]

The superstition that led the Crusaders to rescue the Holy Land from the Infidels, instead of interesting us, appears frigid, if not ridiculous. We cannot be much concerned for the fate of such a crew of fanatics, notwithstanding the magic numbers of a Tasso. . . . we cannot sympathise with Achilles for this loss of his Mistress, when we feel that he gained her by the massacre of her family . . . .

*N*obody considers these things when they read Homer or Shakespear or Dante⌊.⌋

[*Page 37*]

When a Man, where no interest is concerned, no provocation given, lays a whole nation in blood merely for his *glory*; we, to whom his glory is indifferent, cannot enter into his resentment.

False⌊!⌋ All poetry gives the lie to this⌊.⌋

[*Pages 37–8*]

Such may be good poetical characters, of that mixt kind that Aristotle admits; but the most beautiful mixture of light and shade has no attraction unless it warms [or freezes *added by Blake*] the heart. It must have something that engages the sympathy, something that appeals to the [moral sense *altered to*: passions & senses]; for nothing can thoroughly captivate the fancy, however artfully delineated, that does not awake the sympathy and interest the passions [that enlist on the side of Virtue *del*], and appeal to our native notions of right and wrong.

[*Page 39*]

. . . we can go along with the resentment of Ulysses, because it is just, but our *feelings* must tell us that *Achilles* carries his resentment to a savage length, a length where we cannot follow him . . . .

1446

If Homers merit was only in these Historical combinations
& Moral sentiments he would be no better than Clarissa⌊.⌋[1]

[*Page 40*]
It is a contest between barbarians, equally guilty of injustice, rapine,
and bloodshed; and we are not sorry to see the vengeance of Heaven equally
inflicted on both parties.

Homer meant this⌊.⌋

Æneas indeed is a more amiable personage than Achilles; he seems
meant for a perfect character. . . . Æneas, by the connivance of the Gods,
leads the hospitable Queen of Carthage into guilt, and, by the command of
the Gods, *piously* leaves her to ruin and despair.

Every body naturally hates a perfect character because
they all greater Villains than the imperfect as Eneas is
here shewn a worse man than Achilles in leaving Dido⌊.⌋

[*Page 46*]
. . . would he *feel* what vice is in itself . . . let him enter into the passions of
Lear, when he feels the ingratitude of his children; of *Hamlet*, when he
learns the story of his father's murder; of *Othello*, when he shudders at
Iago's tale; . . . and he will know the difference of right and wrong much
more clearly than from all the moralists that ever wrote.

*T*he grandest Poetry is Immoral⌊,⌋ the Grandest charac-
ters Wicke*d*, Very Sata*n*: Capanius⌊,⌋ Othello a murderer,
Prometheus, Jupiter, Jehovah, Jesus a wine bibber⌊.⌋
Cunning & Morality are not Poetry but Philosophy⌊;⌋
the Poet is Independent & Wicked⌊;⌋ the Philosopher is
Dependent & Good⌊.⌋
Poetry is to excuse Vice & shew its reason & necessary
purgation⌊.⌋

[*Page 49*]
The industrious knave cultivates the soil; the indolent good man leaves it
uncultivated. Who ought to reap the harvest? . . . The natural course of
things decides in favour of the villain; the natural sentiments of men in
favour of the man of virtue.

False⌊!⌋

[1] In his letter of 16 July 1804 Blake says, 'I will again read [*Richardson's*] Clarissa
&c⌊;⌋ they must be admirable. I was too hasty in my perusal of them to percieve all
their beauty.'

[*Page 57*]

All that NATURE TEACHES is, that there is a future life, distinguished into different states of happiness and misery . . . .

False⌐!⌐

Nature Teaches nothing of Spiritual Life but only of Natural Life⌐.⌐

[*Page 74*]

Every Sentiment & Opinion as well as Every Principle in Dante is in these Preliminary Essays Controverted & proved Foolish by his Translator If I have any Judgment in Such Things as Sentiments Opinions & Principles⌐.⌐

[*Page 118, HISTORICAL ESSAY OF THE STATE OF AFFAIRS IN THE THIRTEENTH AND FOURTEENTH CENTURIES:* With Respect to the *HISTORY* of *FLORENCE* with a *VIEW* of their *INFLUENCE* on the succeeding *AGES*]

Dante was at this time *Prior* of Florence, and it was he who gave the advice, RUINOUS TO HIMSELF, and PERNICIOUS TO HIS NATIVE COUNTRY, of calling in the heads of the two factions to *Florence*.

Dante was a Fool or his Translator was Not⌐:⌐ That is Dante was Hired or Tr was Not⌐.⌐

It appears to Me that Men are hired to Run down Men of Genius under the Mask of Translators but Dante gives too much Caesar⌐;⌐ he is not a Republican⌐.⌐

[*At the top of the page:*] Dante was an Emperos⌐;⌐ a Caesars Man⌐;⌐

Luther also left the Priest & joind the Soldier⌐.⌐

[*Page 130*]

The fervours of religion have often actuated the passions to deeds of the wildest fanaticism.—The *booted Apostles* of Germany, and the *Crusards* of Florence, carried their zeal to a very guilty degree. But the passion for any thing laudable will hardly carry men to a *proper* pitch, unless it be so strong as sometimes to push them beyond the golden mean.

How very Foolish all this Is⌐.⌐

[*Page 131*]

. . . every well-regulated government, both antient and modern, were SO FAR INTOLERANT, as not to admit the pollutions of every superstition and

EVERY PERNICIOUS OPINION. It was from a regard to the morals of the people, that the Roman Magistrates expelled the Priests of Bacchus, in the first and most virtuous ages of the republic. It was on this principle that the *PERSIANS* destroyed the *TEMPLES OF GREECE WHEREVER THEY CAME.*

If Well regulated Governments act so who can tell so well as the hireling Writer whose praise is contrary to what he Knows to be true⌊?⌋ Persians destroy the Temples & are praised for it⌊.⌋

[*Page 134*]

It was not till the republic was verging to its fall, that Caesar dared in open senate to laugh at the *speculative* opinion of a future state. These were the times of universal toleration, when every pollution, from every clime, flowed to Rome, whence they had carefully been kept out before.

What is Liberty without Universal Toleration⌊?⌋

[*Page 136*]

. . . their decline and fall, at least, may fairly be attributed to irreligion, and to the want of some general standard of morality, whose authority they all allowed, and to which they all appealed. The want of this pole-star left them adrift in the boundless ocean of conjecture; the disputes of their philosophers were endless, and their opinions of the grounds of morality were as different as their conditions, their tastes, and their pursuits.

Yet simple Country Hinds are Moral Enthusiasts Indignant against Knavery without a Moral criterion other than Native Honesty untaught while other country Hinds are as indignant against honesty & Enthusiasts for Cunning & Artifice⌊.⌋

[*Page 148*]

. . . there are certain *BOUNDS* even to *LIBERTY* . . . .

If it is thus the extreme of black is white & of sweet sower & of good Evil & of Nothing Something⌊.⌋

MARGINALIA (?1801–2, 1808–9) : Reynolds, *Works* (1798)

[*Title-page top*]
This Man was Hired to Depress Art⌊.⌋
This is the opinion of Will Blake⌊;⌋ my Proofs of this
Opinion are given in the following Notes⌊.⌋

[*Title-page bottom*]
Advice of the Popes who succeeded the Age of Rafael
Degrade first the Arts if you'd Mankind Degrade.
Hire Idiots to Paint with cold light & hot shade:
Give high Price for the worst, leave the best in disgrace,
And with Labours of Ignorance fill every place⌊.⌋   [

[*Title-page verso*]
Having spent the Vigour of my Youth & Genius under the
Op⌊p⌋ression of Sʳ Joshua & his Gang of Cunning Hired
Knaves Without Employment & as much as could possibly
be Without Bread, The Reader must Expect to Read in all
my Remarks on these Books Nothing but Indignation &
Resentment⌊.⌋ While Sʳ Joshua was rolling in Riches Barry
was Poor & Unemployd except by his own Energy⌊,⌋
Mortimer was calld a Madman & only Portrait Painting
applauded & rewarded by the Rich & Great. Reynolds &
Gainsborough Blotted & Blurred One against the other
& Divided all the English World between them⌊.⌋ Fuseli
Indignant almost hid himself— I am hid⌊.⌋

[*First Contents leaf*]
The Arts & Sciences are the Destruction of Tyrannies

Title-page verso Fuseli's indignation was probably because of the public neglect of
his Milton Gallery in 1799 and 1800.
  Blake explains why he is 'hid in a corner' in 'Public Address' part zz (p. 1053).
Under 'am' ('I am hid') Erdman plausibly sees 'was'.
  Under 'Barry was Poor & Unemployd . . . Rich & Great', Erdman (p. 625)
reads 'Barry was Poor & Independent⌊,⌋ Mortimer was despised & Mocked⌊.⌋
I now despise & Mock in turn although Suffring Neglect'.

or Bad Governments_L._J Why should A Good Government
Endeavour to Depress what is its Chief & only Support_L?_J
The Foundation of Empire is Art & Science_L._J Remove
them or Degrade them & the Empire is No More—
Empire follows Art & Not Vice Versa as Englishmen
suppose_L._J

[*Third Contents leaf*]

'On peut dire que le Pape Léon X*me* en encourageant
les Études donna les armes contre lui-même. J'ai oui
dire à un Seigneur Anglais qu'il avait vu une Lettre du
Seigneur Polus, ou de La Pole, depuis Cardinal, à ce
Pape; dans laquelle, en le félicitant sur ce qu'il etendait
le progrés de Science en Europe, il l'avertissait qu'il
était dangereux de rendre les hommes trop Savan[t]s'—
                    Voltaire Moeurs de Nation[s] Tome 4
O Englishmen! why are you still of this foolish Cardinals
opinion?

Much copying discountenanced.

To learn the Language of Art Copy for Ever is My Rule_L._J

[*Third Contents leaf verso*]

Who will Dare to Say that [fine *del*] Polite Art is En-
couraged or Either Wished or Tolerated in a Nation where
The Society for the Encouragement of Ar*t* Sufferd Barry
to Give the*m* his Labour for Nothing_L,_J A Society Com-
posed of the flower of the English Nobility & Gentry—
A Society Suffering an Artist to Starve while he Supported
Really what They under Pretence of Encouraging were
Endeavouring to Depress.— Barry told me that while he
Did that Work, he Lived on Bread & Apples_L._J

[*Page i*]

O Society for Encouragement of Art—O King &
Nobility of England! Where have you hid Fuseli's Milton_L?_J
Is Satan troubled at his Exposure_L?_J

Third Contents Leaf verso The Society for the Encouragement of Arts, Manufac-
tures, and Commerce was founded in 1754.

TO THE KING.

The regular progress of cultivated life is from necessaries to accommodations, from accommodations to ornaments.

The Bible says That Cultivated Lif*e* Existe[*d*] First— Uncultivate[*d*] Lif*e* comes afterwards from Satans Hirelings ⌞·⌟ Necessaries ⌞,⌟ Accomodation[*s*] & Ornaments are the whole of Life ⌞·⌟ Satan took away Ornament First. Next he took away Accomodations & Then he became Lord & Master of Necessaries ⌞·⌟

[Page ii, Dedication continued]

To give advice to those who are contending for royal liberality, has been for some years the duty of my station in the Academy . . . .

Liberality! we want not Liberality ⌞·⌟ We want a Fair Price & Proportionate Value & a General Demand for Art ⌞·⌟

Let not that Nation where Less than Nobility is the Rewar*d* Pretend that Art is Encouraged by that Nation. Art is First in Intellectuals & Ought to be First in Nations ⌞·⌟

[Page iii]

Invention depends Altogether upon Execution or Organization. *A*s that is right or wrong so is the Invention perfect or imperfect. Whoever is set to Undermine the Execution of Art is Set to Destroy Art ⌞·⌟ Michael Angelos Art Depends on Michael Angelos Execution Altogether ⌞·⌟

[Page viii]

[Some Account of the Life and Writings of Sir Joshua Reynolds]

[As a young man] Raffaelle appeared to him superior to the most illustrious names of ancient or modern time; a notion which he loved to indulge all the rest of his life.

Why then did he not follow Rafaels Track ⌞?⌟

p. i Under 'Ornaments are the whole of Life . . . Necessaries', Erdman (p. 626) reads 'Ornaments are Lifes Wants ⌞·⌟ First were Created Wine & Happiness Good[?] Looks[?] & Fortune. Satan took away Ornament first. ₗNext he took away Accomodations & Then he became Lord & Master of ₗ Necessaries [last *del*]'.

[Page ix footnote]

The better taste introduced by Sir Joshua Reynolds, put an end to Hudson's reign . . . .

> Hudson Drew Correctly⌊·⌋

[Page xiv]

I [*Reynolds*] was informed by the keeper of the Vatican, that many of those whom he had conducted through the various apartments of that edifice, when about to be dismissed, have asked for the works of Raffaelle, and would not believe that they had already passed through the rooms where they are preserved; so little impression had those performances made on them.

> Men who have been Educated with Works of Venetian Artist*s* under their Eyes Cannot see Rafael unless they are born with Determinate Organs⌊·⌋

I remember very well my own disappointment, when I first visited the Vatican; but on confessing my feelings to a brother-student . . . he acknowledged ₐthat‾the works of Raffaelle had the same effect on him, or rather that they did not produce the effect which he expected.

> I am happy I cannot say that Rafael Ever was from my Earliest Childhood hidden from Me. I Saw & I Knew immediately the difference between Rafael & Rubens⌊·⌋

[Page xv]

> Some loo*k* to see the sweet Outlines
> And beauteous Forms that Love does wear⌊;⌋
> Some loo*k* to find out Patche*s*, Pain*t*,
> Bracelets & Stays & Powderd Hair⌊·⌋

. . . on inquiring further of other students, I found that those persons only who from natural imbecility appeared to be incapable of ever relishing those divine performances, made pretensions to instantaneous raptures on first beholding them.

> Here are Mocks on those who Saw Rafael⌊·⌋

I found myself in the midst of works executed upon principles with which I was unacquainted: I felt my ignorance, and stood abashed.

> A Liar⌊;⌋ he never was Abashed in his Life & never felt his Ignorance⌊·⌋

Page xv After 'who Saw Rafael', Erdman (p. 627) sees '[But not Sir Joshua *del*]'.

[*Page xvi*]

I was convinced that I had originally formed a false opinion of the perfection of art . . . .

All this Concession is to prove that Genius is Acquired as follows in the Next page⌐.⌐

[*Page xvii*]

I am now clearly of opinion, that a relish for the higher excellencies of art is an acquired taste, which no man ever possessed without long cultivation, and great labour and attention. . . . we are often ashamed of our apparent dulness; as if it were to be expected that our minds, like tinder, should instantly catch fire from the divine spark of Raffaelle's genius.

A Mock⌐!⌐

. . . but let it be always remembered, that the excellence of his style is not on the surface, but lies deep; and at the first view is seen mistily.

A Mock⌐!⌐

It is the florid style, which strikes at once, and captivates the eye for a time . . . .

A Lie⌐!⌐ The Florid Style such as the Venetian & the Flemi*sh* Never Struck Me at Once nor At-All.

[*Page xviii*]

The Style that Strikes the Eye is the True Style But A Fools Eye is Not to b*e* a Criterion⌐.⌐

I consider . . . *GENERAL COPYING . . . AS A DELUSIVE KIND OF INDUSTRY* . . . .

Here he Condemns Generalizing which he almost always Approves & Recommends⌐.⌐

[*Page xix*]

How incapable of producing any thing of their own, those are, who have spent most of their time in making finished copies . . . .

Finishd. What does he Mean⌐?⌐ Niggling Without the Correct & Definite Outline⌐?⌐ If he means That Copying Correctly is a hindrance he is a Lia*r*, for that is the only School to the Language of Art⌐.⌐

Page xvii   Beside the first paragraph, Erdman (p. 627) reads '[Fool *del*]'.

Page xviii   Before the lines that stand, Erdman (p. 628) sees '[to good Artists *del*]'.

[*Page xxix*]

It is the thoughts expressed in the works of Michael Angelo, Corregio, Raffaelle, Parmegiano, and perhaps some of the old Gothick masters, and not the inventions of Pietro da Cortona, Carlo Maratti, Luca Giordano, and others that I might mention, which we seek after with avidity. From the former we learn to think originally.

Here is an Acknowledgment of all that I could wish But if it is True, Why are we to be told that Masters who Could Think had not the Judgment to Perform the Inferior Parts of Art as Reynolds artfully calls them, But that we are to Learn to Think from Great Masters & to Learn to Perform from Underlings? Learn to Design from Rafael & to Execute from Rubens . . . ? [*One line of about eight words mostly cut off.*]

[*Page xxxiv*]

[*Reynolds*] owed his first disposition to generalize to [*Mr. Mudge, Prebendary of Exeter, who*] was a learned and venerable old man; and as I thought, very much conversant in the Platonick Philosophy . . . .

Slang⌞!⌟

He had been originally a dissenting minister . . . .

Villainy⌞!⌟

[*Page xlii*]

. . . we have been confidently told that they [*the DISCOURSES*] were written by [*Burke.*]

The Contradictions in Reynolds's Discourses are Strong Presumptions that they are the Work of Several Hands But this is no Proof that Reynolds did not Write them⌞·⌟ The Man Either Painter or Philosopher who Learns or Acquires all he Knows from Others, Must be full of Contradictions⌞·⌟

[*Page xlvii*]

Few have passed a more inoffensive or perhaps a more happy life [*than George Michael Moser [d. 1783], Keeper of the Royal Academy*] . . . . He may

Page xxxi By the sentence 'Thus Bacon became a great thinker, by first entering into and making himself master of the thoughts of other man', Erdman (p. 628) sees: '[This is the Character of a Knave *del*]'.

truly be said in every sense to have been the FATHER of the present race of Artists . . . .

I was once looking over the Prints from Rafael & Michael Angelo in the Library of the Royal Academy∟·⌋ Moser came to me & said 'You should not Study these old Hard Stiff & Dry Unfinishd Works of Art. Stay a little & I will shew you what you should Study∟·⌋' He then went & took down Le Bruns & Rubens's Galleries∟·⌋ How I did secretly Rage. I also spoke my Mind [*a line is trimmed mostly away here.*] . . . I said to Moser, 'These things that you call Finishd are not Even Begun∟;⌋ how can they then, be Finishd? The Man who does not know The Beginning, never can know the End of Art∟·⌋'

[*Page xlix*]

I consoled myself, however, by remarking that these ready inventors, are extremely apt to acquiesce *IN IMPERFECTION* . . . .

Villainy∟!⌋ a Lie∟!⌋

[*Page l*]

Metastasio . . . always complained of the great difficulty he found in attaining correctness, in consequence of having been in his youth an *Improvvisatore.*

I do not believe this Anecdote∟·⌋

[*Page liii footnote*]

There is nothing in our art which enforces such continued exertion and circumspection, as an attention to the general effect of the whole. It requires much study and much practice; it requires the painter's entire mind; whereas the *parts* may be finishing by nice touches, while his mind is engaged on other matters: he may even hear a play or a novel read, without much disturbance.

A Lie∟!⌋ Working up Effect is more an operation of Idolence than the Making out of the Parts: as far as Greatest is more than Least∟·⌋

Page xlvii 'Le Bruns & Rubens's Galleries' are probably *La Grande Gallerie de Versailles, et les Deux Salons qui l'Accompagnent*, Peints Par Charles le Brun (Paris, 1742), *Palazzo de Genova . . . di P. Paoli Rubens* delinati (Antwerp, 1672), and *La Gallerie du Palais du Luxembourg* peinte par Rubens (Paris, 1710), vast folios in the Royal Academy Library ([H. R. Tedder], *A Catalogue of Books in the Library of the Royal Academy of Arts*, London [1877]).

I speak here of Rembrandts & Rubens⌐'⌐s & Reynolds's
Effects.—For Real Effec*t* is Making out the Parts & it is
Nothing Else but That∟.⌐

[*Page lvii footnote*]

It is highly probable that the great colourists of former times used certain
methods in mixing and laying on their colours, which they did not com-
municate to others, or at least did not set down in writing . . . [*which have
thus*] been lost.

Oil Colours will not do—

[*Reynolds imitated the Venetian School and*] produced a similar, though perhaps
not quite so brilliant an effect of colour.

Why are we told that Reynolds is a Great Colourist &
yet inferior to the Venetians∟?⌐

[*Page lx footnote*]

A notion prevails concerning this great painter [*Reynolds*], that in the
majority of his works the colours have entirely faded and perished, but this
is by no means the case . . . .

I do not think the Change is so much in the Pictures as in
the Opinions of the Public∟.⌐

[*Page lxx footnote*]

In a Letter to Mr. Baretti, June 10, 1761, Dr. Johnson says—'Reynolds
is without a rival, and continues to add thousands to thousands.'

How much [d]id Barry Get∟?⌐

[*Page lxxii*]

[*Reynolds*] again . . . visited Antwerp and Brussels, and devoted several
days to contemplating the productions of that great painter [*Rubens*].

If Reynolds [h]ad Really admired Mich Angelo he never
would have followd Rubens∟.⌐

Page lxxii   By the reference to the 'works of the Flemish School in the Netherlands
(for I will not gratify our English republicans by calling it BELGIUM)', Erdman
(p. 629) discerns '[why then gratify the Flemish Knaves & Fools *del*]'.

Page lxxxiii   By a footnote saying that 'The original members [*of The Club*] were
Sir Joshua Reynolds, Dr. Johnson, Mr. Burke, Dr. Nugent, Mr. Langton, Mr.
Antony Chamier, Sir John Hawkins, the Hon. Topham Beauclerk, and Dr.
Goldsmith', Erdman (p. 629) makes out: '[Oliver Goldsmith never(?) should have

[Page lxxxix footnote]

[Despite Reynolds's deafness,] When in company with only one person, he heard very well, without the aid of a trumpet.

A Sly Dog⌞!⌟ So can Every body; but bring Two People[e] & the Hearin[g] is Stopped⌞.⌟

[Page xc]

[Beside Goldsmith's poetical epitaph for Reynolds:]

Such Men as Goldsmith [o]ught not to have been Acquainted [w]ith such Men as Reynolds⌞.⌟

[Page xcvi footnote]

. . . it is clear from his manners and his writings that in the character of his eloquence he would have resembled the perspicuous and elegant Lælius, rather than the severe and vehement Galba.

He certainly would have been more like a Fool Than a Wise Man⌞.⌟

[Page xcviii footnote]

He was a great generalizer . . . . But this disposition to abstractions, to generalizing and classification, is the great glory of the human mind . . . .

To Generalize [i]s to be an Idiot⌞.⌟ To Particularize is the Alone Distinction of Merit. General Knowledges are those Knowledges that Idiots possess⌞.⌟

[Page xcix]

Such was his love of his art, and such his ardour to excel, that he often declared he had, during the greater part of his life, laboured as hard with his pencil, as any mechanick working at his trade for bread.

known such knaves *del*]'. As an apprentice at Basire's Blake had seen and admired Goldsmith (Gilchrist [1863], i. 15).

Page lxxxvi By a passage in which Malone speaks of Reynolds's 'ardent love of truth, . . . his strong antipathy to all false pretensions', Erdman (p. 629) plausibly reads '[O Shame False *del*]'.

Page lxxxvii By a note saying 'He had painted, as he once observed to me, *two generations* of the beauties of England', Erdman (p. 629) sees '[God blasts Them As though he(?) were(?) lost Eurydice(?) *del*]'.

Page xci By a comparison of Reynolds to Laelius, Erdman (p. 630) finds: '[Why should Lælius be considered Sir Joshuas Counterpart *del*] [Who dares worship(?) a(?) man(?) Whod have Driven you long Ago Insane *del*]'.

Page xcviii At the end of Blake's note, Erdman (p. 630) reads: '[As do Fools that adore things & ideas(?) x x x of General Knowledge *del*]'.

The Man who does not Labour more than the Hireling
must be a poor Devil⌊.⌋

[*Page ciii footnote*]

[*Lines from Dryden's* ABSALOM AND ACHITOPHEL *may be applied to*]
the *ferocious* and *enslaved* Republick of France . . . .
'These Adam wits, too fortunately free,
'Began to dream they wanted liberty . . . .
'They led their wild desires to woods and caves
'And thought that all but SAVAGES were slaves.'

When France got free Europe 'twixt Fools & Knaves
Were Savage first to France & after: Slaves⌊.⌋

[*Page civ footnote*]

[*Except for the threat of internal violence,*] England is at present in an
unparalleled state of wealth and prosperity, though there is a temporary
distress occasioned by the want of the ordinary circulating medium of com-
merce. . . . the trade of England from 1784 to the present time, has *doubled*
. . . . These FACTS ought to be sounded from one end of England to the
other, and furnish a complete answer to all the SEDITIOUS DECLAMA-
TIONS that have been, or shall be, made on this subject.

This Whole Book was Written to Serve Political Purposes⌊.⌋

[*At the foot of the page:*] [First(?) to(?) Serve(?) Nobility &
Fashionable Taste & Sʳ Joshua *del*]

[*Page cix*]

. . . he died . . . Feb. 23, 1792.

When Sʳ Joshua Reynolds died
All Nature was degraded:
The King dropd a tear into the Queens Ear:
And all his Pictures Faded.

[*Page cxi*]

[*At Reynolds's funeral, the pall was*] borne up by three Dukes, two Marquisses,
and five other noblemen.

A Mock⌊!⌋

Page ciii   These lines are not by Pope, as Malone says, but by Dryden (*Absalom
and Achitophel*, ll. 51–2, 55–6).

Page cxv   By the sentence 'To each of the gentlemen who attended . . . was pre-
sented a print engraved by Bartolozzi', Erdman (p. 631) reads: '[Funeral Granted

[Page cxx]

[Burke said that] Sir Joshua Reynolds was, on very many accounts, one of the most memorable men of his time.

Is not this a Manifest Lie⌊?⌋

Barry Painted a Picture for Burke equal to Rafael or Mich Ang[*elo*] or any of the Italians⌊.⌋ Burke used to shew this Picture to his Friends & to say 'I gave Twenty Guineas for this horrible Dawb & if any one would give . . .'
[Here a line is cropped away]
Such was Burkes Patronage of Art & Science⌊.⌋

[Page 2 DISCOURSE I]

I consider Reynolds's Discourses to the Royal Academy as the Simulations of the Hypocrite who Smiles particularly where he means to Betray. His Praise of Rafael is like the Hysteric Smile of Revenge⌊,⌋ His Softness & Candour, the hidden tra*p*, & the poisoned feast. He praises Michael Angelo for Qualities which Michael Angelo abhorrd; & He blames Rafael for the only Qualities which Rafael Valued, Whether Reynolds knew what he was doing, is nothing to me; the Mischief is just the Same, Whether a Man does it Ignorantly or Knowingly: I always considerd True Art & True Artists to be particularly Insulted & Degraded by the Reputation of these Discourses⌊,⌋ As much as they were Degraded by the Reputation of Reynolds's Paintin*g*s, & that Such Artists as Reynolds, are at all times Hired by the Satans, for the Depression of Art⌊.⌋ A Pretence of Art: To Destroy Art⌊.⌋

[Page 3]

The Neglect of Fuselis Milton in a Country pretending to the Encouragement of Art is a Sufficient Apology for My

to Sir Joshua for having destroyd Art rewarded *del*) for standing Near *del*]'. However the (gentlemen(?) wcrc

Page cxvi By the passage concerning Reynolds's wish to decorate St. Paul's with paintings and its prevention by the Bishop of London, Erdman (p. 631) discerns: '[The Rascals who See(?) Painting want to Destroy Art & Learning *del*]'.

Page 2 Cf. *Jerusalem* pl. 43, l. 35: 'A pretence of Art: to destroy Art!' (p. 509). After Blake's note are three or four erased lines.

Vigorous Indignation if indeed the Neglect of My own
Powers had not been∟⌟ Ought not the ＾Patrons[?] &＾
[*word del*] Employers [Imbecility *del*] of [Folly *del*] Fools to
be Execrated in future Ages∟?⌟ They Will and Shall∟!⌟
Foolish Men∟,⌟ your own real Greatness depends on your
Encouragement of the Arts & your Fall will depend on
[your *del*] Their Negelct & Depression∟⌟ What you Fear
is your tru[e] Interest∟⌟ Leo X was advised not to En-
courage the Arts∟;⌟ he was too Wise to take this Advice∟⌟

[*Page 4*]

The Rich Men of England form themselves into a Societ*y*
to Sell & Not to Buy Pictures∟⌟ The Artist who does not
throw his Contempt on such Trading Exhibition*s* does not
know either his own Interest or his Duty.
When Nations grow Ol*d*, The Arts grow Cold
And Commerce settles on every Tree
And the Poor & the Old can live upon Gold∟,⌟
For all arc Born Poo*r*, Aged Sixty three∟⌟

[*Page 5*]

Reynolds s Opinion was that Genius May be Taught &
that all Pretence to Inspiration is a Lie & a Deceit to say
the least of it∟⌟ [If the Inspiration is Great why Call it
Madness *del*] For if it is a Deceit the whole Bible is Mad-
ness∟⌟ This Opinion originates in the Greeks' Cal[*l*]ing
the Muse[*s*] Daughters of Memory∟⌟
The Enquiry in England is not whether a Man has Talent*s*
& Geniu*s*, But whether he is Passive & Polite & a Vir-
tuous Ass: & obedient to Noblemens Opinions in Art &
Science. If he is; he is a Good Man: If Not he must be
Starved∟⌟

Page 3   For 'Patrons', Erdman (p. 631) reads 'Artists'.

Page 4   The British Institution for Promoting the Fine Arts in the United King-
dom, founded in 1805 (see D. Bindman, 'The dating of Blake's Marginalia to
Reynolds', *Burlington Magazine*, cviii [1966], 522).
   After 'his Duty', Erdman (p. 631) reads: '[Are the Artists who live upon Assassina-
tions of other Men *del*]'. Cf. Blake's remark in his letter of 28 May 1804 that in
London 'Engravers, Painters, Statuaries, Printers, Poets' form 'a City of Assassina-
tions' (pp. 1605–6).

[*Page 7*]

After so much has been done by *His Majesty* . . . .

3 Farthings∟!⌐

[*Page 9*]

Raffaelle, it is ·true, had not the advantage of studying in an Academy; but all Rome, and the works of Michael Angelo in particular, were to him an Academy. On the sight of the Capella Sistina, he immediately from a dry, Gothick, and even insipid manner, which attends to the minute accidental discriminations of particular and individual objects, assumed that grand style of painting which improves partial representation by the general and invariable ideas of nature.

> Minute Discrimination is Not Accidental∟.⌐ All Sublimity is founded on Minute Discrimination∟.⌐
>
> I do not believe that Rafael taught Mich. Angelo or that Mich. Ang: taught Rafael, any more than I believe that the Rose teaches the Lilly how to grow or the Apple tree teaches the Pear tree how to bear Fruit. I do not believe the tales of Anecdote writers when they militate against Individual Character∟.⌐

[*Page 11*]

I would chiefly recommend, that an implicit obedience to the *Rules of Art*, as established by the practice of the great MASTERS, should be exacted from the *young* Students. That those models, which have passed through the approbation of ages, should be considered by them as perfect and infallible guides; as subjects for their imitation, not their criticism.

> Imitation is Criticism∟.⌐

[*Page 13*]

A facility in composing,—a lively, and what is called a masterly, handling of the chalk or pencil, are . . . captivating qualities to young minds . . . .

> I consider The Following sentence is Supremely Insolent for the following Reasons∟:⌐ Why this Sentence Should be begun by the Words 'A Facility in Composing' I cannot tell unless it was to cast a Stigma upon Real Facility in

Page 9 Under 'Pear tree how to bear Fruit', Erdman (p. 632) reads '[Pine tree to bear fruit *del*]' Cf. *Marriage* pl. 9: 'The apple tree never asks the beech how he shall grow'.

Page 13 Under 'a Stigma', Erdman (p. 632) reads '[an Eye *del*]', and for 'Composition' he inaccurately reads 'Execution'.

Composition by Assimilating it with A Pretence to & Imitation of Facility in Execution or are we to understand him to mean that Facility in Composing is a Frivolous pursuit ⌞?⌟ A Facility in Composing is the Greatest Power of Art & Belongs to None but the Greatest Artists i.e. the Most Minutely Discriminating & Determinate ⌞.⌟

[*Page 14*]

By this useless industry they are excluded from all power of advancing in real excellence. Whilst boys, they are arrived at their utmost perfection . . . and make the mechanical felicity the chief excellence of the art, which is only an ornament . . . .

Mechanical Excellence is the Only Vehicle of Genius ⌞.⌟

This seems to me to be one of the most dangerous sources of corruption . . . which has actually infected all foreign Academies. The directors . . . praised their dispatch at the expence of their correctness.

This is all False & Self-Contradictory ⌞.⌟

But young men have not only this frivolous ambition of being thought masters of execution, inciting them on one hand, but also their natural sloth tempting them on the other.

Execution is the Chariot of Genius ⌞.⌟

[*Page 15*]

They wish to find some shorter path to excellence . . . . They must therefore be told again and again, that labour is the only price of solid fame . . . .

This is All Self-Contradictory: Truth & Fals[*e*]hood Jumbled Together ⌞.⌟

When we read the lives of the most eminent Painters, every page informs us, that no part of their time was spent in dissipation.

The Lives of Painters say that Rafael Died of Dissipation ⌞.⌟ Idleness is one Thing & Dissipation Another ⌞.⌟ He who has Nothing to Dissipate Cannot Dissipate ⌞;⌟ the Weak Man may be Virtuous Enough but will Never be an Artist ⌞.⌟

Painters are noted for being Dissipated & Wild.

Page 15 Under 'Painters are . . . Wild', Erdman (p. 633) reads '[What painters have only been dissipated without wildness *del*]'.

[*Page 16*]

When they [*the old masters*] conceived a subject, they first made a variety of sketches; then a finished drawing of the whole; after that a more correct drawing of every separate part—heads, hands, feet, and pieces of drapery they then painted the picture, AND AFTER ALL RE-TOUCHED IT FROM LIFE.

This is False⌞.⌟

The Students, instead of vying with each other which shall have the readiest hand, should be taught to contend who shall have the purest and most correct outline . . . .

Excellent⌞!⌟

[*Page 17*]

The error I mean is, that the students never draw exactly from the living models which they have before them. . . . They . . . make a drawing rather of what they think the figure ought to be, than of what it appears. I have thought this the obstacle that has stopped the progress of many young men of real genius; I very much doubt, whether a habit of drawing correctly what we see, will not give a proportionable power of drawing correctly what we imagine.

This is Admirably Said. Why does he not always allow as much⌞?⌟

[*Page 18*]

He who endeavours to copy nicely the figure before him, not only acquires a habit of exactness and precision, but is continually advancing in his knowledge of the human figure . . . .

Excellent⌞!⌟

[*Page 22*]

The Labourd Works of Journeymen employd by Cor-reggi*o*, Titian⌞,⌟ Veronese & all the Venetians ought not to be shewn to the Young Artist as the Works of original Conception any more than the Engravings of Strange⌞,⌟ Bartolozzi or Woollett. They are Works of Manual Labour⌞.⌟

[*Page 23*]

DISCOURSE II.

THE COURSE AND ORDER OF STUDY.—THE DIFFERENT STAGES OF ART.—
MUCH COPYING DISCOUNTENANCED.—THE ARTIST AT ALL TIMES AND IN ALL

PLACES SHOULD BE EMPLOYD IN LAYING UP MATERIALS FOR THE EXERCISE
OF HIS ART.

What is Layin[g] up materials but Copying⌐?⌐

[*Page 25*]

When the Artist is once enabled to express himself with some degree of
correctness, he must then endeavour to collect subjects for expression;
to amass a stock of ideas . . . to learn all that has been known and done
before . . . .

> After having been a Fool a Student is to amass a Stock
> of Ideas & knowing himself to be a Fool he is to assume
> the Right to put other Mens Ideas into his Foolery⌐.⌐

[*Page 26*]

Though the Student will not resign himself blindly to any single authority,
when he may have the advantage of consulting many, he must still be
afraid of trusting to his own judgment, and of deviating into any track
where he cannot find the footsteps of some former master.

> Instead of Following One Great Master he is to follow
> a Great Many Fools⌐.⌐

[*Page 29*]

A Student unacquainted with the attempts of former adventurers, is
always apt to over-rate his own abilities; to mistake the most trifling ex-
cursions for discoveries of moment, and every coast new to him, for a new-
found country.

> Contemptible Mocks⌐!⌐

The productions of such minds are seldom distinguished by an air of
originality: they are anticipated in their happiest efforts; and if they are
found to differ in any thing from their predecessors, it is only in irregular
sallies, and trifling conceits.

> Thus Reynolds Depreciates the Efforts of Inventive
> Genius⌐.⌐ Trifling Conceits are better than Colouring
> without any meaning at all⌐.⌐

Page 25 Under 'knowing himself . . . Foolery', Erdman (p. 633) reads: '[then to be
insolent in his Foolery *del*]'.

[Page 30 at the foot, below a passage urging students to 'rely' on]
The works of those who have stood the test of Ages . . . .

[wretches(?) Who are born for
it *del*]

[Page 32]
  How incapable those are of producing any thing of their own, who have
spent much of their time in making finished copies, is well known to all
who are conversant with our art. [*See p. xix.*]

This is most False for no one can ever Design till he has
learnd the Language of Art by making many Finishd
Copies both of Nature & Art & of whatever comes in his
way from Earliest Childhood⌊.⌋
   The difference between a bad Artist & a Good One Is
the Bad Artist Seems to Copy a Great Deal. The Good
one Really Does Copy a Great deal⌊.⌋

[Page 33]
The great use in copying, if it be at all useful, should seem to be in learning
to colour; yet even colouring will never be perfectly attained by servilely
copying the model before you.

Contemptible⌊!⌋
   Servile Copying is the Great Merit of Copying⌊.⌋

[Page 34]
  Following these rules, and using these precautions, when you have
clearly and distinctly learned in what good colouring consists, you cannot
do better than have recourse to nature herself, who is always at hand, and
in comparison of whose true splendour the best coloured pictures are but
faint and feeble.

Nonsense—Every Eye Sees differently⌊.⌋ As the Ey*e*, Such
the Object⌊.⌋

[Page 35]
Instead of copying the touches of those great masters, copy only their
conceptions. . . . Labour to invent on their general principles and way of
thinking.

Page 30   Erdman (p. 634) reads 'This is Encouragement for Artists [*about 4 words
illeg*] . . . to those who are born for it'.

Page 32   The first four words here ('This is most False') were first written in
pencil and later confirmed in ink; the rest of the passage is in ink only.

General Principles Again: Unless You Consul*t* Particular*s*, You Canno*t* even Know or See Mich: Ang:° or Rafael or any Thing Else₍.₎

... mere enthusiasm will carry you but a little way ....

Meer Enthusiasm is the All in All!—Bacons Philosophy has Ruind England₍.₎ Bacon is only Epicurus over again₍.₎

[*Page 37*]

Few have been taught to any purpose, who have not been their own teachers.

True₍!₎

[*Page 40*]

A facility of drawing, like that of playing upon a musical instrument, cannot be acquired but by an infinite number of acts.

True₍!₎

[*Page 41*]

I would particularly recommend, that after your return from the Academy ... you would endeavour to draw the figure by memory.

Good Advice₍!₎

Page 35   Before 'Meer Enthusiasm', Erdman (p. 634) reads '[Dam The Fool *del*]'.
See the annotations to Bacons *Essays* (1798), p. 77 (p. 1434): 'Bacon was . . . Evidently an Epicurean'.

Page 36   Beside a description of a 'competition, by . . . making a companion to any picture that you consider as a model . . . and compare them', Erdman (p. 634) sees '[What but a Puppy will dare to do this *del*]'.
By 'a severe and mortifying task', he reads '[Why(?) shou(*l*)d comparing (*or* copying) Great Masters Painfully *del*]'.

Page 37   By a sentence pointing out that comparison of one's work with a great master's 'requires not only great resolution, but great humility', Erdman (p. 634) deciphers: '[Who will or Can endure(?) such(?) Humiliation (either[?] he[?] is[?]) dishonest or(?) he is Insane(?) *del*]'.

Page 38   By 'to choose . . . models, . . . take the world's opinion rather than your own', Erdman (p. 634) reads '[Fools opinions & Endeavours destroy Invention! *del*]'.

But while I mention the port-crayon as the student's constant companion, he must still remember, that the pencil is the instrument by which he must hope to obtain eminence.

Nonsense⌊!⌋

[*Page 42*]

The Venetian and Flemish schools, which owe much of their fame to colouring, have reached the cabinets of the collectors of drawings, with very few examples.

because they could not draw⌊·⌋

[*Page 43*]

Those of Titian, Paul Veronese, Tintoret, and the Bassans, are in general slight and undetermined. Their sketches on paper are as rude as their pictures are excellent in regard to harmony of colouring. Correggio and Baroccio have left few, if any finished drawings behind them. And in the Flemish school, Rubens and Vandyck made their drawings for the most part either in colours, or in chiaro oscuro.

All the Pictures said to be by these Men are the Laboured fabrications of Journey-work⌊·⌋ They could not draw⌊·⌋

[*Page 47*]

. . . he who would have you believe that he is waiting for the inspiration of Genius, is in reality at a loss how to begin; and is at last delivered of his monsters, with difficulty and pain.

A Stroke at Mortimer⌊!⌋

[*Page 48*]

The Man who asserts that there is no Such Thing as Softness in Art & that every thing in Art is Definite & Determinate has not been told this by Practise but by Inspiration & Vision because Vision is Determinate & Perfect & he Copies That without Fatigue⌊,⌋ Every thing being Definite & determinate⌊·⌋ Softness is Produced alone by Comparative Strength & Weakness in the Marking out of the Forms⌊·⌋ I say These Principles could never be found out by the Study of Nature with Con or Innate Science⌊·⌋

[*Page 50* DISCOURSE III]

A work of Genius is a Work 'Not to be obtain'd by the'
'Invocation of Memory & her Syren Daughter*s*, but by'
'Devout prayer to that Eternal Spiri*t*, who can enrich with'
'all utterance & knowledge & sends out his Seraphim'
'with the hallowed fire of his Altar to touch & purify'
'the lips of whom he pleases.'

Milton.

The following [Lecture *del*] Discourse is particularly Inter-
esting to Blockhead*s*, as it Endeavours to prove That there
is No such thing as Inspiration & that any Man of a plain
Understanding may by Thieving from Other*s*, become
a Mich Angelo⌊.⌋

[*Page 52*]

The wish of the genuine painter must be more extensive: instead of en-
deavouring to amuse mankind with the minute neatness of his imitations, he
must endeavour to improve them by the grandeur of his ideas . . . .

Without Minute Neatness of Executio*n* The Sublime can-
not Exist! Grandeur of Ideas is founded on Precision of
Ideas⌊.⌋

[*Page 54*]

The Moderns are not less convinced than the Ancients of this superior
power existing in the art; nor less sensible of its effects.

I wish that this was True⌊.⌋

[*Page 55*]

Such is the warmth with which both the Ancients and Moderns speak of
this divine principle of the art;

And Such is the Coldness with which Reynolds speaks! And
such is his Enmity⌊.⌋

Page 50 This passage is transcribed from Milton's *The Reason of Church-governement
Urg'd against Prelaty* (1641), 41, with minor changes in spelling and punctuation
and the omission of one word ('Dame' in 'Dame Memory').
  For 'Lecture', Erdman (p. 635) reads 'Letter'.
  The quotation marks are Blake's here and on pp. 71 and 180.

but, as I have formerly observed, enthusiastick admiration seldom promotes knowledge.

> Enthusiastic Admiration is the first Principle of Knowledge & its last⌊.⌋
> Now he begins to Degrade⌊,⌋ to Deny & to Mock⌊.⌋

. . . a student by such praise may have his attention roused . . . HE EXAMINES his own mind, and perceives there nothing of that divine inspiration, with which, he is told, so many others have been favoured.

> The Man who on Examining his own Mind finds nothing of Inspiration ought not to dare to be an Artist⌊;⌋ he is a Foo*l* & a Cunning Knave suited to the Purposes of Evil Demons⌊.⌋

[*Page 56*]

He never travelled to heaven to gather new ideas; and he finds himself possessed of no other qualifications than what mere common observation and a plain understanding can confer.

> The Man who never in his Mind & Thoughts traveld to Heaven Is No Artist⌊.⌋
> Artists who are above a plain Understanding are Mockd & Destroyd by this President of Fools⌊.⌋

But on this, as upon many other occasions, we ought to distinguish how much is to be given to enthusiasm, and how much to reason . . . taking care . . . not to lose in terms of vague admiration, that solidity and truth of principle, upon which alone we can reason, and may be enabled to practise.

> It is Evident that Reynolds Wishd none but Fools to be in the Arts & in order to this, he calls all others Vague Enthusiasts or Madmen⌊.⌋
> What has Reasoning to do with the Art of Painting?

[*Page 57*]

. . . most people err, not so much from want of capacity to find their object, as from not knowing what object to pursue.

> The Man who does not know what Object to Pursue is an Idiot⌊.⌋

Page 55 Erdman (p. 636) reads 'Degrade [& *del*] to Deny & ₐtoₐ Mock'.

Page 57 By 'Could we teach taste or genius by rules, they would be no longer taste and genius', Erdman (p. 636) reads: '[This must be how Liars Reason *del*]'.

This great ideal perfection and beauty are not to be sought in the heavens, but upon the earth.

A Lie∟!˩

They are about us, and upon every side of us.

A Lie∟!˩

But the power of discovering what is deformed in nature, or in other words, what is particular and uncommon, can be acquired only by experience;

A Lie∟!˩

[*Page 58*]

and the whole beauty and grandeur of the art consists, in my opinion, in being able to get above all singular forms, local customs, particularities, and details of every kind.

A Folly∟!˩ Singular & Particular Detail is the Foundation of the Sublime∟.˩

All the objects which are exhibited to our view by nature, upon close examination will be found to have their blemishes and defects. The most beautiful forms have something about them like weakness, minuteness, or imperfection.

Minuteness is their whole Beauty∟.˩

. . . This long laborious comparison should be the first study of the painter, who aims at the greatest style. . . . he corrects nature by herself . . . . This idea of the perfect state of nature, which the Artist calls the Ideal Beauty, is the great leading principle by which works of genius are conducted.

Knowledge of Ideal Beauty is Not to be Acquired∟.˩ It is Born with us∟.˩ Innate Idea*s* are in every Man∟,˩ Born with him∟;˩ they are truly Himself∟.˩ The Man who says that we have No Innate Ideas must be a Fool & Knav*e*, Having No Con-Science or Innate Science∟.˩

[*Page 60*]

Thus it is from a reiterated experience, and a close comparison of the objects in nature, that an artist becomes possessed of the idea of that central form . . . from which every deviation is deformity.

One Central Form Composed of all other Forms being Granted∟,˩ it does not therefore follow that all other Forms are Deformity∟.˩

All Forms are Perfect in the Poets Min*d*, but these are not Abstracted nor Compounded from Nature but are from Imagination⌊·⌋

[*Page 61*]

Even the great Bacon treats with ridicule the idea of confining proportion to rules, or of producing beauty by selection.

The Great Bacon he is Calld⌊—⌋ I call him the Little Bacon⌊—⌋ Says that Every thing must be done by Experiment⌊;⌋ his first princip[le] is Unbelief and yet here he says that Art must be producd Without such Method⌊·⌋ He is Like Sr Joshu[a] full of Self-Contradiction & Knavery⌊·⌋

There is a rule, obtained out of general nature, to contradict which is to fall into deformity.

What is General Nature⌊?⌋ is there Such a Thing⌊?⌋ what is General Knowledge⌊?⌋ is there such a Thing⌊?⌋ [Strictly Speaking *del*] All Knowledge is Particular⌊·⌋

[*Page 62*]

To the principle I have laid down, that the idea of beauty in each species of beings is an invariable one, it may be objected, that in every particular species there are various central forms, which are separate and distinct from each other, and yet are undeniably beautiful . . . .

Here he loses sight of A Central For*m* & Gets into Many Central Forms⌊·⌋

[*Page 63*]

It is true, indeed, that these figures are each perfect in their kind, though of different characters and proportions; but still none of them is the representation of an individual, but of a class.

Every Class is Individual⌊·⌋

. . . Thus, though the forms of childhood and age differ exceedingly, there is a common form in childhood, and a common form in age, which is the more perfect, as it is more remote from all peculiarities.

There is na End to the Follies of this Man⌊·⌋ Childhood & Age are Equally belonging to Every Class⌊·⌋

. . . the highest perfection of the human figure . . . is not in the Hercules, nor in the Gladiator, nor in the Apollo; but in that form which is taken from them all . . . .

Here he comes again to his Central Form$_{L\cdot}$

[*Page 64*]

There is, likewise, a kind of symmetry, or proportion, which may properly be said to belong to deformity. A figure lean or corpulent, tall or short, though deviating from beauty, may still have a certain union of the various parts, which may contribute to make them on the whole not unpleasing.

The Symmetry of Deformity is a Pretty Foolery$_{L}$!$_{J}$ Can any Man who Think*s*, [argue *del*] Talk so? Leanness or Fatness is not Deformit*y*, but Reynolds thought Character Itself Extravagance & Deformity$_{L\cdot}$ Age & Youth are not Classes but [Accidents *del*] [Situations *del*] Properties [o]f Each Class$_{L}$;$_{J}$ so are Leanness & Fatness$_{L\cdot}$

[*Page 65*]

When the Artist has by diligent attention acquired a clear and distinct idea of beauty and symmetry; when he has reduced the variety of nature to the abstract idea . . .

What Folly$_{L}$!$_{J}$

[*Page 67*]

. . . the painter . . . must divest himself of all prejudices in favour of his age or country; he must disregard all local and temporary ornaments, and look only on those general habits which are every where and always the same . . . .

Generaliz[ing] in Every th[ing,] the Man w[ould] soon be a Fool bu[t] a Cunning Fool$_{L\cdot}$

[*Page 71*]

Albert Durer, as Vasari has justly remarked, would, probably, have been one of the first painters of his age . . . had he been initiated into those great principles of the art, which were so well understood and practised by his contemporaries in Italy.

What does this mean, 'Would have been' one of the first

Page 65 After 'his next task will be to become acquainted with the genuine habits of nature as distinguished from those of fashion', Erdman (p. 638) sees: '[Is Fashion the concern of Artists   The Knave Calls any thing found in Nature fit for Art *del*]'.

Painters of his Age'ₗ?ⱼ Albert Durer Is! Not would have
been! Besides, let them look at Gothic̄ Figures & Gothic
Buildings & not talk of Dark Ages or of any Age: Ages
are all Equal. But Genius [is Always Above the Age *mostly
cut off.*]

[Page 74]

I should be sorry, if what is here recommended, should be at all under-
stood to countenance a careless or indetermined manner of painting. For
though the painter is to overlook the accidental discriminations of nature,
he is to exhibit distinctly, and with precision, the general forms of things.

Here he is for Determinate & yet for Indeterminateₗ.ⱼ
Distinct General Form Cannot Existₗ.ⱼ Distinctness is
Particular Not Generalₗ.ⱼ

[Page 75]

A firm and determined outline is one of the characteristics of the great
style in painting; and let me add, that he who possesses the knowledge of
the exact form which every part of nature ought to have, will be fond of
expressing that knowledge with correctness and precision in all his works.

A Noble Sentenceₗ!ⱼ
Here is a Sentence Which overthrows all his Bookₗ.ⱼ

To conclude; I have endeavoured to reduce the idea of beauty to general
principles.

. . . [*several words erased*] that Bacons Philosophy makes both
Statesmen & Artists Fools & Knavesₗ.ⱼ

[Page 78 DISCOURSE IV]

The [following Discourse is *del*] Two Following Discourses
are Particularly Calculated for the Setting Ignorant &
Vulgar Artists as Models of Execution in Art. Let him who
will follow such adviceₗ;ⱼ I will not. I know that The Mans
Execution is as his Conception & No betterₗ.ⱼ

Page 71   At the top Erdman (p. 638) makes out: '[Albert Durer would never have
got his Manners from the Nobility *del*]'.

Page 75   The erasure Erdman (p. 638) reads as 'Sir Joshua Proves that'.

[*Page 79*]

The value and rank of every art· is in proportion to the mental labour employed in it, or the mental pleasure produced by it.

Why does he not always allow This⌊?⌋

[*Page 80*]

I have formerly observed that perfect form is produced by leaving out particularities, and retaining only general ideas . . . .

General Ideas again⌊!⌋

Invention in Painting does not imply the invention of the Subject; for that is commonly supplied by the Poet or Historian.

All but Names of Persons & Places is Invention both in Poetry & Painting⌊·⌋

[*Page 82*]

However, the usual and most dangerous error is on the side of minuteness; and therefore I think caution most necessary where most have failed.

Here is Nonsense!

[*Page 83*]

The general idea constitutes real excellence. All smaller things, however perfect in their way, are to be sacrificed without mercy to the greater.

Sacrifice the Parts. What becomes of the Whole⌊?⌋

Even in portraits, the grace, and, we may add, the likeness, consists more in taking the general air, than in observing the exact similitude of every feature.

How Ignorant⌊!⌋ [*In another hand in pencil:* no 'tis true⌊·⌋]

[*Page 86*]

A painter of portraits retains the individual likeness; a painter of history shews the man by shewing his actions.

If he does now Shew the Man as well as the Action he is a poor Artist⌊·⌋

[*Page 87*]

He cannot make his hero talk like a great man; he must make him look like one. For which reason, he ought to be well studied in the analysis of those circumstances, which constitute dignity of appearance in real life.

Here he allows an Analysis of Circumstances⌊.⌋

[*Page 89*]

Certainly, nothing can be more simple than monotony; and the distinct blue, red, and yellow colours which are seen in the draperies of the Roman and Florentine schools . . . have that effect of grandeur which was intended. Perhaps these distinct colours strike the mind more forcibly, from there not being any great union between them; as martial musick . . . has its effect from the sudden and strongly marked transitions from one note to another . . . .

These are Fine & Just Notions⌊.⌋ Why does he not always allow as much⌊?⌋

[*Page 90*]

In the same manner as the historical Painter never enters into the detail of colours, so neither does he debase his conceptions with minute attention to the discriminations of Drapery.

Excellent Remarks⌊!⌋

Carlo Maratti was of opinion, that the disposition of drapery was a more difficult art than even that of drawing the human figure . . . .

I do not believe that Carlo Maratti thought so or that any body can think so, the Drapery is formed alone by the Shape of the Naked⌊.⌋

[*Page 92*]

Though I can by no means allow them [*the Venetians*] to hold any rank with the nobler schools of painting, they accomplished perfectly the thing they attempted. But as mere elegance is their principal object . . . it can be no injury to them to suppose that their practice is useful only to its proper end.

They accomplishd Nothing⌊.⌋ As to Elegance they have not a Spark⌊.⌋

Page 87 At the bottom by 'Those expressions alone should be given to the figures which their respective situations generally produce', Erdman (p. 639) sees '[Nonsense *del*]'.

Page 90 Erdman (p. 639) believes a word was cut away after 'Naked'.

Page 92 The first three words ('They accomplishd Nothing') were first written in pencil and later confirmed in ink; the rest of the passage is in ink only.

[Page 93]

·*[To a question]* on the conduct of Paul Veronese, who . . . had, contrary to the strict rules of art . . . represented the principal figure in the shade, *[it might have been answered:]* 'His intention was solely to produce an effect of light and shadow; . . . and the capricious composition of that picture suited very well with the style which he professed.'

This is not a Satisfactory Answer⌊.⌋ To produce an Effect of True Light & Shadow is Necessary to the Ornamental Style—which altogether depends on Distinctness of Form. The Venetian ought not to be called the Ornamental Style⌊.⌋

[Page 94]

The powers exerted in the mechanical part of the Art have been called *the language of Painters*⋅. . . . The language of Painting must indeed be allowed these masters *[the Venetians.]*

The Language of Painters cannot be allowd them if Reynolds says right at p. 97⌊;⌋ he there Says that the Venetian Will Not Correspond with the Great Style⌊.⌋ The Greek Gems are in the Same Style as the Greek Statues⌊.⌋

[Page 95]

Such as suppose that the great style might happily be blended with the ornamental, that the simple, grave and majestick dignity of Raffaelle could unite with the glow and bustle of a Paolo, or Tintoret, are totally mistaken.

What can be better Said on this Subject? but Reynolds contradicts what he Says Continually⌊.⌋ He makes little Concessions, that he may take Great Advantages⌊.⌋

[Page 97]

However great the difference is between the composition of the Venetian, and the rest of the Italian schools, there is full as great a disparity in the effect of their pictures as produced by colours. . . . yet even that skill, as they

Page 93 This passage was originally written in pencil as follows: 'This is not a Satisfactory Answer⌊.⌋ To produce an Effect of True Light & Shadow Nothing must be sacrificd⌊,⌋ for light & Shadow depends on distinctness of Form'. The passage was then altered in ink to read as above.

have employed it, will but ill correspond with the great style. Their colour-
ing is not only too brilliant, but . . . too harmonious, to produce that . . .
effect, which heroic subjects require . . . .

> Somebody El[se] wrote this pag[e] for Reynolds∟⌐ I think
> th[at] Barry or Fuseli wrote it or dictated it∟⌐

[Page 98]

Michael Angelo . . . after having seen a picture by Titian, told Vasari . . .
'that he liked much his colouring and manner;' but then he added, 'that it
'was a pity the Venetian painters did not learn to draw correctly in their
'early youth, and adopt a better *manner of study.*'
  By this it appears, that the principal attention of the Venetian painters,
in the opinion of Michael Angelo, seemed to be engrossed by the study of
colours, to the neglect of the *ideal beauty of form.*

> Venetian Attention is to a Contempt & Neglect of Form
> Itself & to the Destruction of all Form or Outline Pur-
> posely & Intentionally∟⌐

> [*At the bottom of the page*]
> On the Venetian Painter
>
> He makes the Lame to walk we all agree
> But then he strives to blind those who can see.

But if general censure was given to that school from the sight of a picture of
Titian . . . .

> As if Mich. Ang? had seen but One Picture of Titians∟⌐
> Mich. Ang. Knew & despised all that Titian could do∟⌐

[Page 99]

> If the Venetian['s] Outline was Righ[t] his Shadows would
> destroy it & deform its appearanc[e.]
> > A Pair of Stays to mend the Shape
> > Of crooked Humpy Woman:
> > Put on, O Venus! now thou art,
> > Quite a Venetian Roman.

Page 97 Under 'dictated', Erdman (p. 640) sees 'said'.

Page 98 The poem is in ink only; all the rest of the page is in ink over the same
thing in pencil.

[*Page 100*]

... when I speak of the Venetian painters, I wish to be understood to mean Paolo Veronese and Tintoret, to the exclusion of Titian; for . . . there is a sort of senatorial dignity about him. . . .

> Titian as well as the other Venetians So far from Senatorial dignity appears to me to give always the Characters of Vulgar Stupidity.
> Why should Titian & The Venetians be Named in a discourse on Art_L?_J Such Idiots are not Artists_{L·J}
> Venetian; all thy Colouring is no more
> Than Boulsterd Plasters on a Crooked Whore.

[*Page 101*]

The Venetian is indeed the most splendid of the schools of elegance . . . .

> Vulgarity & not Elegance_L;_J the Word Elegance ought to be applied to Form*s*, not to Colours_{L·J}

[*Page 102*]

. . . painting is not merely a gratification of the sight.

> Broken Colours & Broken Lines & Broken Masses are Equally Subversive of the Sublime_{L·J}

Such excellence, . . . where nothing higher than elegance is intended, is weak and unworthy of regard, when the work aspires to grandeur and sublimity.

> Well Said Enough_L!_J

[*Page 103*]

. . . the Flemish school, of which Rubens is the head, was formed upon that of the Venetian . . . .

> How can that be calld the Ornamental Style of which Gross Vulgarity forms the Principal Excellence_L?_J

[*Page 104*]

Some inferior dexterity, some extraordinary mechanical power is apparently that from which they seek distinction.

> The Words Mechanical Power Should not be thus Prostituted_{L·J}

[Page 106]

An History-Painter paints man in general; a Portrait-painter, a particular man, and consequently a defective model.

A History Painter Paints The Hero, & not Man in General but most minutely in Particular⌊.⌋

[Page 109]

. . . if a portrait-painter is desirous to raise and improve his subject, he . . . leaves out all the minute breaks and peculiarities in the face, and changes the dress from a temporary fashion to one more permanent . . . .

Folly! Of what consequence is it to the Arts what a Portrait Painter does⌊?⌋

[Page 110]

Of those who have practised the composite style . . . perhaps the foremost is Correggio.

There is No Such a Thing as A Composite Style⌊.⌋

[Page 111]

The errors of genius . . . are pardonable . . . .

Genius has no Error⌊;⌋ it is Ignorance that is Error⌊.⌋

[Page 112]

. . . there is but one presiding principle, which regulates, and gives stability to every art. The works . . . which are built upon general nature, live for ever; while those which depend for their existence on particular customs and habits . . . can only be coeval with that which first raised them from obscurity.

All Equivocation & Self-Contradiction⌊!⌋

[Page 114]
DISCOURSE V.

Gainsborough told a Gentleman of Rank & Fortune that the Worst Painters always chose the Grandest Subjects. I desired the Gentleman to Set Gainsborough about one of Rafaels Grandest Subjects⌊,⌋ Namely Christ delivering the Keys to St Peter, & he would find that in Gainsboroughs hands it would be a Vulgar Subject of Poor Fishermen & a Journeyman Carpenter⌊.⌋

The following Discourse is written with the Same End in View, that Gainsborough had in making the Above assertion⌊,⌋ Namely To Represent Vulgar Artists as the Models of Executive Merit⌊.⌋

[*Page 116*]

. . . nothing has its proper luster but in its proper place. That which is most worthy of esteem in its allotted sphere, becomes an object, not of respect, but of derision, when it is forced into a higher, to which it is not suited.

Concessions to Truth for the sake of Oversetting Truth⌊.⌋

[*Pages 117–18*]

If you mean to preserve the most perfect beauty *in its most perfect state*, you cannot express the passions, all of which produce distortion and deformity, more or less, in the most beautiful faces.

[*Page 117*]

What Nonsense⌊!⌋

[*Page 118*]

Passion & Expression is Beauty Itself—The Face that is Incapable of Passion & Expression is deformity Itself⌊.⌋ Let it be Painted & Patchd & Praised & Advertised for Ever⌊,⌋ it will only be admired by Fools⌊.⌋

[*Page 119*]

[*In*] some of the Cartoons and other pictures of Raffaelle . . . the excellent master himself may have attempted this expression of passions above the powers of the art.

If Reynolds could not See variety of Characte[r] in Rafael Others Can⌊.⌋

We can easily, like the ancients, suppose a Jupiter to be possessed of all those powers and perfections which the subordinate Deities were endowed

Page 116 At the bottom, by 'keep your principal attention fixed upon the higher excellencies . . . you may be very imperfect; but still, you are an imperfect artist of the highest order', Erdman (p. 642) sees: '[Caesar said hed rather be the a Village second in Rome was not Caesar Dutch Painter *del*]'.

with separately. Yet, when they employed their art to represent him, they confined his character to majesty alone.

> False⌞!⌟ The Ancien[ts] were chief[ly] attentive to Complicated & Minute Discrimination of Character⌞;⌟ it is the whole of Art⌞·⌟

[*Page 120*]

Reynolds cannot bear Expression⌞·⌟

A statue in which you endeavour to unite stately dignity, youthful elegance, and stern valour, must surely possess none of these to any eminent degree.

> Why not? O Poverty!

The summit of excellence seems to be an assemblage of contrary qualities . . . .

> A Fine Jumble⌞!⌟

[*Page 121*]

If any man shall be master of such a transcendant, commanding, and ductile genius, as to enable him to rise to the highest, and to stoop to the lowest, flight of art, and to sweep over all of them unobstructed and secure, he is fitter to give example than to receive instruction.

> Mocks⌞!⌟

[*Page 123*]

The principal works of modern art are in *Fresco*, a mode of painting which excludes attention to minute elegancies . . . .

> This is False⌞·⌟ Fresco Painting is the Most Minute⌞·⌟ Fresco Painting is Like Miniature Painting; a Wall is a Large Ivory⌞·⌟

[*Page 124*]

Raffaelle . . . owes his reputation . . . to his excellence in the higher parts of the art [Fresco]: . . . though he continually . . . embellished his performances more and more with the addition of those lower ornaments, which entirely make the merit of some painters, yet he never arrived at . . . perfection . . . .

> Folly & Fals[e]hood. The Man who can say that Rafael Knew not the smaller beauties of the Art ought to be contemnd & I accordingly hold Reynolds in Contempt [for this] Sentence in particular⌞·⌟

[*Page 125*]

He never acquired that nicety of taste in colours, that breadth of light and shadow . . . . When he painted in oil, his hand seemed to be so cramped and confined, that he not only lost that facility and spirit, but . . . even that correctness of form . . . .

Rafael did as he Pleased. He who does not admire Rafaels Execution does not Even See Rafael⌞.⌟

I have no desire to degrade Raffaelle from the high rank which he deservedly holds . . . .

A Lie⌞!⌟

[*Page 126*]

Michael Angelo . . . considered the art as consisting of little more than what may be attained by sculpture; correctness of form, and energy of character.

According to Reynolds Mich Angelo was worse still & Knew Nothing at all about Art as an object of Imitation⌞.⌟ Can any Man be Such a fool as to believe that Rafael & Michael Angelo were Incapable of the meer Language of Art & That Such Idiots as Rubens, Correggio & Titian Knew how to Execute what they could not Think or Invent⌞?⌟

He [*Michael Angelo*] never attempted those lesser elegancies and graces in the art.

Damnd Fool⌞!⌟

If any man had a right to look down upon the lower accomplishments as beneath his attention, it was certainly Michael Angelo . . . .

O. Yes!

[*Page 127*]

. . . he has rejected all the false, though specious ornaments, which disgrace the works even of the most esteemed artists . . . .

Here is another Contradiction⌞.⌟ If Mich Ang. Neglected any thing that Titian or Veronese did: He Rejected *it* for Good Reasons. Sʳ Joshua in other Places owns that the Venetian Cannot Mix with the Roman or Florentine⌞.⌟

What then does he Mean when he says that Mich. Ang. & Rafael were not worthy of Imitation in the Lower parts of Art⌊?⌋

[*Page 128*]

Raffaelle had more Taste and Fancy, Michael Angelo more Genius and imagination.

What Nonsense⌊!⌋

[*Page 129*]

Michael Angelo's works have a strong, peculiar, and marked character: they seem to proceed from his own mind entirely . . . . Raffaelle's materials are generally borrowed, though the noble structure is his own.

If all this is True Why does not Reynolds recommend The Study of Rafael & Mich: Angelos Execution⌊?⌋ At page 97 he allows that the Venetian Style will Ill correspond with the great Style⌊.⌋

[*Page 131*]

Such is the great style . . . . in this, search after novelty . . . has no place . . . .

The Great Style is always Novel or New i[n] all its Operatio[ns.]

But there is another style, which . . . has still great merit . . . which may be called . . . the original or characteristical style . . . .

Original & Characteristica[l] are the Two Grand Merits of the Great Style⌊.⌋

[*Pages 131–2*]

One of the strongest-marked characters of this kind . . . is that of Salvator Rosa.

[*Page 131*]

Why should these words be applied to such a Wretch as Salvator Rosa⌊?⌋

[*Page 132*]

Salvator Rosa [W]as precisely [wh]at he Pretended [n]ot to be. His Picture*s* are high Labour⸏d pretensions to Expeditious Workmanship. He was the Quack Doctor of

Painting. His Roughnesses & Smoothnesse*s* are the Pro-
duction of Labour & Trick. As to Imagination he was
totally without Any.

[*Page 133*]

He gives us a peculiar cast of nature, which . . . has that sort of dignity
which belongs to savage and uncultivated nature . . . .

Savages are Fops & Fribbles more than any other Men∟˩

. . . what is most to be admired in him, is, the perfect correspondence
which he observed between the subjects which he chose and his manner of
treating them.

Handling is All that he ha*s*, & we all know thi[*s*.] Hand-
ling is Labo[ur] & Trick∟˩ Salvator Ro[sa] employd
Journeym[en.]

[*Page 134*]

Rubens . . . I think . . . a remarkable instance of the same mind being seen
in all the various parts of the art. The whole is so much of a piece . . . .

All Rubens's Pictures are Painted by Journeymen & so
far from [b]eing all of a Piec*e* are The most wretched
Bunglcs∟˩ [*Note in pencil below in another hand:* He who
could so abuse Rubens's Pictures generally must be
either a fool or madman∟˩]

[*Page 135*]

His Colouring, in which he is eminently skilled, is notwithstanding too
much of what we call tinted.

To My Eye Rubens's Colouring is most Contemptible∟˩
His Shadows are of a Filthy Brown somewhat of the
Colour of Excrement∟;˩ these are filld with tints & me[sses]
of yellow & red∟˩ His lights are all the Colours of the
Rainbow laid on Indiscriminate[ly] & broken one into
another. Altogether his Colouring [is] Contrary to The
Colouring of Real Art & Science∟˩
Opposed to Rubens⌐'⌐s Colouring Sr Joshua has placed
Poussin but he ought to put All Men of Genius who ever

Page 133 Under 'Fops & Fribbles', Erdman (p. 644) reads 'Fribbles & Fops'.
   The last four words are in ink only; the preceding passage is in pencil confirmed
in ink.

Painted. Rubens & the Venetians are Opposite in every thing to True Art & they Meant to be so∟;⌐ they were hired for this Purpose∟·⌐

[*Page 137*]

Poussin in the latter part of his life changed from his dry manner to one much softer and richer . . . as in the Seven Sacraments in the Duke of Orleans Collection, but neither these, nor any of his other pictures in this manner, are at all comparable to many in his dry manner which we have in England.

True∟!⌐

The favourite subjects of Poussin were Ancient Fables; and no painter was ever better qualified to paint such subjects . . . .

True∟!⌐

[*Page 138*]

Poussin seemed to think that the style and the language in which such stories are told, is not the worse for preserving some relish of the old way of painting . . . .

True∟!⌐

[*Page 139*]

. . . if the Figures which people his pictures had a modern air or countenance . . . if the landskip had the appearance of a modern view, how ridiculous would Apollo appear instead of the Sun . . . .

These remarks on Poussin are Excellent∟·⌐

[*Page 141*]

It is certain that the lowest style will be the most popular, as it falls within the compass of ignorance itself . . . .

Well said∟!⌐

[*Page 142*]

. . . our Exhibitions . . . have also a mischievous tendency, by seducing the Painter to an ambition of pleasing indiscriminately the mixed multitude of people who resort to them.

Why then does he talk in other places of pleasing Every body∟?⌐

[*Page 145*]

IMITATION.—GENIUS BEGINS WHERE RULES END.—INVEN-
TION;—ACQUIRED BY BEING CONVERSANT WITH THE
INVENTIONS OF OTHERS.—THE TRUE METHOD OF
IMITATING . . . .

[*Page 144*]

DISCOURSE VI.

When a Man talks of Acquiring Invention & of learning
how to produce Original Conception he must expect to be
calld a Fool by Men of Understanding but such a Hired
Knave cares not for the Few. His Eye is on the Many,
or rather the Money⌊.⌋

[*Page 147*]

Those who have undertaken to write on our art, and have represented it as
a kind of *inspiration* . . . seem to insure a much more favourable disposition
from their readers . . . than he who attempts to examine, coldly, whether
there are any means by which this art may be acquired . . . .

Bacons Philosop[hy] has Destroyd [*word cut away*] Art &
Science⌊.⌋ The Man who says that the Genius is not
Bor*n* b[ut] Taught—Is a Knav[e.]
O Reader behold the Philosophers Grave⌊!⌋
He was born quite a Foo*l*, but he died quite a Knave⌊.⌋

[*Page 149*]

. . . to owe nothing to another, is the praise which men . . . bestow some-
times upon others, and sometimes on themselves; and their imaginary dig-
nity is naturally heightened by a supercilious censure of . . . the servile
imitator.

How ridiculous it would be to se[e] the Sheep Endeavou[r-
ing] to walk like the Do*g*, or the Ox striving to trot like
the Horse⌊;⌋ just as Ridiculou[s] it is to see One Man
Striving to Imitate Another⌊.⌋ Man varies from Man more
than Animal from Anim[al] of Different Speci[es.]

Page 144   The first portion of this passage (up to 'calld a Fool') is in ink only; the
rest is in pencil confirmed in ink.

Page 147   The first sentence is in ink only; the rest is in pencil confirmed in ink.

[*Page 152*]

. . . the *degree* of excellence which proclaims *Genius* is different, in different times and different places . . . .

Never!

and what shews it to be so is, that mankind have often changed their opinion upon this matter.

Never!

[*Page 153*]

These excellencies were, heretofore, considered merely as the effects of genius; and justly, if genius is not taken for inspiration, but as the effect of close observation and experience.

Damnd Fool⌞!⌟

[*Page 154*]

He who first made any of these observations . . . had that merit, but probably no one went very far at once . . . others worked more, and improved further . . . .

If Art was Progressive We should have had Mich Angelo's & Rafaels to Succeed & to Improve upon each other But it is not so. Genius dies with its Possessor & comes not again till Another is Born with It⌞.⌟

[*Page 155*]

. . . even works of Genius, like every other effect, as they must have their cause, must likewise have their rules . . . .

Identities or Things are Neither Cause nor Effect⌞.⌟ They are Eternal⌞.⌟

[*Page 157*]

. . . our minds should be habituated to the contemplation of excellence . . . we should, to the last moment of our lives, continue a settled intercourse with all the true examples of grandeur. Their inventions are not only the food of our infancy, but the substance which supplies the fullest maturity of our vigour.

Reynolds Thinks that Man Learns all that he Knows⌞.⌟ I say on the Contrary That Man Brings All that he has or Can have Into the World with him. Man is Born Like a Garden ready Planted & Sown⌞.⌟ This World is too poor to produce one Seed⌞.⌟

Page 157 The last sentence is in ink only; the rest is in pencil confirmed in ink.

The mind is but a barren soil; a soil which is soon exhausted, and will produce no crop . . . .

> The mind that could have produced this Sentence must have been a Pitiful⌞,⌟ a Pitiable Imbecillity. I always thought that the Human Mind was the most Prolific of All Things & Inexhaustible⌞.⌟ I certainly do Thank God that I am not like Reynolds⌞.⌟

[*Page 158*]

. . . or only one, unless it be continually fertilized and enriched with foreign matter.

> Nonsense⌞!⌟

[*Page 159*]

It is vain for painters or poets to endeavour to invent without materials on which the mind may work . . . . Nothing can come of nothing.

> Is the Mind Nothing?

. . . we are certain that Michael Angelo, and Raffaelle, were equally possessed of all the knowledge in the art which had been discovered in the works of their predecessors.

> If *so*, they knew all that Titian & Correggio knew⌞.⌟ Correggio was two Years older than Mich. Angelo⌞,⌟ Correggio born 1472⌞,⌟ Mich Angelo born 1474⌞.⌟

[*Page 161*]

. . . it is not to be understood, that I advise any endeavour to copy the exact peculiar colour and complexion of another man's mind . . . . His model may be excellent, but the copy will be ridiculous . . . .

> Why then Imitate at all?

[*Page 163*]

Art in its perfection is not ostentatious; it lies hid, and works its effect, itself unseen. It is the proper study and labour of an artist to uncover and find out the latent cause of conspicuous beauties . . . .

> This is a Very Clever Sentence⌞;⌟ who wrote [it] God know[s.]

Page 159 This passage was first written in pencil: 'If *so*, they knew all that Titian & Correggio knew⌞.⌟ Correggio was two Years older than Mich. Angelo⌞,⌟ Correggio born   Mich Angelo   ⌞.⌟' Later these words were confirmed and others added in ink. The erroneous facts are repeated in *Descriptive Catalogue* ¶3 (p. 827).

[*Page 165*]

Peculiar marks, I hold to be, generally, if not always, defects . . . .

Peculiar Mark*s* are the Only Meri[t.]

Peculiarities in the works of art, are like those in the human figure:
. . . they are always so many blemishes . . . .

Infernal Fals[*e*]hood∟!↲

[*Page 166*]

Even the great name of Michael Angelo may be used, to keep in countenance a deficiency or rather neglect of colouring, and every other ornamental part of the art.

No Man who can See Michael Angel*o* can say that he wants Either Colouring or Ornamental parts of Ar*t*, in the highest degre*e*, for he has Every Thing [requisite *del*] of Both∟•↲

[*Page 167*]

. . . there is no defect that may not be excused, if it is a sufficient excuse that it can be imputed to considerable artists . . . .

He who Admires Rafael Must admire Rafaels Execution∟•↲
He who does not admire Rafaels Execution Cannot Admire Rafael∟•↲

[*Page 172*]

. . . want of strength of parts. In this certainly men are not equal . . . .

A Confession∟•↲

[*Page 176*]

In order to encourage you to imitation, to the utmost extent, let me add, that the very finished artists in the inferior branches of the art, will contribute to furnish the mind and give hints . . . .

This Sentence is to Introduce another in Condemnation & Contempt of Alb. Durer.

Page 166   Under 'Thing', Erdman (p. 646) reads 'perquisite', and at the end: '[O what Wisdom & Learning adorn(?) his Superiority—*del*]'.

Page 176   By 'Coypel wanted a simplicity of taste', Erdman (p. 647) sees '[O Yes Coypel indeed *del*]'.

The works of Albert Durer, Lucas Van Leyden, the numerous inventions of Tobias Stimmer, and Jost Ammon, afford a rich mass of genuine materials . . . .

A Polishd Villain who Robs & Murders⌐!⌐

[*Page 178*]

The greatest style, if that style is confined to small figures, . . . would receive an additional grace by the elegance and precision of pencil so admirable in the works of Teniers . . . .

What does Precision of Pencil mean? If it does not mean Outline it means Nothing⌐.⌐

[*Page 179*]

Jan Steen seems to be one of the most diligent and accurate observers . . . if [*he*] . . . had been blessed with Michael Angelo and Raffaelle for his masters . . . he now would have ranged with the great pillars and supporters of our Art.

Jan Stein was a Boor & neither Rafael nor Mich Ang. could have made him any better⌐.⌐

[*Page 180*]

Men . . . although thus bound down by the almost invincible powers of early habits, have still exerted extraordinary abilities . . . and have . . . given . . . great force and energy to their works . . . .

He who Can be bound down is No Genius⌐.⌐ Genius cannot be Bound⌐;⌐ it may be Renderd Indignant & Outrageous⌐.⌐ 'Opression makes the Wise Man Mad⌐.⌐'
Solomon

[*Page 188*]
DISCOURSE VII.

The Purpose of the following discourse is to Prove That Taste & Genius are not of Heavenly Origin & that all who have Supposed that they Are *so* Are to be Considerd as Weak headed Fanatics⌐.⌐ The Obligations Reynolds has laid on Bad Artists of all Classes will at all times make them his Admirers but most especially for this discourse in

Page 180 'Surely oppression maketh a wise man mad' comes from Ecclesiastes 7: 7.

which it is proved that the Stupid are born with Faculties Equal to other Men Only they have not Cultivated them because they thought it not worth the trouble⌊·⌋

[*Page 194*]

We will allow a poet to express his meaning, when his meaning is not well known to himself, with a certain degree of obscurity, as it is one source of the sublime.

Obscurity is Neither the Source of the Sublime nor of any Thing Else⌊·⌋

But when, in plain prose, we gravely talk of courting the muse in shady bowers; waiting the call and inspiration of Genius . . . of attending to times and seasons when the imagination shoots with greatest vigour, . . . sagaciously observing how much the wild freedom and liberty of imagination is cramped by attention to established rules . . . we . . . at best entertain notions not only groundless, but pernicious.

The Ancients & the wisest of the Moderns were of the opinion that Reynolds Condemns & laughs at⌊·⌋

[*Page 195*]

. . . scarce a poet is to be found . . . who . . . continued practising his profession to the very last, whose latter works are not as replete with the fire of imagination, as those which were produced in his more youthful days.

As Replete but Not More Replete⌊·⌋

To understand literally these metaphors or ideas expressed in poetical language, seems to be equally absurd as to conclude . . . .

The Ancients did not mean to Impose when they affirmd their belief in Vision & Revelation⌊·⌋ Plato was in Earnest. Milton was in Earnest. They believd that God did Visit Man Really & Truly[?] & not as Reynolds pretends[?]⌊·⌋

[*Page 196*]

. . . that because painters sometimes represent poets writing from the dictates of a little winged boy or genius, that this same genius really did inform him in a whisper what he was to write; and that he is himself but a mere machine, unconscious of the operations of his own mind.

How very Anxious Reynolds is to Disprove & Contemn Spiritual Perception⌊!⌋

Page 195 The last line is partly cropped off at the bottom.

[*Page 197*]

It is supposed . . . that under the name of genius great works are produced, and under the name of taste an exact judgement is given, without our knowing why, and without our being under the least obligation to reason, precept, or experience.

Who Ever said this⌐?⌐

One can scarce state these opinions without exposing their absurdity . . . .

He states Absurdities in Company with Truths & calls both Absurd⌐.⌐

[*Page 198*]

. . . I am persuaded, that even among those few who may be called thinkers, the prevalent opinion allows less than it ought to the powers of reason . . . .

The Artifice of the Epicurean Philosophers is to Call all other Opinions Unsolid & Unsubstantial than those which are derived from Earth⌐.⌐

We often appear to differ in sentiments from each other, merely from the inaccuracy of terms . . . .

It is not in Terms that Reynolds & I disagree⌐.⌐ Two Contrary Opinions can never by any Language be made alike. I say Taste & Genius are Not Teachable or Acquirable but are born with us⌐;⌐ Reynolds says the Contrary⌐.⌐

[*Page 199*]

We apply the term TASTE to that act of the mind by which we like or dislike, whatever be the subject. . . . we are obliged to take words as we find them; all we can do is to distinguish the THINGS to which they are applied.

This is False⌐;⌐ the Fault is not in Word*s*, but in Things⌐.⌐ Lockes Opinions of Words & their Fallaciousness are Artful Opinions & Fallacious also⌐.⌐

[*Page 200*]

It is the very same taste which relishes a demonstration in geometry, that is pleased with the resemblance of a picture to an original, and touched with the harmony of musick.

Demonstration⌐,⌐ Similitude & Harmony are Objects of Reasoning⌐.⌐ Invention⌐,⌐ Identity & Melody are Objects of Intuition⌐.⌐

[*Page 201*]

Colouring is true, when it is naturally adapted to the eye, from brightness, from softness, from harmony, from resemblance; because these agree with their object, NATURE, and therefore are true; as true as mathematical demonstration . . . .

God forbid that Truth should be Confined to Mathematical Demonstration ! ⌋

But beside real, there is also apparent truth, or opinion, or prejudice. With regard to real truth, when it is known, the taste which conforms to it, is, and must be, uniform.

He who does not Know Truth at Sight is unworthy of Her Notice ⌊ . ⌋

In proportion as these prejudices are known to be generally diffused, or long received, the taste which conforms to them approaches nearer to certainty . . . .

Here is a great deal to do to Prove that All Truth is Prejudice for All that is Valuable in Knowledge is Superior to Demonstrative Science such as is Weighed or Measured ⌊ . ⌋

[*Page 202*]

As these prejudices become more narrow, more local, more transitory, this secondary taste becomes more and more fantastical . . . .

And so he thinks he has proved that Genius & Inspiration are All a Hum ⌊ . ⌋

Having laid down these positions, I shall proceed with less method . . . .

He calls the Above proceeding with Method ⌊ ! ⌋

We will take it for granted, that reason is something invariable and fixed in the nature of things . . . .

Reason or A Ratio of all We have Known is not the Same it shall be when we Know More. *H*e therefore takes a Fals[*e*]-hood for granted to set out with ⌊ . ⌋

[*Page 203*]

. . . we will conclude, that whatever goes under the name of taste, which we can fairly bring under the dominion of reason, must be considered as equally exempt from change.

Now this is Supreme Fooling ⌊ . ⌋

The arts would lie open for ever to caprice and casualty, if those who are to judge of their excellencies had no settled principles by which they are to regulate their decisions . . . .

He may as well say that if Man does not lay down settled Principles The Sun will not rise in a Morning⌊.⌋

[*Page 204*]

My notion of nature comprehends not only the forms which nature produces, but also the nature and internal fabrick and organization . . . of the human mind and imagination.

Here is a Plain Confession that he Thinks Mind & Imagination not to be above the Mortal and Perishing Nature. Such is the End of Epicurean or Newtonian Philosophy⌊;⌋ it is Atheism⌊.⌋

[*Page 208*]

This [*Poussin's 'Perseus and Medusa's Head'*] is undoubtedly a subject of great bustle and tumult, and that the first effect of the picture may correspond to the subject, every principle of composition is violated; . . . I remember turning from it with disgust . . . .

Reynolds's Eye could not bear Characteristic Colouring or Light & Shade⌊.⌋

This conduct of Poussin I hold to be entirely improper to imitate. A picture should please at first sight, and appear to invite the spectator's attention . . . .

Please: Whom? Some Men Cannot See a Picture except in a Dark Corner⌊.⌋

[*Page 209*]

No one can deny, that violent passions will naturally emit harsh and disagreeable tones . . . .

Violent Passions Emit the Real Good & Perfect Tones⌊.⌋

[*Page 214*]

If it be objected that Rubens judged ill at first in thinking it necessary to make his work so very ornamental, this puts the question upon new ground.

Here it is calld Ornamental that the Roman & Bolognian Schools may be Insinuated not to be Ornamental⌊.⌋

[Page 215]

Nobody will dispute but some of the best of the Roman or Bolognian schools would have produced a more learned and more noble work.

Learned & Noble is Ornamental⌐.⌐

This leads us to another important province of taste, that of weighing the value of the different classes of the art . . . .

A Fools Balance is no Criterion because tho it goes down on th[e] heaviest side we ought to look what he puts into it.

[Page 232]

If an European, when he has cut off his beard, . . . or bound up his own natural hair in regular hard knots, as unlike nature as he can possibly make it . . . meets a Cherokee Indian, who has . . . laid on with equal care and attention his yellow and red oker . . . whoever of these two despises the other for this attention to the fashion of his country . . . is the barbarian.

Excellent⌐!⌐

[Page 242]

In the midst of the highest flights of fancy or imagination, reason ought to preside from first to last . . . .

If this is True it is a devilish Foolish Thing to be An Artist⌐.⌐

[Page 244]

DISCOURSE VIII.

Burkes Treatise on the Sublime & Beautiful is founded on the Opinions of Newton & Locke⌐;⌐ on this Treatise Reynolds has grounded many of his assertion*s* in all his Discourses⌐.⌐ I read Burkes Treatise when very Young⌐;⌐ at the same time I read Locke on Human Understanding & Bacons Advance[men]t of Learning⌐;⌐ on Every one of

Page 228   By 'Thus it is the ornaments, rather than the proportions of architecture, which at the first glance distinguish the different orders from each other; the Dorick is known by its triglyphs, the Ionick by its volutes, and the Corinthian by its Acanthus', Erdman (p. 649) makes out: '[He could not tell Ionick from the Corinthian or Dorick or one column from another. *del*]'.

Page 244   Blake's copies of Edmund Burke, *Philosophical Enquiry into the Origin of our Ideas of the Sublime and Beautiful,* John Locke, *An Essay Concerning Human Understanding, The Tvvo Bookes of Francis Bacon,* Of the Profience and aduancement of learning (the first [1605] edition, according to Blake's letter of 23 Aug. 1799) have not survived.

these Books I wrote my Opinions & on looking them over
find that my Notes on Reynolds in this Book are exactly
Similar. I felt the Same Contempt & Abhorrence then;
that I do now. They mock Inspiration & Vision⌞.⌟ In-
spiration & Vision was then & now is & I hope will
always Remain my Element⌞,⌟ my Eternal Dwelling
Place. *How* can I then hear it Contemnd without returning
Scorn for Scorn⌞?⌟

[*Page 245*]

THE PRINCIPLES OF ART, WHETHER POETRY OR PAINTING, HAVE THEIR
FOUNDATION IN THE MIND; SUCH AS NOVELTY, VARIETY AND CONTRAST: THESE
IN THEIR EXCESS BECOME DEFECTS . . . .

Principles according to Sʳ Joshua become defects⌞.⌟

I have recommended in former discourses, that Artists should . . . form an
idea of perfection from the different excellencies which lie dispersed in the
various schools of painting.

In another discourse h[e] says that we cannot Mix the
Florentine & Venetian⌞.⌟

[*Page 251*]

An instance occurs to me of two painters, (Rembrandt and Poussin,) of
characters totally opposite to each other in every respect . . . Rembrandt's
manner is absolute unity . . . Poussin . . . has scarce any principal mass of
light at all . . . .

Rembrand*t* was a Generalizer⌞;⌟ Poussin was a Particu-
larizer⌞.⌟

. . . the works of Poussin . . . [*were*] as much distinguished for simplicity,
as those of Rembrandt for combination.

Poussin knew better that [*i.e. than*] to make all his Pictures
have the same light & shadow⌞.⌟ Any fool may concen-
t[rate] a light in the Middle⌞.⌟

[*Page 256*]

[*In*] the portraits of Titian, . . . dignity . . . has the appearance of an
unalienable adjunct . . . . . ·

Dignity an Adjunct⌞!⌟

Page 245   See Discourse IV, pp. 95, 97 (pp. 1477-8).

[Page 260]

When a young artist is first told, that his composition and his attitudes must be contrasted, . . . and that the eye must be gratified with a variety of colours;—when he is told this, with certain animating words, of Spirit, Dignity, Energy, Grace, greatness of Style, and brilliancy of Tints, he becomes suddenly vain of his newly acquired knowledge . . . .

Mocks⌊!⌋

[Page 262]

The Art in its infancy, like the first work of a Student, was dry, hard, and simple. But this kind of barbarous simplicity, would be better named Penury, as it proceeds from mere want . . . .

Mocks⌊!⌋

. . . their simplicity was the offspring, not of choice, but necessity.

A Lie⌊!⌋

But however they may have strayed, we cannot recommend to them to return to that simplicity . . . but to deal out their abundance with a more sparing hand . . . .

Abundance of Stupidity⌊!⌋

[Page 264]

. . . it is not enough that a work be learned; it must be pleasing . . .

If you Endeavour to Please the Worst you will never Please the Best⌊.⌋ To please All Is Impossible⌊.⌋

[Page 266]

St Paul preaching at Athens in one of the Cartoons, far from any affected academical contrast of limbs, stands equally on both legs, . . . add contrast, and the whole energy and unaffected grace of the figure is destroyed.

Well Said⌊!⌋

[Page 267]

It is given as a rule by Fresnoy, That *the principle figure of a subject must appear in the midst of the picture, under the principal light, to distinguish it from the rest.*

What a Devil of a Rule⌊!⌋

1498

[*Page 272*]

... what those proportions are cannot be so well learnt by precept as by observation on pictures, and in this knowledge bad pictures will instruct as well as good.

Bad Pictures are always Sʳ Joshuas Friends⌐.⌐

It ought, in my opinion, to be indispensably observed, that the masses of light in a picture be always of warm mellow colour, yellow, red, or a yellowish-white; and that the blue, the grey, or the green colours be kept almost entirely out of these masses, and be used only to support and set off these warm colours . . . .

Colouring formed upon these Principles is destructive of All Art because it takes away the possibility of Variety & only promotes Harmony or Blending of Colours one into another⌐.⌐

[*Page 274*]

... the general hue of the picture [*by Poussin*] was inclinable to brown or yellow: which shews sufficiently, that harmony of colouring was not a part of the art that had much engaged the attention of the painter.

Such Harmony of Colouring is destructive of Art⌐.⌐ One Species of General Hue over all is the Cursed Thing calld Harmony⌐;⌐ it is like the Smile of a Fool⌐.⌐

[*Page 275*]

The illuminated parts of objects are in nature of a warmer tint than those that are in the shade . . . .

Shade is always Cold & never as in Rubens & the Colourists Hot & Yellowy Brown.

[*Page 277*]

... that fulness of manner which . . . is found in perfection in the best works of Correggio, and . . . of Rembrandt . . . is produced by melting and losing the shadows in a ground still darker than those shadows . . . .

All This is Destructiv[e] of Art⌐.⌐

[*Page 279*]

The Moon in this picture [*by Rubens*] does not preserve so great a superiority in regard to its lightness over the object which it illumines, as it does in nature . . . . If Rubens had preserved the same scale of gradation of light between the Moon and the objects, which is found in nature, the picture must have consisted of one small spot of light only . . . .

These are Excellent Remarks on Proportiona[l] Colour⌊·⌋

[*Page 281*]

Reason and common sense tell us, that before, and above all other considerations, it is necessary that the work should be seen, not only without difficulty or inconvenience, but with pleasure and satisfaction . . . .

If the Picture ought to be Seen with Ease Surely The Nobler parts of the Picture such as the Heads ought to be Principa[l] but this Never is the Case except in the Roman & Florentine Schools⌊·⌋ Note I include the Germans in the Florentin[e] School⌊·⌋

[*Page 284*]

It is true, sketches, or such drawings as painters generally make for their works, give this pleasure of imagination to a high degree. From a slight undetermined drawing . . . the imagination supplies more than the painter himself, probably, could produce . . . .

What Fals[e]hood⌊!⌋

[*Page 285*]

. . . every thing shall be carefully and distinctly expressed, as if the painter knew, with correctness and precision, the exact form and character of whatever is introduced into the picture.

Excellent & Contrary to his usual Opinion[s!]

[*Page 286*]

Mr. Falconet has observed . . . that the circumstance of covering the face of Agamemnon was probably not in consequence of any fine imagination of the painter, . . . but merely copied from the description of the sacrifice, as it is found in Euripides . . . . Falconet does not at all acquiesce in the praise that is bestowed on Timanthes . . . .

I am of Falconets opinion⌊·⌋

Page 286 Peter Falconet (1741–91) was a portrait painter.

Marginalia (?1818): Spurzheim, *Observations on . . . Insanity* (1817)

[*Page 106*]

In children . . . The disturbances of the [*cerebral*] organization appear merely as organic diseases, because the functions are entirely suppressed.

> Corporeal disease, to which I readily agree. Diseases of the mind: I pity him. Denies mental health and perfection. Stick to this, all is right. But see page 152.

[*Pages 153–4*]

Religion is another fertile cause of insanity. Mr. Haslam, though he declares it sinful to consider religion as a cause of insanity, adds, however, that he would be ungrateful, did he not avow his obligations to Methodism for its supply of numerous cases. Hence the primitive feelings of religion may be misled and produce insanity; that is what I would contend for, and in that sense religion often leads to insanity.

> Methodism, &c. 154. Cowper came to me and said, 'Oh! that I were insane, always. I will never rest. Cannot you make me truly insane? I will never rest till I am so. Oh! that in the bosom of God I was hid. You retain health and yet are mad as any of us all—over us all—mad as a refuge from unbelief—from Bacon, Newton, and Locke.'

Page 106 Page 152 says: 'As the functions depend on the organization, disturbed functions will derange the organization, and one deranged cerebral part will have an influence on others, and so arises insanity. . . . Whatever occupies the mind too intensely or exclusively is hurtful to the brain, and induces a state favourable to insanity, in diminishing the influence of will.'

Pages 153–4 The quotation marks appear in the Ellis & Yeats transcript.

MARGINALIA (*c.* 1820): Berkeley, *Siris* (1744)

[Page 203].

God knoweth all things, as pure mind or intellect, but nothing by sense, nor in nor through a sensory. Therefore to suppose a sensory of any kind, whether space or any other, in God would be very wrong, and lead us into false conceptions of his nature.

Imagination or the Human Eternal Body in Every Man⌊·⌋

[Page 204]

But in respect of a perfect spirit, there is nothing hard or impenetrable: there is no resistance to the deity: Nor hath he any Body: Nor is the supreme being united to the world, as the soul of an animal is to it's body, which necessarily implieth defect, both as an instrument and as a constant weight and impediment.

Imagination is the Divine Body in Every Man⌊·⌋

[Page 205]

Natural phænomena are only natural appearances. . . . They and the phantomes that result from those appearances, THE CHILDREN OF IMAGINA-TION grafted upon sense, such for example as pure space are thought by many the very first in existence and stability, and to embrace and comprehend all beings.

The All in Man The divine Image or Imagination⌊·⌋

[At the foot of the page]

The Four Senses are the Four Faces of Man & the Four Rivers of the Water of Life⌊·⌋

[Page 212]

Plato and Aristotle considered God as abstrated or distinct from the natural world. But the Aegyptians considered God and nature as making one whole, or all things together as making one universe.

They also considerd God as abstracted or distinct from the Imaginative World but Jesus as also Abraham[?] & David considerd God as a Man in the Spiritual or Ima-ginative Vision⌊·⌋

Page 203   Cf. 'Laocoon' (p. 666): 'The Eternal Body of Man is The Imagination'.

[*At the foot of the page*]

Jesus considerd Imagination to be the Real Man & says I will not leave you Orphans and I will manifest myself to you∟;」 he says also the Spiritual Body or Angel as little Children always behold the Face of the Heavenly Father∟.」

[*Page 213*]

The perceptions of sense are gross: but even in the senses there is a difference. Though harmony and proportion are not objects of sense, yet the eye and the ear are organs, which offer to the mind such materials, by means whereof she may apprehend both the one and the other.

Harmony & Proportion are Qualities & Not Things∟.」 The Harmony & Proportion of a Horse are not the Same with those of a Bull∟.」 Every Thing has its own Harmony & Proportion∟,」 Two Inferior Qualities∟,」 in it For its Reality is Its Imaginative Form∟.」

[*Page 214*]

By experiments of sense we become acquainted with the lower faculties of the soul; and from them, whether by a gradual evolution or ascent, we arrive at the highest. Sense supplies images to memory. These become subjects for fancy to work upon. Reason considers and judges of the imaginations. And these acts of reason become new objects to the understanding.

Knowledge is not by deduction but Immediate by Perception or Sense at once∟.」 Christ addresses himself to the Man∟,」 not to his Reason∟.」 Plato did not bring Life & Immortality to Light∟;」 Jesus only did this∟.」

[*Pages 214–15*]

There is according to Plato properly no knowledge, but only opinion concerning things sensible and perishing, not because they are naturally abstruse and involved in darkness: but because their nature and existence is uncertain, ever fleeting and changing.

Jesus supposes every Thing to be Evident to the Child & to the Poor & Unlearned∟.」 Such is the Gospel∟.」

Page 212 For 'Orphans', Erdman (p. 653) reads 'Orphanned'.

Page 214 Cf. 'The Everlasting Gospel' (p. 1054): 'Plato & Cicero did not' bring 'to Light' 'Life & Immortality'.

[At the foot of p. 215]

The Whole Bible is filld with Imaginations & Visions from
End to End & not with Moral Virtues∟;⌐ that is the base-
ness of Plato & the Greek & all Warriors∟.⌐ The Moral
Virtues are continual Accusers of Sin & promote Eternal
Wars & Dominency over others∟.⌐

[Page 217]

Aristotle maketh a threefold distinction of objects according to the three
speculative sciences. Physics he supposeth to be conversant about such
things as have a principle of motion in themselves, mathematics about
things permanent but not abstracted, and theology about being abstracted
and immoveable, which distinction may be seen in the ninth book of his
metaphysics.

God is not a Mathematical Diagram∟.⌐

[Page 218]

It is a maxim of the Platonic philosophy, that the soul of man was originally
furnished with native inbred notions, and stands in need of sensible occa-
sions, not absolutely for producing them, but only for awakening, rousing
or exciting into act what was already preexistent, dormant, and latent in
the soul.

The Natural Body is an Obstruction to the Soul or Spiri-
tual Body∟.⌐

[Page 219]

. . . Whence, according to Themistius, . . . it may be inferred that all beings
are in the soul. For saith he, the forms are the beings. By the form every
thing is what it is. And he adds, it is the soul that imparteth form to
matter . . . .

This is my Opinion but Forms must be apprehended by
Sense or the Eye of Imagination∟.⌐

Page *215* Cf. 'The Everlasting Gospel' part b, ll. 10, 8, 4–6 (p. 1054): 'The Moral
Virtues' are 'the Accusation of Sin'; 'Plato & Cicero . . . wrote . . . These Moral
Virtues'.

Page *217* Cf. 'Laocoon': 'The Gods of Greece & Egypt were Mathematical
Diagrams' (p. 665).

[At the foot of the page:]

Man is All Imagination⌊.⌋ God is Man & exists in us &
we in him⌊.⌋

[Page 241 at the foot]

What Jesus came to Remove was the Heathen or Platonic
Philosophy which blinds the Eye of Imagination⌊,⌋ The
Real Man⌊.⌋

MARGINALIA (?1822): Cennini, *Trattato della Pittura* (1821)

The Pope supposes Nature and the Virgin Mary to be the same allegorical personages, but the Protestant considers Nature as incapable of bearing a child.

MARGINALIA (1826): Wordsworth, *Excursion* (1814)

Wordsworth[1]

It was not the Authors intention formally to announce a System. *I*t was more animating to him to proceed in a different cours*e*, & if he shall Succeed in conveying to the Mind clear thoughts⌞,⌟ lively images & strong feelings the Reader will have no difficulty in extracting the System for himself. And in the mean time the following passag*e*, taken from the Conclusion of the first Book of the Recluse may be acceptable as a Prospectus of the design & scope of the whole Poem⌞.⌟

On Man, on Nature & on Human Life
Musing in solitude I oft percieve
Fair trains of imagery before me rise
Accompanied by feelings of delight
Pur*e*, or with no unpleasant sadness mixd   ⌞
And I am conscious of a[*f*]fecting Thoughts
And dear remembrances whose presence Soothes
Or elevates the Mind intent to weigh
The good & Evil of our Mortal State⌞.⌟
   To these emotions whensoeer they come   ⌞

---

[1] Blake transcribed the whole section of the 'Recluse' and the prose paragraph introducing it (pp. x–xiv). He casually altered punctuation, capitalization, abbreviations ('&' for 'and', 'mixd' for 'mixed', 'tho' for 'though'), and made the following substantive changes: 'It was' (for 'It is'), 'a *kind of* Prospectus', l. 5 'unplea*sing*', l. 10 'when*ceso*'er', l. 44 'hath composed', l. 51 'meer', l. 55 'produc*e*' l. 59 'worse' (for 'more'), l. 85 'inspir'st', l. 87 'on' (for 'of'), l. 97 '*and* Man'.

Whether from breath of outward circumstance
Or from the Soul—an impulse to herself
I would give utterance in numerous Verse⌊.⌋
Of Truth of Grandeur Beauty Love & Hope
And melancholy Fear Subdud by Faith⌊;⌋   [*15*]
Of blessed consolations in distress⌊;⌋
Of moral Strength & intellectual power⌊;⌋
Of joy in widest commonalty spread⌊;⌋
Of the individual Mind that keeps her own
Inviolate retirement subject there   [*20*]
To Conscience only & the Law Supreme
Of that Intelligence which governs all
I sing—'fit audience let me find tho few⌊!⌋'

So prayed⌊,⌋ more gaining than he askd⌊,⌋ the Bard⌊,⌋
Holiest of Men—Urania I shall need   [*25*]
Thy guidance or a greater Muse if such
Descend to Earth or dwell in highest Heaven
For I must.tread on shadowy ground, must sink
Deep —& aloft ascending breathe in worlds
To which the Heaven of Heavens is but a Veil⌊.⌋   [*30*]
All strength, all terror, single or in bands
That ever was put forth in personal Form⌊;⌋
Jehovah—with his thunder & the·choir
Of shouting Angels & the empyreal thrones—
I pass them unalarmd. Not Chao*s*, not   [*35*]
The darkest Pit of lowest Erebus
Nor aught of blinder vancanc*y*, scoopd out
By help of dreams can breed Such fear & awe
As fall upon us often when we look
Into our Mind*s*, into the Mind of Man   [*40*]
My haunt & the main region of my Song⌊.⌋
—Beauty—a living Presence of the Earth

l. 35: Blake told Crabb Robinson that reading 'the preface to the Excursion'
'caused him a bowel complaint which nearly killed him. . . . he very earnestly
asked me— "Is M:ʳ W: a sincere real Christian"? In reply to my answer he said—
"If so what does he mean by the worlds to which the heaven of. heavens is but a
veil— And who is he shall pass Jehovah unalarmed?" ' ' "Does Mʳ Wordsw:
think his mind can *surpass* Jehovah?" ' (*Blake Records*, 325, 321, passages of 19
Feb. 1826, 10 Dec. 1825.)

Surpassing the most fair Ideal Forms
Which craft of delicate spirits have composd
From Earths materials—waits upon my steps⌐;⌐   [₄
Pitches her tents before me as I move
An hourly neighbour. Paradise & groves
Elysian Fortunate Fields—like those of old
Saught in the Atlantic Main—Why should they be
A history only of departed things   [₅
Or a meer Fiction of what never was⌐?⌐
For the discerning intellect of Man
When wedded to this goodly universe
In love & holy passion shall find these
A simple product of the common day   [₅
—*I*, long before the blissful hour arrives
Would chaunt in lonely peace the spousal verse
Of this great consummation—& by words
Which speak of nothing worse than what we are
Would I arouse the sensual from their sleep   [₆
Of death, & win the vacant & the vain
To noble raptures; while my voice proclaims
How exquisitely the individual Mind
(And the progressive powers perhaps no less
(Of the whole Species) to the external World   [₆
Is fitted:—& how exquisitely too,
Theme this but little heard of among Men⌐,⌐
The external World is fitted to the Mind⌐;⌐

You shall not bring me down to believe such fitting & fitted⌐.⌐
I know better & please your Lordship⌐.⌐

And the Creation (by no lower name
Can it be calld) which they with blended might   [₂
Accomplish.—*T*his is our high Argument
—Such grateful haunts foregoing, if I oft
Must turn elsewhere—to travel near the tribes
And fellowships of Men, & see ill sights
Of madding passions mutually inflamd⌐;⌐   [₂
Must hear Humanity in fields & groves
Pipe solitary anguish;

*D*oes not this Fit & is it not Fitting most Exquisitely too but to what⌊?⌋ *N*ot to Mind but to the Vile Body only & to its Laws of Good & Evil & its Enmities against Mind⌊.⌋

　　　　　　　　　　　　or must hang
Brooding above the fierce confederate storm
Of Sorrow barricadoed evermore
Within the walls of cities; may these sounds　　　　　　[*80*]
Have their authentic comment—that even these
Hearing I be not downcast or forlorn.
—Come thou Prophetic Spirit that inspirest
The Human soul of Universal Earth
Dreaming of things to come: & dost possess　　　　　　[*85*]
A Metropolitan Temple in the hearts
Of mighty Poets⌊;⌋ upon me bestow
A gift of genuine Insight; that my Song
With Starlike virtue in its place may shine⌊;⌋
Shedding benignant influence—& secure　　　　　　[*90*]
Itself from all malevolent effect
Of those mutations that extend their sway
Throughout the nether sphere—& if with this
I mix more lowly matter: with the thing
Contemplated describe the Mind of Man　　　　　　[*95*]
Contemplating, & who, & what he was
The transitory Being that beheld
This Vision—when & where & how he lived—
Be not this labour useless. If such theme
May sort with highest objects then dread Power　　　　　　[*100*]
Whose gracious favour is the primal source
Of all Illumination may my life
Express the image of a better time
More wise desires & simpler manners—nurse
My heart in genuine freedom—all pure thoughts　　　　　　[*105*]
Be with me:—so shall thy unfailing Love
Guide & support & chear me to the end⌊.⌋　　　　　　[*107*]

¶ Solomon when he Married Pharohs daughter & became a Convert to the Heathen Mythology Talked exactly in this way of Jehovah as a Very inferior object of Mans Contemplations⌊;⌋

he also passed him by unalarmd & was permitted. Jehovah dropped a tear & followd him by his Spirit into the Abstract Void⌊;⌋ it is called the divine Mercy⌊.⌋ Satan dwells in it but Mercy does not dwell in him⌊;⌋ he Knows not to Forgive⌊.⌋

W Blake

MARGINALIA (1826): Wordsworth, *Poems* (1815)

[Page viii]

The powers requisite for the production of poetry are, first, those of observation and description . . . 2dly, Sensibility . . . 3rdly, Reflection . . . 4thly, Imagination and Fancy . . . 5thly, Invention . . . .

One Power alone makes a Poet—Imagination The Divine Vision⌞.⌟

[Page 1, section title]

POEMS REFERRING TO THE PERIOD OF CHILDHOOD.

I see in Wordsworth the Natural Man rising up against the Spiritual Man Continually & then he is No Poet but a Heathen Philosopher at Enmity against all true Poetry or Inspiration⌞.⌟

[Page 3]

And I could wish my days to be
Bound each to each by natural piety.

There is no Such Thing as Natural Piety Because The Natural Man is at Enmity with God⌞.⌟

[Page 43]

To H.C., SIX YEARS OLD.

This is all in the highest degree Imaginative & equal to any Poet but not Superior⌞.⌟ I cannot think that Real Poets have any Competition⌞.⌟ None are greatest in the Kingdom of Heaven⌞;⌟ it is so in Poetry⌞.⌟

[Page 44]

INFLUENCE OF NATURAL OBJECTS In calling forth and strengthening the Imagination in Boyhood and early Youth; From an unpublished Poem.

Natural Objects always did & now do weaken deaden & Obliterate Imagination in Me⌞.⌟ Wordsworth must Know that what he Writes Valuable is Not to be found in Nature⌞.⌟

Read Michael Angelos Sonnet Vol 2 p 179⌞.⌟

Page 44   Heaven-born, the Soul a heaven-ward course must hold;
Beyond the visible world She soars to seek,

[*Page 341*]

ESSAY, SUPPLEMENTARY TO THE PREFACE.

I do not know who wrote these Prefaces∟;⌐ they are very mischievous & direct contrary to Wordsworths own Practise∟.⌐

[*Page 364*]

In nature every thing is distinct, yet nothing defined into absolute in-dependant singleness. In Macpherson's work it is exactly the reverse; every thing (that is not stolen) is in this manner *defined*, insulated, dislocated, deadened,—yet *nothing distinct*. . . . Now as the Translators of the Bible, Shakespeare, Milton, and Pope, could not be indebted to Macpherson, it follows that he must have owed his fine feathers to them . . . .

I Believe both Macpherson & Chatterton that what they say is Ancient Is so∟.⌐

[*Page 365*]

Yet, much as these pretended treasures of antiquity have been admired, they have been wholly uninfluential upon the literature of the Country. . . . no Author in the least distinguished, has ventured formally to imitate them —except the Boy, Chatterton, on their first appearance.

I own myself an Admirer of Ossian equally with any other Poet whatever∟,⌐ Rowley & Chatterton also∟.⌐

[*Page 375*]

Is it the result of the whole that, in the opinion of the Writer, the judg-ment of the People is not to be respected? The thought is most injurious; . . . to the People . . . his devout respect, his reverence, is due. . . . if he were not persuaded that the Contents of these Volumes, and the Work to which they are subsidiary, evinced something of the 'Vision and the Faculty divine,' . . . he would not, if a wish could do it, save them from immediate destruction . . . .

It appears to me as if the last Paragraph beginning with 'Is it the result' Was writ by another hand & mind from

> (For what delights the sense is false and weak)
> Ideal Form, the universal mould. . . .
> 'Tis sense, unbridled will, and not true love,
> Which kills the soul . . . .

(Wordsworth, *Poems* [1815], ii. 179.) Blake quotes the sonnet in Upcott's Autograph Album on 26 Jan. 1826 (p. 1322).

Page 365 'Rowley' is the supposed fifteenth-century author of Chatterton's poems.

the rest of these Prefaces₍ₗ.₎ Perhaps they arc the opinions of
S͏ʳ G Beaumont the Landscape Painter₍ₗ.₎ Imagination is
the Divine Vision not of The World nor of Man nor from
Man as he is a Natural Man but only as he is a Spiritual
Man₍ₗ.₎ Imagination has nothing to do with Memory₍ₗ.₎

Page 375   The only words Crabb Robinson did not ink over in Blake's notes were
two or three on p. 375 between 'opinions of' and 'Landscape Painter', which
apparently he could not read. Keynes (*The Complete Writings of William Blake*
[1957], p. 783) and Erdman (p. 655) read them unquestioningly as 'a Portrait of',
and I could not do better than to reject this reading. Professor George H. Healey,
Curator of the Cornell Rare Book Department, brilliantly deciphered them as
'S͏ʳ G Beaumont the'. Blake apparently mentioned Beaumont because he had
designed the frontispieces to these volumes.

The quotation marks are Blake's.

[*Title-page*]

I look upon this as a Most Malignant & Artful attack upon the Kingdom of Jesus By the Classical Learned thro the Instrumentality of Dr Thornton∟.⌋ The Greek & Roman Classics is the Antichrist∟.⌋ I say Is & not Are as most expressive & correct too∟.⌋

[*Title-page verso*]

DOCTOR JOHNSON on the Bible.

'The BIBLE is the *most difficult* book in the world *to comprehend*, nor can it be understood at all by the *unlearned*, except through the aid of CRITICAL and EXPLANATORY *notes*.'

Christ & his Apostles were Illiterate Men∟;⌋ Cai[*a*]phas∟,⌋ Pilate & Herod were Learned.

LORD BYRON on the Ethics of CHRIST.

'. . . What made SOCRATES *the greatest of men? His moral truths—his ethics.* What *proved* JESUS CHRIST to be the SON OF GOD, hardly less than *his miracles did? His moral precepts.*'

If Morality was Christianity Socrates was The Savior.[1]

The Beauty of the Bible is that the most Ignorant & Simple Minds Understand it Best— Was Johnson hired to Pretend to Religious Terrors while he was an Infidel or how was it∟?⌋

[*Page (1)*]

Such things as these depend on the Fashion of the Age∟:⌋

In a book where all may Read &	are Equally Right[2] &
In a book which all may read &	that Man who &^{c} is
In a book that all may Read	equally so∟,⌋
	The Man that & the Man which∟.⌋

[1] The same sentence is written in pencil in the middle of the page and also on the 'Laocoon' (p. 664).

[2] 'In a book that all may read' is what Blake wrote in the 'Introduction' to *Innocence* pl. 4 (p. 24).

THE LORD'S PRAYER

(Translated from the Greek,)

BY

DR. THORNTON.

Come let us *worship*, and *bow down*, and *kneel*, before the LORD, OUR MAKER. Psalm xcv.

ΠΑΤΕΡ ἡμῶν ὁ ἐν τοῖς ȣρανιος, ἁγιασθήτω—τὸ ονομα σȣ⌐·⌐ [1]

O FATHER OF MANKIND,

THOU, who dwellest in *the highest of the* HEAVENS, *Reverenc'd be* THY *Name!*

—ἐλθέτω η βασιλεια σȣ γενηθήτω το θέλημα σȣ⌐·⌐

May THY REIGN be, *every where, proclaim'd* so that THY *Will* may be *done* upon *the Earth,* as it is in the MANSIONS of Heaven: GRANT unto *me,* and *the whole world, day* by *day,* an abundant supply of *spiritual* and *corporeal* FOOD:

FORGIVE US OUR TRANSGRESSIONS against THEE, as WE extend OUR *Kindness,* and *Forgiveness,* TO ALL:

O GOD! ABANDON us *not,* when surrounded, by TRIALS; But PRESERVE us from *the Dominion* of SATAN: for THINE only, IS THE SOVEREIGNTY, THE POWER, and THE GLORY, throughout ETERNITY!!!

AMEN.

Men from their *childhood* have been so accustomed *to mouth* the LORD'S PRAYER, that they continue this *through life,* and call it '*Saying their Prayers.*'

It is the learned that Mouth & not the Vulgar⌐·⌐

Lawful Bread Bought with Lawful Money & a Lawful Heaven seen thro a Lawful Telescope by means of Lawful Window Light⌐·⌐ The Holy Ghost [*word del*][2] ⌄& whatever⌄ cannot be Taxed is Unlawful & Witchcraft.

Spirits are Lawful but not Ghosts⌐;⌐ especially Royal Gin is Lawful Spirit⌐·⌐ [real *del*] No Smuggling ⌄real⌄ British Spirit & Truth⌐!⌐

[*Page 2*]

Give us the Bread that is our due & Right by taking away Money or a Price or Tax upon what is Common to all in thy Kingdom⌐·⌐

[1] The Greek here and below is supplied by Blake.
[2] Erdman (p. 658) reads the deletion as 'who'.

[*Page 3*]

Jesus our Father who art in ˄thy˄ Heavns calld by thy
Name the Holy Ghost⌐,⌐ Thy Kingdom on Earth is Not
nor thy Will done but [his *del*]¹ ˄Satans˄ Will ˄who is˄
father & God of this World⌐,⌐ The Accuser. Let his Judg-
ment be Forgiveness that he may be coverd[?]² in his own
Shame[?]⌐·⌐
Give [*word del*] us This Eternal Day our [Ghostly(?) *del*]
˄own right˄ bread [to be(?) *del*.] take away Money or
debt or Tax ˄& Value or Price˄ as [. . . Satan *del*] have
˄all things˄ Common All(?) Things(?) common(?) among
us⌐·⌐ Every thing has as much right to Eternal Life as
God who is the Servant of Man⌐·⌐ The Accusation⌐,⌐ His
Judgment shall be Forgiveness that he may be consumd
in his own Shame⌐·⌐
Leave us not in Parsimony[?]³ [*word del*]⁴ ˄Satans King-
dom⌐;⌐ liberate˄ us from the Natural Man & [*words illeg*]⁵
Kingdom⌐·⌐ For thine is the Kingdom & the Power & the
Glory & not Caesars or Satans⌐·⌐ Amen

[*Page 5*]

Dim at best are the conceptions we have of the SUPREME BEING, who,
as it were, keeps the human race in suspense, neither discovering, nor
hiding HIMSELF . . . .

A Female God⌐!⌐

[*Page 6*]

What is the WILL of GOD *we* are ordered to obey? . . . Let us consider
whose WILL it is . . . . It is the WILL of our MAKER . . . . It is finally the
WILL of HIM, who is *uncontrollably powerful* . . . .

So you See That God is just such a Tyrant as Augustus
Caesar & is not this Good & Learned & Wise & Clas-
sical⌐?⌐

---

¹ Under '[his *del*]', Erdman (p. 658) reads 'Beelzebub'.
² For 'coverd', Erdman (p. 658) reads 'cons[*u*]md'.
³ The word I give as 'Parsimony' looks in fact like 'Persuasion'. Before it
Erdman (p. 658) reads hesitantly '[Poverty and Want *del*]'.
⁴ The deletion is read by Erdman (p. 658) as 'but deliver'.
⁵ The illegible words are read confidently by Erdman (p. 658) as 'want or Jobs'.

[*Page 9*]

REASONS FOR A NEW TRANSLATION OF THE WHOLE BIBLE.

The only thing for Newtonian & Baconian Philosophers to Consider is this_L:_J Whether Jesus did not suffer himself to be Mock'd by Caesars Soldiers Willingly & [I hope they will *del*] to Consider this to all Eternity will be comment Enough_L._J

[*Page 10*]

This is Saying the Lords Prayer Backwards which they say Raises the devil_L._J

Doctor Thorntons ˄Tory˄ Translation Translated out of its disguise in the ˄Classical &˄ Scotch language into [plain *del*] ˄the vulgar˄ English_L:_J
Our Father Augustus Caesar who art in this thy ˄Substantial Astronomical Telescopic˄ Heavens_L,_J[1] Holiness to thy Name ˄or Title & reverence to thy Shadow_L._J˄ Thy Kingship come upon Earth first & then in Heaven_L._J Give us day by day our Real Taxed ˄Substantial˄ Money bought Bread_L;_J [& take . . . have that(?) debt that was owing to him . . . *del*] ˄deliver[?] from the Holy Ghost [so we can pay(?) tax *del*][2] whatever cannot be Taxed ˄for all is debts & Taxes between Caesar & us & one another_L;_J˄ lead us not to read the Bible but let our Bible be Virgil & Shakspeare_L;_J & deliver us from Poverty in Jesus ˄that Evil[?] one˄ For thine is the Kingship ˄or Allegoric Godship˄ & the Power or War & the Glory or Law Ages after Ages in thy descendants ˄for God is only an Allegory of Kings & nothing Else_L._J˄

Amen

I swear that Basileia Βασιλεια is not Kingdom but Kingship_L._J I Nature Hermaphroditic Priest & King Live in Real Substantial Natural Born Man & that Spirit is the Ghost of Matter or Nature & God is The Ghost of

---

[1] There is a descender at the end of this word, which makes it look rather more like 'Harmony' or 'Heaving', but 'Heavens', which seems to be required by the sense, is also possible.

[2] For 'can pay tax', Erdman (p. 658) reads 'call Nature'.

the Priest & King who Exist whereas God exists not except from their[1] Effluvia⌊·⌋

Here is Signed Two Names which are too Holy to be Written⌊·⌋

Thus we see that the Real God is the Goddess Nature & that God Creates nothing but what can be Touchd & Weighed & Taxed & Measured⌊;⌋ all else is Heresy & Rebellion against Ceasiar⌊,⌋ Virgils Only God⌊;⌋ See Eclogue i⌊;⌋ for all this we Thank Dr Thornton⌊·⌋

[1] Under 'their', Erdman (p. 659) sees 'them'.

LETTERS

LETTERS

---

18 OCTOBER 1791

TO 'M̲ᵣ Blake Engraver / Hercules Buildings / Westminster Bridge' [*From Willey Reveley*¹]

M̲ᵣ Reveley's Compᵗˢ to Mᵣ Blake⌊:⌋ if he wishes to engrave any of Mʳ Pars's² drawings for the Antiquities of Athens, & can do them by the end of January Mʳ Reveley will be glad to [*send*] Some to him.

Great Titchfield St
Oct 18³

[OCTOBER? 1791]

TO [*Willey Reveley*]

Mʳ Blakes Compᵗˢ To Mʳ Reveley⌊;⌋ tho full of work [as Mʳ R̲ said he should be by then the plates were put in hand *del*] he is glad to embrace the offer of engraving such beautiful things, & will do what he can by the end of January⌊·⌋

18 Oct. 1791
¹ Willey Reveley (1760–99), architect, edited the third volume of James Stuart and Nicholas Revett's *Antiquities of Athens* (1794), for which Blake engraved three plates after Pars representing 'The . . . battle of the Centaurs and Lapithae'. George Cumberland's later note that he 'Got Blake to engrave for Athens' (*Blake Records*, 189) may indicate that he persuaded Reveley to give the commission to Blake.
² William Pars (1742–82), architectural painter, brother of Henry (1734–1806), whose drawing school Blake attended.
³ The probable year is established by the fact that Blake's plates for the *Antiquities of Athens* are dated 'April 3ᵈ 1792'. The commission was probably given in the preceding autumn. The date of the letter is in some doubt, however, for though Reveley clearly dated the letter 'Oct 18', the numeral in the postmark is equally clearly a '7'. I cannot reconcile these facts.

6 DECEMBER 1795

TO 'G Cumberland¹ Esq / Bishopsgate near Egham / Surrey'

Lambeth
6 Decembʳ 1795²

Dear Sir

[¶*1*] I congratulate you not on any atchievement, because I know that the Genius that produces the Designs can execute them in any manner, notwithstanding the pretended Philosophy which teaches that Execution is the power of One & Invention of Another—Locke says it i[s the] same faculty that Invents Judges, & I say he who can Invent can Execute.

[¶*2*] As to laying on the Wax it is as follows⌊:⌋

Take a cake of Virgins Wax (I dont know What animal produces it³) & stroke it regularly over the surface of a warm Plate (the Plate must be warm enough to melt the Wax as it passes over)⌊,⌋⁴ then immediately draw a feather over it & you will get an even surface which when cold will recieve any impression minutely⌊.⌋

[¶*3*] Note⌊:⌋ The danger is in not covering the Plate *All over*⌊.⌋

[¶*4*] Now You will I hope shew all the family of Antique Borers, that Peace & Plenty & Domestic Happiness is the Source of Sublime Art, & prove to the Abstract Philosophers, that Enjoyment & not Abstinence is the food of Intellect⌊.⌋⁵

Yours Sincerely
Will Blake

[¶*5*] Healt*h* to Mʳˢ Cumberland & family⌊.⌋

The pressure necessary to roll off the lines is the same as when you print, or not quite so great. I have not been able to send

6 Dec. 1795
¹ George Cumberland (1754–1845), painter, engraver, poet, dilettante, lifelong friend of Blake.
² The postmark indicates that the letter was posted between 8 p.m. on 9 Dec. and the evening of 10 Dec.
³ Cumberland called it 'common white wax' when he described the process in his 'Hints on various Modes of Printing from Autographs', *Journal of Natural Philosophy*, xxviii (Jan. 1811), 58.
⁴ This parenthesis is written over an illegible erasure.
⁵ 'Intellect' is written over an erased word which seems to begin with 'H' and end with 'y', perhaps 'Humanity'.

a proof of the bath[6] tho I have done the corrections, my paper not being in order ⌊.⌋

23 DECEMBER 1796

TO [*George Cumberland*] [*Evidently sent in a cover bearing the full address*]

Dear Cumberland

▌   I have lately had some pricks of conscience on account of not acknowledging your friendship to me [before *del*] immediately on the receit of your beautiful book.[1] I have likewise had by me all the Summer 6 Plates which you desired me to get made for you.[2] They have laid on my shelf, without speaking to tell me whose they were or that they were [there *del*] at all & it was some time (when I found them) before I could divine whence they came or whither they were bound or whether they were to lie there to eternity. I have now sent them to you to be transmuted, thou real Alchymist!

▌   Go on Go on. Such works as yours Nature & Providence the Eternal Parents demand from their children ⌊:⌋ how few produce them in such perfection ⌊;⌋ how Nature smiles on them ⌊;⌋ how Providence rewards them. How all your Brethren say, 'The sound of his harp & his flute heard from his secret forest chears us to the labours of life, & we plow & reap forgetting our labour ⌊.⌋'

▌]   Let us see you sometimes as well as sometimes hear from you & let us often See your Works ⌊.⌋

---

[6] Blake's engraving of Cumberland's design after 'Anacreon Ode LII' for Cumberland's *Thoughts on Outline* (1796), pl. 23.

23 Dec. 1796
[1] In Aug. George Cumberland had sent bound copies of his *Thoughts on Outline* (1796) to nineteen friends, including 'Mr Blake' (*Blake Records*, 55).
[2] These six plates have not been identified, but one may be connected with Richard Cosway's suggestion of 27 Dec. 1795 that Cumberland should 'get Blake to make an engraving' of Cumberland's beautiful 'Picture of [*i.e.*, *by*] Leonardo' (*Blake Records*, 49). More probably they were just blank copperplates which Cumberland had asked Blake to buy for him.

Compliments to Mrs Cumberland & Family⌊·⌋

Yours in head & heart

Lambeth   Will Blake

    23 Decemb^r 1796

a Merry Christmas

16 AUGUST 1799

TO [*Dr Trusler*]

To The Revd Dr Trusler[1]

Rev^d: Sir

[¶*1*]   I find more & more that my Style of Designing is a Species by itself & in this which I send you have been compelld by my Genius or Angel to follow where he led⌊;⌋ if I were to act otherwise it would not fulfill the purpose for which alone I liv*e*, which is in conjunction with such men as my friend Cumberland to renew the lost Art of the Greeks⌊·⌋

[¶*2*]   I attempted every morning for a fortnight together to follow your Dictat*e*, but when I found my attempts were in vai*n*, resolvd to shew an independence which I know will please an Author better than slavishly following the track of another however admirable that track may be⌊·⌋ At any rate my Excuse must be: I could not do otherwise, it was out of my power!

[¶*3*]   I know I begged of you to give me your Ideas & promised to build on them⌊;⌋ here I counted without my host⌊·⌋ I now find my mistake⌊·⌋

[¶*4*]   The Design I have Sen*t*, Is

A Father taking leave of his Wife & Chil*d*, Is watchd by Two Fiends incarnat*e*, with intention that when his back is turned they will murder the mother & her infant. If this is not Malevolence[2] with a vengeance I have never seen it on Ear*th*, & If you approve of this I have no doubt of giving you Benevolence with Equal Vigo*r*, as also Pride & Humility, but cannot previously describe in words what I mean to Design for fear I

16 Aug. 1799

     [1] Dr. John Trusler (1735–1820), author of *Hogarth Moralized* and *The Way to be Rich and Respectable*.

     [2] Blake's 'Malevolence' is reproduced in *Blake Records*.

should Evaporate the Spirit of my Invention. But I hope that none of my Designs will be destitute of Infinite Particulars which will present themselves to the Contemplator. And tho I call them Mine I know that they are not Mine being of the same opinion with Milton when he says That the Muse visits his Slumbers & awakes & governs his Song when Morn purples the East,[3] & being also in the predicament of that prophet who says I cannot go beyond the command of the Lord to speak good or bad⌊.⌋[4]

5]   If you approve of my Manner & it is agreeable to you, I would rather Paint Pictures in oil of the same dimensions than make Drawings, & on the same terms. By this means you will have a number of Cabinet pictures, which I flatter myself will not be unworthy of a Scholar of Rembrandt & Teniers, whom I have Studied no less than Rafael & Michael angelo. Please to send me your orders respecting this & In my next Effort I promise more Expedition⌊.⌋

I am Revd Sir
Your very humble Servt
Hercules Build^gs   Willm Blake
Lambeth
Aug^st 16. 1799

23 AUGUST 1799

TO 'Revd Dr Trusler / Englefield Green / Egham / Surrey'[1]

Revd Sir

1]   I really am sorry that you are falln out with the Spiritual

[3] *Paradise Lost*, VII. 29–30. According to the anonymous review of Blake's *Grave* designs in *The Monthly Magazine* (xxvi [1808], 458), 'The author of these designs is an engraver of no mean talents in his art, and is said to receive the conceptions of them from "Visions bright," which, like the Muse of Milton—
       "Visits his slumbers nightly, or when morn
       Purples the East." '

[4] Numbers 24: 13: 'If Balak would give me his house full of silver and gold, I cannot go beyond the commandment of the Lord, to do either good or bad of mine own mind; but what the Lord saith, that will I speak?'

23 Aug. 1799
    [1] The address is endorsed in Cumberland's hand: 'Blake / Dimd with Superstition'.

World Especially if I should have to answer for it∟·⌐ I feel very sorry that your Ideas & Mine on Moral Painting differ so much as to have made you angry with my method of Study. If I am wrong I am wrong in good company. I had hoped your plan comprehended All Species of this Art & Especially that you would not reject that Species which gives Existence to Every other, namely Visions of Eternity∟·⌐ You say that I want somebody to Elucidate my Ideas, But you ought to know that What is Grand is necessarily obscure to Weak men. That which can be made Explicit to the Idiot is not worth my care. The wisest of the Ancients considerd what is not too Explicit as the fittest for Instruction because it rouzes the faculties to act∟·⌐ I name Moses Solomon Esop Homer Plato∟·⌐

[¶2]   But as you have favord me with your remarks on my Design permit me in return to defend it against a mistaken one, which is, That I have supposed Malevolence without a Cause. Is not Merit in one a Cause of Envy in another & Serenity & Happiness & Beauty a Cause of Malevolence? But Want of Money & the Distross of A Thief can never be alledged as the Cause of his Thieving, for many honest people endure greater hard ships with Fortitude∟·⌐ We must therefore seek the Cause else where than in want of Money for that is the Misers passion, not the Thiefs∟·⌐

[¶3]   I have therefore proved your Reasonings Ill proportioned which you can never prove my figures to be; they are those of Michael Angelo∟,⌐ Rafael & the Antique & of the best living Models. I percieve that your Eye is perverted by Caricature Prints, which ought not to abound so much as they do. Fun I love but too much Fun is of all things the most loathsom. Mirth is better than Fun & Happiness is better than Mirth. I feel that a Man may be happy in This World. And I know that This World Is a World of Imagination & Vision∟·⌐ I see Every thing I paint In This World, but Every body does not see alike. To the Eyes of a Miser a Guinea is more beautiful than the Sun & a bag worn with the use of Money has more beautiful proportions than a Vine filled with Grapes. The tree which moves some to tears of joy is in the Eyes of others only a Green thing that stands in the way. Some See Nature all Ridicule & Deformity & by these I shall not regulate my proportion*s*, & Some Scarce see Nature at all⌊.⌋ But to the Eyes of the Man of Imagination Nature is Imagination itself⌊.⌋ As a man is So he Sees. As the Eye is formed such are its Powers⌊.⌋ You certainly Mistake when you say that the Visions of Fancy are not to be found in This World. To Me This World is all One continued Vision of Fancy or Imagination & I feel Flatterd when I am told So. What is it Sets Homer⌊,⌋ Virgil & Milton in so high a rank of Ar*t*? Why is the Bible more Entertaining & Instructive than any other boo*k*? Is it not because they are addressed to the Imagination which is Spiritual Sensation & but mediately to the Understanding or Reason⌊?⌋ Such is True Painting and such was alone valued by the Greeks & the best modern Artists. Consider what Lord Bacon says⌊:⌋ 'Sense sends over to Imagination before Reason have judged & Reason sends over to Imagination before the Decree can be acted'.[2] See Advancem^t of Learning Part 2 P 47 of first Edition⌊.⌋

◄] But I am happy to find a Great Majority of Fellow Mortals who can Elucidate My Visions & Particularly they have been Elucidated by Children who have taken a greater delight in contemplating my Pictures than I even hoped. Neither Youth nor Childhood is Folly or Incapacity⌊.⌋ Some Children are Fools & so are Some Old Men. But There is a vast Majority on the Side of Imagination or Spiritual Sensation⌊.⌋

5] To Engrave after another Painter is infinitely more laborious than to Engrave ones own Inventions. And of the Size you require my price has been Thirty Guineas & I cannot afford to do it for less. I had Twelve for the Head I sent you as a Specime*n*, but after my own designs I could do at least Six times the quantity of labour in the same time which will account for the difference of price as also that Chalk Engraving is at least Six times as laborious as Aqua tinta. I have no objection to Engraving after another Artist. Engraving is the profession I was apprenticed t*o*, & Should never have attempted to live by any thing else If orders had not come in for my Designs & Paintings which I have the pleasure to tell you are Increasing Every Day. Thus If I am a Painter it is not to be

---

[2] The quotation marks are Blake's.

attributed to Seeking after. But I am contented whether I live by Painting or Engraving⌊·⌋

    I am Revd Sir Your very obedient Servant

13 Hercules Buildings   William Blake
   Lambeth
     August 23. 1799

26 AUGUST 1799

TO 'Mr Cumberland / Bishopsgate / Windsor Great Park'

Dear Cumberland

[¶*1*]   I ought long ago to have written to you to thank you for your kind recommendation to Dr Trusler which tho it has faild of success is not the less to be rememberd by me with Gratitude⌊·⌋

[¶*2*]   I have made him a Drawing in my best manner⌊;⌋ he sent it back with a Letter full of Criticisms[1] in which he says It accords not with his Intentions which are to Reject all Fancy from his Work. How far he Expects to please I cannot tell. But as I cannot paint Dirty rags & old Shoes where I ought to place Naked Beauty or Simple ornamen*t*, I despair of Ever pleasing one Class of Men. Unfortunately our authors of books are among this Class⌊;⌋ how soon we Shall have a change for the better I cannot Prophecy. Dr Trusler says '*Your Fancy* from what I have seen of *it*, & I have seen variety at Mr Cumberlands seems to be in the other world or the World of Spirit*s*, which accords not with my Intention*s*, which whilst living in This World Wish to follow *the Nature of it*⌊·⌋'[2] I could not help Smiling at the difference between the doctrines of Dr Trusler & those of Christ. But however for his own sake I am sorry that a Man should be so enamourd of Rowlandsons caricatures as to call them copies from life & manners or fit Things for a Clergyman to write upon⌊·⌋

---

26 Aug. 1799
    [1] Trusler was a neighbour of Cumberland's in Egham, Surrey.
    [2] The quotation marks are Blake's.

3]   Pray let me intreat you to persevere in your Disigning⌐;⌐
it is the only source of Pleasure⌐.⌐ All your other pleasures
depend upon It. It is the Tree⌐,⌐ your Pleasures are the Fruit.
Your Inventions of Intellectual Visions are the Stamina of
every thing you value. Go on⌐,⌐ if not for your own sake yet for
ours who love & admire your works, but above all For the
Sake of the Arts. Do not throw aside for any long time the
honour intended you by Nature to revive the Greek workman-
ship. I study your outlines³ as usual just as if they were antiques.
4]   As to Myself about whom you are so kindly Interested, I
live by Miracle. I am Painting small Pictures from the Bible⌐.⌐
For as to Engraving in which art I cannot reproach myself
with any neglect yet I am laid by in a corner as if I did not
Exist & Since my Youngs Night Thoughts⁴ have been pub-
lishd Even Johnson⁵ & Fuseli⁶ have discarded my Graver.
But as I know that He who Works & has his health cannot
starve, I laugh at Fortune & Go on & on. I think I foresee
better Things than I have ever seen. My Work pleases my
employer & I have an order for Fifty small Pictures at One
Guinea each⁷ which is Something better than mere copying

³ Probably Cumberland's *Thoughts on Outline* (1796).

⁴ Blake's 43 designs for Edward Young's *The Complaint and The Consolation:
or, Night Thoughts* (1797), published by Richard Edwards.

⁵ Joseph Johnson (1738–1809), radical bookseller, regularly employed Blake's
graver from 1780 to 1798, but thereafter the only plates Blake signed for Johnson
were made for his particular friends Henry Fuseli and William Hayley.

⁶ Henry Fuseli (1741–1825), christened Johann Heinrich Füssli in Zürich, was
a splenetic painter of Gothic subjects who seems to have been one of Blake's most
respected friends. Blake had been commissioned to engrave several of Fuseli's
paintings of Miltonic subjects for an edition of Milton to be edited by William
Cowper and published by Joseph Johnson (*Blake Records*, 44, 46–7), but the project
was abandoned because of the apathy of the public and the madness of Cowper.

⁷ The order was evidently from Thomas Butts (1757–1845), clerk, Blake's most
generous patron. By Sept. 1800, when he went to Felpham, Blake had apparently
completed 29 drawings, for he took orders for 21 to Felpham. These included
'The Three Maries' (begun by 20 Oct. 1800, sent 16 Aug. 1803), 'Two Pictures'
sent 22 Nov. 1802, and 'the remaining . . . Eighteen' referred to on 22 Nov. 1802.
Seven of the 18 (including 'The Three Maries') are named on 6 July 1803 and
sent on 16 Aug. 1803. Ten of the 11 unnamed 'Drawings' are listed in Blake's
account with Butts dated 12 May 1805: (1) 'Moses Striking the Rock'; (2) 'Ezekiel's
Wheels'; (3) 'Christ Girding Himself with Strength'; (4) 'The Four and Twenty
Elders'; (5) 'Christ Baptizing' (touched up 12 Dec. 1805); (6) 'Samson Breaking
Bonds'; (7) 'Samson Subdued'; (8) 'Noah and the Rainbow'; (9) 'The Wise and
Foolish Virgins'; (10) 'Hell Beneath Is Moved for Thee' (*Blake Records*, 570–8).
The accounts with Blake suggest that Blake was paid in advance.

after another artist. But above all I feel myself happy & contented let what will come_L;_J having passed now near twenty years in ups & downs I am used to them & perhaps a little practise in them may turn out to benefit. It is now Exactly Twenty years since I was upon the ocean of business[8] & Tho I laugh at Fortune I am perswaded that She Alone is the Governor of Worldly Riche*s*, & when it is Fit She will call on me_L;_J till then I wait with Patience in hopes that She is busied among my Friends.

With Mine & My Wifes best compliments to Mrs Cumberland I remain

Yours Sincerely

Hercules Buildings   Willm Blake
   Lambeth
Augst 26. 1799

18 FEBRUARY 1800

TO [*William Hayley*][1] [*Paraphrase*]

Blake's engravings for Hayley's *Essay on Sculpture* (1800) were 'the occasion of Blake's first coming into direct personal communication with Hayley, to whom he submitted an impression of the plate of *The Death of Demosthenes*, which "has been approved", he writes, February 18th, 1800, "by Mr. Flaxman;"[2] adding his hopes that the young sculptor[3] "will soon be well enough to make hundreds of designs both for the engraver and the sculptor." '

---

[8] Blake was free of his apprenticeship to James Basire in Aug. 1779.

18 Feb. 1800

   [1] William Hayley (1745–1820), poet and patron.

   [2] John Flaxman (1756–1826), sculptor, Blake's intimate friend.

   [3] Hayley's beloved illegitimate son, Thomas Alphonso Hayley (1780–1800), who was dying of a spinal disease. Blake had probably known him at least since 1796, when he was informally apprenticed to Flaxman (*Blake Records*, 51).

1 APRIL 1800

TO 'William Hayley Esqre / Eartham near Chichester / Sussex.'

Dear Sir,

']   With all possible expedition I send you a proof of my attempt to express your & our Much Beloveds Countenance.[1]

']   Mr Flaxman has seen it & approved of my now sending it to you for your remarks. Your sorrows & your dear Sons May Jesus & his Angels assuage & if it is consistent with his divine providence restore him to us & to his labours of Art & Science in this World.

So prays a fellow sufferer
& Your humble servant
Willm Blake

1 April 1800
Hercules Buildings Lambeth

17 APRIL 1800

'To Mr Blake, Engraver / Hercules Buildings / Lambeth / London' [*From William Hayley*]

Thursday April 17 1800

My Dear Blake,

']   You are very good to take such pains to produce a Resemblance of our dear disabled artist—you have improved yr first plate a little, & I believe with a little more alteration it may be more like than the second outline.

1 April 1800
   [1] For some weeks before Blake's letter was written Hayley had been anxiously hoping that 'the dear departing angel [*his son Thomas*] will see his own engraved portrait [*after Flaxman for Hayley's* ESSAY ON SCULPTURE (*1800*)] arrive before his own departure'. When Blake's proof sent with this letter of 1 April arrived, Hayley was mortified to find that it 'exhibits a heavy sullen sulky Head which I can never present to the public Eye as the Image of a Being so tenderly & so justly beloved. I believe I must have a fresh outline & a mere outline instead of it' (*Blake Records*, 63–4).

[¶2]   The great & radical defect I conceive to be this—the engraving is a Head 3 years older than the medallion—the Features by being made *longer* & *more sedate* have lost the *lively juvenility* of *16*—our dear Flaxman's medallion is *very faithful* to that *time of Life*, & certainly *like* tho I cannot say I ever thought it a *very very strong* similitude of the *Individual*.

[¶3]   Truth, precision, & Force of character is that exquisite & subtle essence of art, which is so apt to escape from the finest & ablest Hand in the formation of Portraits, of whatever materials they are formed.

[¶4]   Romney, who was so marvellously happy in *several*, yet has failed egregiously in *many*; & so, I apprehend, has *every* modern artist from the Revival of the Art to the present Hour—perhaps we should think so also of the antients if we saw all their portraits & the originals, altho yr great Connoisseurs presume to say, These said antients were far superior to the moderns in siezing this subtle Truth of Character, particularly in their Gems & Medals.

[¶5]   But to speak of still farther alterations in yr first plate— would it not give a little younger appearance to shorten the space between the nose & the upper lip a little more by representing the mouth rather more open, in the act of speaking which appears to me the Expression of the medallion? I submit the point to you & our dear Flaxman with *proper deference* to yr *superior judgment*; as I do the following Question whether the making the Dot at the corner of the mouth a little deeper, & adding a darker Touch also at the Bottom of the Eye would add a little gay juvenility to the Features without producing (what I by all means wish to avoid) a *Grin* or a *Smirk*—In short I wish the character of the engraving to *harmonise* a *little more*, than *it does at present*, with the following verses towards the conclusion of the Poem, which as *you* are a *kind-hearted Brother of Parnassus*, you will forgive my inserting in this letter to *explain my meaning to you*—

'That youth of fairest Promise, fair as May,
Pensively tender, and benignly gay,
On thy Medallion still retains a Form
In Health exulting, & with pleasure warm.

Teach Thou my Hand, with mutual love, to trace   [5]
His Mind, as perfect, as thy Lines his Face!
For Nature in that Mind' &c[1]   [7]

You will have the goodness not to shew these verses to any one, except to our dear Flaxman, who will, I know, kindly assist you in yr endeavours to catch the exact cast of character, that I wish you to seize— I have to thank Heaven (as I do with my whole Heart) for having been able to *gratify this dear departing angel* with a sight of his *own Portrait united* to the *completion* of a *long, & severely interrupted work*; which *He* most tenderly pressed me to *complete* & which nothing I believe but *his wishes* could have enabled my wounded spirit to pursue under the Heart-rending affliction of seeing a child so justly beloved *perishing by slow Tortures*. His Life may probably not last many days—accept our united Benedictions & believe me dear Blake

your very sincere Friend
W. H.

6 MAY 1800

TO 'William Hayley Esq[re] / Eartham near Chichester / Sussex'

Dear Sir

    I am very sorry for your immense loss,[1] which is a repetition of what all feel in this valley of misery & happiness mixed. I send the Shadow of the departed Ange*l*; hope the likeness is improve*d*; the lip I have again lessened as you advised & done a good many other softenings to the whole—I know that our deceased friends are more really with us than when they were apparent to our mortal part. Thirteen years ago I lost a brother[2] & with his spirit I converse daily & hourly in the Spirit &

17 April 1800
    [1] These lines appear unchanged in Hayley's *Essay on Sculpture* (1800), 160, ll. 97–103. The quotation marks are Hayley's.
6 May 1800
    [1] Thomas Hayley died on 2 May.
    [2] Blake's favourite brother Robert died in Feb. 1787.

See him in my remembrance in the regions of my Imagination.
I hear his advice & even now write from his Dictate. Forgive
me for Expressing to you my Enthusiasm which I wish all to
partake of Since it is to me a Source of Immortal Joy ⌊;⌋ even
in this world by it I am the companion of Angels. May you
continue to be so more & more & to be more & more per-
swade*d*, that every Mortal loss is an Immortal Gain. The
Ruins of Time builds Mansions in Eternity.—I have also sent
A Proof of Pericles[3] for your Remarks thanking you for the
Kindness with which you Express them & feeling heartily your
Grief with a brothers Sympathy
I remain Dear Sir Your humble Servant
Lambeth May 6. 1800. William Blake

2 JULY 1800

TO 'Mr Cumberland / Bishopsgate / Windsor Great Park'

Dear Cumberland

[¶*1*]   I have to congratulate you on your plan for a National
Gallery being put into Execution.[1] All your wishes shall in due
time be fulfilled ⌊;⌋ the immense flood of Grecian light & glory
which is coming on Europe will more than realize our warmest
wishes. Your honours will be unbounded when your plan shall
be carried into Execution as it must be if England continues
a Nation ⌊.⌋ I hear that it is now in the hands of Ministers ⌊,⌋
That the King shews it great Countenance & Encouragement ⌊,⌋
that it will soon be [f *del*] before Parliament & that it *must*
be extended & enlarged to take in originals both of Painting
& Sculpture by considering every valuable original that is
brought into England or can be purchasd Abroad as its objects

---

[3] Blake's unsigned engraving of 'Pericles' for Hayley's *Essay on Sculpture* (1800).

2 July 1800

[1] Cumberland's 'Plan for Improving the Arts in England' (in his *Some Anecdotes
of the Life of Julio Bonasoni* [1793]) called for '*two galleries*' filled with '*plaister casts*',
'one for statues and architectural models, and one for bas-reliefs' (pp. 14, 15),
but it was never carried out. The nucleus of the present National Gallery,
with dimensions more like those Blake describes, was acquired in 1824 from the
J. J. Angerstein collection.

of Acquisition. Such is the Plan as I am told & such must be the plan if England wishes to continue at all worth notice as you have yourself observd⌊,⌋ only now we must possess Originals as well as France or be Nothing⌊.⌋

2] Excuse I intreat you my not returning Thanks at the proper moment for your kind present.[2] No perswasion could make my stupid head believe, that it was proper for me to trouble you with a letter of meer Compliment & Expression of thanks. I begin to Emerge from a deep pit of Melancholy, Melancholy without any real reason for it, a Disease which God keep you from & all good men. Our artists of all ranks praise your outlines & wish for more⌊.⌋ Flaxman is very warm in your commendation & more & more of A Grecian. Mr Hayley has lately mentiond your Work on outline in Notes to [Epistles on Sculpture del] an Essay on Sculpture in Six Epistles to John Flaxman, I have been too little among friends which I fear they will not Excuse & I know not how to apologize for. Poor Fuseli sore from the lash of Envious tongues praises you & dispraises with the same breath⌊;⌋ he is not naturally good natured but he is artificially very ill natured yet even from him I learn the Estimation you are held in among artists & connoisseurs.

3]   I am still Employd in making Designs & little Pictures with now & then an Engraving & find that in future to live will not be so difficult as it has been⌊.⌋ It is very Extraordinary that London in so few years from a City of meer Necessaries or at l[e]ast a commerce of the lowest order of luxuries should have become a City of Elegance in some degree & that its once stupid inhabitants should enter into an Emulation of Grecian manners. There are now I believe as many Booksellers as there are Butchers & as many Printshops as of any other trade⌊.⌋ We remember when a Print shop was a rare bird in London,[3] & I myself remember When I thought my pursuits of Art a Kind of Criminal dissipation & neglect of the main chance which I hid my face for not being able to abandon as a Passion which is forbidden by Law & Religion but now it appears to be Law

---

[2] Perhaps the gift was Cumberland's most recent publication, *The Captive of the Castle of Senaar*, an African Tale (1798).
[3] Blake and James Parker (1750–1805), Blake's fellow apprentice under James Basire, had opened a short-lived print-shop in 1784.

& Gospel to*o*; at least I hear so from the few friends I have dared to visit in my stupid Melancholy. Excuse this communication of sentiments which I felt necessary to my repose at this time. I feel very strongly that I neglect my duty to my Friends but It is not want of Gratitude or Friendship but perhaps an Excess of both⌊.⌋ Let me hear of your welfare. Remember My & My Wifes Respectful Compliments to Mrs Cumberland & Family

                                        & believe me to be for Ever
                                                          Yours
13 Hercules Buildings   William Blake
   Lambeth
   2 July 1800

---

12 SEPTEMBER 1800[1]

TO 'Mr Flaxman / Buckingham Street / Fitzroy Square'

My Dearest Friend
    It is to you I owe All my present Happiness⌊.⌋ It is to you I owe perhaps the Principal Happiness of my life. I have presumed on your friendship in staying so long away & not calling to know of your welfare but hope, now every thing is nearly completed for our removal to Felpham⌊,⌋[2] that I shall see you on Sunday as we have appointed Sunday afternoon to [ca]ll on Mrs Flaxman at Hampstead.[3] I send you a few lines which I hope you will Excuse. And As the time is arrivd when Men shall again converse in Heaven & walk with Angels I know you will be pleased with the Intention & hope you will forgive the Poetry⌊.⌋

12 Sept. 1800
    [1] The letter may be dated from the date-stamp of receipt, 12 Sept. 1800, 2.00 p.m.
    [2] In July 1800 Blake had gone for a short time to Felpham, in order, as Hayley wrote on the 22nd, to take 'a cottage in this little marine village to pursue his art in its various Branches under my auspices' (*Blake Records*, 71).
    [3] Flaxman's house was in Buckingham Street, Fitzroy Square; I don't know why Blake was calling 'on Mrs Flaxman at Hampstead'.

To My Dearest Friend John Flaxman
these lines_L:_J

I bless thee O Father of Heaven & Earth that ever I saw
Flaxmans face_L._J

Angels stand round my Spirit in Heaven, the blessed of Heaven
are my friends upon Earth_L._J

When Flaxman was taken to Italy,[4] Fuseli was giv'n to me for
a season

And now Flaxman hath given me Hayley his friend to be
mine. Such my lot upon Earth_L._J

Now my lot in the Heavens is this; Milton lovd me in childhood
& shewd me his face_L;_J   [5]

Ezra came with Isaiah the Prophet, but Shakespeare in riper
years gave me his hand_L;_J

Paracelsus & Behmen appeard to me, terrors appear'd in the
Heavens above

And in Hell beneath & a mighty & awful change threatend the
Ear[th.]

The American War began_L._J All its dark horrors passd before
my face

Across the Atlantic to France. Then the French Revolution
commencd in thick clouds   [10]

And My Angels have told me that Seeing such visions I could
not Subsist on the Earth

But by my conjunction with Flaxman who knows to forgive
Nervous Fear_L._J   [12]

I remain for Ever Yours
William Blake

Be so kind as to Read & then Seal the Inclosed & Send it on
its much beloved Mission_L._J

14 SEPTEMBER 1800

TO 'Mrs Flaxman'

My Dearest Friend
I hope you will not think we could forget your Services to us,

---

[4] Flaxman was in Italy from 1787 to 1794.

or any way neglect to love & remember with affection even the hem of your garment. *W*e indeed presume on your kindness in neglecting to have calld on you since my Husbands first return from Felpham. We have been incessantly busy in our great removal but can never think of going without first paying our proper duty to you & Mr Flaxman. We intend to call on Sunday afternoon in Hampstea*d*, to take farewell_⌊,⌋ All things being now nearly completed for our setting forth on Tuesday Morning. *I*t is only Sixty Miles & [London *del*] Lambeth was One Hundred for the terrible disart of London was between_⌊.⌋ *M*y husband has been obliged to finish several things necessary to be finishd before our migration_⌊.⌋ *T*he Swallows call us fleeting past our window at this moment. O how we delight in talking of the pleasure we shall have in preparing you a Summer bower at Felpha*m*, & we not only talk but behold the Angels of our journey have inspired a Song to you_⌊:⌋

To my dear Friend Mrs Anna Flaxman

This Song to the flower of Flaxmans joy_⌊,⌋[1]
To the blossom of hope for a sweet decoy_⌊;⌋
Do all that you can or all that you may
To entice him to Felpham & far away_⌊.⌋

Away to Sweet Felpham for Heaven is there_⌊;⌋
The Ladder of Angels descends thro the air_⌊;⌋
On the Turret[2] its spiral does softly descend_⌊,⌋
Thro the village then winds_⌊,⌋ at My Cot is [*i.e. it*] does end_⌊.⌋

You stand in the Village & look up to heaven_⌊;⌋
The precious stones glitter on flights Seventy Seven
And My Brother[3] is there & My Friend & Thine
Descend & ascend with the Bread & the Wine_⌊.⌋

14 Sept. 1800
  [1] Blake described Nancy as 'A little Flower' again in the poem with his Gray designs (1797) (p. 1331).
  [2] Hayley referred to his house as 'The Turret' and himself as the 'Hermit' (see, e.g., *Blake Records*, 70).
  [3] Evidently Blake's favourite brother Robert who died in 1787.

The Bread of sweet Thought & the Wine of Delight
Feeds the Village of Felpham by day & by night
And at his own door the blessd Hermit[2] does stand   [*15*]
Dispensing Unceasing to all the whole Land⌊·⌋   [*16*]

W Blake

Recieve my & my husband*s* love & affection & believe me
    to be Yours affectionately

*H B. Lambeth   Catherine Blake[4]
14 Septr 1800

*[*In another hand:*] Hercules Buildings, Lambeth

16 SEPTEMBER 1800

TO 'William Hayley Esqre / [Eartham near Chichester *del*] at
Miss Pooles^I Lavant / near Chichester / Sussex'

Leader of My Angels
    My Dear & too careful & over joyous Woman has Exhausted
her strength to such a degree with expectation & gladness
added to labour in our removal that I fear it will be Thursday
before we can get away from this ―― City⌊·⌋ I shall not be
able to avail myself of the assistance of Brunos fairie*s*,[2] But I
Invoke the Good Genii that Surround Miss Pooles Villa to
shine upon my journey thro the Petworth road which by your
fortunate advice I mean to take but whether I come on Wednes-
day or Thursday That Day shall be marked on my calendar
with a Star of the first magnitude⌊·⌋
    Eartham[3] will be my first temple & altar⌊·⌋ My wife is like
a flame of many colours of precious jewels whenever she hears

---

[4] Though signed by Catherine, the letter is written in Blake's hand.
16 Sept. 1800
    [1] Harriet Poole (d. 1827) is frequently referred to in Hayley's correspondence
as Lady Paulina and The Lady of Lavant. Hayley went regularly to her house on
the London–Chichester road to get his mail more quickly.
    [2] This may be a reference to the horse Blake seems to have ridden in Felpham;
see the note to 27 April 1804.
    [3] Hayley had been living at Eartham, but he soon moved to the Turret house
in Felpham which he had built for his son.

it named₍ₗ.₎ Excuse my haste & recieve my hearty Love & Respect₍ₗ.₎

H B Lambeth
Sept 16. 1800

I am dear Sir
Your Sincere
William Blake

My fingers Emit sparks of fire with Expectation of my future labours₍ₗ.₎

21 SEPTEMBER 1800

TO 'Mᵣ Flaxman / Buckingham Street / Fitzroy Square / London'

Dear Sculptor of Eternity

[¶1]   We are safe arrived in our Cottage which is more beautiful than I thought it, & more convenient. It is a perfect Model for Cottages & I think for Palaces of Magnificence₍ₗ,₎ only Enlarging not altering its proportions & adding ornaments & not principals. Nothing can be more Grand than its Simplicity & Usefulness. Simple without Intricacy it seems to be the Spontaneous Effusion of Humanity congenial to the wants of Man. No other formed House can ever please me so well nor shall I ever be perswaded I believe that it can be improved either in Beauty or Use.

[¶2]   Mᵣ Hayley recievd us with his usual brotherly affection, I have begun to work₍ₗ.₎ Felpham is a sweet place for Study, because it is more Spiritual than London₍ₗ.₎ Heaven opens here on all sides her golden Gates₍ₗ;₎ her windows are not obstructed by vapours. Voices of Celestial inhabitants are more distinctly heard & their forms more distinctly seen & my Cottage is also a Shadow of their houses. My Wife & Sister[1] are both well, courting Neptune for an Embrace₍ₗ.₎

[¶3]   Our Journey was very pleasant & tho we had a great deal of Luggage No Grumbling₍ₗ;₎ All was Chearfulness & Good Humour on the Road & yet we could not arrive at our Cottage before half past Eleven at Night, owing to the necessary shifting of our Luggage from one Chaise to another₍ₗ;₎ for we had Seven Different Chaises & as many different drivers₍ₗ.₎ We sat out

21 Sept. 1800
    [1] Catherine Blake (b. 1764, died after 1833).

between Six & Seven in the Morning of Thursday, with Sixteen heavy boxes & portfolios full of prints. And Now Begins a New life, because another covering of Earth is shaken off. I am more famed in Heaven for my works than I could well concieve₎.₎ In my Brain are studies & Chambers filld with books & pictures of old which I wrote & painted in ages of Eternity, before my mortal life & those works are the delight & Study of Archangels. Why then should I be anxious about the riches or fame of mortality? The Lord our father will do for us & with us according to his Divine will for our Good₎.₎

⁴] You O Dear Flaxman are a Sublime Archangel My Friend & Companion from Eternity₎;₎ in the Divine bosom is our Dwelling place₎.₎ I look back into the regions of Reminiscence & behold our ancient days before this Earth appeard in its vegetated mortality to my mortal vegetated Eyes. I see our houses of Eternity which can never be separated tho our Mortal vehicles should stand at the remotest corners of heaven from each other₎.₎

⁵] Farewell My Best Friend₎.₎ Remember Me & My Wife in Love & Friendship to our Dear Mʳˢ Flaxman whom we ardently desire to Entertain beneath our thatched roof of rusted gold₎,₎ & believe me for ever to remain

Your Grateful & Affectionate

William Blake

Felpham
Septʳ 21.. 1800
Sunday Morning

22 SEPTEMBER 1800¹

TO 'Mʳ Butts / G! Marlborough Street near / Oxford Street / London'²

Dear Friend of My Angels

ᵇ] We are safe arrived at our Cottage without accident or

22 Sept. 1800
¹ Since the letter was postmarked on its receipt in the London Post Office 'SEP 23 / 1800', and since letters posted in Chichester arrived in London the next day, this letter must have been posted on 22 Sept. Presumably it was written on the day it was posted.
² This letter is docketed, presumably by Butts: 'Mʳ Blake / His Account / & / Correspondence'.

hindrance tho it was between Eleven & Twelve O Clock at night before we could get home, owing to the necessary shifting of our boxes & portfolios from one Chaise to another. We had Seven different Chaises & as many different drivers. All upon the road was chearfulness & welcome ; tho our luggage was very heavy there was no grumbling at all. We traveld thro a most beautiful country on a most glorious day. Our Cottage is more beautiful than I thought it & also more convenient, for tho Small it is well proportiond & if I should ever build a Palace it would be only My Cottage Enlarged. Please to tell Mrs Butts that we have dedicated a Chamber [to h]er Service & that it has a very fine view of the Sea. Mr Hayley recievd me with his usual brotherly affection. My Wife & Sister are both very well & courting Neptune for an Embrace, whose terrors this morning made them afraid but whose mildness is often Equal to his terrors . The Villagers of Felpham are not meer Rustics ; they are polite & modest. Meat is cheaper than in London but the sweet air & the voices of winds trees & birds & the odours of the happy ground makes it a dwelling for immortals. Work will go on here with God speed— A roller & two harrows lie before my window. I met a plow on my first going out at my gate the first morning after my arrival & the Plowboy said to the Plowman: 'Father The Gate is Open'[3]— I have begun to Work & find that I can work with greater pleasure than ever. Hope soon to give you a proof that Felpham is propitious to the Arts.

[¶2]   God bless you. I shall wish for you on tuesday Evening as usual. Pray give My & My wife & sisters love & respects to Mrs Butts; accept them yourself & believe me for ever

Your affectionate & obliged Friend
William Blake

My Sister will be in town in a week & bring with her your account & whatever else I can finish. Direct to Me

Blake: Felpham near Chichester,
Sussex

[3] The quotation marks are Blake's.

[SEPTEMBER 1800][1]

TO [*William Blake from Thomas Butts*] [*Rough draft*]

Marlborough Street

Dear Sir

▌]   I cannot immediately determine whether or no I am dignified by the Title you have graciously conferred on me—you cannot but recollect the difficulties that have unceasingly arisen to prevent my discerning clearly whether your Angels are black white or grey and that on the whole I have rather inclined to the former opinion and considered you more immediately under the protection of the black-guard⌊;⌋ however at any rate I should thank you for an introduction to his Highness⌈'⌉s Court, that when refused admittance into other Mansions I may not be received as a stranger in His⌊.⌋

▌]   I am well pleased with your pleasures feeling no small interest in your Happiness and it cannot fail to be highly gratifying to me and my affectionate Partner to know that a Corner of your Mansion of Peace is asylumd to Her & when invalided & rendered unfit for service who shall say she may not be quarterd on your Cot.—But for the present she is for active Duty and satisfied with requesting that if there is a Snug Berth unoccupied in any Chamber of your warm Heart, that her Portrait may be [suspended *del*] there, at the same time well aware that you like me prefer the Original to the Copy— Your good Wife will permit & I hope may benefit from the Embraces of Neptune but she will presently distinguish betwixt the warmth of his Embraces & yours, & court the former with caution⌊.⌋[2] I suppose you do not admit of a third in that concern or I would offer her mine even at this distance⌊.⌋ Allow me before I draw a Veil over this interesting Subject to lament the

---

[Sept. 1800]

[1] The letter must have been written between the receipt of Blake's letter of 22 Sept., to which it refers, and the writing of Blake's letter of 2 Oct., which alludes to it. The draft begins in a beautiful, clerkly hand, and degenerates, through many deletions which I have ignored, to hasty pencil at the end ('From purest Fountains sip delight') later darkened in ink.

[2] An earlier draft of this sentence read: 'but they [*the Embraces of Neptune*] must be courted with far more caution than yours . . . recollecting that what may be taken by all must be prejudicial to some'.

frailty of the fairest Sex for who alass! of us my good Friend
could have thought that

> So Virtuous a Woman would ever have fled,
> From Hercules' Buildings to Neptunes Bed⌐?⌐³   [⁴

[¶3]   Whether you will be a better Painter or a better Poet from
your changes of ways & means I know not; but this I predict;
that you will be a better Man— *E*xcuse me, as you have been
accustomed from friendship to do, but certain opinions im-
bibed from [indulgence *del*] reading, [rivitted *del*] nourishd
by indulgence, and rivitted by a confined Conversation, and
which have been equally prejudicial to your Interest & Happi-
ness, will [gradually *del*] now I trust, disperse as a Day-break
Vapour, and you will henceforth become a Member of that
Community of which you are at present, in the opinion of the
Archbishop of Canterbury,⁴ but a Sign to mark the residence
of dim incredulity, haggard suspicion, & bloated philosophy—
*W*hatever can be effected by sterling [good *del*] Sense⌐,⌐ by
opinions which harmonize [with *del*] society & beautify cre-
ation, will, in future be exemplified in you & the time I trust
is not distant and that because I truly regard you when you
will be a more valorous Champion of Revelation & Humilia-
tion than any of those who now wield the Sword of the Spirit⌐;⌐
with your natural & acquired Powers nothing is wanting but
a proper direction of them & altho the way is both straight &
narrow I know you too well to fear your want of resolution to
persevere & to pursue it— *Y*ou have the Plough & the Harrow
in full view & the Gate you have been prophetically told is
Open⌐;⌐ can you then hesitate joyfully to enter into it⌐?⌐

[¶4]   I have much to congratulate you on—Meat cheap, Music
for nothing⌐,⌐ a command of the Sea and brotherly affection
fluttering [at your Window *del*] around ye— The Arts have
promised to be propitious and the Graces will courtesy to your
wishes—

---

³ This couplet was first expressed as prose: 'that so [good *del*] virtuous a Woman
would ever have [bartered *del*] exchanged the Buildings of Hercules for the Bed of
Neptune?'

⁴ 'in the opinion of the Archbishop of Canterbury' was added as an afterthought
and therefore scarcely implies that John Moore (Archbishop of Canterbury 1783–
1805) spoke directly about Blake.

Happy, happy, happy Pair,[5]
On Earth, in Sea, or eke in air,
In morn, at noon, & [een all *del*] thro' the Night
From Visions fair receiving light
Long may ye live your Guardians Care,   [5]
And when ye die may not a Hair
Fall to the lot of Demons black⌊,⌋
Be singed by Fire or heard to crack
But may your [friendly *del*] faithful Spirit[s *del*] upward bear
Your gentle Souls to him whose care   [10]
Is ever sure and ever nigh
Those who on Providence rely
And in his Paradise above
Where all is Beauty Truth & Love
O May ye be allowed to chuse   [15]
For your firm Friend [the fairest *del*] a Heaven born Muse⌊,⌋
From purest Fountains sip delight⌊,⌋
Be cloathed in Glory burning bright,
For ever blest for ever free⌊,⌋
The [fairest *del*] loveliest Blossoms on Lifes Tree⌊.⌋   [20]

I have no more Nonsense for you just now but must assure
you that I shall always sincerely devote myself to your service
when my humble endeavours may be useful— Mrs Butts greets
your Wife & charming Sister with a holy Kiss and I with old
Neptune bestow my Embraces there also— *F*or yourself I com-
mend you to the protection of your Guard & am
                              Dear Sir
                                 yours mest Cordially
                                    & faithfully
                                       [*Thomas Butts*]

                    2 OCTOBER 1800

TO 'Mr Butts / Great Marlborough Street'

Friend of Religion & Order
   I thank you for your very beautiful & encouraging Verses
which I account a Crown of Laurels & I also thank you for

---

[5] This line appears in Dryden's 'Alexander's Feast', which was frequently
sung at music festivals.

your reprehension of follies by me fosterd. Your prediction will I hope be fulfilled in me, & in future I am the determined advocate of Religion & Humility the two bands of Society. Having been so full of the Business of Settling the sticks & feathers of my nest, I have not got any forwarder with 'the three Marys'[1] or with any other of your commissions but hope, now I have commenced a new life of industry to do credit to that new life by Improved Works. Recieve from me a return of verses such as Felpham produces by me tho not such as she produces by her Eldest Son.[2] However such as they are, I cannot resist the temptation to send them to you⌊.⌋

To my Friend Butts I write
My first Vision of Light
On the yellow sands sitting⌊.⌋
The Sun was Emitting
His Glorious beams   [5]
From Heavens high Streams⌊.⌋
Over Sea over Land
My Eyes did Expand
Into regions of air
Away from all Care⌊,⌋   [10]
Into regions of fire
Remote from Desire⌊;⌋
The Light of the Morning
Heavens Mountains adorn-
  ing⌊.⌋
In particles bright   [15]
The jewels of Light
Distinct shone & clear—
Amazd & in fear
I each particle gazed
Astonishd Amazed   [20]
For each was a Man
Human formd. Swift I ran⌊,⌋
For they beckond to me

Remote by the Sea
Saying: 'Each grain of
  Sand   [25]
Every Stone on the Land
Each rock & each hill
Each fountain & rill
Each herb & each tree
Mountain hill Earth &
  Sea   [30]
Cloud Meteor & Star
Are Men Seen Afar⌊.⌋'
I stood in the Streams
Of Heavens bright beams
And Saw Felpham sweet   [35]
Beneath my bright feet
In soft Female charms
And in her fair arms
My Shadow I knew
And my wifes shadow too   [40]
And My Sister & Friend⌊.⌋
We like Infants descend
In our Shadows on Earth
Like a weak mortal birth⌊.⌋
My Eyes more & more   [45]

2 Oct. 1800
[1] For the commission and delivery of this drawing, see 26 Aug. 1799.
[2] William Hayley.

Like a Sea without shore
Continue Expanding⌐,⌐
The Heavens commanding⌐,⌐
Till the Jewels of Light⌐,⌐
Heavenly Men beaming
   bright⌐,⌐   [50]
Appeard as One Man
Who Complacent began
My limbs to infold
In his beams of bright gold⌐,⌐
Like dross purgd away   [55]
All my mire & my clay⌐.⌐
Soft consumd in delight
In his bosom Sun bright
I remaind. Soft he smild,
And I heard his voice
   Mild   [60]
Saying 'This is My Fold
O thou Ram hornd with gold

Who awakest from Sleep
On the Sides of the Deep⌐.⌐
On the Mountains around [65]
The roarings resound
Of the lion & wolf⌐,⌐
The loud Sea & deep gulf⌐.⌐
These are guards of My
   Fold⌐,⌐
O thou Ram hornd with
   gold⌐.⌐'   [70]
And the voice faded mild⌐.⌐
I remain'd as a Child⌐.⌐
All I ever had known
Before me bright Shone⌐.⌐
I saw you & your wife   [75]
By the fountains of life⌐.⌐
Such the Vision to me
Appeard on the Sea⌐.⌐   [78]

Mrs Butts will I hope Excuse my not having finishd the Portrait.[3] I wait for less hurried moments. Our Cottage looks more & more beautiful. And tho the weather is wet, the Air is very Mil*d*, much Milder than it was in London when we came away. Chichester is a very handsom[e] City Seven miles from us⌐;⌐ we can get most Conveniences there. *T*he Country is not so destitute of accomodations to our wants as I expected it would be⌐.⌐ We have had but little time for viewing the Country but what we have seen is Most Beautiful & the People are Genuine Saxons⌐,⌐ handsomer than the people about London. Mrs Butts will Excuse the following lines⌐:⌐

To Mrs Butts

Wife of the Friend of those I most rever*e*,
Recieve this tribute from a Harp sincere⌐.⌐
Go on in Virtuous Seed sowing on Mold
Of Human Vegetation & Behold

[3] Blake's miniature of Thomas Butts.

1547

Your Harvest Springing to Eternal life ⌊5

Parent of Youthful Minds & happy Wife⌊!⌋ ⌊6

W B—

I am for Ever Yours

Felpham   William Blake

Octͬ 2ᵈ 1800

26 NOVEMBER 1800

TO [*William Hayley*]

Dear Sir,

[¶*1*]   Absorbed by the poets Milton, Homer, Camoens, Ercilla, Ariosto, and Spenser, whose physiognomies have been my delightful study,[1] *Little Tom*[2] has been of late unattended to, and my wife's illness not being quite gone off she has not printed any more since you went to London. But we can muster a few in colours and some in black which I hope will be no less favour'd tho' they are rough like rough sailors. We mean to begin printing again to-morrow. Time flies very fast and very merrily. I sometimes try to be miserable that I may do more work, but find it is a foolish experiment. Happinesses have wings and wheels; miseries are leaden legged and their whole employment is to clip the wings and to take off the wheels of our chariots. We determine, therefore, to be happy and do all that we can, tho' not all that we would. Our dear friend Flaxman is the theme of my emulation in this of industry, as well as in other virtues and merits. Gladly I hear of his full health and spirits. Happy son of the Immortal Phidias, his

---

26 Nov. 1800

    [1] Blake's heads for Hayley's Library consisted of: (1) Cowper, (2) Spenser, (3) Chaucer (originally Cowley), (4) Cicero, (5) Voltaire, (6) Shakespeare, (7) Dryden, (8) Milton (originally Sappho), (9) Tasso, (10) Camoens, (11) Anacreon (once altered to Ercilla), (12) Pope, (13) Otway (originally Euripides), (14) Dante (originally Ariosto), (15) Demosthenes, (16) Homer, (17) Klopstock (originally Livy or Horace), (18) Thomas Alphonso Hayley (originally Gibbon) (see *Blake Records*, 69). Blake does not seem to have finished the heads of Ercilla or Ariosto.

    [2] Hayley's broadsheet poem, *Little Tom the Sailor*, engraved with two designs by Blake and published 5 Oct. 1800 'by the Widow Spicer of Folkstone for the Benefit of her Orphans'.

lot is truly glorious, and mine no less happy in his friendship and in that of his friends. Our cottage is surrounded by the same guardians you left with us; they keep off every wind. We hear the west howl at a distance, the south bounds on high over our thatch, and smiling on our cottage says, 'You lay too low for my anger to injure.'[3] As to the east and north I believe they cannot get past the turret.

[2]   My wife joins with me in duty and affection to you. Please to remember us both in love to Mr. and Mrs. Flaxman, and

Believe me to be your affectionate,
Enthusiastic, hope-fostered visionary,
William Blake.

Felpham, 26*th November*, 1800

[AUTUMN 1800?]

TO [*Thomas Butts*][1]

I have sent all the sketches of this subject that I ever have produced. The others of the Presentation I have studied, but not yet put on paper. You shall have that in a shorter time than I have taken about this, as I have nearly got rid of engraving, and feel myself perfectly happy. I am full of business thank God, and you and Mr. Flaxman.[2]

---

[3] The quotation marks appear in Gilchrist's transcript.

[Autumn 1800?]
  [1] The unidentified recipient for whom Blake was preparing 'The Presentation [*of Christ in the Temple*]' was probably Thomas Butts, for Butts owned 'Simeon and the Infant Jesus', which is apparently the same as 'The Presentation' (see Luke 2: 25–38) and which he sold at Foster's, 29 June 1853, lot 129 (it is now in the Fogg Art Museum).
  [2] Keynes (ed. *Letters* [1968], 49–50) prints this letter from an anonymous Sotheby catalogue of '3 December 1888 (lot 13)'. This source is apparently an error, for the only Sotheby catalogue of that date known to me (that of Robert Samuel Turner of 23 Nov. 1888 and thirteen following days) contains no Blake MSS. The only other first-hand information about this letter is the following paraphrase from the Sotheby catalogue of H. V. Morten, 5 May 1890, lot 22: 'Sending all the sketches he has ever produced, has studied "The Presentation," but not yet put it on paper, is full of business, and feels perfectly happy, thanks to his correspondents [*sic*] and Mr. Flaxman.'

10 MAY 1801

TO [*Thomas Butts*]

My Dear Sir

[¶*1*]　The necessary application to my Duty as well to my old as new Friends has prevented me from that respect I owe in particular to you. And your accustomed forgiveness of my want of dexterity in certain points Emboldens me to hope that Forgiveness to be continud to me a little long*er*, When I shall be Enabled to throw off all obstructions to Success⌊.⌋

[¶*2*]　Mr Hayley acts like a Prince. I am at complete Eas*e*, but I wish to do my duty especially to you who were the precursor of my present Fortune⌊.⌋ I never will send you a picture unworthy of my present proficiency. I soon shall send you several⌊;⌋ my present engagements are in Miniature Painting⌊.⌋ Miniature is become a Goddess in my Eyes & my Friends in Sussex say that I Excell in the pursuit.[1] I have a great many orders & they Multiply⌊.⌋

[¶*3*]　Now—let me intreat you to give me orders to furnish every accomodation in my power to recieve you & Mrs Butts⌊.⌋ I know my Cottage is too narrow for your Ease & comfort⌊;⌋ we have one room in which we could make a bed to lodge you both & if this is sufficient it is at your servic*e*, but as beds & rooms & accomodations are easily procurd by one on the spot permit me to offer my service in either way either in my cottage or in a lod[*g*]ing in the village as is most agreeable to you if you & Mrs Butts should think Bognor a pleasant relief from business in the Summer. It will give me the utmost delight to do my best⌊.⌋

[¶*4*]　Sussex is certainly a happy place & Felpham in particular is the sweetest spot on Earth⌊,⌋ at least it is so to me & My Good Wife who desires her kindest Love to Mrs Butts & yourself⌊;⌋ accept mine also & believe me to remain

Your devoted

Felpham　　　　　　　　　　　　　　　　Will Blake
May 10. 1801

10 May 1801
　　1 On 13 May 1801 Hayley wrote to David Parker Coke: 'I have recently formed a new artist for this purpose [*the enclosed miniature of Mrs. Hayley*] by teaching a worthy creature (by profession an Engraver) who lives in a little Cottage very near me to paint in miniature' (*Blake Records*, 80).

31 JULY 1801

TO 'William Hayley Esqʳᵉ / Felfham / near Chichester / Sussex'¹ [*From John Flaxman*]

My Dear Blake

I heartily rejoice in Your happiness & I wish you every increase of it for which thanks are due to Divine Providence— The Revᵈ Joseph Thomas of Epsom² desires You will at Your leisure, make a few Sketches of the Same Size, which may be any Size you please from Milton's Comus³ for Five Guineas, he also desires You will make two designs in bister or Indian Ink, from Shakespeare's Troylus & Cressida, Coriolanus, either of the 3 plays of Henry 6ᵗʰ, Richard the 3ᵈ or Henry the 8ᵗʰ, each design for one play for which he will give a Guinea each, the dimensions as follows⌊:⌋ the paper an upright Square of 12 Inches & half by 8 Inches, within this Space leaving a moderate margin, the principal figure not exceeding 6 Inches high⁴— both Mʳˢ Flaxman & myself should delight in Seeing & partaking your Cottage delight*s*,⁵ but I am bound to my sculpture & cannot make my rocks travel with me— however we are happy that You are happy, & are pleased with the reciprocal affection of the Bards, with kindest wishes to Mʳˢ B & Yourself I also remain Your affectionate

J Flaxman

31 July 1801

¹ Flaxman's letter to Hayley concludes: 'I must add a Postscript to our Worthy Blake containing a little commission'.

² The Revd. Joseph Thomas (d. 1811), Rector of Epsom, called on Blake in Felpham, according to Blake's letter of 19 Oct. 1801. In 1805 Nancy Flaxman understood that Thomas 'wishes to collect all B—— has done' (*Blake Records*, 166).

³ Blake's six designs to *Comus* measure *c.* 17·8 × 21·6 cm. They are reproduced in C. H. C. Baker, *Catalogue of William Blake's Drawings and Paintings in the Huntington Library*, rev. R. R. Wark (1957). A smaller duplicate set is in the Boston Museum of Fine Art.

⁴ The strict dimensions were dictated by the fact that the designs were to be among the illustrations (eventually 37) for a second folio Shakespeare (1632) (now in the British Museum Print Room). Blake's illustrations are for *Richard III* (n.d.), *Julius Caesar* (1806), *Hamlet* (1806), *As You Like It* (1806), *Henry VIII* (1809), and 'The Horse of Intellect' (1809) (a copy of the fresco in the *Descriptive Catalogue* [1809] ¶88–9). They are reproduced in W. M. Merchant, 'Blake's Shakespeare', *Apollo*, lxxix (1964), 318–25.

⁵ Blake's invitation is in his letter of 21 Sept. 1800.

11 SEPTEMBER 1801

TO 'Mʳ Butts / Great Marlborough Street / London'

My Dear Sir

[¶*1*]   I hope you will continue to excuse my want of steady perseverance by which want I am still so much your debtor & you so much my Credit-er but such as I can be I will: I can be grateful & I can soon Send you some of your designs which I have nearly completed. In the mean time by my Sisters hands I transmit to Mʳˢ Butts an attempt [to *del*] at your likeness¹ which I hope She who is the best judge will think like⌊·⌋ Time flies faster, (as seems to me), here than in London⌊·⌋ I labour incessantly & accomplish not one half of what I intend because my Abstract folly hurries me often away while I am at work, carrying me over Mountains & Valleys which are not Real in a Land of Abstraction where Spectres of the Dead wander. This I endeavour to prevent & with my whole might chain my feet to the world of Duty & Reality, but in vain! the faster I bind the better is the Ballast for I so far from being bound down take the world with me in my flights & often it seems lighter than a ball of wool rolled by the wind⌊·⌋ Bacon & Newton would prescribe ways of making the world heavier to me & Pitt would prescribe distress for a medicinal potio*n*, but as none on Earth can give me Mental Distress, & I know that all Distress inflicted by Heaven is a Merc*y*, a Fig for all Corporeal⌊!⌋ Such Distress is My mock & scorn. Alas wretched happy ineffectual labourer of times moments that I am! who shall deliver me from this Spirit of Abstraction & Improvidenc*e*? Such my Dear Sir Is the truth of my state & I tell it you in palliation of my seeming neglect of your most pleasant order*s*,² but I have not neglected them & yet a Year is rolled over & only nhw I approach the prospect of sending you some which you may expect soon. I should have sent them by My Sister but as the Coach goes three times a week to London & they [shall *del*] will arrive as safe as with he*r*, I shall have an opportunity of inclosing several together which are not yet

11 Sept. 1801
¹ Blake's miniature of Butts; see 2 Oct. 1800.
² For the nature of this commission, see 26 Aug. 1799.

completed. I thank you again & again for your generous forbearance of which I have need—& now I must express my wishes to see you at Felpham & to shew you Mr Hayleys Library which is still unfinishd but is in a finishing way & looks well. I ought also to mention my Extreme disappointment at Mr Johnsons[3] forgetfulness, who appointed to call on you but did Not. He is also a happy Abstract known by all his Friends as the most innocent forgetter of his own Interests. He is nephew to the late Mr Cowper the Poet ; you would like him much. I continue painting Miniatures & Improve more & more as all my friends tell me, but my Principal labour at this time is Engraving Plates for Cowpers Life, [4] a Work of Magnitude which Mr Hayley is now Labouring with all his matchless industry & which will be a most valuable acquisition to Literature not only on account of Mr Hayleys composition but also as it will contain Letters of Cowper to his Friends, Perhaps or rather Certainly the very best letters that ever were published.

My wife joins with me in Love to you & Mrs Butts hoping that her joy is now increased & yours also in an increase of family & of health & happiness.

I remain Dear Sir
Ever Yours Sincerely
William Blake

Felpham Cottage
of Cottages the prettiest
September 11. 1801

Next time I have the happiness to see you I am determined to paint another Portrait of you from Life in my best manner, for Memory will not do in such minute operations, for I have now discoverd that without Nature before the painters Eye he can never produce any thing in the walks of Natural Painting. Historical Designing is one thing & Portrait Painting another & they are as Distinct as any two Arts can be. Happy would that Man be who could unite them !

---

[3] John Johnson (d. 1833), Cowper's loyal 'Johnny of Norfolk', was a friend of Hayley and an occasional visitor at Felpham.

[4] Hayley's *Life, and Posthumous Writings, of William Cowper, Esq.* (1803, 1804), 3 vols.

[¶4]   P.S. Please to Remember our best respects to Mr Birch^5 & tell him that Felpham Men are the mildest of the human race⌊;⌋ if it is the will of Providence they shall be the wisest⌊.⌋ We hope that he will next Summer joke us face to face—God bless you all⌊!⌋

7 OCTOBER 1801

TO 'William Hayley Esqre / Felfham / near Chichester / Sussex'^1 [*from John Flaxman*]

Dear Blake

I rejoice in Your happiness & contentment under the kind & affectionate auspices of our Friend, Mrs Flaxman & myself would feel no small gratification in a visit of participation in the domestic Innocence & satisfaction of your rural retreat; but the same Providence that has given retirement to You, has placed me in a great City where my employments continually exact an attention neither to be remitted or delayed, & thus the All besto[wing] Hand deals out happiness to his creatures when they are sensible of His Goodness; the little commissions I troubled you with in my last are such as one friend offers unwillingly to another on account of the Scanty recompence, but I know you relieve yourself from more tedious labours by Composition & Design, when they are done let me have them & I will take care to get the money for you, My Wife unites in love to you & Mrs Blak*e*,

with your affectionate
J Flaxman

---

⁵ John Birch (1745?–1815), surgeon and enthusiast for the use of electricity in medicine.

7 Oct. 1801
¹ The letter to Blake is on the back of a letter to Hayley given in *Blake Records*, 82–3.

19 OCTOBER 1801

'TO / Mr Flaxman Sculptor / Buckingham Street / Fitzroy Square / London'[1]

Dear Flaxman

]   I rejoice to hear that your Great Work is accomplishd. Peace[2] opens the way to greater still⌞.⌟ The Kingdoms of this World are now become the Kingdoms of God & his Christ & we shall reign with him for ever & ever.[3] The Reign of Literature & the Arts commences⌞.⌟ Blessed are those who are found studious of Literature & Humane & polite accomplishments. Such have their lamps burning & such shall shine as the stars⌞.⌟

]   Mr Thomas your friend to whom you was so kind as to make honourable mention of me—has been at Felpham & did me the favor to call on me. I have promisd him to send my Designs for Comus[4] when I have done them directed to you⌞.⌟

]   Now I hope to see the Great Works of Art, as they are so near to Felpham⌞,⌟ Paris being scarce further off than London. But I hope that France & England will henceforth be as One Country and their Arts One & that you will Er'e long be erecting Monuments In Paris Emblems of Peace⌞.⌟

    My Wife joins with me in love to You & Mrs Flaxman⌞.⌟ I remain Yours Sincerely

William Blake

Oct 19 1801

---

19 Oct. 1801

[1] Blake's letter is written on a blank leaf of Hayley's letter to Flaxman given in *Blake Records*, 84–5.

[2] '*Downing-street, Oct* 10. The RATIFICATION of the Preliminary Articles of Peace between his Majesty and the French Republick, signed on the Ist instant, were this day exchanged by the Right Hon. Lord Hawkesbury, one of his Majesty's principal Secretaries of State, and M. Otto' (*Gentleman's Magazine*, lxxii [Oct. 1801], 944). The proclamation of peace by George R. is given under 13 Oct., with the terms, which included the issuance of travel passes as soon as possible.

[3] Cf. Revelation 11: 15: 'And the seventh angel sounded; and there were great voices in heaven, saying, The Kingdoms of this world are become the Kingdoms of our Lord, and of his Christ; and he shall reign for ever and ever.'

[4] The commission was given in Flaxman's letter to Blake of 31 July 1801.

10 JANUARY 1802

TO 'Mr Butts / Great Marlborough Street / Oxford Street / London'

Felpham Jany 10. 1802

Dear Sir

[¶*1*]   Your very kind & affectionate Letter & the many kind things you have said in it; calld upon me for an immediate answe*r*, but it found My Wife & Myself so Ill & My wife so very ill that till now I have not been able to do this duty. The Ague & Rheumatism have been almost her constant Enemies which she has combated in vain ever since we have been here, & her sickness is always my sorrow of course⌊.⌋ But what you tell me about your sight afflicted me not a little, & that about your health in another part of your letter makes me intreat you to take due care of both⌊;⌋ it is a part of our duty to God & man to take due care of his Gifts & tho we ought not [*to*] think *more* highly of ourselves, yet we ought to think *As* highly of ourselves as immortals ought to think⌊.⌋

[¶*2*]   When I came down here I was more sanguine than I am at present but it was because I was ignorant of many things which have since occurred & chiefly the unhealthiness of the place⌊.⌋ Yet I do not repent of coming, on a thousand accounts, & M^r H I doubt not will do ultimately all that both he & I wish⌊,⌋ that is to lift me out of difficul*ty*, but this is no easy matter to a man who having Spiritual Enemies of such formidable magnitude cannot expect to want natural hidden ones⌊.⌋

[¶*3*]   Your approbation of my pictures is a Multitude to Me & I doubt not that all your kind wishes in my behalf shall in due time be fulfilled. Your kind offer of pecuniary assistance I can only thank you for at present because I have enough to serve my present purpose here. *O*ur expenses are small & our income from our incessant labour fully adequate to [it *del*] them at present. I am now engaged in Engraving 6 small plates for a New Edition of Mr Hayleys Triumphs of Tempe*r*, from drawings by Maria Flaxman[1] sister to my friend the Sculptor and it seems that other things will follow in course if I do but

10 Jan. 1802
   [1] *The Triumphs of Temper*: A Poem: In Six Cantos. The Twelfth Edition, Corrected. With New Original Designs, by Maria Flaxman (1803).

Copy these well.[2] *But* Patience! if Great things do not turn out it is because such things depend on the Spiritual & not on the Natural World & if it was fit for me I doubt not that I should be Employd in Greater things & when it is proper my Talents shall be properly exercised in Public as I hope they are now in private. *F*or till then I leave no stone unturnd & no path unexplord that tends to improvement in my beloved Arts. One thing of real consequence I have accomplishd by coming into the countr*y*, which is to me consolation enough, namel*y*, I have recollected all my scatterd thoughts on Art & resumed my primitive & original ways of Execution in both painting & engravin*g*, which in the confusion of London I had very much lost & obliterated from my mind. But whatever becomes of my labours I would rather that they should be preservd in your Green House (not as you mistakenly call it dung hill) than in the cold gallery of fashion.—The Sun may yet shine & then they will be brought into open air⌊.⌋

4] But you have so generously & openly desired that I will divide my griefs with you that I cannot hide what it is now become my duty to explain— My unhappiness has arisen from a source which if explord too narrowly might hurt my pecuniary circumstance*s*. As my dependence is on Engraving at present & particularly on the Engravings I have in hand for M*r* H. & I find on all hands great objections to my doing any thing but the meer drudgery of business & intimations that if I do not confine myself to this I shall not live. *T*his has always pursud me. You will understand by this the source of all my uneasiness⌊.⌋ This from Johnson & Fuseli brought me down here & this from M*r* H will bring me back again for that I cannot live without doing my duty to lay up treasures in heaven is Certain & Determined & to this I have long made up my mind & why this should be made an objection to Me while Drunkenness Lewdness Gluttony & even Idleness itself does not hurt other men, let Satan himself Explain. The Thing I have most at Heart! more than life or all that seems to make life comfortable withou*t*, Is the Interest of True Religion & Science & whenever any thing appears to affect that Interes*t* (Especially if I myself

---

² Hayley wrote on 7 Aug. 1803 to Flaxman: 'I am sorry to say that the Ladies (& it is a Ladys Book) find Fault with the Engravings' (*Blake Records*, 121).

omit any duty to my [self *del*] Station as a Soldier of Christ)
It gives me the greatest of torments, I am not ashamed afraid
or averse to tell You what Ought to be Told₍ᶫ,₎ That I am
under the direction of Messengers from Heaven Daily &
Nightly₍ᶫ,₎ but the nature of such things is not as some suppos*e*,
without trouble or care. Temptations are on the right hand &
left₍ᶫ;₎ behind the sea of time & space roars & follows swiftly₍ᶫ;₎
he who keeps not right onward is lost & if our footsteps slide
in clay how can we do otherwise than fear & trembl*e*? but I
should not have troubled You with this account of my spiritual
state unless it had been necessary in explaining the actual
cause of my uneasiness into which you are so kind as to En-
quire₍ᶫ,₎ for I never obtrude such things on others unless ques-
tiond & then I never disguise the truth— But if we fear to
do the dictates of our Angels & tremble at the Tasks set before
u*s*, if we refuse to do Spiritual Act*s*, because of Natural Fears
or Natural Desires! Who can describe the dismal torments of
such a state!—I too well remember the Threats I heard!—
'If you who are organized by Divine Providence for Spiritual
communio*n*, Refuse & bury your Talent in the Earth even tho
you Should want Natural Brea*d*, Sorrow & Desperation pur-
sues you thro life! & after death shame & confusion of face to
eternity— Every one in Eternity will leave you₍ᶫ,₎ aghast at
the Man who was crownd with glory & honour by his brethren
& betrayd their cause to their enemies. You will be calld
the base Judas who betrayd his Friend!'—Such words would
make any Stout man tremble & how then could I be at ease?
But I am now no longer in That State & now go on again with
my Task Fearless and tho my path is difficult. I have no fear
of stumbling while I keep it₍ᶫ.₎

[¶5]   My wife desires her kindest Love to Mʳˢ Butts & I have per-
mitted her to send it to you also. *W*e often wish that we could
unite again in Society & hope that the time is not distant when
we shall do *so*, being determind not to remain another winter
here but to return to London₍ᶫ.₎

I hear a voice you cannot hear that says I must not stay
I see a hand you cannot see that beckons me away₍ᶫ.₎³

³ From Thomas Tickell's 'Lucy and Colin', perhaps quoted from Blake's copy
of Percy's *Reliques of Ancient English Poetry* (1765).

Naked we came here⌞,⌟ naked of Natural things & naked we shall retur*n*,[4] but while clothd with the Divine Mercy we are richly clothd in Spiritual & suffer all the rest gladly⌞.⌟ Pray give my Love to Mʳˢ Butts & your family⌞.⌟ I am Yours Sincerely

William Blake

⁵] P.S. Your Obliging proposal of Exhibiting my two Pictures likewise calls for my thanks⌞.⌟ I will finish the other & then we shall judge of the matter with certainty⌞.⌟

[1802?]

TO [*Thomas Butts?*] [*Paraphrase*]¹

It was when he was one day thus secluded in the dim vaulted solitude of Westminster Abbey² that he saw, as he afterwards records, one of his visions. The aisles and galleries of the old cathedral³ suddenly filled with a great procession of monks and priests, choristers and censer-bearers, and his entranced ear heard the chant of plain-song and chorale, while the vaulted roof trembled to the sound of organ music.

22 NOVEMBER 1802

TO 'Mʳ Butts / Gt Marlborough Street'¹

Felpham Novʳ 22: 1802

Dear Sir

ʹ] My Brother tells me that he fears you are offended with me.

----

⁴ Cf. Job 1:21: 'Naked came I out of my mother's womb, and naked shall I return thither'.

[1802?]

¹ The only known reference to this letter is in [Oswald Crawfurd] 'William Blake: Artist, Poet, and Mystic', *New Quarterly Magazine*, ii (1874), 475: 'An account of this and of several of Blake's earlier visions is given in a letter addressed apparently to Mr. Butts, which was purchased, with others, at a sale in 1861 by a friend of the present writer.'

² The period referred to is towards the end of his apprenticeship to Basire (1772–9). ·   ³ Westminster Abbey is not a 'cathedral'.

22 Nov. 1802

¹ The missing cover in which this letter was enclosed evidently also contained: (2) the continuation of the letter; (3) 'Two Pictures' (called 'two little pictures' in

I fear so too because there appears some reason why you might be so. But when you have heard me out you will not be so⌞.⌟

[¶2]   I have now given two years to the intense study of those parts of the art which relate to light & shade & colour & am Convincd that either my understanding is incapable of comprehending the beauties of Colouring or the Pictures which I painted for You Are Equal in Every part of the Art & superior in One to any thing that has been done since the age of Rafael.— All Sʳ J Reynolds's discourses to the Royal Academy will shew, that the Venetian finesse in Art can never be united with the Majesty of Colouring necessary to Historical beauty, & in a letter to the Revᵈ Mʳ Gilpin author of a work on Picturesque Scenery² he says Thus⌞:⌟ '"It may be worth consideration" "whether the epithet Picturesque is not applicable to the" "excellencies of the inferior Schools rather than to the higher." "The works of Michael Angelo Rafael &ᶜ appears to me to have" "nothing of it: whereas Rubens & the Venetian Painters may" "almost be said to have Nothing Else.—Perhaps Picturesque" "is somewhat synonymous to the word Taste which we should" "think improperly applied to Homer or Milton but very well" "to Prior or Pope. I suspect that the application of these words" "are to Excellencies of an inferior order & which are incom-" "patible with the Grand Style⌞.⌟ You are certainly right in" "saying that variety of Tints & Forms is Picturesque: but it" "must be rememberd on the other hand that the reverse of" "this—('*uniformity of Colour* & a *long continuation of lines*') pro-" "duces Grandeur⌞.⌟"—S[o] Says Sⁱʳ Joshua and So say I for I have now proved that the parts of th[e] art which I neglected to display in those little pictures & drawings which I had the pleasure & profit to do for you are incompatible with the designs— There is nothing in the Art which our Painters do, that

the continuation); (4) an 'Account of Money Recievd & Work done'; (5) 'some Ballads'; (6) 'a letter to my Brother' James Blake. The 'Account' and the letter to James Blake have not been traced.

    ² William Gilpin, *Three Essays*: on Picturesque Beauty; on Picturesque Travel; and on Sketching Landscape (1792, second edition 1794), 34–5. The quotation marks before 'uniformity' are the editor's; the rest are Blake's. Blake opens his quotation with triple quotation marks, but he continues and concludes it with only double quotation marks.

I can confess myself ignorant of⌊.⌋ I also Know & Understand
& can assuredly affirm that the works I have done for You are
Equal to Carrache or Rafael (and I am now Seven years older
than Rafael was when he died) I say they are Equal to Car-
rache or Rafael or Else I am Blind Stupid Ignorant and In-
capable in two years Study to understand those things which
a Boarding School Miss can comprehend in a fortnight. Be
assured My dear Friend that there is not one touch in those
Drawings & Pictures but what came from my Head & my
Heart in Unison, That I am Proud of being their Author and
Grateful to you my Employe*r*, & that I look upon you as the
Chief of my Friends whom I would endeavour to please
because you among all men have enabled me to produce these
things. I would not send you a Drawing or a Picture till I had
again reconsiderd my notions of Art & had put myself back as
if I was a learner⌊.⌋ I have proved that I am Right & shall now
Go on with the Vigor I was in my Childhood famous for⌊.⌋

[3]   But I do not pretend to be Perfec*t*, but if my Works have
faults Carrache Corregio & Rafaels have faults also. *L*et me
observe that the yellow leather flesh of old men⌊,⌋ the ill
drawn & ugly young women & above all the dawbed black &
yellow shadows that are found in most fine⌊,⌋ ay & the finest
picture*s*, I altogether reject as ruinous to Effect tho Connois-
seurs may think otherwise.

[4]   Let me also notice that Carraches Pictures are not like
Correggios nor Correggios like Rafaels & if neither of them
was to be encouraged till he did like any of the others he
must die without Encouragement⌊.⌋ My Pictures are unlike
any of these Painters & I would have them to be so⌊.⌋ I think
the manner I adopt More Perfect than any other⌊;⌋ no doubt
They thought the same of theirs⌊.⌋

[5]   You will be tempted to think that as I improve The Pictures
&ᶜ that I did for you are not what I would now wish them to be.
On this I beg to say That they are what I intended them &
that I know I never shall do better for if I was to do them over
again they would lose as much as they gaind because they were
done in the heat of My Spirits⌊.⌋

[6]   But You will justly enquire why I have not written all this
time to you? I answer I have been very Unhappy & could not

think of troubling you about it or any of my real Friends (I
have written many letters to you which I burnd & did not
send) & why I have not before now finishd the Miniature I
promissd to Mrs Butts? I answer I have not till now in any
degree pleased myself & now I must intreat you to Excuse
faults for Portrait Painting is the direct contrary to Designing
& Historical Painting in every respect— If you have not
Nature before you for Every Touch you cannot Paint Portrait,
& if you have Nature before you at all you cannot Paint
History⌊;⌋ it was Michael Angelos opinion & is Mine. Pray
Give My Wifes love with mine to Mrs Butts⌊,⌋ assure her that
it cannot be long before I have the pleasure of Painting from
you in Person & then that She may Expect a likeness but now
I have done All I could & know she will forgive any failure in
consideration of the Endeavour.

[¶7]   And now let me finish with assuring you that Tho I have
been very unhappy I am so no longer⌊.⌋ I am again Emerged
into the light of day⌊.⌋ I still & shall to Eternity Embrace
Christianity and Adore him who is the Express image of God
but I have traveld thro Perils & Darkness not unlike a Cham-
pion⌊.⌋ I have Conquerd and shall still Go on Conquering⌊.⌋
Nothing can withstand the fury of my Course among the Stars
of God & in the Abysses of the Accuser⌊.⌋ My Enthusiasm is
still what it was only Enlarged and confirmd⌊.⌋

[¶8]   I now Send Two Pictures³ & hope you will approve of
them⌊.⌋ I have inclosed the Account of Money recievd & work
done which I ought long ago to have sent you⌊;⌋ pray forgive
Errors in [*?for* and] omissions of this kind⌊.⌋ I am incapable of
many attentions which it is my Duty to observe towards you
thro multitude of employment & thro hope of soon seeing you
again⌊.⌋ I often omit to Enquire of you But pray let me now
hear how you do & of the welfare of your family⌊.⌋

Accept my Sincere love & respect⌊.⌋

I remain Yours Sincerely
Willm Blake

A Piece of Sea Weed serves for a Barometer⌊;⌋ at [*for* it] gets
wet & dry as the weather gets so⌊.⌋⁴

---

³ For the commission for these pictures see 26 Aug. 1799.
⁴ This postscript is written below the address.

[22 NOVEMBER 1802]

TO [*Thomas Butts, enclosed with the former*]¹

Dear Sir

After I had finishd my Letter I found that I had not said half what I intended to say & in particular I wish to ask you what Subject you choose to be painted on the remaining Canvas which I brought down with me (for there were three) and to tell you that several of the Drawings were in great forward-ness ∟; ⌐ you will see by the Inclosed Account that the remaining Number of Drawings which you gave me orders for is Eigh-teen ∟. ⌐² I will finish these with all possible Expedition if indeed I have not tired you or as it is politely calld Bored you too much already or if you would rather cry out Enough Off Off! *T*ell me in a Letter of forgiveness if you were offended & of ac-customd friendship if you were not. But I will bore you more with some Verses which My Wife desires me to Copy out & send you with her kind love & Respect ∟; ⌐ they were Composed above a twelvemonth ago while Walking from Felpham to Lavant to meet my Sister ∟. ⌐

With happiness stretchd across the hills
In a cloud that dewy sweetness distills ∟, ⌐
With a blue sky spread over with wings
And a mild Sun³ that mounts & sings ∟, ⌐
With trees & fields full of Fairy elves   [5]
And little devils who fight for themselves ∟; ⌐
Remembring the Verses that Hayley sung⁴
When my heart knockd against the root of my tongue ∟; ⌐⁵

[22 Nov. 1802]

¹ We may be confident that the undated continuation belongs with the letter of 22 Nov. 1802 because (1) the former refers to the same 'two little pictures' enclosed with the latter ('Two Pictures'), and (2) the former refers to 'the Inclosed Account' described in the latter as 'the inclosed . . . Account of Money recievd & work done'.

² For the commission for these pictures see 26 Aug. 1799.

³ Cf. *Jerusalem* pl. 19, l. 44: 'With a blue sky spread over with wings and a mild moon' (p. 455).

⁴ These 'Verses that Hayley sung' may be either the beginning of Hayley's translation of Tasso's *Le Sette Giornate del Mondo Creato* called *Genesis* and written out by Blake on paper watermarked 1797, or almost any other of Hayley's volu-minous poetry.

⁵ Beside lines 7–8, which are written sideways in the left margin, Blake wrote:

With Angels planted in Hawthorn bowers
And God himself in the passing hours ⌊,⌋   [1
With Silver Angels across my way
And Golden Demons that none can stay ⌊,⌋
With my Father hovering upon the wind
And my Brother Robert just behind
And my Brother John the evil one   [1
In a black cloud making his mone ⌊;⌋
Tho dead,⁶ they appear upon my path
Notwithstanding my terrible wrath ⌊.⌋
They beg they intreat they drop their tears
Filld full of hopes filld full of fears ⌊;⌋   [2
With a thousand Angels upon the Wind
Pouring disconsolate from behind
To drive them off & before my way
A frowning Thistle implores my stay ⌊.⌋
What to others a trifle appears   [2
Fills me full of smiles or tears
For double the vision my Eyes do see
And a double vision is always with me ⌊.⌋
With my inward Eye 'tis an old Man grey ⌊,⌋
With my outward a Thistle across my way ⌊.⌋   [3
'If thou goest back ⌊,⌋' the thistle said⁷
'Thou art to endless woe betrayd
For here does Theotormon lower
And here is Enitharmons bower
And Los the terrible thus hath sworn   [3
"Because thou backward dost return
Poverty Envy old age & fear
Shall bring thy Wife upon a bier ⌊;⌋
And Butts shall give what Fuseli gave ⌊,⌋
A dark black Rock & a gloomy Cave ⌊.⌋" '   [4

'These 2 lines were omitted in transcribing & ought to come in at X' where 'Re-
membring' is also written.

⁶ Blake's father James died in 1784, and his brother Robert in 1787; this is the
only known reference to the death of his brother John, who had 'run away' to
join the army about 1793 (*Blake Records*, 558).

⁷ ll. 31, 40, 43-52, 59-70: The quotation marks are Blake's except for the second
in l. 31 and the first in l. 40, which are the editor's. There is a stanza-break after
l. 40.

I struck the Thistle with my foot
And broke him up from his delving root⌊·⌋
'Must the duties of life each other cross⌊?⌋'
'Must every joy be dung & dross⌊?⌋'
'Must my dear Butts feel cold neglect'   [45]
'Because I give Hayley his due respect⌊?⌋'
'Must Flaxman look upon me as wild'
'And all my friends be with doubts beguild⌊?⌋'
'Must my Wife live in my Sisters bane'
'Or my Sister survive on my Loves pain⌊?⌋'   [50]
'The curses of Los the terrible shade'
'And his dismal terrors make me afraid⌊·⌋'

So I spoke & struck in my wrath
The old man weltering upon my path.
Then Los appeard in all his power⌊;⌋   [55]
In the Sun he appeard descending before
My face in fierce flames⌊;⌋ in my double sight
Twas outward a Sun: inward Los in his might⌊·⌋[8]

'My hands are labourd day & night'
'And Ease comes never in my sight⌊·⌋'   [60]
'My Wife has no indulgence given'
'Except what comes to her from heaven⌊·⌋'
'We eat little⌊,⌋ we drink less⌊;⌋'
'This Earth breeds not our happiness⌊·⌋'
'Another Sun feeds our lifes streams⌊,⌋'   [65]
'We are not warmed with thy beams⌊;⌋'
'Thou measurest not the Time to me'
'Nor yet the Space that I do see⌊;⌋'
'My Mind is not with thy light arrayd⌊·⌋'
'Thy terrors shall not make me afraid⌊·⌋'   [70]

When I had my Defiance given
Tho Sun stood trembling in heaven⌊,⌋
The Moon that glowd remote below
Became leprous & white as snow⌊,⌋

[8] This is the central action of *Milton* (1804–?8)—see particularly pl. 20, ll. 5–11
(p. 361).

And every Soul of men on the Earth   [7
Felt affliction & sorrow & sickness & dearth⌊.⌋
Los flamd in my path & the Sun was hot
With the bows of my Mind & the Arrows of Thought⌊.⌋
My bow string fierce with Ardour breathes⌊,⌋
My arrows glow in their golden sheaves⌊;⌋   [6
My brothers & father march before⌊;⌋
The heavens drop with human gore⌊.⌋

Now I a fourfold vision see
And a fourfold vision is given to me⌊;⌋
Tis fourfold in my supreme delight   [8
And three fold in soft Beulahs night
And twofold Always. May God us keep
From Single vision & Newtons Sleep⌊!⌋⁹   [8

I also inclose you some Ballads by Mr Hayley¹⁰ with prints to
them by Your Hble Servt I should have sent them before now
but could not get any thing done for You to please myself
for I do assure you that I have truly studied the two little
pictures I now send & do not repent of the time I have spent
upon them⌊.⌋
    God bless you.

Yours
W B

P.S. I have taken the liberty to trouble you with a letter to my
Brother which you will be so kind as to send or give him &
oblige yours W B⌊.⌋

---

  ⁹ In Blake's MS, the poem is in two columns.
  ¹⁰ Butts was charged 10s. for '4 Nos of Hayleys Ballads' under 21 Aug. 1805
in the account between the two men of 3 March 1806 (*Blake Records*, 572). The
fact that Blake had not previously sent Butts any of the *Designs to A Series of Ballads*
published in June, July, Aug., and Sept. suggests that he had not written to him
since May 1802.

30 JANUARY 1803

TO [*James Blake*][1]

Dear Brother   Felpham Jany 30—1803

[¶*1*]   Your Letter mentioning Mr Butts's account of my Ague surprized me because I have no Ague but have had a Cold this Winter. You know that it is my way to make the best of every thing. I never make myself nor my friends uneasy if I can help it. My Wife has had Agues & Rheumatisms almost ever since she has been here[2] but our time is almost out that we took the Cottage for. I did not mention our Sickness to you & should not to Mr Butts but for a determination which we have lately made namely To leave This Place because I am now certain of what I have long doubted Viz t[hat] H[1] is jealous as Stothard[3] was & will be no further my friend than he is compelld by circumstances. The truth is As a Poet[1] he is frightend at me & as a Painter his views & mine are opposite⌊;⌋ he thinks to turn me into a Portrait Painter as he did Poor Romney, but this he nor all the devils in hell will never do. I must own that seeing H. like S Envious (& that he is I am now certain) made me very uneasy, but it is over & I now defy the worst & fear not while I am true to myself which I will be. This is the uneasiness I spoke of to Mr Butts but I did not tell him so plain & wish you to keep it a secret & to burn this letter because it speaks so plain⌊.⌋ I told Mr Butts that I did not wish to Explore too much the cause of our determination to leave Felpham because of pecuniary connexions between H & me— Be not then uneasy on any account & tell my Sister not to be uneasy for I am fully Employd & Well Paid⌊.⌋ I have made it so much H's interest to employ me that he can no longer treat me with indifference & now it is in my power to stay or return or remove

---

30 Jan. 1803

[1] The letter is dirty and fragile, and the original leaf has torn at the fold, making it two leaves. Some letters are invisible, as if rubbed off, and three times the ordinary Black ink has been corrected in a yellowed ink: (1) 'H' appears over an erasure of something like 'arl'; (2) 'Poet' is written over the same word in Black ink; (3) '10 Guineas' was originally '10 G^s'.

[2] Hayley told Nancy Flaxman on 16 Dec. 1802 that 'poor Mrs Blake has suffer'd most severely from Rheumatism but she is reviving' (*Blake Records*, 112).

[3] Thomas Stothard (1755–1834), painter and Blake's intimate friend.

to any other place that I choose because I am getting before hand in money matters⌐.⌐ The Profits arising from Publications are immense⁴ & I now have it in my power to commence publication with many very formidable works, which I have finishd & ready⌐.⌐ A Book price half a guinea may be got out at the Expense of Ten pounds & its almost certain profits are 500 G. I am only sorry that I did not know the methods of publishing years ago & this is one of the numerous benefits I have obtaind by coming here for I should never have known the nature of Publication unless I had known H & his connexions & his method of managing. It now would be folly not to venture publishing. I am now Engraving Six little plates for a little work of Mr H's for which I am to have 10 Guineas each & the certain profits of that work are a fortune such as would make me independent supposing that I could substantiate such a one of my own & I mean to try many⌐.⌐ But I again say as I said before We are very Happy sitting at tea by a wood fire in our Cottage⌐,⌐ the wind singing above our roof & the sea roaring at a distance but if sickness comes all is unpleasant⌐.⌐

[¶2]   But my letter to Mr Butts appears to me not to be so explicit as that to you for I told you that I should come to London in the Spring to commence Publisher & he has offerd me every assistance in his power without knowing my intention. But since I wrote yours we had made the resolution of which we informd him viz to leave Felpham entirely. I also told you what I was about & that I was not ignorant of what was doing in London in works of art. But I did not mention Illness because I hoped to get better (for I was really very ill when I wrote to him the last time) & was not then perswaded as I am now that the air tho warm is unhealthy⌐.⌐

[¶3]   However this I know will set you at Ease. I am now so full of work that I have had no time to go on with the Ballads,⁵ & my prospects of more & more work continually are certain. My Heads of Cowper for Mr H's life of Cowper have pleasd

⁴ Contemporary rumour had it that Joseph Johnson 'paid as much as £10,000 for Hayley's "Life of Cowper"' (Thomas Rees, *Reminiscences of Literary London from 1779 to 1853* [1896], 78).

⁵ On 3 April 1803 Hayley told R. H. Evans: 'he [*Blake*] suspended their publication, that He might proceed, without any Interruption, in his plates for the life of Cowper' (*Blake Records*, 114).

his Relations exceedingly & in Particular Lady Hesketh & Lord Cowper$_L;_J$ to please Lady H was a doubtful chance who almost adord her Cousin the poet & thought him all perfection & she writes that she is quite satisfied with the portraits & charmd by the great Head in particular tho she never could bear the original Picture$_L._J$[6]

4] But I ought to mention to you that our present idea i*s*, To take a house in some village further from the Sea$_L,_J$ Perhaps Lavan*t*, & in or near the road to London for the sake of convenience— I also ought to inform you that I read your letter to M^r H & that he is very afraid of losing me & also very afraid that my Friends in London should have a bad opinion of the reception he has given to me$_L._J$[7] But My Wife has undertaken to Print the whole number of the Plates for Cowpers work which She does to admiration & being under my own eye the prints are as fine as the French prints & please every one.[8] *I*n short I have Got every thing so under my thumb that it is more profitable that things should be as they are than any other wa*y*, tho not so agreeable because we wish naturally for friendship in preference to interest.— The Publishers are already indebted to My Wife Twenty Guineas for work deliverd$_L;_J$ this is a small specimen of how we go on. *T*hen fear nothing & let my Sister fear nothing because it appears to me that I am now too old & have had too much experience to be any longer imposed upon$_L,_J$ only illness makes all uncomfortable & this we must prevent by every means in our power$_L._J$

[6] On 29 Dec. 1802 and 10 and 15 Jan. 1803 Lady Hesketh wrote to Hayley: 'I must tell you I admire Romneys head of all things!'; 'my abhorrence of the Miniature [*by Blake*] is in its full force but this Engraving has an effect totally different from that'—'the print softens it extremely & it has not that distracted and distracting look which prevails in the miniature' (*Blake Records*, 113).

[7] Hayley seems to have reported that the Blakes were moving because of the climate, for on 28 May 1803 Flaxman wrote: 'your account of M^r & Mrs Blake's having suffered so much from a damp Situation concerns me, I earnestly hope what they propose is for the best, you have allways acted with the same bounty & Kindness by them as you do by all' (*Blake Records*, 120).

[8] John Linnell wrote: 'The copper plates which Blake engraved to illustrate Ha[*y*]ley's life of Cowper were as he told me printed entirely by himself and his wife in his own press—a very good one which cost him forty pounds' (*Blake Records*, 461 n. 1). However, Blake does not seem to have printed the plates for the third volume in 1804.

If the rate of pay was the standard one of 6*s*. per hundred pulls (see G. E.

[¶5] I send with this 5 Copies of N4 of the Ballads for Mʳˢ Flax-
man⁹ & Five more two of which you will be so good as to give
to Mʳˢ Chetwynd if she should call or send for them.¹⁰ These
Ballads are likely to be Profitable for we have Sold all that we
have had time to print. Evans the Bookseller in Pallmall says
they go off very well¹¹ & why should we repent of having done
them∟?⌋ *It* is doing Nothing that is to be repented of & not
doing such things as these∟·⌋

[¶6] Pray remember us both to Mʳ Hall when you see him∟·⌋

[¶7] I write in great haste & with a head full of botheration about
various projected works & particularl*y* a work now Proposed
to the Public at the End of Cowpers Lif*e*, which will very likely
be of great consequence∟;⌋ it is Cowpers Milton∟,⌋¹² the same
that Fuselis Milton Gallery was painted for, & if we succeed in
our intentions the prints to this work will be very profitable
to me & not only profitable but honourable at any rate∟·⌋ The
Project pleases Lord Cowpers famil*y*, & I am now labouring
in my thoughts Designs for this & other works equally credi-
table∟·⌋ These are works to be boasted of & therefore I cannot
feel depressd tho I know that as far as Designing & Poetry
are concernd I am Envied in many Quarter*s*, but I will cram
the dogs for I know that the Public are my friends & love
my works & will embrace them whenever they see them∟·⌋ My
only Difficulty is to produce fast enough.

[¶8] I go on Merrily with my Greek¹³ & Lati*n*; am very sorry that
I did not begin to learn languages early in life as I find it very
Eas*y*; am now learning my Hebre*w*: אבנ∟·⌋ I read Greek as

Bentley, Jr., *The Early Engravings of Flaxman's Classical Designs* [1964]), £21 would
pay for 1,750 copies each of the first 4 plates.

    ⁹ The 'Mʳˢ' in 'Mʳˢ Flaxman' is not clear; it could be 'Mʳ'.
    ¹⁰ The three odd copies went to Butts, according to the 1805 entry in Butts's
account with Blake: '3 Hayleys Ballads p Brother' (*Blake Records*, 574).
    ¹¹ On 3 April 1803 Hayley had written to ask whether R. H. Evans thought 'it
will answer to Him to resume the series of Ballads' (*Blake Records*, 114). The quarto
series was abandoned, probably at a net loss to Blake, but a new octavo edition
was undertaken in 1805.
    ¹² On 6 Aug. 1802 Hayley wrote to Johnny Johnson: 'our good Blake . . . has
a great wish . . . [*to*] engrave it [*Abbott's portrait of Cowper*] for the Milton we medi-
tate' (*Blake Records*, 109). Blake signed no plates for Cowper's translation of Milton's
Latin and Italian Poems (1808).
    ¹³ Hayley mentions helping Blake ('who is . . . literally learning the Language')
with his Greek in Nov. 1801 and Feb. 1802 (*Blake Records*, 86, 89).

fluently as an Oxford scholar & the Testament is my chief master⌊;⌋ astonishing indeed is the English Translation⌊,⌋ it is almost word for word & if the Hebrew Bible is as well translated which I do not doubt it is we need not doubt of its having been translated as well as written by the Holy Ghost⌊.⌋

My wife joins me in Love to you both⌊.⌋ I am Sincerely yours
                                        W Blake

25 APRIL 1803

TO 'Mr Butts / Gr^t Marlborough Street'

1] My Dear Sir
    I write in haste having recievd a pressing Letter from my Brother. I intended to have sent the Picture of the Riposo[1] which is nearly finishd much to my satisfaction but not quite⌊;⌋ you shall have it soon. I now send the 4 Numbers for Mr Birch[2] with best Respects to him⌊.⌋ The Reason the Ballads have been suspended is the pressure of other business but they will go on again Soon⌊.⌋

2]   Accept of my thanks for your kind & heartening Letter⌊.⌋ You have Faith in the Endeavours of Me your weak brother & fellow Disciple⌊;⌋ how great must be your faith in our Divine Master. You are to me a Lesson of Humility while you Exalt me by such distinguishing commendations. I know that you see certain merits in me which by Gods Grace shall be made fully apparent & perfect in Eternity. In the mean time I must not bury the Talents in the Earth but do my endeavour to live to the Glory of our Lord & Saviour & I am also grateful to the kind hand that endeavours to lift me out of despondency even if it lifts me too high—

3]   And now My Dear Sir Congratulate me on my return to London with the full approbation of Mr Hayley[3] & with Promise—but Alas!

25 April 1803
    [1] For the commission for 'Riposo' see 26 Aug. 1799.
    [2] Birch took one copy and Butts kept the rest, according to Butts's account with Blake: '3 Ditto [Hayleys Ballads] Mr Birch [paid for by Butts]' (Blake Records, 574).
    [3] On 3 April 1803 Hayley had said that Blake 'is devoted to a life of Industry & Retirement!' (Blake Records, 115), but he may have meant a quiet life rather than a country life.

[¶4]   Now I may say to you what perhaps I should not dare to say to any one else, That I can alone carry on my visionary studies in London unannoyd & that I may converse with my friends in Eternity, See Visions,[4] Dream Dreams & prophecy & speak Parables unobserv'd & at liberty from the Doubts of other Mortals—perhaps Doubts proceeding from Kindness, but Doubts are always pernicious Especially when we Doubt our Friends. Christ is very decided on this Point. 'He who is Not With Me is Against Me.'[5] There is no Medium or Middle state & if a Man is the Enemy of my Spiritual Life while he pretends to be the Friend of my Corporeal, he is a Real Enemy—but the Man may be the friend of my Spiritual Life while he seems the Enemy of my Corporeal but Not Vice Versa.

[¶5]   What is very pleasant Every one who hears of my going to London again Applauds it as the only course for the interest of all concernd in My Works, Observing that I ought not to be away from the opportunities London affords of seeing fine Pictures and the various improvements in Works of Art going on in London.

[¶6]   But none can know the Spiritual Acts of my three years Slumber on the banks of the Ocean unless he has seen them in the Spirit or unless he should read My long Poem descriptive of those Acts for I have in these three years composed an immense number of verses on One Grand Theme Similar to Homers Iliad or Miltons Paradise Lost the Persons & Machinery intirely new to the Inhabitants of Earth (some of the Persons Excepted).[6] I have written this Poem from immediate Dictation twelve or sometimes twenty or thirty lines at a time without Premeditation & even against my Will. The Time it has taken in writing was thus renderd Non Existent, & an immense Poem Exists which seems to be the Labour of a long Life all producd without Labour or Study. I mention this to shew you what I think the Grand Reason of my being brought down here.

---

4 ' "The Visions were angry with me at Felpham^⌐"', he would afterwards say' (A. Gilchrist, *Life of William Blake* [1880], i. 184).

5 Matthew 12: 30. The quotation marks here and below in this letter are Blake's.

6 This is presumably the same poem referred to in the letter of 6 July 1803. Cf. *Jerusalem* pl. 3, ¶1: 'After my three years slumber on the banks of the Ocean, I again display my Giant forms to the Public . . .' (p. 419).

7]   I have a thousand & ten thousand things to say to you. My heart is full of futurity. I percieve that the sore travel which has been given me these three years leads to Glory & Honour. I rejoice & I tremble ⌐:⌐ 'I am fearfully & wonderfully made'.⁷ I had been reading the CXXXIX Psalm⁷ a little before your Letter arrived. I take your advice. I see the face of my Heavenly Father ⌐;⌐ he lays his Hand upon my Head & gives a blessing to all my works ⌐;⌐ why should I be troubled ⌐?⌐ why should my heart & flesh cry ou*t*? I will go on in the Strength of the Lord ⌐;⌐ through Hell will I sing forth his Praise*s*, that the Dragons of the Deep may praise him⁸ & that those who dwell in darkness & in the Sea coasts may be gatherd into his Kingdom. Excuse my perhaps too great Enthusiasm. Please to accept of & give our Loves to Mʳˢ Butts & your amiable Famil*y*, & believe me to be Ever

Yours Affectionately
Felpham   Will. Blake
    April 25. 1803

6 JULY 1803

TO [*Thomas Butts*]

Dear Sir

1]   I send you the Riposo which I hope you will think my best Picture in many respects. It represents the Holy Family in Egypt Guarded in their Repose from those Fiends the Egyptian God*s*, and tho' not directly taken from a Poem of Miltons (for till I had designd it Miltons Poem did not come into my Thoughts) Yet it is very similar to his Hymn on the Nativity which you will find among his smaller Poems & will read with great delight. I have given in the back ground a building which may be supposed the ruin of a Part of Nimrods tower¹

---

⁷ Psalm 139: 'O Lord, thou hast searched me, and known me. . . . I will praise thee; for I am fearfully and wonderfully made . . .'.

⁸ Cf. Psalm 148: 7: 'Praise the Lord from the earth, ye dragons, and all deeps'.

6 July 1803
¹ The tower of Babel.

which I conjecture to have spread over many Countries for he ought to be reckond of the Giant brood$_{\llcorner\lrcorner}$

[¶2]   I have now on the Stocks the following drawings for you$_{\llcorner:\lrcorner}$ 1 Jephthah sacrificing his Daughter 2. Ruth & her mother in Law & Sister 3. The three Maries at the Sepulcher. 4 The Death of Joseph. 5 The Death of the Virgin Mary. 6 St Paul Preaching. & 7 The Angel of the Divine Presence clothing Adam & Eve with Coats of Skins$_{\llcorner\lrcorner}$[2]

[¶3]   These are all in great forwardness & I am satisfied that I improve very much & shall continue to do so while I live which is a blessing I can never be too thankful for both to God & Man$_{\llcorner\lrcorner}$

[¶4]   We look forward every day with pleasure toward our meeting again in London with those whom we have learnd to value by absence no less perhaps than we did by presence for recollection often surpasses every thing. *I*ndeed the prospect of returning to our friends is supremely delightful— Then I am determind that Mrs Butts shall have a good likeness of You if I have hands & eyes lef*t*, for I am become a likeness taker & succeed admirably wel*l*, but this is not to be atchievd without the original sitting before you for Every tou*ch*, all likenesses from memory being necessarily very very defective$_{\llcorner;\lrcorner}$ but Nature & Fancy are Two Things & can Never be joined neither ought any one to attempt it for it is Idolatry & destroys the Soul$_{\llcorner\lrcorner}$

[¶5]   I ought to tell you that Mr H. is quite agreeable to our return & that there is all the appearance in the world of our being fully employd in Engraving for his projected Works Particularly Cowpers Milto*n*, a Work now on foot by Subscription & I understand that the Subscription goes on briskly. This work is to be a very Elegant one & to consist of All Miltons Poems with Cowpers Notes and translations by Cowper from Miltons Latin & Italian Poems. These works will be ornamented with Engravings from Designs from Romne*y*, Flaxman & Y^r hble Servt & to be Engravd also by the last mentiond. The Profits of the work are intended to be appropriated to Erect a Monument to the Memory of Cowper in St Pauls or Westminster Abbey. Such is the Project — & Mr Addington[3]

---

² For the commission for these drawings see 26 Aug. 1799.

³ Henry Addington (1757–1844), Prime Minister (1801–4) between the Pitt Administrations.

& Mr Pitt are both among the Subscribers which are already numerous & of the first rank. The price of the Work is Six Guineas— Thus I hope that all our three years trouble Ends in Good Luck at last & shall be forgot by my affections & only rememberd by my Understanding to be a Memento in time to come & to speak to future generations by a Sublime Allegory which is now perfectly completed into a Grand Poem⌊.⌋ I may praise it since I dare not pretend to be any other than the Secretary⌊;⌋ the Authors are in Eternity⌊.⌋ I consider it as the Grandest Poem that this World Contains. Allegory addressd to the Intellectual powers while it is altogether hidden from the Corporeal Understanding is My Definition of the Most Sublime Poetry; it is also somewhat in the same manner defind by Plato. This Poem shall by Divine Assistance be progressively Printed & Ornamented with Prints & given to the Public.[4] But of this work I take care to say little to Mr H. since he is as much averse to my poetry as he is to a Chapter in the Bible⌊.⌋ He knows that I have writ it for I have shewn it to him & he has read Part by his own desire & has looked with sufficient contempt to inhance my opinion of it. But I do not wish to irritate by seeming too obstinate in Poetic pursuits⌊.⌋ But if all the World should set their faces against This, I have Orders to Set my face like a flint, Ezekiel iii C 9 v, against their faces & set my forehead against their foreheads⌊.⌋[5]

6] As to Mr H I feel myself at liberty to say as follows upon this ticklish subject. I regard Fashion in Poetry as little as I do in Painting. So if both Poets & Painters should alternately dislike (but I know the majority of them will not) I am not to regard it at all⌊;⌋ but Mr H approves of My Designs as little as he does of my Poems and I have been forced to insist on his leaving

---

[4] The descriptions of this poem here and in the letter of 25 April 1803 do not correspond closely to any of the three long poems which survive. It is unlikely that any of them was 'perfectly completed' in 1803; *Vala* and *Jerusalem* are not really 'descriptive of' 'the Spiritual Acts of my three years Slumber on the banks of the Ocean'; and in none were 'the Persons & Machinery intirely [*or largely*] new' to readers (like Butts) of his earlier works. Of the surviving poems, *Milton* seems the most likely candidate, as its central actions take place at Felpham.

[5] Ezekiel 3: 8–9: 'Behold, I have made thy face strong against their faces, and thy forehead strong against their foreheads. As an adamant harder than flint have I made thy forehead; fear them not, neither be dismayed at their looks, though they be a rebellious house.'

me in both to my own Self Will, for I am determind to be no longer Pesterd with his Genteel Ignorance & Polite Disapprobation. I know myself both Poet & Painter & it is not his affected Contempt that can move me to any thing but a more assiduous pursuit of both Arts. Indeed by my late Firmness[6] I have brought down his affected Loftiness & he begins to think I have some Genius, as if Genius & Assurance were the same thing. But his imbecile attempts to depress Me only deserve laughter. I say thus much to you knowing that you will not make a bad use of it But it is a Fact too true That if I had only depended on Mortal Things both myself & my Wife must have been Lost— I shall leave every one in This Country astonishd at my Patience & Forbearance of Injuries upon Injuries & I do assure you that if I could have returnd to London a Month after my arrival here I should have done so, but I was commanded by my Spiritual friends to bear all⌊,⌋ to be silent & to go thro all without murmuring & in fine hope till my three years should be almost accomplishd at which time I was set at liberty to remonstrate against former conduct & to demand Justice & Truth which I have done in so effectual a manner that my antagonist is silencd completely & I have compelld what should have been of freedom⌊,⌋ My Just Right as an Artist & as a Man, & if any attempt should be made to refuse me this I am inflexible & will relinquish any engagement of Designing at all unless altogether left to my own Judgment, As you My dear Friend have always left me for which I shall never cease to honour & respect you⌊.⌋

[¶7]　　When we meet I will perfectly describe to you my Conduct & the Conduct of others toward me & you will see that I have labourd hard indeed & have been borne on angels wings. Till we meet I beg of God our Saviour to be with you & me & yours & mine⌊.⌋ Pray give my & my wifes love to Mrs Butts & Family & believe me to remain

Yours in truth & sincerity

Felpham July 6. 1803　　　　　　　　　　　　　Will Blake

---

[6] Hayley told Flaxman on 7 Aug. 1803 that he had been 'astonished' by the prices Blake was asking for his engravings after Romney (*Blake Records*, 121).

16 AUGUST 1803

TO 'Mr Butts / Gt Marlborough S^t / London'

Felpham August 16. 1803

Dear Sir

*]   I send 7 Drawings¹ which I hope will please yo*u*; this I believe about balances our account— Our return to London draws on apace. *O*ur Expectation of meeting again with you is one of our greatest pleasures. Pray tell me how your Eyes do. I never sit down to work but I think of you & feel anxious for the sight of that friend whose Eyes have done me so much good— I omitted (very unaccountably) to copy out in my last Letter that passage in my rough sketch which related to your kindness in offering to Exhibit my 2 last Pictures in the Gallery in Berners Street⌊;⌋² it was in these Words⌊:⌋ 'I sincerely thank you for your kind offer of Exhibiting my 2 Pictures, the trouble you take on my account I trust will be recompensed to you by him who seeth in secret. *I*f you should find it convenient to do so it will be gratefully rememberd by me among the other numerous kindnesses I have recievd from you'———

*]   I go on with the remaining Subjects which you gave me commission to Execute for you but shall not be able to send any more before my return tho perhaps I may bring some [with m]e finishd. I am at Present in a Bustle to defend my-self against a very unwarrant[able w]arrant from a Justice of Peace³ in Chichester, which was taken out against me by a Private⁴ in Captⁿ Leathes's troop of 1st or Royal Dragoons for an assault & Seditious words. The wretched Man has terribly Perjurd himself as has his Comrade for as to Sedition not one

---

16 Aug. 1803
¹ For the commission for these 7 drawings see 26 Aug. 1799.
² The newly opened '*BRITISH SCHOOL OF PAINTING, BERNER'S-STREET* . . . presents a perpetual exhibition and sale of original paintings by the most eminent living and deceased *British* artists. It consists of modern and original works only, in painting, drawing, architecture, and engraving' (Anon., *The Picture of London for 1804* [1803], 260).
The quotation marks just below are Blake's.
³ The deposition of 15 Aug. is signed by John Quantock (*Blake Records*, 125). For another account of the affair see Blake's 'Memorandum' (pp. 1299–1301).
⁴ John Scofield (d. 1812).

Word relating to the King or Government was spoken by either him or me. His Enmity arises from my having turned him out of my Garden into which he was invited as an assistant by a Gardener[5] at work therein, without my knowledge that he was so invited. I desired him as politely as was possible to go out of the Garden, he made me an impertinent answer₍ₗ.₎ I insisted on his leaving the Garden₍ₗ;₎ he refused₍ₗ.₎ I still persisted in desiring his departure₍ₗ;₎ he then threatend to knock out my Eyes with many abominable imprecations & with some contempt for my Person₍ₗ;₎ it affronted my foolish Pride₍ₗ.₎ I therefore took him by the Elbows & pushed him before me till I had got him out. There I intended to have left him, but he turning about put himself into a Posture of Defiance threatening & swearing at me. I perhaps foolishly & perhaps not, stepped out at the Gate & putting aside his blows took him again by the Elbows & keeping his back to me pushed him forwards down the road about fifty yards₍ₗ,₎ he all the while endeavouring to turn round & strike me & raging & cursing which drew out several neighbours. At length when I had got him to where he was Quarterd, which was very quickly done, we were met at the Gate by the Master of the House, The Fox Inn,[6] (who is [my del] the proprietor of my Cottage) & his wife & Daughter, & the Mans Comrade[7] & several other people₍ₗ.₎ My Landlord compelld the Soldiers to go in doors after many abusive threats [from them del] against me & my wife from the two Soldiers but not one word of threat on account of Sedition was utterd at that time. This method of Revenge was Plannd between them after they had got together into the Stable. This is the whole outline. I have for witnesses: The Gardener who is Hostler at the Fox & who Evidences that to his knowledge no word of the remotest tendency to Government or Sedition was utterd,— Our next door Neighbour a Millers wife[8] who saw me turn him before me down the road & saw & heard all that happend at the Gate of the Inn who

---

[5] We know only the first name of Blake's gardener: William.

[6] Mr. Grinder.   [7] John Cock.

[8] Mrs. Haynes, who is described by Hayley as a 'benevolent, clear-headed woman, (the wife of a millers servant) whose garden adjoined Blakes, & who, by her shrewd Remarks, clearly proved *several impossibilities* in the *false accusation*' (*Blake Records*, 164).

Evidences that no Expression of threatening on account of Sedition was utterd in the heat of their fury by either of the Dragoons. This was the womans own remark & does high honour to her good sense as she observes that whenever a quarrel happens the offence is always repeated. The Landlord of the Inn & His Wife & daughter will Evidence the Same & will evidently prove the Comrade perjurd who swore that he heard me while at the Gate utter Seditious words & D—— the K—— without which perjury I could not have been committed & I had no witness with me before the Justices who could combat his assertion as the Gardener remain in my Garden all the while & he was the only person I thought necessary to take with me. I have been before a Bench of Justices at Chichester this morning, but they as the Lawyer who wrote down the Accusations told me in private are compelld by the Military to suffer a prosecution to be enterd into altho they must know & it is manifest that the whole is a Fabricated Perjury. I have been forced to find Bail. Mr Hayley was kind enough to come forwards & Mr Seagrave the Printer at Chichester, Mr H. in 100£ & Mr S. in 50£ & myself am bound in 100£ for my appearance at the Quarter Sessions[9] which is after Michaelmass. So I shall have the Satisfaction to see my friends in Town before this Contemptible business comes on⌊.⌋ I say Contemptible for it must be manifest to every one that the whole accusation is a wilful Perjury.[10] Thus you see my dear Friend that I cannot leave this place without some adventure. It has struck a consternation thro all the Villages round. Every Man is now afraid of speaking to or looking at a Soldier, for the peaceable Villagers have always been forward in expressing their kindness for us & they express their sorrow at our departure as soon as they hear of it⌊.⌋ Every one oere is my Evidence for Peace & Good Neighbourhood & yet such is the present state of things this foolish accusation

---

[9] According to the official records, Blake's bond was for £100 and those for Hayley and Joseph Seagrave (d. 1808), Hayley's printer, were for £50 apiece (*Blake Records*, 127–8).

[10] 'Mrs Blake used afterwards to tell how, in the middle of the trial, when the soldier invented something to support his case, her husband called out *"False!"* with characteristic vehemence, and in a tone which electrified the whole court and carried conviction with it' (Gilchrist [1863], i. 175).

must be tried in Public. Well I am content⌊,⌋ I murmur not & doubt not that I shall recieve Justice & am only sorry for the trouble & expense. I have heard that my Accuser is a disgraced Sergeant⌊;⌋ [11] his name is John Scholfield; perhaps it will be in your power to learn somewhat about the Man⌊.⌋ [12] I am very ignorant of what I am requesting of you. I only suggest what I know you will be kind enough to Excuse if you can learn nothing about him & what I as well know if it is possible you will be kind enough to do in this matter⌊.⌋

[¶3]   Dear Sir This perhaps was sufferd to Clear up some doubts & to give opportunity to those whom I doubted to clear themselves of all imputation. If a Man offends me ignorantly & not designedly surely I ought to consider him with favour & affection. Perhaps the Simplicity of myself is the origin of all offences committed against me: If I have found this I shall have learned a most valuable thing⌊,⌋ well worth three years perseverance. I have found it! It is certain! that a too passive manner, inconsistent with my active physiognomy had done me much mischief⌊.⌋ I must now express to you my conviction that all is come from the spiritual World for Good & not for Evil.

[¶4]   Give me your advice in my perilous adventure. Burn what I have peevishly written about any friend. I have been very much degraded & injuriously treated, but if it all arise from my own fault I ought to blame myself⌊.⌋

O why was I born with a different face⌊?⌋
Why was I not born like the rest of my race⌊?⌋ [13]
When I look each one starts! when I speak I offend⌊;⌋
Then I'm silent & passive & lose every Friend⌊.⌋

Then my verse I dishonour, My pictures despise⌊,⌋   [5
My person degrade & my temper chastise⌊;⌋

---

[11] At the trial, Private Scolfield said 'he was degraded on account of drunkenness' (*Blake Records*, 142).

[12] As clerk in the office of the Commissary General of Musters, Butts had access to official military records.

[13] These two lines appear in a slightly different form in 'Mary', ll. 21–2 (p. 1308). In Blake's MS, the poem is in two columns. ll. 5–8 are beside ll. 1–4, and ll. 9–10 are centred beneath them.

And the pen is my terro*r*, the pencil my shame⌊;⌋
All my Talents I bury, and dead is my Fame⌊.⌋

    I am either too low or too highly prizd⌊;⌋
    When Elate I am Envyd, When Meek Im Despisd⌊.⌋   [*10*]

5]   This is but too just a Picture of my Present state⌊.⌋ I pray God to keep you & all men from it & to deliver me in his own good time. Pray write to me & tell me how you & your family enjoy health. My much terrified Wife joins me in love to you & Mrs Butts & all your family. I again take the liberty to beg of you to cause the Enclosd Letter to be deliverd to my Brother & remain Sincerely &

Affectionately Yours   William Blake

19 SEPTEMBER 1803

TO [*William Hayley*]

    My admiration of Flaxman's genius is more and more—his industry is equal to his other great powers. [*Speaks of his works in progress in his studio,*[1] *and of various matters connected with art.*]

7 OCTOBER 1803

'To / William Hayley Esqre / Felpham near Chichester / Sussex'

                    London October 7 1803
Dear Sir
    Your generous & tender solicitude about your devoted rebel makes it absolutely necessary that he should trouble you with an account of his safe arrival which will excuse his begging the favor of a few lines to inform him how you escaped the contagion of the Court of Justice—[1] I fear that you have & must

19 Sept. 1803
  [1] The 'studio' and the 'works in progress' are almost certainly Flaxman's.

7 Oct. 1803
  [1] At the Quarter Sessions at Petworth on 4 Oct. 1803, the Grand Jury found that the indictment was a True Bill, and Blake, Hayley, and Seagrave were required to renew their bonds for his appearance at his trial in Jan. 1804.

suffer more on my account than I shall ever be worth—
Arrived Safe in London my wife in very poor health⌊,⌋ still I
resolve not to lose hope of seeing better days. Art in London
flourishes. Engravers in particular are wanted. Every En-
graver turns away work that he cannot execute from his super-
abundant Employment, yet no one brings work to me⌊.⌋ I am
content that it shall be So as long as God pleases⌊.⌋ I know that
many works of a lucrative nature are in want of hands⌊;⌋ other
Engravers are courted. I suppose I must go a Courting which I
shall do awkwardly⌊;⌋ in the mean time I lose no moment to
complete Romney to satisfaction⌊.⌋² How is it possible that a
Man almost 50 Years of Age who has not lost any of his life
since he was five years old without incessant labour & study,
how is it possible that such a one with ordinary common sense
can be inferior to a boy of twenty who scarcely has taken
Saunters about the Playhouses⌊,⌋ who Eats & drinks for business
not for need⌊,⌋ how is it possible that such a fop can be superior
to the Studious lover of Art can scarcely be imagind⌊.⌋ Yet such
is somewhat like my fate & such it is likely to remain. Yet I
laugh & sing for if on Earth neglected I am in heaven a Prince
among Princes & even on Earth beloved by the Good as a
Good Man⌊;⌋ this I should be perfectly contented with but at
certain periods a blaze of reputation arises round me in which
I am considerd as one distinguishd by some mental perfection
but the flame soon dies again & I am left stupefied and aston-
ishd⌊.⌋ O that I could live as others do in a regular succession
of Employment⌊;⌋ this wish I fear is not to be accomplishd to
me— Forgive this Dirge-like lamentation over a dead horse &
now I have lamented over the dead horse let me laugh & be
merry with my friends till Christmas for as Man liveth not by
bread alone I shall live altho I should want bread — nothing is
necessary to me but to do my Duty & to rejoice in the exceed-
ing joy that is always poured out on my Spirit, to pray that
my friends & you above the rest may be made partakers of that
joy that the world cannot concieve that you may still be re-

---

² Blake's head of Romney, referred to here and in his letters of 26 Oct., 13 Dec.
1803, 27 Jan., 23 Feb., 16 March, 4 May, 22 June, 16 July, 28 Sept., 23 Oct., 4,
18, and 28 Dec. 1804, was not printed in Hayley's *Romney* (1809), and no copy of it
is known.

plenishd with the same & be as you always have been a glorious
& triumphant Dweller in immortality. Please to pay for me my
best thanks to Miss Poole⌞;⌟ tell her that I wish her a continued
Excess of Happiness—some say that Happiness is not Good for
Mortals & they ought to be answerd that Sorrow is not fit for
Immortals & is utterly useless to any one⌞;⌟ a blight never does
good to a tree & if a blight kill not a tree but it still bear fruit
let none say that the fruit was in consequence of the blight.
When this Soldier like danger is over I will do double the work
I do now, for it will hang heavy on my Devil who terribly re-
sents it, but I soothe him to peace & indeed he is a good naturd
Devil after all & certainly does not lead me into scrapes. *He*
is not in the least to be blamed for the present scrape as he was
out of the way all the time on other employment seeking amuse-
ment in making Verses to which he constantly leads me very
much to my hurt & sometimes to the annoyance of my friends⌞;⌟
as I percieve he is now doing the same work by my letter I will
finish it wishing you health & joy in God our Saviour⌞.⌟

To Eternity yours
Willm Blake

26 OCTOBER 1803

TO [*William Hayley*]

[*South Molton Street*][1]
October 26th, 1803.

Dear Sir,

I hasten to write to you by the favour of Mr. Edwards.[2] I
have been with Mr. Saunders who has now in his possession all
Mr. Romney's pictures that remained after the sale at Hamp-
stead; I saw *Milton and his Daughters,* and *'Twas where the Seas
were Roaring,* and a beautiful *Female Head.* He has promised to

26 Oct. 1803
   [1] Gilchrist, who is the source of the letter, specifies that 'Blake writes from
South Molton Street'; if the address was on the letter, it provides the first direct
evidence of Blake's occupation of that flat. The italics and quotation marks below
appear in Gilchrist's transcript.
   [2] Perhaps James Edwards (1757–1816), bookseller, brother of Richard Edwards
who published Blake's *Night Thoughts* designs (1797); he was succeeded as a book-
seller by R. H. Evans.

write a list of all that he has in his possession, and of all that he remembers of Mr. Romney's paintings, with notices where they now are, as far as his recollection will serve.[3] The picture of *Christ in the Desert* he supposes to be one of those which he has rolled on large rollers. He will take them down and unroll them, but cannot do it easily, as they are so large as to occupy the whole length of his workshop, and are laid across beams at the top.

[¶2]   Mr. Flaxman is now out of town. When he returns I will lose no time in setting him to work on the same object.

[¶3]   I have got to work after Fuseli for a little Shakespeare.[4] Mr. Johnson the bookseller tells me that there is no want of work. So far you will be rejoiced with me, and your words, '*Do not fear you can want employment!*' were verified the morning after I received your kind letter; but I go on finishing Romney with spirit, and for the relief of variety shall engage in other little works as they arise.

[¶4]   I called on Mr. Evans[5] who gives small hopes of our ballads; he says he has sold but fifteen numbers at the most, and that going on would be a certain loss of almost all the expenses. I then proposed to him to take a part with me in publishing them on a smaller scale, which he declined on account of its being out of his line of business to publish, and a line in which he is determined never to engage, attaching himself wholly to the sale of fine editions of authors and curious books in general. He advises that some publisher should be spoken to who would purchase the copyright: and, as far as I can judge of the nature of publication, no chance is left to one out of the trade. Thus the case stands at present. God send better times. Everybody complains, yet all go on cheerfully and with spirit. The shops in London improve; everything is elegant, clean, and

    [3] On 5 Jan. 1804 William Saunders wrote to Hayley saying: 'Mr Blake calld on me some time ago, saying it was your wish that I should collect the names of as many of Mr Romneys most Capital paintings as I possibly could, & in Whose possession they were . . . I have enclosed a list of what I can recollect' (*Blake Records*, 139).

    [4] Blake engraved two plates (dated 14 Jan. and 12 May 1804) for an edition of *The Plays of William Shakespeare* issued play by play in 1804–5.

    [5] Robert Harding Evans (1778–1857), bookseller and auctioneer, succeeded to the business of James Edwards and was one of the publishers of Hayley's *Designs to A Series of Ballads* (1802).

neat; the streets are widened where they were narrow; even Snow Hill is become almost level and is a very handsome street, and the narrow part of the Strand near St. Clement's is widened and become very elegant.

5]   My wife continues poorly, but fancies she is better in health here than by the seaside. We both sincerely pray for the health of Miss Poole and for all our friends in Sussex, and remain, dear sir,

Your sincere and devoted servants,
W. and C. Blake.

13 DECEMBER 1803

TO 'William Hayley Esqre / Felpham / near Bognor Sussex'

Dear Sir

1]   I write in a violent hurry⌊.⌋ Your Letter has never arrived to me⌊.⌋ Mrs Lambert[1] has been with me which is the first notice I had of the Letter or of the drawing. I have fetchd the drawing from Mr Rose[2] & have shewd it to Mr Flaxman who approves of it wishing only that the Monument itself may be more made out & the other Monument in the back Ground kept in a lower tint.[3] The little oval tablet on the side by Cowpers Monument he tells me is Mrs Unwins⌊;⌋[4] of course that shall be distinguishd⌊.⌋

2]   I have a great many things to say & a great many heartfelt acknowledgments to express particularly for your tens which are hundreds to me nay thousands⌊.⌋ I am going on with success. *B*usiness comes in & I shall be at ease if this infernal business of the soldier can be got over⌊.⌋ I have seen Mr Saunders & enquird of him whether he has any of Mr Romneys [Sketches *del*] Historical Sketches⌊;⌋ he says that he sent a great

13 Dec. 1803

[1] Apparently Mrs. Lambert was a Sussex neighbour of Hayley; in 1801 Johnny Johnson wrote to Hayley in Felpham and asked to be remembered 'to Mrs Lambert and to the good enthusiastic Blake' (*Blake Records*, 81).

[2] Samuel Rose (1767–1804), the friend of Cowper and Hayley, defended Blake at his trial in Jan. 1804.

[3] Blake's engraving of 'A Sketch of the Monument' to Cowper by Flaxman for Hayley's *Cowper* (1804), iii.

[4] The tablet of Cowper's devoted friend Mary Unwin (1724–96) is not distinguished in any of Blake's engravings for Hayley's *Cowper*.

part of them to the North & explaind the North by saying that [Mr Romney *del*] Mr John Romney⁵ has a dwelling in the north— / Mr Flaxman supposes that some if [*i.e. of*] the most distinguishd designs of Mr Romney of which Mr Saunders has a good many were Engravd they would be an appropriate accompaniment to the Life of Romney⌊;⌋ the expense would not be very great & the merit of the designs an object of consequence. /

[¶3]   Mr Saunders will shortly write to you giving you every information in his power with notices of where Mr Romneys best pictures now are & other articles collected from every Fountain he can visit⌊.⌋ I send the five copies of Cowpers Plates which you will recieve with this & have only time to say because I shall be too late for the carriage

God bless you & preserve you
& reward your kindness to me

Tuesday night   Will Blake
13 Decr 1803

[¶4]   P.S My wife is better⌊;⌋ we are very anxious about Miss Pooles health & shall be truly happy to hear that it is perfectly restored. Mr Romneys Portrait goes on with spirit. I do not send a proof because I cannot get one the Printers [being *del*] having been this afternoon unable or unwilling & my Press not yet being put up⌊.⌋

Farewell

14 JANUARY 1804

'To / William Hayley Esqre / Felpham near Chichester / Sussex'

London Jany 14. 1804

Dear Sir

[¶1]   I write immediately on my arriva*l*, Not merely to inform you that I am safe arriv*d*, but also to inform you that in a

---

⁵ George Romney's son John Romney (1758–1832) jealously guarded his father's drawings, papers, and memory, and attacked Hayley's biography in his own *Memoirs . . . of George Romney* (1830).

conversation with an old Soldier who came in the Coach with
me I learned: that no one: not even the most expert horseman:
ought ever to mount a Troopers Horse. They are taught [s]o
many tricks such as stopping short, falling down on their
knees, running sideways, & in various & innumerable ways
endeavouring to throw the rider, that it is a miracle if a
stranger escapes with his Life,— All this I learnd with some
alarm & heard also what the Soldier said confirmd by another
person in the coach. I therefore as it is my duty beg & intreat
you never to mount that wicked horse again[1] nor again trust
to one who has been so Educated. God our Saviour watch
over you & preserve you₍.₎

2]   I have seen Flaxman already as I took to him early this
morning your present to his Scholar₍;₎[2] he & his are all well
& in high spirits & welcomd Me with Kind affection &
generous exultation in my escape from the arrows of darkness.
I intend to See Mrs Lambert & Mr Johnson bookseller this
afternoon. My poor wife has been near the Gate of Death as
was supposed by our Kind & attentive fellow inhabitant, the
young & very amiable Mrs Enoch,[3] who gave my wife all the
attention that a daughter could pay to a mother but my arrival
has dispelld the formidable malady & my dear & good woman
again begins to resume her health & strength. Pray my dear
Sir favour me with a line concerning your health & how you
have escaped the double blow both from the wicked horse &
from your innocent humble servant whose heart & soul are
more & more drawn out towards you & Felpham & its kind
inhabitants₍.₎ I feel anxious & therefore pray to my God &
father for the health of Miss Poole₍;₎ hope that the pang of

14 Jan. 1804

[1] On 1 Jan. 1804 Hayley wrote: 'a new stout & tall Horse fell suddenly in his
Canter & had I not luckily had on a new strong Hat my skull would have been
smashed by a Flint—as it is I have a little Cut on the Forehead'. He told his
doctor: 'you must patch me up very speedily, for living or dying, I must make
a public appearance within a few days at the Trial of our Friend Blake' (*Blake
Records*, 139, 144). At the trial on 11 Jan. 1804, Blake was acquitted.

[2] Flaxman's 'Scholar' may be Thomas Denman, about whom he wrote to
Hayley on 2 Jan. 1804: 'I thank [*you*] kindly for the remembrance of T. Denman₍,₎
he is not my Nephew, he is whole brother to Maria & half brother to My Wife'
(MS in the Pierpont Morgan Library).

[3] There may perhaps be a connection between Mrs. Enoch and Blake's un-
dated engraving of Enoch (c. 1807).

affection & gratitude is the Gift of God for good ⌐.⌐ I am thankful that I feel it ⌐;⌐ it draws the soul towards Eternal life & conjunction with spirits of just men made perfect by love & gratitude ⌐,⌐ the two angels who stand at heavens gate ever open ⌐,⌐ ever inviting guests to the marriage ⌐.⌐ O foolish Philosophy! Gratitude is Heaven itself ⌐;⌐ there could be no heaven without Gratitude ⌐.⌐ I feel it & I know it ⌐.⌐ I thank God & Man for it & above all You My dear friend & benefactor in the Lord ⌐.⌐ [4] Pray give my & my wife's duties to Miss Poole; accept them yourself & believe me to be

Yours in sincerity

Will[m] Blake

27 JANUARY 1804

TO 'William Hayley Esq[re] / Felpham near / Chichester, Sussex'

Dear Sir

[¶*1*]   Your eager expectation of hearing from me compells me to write immediately tho I have not done half the business I wishd owing to a violent cold which confind me to my bed 3 days & to my chamber a week. I am now so well (thank God) as to get out & have accordingly been to M[r] Walkers[1] who is not in town being at Birmingham where he will remain 6 Weeks or 2 Months ⌐.⌐ I took my Portrait of Romney as you desired to shew him, his son was likewise not at home: but I will again call on M[r] Walker Jun[r] & beg him to shew me the Pictures, & make every enquiry of him, If [y]ou think best:— M[r] Sa[u]nders has one or two large Cartoons, The Subjects he does not know. They are folded up on the top of his workshop ⌐,⌐ the rest he packd up & sent into the North. I shewd your Letter to M[r] John Romney to M[r] Flaxman who was perfectly Satisfied with it. I seald & sent it immediately as directed by M[r] Sa[u]nders to Kendall Westmoreland. M[r] Sa[u]nders expects

---

[4] Hayley wrote to Johnny Johnson on 18 Jan. 1804: 'a Letter met me yesterday at Lavant from our good Blake so full of the most cordial Gratitude & Felicity on his safe return to his anxious Wife, that no feeling Mortal can read it without Tears' (*Blake Records*, 148).

27 Jan. 1804
    [1] Adam Walker (1731?–1821), author, lecturer, inventor, friend of Romney.

Mr Romney in town soon. Note, Your Letter to M^r J Romney I sent off the morning after I recievd it from you being then in health⌊·⌋² I have taken your noble present to Mr Rose & left it with charge to the Servant of Great Care⌊;⌋ the Writing looks very pretty⌊·⌋ I was fortunate in doing it myself & hit it off excellently⌊·⌋³ I have not seen Mr Rose, tho he is in town. Mr Flaxman is not at all acquainted with Sr Allan Chambre⌊·⌋⁴ recommends me to enquire concerning him of Mr Rose⌊;⌋ my brother says he believes Sr Allan is a Master in Chancery. — Tho I have calld on Mr Edwards twice for Lady Hamiltons⁵ direction⌊·⌋ was so unfortunate as to find him Out both times⌊·⌋ I will repeat my Call on him tomorrow morning⌊·⌋

2] My Dear Sir I write now to satisfy you that all is in a good train⌊·⌋ I am going on briskly with the Plates⌊·⌋ find every thing promising, Work in Abundance; & if God blesses me with health doubt not yet to make a Figure in the Great Dance of Life that shall amuse the Spectators in the Sky. I thank You for my Demosthenes⁶ which is now become a noble subject— My Wife gets better every Day; hope earnestly that you have entirely escaped the brush of my Evil Star, which I beleive is now for ever fallen into the Abyss. God bless & preserve You & our Good Lady Paulina⁷ with the Good things both of this life & of eternity & with you my much admired & respected Edward the Bard of Oxford⁸ whose verses still sound upon my Ear like the distant approach of things mighty & magnificent⌊·⌋ like the sound of harps which I hear before the Suns rising⌊·⌋ like the remembrance of Felphams waves & of the Glorious &

---

² Hayley's letter of 16 Jan. to John Romney is given in *Blake Records*, 147.

³ This is probably a bank draft enclosed in a complimentary sonnet transcribed by Blake. On 5 May 1804 Samuel Rose wrote to his father-in-law that he had been 'magnificently remunerated by Hayley' 'for my Defense of Blake' (*Blake Records*, 152).

⁴ Sir Alan Chambré (1739–1823), judge, whose portrait Romney painted.

⁵ Emma (1761?–1815), wife of Sir William Hamilton, mistress of Nelson, beloved model for Romney.

⁶ Presumably 'The Death of Demosthenes' engraved by Blake after Thomas Hayley for Hayley's *Essay on Sculpture* (1800).

⁷ Miss Harriet Poole, whose villa was in Lavant.

⁸ Probably Edward Garrard Marsh (1783–1862), then studying for the priesthood at Oxford, who wrote cheerful doggerel to Hayley in which Blake is once mentioned (*Blake Records*, 111). He may be referred to in *Jerusalem* pl. 46, l. 7, as 'Oxford, immortal Bard'.

far beaming Turret, like the Villa of Lavant⌊,⌋ blessed & bless-
ing⌊.⌋ Amen⌊.⌋ God bless you all O people of Sussex around
your Hermit & Bard⌊.⌋ So prays the Emulator of both his &
your mild & happy tempers of Soul your devoted

Will Blake

S^th Molton Street
Friday Jany 27, 1804

23 FEBRUARY 1804

'To / William Hayley Esqre' [*presumably enclosed in a cover
bearing the full address*]

Dear Sir

[¶*1*]   I calld Yesterday on Mr Braithwaite[1] as you desired & found
him quite as chearful as you describe him & by his appearance
should not have supposed him to be near sixty notwithstanding
he was shaded by a green shade over his Eyes. He gives a very
spirited assurance of Mr John Romneys interesting himself in
the great object of his Fathers Fame & thinks that he must be
proud of such a work & in such hands. The Picture from
Sterne[2] which you desired him to procure for you, he has not
yet found where it is. Supposes that it may be in the north &
that he may learn from Mr Romney who will be in town soon—
Mr B. desires I will present his Compliments to you & write
you that he has spoken with Mr Read[3] concerning the Life of
Romney⌊;⌋ he interests himself in it & has promised to procure
dates of premiums⌊,⌋ Pictures &c Mr Read having a number of
Articles relating to Romney either written or printed which
he promises to copy out for your use, as also the Catalogue of
Hampstead Sale. He shewd me a very fine Portrait of M^rs
Siddons (by Romney) as the Tragic Muse half-length that is

23 Feb. 1804
    [1] Daniel Braithwaite of the Post Office was Romney's earliest London patron
and the dedicatee of Hayley's *Life of George Romney* (1809).
    [2] Probably 'The introduction of Doctor Slop, into the parlour of Mr Shandy'
from Sterne's *Tristram Shandy* engraved by William Haines for Hayley's *Romney*,
at p. 31.
    [3] Perhaps Isaac Reed (1742–1807), editor of Shakespeare and book collector,
who was a friend of Romney and Hayley. Reed owned *Poetical Sketches* (F), a
presentation copy from Nancy Flaxman in 1784.

the Head & hand*s*, & in his best Style. He also desires me to express to you his wish that you would give the Public an Engraving of that Medallion by your Sons matchless hand[4] which is placd over his chimney piece between two little pretty pictures correct and enlarged copies from antique Gems of which the center ornament is worthy, he says that it is by far in his opinion the most exact resemblance of Romney he ever saw⌊.⌋ I have furthermore the pleasure of informing you that he knew immediately my Portrait of Romney & assured me that he thought it a very great likeness⌊.⌋

2]   I wish I could give you a Pleasant account of our beloved Counsellor⌊;⌋[5] he Alas was ill in bed when I calld yesterday at about 12 O clock, & the servant said that he remains very ill indeed.

3]   Mr Walker I have been so unfortunate as not to find at home but I will call again in a day or two. Neither Mr Flaxman nor Mr Edwards know Lady Hamiltons address⌊;⌋ the house Sr William livd in in Piccadilly She left some time ago⌊.⌋ Mr Edwards will procure her address for you & I will send it immediately⌊.⌋

4]   I have inclosd for you the 22 Numbers of Fuseli's Shakespeare that are out & the book of Italian Letters from Mrs Flaxman who with her admirable husband present their best Compliments to you⌊;⌋ he is so busy that I believe I shall never see him again but when I call on him for he has never yet since my return to London had the time or grace to call on me⌊.⌋ Mrs Flaxman & her Sisters gave also their testimony to my Likeness of Romney. Mr Flaxman I have not yet had an opportunity of consulting about it but soon will⌊.⌋

5]   I inclose likewise the Academical Correspondence of Mr Hoare[6] the Painter whose note to me I also inclose for I did but express to him my desire of sending you a Copy of his work & the day after I recievd it, with the note Expressing his pleasure [of your *del*] in your wish to see it. You would be much delighted with the Man as I assure myself you will be with his work⌊.⌋

---

[4] The medallion of Romney by Thomas Hayley engraved by Caroline Watson for Hayley's *Romney*.   [5] Samuel Rose.

[6] Prince Hoare (1755–1834), artist (1772–85), popular dramatist, and Honorary Foreign Secretary to the Royal Academy, in which last capacity he published *Academic Correspondence* (1804) with a frontispiece engraved by Blake after Flaxman.

[¶6]   The plates of Cowpers Monument are both in great forward-
ness & you shall have Proofs in another week⌊.⌋ I assure you
that I will not spare pains & am myself very much satisfied that
I shall do my duty & produce two Elegant plates⌊;⌋ there is
however a great deal of work in them that must & will have
time.

'Busy Busy Busy I bustle along
Mounted upon warm Phoebus's rays
Thro the heavenly throng⌊.⌋'[7]

[¶7]   But I hastend to write to you about Mr Braithwaite⌊;⌋ hope
when I send my proofs to give as good an account of M^r
Walker.

My wife joins me in Respects & Love to yo*u*, & desires with
mine to present hers to Miss Poole⌊.⌋

I remain Dear Sir Your Sincere
Will Blake

S^th Molton Street
23 Feby. 1804

12 MARCH 1804

'To / William Hayley Esqre / Felpham near / Chichester /
Sussex'

Dear Sir

[¶1]   I begin with the latter end of your letter & grieve more for
Miss Pooles illhealth than for my failure in sending proofs tho

---

⁷ These lines come from *The Rehearsal* by George Villiers, Duke of Buckingham,
Act v, scene i, in a duet between two kings:

We sail with thunder in our mouth.
In scorching noon-day, whilst the traveller stays;
Busy, busy, busy, busy, we bustle along,
Mounted upon warm Phoebus's rays,
Thro' the heavenly throng,
Hasting to those
Who will feast us at night with a pig's petty-toes.

The Rehearsal was often printed between 1672 and 1777, but it seems likely that
Blake remembered the lines from one of the nine performances in London between
1771 and 1792 (see Morchard Bishop, 'Blake and Buckingham', *Times Literary
Supplement*, 2 April 1964, p. 277).
The quotation marks are Blake's.

I am very sorry that I cannot send before Saturdays Coach. Engraving is Eternal work; the two plates are almost fiinshd⌞·⌟ You will recieve proofs of them for Lady Hesketh, whose copy of Cowpers letters ought to be printed in [le]tters of Gold & ornamented with Jewels of Heaven⌞,⌟ Havilah⌞,⌟ Eden & all the countries where Jewels abound⌞·⌟ I curse & bless Engraving alternately because it takes so much time & is so untractable, tho capable of such beauty & perfection⌞·⌟

2]   My wife desires with me to Express her Love to you Praying for Miss Pooles perfect recovery & we both remain

March 12—   Your Affectionate
1804   Will Blake

16 MARCH 1804

'To / William Hayley Esqre'

Dear Sir

1]   According to your Desire I send proofs of the Monumental Plates tho as you will percieve they have not the last touches especially the Plate of the Monument which I have drawn from Mr Flaxmans Model with all the fidelity I could & will finish with equal care, the writing being exactly copied from the tracing paper which was traced on the marble— The inscriptions to the Plates I must beg of you to send to me that I may Engrave them immediately⌞·⌟

2]   The drawing of the Monument which Mr Johnson sent has the following Inscription— 'Monument Erected to the 'Memory of William Cowper Esqre in St Edmunds Chapel.' 'East Dereham by the Lady Hesketh 1803'—But it strikes me that St Edmunds Chapel East Dereham may be understood to mean a Chapel in East Dereham *Town* & not to Express sufficiently, that the Monument is in *East Dereham Church*.[1] Owing to my determination of sending you Proofs I have not been able to consult Mr Flaxman about the Designs of M^r

16 March 1804
[1] The plate in Hayley's *Cowper* (1804), iii, is inscribed: 'A View of St Edmund's Chapel, in the Church of East Dereham in Norfolk In Memory of William Cowper Esqre Etch'd by W Blake from the original Model by John Flaxman Esqr Sculptor to his Majesty'; it is dated 25 March 1804.
The quotation marks in the letter are Blake's.

Romney which are at Saunders'. I calld once of [*i.e. on*] M^r F: but he was not at home so could not spare more time but will now immediately proceed in that business. The Pleasure I recievd from your kind Letter ought to make me assiduous & it does so. That Mr John Romney is so honest as to expose to you his whole absurd prejudice gives hopes that he may prove worthy of his father & that he should tell such inconsistent surmizes proves that they will soon be eradicated & forgotten⌊.⌋ You who was his fathers best friend will I hope become the most respected object of his love & admiration⌊.⌋

[¶*3*]   I calld on Mr Hoare with your Elegant & Heart lifting Compliment; he was not at home. I left it with a short note, have not seen him since—

[¶*4*]   Mr Rose I am happy to hear is getting quite well. Hope to hear the same good account of our most admirable & always anxiously rememberd Miss Poole⌊.⌋

[¶*5*]   Mr Braithwaite calld on me & brought two Prints which he desires may be sent to you (with His Compliments) (which you will find inclosed) one is a copy from that Miniature you kindly sufferd me to make, from the Picture of Romney which I am now Engraving: & which was lent by Mr Long[2] for the purpose of being Engraved for the European Mag^{ne}⌊.⌋ The other is Mrs Siddons from the Picture by Romney in Mr Braithwaites possession but as much unlike the original as possible⌊.⌋

My Wife joins me in best Affections to you
& I remain Sincerely Yours

16 March 1804   Will Blake

I inclose also N° 23 of the Shakspeare⌊.⌋

21 MARCH 1804

'To / William Hayley Esqre / Felpham' [*probably enclosed in a cover bearing the full address*]

Dear Sir

[¶*1*]   I send two Proofs of Each of the Monumental Plates with the writing, which I hope will please. Should have sent the

---

[2] William Long (1747–1818), surgeon, was an old friend of Flaxman and Hayley.

twelve of each if I had not wishd to improve them still more, & because I had not enough paper in proper order for printing: beg pardon for the omission of Mr Braithwaites two Print*s*, as also for omitting to mention Mr Hoares grateful sensation on His reception of your very beautiful Verses. I now send you his note to Me as I think it will give you a good idea of this good & excellent Man_L._」

²]   I have been able to look at the Drawings & Pictur*e*, but Flaxman has not yet been able to go with me_L._」 Am sorry to inform you that one of the drawings which Mr Romney destined for you is Lost or at least cannot now be found_L ;_」 it is that of the Witch raising the Storm. Mr Romney says that in lieu of the last drawing you shall have choice of either of the remaining ones of which Sa[u]nders says there are severa*l*, but I only saw one more because I would not give much trouble as Flaxman was not with me. The Drawing I saw is of a Female Figure with a Serpent in one hand & a torch in the other, both held above her head & a figure kneeling at her feet. *I*t is a very sublime drawing & would make an Excellent Print but I will not advise any thing till Flaxman sees them_L._」 Th*c* Drawing of Pliny in the Eruption of Vesuvius is very clever & indeed a Sublime but very unfinishd Sketch.—The Picture of the Man on horseback rescuing the drowning people is a beautiful Performance.[1] Mr Saunders says that he has orders from Mr Romney to deliver the Picture & two drawings to any person whom you shall authorize to recieve them_L._」 They are somewhat batterd but not so much as I expected for I remember, & Saunders says, that they never were properly strained upon their straining frames_L._」

¹]   We both rejoice that Miss Poole is better but hope & pray for her intire recovery_L._」

My wife joins me in Sincere love to you_L ;_」 please to remember us both affectionately & gratefully to Miss Poole

& believe me to remain Ever Yours

Sth Molton Street   Will Blake
March 21. 1804

21 March 1804
   [1] Blake made a drawing from this design (BMPR) and an engraving entitled 'Sketch of a Shipwreck' for Hayley's *Romney* (1809).

31 MARCH 1804

'To / William Hayley Esqre / Felpham near Chichester /
Sussex'

Dear Sir

I did not recieve your Letter till Monday of course could not
have got them Printed to send by tuesdays Coach But there is a
real reason equally good why I have not yet sent. I hope you
will believe me when I say that my solicitude to bring them to
perfection has caused this delay as also not being quite sure
that you had Copies ready for them. I could not think of
delivering the 12 Copies[1] without giving the last touches which
are always the best. I have now I hope given them & we
directly go to Printing. Consequently it will be by Tuesdays
Coach that you will recieve 12 of Each. If you do not wish any
more done before I deliver them pray favor me with a lin*e*, that
I may send the Plates to Johnson who wants them to set the
Printer to work upon⌊.⌋

<table>
<tr><td>I remain</td><td>In Engravers hurry</td></tr>
<tr><td></td><td>which is the worst & most unprofitable of hurries</td></tr>
<tr><td>St Molton S^t</td><td>Your Sincere & Affectionate</td></tr>
<tr><td>March 31. 1804</td><td>Will Blake</td></tr>
</table>

2 APRIL 1804

TO [*William Hayley*]

April 2nd, 1804.

* * Mr. Flaxman advises that the drawing of Mr. Rom-
ney's which shall be chosen instead of the Witch (if that cannot
be recovered) be Hecate, the figure with the torch and snake,
which he thinks one of the finest drawings. The twelve im-
pressions of each of the plates which I now send ought to be
unrolled immediately that you receive them and put under
somewhat to press them flat. You should have had fifteen of
each, but I had not paper enough in proper order for printing.

31 March 1804
   [1] Hayley's anxiety about these 12 copies for 'the particular Friends, who we
wish'd to supply with the *utmost Celerity*' is exhibited in *Blake Records*, 149–51.

Letter, 7 April 1804

There is now in hand a new edition of Flaxman's *Homer* with additional designs, two of which I am now engraving.[1] I am uneasy at not hearing from Mr. Dally,[2] to whom I inclosed £15 in a letter a fortnight ago, by his desire. I write to him by this post to inquire about it. Money in these times is not to be trifled with. I have now cleared the way to Romney, in whose service I now enter again with great pleasure, and hope soon to show you my zeal with good effect. Am in hopes that Miss Poole is recovered, as you are silent on that most alarming and interesting topic in both your last letters. God be with you in all things. My wife joins me in this prayer.

I am, dear Sir,
Your sincerely affectionate,
Willm. Blake.

7 APRIL 1804

'To / William Hayley Esq[re] / Felpham near Chichester / Sussex'

Dear Sir

You can have no Idea unless you was in London as I am how much your Name is lovd & respected. I have the Extreme pleasure of transmitting to you one proof of this Respect which you will be pleased with & I hope will adopt & embrace. It comes thro' M[r] Hoare from M[r] Phillips[1] of S[t] Pauls Church Yard. It is as yet an intire Secret between M[r] P, M[r] H, & myself & will remain so till you have given Your Decision— M[r] Phillips is a man of vast spirit & enterprize, with a solidity of character which few have, he is the man who applied to Cowper for that sonnet in favor of a Prisoner at Leicester[2]

2 April 1804

[1] *The Iliad of Homer* Engraved from the Compositions of Iohn Flaxman (1805) had 5 plates more than the edition of 1793, 3 of them engraved by Blake.

[2] R. Dally was evidently a Chichester solicitor, who acted for Blake at his 1804 trial (*Blake Records*, 136–7).

7 April 1804

[1] Richard Phillips (1767–1840), bookseller, publisher of the *Monthly Magazine*, later knighted.

[2] On 18 June 1793 Cowper wrote that he had 'composed a sonnet in . . . favour' of Richard Phillips who was 'now in gaol at Leicester, having been cast

which I believe you thought fit not to Print_{⌊.⌋} So you see he is spiritually adjoind with us. His connections throughout England & indeed Europe & America enable him to Circulate Publications to an immense Exten*t*, & he told Mr Hoare that on the present work which he proposes to commence with your assistance he can afford to expend 2,000 a year. Mr Phillips considers you as the Great Leading Character in Literature & his terms to others will amount to only one Quarter of what he proposes to you. I send Inclosd his Terms as Mr Hoare by my desire has given them to me in writing. Knowing your aversion to Reviews & Reviewing I consider the Present Proposal as peculiarly adapted to your Ideas_{⌊;⌋} it may be calld a Defence of Literature against those pests of the Press & a bulwark for Genius_{⌊,⌋} which shall with your good assistanc*e*, disperse those Rebellious Spirits of Envy & Malignity_{⌊.⌋} In shor*t*, If you see it as I see i*t*, You will embrace this Proposal on the Score of Parental Duty_{⌊.⌋} Literature is your Child. She calls for your assistance! You: who never refuse to assist any how remote soever will certainly hear her Voice. Your answer to the Proposa*l*, you will if you think fit direct to Mr Hoare who is worthy of every Confidence you can place in him_{⌊.⌋}

I am dear Sir

Sth Molton Street   Your anxiously Devoted
  April 7. 1804   Will Blake
    Mr Hoares address is
      To Prince Hoare Esqre
      Buckingham Street
        Strand

27 APRIL 1804

'To / William Hayley Esqre / Felpham near Chichester / Sussex'

Dear Sir

[¶*1*]   I have at length seen Mr Hoare after having repeatedly calld on him every day & not finding him. I now understand

in a prosecution for selling Pain[*e*]'s treasons' (*The Unpublished and Uncollected Letters of William Cowper*, ed. T. Wright [1925], 76), but Rose evidently advised him that it would be legally unwise to communicate it, and Hayley seems to have agreed.

that he recievd your reply to P.s Proposal at Brighton where he has a residenc*e*, from whence he sent it to London to Mr Phillips. *H*e has not seen P. since his return & therefore cannot tell me how he understood your answer. Mr H. appears to me to consider it as a rejection of the Proposal altogether_L._J I took the liberty to tell him that I could not consider it *so*, but that as I understood you, You had accepted the Spirit of P's intention which was to leave the whole Conduct of the affair to you & that you had accordingly nominated one of your Friends & agreed to nominate others. *B*ut if P. meant that you should yourself take on you the drudgery of the ordinary business of a Review his Proposal was by no means a generous one. Mr H. has promised to See Mr Phillips immediately & to know what his intentions ar*e*, but he say*s*, Perhaps Mr P. may not yet have seen your letter to hi*m*, & that his multiplicity of business may very well account for the delay_L._J

2]   I have seen our Excellent Flaxman lately_L;_J he is well in health but has had such a burn on his hand as you had once which has hinderd his working for a fortnight, it is now better. *H*e desires to be most affectionately rememberd to you_L;_J had begun a letter to you a week ago_L;_J perhaps by this time you have recievd it but he is also a laborious votary of Endless Work. Engraving is of so Slow Process I must beg of you to give me the earliest possible notice of what Engraving is to be done fo*r* The Life of Romney_L._J Endless Work is the true title of Engraving as I find by the things I have in hand day and night_L._J

3]   We feel much easier to hear that you have parted with your Horse_L,_J hope soon to hear that you have got a living one of brass_L,_J a pegasus of Corinthian metal & that Miss Poole is again in such health as when she first mounted me on my beloved Bruno_L._J[1]

4]   I forgot to mention that Mr Hoare desires his most respectful compliments to you. Speaks of taking a ride across the country to Felpham as he always keeps a Horse at Brighton_L._J

    *M*y wife joins me in Love to you_L._J

Sth Molton Street	I remain Yours Sincerely
[26 *del*] 27 April 1804	Willm Blake

27 April 1804

    [1] Evidently the horse Blake rode in Felpham; see the note to 16 Sept. 1800.

4 MAY 1804

TO [*William Hayley*]

May 4th, 1804.

Dear Sir,

[¶*1*]   I thank you sincerely for Falconer, an admirable Poet, and the admirable prints to it by Fittler.¹ Whether you intended it or not, they have given me some excellent hints in engraving; his manner of working is what I shall endeavour to adopt in many points. I have seen the elder Mr. Walker. He knew and admired without any preface, my print of Romney, and when his daughter came in he gave the print into her hand without a word, and she immediately said, 'Ah! Romney! younger than I have known him, *but very like indeed*.'² Mr. Walker showed me Romney's first attempt at oil painting; it is a copy from a Dutch picture—Dutch boor smoking; on the back is written, 'This was the first attempt at oil painting by G. Romney.' He shew'd me also the last performance of Romney. It is of Mr. Walker and family, the draperies put in by somebody else. It is a very excellent picture, but unfinished. The figures as large as life, half length, Mr. W., three sons, and I believe two daughters, with maps, instruments, &c. Mr. Walker also shew'd me a portrait of himself (W.), whole length on a canvas about two feet by one and a half; it is the first portrait Romney ever painted. But above all, a picture of *Lear and Cordelia*, when he awakes and knows her,—an incomparable production which Mr. W. bought for five shillings at a broker's shop; it is about five feet by four, and exquisite for expression, indeed it is most pathetic; the heads of Lear and Cordelia can never be surpassed, and Kent and the other attendant are admirable; the picture is very highly finished. Other things I saw of Romney's first works,—two copies, perhaps from Borgognone, of battles; and Mr. Walker promises to collect all he can of information for you. I much admired his mild and gentle, benevolent manners; it seems as if all Romney's intimate friends were truly amiable and feeling like himself.

4 May 1804
¹ William Falconer, *The Shipwreck*, A Poem, ed. J. S. Clarke (1804), with 8 plates engraved by J. Fittler.
² The quotation marks appear in Gilchrist's transcript.

2]   I have also seen Alderman Boydel, who has promised to get the number and prices of all Romney's prints as you desired. He has sent a Catalogue of all his Collection,[3] and a Scheme of his Lottery;[4] desires his compliments to you, says he laments your absence from London, as your advice would be acceptable at all times[5] but especially at the present. He is very thin and decay'd, and but the shadow of what he was; so he is now a Shadow's Shadow; but how can we expect a very stout man at eighty-five, which age he tells me he has now reached? You would have been pleas'd to see his eyes light up at the mention of your name.

3]   Mr. Flaxman agrees with me that somewhat more than outline is necessary to the execution of Romney's designs, because his merit is eminent in the art of massing his lights and shades. I should propose to etch them in a rapid but firm manner, somewhat, perhaps, as I did the *Head of Euler*;[6] the price I receive for engraving Flaxman's outlines of *Homer* is five guineas each.[7] I send the Domenichino, which is very neatly done. His merit was but little in light and shade; outline was his element, and yet these outlines give but a faint idea of the finished prints from his works, several of the best of which I have. I send also the French monuments, and inclose with them a catalogue of Bell's Gallery[8] and another of the Ex-

[3] *An Alphabetical Catalogue of Plates*, engraved by the most esteemed artists, After the Finest Pictures and Drawings of the Italian, Flemish, German, French, English, and other schools, which compose the stock of John and Josiah Boydell, Engravers and Printsellers, No. 90, Cheapside, and at the Shakspeare Gallery, Pall Mall (1803).

[4] By Act of Parliament (43 Geo III c 91), Alderman John Boydell (1719–1804) was allowed to sell 22,000 three-guinea tickets for a lottery of his printselling stock to be held 27 June 1805 (see J. Ashton, *A History of English Lotteries* [1893], 134–8, where the Prospectus for the lottery is quoted).

[5] Hayley had helped to originate Boydell's Shakspeare Gallery.

[6] Leonard Euler, *Elements of Algebra* (1797), with a frontispiece of Euler engraved by Blake.

[7] Flaxman had written to Hayley on 1 May: 'M.' Blake is to have from 5 to 6 Guineas each from Mess.ʳˢ Longman & Rees for the plates of the Homer according to the labor, but what the proper recompense for more finished engraving might be I cannot tell . . . . it might perhaps be advantageous to Romney's life, to adorn the book with two or three bold etchings shadowed on a small scale, in which Blake has succeeded admirably sometimes & to engrave some of the other compositions in outline only for head & tail pieces . . .' (*Blake Records*, 151–2).

[8] The opening of Bell's Gallery of Fine Arts, at the corner of Southampton Street in the Strand, was announced in the *Monthly Magazine* for April 1804

hibition[9] which I have *not* yet seen. I mention'd the pictures from Sterne to Mr. Walker; he says that there were several; one, a garden scene with uncle Toby and Obadiah planting in the garden; but that of Lefevre's Death he speaks of as incomparable, but cannot tell where it now is, as they were scatter'd abroad, being disposed of by means of a raffle. He supposes it is in Westmoreland; promises to make every inquiry about it. Accept also of my thanks for Cowper's third volume, which I got, as you directed, of Mr. Johnson. I have seen Mr. Rose; he looks, tho' not so well as I have seen him, yet tolerably, considering the terrible storm he has been thro'! He says that the last session was a severe labour, indeed it must be so to a man just out of so dreadful a fever. I also thank you for your very beautiful little poem on the King's recovery; it is one of the prettiest things I ever read, and I hope the King will live to fulfil the prophecy and die in peace: but at present, poor man, I understand he is poorly indeed, and times threaten worse than ever. I must now express my sorrow and hopes for our good Miss Poole, and so take my leave for the present with the joint love of my good woman, who is still stiff-knee'd but well in other respects.

> I am, dear Sir,
> Yours most sincerely,
> William Blake.

28 MAY 1804

TO [*William Hayley*]

May 28th, 1804.

Dear Sir,

[¶*1*]   I thank you heartily for your kind offer of reading, &c. I have read the book thro' attentively and was much entertain'd

(p. 274), where it was also stated that Bell offered, at prices lower than those in Paris, such works as Alexander Lenoir's *Museum of French Monuments*; or An Historical and Chronological Description of the Monuments in Marble, Bronze, and Bas-Relief, Collected in the Museum at Paris: Ornamented with Elegant Etchings, Translated from the French by J. R. Griffiths, Volume I [no more published], Paris, 1803.

⁹ Presumably *The Exhibition of the Royal Academy, M.DCCCIV* The Thirty-Sixth (1804), which had just opened.

and instructed, but have not yet come to the *Life of Washington.*[1]
I suppose an American would tell me that Washington did all
that was done before he was born, as the French now adore
Buonaparte and the English our poor George; so the Americans
will consider Washington as their god. This is only Grecian,
or rather Trojan, worship, and perhaps will be revis'd[?] in an
age or two. In the meantime I have the happiness of seeing the
Divine countenance in such men as Cowper and Milton more
distinctly than in any prince or hero. Mr. Phillips has sent a
small poem, he would not tell the author's name, but desired me
to inclose it for you with Washington's Life.

2]   Mr. Carr[2] call'd on me, and I, as you desired, gave him a
history of the reviewing business as far as I am acquainted with
it. He desires me to express to you that he would heartily devote
himself to the business in all its laborious parts, if you would
take on you the direction; and he thinks it might be done with
very little trouble to you. He is now going to Russia; hopes that
the negotiations for this business is not wholly at an end, but
that on his return he may still perform his best, as your assistant
in it. I have delivered the letter to Mr. Edwards, who will give
it immediately to Lady Hamilton. Mr. Walker I have again
seen; he promises to collect numerous particulars concerning
Romney and send them to you—wonders he has not had a line
from you; desires me to assure you of his wish to give every
information in his power. Says that I shall have *Lear and
Cordelia* to copy if you desire it should be done; supposes that
Romney was about eighteen when he painted it; it is therefore
doubly interesting. Mr. Walker is truly an amiable man; spoke
of Mr. Green as the oldest friend of Romney, who knew most
concerning him of any one; lamented the little difference that
subsisted between you,[3] speaking of you both with great affec-

28 May 1804
  [1] John Marshall, *The Life of George Washington* (Printed for Richard Phillips,
1804). The Dedication at the beginning and Advertisement at the end are dated
10 May and the portrait of Washington 15 May, suggesting that the work had
been recently published. Between pp. 176 and 308 the type changes to a distinctly
clearer typeface, though it seems of the same size as the rest.
  [2] John Carr (1772–1832), travel writer, later knighted.
  [3] This 'little difference' concerned the reversion of Romney's picture of 'Flax-
man Modelling the Bust of Hayley' (in which Hayley had a life-interest); Romney
had apparently agreed that it should go to both Flaxman (Hayley's candidate)

tion. Mr. Flaxman has also promised to write all he knows or can collect concerning Romney, and send to you. Mr. Sa[u]nders has promised to write to Mr. J. Romney immediately, desiring him to give us liberty to copy any of his father's designs that Mr. Flaxman may select for that purpose; doubts not at all of Mr. Romney's readiness to send any of the cartoons to London you desire; if this can be done it will be all that could be wished. I spoke to Mr. Flaxman about choosing out proper subjects for our purpose; he has promised to do so. I hope soon to send you Flaxman's advice upon this article. When I repeated to Mr. Phillips your intention of taking the books you want from his shop,[4] he made a reply to the following purpose:—'I shall be very proud to have Mr. Hayley's name in my books, but please to express to him my hope that he will consider me as the sincere friend of Mr. Johnson, who is (I have every reason to say) both the most generous and honest man I ever knew, and with whose interest I should be so averse to interfere that I should wish him to have the refusal first of anything before it should be offered to me, as I know the value of Mr. Hayley's connexion too well to interfere between my best friend and him.'[5] This Phillips spoke with real affection, and I know you will love him for it, and will also respect Johnson the more for such testimony; but to balance all this I must, in duty to my friend Seagrave tell you that Mr. Rose repeated to me his great opinion of Mr. Johnson's integrity while we were talking concerning Seagrave's printing: it is but justice therefore, to tell you that I perceive a determination in the London booksellers to injure Seagrave in your opinion, if possible. Johnson may be very honest and very generous, too, where his own interest is concerned, but I must say that he leaves no stone unturn'd to serve that interest, and often (I think) unfairly; he always has taken care, when I have seen

and Thomas Greene (1737–1810, lawyer for both Hayley and Romney)—see M. Bishop, 'The Poet and the Attorney: The Story of a Legacy', *To Geoffrey Keynes* (1972), 37–47. The breach in 1801 between Hayley and Greene was permanent.

    [4] Evidence from other letters (22 June, 16 July, 28 Sept., 4 Dec. 1804, 19 Jan. 1805) makes it clear that Blake regularly collected, and often read before forwarding, newly published books which Phillips offered to send Hayley.

    [5] The quotation marks here and below appear in Gilchrist's transcript.

him, to rail against Seagrave, and I perceive that he does the same by Mr. Rose. Mr. Phillips took care to repeat Johnson's railing to me, and to say that country printers could not do anything of consequence. Luckily he found fault with the paper which Cowper's *Life* is printed on, not knowing that it was furnish'd by Johnson. I let him run on so far as to say that it was scandalous and unfit for such a work; here I cut him short by asking if he knew who furnish'd the paper, he answered, 'I hope Mr. J. did not.' I assured him that he did, and here he left off; desiring me to tell you that the *Life of Washington* was not put to press till the 3rd of this month (May), and on the 13th he had deliver'd a dozen copies at Stationers Hall, and by the 16th five hundred were out. This is swift work if literally true, but I am not apt to believe literally what booksellers say; and on comparing *Cowper* with *Washington* must assert that *except paper* (which is Johnson's fault) *Cowper* is far the best, both as to type and printing. Pray look at *Washington* as far as page 177, you will find that the type is smaller than from 177 to 308, the whole middle of the book being printed with a larger and better type than the two extremities;[6] also it is carefully hot-pressed. I say thus much being urged thereto by Mr. Rose's observing some defects in Seagrave's work, which I conceive were urged upon him by Johnson: and as to the time the booksellers would take to execute any work, I need only refer to the little job which Mr. Johnson was to get done for our friend Dally. He promised it in a fortnight, and it is now three months and is not yet completed. I could not avoid saying thus much in justice to our good Seagrave, whose replies to Mr. Johnson's aggravating letters have been represented to Mr. Rose in an unfair light, as I have no doubt; because Mr. Johnson has, at times, written such letters to me as would have called for the sceptre of Agamemnon rather than the tongue of Ulysses, and I will venture to give it as my settled opinion that if you suffer yourself to be persuaded to print in London you will be cheated every way; but, however, as some little excuse, I must say that in London every calumny and falsehood utter'd against another of the same trade is thought fair play. Engravers, Painters, Statuaries, Printers, Poets we are not in a field of battle but in

[6] See n. 1, above.

a City of Assassinations.[7] This makes your lot truly enviable, and the country is not only more beautiful on account of its expanded meadows, but also on account of its benevolent minds. My wife joins with me in the hearty wish that you may long enjoy your beautiful retirement.

[¶3]   I am, with best respects to Miss Poole, for whose health we constantly send wishes to our spiritual friends,

Yours sincerely,
William Blake.

[¶4]   P.S.—Mr. Walker says that Mr. Cumberland is right in his reckoning of Romney's age. Mr. W. says Romney was two years older than himself, consequently was born in 1734.

[¶5]   Mr. Flaxman told me that Mr. Romney was three years in Italy; that he returned twenty-eight years since. Mr. Humphry, the Painter,[8] was in Italy the same time with Mr. Romney. Mr. Romney lodged at Mr. Richter's, Great Newport Street, before he went; took the house in Cavendish Square immediately on his return; but as Flaxman has promised to put pen to paper you may expect a full account of all he can collect. Mr. Sa[u]nders does not know the time when Mr. R. took or left Cavendish Square house.

22 JUNE 1804

'To / William Hayley Esq[re] / Felpham near Chichester / Sussex'

Dear Sir

[¶1]   I have got the three Sublime Designs of Romney now in my Lodgings[1] & find them all too Grand as well as too undefined

[7] Hayley quoted this phrase in a letter to Flaxman of 18 June, and on 2 Aug. Flaxman replied: 'with respect to Blake's remark upon "Assassinations" I suppose he may have been acquainted with wretches capable of such practises, but I desire it may be understood that I am not one of them, & tho' I do not deal in "barbarous Stilettos" myself I am willing to acknowledge the benevolence & soundness of Blake's general observation as well as the point & keenness with which it was applied; but this was only a poetic jeu d'esprit which neither did nor intended harm'.(*Blake Records*, 152–3).

[8] Ozias Humphry (1742–1810), miniaturist.

22 June 1804

[1] On 16 June 1804 William Saunders had written to Hayley: 'M[r] Blake calld on me & I have sent him—the three pictures, one the Oil picture, & the two drawings he chose—deliverd them at his house in South Molton S[t]' (*Blake Records*, 153).

for meer outlines, & indeed it is not only my opinion but that of Mr Flaxman & Mr Parker² both of whom I have consulted that to give a true Idea of Romneys Genius nothing less than Some Finishd Engravings will d*o*, as Outline intirely omits his chief beautie*s*, but there are some which may be executed in a slighter manner than other*s*, & Mr Parker whose Eminence as an Engraver makes his opinion deserve notice has advise*d*, that 4 should be done in the highly finished manner & 4 in a less Finishd—& on my desiring him to tell me for what he Would undertake to Engrave One in Each manner the size to be about 7 Inches by 5¼ which is the size of a Quarto printed Pag*e*, he answere*d*: '30 Guineas the finish*d*, & half the sum for the less finishd: but as you tell me that they will be wanted in November I am of opinion that if Eight different Engravers are Employd the Eight Plates will not be done by that time; as for myself (Note Parker now speaks) I have to day turned away a Plate of 400 Guineas because I am too full of work to undertake it, & I know that all the Good Engravers are so Engaged that they will be hardly prevaild upon to undertake more than One of the Plates on so short a notice.' This is Mr Parkers account of the matte*r*, & perhaps may discourage you from the Pursuit of so Expensive an undertaking. *I*t is certain that the Pictures deserve to be Engraved by the hands of Angels & must not by any means be done in a careless or too hasty manner⌊.⌋ The Price M^r· Parker has affixd to each is Exactly what I myself had before concluded upo*n*, Judging as he did that if the Fuseli Shakespeare is worth 25 Guineas, these will be at least worth 30, & that the inferior ones cannot be done at any rate under 15.

[2]   Mr Flaxman advises that the best Engravers should be engaged in the work as its magnitude demands all the Talents that can be procured⌊.⌋

[3]   Mr Flaxman named the following Eight as proper subjects for Prints⌊:⌋

    1 The Vision of Atossa from Eschylus
    2 Apparition of Darius
    3 Black Eyd Susa*n*, a figure on the Sea shore embracing a Corse

        ² James Parker, fellow apprentice with Blake under James Basire.

4 The Shipwreck with the Man on Horseback &^c which I have

5 Hecat*e*, a very fine thing indeed, which I have

6 Pliny very fine but very unfinish*d*, Which I have

7 Lear & Cordelia belonging to Mr Walker

8. One other which I omitted to write down & have forgot but think that it was a Figure with Children which he calld a Charity.

[¶4] I write immediately on recieving the Above Informatio*n*, because no time should be lost in this truly interesting business⌊.⌋

[¶5] Richardson is not yet Published.³ My Head of Romney is in very great forwardness. Parker commends it highly. Flaxman has not yet seen i*t*, but shall soon, & then you shall have a Proof of it for your remarks also. I hope by this time Flaxman has written to you & that you will soon recieve such documents as will enable you to decide on what is to be done in our desirable & arduous task of doing Justice to our admired Sublime Romney. I have not yet been able to meet Mr Braithwaite at home but intend very soon to call again & (as you wish) to write all I can collect from him—be so good as to give me your Earliest decision on what would be safe & not too venturesom[*e*] in the number of projected Engraving*s*, that I may put it into a train to be properly Executed⌊.⌋

[¶6] We both rejoice in the generous Paulinas return with recoverd strength to her delightful Villa⌊;⌋ please to present our sincerest Affections to her. My Wife continues to get better & joins me in my warmest love & acknowledgments to you as do my Brother & Sister⌊.⌋

        I am Dear Sir Yours Sincerely

Sth Molton Street   William Blake

 22. June 1804

³ The publication of *The Correspondence of Samuel Richardson*, ed. Anna Lætitia Barbauld, Six Volumes (London: Printed for Richard Phillips) was announced in Phillips's *Monthly Magazine* of July 1804 (p. 600).

16 JULY 1804

'To / William Hayley Esqre / Felpham near / Chichester / Sussex'

Dear Sir

*] We are both happy to hear that Miss Poole is better, sincerely Pray that she may soon be perfectly restored. I calld on Mr Rose in Chancery Lane on Friday, hear that he is in Sussex & is well⌊,⌋ suppose that he does not tell the worst to his family⌊;⌋ hope that so valuable a life will be preserved in health & strength— I send Richardson accompanied by a Proof of Romney in Still an unfinishd state, but it will have the great advantage to [?of] Time to its completion. I also send a Sketch of the Heroic Horseman as you wishd me to do—the size the Print is to be.[1]

*] Mr Phillips desired I would present his most respectful Compliments to you & inform you that he with Mr Hoare intended to have visited you together—that terrible wet Tuesday but could not for the Deluges of Rain. M^r P was at Brighton with Mr Hoare— fears that So good an opportunity of seeing you may not occur soon again— Mr P. refuses to recieve payment for Books & says that he will not recieve it in Money but in some how else more agreeable still⌊,⌋ of course he means to pursue his court to [his(?) del] Your ∧Coy∧ Muse. I wish him Success⌊.⌋

*] I omitted to get Richardson till last Friday having calld thrice unsuccessfully ∧&∧ before publication have only had time to skim it but cannot restrain myself from speaking of Mrs Klopstocks Letters Vol 3[2]— which to my feelings are the purest image of Conjugal affection honesty & Innocence I ever saw on paper. Richardson has won my heart⌊.⌋ I will again read Clarissa &^c⌊;⌋ they must be admirable⌊.⌋ I was too hasty

16 July 1804
[1] Blake eventually engraved a 'Sketch of a Shipwreck after Romney' for Hayley's *Romney* (1809).
[2] The letters between Richardson and Mrs. Klopstock (*The Correspondence of Samuel Richardson*, ed. A. L. Barbauld [1804], iii. 139–57) were widely admired; according to the *Edinburgh Review*, v (1804), 39, they 'have pleased us infinitely beyond anything else in the collection'.

in my perusal of them to percieve all their beauty. I admire Miss Watsons³ head of Richardson⌐,⌐ it is truly delicate⌐:⌐

'The patient touches of unwearied Art.'⁴

I am now Earnestly employd on the Heroic Horseman endeavoring to do justice to so admirable a Picture⌐.⌐
My Wife joins me in love to you⌐.⌐

I remain Dear Sir

Sth Molton St̲ Your Sincere &
16 July 1804 Obliged Servt
  Will Blake

7 AUGUST 1804

TO [*William Hayley*]

It is certainly necessary that the best artists that can be engaged should be employed on the work of Romney's Life. . . . How can it be that lightness should be wanting in my works, while in my life and constitution I am too light and aërial, is a paradox only to be accounted for by the things of another world. Money flies from me; Profit never ventures upon my threshold, tho' every other man's doorstone is worn down into the very earth by the footsteps of the fiends of commerce. Be it so, as long as God permits, which I foresee is not long. I foresee a mighty change.¹

---

³ Caroline Watson (1764?–1814), engraver.
⁴ Pope, 'The Temple of Fame', ll. 198–9: Virgil
  Finish'd the whole, and labour'd ev'ry Part,
  With patient Touches of unweary'd Art . . . .
The quotation marks in the letter are Blake's.

7 Aug. 1804
  ¹ The Sotheby catalogue of 20 May 1878, lot 22, quotes the first sentence, plus 'Money flies . . . fiends of commerce', without any indication of their relationship. (In this version, a period follows 'from me', a hyphen appears in 'door-stone', and 'Earth' is capitalized.) Everything but the first sentence is quoted above from the Sotheby catalogue of 27 July–1 Aug. 1885, lot 1031, in which the first sentence is omitted. Both catalogues give Hayley as the addressee.

9 AUGUST 1804

TO [*William Hayley*]

[*A letter signed*] W. and C. Blake[1]

28 SEPTEMBER 1804

TO [*William Hayley*] [*presumably enclosed in a cover bearing the address*]

Dear Sir

1]   I hope you will Excuse my delay in sending the Books which I have had some time but kept them back till I could send a Proof of the Shipwreck which I hope will please. It yet wants all its last & finishing touches, but I hope you will be enabled by it to judge of the Pathos of the Picture⌞.⌟

2]   I send Washingtons 2ᵈ Vol:—5 Numbers of Fuselis Shakspeare & two Vol's with a Letter from Mʳ Spilsbury[1] with whom I accidentally met in the Strand. *H*e says that he relinquishd Painting as a Profession, for which I think he is to be applauded, but I concieve that he may be a much better Painter if he pracitises Secretly & for amusement than he could ever be if employd in the drudgery of fashionable dawbing for a poor pittance of money in return for the sacrifice of Art & Genius. *H*e says he never will leave to practise the Art because he loves it & This Alone will pay its labour by Success if not of money yet of True Ar*t*, which is All— I had the pleasure of a call from Mʳˢ Chetwynd & her Brother,[2] a Giant in body

9 Aug. 1804

    [1] The only known reference to the letter is the following passage in the 1878 Sotheby catalogue: 'Two A.L.s signed W. and C. Blake On the subject of "Our Ballads," and other matters connected with art and literature, dated *26th Oct.* 1803, and *9th August*, 1804, respectively, and outline of the "Death of Demosthenes." ' The subject-matter seems to derive exclusively from the October letter, whereas the signature appears to be from that of August (the October letter is signed 'Will. Blake'). Blake's engraving of 'The Death of Demosthenes' for Hayley's *Essay on Sculpture* (1800) is evidently an added item in the lot rather than a subject of discussion in the letters.

28 Sept. 1804

    [1] Jonathan Spilsbury (1737–1812), painter and engraver.

    [2] On 9 Sept. 1801 John Carr wrote to Hayley of Mr. Chetwynd: 'You & Blake have made a Coxcomb of a wretched untutored Artist' (*Blake Records*, 82).

mild & polite in Soul as I have in general found great bodies to be└;┘ they were much pleased with Romneys Designs. Mʳˢ C. sent to me the two articles for you & for the safety of which by the Coach I had some fears till Mʳ Meyer³ obligingly undertook to convey them safe└;┘ he is now I suppose enjoying the delights of the Turret of Lovely Felpham└;┘ please to give my affectionate compliments to him.

[¶3]   I cannot help suggesting an Idea which has struck me very forcibly that the Tobit & Tobias in your bedchamber would make a very beautiful Engraving done in the same manner as the Head of Cowper after Lawrence, The Heads to be finishd & the figures left exactly in imitation of the first strokes of the Painter└.┘ The Expression of those truly Pathetic heads would thus be transmitted to the Public└—┘ a sinuglar Monument of Romneys Genius in that Highest branch of Art└.┘

[¶4]   I must now tell my wants & beg the favor of some more of the needful└;┘ the favor of ten Pounds more will carry me thro this Plate & the Head of Romney for which I am already paid. You shall soon see a Proof of Him in a very advancd state└.┘ I have not yet proved it but shall soon when I will send you one — I rejoice to hear from Mʳ Meyer of Miss Pooles continued recovery└.┘ My wife desires with me her respects to you & her & to all whom we love that is to all Sussex└.┘

Sth Molton St   I remain Your Sincere & Obliged
28 Septʳ 1804   Hble Servant
                                        Will. Blake

To
William Hayley Esqʳᵉ
Felpham

23 OCTOBER 1804

TO [*William Hayley*]

                                            23rd Oct. 1804.

Dear Sir,

[¶1]   I received your kind letter with the note to Mr. Payne,¹ and

³ William Meyer, son of Hayley's friend Jeremiah, the miniaturist.

23 Oct. 1804
    ¹ Thomas Payne [Jr.] (1752–1831), publisher of Hayley's *Romney* (1809).

have had the cash from him. I should have returned my thanks immediately on receipt of it, but hoped to be able to send, before now, proofs of the two plates, the *Head* of R. and the *Shipwreck*, which you shall soon see in a much more perfect state. I write immediately because you wish I should do so, to satisfy you that I have received your kind favour.

2]   I take the extreme pleasure of expressing my joy at our good Lady of Lavant's[2] continued recovery, but with a mixture of sincere sorrow on account of the beloved Councillor.[3] My wife returns her heartfelt thanks for your kind inquiry concerning her health. She is surprisingly recovered. Electricity is the wonderful cause; the swelling of her legs and knees is entirely reduced. She is very near as free from rheumatism as she was five years ago, and we have the greatest confidence in her perfect recovery.

3]   The pleasure of seeing another poem from your hands has truly set me longing (my wife says I ought to have said us) with desire and curiosity; but, however, 'Christmas is a coming.'[4]

4]   Our good and kind friend Hawkins[5] is not yet in town— hope soon to have the pleasure of seeing him—with the courage of conscious industry, worthy of his former kindness to me. For now! O Glory! and O Delight! I have entirely reduced that spectrous Fiend to his station, whose annoyance has been the ruin of my labours for the last passed twenty years of my life. He is the enemy of conjugal love, and is the Jupiter of the Greeks, an iron-hearted tyrant, the ruiner of ancient Greece. I speak with perfect confidence and certainty of the fact which has passed upon me. Nebuchadnezzar had seven times passed over him, I have had twenty; thank God I was not altogether a beast as he was; but I was a slave bound in a mill among beasts and devils; these beasts and these devils are now, together with myself, become children of light and liberty, and my feet and my wife's feet are free from fetters. O lovely Felpham, parent of

---

² The Lady of Lavant is Miss Harriet Poole, Hayley's friend and neighbour.

³ Samuel Rose (1767–1804) defended Blake at his treason trial (Jan. 1804), where he fell ill; he died in the following December.

⁴ The quotation marks appear in Gilchrist's transcript.

⁵ John Hawkins (1758?–1841), dilettante, had been a generous patron of Blake in 1783 (see *Blake Records*, 24–8, 70–2, 99).

Immortal Friendship, to thee I am eternally indebted for my three years' rest from perturbation and the strength I now enjoy. Suddenly, on the day after visiting the Truchsessian Gallery of Pictures,[6] I was again enlighted with the light I enjoyed in my youth, and which has for exactly twenty years been closed from me as by a door and by window-shutters. Consequently I can, with confidence, promise you ocular demonstration of my altered state on the plates I am now engraving after Romney, whose spiritual aid has not a little conduced to my restoration to the light of Art. O the distress I have undergone, and my poor wife with me. Incessantly labouring and incessantly spoiling what I had done well. Every one of my friends was astonished at my faults, and could not assign a reason; they knew my industry and abstinence from every pleasure for the sake of study, and yet—and yet—and yet there wanted the proofs of industry in my works. I thank God with entire confidence that it shall be so no longer:—he is become my servant who domineered over me, he is even as a brother who was my enemy. Dear Sir, excuse my enthusiasm or rather madness, for I am really drunk with intellectual vision whenever I take a pencil or graver into my hand, even as I used to be in my youth, and as I have not been for twenty dark, but very profitable, years. I thank God that I courageously pursued my course through darkness. In a short time I shall make my assertion good that I am become suddenly as I was at first, by producing the *Head of Romney* and the *Shipwreck* quite another thing from what you or I ever expected them to be. In short, I am now satisfied and proud of my work, which I have not been for the above long period.

[¶5] If our excellent and manly friend Meyer is yet with you, please to make my wife's and my own most respectful and affectionate compliments to him, also to our kind friend at Lavant.

> I remain, with my wife's joint affection,
> Your sincere and obliged servant,
> Will. Blake.

---

[6] About 1,000 pictures described in the *Catalogue of the Truchsessian Picture Gallery*, now exhibiting in the New Road, opposite Portland Place (1803).

4 DECEMBER 1804

'To / William Hayley Esqre / Felpham near Chichester / Sussex'

Dear Sir

1]   I have omitted so long to thank you for your kind & admirable Present in hopes to send Proofs of my plates but can no longer wait for them but must express my own & my wifes high gratification in the perusal of your elegant & pathetic Poem. To say that Venusia[1] is as beautiful as Serena is only expressing private opinion which will vary in each [i]ndividual, but to say that She is Your Daughter & is like You⌊,⌋ to say 'tis a Gir*l*, promising Boys hereafter' & to say God bless her for she is a peerless Jewel for a Prince to wear & that we are both highly delighted is what I could not longer omit to say. — Proofs of my Plates will wait on you in a few days. *I*n the mean while I conclude this hasty scrawl with sincere thanks for your kind proposal[2] in your Last Letter. I have not yet been able to meet Phillips. Wilkes[3] was not out when I calld nor any more of Washington. But I have mentiond your Proposal to our Noble Flaxman whose high & generous Spirit relinquishing the whole to me was in some measure to be Expecte*d*, but that he has reasons for not being able to furnish any designs You will readily believe⌊;⌋ he says his engagements are so multiform that he should not be able to do them Justic*e*, but that he will overlook & advise & do all that he can to make my designs

---

4 Dec. 1804

[1] The name, which appears to have been written first as 'Venussia', refers to Hayley's *Triumph of Music* (1804), which is about a girl named Venusia, and of which Hayley seems to have sent Blake a copy.

The quotation marks below are Blake's.

[2] The proposal evidently concerned Hayley's tragedy 'Edward I', with plates to be designed either by Flaxman or by Blake and engraved by Blake. On 12 Aug. 1805 Flaxman wrote to Hayley: 'concerning the Edward the first, I have seen two or three noble sketches by Blake which might be drawn in outline by him in a manner highly creditable to your book & I would overlook them so far as to see that they should be Suitable to the other designs' (*Blake Records*, 165). 'Edward I' has still not been published.

[3] This is probably *The Correspondence of the late John Wilkes, with his Friends*, ed. John Almon, Five Volumes (London: Printed for Richard Phillips, 1805). Evidently Phillips was sending his new publications to Hayley through Blake as Hayley chose them from an announcement list.

(should they ever be attempted) what he can, & I know his
What he Can will be full as much as he pretends so that I
should not fear to produce somewhat in this way that must be
satisfactory⌊;⌋ the only danger will be that I shall put my Name
to his Designs but if it should fall out so he has Enough &
to Spare & the World will know his at once & I shall glory in
the Discover*y*, for Friendship with such a one is better than
Fame! — I was about to have written to you to express my
wish that two so unequal labourers might not be yoked to the
same Plow & to desire you if you could to get Flaxman to do
the whole because I thought it would be (to say the best of
myself) like pulling John Milton with John Bunyan but being
at Flaxmans taking his advice about our Engravings he men-
tiond his having recievd a Letter from you on the same Day I
recievd mine & said somewhat, I cannot tell what, that made
me think you had opend your Proposal to him — I thought at
any rate it would not be premature to tell him what you had
said about the designs for Edward the firs*t*, & he advised it to
be done as above related⌊.⌋

[¶2]   I will soon speak with Phillips about it if you will favor me
with a line of direction how to proceed,— Hope in a few days to
send Proofs of Plates[4] which I must say are far beyond Any
thing I have ever done. For⌊,⌋ O happiness never enough to be
grateful for! I have lost my Confusion of Thought while at
work & am as much myself when I take the Pencil or Graver
into my hand as I used to be in my Youth⌊.⌋ I have indeed
fought thro a Hell of terrors & horrors (which none could know
but mysel*f*) in a divided Existence now no longer divide*d*, nor at
war with myself⌊.⌋ I shall travel on in the strength of the Lord
God as Poor Pilgrim says⌊.⌋[5]

    My wife joins me in Love to You & to our Dear Friend &
Friends at Lavant & in all Sussex⌊.⌋

                I remain dear Sir Your Sincere & obliged

Sth Molton S^t   Will Blake

  4 Dec^r· 1804

    [4] Blake's engravings of Romney's 'Shipwreck' and self-portrait (the latter not
printed) for Hayley's *Romney* (1809).
    [5] In Bunyan's *Pilgrim's Progress*.

18 DECEMBER 1804

TO [*William Hayley*]

[*December 18th, 1804*]¹

Dear Sir,

1]   I send, with some confidence, proofs of my two plates, having had the assistance and approbation of our good friend Flaxman. He approves much (I cannot help telling you so much) of the *Shipwreck*. Mrs. Flaxman also, who is a good co[*n*]noisseur in engraving, has given her warm approbation, and to the plate of the *Portrait*, though not yet in so high finished a state. I am sure (mark my confidence) with Flaxman's advice, which he gives with all the warmth of friendship both to you and me, it must be soon a highly finished and properly finished print; but yet I must solicit for a supply of money, and hope you will be convinced that the labour I have used on the two plates has left me without any resource but that of applying to you. I am again in want of ten pounds; hope that the size and neatness of my plate of the *Shipwreck* will plead for me the excuse for troubling you before it can be properly called finished, though Flaxman has already pronounced it so. I beg your remarks also on both my performances, as in their present state they will be capable of very much improvement from a few lucky or well advised touches. I cannot omit observing that the price Mr. Johnson gives for the plates of Fuseli's *Shakespeare* (the concluding numbers of which I now send) is twenty-five guineas each. On comparing them with mine of the *Shipwreck*, you will perceive that I have done my duty and put forth my whole strength.

2]   Your beautiful and elegant daughter *Venusea* grows in our estimation on a second and third perusal. I have not yet received the *History of Chichester*.² I mention this not because I would hasten its arrival before it is convenient, but fancy it may

---

18 Dec. 1804

¹ Gilchrist (who is the source of the letter) gives its date in his own text, not Blake's.

² Alexander Hay's *History of Chichester* (1804) was dedicated to Hayley, who subscribed for 'four copies, large paper'; one of these he evidently sent to Blake and another to Flaxman, who thanked Hayley for his copy on 1 Oct. 1804 (letter in the Pierpont Morgan Library).

have miscarried. My wife joins me in wishing you a merry Christmas. Remembering our happy Christmas at lovely Felpham, our spirits seem still to hover round our sweet cottage and round the beautiful Turret. I have said *seem*, but am persuaded that distance is nothing but a phantasy. We are often sitting by our cottage fire, and often we think we hear your voice calling at the gate. Surely these things are real and eternal in our eternal mind, and can never pass away. My wife continues well, thanks to Mr. Birch's Electrical Magic, which she has discontinued these three months.

I remain your sincere and obliged,
William Blake.

28 DECEMBER 1804

'To / William Hayley Esqre / Felpham near / Chichester / Sussex'

Dear Sir

[¶*1*]   The Death of so Excellent a Man as my Generous Advocate is a Public Loss which those who knew him can best Estimate & to those who have an affection for him like Yours, is a Loss that only can be repaird in Eternity where it will indeed with such abundant felicity in the meeting Him a Glorified Saint who was a Suffering Mortal that our Sorrow is swallowd up in Hope. Such Consolations are alone to be found in Religion⌞,⌟ the Sun & the Moon of our Journey⌞;⌟ & such Sweet Verses as yours in your last beautiful Poem must now afford you their full reward⌞.⌟

[¶*2*]   Farewell Sweet Rose thou hast got before me into the Celestial City. I also have but a few more Mountains to pass for I hear the bells ring & the trumpets sound to welcome thy arrival among Cowpers Glorified Band of Spirits of Just Men made Perfect⌞.⌟[1]

[¶*3*]   Now My Dear Sir I will thank you for the transmission of ten Pounds to the Dreamer over his own Fortune*s*, for I certainly am that Dreamer, but tho I dream over my own

28 Dec. 1804
   [1] Samuel Rose died on 20 Dec. 1804. The 'spirits of just men made perfect' is from Hebrews 12: 23.

Fortunes I ought not to dream over those of other Men & accordingly have given a look over my account Book in which I have regularly written down Every Sum I have recievd from you, & tho I never can balance the account of obligations with you I ought to do my best at all times &i n all circumstances— I find that you was right in supposing that I had been paid for all I have don*e*, but when I wrote last requesting ten pounds I thought it was Due on the Shipwreck (which it was) but I did not advert to the Twelve Guineas which you Lent Me when I made up 30 Pounds to pay our Worthy Seagrave in part of his Account² — I am therefore that 12 Guineas in your Deb*t*, Which If I had Considerd, I should have used more consideration & more ceremony also in so serious an affair as the calling on you for more Mone*y*, but however your Kind answer to my Request makes me Doubly Thank you⌊·⌋

4] The two Cartoons which I have of Hecate & Pliny are very unequal in point of finishing⌊;⌋ the Pliny in [*is*] a Sketch tho admirably contrived for an Effect equal to Rembrandt. But the Hecate is a finishd Production which will call for all the Engravers nicest attention, indeed it is more finishd than the Shipwreck⌊;⌋ it is every body'[*s*] favourite who has seen it & they regularly prefer it to the Shipwreck as a work of Genius⌊·⌋ As to the [Plates *del*] Price of the Plates Flaxman declares to me that he will not pretend to set a price upon Engraving. I think it can only be done by Some Engraver. I consulted M*r* Parker on the Subject before I decided on the Shipwreck & it was his opinion & he says it still is so that a Print of that Size cannot be done under 30 Guineas if finishd & if a Sketch 15 Guineas⌊;⌋ as therefore Hecate must be a Finishd Plate I consider 30 Guineas as its Price & the Pliny 15 Guineas⌊·⌋

5] Our Dear Friend Hawkins is out of Town & will not return till April. I have sent to him by a parcel from Col Sibthorpes³ your Desirable Poetical Present for M*rs* Hawkins. His address is this — To John Hawkins Esq*r* Dallington near Northampton⌊·⌋ M*r* Edwards is out of Town likewise⌊·⌋

---

² Hayley wrote to the bookseller R. H. Evans on 3 April 1803: 'my worthy Friend Blake . . . has paid a Bill of 30*£* [*presumably to Seagrave*] for paper' for the 1802 *Ballads* (*Blake Records*, 114).

³ Humphrey Sibthorpe, M.P., father of Hester, wife of John Hawkins.

[¶6]   I am very far from shewing the Portrait of Romney as a finishd Proo*f*; be assured that with our Good Flaxmans good help & with your remarks on it in addition I hope to make it a Supernaculum. The Shipwreck also will be infinitely better the next proof. I feel very much gratifid at your approval of my Queen Catherin*e*; beg to observe that the Print of Romeo & the Apothecary annexd to your copy is a shamefully worn out impression but it was the only one I could get at Johnsons.⁴ I left a good impression of it when I left Felpham last in one of Heaths Shakespeare⌊;⌋ you will see that it is not like the same Plate with the worn out Impression — My Wife joins me in love & in rejoicing in Miss Pooles continued health. I am Dear Sir

Sth Molton Street   Yours Sincerely
  28 Decr 1804⁵   Will. Blake

[¶7]   P.S. I made a very high finishd Drawing of Romney as a Companion to my drawing of the head of Cowper (you remember) with which Flaxman is very much satisfied & says that when my print is like that I need wish it no bette*r*, & I am determind to make it so at least. ——————————— W B

19 JANUARY 1805

'To William Hayley Esqre' [*presumably enclosed in a cover bearing the address*]

Dear Sir   Saturday

[¶*1*]   I at length send the Books which I have in vain calld for at the Publishers¹ 3 several time*s*, but his removal from St Pauls to a noble House in Bridge Street Blackfriars perhaps hinderd his sending & perhaps his wish that I might again call. I have

---

⁴ Blake's two plates after Fuseli, of 'Katharine, Griffiths & Patience', and of Romeo and the Apothecary, in *The Plays of William Shakspeare* (1804–5) published by Joseph Johnson and many others.

⁵ The outgoing London postmark of the Inland Mail of 'C·D·E / 29 / 804' indicates that the letter was posted between about 8 p.m. of the 28th and about 6.30 p.m. of the 29th.

19 Jan. 1805
  ¹ Richard Phillips.

however Seen him this morning, & he has in the most open & explicit manner offerd his service to you Expressing his desire that I will repeat to you his regret that your last beautiful Poem[2] was not Publishd in the Extensive way (I speak his own words) that a Poem of Confessedly the first Poet of England ought to be given to the Public (Speaking so I must own he won my heart)⌊.⌋ He said 'I know that Dodsley[3] was Mʳ Hayleys Publisher but hope that as Mʳ D. is dead & if Mʳ H has no Engagement with any London Book-Seller I may myself be appointed by him in so honourable a concern as the Publication of his Labours.' He then Proceeded to find fault with the Printing of our friend the Chichester Printer. Here I considerd it my duty to interfere. I expressd my own respect for our Good Seagrave & said I knew your chief intentions in Employing him were 1ˢᵗ to Encourage a Worthy Man & 2ᵈ For the Honour of Chichester. Mʳ P immediately replie*d*: 'If Mʳ Hayley should think fit to employ me as his Publisher I should have no objection but a pleasure in employing his Printer & have no doubt I could be of service to him in many ways but I feel for the Honour of London Booksellers & consider thcm as losing a great deal of Honour in Losing the first Publication of any work of Mʳ Hayleys & the Public likewise are deprived of the advantage of so extensive a diffusal as would be promoted by the methods which they use to Publish & disperse Copies into all parts to a very great amount⌊.⌋' He then sai*d*: 'If Mʳ Hayley is willing to dispose of this his New Poem I will Purchase it & at his own Price or any other of his Works—For I do assure you I feel it a duty to my Profession that I should do my Endeavour to give Mʳ Hayleys works the first rate Elegance in Printing & Paper as they hold the First in internal value.' I then said 'Is it agreeable to you that I repeat what you have said to me, To Mʳ Hayley or will you yourself for I dare say he will be much pleasd to hear from y*ou*, but' said *I*, 'I will if you wish (as I shall write soon) give him (as near as I can remember) what you have said, & hope that he will see the matter in the light you do.'— He desired I would, expressing (for which I thank him) confidence in my discretion—— Such was our conversation

---

[2] *The Triumph of Music*, 'Chichester Printed by and for J. Seagrave. . . .'
[3] James Dodsley (1724–97).

as near as I can recollect, I thought it best to keep Silent as to any thing like a hint of a proposal relating to Edwd 1st [& *del*] or the Ballads having come from you⌊,⌋ accordingly I did not say that I knew of any Poem but left all to you intirely— I do think from the Liberality of this Enterprizing Man that all Parties⌊,⌋ I mean our Friend Seagrave together with the Author & Publisher (& also the Public)⌊,⌋ may be mutually & extensively benefitted. His connexions are Universal⌊;⌋ his present House is on the most noble scale & will be in some measure a Worthy Town Vehicle for your Beautiful Muse. But Mr Phillips said 'Mr Hayley shall have whatever I publish sent to him if he pleases & he may return them when he has read them—' Such is his determination to do every thing to engage himself to you if possible. He desired I would present you from him with the little volume of poems inclosd⌊;⌋ they are by a Lady of Fortune⌊.⌋ I suppose he sends it as a specimen of Printing— P's chief objection to the manner in which the Triumphs of Music are printed — were the strong Metal Rules at the Ends of the Canto's — but he confessd to me that the first Page of the Poem was beautifully executed & could not be better done⌊.⌋

[¶2]   Pray might I not Shew Phillips the four Numbers of Ballads? or will you write to him? or will you think it best to commission me to answer him? whatever you command I will zealously perform— & Depend upon it I will neither do nor say but as you Direct⌊.⌋

[¶3]   I feel extremely happy that you think My Prints will do me Credit & at the very idea of another Journey to Sweet[?] Felpham. O that I could but bring Felpham to me or go to her in this World as easy as I can in that of Affection & Remembrance. I feel it is necessary to be very circumspect how we advance with Romney⌊;⌋ his best works only, ought to be engraved for your Work⌊.⌋

       Pray accept My & My Wifes Sincerest Affection
         & believe me to remain Yours Sincerely

Sth Molton Street   Will Blake
19 Jany 1805

22 JANUARY 1805

TO [*William Hayley*]

Jan. 22nd, 1805.

Dear Sir,

[1]   I hope this letter will outstrip Mr. Phillips', as I sit down to write immediately on returning from his house. He says he is agreeable to every proposal you have made, and will himself immediately reply to you. I should have supposed him mad if he had not, for such clear and generous proposals as yours to him he will not easily meet from any one else. He will, of course, inform you what his sentiments are of the proposal concerning the three dramas. I found it unnecessary to mention anything relating to the purposed application of the profits, as he, on reading your letter, expressed his wish that you should yourself set a price, and that he would, in his letter to you, explain his reasons for wishing it. The idea of publishing one volume a year he considers as impolitic, and that a handsome general edition of your works would be more productive. He likewise objects to any periodical mode of publishing any of your works, as he thinks it somewhat derogatory as well as unprofitable. I must now express my thanks for your generous manner of proposing the *Ballads* to him on my account, and inform you of his advice concerning them; and he thinks that they should be published *all together* in a volume the size of the small edition of the *Triumphs of Temper*, with six or seven plates. That one thousand copies should be the first edition, and if we choose, we might add to the number of plates in a second edition. And he will go equal shares with me in the expense and the profits, and that Seagrave is to be the printer.[1] That we must consider all that has been printed as lost, and begin anew, unless we can apply some of the plates to the new edition. I consider myself as only put in trust with this work, and that the copyright is for ever yours. I, therefore, beg that you will not suffer it to be injured by my ignorance, or that it should in any

22 Jan. 1805
   [1] The second edition of *Designs to A Series of Ballads* (1802) was printed by Seagrave and published by Phillips as *Ballads* (1805) in a volume the size of Hayley's *Triumphs of Temper* (1803) with five new engravings by Blake dated 18 June 1805. There were no further editions.

way be separated from the grand bulk of your literary property. Truly proud I am to be in possession of this beautiful little estate; for that it will be highly productive, I have no doubt, in the way now proposed; and I shall consider myself a robber to retain more than you at any time please to grant. In short, I am tenant at will, and may write over my door as the poor barber did, 'Money for live here.'[2]

[¶2]   I entreat your immediate advice what I am to do, for I would not for the world injure this beautiful work, and cannot answer P.'s proposal till I have your directions and commands concerning it; for he wishes to set about it immediately, and has desired that I will give him my proposal concerning it in writing.

I remain, dear Sir,
Your obliged and affectionate,
Will. Blake.

22 MARCH 1805

'To / William Hayley Esqre / Felpham near Chichester / Sussex'

Friday[1]

Dear Sir

[¶1]   This Morning I have been with Mr Phillips & have intirely settled with him the plan of Engraving for the new Edition of the Ballads—The Prints 5 in Number I have Engaged to finish by 28 May. They are to be as highly finishd as I can do them⌐,⌐ the Size the same as the Serena plates⌐,⌐[2] the Price 20 Guineas Each⌐,⌐ half to be paid by P—⌐.⌐ The Subjects I cannot do better than those already chosen, as they are the most eminent among Animals Viz The Lion, The Eagle, The Horse, The Dog. Of the Dog Species the Two Ballads are so preeminent

---

² The quotation marks are Blake's.

22 March 1805

¹ Though this letter seems to have been started on 'Friday' 22 March 1805, the outgoing London postmark of the Inland Mail ('A·MR· / 25 / 805') clearly indicates that it was not posted until 3 days later.

² Blake had made 6 plates for Hayley's *Triumphs of Temper* (1803), illustrative of the adventures of the heroine Serena.

& my Designs for them please me so well that I have chosen that design in our Last Number of the Dog & Crocodil*e* & that of the Dog defending his dead Master from the Vultures ⌞;⌟ of these five I am making little high finishd Pictures the Size the Engravings are to b*e*, & am hard at it to accomplish in time what I intend.[3] M^r P— says he will send Mr Seagrave the Paper directly⌞.⌟

⌐2] The Journeymen Printers throughout London are at War with their Masters & are likely to get the better⌞.⌟ Each Party meet to consult against the other, nothing can be greater than the Violence on both sides⌞.⌟ Printing is svspended in London Except at private Presses. I hope this will become a source of Advantage to our Friend Seagrave⌞.⌟[4]

⌐3] The Idea of Seeing an Engraving of Cowper by the hand of Caroline Watson is I assure you a pleasing one to me⌞;⌟ it will be highly gratifying to see another Copy by another hand & not only gratifying but Improvin*g*, which is better⌞.⌟[5]

⌐4] The Town is Mad⌞.⌟ Young Roscius[6] like all Prodigies is the talk of Every Body⌞.⌟ I have not seen him & perhaps never may. I have no curiosity to see him as I well know what is within the compass of a boy of 14, & as to Real Acting it is Like Historical Painting⌞,⌟ No Boys Work⌞.⌟

5] Fuseli is made Master of the Royal Academy. Banks the Sculptor is Gone to his Eternal House. I have heard that Flaxman means to give a Lecture on Sculpture at the Royal

---

[3] On 25 April Phillips wrote to Hayley that 'Mr Blake is forwarding [*i.e. going forward with*] the Plates' 'for the Ballads' (*Blake Records*, 161). These were the 5 subjects engraved for Hayley's *Ballads* (1805).

[4] By 9 March, according to the Master Printers, some 250 pressmen had left their jobs, 'thereby leaving, on their part, all public and private Business nearly at a stand' (*The London Compositor*, ed. E. Howe [1947], 103, 104). For the way in which Blake helped Seagrave to get printing work with Phillips see *Blake Records*, 156 ff.

[5] John Carr wrote to Hayley on 28 March 1805 about a conversation he had had with Blake the day before 'with respect to Caroline Watson's engraving, he observed that his feelings were not wounded, & that he was completely satisfied with your wishes' (*Blake Records*, 161). Caroline Watson re-engraved the Romney frontispiece for the new edition of Hayley's *Cowper* (1806), and later she also engraved 7 of the plates Blake had expected to make for Hayley's *Romney* (1809).

[6] William Henry West Betty (1791–1874), a child prodigy known as 'The Young Roscius' (after the most celebrated Roman actor Quintus Roscius Gallus), had been astonishing London audiences since his first appearance at Covent Garden in the autumn of 1804.

Academy on the Occasion of Banks's Death⌊;⌋[7] he died at the
Age of 75 of a Paralytic Stroke. Now I concieve Flaxman
stands without a competitor in Sculpture⌊.⌋

[¶6]   I must not omit to tell you that on leaving Mr Phillips I
askd if he had any Message to you as I meant to write im-
mediately. *H*e said 'Give my best Respects & tell Mr Hayley
that I wish very much to be at work for him.' But perhaps I
ought to tell you what he said to me previous to this in the
course of our Conversation. His words were 'I feel somewhat
Embarrasd at the Idea of setting a value on any work of M^r
Hayleys & fear that he will wish me to do so.' I asked him how
a Value was set on any Literary work⌊;⌋ he answer'd 'The
Probable sale of the work would be the measure of Estimating
the Profits & that would lead to a Valuation of the Copy
right—⌊.⌋' This may be of no Consequence but I could not
omit telling it you⌊.⌋

[¶7]   My Wife Continues in health & desires to join me in every
Grateful Wish to you & to our Dear Respected Miss Poole⌊.⌋

> I remain
> Yours with Sincerity
> William Blake

[¶8]   P.S. Your Desire that I should write a little Advertisement
at the Beginning of the Ballads has set my Brains to work &
at length producd the following. Simplicity as you desired has
been my first object. I send it for your Correction or Condemna-
tion begging you to supply its deficiency or to New Create it
according to your wish.

[¶9]   The Public ought to be informd that [The following *del*]
These Ballads were the Effusions of Friendship to Countenance

----

[7] After the death of Thomas Banks (1735–2 Feb. 1805), Flaxman wrote to
the Royal Academy on 13 Feb. 'to request that I may deliver a Discourse to the
Academy on the death of Thomas Banks Esqr'; permission was given, and on 16
Feb. 'Mr Flaxman attended and read the heads of his intended Discourse', which
being approved as well, on 27 Feb. 'Mr Flaxman attended & read a Discourse on
the Genius & Character of the late Thomas Banks, Esqr' (Royal Academy Council
Minutes, Vol. iii, pp. 330, 332, 335; Flaxman's Address was 'first published from
the original manuscript' in the second edition of his *Lectures on Sculpture* [1838],
269–94.) Blake's information of *22 March* is evidently considerably out of date.

what their Author is kindly pleased to call Talents for Designing and to relieve my more laborious [employment *del*] engagement of Engraving those Portraits which accompany The Life of Cowper⌞.⌟ Out of a number of Designs I have selected Five [*and*] hope that the Public will approve of my rather giving few highly labourd Plates than a greater number & less finishd. If I have succeeded in these more may be added at Pleasure⌞.⌟[8]

Will Blake

17 MAY 1805

TO [*William Hayley*]

Reading in the Bible of the eyes of the Almighty,[1] I could not help putting up a petition for yours. . . . [*'Speaks of his rough sketch of an advertisement (the diction of which had been improved), and says'*] that if any of my writings should hereafter appear before the Public, they will fall far short of this Specimen.

4 JUNE 1805

TO [*William Hayley*]

June 4th, 1805.
Dear Sir,
I have fortunately, I ought to say providentially, discovered that I have engraved one of the plates for that ballad of *The Horse* which is omitted in the new edition;[1] time enough to save the extreme loss and disappointment which I should have suffered had the work been completed without that ballad's insertion. I write to entreat that you would contrive so as that

---

[8] No Advertisement was printed in the book.

17 May 1805
[1] Perhaps Blake was reading in Zechariah 4: 10 of the 'seven . . . eyes of the Lord, which run to and fro through the whole earth'.

4 June 1805
[1] 'The Horse' was included in the *Ballads* (1805), though Hayley and Lady Hesketh were later amused by it, and D. G. Rossetti said that 'the brute . . . seems absolutely snuffling with propriety' (*Blake Records*, 164).

my plate may come into the work, as its omission would be to me a loss that I could not now sustain as it would cut off ten guineas from my next demand on Phillips, which sum I am in absolute want of; as well as that I should lose all the labour I have been at on that plate, which I consider as one of my best; I know it has cost me immense labour. The way in which I discovered this mistake is odd enough. Mr. Phillips objects altogether to the insertion of my Advertisement, calling it an appeal to charity, and says that it will hurt the sale of the work, and he sent to me the last sheet by the penny (that is the twopenny) post, desiring that I would forward it to Mr. Seagrave. But I have inclosed it to you, as you ought and must see it. I am no judge in these matters, and leave all to your decision, as I know that you will do what is right on all hands. Pray accept my and my wife's sincerest love and gratitude.

Will. Blake.

27 NOVEMBER 1805

TO [*William Hayley*]

Dear Sir

[¶*1*] Mr Cromek[1] the Engraver came to me desiring to have some of my Designs. *H*e namd his Price & wishd me to Produce him Illustrations of The Grave A Poem by Robert Blair. *I*n consequence of this I produced about twenty Designs[2] which pleasd so well that he with the same liberality with which he set me about the drawing*s*, has now set me to Engrave them. He means to Publish them by Subscription with the Poem as you will see in the Prospectus which he sends you in the same

---

27 Nov. 1805

    [1] Robert Hartley Cromek (1770–1812), engraver and literary entrepreneur.

    [2] On 18 Oct. 1805 Flaxman told Hayley: 'Mr Cromek has employed Blake to make a set of 40 drawings from Blair's poem of the Grave 20 of which he proposes [*to*] have engraved by the Designer and to publish them with the hope of rendering Service to the Artist', but the Prospectus (which Cromek sent with Blake's letter and which Blake had clearly not yet seen) described 'Twelve' designs (not 20) which were to be engraved 'by LOUIS SCHIAVONETTI' (not by Blake). The Prospectus announced that 'The Work has been honoured with the Subscriptions and Patronage' of the President and 12 other members of the Royal Academy (*Blake Records*, 168–73). A previous prospectus also of Nov. 1805 had listed Blake as the engraver.

Pacquet with the Letter. You will I know feel as you always do on such occasions, not only warm wishes to promote the Spirited Exertions of my Friend Cromek. You will be pleased to see that the Royal Academy have Sanctioned the Style of work. I now have reason more than ever to lament your Distance from London as that alone has prevented our Consulting you in our Progress, which is but of about two Months Date⌊.⌋ I cannot give you any Account of our Ballads for I have heard nothing of Phillips this Age⌊.⌋ I hear them approved by the best that is the most Serious people & if any others are displeasd it is also an argument of their being Successful as well as Right, of which I have no Doubt for what is Good must Suceed first or last but what is bad owes success to something beside or without itself if it has any⌊.⌋

*] My Wife joins me in anxious wishes for your Health & Happiness desiring to be particularly rememberd by You & our Good Lady Paulina over a dish of Coffee. I long to hear of your Good Health, & that of our dear friend of Lavant & of all our friends (to whom we are grateful & desire to be rememberd) In Sussex⌊.⌋

I am Dear Sir
Yours ever Affectionately
Will. Blake

27 Nov^r
1805

To Mr Hayley

11 DECEMBER 1805

'To / William Hayley Esqre / Felpham near Chichester / Sussex'

Dear Sir

]   I cannot omit to Return you my Sincere & Grateful Acknowledgments, for the kind Reception you have given my New Projected Work.[1] It bids fair to Set me above the difficulties, I have hitherto encounterd. But my Fate has been so

11 Dec. 1805

    [1] This 'kind Reception' probably consisted in subscriptions for *The Grave* (1808) from Hayley and his friends Harriet Poole, W. S. Poyntz, Joseph Seagrave, and Richard Vernon Sadleir.

uncommon that I expect Nothing— I was alive & in health & with the same Talents I now have all the time of Boydells Macklins Bowyers & other Great Works. I was known by them & was lookd upon by them as Incapable of Employment in those Works⌊;⌋[2] it may turn out so again notwithstanding appearances⌊.⌋ I am prepared for it, but at the same time Sincerely Grateful to Those whose Kindness & Good opinion has Supported me thro all hitherto. You Dear Sir are one who has my Particular Gratitude, having conducted me thro Three that would have been the Darkest Years that ever Mortal Sufferd, which were renderd thro your means a Mild & Pleasant Slumber. I speak of Spiritual Things, Not of Natural, Of Things known only to Myself & to Spirits Good & Evil, but Not Known to Men on Earth. It is the passage thro these Three Years that has brought me into my Present State, & *I Know* that if I had not been with You I must have Perish'd. Those Dangers are now Passed & I can see them beneath my feet⌊.⌋ It will not be long before I shall be able to present the full history of my Spiritual Sufferings to the Dwellers upon Earth, & of the Spiritual Victories obtaind for me by my Friends[3]— Excuse this Effusion of the Spirit from One who cares little for this World which passes away, whose Happiness is Secure in Jesus our Lord, & who looks for Sufferings till the time of complete deliverance. In the mean While, I am kept Happy as I used to be, because I throw Myself & all that I have on our Saviours Divine Providence. O What Wonders are the Children of Men! Would to God that they would Consider it⌊,⌋ That they would Consider their Spiritual Life Regardless of that faint Shadow Calld Natural Life, & that they would Promote Each others Spiritual Labours, Each according to its Rank & that they would Know that Recieving

[2] Early in 1792 Robert Bowyer (1758–1834) issued prospectuses announcing that 'W. Blake' was one of the 'eminent Engravers' 'actually engaged' for his 'magnificent' edition of Hume's *History of England*, but when the work was completed in 1806 none of the 195 plates bore Blake's name (*Blake Records*, 46). Blake neither designed nor engraved plates for Thomas Macklin's great Bible (1800), and for *The Dramatic Works of Shakspeare* (1791–1803) published by John (1719–1804) and Josiah Boydell (1752–1817) he engraved only one duplicate plate and designed none.

[3] Probably either *Jerusalem*, which refers (pl. 3) to 'my three years slumber on the banks of the Ocean', or *Milton*, which is set largely in Felpham.

a Prophet As a Prophet is a Duty which If omitted is more Severely Avenged than Every Sin & Wickedness beside⌊.⌋ It is the Greatest of Crimes to Depress True Art & Science⌊.⌋ I know that those who are dead from the Earth & who mockd & despised the Meekness of True Art (and such I find have been the situations of our Beautiful Affectionate Ballads), I Know that such Mockers are Most Severely Punishd in Eternity⌊.⌋ I know it for I see it & dare not help.— The Mocker of Art is the Mocker of Jesus. Let us go on Dear Sir following his Cross⌊;⌋ let us take it up daily Persisting in Spiritual Labours & the Use of that Talent which it is Death to Bur*y*, & of that Spirit to Which we are Called —

2] Pray Present My Sincerest Thanks to our Good Paulina whose Kindness to Me shall recieve recompense in the Presence of Jesus. Present also my Thanks to the Generous Seagra*v*e, In whose debt I have been too long but percieve that I shall be able to Settle with him Soon what is between us.— I have deliverd to Mr Sa[u]nders the 3 Works of Romney as Mrs Lambert told me you wished to have them⌊;⌋ a very few touches will finish the Shipwreck⌊;⌋ those few I have added upon a Proof before I parted with the Picture. It is a Print that I feel proud of on a New inspection. Wishing You & All Friends in Sussex a Merry & a Happy Christmas   I remain Ever Your

Sth Molton Street
Decembr 11. 1805.

Affectionate
Will. Blake &
his Wife Catherine Blake

[?JUNE 1806][1]

TO [*Richard Phillips*]

To the Editor of the Monthly Magazine.

SIR,

1] My indignation was exceedingly moved at reading a criticism in Bell's Weekly Messenger (25th May)[2] on the picture of

[?June 1806]
[1] Since the letter was published on 1 July 1806, it was probably written in June.
[2] According to the anonymous review of Fuseli's 'Ugolino in Prison' in *Bell's Weekly Messenger*, 25 May 1806 (p. 167), we should expect the children to look to their father for assistance, 'the drawing [*of the* young female *in his arms*] is essentially

Count Ugolino, by Mr. Fuseli, in the Royal Academy Exhibition; and your Magazine being as extensive in its circulation as that Paper, and as it also must from its nature be more permanent, I take the advantageous opportunity to counteract the widely diffused malice which has for many years, under the pretence of admiration of the arts, been assiduously sown and planted among the English public against true art, such as it existed in the days of Michael Angelo and Raphael. Under pretence of fair criticism, and candour, the most wretched taste ever produced has been upheld for many, very many years: but now, I say, now its end is come. Such an artist as Fuseli is invulnerable, he needs not my defence; but I should be ashamed not to set my hand and shoulder, and whole strength, against those wretches who, under pretence of criticism, use the dagger and the poison.

[¶2]   My criticism on this picture is as follows:

Mr. Fuseli's Count Ugolino is the father of sons of feeling and dignity, who would not sit looking in their parent's face in the moment of his agony, but would rather retire and die in secret, while they suffer him to indulge his passionate and innocent grief, his innocent and venerable madness, and insanity, and fury, and whatever paltry, cold hearted critics cannot, because they dare not, look upon. Fuseli's Count Ugolino is a man of wonder and admiration, of resentment against man and devil, and of humiliation before God; prayer and parental affection fills the figure from head to foot. The child in his arms, whether boy or girl signifies not, (but the critic must be a fool who has not read Dante, and who does not know a boy from a girl); I say, the child is as beautifully drawn as it is coloured — in both, inimitable! and the effect of the whole is truly sublime, on account of that very colouring which our critic calls black and heavy. The German flute colour, which was used by the Flemings, (they call it burnt bone), has possessed the eye of certain connoisseurs, that they cannot see appropriate colouring, and are blind to the gloom of a real terror.

imperfect', and 'we could have wished that this Picture' were not so 'black and heavy'.
    The quotation marks appear in the *Monthly Magazine* text.

3]   The taste of English amateurs has been too much formed upon pictures imported from Flanders and Holland; consequently our countrymen are easily brow-beat on the subject of painting; and hence it is so common to hear a man say: 'I am no judge of pictures:' but, O Englishmen! know that every man ought to be a judge of pictures, and every man is so who has not been connoisseured out of his senses.

4]   A gentleman who visited me the other day, said, 'I am very much surprised at the dislike that some connoisseurs shew on viewing the pictures of Mr. Fuseli; but the truth is, he is a hundred years beyond the present generation.' Though I am startled at such an assertion, I hope the cotemporary taste will shorten the hundred years into as many hours; for I am sure that any person consulting his own eyes must prefer what is so supereminent; and I am as sure that any person consulting his own reputation, or the reputation of his country, will refrain from disgracing either by such ill-judged criticisms in future. Yours, WM. BLAKE.

MAY 1807

TO [*William Blake from R. H. Cromek*]

64, *Newman Street*
May, 1807

1]   Mr. BLAKE,— Sir, I rec^d, not with^t great surprise, your letter, demanding 4 guineas for the *sketched vignette*, ded^n to the Queen. I have returned the drawing w^h this note, and I will briefly state my reasons for so doing. In the first place I do not think it merits the price you affix to it, *under any circumstances*. In the next place I never had the remotest suspicion that you c^d for a moment entertain the idea of writing *me* to supply money to create an honour in w^h I cannot possibly participate. The Queen allowed *you*, not *me*, to dedicate the work to *her*! The honour w^d have been yours exclus^y, but that you might not be deprived of any advantage likely to contribute to your reputation, I was willing to pay Mr. Schiavonetti *ten* guineas for etching a plate from the drawing in question.

2]   Another reason for returning the sketch is that *I can do without it*, having already engaged to give a greater number of etchings than the price of the book will warrant; and I neither have nor ever had any encouragement from *you* to place you before the public in a more favourable point of view than that which I have already chosen. You charge me w^h *imposing upon you.* Upon my honour I have no recollection of anything of the kind. If the world and I were to settle accounts to-morrow, I do assure you the balance w^d be considerably in my favour. In this respect '*I am more sinned against than sinning.*'¹ But, if I cannot recollect any instances wherein I have imposed upon *you,* several present themselves in w^h I have imposed upon *myself.* Take two or three that press upon me.

[¶3]   When I first called on you I found you without reputation; I *imposed* on myself the labour, and an Herculean one it has been, to create and establish a reputation for you. I say the labour was Herculean, because I had not only the public to contend with, but I had to battle with a man who had pre-determined not to be served. What public reputation you have, the reputation of eccentricity excepted, I have acquired for you, and I can honestly and conscientiously assert that if you had laboured thro' life for yourself as zealously and as earnestly as I have done for you your reputation as an artist w^d not only have been enviable but it would have placed you on an emi-nence that w^d have put it out of the power of an individual, as obscure as myself, either to add to it or take from it. *I also imposed on myself* when I believed what you so often have told me, that your works were equal, nay superior, to a Raphael or to a Michael Angelo! Unfortunately for me as a publisher the public awoke me from this state of stupor, this mental delusion. That public is willing to give you credit for what real talent is to be found in your productions, *and for no more*!

[¶4]   *I have imposed on myself* yet more grossly in believing you to be one altogether abstracted from this world, holding converse w^h the world of spirits!— simple, unoffending, a combination of the *serpent* and the *dove.* I really blush when I reflect how I have been cheated in this respect. The most effectual way of benefiting a designer whose aim is general patronage is to

May 1807
¹ *King Lear* III. ii. 58. The quotation marks here and below appear in the *Gentleman's Magazine* transcript.

bring his designs before the public through the medium of engraving. Your drawings have had the *good fortune* to be engraved by one of the first artists in Europe, and the specimens already shown have already produced you orders that I verily believe you otherwise w^d not have rec^d. Herein I have been gratified, for I was determined to bring you food as well as reputation, tho' from your late conduct I have some reason to embrace your wild opinion, that to manage genius, and to cause it to produce good things, it is absolutely necessary to starve it; indeed, this opinion is considerably heightened by the recollection that your best work, the illustrations of 'The Grave,' was produced when you and Mrs. Blake were reduced so low as to be obliged to live on half-a-guinea a week!

5] Before I conclude this letter, it will be necessary to remark, when I gave you the order for the drawings from the poem of 'The Grave,' I paid you for them more than I could then afford, more in proportion than you were in the habit of receiving, and what you were perfectly satisfied with, though I must do you the justice to confess much less than I think is their real value. Perhaps you have friends and admirers who can appreciate their merit and worth as much as I do. I am decidedly of opinion that the 12 for 'The Grave' should sell at least for 60 guineas. If you can meet with any gentleman who will give you this sum for them, I will deliver them into his hands on the publication of the poem. I will deduct the 20 guineas I have paid you from that sum, and the remainder 40 d° shall be at your disposal.

6] I will not detain you more than one minute. Why sh^d you so *furiously rage* at the success of the little picture of 'The Pilgrimage?' 3,000 people have now *seen it and have approved of it.*[2] Believe me, yours is '*the voice of one crying in the wilderness!*'

7] You say the subject is *low,* and *contemptibly treated.* For his excellent mode of treating the subject the poet has been admired for the last 400 years! The poor painter has not yet the advantage of antiquity on his side, therefore w^h some people an

[2] According to *Bell's Weekly Messenger* for 3 May 1807 (p. 141), 'Stothard's admirable Picture of the Procession of Chaucer's Pilgrims to Canterbury is now exhibiting at No. 344, in the Strand, nearly opposite Somerset House.'
Some of the improbabilities of Cromek's letter are dealt with in *Blake Records,* 184-7.

apology may be necessary for him.³ The conclusion of one of Squire Simkin's letters to his mother in the Bath Guide⁴ will afford one. He speaks greatly to the purpose:

> —— I very well know,
> Both my subject and verse is exceedingly low;
> But if any *great critic* finds fault with my letter,
> *He has nothing to do but to send you a better.*

With much respect for your talents
I remain, sir,
Your real friend and well-wisher,
R. H. CROMEK.

14 OCTOBER 1807

TO 'Richard Phillips Esqʳᵉ / N6 Bridge Street / Black Friars'

Oct 14—

Sir

[¶*1*]   A Circumstance has occurred which has again raised my Indignation⌞.⌟

[¶*2*]   I read in the Oracle & True Briton of Octʳ 13. 1807 — that a Mʳ Blair a Surgeon has *with the Cold fury of Robespierre* caused the Police to sieze upon the Person & Goods or Property of an Astrologer & to commit him to Prison.¹ The Man who can Read the Stars often is oppressed by their Influence, no less than the Newtonian who reads Not & cannot Read is opressed by his own Reasonings & Experiments— We are all

---

³ Stothard's picture had been attacked by unnamed critics for looking too modern; it was defended by Hoppner with arguments very similar to Cromek's in *The Artist* (6 June 1807).

⁴ *The New Bath Guide* (1804 [first published 1766]), 38–9.

14 Oct. 1807

¹ According to the *Daily Advertiser, Oracle and True Briton* for 13 Oct., 'Mr. [*William*] BLAIR [*1766–1822, an eminent surgeon*] concerted with some of the Agents of the Society for the Suppression of Vice, a Strategem to entrap' 'A *Seer* named *Robert Powell*' by having his footman procure a horoscope from Powell. The words Blake underlined do not appear in the newspaper account. Contrary to Blake's implication, Powell was a charlatan who protested with tears gushing from his eyes that 'nothing, save want and the miseries of a wretched family, could have driven him to adopt such a mode of procuring them food. . . . He had no choice between *famine*, *theft*, or *imposture*. . . . The Magistrates, [*though*] obviously affected by this scene', said they had to commit him for trial.

subject to Error: Who shall say Except the Natural Religionists that we are not all Subject to Crime⌊?⌋

¶3]   My desire is that you would Enquire into this Affair & that you would publish this in your Monthly Magazine⌊·⌋ I do not pay the postage of this Letter because you as Sheriff are bound to attend to it—²

William Blake

17 Sᵗʰ Molton Sᵗ.

18 JANUARY [–FEBRUARY] 1808

TO [*Ozias Humphry*]¹

To Ozias Humphry Esqʳᵉ²

¶1]   The Design of The³ Last Judgment,⁴ which I have completed

² Blake was deliberately ignoring the statement on the title-page of the *Monthly Magazine* that the work was published by Richard Phillips 'By whom Communications (Post-paid) are thankfully received.' The letter was not published; it was probably returned to Blake, with a note on the back: 'W. B. Recᵈ Octʳ 27ᵗʰ 1807. With Mʳ P's Comps'.

18 Jan. 1808

   ¹ Blake copied this letter (A) twice, once (B) evidently for the Earl of Egremont or his wife (this copy is still owned by the Earl's great-great-grandson), and the second time (C) in February for Ozias Humphry to send to the Earl of Buchan. On the latter (C), Humphry wrote:

   —The Earl of Buchan—of this Duplicate paper wᶜʰ I have the Honor to inclose I have not been able to read a single Line.—O. H.

With Blake's transcript (C), Humphry sent a letter of his own:

   Not being able to furnish your Lordship with much amusement myself, I have ventured to inclose, (from the Author himself written expressly for the purpose) the subject of an important Composition lately made by W. Blake for the Countess of Egremont, of a final Judgment—

   a Subject so vast, & multitudinous was never perhaps, more happily concievd.—

   The Size of this drawing is but small not exceeding twenty Inches by fifteen or Sixteen (*I guess*) but then the grandeur of its conception, the Importance of its subject, and the sublimely multitudinous masses, & groups, wᶜʰ it exhibits . . . In brief, It is one of the most interesting performanᶜᵉˢ I ever saw; & is, in many respects superior to the last Judgment of Michael Angelo and to give due credit & effect to it, would require a Tablet, not less than the Floor of Westminster Hall.—

   I cannot see to read what I have written . . . [*because of* The unhappy Condition of my Sight.] (*Blake Records*, 186–7)

The variants in copies B and C given in the footnotes below make it clear that they were made independently from copy A (or from the draft for it) with no great effort at identity. I apologize for the cumbrous multiplicity of the footnotes.

   ² '[To Ozias Humphry Esqʳᵉ *del*] [*In another hand above:*] To Ozias Humphrey. R.A.' (B); 'Esqʳᵉ' (C).   ³ 'Design of the' (B).   ⁴ 'Judgment [*no comma*]' (B).

1637

by your recommendation for The Countess of Egremont,[5] it is necessary to give some account of:[6] & its various parts[7] ought to be described,[8] for the accomodation of those who give it the honor of attention.[9]

[¶2]   Christ[10] seated on the Throne of Judgment![11] The Heavens in Clouds rolling before him[12] & around him, like a Scroll[13] ready to be consumed in the fires of the Angels;[14] who descend before his feet with their four trumpets[15] sounding to the four Winds.[16]

[¶3]   Beneath; the Earth is convuls'd[17] with the labours of the Resurrection; In[18] the caverns[19] of the Earth[20] is the Dragon with seven[21] heads & ten horns,[22] Chained[23] by two Angels[24] & above his Cavern[25] on the Earths Surface,[26] is the Harlot[27] also siezed & bound by two Angels[28] with Chains[29] while her Palaces are falling into ruins[30] & her Counsellors[31] & Warriors are descending into the Abyss in wailing & despair⌊.⌋[32]

[5] 'recommendation under a fortunate star, for the [Countess *del*] Earl of Egremont:' (B). Elizabeth Ayliffe (d. 1822) bore seven children to George O'Brien Wyndham (1757–1838), third Earl of Egremont, then married him on 16 July 1801 and bore him an eighth (buried 9 Feb. 1803). Shortly thereafter she separated from him and lived in a handsome establishment set up for her by the Earl in London, where she apparently acted on his behalf occasionally. (Family information derived from Miss D. Beatrice Harris, Secretary, Petworth House.) The uncertainty in the MS as to the origin of the commission for the picture may be due to the fact that the 'Countess' had commissioned it for the Earl. The picture is still in Petworth House.

[6] 'account of;' (B).   [7] 'parts.' (C).

[8] 'described [*no comma*]' (C).   [9] 'attention,' (B); no punctuation in C.

[10] 'Christ,' (C).

[11] 'Throne of Judgment;' (C); no punctuation in B.

[12] 'him' is omitted in B.

[13] 'scroll' (B); 'before his feet & around him, the heavens are rolling like a scroll' (C).

[14] 'Angels [*no semicolon*]' (C).   [15] 'descend with the Four Trumpets' (C).

[16] 'Trumpets sounding to the Four Winds [*no full stop*]' (B); no punctuation in C.

[17] 'Beneath: the Earth is convuls'd' (B); 'Beneath; Earth is convulsed' (C).

[18] 'Resurrection: In' (B); 'Resurrection in' (C).   [19] 'Caverns' (C).

[20] 'Earth,' (B); 'Earth.' (C).   [21] 'Seven' (C).

[22] 'Horns [*no comma*]' (C).   [23] 'chained' (B, C).

[24] 'Angels,' (C).   [25] 'caverns' (B); '[heads(?) *del*] Cavern' (C).

[26] 'Earths Surface [*no comma*]' (B); 'Earths surface [*no comma*]' (C).

[27] 'Harlot,' (B, C).

[28] 'also' omitted in C; 'also chained by two Angels,' (B).

[29] 'chains,' (C).   [30] 'in ruins' (B).   [31] 'councellors' (C).

[32] 'wailings & despair.', no paragraph (B); 'Wailing & despair.', no paragraph (C).

[4]   Hell opens beneath the Harlot's[33] seat on the left hand[34] into
which the Wicked are descending⌊.⌋[35]

[5]   The right hand of the Design[36] is appropriated to the Resur-
rection of The Just;[37] the left hand of the Design[38] is appropriated
to the Resurrection & Fall of the Wicked⌊.⌋

[6]   Immediately before the Throne of Christ is[39] Adam & Eve,
kneeling in humiliation,[40] as representitives[41] of the whole Human
Race;[42] Abraham & Moses kneel on each side beneath them;
from the Cloud on which Eve kneels & beneath Moses & from
the Tables of Stone which utter lightnings;[43] is seen Satan[44]
wound round by the Serpent & falling headlong;[45] the Pharisees
appear on the left hand[46] pleading their own righteousness
before the Throne of Christ:[47] The Book of Death is[48] opend[49]
on Clouds[50] by two Angels;[51] many groupes of Figures are falling
from before the Throne & from the[52] Sea of Fire[53] which flows[54]
before the Steps of the Throne;[55] on which are seen the Seven[56]
Lamps of the Almighty[57] burning before the Throne.[58] Many
Figures chaind[59] & bound together fall[60] thro' the air,[61] & some
are scourged by Spirits[62] with flames of fire into the Abyss of
Hell[63] which opens to recieve them beneath,[64] on the left hand
of the Harlot's seat;[65] where others are howling & descending
into the flames, &[66] in the act of dragging[67] each other into
Hell & of[68] contending in fighting with each other on the
brink of Perdition⌊.⌋[69]

---

[33] 'Harlots' (B, C).   [34] 'left hand,' (B); 'left hand;' (C).
[35] 'descending while others rise from their Graves on the brink of the Pit.'(B).
[36] 'Design,' (C).   [37] 'the Just. The' (B); 'the Just: the' (C).
[38] 'Design,' (C).   [39] 'Christ, is' (C).
[40] 'humiliation;' (B); no punctuation in C.   [41] 'representatives' (B).
[42] 'Human Race:' (B); 'Human Race,' (C).   [43] 'lightnings.' (B).
[44] 'Eve kneels, is seen Satan,' (C).   [45] 'headlong. The' (B).
[46] 'left hand,' (C).   [47] 'of Christ.' (B, C).
[48] '& before the Book of Death which is' (C).   [49] 'opened' (B).
[50] 'on clouds' (C).   [51] 'Angels,' (C); no punctuation in B.
[52] 'Throne, & from before the' (C).   [53] 'fire' (B).   [54] 'burns' (B).
[55] 'Steps of the Throne,' (B); 'steps of the Throne;' (C).
[56] 'is seen the seven' (C).   [57] 'almighty,' (B).   [58] 'Throne:' (C).
[59] 'Many Figures chained' (B); 'many Figures chained' (C).
[60] 'together & in various attitudes of Despair & Horror: fall' (C).
[61] 'thro the air:' (B); 'thro the air;' (C).   [62] 'by spirits' (B).
[63] 'of Hell,' (C).   [64] 'opens beneath,' (C); no punctuation in B.
[65] 'Harlots seat,' (B); 'Harlots Seat;' (C).   [66] 'flames &' (B).
[67] 'howling & dragging' (C).   [68] 'Hell and of' (B); 'Hell & in' (C).
[69] 'the very brink of Perdition [no full stop]' (B); 'the brink of Perdition.' (C).

[¶7]   Before the Throne of Christ on the right hand[70] the Just in Humiliation[71] & in exultation, rise thro' the air, with[72] their Children & Families;[73] some of whom are bowing before the Book of Life[74] which is opend by two Angels on Clouds;[75] many Groupes[76] arise with Exultation;[77] among them is a Figure crowned[78] with Stars & the moon[79] beneath her feet[80] with six infants around her⌊;⌋[81] She represents the Christian Church; The Green Hills[82] appear beneath:[83] with the Graves of the Blessed, which are seen bursting with their births of immortality;[84] Parents & Children embrace[85] & arise together[86] & in exulting attitudes tell[87] each other, that[88] The New Jerusalem is ready to descend upon Earth; they[89] arise upon the air[90] rejoicing![91] Others newly awakend from the Grave[92] stand upon the Earth embracing & shouting to the Lamb who cometh in the Clouds with Power[93] & great Glory.[94]

[¶8]   The whole[95] upper part of the Design is a view[96] of Heaven opened;[97] around the Throne of Christ, Four[98] Living Creatures filled with Eyes,[99] attended by seven[100] Angels with Seven Vials[101] of the Wrath of God,[102] & above these Seven Angels[103] with the Seven Trumpets compose the Cloud,[104] which by its rolling away displays the opening Seats of the Blessed,[105] on the right

[70] 'right hand,' (B); 'Right hand.' (C).
[71] 'humiliation' (B, C).
[72] 'exultation rise thro the air with' (B); 'exultation rise thro the Air with' (C).
[73] 'Families,' (B); 'Families:' (C). [74] 'Book of Life,' (B).
[75] 'opened by two Angels, on clouds;' (B); 'opend on clouds by two Angels;' (C).
[76] 'groupes' (C). [77] 'arise in exultation,' (C); 'arise in joy;' (B).
[78] 'crownd' (C). [79] 'Moon' (B, C). [80] 'her feet,' (B).
[81] 'around her:' (B); 'around her.' (C).
[82] 'Christian Church. Green Hills' (B); 'Christian Church; Green hills' (C).
[83] 'beneath [no colon]' (B, C). [84] 'immortality:' (B, C).
[85] 'Children. Wives & Husbands embrace' (C). [86] 'together,' (B).
[87] 'attitudes of great joy tell' (C). [88] 'other that the' (C).
[89] 'Earth. they' (B); 'Earth they' (C). [90] 'Air' (C).
[91] 'rejoicing:' (B, C). [92] 'Grave;' (B); 'Grave,' (C).
[93] 'in Power' (C). [94] 'Glory [no full stop]' (B). [95] 'Whole' (C).
[96] 'View' (C). [97] 'opened [no semicolon]' (B, C).
[98] 'Christ. Four' (B); 'Christ: in the Cloud which rolls away, are the Four' (C).
[99] 'Eyes [no comma]' (B). [100] 'Seven' (B, C).
[101] 'with the Seven Vials' (B, C). [102] 'of God;' (C).
[103] 'these are Seven Angels' (B).
[104] 'Trumpets, altogether composing the Cloud [no comma]' (B); 'Trumpets, these compose the Cloud [no comma]' (C).
[105] 'seats of the Blessed.' (B).

& the left[106] of which are seen the Four & Twenty Elders[107] seated on Thrones to Judge the Dead.[108]

9] Behind the Seat & Throne of Christ appears the Tabernacle with its Veil opened;[109] the Candlestick on the right; the Table with Shew Bread, on the left; & in the midst,[110] the Cross[111] in place of the Ark, with the[112] two Cherubim[113] bowing over it.

0] On the right[114] hand of the Throne of Christ is Baptism, On his left[115] is the Lords Supper;[116] the two introducers into Eternal Life.[117] Women with Infants approach the Figure of an aged apostle[118] which represents Baptism;[119] & on the left hand the Lords Supper is administerd by Angels,[120] from the hands of another aged Apostle;[121] these kneel on each side of the Throne which is surrounded by a glory,[122] in the glory many Infants appear, representing Eternal[123] Creation flowing from The Divine[124] Humanity in Jesus;[125] who opens the Scroll of Judgment upon his knees before the Living & the Dead.[126]

1] Such is the Design[127] which you my Dear[128] Sir have been the cause of my producing & which;[129] but for you might[130] have slept till the Last Judgment.[131]

William Blake.[132]

18 January 1808.[133]

---

[106] '& left' (C).   [107] 'twenty Elders' (B); 'twenty Elders,' (C).
[108] 'Dead [*no full stop*]' (B).   [109] 'opened;' (C).
[110] '& the Candlestick on the right: The Table with the Shew Bread, on the left, & in the midst [*no comma*]' (B); 'the Candlestick on the right: the Table with the Shew Bread on the left; in midst [*no comma*] is' (C).
[111] 'The Cross,' (B).   [112] 'Ark. with the' (B); 'Ark. the' (C).
[113] 'Cherubim[s *del*]' (C).   [114] 'Right' (C).
[115] 'Christ is, Baptism: On his left:' (B); 'Baptism on the left' (C).
[116] 'The Lords Supper:' (B); 'the Lords Supper.' (C).
[117] 'Life:' (C).   [118] 'Apostle.' (B); 'Aged Apostle' (C).
[119] 'Baptism.' (B); 'Baptism,' (C).   [120] 'by Angels [*no comma*]' (B, C).
[121] 'another Apostle.' (C).
[122] 'glory:' (B); 'Glory [*no punctuation*]' (C).
[123] 'appear. representing Eternal' (B); 'many Infants appear in the Glory representing the Eternal' (C).
[124] 'the Divine' (B, C).   [125] 'in Jesus:' (B); 'in Jesus,' (C).
[126] 'Dead [*no full stop*]' (B).   [127] 'design' (C).   [128] 'dear' (C).
[129] 'which:' (B); no punctuation in C.   [130] 'you. might' (C).
[131] 'Judgment:' (B); 'Judgment [*no punctuation*]' (C).
[132] 'Blake [*no full stop*]' (B).
[133] '18 January 1808 [*no full stop*]' (B); 'Feby 1808' (C).

18 DECEMBER 1808

TO 'G. Cumberland Esqʳ Junʳ / N64 Neman Street / Oxford Street / London' [*From George Cumberland*]

¹your Line Dr George is at the end of the Street

Dear Blake,

[¶*1*]   A gentleman of my acquaintance to whom I was shewing your incomparable etchings last night, was so charmed with them, that he requested me to get him a compleat Set of all you have published in the way of *Books* coloured as mine are;²— and at the same time he wishes to know what will be the price of as many as you can spare him, if all are not to be had, being willing to wait your own time in order to have them as those of mine are.

[¶*2*]   With respect to the money I will take care that it shall be reced[?] and sent to you through my Son as fast as they are procured.

[¶*3*]   I find by a Letter from my son that the picture you sent, he asked you for,³ which is what I do not approve, as I certainly had no such thing in contemplation when I sent you those very slight sketches from Raffael,— I Am glad however that you found them acceptable, and shall certainly send you a few more as soon as I can light on them among my papers.— The Holy family⁴ is like all your designs full of Genius and originality— I shall give it a handsome frame and shew it to all who come to my house.

[¶*4*]   — When you answer this pray tell me if you have been able to do any thing with the Bookseller.— Something of that kind would be no bad thing, and might turn out a great one if a

---

18 Dec. 1808

¹ The letter to Blake is part of George Cumberland's letter to his son.

² Cumberland owned *Thel* (A), *Visions* (B), *America* (F), *Songs* (F), *Europe* (D), *Song of Los* (D), as well as *Poetical Sketches* (D), *For Children* (C), Blair's *Grave* (1808), *Descriptive Catalogue*, and *Job*.

³ On 1 Dec. 1808 Cumberland had sent to his son for 'Mr Blake a few old Tracings [rude sketches only] from Raffaels Pictures in Fresco', and his son replied on 4 Dec.: 'Mr Blake was very much pleased with the traicings ; I thought it a good opportunity to ask him for the Holy Family, which he gave very readily' (*Blake Records*, 209, 210).

⁴ Blake's 'Holy Family' has not been traced.

competition could be raised by this means among the genuine
appre[*cia*]ters of talents of every sort— —You talked also of
publishing your new method of engraving—send it to me and
I will do my best to prepare it for the Press.— *P*erhaps when
done you might with a few specimens of Plates make a little
work for subscribers of it — as Du Crow⁵ did of his Aqua
tinta — selling about 6 Pages for [half *del*] a guinea to non
Subscribers — but if you do not chuse this method, we might
insert it in Nicholsons Journal⁶ or the Monthly Magazin*e* —
with reference to you for explanations— *W*ith best regards to
you & yours I am always

Your sincere friend

Culvert St 18 Dec. 1808—   G Cumberland

Dear George
  [Take the above to Mr Blake, and *del*] Go on receit of this
to Black Friars & when You have been to Sr. R Phillips to
know if he got my 24 Pages of Biography sent by *Fromonts*
Coach carriage Paid & booked on Wednesday last — take the
above to Mr Blake and get him to answer it *directly* on the
Sheet of Paper on which you write your answer as to the receit
of the Biography of Grignion⁷—but say nothing to his Brother
as to where I publish it as yet. I shall ret? his Papers. All well
& all desire love. Yours

GC.

PS. If you have my Lett. through S. R Phillips—it is come
safe∟.⌋⁸

---

  ⁵ Probably Pierre Ducros (1745–1810), popular painter and engraver of land-
scapes. See 'A Work on Art', pp. 1680–2.
  ⁶ Cumberland did not describe Blake's process in his letter ('Hints on various
Modes of Printing from Autographs') to William Nicholson's *Journal of Natural
Philosophy*, xxviii (Jan. 1811), 56–9, though he did say that '*Blake* . . . alone excels
in that art' of writing or perusing backwards.
  ⁷ Cumberland's unsigned 'Sketch of the Biography of Charles Grignion, Esq.'
appeared in the *Monthly Magazine*, xxvi (Jan. and Nov. 1809), 548–53 and 377–9.
  ⁸ That is, if George received this letter, which his father had enclosed with the
parcel to Phillips, he could assume that the parcel with the biography had also
'come safe'.

19 DECEMBER 1808

TO [George Cumberland]

Dear Cumberland

I am very much obliged by your kind ardour in my cause &
should immediately Engage in reviewing my former pursuits of
printing if I had not now so long been turned out of the old
channel into a new one that it is impossible for me to return to
it without destroying my present course⌊.⌋ New Vanities or
rather new pleasures occupy my thoughts⌊.⌋ New profits seem
to arise before me so tempting that I have already involved
myself in engagements that preclude all possibility of promising
any thing. I have however the satisfaction to inform you that
I have Myself begun to print an account of my various In-
ventions in Art for which I have procured a Publisher[1] & am

19 Dec. 1808

[1] This presumably refers to *A Descriptive Catalogue of Pictures*, Poetical and His-
torical Inventions . . . Printed by D. N. Shury (1809).

Blake and Cumberland had previously discussed these publishing plans, for in
the summer of 1807 Cumberland recorded in his notebook that 'Blake . . . Intends
to publish his new method through means[?] of stopping lights'; later, apparently
just before he wrote to Blake in Dec. 1808, he wrote in another notebook: 'Blakes
new Mode of Engraving to be Published by me at his desire [*in another ink:*] He
will publish it' (*Blake Records*, 187, 211 n. 3).

Cumberland twice described Blake's techniques. The first is on the last leaf of
his commonplace book, in my possession, n.d.:

Blakes Instructions to Print Copper Plates

Warm the Plate a little and then fill it with Ink by dabbing it all over two or
three times.—*Then* wipe off the superfluous Ink till the surface is clean—then
with the palm of the hand *beneath the little finger* rubbed over with a little of the
Ink, & smoothed with whiting by rubbing it on a Ball of *it*, Wipe the surface
of the Plate till it shines all over—then roll it through the Press with 3 blankets
above the Plate, and pastboards beneath it next the Plank—Paper may be used
instead of Pastboard.

The second is directions for making lithographs, found on the verso of a copy of
Blake's only lithograph, of 'Enoch' (?1807), in the possession of Mr. Edward
Croft-Murray (a photograph of which the owner generously sent to me):

White Lyas—is the Block⌊;⌋ draw with Ink composed of Asphaltum dissolved
in dry Linseed Oil—add fine venetian Tripoli and Rotten Stone Powder. Let it
dry. *W*hen dry saturate the stone with water and Dab it with the broad Dabber,
and cover very thinly with best Printers Ink—and Print as a block—of Blake.

Lias is a limestone rock found in the South of England, which C. Hullmandel,
The Art of Drawing on Stone (1824), 2, says 'is too soft and porous' for printing, com-

determind to pursue the plan of publishing[2] what I may get printed without disarranging my time which in future must alone be devoted to Designing & Painting [alone *del*]└;┘ when I have got my Work printed I will send it you first of any body└;┘ in the mean time believe me to be

Your Sincere Friend

19 Dec[r] 1808   Will Blake

[MAY? 1809][1]

TO 'Ozias Humphrey Esq[re] / Sloane Street'[1]

Dear Sir

[1]   You will see in this little work[1] the cause of difference between you & me. *Y*ou demand of me to Mix two things that Reynolds has confessed cannot be mixed. You will percieve that I not only detest False Art but have the Courage to say so Publickly & to dare all the Power on Earth to oppose — Florentine & Venetian Art cannot exist together└.┘ Till the Venetian & Flemish are destroyd the Florentine & Roman cannot Exist, this will be shortly accomplishd. *T*ill then I remain Your Grateful altho seemingly otherwise I say Your Grateful & Sincere

William Blake

[2]   I inclose a ticket of admission if you should honour my Exhibition with a Visit└.┘[2]

pared with the German stone; 'Tripoli' or 'rotten stone' is a fine earth used as a powder for polishing metals. The ink here seems very unusual.

    In the advertisement to his Exhibition (1809), Blake said that the lost technique of fresco painting 'will be told . . . in a Work on Art, now in the Press' (p. 822), but neither the *Descriptive Catalogue* (1809) nor any other known work describes in detail his techniques of fresco painting or Illuminated Printing.

    [2] In a draft in his Notebook (p. 1050), Blake addressed himself 'To the Society for Encouragement of Arts . . . requesting their Consideration of my Plan' for decorating public buildings with paintings and sculpture.

[May? 1809]

    [1] The sheet on which the letter is written is addressed merely to 'Ozias Humphrey Esq[r]', but it was clearly enclosed with his *Exhibition of Paintings in Fresco* (1809) (A), which is addressed to 'Ozias Humphrey Esq[re] / Sloane Street'. Since the *Exhibition* is dated in MS 'May 15, 1809', this letter is probably of approximately the same date.

    [2] The Exhibition was open 1809–10 in his brother's house at 28 Broad Street.

AUGUST? 1810

TO [*Charles Henry Bellenden Ker*]

About August 1810, Charles Henry Bellenden Ker[1] wrote to George Cumberland that 'the other Day', in reply to a letter from Ker, Blake 'sent me home the 2 Drawings',[2] with a covering 'note [*in which* he desired] that the money [£*21*] was paid in a fortnight or part of it — intimating he should take hostile Mode[?] if it were not . . . .'[3]

AUGUST? 1810

TO [*William Blake from Charles Henry Bellenden Ker*]

In a letter to George Cumberland postmarked 27 August 1810, C. H. B. Ker summarized the rest of the correspondence:

Blake— I wrote at last to propose 15 Gs. *No*— *T*hen to pay

[Aug.? 1810]

[1] C. H. B. Ker (?1785–1871) was the son of John Gawler (?1765–1842) who, on 5 Nov. 1804, took the name of John Ker Bellenden, though he was always known as John Bellenden Ker. John's second cousin, William, 7th Baron Bellenden and 4th Duke of Roxburgh, tried to divert his entailed estate and his title to John Bellenden Ker. After the Duke's death in 1805, the Roxburgh Cause was taken to the House of Lords, where the case against John Ker was summed up on 15–20 June 1809 and decided against him on 11 May 1812.

[2] The two unidentified Blake drawings were ordered 'Near 3 Y.ʳ ago', when, as C. H. B. Ker said in this letter, 'we (meaning my father) are so near getting the Roxburgh Cause'; they must have been commissioned before the case was decided in 1812 and probably before 1809 when it was summed up against the Kers.

[3] In his letter to Cumberland, Ker went on:

Now I was I assure you thunderstruck as you as well as he must know that in my present circumstances it is ludicrous to fancy I can or am able to pay 20 Gs. for 2 Drawings not Knowing Where in the World [*to*] get any money. Nor do I at all conceive I am obliged to pay for them . . . . *N*ow if he thinks proper to pursue the latter [*take legal action,*] he is welcome and I wish you to call on him and shew him this and also that he may be informed of the grounds on which I meant to resist the payment ͺ;ͺ first as to the time when they were ordered which in his letter to me he admits was even then 2 years ago—therefore at that time I was not of age—next a young gentleman who can prove the terms on which they were ordered—these will be the grounds on which I shall rest if he insists on immediate payment and you can tell him my Attorney . . . is Mr Davis 20, Essex Street Strand—but of course the moment either by any success[?] of my father &.ᶜ I am enabled I shall pay him. You will act as you think best ͺ.ͺ

I trouble you with this as from some[?] peculiar misfortunes I am not able to attend to any thing ͺ.ͺ

the price any mutual friend or friends shᵈ put on them— *No—*
*T*hen I proposed to pay 10! first & 10! 3 months afterwᵈˢ *No*⌊.⌋¹

29 JULY 1815

TO 'Mʳ Blake / 17 South Molton St' [*From Josiah Wedgwood*]¹

Sir   Etruria 29 July 1815

1]   I return the drawing you have been so good to send me
which I entirely approve in all respects. I ought to have men-
tioned when the Terrine was sent you that the hole for the
ladle in the cover should not be represented & which you will
be so good to omit in the engraving.

2]   I presume you would make a drawing of each article that is
to be engraved & if it will be agreeable to you to complete the
drawings before the engraving is begun I think it may enable
me to make the best arrangement of the articles on the copper
plates, but if this is not quite as agreeable to you as going on
with the drawing & engraving together, I will only beg you
to make two or three drawings⌊.⌋ I will in that case in the mean
time consider of the arrangement. I have directed a Terrine to
be sent you, presuming you will prefer having only one vessell
at a time. If you would have more be so good as to let Mr
Mowbray at my house know who has a list of more articles.

I am Sir
Your mo obt Servᵗ
Josiah Wedgwood

Mʳ Blake 17 South Molton St

[Aug.? 1810]
    ¹ Ker continued: 'and then he arrested me—and then defended the action and
now perhaps [*?his*] obstinacy will never get a shilling of the 20 L. [*he ori*]ginally
intended to defraud me of'. (It is not clear whether the exchanges after the first
sentence were written or verbal.) In the event, as Ker reported in an undated letter
to Cumberland, 'Blake . . . made me pay 30 [*sic*] Guineas for 2 Drawings which on
my word were never ordered and which were as [*word illeg:*] unportus[?] as they
are infamously done' (*Blake Records*, 228). No record of his arrest has been traced.

29 July 1815
    ¹ Josiah Wedgwood [Jr.], son of the founder of the Staffordshire pottery works,
to whom Blake had been introduced by Flaxman. Blake was commissioned to
make engravings of 189 china figures for the Wedgwood sales catalogue, for which
he was paid £30 in Nov. 1816 (*Blake Records*, 239–41).

8 SEPTEMBER 1815

'To / Josiah Wedgwood Esqre'

Sir

[¶*1*]   I send Two more Drawings with the First that I did, altered: having taken out that part which expressed the hole for the ladle.

[¶*2*]   It will be more convenient to me to make all the drawings firs*t*, before I begin Engraving them as it will enable me also to regulate a System of working that will be uniform from beginning to end. Any Remarks that you may be pleased to make will be thankfully recievd by Sir

17 South Molton Street   Your humble Servant
8 Septemb^r 1815   William Blake

9 JUNE 1818

'To / Dawson Turner¹ Esqre / Yarmouth / Norfolk'

Sir

[¶*1*]   I send you a List of the different Works you have done me the honour to enquire after — unprofitable enough to me tho Expensive to the Buyer⌊.⌋ Those I Printed for Mr Humphry² are a selection from the different Books of Such as could be Printed without the Writing³ tho to the Loss of some of the best things For they when Printed perfect accompany Poetical Personifications & Acts without which Poems they never could have been Executed⌊.⌋

		£	s	d
America	18 Prints folio.	5	5	0
Europe	17 do⁴ folio	5.	5.	0
Visions &^c	8 do⁵ folio	3.	3.	0

9 June 1818
  ¹ Dawson Turner (1775–1858), banker, botanist, and antiquary.
  ² Ozias Humphry (1742–1810), painter.
  ³ The collection of colour prints with the texts omitted known as the Large (A, 8 plates) and Small Books of Designs (A, 23 plates) made about 1796.
  ⁴ Copies A–G, I, L, M of *Europe* (watermarked 1794–1832) have 17 plates, but copies H and K (the latter watermarked 1818, 1819, and sold to Linnell in 1821) have 18 plates.
  ⁵ All 16 copies of the *Visions* have 11 plates, and all copies of *Thel* but E have

	[£ s d]
Thel 6 do[6] Quarto	2. 2. 0
Songs of Innocence 28 do.[6] Octavo	3. 3. 0
Songs of Experience 26 do[6] Octavo	3. 3. 0
Urizen 28 Prints[7] Quarto	5. 5. 0
Milton 50 do[8] Quarto	10.10. 0[9]

12 Large Prints∟,⌐ Size of Each⎫
about 2 feet by 1 & 1/2 Historical⎪
& Poetical∟,⌐ Printed in Colours ⎬
                     Each ⎭   5. 5. 0

These last 12 Prints are unaccompanied by any writing∟.⌐[10]

[2] The few I have Printed & Sold are sufficient to have gained me great reputation as an Artist which was the chief thing Intended But I have never been able to produce a Sufficient number for a general Sale by means of a regular Publisher∟.⌐ It is therefore necessary to me that any Person wishing to have any or all of them Should Send me their Order to Print them on the above terms & I will take care that they shall be done at least as well as any I have yet Produced∟.⌐

[3] I am Sir with many thanks for your very Polite approbation of my works

Your most obedient Servant

9 June 1818   William Blake
17 South Molton Street

8 plates; Blake's descriptions of these books only fit if for 'Prints' we read 'Plates with substantial designs'.

[6] Only *Songs* (*B–D, L–M*) consist of 28 plates in *Innocence* and 26 in *Experience*.

[7] Copies A–B of *Urizen* (the second watermarked 1794) have 28 plates, but all the rest (watermarked 1794–1815) have only 3 to 27 plates.

[8] Only *Milton* D (watermarked 1815) has 50 plates; the other copies (watermarked 1808) have 45 or 49 plates.

[9] These prices indicate that the copies were to be coloured. For other lists of prices see Blake's Prospectus of 10 Oct. 1793 and his letter of 12 April 1827 (pp. 202–3, 1668).

[10] These 12 large colour prints are: (1) 'Good and Evil Angels'; (2) 'The House of Death'; (3) 'God Judging Adam'; (4) 'Lamech'; (5) 'Nebuchadnezzar'; (6) 'Newton'; (7) 'God Creating Adam'; (8) 'Christ Appearing to the Apostles'; (9) 'Ruth Parting from Naomi'; (10) 'Satan Exulting over Eve'; (11) 'Pity'; and (12) 'Hecate', the first 8 of which appear in Blake's account with Butts for 1805 (*Blake Records*, 572–3).

11 OCTOBER 1819

TO [*John Linnell?*][1]

Dear Sir

I will have the Pleasure of meeting you on Thursday at 12 OClock⌊;⌋ it is quite as Convenient to me as any other day. It appears to me that neither Time nor Plac*e* can make any real difference as to perfect Independence of Judgmen*t*, & If it is more Convenient to Mr Heaphy[2] for us to meet at his House let us accomodate him in what is Indifferent but not at all in what is of weight & moment to our Decision. *H*oping that I may meet you again in perfect Health & Happiness

	I remain Dear Sir
Oct. 11 1819	Yours Truly
Monday Evening	William Blake

25 MARCH 1823

Memorandum of Agreement[1]

between William Blake and

John Linnell.

March 25th 1823.

W. Blake agrees to Engrave the set of Plates from his own designs of Job's captivity in number twenty,[2] for John Linnell — and John Linnell agrees to pay William Blake five Pounds p^r Plate or one hundred Pounds for the set part before and the remainder when the Plates are finished as Mr Blake may require it, besides which J. Linnell agrees to give

---

11 Oct. 1819

[1] John Linnell (1792–1882), painter, who met Blake in 1818 and became a most generous patron to him.

[2] Thomas Heaphy (1775–1835), water-colour painter.

25 March 1823

[1] Since this is a 'Memorandum', there is no address. The document is in Linnell's hand except for Blake's signature, which is rather shaky. The verso is docketed 'Blakes / Mem– &c', with a receipt: '1823. / March 25th / Cas*h* on acc^!/ of Plates in the foregoing / agreement——£.o.o / WB'.

[2] Eventually there were 22 plates, including the title-page.

W. Blake one hundred pounds more out of the Profits of the
work as the receipts will admit of it.
   signed J. Linnell
Willm Blake

N.B. J. L. to find copper Plates.

[4 AUGUST 1824?][1]

TO [*C. H. Tatham*]

M^r C Tatham
  The humble is formed to adore; the loving to associate[2]

with eternal Love
C Blake

[MARCH 1825?][1]

TO 'J Linnell Esqre / Cirencester Place / Fitzroy Square'

Dear Sir
  A return of the old Shivering fit came on this Morning as
soon as I awaked & I am now in Bed.—Better & as I think
almost well⌊.⌋ If I can possibly I will be at Mr Lahees to-
morrow Morning, these attacks are too serious at the time to
permit me to be out of Bed, but they go off by rest which seems

---

[4 Aug. 1824?]
  [1] The note is on the back of Blake's engraving of Robert Hawker, which was
'Published 1st May 1820'. The speculative date for the note is based upon the
fact that the only occasion when Blake and C. H. Tatham (1772–1842, architect)
are known to have been together after 1820 was on 4 Aug. 1824 when they went to
a dinner at Linnell's (*Blake Records*, 288) but see p. 1660 below.
  [2] The message is no. 69 of Lavater's aphorisms (see p. 1355).

[March 1825?]
  [1] The reference to being 'at Mr Lahees tomorrow Morning' suggests that the
date is March 1825, for Linnell went on Saturday '*March* 5. With Mr Blake to
Lahee's proving Job'. As late as 3 March they had been taking proofs on Mr.
Dixon's press (*Blake Records*, 300, 588).
  The letter is written in pencil.

to be All that I want— I send the Pilgrims² under your Care with the Two First Plates of Job⌞.⌟

I am Yours Sincerely

12 O Clock   Willᵐ Blake

Wednesday

[7 JUNE 1825]¹

TO 'Mʳ Linnell / 6 Cirencester Place / Fitzroy Square'

Dear Sir

I return you thanks for The Two Pounds you now send me⌞.⌟ As to Sʳ T. Lawrence I have not heard from him as ye*t*, & hope that he has a good opinion of my willingness to appear grateful² tho not able on account of this abominable Ague or whatever it is⌞.⌟ I am in Bed & at Work⌞;⌟ my health I cannot speak of for if it was not for the Cold weather I think I should soon get about again. Great Men die equally with the little⌞.⌟ I am sorry for Lᵈ L.³ he is a man of very singular abilities⌞,⌟ as also for the D of Cᴵ but perhaps & I verily believe it Every Death is an improvement of the State of the Departed. I can

---

² Probably a copy of Blake's engraving of Chaucer's Canterbury Pilgrims (1810), or, as Dr. James Wills suggests, Blake's designs (?1824) to *Pilgrim's Progress*.

[7 June 1825]

¹ The date is established by the reference to the death of Gerrard Andrewes (1750–1825), 'the D[*ean*] of C[*anterbury*]', who died on 2 June 1825; Blake's letter was evidently written on the following Tuesday, the 7th.

² Perhaps Blake was grateful to Sir Thomas Lawrence (1769–1830) for his purchase of two drawings ('The Wise and Foolish Virgins' and 'The Dream of Queen Catherine') for £31. 10*s*. (*Blake Records*, 339, 400; see also 468 n. 3). Or this gratitude may have come from the incident referred to in the letter written by Thomas Campbell to William Etty on 25 March 1830:

> Mr. Blake, the artist . . . . was a year or two ago in great pecuniary distress, which came to the knowledge of Sir Thomas, and he, Mʳ Blake, came to a friend's of mine, who lives near Charing Cross, one morning, with tears of joy and gratitude in his eyes—on being asked the cause, he told my friend that Sir Thomas had sent him a 100£ bills that [*sic*] which had relieved his distresses, and made him and his wife's heart leap for joy.—

(Quoted from a reproduction of the MS generously sent me by its owner, Professor Robert Essick.) Etty's date of 'a year or two ago' (1828–9) is clearly wrong, for Blake died three years before, in 1827.

³ Probably Lord Lilford, who died 4 July 1825.

draw as well aBed as Up & perhaps better but I cannot En-
grave⌊·⌋ I am going on with Dante[4] & please myself.

I am d͏ͬ Sir yours Sincerely

Tuesday Night William Blake

11 OCTOBER 1825[1]

TO 'M͏ͬˢ Linnell / Collins s Farm North End / Hampstead'[2]

Dear Madam

I have had the Pleasure to See M͏ͬ Linnell set off safe in a
very comfortable Coa*ch*, & I may say I accompanied him part
of the way on his Journey in the Coach for we both got in
together & with another Passenger enterd into Conversation
when at length we found that we were all three proceeding on
our Journe*y*, but as I had not paid & did not wish to pay for
or take so long a Rid*e*, we with Some difficulty made the
Coachman understand that one of his Passengers was unwilling
to G*o*, when he obligingly permitted me to get out to my
great joy. *H*ence I am now enabled to tell you that I hope to
see you on Sunday morning as usual[3] which I could not have
done if they had taken me to Gloucester⌊·⌋

Tuesday I am D͏ͬ Madam yours Sincerely
11 October 1825 William Blake

10 NOVEMBER 1825

TO 'John Linnell, Esq͏ͬ / Cirencester Place / Fitzroy Square'

Dear Sir

I have I believe done nearly all that we agreed on &͏ᶜ⌊·⌋
If you should put on your considering Cap just as you did last

---

[4] Blake was making 101 designs from Dante's *Divine Comedy* for Linnell.

11 Oct. 1825

[1] The postmark indicates that the letter was posted between 8 p.m. of the 11th
and the evening of the 12th.

[2] Linnell moved with his family to Hampstead in 1824, but he kept a studio
in Cirencester Place, to which most of Blake's letters to him are addressed.

[3] Blake evidently spent Sundays regularly with the Linnells at Hampstead.
Mrs. Linnell wrote to her husband about Blake's letter on the 13th (*Blake Records*,
364).

time we met I have no doubt that the Plates would be all the better for it— I cannot get Well & am now in Bed but seem as if I should be better tomorrow⌊;⌋ rest does me good— Pray take care of your health this wet weather & tho I write do not venture out on such days as to day has been. I hope a few more days will bring us to a conclusion⌊.⌋

Thursday Evening   I am dear Sir
10 Novr 1825   Yours Sincerely
   Fountain Court   William Blake
   Strand

31 JANUARY 1826[1]

'To / John Linnell Esqre / N6 Cirencester Place / Fitzroy Square'

Dear Sir

[¶*1*]   I am forced to write because I cannot come to you & this on two accounts⌊:⌋ First I omitted to desire you would come & take a Mutton chop with us the day you go to Cheltenham & I will go with you to the to the [*sic*] Coach⌊;⌋ also I will go to Hampstead to see Mrs Linnell on Sunday but will return before dinner (I mean if you set off before that) & Second I wish to have a Copy of Job to shew to Mr Chantry⌊.⌋[2]

[¶*2*]   For I am again laid up by a cold in my stomach⌊;⌋ the Hampstead Air as it always di*d*, so I fear it always will do [it *del*] this Except it be the Morning air & that; in my Cousins[3] time⌊,⌋ I found I could bear with safety & perhaps benefit. I believe my Constitution to be a good one but it has many peculiarities that no one but myself can know. When I was young Hampstead Highgate Hornsea Muswell Hill & even Islington & all places North of London always laid me up the day after & sometimes two or three days with precisely the same Complaint & the same torment of the Stoma*c*h, Easily

31 Jan. 1826
    [1] The postmark of '31 JA[*NUARY*]' clearly indicates that Blake had postdated his letter.
    [2] Francis Leggatt Chantrey (1781–1841, later knighted), sculptor, paid for his proof copy of *Job* on 29 April 1826 (*Blake Records*, 591).
    [3] This is the only known reference to Blake's cousin.

removed but excruciating while it lasts & enfeebling for some time after⌊.⌋ Sr Francis Bacon would say it is want of discipline in Mountainous Places. Sr Francis Bacon is a Liar. No discipline will turn one Man into another even in the least particle & such discipline I call Presumption & Folly⌊.⌋ I have tried it too much not to know this & am very sorry for all such who may be led to such ostentatious Exertion against their Eternal Existence itself because it is Mental Rebellion against the Holy Spirit & fit only for a Soldier of Satan to perform⌊.⌋

¶3] Though I hope in a morning or two to call on you in Cirencester Place I feard you might be gone or I might be too ill to let you know how I am & what I wish⌊.⌋

                                               I am dear Sir
Feby 1. 1826   Yours Sincerely
                                               William Blake

[5 FEBRUARY 1826?]¹

TO [*Mrs. John Linnell?*]

                                    London Sunday Morning
Dear Madam
    Mr Linnell will have arrived at his Journeys end before the time I now write, he set off Last night before Eight O Clock from the Angel Inn near St Clements Church Strand on one of the Strongest & Handsomest Built Stages I ever Saw⌊.⌋ I should have written Last Night but as it would not come before now I do as Mr Linnell desired I would do by the First Stage⌊.⌋²
My Wife desires her kindest remembrances to you & I am

                                               Yours Sincerely
                                               Willm Blake
Excuse the writing⌊.⌋
I have delayed too long⌊.⌋

[5 Feb. 1826?]
    ¹ In his letter of Tuesday 31 Jan. Blake said he would go with Linnell 'to the Coach' and thereafter 'I will go to Hampstead to see Mrs Linnell on Sunday'. His undated letter, evidently written because he was not well enough to go to Hampstead with the news himself, describes the stagecoach in which Linnell set off and was probably therefore written on Sunday 5 Feb. 1826.
    ² Since Linnell 'set off Last night [?*a little*] before Eight O Clock', the hour when the Twopenny Post Office receiving-houses closed, Blake's letter could not in any case go out until the next morning.

31 MARCH 1826

TO 'John Linnell Esqre / Cirencester Place'¹

Friday Evening
March 31. 1826

Dear Sir

[¶*1*]   I have been very ill since I saw you but am again well enough to go on with my work but not well enough to venture out⌊;⌋ the Chill of the weather soon drives me back into that shivering fit which must be avoided till the Cold is gone.

[¶*2*]   Mr Robinson certainly did Subscribe for Prints only & not for Proofs for I remember that he offerd to pay me Three Guineas for each of the Copies⌊.⌋²

[¶*3*]   However if the weather should be warm I will endeavour to come to you before Tuesday but much fear that my present tottering state will hold me some time yet⌊.⌋

I am dear Sir yours Sincerely
Willm Blake

[APRIL 1826?]¹

TO 'John Linnell Esqr / Cirencester Place / Fitzroy Square'

Dear Sir

[¶*1*]   I am still far from recoverd & dare not get out in the cold

---

31 March 1826
¹ The letter is written on an oddly shaped piece of paper, half as wide as it is high (10·3 × 19·9 cm), which is pasted on to another sheet. A scrap of paper bearing the address is pasted above the letter.
² Henry Crabb Robinson (1775–1867), diarist, paid Blake £3 on 6 Jan. 1826 as deposits for plain copies of *Job* for himself, George Proctor, and Basil Montagu (1770–1831), author, and on 15 April 1826 he paid the balance of £6. 9*s.* (*Blake Records*, 320, 599).

[April 1826?]
¹ The letter may be cautiously dated April 1826, when Blake was unwell (31 March: 'I have been very ill'; 19 May: 'I have had another desperate Shivering Fit'), when he was working on his Dante engravings, and when Butts paid, about 29 April, £3. 3*s.* for his copy of *Job*. Proof copies were ordinarily five guineas, but Butts got a special price (as Linnell's account book records) 'because he lent the Drawing to Copy'. For such a favour, Blake and Linnell probably would have given Butts a proof copy free, had Butts not made the 'decision quite in Character' 'to have a Proof Copy for Three Guineas' (*Blake Records*, 591, 599).

air. Yet I lose nothing by it⌊.⌋ Dante goes on the better which is all I care about⌊.⌋

¶2] Mr Butts is to have a Proof Copy for Three Guineas⌊;⌋ this is his own decision quite in Character⌈;⌋ he calld on me this Week⌊.⌋

Yours Sincerely,
William Blake

19 MAY 1826

'To / John Linnell Esqre / N6 Cirencester Place / Fitzroy Square'

Dear Sir

I have had another desperate Shivering Fit. *It* came on yesterday afternoon after as good a morning as I ever experienced. It began by a gnawing Pain in the Stomach & soon spread a deathly feel all over the limbs which brings on the Shivering fit when I am forced to go to bed where I contrive to get into a little Perspiration which takes it quite away⌊.⌋ It was night when it left me so I did not get up but just as I was going to rise this morning the Shivering fit attackd me again & the pain with its accompanying deathly feel⌊.⌋ I got again into a perspiration & was well but so much weakend that I am still in bed. This intirely prevents me from the pleasure of seeing you on Sunday at Hampstead as I fear the attack again when I am away from home⌊.⌋

I am d^r Sir

Friday Evening   Yours sincerely
May 19 1826   William Blake

2 JULY 1826

'To / John Linnell Esqre / N6 Cirencester Place / Fitzroy Square'

My dearest Friend

¶1] This sudden Cold Weather has cut up all my hopes by the roots. Every one who knows of our intended flight into your delightful Country concur[s] in saying 'Do not Venture till

Summer appears again'. I also feel Myself weaker than I was aware, being not able as yet to set up longer than six hours at a time & also feel the Cold too much to dare venture beyond my present precincts— My heartiest Thanks for your care in my accomodation & the trouble you will yet have with me⌊.⌋ But I get better & stronger every day tho weaker in muscle & bone than I supposed.— As to pleasantness of Prospect it is All pleasant Prospect at North End. Mrs Hurds[1] I should like as well as any — But think of the Expense & how it may be spared & never mind appearances⌊.⌋

[¶2]   I intend to bring with me besides our necessary change of apparel, Only My Book of Drawings from Dante & one Plate shut up in the Book. All will go very well in the Coach which at present would be a rumble I fear I could not go thro'. So that I conclude another Week must pass before I dare Venture upon what I ardently desire — the seeing you with your happy Family once again & that for a longer Period than I had ever hoped in my health full hours⌊.⌋

I am dear Sir
Yours most gratefully
William Blake

5 JULY 1826

TO 'John Linnell Esqre / Cirencester Place'

5 July 1826

Dear Sir

[¶1]   I thank you for the Receit of Five Pounds this Morning & Congratulate you on the receit of another fine Boy⌊;⌋ am glad to hear of Mrs Linnells health & safety⌊.⌋

[¶2]   I am getting better every hour⌊;⌋ my Plan is diet only & if the Machine is capable of it shall make an old man yet: I go on Just as If perfectly well which indeed I am except in those paroxysms which I now believe will never more return⌊.⌋ Pray let your own health & convenience put all solicitude concern-

---

2 July 1826
[1] Linnell's landlady before he moved to Hampstead.

ing me at rest⌊.⌋ You have a Family⌊,⌋ I have none⌊;⌋ there is
no comparison between our necessary avocations⌊.⌋

Believe me to be d^r Sir
Yours Sincerely
William Blake

14 JULY 1826

'To / John Linnell / Cirencester Place / Fitz Ro*y* Square'

Dear Sir
I am so much better that I have hopes of fulfilling my ex-
pectation & desire of Visiting Hampstead⌊.⌋ I am never the
less very considerably weakend by the Last severe attacks⌊.⌋
Pray remember me with Kind Love to Mrs Linnell & her
lovely Family⌊.⌋

Yours Sincerely
July 14: 1826   William Blake

To Mr John Linnell — July 14: 1826
I hereby Declare, That Mr John Linnell
has Purchased of M*e*, The Plates & Copy-right
of Job; & the same is his sole Property[1]
Witness   William Blake
Edwd Jno Chance[2]
14 July 1826

[1] Blake signed a receipt to the same purpose:
London July 14: 1826
Recievd of Mr John Linnell, the Sum of One Hundred & fifty Pounds for
the copy-right & Plates (Twenty-two in number) of the Book of Job. Publishd
March 1825 by Me: William Blake Author of the Work.
N° 3 Fountain Court Strand
Witness: *Edwd Jno Chance*
Confusion over the ownership may have arisen because the March 1825 inscription
on the plates listed Blake as the publisher, while the label of March 1826 (when
the work was in fact published) listed Blake and Linnell as joint publishers. On
24 April 1826 Robert Balmanno had implicitly questioned Linnell's rights in *Job*
(*Blake Records*, 582, 329, 583).
[2] The signature of Linnell's nephew Edward John Chance is, of course, in
a different hand from the copybook writing that precedes it. The document is a
folded leaf, with the message on the first page and the copyright statement on the
third.

16 JULY 1826[1]

'To / John Linnell Esqre / Cirencester Place / Fitzroy Square'

Dear Sir

I have been ever since taking Dr Youngs[2] Addition to Mr Finchams Practise with me ([it *del*] the Addition is dandelion) In a Species of Delirium & in Pain too much for Thought₎.₎ It is now passed as I hope But the moment I got ease of Body began Pain of Mind [it is(?) *del*] & that not a Small one₎.₎ It is about The Name of the Child which Certainly ought to be Thoma*s*, after Mrs Linnells Father₎.₎[3] It will be brutal not to say Worse for it is worse In my opinion & on my Part. Pray Reconsider it if it is not too late₎.₎ It very much troubles Me as a Crime in which I shall [*be*] [a *del*] The Principal. Pray Excuse this hearty Expostulation & believe me to be Yours Sincerely

Sunday Afternoon[1]   William Blake
July 16. 1826

P.S. Fincham is a Pupil of Abernathys₎;₎[4] this is what gives me great pleasure₎.₎ I did not know it before yesterday from Mr Fincham₎.₎

29 JULY 1826

TO 'Mr Linnell / 6, Cirencester Place / Fitzroy Square'

Dear Sir

Just as I had become Wel*l*, that is Subdued the disease, tho not its Effects Weakness &^c Comes Another to hinder my Progress calld The Piles which when to the degree I have had

16 July 1826

[1] The postmark indicates that the letter was posted between 8 p.m. of the 16th and the evening of the 17th.

[2] Perhaps Dr. Thomas Young (1773–1829), sometime student of John Hunter, physician and polymath, called 'Phenomenon Young'.

[3] Linnell had unhesitatingly written '3^d son—William Born ½ past 3 morning' in his Journal for 3 July 1826, but this son was later named James and the next one William.

[4] John Abernethy (1764–1831), eminent surgeon, disciple of John Hunter.

them are a most sore plague & on a Weak Body truly afflic-
tive. These Piles have now also as I hope run their Period, &
I begin to again feel returning Strength, on these accounts I
cannot yet tell when I can start for Hampstead like a young
Lark without feathers. Two or Three days may be sufficient
or not, all now will depend on my bones & sinews⌊.⌋ Muscle
I have none but a few days may do & have done miracles in the
Case of a Convalescent who prepares himself ardently for his
return to Life & its Business among his Friend[s]

With whom he makes his first Effort⌊.⌋

29 July 1826   Dear Sir Yours Ever
                                              William Blake

Tuesday 1 AUGUST 1826[1]

'To / Mr Linnell / Cirencester Place / Fitzroy Square'

Dear Sir

If this Notice should be too short for your Convenience
please to let me know. But finding myself Well enough to
come I propose to set out from here as soon after ten as we
can on Thursday Morning⌊.⌋[2] Our Carriage will be a Cabriolet,
for tho getting better & stronger I am still incapable of riding
in the Stage & shall be I fear for Some time being only bones &
sinews⌊,⌋ All strings & bobbins like a Weavers Loom. Walking
to & from the Stage would be to me impossible tho I seem well
being entirely free from both pain & from that Sickness to
which there is no name. Thank God I feel no more of it & have
great hopes that the disease is Gone⌊.⌋

                                  I am dear Sir Yours Sincerely
Augst 1. 1826   William Blake

---

1 Aug. 1826

[1] The postmark indicates that the letter was posted between 8 p.m. of the 1st
and the evening of the 2nd.

[2] 'Mrs. Collins, of the Farm, still [in 1863] remembers Blake as "that most de-
lightful gentleman!" . . . During this visit [of 3 August 1826] he was at work upon
the Dante. A clump of trees on the skirts of the heath is still known to old friends
as the "Dante wood." ' (Gilchrist [1863], i. 353.)

4 NOVEMBER 1826

TO 'Mr Blake' [*From Sir Edward Denny*] [*Enclosed in a letter to Linnell*]¹

Sir

If you have a copy of Blair's Grave, with your illustrations, to dispose of, I should be much obliged to you if you could let me have it, or if you have not one yourself, would it be asking too muc*h* to request you would be so kind as to procure a copy for me,² and if you will send to me directed to me '*at Barbourne House, Worcester*' I shall feel particularly thankful to you— I hope you will be very particular in letting it be as good an impression as you can, as I am very much interested in it, I was shewn the work a day or two ago, and think it one of the most beautiful and interesting things I have seen of your's— I am also much interested in the progress of your illustrations of the Book of Job, having seen the unfinished plates some time since in the possession of Mr. Linnell, and hope you will tell me how it is going on, and when it is likely to be completed, perhaps also you would let me know whether you are engaged in any other performance at present—

Believe me, Sir,
Your's very truly obliged
Edward Denny

Barbourne House—Worcester
November 4th 1826—

4 Nov. 1826

¹ The lack of address is explained by the following letter addressed to 'Mr J. Linnell / N° 6 Cirencester Place / Titchfield Street / London' (in the Ivimy MSS) in which the one to Blake was enclosed:

Dear Sir

I do not know exactly Mr Blake's residence, and therefore I have enclosed this letter to you, hoping that you will be so obliging as to deliver it to him— I should be very much obliged if you could write me a line to tell me when the Book of Job will be completed, and whether Mr Blake is engaged in any other work— I think I remember your telling me, that he had some notion of illustrating Dante, I should be glad to know if he has begun it yet, or whether he ever intends to do so . . . . [*sic*]

The quotation marks are Denny's.

² Linnell's grandson A. H. Palmer claimed that Blake never received the letter; 'Linnell suppressed the letter to Blake & supplied a copy of The Grave himself thus robbing Blake of the profit' (*Blake Records*, 335 n. 3). However, Blake was ill at the time, and Linnell may have been simply saving his friend trouble. Since Linnell owned the *Job* copyright, and Ackermann that to Blair, there may have been no profit for Blake involved in any case.

Will you let me know the price of the Grave, at the same time that you send it to me⌊?⌋[3]

29 DECEMBER 1826

TO 'M[rs] Ade[*r*]s[1] Euston Square'

M[r] Blakes respectful Compliments to M[rs] Ade[*r*]s⌊,⌋ is sorry to say that his Illness is so far from gone that the least thing brings on the symptoms of the original complaint. *H*e does not dare to leave his room by any means. *H*e had another desperate attack of the Aguish trembling last night & is certain that at present any venture to go out must be of bad⌊,⌋ perhaps of fatal consequence⌊;⌋ Is very sorry indeed that he is deprived of the happiness of visiting again & also of seeing again those Pictures of the old Masters but must Submit to the necessity & be Patient till warm weather Comes⌊.⌋

3 Fountain Court Strand
29 [Jan[y] *erased*] Dec[r] 1826

[3] Linnell replied for Blake, and on 20 Nov. Denny wrote to Linnell (Ivimy MSS) in terms evidently intended for Blake also:

Dear Sir
I thank you for your ready compliance with my wishes, and beg you will pardon my tardiness in writing to you—I am much obliged by your letter, and the very interesting information it contains— What shall I say, what *can* I say of the book of Job— I can only say that it is a *great work*—and tho' I can not venture to pass my humble comments upon any thing so truly sublime—I do indeed feel its exquisite beauty and marvellous grandeur— It is a privilege to possess such a work and ‸still greater to‸ be able to feel it— it is, I think, the most perfect thing I ever have seen from the hands of M[r] Blake, and if his Dante is superior, he will, I may almost say, outdo himself— I hope indeed he may complete this valuable work—
I am very sorry to hear that M[r] Blake has been in danger, and sincerely hope that he is now in perfect health—. . . .
I send you a draft upon Puget & Bambridge for £7. 17. 6 the price of the Job and the Grave—and will you oblige me by informing me of your having received it⌊?⌋

29 Dec. 1826
[1] Eliza, daughter of the engraver J. R. Smith, married Charles Aders, and became a friend and patron of Blake.

27 JANUARY 1827

TO 'Mr Linnell / 6 Cirencester Place / Fitzroy Square'

Dear Sir

I ought to have acknowledgd the Rec[e]it of Five Pounds from you on 16 Jany 1827.¹ That part of your Letter in which you desired I would send an acknowledgd it [*sic*] I did not see till the next morning owing to its being writ on the outside double of your letter. Nevertheless I ought to have sent it but must beg you to Excuse such Follies which tho I am enough ashamd of & hope to mend can only do so at present by owning the Fault⌊.⌋

I am dear Sir yours Sincerely

Saturday Night
Jany 27 1827

William Blake

[FEBRUARY 1827?]¹

TO 'Mr Linnell / Cirencester Place / Fitzroy Square'

Dear Sir

[¶*1*]   I thank you for the Five Pounds recievd to Day⌊;⌋¹ am getting better every Morning but slowl*y*, as I am still feeble & totterin*g*, tho all the Symptoms of my complaint seem almost gone as the fine weather is very beneficial & comfortable to me⌊.⌋ I go on as I think improving my Engravings of Dante more & more & shall Soon get Proofs of these Four which I have & beg the favor of you to send me the two Plates of Dante which you have that I may finish them sufficiently to make some Shew of Colour & Strength⌊.⌋

[¶*2*]   I have Thought & thought of the Remova*l*,¹ & cannot get my

27 Jan. 1827
   ¹ According to Linnell's account book, this was paid on 18 Jan. (*Blake Records*, 593).

[Feb. 1827?]
   ¹ The date and 'the Removal' may be those referred to in Linnell's Journal: '*February* 7 [*1827*]. To Mr Blake to speak to him @ living at C[*irencester*] P[*lace*]', in which Linnell had a study and where Blake's brother James lived. On the other hand, Linnell had proposed in the summer of 1826 that the Blakes should move nearer to his Hampstead cottage, and his records of payments of £5 to Blake in

Mind out of a State of terrible fear at such a Step. The more I think the more I feel terror at what I wishd at first & thought it a thing of benefit & Good hope$_{\llcorner}$;$_{\lrcorner}$ you will attribute it to the right Cause Intellectual Peculiarity that must be Myself alone shut up in Myself or Reduced to Nothing. I could tell you of Visions & Dreams upon the Subject$_{\llcorner}$.$_{\lrcorner}$ I have asked & intreated Divine help but fear continues upon me & I must relinquish the step that I had wished to take & still wish but in vain$_{\llcorner}$.$_{\lrcorner}$

Your Success in your Profession is above all things to me

3] most gratifying. May it go on to the Perfection you wish & more$_{\llcorner}$.$_{\lrcorner}$ So wishes also Yours Sincerely

William Blake

[FEBRUARY 1827?][1]

TO 'J Linnell Esqre'[2]

Dear Sir

I calld this Morning for a Walk & brought my Plates with me to prevent the trouble of your Coming thro Curiosity to See what I was about$_{\llcorner}$.$_{\lrcorner}$ I have Got on very forward with 4 Plates & am getting better — or I could not have Come at all$_{\llcorner}$.$_{\lrcorner}$ Yours Willm Blake

15 MARCH 1827

TO 'Mr Linnell / Cirencester Place / Fitzroy Square'

Dear Sir

This is to thank you for Two Pounds now by me recievd on account$_{\llcorner}$.$_{\lrcorner}$ I have recievd a Letter from Mr Cumberland[1] in

July and 29 Aug. 1826 and 9 Jan. 1827 suggest alternative dates for this letter (*Blake Records*, 338, 592).

[Feb. 1827?]
  [1] The approximate date is established by the reference to getting 'forward with 4 Plates', an echo of the sentence in the other letter of ?Feb 1827: 'I go on as I think improving my Engravings of Dante more & more & shall Soon get Proofs of these Four which I have'.
  [2] This note, on a long thin strip of torn paper (28·5 × 4·1 cm) without address, was probably left by Blake at Linnell's studio when he 'calld this Morning for a Walk' and found no one there.

15 March 1827
  [1] George Cumberland noted in his diary for 5 March 1827 that he had 'Sent . . .

which he says he will take one Copy of Job for himself but
cannot as yet find a Customer for one but hopes to do some-
what by perseverance in his Endeavours∟;⌋ he tells me that it is
too much Finishd or over Labourd for his Bristol Friends as they
think∟.⌋ I saw Mʳ Tatham Senʳ yesterday∟;⌋[2] he sat with me
above an hour & lookd over the Dante∟;⌋ he expressd himself
very much pleasd with the designs as well as the Engravings∟.⌋
I am getting on with the Engravings & hope soon to get Proofs
of what I am doing∟.⌋

I am dear Sir Yours Sincerely

15 March 1827   William Blake

[?18 MARCH 1827]

'To / Miss Denman[1] / Buckingham Street / Fitzroy Square'

Mʳ Blakes respectful Compliments to Miss Denman∟;⌋ has
found 15 Proofs of The Hesiod∟;⌋[2] as they are duplicates to
others which he has, they are intirely at Miss Denmans Service
if she will accept of them∟;⌋ what Proofs he has remaining are[3]
all Printed on both sides of the Paper & so are unfit for to make
up a Set especially as many of the backs of the paper have on
them impressions from other Plates for Booksellers[4] which he
was employd about at the same time∟.⌋

Wednesday Morning
   18 March 1827[5]
3 Fountain Court Strand

[a] Lett[er] . . . to *Blake*' (*Blake Records*, 340). His subsequent efforts and ill success
are described in his letter to Catherine of 25 Nov. 1827.

   [2] Charles Heathcote Tatham (1772–1842), architect, father of Frederick (1805–
78), Blake's disciple.

[?18 March 1827]
   [1] Maria Denman, Flaxman's sister-in-law and executrix.
   [2] Flaxman's *Compositions from the Works Days and Theogony of Hesiod* (1817), with
37 plates by Blake.
   [3] 'are' is altered from 'all'.
   [4] The only other plates Blake is known to have been employed upon at this
time (1814–17) were for Rees's *Cyclopaedia* (1816–19) and Wedgwood's *Catalogue*
(1815–16).
   [5] The date is actually written '1[7 *del*]827'. Since 18 March 1827 was a Sunday
(not 'Wednesday'), and since the letter is not postmarked, we can only guess that it
was written on Wednesday, 14 or 21 March 1827.

12 APRIL 1827

TO 'George Cumberland Esqre / Culver Street / Bristol'

Dear Cumberland

1]   I have been very near the Gates of Death & have returned
very weak & an Old Man feeble & tottering, but not in Spirit
& Life not in The Real Man The Imagination which Liveth
for Ever. In that I am stronger & stronger as this Foolish
Body decays. I thank you for the Pains you have taken with
Poor Job.[1] I know too well that a great majority of Englishmen
are fond of The Indefinite which they Measure by Newtons
Doctrine of the Fluxions of an Ato*m*, A Thing that does not
Exist. These are Politicians & think that Republican Art is
Inimical to their Atom. For a Line or Lineament is not formed
by Chance⌐;⌐ a Line is a Line in its Minutest Subdivisions⌐;⌐
Strait or Crooked It is Itself & Not Intermeasurable with or
by any Thing Else⌐.⌐ Such is Job but since the French Revolu-
tion Englishmen are all Intermeasurable One by Another⌐,⌐
Certainly a happy state of Agreement to which I for One do
not Agree. God keep me from the Divinity of Yes & No too⌐,⌐
The Yea Nay Creeping Jesus⌐,⌐[2] from supposing Up & Down
to be the same Thing as all Experimentalists must suppose⌐.⌐

2]   You are desirous I know to dispose of some of my Works &
to make them Pleasin[*g*.] I am obliged to you & to all who do so
But having none remaining of all that I had Printed I cannot
Print more Except at a great loss for at the time I printed those
things I had a whole House to range in⌐;⌐[3] now I am shut up
in a Corner therefore am forced to ask a Price for them that I
scarce expect to get from a Stranger. I am now Printing a Set
of the Songs of Innocence & Experience for a Friend[4] at Ten
Guineas which I cannot do under Six Months consistent with

12 April 1827

[1] Cumberland's pains with *Job* are described in his letter of 25 Nov. 1827.

[2] A Sussex expression meaning a servile hypocrite; see 'The Everlasting Gospel',
part K, l. 59 (p. 1067).

[3] Blake only 'had a whole House to range in' when he lived in Hercules Build-
ings, Lambeth (1790–1800) and in Felpham (1800–3).

[4] The Friend is probably Thomas Griffiths Wainewright (1794–1852), dil-
ettante and poisoner, who told Linnell on 22 Feb. 1827 that he had asked Blake
to let him have a coloured copy of the *Songs* (X) (*Blake Records*, 339).

my other Work, so that I have little hope of doing any more of such things. The Last Work I produced is a Poem Entitled Jerusalem the Emanation of the Giant Albion, but find that to Print it will Cost my Time the amount of Twenty Guineas. One I have Finishd⌊.⌋ It contains 100 Plates but it is not likely that I shall get a Customer for it⌊.⌋[5]

[¶3] As you wish me to send you a list with the Prices of these things they are as follows

	£	s	d
America ———————	6.	6.	0
Europe	6.	6.	0
Visions &c	5.	5.	0
Thel	3.	3.	0
Songs of Inn. & Exp.	10.	10.	0
Urizen	6.	6.	0[6]

[¶4] The Little Card[7] I will do as soon as Possible but when you Consider that I have been reduced to a Skeleton from which I am slowly recovering you will I hope have Patience with me⌊.⌋

[¶5] Flaxman is Gone[8] & we must All soon follow⌊,⌋ every one to his Own Eternal House Leaving the Delusive Goddess Nature & her Laws to get into Freedom from all Law of the Members into The Mind in which every one is King & Priest in his own House⌊.⌋ God send it so on Earth as it is in Heaven⌊.⌋

I am Dear Sir Yours Affectionately
William Blake

12 April 1827
N 3 Fountain Court Strand[9]

[5] *Jerusalem* (E) was not sold when Blake died, and passed to Catherine and then (1831) to Frederick Tatham.

[6] These prices indicate that the copies were coloured. For other lists of prices see Blake's Prospectus of 10 Oct. 1793 and his letter of 9 June 1818 (pp. 202–3, 1648–9).

[7] This Message Card, which Cumberland said he 'sent up to have a few ornaments engraved or etched round my Name', was not quite finished when Blake died (*Blake Records*, 360, 365).

[8] Flaxman died 7 Dec. 1826.

[9] To the third page of this folded leaf, Cumberland appended the card which Blake had engraved for him and the following note:

He died aug 12: 1827 in the back room of the first floor of N 3 Fountain Court in the Strand, and was buried in Bunhill fields burying ground on the 17 aug 25 feet from the north wall N 80. *T. Smith* [*NOLLEKENS AND HIS TIMES*

25 APRIL 1827

TO 'Mr Linnell / 6 Cirencester Place / Fitzroy Square'

Dear Sir

I am going on better Every day as I think both in hea[l]th & in work⌊.⌋ I thank you for The Ten Pounds which I recievd from you this day which shall be put to the best use as also for the prospect of Mr Ottleys[1] advantageous acquaintance⌊.⌋ I go on without daring to consider Futurity, which I cannot do without Doubt & Fear that ruins Activity & are the greatest hurt to an Artist such as I am. As to Ugolino[2] &c I never supposed that I should sell them⌊;⌋ my Wife alone is answerable for their having Existed in any finishd State⌊.⌋ I am too much attachd to Dante to think much of any thing else— I have Proved the Six Plates & reduced the Fighting devils ready for the Copper⌊.⌋[3] I count myself sufficiently Paid If I live as I now do & only fear that I may be Unlucky to my friends & especially that I may not be so to you.

I am Sincerely yours

25 April 1827   William Blake

3 JULY 1827

TO 'Mr Linnell / 6 Cirencester Place / Fitzroy Square'

Dear Sir

I thank you for the Ten Pounds you are so kind as to send

(*1828*)], says his desease was the bile mixing with his blood—in his random way of writing—and considering the malignity of this Smith in his infamous biography of Nollekens it is fortunate that he speaks no ill of him.
my little message card was the last thing he executed and he dates it thus—

W. Blake inv & sc.

A Æ 70 1827.

The widow charged me 3.3 for it and £3. 3. – for the Job⌊.⌋

25 April 1827

[1] William Young Ottley (1771–1836), art amateur. On 17 April, according to his Journal, Linnell went 'To Mr Ottley with Mr Blake' and on 11 Aug., the day before Blake died, Ottley paid £5. 5s. for an uncoloured copy of *Jerusalem* (*Blake Records*, 341, 594).

[2] Evidently the tempera of 'Ugolino and his Sons and Grandsons in Prison'.

[3] The engraving was partly finished before his death.

me at this time.¹ My journey to Hampstead on Sunday brought on a relapse which is lasted till now. I find I am not so well as I thought⌊.⌋ I must not go on in a youthful Style— however I am upon the mending hand to day & hope soon to look as I did for I have been yellow accompanied by all the old Symptoms⌊.⌋

I am dear Sir
Yours Sincerely

3 July 1827   William Blake

25 NOVEMBER 1827

TO 'M⁏ˢ Blake at M⁏ Linnells 6 Cirencester Place' [*From George Cumberland*]

Bristol 25. Nov. 1827.¹

My Dear Madam.

[¶*1*]   It was only very lately that I heard of the death of my excellent friend, your departed husband;² and this week by an enclosure from my Son I find a Lett⁏ to him from Mr Linell stating that the card plate was ready for me, and that it will be expected that I pay for the Book of Job at the same time.—³ I have in consequence written to him, by this conveyance, to call for the Card Plate, and now assure you, that if I do not succeed in Selling the Job (which was sent to me for that purpose from Mr Blake,) I shall certainly take it for myself and remit you the money as soon as I conveniently can.

[¶*2*]   That elaborate work, I have not only shewn to all our amateurs and artists here without success but am now pushing it through Clifton, by means of *Mr Lane* the Bookseller there, having previously placed it with Mr *Tyson*, Mr *Trimlet*, and

---

3 July 1827
  ¹ According to Linnell's account book, he sent Blake £10. 10s. on 26 June (*Blake Records*, 594).

25 Nov. 1827
  ¹ In his diary Cumberland mistakenly recorded the date when he 'Wrote to . . . Mrs Blake' as 27 Nov. (*Blake Records*, 359 n. 2).
  ² Blake died 12 Aug. 1827.
  ³ Linnell's letter of 12 Nov. and the undated letter of George Cumberland, Jr., together with George Jr.'s undated letter to Linnell enclosing his father's letter to Catherine Blake, are given in *Blake Records*, 357–8.

another of our Print Sellers here without success — and as that
is the case, and that even those who desired me to write to
my friend for a List of his works and prices, (among whom
were his great admirers from having seen what I possessed —
viz. Dr King of Clifton & Mr Rippengale the Artis*t*) declined
giving him any orders, on account, as they said, of the prices[4] —
I should not recommend you to send any more here — but
rather to fix a place in London where all his works may be
disposed of offering a complete set for Sale to the British
Museum Print room,[5] as that will make them best know*n*—
better even than their independant author who for his many
virtues most deserved to be so — a Man who has stocked the
english school with fine ideas,— above trick, fraud, or servility.

> With my best wishes for your happiness I
> I am My dear Madam
> Yours very truly
> G. Cumberland.

PS.

[3]   The reason I did not continue to purchase everything Mr
Blake engraved, was that latterly I have not only been unable
to continue Collecting but have even sold all I had Collected —
yet still preserving all I possessed of his graver⌞.⌟

[4]   If you have occasion to write, let the Lett^r be left for me with
my Son George at the army Pay Office and he will get it
franked.

---

4 Blake's prices are given in his letter to Cumberland of 12 April 1827.

5 The British Museum apparently did not acquire its first Blake until many
years after 1827. Indeed, no contemporary collection is known to have compre-
hended 'a complete set' of Blake's works.

LOST WORKS

LOST WORKS

INTRODUCTION

In this section are descriptions of works alluded to in Blake's writings or elsewhere of which no significant text is known. Some may be titles of works never written, some may be alternative titles for known works, and others may have been written but lost.

Blake told Crabb Robinson: 'I have written more than Voltaire or Rousseau—Six or Seven Epic poems as long as Homer and 20 Tragedies as long as Macbeth.'[1] At his death he 'left volumes of verse, amounting, it is said, to nearly an hundred, prepared for the press'.[2] No manuscript works 'prepared for the press' survive, but the bulk of unpublished writings was apparently at one time formidable.

Many manuscripts seem to have been destroyed by Blake's friends. Blake himself told Crabb Robinson on 18 February 1826:

'I have been tempted to burn my MSS but my wife wont let me⌞.⌟'
'She is right⌞,⌟' said I— 'You have written these, not from yourself but by a higher order⌞.⌟ The MSS. are theirs not your property— You cannot tell what purpose they may answer; unforeseen to you⌞.⌟' He liked this And said he wo^d not destroy them⌞,⌟'[1]

Even if Blake kept his word, poverty may have forced his widow to discard some of his works which no one else seemed to want.

At the death of Catherine Blake, almost all Blake's drawings, copperplates, books, and manuscripts evidently passed into the possession of their devoted friend Frederick Tatham. Tatham

---

[1] *Blake Records*, 322. No completed tragedy survives, and none of his epics is as long as Homer's.
[2] A. Cunningham, *Lives* (1830) (*Blake Records*, 506–7).

printed a few of the works in Illuminated Printing in the 1830s and sold them along with a good many of the drawings. Later Tatham became 'a zealous Irvingite' and was persuaded 'by some very influential members of the Sect . . . that Blake was inspired . . . by Satan himself—and was to be cast out as an "unclean spirit" ' ⌐.⌐[1] Though Edward Calvert implored Tatham not to destroy Blake's works,[2] 'Tatham . . . enacted the holocaust of Blake manuscripts—not designs, I think, as I have heard from his own lips'.[1] The destruction was not complete, for about 1860 he said 'that he had destroyed some of Blake's manuscripts and kept others by him, which he had sold from time to time'.[3] The only manuscript he is known to have kept by him was the 'Ballads MS', which he sold about 1864.

Others also apparently destroyed Blake manuscripts of less importance. When D. G. Rossetti acquired the *Notebook* in 1847, 'there were many loose papers in the book. . . . Many of these loose sheets contained verses which were so bad that Rossetti threw them into his waste-basket, from which Swinburne rescued a few fragments not quite so worthless as the rest.'[4] Mrs. Gilchrist wrote to W. M. Rossetti about the Blake manuscripts 'your brother destroyed', but W. M. Rossetti did 'not distinctly recollect' such an action.[5] Mrs. Gilchrist herself had 'a long thing which I really believe even Mr Swinburne will pronounce pure rubbish'.[5] W. M. Rossetti described it as

a prose narrative of a domestic, and also fantastic, sort, clearly intended by its author to count as humouristic or funny, and somewhat in the Shandean vein. I read this performance, and heartily confirmed Mrs Gilchrist in the conviction of its being rubbish; yet I was startled to learn soon afterwards that, on receiving my letter, she had burned the MS. The thing was stupid, but it was Blake's, and a curiosity.[5]

[1] As Anne Gilchrist reported in a letter of 9 Nov. 1862 in *Anne Gilchrist: Her Life and Writings*, ed. H. H. Gilchrist (1887), 129–30.

[2] [S. Calvert] *A Memoir of Edward Calvert Artist* (1893), 59.

[3] A. Symons, *William Blake* (1907), 241, reporting a conversation between Dr. Garnett and Tatham.

[4] E. J. Ellis, *The Real Blake* (1907), 299, quoting an unnamed 'friend of D. G. Rossetti'. Perhaps one of the fragments was part of 'The Everlasting Gospel' which Swinburne printed in *William Blake* (1868), 175–6.

[5] *Rossetti Papers* 1862 to 1870, ed. W. M. Rossetti (1903), 41–2.

It seems likely, therefore, that Blake's friends destroyed many manuscript works by Blake of which we have no knowledge. The fragments below[1] are all apparently quite minor, with the possible exception of the 'Work on Art'.

'Barry a Poem' (?1808)

On *Notebook* p. 60 (?1808) (p. 958), Blake wrote fourteen satirical lines 'to come in Barry a Poem', but no other reference to the work is known. Their subject and style are similar to other poems in the *Notebook* of about 1808.

'The Bible of Hell' (?1793)

In the *Marriage* (?1790–3) pl. 24 (p. 97), Blake wrote that he had 'The Bible of Hell: which the world shall have whether they will or no.' He evidently seriously intended to produce such a work, for he made a tentative draft title-page for it (see p. 1323): 'The Bible of Hell, in Nocturnal Visions collected Vol. I. Lambeth'. The date must be 1790–1800, when he was living in Hercules Buildings, Lambeth.

No other direct reference to the work has survived.[2] Perhaps it became *Vala* (?1796–?1807), which is subtitled 'a Dream of Nine Nights'. Alternatively, this promise, on one of the first plates (?1790) etched for the *Marriage*, to produce 'The Bible of Hell' may have been fulfilled in the 'Proverbs of Hell' on *Marriage* pl. 7–10, which were apparently etched rather later (?1793).

Descriptions of *Comus* Designs (?1801)

Among the property of Thomas Butts was 'Milton's Comus, 8 [*drawings*], with the artist's descriptions',[3] but there is no other evidence that Blake made descriptions of the drawings. In his letter of 19 October 1801 Blake spoke of sending his 'Designs for Comus' to the Revd. Joseph Thomas. If the Descriptions existed, they were probably written at this time.

---

[1] They are given in alphabetical order because their dates are so uncertain.
[2] Unless it is related to 'For Children[:] the Gates of Hell' (?1793), below.
[3] Sold at Foster's, 29 June 1853, lot 98.

'For Children the Gates of Hell' (?1793)

Blake drafted a title-page for a work to be called 'For Children∟:⌋ the Gates of Hell' (see p. 1323), but no more of the work is known. It is clearly analogical to *For Children: The Gates of Paradise* (1793) and perhaps related to 'The Bible of Hell' (?1793), above.

'The History of England' (?1793)

In his Prospectus of 10 October 1793 Blake offered 'The History of England, a small book of Engravings. Price 3*s*.' Evidently it was not to be printed in colours, for it is not described as 'in Illuminated Printing' as *Thel* (1789), *Visions* (1793), *America* (1793), and the *Songs* (1789–94) are. On the other hand, Blake may have intended to include some text, as he did in *For Children* (1793), which is also described in the Prospectus as 'a small book of Engravings. Price 3*s*.' The identity in price of the two works may suggest that the 'History of England' was to have about eighteen plates, like *For Children*. On p. 116 (?1793) of the *Notebook* (pp. 1002–4) Blake made a list of about twenty subjects (to which five were later added) dealing with the history of England, with a 'frontispiece' to represent 'The Ancient Britons according to Caesar'. Probably the subjects in this list were intended for the work advertised in the Prospectus, but none of the subjects is known to have been engraved.

Names of Gods (?1783)

W. M. Rossetti described a 'scrap of paper in the same [*Blake's*] handwriting, giving a few details about names of Gods in different mythologies. It is a mere memorandum. . . . The spelling is very bad, & must belong to B's youth.'[1] The piece sounds somewhat similar to 'then she bore Pale desire' (?1783) (pp. 869–73), which deals with the origins of the passions and which W. M. Rossetti owned. No other reference is known to Blake's 'memorandum' 'about names of Gods in different mythologies'.

[1] *Letters of William Michael Rossetti*, ed. C. Gohdes & P. F. Baum (1934), 131, 132.

'Outhoun' (?1793)

Catherine Blake offered to James Ferguson, probably after Blake's death (1827–31), 'A work called Outhoun. 12 Plates, 6 inches more or less. Price £2 2s. od.'[1] This work sounds rather like *Visions of the Daughters of Albion* (1793), in which Oothoon is the chief character.

The details, however, do not fit the *Visions* very precisely. It has eleven plates (not '12'), the leaves are 11" to 15" high, the plate size is about $4\frac{3}{4}" \times 6\frac{3}{4}"$ (though this could, I suppose, be '6 inches more or less'), and the price in Blake's letter of 12 April 1827 was £5. 5s. (not £2. 2s.). Probably 'Outhoun' is the *Visions* rather inaccurately described.

'Twelve Good Rules' (?1803)

From May 1803 to 1808 George Cumberland regularly made notes to himself in his pocket-book to discover 'who has Plate of the 12 good Rules [engraved] by Blake lost'.[2]

Perhaps the work is related to 'King Charles' "Twelve Good Rules" ', which normally consisted of a decorative design, such as the King's execution, and the following uplifting maxims: (1) Urge no healths; (2) Profane no divine ordinances; (3) Touch no state matters; (4) Reveal no secrets; (5) Pick no quarrels; (6) Make no comparisons; (7) Maintain no ill opinions; (8) Keep no bad company; (9) Encourage no vice; (10) Make no long meals; (11) Repeat no grievances; (12) Lay no wagers. These 'Twelve Good Rules' of King Charles were very popular among country people. They are referred to by Goldsmith in *The Deserted Village* and by Crabbe in *The Parish Register* (ll. 51–2), and Thomas Bewick (1753–1828) said they were 'common to be seen when I was a boy in every cottage and farm house throughout the country'.[3]

If Blake had wanted to deal with a popular subject, particularly when he was living in the country, in Felpham (1800–3), he might have engraved 'King Charles' "Twelve Good Rules" ' for sale among his rural neighbours. To save money and trouble,

---

[1] Gilchrist (1863), ii. 262.   [2] *Blake Records*, 118 & n. 4.
[3] *A Memoir of Thomas Bewick*, ed. A. Dobson (1887), 261.

he may have engraved them on pewter by the process which he described in his *Notebook* and recommended to his friends.[1] If so, they may be related to the 'Illustrations by W. Blake—pewter-types 13' which are recorded in a sale catalogue[2] but are untraced.

No other reference to Blake's 'Twelve Good Rules' is known.

'Version of Genesis' (date unknown)

Crabb Robinson reported that on 18 February 1826 Blake 'shewed me his Version (for so it may be called) of Genesis—"as understood by a Christian Visionary" in which in a style resembl^g the Bible—The spirit is given⌞.⌟ *He* read a passage at random⌞.⌟ It was striking⌞.⌟'[3] Nothing like such a work has survived.[4] It probably gave the 'infernal or diabolical sense' of the Bible, a work which he promised in the *Marriage* (?1790–3) pl. 24 (p. 97) 'the world shall have if they behave well'. The date could be almost any time between 1793 and 1826.

'A Work on Art' (?1809)

Several references are known to Blake's unpublished 'Work on Art'. As early as 10 January 1802 he had, as he wrote to Butts, 'recollected all my scatterd thoughts on Art', and perhaps from this date he began to cast about for ways of publishing them. When he returned to London in 1803 he evidently talked to his friends about this project. In the summer of 1807 George Cumberland wrote in his Diary that Blake 'Intends to publish his new method [*of engraving*] through means[?] of stopping lights', and next spring he wrote more specifically: 'Blakes

[1] *Notebook* p. 10 (p. 927). On 12 April 1813 Blake 'recommended [*to George Cumberland*] Pewter to Scratch on with the Print' (*Blake Records*, 232).

[2] Sale of Mrs. Steele's collection at Christie's, 7 February 1893, lot 186.

[3] When he revised this passage in his 'Reminiscences', Robinson said Blake 'read a wild passage in a sort of Bible Style' from his '[Vision . . . *del*] Version of Genesis' (*Blake Records*, 322, 547).

[4] The Illuminated Genesis Manuscript (1827) gives the Bible literally, and the 'Genesis' manuscript, a translation (probably by Hayley) of Tasso's *Sette Giornate del Mondo Creato*, is not by Blake (but was transcribed by him), is not 'striking', and is not 'in a style resembl^g the Bible'. Perhaps the 'Version of Genesis' is related to 'The Bible of Hell' above.

new mode of Stopping lights to be published in Nicholson'. That autumn he wrote again: 'Blakes new Mode of Engraving to be Published by me at his desire',[1] and on 18 December 1808 he wrote to Blake proposing this:

> You talked also of publishing your new method of engraving—send it to me and I will do my best to prepare it for the Press.—Perhaps when done you might with a few specimens of Plates make a little work for subscribers of it—as Du Crow [*Ducros*] did of his Aqua Tinta—selling about 6 Pages for a guinea to non Subscribers—but if you do not chuse this method, we might insert it in Nicholsons Journal [OF NATURAL PHILOSOPHY, CHEMISTRY, AND THE ARTS] or the Monthly Magazine—with reference to you for explanations⌊.⌋

On the 19th Blake replied declining Cumberland's offer: 'I have Myself begun to print an account of my various Inventions in Art for which I have procured a Publisher[2] & am determind to pursue the plan of publishing what I may get printed without disarranging my time'.

The work is described further in the advertisement of his exhibition (15 May 1809, p. 822):

> Fresco Painting is properly Miniature, or Enamel Painting; every thing in Fresco is as high finished as Miniature or Enamel, although in works larger than Life. The Art has been lost: I have recovered it. How this was done, will be told, together with the whole Process, in a Work on Art, now in the Press.

And in the *Descriptive Catalogue* (1809), ¶9 (p. 829), are more details:

> Whether Rubens or Vandyke, or both, were guilty of this villa⌊i⌋ny [*first bringing* oil Painting into general opinion and practice], is to be enquired in another work on Painting, and who first forged the silly story and known fals[e]hood, about John of Bruges inventing oil colours . . . .

Thus Blake twice says positively that the work is actually being printed. It seems at least possible that it was published,

---

[1] *Blake Records*, 187, 188, 211 n. 3.

[2] This phraseology suggests that Blake was printing the work at his own expense and planned to distribute it through a bookseller selling on commission. Blake may be referring here to the *Descriptive Catalogue* (1809).

for in 1828 J. T. Smith wrote that Blake 'proposed an engraving from his fresco picture [*of the Canterbury Pilgrims*], which he publicly exhibited in his brother James's shop window, at the corner of Broad-street [*an address James Blake left in 1812*], accompanied with an address to the public, stating what he considered to be improper conduct'.[1] If it was printed, however, no copy has been traced. Perhaps the 'Public Address' (pp. 1029–53) was part of the text.

---

[1] *Blake Records*, 465. Smith may be referring to the *Descriptive Catalogue* (1809), which does complain in passing of 'improper conduct' and mentions the Chaucer engraving, but it cannot accurately be described as a prospectus for the engraving. The advertisements for the engraving, on the other hand, do not contain accusations of 'improper conduct'.

BIBLIOGRAPHICAL NOTES

BIBLIOGRAPHICAL NOTES

Poetical Sketches (1783)

(Text pp. 749–99)

COPY-TEXT: Copy C (Huntington).

COLLATION: 4° (half sheet imposition): [A1–2], B–K4 (*J omitted*); signed on first two leaves of each quire except in quire A; 38 leaves, 76 pp. K4 present in copies B, C, E, G, H, I, R.

CONTENTS: Title-page ([A1]ʳ), 'Advertisement' ([A2]ʳ), 'Miscellaneous Poems': 'To Spring' (B1ʳ⁻ᵛ), 'To Summer' (B1ᵛ), 'To Autumn' (B2ʳ), 'To Winter' (B2ᵛ), 'To the Evening Star' (B3ʳ), 'To Morning' (B3ᵛ), 'Fair Elenor' (B4ʳ–C1ᵛ), 'Song [How sweet I roam'd]' (C1ᵛ), 'Song [My silks and fine array]' (C2ʳ), 'Song [Love and harmony combine]' (C2ᵛ), 'Song [I love the jocund dance]' (C3ʳ), 'Song [Memory, hither come]' (C3ᵛ), 'Mad Song' (C4ʳ), 'Song [Fresh from the dewy hill]' (C4ᵛ), 'Song [When early morn walks forth]' (D1ʳ), 'To the Muses' (D1ᵛ), 'Gwin, King of Norway' (D2ʳ–D4ʳ), 'An Imitation of Spencer' (D4ᵛ–E1ᵛ), 'Blind-Man's Buff' (E1ᵛ–E2ᵛ); 'King Edward the Third' (E3ʳ–H4ʳ), 'Prologue, intended for a dramatic piece of King Edward the Fourth' (H4ᵛ), 'Prologue to King John' (I1ʳ–I1ᵛ), 'A War Song to Englishmen' (I1ᵛ–I2ʳ), 'The Couch of Death' (I2ᵛ–I3ᵛ), 'Contemplation' (I4ʳ⁻ᵛ), 'Samson' (14ᵛ–K3ᵛ); [A1]ᵛ, [A2]ᵛ, K4ʳ⁻ᵛ blank.

LEAF-SIZE: 13·9 × 22·3 cm (R).

WATERMARK: Chain lines 2·8 cm apart. Paper defective, perhaps an odd lot.

PAGE NUMBERING: Pages numbered correctly 2–70 (B1ᵛ–K3ᵛ) at the outside corners of pages with running heads; in square brackets in the middle of the top margin when the first line of the page is the title of the piece that follows (except that pp. 15–16 are in round brackets).

RUNNING TITLES: Correct, except for p. 26, 'BLIND-MAN'S BUFF.', which should be 'AN IMITATION OF SPENCER.', and p. 58, 'A WAR SONG TO ENGLISHMEN.', which should be 'PROLOGUE TO KING JOHN.'

CATCHWORDS: Correct, except for p. 43, '*Prince*' which should be '*Prince*.' and p. 55, 'PROLOGUE' which should be 'PROLOGUE,'.

PRESS FIGURES: None.

ORNAMENT: p. 10.

FACSIMILE PAGES:[1] H1–K4 (in copies K, L, U), I1–K4 (in copy P), [A2] (in copy Q).

The facsimile pages were printed on paper watermarked 'MICHALLET',[2] sometime before 1887, when they were described in a Pearson catalogue, and probably before the death in 1883 of Francis Bedford, who bound copies K and U.

PUBLICATION: According to J. T. Smith (1828), John Flaxman and A. S. Mathew paid for the printing of Blake's *Poetical Sketches* and gave the copies 'to Blake to sell to friends, or publish, as he might think proper'.[3] He did not show much interest in the thirty-eight leaves stitched into bluish-Grey wrappers. A few copies he evidently gave away himself: George Cumberland probably received his copy (D) about 1783; Thomas Butts is likely to have acquired a copy (B) soon after he became Blake's patron about 1795; and Charles Tulk was presumably given his copy (C) after 1810 when, at the age of twenty-four, he began working with John Flaxman in the interest of Swedenborg. Other copies were given away by the Flaxmans in Blake's interest; Flaxman gave one copy (S) to William Hayley on 26 April 1784,[4] and another (E) to William Long, almost certainly at the same time,[4] while Nancy Flaxman gave copy F away on 15 May 1784, perhaps to Isaac Reed.

CORRECTIONS: In all these copies which were given away by or for Blake, the author made neat corrections in ink in a kind of printing hand. Apparently he corrected copies unsystematically, as he happened to notice

Incidence of Manuscript Changes in Poetical Sketches

Copy	Pages																		Totals
	2	4	5	7	9	12	15^a	15^b	20	24^a	24^b	25	28	29	44	46	64^a	64^b	
B		*			*		*	*											4
C		*		*	*			*											4
D			*					*											2
E		*		*	*		*	*											5
F		*			*		*	*		*									5
O		*			*	*		*											4
Q		*		*	*	*	*	*			*	*	*	*					10
S		*		*	*			*		*	*								6
T		*					*	*			*				*	*	*		7
V		*		*		*	*	*							*	*	*	*	9
W	*	*			*		*	*	*										6
11	1	10	1	5	8	3	7	11	1	2	3	1	1	1	2	2	2	1	

[1] The clearest indication of the facsimile is in the last words on p. 59, where the penultimate 'Prepare' is under the 'w' of 'welcome' in genuine copies and under the 'c' in the facsimile.

[2] Oddly enough, the 1890 Griggs facsimile of the *Poetical Sketches*, which is typographically quite distinct from the inserted facsimile leaves, is also printed on paper watermarked 'MICHALLET', and a fly-leaf in copy X is on the same paper.

[3] *Blake Records*, 456. Keynes (*Blake Studies* [1949], 26) calculated that they probably paid about £6 to have fifty copies printed.

[4] *Blake Records*, 27–8. Crabb Robinson owned two copies (?A, ?O).

errors afresh. In all copies which he improved, Blake corrected the mis-
spelling on page 15, and in all but one he made the same deletion on page
4, but the other changes seem almost random.[1]

UNCORRECTED COPIES: At his death Blake left a number of copies as they
had come to him from the printer, unstitched, uncut, and uncorrected.
Five copies (G–I, ?N, R) seem to have come into Samuel Palmer's hands
in this pristine state.[2] Copies K, L, P, U probably survived in the original
sheets until the last three or four quires were accidentally damaged, for in
each copy these last quires were supplied in facsimile. All these copies
(G, H, I, K, L, P, R, U) are uncorrected, and with them may be associated
copies A, M, N, and X which also lack changes by Blake. Copies A, G, H,
I, K, L, M, N, P, R, U, X were probably all in Blake's possession at his
death and are, therefore, in a sense, 'posthumous' copies.

Dates at which Poetical Sketches *left Blake's hands*

Date	Copies
1783–4	D, E, F, S
c. 1795	B
c. 1810	C
1783–1827	O, Q, V, W
Posthumous	A, G, H, I, K, L, M, N, P, R, T (1831), U, X

ERRATA:[3] (**1**) p. 4, l. 11, there is an extra 'in'; (**2**) p. 7, l. 6, 'cheeks' should
be singular; (**3**) p. 12, l. 16 'her' should be 'his'; (**4**) p. 14, ll. 6, 8 are not
indented like ll. 14, 16; (**5**) p. 15, l. 4, 'unfold' should be 'infold'; (**6**) p. 15,
l. 7, 'beds' should be 'birds'; (**7**) p. 18, l. 6, 'greeen'; (**8**) p. 18, l. 9, 'chrystal';
(**9**) p. 22, ll. 78, 80, 'doth' should be 'do'; (**10**) p. 24, 'Spencer' is mis-
spelt; (**11**) p. 24, l. 8, 'yields' should be 'yieldst'; (**12**) p. 24, l. 14, 'others'
should be singular; (**13**) p. 24, l. 15, 'cares' probably should be 'ears';
(**14**) p. 26, l. 1, 'Snow' should be lower case; (**15**) p. 27, ll. 30, 40, the closing
quotation marks are omitted; (**16**) p. 28, l. 64, there is an extra full stop;
(**17**) p. 28, l. 66, the semicolon should probably be a comma; (**18**) p. 29, the

[1] Blake evidently made corrections in some copies well before they were dis-
posed of, for copy T, which Linnell bought from his widow in 1831 (*Blake Records*,
596), has extensive corrections.

[2] According to a note in copy G by '*John Linnell jun.*', 'I found in Mr S. Palmer's
store room at Furze Hill House [*where Palmer lived from 1862 until his death in 1881*],
3 copies of this book *in sheets*, (one [*?copy U*] not quite perfect)— S. P. told me to
take one [*copy G*] for my self . . .'. A. H. Palmer sold 'two [*?more*] copies of Blake's
"Poetical Sketches" ' which he had found 'among my father's papers and books'
to the dealer Pearson (according to his note with copy N), perhaps copies H and R.
Palmer also probably gave copy I to Gilchrist.

[3] This Errata List omits defects of type such as p. 27, l. 49, p. 42, l. 182; the
defective 't', p. 31, l. 7; the defective 'g', p. 45, l. 253; the defective 't' in 'tir'd'.
The conventionality of the spelling, punctuation, and capitalization, compared
with Blake's usual later practice, suggests that someone corrected the printer's
copy fairly carefully.

Dramatis Personae omits the 'Minstrel' and 'Warriors'; (**19**) p. 29, in the scene heading '*Nobles before it*' should evidently omit the last two words; (**20**) p. 32, l. 20, 'phlosophic'; (**21**) p. 35, '*Cressey*' for '*Cressy*'; (**22**) p. 36, l. 10, 'ere' for 'e'er'; (**23**) p. 43, '*Exeunt*' should be '*Exit*'; (**24**) p. 44, l. 235, 'her' should be 'his'; (**25**) p. 46, l. 291, 'them' should be 'him'; (**26**) p. 50, the direction '—*to him*' is misplaced; (**27**) p. 56, l. 1, 'For' should be lower case; (**28**) p. 60, 'on' should be 'an'; (**29**) pp. 63–4, the first speech should have quotation marks all down the left margin, like the second speech; (**30**) p. 64, 'in the house when I grew up; he was my schoolfellow' should be repunctuated; (**31**) p. 65, 'ly'is misspelt; (**32**) p. 67, 'withs' for 'withes'; (**33**) p. 67, 'falshood'.

The French Revolution (1791)

(Text pp. 800–18)

COPY-TEXT: Copy A (Huntington).

COLLATION: 4°: [A1–2], B1–C[4]; B1–2, C1–2 signed; 10 leaves, 20 pages.

CONTENTS: Title-page ([A1]ʳ), 'Advertisement' ([A2]ʳ), 'Book the First' (B1ʳ–C4ᵛ); [A1]ᵛ, [A2]ᵛ blank. No fly-leaves or half-title.

LEAF-SIZE: 22·2 × 29·6 cm.

WATERMARK: None.

PAGE NUMBERING: Pages 2–16 are correctly numbered in the middle of the top margin within square brackets.

RUNNING TITLES: None.

CATCHWORDS: Correct throughout.

PRESS FIGURES: B1ᵛ '1'; C1ᵛ '2'.

ORNAMENTS: None.

PUBLICATION: Not published. There are a number of reasons[1] for believing that *The French Revolution* never got beyond the stage of proof: (1) Only one copy has been traced; (2) The register is defective, suggesting that the formes were never quite ready to be printed; (3) The impression of the type is extraordinarily heavy, occasionally nearly piercing the thin paper; (4) Thumb marks, presumably of the printer, may be seen on some pages; (5) The inking is uneven, and the ends of the lines are often somewhat blurred; (6) The last words, 'END OF THE FIRST BOOK', are not properly centred; (7) A number of simple misprints, such as 'Eeternally' (l. 46), 'were away' for 'wear away' (l. 76), the '8' upside-down on p. 8, have not been corrected; (8) None of the other 'seven books' promised on the title-page is known.

[1] These points are largely summarized from the notes of Horace Hart in *The Poetical Works of William Blake*, ed. J. Sampson (1925), xxxii, li.

Perhaps the book was suppressed by author or publisher because of fear of public prosecution or because events in France took a turn not envisaged in the poem.

CONTEMPORARY OWNER: John Linnell.

CORRECTIONS: None.

ERRATA:[1] (**1**) l. 40, 'spiders' should be 'spiders' ': (**2**) l. 46, 'Eeternally'; (**3**) l. 74, 'bonds' perhaps should be 'bands'; (**4**) l. 76, 'were away' should be 'wear away'; (**5**) l. 82, 'antientest' should be 'ancientest'; (**6**) l. 92 'is' should be 'are'; (**7**) ll. 114, 125, 'Neckar' should be 'Necker'; (**8**) l. 147, 'Is' should be 'Are'; (**9**) l. 159, 'When' should be lower case; (**10**) ll. 162–4, the punctuation seems wrong; (**11**) l. 176, the punctuation seems wrong; (**12**) l. 203, the comma and semicolon should be reversed; (**13**) l. 208, though 'vallies' is a Blakean spelling, yet 'valleys' is spelled conventionally in ll. 220, 224; (**14**) l. 208, 'is' should be 'are'; (**15**) l. 219, the full stop should be an exclamation mark or a question mark; (**16**) ll. 273–4 seem to be mispunctuated; (**17**) l. 283, 'war-living' should probably be 'war, living' or 'war—living'.

Excerpt from Malkin's *Memoirs* (1806)
(Text pp. 818–19)

TITLE: A / FATHER'S MEMOIRS / OF / HIS CHILD. / BY / *BENJ. HEATH MALKIN, ESQ.*/ M.A. F.A.S. / = / Great loss to all that ever him did see; / Great loss to all, but greatest loss to me. / ASTROPHEL. / = / LONDON: / PRINTED FOR LONGMAN, HURST, REES, AND ORME, / PATERNOSTER ROW; / *BY T. BENSLEY, BOLT COURT, FLEET STREET.* / 1806.

PUBLICATION: Bensley printed 1,000 copies of Malkin's *Memoirs* for the author in January 1806[2] with four plates probably engraved by R. H. Cromek (only the first is so signed), the frontispiece after Blake's design of Malkin's son, the other three after the son himself. Between 7 February 1806 and 1810, Malkin took 52 copies of the book himself;[3] in August 1811 450 copies were pulped;[4] and by June 1815 445 copies had been sold, leaving 53 on hand.[4] The book was scantly noticed in the public press,[5] and clearly it sold very slowly—about 45 copies a year for ten years.

CONTEXT: In the introductory letter to Thomas Johnes, M.P. (pp. xvii–xli), dated 4 January 1806, Malkin gives an account of Blake, including

[1] The regularity of the capitalization, of the spelling, and (on the whole) of the punctuation, suggests that these aspects of Blake's manuscript were considerably revised in the printing-house.

[2] Longman Impression Book No. 3, f. 14, with the firm of Longman Green & Co., London.

[3] Longman Commission and Divide Ledger, ff. 187, 302, Commission Ledger I, f. 30.

[4] Longman Commission Ledger I, f. 30.   [5] *Blake Records*, 181, 182.

the reprinting of some of his poems.[1] Blake's passage (on pp. 33–4) is introduced thus by Malkin:

> Yet, as my panegyric on such a subject [*his dead six-year-old son's drawings*] can carry with it no recommendation, I subjoin the testimony of Mr. Blake to this instance of peculiar ingenuity, who has given me his opinion of these various performances in the following terms.

'To the Queen' (April 1807) from Blair's *Grave* (1808)
[Text pp. 819–20]

PRINTED TITLE: THE / GRAVE, / A POEM. / BY / ROBERT BLAIR. / — / ILLUSTRATED BY / Twelve Etchings / EXECUTED FROM / ORIGINAL DESIGNS. / — / LONDON: / *PRINTED BY T. BENSLEY, BOLT COURT*, / FOR THE PROPRIETOR, R. H. CROMEK, Nº 64, NEWMAN STREET; / AND SOLD BY / CADELL AND DAVIES, J. JOHNSON, T. PAYNE, J. WHITE, LONGMAN, HURST, REES, AND / ORME, W. MILLER, J. MURRAY, AND CONSTABLE AND CO. EDINBURGH. / 1808.

ENGRAVED TITLE: THE / GRAVE, / A Poem. / Illustrated by twelve Etchings / Executed by / Louis Schiavonetti, / From the Original / Inventions / OF / WILLIAM BLAKE. / 1808.

COMPOSITION: The publication of Blake's designs for Blair's *Grave* was evidently first undertaken by R. H. Cromek in September 1805 (see Blake's letter of 27 November 1805, p. 1628), and the first proofs are dated February and June 1806. According to a letter from Cromek to James Montgomery, between the 17th and the 20th of April 1807,

> Blake's Drawings for 'The Grave . . . [*were*] presented to the Queen & Princess at Windsor— I received a Letter . . . stating Her Majesty's wish that Mʳ Blake would dedicate the Work to Her— This circumstance has so much pleased Blake that he has already produced a *Design* for the Dedication & a poetic Address to the queen marked with his usual Characteristics—Sublimity, Simplicity, Elegance and Pathos, his wildness *of course*.[2]

Cromek goes on to 'transcribe the Lines' in a form which differs from the published version only in accidentals and in the insertion above Blake's name of the words 'Your Majesty's devoted Subject and Servant'.[3]

---

[1] *Blake Records*, 421–31.

[2] Cromek's letter (written 17 April 1807, with the above postscript on the 20th) is in the Sheffield Public Library.

[3] A similar contemporary manuscript copy, called 'dedication to the Grave', is among the poetry collections of Nancy Flaxman (BM Add. MSS 39788, f. 89, not in Blake's hand). Except for accidentals, it differs from the printed version only in l. 7 inserted in pencil in the right margin, 'Region' for 'regions' in l. 15, and the termination of the quotation marks at the end of l. 18.

L. Binyon (*Catalogue of Drawings by British Artists . . . in the British Museum* [1898]),

Bibliographical Notes

PUBLICATION: Six hundred and eighty-eight copies of the quarto edition were published in August 1808 for 578 subscribers, ordinary copies at £2. 12s. 6d., proof copies at £5. 5s. A folio edition was published in the same year. The whole work was republished in 1813[1] and ?1874 without significant change in the text of Blake's poem.[2] 'To the Queen' did not accompany the reduced editions of the work published in 1847 and 1858 or the reissue of the plates with a poem by Jose Joaquin de Mora in 1826.

The only known published contemporary comment on the poem complained that

> The dedication of this edition of the Grave to the Queen, written by Mr. Blake, is one of the most abortive attempts to form a wreath of poetical flowers that we have ever seen. Should he again essay to climb the Parnassian heights, his friends would do well to restrain his wanderings by the strait waistcoat. Whatever licence we may allow him as a painter, to tolerate him as a poet would be insufferable.[3]

'Exhibition of Paintings in Fresco' (1809)

(Text pp. 820–3)

COPY-TEXT: Copy A (Huntington).

COLLATION: Folio: [A1–2], 1 sheet, 4 pages.

CONTENTS: 'Exhibition of Paintings in Fresco . . . Watts & Co. Printers, Southmolton St.' ([A1]^r), 'The Invention of a Portable Fresco' ([A1]^v); [A2]$^{r-v}$ blank. Copy B lacks [A2].

LEAF-SIZE: 18·0 × 23·8 cm.

WATERMARKS: N HENDON[?] / 1802 (copy A).

PAGE NUMBERING: None.

RUNNING TITLES: None.

i. 128) reports that the first six lines (' "The Door of Death . . . golden Keys," &c.') were 'just decipherable' in pencil on Blake's sketch for the dedication to *The Grave*, but seventy years later I can only make out the first two words. Blake's water-colour (23·6 × 30·0 cm) represents a body at the foot of the page, from which the soul, bearing two keys, floats up toward a golden double-door with two locks (see the reproduction in *Blake Records*, 184).

[1] The 1813 title-page is expanded with the information: TO WHICH IS ADDED / A LIFE OF THE AUTHOR. / = / LONDON: / *PRINTED BY T. BENSLEY, BOLT COURT,* / FOR THE PROPRIETOR, R. ACKERMANN, 101, STRAND; / AND SOLD BY / CADELL AND DAVIES, J. JOHNSON, T. PAYNE, J. WHITE, LONGMAN, HURST, REES, AND / ORME, W. MILLER, J. MURRAY, AND CONSTABLE AND CO. EDINBURGH. / 1813. This edition was imitated *c.* 1874.

[2] The poem appears on an unsigned leaf in all three contemporary editions.

[3] Anon., review of *The Grave* in *Antijacobin Review and Magazine*, xxxi (1808), 234; see *Blake Records*, 208.

CATCHWORDS: None.

PRESS FIGURES: None.

PUBLICATION: This flyer was apparently sent out by Blake in May 1809 (the date he added at the end) to his friends, for the only surviving copies were folded to make envelopes and sealed with wafers, and copy A was addressed to Ozias Humphry and sent with a letter by Blake.

CORRECTIONS: [A1]$^{r-v}$.

ERRATA: (1) ¶5 'discriptive'; (2) ¶10 'Gentleman' should be plural (3) ¶11 'exluded'; (4) ¶11 'Exbibition'.

'Blake's Chaucer: The Canterbury Pilgrims' (1809)
(Text pp. 823–4)

COPY-TEXT: Copy A (BMPR).

COLLATION: Broadsheet: [A1], 1 sheet.

CONTENTS: 'Blake's Chaucer: The Canterbury Pilgrims' ([A1]^r); [A1]^v blank.

LEAF-SIZE: 18·7 × 22·8 cm.

WATERMARK: 1807 (as in the *Descriptive Catalogue* [1809]).

PUBLICATION: Blake probably sent copies of this prospectus to his friends in May 1809, as he did those advertising his exhibition and *Descriptive Catalogue* (1809), but only one copy is known to have survived.

ERRATUM: 'dissemminated' (¶2).

'A Descriptive Catalogue' advertisement (1809)
(Text p. 825)

COPY-TEXT: Copy A (Glasgow University Library).[1]

COLLATION: Broadsheet, text [A1]^r, verso blank: 1 sheet, 2 pages.

CONTENTS: Text on [A1]^r.

LEAF-SIZE: 13·8 × 16·5 cm.

WATERMARK: None.

PUBLICATION: Blake probably sent copies of his advertisement for the *Descriptive Catalogue* (1809) to his friends, such as Thomas Butts, in the spring of 1809, as he had the flyer for the exhibition itself (pp. 820–3, 1692).

---

[1] The only known copy of this flyer is bound with *Descriptive Catalogue* (O) and reproduced by Keynes, *Blake Studies* (1949). The printers of 'A Descriptive Catalogue', '[*Ann*] Watts & [*Edward*] Bridgewater, [*31*] Southmolton-street', were at this address about 1807–10 (W. B. Todd, *A Directory of Printers . . . 1800–1840* [1972], 206), not far from Blake, who was at 17 South Molton Street about 1803–21.

Bibliographical Notes

A Descriptive Catalogue (1809)

(Text pp. 826–63)

COPY-TEXT: Copy D (Huntington).

COLLATION: 12mo in half-sheet imposition: [A]² (= G3–4) B–G⁶ (−G3–4), signed on the first three leaves of each quire (but G3 is unsigned); 36 leaves, 72 pages.

Note: In a 12mo in sixes, the first leaf of each gathering is conjugate with the sixth, the second with the fifth, and the third with the fourth, the third and fourth being cut free to insert between $1–2 and $5–6. In Signature G, the 'Index' was printed as G6, for it is conjugate with G1 in copy N.¹ However, the Index was, at least occasionally, a separate leaf, for the advertisement for 'A Descriptive Catalogue' (p. 825) offers '*an Index to the Catalogue gratis*' to those paying the price of admission but not buying a catalogue.

CONTENTS: Title-page ([A1]ʳ), 'Conditions of Sale' ([A1]ᵛ), 'Preface' ([A2]ʳ⁻ᵛ), 'Descriptive Catalogue, &c. &c.': 'Number I' (B1ʳ), 'Number II' (B1ᵛ–B4ʳ), 'Number III' (B4ʳ–D5ᵛ), 'Number IV' (D6ʳ–E1ᵛ), 'Number V' (E2ʳ–F2ʳ), 'Number VI' (F2ʳ), 'Number VII' (F2ᵛ), 'Number VIII' (F2ᵛ–F3ʳ), 'Number IX' (F3ᵛ–F6ʳ), 'Number X' (F6ʳ), 'Number X' (F6ʳ), 'Number[*s*] XI', 'XII', 'XIII' (F6ᵛ), 'Number XIV' (F6ᵛ–G1ʳ), 'Number XV' (G1ʳ–G2ᵛ, G5ʳ), 'Number XVI' (G5ʳ⁻ᵛ), 'Index' (G6ʳ⁻ᵛ); no blank pages.

LEAF-SIZE: about 11·5 × 19·0 cm uncut (copies C, E, G), probably Medium paper.

WATERMARK: '1807 AP' edgemark, visible only in $1, $3 (in about half the gatherings, as we would expect in a 12mo in half-sheet imposition).

PAGE NUMBERING: Pages correctly numbered: iv ([A2]ᵛ) at the top left corner of the page; 2–66 (B1ᵛ–G5ᵛ) at the top middle of the page.

RUNNING TITLE: None except for the correct second page of the 'INDEX'.

CATCHWORDS: None.

PRESS FIGURES: None.

PUBLICATION: Probably very few copies of the *Descriptive Catalogue* were printed, perhaps fifty or a hundred. Only sixteen have been traced, and there are records of a few more copies. They were issued in unlabelled greyish-Blue wrappers (still preserved with copies C, G, K) to the 'Fit audience . . . tho' few' who paid 2*s*. 6*d*. to see Blake's exhibition in 1809–10.

CORRECTIONS: By an oversight, the crucial fact that the exhibition could be seen 'At N 28 Corner of Broad Street Golden Square' was left off the

---

¹ I am deeply grateful to Mr. Paul Needham of the Pierpont Morgan Library for help with this description. Keynes (1921) gives '[A]⁴, B–F⁶, G⁴', with blanks at [A]¹ and G⁴ and the 'Index' after the 'Preface' rather than as the last leaf.

title-page. Blake corrected this error and another on p. 64 in Black ink, probably in most of the copies that were distributed at the exhibition (copies B¹–D, F–H, J, L, O). The copies without these corrections (A, E, I, K, M, N, P) probably were not disposed of until years later. Some confirmation of this conjecture may be seen in the facts that copy I was apparently not bound before 1818, copy P, also uncorrected, was evidently a gift to 'Frederick Tatham / from the Author, June 12, 1824', and copy K was sold to Linnell by Blake's widow in 1831.[2]

DISTRIBUTION DATES: This suggests that copies left Blake's hands:

In 1809–10:	B, C, D, F, G, H, J, L, O
After 1810:	A, E, M, N
After 1818:	I
In 1824:	P
In 1831:	K

ERRATA:[3] (1) Title-page, 'At N 28 Corner of Broad Street Golden Square' omitted; (2) ¶4, the question mark belongs at the end of the sentence, and the extra 'he' should be removed; (3) ¶5, sentences one and two evidently should be one sentence; (4) ¶5, in the last sentence 'We' should be lower case; (5) ¶7, sentences one and two should be one sentence; (6) ¶9, 'villany'; (7) ¶9 'falshood'; (8) ¶10, 'Hercules, Farnese' should have no comma; (9) ¶12, 'changing yellow' was perhaps meant to be 'changing to yellow'; (10) ¶14, there is an extra set of quotation marks in line 2 of the first quotation (this convention of extra quotation marks is used elsewhere in the volume only in ¶21); (11) ¶14, the semicolon after 'cavalcade' should evidently be a comma; (12) ¶21, the second set of quotation marks is redundant (see ¶14 above); (13) ¶24, the second full stop should evidently be a comma; (14) ¶26, the 'b' dropped out of 'but'; (15) ¶31, the first word, 'For', serves no purpose; (16) ¶34, the full stop after 'dispute' should evidently be a question mark; (17) ¶34, the closing double quotation mark is misprinted as an apostrophe and a single quotation mark; (18) ¶41, a Black quad shows in the left margin; (19) ¶48, the last sentence should evidently be two sentences, divided after 'temper'; (20) ¶50, 'Ruben's' should be 'Rubens' '; (21) ¶54, the closing quotation marks are omitted; (22) ¶57, 'The' in 'The Reeve' should not be capitalized; (23) ¶59, the last full stop should be a question mark; (24) ¶64, 65, 67, quotation marks are omitted at the beginnings and ends of the quotations; (25) ¶68, the hyphen in

---

[1] B lacks the title-page alteration.

[2] *Blake Records*, 596. Thomas Boddington, who bought *For the Sexes* (D) in 1833, may have acquired his copy of *Descriptive Catalogue* (E) at the same time.

[3] This Errata List omits minor eccentricities of punctuation and capitalization (which presumably reflect Blake's text), defects of type (e.g. ¶21, the initial quotation marks are defective; ¶34, the first *i* of 'sublimity' is broken; ¶59, the 'f' in the last 'of' is in the wrong fount), and the fact that pp. 44 and 47 have more lines than pp. 45–6. Keynes (ed., *The Complete Writings of William Blake* [1957], 913) says the book 'was on the whole carefully printed', but the above lapses on the part of compositor and proofreader might justify another conclusion.

'statues' at the end of page 36 appears to be broken; (**26**) ¶68, 'God's' should apparently be 'gods'; (**27**) ¶68, the last exclamation mark probably should be a question mark; (**28**) ¶72, '*sat*' should be '*set*'; (**29**) ¶73, 'histori ans'; (**30**) ¶74, 'thin g'; (**31**) ¶77, 'The antiquities . . . is' should be 'The antiquities . . . are'; (**32**) ¶77, the semicolon after 'Voltaire' should be a comma; (**33**) ¶77, 'opinions' should be 'opinion'; (**34**) ¶78, there should be a mark of punctuation after 'remains of antiquity'; (**35**) ¶78, 'Painting and Sculpture as it exists . . . is Inspiration . . . it is perfect' should be 'Painting and Sculpture as they exist . . . are Inspiration . . . they are perfect'; (**36**) ¶80, 'The face and limbs that deviates or alters . . . is' should be 'The face and limbs that deviate or alter . . . are'; (**37**) ¶85, there is a Black quad between 'among' and 'the'; (**38**) ¶87, there should be a question mark after 'go naked'; (**39**) ¶110, 'idea of want' should be 'want of idea'; (**40**) ¶110, after 'intentions' there should be a question mark, not a full stop; (**41**) ¶110, 'line' is spelt 'lne'.

'Blake's Chaucer: An Original Engraving' (1810)
(Text pp. 863–6)

COPY-TEXT: Copy C (Harvard).

COLLATION: 4°: [A1–2]; one sheet, four pages.

CONTENTS: 'Blake's Chaucer: An Original Engraving' ([A1]ʳ–[A2]ʳ); [A2]ᵛ blank.

SHEET-SIZE: 25·3 × 20·1 cm.

WATERMARK: H WILLMOTT / 1810 (B, C).

PAGE NUMBERING: Pages 2–3 are correctly numbered in round brackets in the middle of the top margin.

RUNNING TITLE: None.

CATCHWORDS: Correct, except for 'ing's' (p. 1), which corresponds, not to the top line of p. 2 ('Cook'), but to l. 6 of p. 2 ('[morn-]ing's draught').

ORNAMENTS: None.

PUBLICATION: Blake probably sent copies of this leaflet to his friends such as Thomas Butts in 1810,[1] as he had the flyers advertising his exhibition and *Descriptive Catalogue* (1809). Only three copies are known to have survived.

ERRATA: (**1**) ¶3 'Squires and' should be 'Squire's'; (**2**) ¶4 'Tapster' should be 'Tapiser'; (**3**) ¶7, 'ef'; (**4**) ¶8, 'horrizon'; (**5**) ¶9, 'end' should be 'and'; (**6**) ¶9, 'Leneaments'.

---

[1] The watermark of 1810 gives an initial terminus, and the publication of the engraving on 8 Oct. 1810 gives a probable final terminus.

'then she bore Pale desire' (?1783) and 'Woe cried the muse (?1783)

(Text pp. 869–74)

COLLECTION: The Berg Collection of the NEW YORK PUBLIC LIBRARY.

WATERMARK: Vertical chain lines 2·7 cm apart, as in *Poetical Sketches* (1783).

LEAF-SIZE: 12·0 × 19·0 cm.

DATE: *c.* 1783.

There is general agreement that the works were written in the 1770s or 1780s and that they are the earliest of Blake's manuscripts which have survived. The handwriting is early, the mythology unformed, the metrical style uncertain, the subject-matter conventionally sentimental (reminiscent of 'Fair Elenor' in *Poetical Sketches* [1783]). One indication of date may be the reference to the death of the Roman Empire, 'A sacrifice done by a Priestly hand' (p. 2), apparently echoing similar assertions in Gibbon's *Decline and Fall of the Roman Empire* (vols. i–iii, 1776, 1781). The 'Envy that Inspires my Song' (p. 3) may be associated with the envy expressed by Quid–Blake in the *Island in the Moon* (?1784)—'they envy me my abilities' (p. A—p. 899)— and with Flaxman's envious 'blasting my character as an Artist to Macklin my Employer' ('Public Address' in the *Notebook* p. 53— p. 1032) in 1782–3,[1] perhaps corresponding to the time in 'Woe cried the muse' when 'Grief perch't upon my brow'. The date 1783 for 'then she bore Pale desire' and 'Woe cried the muse' is, however, admittedly very tentative.

DESCRIPTION: The manuscript consists of four leaves mounted on larger leaves. The last leaf is pasted down so that the verso (p. 8) is invisible. There are horizontal creases in the pages. The first words on p. 1 suggest that a preceding section is missing.

Order: Though the four leaves are now detached and separate, it can be seen[2] that leaves 2 and 3 were originally conjugate, because the missing *e* of 'Shame in a mist' on 2ᵛ (p. 4) is to be found on 3ʳ (p. 5), and the *l* of 'Smoul-dring' on 2ᵛ is also visible on 3ʳ. This leaves no difficulty in establishing the order of leaves 1–3ʳ (pp. 1–5), for 'then she bore Pale desire', followed by 3ᵛ (p. 6) with 'Woe cried the muse'. Various symbols link the isolated fragments on 4ʳ (p. 7) to pp. 4, 5, 6. A flourish 4·5 cm from the bottom of 3ʳ (p. 5) separates 'then she bore Pale desire' from 'Woe cried the muse' on 3ᵛ (p. 6), while a stroke 2·4 cm from the bottom of p. 6 in turn separates 'Woe cried the muse' from the additions on p. 7. (For p. 7, see the footnotes to the text.)

[1] Blake's plates for Macklin are dated 10 and 21 Aug. 1782, 30 March and 1 Oct. 1783.

[2] D. V. Erdman, 'A Blake Manuscript in the Berg Collection: "then She bore Pale desire" and "Woe cried the Muse" ', *Bulletin of the New York Public Library*, lxii (1958), 191–201.

Writing and Ink: The pages are written to the very margin in Blake's usual hand. The ink is Brown up to p. 3; after 'Solid Ground' on that page the ink becomes Grey; at the top of p. 5, beginning with the word 'Hate', the same Brown ink as on the first three pages recurs. All of p. 6 ('Woe cried the muse') is written in Black ink with a sharp pen. On p. 7, the first insertion ('She brings humility . . . to know—&ᶜ &ᶜ') is in dark Brown ink; the second ('Conceit . . . around the World') is in pencil; the third ('then Shame bore . . . with Pride', the first word converted in ink to 'And') in pencil; and the fourth ('Swift as the . . . Infant Bud' for p. 6) in the same Black ink and sharp pen as p. 6. A correction on p. 1 ('observ[d and *del*]ing inly') and an insertion on p. 4 ('in the darkning Storm') are in Black ink. On p. 6 'Shadowy' and on p. 7 'humility, her Daughter' are deleted in pencil, and the 'awful' replacing 'Shadowy' is written in pencil. For other pencil insertions see p. 872, n. 8.

Lineation: The actual lineation of Blake's prose text may be seen in Erdman's transcript.[1] W. M. Rossetti, the first editor of the work,[2] persuaded himself that the metrical prose was intended as verse, and he put slash marks on to Blake's manuscript (together with two notes on the last page) to direct his printer how to set up the text as iambic pentameter. The text here of course ignores these tamperings.

An Island in the Moon (?1784)

(Text pp. 875–900)

COLLECTION: FITZWILLIAM MUSEUM.

WATERMARKS: A design 7·1 × 11·3 cm on pp. 3–16, O–P represents a fleur-de-lis above a rectangular shield in a triple border, divided into four compartments. In the bottom left compartment are sheep, and in the bottom right one a harp.

The *countermark* (2·8 × 3·9 cm) on pp. 1–2, A–N consists of 'G R' under a small crown.[3]

See diagram on page 1698.

SIZE: 18·3 × 30·8 cm.

DATE: ?Autumn 1784. The date of the *Island in the Moon* is a vexed and difficult question. A number of internal references point to the autumn of 1784.

'Holy Thursday' was first celebrated in St. Paul's Cathedral (as it is in

---

[1] See note 2, p. 1696.

[2] ' "The Passions": An Unpublished Poem by William Blake', ed. W. M. Rossetti, *Monthly Magazine*, xii (1903), 123–9.

[3] The marks are similar to but distinct from figures 19 and 25 in Thomas Balston, *James Whatman, Father and Son* (1957). Miss Phyllis M. Giles, Librarian of the Fitzwilliam Museum, has provided me with a great deal of information about the watermarks in the *Island*.

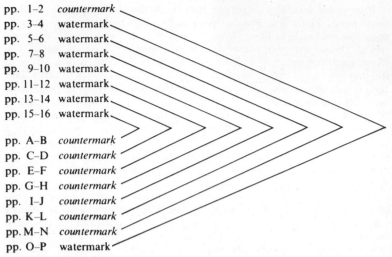

pp. 1–2   *countermark*
pp. 3–4   watermark
pp. 5–6   watermark
pp. 7–8   watermark
pp. 9–10   watermark
pp. 11–12   watermark
pp. 13–14   watermark
pp. 15–16   watermark

pp. A–B   *countermark*
pp. C–D   *countermark*
pp. E–F   *countermark*
pp. G–H   *countermark*
pp. I–J   *countermark*
pp. K–L   *countermark*
pp. M–N   *countermark*
pp. O–P   watermark

the poem in Chap. 11) on Ascension Day, 2 May 1782,[1] and the poem must therefore have been composed after 2 May 1782. The impulse to 'Hang Italian songs' in favour of 'English Genius forever' and the references to the commercial success of 'Doctor Clash And Signior Falalasole' (Chaps. 9, 11) may have arisen from the Handel Festival of May 1784.[2] The allusion to a new method of printing (p. A) may be connected with George Cumberland's experiments on the subject between January and October 1784.[3] Jacko in Chap. 8 may have been inspired by the monkey of that name which was brought to Astley's circus in 1784.[2] The reference to 'Vauxhall & Ranelagh' (¶27) suggests the warm months when those gardens were open; the fact that Suction plans to 'knock them all up' in the May Royal Academy exhibition 'next year' implies that the setting, and perhaps the time of writing, are between June and December;[4] and the 'swallows . . . on their passage' (¶3) seem to point to autumn.

The most precise contemporary references come from the fashionable Miss Gittipin's envy of 'Miss Filligreework . . . & her maids & Stormonts & Balloon hats & a pair of Gloves every day & the sorrows of Werter & Robinsons & the Queen of Frances Puss[5] colour' (Chap. 8).[6] These fashions

[1] *European Magazine*, i (June 1782), 388: 'This day one of the noblest spectacles in the world was exhibited in St. Paul's cathedral. Upwards of 6000 charity children were arranged under the dome . . .'.

[2] See D. V. Erdman, *Blake: Prophet Against Empire* (1969).

[3] See his articles in *New Review*, vi (Oct. 1784), 318–19 and *European Magazine*, vi (Nov. 1784), 345.

[4] Blake himself exhibited at the Royal Academy in 1780, 1784, 1785, and 1799.

[5] The first use of the word 'puce' recorded in the *Oxford English Dictionary* is in 1787.

[6] As Palmer Brown has shown in unpublished studies made about 1951.

were of a butterfly longevity, as Miss Gittipin clearly knew, and as Blake may have learned from his engraving work.[1] 'Robinsons' may have been Robinson Gowns (*Lady's Magazine*, xiv [April 1783], 187) or Robinson Chapeaux and Hats (*Lady's Magazine*, xiv [May, Dec. 1783], 268, 650; xv [March, June 1784], 154, 303), but they are unlikely to have long survived the fall from fashion on 13 January 1785 (*Gazetteer*) of Perdita Robinson, who inspired them.

The first manned balloon ascents created a brief rage for balloon fashions. The first '*chapeaux au ballon*' appeared in Paris, and a contributor to the *European Magazine*, iv (Dec. 1783), 406, hoped 'that this whimsical mode will not be introduced among the people of England', but in fact, according to the *Lady's Magazine*, xiv (Dec. 1783), 650, 'The *Balloon* hat' had already appeared in London. A correspondent of the *Gazetteer* of 19 February 1784 hoped that 'balloon fashions are about their zenith, and must soon burst and be forgotten!', but the mode persisted at least through the spring of 1784. However, by 18 September 1784, according to the *Morning Herald*, 'Balloon' was losing its influence as a name in the fashionable world, and the same styles were thenceforth to be denominated 'Lunardis' (after the balloonist who electrified London by his ascent on 15 September). By next summer, all these fashions had dispersed, according to the *Gazetteer* of 26 July 1785: 'The balloon hat has had its day;—the Werter, Lunardi [*also*] . . .'.

The ephemeral nature of these fashions means that Miss Gittipin's allusions and Blake's satire would have been virtually meaningless after 1785. The period when these fashionable Robinsons, Werters, and Balloon Hats were flourishing, in 1784, is almost certainly the period as well when Blake was writing his *Island in the Moon*.

DESCRIPTION: The manuscript consists of sixteen unnumbered leaves, thirty-two pages. Apparent gaps in the text and in the watermark–countermark pattern suggest that two or more leaves are missing between the eighth and ninth leaves. I have therefore numbered the pages 1–16 and A–P. The text of the *Island* is on pp. 1–16, A; pp. B–O are blank; while p. P (the verso of the sixteenth leaf) is a jumble of sketches, including six horses' heads, a lion lying down with a lamb (drawn twice), the head of a man, in the middle 'Numeration', and scattered round it six 'n's, an 'm', 'nu', 'B', 't' twice, 'Bla' written backwards, and 'William Blake' three times. Before these sixteen leaves are three others (one with proofs from Blake's woodcuts for Thornton's Virgil [1821] and one with A. H. Palmer's statement of the provenance of the proofs), and at the end are two more, all the extra leaves watermarked 'VAN GEL[DER?]'.

Page 16 ends with a song by Sipsop as the last of a series of burlesques of Italian opera. Page A begins abruptly with 'thus Illuminating the Manuscript' and ends abruptly half-way down the page. There is no context for p. A, and the immediately preceding pages may have been removed

---

[1] For example, his plate for the *Lady's Pocket Book* of Nov. 1782 shows '*A Lady in the full Dress, & another in the most fashionable Undress now worn*'.

because they reveal too directly or too inaccurately Blake's secret method of Illuminated Printing. If the manuscript was originally a bound gathering of leaves issued as a notebook, it may have consisted of eight or ten sheets, or a multiple thereof. Pages O–P are sewn in separately and may once have been in a different position, though their watermark corresponds neatly to the countermark on pp. 1–2. There are the same number of leaves with watermarks (pp. 3–16, O–P) and with countermarks (pp. 1–2, A–N), so that no conclusion can be drawn from an imbalance there. If anything was removed, it probably consisted of at least one sheet, two leaves bearing watermark and countermark. Thus it seems likely that at least four pages are missing between p. 16 and p. A of the *Island in the Moon*.

Inks: There are three shades of ink used in the manuscript, suggesting seven periods of work on it: (1) *Brown*, p. 1 to p. 8 middle; (2) *Grey*, p. 8 (from 'are always talking . . .' [¶27]) to p. 9, ¶30; (3) *Brown*, p. 10 ('Chap 9' [¶31]) to p. 12 ('. . . its a shame' [¶41]); (4) *Grey*, p. 12 (including the deletion of the last two-and-a-half Brown lines) to p. 14 (the first line after 'Holy Thursday', '. . . & Mrs Sistagatist' [¶51]); (5) *Brown*, p. 14 (including the deletion and replacement of the last three words) to p. 16 ('in such a serious humour' [¶55]); (6) *Black*, the rest of p. 16; (7) *Brown*, p. A. *Deletions and Corrections* are in the same ink as the original except for the following changes in *Grey* ink: p. 3, ¶6 '[Ass *del*] Arse' is deleted and 'Ass' restored; pp. 5, ¶15, 8, ¶25, the deletions ('what is this gim' and 'O what a scene . . . disguise'); p. 15, ¶53, 'turd' deleted and 'tansy' substituted.

Title: The conventional title, *An Island in the Moon*, is an adaptation of the first words of the work.

All Blake's lines begin at the left margin, and it is therefore sometimes difficult to know where he intended a new paragraph to begin.

List of Speakers

Aradobo the dean of Morocco
Etruscan Column the Antiquarian
Gibble Gabble, the wife of Inflammable Gass, and cousin of Miss Gittipin
Mrs. Gimblett
Miss Gittipin, cousin of Gibble Gabble
Inflammable Gass the Windfinder, husband of Gibble Gabble
Mrs. Nannicantipot
Obtuse Angle the Mathematician
Quid the Cynic, a painter, one of the Island's Three Philosophers
Little Scopprell
Mrs. Sinagain (perhaps the same as Mrs. Sistagatist)
Sipsop the Pythagorean, evidently an apprentice surgeon, one of the Island's Three Philosophers
Mrs. Sistagatist (perhaps the same as Mrs. Sinagain)
Steelyard the Lawgiver
Suction the Epicurean, one of the Island's Three Philosophers
Tilly Lally the Siptippidist.

'Songs by Shepherds' (?1787)

(Text pp. 900–1)

COLLECTION: The original MS is not known. A contemporary transcript is on two fly-leaves of *Poetical Sketches* (F) in the Alexander Turnbull Library, Wellington, New Zealand (reproduced in D. F. McKenzie, 'Blake's *Poetical Sketches* [1783]', *Turnbull Library Record*, i, no. 3 [March 1968], at pp. 8–9).

WATERMARK: Chain lines 2·8 cm apart, like those in *Poetical Sketches*, but the paper is slightly heavier and darker.

LEAF-SIZE: 13 × 20·5 cm, as in *Poetical Sketches* (F).

DATE OF COMPOSITION: c. 1787.

One of the manuscript poems was etched in a modified form for *Songs of Innocence* (1789), which were evidently composed 1784–9. 1787 is little more than a guess within this period.

DATE OF TRANSCRIPTION: *c.* 1787.

The printed leaves of *Poetical Sketches* (F), stabbed in incorrect order through three holes, were a 'present from Mrs Flaxman May 15, 1784' (according to an inscription on the title-page), perhaps to the Flaxmans' friend Isaac Reed. Later, the mistaken order of the sheets was pointed out in an unknown hand[1] which also transcribed Blake's poems on two un-stabbed leaves. It seems likely, therefore, that the poems were transcribed before the sheets were put into their present binding. Since a contemporary hand has written 'Reeds Sale 1807' at the top of f. 2^r (bearing a Blake poem), it seems clear that this binding took place before 1807. The poems must, then, have been transcribed and bound between 1784 and 1807; once again, 1787 is little more than a guess.

DESCRIPTION: Two fly-leaves have been added at the beginning and two more at the end of *Poetical Sketches* (F). The 'Songs by Mr Blake' are on the verso of the first leaf (which is pasted to the marbled endpaper) and on recto and verso of the second leaf. There are four distinct hands affecting Blake's text in the volume: (1) Blake's neat ink corrections to the printed text; (2) Other corrections in a different hand and ink; (3) The pencil corrections to the text; and (4) The manuscript poems. The last three hands have not been identified.

Tiriel (?1789)

(Text pp. 902–20)

COLLECTION: BRITISH MUSEUM Department of Manuscripts.[2]

WATERMARK: Britannia type, with the countermark 'G R'.[2]

---

[1] Comparison with MSS of Isaac Reed dated 1762, 1773, 1776, 1781, 1790, 1800 (in the Folger Shakespeare Library) makes it clear that the hand is not that of Reed. Nor is it that of Blake or John Flaxman. I do not agree with McKenzie (see above) that the poems are in the hand of the presentation inscription.

[2] The manuscript, watermark, and traceable designs are reproduced in the 1967 edition of *Tiriel*, from which some descriptions are repeated here.

Bibliographical Notes

SIZE OF TEXT-LEAVES: 15·7 × 21·0 cm.

SIZE OF DRAWINGS: *c.* 18·0 × 27·0 cm.

DATE: ?1789.

Some indications of an early date, preceding Blake's confident adoption of his technique of Illuminated Printing about 1789, are as follows: (1) The characters of the handwriting and the drawing are early; (2) The poem is incomplete, with some lines left unfinished; (3) The characters and events of the poem were scarcely used in Blake's later myth; (4) The work was never etched for publication; (5) The designs are physically separate from the text and quite different in shape and character from the illuminations for his etched works; (6) ll. 360, 370 are repeated in *Thel* (1789) and the *Marriage* (?1790–3). The time of composition might, however, range from 1785 to 1793.

DESCRIPTION: The manuscript consists of eight leaves enclosed within light bluish-Grey wrappers inscribed, perhaps by Blake: 'Tiriel / MS by Mʳ Blake'. The rectos are correctly foliated in pencil 2–9 at the top right corners of pp. 1, 3, 5, 7, 9, 11, 13, 15, and there are section numbers (1–8) on pp. 1, 3, 5, 7, 10, 11, 13, 14. Most pages on which a section ends (pp. 2, 6, 9, 12, 13, 15) are only partly filled with writing.

Ink and Writing: The same greyish-Black ink is used throughout the poem, with very minor changes. The hand is clear but not copperplate, and there are numerous changes in the text, including some thirty-nine deleted lines, but there are few enough minor alterations to make one wonder whether this was intended as a fair copy.

DRAWINGS: Twelve separate finished drawings for *Tiriel* are known,[1] but only nine of them have been traced,[2] as follows:

Drawing	Collection	Lines illustrated	Subject
1	Mr. *Paul Mellon*	19–20	Tiriel Supporting Myratana[3]
2	FITZWILLIAM	59–60?	Har and Heva Bathing
3	*UNTRACED*[4]	75–84?	Har Addressing Mnetha
4	BMPR	84–6	Har Blessing Tiriel
5	*UNTRACED*[4]	123?	Har and Heva Playing Harps
6	*Robert N. Essick*	149–52	Tiriel Leaving Har and Heva
7	VICTORIA & ALBERT	215–33	Tiriel Carried by Ijim
8	Sir *Geoffrey Keynes*	257–61	Tiriel Denouncing his Four Sons and Five Daughters

[1] Southgate & Barrett sale, 8 June 1854, lot 643, 'Twelve elaborate Subjects'; Sotheby sale, 1 May 1863, lots 377–88; A. Gilchrist, *Life of William Blake* (1863), ii. 253, (1880), ii. 273—1863 somewhat different from 1880 in details.

[2] See note 2, p. 1701.

[3] A sheet bearing pencil sketches for this design in the Tate Gallery is reproduced in M. Butlin, *William Blake* (1971), 29.

[4] Nos. 3, 5, and 9 are last known from the references by W. M. Rossetti in Gilchrist.

Drawing	Collection	Lines illustrated	Subject
9	*UNTRACED*[1]	271–7	Tiriel's Sons Awed by their Father's Curse
10	*Mrs. Louise Y. Kain*	321–7	Har Walking with Hela
11	Sir *Geoffrey Keynes*	347–8	Har and Heva Asleep
12	*T. E. Hanley*	393	Tiriel Dead before Hela

There can be no doubt that the twelve designs form a sequence, for the characterization is quite consistent.[2] In Drawings 1, 4, 6–8, 10 12, Tiriel is shown as a 'blind' old man, 'bald' except for a fringe of white hair at the ear-line (ll. 28, 29), with a White beard, and a long-sleeved, unbelted, loose-fitting gown that reaches to his ankles. Har in Drawings 2, 4, 6, 11 is an old man of about the same apparent age as Tiriel, with a smooth, trouble-free face, and 'very long' silvery hair and beard (l. 114). In Drawings 1, 7–8, one of the sons addressed by Tiriel, evidently Heuxos, has a fair curling beard and wears a knee-length dark gown, a pale mantle, and a strange, spiked crown. In Drawings 7–8, 10–12, Hela has 'dark hair' (l. 321) and a clinging, belted gown which leaves her knee and right breast bare. Since this characterization is consistent in all nine drawings which have been traced, we may be confident that the designs belong together.

Further, it is clear that Drawings 1, 4, 6–8, 10, 12 are closely related to the text of *Tiriel*, sometimes illustrating it quite literally. A few designs are difficult to relate to Blake's poem, but since the characters in them are demonstrably the same as those in the closely related drawings, we must conclude that Blake meant them all to illuminate *Tiriel*.[3]

CATCHWORDS: None.

[1] See note 4, p. 1702.

[2] There are as well some remarkable inconsistencies. Tiriel's hair and beard are described as 'grey' in the text (ll. 14, 196) but are conspicuously White in the designs. Har says Tiriel's beard is 'shriveld' (l. 88), but the designs show it full and cut straight across the bottom. There are frequent references in the text to the countless wrinkles of Tiriel's face (ll. 14, 88, 93, 115, 135, 315, 334), but such wrinkles are not conspicuous in the designs. Har says Tiriel has 'no teeth' (l. 89), but the designs do not show him with the fallen cheeks of toothless age. Tiriel is not 'outstretchd at Har & Hevas feet' (l. 393) in Drawing 12 but at Hela's feet.

More puzzling is the inconsistent representation of Heva and Mnetha, who are 'aged' women in the text (ll. 58, 63) and in Drawings 4–6 but are beautiful young women with clear foreheads, smooth necks, and firm breasts in Nos. 2 and 11.

[3] In the British Museum Print Room are two drawings of about the time of *Tiriel* which have sometimes been associated with the poem. One represents a Black-bearded man embracing a dark-haired woman (in a position like that in *Tiriel* Drawing 2, reversed), as they kneel on a rug and bolster before a figured curtain. The second represents the same couple kneeling as they warm their hands before a fire in the forest. In details of appearance and situation, they bear no other close resemblance to the characters or actions of *Tiriel*.

Bibliographical Notes

ORDER: Pp. 1–15.

The order of the pages is given clearly by Blake's ink section numbers and by the narrative continuity of the poem. The order and position of the Drawings is much more problematical.

ERRATA: 'was' for 'were' (l. 154); 'the[*e*]' (ll. 170, 297, 310); '&' for 'as' (l. 239); 'here' for 'hear' (l. 255).

Notebook (?1793–?1818)

(Text pp. 921–1069)

COLLECTION: BRITISH MUSEUM Department of Manuscripts.

WATERMARKS: Pages 1–116 have chain lines 2·65 cm apart, plus a circular watermark with a radius of about 1·5 cm perhaps representing a fleur-de-lis. The top, partly triangular, section of the watermark is visible on twenty-eight leaves, while the bottom, more curvilinear part, is on thirty leaves. Arranging the pages as they were when Blake wrote on them[1] the pattern of gatherings seems to be as follows ('Top' and 'Bottom' referring to the portion of the watermark visible):

Gatherings:	2 leaves	6 leaves	12 leaves	12 leaves	12 leaves	12 leaves	4 leaves
Top: pp.	9–10	1–4, 15–16	25–36	49–60	73–84	97–108	*8 pages missing*
Bottom: pp.	5–6	13–14, 11–12, 7–8	17–24 *4 pages missing*	37–48	61–72	85–96	109–16

The eight pages missing at the end could not well have been after p. 116 when Blake was using the book, for p. 116 is dirty from use as an outside cover; nor could they have been between p. 108 and p. 109, for these pages are linked by transferred blobs of Blake's ink. It seems likely, therefore, that the eight pages missing at the end were removed before William Blake began using the *Notebook*. By analogy, it seems likely that the four pages missing from pp. 17–24 and the unknown number probably missing from pp. 1–16 were also removed before the poet used the book.

Pages 117–20 have neither chain lines nor watermark.

The fragment of a leaf pasted on p. 8 has part of a circular watermark very much larger than that on pp. 1–116.

---

[1] See the ORDER below. The side facing the mould when the paper was made is indented with the lines of the mould, and the verso facing the felt is smooth. When a sheet or group of sheets is folded once, all the mould-sides will uniformly face either towards or away from the fold, thus: pp. 1–2 (mould–felt) FOLD pp. 3–4 (felt–mould). In every leaf of the *Notebook*, the felt- and mould-marks confirm the watermark pattern above and indicate that (whatever the sequence of leaves) the present rectos were all rectos when Blake first used the *Notebook*. (This line of argument was privately conveyed by Mr. Howard Nixon to Mr. Erdman and thence to me.)

LEAF-SIZE: 15·7 × 19·5 cm, irregular. A fragment 7·4 × 11·3 cm was cut from the top outer corner of pp. 71–2, probably by 1847.[1]

DATES:

(1) *By 1787*: Sketches *by Robert Blake* (d. 1787) on pp. 5, 7–9, 11, 13.

(2) *About 1793*: Poems (pp. 4, ?78, 98–101, 103, 105–9, 111, 113–15, including *Songs of Experience* [1794] on pp. 101, 103, 105–9, 111, 113–15); prose (pp. 10 [June 1793], ?92, 116); vignettes (pp. 2, 8, 15–37, 39–61, 63, 65, 67–75, 77–9, 81, 83–9, 91–102, 106–8, 110–12, including *For Children* [1793] on pp. 15, 17, 19, 34, 40, 45, 52, ?58, 59, 61, 63, 68–9, 71, 75, 91, 93–5, ?98, *Marriage* [?1790–3] on pp. 44, 48, 'Job' [1793] on p. 20, *Visions* [1793] on pp. 28, 30, 32, ?50, 74, 78, 81, 92, *America* [1793] on pp. ?29, ?49, ?75, ?77, *Songs of Experience* [1794], on pp. 43, 54, 57, 65, 74, *Europe* [1794] on pp. 8, 25, 74–5, ?77, 96, ?97, ?98, *Urizen* [1794] on pp. ?15, 74, *Song of Los* [1795] on pp. ?13, ?60, 'Elohim Creating Adam' [?1795] on p. 54, 'Satan Exulting over Eve' [?1795] on p. 112).

(3) *1801–3*: Poems (pp. 2–3, ?5, 6–7, 12, 14, 46 [for *Jerusalem* (1804–?20)], 56, 93) and sketches (pp. 2–4, 6, 12, 16, 19, 21, 38, 40, 47, 54, 66–7, 69–70, 73–6, 80–2, 90, 92, including Hayley's *Designs for A Series of Ballads* [1802], on pp. 6, 73, 92, portrait-like sketches on pp. 2–4, 12, 19, 21, 40, 47, 54, 66–7, 69–70, 74, 82, *Vala* [?1796–?1807] on p. ?90, *Jerusalem* [1804–?20] on pp. 16, 76, 80).

(4) *1807*: Prose (pp. 10 [20 Jan.], 64, 88–9 [Aug.]); poems (pp. 54, 96–7); and a sketch for *Paradise Lost* (?1807) (p. 104).

(5) *1809*: Poem (p. 40).

(6) *1810*: 'Vision of the Last Judgment' ('For the Year 1810') (pp. 68–72, 76–87, 90–5 (see pp. 1009–28); miscellaneous prose (pp. 67 [23 May], 72); and a poem (p. 87).

(7) *1810–11*: 'Public Address' (pp. 1, 17–21, 23–5, 38–9, 44, 46–7, 51–3, 55–67, 71, 76, 78, 86; see pp. 1029–53); poems associated with the 'Public Address' (pp. 21, 23–43, 47, ?50, 52, 60–3, 65, 70, 73, 79, 89); a translation (p. 64); a transcript (p. 59 [4 Aug. 1811]); and 'Blake's Chaucer' (pp. 117–19).

(8) *1812*: Poems (pp. 6, 22).

(9) *?1818*: 'The Everlasting Gospel' (pp. 21, 33, 48–54, 98, 100–1, 120; see pp. 1054–69).

DESCRIPTION:

Title: The volume now generally known as the *Notebook* was for many

[1] The date is established by the fact that the words cut out are missing from the early transcripts by D. G. Rossetti, one in manuscript made shortly after he acquired the book in 1847 on paper watermarked 1844 and bound with the *Notebook*, another printed in Gilchrist (1863), ii. 161 ff.
On 27 November 1864 W. M. Rossetti wrote to Horace Scudder: 'if I can find a convenient little bit to snip out [*of the NOTEBOOK*], I shall have great pleasure in sending it to you, just as a specimen of writing' (MS in Harvard). S. F. Damon (*A Blake Dictionary* [1965], 437) supposes that the bit snipped off may have been from pp. 71–2 of the *Notebook*, but the chronology above invalidates the suggestion.

years called 'The Rossetti Manuscript', from its best-known owner, D. G. Rossetti, who owned it between 1847 and 1882.

CONTENTS: The *Notebook* is made up of fifty-eight leaves[1] (pp. 1–116) with the same watermark, plus two leaves (one sheet, pp. 117–120) consisting of the inner margin of pp. 45–6 of William Hayley's *Designs to A Series of Ballads* (9 September 1802).[2] These sixty leaves are mounted on stubs, interleaved, and bound with thirty-three leaves of Dante Gabriel Rossetti's transcript of the *Notebook* in half morocco over marbled boards, with an older leather spine lettered 'BLAKE / M.S.' When the leaves were disbound, they were not trimmed, for the writing goes quite to the three outer margins, and sewing holes are still visible in the inner margin, sometimes overlapping with the designs and some writing (e.g. p. 10).

Pages 1 and 116 are very dirty, suggesting that the leaves may once have been without a cover and that pp. 117–120 (which are separately hinged and much cleaner) were not added to the others until they were bound. The writing throughout the *Notebook*, especially that in pencil, appears to have faded noticeably since the facsimile of 1935 was made. The outer margins of all the leaves are dirty, and a few chips have broken off the outer edges.

On p. 8 has been pasted a roughly L-shaped fragment (9·6 × 7·3 cm at the largest dimensions) with a sketch for *Europe* (1794) pl. 5, and, on the verso, lines for a much larger sketch.

The *Notebook* was paginated 1–120 in the upper outer corners in the present order by W. A. White,[3] who owned it from 1887 to 1927.

ORDER: In the original order of the *Notebook*, the designs apparently by Robert Blake (pp. 5, 7–9, 11, 13) were evidently at the front, in the following order: pp. 5–6?, 9–10,[4] 13–14,[4] 11–12?, 7–8,[5] 1–2,[5] 3–4,[6] 15–20,[6] 21–116.[7]

---

[1] For evidence that there may have been at least twelve pages more at one time, see the *Watermark* description above.

[2] The paper can be identified from the fragments of printing on pp. 118 and 120. Blake designed, engraved, and printed the plates for the book, and was given the printed sheets to sell for his own benefit. In later years he used the unsold sheets for scrap paper, for example in 'The Ballads MS', pp. 1302–18, 1733

[3] *The Poetical Works of William Blake*, ed. J. Sampson (1905), 138.

[4] A stain in the top margin 4·2 cm from the outside appears on pp. 10 and 13, indicating that pp. 9–10, 13–14 were sequential.

[5] A chip is missing in the top inner margin on pp. 7–8, 1–2, indicating that these pages were once sequential.

[6] A large ink or *aqua fortis* blob at the top outer corner appears in steadily diminishing size on pp. 1–2, 3–4, 15–16, 17–18, 19–20, indicating clearly that these pages were once sequential: 1–4, 15–20. Further, there is a clear offset of writing from p. 4 to p. 15, and a probable offset from p. 2 to p. 3. In addition, transferred blobs of ink indicate the relationship of pp. 14–11 24–25, 48–49, 54–55, 59–61, 78–89, 80–81, 90–91, 96–97, 98–99, 106–107, 108–109, 110–111, 112–113.

[7] Erdman (pp. 768, 774–5, 781) suggests this order; some of the evidence given here was pointed out privately by Erdman. I have not observed evidence which demonstrates the position of pp. 6–9, and 12–17 in this sequence. Page 116 is smudged, as if it had been the outside page for some time.

Bibliographical Notes

Later, perhaps when pp. 117–20 were added to the others, the leaves were rearranged and rebound in their present order: pp. 1–120. The alteration is now of considerable venerability, for p. 1 is much dirtier than the other pages, the tiger on p. 6 has offset on p. 7, the design on p. 9 has offset on p. 8, and some words on p. 10 have offset on p. 11. The pages were presumably in this new order in 1847 when D. G. Rossetti bought the *Notebook* and inscribed the fly-leaf. The pages of the *Notebook* are here numbered in the order of the present binding.

COMPOSITION: The first user of the book was evidently Robert Blake, who started making designs at the front. After his death in 1787, William Blake made sketches in it from front to back in about 1792 and 1793. Then he turned the book round and wrote lyrics in it, starting at the back, in approximately 1793 and 1794. Some years later he picked it up again, and began making memoranda and drafting poems and prose starting at the front, in about the years 1801–3, 1807, 1809–11, and 1818.

ORDER OF PRINTING: The Order of Printing in the present work is from front to back (pp. 1–120), with two kinds of exceptions: (1) long poems written back to front (as it were) on two pages are printed of course with the second page first (pp. 3–2, 99–98, 109–108); and (2) three long works, the 'Vision of the Last Judgment', the 'Public Address', and 'The Everlasting Gospel', which are scattered through the *Notebook* (pp. 1, 17–21, 23–5, 33, 38–9, 44, 46–72, 76–87, 90–5, 98, 100–1, 120), are printed separately in the present edition, after the main text of the *Notebook* (see pp. 1007–28, 1029–53, 1057–69). With these exceptions, the text of the *Notebook* is printed from start to finish in the order in which it appears in the manuscript (pp. 1–116).

When the MS is complicated, a note attempts to explain the physical appearance of the page. The Order of Composition given in the notes is often quite tentative. The approximate chronological order of the contents can be reconstructed from the table of dates above.

The text is in ink and the designs in pencil unless otherwise specified. The designs are separately described below.

VARIANTS: The text of the *Notebook* printed here has been compared carefully with that of Erdman (1967), and those alternative readings which seem possible to me are reported in footnotes.

NOTEBOOK Designs

* Means there is no writing on the page except inscriptions for the designs (pp. 8–9, 11, 13, 15–16, 45, 102, 104, 110, 112).

Undecipherable designs are on pp. 15 (bottom), 16 (bottom), 25 (bottom), 32 (bottom), 50 (top), 53, 59 (bottom), 64 (erased), 66 (middle), 79 (numbered '[8 *del*] 12'), 89 (numbered '21[?]'), 99 (erased), 107 (in the centre, small), 114 (sideways).

No designs appear on pp. 1, 10, 14, 62, 74–5, 103, 105, 109, 113, 115–20.

Bibliographical Notes

All sketches, numbers, and inscriptions are *in pencil* unless otherwise specified.

p. 2   A woman is apparently turning into a tree; a more finished version is on p. 36, and a third version is in the British Museum. *Upside-down* at the bottom is a face.

p. 3   A naked man(?) bending to the right is at the top of the page. Below is the head of a man in a fez-like hat facing left.

p. 4   At the top are two unfinished profiles. In the middle, partly obliterated by the sketch, is: 'Ideas / of / Good & Evil'. Below are a man(?) lying in bed and a woman(?) sitting on the edge of the bed taking off long stockings.[1]

p. 5   *Sideways* at the bottom is a tall figure with its arms raised, with other erased figures above it, perhaps *by Robert Blake*.[2]

p. 6   Most of the page is taken up by a pencil sketch confirmed in ink of a tiger (quite finished) and a fleeing man (somewhat rough) for Blake's second plate (not reversed) for Hayley's *Designs to A Series of Ballads* (1 July 1802). Below these is a finished head of the tiger approximately in the attitude of the 1802 tiger.[3]

p. 7   *Sideways* in the middle are three large, rather stiff robed figures which may be *by Robert Blake*.[4]

*p. 8   Three faint, tall figures facing a smaller one drawn *sideways* may be *by Robert Blake*. Pasted on to the bottom of the page was an irregularly shaped scrap of paper with the three struggling figures etched in *Europe* (1794) pl. 5. (On the verso of the scrap are lines of a larger sketch; the scrap was listed and mounted separately after 1966.)

*p. 9   The page is entirely filled *sideways* with an ink-and-Grey-wash drawing of a poorly proportioned knight, apparently with a drawn sword, rushing from a Gothic cloister after a woman into a wood; it may be *by Robert Blake*.[4]

*p. 11   Drawn *sideways* is a crowned figure in a long robe with arms outstretched towards another figure which turns away. Behind them are groups of other, smaller figures. At the bottom are two children by a recumbent figure. All are probably *by Robert Blake*.[4]

p. 12   In the middle is a pudgy boy, perhaps Henry VIII aged about eight. Below, to the right, is a different face.

---

[1] The sketch may be related to the couplet at the bottom of the page:
> When a Man has Married a Wife he finds out whether
> Her knees & elbows are only glued together⌊.⌋

[2] Suggested by Keynes (ed., *The Note-Book* [1935], 149).
[3] Its attitude is not that of the beast in 'The Tyger' (*Songs* [1794] pl. 42—p. 185).
[4] Suggested by Keynes (ed. *The Note-Book* [1935], 149, 150).

*p. 13 The page is taken up with a full-page ink-and-Grey-wash sketch of a crowned king and queen on a flower, with angelic figures hovering over them, probably *by Robert Blake*.[1] This design was copied on the cover of the 1880 Gilchrist; a similar design was used in *Song of Los* (1795) pl. 5 (p. 289).

*p. 15 In the centre is the design for *For Children* (1793) pl. 16 (p. 657), numbered '39' and entitled: 'The traveller hasteth in the Evening'. Above this is a rough, winged man carrying a tiny man in his mouth,[2] which is repeated twice more below the first sketch, and on pp. 16–17. In the top left corner is the back of a man standing with his legs apart and urinating. (An offset of this design appears on p. 14.) In the bottom left corner is a dog looking up at a man, perhaps related to *Urizen* (1794) pl. 26 (p. 280). Other lines seem indecipherable. At the bottom is some offset ink writing, not in Blake's hand, which may read: 'sweet of them'.

*p. 16 At the top centre are two sketches of the flying man with a tiny human figure in his mouth attempted on pp. 15, 17. At the bottom left side is the back of a nude man. To his right is a woman with outspread arms sheltering three(?) children, similar to the design on pp. 76 and 80 for *Jerusalem* (1804–?20) pl. 32 (p. 485). Other lines are indecipherable.

p. 17 At the top are two sketches of the mouth of the giant with a man in his mouth, more fully given on pp. 15–16. In the centre, a man walks forward, perhaps through a door, and meets a skeleton.[3] The design is numbered '40' and entitled 'Are glad when they can / find the grave'.[4]

p. 18 A man on horseback followed by another figure (a woman?) carrying something is numbered '34'.

p. 19 In the top left corner is a man's left profile, like the bearded profile on p. 21. In the centre is a sketch for *For Children* (1793) pl. 9 (p. 652), numbered '[6 *del*] 8' and inscribed:

> Ah luckless babe born under cruel star
> And in dead parents baleful ashes bred⌊,⌋
> Full little weenest thou what sorrows are
> Left thee for portion of thy livelihed⌊.⌋
> Spenser [*FAERIE QUEENE, II. ii. 2. 1–4*]

p. 20 Four(?) figures sitting round a fifth who is looking at the sky are reminiscent of the engraving of 'Job' ('18 August 1793').

[1] See note 4, p. 1708.
[2] Cf. p. 22, ll. 5–6: 'Not only in his Mouth his own Soul lay But my Soul also'.
[3] A related design was used in *For Children* (1793) pl. 17 (p. 658), *America* (1793) pl. 14 (p. 131), Blair's *Grave* (1808), and *Jerusalem* (1804–?20) pl. 1 (p. 416); it is repeated on p. 71.
[4] Job 3 : 22.

p. 21   At the top left is a fine bearded profile, very like the beardless profile on p. 19. In the top middle are three studies of lips, as on p. 33. In the centre is a man looking up at a woman springing from a flower (not unlike *Songs* [1794] pl. 39—p. 181), and below it are lines from Shakespeare's Sonnet XV:

> Every thing that grows
> Holds in perfection but a little [*moment.*]

p. 22   Two figures stand on either side of a seated one, before whom kneels a fourth, while a fifth turns away; the very faint sketch is numbered '17'.

p. 23   A cage hanging from a tree holds a crouching person; the design is numbered '30[?]'.

p. 24   Two figures in a wood are threatened by a bearded man; the scene, numbered '18', may perhaps be Adam and Eve driven from Paradise.

p. 25   In the centre, numbered '[32 *del*] 23', are five despairing figures; the three at the left were used for *Europe* (1794) pl. 10 (p. 213), the third from the left reversed.

p. 26   A large, complicated sketch seems to represent naked soldiers with shields, standards, and swords, landing from a boat; they may be connected with the proposed engraving (*Notebook*, p. 116) of 'The Landing of Julius Caesar'.[1]

p. 27   Two(?) smudged figures looking down on a prostrate man are numbered '[33(?) *del*] 24' and inscribed with a quotation from Milton's Sonnet XVII, to Sir Henry Vane:

> [*Whether to settle peace, or to unfold*]
> The drift of hollow state*s*, hard to / be spelld ⌊.⌋

p. 28   In the centre is a large sketch for *Visions* (1793) pl. 3 (p. 103), reversed.

p. 29   A slight figure hovering in the air over a prostrate person, numbered '[32(?) *del*] 19', may be related to *America* (1793) pl. 2 (p. 119).

p. 30   Four faint figures dancing in the air (for *Visions* [1793] pl. 2, reversed [p. 101]) are inscribed:

> A fairy vision of some gay
> Creatures of the element who
> In the colours of the rainbow live
>   Milton[2]

p. 31   A figure apparently standing on a cloud and going through a door to be received by three waiting people is numbered '35'.

---

[1] Suggested by M. Wilson, *Life of William Blake* (1948).

[2] *Comus*, ll. 298–300: 'I took it for a faëry vision / Of some gay creatures of the element / That in the colours of a Rainbow live . . .'.

Bibliographical Notes

p. 32   In the centre is a large clear sketch for *Visions* (1793) pl. 6 (p. 108), reversed.

p. 33   At the top are two pairs of lips, as on p. 21. In the centre is an indistinct figure lying on a bed, with another holding a child(?) kneeling beside the bed.

p. 34   The rough sketch for *For Children* (1793) pl. 10 (p. 653) is numbered '16' and inscribed, as on the print: 'My son My son'.

p. 35   A woman standing on a cloud and leading two children with each hand is numbered '[2 *del*] 13'.

p. 36   A woman reaching upwards and turning into a tree (like the design on p. 2) is inscribed: 'As Daphne was root bound / Milton.'[1]

p. 37   A group of five(?) people gathered round a figure on a bed is numbered '[10 *del* 25 (?) *del*] 26'.

p. 38   In the centre is a rough sketch of muscular shoulders. In the middle of the right margin is a pointing index finger darkened in ink (perhaps related to Hand—see *Milton* [1804–?8] pl. 17—p. 356).

p. 39   Three figures looking down at a fourth lying in bed (not like the sketch on p. 37) is somewhat like Blake's second plate for Mary Wollstonecraft's *Original Stories* (1791);[2] it is numbered '[26 *del* 26 del* 14 *del*] 25'.

p. 40   In the centre is a faint sketch used in *For Children* (1793) pl. 11 (p. 654), reversed. In the bottom right is a smudged and scribbled-over miniature portrait; a similar head is on p. 47.

p. 41   In front of a Gothic door a man and a woman are kissing, respectively, a girl and a boy; the drawing is numbered '[32 *del* 14 *del* 27 *del*]'.

p. 42   An old man leaning on a stick reaches for a butterfly.

p. 43   A vague sketch for *Songs* (1794) pl. 29 (p. 173), reversed, is numbered '[15 *del*] 28'.

p. 44   In the centre is a clear sketch for the *Marriage* (?1790–3) pl. 24 (p. 97) reversed, as on p. 48.

*p. 45   Below the rough sketch for *For Children* (1793) pl. 18 (p. 658), numbered '[13 *del* 7(?) *del*] 1', is the title: 'I have said to corruption thou art / my father, to the worm thou art / my mother & my Sister⌊.⌋ / Job' (17: 14)[3]

p. 46   A man sitting on the edge of a bed and looking apprehensively upward is entitled: 'Murder⌊.⌋'

---

[1] *Comus*, ll. 659–62: 'Nay Lady sit; if I but wave this wand, / Your nervs are all chain'd up in Alabaster, / And you a statue; or as *Daphne* was / Root-bound, that fled *Apollo*.'

[2] Suggested by Keynes (ed., *The Note-Book* [1935], 154).

[3] The etched title is: 'I have said to the Worm Thou art my mother & my sister'.

p. 47 Two figures with outstretched arms are springing upwards, and between their arms are two other figures also rising up; the sketch is numbered '2[?] 29[?]'. Below them, in the bottom margin and somewhat overlapping them, is a clear face with an elaborate head-dress, not unlike that on p. 40.

p. 48 In the centre is a faint sketch for the *Marriage* (?1790–3) pl. 24 (p. 97), reversed, as on p. 44.

p. 49 A rough figure standing with his hands to his head beside another prostrate on the ground (similar to the standing man in *America* [1793] pl. 3—p. 120— or to 'Cain Standing over the Body of Abel') is numbered '[4(?) *del* 21 (?) *del* 23 *del*] 15'.

p. 50 In the centre is a naked man falling, apparently after having stabbed himself; a very similar design is on p. 75, and the general attitude is like that of the bottom figure in *Visions* (1793) pl. 2 (p. 101).

p. 51 In the centre, numbered '[40 *del*] 42', are five rough figures dancing in a circle at the foot of a tree. At the top of the tree there seems to be seated a larger figure blowing a curling horn; this musician is repeated on a larger scale at the bottom left corner.

p. 52 The clear sketch for *For Children* (1793) pl. 13 (p. 655) is labelled, like the etched plate: 'Aged Ignorance'.

p. 54 At the top is a fine, fairly finished head. In the middle is the design etched in *Songs* (1794) pl. 46 (p. 190), reversed. At the bottom is a fine sketch for the colour print which Blake called 'Elohim creating Adam' (?1795).

p. 55 A very faint child kneeling before a seated figure is numbered '5[?]'.

p. 56 A figure running over the edge of a cliff is held by the ankle by another person (of whom only the head and restraining arm are visible).

p. 57 A sketch for *Songs* (1794) pl. 30 (p. 174), reversed, is numbered '[8(?) *del*] 34'.

p. 58 A faint sketch, perhaps that used in *For Children* (1793) pl. 12 (p. 654), is numbered '[45 *del*] 33'; another sketch may be for pl. 11 of the same work; a third is undecipherable.

p. 59 The design used in *For Children* (1793) pl. 14 (p. 656) is numbered '[44 *del* 29 *del*] 30'.

p. 60 A man kissing, from behind, the neck of a woman running away from him, numbered '[29 *del*]', is similar to that in *The Song of Los* (1795) pl. 4 (p. 288).

p. 61 The sketch (numbered '[26 *altered to* 29 *del*] 31') used in *For Children* (1793) pl. 15 (p. 656), reversed, is inscribed: 'What we hope to See'.[1]

    [1] The etched plate is called 'Fear & Hope are—Vision'.

p. 63   The pencil, ink, and wash design used in *For Children* (1793) pl. 3 (p. 646), reversed, is numbered '[10 *del*] 15' and entitled: 'I found him beneath a tree in the Garden'.[1] Beneath is a second sketch of the mandrake.

p. 65   The pencil, ink, and wash sketch (numbered '[45(?) *del*] 46') for *Songs* (1794) pl. 41 (p. 183), reversed, does not show the wings of the etched version.

p. 66   At the top is a profile face like that on p. 67, evidently representing Blake himself.

p. 67   At the top is a clear profile like that on p. 66. In the centre are two rough figures standing before a door, numbered '[48(?) *del*] 47'.

p. 68   The sketch labelled above 'Frontispiece', for *For Children* (1793) pl. 1 (p. 644), seems to be very faintly inscribed:

    What is Man that thou shouldest / Magnify him & that
    thou shouldest set / Thine heart upon him⌊?⌋ / Job' [7: 17.][2]

p. 69   The sketch used in *For Children* (1793) pl. 8 (p. 651) is numbered '[5 *del*]' and labelled:

    At length for hatching ripe he breaks / the Shell Dryden.[3]
    Above this is a rough head.

p. 70   At the top left is a face in ink; a related sketch is on p. 74. Below are two adults surrounded by three children.

p. 71   The design, numbered '35', is labelled, as it is in *For Children* (1793) pl. 17 (p. 658 above; see *Notebook* p. 17): 'Deaths Door'.

p. 72   In the centre is a figure with upraised arms numbered '48'.

p. 73   At the top and left are three sketches of the eagle bearing a child used as pl. 7 of Hayley's *Designs to A Series of Ballads* (1 July 1802). In the centre a woman holding a baby in her arms is numbered '[18(?) *del*] 36' and inscribed:

    Yet can I not persuade / me thou art dead
           Milton ['*Death of a Fair Infant*', *l. 29*.]

p. 74   There are approximately five horizontal rows of sketches. In the top middle is a left profile.

[1] The etched plate omits the last three words.
[2] Only the first three words are inscribed under the etching itself.
[3] Translation of Chaucer's Knight's Tale, Book III (Dryden, *Fables Ancient and Modern* [1700], 87, reprinted in E. Bysshe, *The Art of English Poetry* [1710]):

    So Man, at first a Drop, dilates with Heat,
    Then form'd, the little Heart begins to beat;
    Secret he feeds, unknowing in the Cell;
    At length, for Hatching ripe, he breaks the Shell,
    And struggles into Breath, and cries for Aid;
    Then, helpless, in his Mothers Lap is laid.

The first figure in the second row (repeated as the second figure in the third line) is the bowed figure in *Visions* (1793) pl. 7, 10 (pp. 109, 114). The second figure in the second row is the woman etched reversed in *Songs* (1794) pl. 33 (p. 177). The third sketch is a finished head related to that on p. 70. The fourth is a standing figure clasping another person, used in *Urizen* (1794) pl. 21 (p. 272).

The first figure in the third row is flying with outstretched arms and a robe whirling upward; it is perhaps related to the flaming god in *Visions* pl. 2 (p. 101). The third sketch in this row is a left profile portrait.

In the fourth row the first and second figures kneel or sit with bowed heads, like the central woman in *Visions* pl. 10 (p. 114). The third figure in the row is for *Songs* pl. 28 (p. 172).

The first figure in the fifth row, tormented, with his arms clutched round his shoulders, is apparently that used for the bat-winged figure at the bottom of *Europe* (1794) pl. 4 (p. 207); it seems to be repeated on p. 75. The second figure in this row, quite similar, seems to be the model for the flaming god at the bottom of *Visions* pl. 2 (p. 101).

p. 75   Three rows of sketches fill the page. At the top left is a bowed figure related to that for *Europe* (1794) pl. 4 (p. 207) on p. 74. To the right is a seated figure with head bowed, like the left person in *For Children* (1793) pl. 14 (p. 656). In the top right corner two tormented figures falling, related to *America* (1793) pl. 7 (p. 124), are inscribed: 'A vision of fear'. To the left of the next row is a man falling backward, very like the figure on p. 50.

In the centre, a sketch of two embracing figures on their knees with a child between them is inscribed to the right: 'A vision of hope'. Below, in the bottom row at the left, there are faint lines apparently representing a bearded figure. In the middle of the bottom row is a sketch for *For Children* pl. 5 (p. 648; see *Notebook* p. 93), numbered '[16 *del*] 38'.

p. 76   Three faint adults with children on either side (like the designs on p. 80 and *Jerusalem* [1804–?20] pl. 32—p. 485) fill most of the page.

p. 77   In the centre is a flying child, with an illegible deleted number. At the bottom, partly razored out after the writing was added to the verso, is a prostrate child related to those etched reversed in *America* (1793) pl. 11, and *Europe* (1794) pl. 9 (pp. 128, 212).

p. 78   A large sketch for *Visions* (1793) pl. 11 (p. 117), reversed, fills most of the page.

p. 80   The clear design of a woman sheltering a group of children is like those on p. 76 and *Jerusalem* (1804–?20) pl. 32 (p. 485).

p. 81   The figure, numbered '[14 *del*] 32', was used, reversed, for the top right one, in *Visions* (1793) pl. 2 (p. 101).

Bibliographical Notes

p. 82   At the bottom, *upside-down*, is a head, perhaps of Catherine Blake,[1] perhaps of a man.

p. 83   A clear seated woman with a rigid child on her knees is numbered '37' and inscribed:

> Sweet rose⌊,⌋ fair flower⌊,⌋ untimely pluckd⌊,⌋ soon faded⌊,⌋
> Pluckd in the bud & faded in thine Spring⌊.⌋[2]

p. 84   Two figures near a corpse walk beneath a crescent moon.

p. 85   A man, manacled(?) and seated before a rock(?), is numbered '[20 *del* 2 *del*] 2' and inscribed:

> Whose changeless brow
> Neer smiles nor frowns
> Donne[3]

p. 86   Three faint women extend *sideways* from margin to margin.

p. 87   A faint standing figure beside one reclining is numbered '6'.

p. 88   A large faint *sideways* sketch represents a standing figure holding his hand over another person engulfed in serpent coils.

p. 90   A *sideways* sketch of a reclining man looking upward is rather like that on *Vala* (?1796–?1807) p. 48.

p. 91   The design, reversed in *For Children* (1793) pl. 7 (p. 650), is numbered '[4 *del*] 6' and inscribed:

> [Forthwith upright *del*] he rears from off the pool
> His mighty stature
> Milton [*PARADISE LOST, I, 221–2.*]

p. 92   At the top is a sketch for the doorway (like that on p. 6) etched for pl. 2 of Hayley's *Designs to A Series of Ballads* (1 June 1802). Below is the design reversed in *Visions* (1793) pl. 7 (p. 109).

p. 93   The design, reversed in *For Children* (1793) pl. 5 (p. 648; see *Notebook* p. 75), is numbered '3' and '2' and inscribed: 'Rest Rest perturbed Spirit / Shakespeare' (*Hamlet*, i. v. 183).[4]

p. 94   Two sketches for the figure in *For Children* (1793) pl. 6 (p. 649; see *Notebook* p. 98) show his elbows in different positions; the central one in ink-and-wash is numbered '5' and inscribed:

> Thou hast set thy heart as / the heart of God
> Ezekiel.[5]

---

[1] Suggested by Keynes (ed. *The Note-Book* [1935], 159).

[2] 'The Passionate Pilgrim', ll. 131–2 (accurate except for 'the spring'); '*faded* is always spelt *vaded*' in Jacobean printings (*The Plays and Poems of William Shakspeare*, ed. E. Malone [1790], x. 326).

[3] 'The Progress of the Soule', ll. 35–6: 'Great Destiny . . . whose changelesse brow Ne'r smiles nor frownes . . .' Blake made a large drawing of the subject, called 'Fate' (*The Note-Book*, ed. G. Keynes [1935], 160).

[4] The words are those Hamlet speaks to his father.

[5] Ezekiel 28: 6–7: 'Thus saith the Lord God; because thou hast set thine heart as the heart of God . . . thou shalt die . . .'.

p. 95　　The design used in *For Children* (1793) pl. 4 (p. 647) is numbered '[*number del and illeg*] 4' and inscribed:

O that the Everlasting had not fixd
His canon gainst self-slaughter
　　　　Shakespeare [*HAMLET, I. ii. 131–2; the first
　　　　　　　　　　　　　　word should be 'Or'.*]

p. 96　　The rough *sideways* sketch for *Europe* (1794) pl. 1 (p. 204) is inscribed at the right side from *Europe* pl. 5 (p. 208):

Who shall bind / the Infinite[?]

p. 97　　The crouching man with a knife, numbered '[20(?) *del* 32 *del*] 33', is related to the ones in *Europe* (1794) pl. 4 (p. 207) and in the picture called 'Malevolence'[1] which Blake described in his letter of 16 August 1796.

p. 98　　The *sideways* figure with his hands clasped over his head and numbered '5' at the top left may be related to the one in *For Children* pl. 6 (p. 649; see *Notebook* p. 94), or to the one in the top right corner of *Europe* (1794) pl. 5 (p. 208).

p. 100　　The half-reclining figure gazing beneath his hand fills the whole page *sideways*.

p. 101　　The faint man pushing a woman from him is numbered '[26 *del*] 50' and inscribed:

Begone & trouble me no / more

*p. 102　　The stiff nude man and woman, with lines as if of trees beside them, almost fill the page *sideways*.

*p. 104　　Christ, with arms outspread, flies to kiss God, who sits with bowed head, while over him broods the Holy Ghost, with wings spread. Similar large designs are on pp. 106 and 108 and were repeated in Blake's *Paradise Lost* illustration (1807?).

p. 106　　A large, very rough, *sideways* design may be for the Trinity, as on pp. 104, 108.

p. 108　　The large, almost undecipherable *sideways* sketch may be for the Trinity, as on pp. 104, 106.

*pp. *110–11　　These pages were used *sideways* for a single sketch representing a robed figure on the right inclining toward a seated figure, with, below them on p. 111, another naked figure falling. The subject may be God, Christ, and Satan.

*p. 112　　The *sideways* sketch of Satan for the colour print of 'Satan Exulting over Eve' (?1795) entirely fills the page.

------

[1] Reproduced in *Blake Records*, pl. x.

DESIGN NUMBERS: The decipherable numbers attached to the drawings are both so incomplete and so redundant as to make it very difficult to draw any reliable conclusions from them. In the following list, numbers in brackets are deleted.

Design number	Found on page number									
1			45							
2		[35]	?47				85	[85]	93	
3									93	
4			[?49]					[91]	95	
5				?55	[69]			94	98	
6	[19]						87		91	
7			[?45]							
8	19			[?57]		[79]				
9										
10		[37]			[63]					
11										
12						79				
13		35	[45]							
14		[39]	[41]				[81]			
15			[43] 49		63					
16		34				[75]				
17	22									
18	24					[?73]				
19	29									
20							[85]	[?97]		
21			[?49]				?89			
22										
23		25	[49]							
24		27								
25		[?37] 39								
26		37 [39]			[61]					[101]
27			[41]							
28			43							
29			?47	[59]	[60, 61]					
30	?23			59						
31					61					
32		[25, ?29]	[41]				81	[97]		
33		[?27]		58				97		
34	18			57						
35		31				71				
36						73				
37							83			
38						75				
39	15									
40	17				[51]					
41										
42					51					
43										
44					[59]					

Design number	Found on page number		
45		[58] [?65]	
46		65	
47		67	
48		[?67]	72
49			
50			101

The facts that pl. 3–9 of *For Children* are numbered approximately accurately (though pl. 12, 14–18 are inaccurate) and that several numbers are duplicated suggest that more than one series of numbers may be included here.

'Vision of the Last Judgment'
(Text pp. 1007–28)

MANUSCRIPT: *Notebook* pp. 68–72, 76–87, 90–95.

DATE: 1810 (part c is headed 'For the Year 1810').

Blake made a design of the Last Judgement about 1805 for Blair's *Grave* (published in 1808). He made another for the wife of Lord Egremont, which he described in his letter of 18 January 1808 to Ozias Humphry. Cumberland's sons saw a third overworked water-colour of the Last Judgement on 21 April 1815.[1] Just before he died in 1827 he was preparing yet a fourth drawing of the Last Judgement 'containing upwards of one thousand figures' for the 1828 exhibition of the Royal Academy.[2] Blake probably began the present description about 1810, perhaps with the intention of including it with a new edition of his *Descriptive Catalogue*. It may have been written over an extended period of time, for some parts (e, k, l, s, pp. 71, 76, 78) precede the 'Public Address' of 1810–11 and one (part u, p. 86) succeeds it.

DESCRIPTION: The parts of the 'Vision of the Last Judgment' scattered through the *Notebook* are linked largely by a common subject-matter, a description of the Last Judgement design and of the nature of eternity. The same title has been supplied by all editors. In parts a–e, k–l, m–o, w–x, each group was probably written continuously. The other parts may have been written at separate times. The order of the parts as printed here is the same as in Keynes and in Erdman.

Before the 'Vision of the Last Judgment', the 'Public Address', and 'The Everlasting Gospel' were written, much of the *Notebook* was still empty. Pages 1, *8–9*, *11*, *13*, *15–16*, 17–20, ?23, 49, 51–53, 55, 57–60, 62, 66–70, *74–75*, 76–77, 80–86, 90–96 (forty-six pages) were occupied only by designs and their inscriptions, and the page-numbers italicized above still have no other writing.

---

[1] *Blake Records*, 235.   [2] Ibid. 467, quoting J. T. Smith.

Bibliographical Notes

'Public Address'

(Text pp. 1029–53)

MANUSCRIPT: *Notebook* pp. 1, 17–21, 23–25, 38–39, 44, 46–47, 51–53, 55–67, 71, 76, 78, 86.

DATE: *c.* 1811. Many indications of date are quite clear. Some parts (y, bb–dd, pp. 71, 76, 78) were clearly written after the 'Vision of the Last Judgment' of 1810, and one (part ee, p. 86) precedes part of it. Part g precedes 4 August 1811, parts z, aa are before 23 May 1810, part j is after June 1810 (see pp. 1038 [cf. p. 957], 1043 [cf. p. 960], 1040 below).

Other indications are more general. Blake refers, in part b, to his plates after Stothard (1780–3) made twenty-five years before. He complains in part b of attacks made on him for the last thirty-two years, but we do not know the date of the first of these attacks (?1779). His references to forty years of engraving (part gg) and of commerce (part b) suggest the years 1772 (when his apprenticeship began) to 1812. Part b precedes 'The Everlasting Gospel' of ?1818.

It is indeed possible that the 'Public Address' was printed (see 'A Work on Art', pp. 1680–2 above), but, if so, no copy has been found. Blake may alternatively have intended to publish it with *The Prologue and Characters of Chaucer's Pilgrims* (1812), which was printed to make known Blake's Chaucer engraving.

DESCRIPTION: The parts of the 'Public Address' scattered through the *Notebook* are linked largely by a common subject-matter, a description of his 'Canterbury Pilgrims' engraving and an attack upon the colourists. Blake refers to the work as 'this Public Address' (part c), and it has been known thus since it was first published by Gilchrist in 1863.

In parts ff–gg, ii–kk, tt–uu, each group was probably written continuously. The other parts may have been written at separate times. The parts up to p. 47 were probably written after those on pp. 51–86. The order of the parts printed here is the same as in Keynes (who is followed by Erdman), except that Keynes puts (1) the first two sentences of part c before the last paragraph of part b and the rest of part c after part f; (2) part kk after part ss; (3) part nn after part mm; (4) part vv after part uu; Keynes also (5) omits part ddd, and (6) lumps parts ccc, eee–ggg together as 'Additional Passages'.

'The Everlasting Gospel'

(Text pp. 1054–69)

MANUSCRIPT: ROSENBACH FOUNDATION and *Notebook* pp. 33, 48–54, 98, 100–101, 120.

SIZE: 9·6 × 16·2 cm (for the Rosenbach MS; for the *Notebook*, see above, p. 1705).

WATERMARK: '1818' plus chain lines 2·5 cm apart (for the Rosenbach MS; for the *Notebook*, see above, p. 1704).

DATE: *c.* 1818 The date of the Rosenbach MS is shown by the watermark to be in or after 1818. Internal consistency[1] suggests that the Rosenbach MS preceded the *Notebook* drafts, so all 'The Everlasting Gospel' must come in or after 1818. Similarities of phraseology between 'The Everlasting Gospel' and *For the Sexes* (?1818), the marginalia (*c.* 1820) to Berkeley's *Siris*, and 'Laocoön' (?1820) (see pp. 1502–5,) suggest *circa* 1818 as the date for all the drafts of 'The Everlasting Gospel'.

DESCRIPTION: The Rosenbach MS consists of a single leaf, folded to make four pages,[2] with four stab holes (1·5, 4·0, 2·3 cm apart) down the central crease. The prose (p. 1) is written in pencil; the rest is in Black ink.

The parts of the poem scattered through the Rosenbach MS and the *Notebook* have been given letters[1] for convenience of reference. The poem was repeatedly drafted but never finished. It is printed here in approximate chronological order.

'A Fairy leapt' (?1793)
(Text p. 1070)

COLLECTION: LIBRARY OF CONGRESS.

WATERMARK: None.

LEAF-SIZE: 14·1 × 18·9 cm.

DATE: About 1793.

The date is somewhat uncertainly derived from the style of the poem, the form of the handwriting, and the hypothetical date of the drawing on the verso.

DESCRIPTION: The text, on one side of a single leaf, is in pencil and is quite difficult to read; the words 'Disguser', 'paltry', 'poisnous', 'hides', and 'Storm' are particularly doubtful.

On the verso is the drawing known as 'The Infant Hercules Throttling Serpents'.[3]

'I asked a thief' (1796)
(Text p. 1071)

COLLECTION: PRINCETON.

WATERMARK: Chain lines 3·3 cm apart, slightly crooked.

LEAF-SIZE: 13·5 × 12·3 cm.

---

[1] See *The Complete Writings of William Blake*, ed. G. Keynes (1966) and D. V. Erdman, ' "Terrible Blake in his Pride": An Essay on *The Everlasting Gospel*', *From Sensibility to Romanticism*; Essays Presented to Frederick A. Pottle (1965), 331–56.

[2] The four pages thus formed might perhaps have been folded differently to give the order: 3, 4, 1, 2.

[3] Reproduced in G. Keynes, *Blake's Pencil Drawings*: Second Series (1956), no. 5, where the drawing is dated 1793.

Bibliographical Notes

DATE: Dated '1796' by Blake.

DESCRIPTION: The poem is written in Brown ink on one side of the leaf. The first line is smudged, and the paper has three folding creases. The poem is copied with no verbal changes from the draft on p. 114 of the *Notebook* (p. 996).

Vala or *The Four Zoas* (?1796–?1807)
(Text pp. 1072–1297)

COLLECTION: BRITISH MUSEUM Department of Manuscripts (Add. MSS 39764).

WATERMARKS: 1794 J WHATMAN[1] on (1–2) (9–10) (23–4) (25–6) (31–2) (39–40) (41–2) (51–2) (67–8) (77–8) (79–80) (81–2) 137–8).

[*LE*] PARD[2] on (97–8) (109–10) (119–20).

... R (perhaps I TAYLOR) on (141–2).

LEAF-SIZES: $31\cdot3\times$ $39\cdot7$ cm (1–2)
$31\cdot3\times c.41\cdot3$ cm (3–4) (21–2)[3]
$c.32\cdot8\times c.41\cdot4$ cm (5–6)[4] (9–10) (25–6) (111–12) (127–8)[5]
$c.31\cdot9\times c.40\cdot9$ cm (7–8) (13–14) (15–16) (29–30) (31–2)
(37–8) (85–6)[6] (121–2)
$c.32\cdot4\times c.41\cdot2$ cm (11–12)[7] (17–18) (23–4) (27–8) (47–8)[4]
(73–4) (77–8) (81–2) (117–18) (133–4)[5]
$33\cdot3\times$ $25\cdot4$ cm (19–20)[3]

[1] Pages 1–18, 23–86, 91–6, 99–108, 111–18, 121–40 seem to be the same 1794 J WHATMAN paper, of which pp. 43–86, 91–140 were used for *Night Thoughts* proofs. On 24 June 1796 Fuseli reported that Richard Edwards, who had commissioned the *Night Thoughts* proofs, had supplied Blake with 'ab.t 900 pages' of 'large half sheet[s] of paper' (*Blake Records*, 52), clearly this 1794 J WHATMAN paper.

[2] Paper watermarked 'LE[P]ARD 1803' was used in proofs of Flaxman's then unpublished designs for the *Divina Commedia* (1793), probably in preparation for the 1807 Longman edition (G. E. Bentley, Jr., *The Early Engravings of Flaxman's Classical Designs* [1964], 49).

[3] Pages 19–22 are two halves of a large, vague sketch. The paper has chain lines. The bottom of pp. 19–20 was evidently cut off.

[4] Pages 5–6 have a curious wavy crease, made after the writing, as if from a heavy weight. Pages 45–6 were creased horizontally and pp. 47–8 (q.v.) vertically *after* the *Night Thoughts* engravings were printed but *before* the sketches were completed.

[5] Made of two halves of overlapping leaves, with widths of 21·3 cm (95–6) (127–8) (131–2), 20·8 cm (95–6) (123–4) (133–4), 20·6 cm (both in 103–4) (133–4), 19·7 cm (105–6), 21·0 cm (105–6) (135–6), 21·1 cm (123–4), 20·2 cm (125–6) (129–30), 21·6 cm (125–6) (127–8) (135–6), 20·3 cm (129–30), 20·5 cm (131–2). The leaves were joined before the *Night Thoughts* engravings were printed on them.

[6] Pages 85–6 have a small patch at the side, 5·4×3·0 cm.

[7] Pages 11–12 seem to have been trimmed at the top, for several letters go off p. 12 *and return*.

$c.32\cdot8 \times c.40\cdot5$ cm $(33-4)$ $(93-4)$ $(123-4)^1$ $(125-6)^1$ $(135-6)^1$
$c.32\cdot8 \times c.42\cdot2$ cm $(35-6)$ $(39-40)$ $(41-2)$ $(43-4)$
$c.33\cdot0 \times c.39\cdot5$ cm $(45-6)^2$ $(97-8)$ $(109-10)$ $(119-20)$
$c.32\cdot4 \times c.40\cdot8$ cm $(49-50)$ $(51-2)$ $(53-4)$ $(61-2)$
$c.32\cdot3 \times c.39\cdot4$ cm $(55-6)$ $(67-8)$ $(113-14)$ $(129-30)^1$ $(137-8)$
$\quad 32\cdot4 \times c.42\cdot0$ cm $(57-8)$ $(71-2)$
$\quad 32\cdot9 \times \quad 41\cdot0$ cm $(59-60)$
$c.32\cdot3 \times c.40\cdot4$ cm $(63-4)$ $(65-6)$ $(69-70)$ $(83-4)$ $(89-90)^3$
$\qquad\qquad\qquad\quad (91-2)$ $(95-6)^1$ $(131-2)^1$
$\quad 33\cdot2 \times \quad 42\cdot2$ cm $(75-6)$
$\quad 32\cdot2 \times \quad 32\cdot5$ cm $(79-80)$
$\quad 31\cdot4 \times \quad 40\cdot5$ cm $(87-8)^3$
$\quad 32\cdot9 \times \quad 37\cdot0$ cm $(99-100)$
$\quad 33\cdot5 \times \quad 36\cdot4$ cm $(101-2)^4$
$\quad 32\cdot6 \times c.39\cdot9$ cm $(103-4)^1$ $(105-6)^1$
$\quad 33\cdot3 \times \quad 37\cdot1$ cm $(107-8)$
$\quad 30\cdot6 \times \quad 41\cdot6$ cm $(115-16)$
$\quad 31\cdot8 \times \quad 37\cdot3$ cm $(139-40)$
$\quad\; 9\cdot7 \times \quad 16\cdot6$ cm $(141-2)$
$\quad 16\cdot2 \times \quad 10\cdot4$ cm $(143-4)$ irregular
$\quad 14\cdot4 \times \quad 23\cdot3$ cm $(145-6)$

DATES:

(1) ?1796–7 *Vala* probably drafted in a notebook.

(2) 1797 Copperplate fair copy (pp. 1–18, 23–42) plus perhaps drafts of Nights IV–IX.

(3) ?1797–1802 revised.

(4) ?1802 fair copy (pp. 43–84, 112) plus perhaps drafts of Nights VIIb–IX.

(5) ?1803–7, revised, pp. 19–22, 85 ff. transcribed, pp. 99–118 recopied again, title changed to *The Four Zoas*.

(1) It is likely that *Vala* was drafted on separate pages, perhaps in a note-book like pp. 141–4 (though no such pages are known to survive), for the earliest surviving draft is clearly a fair copy, the original of which must have been written elsewhere. This lost draft was probably composed between 1795,[5] when *Ahania* and *The Book of Los* were etched, and 1797, when the fair copy was dated.

(2) The fair copy was first transcribed in the Copperplate Writing on large blank sheets and dated '1797'[6] on the title-page. This date presumably

[1] See note 5, p. 1721.   [2] See note 4, p. 1721.

[3] Pages 87–90 are two halves of Blake's engraving called 'Edward & Elinor', from which *c.* 8 cm were removed when they were separated.

[4] The top of the engraving is missing in pp. 101–2.

[5] It may be related to 'The Bible of Hell: which the world shall have whether they will or no' announced in the *Marriage* (?1790–3) pl. 24, ¶89, and to 'The Bible of Hell, In Nocturnal Visions collected' (?1793) for which he made a separate title-page (see pp. 97, 1323).

[6] It is unlikely that Blake would have used the WHATMAN paper supplied him

applies to the pages originally in the Copperplate Hand (pp. 1–14, 17–18, 23–30) plus pp. 15–16[1] in the Modified Copperplate Hand, which were all stitched together. Probably in the same year, pp. 31–42 were transcribed in the Modified Copperplate Hand and stitched with pp. 1–18, 23–30 through a distinct set of stab holes. (Probably the rest of the poem was also transcribed from the hypothetical notebook on to other leaves later discarded and now lost.)

The other pages of *Vala* are quite distinct from pp. 1–18, 23–42 in handwriting, in being written on sheets previously used for proofs (chiefly for *Night Thoughts*[2]) or sketches, and in stab holes. Pages 1–18, 23–42 in the Copperplate Hands were heavily revised, with about eight deleted lines and twelve added lines to a page, compared to pp. 19–22, 43–139, which have only about one deleted line and three and a half added ones to a page. This suggests that pp. 1–18, 23–42 were first transcribed in their present form earlier than the rest.[3]

(*3*) The whole poem was probably revised extensively between 1797 and about 1802. In the process, some pages, such as pp. 4–8, became difficult to read. Blake partially transcribed at least pp. 7–8 in a little notebook, of which only pp. 144, 143 survive.

(4) Blake transcribed p. 48, and probably the rest of the poem, after June 1802.

The evidence for the date of p. 48 is relatively simple, for underneath ll. 11–29 is a mirror-image of the type from [William Hayley] *Designs to A Series of Ballads* (1 June 1802) p. 9. The image was transferred when Blake used his *Night Thoughts* proof sheet as a backing in printing his engraving on p. 9 of Hayley's *Ballad*.[4] *Vala* p. 48 must, then, have been written after 1 June 1802.

Page 48 is similar in character to pp. 43–7, 49–86, 91–140 in being written on *Night Thoughts* proofs in the Usual Hand, and all three pages differ from pp. 1–18, 23–42 in these respects and in stab holes and symbolism. Probably, therefore, pp. 43–140[5] were all transcribed after June 1802.

for his *Night Thoughts* work (see Watermarks above) for his fair copy of *Vala* before June 1797, when the *Night Thoughts* was published (*Blake Records*, 59).

[1] Pages 15–16 differ from pp. 1–14, 17–18 in handwriting, in a stab holes, and in their omission from the earliest page- and line-numeration.

[2] Like *Night Thoughts*, *Vala* is organized in nine Nights.

[3] An alternative hypothesis is that Blake first (?*c.* 1796) copied out the whole poem in the Usual Hand and then in 1797 recopied as far as mid Night III in the Copperplate Hands, discarding originals as they were copied. However, this hypothesis cannot, it seems to me, satisfactorily account for such diverse factors as symbolism, stab holes, corrections, and handwriting.

[4] At the bottom of *Vala* p. 48 is an indentation the size (11·5 × 8·0 cm) of Blake's engraving of an elephant for *Ballads* (1802) p. 9.

[5] Pages 87–90 seem from other evidence to be even later than the immediately preceding pages. Since pp. 85–6 with the first 'End of the Seventh Night' were not stabbed, they presumably replace pages ending Night VIIa which were stabbed and then discarded.

Pages 43–84, 111–12 were once stabbed together (p. 112 evidently as an illustration for Night IV), separate from the other leaves, from which they also differ in symbolism. Probably they are all that survive of the 1802 transcript.

(5) Pages 19–22, 85 ff.,[1] and revisions of the whole were probably made from 1803 to about 1807. The evidence for these dates is of several kinds.

On *Vala* p. 3 Blake wrote two passages in Greek. He learned Greek from Hayley in 1801–3,[2] and by 30 January 1803 he felt that he could 'read Greek as fluently as an Oxford scholar'. The Greek is therefore likely to have been added after 1802.

Further, the Greek passages are from the New Testament and deal with the nature of Christ and the mission of his disciples. Such enthusiastic Christian references are scarcely visible in the earliest surviving drafts of Nights I–VIIa or in Blake's letters much before 1803. However, after 1803 Blake's letters and poetry take on an explicitly Christian character. On 23 October 1804 he wrote:

> Suddenly, on the day after visiting the Truchsessian Gallery of pictures, I was again enlightened with the light I enjoyed in my youth, and which has for exactly twenty years been closed from me as by a door and by window-shutters.

This renewed revelation probably accounts for the Hebrew and Christian symbolism found in the additions to pp. 1–18, 23–84 (Nights I–VIIa). However, such symbolism is found in the earliest surviving lines of Nights VIIb–IX, suggesting that they were transcribed in their present form after Nights I–VIIa had been revised. This distinction in symbolism in Nights VIIb–IX is confirmed by the fact that I–VIIa were stabbed, whereas VIIb–IX were not. The present drafts of VIIb–IX seem, then, to be later than 1803.[3]

The growing explicitness of the Christian and Hebrew symbolism suggests that the surviving drafts were written in this order: VIIa, VIIb, IX, VIII.[4] The present Night VIII must replace a discarded draft[5] of the time of VIIb or IX (that is, of perhaps 1803–5).[6]

Pages 19–21 are an insertion into Night I which incorporates references to 'the Council of God', which is found elsewhere only as additions to

---

[1] With the exception of pp. 19–20, 111–12, none of these pages was ever stabbed with pp. 1–18, 23–42 or with pp. 43–84.

[2] *Blake Records*, 86, 89.

[3] Most of Nights VIIb–IX (pp. 95–110, 115–16, 121–36, 139–40) are made of leaves which are odd sizes (pp. 99–102, 107–8, 115–16, 139–40), patched together (pp. 95–6, 103–6, 123–36), or creased (pp. 97–8, 109–10, 121–2). Pages 111–14, 117–18 are even later additions to Nights VIII–IX.

[4] For detailed evidence for these conclusions, see *Vala* (1963), 162–5.

[5] Page 145 seems to be notes for the revision of this earlier draft.

[6] Over 120 lines in the earliest surviving forms of I–VIIb and IX were moved from *Vala* to *Jerusalem* (1804–?20), but the traffic seems to have gone from *Jerusalem* to *Vala* in lines from the earliest surviving form of Night VIII (see especially p. 105, ll. 31–54) and in additions to other Nights.

pp. 55–6; this plus their Hebrew, Christian, and Druid symbolism suggests that they were the last complete pages added to the poem.

One of the last changes was the substitution in the title of *The Four Zoas* for *Vala*; its lateness is demonstrated by the facts that each chapter is still headed 'Vala' rather than 'The Four Zoas' and that the word 'Zoa' never appears in the text of the poem at all.[1] The date must be about 1807, for the word 'Zoa' is found in *Milton* (1804–?8) and *Jerusalem* (1804–?20), zoas are clearly depicted in Blake's drawings for *Paradise Lost* (1807–8), and they are described in his letter of 18 January 1808 and in his *Descriptive Catalogue* (1809) ¶75, where *Vala* is apparently referred to.

DESCRIPTION: The manuscript consists of seventy-three leaves (146 pages), of which pp. 66, 76, 89, 112, 114, 140, and 146 have no writing and pp. 2, 88 have only prose perhaps not integral to *Vala*. The writing is in Black ink except for a few noted Brown ink lines and seventy-three lines in pencil, including all of pp. 2, 20, 142.

The text is written on five different kinds of paper which represent roughly chronological divisions of the work. (1) Pages 1–18, 23–42 are on blank 1794 J WHATMAN paper, meticulously written in the Copperplate Hands, with light strokes to keep the writing level,[2] careful punctuation, catchwords,[3] and sketches on all but p. 34.

(2) Pages 43–86, 91–140 are written in the Usual Hand mostly on the same paper, on which Blake had previously pulled proofs of his engravings for Young's *Night Thoughts* (1797). These engravings were designed to leave a space in the centre for Young's text; in this blank centre of the proofs and on the versos Blake wrote Nights IV–IX of *Vala*. The proof is regularly on the recto, except for pp. 113–14, 139–40, where the proofs on the versos are title-pages which scarcely left room for writing. In general, the *Night Thoughts* engravings seem to have had little effect upon the text and designs of *Vala*.

(3) Pages 87–90 were originally one leaf bearing Blake's engraving of 'Edward & Elinor' (18 Aug. 1793), which was cut in two; the engraving is on pp. 87–8.

(4) Pages 19–22 are written on a leaf which originally contained a large, vague sketch, which was cut in two.

(5) Pages 141–6 are scraps of paper with related texts not integral to the present form of *Vala*; pp. 141–2 are probably drafts of the poem but they are not used in the surviving text; pp. 143–4 are revisions of pp. 7–8; and p. 145 is a revision for Night VIII.

There is some confusion about the headings to five Nights. Night I (p. 3) is headed 'Night the First', Night II (p. 23) is also 'Night the [First

---

[1] The addition of 'Albion' on the title-page is also late, for 'Albion' is found only in added passages and is not found after p. 56.

[2] Pages 2–9 have no strokes, probably because p. 2 was not meant for text and pp. 3–9 were obscured by repeated erasures.

[3] There are catchwords on pp. 3–6, 8–10, 12–13, 15–17, 26, 28–9, 32, 37–8, 40, 42.

del] ∧∧*First∧∧', and p. 8 has an inserted 'Night the Second' though pp. 18–19 each still have 'End of The First Night'. Night III (p. 37) is headed 'Night the [Fourth(?) *del*] Third'. The present order of Nights I–III is clear, but Blake's original intentions are matters for speculation.

Blake left two Nights headed 'Night the Seventh', one (pp. 77–90) called here Night VIIa and the other (pp. 91–9) called here Night VIIb. They seem to form a continuous narrative, but the evidence of stab holes and symbolism suggests that Night VIIa was transcribed distinctly before Night VIIb.

PROOFS OF YOUNG'S *Night Thoughts* (1797)
USED IN *Vala*

Vala Page	Night Thoughts Page	Vala Page	Night Thoughts Page	Vala Page	Night Thoughts Page
43	63	75	75	111	*73
45	*90	77	12¹	114	*65²
47	49¹	79	55	115	73
49	12¹	81	* 8¹	117	*41³
51	33¹	83	*54³	119	*86
53	* 7¹	85	*93²	121	*40⁴
55	87	91	*15¹	123	*16¹
57	*70¹	93	*57	125	31¹
59	73	95	*35¹	127	25¹
61	86	97	*90	129	*37
63	23¹	99	*24¹	131	*40⁴
65	*80²	101	*13¹	133	* 8¹
67	*72²	103	*27¹	135	*26¹
69	92	105	*19¹	137	*88²
71	* 7¹	107	* 4¹	140	Title-page¹
73	43	109	*95		

* indicates a proof state; for the differences between proof and published states, see *Vala* (1963), 209.

N.B. Pulls of all the *Night Thoughts* plates were used except for pl. 1, 10, 17, 46. Pages 7–8, 12, 40, 86, 90 were used twice and p. 73 thrice. No *Night Thoughts* proof in *Vala* is dated after 27 June 1796.

Most of *Vala* is clearly fair copy, but the text is sometimes overwhelmed with corrections, inversions, deletions, and additions, and a number of passages are obviously incomplete, with crucial words deleted, for example, or with directions to add otherwise unknown passages. As it stands, the

¹ The published imprint is 27 June 1796. *Vala* pp. 53, 57, 71, 81, 91, 105, 123, 133 are proofs before date.
² The published imprint date of 1 June 1797 was not yet engraved in *Vala* pp. 65, 67, 85, 114, 137.
³ The published imprint date of 22 March 1797 is missing in both proofs in *Vala* (pp. 83, 117).
⁴ The published imprint date of 4 January 1797 is missing in both proofs in *Vala* (pp. 121, 131).

poem is clearly unfinished, and its transcription is especially complex. Through most of its revisions Blake called it *Vala*, but eventually he changed the title to *The Four Zoas*. For convenience, it is consistently referred to in this edition as *Vala*.

There is no known reference to *Vala* by Blake's contemporaries, and the first printed mention of it is in the catalogue in Gilchrist's *Life* (1863). The text was first transcribed and partly reproduced in Blake's *Works*, ed. E. J. Ellis & W. B. Yeats (1893); independent transcripts of a more satisfactory kind were made in *The Writings*, ed. G. Keynes (1925 . . . 1972), *The Prophetic Writings*, ed. D. J. Sloss & J. P. R. Wallis (1926), in *Vala*, ed. H. M. Margoliouth (1956), with the complete facsimile (1963), and in *Poetry and Prose*, ed. D. V. Erdman (1967). The present text is essentially that of 1963.[1]

HANDWRITING: Blake used three discrete styles of handwriting in *Vala*, probably at discrete times.[2] In general, the more careless the handwriting, the later it was used.

(1) The Copperplate Hand is large, elaborate, beautiful, and clear, apparently a fair copy with about 16 lines to a page on pp. 1–14, 17–18, 23–30. It is rarely used to replace a later hand.[3] (2) The Modified Copperplate Hand is hastier, exhibits fewer punctilios of punctuation, and also has about 16 lines to a page on pp. 15–16, 31–42 and revisions to pp. 4–5, 14, 18. It is rarely substituted for the Usual Hand. (3) The Usual Hand which Blake used for his correspondence is hastily written; individual words are often hard to decipher, there is very little punctuation, and stanza breaks are sometimes hard to identify. About seven-eighths of the poem is in this hand, including all of pp. 19–22, 43–145 and revisions and additions to early pages, with about 30–37 lines to a page. There is a reduced and hurried form of the Usual Hand on pp. 85 (l. 32)–90, 113, 142.

Blake raised lower-case initial letters to capitals on p. 7, l. 6 ('Cruelty'), l. 18 ('Caves'); p. 14, l. 14 ('Men'), l. 16 ('Valleys'), l. 22 ('Children'); p. 15, l. 8 ('Human'), l. 11 ('Horse'); p. 19, l. 9 ('Seven'); p. 20, l. 8 ('Gates'); p. 21, l. 4 ('One'), l. 9 ('He'), l. 13 ('Beulah'); p. 27, l. 1 ('Great'); p. 28, l. 26 ('Globe'), l. 31 ('Sons'); p. 30, l. 19 ('Mountains'); p. 33, l. 4 ('Cubes'), l. 6 ('World'), l. 17, ('Body', 'Abyss'); p. 34, l. 15 ('Elemental'); p. 40, l. 2 ('Man'), l. 3 ('Shadow'); p. 41, l. 7 ('Eyes'), l. 12 ('Love'); p. 52, l. 10 ('Trumpets Horns & Clarions'); p. 60, l. 2 ('Extinction'); p. 63, l. 10 ('Golgonooza'); p. 67, l. 17 ('Woman'); p. 80, l. 30 ('When'); p. 81, l. 15 ('Men'); p. 82, l. 24 ('Tree'), l. 34 ('Orc'); p. 85, l. 2 ('Embracing'); p. 92, l. 24 ('Cisterns'); p. 122, l. 32 ('Eyes'); p. 135, l. 39 ('Odors'); p. 136, l. 10 ('Yet'), l. 35 ('Nettle'). I have not observed a place where Blake reduced an initial capital letter to lower case.

---

[1] I am grateful for advice, particularly about drawings in *Vala*, from Mr. Wm. R. Hughes.

[2] A table of the handwriting on each page may be found in *Vala* (1963), 210–13.

[3] The Modified Copperplate Hand turns into the most beautiful Copperplate Hand at p. 42, l. 10.

DRAWINGS: Eighty-four pages have *Vala* sketches, most of which seem to have been made after the text was transcribed. The majority of the drawings were begun in pencil;[1] some were confirmed in ink[2] or crayon;[3] and a few were continued in water-colour wash.[4]

Nights III–VIIa (pp. 37–90) originally ended after nine pages of text, and the tenth page (pp. 46, 56, 66, 76, 86) was left blank for a design. In Nights III, V–VIIa Blake completed the designs in the spaces he had left for them, but on p. 55 in Night IV he made a note to himself to 'Bring in here the Globe of Blood as in the B of Urizen'; he erased 'The End of the Fourth Book' and added thirty-two more lines which filled the space he had left for a design on p. 56. Apparently he then made a design on a separate leaf (now p. 112) illustrating the passage to be borrowed on p. 55 from *Urizen*, and stabbed pp. 111–12 with pp. 43–84. (Later, when he needed paper for additions to Night VIII, he used the recto of this drawing. Therefore p. 111 belongs in Night VIII and p. 112 apparently with Night IV.)

The text on pp. 16, 19, 22, 54, 58 is written *over* large, vague sketches which precede and are presumably not related to the poem. The large drawings on pp. 16, 58 (q.v.) are for *Night Thoughts* (1797) p. 65 and probably not for *Vala* at all.[5] Pages 20, 126, 132 have childish scrawls *over* the text[6] which presumably do not illustrate *Vala*.

PAGE-NUMBERS: Blake wrote ink numbers (1–9, 11–14) on pp. 3–11, 13–14, 17–18. All the rest of the numbers are in pencil; most were demonstrably added after 1893, and all probably lack Blake's authority.[7]

LINE-NUMBERS: Blake numbered the lines of Nights I–II early in pencil by hundreds and then later, after many revisions, in ink by fifties. The rest of the Nights were generally numbered early in ink in fifties (including the last line) and later in pencil in fives or tens. Since both pencil and ink line-numbers include some added lines but omit others added still later, it

---

[1] The sketches on pp. 1–2, 10–12, 16, 19, 21–2, 30, 39–41, 48, 89, 96, 139, 144 are in pencil only.

[2] The sketches on pp. 3–5, 50, 116, 128 are in ink as well as pencil.

[3] Pages 6–9, 13–14, 17–18, 20, 23–4, 26–9, 31–2, 35–6, 38, 42, and all the rest to p. 138 (save pp. 48, 70, 84, 88, 90, 96, 114) are in Black crayon as well as pencil; on pp. 14, 60, 62, 68, 86, 98, 100, 102, 104, 106, 108, 110, 118, 122, 130, 134, 136 the background is shaded in crayon; pp. 25, 31, 37 are in crayon only.

[4] There are water-colour washes on pp. 3 (Brown, Blue, Grey, Black), 4 (Grey, Brown, Black), 5 (Blue, Grey, Pink, Brown, Black), 7 (Black, Grey), 15 (Brown), 31 (Grey, Brown), and 128 (Blue, pinkish-Purple, Brown). Some lines are deleted in Grey wash (e.g. pp. 6, 8) even though Grey wash is not used in the designs on these pages.

[5] The *Night Thoughts* engravings found in *Vala* do not seem to have exerted an appreciable effect upon the text or designs.

[6] Perhaps these scrawls are by John Linnell's children. The erasures of erotic drawings might have been made by Blake, by Linnell, or by Linnell's children.

[7] For fuller details of the pencil page-numbers, see *Vala* (1963), 197, 207.

seems fairly clear that Blake added the line-numbers during the course of his revisions.[1]

The ink line-numbers link pp. 3–18, 23–32, 33–6, 37–46, 47–54, 55–6,[2] 57–66, 67–76, 77–84, 91–8, 99–110, 117–39. Pages 19–22, 87–90, 111–16 have no line-numbers.

STAB-HOLES: Pages 1–20, 23–42 seem to have been stitched four times through seven stab holes; the First is *c.* 9·1 cm from the top, the Second 0·24 cm lower, the Third *c.* 1·1 cm lower, the Fourth *c.* 7·5 cm lower, the Fifth 0·8 cm lower, the Sixth *c.* 7·2 cm lower, and the Seventh *c.* 5·1 cm lower. (1) First pp. 1–18, 23–30 were stitched through the Second, Fifth, and Seventh holes. (2) Second, pp. 31–42 were added to these pages (pp. 16–15 now reversed) through the First, Fourth, and Sixth holes.[3] (3) Third, to put pp. 15–16 right,[4] pp. 1–18, 23–42 were stitched through the First, Fifth, and Seventh holes. (4) Fourth, pp. 19–20 were stitched with pp. 1–14, 17–42 through the First and Third holes.[5]

Pages 43–84, 111–12 were separately stabbed through three holes about 15 cm from the top and 4·15, 4·8 cm apart. The two sections (pp. 1–20, 23–42 and pp. 43–84, 111–12) were never stitched together.

N.B. Pages 21–2, 85–110, 113–40 were never stabbed at all.

CATCHWORDS: The catchwords are 'In' (pp. 3, 40), '[Enion *del*] ⌃So⌃' (p. 4), '[Where[6] *del*] ⌃Reard⌃' (p. 5), '[And(?) *del*] [Till (?) *del*]' (p. 6), '[Why *del*]' (p. 8), '[But (?) *del*]' (p. 9), 'I' (p. 10), 'They' (pp. 12, 15), 'Stretch' (p. 13), 'Enion' (p. 16), 'Why' (p. 17), 'And' (p. 26), 'That' (p. 28), 'Spread' (p. 29), 'The' (p. 32), 'Infolded' (p. 37), 'Raise' (p. 38), '[Leaping (?) *del*]' (p. 42, after l. 20). All the catchwords match the following pages in the present order except for replaced catchwords and pp. 6, 8, 42. Pages 9, 43 begin with additions in a hand different from the catchwords, and the lines to which the catchwords refer are evidently lost. Apparently the page beginning with words to match the catchword on p. 6 is also lost.

The catchwords associate pp. 3–4, 5–6, 9–14, 15–18, 25–30, 31–4, 37–42.

ORDER: Pages 1–18, 21–2, 19(–20), 23–104, 113–16, 105–12, 117–39.

In 1889, when Ellis & Yeats began to transcribe *Vala*, 'it was unpaged and unsorted'.[7] How had Blake arranged it?

---

[1] For detailed arguments about which lines are counted and which omitted in the line-numeration, see *Vala* (1963), 202–6.

[2] The line-number joining p. 55 with p. 54 is wrong by only one, and the sense joins the two pages perfectly.

[3] The first hole does not appear in pp. 15–16.

[4] The catchword demonstrates that the order should be 15–16.

[5] In pp. 1–2, 33–4, 37–8, the Third stab hole missed the paper. This accounts for all the stab holes in these pages, but other explanations might suffice. For details of the stab holes in each leaf, see *Vala* (1963), 214–15. There are from one to thirteen holes in the top margin of pp. 47–50, 53–4, 57–8, 91–6, 99–108, 117–18, 121–2, 125–6, 129–30, 133–40, which do not seem to have been used for stitching.

[6] ?Or 'When'.

[7] *The Poetical Works of William Blake*, ed. E. J. Ellis & W. B. Yeats (1893),

Pages 3–18, 23–36, 37–46, 47–56, 57–66, 67–76, 77–84, 91–8, 99–110, 117–39 are linked by Blake's *page-numbers* (pp. 3–11, 13–14, 17–18), by his *line-numbers* (pp. 3–18, 23–32, 33–6, 37–46, 47–56, 57–66, 67–76, 77–84, 91–8, 99–110, 117–39), and by his *catchwords* (pp. 3–4, 5–6, 9–14, 15–18, 25–30, 31–4, 37–42). If we further link the title-page (p. 1) and 'The End' of one Night with the beginning of the next, the pattern becomes pp. 1–18, 23–84, 91–110, 117–39.

Pages 19–22, 85–90, 111–16, which are missing from this sequence, can be fitted in without great difficulty. Since 'messengers from Beulah' arrive on p. 21 (l. 6) and finish their message on p. 19 (l. 6), p. 19 seems to follow pp. 21–2. Page 19 concludes with 'End of The First Night', so pp. 21–2, 19 presumably come after the 'End of The First Night' on p. 18.[1] Page 20 does not fit well with p. 19 or with any other passage; it seems to be an additional fragment never integrated with the rest of the poem.

Page 84 is strongly linked to p. 85 by narrative continuity. Pages 87–90 are written on two halves of a large leaf in the hand in which the last additions were made to p. 86 and continue its narrative. The text on pp. 85–7, 90 is essentially a single addition to Night VIIa.

Page 112 bears a design which apparently illustrates a passage to be added on p. 55. The text on the recto (p. 111) seems intended as a replacement for p. 110, ll. 29–37 which were deleted. Probably yet later p. 110, ll. 38–41 were added to replace p. 111; if so, p. 111 was abandoned and, like pp. 20, 141–5, is not integral to *Vala*.

According to inserted directions, the top passage on p. 113 was to be entered on p. 104 and the bottom passage on p. 113 plus its continuation on p. 115[2] was to be entered on p. 106. The direction on p. 106 to 'turn back three leaves' to p. 113 and the one on p. 116 to 'turn over leaf' to p. 106 clearly indicate that the order here was pp. 103–4, 113–16, 105–6. The over-all order then should be pp. 1–18, 21–2, 19 (–20), 23–104, 113–16, 105–12, 117–39.[3]

Pages 141–6 were small leaves apparently never bound by Blake with pp. 1–140. The order of the text indicates that p. 144 should precede p. 143 and that they are presently bound backwards.

ERRATA:[4] 'has[*t*]' (p. 4, l. 12)
'des[*c*]ending' (p. 5, l. 41)
'Speterous' for 'Spectrous' (p. 9, l. 8)

ii. 300. The page-numbers of *Vala* refer to the order of pages as bound in the British Museum.

[1] However, D. J. Sloss & J. P. R. Wallis (ed., *The Prophetic Works of William Blake*) rather awkwardly add pp. 21–2, 19–20 to the apparent end of Night I on p. 9.

[2] Page 113 ends with Los saying 'Hear me repeat my Generations' and p. 115 begins with a list of 'the Sons of Los & Enitharmon'.

[3] At a late stage, Blake turned Night VIIb inside out, so that the order there should be pp. 95 (l. 15)–8, 91–5 (l. 14).

[4] Ignoring oddities in overly or insufficiently deleted passages.

'warr' (p. 12, l. 28)
'Luvah['s]' (p. 13, l. 9)
'let'?for 'led' (p. 19, l. 3)
'As[c]ending' (p. 30, l. 34)
'hum[m]ing' (p. 34, l. 73)
'su[l]phuireous' (p. 44, l. 7)
'gnasshing' (p. 44, l. 16)
'strugg[l]ing' (p. 50, l. 21)
'ribbs' (p. 54, l. 13)
'& &' (p. 58, l. 9)
'firma[m]ent' (p. 58, l. 25)
'wire' for 'were' (p. 70, l. 31)
'stre[t]chd' (p. 73, l. 34)
'his' for 'him' (p. 75, l. 11)
'excentric' (p. 75, l. 28)
'be' for 'you' or 'ye' (p. 80, l. 3)
'Urizen['s]' (p. 90, l. 59)
'crumb[l]ing' (p. 91, l. 7)
'trapppings' (p. 91, l. 29)
'in' for 'on' (p. 94, l. 33)
'Mo[u]rning' (p. 95, l. 3)
'B[r]other' (p. 95, l. 6)
'to' apparently omitted (p. 95, l. 32)
'the[e]' (p. 98, l. 28)
'writ[h]ing' (p. 101, l. 12)
'deci[e]t' (p. 101, l. 26)
'fal[l]ing' (p. 102, l. 29)
?'come' omitted (p. 103, l. 17)
'num[m]ing'[1] (p. 103, l. 30)
'Jerusa[le]m' (p. 104, l. 1)
'divin[e]' (p. 104, l. 53)
'Fo[r]lorn' (p. 104, l. 65)
'rec[iev]ing' (p. 105, l. 57)
'dec[i]etful' (p. 106, l. 34)
'forn' for 'form' (p. 106, l. 47)
'Eyes' for 'Eye' (p. 107, l. 9)
'whereever' (p. 110, l. 26)
'thou[sa]nd' (p. 113, l. 27)
'wherefor[e]' (p. 115, l. 13)
'des[c]ended' (p. 115, l. 26)
'infinitie' for 'infinite' or 'infinity' (p. 122, l. 24)
'ou[t]braving' (p. 123, l. 3)
'hipocrisy' (p. 123, l. 31)
'ornaminted' (p. 124, l. 11)
'horse[s]' (p. 124, l. 15)

---

[1] 'numming' is Blake's ordinary spelling for 'numbing'.

'ha[n]d' (p. 124, l. 26)
'vall[e]y' (p. 128, l. 19; p. 129, l. 12)
'mour[n]d' (p. 129, l. 18)
'fa[i]nt' (p. 129, l. 30)
'l[i]ght' (p. 129, l. 36)
'roon' for 'room' (p. 135, l. 8)
'wodd' for 'wood' (p. 137, l. 25)
'beholds' for 'beheld' (p. 138, l. 25)

'The Riddle Manuscript' (?1802)

(Text p. 1298)

COLLECTION: *G. E. Bentley, Jr.*

LEAF-SIZE: 10·6 × 15·5 cm.

WATERMARK: None.

DATE: ?Summer 1802. See below.

DESCRIPTION: On the verso of the 'Riddle MS' is a proof before letters of Blake's 14th engraving, dated 9 September 1802 in the published state, for Hayley's *Designs to A Series of Ballads*. The leaf was trimmed to conform to the proof, and this trimming has removed the beginnings of the lines and perhaps some lines at the top (the letters at the top and left are transcribed here with some hesitation) of the text written the other way up on the recto. Since the MS fairly clearly preceded the print, September 1802 is the latest likely date. Since Blake is unlikely to have taken much pains to preserve such a trifle, September 1800, when he moved to Felpham, is the earliest likely date. Summer 1802 seems a good guess.

The page may be a list of riddles playing with words—'Love lie Girl' may equal 'Lovely Girl', 'Love Errs' equals 'Lovers', 'Isinglass' equals 'Eyes in Glass', 'an Ell ["*L*"] taken from London is Undone [*ondon*]'.

'Blake's Memorandum' (?August 1803)

(Text pp. 1299–130)

COLLECTION: *UNTRACED*. A transcript, apparently by a contemporary from Blake's original, is in Trinity College, Hartford, Connecticut.

WATERMARK: '1802', with a Britannia-type crowned shield.

DATE: ?Late August 1803.

Blake's 'Refutation' was clearly prepared after the Deposition of 16 Aug. and before Blake appeared at the Quarter Sessions on 4 Oct. 1803 to answer the charge of sedition.[1] Probably Blake collected his thoughts on the evidence shortly after the Depositions were made, in late August 1803, and

---

[1] *Blake Records*, 122–37.

communicated them to his lawyer (?R. Daly), who had them transcribed for his own use.

DESCRIPTION: On a folded sheet are two documents apparently collected for the use of Blake's lawyer at his trial for sedition. The manuscript consists of: 1ʳ 'The Information and Complaint of John Scolfield';[1] 1ᵛ–2ᵛ 'Blake's Memorandum'.

'The Ballads [Pickering] Manuscript'
(? after 1807)
(Text pp. 1302–18)

COLLECTION: PIERPONT MORGAN LIBRARY.

WATERMARK: None. The paper is that used in Hayley's *Designs to A Series of Ballads* (1802).[2]

LEAF–SIZE: 12·5 × 18·4 cm.

DATE: ?after 1807.

The earliest possible date, as shown by the use of leaves from Hayley's *Ballad* of 1 July 1802, is June or July 1802. Three of the poems ('Mary', 'The Grey Monk', and 'The Golden Net') seem to be copied from drafts of 1803. Other leaves from unsold copies of the *Ballads* (1802) were apparently used between 1807 and 1824.[3]

This evidence suggests that the Ballads Manuscript poems were transcribed in their present form after 1805, when publication of the separate quarto *Ballads* (1802) was abandoned (see Blake's letter of 22 Jan. 1805), and probably after 1807. The dates of original composition may well be 1800–4 for the Ballads Manuscript poems.

DESCRIPTION: The manuscript consists of 22 pages (11 leaves) numbered 1–22 in the top outer corners of the pages in the Black ink in which the text is written. The text is fairly copied in ink which is uniformly Black[4] except for some corrections recorded in the notes. There are faint offsets from the writing on many pages.

¹ *Blake Records*, 122–37.
² At the bottom left of p. 16 appear fragments of an erased printed word which is evidently the catchword 'With' on p. 20 of Hayley's *Designs to A Series of Ballads* for which Blake made engravings published on 1 July 1802. Blake's Ballads Manuscript paper was obtained by taking the abandoned *Ballads* (1802) sheets and cutting off the sections bearing Hayley's text and the '1802' watermark, leaving the wide inner margins for Blake's own poems.
³ See 'The Date of Blake's Pickering Manuscript', *Studies in Bibliography*, xix (1966), 232–43.
⁴ The initial letters in the following words were originally written as lower case and were altered to capitals in the same Black ink: 'Frown' ('The Smile' l. 5), 'Eyes' ('The Golden Net' l. 8), 'Reap' and 'Every' ('The Mental Traveller' ll. 7, 96), 'Fair', 'Golden', 'Envious Race', and 'Evening' ('Mary' ll. 2, 6, 22, 36), 'Rising' and 'Winners' ('Auguries of Innocence' ll. 18, 117).

TITLE: The manuscript has long been called 'The Pickering Manuscript', after B. M. Pickering, who owned it for a few years, but 'The Ballads Manuscript' seems a more useful title, since it describes both the poems themselves and the paper on which they are written.

'The Order' of the *Songs* (?after 1807)

(Text pp. 1319–20)

COLLECTION: LIBRARY OF CONGRESS.[1]

WATERMARK: None.

LEAF-SIZE: 19·6 × 27·1 cm.

DATE: ?after 1818.

The only copy of the *Songs* arranged in the order given in 'The Order' (copy V) is on paper watermarked '1818'. Therefore 'The Order' was probably produced after 1818.

DESCRIPTION: The manuscript consists of a sheet of paper, folded to make four pages, with stitching marks in the inner margin and the number '102' at the top of p. 1 added when the sheet was part of a volume of Blakeana formed about 1853. A note on the first page describes its provenance, the text is on pp. 2–3, and p. 4 is blank and somewhat dirty. The text is in Black ink.

There are two series of checks in the margins by most numbers. The left-hand series includes all the numbers but 1 and 44, corresponding to no known copy of the *Songs*. The right-hand series includes all but nos. 17–18, 23, 28–34, 46–9, 51–4 (with Xs before nos. 1, 5–6), corresponding to copy F of *Innocence*, except that F has no. 23.

Upcott's Autograph Album (16 January 1826)

(Text pp. 1321–2)

COLLECTION: Berg Collection of the NEW YORK PUBLIC LIBRARY.[2]

WATERMARK: None on Blake's page.

LEAF-SIZE: 21·0 × 27·0 cm.

DATE: 16 January 1826 is the date of Blake's autograph. The signatures with which it is bound are dated from 1820 to 1828; the portraits which illustrate the signatures (including Phillips's portrait of Blake engraved

---

[1] A lithographic facsimile was published with the Muir facsimile of the *Marriage* (1885).

[2] The MS is reproduced in D. V. Erdman, 'Reliques of the Contemporaries of William Upcott, "Emperor of Autographs" ', *Bulletin of the New York Public Library*, lxiv (1960), 581–7. William Upcott (1779–1845) was the natural son of Ozias Humphry and was, like his father, a friend and patron of Blake.

for Cunningham's *Lives* [1830]) have dates running into the 1830s; the index[1] is dated 27 September 1833; and the title-pages are dated 1833. It is clear that Blake's signature was secured on 16 January 1826, and that the materials were arranged in volumes, indexed, and bound in 1833.

DESCRIPTION: Blake's autograph appears below that of B. R. Haydon on a leaf inserted in Volume II of a two-volume collection of autographs. The hand-lettered title-page of Volume II reads: 'RELIQUES / OF MY / CONTEMPORARIES. / — / WILLIAM UPCOTT. / — / WITH PORTRAITS. / AUTHORS, ARTISTS, FOREIGNERS & MISCEL-LANEOUS. / My Life steals on:— / ROGERS. / 1833'; the title to the first volume is the same in substance except for a motto from Crabbe.

MS INSCRIPTIONS ON DESIGNS

'Father & Mother . . .' (?1793)
(Text p. 1323)

DATE: ?1793, Mr. Martin Butlin's estimate for the date of the drawing.

DESCRIPTION: The faint sketch of a woman with butterfly wings is numbered '11 [9 *del* 10 *del* 13 *del*]'. The intention of the drawing and its relation to the words on the page are not clear. On the verso is a sketch for *Milton* pl. 45.

'The Bible of Hell' (?1793)
(Text p. 1323)

DATE: ?1793; see p. 1677.

DESCRIPTION: The words are written 'in title-page form' on the back of 'A drawing', according to E. J. Ellis and W. B. Yeats (*The Works of William Blake* [1893], i. 46). For the possible context for this unknown work, see p. 1677.

'Is all joy forbidden' (?1793)
(Text p. 1323)

DATE: ?1793. Embracing figures at the top left are similar to those at the bottom of the title-page of the *Marriage* (?1790–3).

DESCRIPTION: The pencil drawing (related to *For Children* [1793] pl. 14— p. 656—and reproduced in *Pencil Drawings* [1927], pl. 7) represents an old man brooding over a book, as one weeping child stands at the left and two more lie at the right. The inscription is at the top.

---

[1] In the index appears: 'Blake (William) artis*t* & author of designs for Blair's Grave &c.—[*Page*] 19'.

'How I pity' (?1793)
(Text p. 1323)

DATE: ?1793.

DESCRIPTION: At the centre of concentric circles, like a web, in a pencil design similar to *For Children* (1793) pl. 14 (p. 656), an old man crouches before two smaller, prone, childish figures, who seem to be wrapped in webs.

'Visions of Eternity' (?1793)
(Text p. 1323)

DATE: ?1793, like *Visions* (1793).

DESCRIPTION: On the verso is a rough sketch of a standing man with outspread arms; on the recto is a sketch of a title-page, with branches and flying figures around the inscription.

'For Children The Gates of Hell' (?1793)
(Text p. 1323)

DATE: ?1793, like *For Children: The Gates of Paradise* (1793).[1]

DESCRIPTION: The text is the title on a sketched title-page. Nothing more is known of the work.

'Behold your King' (?1795)
(Text p. 1323)

DATE: ?1795. Perhaps it is related to the Bible series for Butts of 1795 ff.

DESCRIPTION: A figure (?Pilate) in a conical hat at the left of a rough sketch points to another figure (?Christ) at the top right and says, according to the pencil inscription at the bottom: 'Behold your King'.

Gray Designs (1797)
(Text pp. 1324–31)

DATE: 1797.

In a letter of *c.* 1–4 November 1797,[2] Nancy Flaxman said that 'Flaxman has employ'd him [*Blake*] to Illuminate the works of Grey for my library'.

---

[1] G. Keynes (*The Gates of Paradise* [1968], i. 3) suggests that the date is 'perhaps about 1818', when Blake was revising *For Children* as *For the Sexes*.

[2] BM Add. MSS 39790, ff. 3–4. For the date see M. K. Woodworth, 'Blake's Illustrations for Gray's Poems', *Notes and Queries*, ccxv (1970), 312–13.

Cumberland reported that Blake asked only ten guineas for the designs,[1] which is the price of friendship, not of commerce.

DESCRIPTION: The leaves of the title-page and pp. 43–158 of POEMS / BY / MR. GRAY / [*in pencil:* DRAWINGS / by / WILLIAM BLAKE] / — / A NEW EDITION. / — / LONDON: / PRINTED FOR J. MURRAY, (No. 31.) FLEET- / STREET. / MDCCLXXXX [*1790*] (watermarked with chain lines and about 8.6×14.7 cm) are inset into fifty-eight much larger leaves of 1794 / J WHATMAN paper. On each of the larger leaves is a drawing by Blake in illustration of Gray's poems, and on the verso of the last leaf of each poem is a manuscript list by Blake of the lines illustrated by, or the titles of, the drawings for the succeeding poem. Occasional mistakes indicate that: (1) The centres of the WHATMAN sheets were cut out; (2) The leaves of POEMS BY MR. GRAY were inset, with the recto of the text leaves always overlapping at the outer margin and the verso always partly obscured by the larger sheet; (3) A Red border was carefully drawn on the larger sheet just outside the incision and occasionally showing on the inner sheet; (4) Often while this Red border was still wet, the surrounding designs were drawn in pencil and water-coloured;[2] (?5) The design titles and the poems were written;[3] (?6) The pages were numbered in ink at the top outer corners; (7) The work was bound in contemporary three-quarter calf over marbled boards[4] and has been repeatedly rebacked since then[5] without being trimmed or gilt; (8) A drawing lettered 'William Blake / Drawn by John Flaxman' was pasted, to the fly-leaf facing the title-page, *over* an offset of the Red border from the title-page, probably long after the volume was bound. There are clear Brown fingerprints on the title-page, pp. 58, 158, and occasionally elsewhere on the designs.

Numbers: The *page-numbers* given here are those of the printed text of Gray. The ordinary design numbers for each poem were made by Blake. The design numbers [*in square brackets*] are an editorial interpolation incorporating all the designs in one series. Each large page is also numbered by Blake in the top outer margin in ink.

---

[1] *Blake Records*, 187.

[2] Occasionally the pencil or water-colour overlaps the wide border or the inset page (e.g. pp. 67, 71, 75, 126, 134, 148, 150, 153, 155) or the water-colour has made the Red border run (e.g. p. 131).

[3] The pencil Xs by the lines illustrated may or may not have been made by Blake. Similar symbols, some of them probably not by Blake, are used in the drawings for Young's *Night Thoughts*.

[4] The designs are coloured so close to the inner margins that they could not have been bound when Blake was colouring them. Further, the water-colours when wet have occasionally blurred on to pages not now facing each other.

[5] The two fly-leaves in front and the one in the back all have different watermarks.

Title-page for Blair's *Grave* (1806)
(Text p. 1331)

DATE: 1806.

DESCRIPTION: At the sides of a tomb are two women, one, at the left, with bat wings and one with heavy, moth wings, while from the top of it rises a thinly draped woman with clasped hands. The inscription is on the tomb.

'The Fall of Man' (1807)
(Text p. 1332)

DATE: '1807 W Blake inv' is inscribed on the drawing and presumably applies to the words on the back of the drawing as well.

DESCRIPTION: On the cardboard back of his water-colour-and-ink drawing of 'The Fall of Man' Blake has written his description in his Copperplate Hand in pencil.

'Epitome of Hervey's *Meditations*' (after 1808)
(Text p. 1332)

DATE: After 1808, like the drawing.[1]

DESCRIPTION: Blake's water-colour called 'Epitome of Hervey's *Meditations among the Tombs*' has many inscriptions identifying the figures as they rise toward or fall from heaven.

L'Allegro and *Il Penseroso* (?1816)
(Text pp. 1332–8)

DATE: *c.* 1816.

The *L'Allegro* and *Il Penseroso* designs were probably made about 1816, and their descriptions are presumably from the same date. At the same time Blake engraved 'Mirth' from *L'Allegro* and called on Thomas Frognall Dibdin to discuss 'Milton's minor poems'.[2]

DESCRIPTION: Blake wrote descriptions of his six *L'Allegro* and six *Il Penseroso* drawings, one each on twelve sheets of paper, and numbered them 1–12. The titles, given here in brackets, are on one side (now pasted down on larger leaves and only legible against strong light), and the descriptions on the other. Each description leaf seems to have a horizontal crease near the top, as if it had been folded.

---

[1] M. Butlin, *William Blake*: a complete catalogue of the works in the Tate Gallery (1971), 45–6.
[2] *Blake Records*, 242.

'Return Alpheus' (?1816)

(Text p. 1338)

DATE: ?1816, like *L'Allegro* and *Il Penseroso*.

DESCRIPTION: At the bottom of a very rough sketch, which may represent a river god lifting his head from the waves while the personified valleys scatter flowers, is the inscription.

'All Genius varies . . .' (?1819)

(Text p. 1339)

DATE: ?1819, when Blake's interest in the Visionary Heads was raised by Varley and his interest in phrenology was re-aroused by Spurzheim (see p. 1501). The drawing survives with a collection of Visionary Heads and may therefore be associated with them in time.

DESCRIPTION: Blake's words are inscribed at the bottom of a drawing of Nine Grotesque Heads.

List of Apostles (?1823)

(Text p. 1339)

DATE: ?1823.

The date could be almost any time from 1802, when the *Ballads* (1802) leaves came into Blake's hands, until his death in 1827. They were probably used after 1805, when publication of the 1802 *Ballads* was officially abandoned, and before 1824, when the *Job* pencil sketches which they accompany must have been completed and, when Blake had made his engravings, given to Linnell. The '1823' below Blake's initials may date the apostles as well.

DESCRIPTION: Pages iii–iv, 37–81 of the 1802 *Ballads* were used as a wrapper for Blake's *Job* sketches 'Done for me John Linnell' (according to the inscription on the innermost wrapper) probably about 1824. They bear fifty versions of the initials WB, including Blake's usual monogram:

There is also an A D like Dürer's, a sketch of a head for *Job*, two rough sketches of the dog on *Job* pl. 3, 22, and the list of disciples.

The list could be for subjects of a series of paintings—or it could have served a great many other purposes.

---

¹ The two leaves were folded and are now divided along the creases into four leaves; p. 38, the dirtiest page, was probably the outside wrapper.

Dante Designs (1824–7)

(Text pp. 1339–44)

DATE: 1824–7.

Blake was at work on his 102 designs and his seven engravings for Dante's *Divine Comedy* from 1824 to 1827.[1]

DESCRIPTION: Blake's identifications and comments quoted here appear chiefly in pencil on parts of the designs which might otherwise have been obscure.

Most of the Dante designs have as well an ink inscription by Blake at the bottom saying something like 'HELL Canto 4' (as on No. 7), the same thing (often erased) in pencil, frequently at the bottom right; something similar in pencil on a corner of the verso; and perhaps the same thing in pencil erased in the middle of the verso. These hundreds of working identifications are omitted in the present text.

All the Dante designs are reproduced in *Illustrations to the Divine Comedy of Dante by William Blake* (1922) and in A. S. Roe, *Blake's Illustrations to the Divine Comedy* (1953); the latter is the source of the uniform numeration and of much of the scholarly information given here.

Illuminated Genesis Manuscript (1827)

(Text pp. 1344–5)

DATE: 1827, the date given by Gilchrist,[2] is confirmed by the very tentative nature of the latter part of the transcription and designs.

DESCRIPTION: The eleven leaves of Blake's illuminated transcription of Genesis consist of one tentative and one fairly finished sketch of a title-page plus nine leaves of illuminated text. The text is in pencil confirmed in Green ink at first (through 2: 5, except for the title of Chapter 2). The ruled portion of leaf 11 is mostly blank.

In transcribing Genesis, Blake frequently altered punctuation and capitalization, changed 'and' to '&', and omitted the 'e' in the past tense; he often shortened 'unto' to 'to' (2: 19, 24; 3: 6, 17 ['to the voice']; 4: 5, 7) and reversed 'shalt' and 'thou' (3: 16, 19 [twice]; 4: 12). The most significant addition is 'Adamah' written over (2: 7, 19), or in parentheses after, 'the ground' (2: 9; 3: 19; 4: 10, 11, 12). His other changes in the text, many of them apparently accidental, are indicated in the footnotes, the unrevised King James version in square brackets, Blake's additions *in italics*.

MS INSCRIPTIONS ON DESIGNS

(Text pp. 1323–45)

The inscriptions printed in the present text are written on the designs themselves.

For titles and descriptions of other pictures see the *Notebook* (?1793–?1818) (pp. 1708–16), 'The Accusers' (1793) (p. 162), *America* (1793) pl. 2–3

---

[1] *Blake Records*, 290 ff.   [2] Gilchrist (1863), 246; (1942), 259.

Bibliographical Notes

(p. 136 n.), The Small Book of Designs (?1795),[1] The Large Book of Designs (?1795),[2] 'Albion Rose' (?1796) (p. 315), *Vala* (?1796–?1807) p. 100, l. 4 (p. 1223 n.), *Jerusalem* (1804–?20) pl. 97 (pp. 633–4 n.), 'To the Queen' (1807) (pp. 1690–1), *Descriptive Catalogue* (1809) ¶6, 8 (pp. 828–9), 'Joseph of Arimathea' (?1809) (pp. 642–3), 'Mirth' (?1820) (p. 662), and 'Laocoon' (?1820) (pp. 663–6).

This section yet omits most of the simple titles Blake wrote on his pictures. Some of these are:

'Death of Earl Goodwin' (Royal Academy, 1780)
'A breach in a city, the morning after a battle' (Royal Academy, 1784)
'War unchained by an angel, Fire, Pestilence, and Famine following' (Royal Academy, 1784)
'Joseph making himself known to his brethren' (Royal Academy, 1785)
'Joseph ordering Simeon to be bound' (Royal Academy, 1785)
'Joseph's brethren bowing before him' (Royal Academy, 1785)
'The Bard, from Gray' (Royal Academy, 1785)
'Edward & Elinor' (engraving, 1793)
'Job / What is Man That thou shouldest Try him Every Moment? Job vii C 17 & 18' (engraving, 1793)
'Ezekiel / I take away from thee the Desire of thine Eyes, Ezekiel xxiv C 16' (engraving, 1794)
'Newton' (?1795)[3]
'Nebuchadnezzar' (?1795)[3]
'Elohim creating Adam' (?1795)[3]
'God speaking[?] to Adam' (?1795)[3]
'Lamech and his two Wives' (?1795)[3]
'The House of Death Milton' (?1795)[3]
'The last supper⌊:⌋ "Verily I say unto you, that one of you shall betray me." Matt. chap. 26. ver. 21' (Royal Academy, 1799)
'The loaves and fishes' (Royal Academy, 1800)
Hebrew for 'And Enoch walked with God, and he was not: for God took him', Genesis v. 24 (engraving, *c.* 1807)
'Jacob's Dream: Vide Genesis, chap. xxviii. ver. 12' (Royal Academy, 1808)
'Christ in the sepulchre, guarded by angels' (Royal Academy, 1808)
'Adam and Eve' (?1809)[4]
'Canute Dark Hair & Eyes' (?1819)[5]
'The Egyptian Taskmaster who was killed and Buried by Moses' (?1819)[6]

---

[1] i.e. *Marriage* (?1790–3) pl. 11, 14, (pp. 85, 88), *Visions* (1793) pl. 2, 10 (pp. 102 n., 115 n.), *Urizen* (1794) pl. 1–2, 5, 9–10, 12 (pp. 239 n., 240 n., 244 n., 247 n., 253 n.).   [2] *Urizen* pl. 22 (p. 271 n.).

[3] M. Butlin, *William Blake* (1971), colour prints in the Tate.

[4] *Blake's Pencil Drawings*, ed. G. Keynes (1956).

[5] C. H. Collins Baker, *Catalogue of William Blake's Drawings and Paintings in the Huntington Library*, rev. R. R. Wark (1957).

[6] *The Blake Collection of W. Graham Robertson*, ed. K. Preston (1952).

'Saul King of Israel somewhat influenced by the Evil Spirit' (?1819)[1]
'Corinna the Rival of Pindar', 'Corinna the Grecian Poetess' (?1819)[2, 1]
'The Three Tabernacles / The Lamb of God'[2]
'The Church Yard'[2]
'Death'[2]
'Mirth'[2, 3]
'Hope'[2]
'Pilgrim's Progress', 'Christian returning home', 'Apollyon' (?1824)[4]
'Here Lieth Thomas Day aged 100' (*Night Thoughts* drawing [?1797] for
    Night IX, p. 6, British Museum Print Room)

MARGINALIA (?1788): Swedenborg, *Heaven and Hell* (1784)
(Text p. 1349)

TITLE: A / TREATISE / CONCERNING / HEAVEN AND HELL, /
AND OF THE / Wonderful Things therein, / AS / HEARD AND SEEN, /
BY THE HONOURABLE AND LEARNED / EMANUEL SWEDEN-
BORG, / Of the SENATORIAL ORDER of NOBLES in the Kingdom of SWEDEN.
/ — / TRANSLATED FROM THE ORIGINAL LATIN [by William Cookworth &
Thomas Hartley]. / — / THE SECOND EDITION. / — / Where there is
no Vision, the people perish. Prov. xxix. 18. / The invisible things of Him
from the creation of the world are clearly / seen, being understood by the
things that are made. Rom. i. 20. / He that hath ears to hear, let him hear.
Luke xiv. 35. / = / London: Printed by R. HINDMARSH, No. 32, Clerken-
well-Close; / And Sold by T. EVANS, AND T. BUCKLAND, Paternoster-Row; /
J. DENIS and SON, New-Bridge-Street, Fleet-Street; / I. CLARK, Manchester;
T. MILLS, Wine-Street, Bristol; / S. HAZARD, Bath; and by all the other
Booksellers in Town / and Country. / M.DCC.LXXXIV.

COLLECTION: HARVARD.

DATE: ?1788.

The reference to a book of 1787 provides the earliest date for Blake's
marginalia. The latest is probably 1790, when such eager interest as the
comments suggest was modified by disillusionment. 1788 is a plausible guess
between the two.

DESCRIPTION: On the title-page is the signature 'William Blake'. Another
hand has made a note on the half-title on which in turn Blake comments
vigorously, indicating that Blake was not the first annotator.[5]

[1] *Pencil Drawings by William Blake*, ed. G. Keynes (1927).
[2] See note 6, p. 1741.   [3] See note 4, p, 1741.
[4] These titles appear on designs no. 1, 11, 20 for Bunyan's *The Pilgrim's Progress*
(watermarked J WHATMAN / 1824) in the Frick Collection, New York. The wicket
gate in no. 10 is marked 'KNOCK AND IT SHALL BE OPENED'. Most of
the drawings in the series bear other inscriptions, which I believe to be by Tatham;
'Apollyon' (above) may be in Tatham's hand as well.
[5] ¶333–4 are quoted by Erdman (p. 591) because they were 'scored' as 'by [a]
fingernail', but he does not say how he knows the finger-nail was Blake's.

MARGINALIA (1788): Lavater, *Aphorisms* (1788)

(Text pp. 1350–87)

TITLE: APHORISMS ON MAN / TRANSLATED [by J. H. Fuseli] / FROM THE ORIGINAL MANUSCRIPT / OF / THE REV. JOHN CASPAR LAVATER, / CITIZEN OF ZURIC. / — / — è cœlo descendit γνωθι σεαυτον / Juv. Sat. IX. / — / LONDON: / PRINTED FOR J. JOHNSON, / ST. PAUL'S CHURCH-YARD. / — / MDCCLXXXVIII.

COLLECTION: HUNTINGTON LIBRARY.

DATE: 1788.

From the facts that Blake engraved the frontispiece for this edition of Lavater's *Aphorisms*, and that his friend Fuseli made the translation, it may be confidently concluded that Blake read and annotated the volume in the year of publication.

DESCRIPTION: On the title-page Blake wrote '*Will.ᵐ Blake*' below 'LAVATER' and drew a heart around the two names in ink, and at the top of p. 1 he wrote 'Will. Blake' in the same ink as the notes. The notes on some paragraphs (e.g. 11, 39, 97, 98, 163, 410), the change from pencil to ink, and the change in pen-points indicate that Blake went through the book making comments several times.

Offsets: Faint impressions left by the ink before it dried appear in the normal way on the following facing pages: 42–3, 118–19, 156–7, 162–3, 170–1, 172–3, 174–5, 180–1, 188–9, 190–1, 204–5, 218–19, 220–1, 222–3, and the notes on these pages may have been made after the book was bound. Other offsets, however, were transferred from pages which do not at present face one another, and therefore the notes must have been made when the sheets were unbound. These are: 97 (G1ʳ)–100 (G2ᵛ); 115 (H2ʳ)–120 (H4ᵛ); 135 (I4ʳ)–82(F1ᵛ); 224 (O8ᵛ)–208 (N8ᵛ); *upside-down*: 64 (D8ᵛ)–66 (E1ᵛ), 139 (I6ʳ)–209 (O1ʳ); 207 (N8ʳ)–134 (I3ᵛ). Clearly the sheets were stacked on each other, higgledy-piggledy, when the ink of the annotations was still fresh and before the sheets were bound.

Erasures: There are illegible erasures by ¶ 70, 342, 452, 533, 612 ('?for . . . persons'), 638.

*X*s: There are Xs in the margin[1] beside ¶21, 32, 36, 37, 39, 54, 70, 71, 86, 92, 96–8, 121, 141, 150–1, 163–4, 168, 219, 226, 261, 276, 308, 338, 385–6, 389, 410, 414, 440, 444, 449, 460, 465, 486, 514, 518, 526, 543, 577, 588, 602 (?under the writing), 607, 619, 624, 638.

Pencil and Pen: Blake's comments on ¶10, 285, 287, 502, and 532 are in pencil; the rest are in ink. A dull pen is superseded by a conspicuously sharper one in ¶68, 71 (at the full stop), 124, 309 (at 'mark'), 334, 409 (after 'Noble'), 526, 539 (at 'mans female').

---

[1] Erdman (pp. 573–90) gives these as if they were by Blake. He says as well that the horizontal line in the margin beside ¶25 and the daggers by ¶289, 343 are by Blake. He seems sure that the pencil comments to ¶20, 503 are 'by two different writers', but Keynes (1957) and I think they are by Blake.

Corrections: The substantive misprints identified in the printed Errata list have been corrected.

Notes by Others: After Blake's comment on ¶21, 'See 384'¹ is written in a yellowed ink; after ¶280 is '115'; and after ¶ 384 is 'See 20 & 21'¹ in the same ink. ¶ 165 has parallel lines beside it in the margin in an ink somewhat different from that of Blake's comments. At the top of p. 220 (¶633) an unknown hand has written in pencil: 'Not an Apho[*rism*]'.

MARGINALIA (?1789): Swedenborg, *Divine Love and Divine Wisdom* (1788)

(Text pp. 1388–99)

TITLE: THE / WISDOM / OF / *ANGELS,* / CONCERNING / DIVINE LOVE / AND / DIVINE WISDOM. / — / TRANSLATED FROM THE ORIGINAL LATIN / OF THE / *Hon. EMANUEL SWEDENBORG* [by Dr. N. Tucker]. / — / LONDON: / PRINTED BY W. CHALKLEN, GROCERS COURT, POULTRY. / M.DCC.LXXXVIII.

COLLECTION: BRITISH MUSEUM.

DATE: ?1789.

The relatively uncritical nature of Blake's comments suggests that they were written before his disillusionment with Swedenborg about 1790, while the reference to what 'was asserted in the society' (p. 429), which Blake and his wife joined in April 1789,² implies a date after the spring of 1789.

DESCRIPTION: A note on the half-title says 'the Volume came' from 'Mr Tatham'. Blake's comments are in pencil, many of them, particularly those on the fly-leaf, very dim indeed.³ The annotations continue through the volume quite steadily except for gaps between pp. 58 and 131, between 146 and 181, between 233 and 268, and between 295 and 410.

MARGINALIA (?1790): Swedenborg, *Divine Providence* (1790)

(Text pp. 1400–3)

TITLE: THE / WISDOM / OF / *ANGELS* / CONCERNING THE / DIVINE PROVIDENCE. / — / TRANSLATED FROM THE LATIN / OF THE / *Hon. EMANUEL SWEDENBORG* [by Dr. N. Tucker]. / — / Originally Published at AMSTERDAM, Anno 1764. / = / *LONDON:* / Printed and Sold by R. Hindmarsh, / PRINTER TO HIS ROYAL HIGHNESS THE PRINCE OF WALES, / No. 32, *CLERKENWELL-CLOSE,* / And

---

¹ See note 1, p. 1743. ² *Blake Records*, 35.
³ Erdman (p. 597) prints ¶336 because he assumes that the cross beside it is by Blake.

may be had by giving Orders to any of the Booksellers / in Town or Country. /
M.DCC.XC.

COLLECTION: *Sir Geoffrey Keynes.*

DATE: ?1790.

Blake was clearly sympathetic to Swedenborg's New Jerusalem Church
when he joined it in April 1789[1] and sharply critical when he wrote the
Marriage (?1790–3). The vigour of Blake's indignation with Swedenborg's
'Cursed Folly' (p. 434) in the *Divine Providence* implies a recent disillusion-
ment and a date for Blake's marginalia shortly after the book's publication
in 1790.

DESCRIPTION: 'William Blake' appears on the half-title. All the notes are in
pencil. The original boards and label are still present, though rather bat-
tered. The leaves are not trimmed. At one time Samuel Palmer owned the
volume.

MARGINALIA (1798): Watson, *Apology for the Bible* (1797)

(Text pp. 1404–24)

TITLE: AN / APOLOGY / FOR THE / BIBLE, / IN A / SERIES OF
LETTERS, / ADDRESSED TO / *THOMAS PAINE,* / Author of a Book
entitled, The Age of Reason, Part the Second, / being an Investigation of
True and of Fabulous Theology. / — / BY R. WATSON, D.D. F.R.S. /
LORD BISHOP OF LANDAFF, AND REGIUS / PROFESSOR OF
DIVINITY IN THE UNIVERSITY OF CAMBRIDGE. / — / EIGHTH
EDITION. / — / LONDON: / Printed for T. EVANS, in Paternoster-
Row. / — / 1797. / — / Price One Shilling, or Fifty Copies for Two Pounds,
stitched. / *Entered at Stationers' Hall.*

COLLECTION: HUNTINGTON LIBRARY.

DATE: 1798.

The reference to 'this year 1798' (title-page verso) gives the date un-
equivocally.

DESCRIPTION: At the top of the title-page is the signature of 'S. Palmer'.
The front and back of the text are very dirty. On the early pages the margins
are regularly filled to overflowing with Blake's comments. The notes to the
Preface and pp. 31, 34, 95 are in pencil, the rest in ink.

MARGINALIA (?1798): Bacon, *Essays* (1798)

(Text pp. 1425–45)

TITLE: ESSAYS / MORAL, ECONOMICAL, / AND / POLITICAL. /
BY / *FRANCIS BACON,* / BARON OF VERULAM, / AND / VISCOUNT

---

[1] *Blake Records,* 35.

ST. ALBANS. / = / LONDON: / PRINTED BY T. BENSLEY / FOR J. ED-
WARDS, PALL MALL, AND T. PAYNE, / MEWS GATE. / — / 1798.

COLLECTION: *Sir Geoffrey Keynes.*

DATE: ?1798.

The tenor of the comments, particularly the frequent comparison of
Bacon's advice to Christ's, suggests a date not long after publication for
Blake's annotations.

DESCRIPTION: The first endpaper is inscribed 'Samuel Palmer / 1833'.
All the notes are in pencil. There are no notes on pp. 240–70.

MARGINALIA (?1800): Dante, *Inferno*, tr. Boyd (1785)
(Text pp. 1446–9)

TITLE: A / TRANSLATION / OF THE / INFERNO / OF / *DANTE
ALIGHIERI*, / IN ENGLISH VERSE. / WITH / HISTORICAL NOTES,
AND THE LIFE OF *DANTE*. / TO WHICH IS ADDED, / A SPECIMEN
OF A NEW TRANSLATION / OF THE / ORLANDO FURIOSO / OF /
ARIOSTO. / — / BY HENRY BOYD, A. M. / = / DUBLIN: / PRINTED
BY P. BYRNE. 1785.

COLLECTION: *Sir Geoffrey Keynes.*

DATE: ?1800.

In the subscription list is 'William Hayley, Esq. 7 sets'. Hayley may have
given Blake a set soon after Blake moved to Felpham to work with him in
September 1800. Blake's concern for political liberty in his comments is
consistent with a date of 1800.

DESCRIPTION: The first endpaper is inscribed by A. H. Palmer, 'Samuel
Palmer's copy' and

This volume as far back as I can remember, stood upon one of my
father's book-shelves by the side of books annotated or illustrated by
Blake. Among them was the now well-known copy of Lavater's 'Apho-
rism*s*' . . . Bacon's Essays with Blake's notes were there, Hayley's Ballads,
and a Copy of Thornton['*s Virgil*.]

Up to p. 131 Blake's comments are in ink; thereafter they are in pencil.
There is an erasure on p. 209. In addition to Blake's annotations, there are a
number of corrections to the text[1] as follows: p. 193, 'His look' to 'Her look';
p. 207, 'wand'ring son' to 'wand'rings on'; pp. 312, 316, 'noisome frogs' to
'noisome fogs'; p. 313, 'Hide' to 'Hid'; p. 360, 'her' to 'his'; p. 326, in the
sentence 'Epicurus . . . thought the Louban air of fleeting breath' the strange
noun was changed to 'Soul an'.

[1] There is no Errata list. Erdman (p. 801) says the corrections are 'not [*by*]
Blake', but he does not say how he knows. In addition, he says that on p. 187 Blake
added the Italian above the English text: 'Nel mezzo del cummin de nostra vita'.

MARGINALIA (?1801–2, 1808–9): Reynolds, *Works* (1798)

(Text pp. 1450–1500)

TITLE: THE / WORKS / OF / SIR JOSHUA REYNOLDS, KNIGHT; / LATE PRESIDENT OF THE ROYAL ACADEMY: / CONTAINING / HIS DISCOURSES, IDLERS, / A JOURNEY TO FLANDERS AND HOLLAND, / AND HIS COMMENTARY ON DU FRESNOY'S ART OF / PAINTING; / PRINTED FROM HIS REVISED COPIES, / (WITH HIS LATEST CORRECTIONS AND ADDITIONS,) / *IN THREE VOLUMES.* / TO WHICH IS PREFIXED / AN ACCOUNT OF THE LIFE AND WRITINGS OF THE / AUTHOR, / BY EDMOND MALONE, ESQ. / ONE OF HIS EXECUTORS. / THE SECOND EDITION CORRECTED. / —QUASI NON EA PRÆCIPIAM ALIIS, QUÆ MIHI IPSI DESUNT. CICERO. / — / VOLUME THE FIRST. / — / *LONDON:* / PRINTED FOR T. CADELL, JUN. AND W. DAVIES, IN THE STRAND. / 1798.

COLLECTION: BRITISH MUSEUM.

DATE: ?1801–2, 1808–9.

Blake's annotations to Reynolds were probably written at two distinct periods, perhaps first about 1801–2 and second in 1808–9.[1]

Twice in his letters he cites the opinions of Sir Joshua, and on each occasion he had been making a prolonged and careful study of theories of colouring. On 22 November 1802 he told Butts:

> I have now given two years to the intense study of those parts of the art which relate to light & shade & colour . . . . All Sʳ J Reynolds's discourses to the Royal Academy will shew, that the Venetian finesse in Art can never be united with the Majesty of Colouring necessary to Historical beauty⌊.⌋[2]

Perhaps during these two years (1801–2) Blake made the series of pencil comments in his copy of Reynolds's *Works*. These pencil notes seem rather more temperate and less personal than those he made later.

In May 1809 Blake told Ozias Humphry:

> you demand of me to Mix two things that Reynolds has confessed cannot be mixed. . . . Florentine & Venetian Art cannot exist together⌊.⌋

For some time he had been brooding over his wrongs at the hands of Cromek and the scant public patronage he had attracted and preparing 'an account of my various Inventions in Art'.[3] Probably at this time (1808–9)

---

[1] Blake probably heard some of the lectures delivered from the time when he became a student at the Royal Academy in 1779, and he could also have read them as they were individually printed before the collected editions of 1797 and 1798. The references to Fuseli's Milton Gallery (1799–1800) on the title-page verso and pp. i, 3 suggest a date after 1800.

[2] See Reynolds pp. 95, 97 (pp. 1477–8.).

[3] As he told Cumberland on 19 Dec 1809. The reference in ink on p. 4 to the British Institution must be after that society was founded in 1805. A note on

he went through Reynolds's *Works* once again, confirming many of the old pencil comments in ink, and making a great many new ones. The ink notes are distinguished from those written originally in pencil by their virulence, by the personal rancour they display against 'Sʳ Joshua & his Gang of Cunning Hired Knaves' (title-page verso), and by their concern for Venetian colour. These differences are also reflected in various forms in Blake's *Descriptive Catalogue* (1809), in his 'Public Address' (?1810–11), and in several poems in the *Notebook* apparently written just before or during the composition of the two former, particularly one replying directly to Reynolds's last Lecture (see p. 944).

Even if the two dates, 1801–2 and 1808–9, are accepted, it is possible that a few of the annotations were made between 1802 and 1808 or after 1809. Some of the ink comments may have been made before 1808, and some of the pencil comments (e.g. on pp. 144, 147) were certainly made after the ink notes on the same pages.

DESCRIPTION: The three volumes are now in uniform modern bindings heavily trimmed on all sides,[1] but only the first volume (containing Malone's 'Life' and Reynolds's first eight Discourses) has Blake's annotations or any indication of his ownership. Some of the poems in Blake's *Notebook* (e.g. p. 944) were directly stimulated by Discourses in the second volume of Reynolds's *Works*, but there is no direct evidence that Blake owned and annotated any volume except the first.[2] The comment on p. xlvii is so far into the inner margin that it must have been written before the sheets were bound.

Pencil and Ink: The first notes seem to have been made in *pencil only* on pp. ix, xxxiv, xlvii, lx, xcvi, civ (erasure), cxx, 13, 30, 48, 61, 65, 67, 75 bottom, 92 (all but the top three words), 93 bottom, 98 bottom, 99, 100 top and bottom, 133 bottom, 144 top, 147 top seven words, 152 top, 158, 159 top, 180, 209, 256, 260, 262, 264, 266–7, 272, 274–5, 277, 281, 284, 285 (that is, from 256 on except for pp. 279, 286).

Later many *pencil notes were darkened in ink* on the title-page verso, Contents [1], [iii]–[v]; i–ii, xiv–xix, xxix, xlii, lvii, lxxxix–xc, xcviii–xcix, ciii–civ, cxi, [2]–5 top, 9, 26, 32 top four words, 35, 37, 40, 41 top, 47, 52, 55–6, 58, 60, 62–4, 71, 74–5 top, 78–80, 83 bottom, 89–90, 92 top three words, 93³–5, 98 (all but the poem), 100 (middle only), 106, 109–10, 114, 118–20, 123–7, 129, 132–3 (all but the last four words), 134, 144 (the pencil begins with 'by Men'), 147 (but not the top seven words), 152 (but not the top), 157 (but not the last sentence), 159 (all but the first paragraph, the numbers,

p. 159 was incorporated in the *Descriptive Catalogue* (1809), ¶3, and another on p. 2 in *Jerusalem* (1804–?20) pl. 43, l. 35 (pp. 827, 509).

[1] A number of letters and words from Blake's marginalia were cropped off in the process.

[2] The reference (title-page verso) to 'my Remarks on these Books', plural, might suggest that he annotated vols. ii and iii as well. If so, they were separated from vol. i by 1865, when the above set entered the British Museum.

[3] The pencil passage on p. 93 is inked over only as far as 'Form'.

and the second 'born', for which read '. . .'), 165–7, 172, 176, 178–9, 196, 208 bottom, 245 bottom, 251 bottom. Sometimes of course he changed the text a little when confirming it in ink.

The notes *in ink only*[1] are in effect additions to the title-page, iii, viii, xlix, l, liii, lxx, lxxii, cix, 5 bottom, 7, 11, 14–18, 22–3, 25, 29, 32 (all but the top four words), 33–4, 42–3, 50, 54, 57, 82, 83 top, 86–7, 92 bottom, 93 bottom, 98 bottom, 99, 100 bottom, 101–4, 111–12, 116–17, 121, 128, 131, 133 bottom, 135, 137–9, 141–2, 144 top, 147 top, 149, 152 top, 153–5, 157 bottom, 159 some, 161, 163, 188, 194–5, 197–204, 208 top, 214–15, 232, 242, 244–5 top, 251 top, 279, 286. For a discussion of the implications of these writing variations see the DATE above.

Erasures: There are erasures on pp. civ footnote, 30, 36, 38, 75, 87.

A misprint ('reserved' for 'reversed') is corrected on p. 273.

Comments in other hands are written after Blake's on pp. 83, 134.

MARGINALIA (?1818): Spurzheim, *Observations on . . . Insanity* (1817)

(Text p. 1501)

TITLE: OBSERVATIONS / ON THE / DERANGED MANIFESTA-TIONS / OF / THE MIND, / OR / INSANITY. / = / BY / J. G. SPURZ-HEIM, M.D. / LICENTIATE OF THE COLLEGE OF PHYSICIANS OF LONDON, PHYSICIAN TO THE / AUSTRIAN EMBASSY, AUTHOR OF THE 'PHYSIOGNOMICAL SYSTEM / OF DRS. GALL AND SPURZHEIM,' ETC. / — / WITH FOUR COPPER PLATES. / — / 'NOTHING TENDS MORE TO THE CORRUPTION OF SCIENCE THAN / TO SUFFER IT TO STAGNATE.' / = / LONDON: / PRINTED FOR BALDWIN, CRADOCK, AND JOY, / 47, PATER-NOSTER-ROW. / — / 1817.

COLLECTION: *UNTRACED*; see below.

DATE: ?1818.

Blake's long interest in phrenology was probably stimulated anew by Spurzheim's book shortly after it was published in June 1817. Not long thereafter, he began producing his Visionary Heads for Varley, which are clearly related to the phrenological theories of Spurzheim, Lavater, and others.

DESCRIPTION: The only direct information about Blake's notes to Spurz-heim is to be found in *The Works of William Blake*, ed. E. J. Ellis & W. B. Yeats (1893), i. 154–5:

A fragment of paper, seemingly torn off to make a hasty memorandum

---

[1] Erdman (p. 801) treats all these 'notes in ink only . . . as additions'. I have carefully examined the MS to check the erasures, etc., read by Erdman and recorded in the footnotes. In all cases relegated to the notes, I could not read the text with confidence; in some cases, I could not even *find* the erasures.

of the incident, is preserved by the Linnell brothers among the sheets of the Vala MS.[1] It is in Blake's handwriting, and bears no sign of having been of the nature of a letter. . . . It is a note made while reading Spurzheim, in a copy[2] where marginal pencillings were either not permitted, or insufficient. The words are as follows:—'Methodism, &c. 154 . . . .' And to a previous page, 106, he has, on the same piece of paper, 'Corporeal disease . . . .'

The passages from Spurzheim to which Blake evidently refers are not given by Ellis & Yeats.

MARGINALIA (*c.* 1820): Berkeley, *Siris* (1744)
(Text pp. 1502–5)

TITLE: *SIRIS:* / A CHAIN OF / Philosophical Reflexions / AND / IN-QUIRIES / Concerning the VIRTUES of / *TAR WATER,* / And divers other *Subjects* connected together / and arising one from another. / — /By G.L.B.O.C.[3] / — / *As we have opportunity let us do good unto all men.* / Gal. vi. 10. / *Hoc opus hoc studium parvi properemus et ampli.* / HOR. / ☰ / DUBLIN: Printed by MARG[T]. RHAMES, / For R. GUNNE, Bookseller in *Capel-street,* / M DCC XLIV.

COLLECTION: TRINITY COLLEGE, Cambridge.

DATE: *c.* 1820.

The concern in the notes for the divinity of imagination and the conflict between it and mathematics suggest a date close to that of 'The Everlasting Gospel' (?1818) parts k, l and to that of 'Laocoon' (?1820) (pp. 1065–9, 663–6) in which very similar ideas are expressed.

DESCRIPTION: The flyleaf is inscribed 'From the Author', i.e. from Berkeley. Blake's annotations are in ink. In the middle of p. 51 is a pencil comment in another hand: 'the same Effects were produced by oxygen gass—vital air'.

'*In* 1833' the volume belonged to Samuel Palmer (Keynes, *The Complete Writings of William Blake* [1957]).

MARGINALIA (?1822): Cennini, *Trattato della Pittura* (1821)
(Text p. 1506)

TITLE: DI CENNINO CENNINI / TRATTATO / DELLA PITTURA / MESSO IN LUCE LA PRIMA VOLTA / CON ANNOTAZIONI / DAL

---

[1] The Spurzheim note is not now with the *Vala* MS in the British Museum.

[2] Perhaps the copy Blake saw was Linnell's, bought from Spurzheim on 14 June 1817, according to Linnell's Ledger (Ivimy MS).

[3] That is, George, Lord Bishop of Cloyne.

CAVALIERE / GIUSEPPE TAMBRONI / SOCIO ONORARIO DELL'ACCADEMIA DI S. LUCA / DELLA I. R. DELLE BELLE ARTI DI VIENNA / DELL'ARCHEOLOGICA DI ROMA / DELLA R. DI SCIENZE LETTERE ED ARTI DI PARIGI EC. / — / ROMA / CO' TORCHJ DI PAOLO SALVIUCCI / 1821 / *Con Approvazione*.

COLLECTION: *UNTRACED*; see below.

DATE: ?1822.

From Linnell's comment (below) it is clear that Blake must have been reading Cennini's book soon after it was published in 1821.

DESCRIPTION: The text derives from E. J. Ellis, *The Real Blake* (1907), 420, who says merely that Blake's comments are 'In the margin of a copy of Cennini's book on fresco painting'.[1] On 10 December 1862 Linnell wrote to Anne Gilchrist:

> I believe that the first copy of Cennino Cennini seen in England was the copy I obtained from Italy & gave to Blake who soon made it out & was gratified to find that he had been using the same materials & methods in painting as Cennini describes—particularly the Carpenters glue ⌊.⌋[2]

MARGINALIA (1826): Wordsworth, *Excursion* (1814)

(Text pp. 1506–10)

TITLE: THE EXCURSION, / BEING A PORTION OF / THE RE-CLUSE, / *A POEM*. / — / BY / WILLIAM WORDSWORTH. / — / LONDON: / PRINTED FOR LONGMAN, HURST, REES, ORME, AND BROWN, / PATERNOSTER-ROW. / 1814.

COLLECTION: No copy of *The Excursion* with Blake's notes is known; see below.

DATE: 1826.

On 18 February 1826 'He [*Blake*] gave me [*Crabb Robinson*] copied out by himself Wordsworths preface to his Excursion'.[3] Blake had remarked on this passage when he first met Robinson on 10 December 1825,[4] and shortly thereafter 'I [*Robinson*] lent him the copy of Wordsworths poems which occasiond this Extract'.[5] The loan was between 10 December 1825, when

---

[1] Erdman (p. 803) argues that the notoriously inaccurate Ellis intended not Cennini's *Trattato della Pittura* but Benvenuto Cellini's *Trattato dell'Oreficeria*.

[2] MS with the Ivimy MSS. Keynes ([1921], p. 54) says that Blake transcribed an extract from Cennini in a sketch-book (watermarked 1824) used by George Richmond. (The sketch-book, also used by Palmer, C. H. Tatham, and Calvert, was described, without reference to the Blake passage, in the Sotheby catalogue of 28 July 1920, lot 162. Sir Geoffrey tells me that the book contained as well a sketch by Blake of a Vision of Hercules inked over by Richmond.)

[3] *Blake Records*, 321. [4] Ibid., 312.

[5] This is Crabb Robinson's note on the folder in which he kept Blake's transcript. Robinson transcribed it in his Diary for 18 Feb. 1826 and in his letter to Dorothy Wordsworth of 19 Feb.

Robinson met Blake, and 18 February 1826. Blake's notes are almost certainly of 1826.

DESCRIPTION: Crabb Robinson's copy of *The Excursion* which Blake read has not been traced, but Blake gave a copy of his notes to Crabb Robinson on 18 February 1826, and this copy has been preserved.[1] The unwatermarked leaves on which Blake's ink notes are written are of slightly different size (11·8×21·4 for the first, 11·2×19·8 for the second), and there are no stab holes in them. The four sides are quite filled.

MARGINALIA (1826): Wordsworth, *Poems* (1815)
(Text pp. 1511–13)

TITLE: POEMS / BY / WILLIAM WORDSWORTH: /INCLUDING/ LYRICAL BALLADS, / AND THE / MISCELLANEOUS PIECES OF THE AUTHOR. / WITH ADDITIONAL POEMS, / A NEW PREFACE, AND A SUPPLEMENTARY ESSAY. / = / IN TWO VOLUMES. / = / VOL. I. / — / LONDON: / PRINTED FOR LONGMAN, HURST, REES, ORME, AND BROWN, / PATERNOSTER-ROW. / — / 1815.

COLLECTION: CORNELL.

DATE: 1826.

Crabb Robinson lent his set of Wordsworth's *Poems* (1815) to Blake between 10 December 1825, when he first met him, and 26 January 1826, when Blake transcribed a portion of the Michelangelo sonnet in Upcott's Autograph Album (see p. 1322). Blake probably made his notes soon after he received the volume.

DESCRIPTION: Both volumes are inscribed at the tops of the title-pages 'H. C. Robinson', though in vol. i the name is largely trimmed off. Blake's notes are entirely in vol. i.

In a letter of 10 August 1848 (now in Dove Cottage, Grasmere), Crabb Robinson wrote: 'I had lent him when he died the 8vo Edit in 2 Vols: of W. Ws poems— They were sent me by his widow with pencil marginalia which I inked over' lest they should be lost, except for the passage on p. 375 which he could not decipher.

MARGINALIA (1827): Thornton, *Lord's Prayer* (1827)
(Text pp. 1514–18)

TITLE: THE / LORD'S PRAYER, / NEWLY TRANSLATED / *FROM THE ORIGINAL GREEK*, / WITH CRITICAL AND EXPLANATORY NOTES, / BY / ROBERT JOHN THORNTON, M.D. / OF TRINITY

[1] In Dr. Williams's Library, ff. 101–2 in the volume containing Robinson's letters 1864–7.

COLLEGE, CAMBRIDGE, AND MEMBER OF THE ROYAL LON-DON COLLEGE / OF PHYSICIANS. / WITH A FRONTISPIECE / FROM A DESIGN BY HARLOW, / OF THE ACADEMY OF ST. LUKE, AT ROME, AND OF THE ACADEMY OF FLORENCE. / *ADDRESSED TO THE BIBLE SOCIETIES / FOR DISTRIBUTION. / — / Stereotyped and printed by J. M'Gowan and Son, 16, Great Windmill Street, Haymarket.* / PUBLISHED BY SHERWOOD AND CO., PATERNOSTER ROW; COX, ST. THOMAS STREET, BOROUGH; AND DR. THORNTON, / 52, GREAT MARLBOROUGH STREET; AND SOLD BY ALL BOOKSELLERS, 1s. 6d. INCLUDING A PRINT / FROM THE FAMOUS PAINTER HARLOW, BY COOK. / — / 1827.

COLLECTION: HUNTINGTON LIBRARY.

DATE: 1827, between 31 March, the imprint on the frontispiece, and 12 August, when Blake died.

DESCRIPTION: The little pamphlet is stitched through the original Blue paper wrappers (with the original label) *and* through modern cardboard covers. The two leaves with the title-page and the 'Reasons for a New Translation of the Whole Bible' are misbound behind the other four leaves.

Blake's comments were evidently of some interest to Blake and his friends.[1] All but that on p. 2 were first written in pencil, and later all were confirmed in ink (except for those on pp. 3 and 10). Those on p. 10 were carefully transcribed by someone—not Blake—on the inside of the back Blue wrapper. These transcriptions were apparently made at different times, for one sentence at the bottom of the title-page verso is in Brown ink, and one in Black. The faintness of the pencil and the overwriting in ink have made some of the words exceedingly difficult to read.

Letters (1791–1827)
(Text pp. 1521–1671)

Between 1790 and 1830, a letter could be posted from London to a recipient in England in one of three ways:

1. If destined for a place over fifteen miles from London, it could be taken before 5 p.m. to an Inland Mail receiving-house (often doubling as a shop), in which case it would be stamped with a rectangular receiving-house stamp (e.g. 'BRIDGE / WESTMINSTER', letter of 16 September 1800). If the recipient was in or near London, it could be taken before 8 p.m. to a receiving-house of the Twopenny Post,[2] where it was given a receiving-house postmark shaped like a stunted, upside-down T (e.g. 'T.P/STRAND', letters of 1825–6). After 8 p.m., a London letter could be put through a hole

---

[1] On 29 Aug. 1828 Samuel Palmer wrote to Linnell: 'My Father . . . would be very much amused by a sight of Mr. Blake's annotations on Dr. T.s Lord's Prayer' (*Blake Records*, 369).

[2] The Twopenny Post was instituted in 1801; before that time it was the Penny Post.

in the shutter of one of the Twopenny Post receiving-houses, in which case it would not be stamped and delivered until the next day. Letters handed in at Inland Mail and Twopenny Post receiving-houses were transferred from there to the main Post Offices.

2. Inland Mail could be given to one of the Inland Mail postmen who went through the streets ringing a bell, from the closing of the Inland Mail receiving-houses at 5 p.m. until 6.30 p.m. The postmen took these letters directly to a main Post Office.

3. For both Inland Mail and Twopenny Post, a letter could be taken directly to one of the two main Post Offices in London (Lombard Street) or Westminster (Gerrard Street).

However an outgoing letter reached the main Post Office, it was there postmarked with a circular, dated, 'evening duty' stamp giving the day and, for the Twopenny Post, the hour when it was received. All mail bound for outside the city left the main Post Offices at 8 p.m. Letters which were not mailed at a receiving-house bear only one stamp, which is dated. Letters leaving London were not stamped in the towns where they were received; only London and a few other cities such as Oxford and Edinburgh had dated postmarks; the place is always indicated in the date-stamp except in London.

Thus we can tell that most of Blake's letters which are known to have gone through the Twopenny Post were mailed at the branch receiving-house in the Strand, the closest one to his home in Fountain Court, Strand. From there they were taken to the Gerrard Street Post Office—the Westminster Post Office in Gerrard Street gave the day before the month in its date-stamp, whereas the one in Lombard Street, London, gave the month before the day.[1] Evidently the letters of 11 October, 10 November 1825, 16 July, and 1 August 1826 were mailed between 8 p.m. and the time the offices opened next morning, since they are date-stamped a day later than the date Blake put on his letter.

Letters posted in the country to London[2] were handed in to the village postmaster, who scrawled on them the fee appropriate to the number of sheets of paper used and the distance from London—'6' pence from Chichester to London. The postmaster also stamped the letter with the name of the town and its distance from London—'CHICHESTER / 63'. There was no sub-post-office in Felpham where Blake lived from 1800 to 1803, so his letters during these years had to be taken to Chichester. Letters left Chichester for London daily at 4 p.m. and arrived next day; letters from London arrived in Chichester at 11 a.m.[3] When country letters reached

---

[1] The letter of 11 Oct. 1825 seems to have a stamp of both the Westminster Office ('8·MORN·8 / 12·OC / 1825') and the London Office ('10[?]·F·NO[ON?] . . . / OC·12 / 1825').

[2] Those in the Table below of 1794, Jan., Feb., May 1796, 17 April 1800, 21 Sept. 1800 to 16 Aug. 1803 (except for Sept. 1800, 7 Oct. 1801), 18 Dec. 1808, 29 July 1815, 4 Nov. 1826, 25 Nov. 1827.

[3] J. Cary, *Cary's New English Atlas* (1793). The fee given by Cary and on the letters was sixpence. Cary gives the post distance as 63 miles.

London, the postal charges were checked and the letters were date-stamped on receipt with a 'morning duty' stamp.[1] Delivery began at 10 a.m., the postman ordinarily collecting the postal fee from the recipient.

Thus the dates stamped on letters of this period mean different things depending on where the letters were posted. Those mailed *in London* bear a round, outgoing, 'evening duty' stamp dated the day the letter left the London Post Office, whereas letters coming *to London* bear a round, incoming, 'morning duty' stamp dated the day the letter arrived in the London Post Office and distinguished from the former by having a single rim rather than a double one. In the case of Blake's letters, there is no confusion between the two. (We do not need to consider the cases of letters going through London, or not touching London, for all Blake's known correspondence was directed either to or from London.)

Many of Blake's letters bear no postmark, presumably because they were either delivered by messenger or enclosed in another sheet (bearing the address) which has since disappeared. Since an ordinary letter consisted of a single sheet folded so as to form its own envelope, the opening of the letter entailed tearing it, and consequently one or more of the postmarks may be hard to read or even torn off entirely. Naturally, for letters for which the manuscripts have not been traced, there is no information as to postmark or watermark in the Table below.

Table

Symbols

(Ph)   Transcribed from a Photograph, Photostat, or Microfilm; all other manuscripts are transcribed from originals.

(Gilchrist)   Transcribed from Alexander Gilchrist,[2] *Life of William Blake* (1880), i, 143, 163–4, 194–5, 205–6, 209–13, 215–16, 218–20, 222–3, because the manuscripts have not been traced.

(Sotheby)   Transcribed from the Sotheby catalogue of Hayley Correspondence, 20 May 1878, lots 4, 21, 22, 25, 32, because the manuscripts have not been traced.

[1] 'In addition to the date the stamp contained a letter of the alphabet which indicated the table in the post office at which the letter was processed' (K. N. Cameron, *Shelley and his Circle* [1961], ii. 918 n. 11; this work is the source of most of the information above). Such a 'morning duty' stamp may be seen on Blake's letter of 19 Oct. 1801: 'F / OCT 21 / 1801'.

[2] A comparison of the Gilchrist transcripts with the manuscripts of the traceable letters which he quotes reveals that he consistently normalized capitalization, spelling ('conceived' for 'Concievd'), punctuation, grammar ('you were' for 'you was', 7 April 1804), and paragraphing, and expanded contractions ('&' to 'and', 'tho' to 'though'). Occasionally such changes significantly affect meaning. Additionally, the Gilchrist transcripts were often startlingly casual. For example, in the letter of 14 Jan. 1804, ten words were omitted in the first sentence, plus five in the last; 'Mrs Lambert' became 'Mr. Lambert', and 'wicked' changed twice into 'wretched'. Presumably he made similar changes in the letters for which the original manuscripts have not been traced.

  *   A *wafer* sealed the letter.

  +   A *wax seal* is on the letter. The only clear seal (19 Oct. 1801) represents an owl on a perch. That of 27 Jan. 1804 seems to represent a classical head.

1791 Oct. 18   *Dates in italics* indicate the letter is written *to* Blake.

Date	Postmark	Watermark	Collection	Page
1791 Oct. 18	C OCT / 7 / ...[1]	CURTEIS & SON	HUNTINGTON	1521
[*1791 Oct.?*]			*UNTRACED*[2]	1521
[*1794 Oct.*]			*UNTRACED*[3]	
[*1794 Nov.*]			*UNTRACED*[3]	
1795 Dec. 6	*C DE / 10 / 95	[ ]TH	BM	1522–3
[*1796 Jan.*]			*UNTRACED*[3]	
[*1796 Feb.*]			*UNTRACED*[3]	
[*1796 May*]			*UNTRACED*[3]	
1796 Dec. 23	——	*chain lines*	BM	1523–4
1799 Aug. 16	——	*design*	BM	1524–5
[*1799 Aug.*]			*UNTRACED*[4]	
1799 Aug. 23	*BRIDGE.ST / WEST-MINSTER B·AU· / 28 / ·99[5]	*chain lines*	BM	1525–8
1799 Aug. 26	*BRIDGE ST / ... AU / ... / 99	*chain lines*	BM	1528–30
1800 Feb. 18			(Gilchrist)	1530
1800 April 1	+BRIDGE / WEST-MINSTER A / 1 / 1800	*design*	*Lady Radcliffe*	1531
1800 April 17	CHICHESTER		*G. Keynes*[6]	1531–3
1800 May 6	+C·MA· / 6 / 800	*design*	HARVARD	1533–4
1800 July 2	*C JY / 2 / 800	*design*	LC	1534–6
1800 Sept. 12	2 o'Clock / 12·SP / 1800 A·N O[?] Unpaid	*design*	MORGAN	1536–7
1800 Sept. 14	——	1798	MORGAN	1537–9
1800 Sept. 16	*BRIDGE / WEST-MINSTER A·S·E· / 16 / 800	179[ ]	HUNTINGTON	1539–40
1800 Sept. 21	*CHICHESTER	*design*	YALE	1540–1
1800 Sept. 22	+CHICHESTER SEP 23 / 1800	*design*	WESTMINSTER PUBLIC LIBRARY	1541–2
[*1800 Sept.*]	——	1798	WESTMINSTER PUBLIC LIBRARY[7]	1543–5
1800 Oct. 2	*——	1798	WESTMINSTER PUBLIC LIBRARY	1545–8
1800 Nov. 26			(Gilchrist)	1548–9
[*1800 Autumn?*]			*UNTRACED*[8]	1549

[1] The only really clear part of the postmark is the '7', which seems to contradict the written date of 'Oct 18'.

[2] The draft of Blake's letter to Reveley is on the verso of Reveley's letter to Blake; the fair copy sent has not been traced.

[3] In his Journal, Captain John Gabriel Stedman included 'Blake' in a list of letters he wrote in October 1794; 'I wrote to ... Blake' in November 1794; in 'January and February [*1796*] I write ... to Blake—3 times—d⁰ [*i.e. in London*]'; and under '*Correspondence*' for May 1796 he noted '12 letters to Blake' (*Blake Records*, 48, 50, 51), but none of these letters has been traced.

[4] Dr. Trusler's untraced letter to Blake is known only from the references in Blake's letter of 26 Aug. 1799.

[5] The clear postmark date of 28 Aug. (which contradicts the clear written date of 23 Aug.) must be a mistake.

[6] Quoted from *The Letters of William Blake*, ed. G. Keynes (1956).

[7] Butts's letter to Blake is known only from his rough draft.

[8] The last known location is the Sotheby catalogue of H. V. Morten, 5 May 1890, lot 22. Keynes (*Letters* [1968], 49–50) prints this letter from an anonymous Sotheby catalogue of 3 Dec. 1888, lot 13, which I cannot trace.

Bibliographical Notes

Date	Postmark	Watermark	Collection	Page
1801 May 10	*——	design	WESTMINSTER PUBLIC LIBRARY	1550
1801 July 31	AJY / 31 / 801	——	FOLGER (Ph)	1551
1801 Sept. 11	*——	F HAYES / 1798	WESTMINSTER PUBLIC LIBRARY	1552–4
1801 Oct. 7	+. . . [1]801	design	FITZWILLIAM	1554
1801 Oct. 19	+CHICHESTER / 63[?] F / OCT 21 / 1801	BUTTANSHAW / 18[00?]	MORGAN	1555
[1801 Autumn]			UNTRACED[9]	
1802 Jan. 10	*CHICHESTER	A BLACKWELL / 1798	WESTMINSTER PUBLIC LIBRARY	1556–9
[1802?]			UNTRACED[10]	1559
1802 Nov. 22	——	F HAYES / 1798	WESTMINSTER PUBLIC LIBRARY	1559–62
1802 Nov. 22	——	design	WESTMINSTER PUBLIC LIBRARY	1562–9
[1802 Nov.]			UNTRACED[11]	
[1803 Jan.?]			UNTRACED[12]	
1803 Jan. 30	——	chain lines	LC	1567–71
[1803 April]			UNTRACED[13]	
1803 April 25	+——	A BLACKWELL / 1798	WESTMINSTER PUBLIC LIBRARY	1571–3
1803 July 6	——	A BLACKWELL / 1798	WESTMINSTER PUBLIC LIBRARY	1573–6
1803 Aug. 16	+——	F HAYES / 1798	WESTMINSTER PUBLIC LIBRARY	1577–81
1803 Sept. 19			(Sotheby)	1581
1803 Oct. 7	——	A B[LACKWELL?]	Mrs D. F. Hyde	1581–3
1803 Oct. 26			(Gilchrist)	1583–5
1803 Dec. 13	+——	A BLA[CKWELL] / 1798	MAINE HISTORICAL SOCIETY (Ph)	1585-6
1804 Jan. 14	*JA / 16[?] / . . .	A BLACKWELL / 1798	HARVARD	1586 8
1804 Jan. 27	+B·JA· / 27 / 804	A BLACKWELL / 1798	HARVARD	1588–90
[1804 Feb.]			UNTRACED[14]	
1804 Feb. 23	*——	design	BM	1590–2
1804 March 12	*B·M·R / 12 / 804	design	Malone	1592–3
[1804 March]			UNTRACED[15]	
1804 March 16	——	design	MORGAN	1593–4
[1804 March 19?]			UNTRACED[16]	
1804 March 21	——	design	PENNSYLVANIA HISTORICAL SOCIETY (Ph)	1594–5
1804 March 31	+C MR / 31 / 804	design	TRINITY COLLEGE (Hartford, Conn.)	1596
1804 April 2			(Gilchrist)	1596–7
1804 April 2			UNTRACED[16]	
1804 April 7	*A AP / 7 / 804	design	HARVARD	1597–8
1804 April 27	*C·AP / 27 / 804	design	MORGAN	1598–9
1804 May 4			(Gilchrist)	1600–2
1804 May 28			(Gilchrist)	1602–6
1804 June 22	+B·JU· / 22 / 04	design	MORGAN	1606–8
1804 July 16	*——	design	F. W. Hilles (Ph)	1609–10

[9] Butts's letter is referred to in Blake's of 10 Jan. 1802.
[10] [O. Crawfurd] 'William Blake: Artist, Poet, and Mystic', New Quarterly Magazine, ii (1874), 475.
[11] Blake's untraced letter to his brother James was enclosed in his letter of 22 Nov. 1802.
[12] Blake's letter from his brother is mentioned in the letter of 30 Jan. 1803.
[13] James Blake's 'pressing letter' is mentioned in William's of 25 April 1803.
[14] Prince Hoare's letter is mentioned in Blake's of 23 Feb. 1804.
[15] On 16 March Blake refers to Hayley's letter to him.
[16] On 2 April 1802 Blake said he sent letters to his solicitor, Mr. R. Dally, 'a fortnight ago' and 'by this post'.

Date	Postmark	Watermark	Collection	Page
1804 Aug. 7			(Sotheby)	1610
1804 Aug. 9			(Sotheby)	1611
1804 Sept. 28	——	*design*	LC	1611–12
[*1804 Oct.*]			*UNTRACED*[17]	
1804 Oct. 23			(Gilchrist)	1612–14
[*1804 Nov.*]			*UNTRACED*[18]	
1804 Dec. 4	+B[?]·D·E· / 4 / 80[ ]	W D[AC]IE & CO. / 1804	LC (Ph)	1615–16
1804 Dec. 18			(Gilchrist)	1617-18
1804 Dec. 28	C·D·E· / 29 / 804	——	PENNSYLVANIA HISTORICAL SOCIETY (Ph)	1618–20
1805 Jan. 19	——	*design*	HAVERFORD COLLEGE (Ph)	1620–2
1805 Jan. 22			(Gilchrist)	1623-4
1805 March 22	+A·MR· / 25 / 805	W DA[CI]E / 1803	HARVARD	1624–7
1805 May 17			(Sotheby)	1627
1805 June 4			(Gilchrist)	1627–8
1805 Nov. 27	——	*design*	HARVARD	1628–9
1805 Dec. 11	+[ ] DE / 11 / 805	*design*	G. Keynes	1629–31
[*1806 June?*]			*UNTRACED*[19]	1631–3
1807 May			*UNTRACED*[20]	1633–6
1807 Oct. 14	*TWO PENNY / POST / . . . . . . OC / 1807	180[2?]	BOSTON PUBLIC LIBRARY (Ph)	1636–7
1808 Jan. 18 [A]	——	IVY MILL / 1806	R. W. Barrett	1637–41
1808 Jan. 18 [B]	——	IVY MILL / 1806	Lord *Egremont* (Ph)	1637–41
1808 Feb. [C]	——	IVY MILL / 1806	Lord *Cunliffe*	1637-41
1808 Dec. 18	*[2 indecipherable round stamps]	1806	BM	1642–3
1808 Dec. 19		——	BM	1644–5
[*1809 May?*]	+——	*design*	TRINITY COLLEGE (Hartford, Conn.) (Ph)	1645
[*1810 July?*]			*UNTRACED*[21]	
[*1810 Aug.?*]			*UNTRACED*[22]	1646
[*1810 Aug.?*]			*UNTRACED*[23]	1646–7
1815 July 29			*UNTRACED*[24]	1647
1815 Sept. 8	——	——	WEDGWOOD MUSEUM (Ph)	1648
1818 June 9	R J[U?] / 9 / 1818	*design*	ROSENBACH FOUNDATION[25]	1648–9
1819 Oct. 11	——	——	UNIVERSITY OF TEXAS (Ph)	1650
1823 March 25	——	*design*	YALE	1650–1
[*1824 Aug. 4?*]	——		LC	1651

[17] Blake's letter of 23 Oct. 1804 mentions Hayley's letter to him.

[18] Blake's letter of 4 Dec. 1804 mentions Hayley's letter to him.

[19] *Monthly Magazine*, xxi (1 July 1806), 520–1.

[20] Anon., 'The Life and Works of Thomas Stothard, R.A.', *Gentleman's Magazine*, N.S., xxxvii (1852), 149–50.

[21] C. H. B. Ker wrote to George Cumberland, probably in August 1810, that he had 'some time before written to him [*Blake*]' (BM Add. MSS 36516, f. 56—*Blake Records*, 227).

[22] Blake's reply to Ker is summarized in the letter above.

[23] In another letter to Cumberland, postmarked 27 Aug. 1810, C. H. B. Ker mentioned what 'I wrote' to Blake (BM Add. MSS 36502, f. 273—*Blake Records*, 228). In this letter Ker refers to a series of exchanges with Blake which may have been verbal or may represent further lost letters.

[24] My transcript derives from a photostat of the office copy on flimsy paper watermarked 'WATTS & CO. SOHO / STAFFORDSHIRE' in the Wedgwood Museum. The original has not been traced.

[25] A beautiful manuscript copy on unwatermarked paper was made by Dawson Turner, bound in a volume with an index (identifying it as a 'copy') dated 1837, and given in 1890 to Trinity College, Cambridge.

Date	Postmark	Watermark	Collection	Page
[1825 March?]	*——	1818	HUNTINGTON	1651–2
[1825 June 7]	*——	chain lines	HUNTINGTON	1652–3
1825 Oct. 11	*TP STRAND CO 8·MORN·8 / 12·OC / 1825 10[?]·F·NO[ON?] . . . / OC·12 / 1825	probably none[26]	HUNTINGTON	1653
1825 Nov. 10	*TP / STRAND CO 8·MORN·8 / 11·NO / 1825	design	HUNTINGTON	1653–4
1826 Jan. 31	*T·P / STRAND CO 4[?]·EVEN / 31 JA / 18[ ]	RUSE & TURNERS / 1810	HUNTINGTON	1654–5
[1826 Feb. 5?]	——	chain lines[27]	HUNTINGTON	1655
1826 March 31	——	chain lines[27]	MORGAN	1656
[1826 April?]	——	——	YALE	1656–7
1826 May 19	*T·P / STRAND CO 10·F[?]·NOON·10 / [ ]Y / 1826	chain lines[27]	HUNTINGTON	1657
1826 July 2	*T·P / STRAND CO 12 NOON· / 2·JY / 1826	chain lines[27]	ST. JOHN'S SEMINARY	1657–8
1826 July 5	——	chain lines[27]	HUNTINGTON	1658–9
1826 July 14	——	SMITH & ALL-NUTT / 1815	MORGAN	1659
1826 July 16	*T·P / STRAND CO 10[?]·NOON·10 / 17·JY / 1826	RUSE & TURNERS / 1810	HUNTINGTON	1660
1826 July 29	*T·P / STRAND CO 2·A·NOON·2 / 29·JY / 1826	chain lines[27]	HUNTINGTON	1660–1
1826 Aug. 1	*T·P / STRAND CO 10·F·NOON·10 / 2·AU / 1826	chain lines[27]	HUNTINGTON	1661
1826 Nov. 4	WORCESTER / NO 3 D2 / 117 D / PAID / 4NO4 / 1826	R BARNARD / 1825	*Miss J. L. Ivimy*[28]	1662–3
1826 Dec. 29	*——	——	TEXAS *UNTRACED*[29]	1663
[*1827 Jan.*]				
1827 Jan. 27	*——	chain lines[27]	HUNTINGTON	1664
[1827 Feb.?]	——		HUNTINGTON	1664–5
[1827 Feb.?]	*——	chain lines	LC	1665
1827 March 5			*UNTRACED*[30]	
1827 March 15	*——	chain lines[27]	FITZWILLIAM	1665–6
[1827 March 18?]	*——	chain lines[27]	BERG COLLECTION (NYP)	1666
1827 April 12	*——	RUSE & TURNERS / 1810	FITZWILLIAM	1667–8
1827 April 25	*——	chain lines[27]	HUNTINGTON	1669
1827 July 3	*——	chain lines[27]	HUNTINGTON	1669–70
1827 Nov. 25			*Miss J. L. Ivimy*	1670–1

[26] The letter is mounted on linen, and the watermark is therefore obscured.

[27] The chain lines in Blake's otherwise unwatermarked letters of 1826–7 are the same distance apart as those in his letters bearing the watermark RUSE & TURNERS / 1810. All the letters of 1826–7 (except that of 14 July 1826) may therefore be on the same paper.

[28] The postmark is on the letter to Linnell (also with the Ivimy MSS) in which the letter to Blake was enclosed.

[29] Blake mentions Linnell's letter in his of 27 Jan. 1827.

[30] Cumberland wrote on 5 March 1827 that he 'Sent . . . [a] Lett[er] . . . to Blake' (*Blake Records*, 340), which has not been traced.

TABLE OF COLLECTIONS OF CONTEMPORARY COPIES OF BLAKE'S WRITINGS

† Means that I have not seen the original and have worked from a reproduction. Footnotes record those who have generously sent me vital information. Public collections are indicated in SMALL CAPITALS, private collections in *italics*.

Anonymous	ILLUMINATED WORKS: *Thel* (A), *For Children* (C), *Innocence* (J, M), *Jerusalem* pl. 4, 18–19, 28, 35, 37, *Songs* (P, X) MS: ALS, 12 March 1804
ASHMOLEAN MUSEUM, Oxford	Dante design no. 86
AUCKLAND PUBLIC LIBRARY, New Zealand	*America* (N), *Europe* (I)
Barrett, Mr. Roger W. Chicago	ALS: 18 Jan. 1808 (A)
Baskin, Mr. Leonard Northampton, Massachusetts	*Europe* (c, pl. 1^b, 4^a, 5^a)
Bentley, G. E., Jr. Toronto	ILLUMINATED WORKS: *Songs* electrotypes, plus (copy o, pl. 39), pl. 22, 28, 30, 40, 44–6, 48^{a–b} MS: 'Riddle MS'
BERG COLLECTION: see NEW YORK PUBLIC LIBRARY	
BIRMINGHAM CITY MUSEUM AND ART GALLERY	Dante design no. 3
Blunt, Sir Anthony London	*Songs* (J), pl. 28
BODLEIAN LIBRARY, Oxford	ILLUMINATED WORKS: 'The Accusers' (B); *Thel* (I); *Marriage* (B); *Innocence* (L) TYPE-PRINTED WORKS: *Descriptive Catalogue* (H), 'Exhibition' (B)
BOSTON MUSEUM OF FINE ARTS	'The Accusers' (D)

Table of Collections

---

[1] Ellen M. Oldham (Curator of Classical Literature).

Table of Collections

CINCINNATI ART MUSEUM	ILLUMINATED WORKS: *Thel* (N); *Innocence* (S); *Songs* (S) TYPE-PRINTED WORKS: *Poetical Sketches* (D)
CORNELL UNIVERSITY, Ithaca, N.Y.	MS, MARGINALIA: Wordsworth, *Poems* (1815)
Crawford and Balcarres, Earl of, Colinsburgh, Scotland	*Europe* pl. 2; *Jerusalem* pl. 24; *Songs* (H)
Cunliffe, Lord, London	ILLUMINATED WORKS: *America* (G); *Europe* (B); *Jerusalem* (B); *Songs* (i); *Visions* (C) MS, ALS: Feb. 1808 (C)
Dennis, Mrs. Seth, New York	*Songs* (Q)
DOHENY MEMORIAL LIBRARY: see ST. JOHN'S SEMINARY	
Drysdale, Mrs. William, Radley, Berkshire	*Songs* (c)
Egremont, Lord,[1] Petworth, Sussex	ALS: 18 Jan. 1808 (B)†
Essick, Professor *Robert N.,* Pasadena, California	*Tiriel* drawing no. 6†
FITZWILLIAM MUSEUM, Cambridge, England (The bulk of the Keynes Collection is promised to the Fitzwilliam)	ILLUMINATED WORKS: *America* (O, P); *Thel* (G); *Europe* (K, M); *Jerusalem* (H); *Marriage* (H, I, K); *Songs* (R, AA), electrotypes; *Visions* (P) TYPE-PRINTED WORKS: *Descriptive Catalogue* (G) MSS: *An Island in the Moon*; INSCRIPTION: List of Apostles; ALS: 15 March, 12 April 1827; *To Blake*: 7 Oct. 1801 *Tiriel* drawing no. 2
FOGG MUSEUM,[2] Cambridge, Massachusetts: see also HARVARD	MS: Dante no. 7†, 17
FOLGER SHAKESPEARE LIBRARY, Washington, D.C.	ALS: 31 July 1801
GLASGOW UNIVERSITY LIBRARY	*Descriptive Catalogue* (O)

[1] Mr. Francis W. Steer of the Sussex County Record Office.
[2] Mrs. Carol C. Gillham (Drawing Department).

Table of Collections

[1] Mrs. Elizabeth B. Tritle (Secretary to the Curator, Quaker Collection).
[2] The collector himself has generously assisted me by correspondence.

Table of Collections

MSS Inscriptions: Blair's *Grave* title-page;
Illuminated Genesis MS; ALS: [Oct. 1791];
16 Sept. 1800; May 1809 (address only);
[March 1825]; [7 June 1825]; 11 Oct., 10
Nov. 1825; 31 Jan., [5 Feb.], 19 May, 5, 16,
29 July, 1 Aug. 1826; 27 Jan., [Feb.], 25
April, 3 July 1827; *To Blake*: 17 Oct. 1791;
Marginalia: Lavater, *Aphorisms* (1788);
Thornton, *Lord's Prayer* (1827); Watson,
Apology for the Bible (1798)

Hyde, Mrs. Donald F.,
Somerville, New Jersey

ALS: 7 Oct. 1803

Ivimy, Miss Joan; see
Mrs. Burton

Juel-Jensen, Dr. B.,[1]
Oxford

Songs pl. 7, 10, 33, 44†

Kain, Mrs. Louise Y.,
Louisville, Kentucky

Tiriel drawing no. 10†

Keynes, Sir *Geoffrey*,[1]
Brinkley, Suffolk
(Mostly promised to the
Fitzwilliam[2])

Illuminated Works: 'The Accusers' (E);
All Religions are One pl. 1; *America* pl. 3, 6, 10;
Ahania (Ba); 'Ancient of Days' (C); *Europe*
pl. 1, 2, 4–7, 10, 12; *Urizen* pl. 1, 3, 25; *For
the Sexes* (L), pl. 3, 6–7; *The Ghost of Abel* (B);
Jerusalem pl. 1, 37, 51, 100; 'Joseph of
Arimathea' (A, D, E); 'Laocoon' (A);
Marriage pl. 3–4, (E); 'Mirth' (B); *On
Homer* (B); *Innocence* (R); *Songs* (G, pl. 30–2,
37–8, 42–3, 47, 50–1, b, k, l, m), pl. 9–10, 51;
No Natural Religion (L²); *Visions* pl. 6, 10
Type-Printed Works: 'Blake's Chaucer:
An Original Engraving' (B); *Descriptive
Catalogue* (C)
MSS 'For Children The Gates of Hell';
ALS: 11 Dec. 1805; *To Blake*: 17 April
1800; Marginalia: Bacon, *Essays* (1798);
Dante, *Inferno* (1785); Swedenborg, *Divine
Providence* (1790)
Tiriel drawings nos. 8, 11

[1] See note 2, p. 1763.
[2] Sir Geoffrey has 'promised to bequeath' to the Fitzwilliam Museum all these
works except *Ahania* (Ba); 'Ancient of Days' (C); *Descriptive Catalogue* (C); *Ghost*
(B); 'Laocoon'; *Marriage* (E); 'Mirth' (B); *On Homer* (B); *Songs* pl. b, according to
William Blake: Catalogue of the Collection in the Fitzwilliam Museum, Cambridge,
ed. David Bindman (1970), 60.

1764

Table of Collections

---

[1] Mr. John C. Broderick (Specialist, American Cultural History).
[2] Marion R. Small (Assistant Librarian).

Table of Collections

METROPOLITAN MUSEUM OF ART, New York — *Jerusalem* pl. 1; *Songs* (Y)

MORGAN (J. Pierpont) LIBRARY, New York — ILLUMINATED WORKS: *America* (A–B), pl. 4; *Ahania* (Bc); *Book of Los* (B); *Thel* (a, C); *Europe* (b); *Urizen* (B, I), pl. 12; *For the Sexes* (D, G); *Jerusalem* (F), pl. 28, 45, 56, 74; *Marriage* (C, F); *On Homer* (F); *Song of Los* (C); *Innocence* (D); *Songs* (K, V, e, n); *No Natural Religion* (G$^{1-2}$, I, L^1), pl. a1; *Visions* (F)
TYPE-PRINTED WORKS: *Descriptive Catalogue* (N, P); *Poetical Sketches* (X)
MSS: *L'Allegro* and *Il Penseroso* descriptions; ALS: 12, 14 Sept. 1800; 19 Oct. 1801; 16 March, 27 April, 22 June 1804; 31 March, 14 July 1826; 'Ballads (Pickering) MS'

NATIONAL GALLERY OF AUSTRALIA, Canberra — *Europe* pl. 1^{a-b}, 2^a, *Jerusalem* pl. 25, 32, 41

NATIONAL GALLERY OF CANADA, Ottawa — *Songs* (T$^{1-2}$ pl. 29–31, 38, 41, 43, 46–7, 49–51)

NATIONAL GALLERY OF VICTORIA, Melbourne, Australia — ILLUMINATED WORKS: *Europe* pl. 11; *Urizen* pl. 21; *Jerusalem* pl. 51
MSS: Dante no. 15–16, 36, 51, 56, 90, 99

NEWBERRY LIBRARY, Chicago — *Europe* (c, pl. 4^b, 9^b, 11^b, 16, 17^{a-b})

Newton, Miss Caroline Daylesford, Pennsylvania — *America* (D); *Urizen* pl. 9; *For the Sexes* (J); *Marriage* pl. 11; *Songs* (j) (bequeathed to Princeton)

NEW YORK PUBLIC LIBRARY — *Milton* (C)

(Berg Collection) — ILLUMINATED WORKS: *America* (L); *Thel* (M); *Europe* (F); *Innocence* (E); *Visions* (K)
MSS: 'then She bore Pale desire'; 'Woe cried the muse'; Upcott's Autograph Album; ALS: 18 March 1827

NEW YORK UNIVERSITY — *Europe* (c pl. 6–7, 15^a); *On Homer* (E)

PENNSYLVANIA HISTORICAL SOCIETY,[1] Philadelphia — ALS: 21 March, 28 Dec. 1804†

PFORZHEIMER (The Carl and Lily) FOUNDATION, Room 815, 41 East 42nd Street, New York — ILLUMINATED WORK: *Innocence* (K)
TYPE-PRINTED WORK: *Poetical Sketches* (H)

[1] Mr. R. N. Williams (Director).

Table of Collections

¹ See note 2, p. 1763.

Table of Collections

TEXAS CHRISTIAN UNIVERSITY,[1] Fort Worth, Texas

Poetical Sketches (V)†

TEXAS, UNIVERSITY OF,[2] Austin, Texas

ILLUMINATED WORKS: *Urizen* pl. 5;† *Innocence* (O)
TYPE-PRINTED WORK: *Poetical Sketches* (O)
MSS, ALS: 11 Oct. 1819; 29 Dec. 1826

Thorne, Mrs. Landon K., New York

Europe (G)

TORONTO, UNIVERSITY OF

Poetical Sketches (K)

TRINITY COLLEGE, Cambridge

TYPE-PRINTED WORK: *Poetical Sketches* (L)
MS, MARGINALIA: Berkeley, *Siris* (1744)

TRINITY COLLEGE, Hartford, Connecticut

ILLUMINATED WORKS: *Europe* pl. 2, 18; *For the Sexes* pl. 14; *The Ghost of Abel* (D); 'Joseph of Arimathea' (H); *On Homer* (D); *No Natural Religion* (J)
MSS: Blake's Memorandum; ALS: 31 March 1804; May 1809 (message only)

TURNBULL (Alexander) LIBRARY, Wellington, New Zealand

TYPE-PRINTED WORK: *Poetical Sketches* (F)
MS: 'Songs by Shepherds'

UNIVERSITY COLLEGE, London

Poetical Sketches (W)

Vanderhoef, Mr. F. Bailey, Ojai, California

MS: 'All Genius varies'

VICTORIA AND ALBERT MUSEUM, London

ILLUMINATED WORKS: *All Religions are One* pl. 1; *Jerusalem* pl. 9, 11; *Songs* electrotypes; *No Natural Religion* (M)
TYPE-PRINTED WORK: *Descriptive Catalogue* (E)
MS: 'Theotormon woven' [see *Vala* p. 100]; 'The Fall of Man'
Tiriel drawing no. 7

VIVIAN (Glynn) ART GALLERY, Swansea, Wales

America pl. 2, 5, 15; *Europe* pl. 6–7, 12; *Jerusalem* pl. 35

WEDGWOOD MUSEUM, Barlaston, Stoke-on-Trent, Staffordshire

ALS: 8 Sept. 1815; *To Blake*: 29 July 1815 (copy)

---

[1] C. G. Sparks (Librarian), Dr. Lyle Kendall (Department of English, Texas Christian University).

[2] Mr. William A. Robinson (Research Associate, Iconography Collection, Humanities Research Center).

Table of Collections

TABLE OF
AMBIGUOUSLY BROKEN WORDS

TABLE OF REPEATED LINES

Table of Repeated Lines

Vala (?1796–?1807) pp. 1, 4–13, 16, 18–19, 21–3, 25–6, 30, 33–6, 39–42, 44, 48, 50–1, 53–6, 58–60, 64, 68, 71–3, 75, 78, 80, 84–5, 87, 91–3, 95, 99–101, 103–6, 108, 110, 113, 115, 117–20, 129, 132–4, 136–8, 143–5
Visions of the Daughters of Albion (1793) pl. 4–5, 7–11

TABLE OF REPEATED DESIGNS

MAPS I–II: BLAKE'S LONDON

pp. 1821 and 1822

KEY

'London coverd the whole Earth' (*Jerusalem* pl. 79, l. 22). (*N.B.* In the map-references below, 'I' refers to the map primarily of London and 'II' to the map showing the villages round London. Many references from Blake's correspondence are omitted here.)

Battersea (I: 5B) (Catherine Blake's birthplace)   *Jerusalem* 21, 33
Billingsgate (I: 3D)   *Jerusalem* 82
Blackheath (I: 5F, II: 4E–F)   *Milton* 4, 26, 35, *Jerusalem* 42
Bow (Old) (I: 2F)   *Milton* 4, *Jerusalem* 27, 41, 84
Broad Street (I: 3B) (Blake's birthplace)   'Exhibition of Paintings', 'A Descriptive Catalogue', 'Blake's Chaucer: An Original Engraving', *Descriptive Catalogue*, *Jerusalem* 84
Brockley Hills (II: 4E)   *Jerusalem* 90

Camberwell (I: 5D, II: 3D–E)   *Milton* 35, *Jerusalem* 47, 68, 84, 92
Chelsea (I: 4B)   *Jerusalem* 8, 21, 33
Chelsea Pensioners' Hospital (I: 4B)   *Jerusalem* 8
Cromwell's Gardens (I: 4A)   *Jerusalem* 8

Esher (II: 5A)   *Jerusalem* 68

Finchley (II: 1C)   *Milton* 4, *Jerusalem* 16, 42
Fountain Court [Strand] (I: 3C) (Blake's home 1821–7)   Letters

Great George Street (I: 4B)   *Europe* 15
Great Queen Street (I: 3C) (see Queen Street)
Green Man (I: 2B)   *Jerusalem* 27

Hackney (I: 1E, II: 2E)   *Jerusalem* 21, 31, 84
Hampstead (II: 2C–D)   *Milton* 4, 34, *Jerusalem* 16, 84, Letters
Harrow (II: A–B)   *Milton* 35
Hendon (II: 1C)   *Jerusalem* 16
Hercules Buildings [Lambeth] (I: 4C) (Blake's home 1791–1800)   'To the Public', *For Children* 1
Highgate (II: 1C–D)   *Milton* 4, 35, 40, *Jerusalem* 16, 31, 47, 83–4, 90, Letter 31 i 1826

Holloway (I: 1C) *Milton* 40, *Jerusalem* 21, 31
Hounslow (II: 3A–B) *Milton* 4, 26, *Jerusalem* 42
Hyde Park (I: 3B) *Milton* 4, 9, *Jerusalem* 38, 44

Isle of Leuthas Dogs (I: 4E–F) *Jerusalem* 31
Islington (I: 1C) *Jerusalem* 27, 41, 84, Letter 31 i 1826

Jew's Harp House (I: 2B) *Jerusalem* 27

Kensington Gardens (I: 3A) *Milton* 4, *Jerusalem* 29
Kentish Town (I: 1B) *Jerusalem* 27

Lambeth (I: 4C) (see Hercules Buildings) *Notebook*, *America* 2, 'To
  the Public', *For Children* 2, *Urizen* 2, *Europe* 2, *Song of Los* 2,
  Ahania 2, *Book of Los* 2, *Vala* 25, *Milton* 4, 11, 20, 25, 35–6, *Jerusalem*
  12, 19–20, 27, 41, 65, 84, 92, Letters
Lambeth's Vale (I: 4C) *Vala* 2, *Milton* 4, 13, 35, 42, *Jerusalem*
  19–20, 26, 41, 65, 92
Lincoln's Inn (I: 3C) *Jerusalem* 84
London (I, II) *Poetical Sketches*, *Island*, *Songs* 19, 46, *Marriage* 26,
  Europe 15, 'Ballads MS', *Milton* 4, 18, 40, 44, *Descriptive Catalogue*,
  Jerusalem 5, 10, 15, 24, 30–3, 38, 41, 46, 53, 57, 59, 63, 65–6, 72–4,
  82–4, Letters
London Stone (I: 3D) *Milton* 4, *Descriptive Catalogue*, *Jerusalem* 8,
  27, 29, 31, 42, 57–8, 66, 74, 79, 94
London Street (I: 3A) *Jerusalem* 58

Malden (II: 5B) *Jerusalem* 21, 27, 41, 57, 65, 68, 90, 94
Marybone (i.e. Marylebone) (I: 2–3B) *Jerusalem* 27, 31, 41, 65
Middlesex (II: 2A–E . . .) *Milton* 26, *Jerusalem* 16, 30–2, 34, 56, 58,
  71, 90
Mile End Road (I: 2E) *Milton* 4
Muswell Hill (II: 1D) *Jerusalem* 16, Letter 31 i 1826

Narrow Street (I: 3E) *Jerusalem* 31
Norwood (II: 4D, 5E) *Milton* 4, *Jerusalem* 42

Old Bow (I: 2F) (see Bow)
Old Stratford (I: 1F) *Milton* 4, *Jerusalem* 31
Oxford Street (I: 3B–C) *Jerusalem* 38

Paddington (I: 2A, II: 2C) *Jerusalem* 12, 27, 84
Pancrass (I: 2B–C) *Jerusalem* 27, 41

MAPS III–IV: BLAKE'S BRITAIN

pp. 1823 and 1824

KEY

'England encompassd the Nations: And all the Nations of the Earth were seen in the Cities of Albion'; '(I call them by their English names: Englis*h*, the rough basement. . . .)' (*Jerusalem* pl. 79, ll. 22–3 [cf. pl. 24, l. 44], pl. 40, l. 58)

(*N.B.* In the map-references below, 'III' refers to the map of all Britain and 'IV' to the map of England and Wales.)

Ab[e]rdeen[shire] (III: 3C–D)   *Jerusalem* 16
Anglesey (Mona) (III: 5C)   *Jerusalem* 16
Annandale (III: 4C)   *Milton* e, *Jerusalem* 63, 65
Antrim (III: 4B)   *Jerusalem* 72
Argyll[shire] (III: 3C)   *Jerusalem* 16
Armagh (III: 4B)   *Jerusalem* 72
Asaph (IV: 3B)   *Jerusalem* 46
Atlantic (III: 1–6A–C)   *French Revolution, Marriage* 25, *America* 5–6, 12, 15–16, 18, a–b, *Europe* 14, *Vala* 22, 25, 42, *Milton* 17, 22, 28, 31, 35, *Notebook, Descriptive Catalogue* ¶76, 'Vision of the Last Judgment', *Jerusalem* 4, 23–4, 27, 34, 36, 44, 48–50, 57, 59, 71, 83, Letter 12 ix 1800
Ayr[shire] (III: 4C)   *Jerusalem* 16

Baltimore, Ireland (III: 6A)   *Jerusalem* 49
Banff[shire] (III: 2C–D)   *Jerusalem* 16
Bangor (IV: 3B)   *Jerusalem* 46
Bath (IV: 5C)   *Milton* 40, *Descriptive Catalogue* ¶14, 46, 58, *Jerusalem* 17, 40–1, 43–6, 57, 65, 71, 75, 79, 82, Letters
Bedford[shire] (III: 5E)   *Jerusalem* 16, 71
Berkshire (III: 5–6D)   *Jerusalem* 16, 71
Berwi[c]k (III: 3D)   *Jerusalem* 16
Bognor (IV: 6D)   *Milton* 40, Letter 10 v 1801
Breckno[c]kshire (III: 5C)   *Jerusalem* 16
Bristol (IV: 5C)   *Island, America* 17, *Jerusalem* 40, 43, 67, Letter 15 iii 1827
Buckingham[shire] (III: 5D–E)   *Jerusalem* 71
Bute (III: 3C)   *Jerusalem* 16

Heref(ordshire) (III: 5D) *Jerusalem* 16, 71
Hertfordshire (III: 5E) *Jerusalem* 16, 31
Humber River (IV: 3D) *Jerusalem* 16, 66
Hunt(in)g(do)n[shire] (III: 5E) *Jerusalem* 16, 71

Invernes[s-shire] (III: 2C–3C) *Jerusalem* 16
Ireland (III: 4–5A–B) *America* 17, *Milton* 4, 40, *Descriptive Catalogue* ¶74, *Jerusalem* 16, 29, 34, 49, 63, 67, 71–2, 83, 89
Irish Sea (III: 4–5B) *Jerusalem* 90
Isle of Man (III: 4C) *Jerusalem* 71

John Groat's House (III: 2C) *Milton* 26
Jura, see Dura

Kent (III: 6E) *America* 4, *Jerusalem* 16, 29, 71, Letter 4 v 1804
Kerry (III: 5A) *Jerusalem* 72
Kildare (III: 5B) *Jerusalem* 72
Kilkenny (III: 5B) *Jerusalem* 72
Kincard[ine] (III: 3D) *Jerusalem* 16
King's County (III: 5B) *Jerusalem* 72
Kinros[s] (III: 3C–D) *Jerusalem* 16
Kirk[c]udbri[g]ht[shire] (III: 4C) *Jerusalem* 16
Kromarty (i.e. Cromarty) (III: 2C) *Jerusalem* 16

Lanark, see Lanerk
Lancashire (III: 4D) *Jerusalem* 16, 90
Landaff (i.e. Llandaff) (IV: 5B) *Jerusalem* 46
Lanerk (i.e. Lanark) (III: 3C) *Jerusalem* 16
Legions (i.e. Caerleon) (IV: 5B) *Milton* 40, *Jerusalem* 41
Leicester(shire) (III: 5D) *Jerusalem* 16, 71
Leinster (III: 5B) *Jerusalem* 72
Leitrim (III: 4B) *Jerusalem* 72
Limerick (III: 5A) *Jerusalem* 72
Lincoln (IV: 3D) *Jerusalem* 5, 21, 46, 66, 71
Lincoln(shire) (III: 5E) *Jerusalem* 16
Linlithgo (III: 3C) *Jerusalem* 16
Litchfield (IV: 5C) *Jerusalem* 46
Liverpool (IV: 3C) *Jerusalem* 21
Lizard Point (IV: 6A) *Milton* 4, 26, *Jerusalem* 83
London (III: 6E, IV: 5D, also I, II) *Poetical Sketches*, *Island*, *Songs* 19, 46, *Marriage* 26, *Europe* 15, 'Ballads MS', *Milton* 4, 18, 40, 44, *Descriptive Catalogue*, *Jerusalem* 5, 10, 15, 24, 30–3, 38, 41, 46, 53, 57, 59, 63, 65–6, 72–4, 82–4, Letters

Londonderry (III: 4B) *Jerusalem* 72
Longford (III: 4B) *Jerusalem* 72
Lowth (i.e. Louth) (III: 4B) *Jerusalem* 72

Malden (IV: 5D) *Jerusalem* 21, 27, 41, 57, 65, 90, 94
Malden's Cove (IV: 5E) *Jerusalem* 68
Malvern (IV: 4C) *Jerusalem* 4, 21
Mam-Tor (Derbyshire) (IV: 3C) *Jerusalem* 34, 82, 93
Managhan, see Monaghan
Manchester (IV: 3C) *Jerusalem* 21
Mayo (III: 4A) *Jerusalem* 72
Medway (IV: 5D–E) *Jerusalem* 4, 63, 79
Merionethshire (III: 5C) *Jerusalem* 16
Mersey River (IV: 3C) *Jerusalem* 90
Middlesex (III: 6E) *Milton* 26, *Jerusalem* 16, 30–2, 34, 56, 58, 71, 90
Mona (Anglesey) (III: 5C) *Jerusalem* 66
Monaghan (III: 4B) *Jerusalem* 72
Monmouth [city] (IV: 5C) *Jerusalem* 21
Monmouth[shire] (III: 5D) *Jerusalem* 16
Montgomeryshire (III: 5C) *Jerusalem* 16
Moray, see Murra
Munster (III: 5A–B) *Jerusalem* 72
Murra (i.e. Moray) (III: 2C) *Jerusalem* 16

Nairn[shire] (III: 2C) *Jerusalem* 16
Norfolk (III: 5E) *Jerusalem* 16, 72
Northampton[shire] (III: 5D) *Jerusalem* 16, 71
Northumberland (III: 4D) *Jerusalem* 16, 71
Norwich (IV: 4E) *Milton* 40, *Jerusalem* 5, 21, 46
Nott(in)gham(shire) (III: 5D) *Jerusalem* 16, 71

Orkney (III: 2D–E) *Jerusalem* 16
Oxford (IV: 5C) *Vala* 25, *Milton* 11, 40, *Descriptive Catalogue* ¶14, *Jerusalem* 5, 16, 29, 42, 45–6, 66, 71, 82–3, Letters 30 i 1803, 27 i 1804
Oxfordshire (III: 5D) *Jerusalem* 16

Peak, The, (Derbyshire) (IV: 3C) *Jerusalem* 21, 57, 64
Peebles (III: 3C–D) *Jerusalem* 16
Pembrokeshire (III: 5C) *Jerusalem* 16
P[a]enmaenmawr (III: 5C) *Vala* 25
Pentland [Firth] (III: 2C) *Milton* 26

Perth[shire] (III: 3C) *Jerusalem* 16
Peterboro (IV: 4D) *Jerusalem* 46
Plinlimmon (IV: 4B) *Jerusalem* 4, 66

Queen's County (III: 5B) *Jerusalem* 72

Radnorshire (III: 5C) *Jerusalem* 16
Rathlin (III: 4B) *Jerusalem* 49
Renfru (i.e. Renfrewshire) (III: 3C) *Jerusalem* 16
Ribble River (IV: 2–3C) *Jerusalem* 90
Rochester (IV: 5E) *Jerusalem* 46, 67
Rosamund's Bower (IV: 4C) *Jerusalem* 57
Roscommon (III: 4B) *Jerusalem* 72
Roxbro (i.e. Roxburghshire) (III: 4D) *Jerusalem* 16
Rutland (III: 5D–E) *Jerusalem* 16, 71

Saint David's (IV: 4A) *Jerusalem* 46
Salisbury (IV: 5C) *Jerusalem* 40, 67
Salisbury Plain (IV: 5C) *Vala* 25, *Jerusalem* 63–7, 80
Scotland (III: 1–4B–D) *America* 17, *Milton* 40, *Notebook*, *Descriptive Catalogue* ¶74, *Jerusalem* 5, 16, 23, 29, 66, 71–2
Selkirk (III: 3D) *Jerusalem* 16
Selsey (IV: 6D) *Jerusalem* 40, 71
Severn (IV: 4B–C) *Vala* 25, *Jerusalem* 66, 75, 79, 89
Shetland (III: 1D) *Jerusalem* 16
Shrops(hire) (III: 5D) *Jerusalem* 16, 71
Skiddaw (IV: 2B) *Jerusalem* 80, 82, 90
Skye (III: 2B–3B, C) *Jerusalem* 16
Sligo (III: 4A–B) *Jerusalem* 72
Snowdon (IV: 3B) *Vala* 19, 21, 25, *Descriptive Catalogue* ¶76, *Jerusalem* 4, 66
Sodor (III: 4C) *Jerusalem* 16, 46
Somerset (III: 6C–D) *Jerusalem* 16, 71
Stafford[shire] (III: 5D) *Jerusalem* 16, 71
Sterling (i.e. Stirlingshire) (III: 3C) *Jerusalem* 16
Stone-henge (IV: 5C) *Descriptive Catalogue* ¶86, *Jerusalem* 57–8, 66, 68, 94
Strathness, perhaps the strath (valley) of the River Ness (III: 2C) *Jerusalem* 90
Suffolk (III: 5E) *Jerusalem* 16, 71
Surrey (III: 6E) 'Ballads MS', *Milton* 4, 28, 44, *Jerusalem* 4, 16, 30–1, 41, 53, 71, 79, 83, 90

MAP V: BLAKE'S HOLY LAND

p. 1825

KEY

'here all the Tribes of Israel I behold Upon the Holy Land' (*Jerusalem* pl. 86, ll. 17–18)

Abarim, Mountains of (5D)   *Milton* 16
Amalek (6B)   *Vala* 105, *Milton* 16, 21, 23, *Jerusalem* 5, 13, 29, 43, 61, 63, 68, 74, 80, 82–3, 86, 92
Ammon (4D–E)   *Milton* 37, *Jerusalem* 5, 62, 86, 89, 92
Aram (1E)   *Milton* 16, *Descriptive Catalogue* ¶10, *Jerusalem* 5, 7, 49, 54, 89
Arnon River (originally Pison) (5D)   *Vala* 113, *Milton* 17, 34, 40, 42, *Jerusalem* 61, 80, 89

Bashan (2D)   *Milton* 16, 'Vision of the Last Judgment', *Jerusalem* 34, 48, 63, 74
Bethlehem (or Ephratah) (5C)   *Jerusalem* 31
Beth Peor (4D) (see Valley of Beth Peor)   *Vala* 21, *Milton* 17, *Jerusalem* 67
Bohan (4C)   *Jerusalem* 34

Cabul (2C)   *Jerusalem* 74, 79
Calvary (Golgotha) (2G)   *Milton* 2, *Jerusalem* 12, 16, *Ghost* 2
Canaan (2–5A–C)   *Vala* 105, 145, *Milton* C, 16–18, 23, 42, *Jerusalem* 5, 13, 15, 29, 43, 54, 58, 60, 63–4, 66, 68–9, 71, 74, 80, 82–3, 85, 89, 92, 'Everlasting Gospel', Watson marginalia
Carmel, Mount (3B–3C)   *Milton* 17

Damascus (1E)   *Milton* 37, *Jerusalem* 38, 89
Dan (1D)   *Vala* 115, *Jerusalem* 16, 67, 72, 74, 79
Dead Sea (5–6C)   *Milton* 34, *Jerusalem* 89

Ebal, Mount (4C)   *Vala* 105, *Jerusalem* 68
Edom (6C–D)   *Marriage* 3, *Milton* 16, *Descriptive Catalogue* ¶10, *Jerusalem* 7, 49, 92, 96
Ephraim (4B–C)   *Vala* 14, 19, 105, *Milton* 17–18, 23, *Jerusalem* 67–8, 72, 79, 85
Ephratah (or Bethlehem) (5C)   *Jerusalem* 29

Map V: Blake's Holy Land

Fishpools of Heshbon (4D) (see Heshbon) *Jerusalem* 89

Gad (3D)　*Vala* 105, *Milton* 17, 23, *Jerusalem* 16, 67, 74, 79
Gaza (5A)　*Jerusalem* 63, 89
Gihon (4G)　*Jerusalem* 61, 89
Gilead (3–4D)　*Vala* 8, 19, 21, 99, 105, *Jerusalem* 5, 36, 48, 68, 79
Gilgal (4C)　*Jerusalem* 36
Golgotha (Calvary) (2G)　*Jerusalem* 12, 38, 63, 92
Gomorr(h)a (6C)　*Milton* 37, *Jerusalem* 67, 89
Goshen (5B)　*Jerusalem* 79

Hazor (2D)　*Milton* 19
Hebron (5C)　*Jerusalem* 74
Hermon, Mount (1D)　*Vala* 8, 99, *Milton* 16, *Jerusalem* 85
Heshbon, Heshbon's Wall (4D) (see Fishpools of Heshbon)　*Jerusalem* 36, 79, 82, 89
Hinnoms Vale (4G)　*Jerusalem* 50, 53

Israel (1–4B–C)　*Poetical Sketches, Marriage* 12, *Notebook, Milton* 42, *Jerusalem* 27, 86, 89, 'Laocoon', Watson marginalia

Jerusalem (the place, not the woman) (4C)　'Then she bore', *Song of Los* 3, 7, *Vala* 42, 104, 117, 122, 123, *Milton* 2, *Jerusalem* 27, 33, 57, 76, 84, 92
Jordan (4C–D)　*Jerusalem* 34, 36
Jordan River (1–4C–D)　*Milton* 17, *Jerusalem* 58, 61, 79
Judea (5B–C)　*Song of Los* 7, *Jerusalem* 67, 79

Kanah River (4B–C)　*Vala* 105, *Jerusalem* 67
Kishon (2–3C)　*Jerusalem* 79

Lebanon, Mount (1C)　*Jerusalem* 36

Machpelah (5C)　*Jerusalem* 64
Mahenaim (4D)　*Milton* 17
Manasseh (also Manazzoth, Menassheh) (3B–C)　*Vala* 105, *Milton* 18, 23, *Jerusalem* 67, 72, 79
Moab (5D)　*Vala* 105, 145, *Milton* 16, 23, 37, *Descriptive Catalogue* ¶10, *Jerusalem* 5, 13, 20, 29, 36, 43, 49, 62, 80, 82–3, 86, 89, 92
Mount Ebal (4C), see Ebal
Mount Ephraim (4B), see Ephraim
Mount Gilead (4D), see Gilead
Mount Hermon (1D), see Hermon

Mount Lebanon (1C), see Lebanon
Mount Olivet (3J), see Olivet
Mount Zion (4G), see Zion

Nazareth (2C)   *Poetical Sketches* ('Samson'), *Jerusalem* 61

Og (2D)   *Vala* 22, 113, *Milton* 18, 20, 31, 37, 'Vision of the Last
   Judgment' (*Notebook* 76–7, 93), *Jerusalem* 13, 27, 48, 49, 73, 79, 89
Olivet, Mount (3J)   *Jerusalem* 16

Palestine (1–5A–C)   *Poetical Sketches* ('Samson'), *Milton* 37, *Jerusalem*
   72
Peor, see Beth Peor
Philist(h)(e)a (5A–B)   *Poetical Sketches* ('Samson'), *Milton* 42, *Jeru-
   salem* 49, 68, 74, 78–79, 86, 89, 92
Pison River (later Arnon) (5D)   *Jerusalem* 61, 89

Rabbath (4D)   *Jerusalem* 89
Rephaim's [Giant's] vale (5C)   *Milton* 17, *Jerusalem* 48, 64, 68,
   92

Shechem (4C)   *Vala* 105, *Jerusalem* 68, 74
Shiloh (4C)   *Vala* 19, 21, *Jerusalem* 49, 55, 79, 85–86, 92
Sidon (1C)   *Milton* 37, *Jerusalem* 89
Sodom (6C)   Lavater marginalia, *Milton* 37, *Jerusalem* 67, 89
Storge, see Arnon
Succoth (4D)   *Milton* 17, *Jerusalem* 34

Tyre (1C)   'then she bore', *Milton* 7, 37, *Jerusalem* 63, 86, 89

Valley of (Beth) Peor (4D)   *Milton* 17, *Jerusalem* 49

Zaretan (3D)   *Jerusalem* 34
Zion (4G)   *Vala* 14, 99, *Jerusalem* 8, 12, 24, 27, 29, 77–80, 82
Zion, Mount (4G)   *Vala* 14, 99, *Jerusalem* 24, 78–80
Zion's Hill (4G)   *Jerusalem* 8, 12, 27, 29, 80, 82, 'Everlasting Gospel'

INDEX

OF TITLES, FIRST LINES, AND EDITORIAL MATTER

The Index includes the titles of all Blake's literary works, the first lines of individual poems (even when among prose, as in the *Island in the Moon*), and editorial matter.

Exclamations such as 'O' and 'Oho' and prepositions (To, From) are indexed, but articles (The, An) are not. Page numbers for Blake's works themselves are in **bold-face type**; other references to them are in plain roman type. For references within Blake's text, see the Blake *Concordance* (1967).

Index entries for editorial matter are primarily for names of persons and places and for titles of Blake's writings, prints, and drawings referred to in the footnotes and in the Bibliographical Notes. For place-names in London, Britain, and the Holy Land, see the Tables on pp. 1774–86, and for Collections of Blake's Writings, see the Table on pp. 1760–9.

N.B. Volume II begins at p. 747.

Index of Titles, First Lines, and Editorial Matter

Index of Titles, First Lines, and Editorial Matter

Index of Titles, First Lines, and Editorial Matter

Index of Titles, First Lines, and Editorial Matter

Index of Titles, First Lines, and Editorial Matter

Index of Titles, First Lines, and Editorial Matter

Index of Titles, First Lines, and Editorial Matter

Index of Titles, First Lines, and Editorial Matter

Index of Titles, First Lines, and Editorial Matter

Index of Titles, First Lines, and Editorial Matter

Index of Titles, First Lines, and Editorial Matter

MAP 1. Blake's Britain

MAP 2. Blake's England and Wales

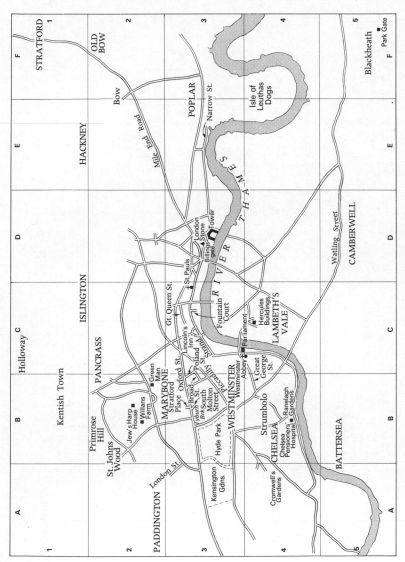

MAP 3. Blake's London

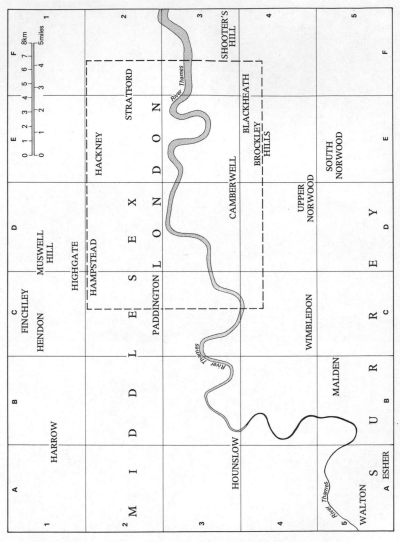

MAP 4. Blake's London (outlying villages)

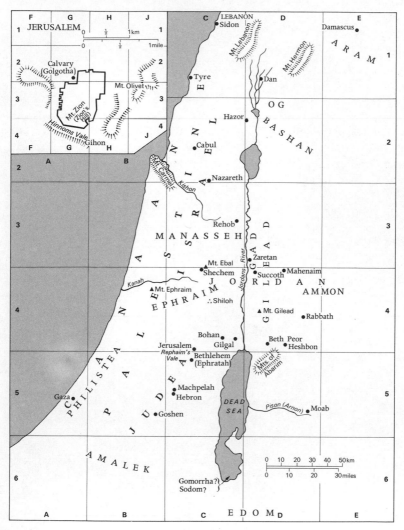

MAP 5. Blake's Holy Land